SEVENTH EDITION

# TRADITIONS & ENCOUNTERS

## A GLOBAL PERSPECTIVE ON THE PAST

**Jerry H. Bentley**
UNIVERSITY OF HAWAI'I

**Heather E. Streets-Salter**
NORTHEASTERN UNIVERSITY

**Herbert F. Ziegler**
UNIVERSITY OF HAWAI'I

**Craig Benjamin**
GRAND VALLEY STATE UNIVERSITY

AP CONTRIBUTORS

**Monty Armstrong**
CERRITOS HIGH SCHOOL

**Mary Jo Jepson**
BRIGHTON CENTRAL SCHOOLS

**Amy R. Caldwell**
CALIFORNIA STATE UNIVERSITY, CHANNEL ISLANDS

**Lenore Schneider**
NEW CANAAN HIGH SCHOOL

mheonline.com/advancedplacement

Send all inquiries to:
McGraw Hill
8787 Orion Place
Columbus, OH 43240

ISBN: 978-1-26-654532-0
MHID: 1-26-654532-8

Printed in the United States of America.

1 2 3 4 5 6 7 8 9 LWI 30 29 28 27 26 25 24 23 22

# Brief Contents

# Contents

## CHAPTER 10

### Transoceanic Encounters and Global Connections 313



## CHAPTER 11

### The Transformation of Europe 345



## CHAPTER 12

### The Integration of the Americas and Oceania with the Wider World 378

## CHAPTER 24

### New Conflagrations: World War II and the Cold War 787



## CHAPTER 25

### The End of Empire in an Era of Cold War 825

## CHAPTER 26

### Into the Twenty-First Century 857



## PART 4 CLOSER

### Global Conflict, Cold War and Decolonization, and Globalization, 1900 to present 896

# Preface

## DESIGNED FOR AP SUCCESS

### How do the themes of traditions and encounters continue to help make sense of the entire human past in the twenty-first century?

As Jerry Bentley and Herb Ziegler noted in their original Preface to this book, world history is about both diversity and connections. They began this text with a simple goal: to help students understand the unique histories of the world's rich variety of peoples, while at the same time allowing them to see the long histories of connections and interactions that have shaped all human communities for millennia. To do this, the authors wrote a story around the dual themes of traditions and encounters to highlight the many different religions and customs embraced by the world's peoples while also exploring the encounters with other cultures that brought about inevitable change.

It is the interaction of these traditions and encounters that continues to provide the key to making sense of our past. Human communities furthered themselves not by remaining isolated, but by interacting with others and exploring the benefits and risks of reaching out. The vitality of history—and its interpretation—lies in understanding the nature of individual cultural traditions and the scope of encounters that punctuated every significant event in human history.

### For the AP World History: Modern Classroom

Developed exclusively for the AP classroom, the *Traditions & Encounters: A Global Perspective on the Past,* 7th Edition, Student Edition Part and Chapter structure aligns with the chronological periods in the AP World History: Modern framework. Additionally, the program comprehensively incorporates AP Historical Thinking Skills and Reasoning Processes, which are central to the study and understanding of world history. These skills and processes are embedded in every chapter through features that utilize historical primary and secondary sources, historical analysis, and historical argumentation. AP style exam practice, at both the chapter and unit levels, and a complete practice exam help students prepare for the AP World History: Modern Exam.

An array of valuable resources developed specifically to support teaching and learning in the context of the AP World History: Modern course framework are integrated throughout the print and digital courses. The Student Edition features include:

- 12 Sources from the Past features throughout the course
- 4 Connecting the Sources features throughout the course
- 95 Interpreting Images features throughout the course
- 26 AP style, 10-question exam practice covering content on the chapter level
- 4 AP style, 22-question exam practice covering content on the unit level
- Full AP Practice Exam structured to mirror the written AP World History: Modern Exam

The *Traditions & Encounters* Teacher Manual is constructed with the AP Curriculum Framework at the forefront and focuses on activities designed around Historical Thinking Skills and Reasoning Processes. Exam tips are paired with thoughtful activities to help students apply and retain effective strategies for success on the AP Exam.

### AP Test Prep

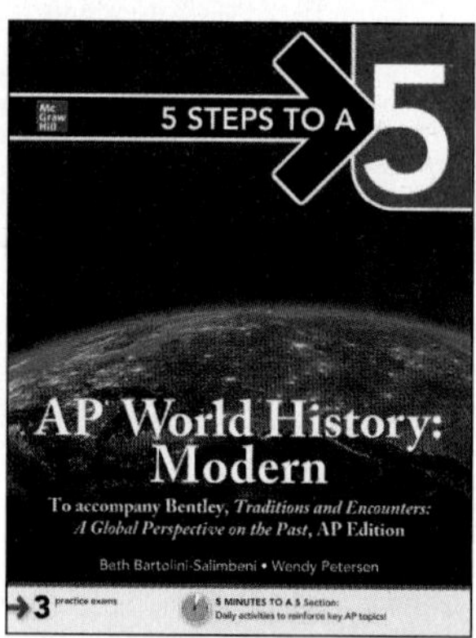


*5 Steps to a 5: World History: Modern* is available to accompany *Traditions & Encounters.* The test prep workbook guides students through an easy to follow, effective 5-step study plan to help them build the skills, knowledge, and test-taking confidence for AP Exam success. Expertly authored by veteran AP teachers and presented in lock-step alignment to the College Board framework, *5 Steps to a 5* provides support to reinforce the retention of concepts and skills covered in *Traditions & Encounters: A Global Perspective on the Past.*

# HOW TO USE YOUR *Traditions & Encounters* AP STUDENT EDITION

## Prelude: An Introduction to Modern World History

The Prelude sets the context for the World History: Modern course as students are invited to explore how ancient history has shaped the development of cultures and civilizations of the Modern era.

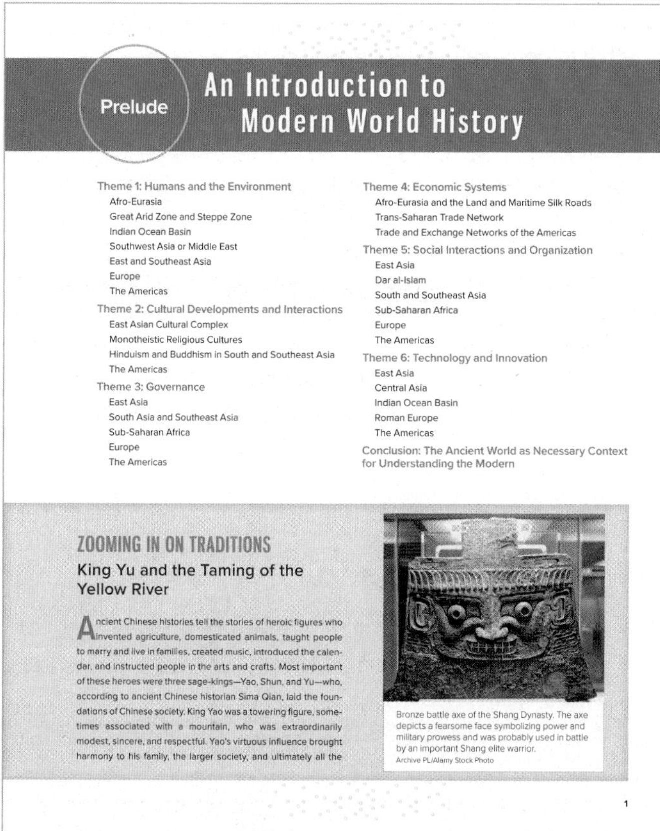

Prelude

An Introduction to Modern World History

Theme 1: Humans and the Environment
- Afro-Eurasia
- Great Arid Zone and Steppe Zone
- Indian Ocean Basin
- Southwest Asia or Middle East
- East and Southeast Asia
- Europe
- The Americas

Theme 2: Cultural Developments and Interactions
- East Asian Cultural Complex
- Monotheistic Religious Cultures
- Hinduism and Buddhism in South and Southeast Asia
- The Americas

Theme 3: Governance
- East Asia
- South Asia and Southeast Asia
- Sub-Saharan Africa
- Europe
- The Americas

Theme 4: Economic Systems
- Afro-Eurasia and the Land and Maritime Silk Roads
- Trans-Saharan Trade Network
- Trade and Exchange Networks of the Americas

Theme 5: Social Interactions and Organization
- East Asia
- Dar al-Islam
- South and Southeast Asia
- Sub-Saharan Africa
- Europe
- The Americas

Theme 6: Technology and Innovation
- East Asia
- Central Asia
- Indian Ocean Basin
- Roman Europe
- The Americas

Conclusion: The Ancient World as Necessary Context for Understanding the Modern

ZOOMING IN ON TRADITIONS

King Yu and the Taming of the Yellow River

Ancient Chinese histories tell the stories of heroic figures who invented agriculture, domesticated animals, taught people to marry and live in families, created music, introduced the calendar, and instructed people in the arts and crafts. Most important of these heroes were three sage-kings—Yao, Shun, and Yu—who, according to ancient Chinese historian Sima Qian, laid the foundations of Chinese society. King Yao was a towering figure, sometimes associated with a mountain, who was extraordinarily modest, sincere, and respectful. Yao's virtuous influence brought harmony to his family, the larger society, and ultimately all the

Bronze battle axe of the Shang Dynasty. The axe depicts a fearsome face symbolizing power and military prowess and was probably used in battle by an important Shang elite warrior.
Archive PL/Alamy Stock Photo

1

**Themes** Students are introduced to the 6 AP World History: Modern themes and guided through an overview of ancient history to provide a basis for understanding the world at 1200, the start date of the AP World History: Modern course. The same 6 themes reappear in the post-1200 coverage, connecting cultures, events, and movements throughout world history.

**Chronology** Beginning with the Prelude, each chapter includes a table of key events in World History. These provide chronological structure for the chapter and may be used as a study tool for understanding the sequence of major events.

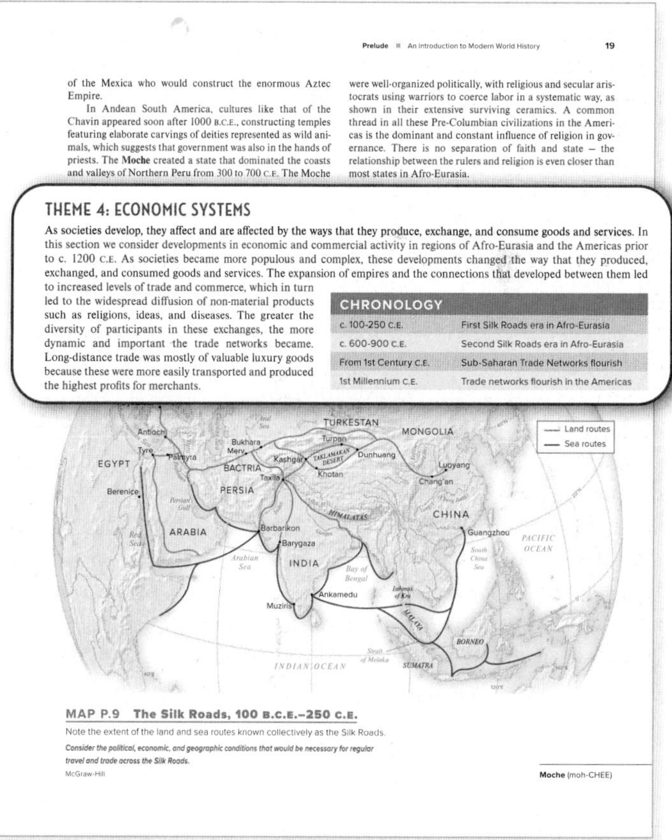

Prelude ■ An Introduction to Modern World History 19

of the Mexica who would construct the enormous Aztec Empire.

In Andean South America, cultures like that of the Chavin appeared soon after 1000 B.C.E., constructing temples featuring elaborate carvings of deities represented as wild animals, which suggests that government was also in the hands of priests. The **Moche** created a state that dominated the coasts and valleys of Northern Peru from 300 to 700 C.E. The Moche were well-organized politically, with religious and secular aristocrats using warriors to coerce labor in a systematic way, as shown in their extensive surviving ceramics. A common thread in all these Pre-Columbian civilizations in the Americas is the dominant and constant influence of religion in governance. There is no separation of faith and state – the relationship between the rulers and religion is even closer than most states in Afro-Eurasia.

THEME 4: ECONOMIC SYSTEMS

**As societies develop, they affect and are affected by the ways that they produce, exchange, and consume goods and services.** In this section we consider developments in economic and commercial activity in regions of Afro-Eurasia and the Americas prior to c. 1200 C.E. As societies became more populous and complex, these developments changed the way that they produced, exchanged, and consumed goods and services. The expansion of empires and the connections that developed between them led to increased levels of trade and commerce, which in turn led to the widespread diffusion of non-material products such as religions, ideas, and diseases. The greater the diversity of participants in these exchanges, the more dynamic and important the trade networks became. Long-distance trade was mostly of valuable luxury goods because these were more easily transported and produced the highest profits for merchants.

| CHRONOLOGY | |
|---|---|
| c. 100-250 C.E. | First Silk Roads era in Afro-Eurasia |
| c. 600-900 C.E. | Second Silk Roads era in Afro-Eurasia |
| From 1st Century C.E. | Sub-Saharan Trade Networks flourish |
| 1st Millennium C.E. | Trade networks flourish in the Americas |



MAP P.9 The Silk Roads, 100 B.C.E.–250 C.E.

Note the extent of the land and sea routes known collectively as the Silk Roads.

***Consider the political, economic, and geographic conditions that would be necessary for regular travel and trade across the Silk Roads.***

McGraw-Hill

**Moche** (moh-CHEE)

**Regional Maps** Maps from different regions and time periods situate history in time and place to help students develop geospatial awareness as it relates to cross-cultural contacts, economic systems, trade routes, and migrations.

# HOW TO USE YOUR
# *Traditions & Encounters* AP STUDENT EDITION

## Part Openers

The part openers make thematic connections among the chapters' content and help students see the big picture for each time period.

**Learning Objectives** establish the framework for the learning ahead by focusing on the chapters' key takeaways and setting clear expectations for what students should know and be able to demonstrate by the end of the Part. Overarching themes emphasize the connections between the chapters.

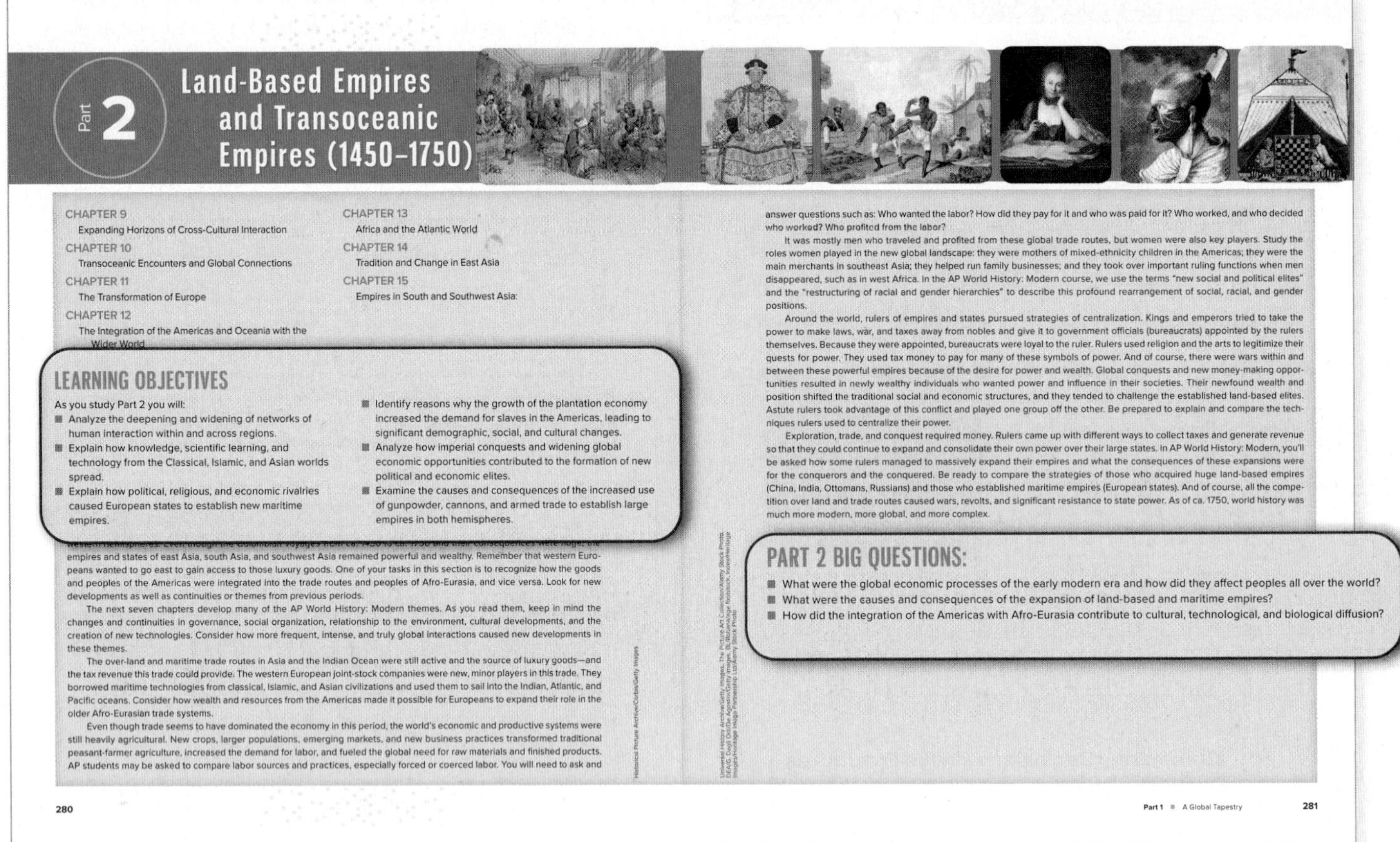

Part 2 Land-Based Empires and Transoceanic Empires (1450–1750)

CHAPTER 9 Expanding Horizons of Cross-Cultural Interaction
CHAPTER 10 Transoceanic Encounters and Global Connections
CHAPTER 11 The Transformation of Europe
CHAPTER 12 The Integration of the Americas and Oceania with the Wider World
CHAPTER 13 Africa and the Atlantic World
CHAPTER 14 Tradition and Change in East Asia
CHAPTER 15 Empires in South and Southwest Asia:

LEARNING OBJECTIVES

As you study Part 2 you will:

- Analyze the deepening and widening of networks of human interaction within and across regions.
- Explain how knowledge, scientific learning, and technology from the Classical, Islamic, and Asian worlds spread.
- Explain how political, religious, and economic rivalries caused European states to establish new maritime empires.
- Identify reasons why the growth of the plantation economy increased the demand for slaves in the Americas, leading to significant demographic, social, and cultural changes.
- Analyze how imperial conquests and widening global economic opportunities contributed to the formation of new political and economic elites.
- Examine the causes and consequences of the increased use of gunpowder, cannons, and armed trade to establish large empires in both hemispheres.

empires and states of east Asia, south Asia, and southwest Asia remained powerful and wealthy. Remember that western Europeans wanted to go east to gain access to those luxury goods. One of your tasks in this section is to recognize how the goods and peoples of the Americas were integrated into the trade routes and peoples of Afro-Eurasia, and vice versa. Look for new developments as well as continuities or themes from previous periods.

The next seven chapters develop many of the AP World History: Modern themes. As you read them, keep in mind the changes and continuities in governance, social organization, relationship to the environment, cultural developments, and the creation of new technologies. Consider how more frequent, intense, and truly global interactions caused new developments in these themes.

The over-land and maritime trade routes in Asia and the Indian Ocean were still active and the source of luxury goods—and the tax revenue this trade could provide. The western European joint-stock companies were new, minor players in this trade. They borrowed maritime technologies from classical, Islamic, and Asian civilizations and used them to sail into the Indian, Atlantic, and Pacific oceans. Consider how wealth and resources from the Americas made it possible for Europeans to expand their role in the older Afro-Eurasian trade systems.

Even though trade seems to have dominated the economy in this period, the world's economic and productive systems were still heavily agricultural. New crops, larger populations, emerging markets, and new business practices transformed traditional peasant-farmer agriculture, increased the demand for labor, and fueled the global need for raw materials and finished products. AP students may be asked to compare labor sources and practices, especially forced or coerced labor. You will need to ask and answer questions such as: Who wanted the labor? How did they pay for it and who was paid for it? Who worked, and who decided who worked? Who profited from the labor?

It was mostly men who traveled and profited from these global trade routes, but women were also key players. Study the roles women played in the new global landscape: they were mothers of mixed-ethnicity children in the Americas; they were the main merchants in southeast Asia; they helped run family businesses; and they took over important ruling functions when men disappeared, such as in west Africa. In the AP World History: Modern course, we use the terms "new social and political elites" and the "restructuring of racial and gender hierarchies" to describe this profound rearrangement of social, racial, and gender positions.

Around the world, rulers of empires and states pursued strategies of centralization. Kings and emperors tried to take the power to make laws, war, and taxes away from nobles and give it to government officials (bureaucrats) appointed by the rulers themselves. Because they were appointed, bureaucrats were loyal to the ruler. Rulers used religion and the arts to legitimize their quests for power. They used tax money to pay for many of these symbols of power. And of course, there were wars within and between these powerful empires because of the desire for power and wealth. Global conquests and new money-making opportunities resulted in newly wealthy individuals who wanted power and influence in their societies. Their newfound wealth and position shifted the traditional social and economic structures, and they tended to challenge the established land-based elites. Astute rulers took advantage of this conflict and played one group off the other. Be prepared to explain and compare the techniques rulers used to centralize their power.

Exploration, trade, and conquest required money. Rulers came up with different ways to collect taxes and generate revenue so that they could continue to expand and consolidate their own power over their large states. In AP World History: Modern, you'll be asked how some rulers managed to massively expand their empires and what the consequences of these expansions were for the conquerors and the conquered. Be ready to compare the strategies of those who acquired huge land-based empires (China, India, Ottomans, Russians) and those who established maritime empires (European states). And of course, all the competition over land and trade routes caused wars, revolts, and significant resistance to state power. As of ca. 1750, world history was much more modern, more global, and more complex.

PART 2 BIG QUESTIONS:

- What were the global economic processes of the early modern era and how did they affect peoples all over the world?
- What were the causes and consequences of the expansion of land-based and maritime empires?
- How did the integration of the Americas with Afro-Eurasia contribute to cultural, technological, and biological diffusion?

Historical Picture Archive/Corbis/Getty Images

280

Part 1 ■ A Global Tapestry 281

**Part Opening Narrative** provides an overview of the time period and major themes in the chapters to make connections among historical events, people, and places.

**Big Questions** guide students as they study historical events, people, and places within thematic contexts. Students should keep these questions in mind as they progress through the Part material, helping them to identify patterns throughout world history. Students should revisit the Big Questions at the end of each Part.

# HOW TO USE YOUR
# *Traditions & Encounters* AP STUDENT EDITION

## Chapter Openers

Engaging historical stories about individuals and events from world regions and time periods brings history to life. This followed by an overview of AP Historical Developments, Reasoning Processes, and Historical Thinking Skills to prepare students to learn historical content and skills.

The **Chapter Focus** lists key developments during the period covered in the chapter to give student a preview of the key content and concepts.

The Exploration of the World's Oceans
- The Technology of Exploration
- Motives for Exploration
- European Voyages of Exploration: From the Mediterranean to the Atlantic
- European Voyages of Exploration: From the Atlantic to the Pacific

Ecological Exchanges
- The Columbian Exchange
- The Origins of Global Trade

Trade and Conflict in Early Modern Asia
- Trading-Post Empires
- European Conquests in Southeast Asia
- Foundations of the Russian Empire in Asia
- Commercial Rivalries and the Seven Years' War

ZOOMING IN ON ENCOUNTERS

Vasco da Gama's Search for Spices

On 8 July 1497 the Portuguese mariner **Vasco da Gama** led a small fleet of four armed merchant vessels with 170 crewmen out of the harbor at Lisbon. His destination was India, which he planned to reach by sailing around the continent of Africa and through the Indian Ocean, and his goal was to enter the highly lucrative trade in spices dominated in Europe by the merchants of Venice. He carried letters of introduction from the king of Portugal as well as cargoes of gold, pearls, wool textiles, bronzeware, iron tools, and other goods that he hoped to exchange for spices in India.

Before there would be an opportunity to trade, however, da Gama and his crew had a prolonged voyage through two oceans. They sailed south from Portugal to the Cape Verde Islands off the west coast of Africa, where they took on water and fresh provisions. On 3 August they headed south into the Atlantic Ocean to take advantage of the prevailing winds. For the next ninety-five days, the fleet saw no land as it sailed through some six thousand nautical miles of open ocean. By October, da Gama came across westerly winds in the southern Atlantic, which helped propel him around the Cape of Good Hope and into the Indian Ocean. The fleet slowly worked its

Vasco da Gama's flagship on the journey to India in 1497, the *San Rafael*.
Photo Researchers/Science History Images/Alamy Stock Photo

**Vasco da Gama** (VAHS-koh duh GAHM-uh)

313

way up the east coast of Africa, engaging in hostilities with local authorities at Mozambique and Mombasa, as far as Malindi, where da Gama secured the services of an Indian Muslim pilot to guide his ships across the Arabian Sea. On 20 May 1498—more than ten months after its departure from Lisbon—the fleet anchored at Calicut in southern India.

In India the Portuguese fleet encountered a wealthy, cosmopolitan society. Upon their arrival local authorities in Calicut dispatched a pair of Tunisian merchants who spoke Spanish and Italian to serve as translators for the newly arrived party. The markets of Calicut offered not only pepper, ginger, cinnamon, and other spices sought so eagerly by da Gama, but also rubies, emeralds, gold jewelry, and fine cotton textiles. But apart from gold and some striped cloth, the merchants at Calicut thought the goods that da Gama had brought to trade were worthless and showed no interest in them. Nevertheless, da Gama managed to exchange gold for a cargo of pepper and cinnamon that turned a handsome profit when the fleet returned to Portugal in August 1499. Da Gama's expedition opened the door to direct maritime trade between European and Asian peoples and helped to establish permanent links between the world's various regions.

CHAPTER FOCUS

- Globalization begins in 1492.
- Maritime technologies from Asia and *Dar al-Islam* enabled western European exploration and increasing integration.
- Portuguese, Dutch, English, and French explorers sailed around Africa and into the Indian Ocean basin, setting up coastal trading posts financed by joint-stock companies.
- Columbus sailed west to reach the "East Indies," and ended up in the Caribbean instead. This new connection had massive environmental and demographic effects—the first *global* exchange of people, animals, plants, and diseases, known as the Columbian Exchange.
- Magellan, first to circumnavigate the global, claimed all "unknown" lands for the Spanish King Philip II, including the newly named Philippine Islands, which gave Spanish merchants a critical base to trade with the Chinese.
- Pay particular attention to how historical narratives shifted. What is "known" and "unknown," and whose knowledge takes precedence? How does that affect our historical understanding even today?

Historical Developments

- Knowledge, scientific learning, and technology from the Classical, Islamic, and Asian worlds spread, facilitating European technological developments and innovation.
- The developments included the production of new tools, innovations in ship designs, and an improved understanding of regional wind and currents patterns—all of which made transoceanic travel and trade possible.
- Portuguese development of maritime technology and navigational skills led to increased travel to and trade with Africa and Asia and resulted in the construction of a global trading-post empire.
- Northern Atlantic crossings were undertaken under English, French, and Dutch sponsorship, often with the goal of finding alternative sailing routes to Asia.
- The new connections between the Eastern and Western Hemispheres resulted in the exchange of new plants, animals, and diseases, known as the Columbian Exchange.
- Populations in Afro-Eurasia benefited nutritionally from the increased diversity of American food crops.
- Empires achieved increased scope and influence around the world, shaping and being shaped by the diverse populations they incorporated.

Reasoning Processes

- **Developments and Processes** Explain the Columbian Exchange and its consequences in the Americas and Afro-Eurasia.
- **Source Claims and Evidence** Identify the evidence used to support the claim that the voyages of Christopher Columbus and Vasco da Gama were motivated by commerce.
- **Contextualization** Identify the historical context of the Seven Years' War.
- **Making Connections** Identify patterns among or connections between the Spanish, English, Dutch, Portuguese, and Russian empires in Asia.
- **Argumentation** Make a historically defensible claim that explains the motives of Spanish and Portuguese voyages of exploration.

Historical Thinking Skills

- **Causation** Describe the causes and effects of the Columbian Exchange.
- **Continuity and Change** Explain patterns of continuity and change in European economic systems from the fifteenth to the eighteenth century.

314

**Zooming in On Traditions** or **Zooming in On Encounters** features open each chapter with a historical vignette profiling a person, place, or event that sets up the major themes of the chapter. The stories represent diverse points of view.

**Historical Developments** focuses on important themes and patterns, tying the chapter content into the broader focus of each Chapter and Part.

**Historical Thinking Skills** and **Reasoning Processes** contextualize the chapter topics to help students evaluate and analyze historical developments and explain historical relationships and situations.

# HOW TO USE YOUR *Traditions & Encounters* AP STUDENT EDITION

## Hallmark Features to Support AP Success

The 7th edition of *Traditions & Encounters: A Global Perspective on the Past* fully aligns with the AP World History: Modern Framework and supports mastery of knowledge and skills students require for success in the course and on the AP Exam. The narrative is brought to life through rich visuals, images, graphics, and accessible features that bring discrete focus to the most critical content and concepts of the AP course.

## Source Analysis Skills

Students analyze text and visual primary sources from diverse viewpoints and time periods, think about about silenced historical voices, and synthesize historical material to make historical arguments to demonstrate an understanding of the complexity of world history.

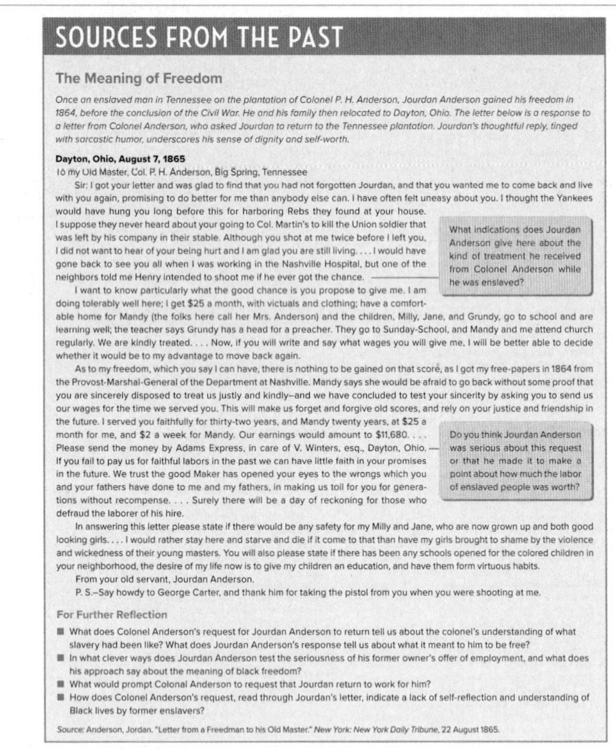

SOURCES FROM THE PAST

The Meaning of Freedom

*Once an enslaved man in Tennessee on the plantation of Colonel P. H. Anderson, Jourdan Anderson gained his freedom in 1864, before the conclusion of the Civil War. He and his family then relocated to Dayton, Ohio. The letter below is a response to a letter from Colonel Anderson, who asked Jourdan to return to the Tennessee plantation. Jourdan's thoughtful reply, tinged with sarcastic humor, underscores his sense of dignity and self-worth.*

**Dayton, Ohio, August 7, 1865**

To my Old Master, Col. P. H. Anderson, Big Spring, Tennessee

Sir: I got your letter and was glad to find that you had not forgotten Jourdan, and that you wanted me to come back and live with you again, promising to do better for me than anybody else can. I have often felt uneasy about you. I thought the Yankees would have hung you long before this for harboring Rebs they found at your house. I suppose they never heard about your going to Col. Martin's to kill the Union soldier that was left by his company in their stable. Although you shot at me twice before I left you, I did not want to hear of your being hurt and I am glad you are still living. . . . I would have gone back to see you all when I was working in the Nashville Hospital, but one of the neighbors told me Henry intended to shoot me if he ever got the chance.

What indications does Jourdan Anderson give here about the kind of treatment he received from Colonel Anderson while he was enslaved?

I want to know particularly what the good chance is you propose to give me. I am doing tolerably well here; I get $25 a month, with victuals and clothing; have a comfortable home for Mandy (the folks here call her Mrs. Anderson) and the children, Milly, Jane, and Grundy, go to school and are learning well; the teacher says Grundy has a head for a preacher. They go to Sunday-School, and Mandy and me attend church regularly. We are kindly treated. . . . Now, if you will write and say what wages you will give me, I will be better able to decide whether it would be to my advantage to move back again.

As to my freedom, which you say I can have, there is nothing to be gained on that score, as I got my free-papers in 1864 from the Provost-Marshal-General of the Department at Nashville. Mandy says she would be afraid to go back without some proof that you are sincerely disposed to treat us justly and kindly–and we have concluded to test your sincerity by asking you to send us our wages for the time we served you. This will make us forget and forgive old scores, and rely on your justice and friendship in the future. I served you faithfully for thirty-two years, and Mandy twenty years, at $25 a month for me, and $2 a week for Mandy. Our earnings would amount to $11,680. . . . Please send the money by Adams Express, in care of V. Winters, esq., Dayton, Ohio. If you fail to pay us for faithful labors in the past we can have little faith in your promises in the future. We trust the good Maker has opened your eyes to the wrongs which you and your fathers have done to me and my fathers, in making us toil for you for generations without recompense. . . . Surely there will be a day of reckoning for those who defraud the laborer of his hire.

Do you think Jourdan Anderson was serious about this request or that he made it to make a point about how much the labor of enslaved people was worth?

In answering this letter please state if there would be any safety for my Milly and Jane, who are now grown up and both good looking girls. . . . I would rather stay here and starve and die if it come to that than have my girls brought to shame by the violence and wickedness of their young masters. You will also please state if there has been any schools opened for the colored children in your neighborhood, the desire of my life now is to give my children an education, and have them form virtuous habits.

From your old servant, Jourdan Anderson.

P. S.–Say howdy to George Carter, and thank him for taking the pistol from you when you were shooting at me.

For Further Reflection

- What does Colonel Anderson's request for Jourdan Anderson to return tell us about the colonel's understanding of what slavery had been like? What does Jourdan Anderson's response tell us about what it meant to him to be free?
- In what clever ways does Jourdan Anderson test the seriousness of his former owner's offer of employment, and what does his approach say about the meaning of black freedom?
- What would prompt Colonal Anderson to request that Jourdan return to work for him?
- How does Colonel Anderson's request, read through Jourdan's letter, indicate a lack of self-reflection and understanding of Black lives by former enslavers?

*Source:* Anderson, Jordan. "Letter from a Freedman to his Old Master." *New York: New York Daily Tribune*, 22 August 1865.

**SOURCES FROM THE PAST** features invite students to dive deep into primary source documents that illuminate historical figures, events, and places. Annotations support students in developing the skills to effectively analyze the sources and critical thinking questions present opportunities to apply and hone their skills.

A new feature in the 7th edition, **WHAT'S LEFT OUT,** highlights neglected or silenced historical voices, challenging students to think about multiple perspectives in historical narratives and how our understanding of history can evolve to reveal new interpretations.

**What's Left Out?**

In textbook overviews such as this, women in the empires of south and southwest Asia tend to appear only briefly, usually in the context of imperial harems. There is a reason for this: Extensive records were kept about (and sometimes by) the elite women who inhabited these harems. But it would be a mistake to imagine that the lives of most women in the Ottoman, Mughal, and Safavid empires were similar to the lives of women in imperial harems. If we take the Ottoman Empire during the seventeenth century as an example, we would see that only a tiny proportion of Ottoman women lived in the secluded and isolated conditions of harems. Instead, Ottoman women were visible in multiple contexts, though their visibility depended upon their social class and geographical location. Elite women, as was the case in many parts of the world, were more constrained in their mobility than those from laboring classes but nevertheless could be seen moving through towns and cities with their bodies covered. Women of the farming and agricultural classes, in contrast, were integral to family labor and were visible in the fields driving horses and threshing grain. In cities and large towns, laboring women could be seen selling crafts on the streets. And in both rural and urban areas, slave women were constantly visible in public while they performed a wide variety of tasks for their owners. In the realm of law, Ottoman women were highly visible in the courts, where they frequently brought suits against others. Additionally, Ottoman law allowed women to own property in their own names and to dispose of it as they pleased. Thus, while it is important to remember that Ottoman women were not considered equal to men (such a status did not exist anywhere in the world at this time), they also were not the invisible, secluded, highly controlled creatures that images of the harem tend to suggest.

*Source:* Ebru Boyar and Kate Fleet, eds. *Ottoman Women in Public Space* (Leiden: Brill, 2016).

**Thinking Critically About Sources**

1. The passage emphasizes that Ottoman, Mughal, and Safavid women were "highly visible." What examples are provided?
2. Is it only one class of women who were visible in these societies?
3. What were various roles these women performed, outside the home?

**Thinking Critically About Sources** questions encourage students to critically engage with not only what sources historians use, but also how historians' point of view affects how the sources are used.

## Connecting the Sources

These features guide students through an analysis of multiple primary sources in historical contexts and offer a rich diversity of perspectives. They provide analysis, comparison, and synthesis skills practice necessary for successfully answering the Document-based question on the AP Exam.

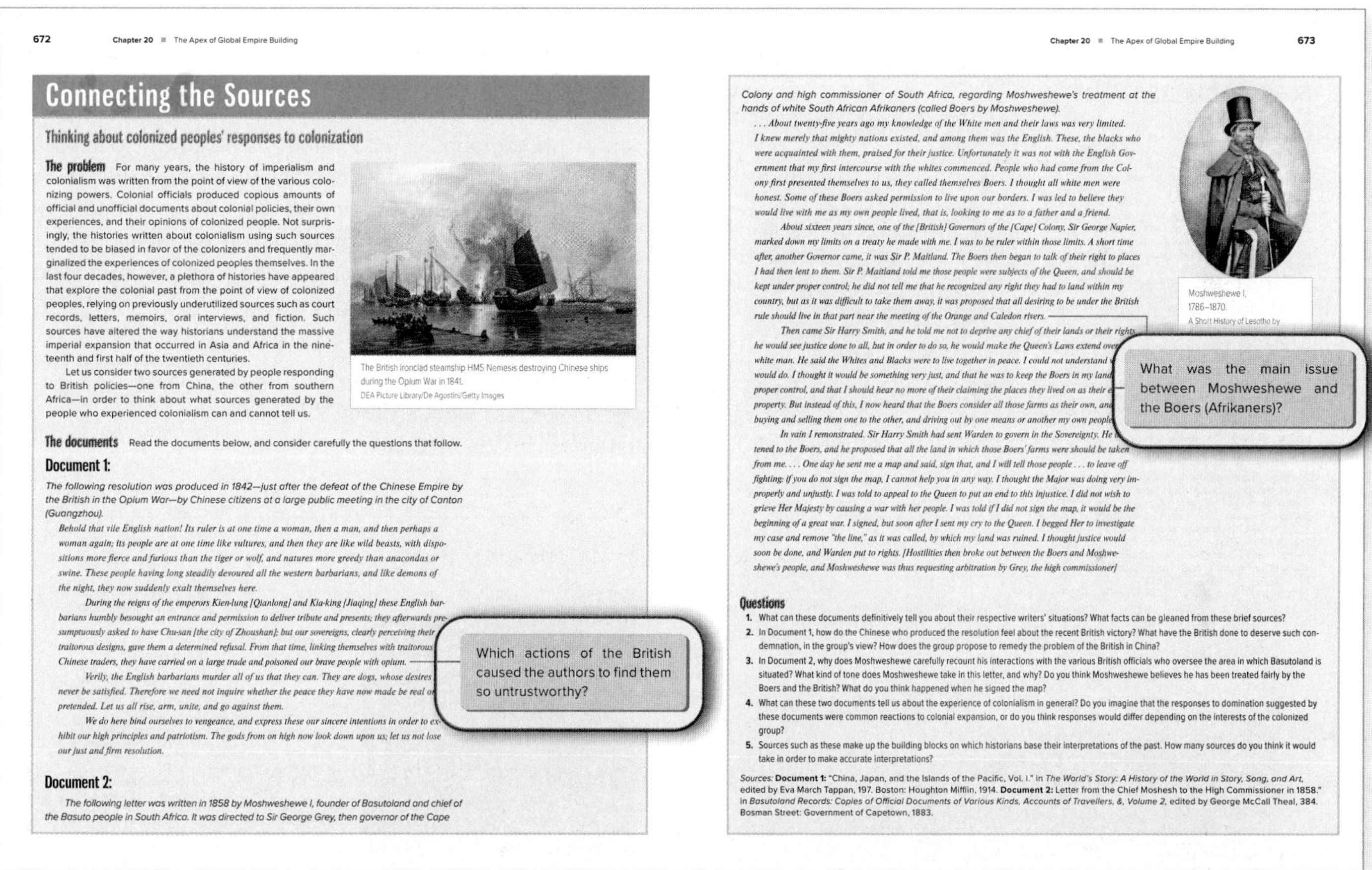

672 Chapter 20 ■ The Apex of Global Empire Building

# Connecting the Sources

## Thinking about colonized peoples' responses to colonization

**The problem** For many years, the history of imperialism and colonialism was written from the point of view of the various colonizing powers. Colonial officials produced copious amounts of official and unofficial documents about colonial policies, their own experiences, and their opinions of colonized people. Not surprisingly, the histories written about colonialism using such sources tended to be biased in favor of the colonizers and frequently marginalized the experiences of colonized peoples themselves. In the last four decades, however, a plethora of histories have appeared that explore the colonial past from the point of view of colonized peoples, relying on previously underutilized sources such as court records, letters, memoirs, oral interviews, and fiction. Such sources have altered the way historians understand the massive imperial expansion that occurred in Asia and Africa in the nineteenth and first half of the twentieth centuries.

Let us consider two sources generated by people responding to British policies—one from China, the other from southern Africa—in order to think about what sources generated by the people who experienced colonialism can and cannot tell us.

The British ironclad steamship HMS Nemesis destroying Chinese ships during the Opium War in 1841.
DEA Picture Library/De Agostini/Getty Images

**The documents** Read the documents below, and consider carefully the questions that follow.

### Document 1:

*The following resolution was produced in 1842—just after the defeat of the Chinese Empire by the British in the Opium War—by Chinese citizens at a large public meeting in the city of Canton (Guangzhou).*

*Behold that vile English nation! Its ruler is at one time a woman, then a man, and then perhaps a woman again; its people are at one time like vultures, and then they are like wild beasts, with dispositions more fierce and furious than the tiger or wolf, and natures more greedy than anacondas or swine. These people having long steadily devoured all the western barbarians, and like demons of the night, they now suddenly exalt themselves here.*

*During the reigns of the emperors Kien-lung [Qianlong] and Kia-king [Jiaqing] these English barbarians humbly besought an entrance and permission to deliver tribute and presents; they afterwards presumptuously asked to have Chu-san [the city of Zhoushan]; but our sovereigns, clearly perceiving their traitorous designs, gave them a determined refusal. From that time, linking themselves with traitorous Chinese traders, they have carried on a large trade and poisoned our brave people with opium.*

*Verily, the English barbarians murder all of us that they can. They are dogs, whose desires never be satisfied. Therefore we need not inquire whether the peace they have now made be real or pretended. Let us all rise, arm, unite, and go against them.*

*We do here bind ourselves to vengeance, and express these our sincere intentions in order to exhibit our high principles and patriotism. The gods from on high now look down upon us; let us not lose our just and firm resolution.*

Which actions of the British caused the authors to find them so untrustworthy?

### Document 2:

*The following letter was written in 1858 by Moshweshewe I, founder of Basutoland and chief of the Basuto people in South Africa. It was directed to Sir George Grey, then governor of the Cape*

Chapter 20 ■ The Apex of Global Empire Building 673

*Colony and high commissioner of South Africa, regarding Moshweshewe's treatment at the hands of white South African Afrikaners (called Boers by Moshweshewe).*

*. . . About twenty-five years ago my knowledge of the White men and their laws was very limited. I knew merely that mighty nations existed, and among them was the English. These, the blacks who were acquainted with them, praised for their justice. Unfortunately it was not with the English Government that my first intercourse with the whites commenced. People who had come from the Colony first presented themselves to us, they called themselves Boers. I thought all white men were honest. Some of these Boers asked permission to live upon our borders. I was led to believe they would live with me as my own people lived, that is, looking to me as to a father and a friend.*

*About sixteen years since, one of the [British] Governors of the [Cape] Colony, Sir George Napier, marked down my limits on a treaty he made with me. I was to be ruler within those limits. A short time after, another Governor came, it was Sir P. Maitland. The Boers then began to talk of their right to places I had then lent to them. Sir P. Maitland told me those people were subjects of the Queen, and should be kept under proper control; he did not tell me that he recognized any right they had to land within my country, but as it was difficult to take them away, it was proposed that all desiring to be under the British rule should live in that part near the meeting of the Orange and Caledon rivers.*

*Then came Sir Harry Smith, and he told me not to deprive any chief of their lands or their rights, he would see justice done to all, but in order to do so, he would make the Queen's Laws extend over white man. He said the Whites and Blacks were to live together in peace. I could not understand would do. I thought it would be something very just, and that he was to keep the Boers in my land proper control, and that I should hear no more of their claiming the places they lived on as their property. But instead of this, I now heard that the Boers consider all those farms as their own, and buying and selling them one to the other, and driving out by one means or another my own people*

*In vain I remonstrated. Sir Harry Smith had sent Warden to govern in the Sovereignty. He tened to the Boers, and he proposed that all the land in which those Boers' farms were should be taken from me. . . . One day he sent me a map and said, sign that, and I will tell those people . . . to leave off fighting: if you do not sign the map, I cannot help you in any way. I thought the Major was doing very improperly and unjustly. I was told to appeal to the Queen to put an end to this injustice. I did not wish to grieve Her Majesty by causing a war with her people. I was told if I did not sign the map, it would be the beginning of a great war. I signed, but soon after I sent my cry to the Queen. I begged Her to investigate my case and remove "the line," as it was called, by which my land was ruined. I thought justice would soon be done, and Warden put to rights. [Hostilities then broke out between the Boers and Moshweshewe's people, and Moshweshewe was thus requesting arbitration by Grey, the high commissioner]*

Moshweshewe I,
1786–1870.
A Short History of Lesotho by

What was the main issue between Moshweshewe and the Boers (Afrikaners)?

**Questions**

1. What can these documents definitively tell you about their respective writers' situations? What facts can be gleaned from these brief sources?
2. In Document 1, how do the Chinese who produced the resolution feel about the recent British victory? What have the British done to deserve such condemnation, in the group's view? How does the group propose to remedy the problem of the British in China?
3. In Document 2, why does Moshweshewe carefully recount his interactions with the various British officials who oversee the area in which Basutoland is situated? What kind of tone does Moshweshewe take in this letter, and why? Do you think Moshweshewe believes he has been treated fairly by the Boers and the British? What do you think happened when he signed the map?
4. What can these two documents tell us about the experience of colonialism in general? Do you imagine that the responses to domination suggested by these documents were common reactions to colonial expansion, or do you think responses would differ depending on the interests of the colonized group?
5. Sources such as these make up the building blocks on which historians base their interpretations of the past. How many sources do you think it would take in order to make accurate interpretations?

*Sources:* **Document 1:** "China, Japan, and the Islands of the Pacific, Vol. I." in *The World's Story: A History of the World in Story, Song, and Art,* edited by Eva March Tappan, 197. Boston: Houghton Mifflin, 1914. **Document 2:** Letter from the Chief Moshesh to the High Commissioner in 1858." in *Basutoland Records: Copies of Official Documents of Various Kinds, Accounts of Travellers, &, Volume 2,* edited by George McCall Theal, 384. Bosman Street: Government of Capetown, 1883.

**Annotations** guide students to key ideas in the text to give them practice and models of how to ask questions, analyze sources in conversation with one another, and develop complex historical arguments.

**Questions** encourage a deep examination of each source individually and then provide multiple opportunities to synthesize source material to construct a historical argument and understand continuity and change in world history.

# HOW TO USE YOUR
# *Traditions & Encounters* AP STUDENT EDITION

## Interpreting Images

Art, artifacts, and historical photographs are historical sources that can be read and interpreted just like text sources. Students delve deep into historical images supported with extended captions and questions to guide their analysis.

Exclusive to the 7th AP edition, **INTERPRETING IMAGES** features help students understand that images, like texts, are a channel for communication and that art and photographs can be "read" as historical sources. This feature gives students multiple opportunities to move beyond identifying image sources and apply more sophisticated skills by providing explanations of why the source matters and connecting the source to an effective, nuanced argument.

Chapter 2 ■ The Expansive Realm of Islam 83

Nishapur, Bukhara, and Samarkand were long-established commercial centers, and they made it possible for Muslim merchants to trade over a revived Silk Roads network extending from China in the east to the Mediterranean in the west. Thus Muslim merchants were able to take advantage of the extensive road networks originally built during the ancient era by imperial authorities in India, Persia, and the Mediterranean basin. Umayyad and Abbasid rulers maintained the roads that they inherited because they provided splendid routes for military forces and administrative officials traveling through the *dar al-Islam*. But those same roads also made excellent highways for merchants as well as missionaries and pilgrims. Travel along the roads could be remarkably speedy and efficient. After the tenth century, for example, the Muslim rulers of Egypt regularly imported ice from the mountains of Syria to their palace in Cairo. Even during the summer months, they received five camel loads of ice weekly to cool their food and drink.

**Camels and Caravans** Overland trade traveled mostly by camel caravan. Although they can be difficult to manage, camels endure the rigors of desert travel much better than oxen, horses, or donkeys. Moreover, when fitted with a well-designed saddle, camels can carry heavy loads. During the early centuries C.E., the manufacture of camel saddles spread throughout Arabia, north Africa, southwest Asia, and central Asia, and camels became the favored beasts of burden in deserts and other dry regions. As camel transport became more common, the major cities of the Islamic world and central Asia built and maintained caravanserais—inns offering lodging for caravan merchants as well as food, water, and care for their animals.

**Maritime Trade** Meanwhile, innovations in nautical technology contributed to a steadily increasing volume of maritime trade in the Red Sea, Persian Gulf, Arabian Sea, and Indian Ocean. Arab and Persian mariners borrowed the compass from its Chinese inventors and used it to guide them on the high seas. From southeast Asian and Indian mariners, they borrowed the lateen sail, a triangular sail that increased a ship's maneuverability. From the Hellenistic Mediterranean

INTERPRETING IMAGES

A map produced in the eleventh century by the Arab geographer al-Idrisi shows the lands known and reported by Muslim merchants and travelers. Note that, in accordance with Muslim cartographic convention, this map places south at the top and north at the bottom.

**Analyze** *Why did Muslim cartographers place the south at the top of the map and the north at the bottom? How might this understanding affect the ways that Muslim thinkers perceived the world they traveled and lived in?*

World History Archive/Alamy Stock Photo

Practice analyzing **art** supports students' success working with visual stimuli on the AP Exam.

Chapter 18 ■ The Americas in the Age of Independence 595

INTERPRETING IMAGES

Italian migrants construct a railway in New York. Italians were just one of many migrant groups coming to the Americas in the nineteenth century, including Irish and Chinese.

**Analyze** *When you think about the impacts of new waves of immigration to the Americas, how do you connect these migrants to the histories of their countries of origin? What does a world history perspective offer to histories of migration? How might this context help us tell a more accurate story about the history of the United States?*

Michael Maslan/Corbis Historical/Getty Images

when officials of the Qing government permitted foreigners to seek indentured laborers in China and approved their migration to distant lands. Between 1852 and 1875 some two hundred thousand Chinese migrated to California alone. Some, like Fatt Hing Chin, negotiated their own passage and sought

Brazilian government paid Italian migrants to cross the Atlantic and work for coffee growers, who experienced a severe labor shortage after the abolition of slavery in 1888. Many Italian workers settled permanently in Latin America, especially Argentina, but some, popularly known as *golondrinas* ("swal-

Students Practice analyzing **historical photographs** like the ones they will encounter in the DBQ and with Multiple Choice questions on the AP Exam.

454 Chapter 14 ■ Tradition and Change in East Asia

INTERPRETING IMAGES

Portrait of Howqua (Wu Bingjian—1769–1843) in the early nineteenth century. His elegant clothing and surroundings suggest the great wealth of merchants in late imperial China.

**Analyze** *Compare this portrait with that of Emperor Kangxi on page 447. They were painted in the same century. How are they different? Who is the audience for each portrait and what are they trying to convey about the subject?*

IanDagnall Computing/Alamy Stock Photo

that manufacturing and commerce had become much more economically important than in ancient times.

entertainers, prostitutes, and other marginal groups such as the "beggars of Jiangsu" and the "boat people of Guangdong."

THE CONFUCIAN TRADITION AND NEW CULTURAL INFLUENCES

The Ming and Qing emperors looked to Chinese traditions for guidance in framing their cultural as well as their political and social policies. They provided generous support for Confucianism, particularly in the form of neo-Confucianism articulated by the twelfth-century scholar **Zhu Xi**, and they ensured that formal education in China revolved around Confucian thought and values. Yet the Confucian tradition was not the only cultural alternative in Ming and Qing China. Demographic and urban growth encouraged the emergence of a vibrant popular culture in Chinese cities, and European missionaries reintroduced Roman Catholic Christianity to China and introduced Chinese intellectuals to European science and technology as well.

**Neo-Confucianism and Pulp Fiction**

Imperial sponsorship of Chinese cultural traditions meant primarily support for the Confucian tradition, especially as systematized by the Song dynasty scholar Zhu Xi, the most prominent architect of neo-Confucianism. Zhu Xi combined the moral, ethical, and political values of Confucius with the logical rigor and speculative power of Buddhist philosophy. He emphasized the values of self-discipline, filial piety, and obedience to established rulers, all of which appealed to Ming and Qing emperors seeking to maintain stability in their vast realm. Cultural policies of the Ming and Qing dynasties made the neo-Confucian tradition the reigning ... from the fourteenth to the early twentieth

...ucation To promote Confucian values, the emperors supported educational programs at ...hey funded the Hanlin Academy, a research ...nfucian scholars in Beijing, and maintained ...schools throughout China where promising students could study for the civil service examinations. The exams themselves encouraged the cultivation of Confucian

**Analyze** questions walk students through the process of analyzing source images.

# HOW TO USE YOUR
# *Traditions & Encounters* AP STUDENT EDITION

## AP Exam Prep and Practice

End-of-chapter practice questions help students build mastery adn confidence for AP Exam success.

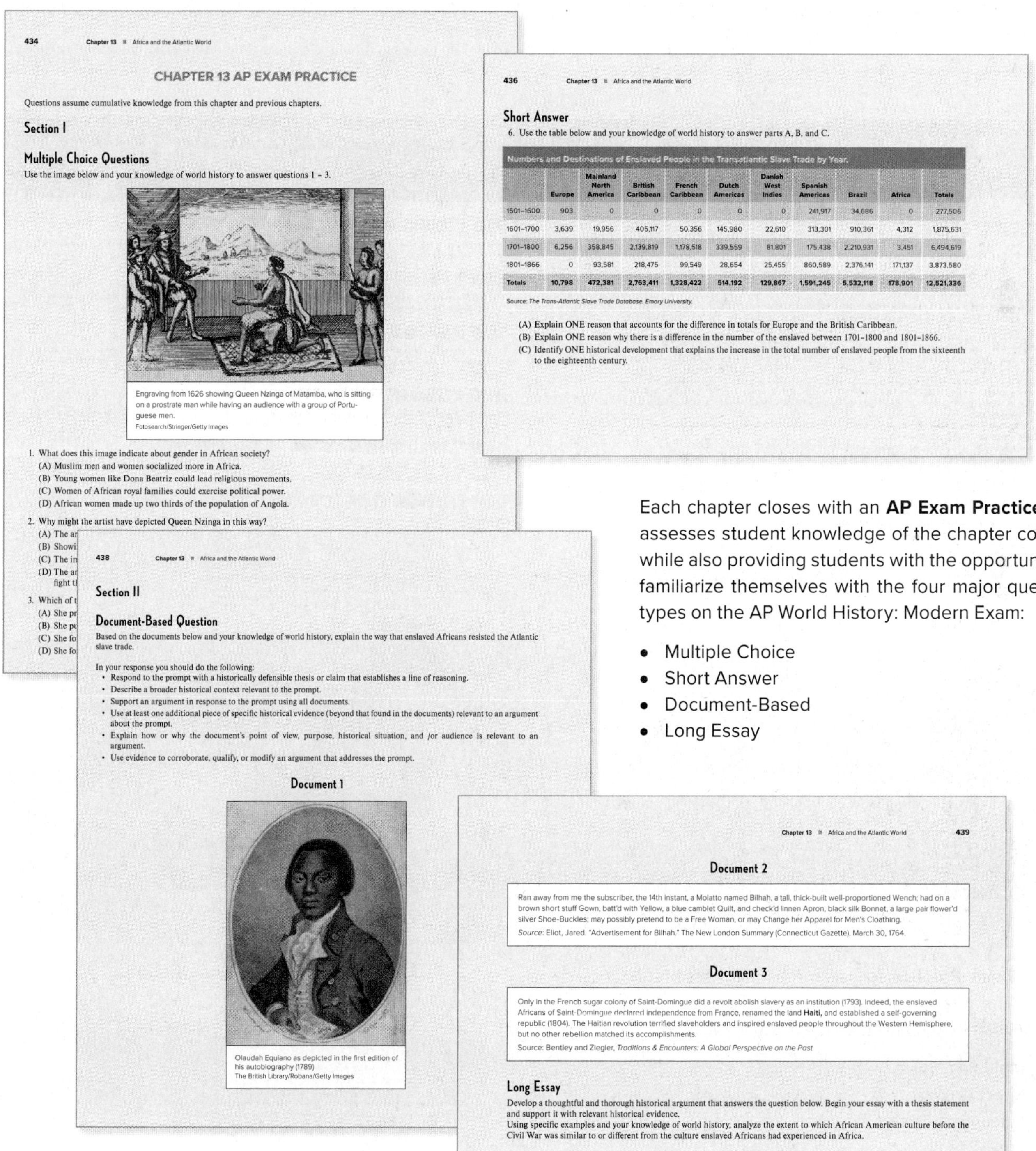

434 Chapter 13 ■ Africa and the Atlantic World

CHAPTER 13 AP EXAM PRACTICE

Questions assume cumulative knowledge from this chapter and previous chapters.

Section I

Multiple Choice Questions

Use the image below and your knowledge of world history to answer questions 1 - 3.

Engraving from 1626 showing Queen Nzinga of Matamba, who is sitting on a prostrate man while having an audience with a group of Portuguese men.
Fotosearch/Stringer/Getty Images

1. What does this image indicate about gender in African society?
   (A) Muslim men and women socialized more in Africa.
   (B) Young women like Dona Beatriz could lead religious movements.
   (C) Women of African royal families could exercise political power.
   (D) African women made up two thirds of the population of Angola.
2. Why might the artist have depicted Queen Nzinga in this way?
   (A) The ar
   (B) Showi
   (C) The in
   (D) The ar
   fight th
3. Which of t
   (A) She pr
   (B) She pu
   (C) She fo
   (D) She fo

436 Chapter 13 ■ Africa and the Atlantic World

Short Answer

6. Use the table below and your knowledge of world history to answer parts A, B, and C.

Numbers and Destinations of Enslaved People in the Transatlantic Slave Trade by Year.

| | Europe | Mainland North America | British Caribbean | French Caribbean | Dutch Americas | Danish West Indies | Spanish Americas | Brazil | Africa | Totals |
|---|---|---|---|---|---|---|---|---|---|---|
| 1501–1600 | 903 | 0 | 0 | 0 | 0 | 0 | 241,917 | 34,686 | 0 | 277,506 |
| 1601–1700 | 3,639 | 19,956 | 405,117 | 50,356 | 145,980 | 22,610 | 313,301 | 910,361 | 4,312 | 1,875,631 |
| 1701–1800 | 6,256 | 358,845 | 2,139,819 | 1,178,518 | 339,559 | 81,801 | 175,438 | 2,210,931 | 3,451 | 6,494,619 |
| 1801–1866 | 0 | 93,581 | 218,475 | 99,549 | 28,654 | 25,455 | 860,589 | 2,376,141 | 171,137 | 3,873,580 |
| **Totals** | **10,798** | **472,381** | **2,763,411** | **1,328,422** | **514,192** | **129,867** | **1,591,245** | **5,532,118** | **178,901** | **12,521,336** |

Source: *The Trans-Atlantic Slave Trade Database. Emory University.*

(A) Explain ONE reason that accounts for the difference in totals for Europe and the British Caribbean.
(B) Explain ONE reason why there is a difference in the number of the enslaved between 1701–1800 and 1801–1866.
(C) Identify ONE historical development that explains the increase in the total number of enslaved people from the sixteenth to the eighteenth century.

438 Chapter 13 ■ Africa and the Atlantic World

Section II

Document-Based Question

Based on the documents below and your knowledge of world history, explain the way that enslaved Africans resisted the Atlantic slave trade.

In your response you should do the following:
- Respond to the prompt with a historically defensible thesis or claim that establishes a line of reasoning.
- Describe a broader historical context relevant to the prompt.
- Support an argument in response to the prompt using all documents.
- Use at least one additional piece of specific historical evidence (beyond that found in the documents) relevant to an argument about the prompt.
- Explain how or why the document's point of view, purpose, historical situation, and /or audience is relevant to an argument.
- Use evidence to corroborate, qualify, or modify an argument that addresses the prompt.

Document 1

Olaudah Equiano as depicted in the first edition of his autobiography (1789)
The British Library/Robana/Getty Images

Chapter 13 ■ Africa and the Atlantic World 439

Document 2

Ran away from me the subscriber, the 14th instant, a Molatto named Bilhah, a tall, thick-built well-proportioned Wench; had on a brown short stuff Gown, batt'd with Yellow, a blue camblet Quilt, and check'd linnen Apron, black silk Bonnet, a large pair flower'd silver Shoe-Buckles; may possibly pretend to be a Free Woman, or may Change her Apparel for Men's Cloathing.

*Source*: Eliot, Jared. "Advertisement for Bilhah." The New London Summary (Connecticut Gazette), March 30, 1764.

Document 3

Only in the French sugar colony of Saint-Domingue did a revolt abolish slavery as an institution (1793). Indeed, the enslaved Africans of Saint-Domingue declared independence from France, renamed the land **Haiti,** and established a self-governing republic (1804). The Haitian revolution terrified slaveholders and inspired enslaved people throughout the Western Hemisphere, but no other rebellion matched its accomplishments.

Source: Bentley and Ziegler, *Traditions & Encounters: A Global Perspective on the Past*

Long Essay

Develop a thoughtful and thorough historical argument that answers the question below. Begin your essay with a thesis statement and support it with relevant historical evidence.
Using specific examples and your knowledge of world history, analyze the extent to which African American culture before the Civil War was similar to or different from the culture enslaved Africans had experienced in Africa.

Each chapter closes with an **AP Exam Practice** that assesses student knowledge of the chapter content while also providing students with the opportunity to familiarize themselves with the four major question types on the AP World History: Modern Exam:

- Multiple Choice
- Short Answer
- Document-Based
- Long Essay

# HOW TO USE YOUR
# *Traditions & Encounters* AP STUDENT EDITION

## Part Closers

Students are asked to reflect on the material from the preceding chapters in the larger context of each Part. By reframing the chapters within this broader context, they can think thematically and use the Reasoning Processes of Causation, Comparison, and Continuity and Change to re-examine the content as a whole.

Part 1 A Global Tapestry c. 1200–c. 1450

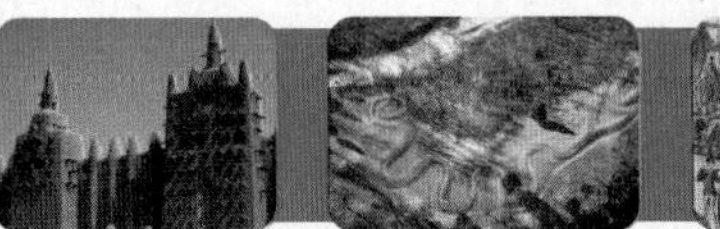

It should be clear from reading the preceding chapters that the reasons for and consequences of increasing trade, contact, and wealth are a critical part of understanding this era of world history. It's also important not to forget the people. As you reflect on these post-classical "Global Tapestry" chapters, think about what sort of people functioned in which roles:

- Who were the merchants, the workers, the bankers, the soldiers and sailors, the enslaved?
- Where did these people and their work "fit" into society?
- How was one's position on the social ladder determined?
- How did women fare in these postclassical societies?
- What was considered "women's work," and how much influence did women of different classes or castes have on "men's work"?
- Did newly introduced religious beliefs improve or suppress the influence of women in a society?

Think especially about the pastoralist peoples—the Mongols, the Bantu, the Arabs, and Berbers: their roles in trade, cultural exchange, and conquest will continue to impact the development of societies and the global system.

More written documents have survived from the postclassical era than from earlier periods, and those highlighted in AP World History tend be travelers' writings. Why? Because travelers in foreign lands commented on the people and their social practices, telling us how much or how little intercultural knowledge and understanding existed. When you think back on the travel accounts you read in Part 1, what kinds of things stood out to you? What did the writers notice about the societies they encountered? What elements are common between these accounts? In contrast, what differs between the accounts? What do those differences tell us about the cultures that produced these travelers?

Another significant pattern highlighted in this period—and critical to your understanding of AP World History and its themes—is the continuing importance of cities and their enormous growth.

- Why did they rise and fall? Did religious leaders in a region locate themselves in cities, and, if so, why?
- Who ruled the cities, and were the cities important because they were political centers (capitals), or commercial or religious centers?
- Who lived in the cities, and where did they come from? Were the cities centers of learning and the arts?

You will want to be able to explain the religious, commercial (trade), governmental, and cultural functions of at least two major cities in this period, as this will help you prepare for questions that might arise on the AP exam.

As you review what you have learned, consider how the AP World History themes were demonstrated through these chapters.

270

### THEME 1: HUMANS AND THE ENVIRONMENT (ENV)

The environment shapes human societies, and as populations grow and change, these populations in turn shape their environments. (This also includes geography. The history of India would be much different had there not been the Khyber Pass.)

### THEME 2: CULTURAL DEVELOPMENTS AND INTERACTIONS (CDI)

The development of ideas, beliefs, and religions illustrates how groups in society view themselves, and the interactions of societies and their beliefs often have political. social, and cultural implications.

### THEME 3: GOVERNANCE (GOV)

A variety of internal and external factors contribute to state formation, expansion, and decline. Governments maintain order through a variety of administrative institutions, policies, and procedures, and governments obtain, retain, and exercise power in different ways and for different purposes. (Pay attention to the reasons for the rise and fall of governments/dynasties/empires.)

### THEME 4: ECONOMIC SYSTEMS (ECN)

As societies develop, they affect and are affected by the ways that they produce, exchange, and consume goods and services. (The major focus of this theme before 1750 is going to be trade, which is a constant item on the AP exam.)

### THEME 5: SOCIAL INTERACTIONS AND ORGANIZATION (SIO)

The process by which societies group their members and the norms that govern the interactions between these groups and between individuals influence political, economic, and cultural institutions and organization.

### THEME 6: TECHNOLOGY AND INNOVATION (TEC)

Human adaptation and innovation have resulted in increased efficiency, comfort. and security, and technological advances have shaped human development and interactions with both intended and unintended consequences. (Quick definition: technology is anything that

**PART 3 AP EXAM PRACTICE**

Questions assume cumulative knowledge from this Part.

**Section I**

**Multiple Choice Questions**

Questions 1–3 have no stimulus.

1. Which of the following was NOT and environmental factor that contributed to industrialization?
   (A) Access to rivers and canals
   (B) Lack of humidity
   (C) Access to coal, iron, and timber
   (D) Agricultural productivity
2. What did Fukuzawa Yukichi do for Japan?
   (A) He traveled to the United States and wrote about constitutional government.
   (B) He organized the overthrow of the Tokugawa *bakufu*.
   (C) He wrote the slogan "Revere the emperor, expel the barbarians."
   (D) He built the Japanese railroad system.
3. The religious movement associated with the Enlightenment is known as
   (A) Transcendentalism
   (B) Stoicism
   (C) Deism
   (D) Dispensationalism

Using the map below and your knowledge of world history, answer questions 4–6.

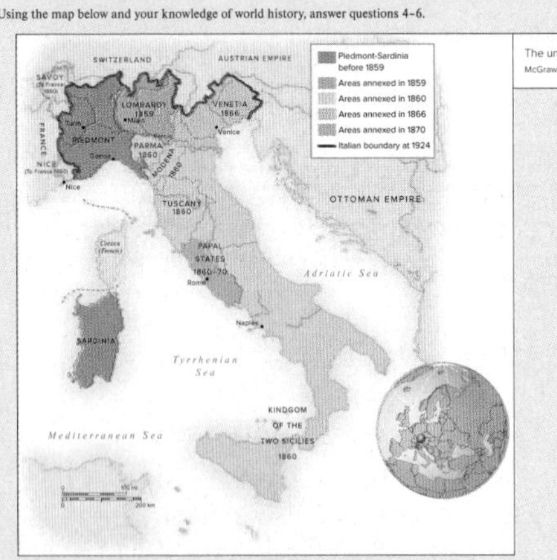


The unification of Italy
McGraw Hill

4. Why did the Congress of Vienna give northern Italy to Austria?
   (A) The Congress wanted to give Austria control of the mountain passes to Switzerland.
   (B) They planned to let Austria invade the whole Italian peninsula.
   (C) They wanted the German-speaking people of the Italian Alps to be ruled by a German-speaking state.
   (D) They wanted a strong, unified state near the French border to prevent further war.
5. What kind of nationalism was promoted by Giuseppe Mazzini and the Young Italy movement?
   (A) Political nationalism
   (B) Imperial nationalism
   (C) Cultural nationalism
   (D) Socialist nationalism
6. What did Camillo di Cavour contribute to the unification of Italy?
   (A) He made and alliance with France to expel the Spanish from Italy.
   (B) He made an alliance with France to expel the Austrians from Italy.
   (C) He persuaded to British parliament to support Giuseppe Garibaldi's revolutionaries.
   (D) He led an army of one thousand soldiers wearing red shirts to liberate Sicily.

685

**AP Exam Practice** for each Part provides students with the opportunity to use content-based excerpts and images to answer AP Exam style questions:

- Multiple Choice
- Short Answer
- Document-Based
- Long Essay

# HOW TO USE YOUR

# *Traditions & Encounters* AP STUDENT EDITION

## Full Document-Based Question with Each Part Closer

Students apply what they learned in each Part with a culminating DBQ offering 7 documents with various perspectives on a historical development or process.

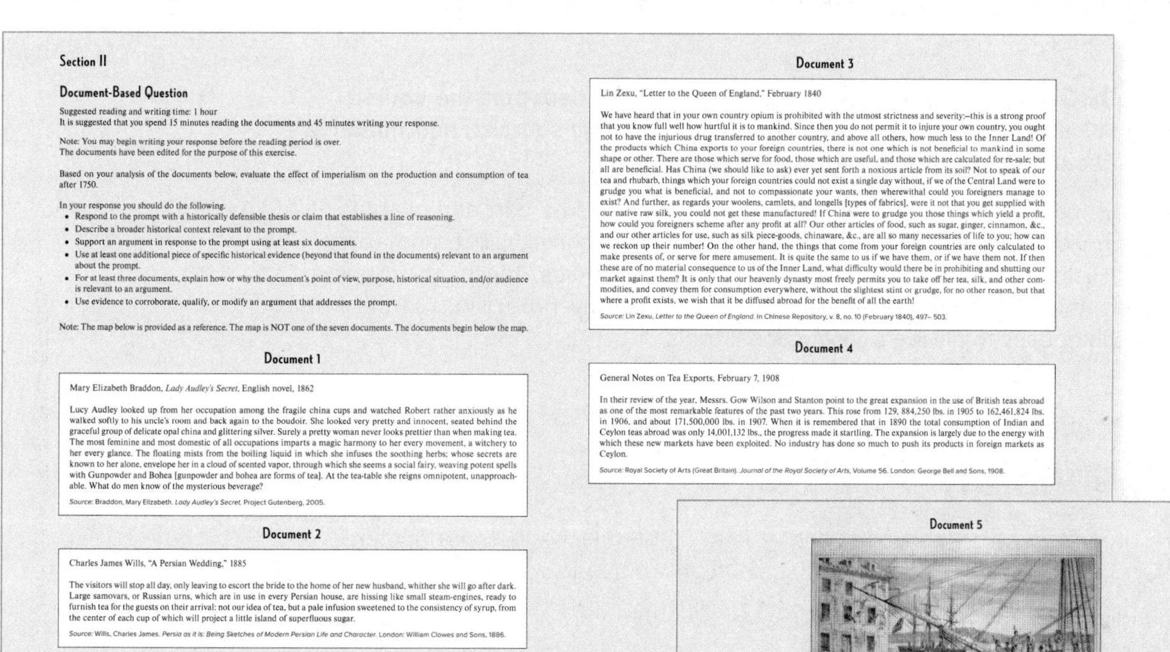

**Section II**

**Document-Based Question**

Suggested reading and writing time: 1 hour
It is suggested that you spend 15 minutes reading the documents and 45 minutes writing your response.

Note: You may begin writing your response before the reading period is over.
The documents have been edited for the purpose of this exercise.

Based on your analysis of the documents below, evaluate the effect of imperialism on the production and consumption of tea after 1750.

In your response you should do the following.

- Respond to the prompt with a historically defensible thesis or claim that establishes a line of reasoning.
- Describe a broader historical context relevant to the prompt.
- Support an argument in response to the prompt using at least six documents.
- Use at least one additional piece of specific historical evidence (beyond that found in the documents) relevant to an argument about the prompt.
- For at least three documents, explain how or why the document's point of view, purpose, historical situation, and/or audience is relevant to an argument.
- Use evidence to corroborate, qualify, or modify an argument that addresses the prompt.

Note: The map below is provided as a reference. The map is NOT one of the seven documents. The documents begin below the map.

**Document 1**

Mary Elizabeth Braddon, *Lady Audley's Secret*, English novel, 1862

Lucy Audley looked up from her occupation among the fragile china cups and watched Robert rather anxiously as he walked softly to his uncle's room and back again to the boudoir. She looked very pretty and innocent, seated behind the graceful group of delicate opal china and glittering silver. Surely a pretty woman never looks prettier than when making tea. The most feminine and most domestic of all occupations imparts a magic harmony to her every movement, a witchery to her every glance. The floating mists from the boiling liquid in which she infuses the soothing herbs; whose secrets are known to her alone, envelope her in a cloud of scented vapor, through which she seems a social fairy, weaving potent spells with Gunpowder and Bohea [gunpowder and bohea are forms of tea]. At the tea-table she reigns omnipotent, unapproachable. What do men know of the mysterious beverage?

Source: Braddon, Mary Elizabeth. *Lady Audley's Secret*. Project Gutenberg, 2005.

**Document 2**

Charles James Wills, "A Persian Wedding," 1885

The visitors will stop all day, only leaving to escort the bride to the home of her new husband, whither she will go after dark. Large samovars, or Russian urns, which are in use in every Persian house, are hissing like small steam-engines, ready to furnish tea for the guests on their arrival: not our idea of tea, but a pale infusion sweetened to the consistency of syrup, from the center of each cup of which will project a little island of superfluous sugar.

Source: Wills, Charles James. *Persia as it is: Being Sketches of Modern Persian Life and Character*. London: William Clowes and Sons, 1886.

691

692

**Document 3**

Lin Zexu, "Letter to the Queen of England," February 1840

We have heard that in your own country opium is prohibited with the utmost strictness and severity:—this is a strong proof that you know full well how hurtful it is to mankind. Since then you do not permit it to injure your own country, you ought not to have the injurious drug transferred to another country, and above all others, how much less to the Inner Land! Of the products which China exports to your foreign countries, there is not one which is not beneficial to mankind in some shape or other. There are those which serve for food, those which are useful, and those which are calculated for re-sale; but all are beneficial. Has China (we should like to ask) ever yet sent forth a noxious article from its soil? Not to speak of our tea and rhubarb, things which your foreign countries could not exist a single day without, if we of the Central Land were to grudge you what is beneficial, and not to compassionate your wants, then wherewithal could you foreigners manage to exist? And further, as regards your woolens, camlets, and longells [types of fabrics], were it not that you get supplied with our native raw silk, you could not get these manufactured! If China were to grudge you those things which yield a profit, how could you foreigners scheme after any profit at all? Our other articles of food, such as sugar, ginger, cinnamon, &c., and our other articles for use, such as silk piece-goods, chinaware, &c., are all so many necessaries of life to you; how can we reckon up their number! On the other hand, the things that come from your foreign countries are only calculated to make presents of, or serve for mere amusement. It is quite the same to us if we have them, or if we have them not. If then these are of no material consequence to us of the Inner Land, what difficulty would there be in prohibiting and shutting our market against them? It is only that our heavenly dynasty most freely permits you to take off her tea, silk, and other commodities, and convey them for consumption everywhere, without the slightest stint or grudge, for no other reason, but that where a profit exists, we wish that it be diffused abroad for the benefit of all the earth!

Source: Lin Zexu, *Letter to the Queen of England*. In Chinese Repository, v. 8, no. 10 (February 1840), 497– 503.

**Document 4**

General Notes on Tea Exports, February 7, 1908

In their review of the year, Messrs. Gow Wilson and Stanton point to the great expansion in the use of British teas abroad as one of the most remarkable features of the past two years. This rose from 129, 884,250 lbs. in 1905 to 162,461,824 lbs. in 1906, and about 171,500,000 lbs. in 1907. When it is remembered that in 1890 the total consumption of Indian and Ceylon teas abroad was only 14,001,132 lbs., the progress made it startling. The expansion is largely due to the energy with which these new markets have been exploited. No industry has done so much to push its products in foreign markets as Ceylon.

Source: Royal Society of Arts (Great Britain). *Journal of the Royal Society of Arts*, Volume 56. London: George Bell and Sons, 1908.

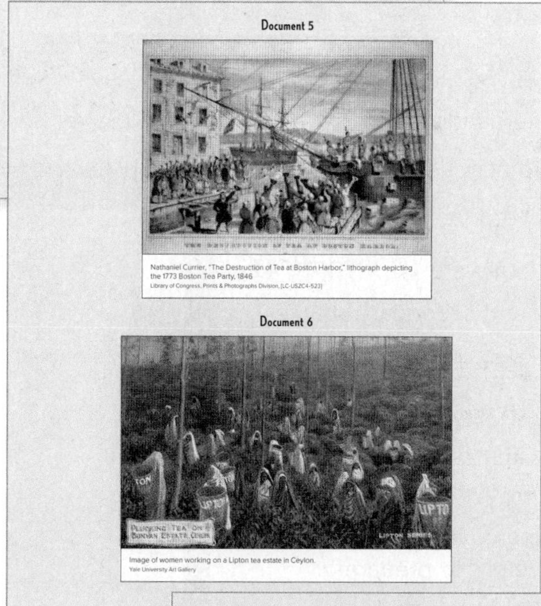

**Document 5**

Nathaniel Currier, "The Destruction of Tea at Boston Harbor," lithograph depicting the 1773 Boston Tea Party, 1846

Library of Congress, Prints & Photographs Division, [LC-USZC4-523]

**Document 6**



Image of women working on a Lipton tea estate in Ceylon.

Yale University Art Gallery

**Document 7**

Kakuzo Okakura *The Book of Tea*, Japan, 1906.

Perhaps I betray my own ignorance of the Tea Cult by being so outspoken. Its very spirit of politeness exacts that you say what you are expected to say, and no more. But I am not to be a polite Teaist. So much harm has been done already by the mutual misunderstanding of the New World and the Old, that one need not apologise for contributing his tithe to the furtherance of a better understanding. The beginning of the twentieth century would have been spared the spectacle of sanguinary warfare if Russia had condescended to know Japan better. What dire consequences to humanity lie in the contemptuous ignoring of Eastern problems! European imperialism, which does not disdain to raise the absurd cry of the Yellow Peril, fails to realise that Asia may also awaken to the cruel sense of the White Disaster. You may laugh at us for having "too much tea," but may we not suspect that you of the West have "no tea" in your constitution?

Let us stop the continents from hurling epigrams at each other, and be sadder if not wiser by the mutual gain of half a hemisphere. We have developed along different lines, but there is no reason why one should not supplement the other. You have gained expansion at the cost of restlessness; we have created a harmony which is weak against aggression. Will you believe it?—the East is better off in some respects than the West!

Strangely enough humanity has so far met in the tea-cup. It is the only Asiatic ceremonial which commands universal esteem. The white man has scoffed at our religion and our morals, but has accepted the brown beverage without hesitation. The afternoon tea is now an important function in Western society. In the delicate clatter of trays and saucers, in the soft rustle of feminine hospitality, in the common catechism about cream and sugar, we know that the Worship of Tea is established beyond question. The philosophic resignation of the guest to the fate awaiting him in the dubious decoction proclaims that in this single instance the Oriental spirit reigns supreme.

Source: Okakura, Kakuzo. *The Book of Tea*. Project Gutenberg, 1997.

Each Part Closer AP Exam Practice features a full **document-based question** with seven new stimuli to give students more opportunities to master analysis, historical reasoning, writing, and argumentation skills in preparation for the AP exam. Students deepen their understanding of historical perspectives as they practice contextualizing and synthesizing primary souce documents to successfully construct complex historical arguments.

# Personalized, Adaptive, and Dynamic **Digital Resources**

***Traditions & Encounters*** **is enriched with resources that support the course Framework including AP practice test banks, primary and secondary sources, and adaptive learning tools that lead students to content and concept mastery.**

Authored by the world's leading subject matter experts and organized by part and chapter levels, the resources provide students with multiple opportunities to contextualize and apply their understanding of Historical Thinking Skills and Reasoning Processes. Teachers can save time, customize lessons, monitor student progress, and make data-driven decisions in the classroom with the flexible, easy-to-navigate instructional tools.

## Intuitive Design

Resources are organized at the part and chapter levels. To enhance the core content, teachers can add assignments, activities, and instructional aides to any lesson.

The chapter landing page gives students access to:

- assigned activities
- interactive eBook
- adaptive, assignable ***SmartBook®***
- primary and secondary sources
- AP test prep and practice
- interactive map activities
- primary and secondary source libraries
- resources covering pre-1200 world history to prepare students for the AP World History start date

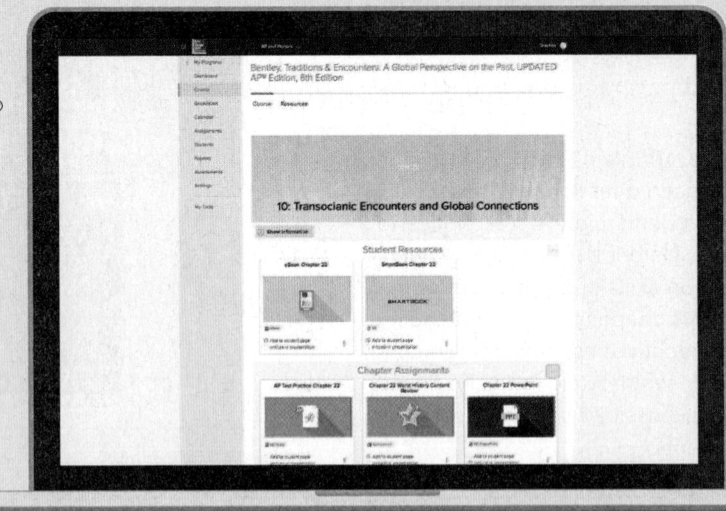


**Chapter landing page** links students to resources that support success.

**Mobile Ready** Access to course content on-the-go is easier and more efficient than ever before with the *ReadAnywhere* mobile app.

Because learning changes everything.®

## Adaptive Study Tool

SMARTBOOK® is the assignable, adaptive study tool. The interactive features personalize learning with self-guided tools that:

- assess proficiency and knowledge
- track which topics have been mastered
- identify areas that need more study
- deliver meaningful practice with guidance and instant feedback
- recharge learning with previously completed assignments and personalized recommendations
- allow teachers to assign material at the topic level.

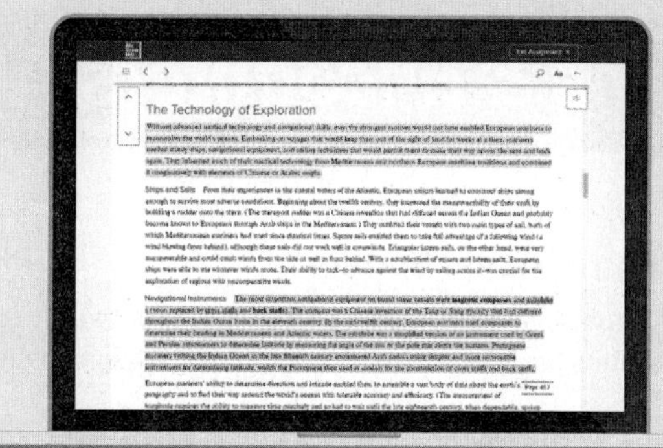


**Highlighted content** continuously adapts as students work through exercises.

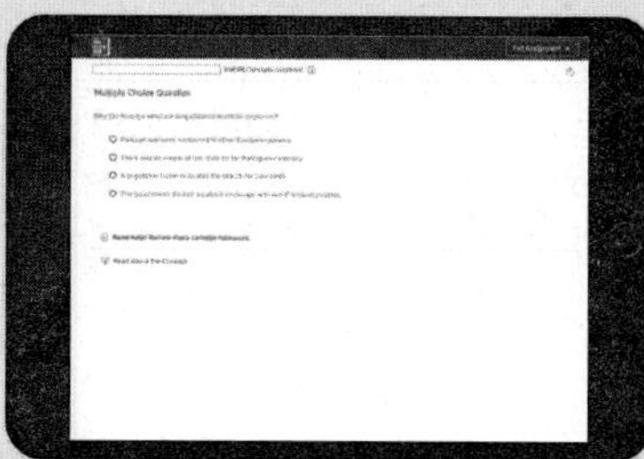

**Practice sets** measure depth of understanding and present a personalized learning path based on student responses.

## Teacher Resources

Teachers have access to the interactive eBook, adaptive *SmartBook®*, plus a wealth of customizable part and chapter resources and powerful gradebook tools including:

- a *Teacher Manual* with a chapter to help with the transition to the 1200 course start date, teaching suggestions, and pacing guides
- student performance reports to help teachers identify gaps, make data-driven decisions, and adjust instruction
- customizable PowerPoint presentations
- labeled visual aids and additional ideas for lecture enrichment
- AP-style test practice and test banks

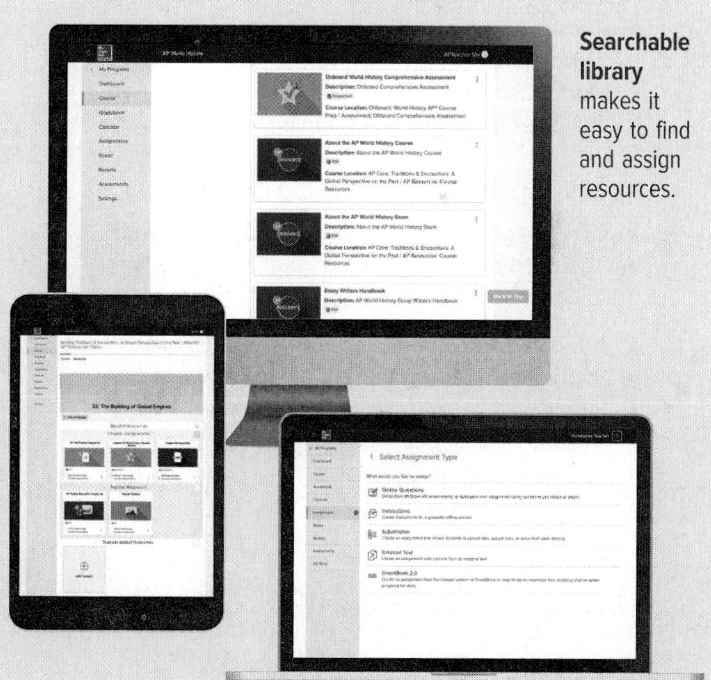

**Searchable library** makes it easy to find and assign resources.

**Customizable assignments** and **quiz banks** are automatically graded and populate easy-to-read reports.

Harness technology, unlock success with the digital resources for *Traditions & Encounters* **Visit My.MHEducation.com**

# HOW TO USE YOUR
# *Traditions & Encounters* AP TEACHER MANUAL

## Unmatched Instructional Support

The AP Teacher Manual, available in print and online, coupled with powerful digital resources provide unparalled support and guidance for teaching the themes and skills within the Modern time span.

The Teacher Manual contains 4 **Part Guides,** helping teachers thematically conceptualize the content for each Part, suggesting broader connections and discussion starters for classroom instruction.

Each chapter contains a variety of activities to accompany the Student Edition content utilizing **Historical Thinking Skills** and **Reasoning Processes**. Each activity is categorized with the Historical Thinking Skill or Reasoning Process it supports. Chapters also include **AP Key Terms** and locations for **geographical mapping activities.**

**Answer Keys** in the Teacher Manual include answers and detailed rubrics for both chapter and part exam practice. They include:

- An Answer Key for Multiple Choice questions
- Suggested evidence for Short Answer questions
- Suggested theses, evidence, and analysis for Document-Based and Long Essay questions

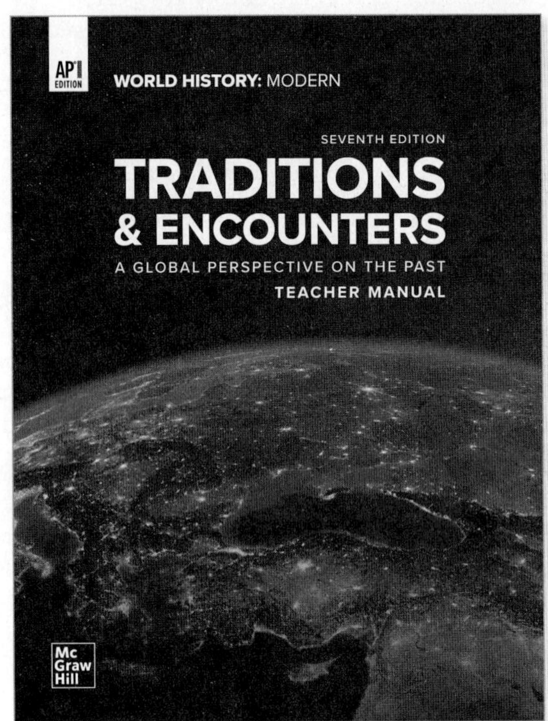

# Maps

# Sources from the Past

# Connecting the Sources

# 7th Edition

This Seventh Edition of *Traditions & Encounters: A Global Perspective on the Past* provides a genuinely global vision of history that is increasingly meaningful in the shrinking world of the twenty-first century. The theme of *traditions* draws attention to the formation, maintenance, and sometimes collapse of so many distinctive, individual societies. Because the world's peoples have also interacted regularly with one another since the earliest days of human history, the theme of *encounters* directs attention to communications, interactions, networks, and exchanges that have linked individual societies to their neighbors and others in the larger world. Despite many changes in the way world historians have tried to conceptualize the past and present since the appearance of the first edition of *Traditions and Encounters* decades ago, the twin themes of traditions and encounters remain at the heart of every chapter in the text, no matter how extensive revisions might have been. They provide a lens through which to interpret the affairs of humankind and the pressures that continue to shape history. All aspects of the text support these themes—from the organization of chapters, engaging stories of the world's peoples, to the robust map program, updated primary sources, and critical-thinking features that permeate the text.

Some of the changes authors Heather Streets-Salter and Craig Benjamin have introduced to the Seventh Edition of *Traditions and Encounters* include the following:

We have worked hard to eliminate any gendered or out-of-date language throughout the book, in line with most historical writing being done today.

We have changed the old Eyewitness feature to *Zooming in on Traditions* or *Zooming in on Encounters* to further emphasize the key organizational lens of the book. And we have streamlined the opening stories featured in these *Zooming* features to give greater voice to the many individuals from the past they include. We have also separated these stories from a new *Chapter Overview* that helps better prepare readers for the contents of the chapter that follows.

We have changed the titles of a number of chapters to reflect recent thinking within the field and, in some cases, to be more geographically and politically inclusive. We have also made numerous changes to headers and subheaders throughout, both to reflect new interpretations of how we should "label" various peoples and historical processes and also to make the structure of each chapter clearer.

We have replaced and updated a number of sources in the *Sources from the Past* and *Connecting the Sources* features and have also selected many new images to better illustrate the text. We have added in-line comprehension questions to the sources and also updated reflection questions on most sources, maps, and images to help students practice both their comprehension and analytical thinking skills.

We have changed the old *Reverberations* feature to *How the Past Shapes the Future*, both to further enhance the flow of historical processes and also to more clearly emphasize the continuing relevance of each of the themes explored to the global world of today.

We have changed the old *Summary* feature to a *Conclusion* and modified the language in each to more succinctly sum up the developments described in the chapter. We have also moved the *Chronology* section earlier in the chapter and updated it to incorporate recent date revisions by historians and added new and more relevant secondary courses to the *For Further Reading* section at the end of each chapter.

**New to this edition**, we have added a feature called *What's Left Out?* to call attention to issues most texts do not usually have space to discuss. Its purpose is to remind students that history is far more complicated and nuanced than any brief narrative can provide. For example, in chapter 15 the authors give greater context on non-elite women in Southwest Asia because most textbooks focus on elite women associated with the imperial harem, while in chapter 25 they help students understand that the rivalries of the Cold War in fact originated much earlier in the interwar period.

## CHAPTER-BY-CHAPTER CHANGES

The following is a chapter-by-chapter list of topics that are new to this edition or elements that have been substantially revised or updated.

### Chapter 1: The Resurgence of Empire in South Asia

- Updated geographical locations throughout (e.g., of Xuanzang's journey).
- Added language to emphasize continuity of certain Tang and Song social practices into modern Chinese society.
- Defined religious terms like *scriptoria* and *stupa*.
- Included reference to female ruler of Korean Silla state, Queen Seondeok.
- Included references to Soga in discussion of Japanese clans.
- Added a "What's Left Out?" on history and evolution of role of concubines in Chinese society.

### Chapter 2: The Expansive Realm of Islam

- Added definitions and clarifications of various Islamic and Arabic terms (*ibn*, *hadith*, *jihad*, etc.).
- Added language to help clarify the disagreements over succession following the death of the Prophet Muhammad.

- Added some language to provide a more nuanced discussion of attitudes toward women, including role of female Sufis.
- Added language throughout to emphasize continuing relevance of the expansion of Islam to the modern world.
- Added a "What's Left Out?" about why an otherwise obscure and out-of-the way trading town named Mecca became so central to the Islamic faith, as well as the relevance of Ka'ba.

## Chapter 3: India and the Indian Ocean Basin

- Added more careful descriptors of relevant groups such as White Huns (Hephthalites), Turkic-Mongols, Turkic-Iranian, etc.
- Added new phrasing about climatic causes of monsoon winds.
- Added language reminding readers that Indian Ocean Basin trade had also flourished back in the First Silk Roads Era.
- Defined terms such as *emporia*.
- Added language emphasizing how religious developments during the first millennium C.E. are still influencing South Asia today.
- Added new sources to provide a more balanced view of trade and exchange in the Indian Ocean Basin and Southeast Asia during the era, including Chinese observations of Nanhai trade, Chinese reports on a wealthy Javanese commercial kingdom, and Marco Polo on the flourishing port of Quanzhou (Zaiton).
- Added a "What's Left Out?" on Queen Pwa Saw, the power behind the throne in Myanmar in the thirteenth century.

## Chapter 4: Eastern and Western Europe in the Early Medieval Period

- Changed chapter title to reflect more recent thinking and emphasize continuing relevance today of the emergence of "two Europes" during the first millennium C.E.
- Through new subheaders and language, added further emphasis of the different ways of comparing the two halves of Europe using different lenses–political, economic, cultural, etc.
- Added General Belisarius to discussion of Justinian's attempts to reconstitute the Roman Empire; added reference to Saracens.
- Added a "What's Left Out?" on Anna Comnena and Hildegard of Bingen as a final way of comparing the two halves of early Medieval Europe–this time through the lives of elite women.

## Chapter 5: Nomadic Empires and Eurasian Integration

- Streamlined and updated the opening story.
- Updated the introductory paragraphs for both "Sources from the Past."
- Added a "What's Left Out?" about problems of language and translation in Mongol sources.
- Updated information on the controversial legacies of Mongol invasions.

## Chapter 6: States and Societies in Sub-Saharan Africa

- Updated and streamlined the opening story based on new information about Sundiata.
- Replaced the term *Bantu-speaking peoples* throughout to reflect updated scholarly understanding.
- Updated information on kin-based societies to reflect current scholarly understanding.
- Moved the section on Islamic Kingdoms and Empires so that it now follows the section on African Society and Cultural Development to improve the flow of the chapter.
- Updated the section on gender to more accurately reflect current scholarship.
- De-emphasized exoticism of African religions throughout.
- Added a "What's Left Out?" on academic contributions to stereotypes about Africa's pre-colonial past.

## Chapter 7: The Increasing Integration of Europe with the Wider World

- Changed title to emphasize Europe's outlier position in world history at the time.
- Added a "What's Left Out?" on the everyday lives of peasants in medieval Europe.
- Added a new "Sources from the Past" on Margery Kempe to emphasize the role of women.
- Clarified the origins of the Holy Roman Empire.
- Clarified events regarding the Norman conquest of England.

## Chapter 8: Worlds Apart: The Americas and Oceania

- Deleted long quote in-text by Bernal Diaz.
- Streamlined and clarified the section on Mexica.
- Widened discussion on Mexica religion and Mexica culture.
- Changed language in subhead from Inca Gods to Inca Religion.
- Deleted information on Easter Island because it is now disputed by scholars.
- Added a "What's Left Out?" about the difficulties of interpreting Nahuatl sources sponsored by Spanish conquerors.

## Chapter 9: Expanding Horizons of Cross-Cultural Interaction

- Streamlined opening vignette.
- Added a "What's Left Out?" about the motivations behind becoming a eunuch.
- Clarified and streamlined section on the slave trade.

## Chapter 10: Transoceanic Encounters and Global Connections

- Reversed subsections in the first section so that Technology of Exploration precedes Motives of Exploration.
- Reversed the sections on Trade and Conflict in Early Modern Asia and Ecological Exchanges so that Ecological Exchanges comes first.
- Added a "What's Left Out?" on the reasons spices were so coveted in European societies.
- Deepened the context for the "Sources from the Past" about Christopher Columbus.
- Added a new "Sources from the Past" by James Cook.
- Updated section on Ecological Exchanges to reflect current scholarship.

## Chapter 11: The Transformation of Europe

- Changed title of section on Western Christendom to Western European Christendom to be more specific.
- Clarified relationship between gender and witch-hunting in early modern Europe.
- Added a "What's Left Out?" on the desperate conditions for ordinary Europeans caused by the Thirty Years' War.

## Chapter 12: The Integration of the Americas and Oceania with the Wider World

- Changed title to emphasize the relations of these regions with the rest of the world.
- Changed the subsection on the Conquest of Mexico and Peru to simply Mexico and Peru to de-emphasize the idea that conquest was inevitable.
- Changed introductory vignette on Doña Marina to complicate her story.
- Emphasized the critical role of epidemic disease in the devastation of the populations of the Americas.
- Added more detail on the Taíno people so they don't appear passive at the moment of Spanish contact.
- Emphasized previous Spanish practices with slavery and sugar production in the Azores and Canary Islands for informing practices in the Americas.
- Emphasized the brutal treatment of native American peoples by European conquerors and settlers, as well as resistance to such treatment.
- Added a "What's Left Out?" on the widespread practice of British settlers enslaving native American peoples in the eastern colonies.
- Added a new "Sources from the Past" by Miantanamo.
- Streamlined and clarified section on Colonial Society in the Americas to reflect current scholarship.
- Updated the section on slavery in Brazil to reflect current scholarship.
- Added clarity regarding competition among native American groups in North America.

## Chapter 13: Africa and the Atlantic World

- Removed several instances of Eurocentric text.
- Brought the sections on the trans-Saharan slave trade and Atlantic slave trade up to date.
- Updated section on consequences of the Atlantic slave trade in Africa to reflect current scholarship.
- Updated section on the African diaspora to reflect current scholarship.
- Added a "What's Left Out?" on the ways women experienced slavery differently than men.
- Updated the section on African diaspora cultures to reflect current scholarship.

## Chapter 14: Tradition and Change in East Asia

- Clarified and updated section on foot-binding.
- Added a "What's Left Out?" on the parallels between Chinese foot-binding and the use of corsets in western Europe.
- Streamlined material on Zheng He.
- Rewrote the section on Government and Technology to minimize Eurocentrism.
- Eliminated comparisons of Chinese and European merchants to eliminate Eurocentrism.

## Chapter 15: Empires in South and Southwest Asia

- Changed title to de-emphasize Islam for a focus on the region.
- Reversed the two subheads in the section on Empires in Transition to tell the story more clearly.
- Clarified the section on the Battle of Chaldiran.
- Significantly updated the section on the Dynastic State to reflect current thinking on succession.
- Reversed subheads on Steppe Traditions and Women in Politics in the section on the Dynastic State.
- Added a new "Sources from the Past" by Emperor Akbar of the Moghul dynasty.
- Added a "What's Left Out?" on the lives of ordinary Muslim women in the Ottoman Empire.
- Added detail to section on Food Crops.
- Significantly updated section on Economic Difficulties and Military Decline to reflect current scholarship.

- Deleted section on Cultural Conservatism because of Eurocentrism and bias.

## Chapter 16: Revolutions and National States in the Atlantic World

- Changed title of first section to Revolutionary Ideas.
- Added a new section on Revolutions to cover the American, French, Haitian, and Latin American revolutions.
- Added a new heading called Consequences and Implications of the Revolutions.
- Changed first subhead under the Consequences section to The Emergence of New Ideologies.
- Changed final section to New Nations and Nationalism in Europe.
- Rewrote chapter overview to reflect extensive changes in the chapter.
- De-emphasized the revolutionary potential of ideas and emphasized the importance of war as a factor in instigating the revolutions of this period.
- Rewrote the subhead on Tightened British Control of the Colonies to reflect the importance of the experience of war.
- Clarified the reasons behind the start of the American Revolution.
- Rewrote the section on why the British lost the American Revolution, with an emphasis on the role of the French.
- Clarified that the French philosophes were deeply inspired by the American Revolution.
- Updated section on the Haitian Revolution.
- Wrote introduction to new section on the consequences of the revolutions.
- Added a "What's Left Out?" on women's participation in the revolutions.

## Chapter 17: The Making of Industrial Society

- Added more on the environmental impact of the Industrial Revolution.
- Updated section on the origins of the Industrial Revolution, especially subheads on Ecological Relief and Mechanization, to reflect current scholarship.
- Added a new "Sources from the Past" on Ned Ludd.
- Added a "What's Left Out?" on the introduction of clock time.
- Revised subheads on Big Business and Corporations for greater clarity.
- Deleted claim about the strong link between industrialization and the abolition of slavery.
- Updated and clarified subheads on New Social Classes and Work and Play.
- Updated subheads on women and gender to reflect current scholarship.
- Updated and rewrote subhead on the Global Division of Labor and Economic Interdependence to reflect current scholarship.

## Chapter 18: The Americas in the Age of Independence

- Added more in-depth indigenous perspectives to chapter content.
- Clarified and streamlined lead-up to the U.S. Civil War.
- Clarified the process of Canada gaining dominion status.
- Updated and streamlined subhead on Mexico.
- Rewrote the introduction to American Economic Development.
- Significantly rewrote the Section on Latin American Investments.
- Added a "What's Left Out?" on child removal in Australia, Canada, and the United States.
- Updated the section on Societies in the United States to reflect recent scholarship.

## Chapter 19: Societies at Crossroads

- Changed section title from The Ottoman Empire in Decline to The Weakening of the Ottoman Empire.
- Changed subhead in this section from The Nature of Decline to Sources of Ottoman Weakness.
- Significantly rewrote opening story on Taiping Rebellion and the Chapter Overview.
- Updated subhead on Ottoman military problems to reflect current scholarship.
- Added a "What's Left Out?" on the global importance of the Russo-Japanese War.
- Updated section on Opium War in China.

## Chapter 20: The Apex of Global Empire Building

- Changed title to reflect content changes in chapter.
- Changed subhead under Legacies of Imperialism from Nationalism and Anticolonial Movements to Anticolonial and Nationalist Movements.
- Wrote a new introductory story on Menelik II of Ethiopia.
- Rewrote the Chapter Overview to reflect content changes in the chapter.
- Changed subhead on Political Motives for Imperialism to Geopolitical Motives for Imperialism.
- Substantially rewrote subheads on Geopolitical Motives for Imperialism, Economic Motives for Imperialism, and Cultural Justifications for Imperialism.
- Moved subheads within the section on Foundations of Empire for better flow.

- Rewrote most of the section on the Indian Mutiny.
- Added two new "Sources from the Past," by Raden Kartini and Queen Lili'uokulani.
- Deleted some material on European explorers in Africa and added material on King Leopold's Congo.
- Added material on the British conquest of Egypt and the South African War.
- Updated section on The Emergence of New Imperial Powers to reflect current scholarship.
- Added material on the Can Vuong anti-French movement in Vietnam.
- Updated subhead on Scientific Racism to reflect current scholarship.
- Added a "What's Left Out?" on the unintended consequences of colonialism on gender relations.

## Chapter 21: The Great War: The World in Upheaval

- Under the section Global War; added sections on Battles in Southwest Asia and Africa and Africans in the War.
- Streamlined and clarified introductory story.
- Clarified introduction to the section on Understandings and Alliances.
- Clarified the establishment of the Western Front.
- Updated the subhead on Women at War to reflect current scholarship.
- Added a "What's Left Out?" on the German Committee for Indian Independence.
- Added material on battles in Southwest Asia.
- Added material on Africa in the war (originally in chapter 35).
- Clarified section on the mandate system.

## Chapter 22: Anxieties and Experiments in Postwar Europe and the United States

- Changed title to reflect content within chapter.
- Changed section on Probing Cultural Frontiers to New Intellectual Frontiers.
- Shortened introductory story on Hitler.
- Significantly rewrote the section on Communism in Russia.
- Added a "What's Left Out?" on the popularity of eugenics in the United States.

## Chapter 23: Revolutionaries and Nationalists in the Colonial and Neocolonial World

- Changed title to reflect new content in the chapter.
- Changed section on Asian Paths to Autonomy to Paths to Autonomy in East and Southeast Asia.
- Changed subhead on China's Search for Order to China's Campaigns to End Foreign Domination.
- Added a new "Sources from the Past" by M.N. Roy.
- Changed section on Africa under Colonial Domination to Sub-Saharan Africa under Colonial Domination.
- Deleted section on Africa and Africans in the Great War.
- Significantly rewrote the material on China and India to reflect current scholarly understandings.
- Updated section on sub-Saharan Africa to reflect current scholarship.
- Added a "What's Left Out?" on the League Against Imperialism.
- Updated and clarified subhead on Neighborly Cultural Exchanges.
- Added a new ending to chapter.

## Chapter 24: New Conflagrations: World War II and the Cold War

- Updated subhead on Chinese resistance to Japanese invasion to reflect current scholarship.
- Updated subhead on Italian and German Aggression by adding material on Ethiopian invasion.
- Updated and clarified subhead on Peace for Our Time by nuancing the philosophy of appeasement.
- Clarified and rewrote chain of events on the German conquest of western Europe.
- Added to subhead on Women's Roles by adding information about Soviet women.
- Added a "What's Left Out?" on the long history of anti-communism.
- Added material in the section on Cold War that clarifies Soviet perspective.
- Updated section on Cracks in the Soviet-Chinese Alliance to reflect current scholarship.

## Chapter 25: The End of Empire in an Era of Cold War

- Changed title to reflect importance of Cold War in decolonization.
- In section on After Independence, added Pan-Arab to the subhead on Islamic Resurgence in Southwest Asia and North Africa.
- Streamlined introductory story on Gandhi and significantly rewrote the chapter overview to reflect new content in the chapter.
- Rewrote introduction to Independence in Asia.
- Rewrote material on Partition in India.
- Rewrote section on nationalism in Vietnam.
- Updated section on Palestine to reflect recent scholarship.

- Rewrote section on the Suez Crisis.
- Substantially rewrote the section on French decolonization in North Africa.
- Added material on the Mau Mau Rebellion in Kenya.
- Added material on apartheid in South Africa.
- Streamlined and updated the material on Mao's China.
- Updated material on postcolonial India to reflect current scholarship.
- Updated material on Islamism and the Iranian Revolution.
- Deleted text on African disunity.
- Added "Sources from the Past" on China's Marriage law (originally in chapter 38).
- Added a "What's Left Out?" on the combination of decolonization and the Cold War in Angola.

## Chapter 26: Into the Twenty-First Century

- Changed title to make it sound more current.
- Updated all dates and material to bring it current with second decade of twenty-first century.
- Changed title of section on The End of the Cold War to The End of the Cold War and the Emergence of a Unipolar World.
- Added subhead under this section called The Unipolar Moment.
- Moved the subhead on International Organizations to the section on Cross-Cultural Exchanges.
- Renamed the section on Global Problems to Urgent Global Issues in the Twenty-First Century.
- Added subheads in this section on The Continuing Inequality of Women, Migration, and Global Diseases.
- Deleted final section on Crossing Boundaries.
- Rewrote Chapter Overview to reflect content changes in the chapter.
- Added a new introduction to the section on the End of the Cold War.
- Added new text on the end of the Cold War through 2020.
- Clarified information on GATT and WTO.
- Updated section on the Rise of China.
- Added new material on the EU to Brexit.
- Updated material on OPEC.
- Deleted subhead on Pan-American culture and added material on cultural globalization.
- Deleted subhead on the Age of Access and added material on the Networked World.
- Deleted subheads on the Prominence of the English Language and Adaptations of Technology.
- Updated information on population pressure.
- Added material on climate change.
- Added new material on global diseases, specifically the COVID-19 pandemic, to bring content up to the present.
- Updated material on global terrorism.
- Added new material on women's inequality globally.
- Added a new "Sources from the Past" by Malala.
- Added a "What's Left Out?" on the difficulties about writing the history of the very recent past.
- Added new material on migrants in a global context.

## NEW AP 7TH EDITION

The updated Seventh Edition of *Traditions & Encounters: A Global Perspective on the Past* provides the essential tools to understand world history and has been thoroughly updated in collaboration with the authors, veteran AP teachers, and consultants to fully align with the Advanced Placement World History: Modern Curriculum Framework.

Changes from the Sixth Edition include:

- New Chapter Structure to Align to the World History: Modern course
- New Prelude Chapter organized around the AP World History: Modern themes
- New Part Openers to set the context for the time period
- New Chapter Openers
- New Interpreting Images features
- New AP Exam Practice
- New Part AP Exam Practice
- New Full Document-Based Questions for each Part with 7 new documents specifically selected for the question
- New Full AP Practice Exam

# About the Authors

**Jerry H. Bentley** was professor of history at the University of Hawai'i and editor of the *Journal of World History.* His research on the religious, moral, and political writings of the Renaissance led to the publication of *Humanists and Holy Writ: New Testament Scholarship in the Renaissance* (Princeton, 1983) and *Politics and Culture in Renaissance Naples* (Princeton, 1987). More recently, his research concentrated on global history and particularly on processes of cross-cultural interaction. His book *Old World Encounters: Cross-Cultural Contacts and Exchanges in Pre-Modern Times* (New York, 1993) examines processes of cultural exchange and religious conversion before the modern era, and his pamphlet *Shapes of World History in Twentieth-Century Scholarship* (1996) discusses the historiography of world history. His most recent publication is *The Oxford Handbook of World History* (Oxford, 2011), and he served as a member of the editorial team preparing the forthcoming *Cambridge History of the World.* Jerry Bentley passed away in July 2012, although his legacy lives on through his significant contributions to the study of world history. The World History Association recently named an annual prize in his honor for outstanding publications in the field.

**Herbert F. Ziegler** is an associate professor of history at the University of Hawai'i. He has taught world history since 1980; he previously served as director of the world history program at the University of Hawai'i as well as book review editor of the *Journal of World History.* His interest in twentieth-century European social and political history led to the publication of *Nazi Germany's New Aristocracy: The SS Leadership, 1925-1939* (Princeton, 1990) and to his participation in new educational endeavors in the history of the Holocaust, including the development of an upper-division course for undergraduates. He is at present working on a study that explores from a global point of view the demographic trends of the past ten thousand years, along with their concomitant technological, economic, and social developments. His other current research project focuses on the application of complexity theory to a comparative study of societies and their internal dynamics.

**Heather Streets-Salter** is Professor and Director of World History Programs at Northeastern University in Boston, Massachusetts. She is the author of *World War One in Southeast Asia: Colonialism and Anticolonialism in an Era of Global Conflict* (Cambridge University Press, 2017); *Martial Races: The Military, Martial Races, and Masculinity in British Imperial Culture, 1857-1914* (Manchester University Press, 2004); and *Empires and Colonies in the Modern World* (Oxford University Press, 2015) with Trevor Getz. Her next book is called *The Chill Before the Cold War: Communism and Anti-Communism in Colonial Southeast Asia in the Interwar Period.*

**Craig Benjamin** is a Professor of History in the Frederik J. Meijer Honors College at Grand Valley State University in Michigan. He is the author of *The Yuezhi: Origin, Migration and the Conquest of Northern Bactria* (Brepols, 2007); *Empires of Ancient Eurasia. The First Silk Roads Era 100 BCE-250 CE* (Cambridge University Press, 2018); and *Big History: Between Nothing and Everything* (McGraw-Hill, 2014) with David Christian and Cynthia Stokes Brown. He is the editor of Volume 4 of the *Cambridge History of the World* (Cambridge University Press, 2015) and *The Routledge Companion to Big History* (Routledge, 2019) with Esther Quaedackers and David Baker. His next book is called *Eurasia Reconnected. The Second Silk Roads Era 600-1000 CE.*

## AP CONTRIBUTORS

**Monty Armstrong** (BA, California State University; MEd, University of San Francisco) taught both AP World History and AP European History at Cerritos High School. He has served as a Consultant for the College Board for AP World History, leading AP Summer Institutes and over 60 one-day workshops. He served as a Reader for AP European History from 1996 to 2000 and in leadership roles as both a Table and Question Leader for AP World History from 2001–2018. He is also an author and contributor to several publications on teaching world history, and serves as a moderator for the AP Teacher Community. His work on this volume was assisted by his son, James Armstrong (Northwood High School, Irvine, CA), an "intrepid editor and intellectually curious" student who provided feedback on exam review materials.

**Amy R. Caldwell** (PhD, UC Santa Barbara) is a lecturer of history at California State University, Channel Islands, where she teaches world history. Since 2008, she has participated in the annual AP World History Reading as a reader and scoring leader. Her research concentrates on religion, diplomacy, and gender in the Protestant Reformation, and she regularly presents her work at national and international conferences. She is also the co-founder of H-HRE: an H-Net discussion network on the history of the Holy Roman Empire.

**Mary Jo Jepson** (MA, University of Rochester) has more than 34 years of teaching experience focused on secondary social studies. She has specialized in world history and cultural studies and provided instruction at the regents and honors levels in U.S. history, Advanced Placement European history, government, and psychology. In addition, Mary Jo has served for three years as an Advanced Placement European History reader and rater. She continues to prepare students for college, serving for more than 20 years as a Continuing Education instructor for the PSAT, SAT, and ACT (both online and in-person). Mary Jo earned her Bachelor of Arts in Social Studies Education from Syracuse University, and her Master of Arts in Secondary Education, Social Science, from the University of Rochester. She also received a National Science Foundation grant to study aging and has completed more than 100 hours of in-service courses covering content, pedagogy, and technology.

**Lenore Schneider** (MA, Duke; PhD, Carnegie Mellon) has taught AP World History for fifteen years at New Canaan High School in Connecticut and has served as Reader and Table Leader for the AP Exam essays for many years. She has taught AP workshops and institutes at over twenty sites, including several institutes in Europe, Japan, and China, and has traveled to fifty-three countries. She has also taught AP European History for many years, has served on the AP European History Test Development Committee, and in 2016, the AP European History Standards Setting Committee. She has also mentored AP teachers and College Board consultants and served on the College Board Advisory Board. Her specialties include writing skills to help students succeed on the essays, performance assessments, and student-centered activities such as simulations and role play.

# Acknowledgments

Many individuals have contributed to this book, and the authors take pleasure in recording deep thanks for all the comments, criticism, advice, and suggestions that helped to improve the work. The editorial, marketing, and production teams at McGraw Hill did an outstanding job of seeing the project through to publication. Special thanks go to Jason Seitz, Stephanie Ventura, and Sandy Wille, who provided crucial support by helping the authors work through difficult issues and solve the innumerable problems of content, style, and organization that arise in any project to produce a history of the world. Many colleagues at the University of Hawai'i at Mānoa, most notably Professor Margot A. Henriksen, and elsewhere aided and advised the authors on matters of organization and composition. Finally, we would like to express our appreciation for the advice of the following individuals, who read and commented on the Seventh Edition, as well as previous editions of *Traditions & Encounters.*

Brian C. Black, *Pennsylvania State University*
Beau Bowers, *Central Piedmont Community College*
Erika Briesacher, *Worcester State University*
Stanley Burstein, *California State University, Los Angeles*
David Eaton, *Grand Valley State University*
David Fahey, *Miami University of Ohio*
Amy Forss, *Metropolitan Community College, Omaha*
Melissa Gayan, *Georgia Southern University*
Aimee Harris-Johnson, *El Paso Community College*
Matthew Herbst, *University of California San Diego*
Mark Lee, *University of Nebraska*
Emily G. Miller, *University of Indianapolis*
William Plants, *University of Rio Grande*
Annie Tracy Samuel, *University of Tennessee at Chattanooga*
Pamela Sayre, *Henry Ford Community College*
William Schell Jr., *Murray State University*
Scott Seagle, *University of Tennessee at Chattanooga*
David Simonelli, *Youngstown State University*
Adam Stanley, *University of Wisconsin at Platteville*
Ryan Thompson, *Cleveland State Community College*

Special thanks and gratitude to the McGraw Hill Academic Integrity Board of Advisors who were instrumental in providing guidance on chapter content, illustration program, and language and conventions. Our advisors include:

Susan Bragg, *Georgia Southwestern State University*
Jennifer Epley Sanders, *Texas A & M*
Eileen Ford, *California State University, Los Angeles*
Nicholas Fox, *Houston College*
Rudy Jean-Bart, *Broward Community College*
Darnell Morehand-Olufade, *University of Bridgeport*
Sharon Navarro, *University of Texas at San Antonio*
Jeffrey Ogbar, *University of Connecticut*
Andrea Oliver, *Tallahassee Community College*
Birte Pfleger, *California State University, Los Angeles*
Linda Reed, *University of Houston*

# About the AP World History: Modern Course

The Advanced Placement (AP) program was created by the College Board, which also developed other standardized tests taken in high school, including the PSAT/NMSQT and the SAT. The AP World History: Modern course description and AP Exams are written by the AP World History Development Committee, which consists of college history professors and high school teachers who are experienced AP World History course teachers. This committee has studied world history course descriptions from hundreds of university professors to determine which concepts to include in the AP World History course and exam.

| Historical Periods and Dates | Weight on AP Exam | Chapters in *Traditions & Encounters* |
|---|---|---|
| **Regional and Interregional Interactions (c. 1200 to c. 1450)** | | |
| 1. The Global Tapestry<br>2. Networks of Exchange | 8–10%<br>8–10% | 1, 2, 3, 4, 5, 6, 7, 8 |
| **Global Interactions (c. 1450 to c. 1750)** | | |
| 3. Land-Based Empires<br>4. Trans-Oceanic Interconnections | 12–15%<br>12–15% | 9, 10, 11, 12, 13, 14, 15 |
| **Industrialization and Global Integration (c. 1750 to c. 1900)** | | |
| 5. Revolutions<br>6. Consequences of industrialization | 12–15%<br>12–15% | 16, 17, 18, 19, 20 |
| **Accelerating Global Change and Realignments (c. 1900 to the present)** | | |
| 7. Global Conflict<br>8. Cold War and Decolonization<br>9. Globalization | 8–10%<br>8–10%<br>8–10% | 21, 22, 23, 24, 25, 26 |

## HISTORICAL PERIODS

The AP World History: Modern course is divided into four historical periods spanning from c. 1200 C.E. to the present. These historical periods are organized into nine units, and form the backbone of the AP World History: Modern course. The breakdown of these Periods, along with their weight on the AP Exam and corresponding chapters in *Traditions & Encounters*, are shown above. To encourage flexibility with dates, note that *c.* or *circa*—meaning "about"– has been added as a prefix to all the dates in all the Periods. Organizing historical information chronologically helps you compare what was happening in one region to what was happening *at the same time* in other regions. As shown in the table, the first period covers events from c. 1200 to c. 1450, just before the age of Atlantic exploration starting with Columbus.

## HISTORICAL DEVELOPMENTS

Each Period is defined by Historical Developments that help teachers and students focus on the most important information in a particular Period. Global in nature, the Historical Developments help you tie specific events to larger global processes. The required content you need to know for the AP Exam is indicated in each Historical Development in the AP World History: Modern Full Course Description College Board site.

## THEMES

Not only does the College Board organize AP World History: Modern information chronologically, it also gives you a way to compare information *across* Periods. Six overarching themes provide categories to make comparisons as well as to recognize continuities and changes over time:

Theme 1: Humans and the Environment (ENV)
Theme 2: Cultural Development and Interactions (CDI)
Theme 3: Governance (GOV)
Theme 4: Economic Systems (ECN)
Theme 5: Social Interactions and Organization (SIO)
Theme 6: Technology and Innovation (TEC)

Learning Objectives for the AP World History: Modern course and AP Exam support the six themes above. Learning to think in terms of themes can help you recognize patterns and trends that developed over thousands of years and around the globe. Thinking "thematically" can also help you organize large amounts of information. The books four Part Openers and Part Closers highlight these themes, providing questions to help you think about how each one plays out as you study the chapters.

## HISTORICAL THINKING SKILLS AND REASONING PROCESSES

The AP World History: Modern course and AP Exam evaluate not merely your content knowledge but also how well you have developed the application of historical thinking skills and reasoning processes. These skills and processes are best developed by investigating the past through exploration and interpretation of primary sources and secondary texts as well as through the regular development of historical argument in writing. Every question on the Exam will require you to respond using one or more of these practices and skills.

### Historical Thinking Skills

**Skill 1: Developments and Processes** Identify and explain historical development and processes.

**Skill 2: Sourcing and Situation** Identify and explain the point of view, purpose, historical situation, and/or audience of primary and secondary sources and their significance.

**Skill 3: Claims and Evidence in Sources** Identify and describe a claim or argument in a text or non-text source and identify the evidence used to support an argument; compare the arguments in two or more sources; explain how claims or evidence support, modify, or refute a source's argument.

**Skill 4: Contextualization** Identify and describe a historical context for historical developments and process and explain historical developments and processes within a broader historical context.

**Skill 5: Making Connections** Identify patterns and connections among historical developments and processes and how a development or process relates to another development or process.

**Skill 6: Argumentation** Make a historically defensible claim in the form of an evaluative thesis, specific and relevant evidence to support the argument; use historical reasoning to explain relationships among pieces of evidence; and consider diverse or alternative evidence that could be used to corroborate, qualify, or modify an argument.

### Reasoning Processes

**Reasoning Process 1: Comparison** This reasoning skill requires you to describe and explain relevant similarities and/or differences between different historical developments or processes and explain the relative historical significance of the similarities and/or differences.

**Reasoning Process 2: Causation** You need to be able to describe causes and effects and explain the relationship between causes and effects of a specific historical development or process. You also must be able to explain the relative historical significance of different causes and/ or effects and explain the differences between primary and secondary causes, and between short- and long-term effects.

**Reasoning Process 3: Continuity and Change** You must be able to describe and explain patterns of continuity and/or change over time and explain the relative historical significance of specific historical developments in relation to a larger pattern of continuity and/or change.

# About the AP World History: Modern Exam

The AP World History: Modern Exam is 3 hours and 15 minutes long. There are four sections to the AP World History: Modern Exam: a multiple-choice section, a short-answer section, a document-based question, and a long essay. All questions will test students' proficiency in AP Historical Thinking Skills and Reasoning Processes, as well as the Thematic Learning Objectives and Historical Developments of the AP World History course.

| Section | Question Type | Number of Questions | Timing | Percentage of Total Exam Score |
|---|---|---|---|---|
| I | Part A: Multiple-choice questions | 55 Questions | 55 minutes | 60 minutes |
| | Part B: Short-answer questions | 3 Questions | 40 minutes | 40 minutes |
| II | Part A: Document-based question | 1 Question | 60 minutes | 25% |
| | Part B: Long essay question | 1 Question | 40 minutes | 15% |

## UNDERSTANDING THE FORMAT

### Multiple-Choice Questions

There are 55 multiple-choice questions with four answer choices (A–D). Only one answer is correct for each question, and there is no penalty for guessing incorrectly, so answer every question even if you don't know the answer or feel uncertain about your choice. Students are given 55 minutes to complete this section. The multiple-choice questions are stimulus-based, which means that a primary or secondary source (excerpts, photos, maps, charts, etc.) is provided, followed by between two and five questions based on that stimuli.

### Short-Answer Questions

The short-answer section of the Exam includes four questions closely aligned with the course skills that must be answered within 40 minutes (roughly 13 minutes for each question). Students are required to answer the first two questions but can choose between two options for the final required short-answer question, each focused on a different time period. Each question will have three parts and is worth three points. At least two of the short-answer questions are accompanied with stimulus material. There will be a finite amount of space in which student answers must be contained, and no credit will be given for writing outside of this finite area. Student answers must be in complete sentences (bulleted answers will not receive credit), but a thesis statement is not required. Students must be extremely careful to follow the directions and explicitly answer the question they are asked.

### Document-based Questions (DBQ)

The DBQ requires students to analyze and interpret historical documents, and then use the documents as well as outside information to support a well-developed thesis statement that directly answers the question and takes a position. Thesis statements that simply restate the prompt as a statement will not receive credit. DBQs will contain seven historical documents. You begin the DBQ with a recommended 15-minute reading period intended for you to read and analyze the documents. After the reading period ends, you will have 85 minutes to complete the DBQ *and* the long essay, so plan to take 45 minutes of this time to answer the document-based question.

**Tips for writing the DBQ essay:**

1. **Read the prompt (essay question) carefully and thoroughly.** Mark it to indicate the key words, phrases, or tasks required. Do not begin any other step until you know what the question is asking.
2. **Jot down your thoughts as you begin to read the source documents.** You should begin to see some connections or contradictions among the documents. Underline or circle key ideas in each document. You can refer to these marks after you begin to write your essay. Begin a list of these ideas in the margins of your test booklet so you can refer to them later.
3. **Draft a clear 1- or 2- sentence thesis paragraph that fully addresses the prompt,** is historically defensible, and establishes a line of reasoning. Position the thesis paragraph at the start or the end of the essay so readers do not need to hunt for it.
4. **Use your thesis as a map for putting the essay together.** Use words from your thesis in each body paragraph topic sentence. Follow your thesis order to organize each body paragraph and to answer the prompt.

5. **Provide historical context.** Connect your response to related broader historical events, developments, or processes that occurred before, during, or continued after the time frame in question.

6. **Always cite the documents.** You should cite each document every time you use it. Putting a (Doc. 1) or a (1), for example, after each usage is fine.

7. **Use documents to support your argument in response to the prompt.** Your response must accurately describe—rather than simply quote—the content of the documents to support your argument. You must also describe additional evidence from documents not given to you in the DBQ to support your argument.

8. **For the source documents, analyze point of view, the intended audience, the author's purpose, or historical context.** Practice these analytical skills with your teacher's help and feedback.

9. **Demonstrate a complex understanding of historical developments.** You should be able to analyze multiple variables, explain similarities and differences or continuity and change or causes and effects, explain connections within and across time periods, corroborate multiple perspectives across themes, or consider diverse or alternative views or evidence as part of your argument.

## Scoring the DBQ

The DBQ will be scored on a 0-7 scale using an analytic rubric. The key elements of the rubric are:

1. (0–1 point) **Thesis/Claim**
   - (1 point) Responds to the prompt with a historically defensible thesis/claim that establishes a line of reasoning.

2. (0–1 point) **Contextualization**
   - (1 point) Describes a broader historical context relevant to the prompt.

3. (0–3 points) **Evidence**
   a. **Evidence from the Documents**
      - (1 point) Uses the content of at least **three** documents to address the topic of the prompt.
      **OR**
      - (2 points) Supports an **argument** in response to the prompt using at least six documents.

   b. **Evidence beyond the Documents**
      - (1 point) Uses at least one additional piece of the specific historical evidence (beyond that found in the documents) relevant to an argument about the prompt.

4. (0–2 points) **Analysis and Reasoning**
   - (1 point) For at least three documents, explain how or why the document's point of view, purpose, historical situation, and/or audience is relevant to an argument.
   - (1 point) Demonstrates a complex understanding of the historical development that is the focus of the prompt, using evidence to corroborate, qualify, or modify an argument that addresses the question.

## Long Essay Question

You will have the choice of answering one of three long essay questions. All three essays will test the same theme but focus on different chronological periods, so you can choose which period you are most prepared to write about.

The long essay is designed to measure your ability to use historical reasoning through the demonstration of thesis development, organized presentation of historical argument, and evidence given to support the argument. You will have 40 minutes to write the long essay.

**Tips for writing the Long Essay:**

1. **Read the prompt (essay question) carefully and thoroughly.** Mark it to indicate key words, phrases, or tasks required. Especially note the reasoning processes required: *Comparison, Causation,* or *Continuity and Change.* Do not begin any other step until you know what the question is asking.

2. **Write a 1- or 2- sentence thesis that contains a claim (position, premise, or idea) that you can support and that will guide the rest of your essay.** Your thesis should identify and quantify comparisons (similarities/differences), change/continuities, or causes/effects. In other words, your thesis must have some value-added concepts, which means you must demonstrate some applicable knowledge. Do not just repeat the prompt.

3. **Follow your thesis order for your paragraph order.** This will keep you on track and reduce the time required to write the essay because you will not be wondering what to write about next.

4. **Provide historical context.** Similar to the DBQ, connect your response to related broader historical events, developments, or processes that occurred before, during, or continued after the time frame in question.

5. **Use historical evidence to support each part of the argument in your topic sentences.** Although you might know more about one aspect of the essay than another, use ample historical evidence to support each element in your topic sentence.

6. **Remember this mantra: *Describe examples, then analyze and explain.*** If the reasoning process is Comparison, list similarities and differences and then analyze and explain the reasons for them. If the reasoning process is Causation, describe causes and/ or effects and then analyze and explain them. If the reasoning process is Continuity and Change, list examples of things that stayed the same and analyze and explain them. Then list examples of things that changed and analyze and explain them.

7. **Demonstrate a complex understanding of historical developments using reasoning processes.** Use reasoning processes to structure your argument. Also, as in the DBQ, analyze multiple variables, explain similarities and differences or continuity and change or causes and effects, explain connections within and across time periods, corroborate multiple perspectives across themes, or consider diverse or alternative views or evidence as part of your argument to demonstrate a complex understanding.

## Scoring the Long Essay

The Long Essay will be scored on a 0–6 scale using an analytic rubric. The key elements of the rubric are:

1. (0–1 point) **Thesis/Claim**
   - Responds to the prompt with a historically defensible thesis/claim that establishes a line of reasoning.
2. (0–1 point) **Contextualization**
   - Describes a broader historical context relevant to the prompt.
3. (0–2 points) **Evidence**
   - (1 point) Provides specific examples of evidence relevant to the topic of the prompt.

     **OR**
   - (2 points) Supports an argument in response to the prompt using specific and relevant examples of evidence.
4. (0–2 points) **Analysis and Reasoning**
   - (1 point) Uses reasoning processes (e.g. comparison, causation, continuity and change) to frame or structure an argument that addresses the prompt.

     **OR**
   - (2 points) Demonstrates a complex understanding of the historical development that is the focus of the prompt, using evidence to corroborate, qualify, or modify an argument that addresses the question.

## Grading of the AP Exam

Colleges and universities often grant credits equivalent to what is offered for their introductory World History survey course to those students who successfully complete the AP Exam. The criteria for receiving credit vary widely from institution to institution and you should find out from each college and university you plan to apply to what their standards are. You may also choose to have your scores sent to colleges and universities to which you are applying. The AP Exam is scored on the following 5-point scale: 5 is "extremely well qualified"; 4 is "well qualified"; 3 is "qualified"; 2 is "possibly qualified"; 1 is "no recommendation."

Prelude

# An Introduction to Modern World History



## ZOOMING IN ON TRADITIONS

### King Yu and the Taming of the Yellow River

Ancient Chinese histories tell the stories of heroic figures who invented agriculture, domesticated animals, taught people to marry and live in families, created music, introduced the calendar, and instructed people in the arts and crafts. Most important of these heroes were three sage-kings—Yao, Shun, and Yu—who, according to ancient Chinese historian Sima Qian, laid the foundations of Chinese society. King Yao was a towering figure, sometimes associated with a mountain, who was extraordinarily modest, sincere, and respectful. Yao's virtuous influence brought harmony to his family, the larger society, and ultimately all the

Bronze battle axe of the Shang Dynasty. The axe depicts a fearsome face symbolizing power and military prowess and was probably used in battle by an important Shang elite warrior.
Archive PL/Alamy Stock Photo

states of China. King Shun succeeded Yao and continued his work by ordering the four seasons of the year and instituting uniform weights, measures, and units of time.

Most dashing of the sage-kings was Yu, a vigorous and tireless worker who rescued China from the raging waters of the flooding Yellow River. Before Yu, according to the stories, experts tried to control the Yellow River's floods by building dikes to contain its waters. The river was much too large and strong for the dikes, however, and it unleashed massive floods when it broke through. Yu abandoned the effort to dam the Yellow River and organized two alternate strategies. He dredged the river to deepen its channel and minimize the likelihood of overflows, and he dug canals parallel to the river so floodwaters would flow to the sea without devastating the countryside.

According to Sima Qian, Yu worked on the river for thirteen years without ever returning home. Because he tamed the Yellow River and made it possible to cultivate rice and millet, Yu became a popular hero. Poets praised the man who protected fields and villages from deadly and destructive floods. Historians such as Sima Qian reported that "he led the waters to the sea in a manner as orderly as lords proceeding to a formal reception." Eventually, Yu succeeded King Shun as leader of the Chinese people, and according to Sima Qian, he founded the Xia dynasty, which many believe to have been the first ruling house of ancient China.

The legends of Yao, Shun, and Yu no doubt exaggerated the virtues and deeds of the sage-kings. Agriculture, arts, crafts, marriage, family, government, and means of water control developed over an extended period of time, and no single individual was responsible for introducing them into China. Yet legends about early heroic figures reflected the interest of a people in the traditions that defined their society. At the same time, the moral thinkers who transmitted the legends used them to advocate values they considered beneficial for their society. By exalting Yao, Shun, and Yu as exemplars of virtue, Chinese moralists promoted values of social harmony and selfless, dedicated work that the sage-kings represented.

# CHAPTER FOCUS

- The College Board's Advanced Placement World History: Modern course begins around the year 1200 C.E.
- This chapter will introduce you to the course, providing context for the historical developments explored in the coming chapters. It includes a brief overview of the major events and trends that played out across the tens of thousands of years of human history that preceded the time span covered in the AP course.
- The chapter will help you develop a solid geographical and chronological foundation on which to build your content knowledge and historical thinking skills.

## Thematic Structure

The AP World History: Modern course is structured around six themes:

- Humans and the Environment (ENV)
- Cultural Developments and Interactions (CDI)
- Governance (GOV)
- Economic Systems (ECN)
- Social Interactions and Organization (SIO)
- Technology and Innovation (TEC)

To help you learn the material required in the AP World History: Modern course, this introduction is also structured around the same six AP world history themes. Studying history through the lens of these themes will help you see interconnections, changes over time, and causes and effects across the vast time spans of world history.

## THEME 1: HUMANS AND THE ENVIRONMENT

Environments shape human societies, and as populations grow and change, these populations in turn shape their environment. In this section we explore the environments and geography of the world's major regions. The world is divided into four large world-zones: Afro-Eurasia, the Americas, Australasia and the Pacific. The most populous of these zones have always been Afro-Eurasia and the Americas. From the beginning of human history, environments have played a crucial role in the way humans lived. It has determined what types of plants and animals could be domesticated by early farmers, where land and maritime trade and migration routes could be established, and what types of flora and fauna could be turned into valuable commercial exports. For groups who lived as pastoral nomads, the environment of the steppe made possible the creation of a brand-new lifeway.

| CHRONOLOGY | |
|---|---|
| 250-200,000 B.C.E. | Early evolution of homo sapiens in Sub-Saharan Africa |
| c. 90,000 B.C.E. | Migration of humans out of Africa |
| c. 15,000 B.C.E. | Migration of humans into the Americas |
| 10,000-8,000 B.C.E. | Early experimentation with agriculture |
| 8000 B.C.E. | Appearance of agricultural villages |
| 4000-3500 B.C.E. | Appearance of first cities |
| 4000 B.C.E. | Domestication of horses by pastoral nomads |

### Afro-Eurasia

Afro-Eurasia is a vast geo-political world zone that includes all of Asia, Europe, and Africa. Afro-Eurasia was home to all of the world's earliest civilizations, many of which were connected for thousands of years by exchange networks such as the **Silk Roads**. While you do not need to know details of these various civilizations for the AP World History: Modern course, knowledge of the range and diversity of environments within Afro-Eurasia provides important context for events and cultural developments that occur after 1200 C.E. The Afro-Eurasian world zone can be divided into several environmental sub-zones.

**Great Arid Zone and Steppe Zone** The Great Arid Zone is a combination of deserts, semi-deserts, and mountainous terrain that stretches from the Atlantic Coast of Africa to East Asia. From west to east, the Great Arid Zone includes the Sahara Desert of North Africa, the deserts of the Middle East and Iranian Plateau, the Great Thar Desert of South Asia, and the deserts of Inner Eurasia such as the Kara Kum, the Taklamakan, and the Gobi.

To the north of this long expanse of deserts is the Eurasian Steppe, characterized by extensive grasslands that stretch from Eastern Europe to Mongolia and beyond. Because of the abundance of grass, all the major pastoral nomadic groups in Afro-Eurasian history were based in the steppe, where the grass provided food for their animals. Pastoral nomads had a significant impact on many of the sedentary states and civilizations of Afro-Eurasia. Pastoralists generally follow a nomadic lifeway, moving across the steppe with their herds and flocks. Yet in some locations on the steppe, irrigation-based agriculture also flourished, allowing for the appearance of towns and cities that became important centers of Silk Roads commerce.

The Mongols make their appearance in the early 1200s, so it is important to understand something about pastoral nomadic lifestyles. Nomads were able to produce most of what they needed from their animals, but not all, which means they regularly interacted with sedentary peoples through trading or raiding. Pastoral nomads also interacted with merchants across both the Great Arid and the Great Steppe Zones, often functioning as important intermediaries in facilitating trade across the Sahara and along the Silk Roads. Pastoral nomads depended on a range of animals for survival, but of critical importance were the horse, upon which nomadic armies rode, and the camel, which carried the bulk of commercial goods along these major Afro-Eurasian trade routes. The nomadic military consisted mostly of fast moving, horse-mounted cavalry soldiers skilled with the bow and arrow, which made them formidable foes for sedentary armies. Socially, nomadic communities were a lot more egalitarian than sedentary societies, and women had more equality with men.

**Indian Ocean Basin** Thousands of years ago merchants discovered another way of moving their goods long distances across Afro-Eurasia - by sea. Maritime trade across the Indian Ocean Basin was made possible by **monsoon** weather patterns. From April to September monsoon winds blow eastwards from Africa and across the Arabian Sea towards South and Southeast Asia, often bringing torrential rains to those regions. From November to February the winds blow in the opposite direction, from the arid regions of Tibet and the Himalaya across South Asia and back out into the Arabian Sea. During this cycle rainfall is sparse and drought was and is often severe on the Indian Subcontinent.

These monsoon wind patterns were exploited by merchants trading across the Indian Ocean Basin from Roman times and even earlier. When the winds blew from Africa eastwards across the Arabian Sea, commercial fleets would sail from ports in Egypt and the Arabian Peninsula bringing valuable trade goods to India. When the winds blew in the opposite direction, these same merchant fleets, now laden with cargo from South Asia, would sail back across the Arabian Sea to ports in the Persian

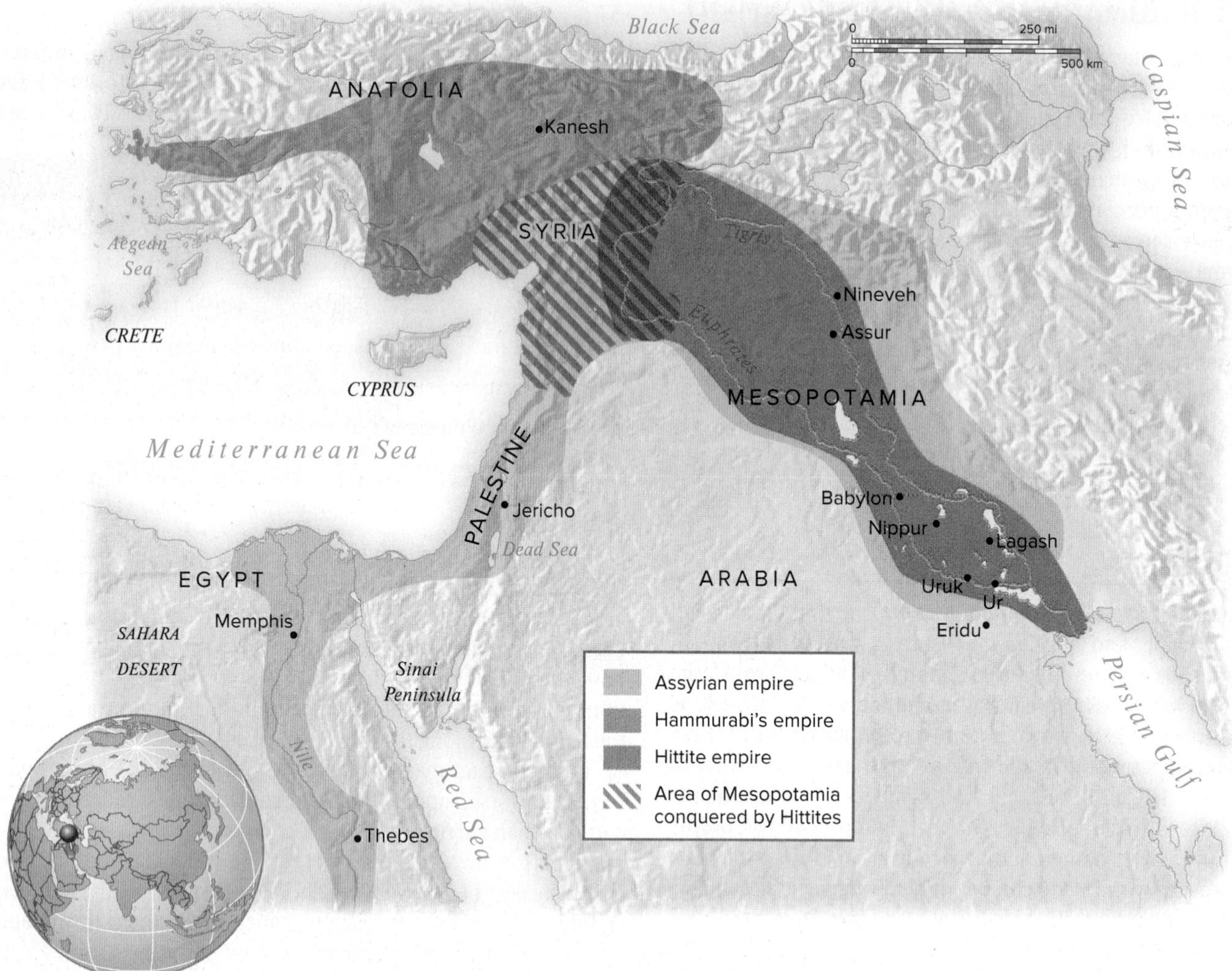


**MAP P.1 Mesopotamian empires, 1800-600 B.C.E.**

Note the locations of Mesopotamian cities in relation to the Tigris and Euphrates rivers.

***In what ways did the environment of Southwest Asia facilitate the emergence of complex societies in the region?***

McGraw-Hill

Gulf and Red Sea. These sea routes were so important they are often termed the 'Maritime Silk Roads'.

We can sub-divide Indian Ocean maritime trade into three sub-zones, in which sailors and merchants from different cultures dominated commerce in a range of regionally specific goods, generally products of the flora and fauna native to each region. In the Western Indian Ocean, commerce was dominated by merchants and sailors from East Africa, the Arabian Peninsula, the Persian Gulf, and South Asia. Arabian and African products such as gold, copper, ivory, and coffee were exchanged for South Asian cotton textiles, dyes, and pepper. Between the Indian Subcontinent and Southeast Asia, South and Southeast Asian merchants and sailors conducted trade in products produced in the two regions, including a range of spices and scented woods. A third zone operated between Southeast and East Asia, dominated by Chinese and Southeast Asian merchants and sailors. The Chinese merchants exported silk textiles, tea, sugar, and luxury goods such as porcelain, in exchange for spices and scented woods. In each of these zones, port cities emerged to facilitate exchanges, often located at the intersection of these sub-zones. Merchants rarely if ever made the entire voyage from East Asia to East Africa, but their goods regularly did.

Central to the Indian Ocean Monsoon Zone is the Indian Subcontinent, which is separated from the Arid and Steppe Zones by the various ranges of the Himalaya Mountains. The Subcontinent is dominated by two major river systems, the Indus and Ganges, and by the Vindhya Mountains which rise up in an east-west direction across the modern nation of India at roughly its halfway point. Because the Indian Subcontinent is impacted by the monsoon systems, it has very arid regions, and also regions that receive a tremendous amount of rainfall.

**Southwest Asia or Middle East** These two terms are often used interchangeably, which can be confusing. Southwest Asia is a geographical designation, while the Middle East is a geo-political and cultural designation. The term "Middle East" is a Eurocentric descriptor which dates from the nineteenth century, when European diplomats and geographers described China, Korea, and Japan as the "Far East," because they were far to the east from Europe. They used the term "Near East" to describe the lands of the Eastern Mediterranean, and the regions halfway between Europe and East Asia were termed the "Middle East." Southwest Asia was the cradle of the world's earliest civilizations which arose in what is Iraq today, along the valleys of the Tigris and Euphrates Rivers, and in Egypt, along the valley of the **Nile River**.

Thousands of years later this same region was where Islam first emerged. As the heartland of Islamic civilization, Southwest Asia functioned as an enormous transit zone between all the regions of Afro-Eurasia where goods, ideas, crops, technologies, and peoples regularly passed. Geographically, Southwest Asia is dominated by arid zones, some low mountain ranges, extensive coastlines of the Mediterranean Sea, Persian Gulf, and Arabian Sea, and major rivers including the Tigris, Euphrates, and Nile.

**East and Southeast Asia** This enormous region includes China, the Korean Peninsula, the Japanese archipelago, and all of Southeast Asia including many islands such as Taiwan and the Philippines. Although these regions are geographically diverse, they have long been unified culturally through the widespread adoption of Chinese ideologies such as **Confucianism, Daoism,** and **Legalism,** and the imported South Asian ideology of **Buddhism.** We'll discuss these ideologies more later in the chapter.

Geographically China is dominated by two major river systems, those of the Huang He (or Yellow River) in the north, and the **Yangzi** (or Chang Jian) in the south. Because of its enormous size, China has a wide range of topography, climate, and vegetation. The eastern regions consist of alluvial plains built up by the two great rivers, so this is where most of China's food has been grown, and where all the early states were located. In the north, China merges with the Great Steppe Zone, and it is here that interactions between Chinese states and pastoral nomads regularly occurred. The southern regions of China are hilly and receive a great deal of rainfall, ideal for the cultivation of rice. Most of western China consists of very high mountain ranges and arid deserts, terrain that formed a barrier to Chinese interaction with Central Asia until the opening up of the Silk Roads late in the second century B.C.E.

Korea is a peninsula jutting out from the East Asian mainland; it features rugged mountains, many fast-flowing rivers, and a long coastline. Japan is an archipelago of many islands, with a wide range of climates, high mountains, and a long coastline. Southeast Asia, including the many islands, has an enormous coastline, and inland is influenced by major rivers like the Mekong, along with steep mountains and tropical forests.

**Europe** Although Europe has for centuries traditionally been referred to as a continent, the region would more accurately be considered a sub-continent, much like the Indian Subcontinent. The practice of describing Europe as a continent is another Eurocentric decision. There are no significant geographical boundaries that separate Europe from Asia. Neither the Ural Mountains nor the Caucasus Mountains form appreciable barriers to movement, as shown by the sheer number of migrations and invasions of Europe by peoples from Asia, including Inner Eurasian nomads such as the Mongols.

Europe consists of, in part, a series of peninsulas, including Scandinavia, Jutland, Brittany, Iberia (Spain and Portugal), Italy, the Balkans, the Peloponnesus, and Crimea. These peninsulas jut into major surrounding seas, such as the Atlantic Ocean and North Sea in the west, and the Mediterranean and Black Seas in the south. Within these large bodies of water lie many important islands, including Iceland, the Faroe Islands, the British Isles, the Balearic Islands, Sardinia, Corsica, Sicily, Malta, Cyprus and the islands of the **Aegean Sea**. Given the predominance of seas surrounding Europe, it is not surprising that early cultures and civilizations emerged along the coastlines, and that maritime cities such as Venice, Genoa and the Hanseatic cities later became wealthy and powerful.

The Mediterranean and Black Sea regions form an interconnected geographic zone. The region is shielded from cold Arctic winds by mountain ranges such as the Alps and Pyrenees, while hot winds from the Sahara Desert of North Africa blow north across the sea. The ancient Greeks, who extensively colonized much of the Mediterranean and Black Sea coasts, developed patterns of agriculture that are still prevalent today, including the cultivation of olives and grapes. Further north, the coastal regions of the Atlantic Ocean including the North and Baltic Seas experience much harsher weather, but this did not prevent the emergence of major ports and trading leagues.

Separated from Southern Europe by the Pyrenees, Alps, and Carpathians, much of central and eastern Europe is located in a geographic zone known as the Great European Plain. Historically this region has been dominated by vast forests, rich soil, swamps, and major rivers, and it was within the Great European Plain that Germanic and Slavic civilizations emerged. During the Middle Ages many of the forest

**Confucianism** (kuhn-FYOO-shuhn-iz'm)
**Daoism** (DOW-i'zm)
**Buddhism** (BOO-diz'm)
**Yangzi** (YAHNG-zuh)

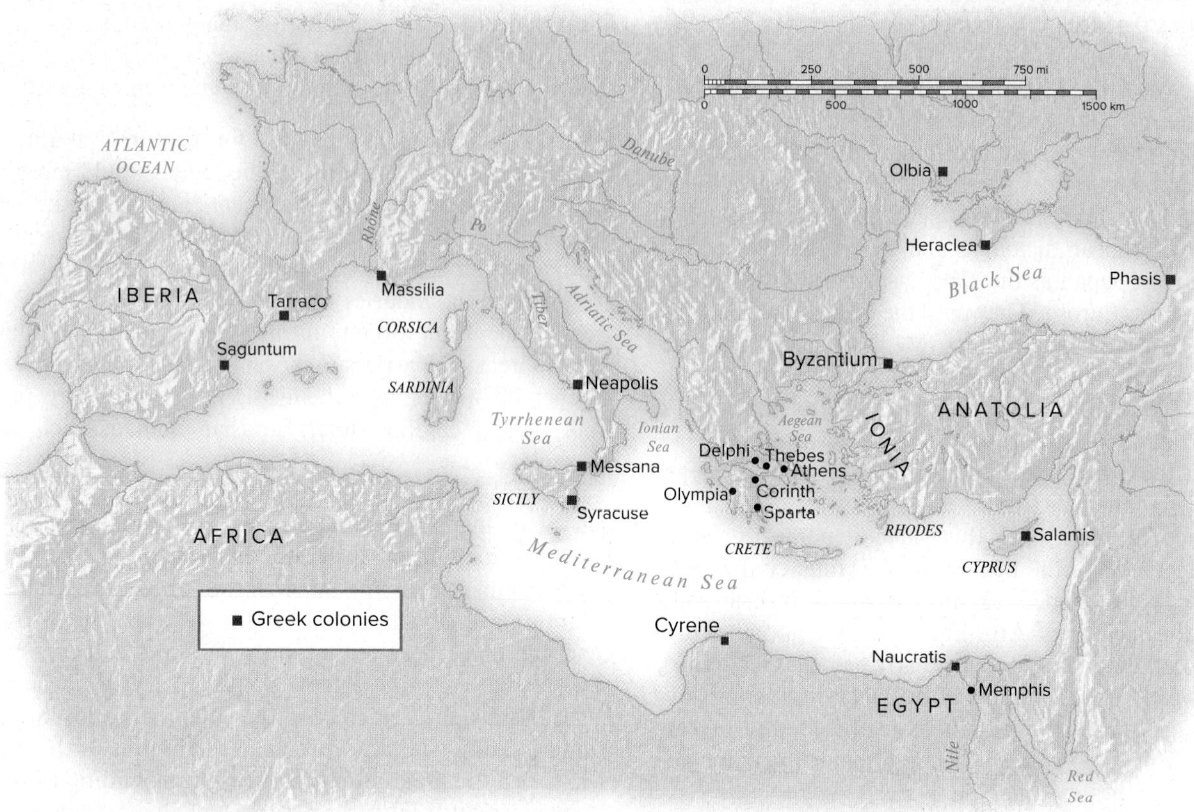


**MAP P.2 Classical Greece and the Mediterranean basin, 800-500 B.C.E.**

All the Greek colonies were located on the coastlines of the Mediterranean Sea and the Black Sea.

***What impacts did Greek colonization have on the peoples already living along the shores of the Mediterranean and Black seas?***

McGraw-Hill

were cleared to make way for farming, a process in which Christian monastic communities played a major role. Although the soils were often difficult to farm, crops such as wheat, barley and rye flourished, and became the staple crops throughout the Middle Ages. The Great European Plain is crossed by major rivers such as the Danube and Rhine, and important towns and cities formed along these rivers at crossing points or at the confluence of trade routes.

## The Americas

The continents of North and South America, and the **Mesoamerican** isthmus that connects them, constitute another vast world zone made up of many different environments. Major environmental zones of North America include the Southwest interior, located east of the Great Basin and west of the Rocky Mountains. This zone, which extends south into modern Mexico, is a harsh environment consisting mostly of deserts and semi-deserts. Control of water has been critical throughout the history of the region. It was the home to the Anasazi, the ancestors of the Puebloan peoples, and the Hohokam and Mogollon cultures. A second important environmental region of North America is the vast Mississippi River Basin, including its many tributaries and the adjacent Southeast Woodlands. This region has historically featured forests and rich agricultural soils. The rivers facilitated communication and exchange between early inhabitants, including several mound building cultures. Early farmers grew a trio of crops known as the "three sisters" - corn, beans and squash - and also practiced extensive hunting.

Mesoamerica also has a diverse range of environments, including chains of active and dormant volcanoes, tropical rainforests, and extensive coastlines. Historically important regions include the Valley of Mexico, the Oaxaca Valley, the Yucatan, the Guatemalan Highlands, and the coasts of Veracruz. Mesoamerica was the location of the first complex

**Mesoamerica** (mez-oh-uh-MER-i-kuh)

cultures and states to appear in the Americas. Successful agriculture in these challenging environments led to increased populations and social complexity, resulting in the emergence of sophisticated cultures such as the **Olmecs**, **Teotihuacan**, **Maya**, and Aztecs.

South America is another enormous continent with a wide range of environments, from tropical rainforest (particularly in Amazonia), steppe-like grasslands (known as *pampas* in modern Argentina) and sub-polar regions in the far south. Of most importance historically is the Andean region, which stretches almost the entire length of the Pacific Coast of the continent. It includes high mountains, coastal deserts, and a narrow strip of fertile coastland. Early farmers in the Andes region were able to make use of the different plants and animals that flourished at different altitudes in this land of vertical zonation. At sea level humans accessed extensive marine resources and limited plant domesticates. At the intermediate level farmers grew corn and herded llamas and alpacas. This zone supported the densest populations. At higher altitudes farmers successfully domesticated hundreds of varieties of potatoes. Extensive trade occurred between all three zones, and successful states like the Inca were able to take control of each of these zones to support large populations and construct an extensive empire.

## THEME 2: CULTURAL DEVELOPMENTS AND INTERACTIONS

The development of ideas, beliefs, and religions illustrates how groups in society view themselves, and the interactions of societies and their beliefs often have political, social and cultural implications. In this section we consider major cultural, ideological, and religious developments in the regions of the world, from ancient times up to c.1200 C.E. Sometimes when viewing history on the macro scale what becomes most immediately apparent is the commonality of human experiences rather than the differences. But humans have come up with an astonishing range of ideologies and religions which continue to profoundly affect human beliefs and relationships between nations today.

| CHRONOLOGY | |
|---|---|
| c. 1300 B.C.E | Hebrews settle in Palestine |
| 563-483 B.C.E | Life of Siddhartha Gautama, the Buddha |
| 551-479 B.C.E | Life of Confucius |
| 3rd Century B.C.E | Spread of Buddhism and Hinduism to Southeast Asia |
| 1st Century B.C.E | Introduction of Buddhism to China |
| 4 BCE – early 30s C.E | Life of Jesus of Nazareth |
| 1st Century C.E | Life of Paul of Tarsus |
| 300-1100 C.E | Mayan society |
| 570-632 C.E | Life of Muhammad |
| 650s | Compilation of the Quran |

### East Asian Cultural Complex

The East Asian Cultural Complex includes China, Korea, Japan, and regions of Southeast Asia, particularly Vietnam. As we mentioned earlier in the chapter, the entire region was heavily influenced by Chinese cultural practices, but Korea, Japan, and Vietnam were also able to maintain their cultural distinctiveness. Chinese traditions influenced the entire region, including the beliefs and practices of the core Chinese ideologies of Confucianism, Daoism, and Legalism. These ideologies are responsible for cultural traditions that for thousands of years have affected ideas about social organization, gender relations, and government and bureaucracy. We discuss some of these effects in relevant thematic sections later in the chapter. Having some knowledge of these ancient traditions will help you understand developments after 1200 C.E.

Another important ideology that has been widely influential in the East Asian Cultural Complex is Buddhism, which originated in South Asia but spread to China during the **Han Dynasty** in the centuries on either side of the B.C.E/C.E. divide. Buddhism went through periods of acceptance and persecution during the centuries that followed. During the Song Dynasty, the ideology of Neo-Confucianism emerged, which was partly an attempt to reject the "foreign ideology" of Buddhism. Neo-Confucianism was highly influential on Chinese culture through the twentieth century.

Korean culture was influenced by all these Chinese ideologies, but also developed its own distinctive cultural practices and invented Hangul as an original Korean writing system. Japanese culture maintained its indigenous Shinto religion, although this was also synthesized with elements of Buddhism. Vietnamese elites were assimilated into Chinese culture through their adoption of the Confucian educational system, but the rejection of some of the gender implications of Confucian ideology meant that women in Vietnamese society enjoyed much greater freedoms and equality with men than was the case in China, Korea, or Japan.

**Teotihuacan** (tay-uh-tee-wah-KAHN)
**Maya** (Mye-uh)

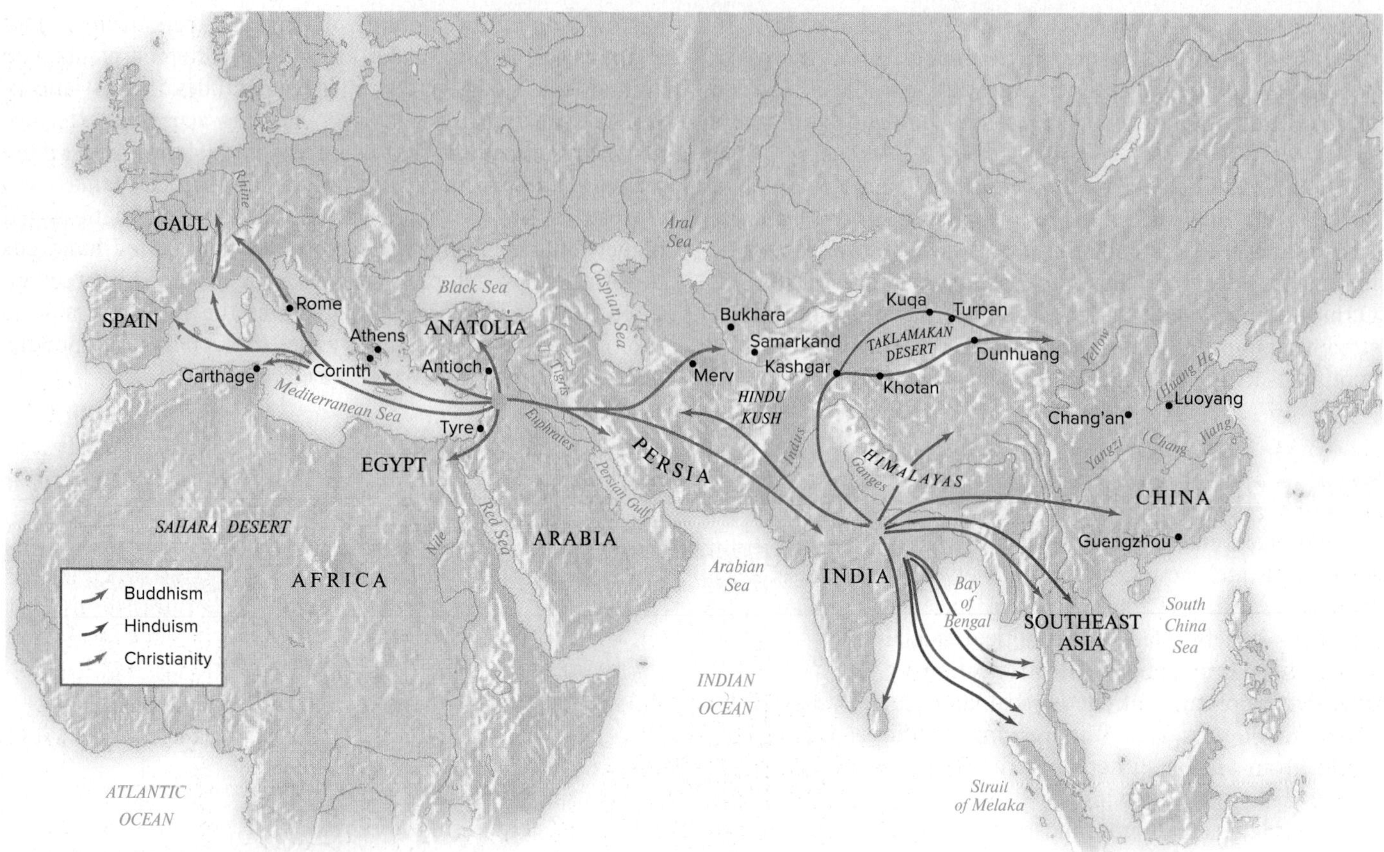


**MAP P.3 The spread of Buddhism, Hinduism, and Christianity, 200 B.C.E.–400 C.E.**

Compare the routes taken by Buddhism, Hinduism, and Christianity with the routes followed by merchants on Silk Roads depicted on Map 12.1.

***What role did Silk Roads trade play in the diffusion of these religions?***

McGraw-Hill

## Monotheistic Religious Cultures

By 1200 C.E. millions of people in Afro-Eurasia were practicing one of the three major **monotheistic** religions - Judaism, **Christianity**, and **Islam**. Of the three religions Judaism is the oldest, and by 1200 Jewish communities were dispersed widely across Afro-Eurasia, particularly in Europe, Kievan Rus', Ethiopia, and Southwest Asia. The **Jews** were a diasporic community (from the Greek word for scattering), which meant that many Jewish communities were often isolated and thus more easily persecuted, particularly in parts of Europe. In the Islamic world, Jews were often protected. Despite their small numbers and the isolated nature of their communities, Jewish people were united by their religion, and gained great influence intellectually and commercially throughout much of Afro-Eurasia.

Christianity emerged more recently than Judaism. It originated in Southwest Asia as a minor sect within Judaism. But during the first two centuries of the Common Era, dedicated Christian missionaries, such as **Paul of Tarsus**, used the land and maritime trade routes of the Eastern Mediterranean to spread Christianity throughout much of the **Roman Empire**. Beyond the Roman world, Christian merchants and missionaries also carried their faith into Arabia, **Nubia**, Ethiopia, the Caucasus, India, the **Sasanians**, Central Asia, and East Asia.

Major splits occurred in Christian theology during the first millennium CE, particularly between the Latin (Roman) Church and the Greek Orthodox Church. An important early break-away group were the **Nestorians**, who were declared heretics by the mainstream church, but who had great influence in the wider Muslim world, and later in the Mongol Empire. Nestorian communities were established along trade routes that connected Europe and Southwest Asia with India and China. Another important development in Christianity was the Great Schism of 1054, which was a reaction against the

**Nubia** (NOO-bee-uh)
**Sasanians** (suh-SAHN-iens)
**Nestorian** (neh-STOHR-ee-uhn)

expansion of the papacy in Italy to something more than a religious institution. During the Middle Ages in Western Europe, the power of the pope and of the Church in general rivaled even the power of secular princes and kings.

The Catholic and Orthodox churches also developed different forms of monasticism. Monks in the Orthodox tradition saw their practice as a retreat from the world, whereas Western monasticism, which was founded under the influence of St. Benedict, tended to engage with the world. After the disintegration of the Western Roman Empire, monasteries effectively replaced many former governmental institutions such as schools, orphanages, and social welfare providers. Western monasteries also became places of great learning focused on the preservation of knowledge from the Greek and Roman worlds, while Eastern monasteries were places of contemplation.

The most recent of the monotheistic religions is Islam, which emerged in the Arabian Peninsula in the seventh century and rapidly spread across vast regions of Afro-Eurasia. The key figure in early Islam is the Prophet Muhammad, who Muslims believe received messages from a single god named Allah. These messages were written down in a book called the Quran ("Recitations"). After Muhammad's death, his successors as heads of government and the faith were named caliphs (which means "deputies"). The early caliphs and the dynasties that followed spread the religion all across Southwest Asia, North Africa, and deep into Central Asia. By 1200 Islamic communities were located widely across Afro-Eurasia, from Southwest Asia and China to North Africa and the Iberian Peninsula of Europe.

Islam spread because of a range of factors, including military campaigns, trade, and missionary activities carried out particularly effectively by missionaries known as the Sufis. As was the case with Christianity, Islam suffered a major ideological split between the Sunni and Shia interpretations of the faith. Non-Arab converts to Islam gravitated towards Shia, which was more welcoming of outsiders, and this explains the existence today of nations in Central and Southwest Asia that are either Sunni or Shia, and which often have tense relations with each other.

Finally, it is worth noting the influence of the ancient Greek philosopher Aristotle on these three monotheistic religions. Major intellectuals such as the Jewish thinker Maimonides (1138-1204), the Islamic intellectual Ibn Rushd (also known as Averroes, 1126-1198), and the Christian philosopher St. Thomas Aquinas (1225-1274) all helped integrate Aristotelian thinking into these religions, and into their monotheistic societies more widely.

Aristotle (322-384 B.C.E.)
Michele Ursi/Alamy Stock Photo

Moses Maimonides (1138-1204)
Ken Welsh/Age Fotostock

St. Thomas Aquinas (1225-1274)
Art Collection 2/Alamy Stock Photo

## Hinduism and Buddhism in South and Southeast Asia

Early religious beliefs and practices in South Asia revolved around ritual sacrifices offered by elite **brahmin** priests, the highest group in the rigidly hierarchical **caste** system that emerged early in the first millennium B.C.E. But during the mid-first millennium B.C.E., new spiritual ideas emerged that challenged the old beliefs, and also the pretensions of the **brahmins**. One of the influential new religions was **Jainism**, which advocated the principle of ***ahimsa*** or nonviolence to all other living souls. Jains rejected the caste system which divided humans into different social classes, arguing that all souls were of equal importance.

Vardhamana Mahavira with one of his disciples. Representations of the early Jains often depicted them in the nude because of their rejection of material culture. Eleora Caves, South Asia, tenth century.
Stuart Forster India/Alamy Stock Photo

The next important spiritual ideology to emerge was Buddhism, which also rejected the caste system. Buddhism is closely associated with the life of **Siddhartha Gautama**, a sixth century prince who abandoned his wealthy life to become a wandering ascetic, seeking answers to the question of human suffering. Eventually Siddhartha came to understand that the cause of human suffering is desire or unchecked ambition, and this could be controlled by leading a decent, non-violent and meditative life. Siddhartha, now known as the Buddha, attracted many disciples whom he organized into an effective monastic order. Over the centuries that followed, Buddhism became the most important spiritual ideology in South Asia. A more accessible version of Buddhism emerged in the late centuries B.C.E. - **Mahayana** or "greater vehicle" Buddhism - and this spread along the land and maritime Silk Roads to Central Asia, China, Korea, Japan, and much of Southeast Asia.

A painting produced in the late fifth century C.E. depicts the Buddha seated under a pavilion as servants attend to his needs and anoint him with holy water.
NiKreative/Alamy Stock Photo

As Buddhism became increasingly popular, followers of the original South Asian religion made major reforms to help it compete with Buddhism, and this led to the development of Hinduism. Hindus blended ancient practices with new ideas drawn from great secular works of prose and poetry to create a syncretic religion that better addressed the needs and interests of ordinary people. Unlike Jainism and Buddhism,

**Brahmins** (BRAH-minz)
**Jainism** (JEYEN-iz'm)
**Ahimsa** (uh-HIM-suh)
**Siddhartha Gautama** (sih-DHAR-tuh GOW-taumah)
**Mahayana** (mah-huh-YAH-nah)

A tenth-century sculptural representation of three of the major Hindu gods, from left to right, Vishnu (preserver), Shiva (destroyer), and Brahma (creator). Gift of Ramesh and Urmil Kapoor/Los Angeles County Museum of Art.

Hinduism actively supports the caste system, arguing that only by accepting one's caste position and duties is one able to play an active role in the world, enjoy material, social and physical success, and still obtain salvation. The transformed religion of Hinduism was tremendously successful in South Asia and parts of Southeast Asia, and completely eclipsed Buddhism in India.

By 1200 C.E. Hinduism was flourishing in India and had further evolved due to the rise of devotional cults amongst the lower castes that focused on two gods in particular, **Vishnu** and Shiva. Buddhism in India was largely extinct, a process helped by the destruction of Buddhist temples and religious complexes that had occurred at the hands of expanding Islamic armies in the preceding centuries. Buddhism also lost support amongst state governments in India, although it was strongly supported by states in areas of East Asia such as Korea and Japan, and in Vietnam and Cambodia. New more mystical forms of Buddhism also appeared, such as Vajrayana, which flourished in parts of Central Asia and Tibet.

## The Americas

Human societies in the Americas developed their own rich and complex religions and ideologies. Early Mesoamerican cultures such as the Olmec built ceremonial centers and constructed **colossal human heads**, although what sort of beliefs and rituals these represented is unclear. The Maya followed an elaborate creation story known as the **Popol Vuh**, which describes how the gods made humans out of **maize** and water.

The Maya also supported a large class of priests whose job it was to conduct rituals that included **bloodletting rituals** as a way of asking the gods to send rain. Early South American societies like that of the **Chavín culture** also constructed temples to worship their gods, which were represented in carved stones as a mix of human and wild animal features, including jaguars and snakes. By 1200 C.E. numerous cultures had emerged, thrived and disappeared in various locations across North, Central, and South America, and many aspects of daily life in each of those cultures were influenced by local religious beliefs and practices.

---

**Vishnu** (VIHSH-noo)
**Popol Vuh** (paw-pawl vuh)

# SOURCES FROM THE PAST

## The Creation of Humanity According to the Popol Vuh

*The Popol Vuh, a Mayan creation myth, describes how, after several failed attempts, the Mayan gods finally created humans out of maize and water. The following excerpt from the myth concludes by naming the first four humans, describing them as "our first mothers and fathers." The version of the work that survives today dates from the mid-sixteenth century, but it reflects beliefs of a much earlier era.*

THIS, then, is the beginning of the conception of humanity, when that which would become the flesh of mankind was sought. Then spoke they who are called She Who Has Borne Children and He Who Has Begotten Sons, the Framer and the Shaper, Sovereign and Quetzal Serpent:

Who or what are the characters being referred to in this paragraph?

"The dawn approaches, and our work is not successfully completed. A provider and a sustainer have yet to appear—a child of light, a son of light. Humanity has yet to appear to populate the face of the earth," they said.

Thus they gathered together and joined their thoughts in the darkness, in the night. They searched and they sifted. Here they thought and they pondered. Their thoughts came forth bright and clear. They discovered and established that which would become the flesh of humanity. This took place just a little before the appearance of the sun, moon, and stars above the heads of the Framer and the Shaper.

It was from within the places called Paxil and Cayala that the yellow ears of ripe maize and the white ears of ripe maize came.

THESE were the names of the animals that obtained their food—fox and coyote, parakeet and raven. Four, then, were the animals that revealed to them the yellow ears of maize and the white ears of maize. They came from Paxil and pointed out the path to get there.

Thus was found the food that would become the flesh of the newly framed and shaped people. Water was their blood. It became the blood of humanity. The ears of maize entered into their flesh by means of She Who Has Borne Children and He Who Has Begotten Sons.

Thus they rejoiced over the discovery of that excellent mountain that was filled with delicious things, crowded with yellow ears of maize and white ears of maize. It was crowded as well with pataxte and chocolate, with countless zapotes and anonas, with jocotes and nances, with matasanos and honey. From within the places called Paxil and Cayala came the sweetest foods in the citadel. All the small foods and great foods were there, along with the small and great cultivated fields. The path was thus revealed by the animals.

What is the path that has been revealed to humans in this paragraph?

The yellow ears of maize and the white ears of maize were then ground fine with nine grindings by Xmucane. Food entered their flesh, along with water to give them strength. Thus was created the fatness of their arms. The yellowness of humanity came to be when they were made by they who are called She Who Has Borne Children and He Who Has Begotten Sons, by Sovereign and Quetzal Serpent.

Thus their frame and shape were given expression by our first Mother and our first Father. Their flesh was merely yellow ears of maize and white ears of maize. Mere food were the legs and arms of humanity, of our first fathers. And so there were four who were made, and mere food was their flesh.

These are the names of the first people who were framed and shaped: the first person was Balam Quitze, the second was Balam Acab, the third was Mahucutah, and the fourth was Iqui Balam. These, then, were the names of our first mothers and fathers.

### For Further Reflection

- According to the text, what was the origin of the foods the Maya depended on?
- What was the relationship between food and humans?
- How might this account of creation have influenced the religious beliefs and rituals that emerged in Mayan society?

*Source:* Alan J. Chistenson, *Popol Vuh: The Sacred Book of the Maya.* Originally published by O Books, Alresford, Hants, U.K. Copyright 2003 by Allen Christenson. Oklahoma edition published 2007 by the University of Oklahoma Press. Reprinted by permission. All rights reserved.

## THEME 3: GOVERNANCE

A variety of internal and external factors contribute to state formation, expansion, and decline. Governments maintain order through a variety of administrative institutions, policies, and procedures, and governments obtain, retain, and exercise power in different ways and for different purposes.

In this section we outline the various political and administrative structures put in place by states to govern their societies in the major regions of Afro-Eurasia and the Americas prior to c. 1200 C.E. Humans have been experimenting with different forms of governance for thousands of years and have constructed a wide range of state-like structures, most of which have facilitated the organization of large human populations by a relatively small number of secular and religious elites.

| CHRONOLOGY | |
|---|---|
| 3200-2350 B.C.E. | Sumerian dominance in Southwest Asia |
| 2300-1600 B.C.E. | Babylonian dominance in Southwest Asia |
| 1000-612 B.C.E. | Assyrian dominance in Southwest Asia |
| 2660-760 B.C.E. | Egyptian civilization flourishing in Northwest Africa |
| 2100-1600 B.C.E. | Xia Dynasty in East Asia |
| 1600-1050 B.C.E. | Shang Dynasty in East Asia |
| 1200-100 B.C.E. | Olmec society in Mesoamerica |
| 1050-256 B.C.E. | Zhou Dynasty in East Asia |
| 558-330 B.C.E. | Achaemenid Persian Empire in Central and Southwest Asia |
| 509 B.C.E. | Establishment of Roman Republic in Europe |
| 321-185 B.C.E. | Mauryan Dynasty in South Asia |
| 206 B.C.E.-220 C.E. | Han Dynasty in East Asia |
| 27 B.C.E.-476 B.C.E. | Traditional dates of Roman Empire in Europe |
| 300-700 C.E. | Moche Culture in Andean South America |
| 300-1100 C.E. | Mayan society in Mesoamerica |
| 320-550 C.E. | Gupta Dynasty in South Asia |
| 313-1452 C.E. | Byzantine Empire in Eastern Europe |
| c. 500-1500 C.E. | Medieval era in Western Europe |
| 618-907 C.E. | Tang Dynasty in East Asia |
| 661-750 C.E. | Umayyad Dynasty in Central and Southwest Asia |
| 670-1025 C.E. | Srivijaya Kingdom in Southeast Asia |
| 800-1100 C.E. | Kingdom of Ghana flourishing in sub-Saharan Africa |

### East Asia

By 1200 C.E. much of East Asia—China in particular—had experienced thousands of years of effective and quite sophisticated government. Early Chinese states had been structured as regional kingdoms, but during the second millennium B.C.E., many of these kingdoms were gradually brought under the control of dynasties (essentially a state ruled by members of the same family). The first of these was probably the **Xia**, followed by the **Shang** and **Zhou** Dynasties. The Zhou later claimed the "**Mandate of Heaven**" as justification for their overthrow of the Shang, the idea that heaven can bestow and remove power from rulers based on their effectiveness, and this became one of the defining ideals of Chinese dynastic government.

During the Later Zhou (770-221 B.C.E.) the dynasty fell apart and China was divided into a number of warring states. In these troubled times different ideologies emerged that went on to strongly influence approaches to political administration for millennia, in China and East and Southeast Asia. The most important of these ideologies was Confucianism, which advocated for the use of advanced education to produce intelligent, ethical bureaucrats that would run government efficiently and fairly. Candidates for high government office were chosen on the basis of an exam which tested their knowledge

**Xia** (shyah)
**Zhou dynasty** (JOH)

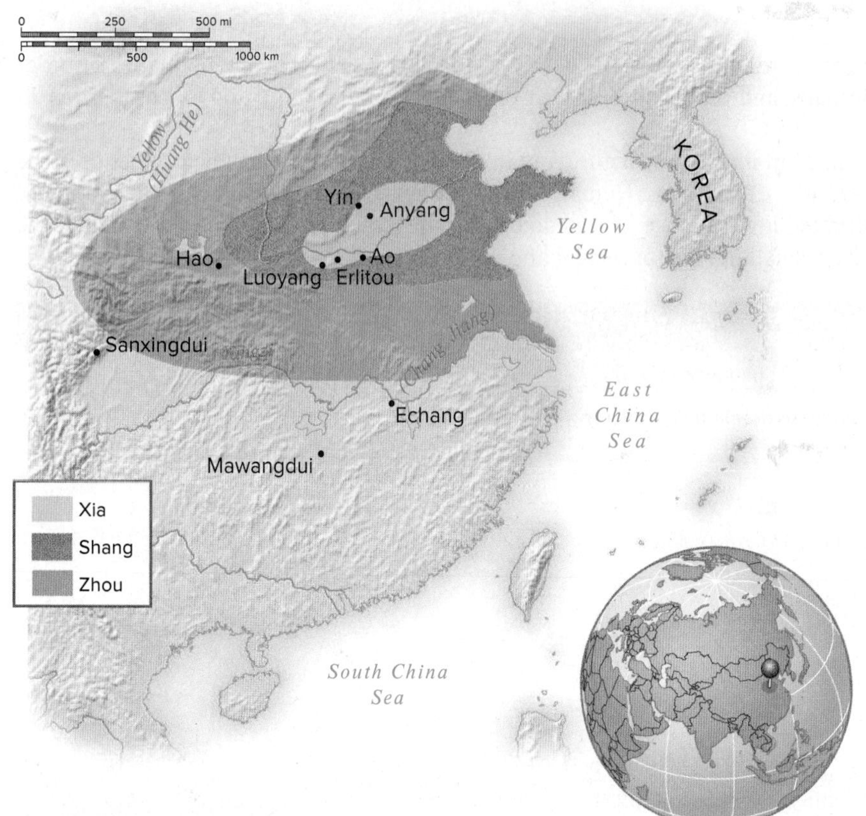


**MAP P.4 The Xia, Shang, and Zhou dynasties, 2100–256 B.C.E.**

Note that the three dynasties extended their territorial reach through time.

***What role did technology play in the increasing size of early Chinese states?***

McGraw-Hill

of Confucian ideology and the classics of Chinese literature. Although it was the **Qin** Dynasty, using the much harsher ideology of Legalism, that in 221 B.C.E. brought an end to the **Warring States period** and restored unity to China, most of the dynasties that followed were modeled on Confucian ideals. The most important of these subsequent dynasties were the Han (206 B.C.E.-220 C.E.) and Tang (618-907). It was the collapse of the Tang that led to the emergence of the Song Dynasty, which you will read more about in Chapter 1.

All these Chinese dynasties were forced to deal with powerful nomadic confederations that occupied the Great Steppe to the north. The Great Wall of China was built to try and keep these militarized nomads out of China. By 1200 C.E groups such as the Khitan and Jurchen had caused enormous problems for the Song, a situation that would only worsen with the rise of the Mongols.

The East Asian Zone also includes those neighboring civilizations and states that fell under Chinese cultural and political influence, notably Korea, Japan, and Vietnam. Each of these countries was influenced by Chinese ideas about government, but as we saw earlier in the chapter, they also managed to find ways to maintain their cultural distinctiveness. Nonetheless, in each country the Confucian exam system was, at various times, used to recruit qualified men for government, although access to the exam was often restricted to the sons of elite families. The Chinese Tang Dynasty was particularly influential on political life in Korea and Japan; both countries constructed capital cities modelled on the Tang capital of **Chang'an**, for example. In Vietnam, political elites adopted Chinese approaches to government, but at the local level the Vietnamese largely resisted attempts at **sinicization**.

## South Asia and Southeast Asia

For most of the history of South Asia (which includes the modern states of India, Pakistan, Bangladesh, and Sri Lanka) government was in the hands of regional rulers known as ***rajas*** (kings) rather than centralized imperial rulers. Large regions of South Asia were unified under imperial control twice, first by the **Mauryan empire** (321-185 B.C.E.) and later by the **Gupta dynasty** (320-550 C.E.). Like their counterparts in East Asia, the Gupta kings were forced to deal with powerful militarized nomads along their northern frontier, and after their empire collapsed, South Asia reverted again to regional government. But despite these long periods of fragmented government, the caste system and

The Great Wall of China, the first version of which was constructed by the first emperor of the Qin, stretches across the mountains of northern China.
axz700/Shutterstock

**Qin** (chihn)
**Chang'an** (chahng-ahn)
**Gupta** (GOOP-tah)

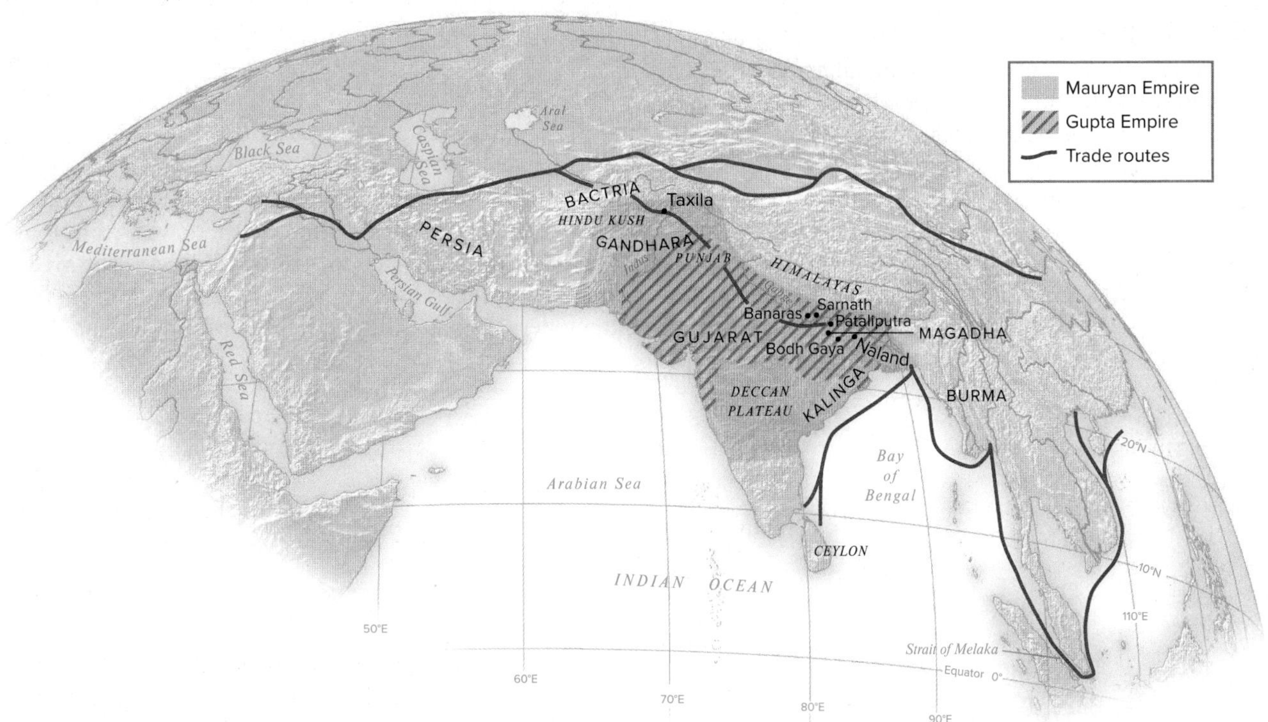


**MAP P.5 The Mauryan and Gupta empires, 321 B.C.E.–550 C.E.**

The Mauryan and Gupta dynasties both originated in the kingdom of Magadha.

***What geographical and political advantages did Magadha enjoy that gave it advantages over other regions of the subcontinent?***

McGraw-Hill

Hindu religion helped create cultural, social, and political stability.

In the eighth century Muslim warriors and merchants expanded into South Asia, and although Muslim outposts established in the region remained on the fringes of the Umayyad and Abbasid empires, Muslim merchants dwelling in coastal Gujarat became important participants in Indian Ocean trade. Late in the twelfth century Muslim administrators placed more of northern India under their control, a process that led to the establishment of the Sultanate of Delhi in 1206. Southern India and Sri Lanka was controlled by the Hindu Chola Kingdom from 850 to 1267, which at various times extended its control to parts of South East Asia.

While government in Vietnam was influenced by Chinese ideas, other parts of Southeast Asia were influenced by South Asian and later Muslim practices. The geography of the region played a key role in the formation of states. One example of this is the fifth century C.E. state of Funan, which grew wealthy through controlling the narrow Isthmus of Kra in the Malay Peninsula, which allowed merchants to transport their goods overland and avoid a long sea voyage. The rulers of Funan called themselves *rajahs*, and worshipped Hindu gods. After the fall of Funan the Kingdom of Srivijaya, based on the island of Sumatra, used its powerful navy to control much of Southeast Asia, from 670 to 1025. On the mainland of modern Cambodia, the Khmer ruled a substantial state into the fifteenth century, its wealth generated by successful rice cultivation. Khmer rulers constructed a magnificent capital at Angkor Thom that featured a superb temple complex influenced by both Hindu and Buddhist architecture.

## Sub-Saharan Africa

The vast continent of Africa was home to a wide range of states prior to 1200 C.E. Most of Saharan Africa was part of the *Dar al-Islam* and incorporated to varying degrees into the empires of the Umayyads and Abbasids. South of the Sahara, Arab traders established an early commercial society in modern Ethiopia, which evolved into the state of Aksum that dominated maritime trade in the Red and Arabian Seas through the fifth century. Aksum was followed by the state of Zagwe, whose rulers carved Christian churches into solid rock. On the western side of the African continent, successful agriculture and trade led to the emergence of states along the Niger River, and also in Ghana. By 800 C.E. the Kingdom of Ghana was powerful and wealthy because of trans-Saharan trade in gold, salt, and enslaved people. By the eleventh century the King of Ghana, who controlled an army of 200,000 warriors, was believed by his people to be divine. During the thirteenth century the Kingdom of Ghana was replaced by the wealthy Mali Empire, a process discussed in more detail in Chapter 18.

On the east coast of Africa hundreds of small states appeared, all based on Indian Ocean maritime trade, often of products produced in the interior of Sub-Saharan Africa. These communities were linked by a common language and culture called Swahili, and were ruled by kings or sultans. Evidence of the wealth these states acquired can be seen in the impressive remains of the Palace of Kilwa, built right on the edge of the Indian Ocean. In Central and South Africa small agricultural states formed, the elites of which grew wealthy by accumulating herds of cattle. Two of these states became particularly impressive - Mapungubwe and Great Zimbabwe. The rulers demonstrated their wealth and power by constructing impressive stone buildings.

## Europe

Government in Europe became increasingly fragmented following the disintegration of the Western Roman Empire in the fifth century CE. The period that followed, from roughly 500-1500, is often referred to as the Middle Ages or Medieval period of European history, a sort of bridge between ancient and modern times. Although the western Roman Empire

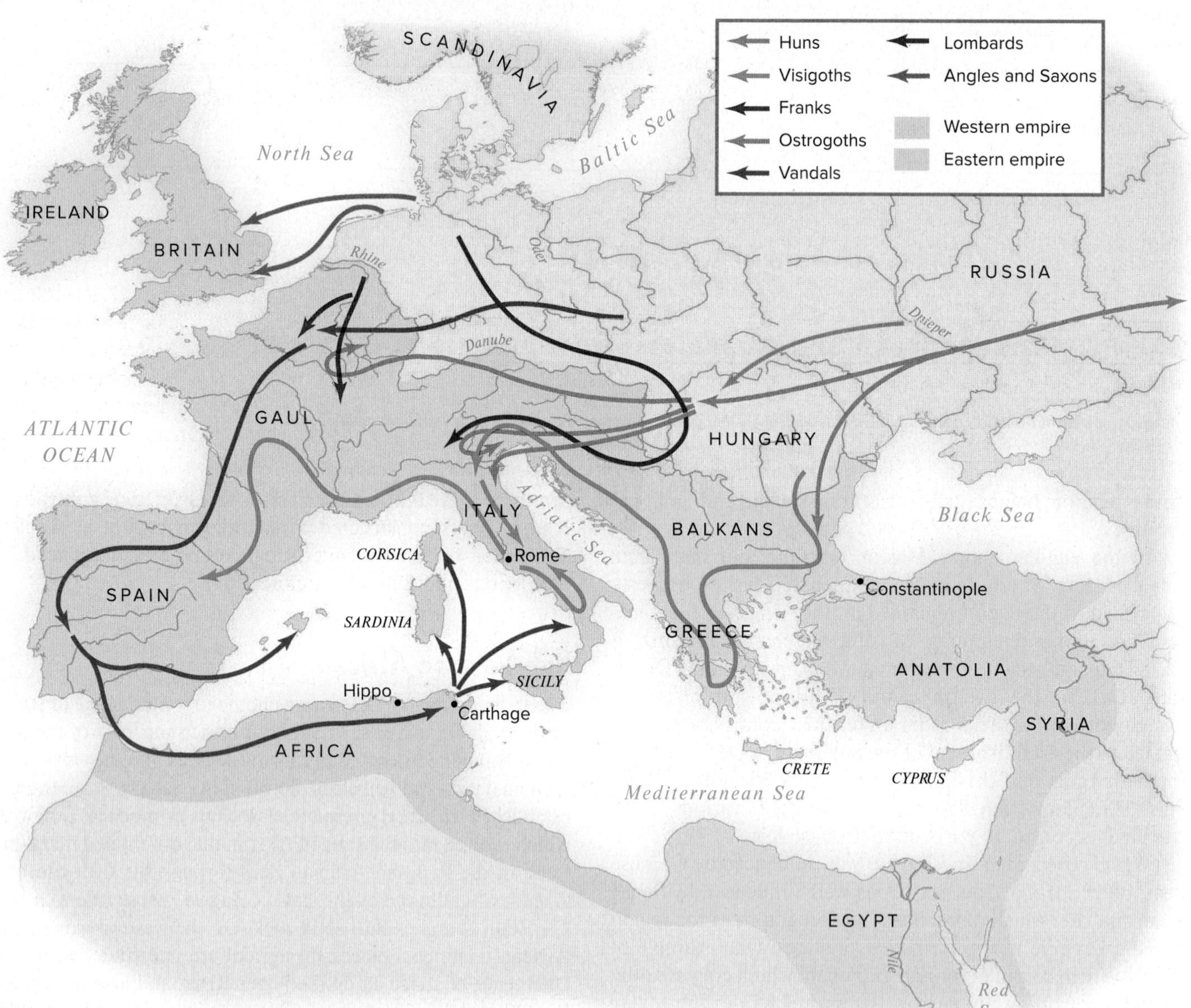


**MAP P.6 Germanic invasions and the collapse of the Western Roman Empire, 450–476 C.E.**

Many different groups invaded the Roman Empire following many different routes.

***What has been the long-term impact on Europe and the Mediterranean Basin due to the invasions of the Roman Empire by Germanic peoples?***

McGraw-Hill

collapsed, the Eastern empire transitioned to the **Byzantine Empire**, so it makes sense to consider Eastern and Western Europe as two distinct regions during the Medieval period.

In Western Europe the institutions of Roman imperial government were gradually replaced by a series of Germanic states and kingdoms. The most successful of these were constructed by the Franks who by the early sixth century had conquered most of Roman **Gaul** (modern France). In the eighth century the Carolingians, named after their most successful ruler Charlemagne (Charles the Great), extended Frankish power into much of northern and central Europe and modern Italy, and also stopped the attempted expansion of Muslim armies north out of Spain. But Carolingian attempts to reunify much of Western Europe failed. Thereafter, government throughout non-Muslim Western Europe was essentially in the hands of aristocrats who swore personal loyalty to regional kings and princes, who rewarded their supporters with gifts of land, the origins of the system known as feudalism. During this period the Catholic Church became increasingly powerful, and regional rulers forged alliances with the Church as a way of reinforcing their power.

The colossal head of Constantine is one of the few remaining fragments from a marble statue that originally stood about 14 meters (46 feet) tall.

Deco Images/Alamy Stock Photo

In the ninth and tenth centuries these Western European kingdoms were forced to deal with dangerous invasions by Muslim raiders called Saracens, Central Asian nomads known as the Magyars, and Scandinavian seafarers known as Vikings. This led to an extension of the feudal system, because rulers of regional kingdoms were not strong enough to defend their state without the support of local aristocratic military forces, including knights. These developments further fragmented much of Western Europe, leading to competition between monarchs and other aristocrats for regional power. The Vikings settled in parts of England and France, and created their own kingdoms, which further fueled the competition between aristocrats and monarchs. This fragmented, decentralized system of government was still very much in place in 1200 C.E.

The situation was very different in Eastern Europe. During the fourth century C.E., Roman Emperor **Constantine** had established a new capital at Constantinople, and turned what had been a small town into a magnificent imperial capital. The original town was named Byzantion, and although Constantine's successors continued to see themselves as rulers of the Eastern Roman Empire, historians have labelled the realm governed by Constantinople the Byzantine Empire in honor of the original town. The Byzantine emperors combined religious and secular power, and presented themselves to their people as exalted, absolute monarchs. The emperor was supported by a highly educated bureaucracy, a professional military, and an elaborate law code that has influenced most western law codes ever since, including that of the United States of America. The Byzantine Empire lasted until its capital city of Constantinople was captured by the Ottoman Turks in 1453; they renamed the city Istanbul, the name it retains to this day.

So the tale of government in Europe from the end of the ancient period through to the thirteenth century is truly a tale of two Europes. In the west, the disintegration of the Roman Empire led to fragmentation and the appearance of numerous small states and kingdoms ruled through the system of feudalism. In the east, the citizens of the Byzantine Empire believed that their unified, centralized state was a continuation of the Roman Empire, a situation that continued for another thousand years.

## The Americas

As we noted earlier, the vast world zone of the Americas had been home to a wide array of cultures and states by 1200 C.E. The Olmec ("rubber people") constructed the first complex society in Mesoamerica, although little is known of its political structure. Given the amount of monumental architecture created by the Olmec, including huge carved stone heads and impressive ceremonial buildings at sites such as San Lorenzo and La Venta, the Olmec state was probably authoritarian, with elites using coerced labor to carry out these projects. After 400 C.E. the Maya constructed their own sophisticated culture which spread extensively through much of Mesoamerica. The Maya never constituted a centralized state, but instead organized themselves politically into scores of small city-kingdoms, including **Tikal**, Palenque, and **Chichén Itzá**. Mayan

**Byzantine empire** (BIHZ-ann-teen)
**Tikal** (tee-KAHL)
**Chichén Itzá** (chee-CHEN eet-SAH)

## MAP P.7 Early Mesoamerican societies, 1200 B.C.E.–1100 C.E.

Describe the different geographic settings of the early Mesoamerican societies represented here.

***What role did environmental conditions in Mesoamerica play in determining the location and size of these different societies?***

McGraw-Hill

kings reinforced their status by giving themselves menacing names such as Smoking Frog and Stormy Sky. By 800 C.E. Mayan society was in decline, perhaps caused by civil war, invasion, or environmental problems.

Another impressive Mesoamerican society emerged centered on the huge city of Teotihuacan, which flourished between 200 and 500 C.E. in the highlands of Mexico. Much is unclear about the organization of this society, but obviously the administration of a city of up to 50,000 residents required some source of authority, perhaps in the form of an alliance between priests and secular leaders. By 650 C.E. the city of Teotihuacan had been sacked and burned by unknown invaders. In the centuries that followed, small local cultures dotted the landscape until the arrival of the Toltecs, who used their powerful army to maintain a compact regional empire through to the mid-twelfth century, paving the way for the arrival

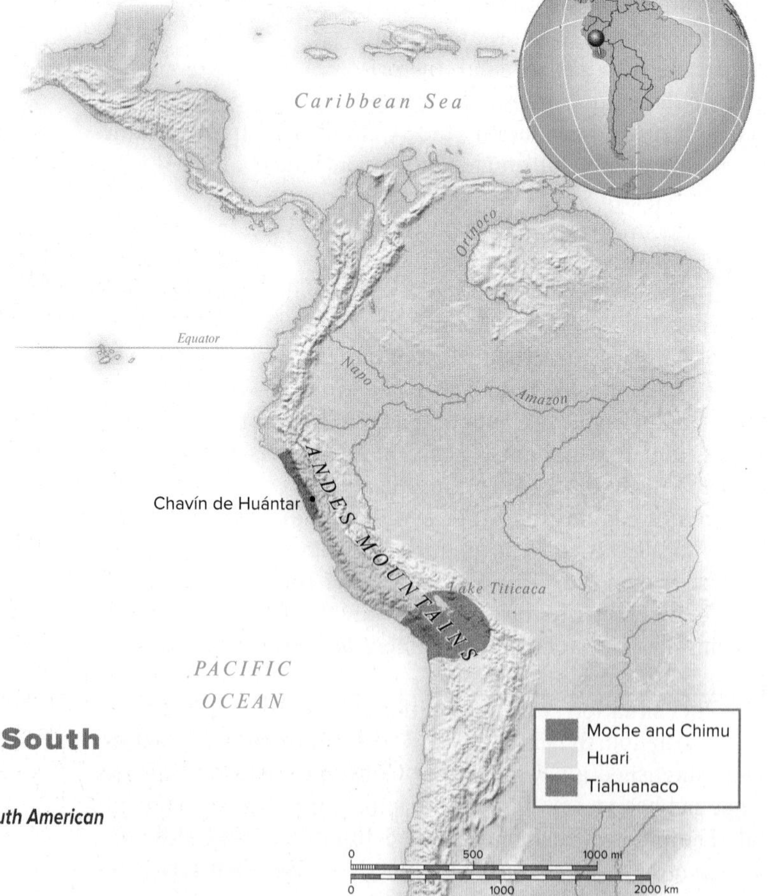


## MAP P.8 Early societies of Andean South America, 1000 B.C.E.–700 C.E.

***What geographical factors explain the location and shape of these early South American societies?***

McGraw-Hill

of the Mexica who would construct the enormous Aztec Empire.

In Andean South America, cultures like that of the Chavin appeared soon after 1000 B.C.E., constructing temples featuring elaborate carvings of deities represented as wild animals, which suggests that government was also in the hands of priests. The **Moche** created a state that dominated the coasts and valleys of Northern Peru from 300 to 700 C.E. The Moche were well-organized politically, with religious and secular aristocrats using warriors to coerce labor in a systematic way, as shown in their extensive surviving ceramics. A common thread in all these Pre-Columbian civilizations in the Americas is the dominant and constant influence of religion in governance. There is no separation of faith and state – the relationship between the rulers and religion is even closer than most states in Afro-Eurasia.

## THEME 4: ECONOMIC SYSTEMS

As societies develop, they affect and are affected by the ways that they produce, exchange, and consume goods and services. In this section we consider developments in economic and commercial activity in regions of Afro-Eurasia and the Americas prior to c. 1200 C.E. As societies became more populous and complex, these developments changed the way that they produced, exchanged, and consumed goods and services. The expansion of empires and the connections that developed between them led to increased levels of trade and commerce, which in turn led to the widespread diffusion of non-material products such as religions, ideas, and diseases. The greater the diversity of participants in these exchanges, the more dynamic and important the trade networks became. Long-distance trade was mostly of valuable luxury goods because these were more easily transported and produced the highest profits for merchants.

| CHRONOLOGY | |
|---|---|
| c. 100-250 C.E. | First Silk Roads era in Afro-Eurasia |
| c. 600-900 C.E. | Second Silk Roads era in Afro-Eurasia |
| From 1st Century C.E. | Sub-Saharan Trade Networks flourish |
| 1st Millennium C.E. | Trade networks flourish in the Americas |

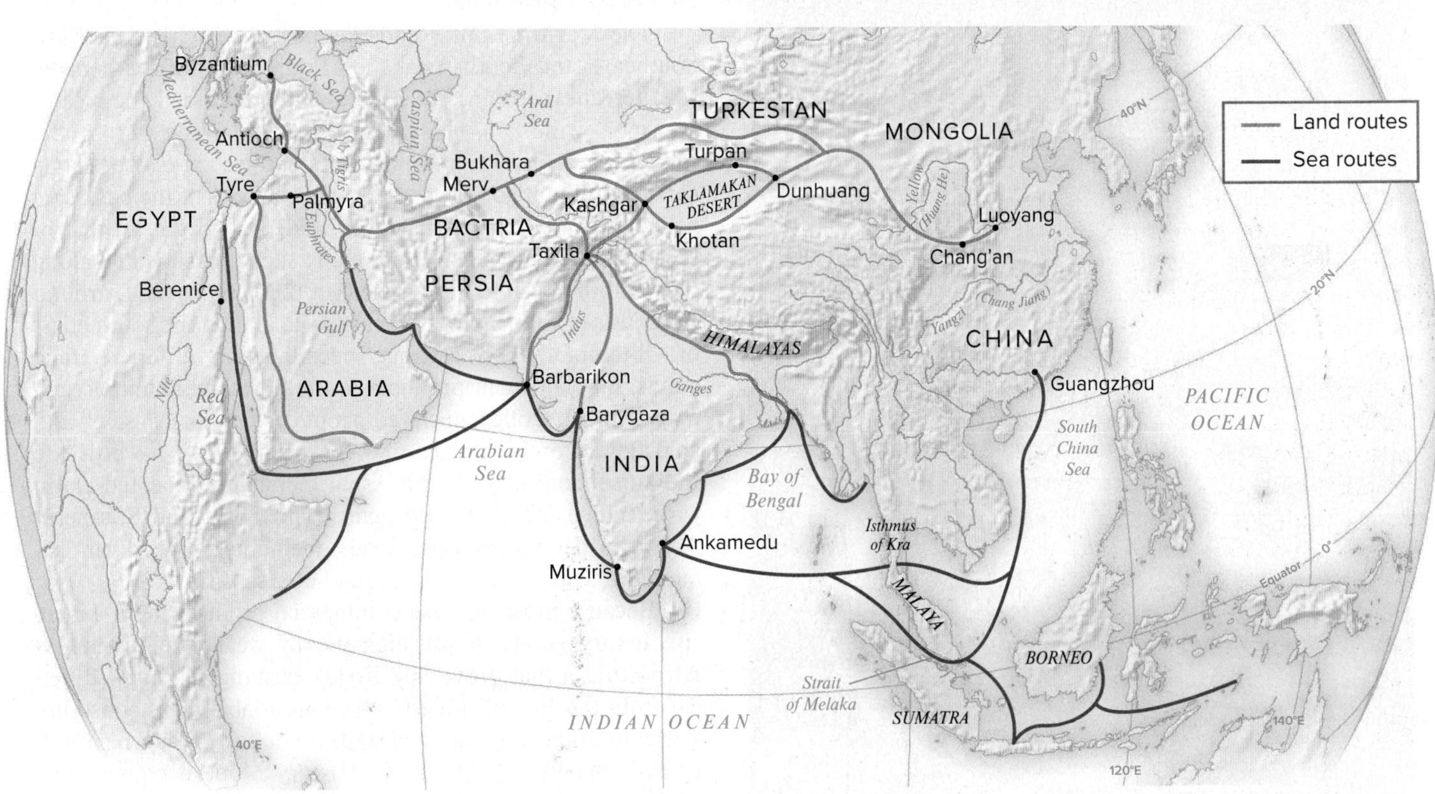


**MAP P.9 The Silk Roads, 100 B.C.E.–250 C.E.**

Note the extent of the land and sea routes known collectively as the Silk Roads.

***Consider the political, economic, and geographic conditions that would be necessary for regular travel and trade across the Silk Roads.***

McGraw-Hill

**Moche** (moh-CHEE)

## Afro-Eurasia and the Land and Maritime Silk Roads

As powerful states such as the Han and Tang Dynasties of China, the Roman, **Kushan**, and Persian Empires, and the Islamic caliphates, took political control of large regions of Afro-Eurasia this led to a significant increase in trade within these empires, but also between them. These imperial states established a broad zone of communication and exchange throughout much of Afro-Eurasia, bringing together a diverse range of participants in the most important exchange network of the ancient world, which historians have dubbed the Silk Roads because the trade in Chinese silk was such an important part of the system.

The Silk Roads consisted of a complex network of land and maritime routes which facilitated high levels of material and non-material exchange. The Silk Roads did not operate continuously, but rather waxed and waned. The First Silk Roads Era flourished between roughly 100 B.C.E. and 250 C.E., but the network then went into decline for several centuries following the collapse of three of the empires that had sustained it. The appearance of the Chinese Tang Dynasty in the early seventh century, and the expansion of the *Dar al-Islam* in the eighth, led to a Second Silk Roads Era that continued through to the tenth century. The Silk Roads flourished again under the Mongols in the thirteenth and fourteenth centuries.

Tomb figure of a camel and a foreign rider. The majority of the Silk Road trade was handled by the nomadic peoples of central and west Africa.

Werner Forman/Universal Images Group/Getty Images

Throughout each of these Silk Roads eras, land routes connected East Asia with Central Asia, the Middle East, Africa and Europe. Crucial to the land routes was the Bactrian camel, a two-humped camel that could carry heavy loads long distances across harsh desert and mountainous terrain. The luxury goods that moved back and forth along the Silk Roads were literally carried on the backs of these camels. Flourishing land-based trade also led to the expansion of major commercial cities in Central Asia, such as Kashgar, Samarkand, Bukhara, and Merv. Within these cities dwelt merchant communities of groups like the Sogdians, who were key trade intermediaries in the first two Silk Roads eras. Commercial exchanges on the Silk Roads were further enhanced by the development of infrastructure such as caravanserais (wayside inns for travelers and their animals), and financial instruments such as letters of credit, banking systems and eventually paper money.

The Maritime Silk Roads connected merchants in East, Southeast, and South Asia, the Middle East, Africa and the Mediterranean Basin. We have already discussed the role of monsoon winds in facilitating maritime trade across the Indian Ocean Basin, and how different groups of merchants carried different goods across the three zones of the basin. As with land-based trade, maritime trade led to the growth of commercial ports. There were many such ports located along the Swahili coast of East Africa, in the Persian Gulf, around the coasts of India and Southeast Asia, and on the south coast of China. Different regions specialized in different trade goods, most of them products of the flora and fauna of each environment. Coffee, enslaved people, ivory, horses, steel, and gold flowed out of Africa and the Middle East towards the Indian subcontinent. South Asian merchants exported cloth, yarn, indigo, peppers, and gems; while East and Southeast Asia provided spices, rare woods, medicines, rice, silver, lacquer, tea, sugar, porcelains, and, of course, silk.

Because most of these commercial products were expensive luxury goods, it was demand by wealthy elites across Afro-Eurasia that drove Silk Roads exchanges. This is different from the sort of trade in more affordable mass-consumption goods that characterized trade in the early modern period, as explored in the AP World History Modern course. The trade networks also led to the establishment of various diasporic commercial communities throughout the network, including Jewish, Swahili, Nestorian, Muslim, Chinese, Italian, and German merchants. The Silk Roads were the most important trade network of the pre-modern world; they connected much of Afro-Eurasia into a single system of exchanges that was the forerunner to the phenomenon of globalization that has so characterized the modern world.

## Trans-Saharan Trade Network

Although the Sahara Desert might appear to be a formidable barrier to trade and exchange, groups of nomads have survived there for at least 5,000 years, and even in ancient times merchants organized commercial expeditions through the desert. Crucial to trans-Saharan trade was the dromedary (or one-humped) camel, which like its cousin the Bactrian, is able to carry heavy loads long distances across very harsh terrain. The availability of the camel made possible the transportation of valuable export commodities produced on the fringes of the desert, or in Sub-Saharan Africa, to the Mediterranean coast, and on to Europe or the Middle East.

During the Roman Empire the Berber people of the Sahara facilitated trade, although they were also fierce enemies of the Romans at times. When Arab conquerors incorporated much of North Africa into the Dar al-Islam in the seventh and eighth centuries, they expanded the pre-existing trade routes and infrastructure, which led to a significant increase in the export of gold, ivory and slaves from Sub-Saharan Africa to the Mediterranean and throughout the Islamic world. This greatly increased the wealth of Muslim merchants, but also of strategically located states such as those in Ghana and Mali, discussed earlier in the chapter. Much like the Silk Roads, the Trans-Saharan trade networks connected much of the African continent to the rest of Eurasia, allowing for high levels of trade and exchange despite the challenging geography of the routes.

## Trade and Exchange Networks of the Americas

Although trade and exchange occurred in the ancient Americas, it was on a much smaller scale, and had less impact on historical development there compared to Afro-Eurasia. Mesoamerican exchange networks reached from Central America north to the Mississippi river, as evidenced by the diffusion of the Mesoamerican invention of corn agriculture. And there were also tenuous links between Andean and Mesoamerican regions, maintained perhaps by the use of large, ocean-going canoes. Well-built canoes also glided the length of the rivers of eastern North America and of the Amazon Basin, and along both coasts of Central America. The Maya had dugout canoes that could hold up to fifty people. Caribbean peoples also built ocean-going canoes, as did the Chincha along the Peruvian coast, so canoe technology was probably used to link ancient American states and civilizations into a loosely interacting exchange network.

American networks of exchange were thus geographically extensive, but these networks were much smaller in trade volumes and also considerably less varied than those of Afro-Eurasia. The geographical challenges of the rainforests of Mesoamerica, the height of the Andes and the arid deserts of the southwest of North America were simply too challenging to permit large-scale commerce. Within the various communities and states that flourished in the Americas prior to 1200 CE, internal trade flourished and local markets sold both local products and also some items brought in from wider regions. And some Mesoamerican cities such as Tikal and Teotihuacan did become hubs for regional trade. But there was nothing in the ancient Americas to compare to the vast and dynamic exchange networks of Afro-Eurasia, and this would have significant consequences once the two world zones collided in the fifteenth and sixteenth centuries.

# THEME 5: SOCIAL INTERACTIONS AND ORGANIZATION

The process by which societies group their members and the norms that govern the interactions between these groups and between individuals influence political, economic, and cultural institutions and organization. In this section we consider developments in social interactions and organization in Afro-Eurasia and the Americas up to c. 1200 C.E. In general we can see that societies became increasingly hierarchical, with small, wealthy elite groups using their resources to maintain a privileged position in society, while the great majority of humans occupied lower positions such as peasant farmers. Over time a middle class of artisans and merchants began to gain enough resources to challenge the status of elites, and even some freed slaves in ancient Rome grew fabulously wealthy, but this was the exception rather than the rule. We can also say that most ancient societies became increasingly patriarchal, with public power vested in the hands of men, a trend reinforced by secular and religious laws.

| CHRONOLOGY | |
|---|---|
| 1050-256 B.C.E | Zhou Dynasty in East Asia |
| 558-330 B.C.E | Achaemenid Persian Empire in Central and Southwest Asia |
| 509 B.C.E | Establishment of Roman Republic in Europe |
| 321-185 B.C.E | Mauryan Dynasty in South Asia |
| 206 B.C.E-220 C.E | Han Dynasty in East Asia |
| 27 B.C.E-476 C.E | Traditional dates of Roman Empire in Europe |
| 300-700 C.E | Moche Culture in Andean South America |
| 300-1100 C.E | Mayan society in Mesoamerica |
| 320-550 C.E | Gupta Dynasty in South Asia |
| 313-1452 C.E | Byzantine Empire in Eastern Europe |
| c. 500-1500 C.E | Medieval era in Western Europe |
| 618-907 C.E | Tang Dynasty in East Asia |
| 661-750 C.E | Umayyad Dynasty in Central and Southwest Asia |
| 670-1025 C.E | Srivijaya Kingdom in Southeast Asia |
| 800-1100 C.E | Kingdom of Ghana flourishing in sub-Saharan Africa |

# CONNECTING THE SOURCES

## Prescriptive literature and the lives of Chinese women during the Han dynasty

**The problem** Writing about culture and social relationships in the distant past poses specific challenges for historians. Even in societies like China, where literary traditions were already highly sophisticated by the time of the Han dynasty (206 B.C.E.–220 C.E.), available sources illuminating particular cultural attitudes or social relations were nevertheless limited. Existing textual sources tended to be written by educated elites rather than by the peasant farmers or laborers who made up the majority of the population. As a result, historians often have to rely on sources that tell us what educated people said about the ways culture and social relationships should be. Historians call these types of texts prescriptive literature because they *prescribe* how things should be, at least according to their authors. But what can prescriptive literature tell us about how real people actually interacted? Did prescriptive literature *reflect* what culture and social relationships were like for ordinary people, or did people write prescriptive literature in order to *shape* those aspects of society? These are the sorts of questions historians need to address every day as they seek to understand what people's lives were really like in the ancient world.

When exploring the effects of Confucianism on women's lives in Han China, for example, historians must rely on a relatively small body of textual sources. Two of the most commonly known of these sources—the *Analects* of Confucius and Ban Zhao's *Lessons for Women*—were written by highly educated elites (one male and one female) centuries apart from one another. Read the following two documents and think about what historians can and cannot understand about the lives of women in Han China by reading prescriptive literature.

**The documents** Read the documents below, and consider carefully the questions that follow.

### Document 1:

*The* Analects *of Confucius do not specifically address the subject of women in many places, although women were implicitly included in Confucius's vision of a moral and ethical society. This short selection, titled "On Women and Servants," is one place where women are mentioned explicitly.*

*The text reads:*

*17:25 Women and servants are most difficult to nurture. If one is close to them, they lose their reserve, while if one is distant, they feel resentful.*

### Document 2:

*This is an excerpt from Ban Zhao's* Lessons for Women, *written in about 80 C.E.*

*The text reads:*

Being careless, and by nature stupid, I taught and trained my children without system...

But I do grieve that you, my daughters, just now at the age for marriage, have not at this time had gradual training and advice; that you still have not learned the proper customs for married women. I fear that by failure in good manners in other families you will humiliate both your ancestors and your clan . . . in order that you may have something wherewith to benefit your persons, I wish every one of you, my daughters each to write out a copy for yourself.

From this time on every one of you strive to practice these lessons.

According to this section of the text, what is Ban Zhao's specific purpose in writing *Lessons for Women*?

**HUMILITY**

On the third day after the birth of a girl the ancients observed three customs: first to place the baby below the bed; second to give her a potsherd [pottery piece] with which to play; and third to announce her birth to her ancestors by an offering. Now to lay the baby below the bed plainly indicated that she is lowly and weak, and should regard it as her primary duty to humble herself before others. To give her potsherds with which to play indubitably signified that she should practice labor and consider it her primary duty to be industrious. To announce her birth before her ancestors clearly meant that she ought to esteem as her primary duty the continuation of the observance of worship in the home.

...

These three ancient customs epitomize woman's ordinary way of life and the teachings of the traditional ceremonial rites and regulations. Let a woman modestly yield to others; let her respect others; let her put others first, herself last. Should she do something good, let her not mention it; should she do something bad let her not deny it. Let her bear disgrace; let her even endure when others speak or do evil to her. Always let her seem to tremble and to fear. When a woman follows such maxims as these then she may be said to humble herself before others.

. . .

No woman who observes these three fundamentals of life has ever had a bad reputation or has fallen into disgrace. If a woman fails to observe them, how can her name be honored; how can she but bring disgrace upon herself?

What might be Ban Zhao's purpose in encouraging women to be humble?

**WOMANLY QUALIFICATIONS**

A woman ought to have four qualifications: (1) womanly virtue; (2) womanly words; (3) womanly bearing; and (4) womanly work. Now what is called womanly virtue need not be brilliant ability, exceptionally different from others. Womanly words need be neither clever in debate nor keen in conversation. Womanly appearance requires neither a pretty nor a perfect face and form. Womanly work need not be work done more skillfully than that of others.

To guard carefully her chastity; to control circumspectly her behavior; in every motion to exhibit modesty; and to model each act on the best usage, this is womanly virtue.

To choose her words with care; to avoid vulgar language; to speak at appropriate times; and nor to weary others with much conversation, may be called the characteristics of womanly words.

To wash and scrub filth away; to keep clothes and ornaments fresh and clean; to wash the head and bathe the body regularly, and to keep the person free from disgraceful filth, may be called the characteristics of womanly bearing.

With whole-hearted devotion to sew and to weave; to love not gossip and silly laughter; in cleanliness and order to prepare the wine and food for serving guests, may be called the characteristics of womanly work.

These four qualifications characterize the greatest virtue of a woman. No woman can afford to be without them. In fact they are very easy to possess if a woman only treasure them in her heart.

## Questions

1. What can these sources definitively tell you about the lives of the people who wrote them? What *facts* can be gleaned from these sources?
2. In Document 1, why did Confucius group women together with servants when describing the difficulty of nurturing both?
3. In Document 2, what is the primary role of women, according to Ban Zhao? What kinds of behaviors should women cultivate if they wish to maintain good virtue and harmonious relationships with others?
4. Taking both documents together, what can they tell us about the effects of Confucianism on the lives of actual women in Han China?
5. Sources such as these can help historians understand attitudes about women in Han China, especially when read in conjunction with other textual and material evidence. But what other forms of evidence would historians need to understand the experiences of the majority of women in China, not just those in the elite classes?

*Source Website:* **Document 1:** http://afe.easia.columbia.edu/ps/cup/confucius_women_servants.pdf **Document 2:** http://acc6.its.brooklyn.cuny.edu/~phalsall/texts/banzhao.html

## INTERPRETING IMAGES

Han Dynasty painting of peasants working in a rice field. The figures above are walking on a path through the flooded rice fields carrying rice sprouts, which the figures in the foreground are planting.

**Analyze** *What can you determine about the people in the picture? Are there social hierarchies present? What might the artist have been trying to convey through this painting?*

The Art Archive/Shutterstock

## East Asia

During the early millennia of East Asian history successful agriculture gradually led to the accumulation of more resources by some individuals and families. By the period of the Shang and Zhou dynasties in China, powerful elites had emerged, including royal families. Elites dominated the production of bronze and jade, and rulers would often give these to regional aristocrats as a way of rewarding them for their support. Below the elites was a small class of free artisans and craftsmen who worked for the elites. But by far the largest group in Chinese society has always been peasant farmers. They did not own any land themselves, but provided agricultural, military and labor service for their lords in return for plots to cultivate, security and a portion of the harvest. East Asian society was patriarchal, with authority vested principally in elderly males as heads of their households, although we do know of some exceptional women that gained great status as warriors and consorts. These same general developments also occurred in ancient Korea and Japan.

As we have discussed, during the Late Zhou warring states period, new ideologies emerged that have influenced East Asian social organization ever since, particularly Confucianism, Daoism, and Legalism. Confucians focused on education as a way of improving government and public behavior, Daoism on creating social harmony through introspection and disengagement, and Legalism on creating order through strict laws and harsh punishments. These three ideologies were also influential on society more widely throughout East Asia, particularly Confucianism, which helped create an elite class of scholar-bureaucrats to administer the affairs of state.

There were some noticeable differences, however. In Korea aristocrats dominated society, not the scholar-bureaucrats. In Japan the scholar-bureaucrats lost influence and were replaced by a land-owning elite, especially the samurai and their daimyo. In Vietnam, the Sinicized elite was often confined to the urban areas leaving the village elders and women to run villages and local markets. What was common in all of East Asia prior to 1200 was the harsh lives of the peasants. Peasant unrest has been responsible for the collapse of most of the dynasties, kingdoms and states of East Asian history, which were brought down by rebellions led by hungry and oppressed peasant armies.

## Southwest and Central Asia

In early **Mesopotamian** society during the third millennium BCE, a ruling class of kings and nobles gradually emerged, which enjoyed high status and amassed considerable wealth. Closely allied to the ruling elites were priests and priestesses, often the younger relatives of the nobles. Below these elite groups were free commoners, most of whom worked as farmers, although some worked in the cities as builders and craft workers. Further down the social hierarchy were dependent clients who possessed no property but worked on the estates owned by the elites. Both free commoners and dependent clients also provided labor services for large-scale construction projects such as roads, city walls, temples and irrigation systems. Mesopotamian society was patriarchal in that men dominated public life and had power over the lives of women, as laid out in **Hammurabi's Code** for example. Yet, despite their status of being legally subordinate to men,

**Hammurabi's Code** (hahm-uh-RAH-beez)

# SOURCES FROM THE PAST

## Hammurabi's Laws on Family Relationships

*By the time of Hammurabi, Mesopotamian marriages had come to represent important business and economic relationships between families. Hammurabi's laws reflect a concern to ensure the legitimacy of children and to protect the economic interests of both marital partners and their families. While placing women under the authority of their fathers and husbands, the laws also protected women against unreasonable treatment by their husbands or other men.*

**[128]** If a man take a woman to be his wife, but has no intercourse with her, this woman is no wife to him.

**[129]** If a man's wife be surprised having sexual relations with another man, both shall be tied and thrown into the water, but the husband may pardon his wife and the king may spare her.

What are the differences in punishments for a man and a woman for the crime of adultery?

**[130]** If a man violates the wife (betrothed or child-wife) of another man, who has never known a man, and still lives in her father's house, and sleeps with her and be surprised, this man shall be put to death, but the wife is blameless.

What is the punishment for rape?

**[131]** If a man brings a charge against his wife, but she is not surprised with another man, she must take an oath and then may return to her house.

**[138]** If a man wishes to separate from his wife who has borne him no children, he shall give her the amount of her purchase money and the dowry which she brought from her father's house, and let her go.

**[139]** If there was no purchase price he shall give her one mina of gold as a gift of release.

**[140]** If he be a freed man he shall give her one-third of a mina of gold.

**[141]** If a man's wife, who lives in his house, wishes to leave it, plunges into debt, tries to ruin her house, neglects her husband, and is judicially convicted: if her husband offer her release, she may go on her way, and he gives her nothing as a gift of release. If her husband does not wish to release her, and if he takes another wife, she shall re-main as servant in her husband's house.

**[142]** If a woman quarrels with her husband, and says: "You are not congenial to me," the reasons for her prejudice must be presented. If she is guiltless, and there is no fault on her part, but he leaves and neglects her, then no guilt attaches to this woman, she shall take her dowry and go back to her father's house.

**[143]** If she is not innocent, but leaves her husband, and ruins her house, neglecting her husband, this woman shall be cast into the water.

What is the process for separation or divorce, according to the laws?

### For Further Reflection

- What family relationship is the main focus of these laws?
- What do these laws suggest about the complexity of married life in ancient Babylon?
- Do these laws seem to favor one gender over another?

*Source:* James B. Pritchard, ed. *Ancient Near Eastern Texts Relating to the Old Testament.* Princeton: Princeton University Press, 1955, pp. 171–72.

women in Mesopotamia had many more options available to them than women in other ancient societies. We know that some women became powerful high priestesses for example, others achieved high levels of education, some became slaves, while others worked as midwives, shopkeepers, bakers and brewers.

In the first millennium B.C.E. the **Achaemenid** Persians created a vast cosmopolitan empire that incorporated all of Southwest Asia and most of Central Asia. To administer the complex affairs of this multicultural empire a new class of educated bureaucrats emerged, similar to the Confucian scholar-bureaucrats of East Asia. This group constituted an elite just below the status of the nobility. Persian cities were home to masses of administrators, tax collectors and record

**Achaemenid empire** (ah-KEE-muh-nid)

keepers. Below the nobility and bureaucrats were individuals who were free but of lesser status, including artisans, craft workers, merchants and low ranking civil servants, and in the countryside peasant farmers. Like the Mesopotamians, the Persians also treated women with more respect than most other ancient societies. Persian armies included female fighters, some women became managers of large construction projects, and where a profession was available for both men and women, their payment in rations was more or less equal.

## South and Southeast Asia

For more than three thousand years the caste system has regulated social interactions in South Asia. The population is divided into five distinct castes, or ***varnas*** as they are called in India. From top to bottom these are the *brahmins* (priests), ***kshatriyas*** (warriors and aristocrats), ***vaishyas*** (peasants and merchants), ***shudras*** (serfs) and **untouchables** (who handle the flesh or skin of dead animals). As trade and manufacturing activity increased over the millennia, different guilds based on

## SOURCES FROM THE PAST

### Caste Duties According to the *Bhagavad Gita*

*As we noted earlier in the chapter, the* Bhagavad Gita *("song of the lord") is a short poetic work that illustrates the expectations that Hinduism made of individuals and also the promise of salvation that it held out to them. It is presented in the form of a dialogue between Arjuna, a kshatriya warrior who is reluctant to enter battle, and his charioteer Krishna, who was in fact a human incarnation of the god Vishnu. In urging Arjuna to enter battle, Krishna pointed out that Arjuna could not harm the immortal souls of his family and friends on the other side. Beyond that, however, Krishna emphasized the duty to fight that Arjuna inherited as a member of the kshatriya caste.*

**As a man, casting off** old clothes, puts on others and new ones, so the embodied self, casting off old bodies, goes to others and new ones. Weapons do not divide the self into pieces; fire does not burn it; waters do not moisten it; the wind does not dry it up. It is not divisible; it is not combustible; it is not to be moistened; it is not to be dried up. It is everlasting, all-pervading, stable, firm, and eternal. It is said to be unperceived, to be unthinkable, to be unchangeable. Therefore knowing it to be such, you ought not to grieve. But even if you think that the self is constantly born, and constantly dies, still, O you of mighty arms, you ought not to grieve thus. For to one that is born, death is certain; and to one that dies, birth is certain. Therefore about this unavoidable thing, you ought not to grieve. . . .

According to Krishna, why is it pointless to grieve for the dead?

Having regard to your own duty, you ought not to falter, for there is nothing better for a kshatriya than a righteous battle. Happy those kshatriyas who can find such a battle—an open door to heaven! But if you will not fight this righteous battle, then you will have abandoned your own duty and your fame, and you will incur sin. All beings, too, will tell of your everlasting infamy; and to one who has been honored, infamy is a greater evil than death. Warriors who are masters of great chariots will think that you have abstained from the battle through fear, and having been highly thought of by them, you will fall down to littleness. Your enemies, too, decrying your power, will speak much about you that should not be spoken. And what, indeed, could be more lamentable than that? Killed, you will obtain heaven; victorious, you will enjoy the earth. Therefore arise, resolved to engage in battle. Looking on pleasure and pain, on gain and loss, on victory and defeat as the same, prepare for battle, and thus you will not incur sin. . . .

What arguments is Krishna making to urge Arjuna not to shirk his duties in battle?

***Varna*** (VAHR-nuh)
**Kshatriayas** (KSHAHT-ree-uhs)
**Vaishyas** (VEYES-yuhs)
**Shudras** (SHOO-druhs)

The state of mind that consists in firm understanding regarding steady contemplation does not belong to those who are strongly attached to worldly pleasures and power, and whose minds are drawn away by that flowery talk that is full of specific acts for the attainment of pleasures and power, and that promises birth as the fruit of actions—that flowery talk uttered by unwise ones who are enamored of Vedic words, who say there is nothing else, who are full of desires, and whose goal is heaven. . . .

Your business is with action alone, not by any means with the fruit of the action. Let not the fruit of action be your motive to action. Let not your attachment be fixed on inaction. Having recourse to devotion, perform actions, casting off all attachment, and being equable in success or ill success.

### For Further Reflection

- What attitude does Krishna urge Arjuna to adopt when performing his caste duties?
- How does the approach of Krishna to warfare and battle compare to that of Ashoka in his 13th Rock Edict?
- As you continue your study of world history, consider how these reflections on caste duty compare to the arguments made by Confucius about the behavior of leaders, as discussed in Chapter 5? Revisit this question after you read Chapter 5.

*Source: The Bhagavad Gita.* Trans. by Kashinath Trimbak Telang. In F. Max Müller, ed., *The Sacred Books of the East,* vol. 8. Oxford: Clarendon Press, 1908, pp. 45–48. (Translation slightly modified.)

occupation appeared that functioned as subcastes. Known as ***jati***, it was these guilds that maintained social order throughout the subcontinent, organizing courts, resolving differences, and regulating community affairs. This tendency for families to associate closely with others of the same occupation remained a prominent and distinctive feature of South Asian society well into modern times.

Gender relations in South Asia were strongly influenced by patriarchal attitudes. As ancient society became more urban and commercial, traditionalists sought to promote stability by encouraging respect for strong patriarchal families. Classic works of literature do depict some women as strong and independent, but also as devoted to their husbands. During the early centuries of the Common Era patriarchal dominance became more prominent. Child marriage became widespread and this placed young wives under the direct control of older men who encouraged women to devote themselves to family matters and keep out of playing a more public role in society.

Although societies in Southeast Asia were influenced by early South Asian ideas, and in the case of Vietnam by Chinese ideologies, they generally did not adopt the caste system and women played a more prominent role in society. The Viets and other peoples of Southeast Asia favored the nuclear family over the much larger extended family preferred by the Chinese, and the Viets developed the strong clan associations that characterized Chinese, Korean, and particularly Japanese society. Vietnamese and other Southeast Asian women had much greater freedom and influence on public life than women in China or South Asia ever enjoyed. It was women that ran most of the markets, a practice that continues today.

## Sub-Saharan Africa

Early Sub-Saharan societies did not develop elaborate social hierarchies or bureaucracies but organized themselves through family and kinship groups instead. People generally lived in villages of about 100 people, and the older male heads of families constituted a ruling council. The most prominent of these family head males was recognized as chief, and he represented the village in negotiations with neighboring peoples. Over time, large networks of kin-based societies appeared which organized the public affairs of many thousands of people. After about 1000 C.E. conflicts arose between many of these networks, leading to the emergence of very powerful chiefs supported by military contingents based in urban centers. But at the village level, family relationships continued to regulate social interactions.

Work roles were determined by gender. Men dominated leather tanning and iron working, and also the heavier tasks associated with agriculture. Women contributed most of the labor associated with planting and harvesting the crops. Despite these clear distinctions, women in Sub-Saharan Africa had more opportunities available to them than in most of the other regions of the world we have been discussing. We know that women merchants commonly traded at markets, that female military contingents were formed, and that some aristocratic women rose to positions of political prominence in their societies.

## Europe

Earlier in the chapter we discussed the very different political experiences of people and states in eastern and western Europe during the Middle Ages. Social relations in these two regions were also distinctly different, so here again it makes sense to think of two Europes.

In the Byzantine Empire that controlled parts of eastern Europe and the Middle East, society was dominated by large, prosperous, cosmopolitan cities such as Constantinople, **Alexandria** (in Egypt) and Damascus (in modern Syria). In these cities, particularly the capital Constantinople, aristocrats lived in enormous palaces. We know there were 4,338 such palaces in Constantinople alone by the fifth century, as well as many other imperial and princely palaces. Women lived in separate apartments from men, did not participate much in banquets and parties, and wore veils in public to discourage the attention of men outside of their household.

Further down the ranks of Byzantine society, artisans and crafts workers commonly lived in rooms above their shops, while clerks and government officials lived in multistory apartment complexes. Workers and the poor lived in rickety tenements where they shared kitchens and toilets with their neighbors.

In contrast to the Byzantine Empire, Medieval Western Europe was largely a rural society, a situation that developed as a result of the disintegration of the Western Roman Empire in the mid-first millennium C.E. Invasions of the empire by the **Huns** in the fifth century C.E., followed by various Germanic-speaking peoples, led to the collapse of Roman institutions and the abandonment of the towns and cities that had been central to commerce and social life. At the height of the Roman Empire merchants brought delicacies and luxury items from all parts of the Roman Empire to these towns and cities - Spanish hams, British oysters, fine woolen cloaks from Gaul, and nuts, dates and figs from Syria. Roman engineers worked to provide abundant supplies of fresh water, and all sizeable towns had public baths with hot and cold water. The increasing wealth of many Roman urban dwellers led to the emergence of new classes that accumulated enough wealth through commerce or construction to rival the old **patrician** nobility for prominence. At the other end of the social spectrum was a huge class of enslaved peoples that might have numbered up to one third of the population of the Roman Empire. In the late Roman Empire most enslaved people were employed as agricultural laborers on fortified estates known as ***latifundia***. When the western empire disintegrated in the fifth and sixth centuries, these enslaved peoples were left to fend for themselves as invading military leaders established small states all over Western Europe, events discussed in Chapter 7.

Roman society during both the Republican and imperial periods was decidedly patriarchal, as Roman law invested immense authority in male heads of families. The eldest male in an extended household ruled as ***paterfamilias*** ('father of the family'), and had the right to arrange marriages, designated duties and mete out punishment as he saw fit. But in reality, Roman women usually supervised domestic affairs, and by the time they reached middle age, generally wielded considerable influence within their families. We even know of gender revolts at different periods in Roman history, as women demanded certain rights or the end to restrictive laws. As was the case with many ancient civilizations then, although women were denied a role in public life, they were often able to influence society around them in subtle ways, and sometimes force the government to pass laws that offered them at least basic rights and some level of protection, even if they never resembled equality.

## The Americas

Society in Mesoamerica was rigidly hierarchical, particularly under the Maya. At the top were the kings and their families, followed by a hereditary nobility that owned most of the land and cooperated with the kings and priests by organizing military forces and participating in religious rituals. Mayan merchants seem to have come from the noble class, and as they traveled from city-state to city-state their role was often as much diplomatic as it was commercial.

There were several other distinct classes in Mayan society. Professional architects and sculptors oversaw the construction of large monuments and public buildings. Artisans specialized in the production of pottery, tools and cotton textiles. Large groups of peasants and slaves fed the entire society, and also provided physical labor for the construction of cities and monuments. Priests also constitute a distinct class in Mayan society, presiding over religious ceremonies, studying astronomy and mathematics, and maintaining the complex calendar and writing system of the Maya. And while society was patriarchal women seem to have had some roles outside of the home including in the market place, and as midwives and priestesses.

---

**Latifundia** (LAT-ih-FOON-dee-uh)
***Paterfamilias*** (PAH-tur fuh-MEE-lee-ahs)

## THEME 6: TECHNOLOGY AND INNOVATION

| CHRONOLOGY | |
|---|---|
| 461-429 B.C.E | Periclean era in ancient Athens |
| 206 B.C.E-220 C.E | Han Dynasty |
| 2nd Century C.E | Invention of paper |
| 57-935 C.E | Silla Dynasty in Korea |
| 200-750 C.E | Teotihuacan society |
| 300-1100 C.E | Mayan society |
| 710-794 C.E | Nara Period in Japan |

Human adaption and innovation have resulted in increased efficiency, comfort, and security, and technological advances have shaped human development and interactions with both intended and unintended consequences. In this final section of the chapter we outline some of the developments in technology and innovation in the major regions of the planet prior to c. 1200 C.E. In general what we see is humans gaining increasing knowledge of and mastery over nature in order to assist their own species. This can be traced back to the invention in the Paleolithic Era of more sophisticated stone spear points and bows and arrows as aids to hunting, and then to the development of irrigation agriculture in the Neolithic Era to make possible the transition to a sedentary agricultural lifestyle. The technological achievements of ancient and medieval peoples in all of the world's regions are incredibly impressive, and helped drive our species into the pre-modern and industrial worlds explored in the AP World History Modern course. In this section we offer a very brief survey of some of the most important innovations.

### East Asia

Societies in East Asia have a long history of technological innovation. Perhaps the most impressive Chinese dynasty of all in this context was the Han, which invented the world's first padded collar to assist with plowing, the first wheelbarrow, the first water mill to help with the grinding of grain, a type of seismograph to measure the strength of earthquakes, a piston bellows to assist in the manufacture of high quality steel, and paper! Their successors the Tang invented fixed and moveable type printing, and by the time of the Song the invention of gunpowder could be added to the list of Chinese innovation, which also included the construction of monumental buildings, most famously the Great Wall of China.

During the Silla Dynasty in Korea, which ruled until 925 CE, a scholar named Kim Taemun used advanced mathematics to construct a superbly accurate celestial observatory in the capital of Kyongju. Math in Korea was also put to good practical use in the construction of Buddhist temples that were carefully designed to allow maximum air flow to prevent damage from the build-up of moisture. Wood-block printing was also highly advanced in Korea, used to print long and complex Buddhist sutras. During the eighth century Nara Period in Japan, Japanese architects also demonstrated their skills in practical mathematics by constructing Buddhist pagodas around a central pole that was unconnected to the surrounding wooden bracketing, thus allowing the building to shake during earthquakes without collapsing.

### Central Asia

One of the major challenges for merchants and travelers on the Silk Roads was access to water and to supplies of food, which meant that the establishment of villages and towns in which successful irrigation agriculture was being practiced was critically important. The towns that emerged around the edges of the harsh Taklamakan Desert in the Tarim Basin were able to sustain themselves through the invention of sophisticated irrigation systems later known as a ***qanat***, a Persian word that describes an underground channel to store and distribute water. The *qanats* are connected to aquifers or to other sources of water (such as streams regularly swollen by melting snow), and use a series of vertical shafts and horizontal underground channels to move water to agricultural fields.

This sort of system has operated in the Turpan Basin on the northern edge of the Taklamakan for millennia, including during all the major Silk Roads eras. The irrigation system is

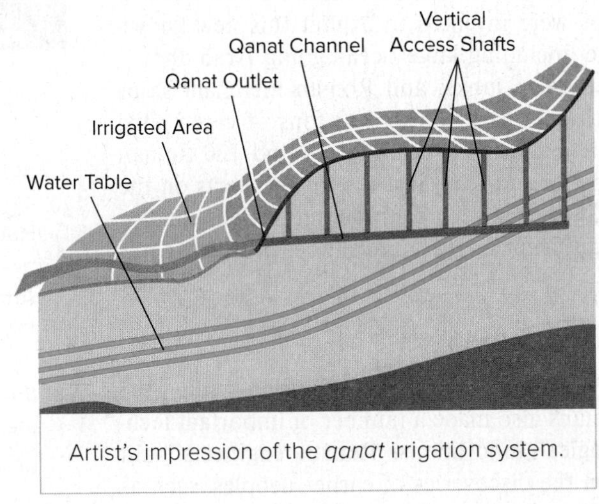


Artist's impression of the *qanat* irrigation system.

***Qanat*** (kah-NAHT)

called a *karez* in the local Uyghur language. The Turpan *karez* consists of a series of vertical shafts that are connected together by horizontal underground canals to collect melting snow water from the surface that has come down from the nearby Tian Shan Mountains. Because Turpan is a low basin, the underground canals use gravity to bring the water into dams closer to the community, and being underground they also protect from water loss by evaporation. Today there are still some 1100 karez in operation in the basin, and the modern city of Turfan has even built a Water Museum to celebrate the extraordinary technology that made living in this harsh desert environment possible. The availability of abundant supplies of water and food meant that communities right across the Tarim Basin were able to accommodate large numbers of merchants, along with their agents, camels and camel drivers, for days and weeks at a time, thus making the Silk Roads network viable.

## Indian Ocean Basin

We have already discussed the discovery by unknown ancient mariners of the monsoon wind patterns that prevail across the Indian Ocean Basin. Before that discovery maritime trade had been much smaller in scale, as small flat-bottomed boats had made their way from port to port by hugging the coast. The discovery of monsoon wind patterns meant that it was now possible to send much larger ships across the deeper reaches of the Indian Ocean, from the coast of Africa and the Persian Gulf to South Asia, and on to Southeast and East Asia. So new types of ships were invented to exploit this new knowledge, including large ocean-going Arab dhows, East Asian junks, and Roman merchant ships that could carry up to 300 tons of cargo. One Roman source reports that around 120 Roman ships set sail from just one of the ports on the Red Sea each year, so these innovations enabled a significant increase in volumes of trade.

## Roman Europe

As with their counterparts in Han China, the Romans also made a number of important technological innovations. Roman engineers built upon the discoveries of earlier peoples, such as the Egyptians and Babylonians who constructed

### INTERPRETING IMAGES

A marble relief sculpture of about 100 C.E. depicts a crew of men working in a treadmill that powers a crane used in construction of a Roman temple, demonstrating the extraordinary technological and engineering skills of the Romans. The relief is part of a tomb for the Haterii, a family of builders who constructed some of the most iconic pieces of Roman architecture from the second century C.E.

**Analyze** *Why is it important to know that this relief comes from a tomb? What does it tell you that the family chose a scene like this for their memorial? What do you think they were trying to convey to future generations about their role in Roman society, and do you think they anticipated their legacy being so important even two millennia after they lived?*

DEA/G. NIMATALLAH/De Agostini/Getty Images

monumental buildings like **ziggurats** and pyramids, and the Greeks who constructed the Parthenon and other magnificent buildings in the Acropolis complex in **Athens**. The gigantic stadiums of the Circus Maximus and Colosseum are some of Rome's most famous buildings, and are testament to the skills of Roman engineers, but these engineers also built impressive monumental structures all over the Empire - aqueducts, temples, bridges, and a vast road network. The speed of travel on the 50,000 miles of constructed roadways the Romans built was not surpassed until the nineteenth century.

Roman engineers were methodical in their construction of bridges and aqueducts, like the Pont du Gard in southern France, all of which incorporated the stone arch in their design. Their designs were so solid that tiers of arches could be placed one on top of another. The arch allowed the Romans to build bridges and aqueducts with very long spans, and also to lay their road network across the landscape with little regard for the course of rivers. In the capital, aqueducts had the capacity to supply up to 50 gallons per day for each of the one million citizens of Rome during the Antonine Age.

Another important Roman construction innovation was the invention of concrete, which made it possible to pour formworks to create walls, vaults and domes. Even today when builders use forms of timber to contain poured concrete they are essentially emulating the original Roman technique. Dried concrete is very strong, which means once set it could be used to make huge vaulted domes that did not need supports. The classic example of this is the gigantic Pantheon in Rome, which has a diameter of about 130 feet, much larger than the domes of St. Peter's in Rome, or St. Paul's in London, even though these structures were built many centuries later.

## The Americas

Early societies in the Americas also developed impressive scientific and technological skills. The Olmec constructed pyramid tombs up to 100 feet high, and also carved enormous stone heads weighing up to 20 tons out of basalt. The city of Teotihuacan was a carefully planned urban center that housed up to 150,000 people by 500 C.E., making it one of the six largest cities in the world at that time. The city featured two massive stepped temples, the Pyramids of the Moon and the Sun, two of the most impressive engineering achievements anywhere in the world prior to the industrial age.

The Maya developed one of the most sophisticated mathematical systems anywhere in the ancient world, and like their counterparts in South Asia also invented the concept of zero. This allowed them to acquire a sophisticated understanding of the movement of planets, and also of time, which they expressed in different types of calendars. The Pyramid of Kukulkan, built by the Mayan engineers at Chichén Itzá between the eighth and twelfth centuries, is a striking example of the application of mathematical and astronomical knowledge to construction. The temple itself was used as a calendar. It featured four stairways, each with 91 steps and a platform at the top, making a total of 365, equivalent to the number of days in a calendar year.

In both Afro-Eurasia and the Americas, in the many millennia of human history that occurred before 1200 C.E., humans invented complex mathematical systems that allowed them to understand and take control of much of the natural world and leave behind some of the most impressive monuments and roads in world history.

**Ziggurats** (ZIG-uh-rahts)

Mayan Temple at Chichen Itza, known as El Castillo today.
Kitti Boonnitrod/Getty Images

## CONCLUSION: THE ANCIENT WORLD AS NECESSARY CONTEXT FOR UNDERSTANDING THE MODERN

This chapter has offered an introduction to the AP World History: Modern course, providing historical information and context for the events that occur after c.1200. The chapter gives students a solid geographical, cultural, political foundation as well as chronological framework on which to build their content knowledge and historical thinking skills. Like the AP course, this introduction is structured around the six AP world history themes. Some of the key points to remember about these themes are:

### Humans and the Environment (ENV)

From the beginning of human history the environment has played a crucial role in the way humans lived. It has determined what types of plants and animals could be grown by early farmers, where land and maritime trade and migration routes could be established, and what types of plants and animals could be turned into valuable commercial exports. The environment of the steppe made possible the creation of a brand new lifeway, that of pastoral nomadism, that was destined to play a crucial role in world history, particularly with the rise of the Mongols.

## Cultural Developments and Interactions (CDI)

Sometimes when viewing history on the macro scale what is most apparent is the commonality of human experiences, rather than the differences. But humans have come up with an astonishing range of ideologies and religions which continued to profoundly affect human beliefs and relationships between nations in the centuries after 1200 C.E.

## Governance (GOV)

Humans have been experimenting with different forms of governance for thousands of years, and have constructed a wide range of state-like structures, most of which have facilitated the organization of large human populations by a relatively small number of secular and religious elites. You will certainly see this trend continue after 1200 C.E.

## Economic Systems (ECN)

As societies became more populous and complex, this changed the way that they produced, exchanged, and consumed goods and services. In particular the expansion of empires and the connections that developed between them led to increased levels of trade and commerce, which in turn led to the widespread diffusion of non-material products such as religions, ideas and diseases. The greater the diversity of participants in these exchanges, the more dynamic and important the trade networks became, and this is particularly true of the Silk Roads. A key development in this theme post-1200 is the connection of regional exchange networks into a genuinely global network.

## Social Interactions and Organization (SIO)

During the millennia leading up to 1200 C.E. societies became increasingly hierarchical, with small, wealthy elite groups using their resources to maintain a privileged position in society, while the great majority of humans occupied lower positions such as peasant farmers. Over time a middle class of artisans and merchants began to gain enough resources to challenge the status of elites. Most ancient and medieval societies were also patriarchal, with public power vested in the hands of men, a situation reinforced by secular and religious laws. All these trends continue after 1200, and indeed some of them have only been challenged very recently in human history.

## Technology and Innovation (TEC)

Since humans first appeared we have been gaining increasing knowledge of and mastery over nature in order to assist our own species. We can trace this all the way back to the Paleolithic Era, and the invention of more sophisticated stone spear points and bows and arrows as aids to hunting; and more recently to the Neolithic and the development of irrigation agriculture which made possible the transition to a sedentary lifestyle. The achievements of ancient and medieval peoples in all of the world's regions are incredibly impressive, and helped drive our species into the pre-modern and industrial worlds explored in the AP World History Modern course.

There is a well-known history cliché that goes something like this: "You can't know where you are going if you don't know where you've been." An awful lot of history happened between the emergence of the human species some 250,000 years ago, and the events that occurred after the year 1200 CE, a mere 800 years ago. It is impossible in a single chapter to do justice to the myriad of events and human actions that shaped history up to 1200 CE. But it is our hope as authors that this introduction will give you some sense of the remarkable achievements of human societies, and help you make better sense of the events and people that you will be learning about in the AP World History: Modern course.

## KEY TERMS

Achaemenid (25)
Aegean Sea (6)
*ahimsa* (10)
Alexandria (28)
Athens (30)
bloodletting rituals (11)
brahmins (10)
Buddhism (5)
Byzantine Empire (17)
caste (10)
Chang'an (14)
Chavín culture (11)
Chichén Itza (17)
Christianity (8)
colossal human heads (11)
Confucianism (5)
Daoism (5)
Gupta (14)
Hammurabi's Code (24)
Han dynasty (7)
Huns (28)
Islam (8)
Jainism (10)
*jati* (27)
Jews (8)
*kshatriyas* (26)
Kushan empire (20)
*latifundia* (28)
Legalism (5)
Mahayana (10)
maize (11)
Mandate of Heaven (13)
Mauryan empire (14)
Maya (7)
Mesoamerica (6)
Mesopotamia (24)
Moche (19)
monotheism (8)
Monsoon system (3)
Nestorian (8)
Nile River (5)
Nubia (8)
Olmecs (7)
*paterfamilias* (28)
patrician (28)
Paul of Tarsus (8)
Popol Vuh (11)
Qin dynasty (14)
*rajas* (14)
Roman Empire (8)
Sasanians (8)
Shang dynasty (13)
*shudras* (26)
Siddhartha Gautama (10)
Silk Roads (3)
sinicization (14)
Teotihuacan (7)
Tikal (17)
untouchables (26)
*vaishyas* (26)
*varnas* (26)
Vishnu (11)
Warring States period (14)
Xia dynasty (13)
Yangzi (5)
Yellow River (6)
Zhou dynasty (13)
ziggurats (31)

## FOR FURTHER READING


Lindsay Allen. The Persian Empire. Chicago, 2005. A valuable survey of the Achaemenid empire with special attention to archaeological discoveries.

David W. Anthony. The Horse, the Wheel, and Language: How Bronze- Age Riders from the Eurasian Steppes Shaped the Modern World. Princeton, 2007. Brilliant study of early Indo-European speakers and the uses they made of domesticated horses.

Karen Armstrong. Buddha. New York, 2001. An accessible introduction to the Buddha by a prominent scholar of South Asian religions.

Jeannine Auboyer. Daily Life in Ancient South Asia. Trans. by S. W. Taylor. London, 2002. An excellent introduction to South Asian social history during the classical era.

A. L. Basham. The Origins and Development of Classical Hinduism. Oxford, 1989. Classic account of the origins and development of classical Hinduism by one of the world's leading ancient South Asian scholars.

C. Benjamin. Empires of Ancient Eurasia: The First Silk Roads Era 100 b.c.e.–250 c.e. Cambridge, 2017. Neat synthesis of the history of ancient China and the other Eurasian empires of the Silk Roads Era, through to the collapse of the Later Han Dynasty.

Jerry H. Bentley. Old World Encounters: Cross-Cultural Contacts and Exchanges in Pre-Modern Times. New York, 1993. Studies the spread of cultural and religious traditions before 1500 c.e.

Mary T. Boatwright. The Romans: From Village to Empire: A History of Rome from Earliest Times to the End of the Western Empire. Oxford, 2013. Vividly written and accessible, The Romans traces Rome's remarkable evolution from village to monarchy, to republic, to one-man rule by an emperor.

Michael Coe. The Maya. New York, 2005. Scholarly and readable account of the history and culture of the Maya from one of the world's leading experts on ancient Mesoamerica.

Basil Davidson. Lost Cities of Africa. Rev. ed. Boston, 1970. Popular account with discussions of Kush and Meroë.

Touraj Daryaee. Sasanian Persia: The Rise and Fall of an Empire. London, 2010. Lucid history of the Sasanian empire by a leading Persian historian.

Nicola di Cosmo. Ancient China and Its Enemies: The Rise of Nomadic Power in East Asian History. Cambridge, 2002. An insightful study analyzing the emergence of pastoral nomadism and relations between Chinese cultivators and nomadic peoples in ancient times.

Richard A. Diehl. The Olmecs: America's First Civilization. London, 2004. The best brief introduction to Olmec society.

Patricia Ebrey. The Cambridge Illustrated History of China. Cambridge, 2000. A splendid collection of images and superb text makes this one of the finest resources available on Chinese history and culture.

Christopher Ehret. The Civilizations of Africa: A History to 1800. Charlottesville, 2001. An important contribution that views Africa in the context of world history.

Israel Finkelstein and Neil Asher Silberman. The Bible Unearthed: Archaeology's New Vision of Ancient Israel and the Origin of Its Sacred Texts. New York, 2001. Interprets the Hebrew scriptures and early Israelite history in light of numerous archaeological discoveries.

Richard C. Foltz. Spirituality in the Land of the Noble: How Iran Shaped the World's Religions. Oxford, 2004. Includes an accessible discussion of the Zoroastrian faith.

W. V. Harris, ed. Rethinking the Mediterranean. New York, 2005. A collection of scholarly essays exploring issues that linked the various lands bordering the Mediterranean in premodern times.

Peter Hiscock. Archaeology of Ancient Australia. London, 2008. The most up-to-date account of the key archaeological evidence for Australia's ancient peoples by one of the foremost specialists in the field.

K. R. Howe. The Quest for Origins: Who First Discovered and Settled the Pacific Islands? Honolulu, 2003. Reviews the numerous theories advanced to explain the arrival of human populations and the establishment of human societies in the remote islands of the Pacific Ocean.

Gwendolyn Leick. Mesopotamia: The Invention of the City, London, 2004. A refreshing look at ancient Mesopotamia through the lens of its major cities.

Michael E. Mosley. The Incas and Their Ancestors: The Archaeology of Peru. Rev. ed. London, 2001. A comprehensive survey of Andean history through the era of the Incas.

Sarah B. Pomeroy. Goddesses, Whores, Wives, and Slaves: Women in Classical Antiquity. New York, 1975. Outstanding study analyzing the status and role of women in classical Greece and Rome.

William Ruddiman. Plows, Plagues, and Petroleum: How Humans Took Control of Climate, Princeton, NJ: Princeton University Press, 2005. An extraordinary deep historical overview of the relationship between humans and the environment from the earliest periods of human history through to the present.

Romila Thapar. Early India: From the Origins to a.d. 1300. Berkeley, 2003. A fresh view by one of the leading scholars of early Indian history.

Jan Vansina. Paths in the Rainforests: Toward a History of Political Tradition in Equatorial Africa. Madison, 1990. A brilliant synthesis concentrating on central Africa by one of the world's foremost historians of Africa.

Arthur Waldron. The Great Wall of China: From History to Myth. Cambridge, 1989. Places the modern Great Wall in the tradition of Chinese wall building from Qin times forward.

# Part 1 A Global Tapestry c. 1200–c. 1450

CHAPTER 1
The Resurgence of Empire in East Asia

CHAPTER 2
The Expansive Realm of Islam

CHAPTER 3
India and the Indian Ocean Basin

CHAPTER 4
Eastern and Western Europe in the Early Medieval Period

CHAPTER 5
Nomadic Empires and Eurasian Integration

CHAPTER 6
States and Societies of Sub-Saharan Africa

CHAPTER 7
The Increasing Integration of Europe with the Wider World

CHAPTER 8
World Apart: The Americas and Oceania

## LEARNING OBJECTIVES

As you study Part 1 you will:

- Explain Chinese systems of government, cultural traditions, and innovation of economy over time.
- Analyze how systems of belief and their practices affected society in the period from c. 1200 to c. 1450.
- Identify the causes and effects of the rise of Islamic states and the effects of intellectual innovation in Dar al-Islam.
- Explain how and why states in the Americas developed and changed over time.
- Interpret the causes and the consequences of political decentralization and agriculture in Europe from c. 1200 to c. 1450.
- Analyze the similarities and differences in the processes of state formation from c. 1200 to c. 1450.

The first unit of the AP curriculum addresses the various societies and cultures of the world that made up a "Global Tapestry" from roughly 1200–1450 C.E. Historians often call this period the "postclassical" era because it follows the classical era civilizations, such as Rome, Persia, the Han Dynasty, and the Maya. These "classical" empires in Eurasia and the Americas had all collapsed by ca. 600 C.E. Some were replaced by improved versions of the old classical empires. Many postclassical imperial governments were reassembled along almost the same lines as the classical empires—with social structures, written languages, art forms, and religions remaining relatively the same. These "new-and-improved" postclassical empires came with new technologies, new forms of taxation and other governmental powers, tweaks to religious institutions, and much more trade and contact with other empires and regions.

The chapters in Part 1 offer many examples of the AP World History themes. As you read these next eight chapters, consider the similarities and differences between governance, social organization, relationship to the environment, cultural developments, and the creation of new technologies. One way to approach this is to consider how these elements of empire were affected by the growth of economic systems through increasingly connected trade.

The exchange of goods for items of similar value is something everyone can understand. From China to the Indian Ocean to the Vikings and the Mongols to the growth of Europe, trade played a vital role in both the development of societies and building connections between them. As you read through these first eight chapters, keep an eye on who is buying and selling and what they are buying and selling.

From here, we move into the details. Part 1 is going to take you around the world, starting with East Asia and ending with the Americas and Oceania. While the first chapters cover historical events that occurred before the timeframe for this course, it is important to have a sense of where the developments of the later chapters began. This will also help you do better on the exam.

In some places, different types of states formed. City-states flourished in the Mediterranean region, on the east coast of Africa, in Mesoamerica, and in southeast Asia. People on the Arabian Peninsula launched massive wars of conquest, creating an Arab-speaking, predominantly Muslim world (called *dar al-Islam*) that stretched from the Iberian Peninsula to western China—entire areas ruled, for a while, by a caliph. Ruled by interrelated khans, the Mongols (central Asian pastoralists) controlled much of Eurasia for a time. Nothing so grand replaced the fallen empires of western Rome and Gupta India. People settled on small

Henry Westheim Photography/Alamy Stock Photo

kingdoms or principalities rather than an empire. You will need to know the locations and other specifics of how these states were ruled, as well as the relationships the states had with one another.

Trade intensified during this period. Although people in Afro-Eurasia and the Americas remained separate from each other, within each hemisphere many more people and much more merchandise moved along the old, and some new, trade routes. Know the specifics of who and what was moving along these routes, and why, and study the maps. What were the new agricultural and transportation technologies and products? Who were the wealthy consumers with tastes for luxury goods? Who were the innovative merchants and trade organizations? Which governments sponsored commercial policies (minting coins and paper money, for example) and advantageous infrastructure projects, like roads and canals? Scrutinize the roles the invaders—peoples like the Vikings, the Mongols, the Arabs, the Turkic peoples, the European Crusaders, the Mexica/Aztec—played in shaping world history.

It might be useful to think of a spider's web when you evaluate the effects of massively increasing trade, which are both far-reaching and interconnected. For example, powerful new trading cities were created in which foreign merchants set up communities; therefore, a cross-fertilization of artistic, religious, linguistic, and cultural traditions occurred between newcomers and inhabitants.

Technology and science spread to new lands, creating powerful changes. Mongol conquests through *dar al-Islam* spread gunpowder weapons from China, and from there into western European militaries. Indian, Persian, Arab, and Greek science, math, and technologies from universities and libraries within *dar al-Islam* slowly trickled into western Europe via merchants and scholars and formed the backbone of the Renaissance. Foods, animals, and diseases were transported by merchants from their places of origins to new lands, altering agriculture and often dramatically affecting birth and death rates.

Merchants, missionaries, migrants, and military conquerors (the four Ms) spread religions and languages from their 'homelands' to new places where they were synthesized and reinterpreted by the people in the visited or conquered lands. For example, the new language of Swahili was a blend of east African Bantu and Arabic created over centuries because of close trade connections. There are many examples of cultural synthesis in the postclassical period, and AP students are frequently asked to explain the how, why, and significance of these syncretic processes. Wonderfully written architectural, literary, and artistic documents illustrate this blending and are important to AP World History, so watch for them in photographs and text.

The "Global Tapestry" unit of AP World History sees the growth of old structures and the introduction of some new historical players. People in the western and eastern hemispheres didn't know of each other's existence. This period sets the stage for eastern hemisphere peoples—mostly merchants and governments—to develop the science, technologies, and funding to support more intensive maritime explorations that will lead to the Columbian voyages. Before you begin this journey into world history, this is a good time for you and your AP teacher to review each of the themes, historical thinking skills, and reasoning processes you will be faced with in this unit and for the rest of the course.

## PART 1 BIG QUESTIONS:

- How does buying and selling affect people's lives and the development of societies?
- How is religion related to trade?
- What is the relationship between trade, technology, and the growth of societies in Eurasia, Africa, and the Americas?

Explorer/Science Source, Georg Gerster/Science Source, Album/Alamy Stock Photo

Chapter 1

# The Resurgence of Empire in East Asia



## ZOOMING IN ON ENCOUNTERS

### Xuanzang: A Young Monk Hits the Road

Early in the seventh century C.E., the emperor of China issued an order forbidding his subjects to travel beyond Chinese borders into central Asia. In 629, however, in defiance of the emperor, a young Buddhist monk slipped past imperial watchtowers under cover of darkness and made his way west. His name was **Xuanzang,** and his destination was South Asia, homeland of Buddhism. Although educated in Confucian texts as a youth, Xuanzang had followed his older brother into a monastery where he became devoted to Buddhism. While studying the Sanskrit language, Xuanzang noticed that Chinese writings on Buddhism contained many teachings that were

Panels from the twelfth-century Qingming scroll, depicting cosmopolitan life in the city of Kaifeng during the Northern Song dynasty.
Werner Forman Archive/Palace Museum, Beijing/Heritage Image Partnership Ltd/Alamy Stock Photo
Heritage Image Partnership Ltd/Alamy Stock Photo

**Xuanzang** (SHWEN-ZAHNG)

confusing or even contradictory to those in the original Buddhist texts. He decided to travel to the Indian subcontinent, visit the holy sites of Buddhism, and study with the most knowledgeable Buddhist teachers and sages to learn about Buddhism from the purest sources.

Xuanzang could not have imagined the difficulties he would face. Immediately after his departure from China, his guide abandoned him in the Gobi desert. After losing his water bag and collapsing in the heat, Xuanzang made his way to the oasis town of Gaochang in the Turpan Depression, a key town on the Silk Roads. The Buddhist ruler of Gaochang provided the devout pilgrim with travel supplies and rich gifts to support his mission. Among the presents were twenty-four letters of introduction to rulers of lands on the way to India, each one attached to a bolt of silk, five hundred additional bolts of silk and two carts of fruit for the most important ruler, thirty horses, twenty-five laborers, and yet another five hundred bolts of silk along with gold, silver, and silk clothes for Xuanzang to use as travel funds. After departing from Turpan, Xuanzang crossed three of the world's highest mountain ranges—the Tian Shan, Hindu Kush, and Pamir ranges—and lost one-third of his party to exposure and starvation in the Tian Shan. He crossed yawning gorges thousands of meters deep on footbridges fashioned from rope or chains, and he faced numerous attacks by bandits.

Yet Xuanzang persisted and arrived in the northern region of the Indian subcontinent in 630. He lived there for more than twelve years, visiting the holy sites of Buddhism and devoting himself to the study of languages and Buddhist doctrine, especially at Nalanda, the center of advanced Buddhist education in the Ganges Valley. He also amassed a huge collection of relics and images as well as 657 books, all of which he packed into 527 crates and transported back to China to advance the understanding of Buddhism in his native land.

By the time of his return in 645, Xuanzang had logged more than 16,000 kilometers (10,000 miles) on the road. News of the holy monk's efforts had reached the imperial court, and even though Xuanzang had violated the ban on travel, he received a hero's welcome and an audience with the emperor. Until his death in 664, Xuanzang spent his remaining years translating Buddhist treatises into Chinese and clarifying their doctrines. His efforts helped to popularize Buddhism throughout China.

## CHAPTER FOCUS

- China endured 350 years of warlord fighting before the Sui dynasty prevailed—beginning almost 700 years of stability, peace, and prosperity in China through three dynasties. Historians study the reasons for this stability and analyze how China became the driver of the entire Eurasian economy in this period. The Tang era was a historic golden age for the Chinese.
- Japan and Korea, part of the east Asian region, and Vietnam, part of the southeast Asian region, fell under China's tributary control in the Tang dynasty. These kingdoms benefited from trade with China while nurturing their own cultures.
- Buddhism was accepted by some, while others merged Buddhist philosophies with Confucian beliefs to create neo-Confucianism.

## Historical Developments

- Empires and states in Afro-Eurasia and the Americas demonstrated continuity, innovation, and diversity in the 13th century. This included the Song Dynasty of China, which utilized traditional methods of Confucianism and an imperial bureaucracy to maintain and justify its rule.
- Chinese cultural traditions continued, and they influenced neighboring regions.
- Buddhism and its core beliefs continued to shape societies in Asia and included a variety of branches, schools, and practices.
- The economy of Song China became increasingly commercialized, while continuing to depend on free peasant and artisanal labor.
- The economy of Song China flourished as a result of increased productive capacity, expanding trade networks, and innovations in agriculture and manufacturing.

## Reasoning Processes

- **Developments and Processes** Identify the ways in which states in East Asia experience demographic and economic growth.
- **Sourcing and Situation** Explain the impact of the Tang Dynasty Wars and the operations of the Tang Economy using primary source accounts.
- **Contextualization** Explain the larger historical context for the spread of Buddhism in East Asia.
- **Making Connections** Identify and explain the significance and nature of China's connections to Korea, Japan, and Vietnam.

## Historical Thinking Skills

- **Continuity and Change** Explain Patterns of Continuity and Change in China from the Sui through the Song Dynasties.
- **Comparison** Describe similarities and/or differences between the branches of Buddhism and how various East Asian societies adopted Buddhist traditions.

## CHAPTER OVERVIEW

Xuanzang undertook his journey at a fortunate time. For more than 350 years after the fall of the Han dynasty, war, invasion, conquest, and foreign rule disrupted Chinese society. Toward the end of the sixth century, however, centralized imperial rule returned to China. The Sui and Tang dynasties restored order and presided over an era of rapid economic growth in China. Agricultural yields rose dramatically, and technological innovations boosted the production of manufactured goods. China ranked with the Abbasid and Byzantine empires as a political and economic anchor of the Afro-Eurasian world zone.

For China the later first and early second millennia CE was an age of intense interaction with other peoples. Chinese merchants participated in trade networks that linked most regions of the eastern hemisphere. **Buddhism** spread beyond its homeland of India, attracted a large popular following in China, and even influenced the thought of Confucian scholars. A resurgent China made its influence felt throughout east Asia: diplomats and armed forces introduced Chinese ways into Korea and Vietnam, and rulers of the Japanese islands looked to China for guidance in matters of political organization. Korea, Vietnam, and Japan retained their distinctiveness, but all three lands drew deep inspiration from China and participated in a larger east Asian society centered on China.

| CHRONOLOGY | |
|---|---|
| 589–618 | Sui dynasty (China) |
| 602–664 | Life of Xuanzang |
| 604–618 | Reign of Sui Yangdi |
| 618–907 | Tang dynasty (China) |
| 627–649 | Reign of Tang Taizong |
| 669–935 | Silla dynasty (Korea) |
| 710–794 | Nara period (Japan) |
| 755–757 | An Lushan's rebellion |
| 794–1185 | Heian period (Japan) |
| 875–884 | Huang Chao's rebellion |
| 960–976 | Reign of Song Taizu |
| 960–1279 | Song dynasty (China) |
| 1024 | First issuance of government-sponsored paper money |
| 1130–1200 | Life of Zhu Xi |
| 1185–1333 | Kamakura period (Japan) |
| 1336–1573 | Muromachi period (Japan) |

## THE RESTORATION OF CENTRALIZED IMPERIAL RULE IN CHINA

During the centuries following the Han dynasty, several regional kingdoms made bids to assert their authority over all of China, but none possessed the resources to dominate its rivals over the long term. In the late sixth century, however, **Yang Jian,** an ambitious ruler in northern China, embarked on a series of military campaigns that brought all of China once again under centralized imperial rule. Yang Jian's Sui dynasty survived less than thirty years, but the tradition of centralized rule outlived his house. The Tang dynasty replaced the Sui, and the Song succeeded the Tang. The Tang and Song dynasties organized Chinese society so efficiently that China became a center of exceptional agricultural and industrial production. Indeed, much of the eastern hemisphere felt the effects of the powerful Chinese economy of the Tang and Song dynasties.

**Yang Jian** (yahng jyahn)

## The Sui Dynasty

**Establishment of the Dynasty** Like Qin Shihuangdi some eight hundred years earlier, Yang Jian imposed tight political discipline on his state and then extended his rule to the rest of China. Yang Jian began his rise to power when a Turkish ruler appointed him duke of Sui in northern China. In 580 Yang Jian's patron died, leaving a seven-year-old son as his heir. Yang Jian installed the boy as ruler but forced his abdication one year later, claiming the throne and the "mandate of heaven" (chapter 5) for himself. During the next decade Yang Jian sent military expeditions into central Asia and southern China. By 589 the house of Sui ruled all of China.

Like the rulers of the Qin dynasty, the emperors of the **Sui dynasty** (589–618 C.E.) placed enormous demands on their subjects in the course of building a strong, centralized government. The Sui emperors ordered the construction of palaces and granaries, carried out extensive repairs on defensive walls, dispatched military forces to central Asia and Korea, levied high taxes, and demanded compulsory labor services.

**The Grand Canal** The most elaborate project undertaken during the Sui dynasty was the construction of the **Grand Canal,** which was one of the world's largest waterworks projects before modern times. The second emperor, **Sui Yangdi** (reigned 604–618 C.E.), completed work on the canal to facilitate trade between northern and southern China, particularly to make the abundant supplies of rice and other food crops from the Yangzi River valley available to residents of northern regions. The only practical and economical way to transport food crops in large quantities was by water. But since Chinese rivers generally flow from west to east, only an artificial waterway could support a large volume of trade between north and south.

The Grand Canal was really a series of artificial waterways that ultimately reached from Hangzhou in the south to the imperial capital of Chang'an in the west to a terminus near modern Beijing in the north. Sui Yangdi used canals dug as early as the Zhou dynasty, but he linked them into a network that served much of China. When completed, the Grand Canal extended almost 2,000 kilometers (1,240 miles) and reportedly was forty paces wide, with roads running parallel to the waterway on either side.

Though expensive to construct, Sui Yangdi's investment in the Grand Canal paid enormous dividends for the future. It integrated the economies of northern and southern China, thereby establishing an economic foundation for political and cultural unity. Until the arrival of railroads in the twentieth century, the Grand Canal served as the principal conduit for internal trade. Indeed, the canal continues to function even today, although modern forms of transport have diminished its significance as a trade route.

Sui Yangdi's construction projects served China well over the long term, but their dependence on high taxes and forced labor generated hostility toward his rule. The Grand Canal alone required the services of conscripted laborers by the millions. But it was disastrous military expeditions into Korea that ultimately prompted discontented subjects to revolt against Sui rule. During the late 610s, rebellions broke out in northern China when Sui Yangdi sought additional resources for his Korean campaign. In 618 a disgruntled minister assassinated the emperor and brought the dynasty to an end.

## The Tang Dynasty

Soon after Sui Yangdi's death, a rebel leader seized Chang'an and proclaimed himself emperor of a new dynasty that he named the **Tang dynasty** after his hereditary title. The dynasty survived for almost three hundred years (618–907 C.E.), and Tang rulers organized China into a powerful, productive, and prosperous society.

**Tang Taizong** Much of the Tang's success was due to the energy, ability, and policies of the dynasty's second emperor, **Tang Taizong** (reigned 627–649 C.E.). Taizong was both ambitious and ruthless: in making his way to the imperial throne, he murdered two of his brothers and pushed his father aside. Once on the throne, however, he displayed a high sense of duty and strove conscientiously to provide an effective, stable government. He built a splendid capital at Chang'an, and he saw himself as a Confucian ruler who heeded the interests of his subjects. Contemporaries reported that banditry ended during his reign, that the price of rice remained low, and that taxes levied on peasants amounted to only one-fortieth of the annual harvest—a 2.5 percent tax rate—although required rent payments and compulsory labor services meant that the effective rate of taxation was somewhat higher. These reports suggest that China enjoyed an era of unusual stability and prosperity during the reign of Tang Taizong.

Three policies in particular help to explain the success of the early Tang dynasty: maintenance of a well-articulated transportation and communications network, distribution of land according to the principles of the equal-field system, and reliance on a bureaucracy based on merit. All three policies originated in the Sui dynasty, but Tang rulers applied them more systematically and effectively than their predecessors had.

**Transportation and Communications** Apart from the Grand Canal, which served as the principal route for long-distance transportation within China, Tang rulers maintained an extensive communications network based on roads, horses, and sometimes human runners. Along the main routes, Tang officials maintained inns, postal stations, and stables, which provided rest and refreshment for travelers, couriers, and their mounts. Using couriers traveling by horse, the Tang court could communicate with the most distant cities in the empire in about eight days. Even human runners provided impressively speedy services: relay teams of some 9,600 runners supplied

**Sui Yangdi** (sway yahng-dee)
**Tang Taizong** (TAHNG TEYE-zohng)

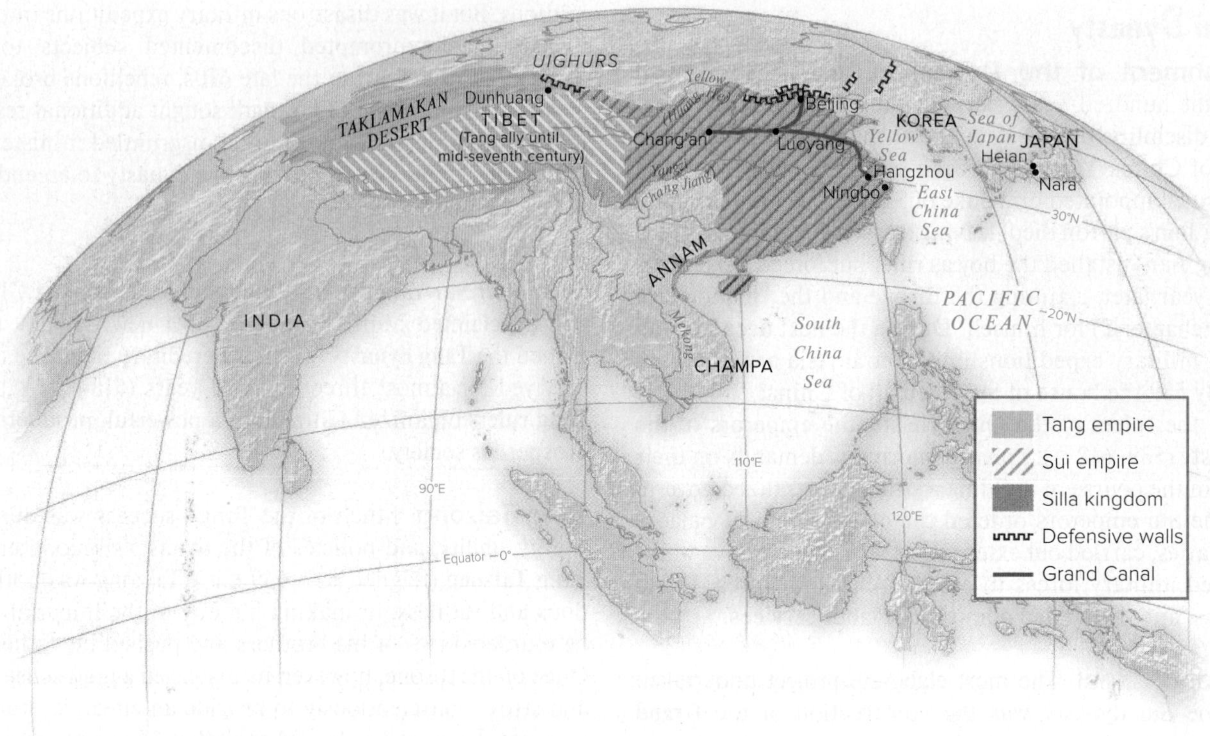


## MAP 1.1 The Sui and Tang dynasties, 589–907 C.E.

Compare the size of the Sui and Tang empires.

***What impact did the Grand Canal have on helping reunify China after 350 years of disunity?***

***What techniques did the Tang Dynasty use that allowed it to create such a vast tributary empire in East and Central Asia?***

the Tang court at Chang'an with seafood delivered fresh from Ningbo, more than 1,000 kilometers (620 miles) away.

**The Equal-Field System** The **equal-field system** governed the allocation of agricultural land. Its purposes were to ensure an equitable distribution of land and to avoid the concentration of landed property that had caused social problems during the Han dynasty. The system allotted land to individuals and their families according to the land's fertility and the recipients' needs. About one-fifth of the land became the hereditary possession of the recipients, and the rest remained available for redistribution when the original recipients' needs and circumstances changed.

For about a century, administrators were able to apply the principles of the equal-field system relatively consistently. By the early eighth century, however, the system showed signs of strain. A rapidly rising population placed pressure on the land available for distribution. Meanwhile, through favors, bribery, or intimidation of administrators, influential families found ways to retain land scheduled for redistribution. Furthermore, large parcels of land fell out of the system altogether when Buddhist monasteries acquired them. Nevertheless, during the first half of the Tang dynasty, the system provided a foundation for stability and prosperity in the Chinese countryside.

**Bureaucracy of Merit** The Tang dynasty also relied heavily on a bureaucracy based on merit, as reflected by performance on imperial civil service examinations. Following the example of the Han dynasty, Sui and Tang rulers recruited government officials from the ranks of candidates who had progressed through the Confucian educational system and had mastered a sophisticated curriculum concentrating on the classic works of Chinese literature and philosophy. During the early Tang dynasty, most officeholders were aristocrats. By the late Tang era, however, when educational opportunities were more widely available, officeholders came largely from the ranks of common families. The Confucian educational system and the related civil service served Chinese governments so well that, with modifications and an occasional interruption, they survived for thirteen centuries, disappearing only after the collapse of the Qing dynasty in the early twentieth century.

**Military Expansion** Soon after its foundation, the powerful and dynamic Tang state began to flex its military muscles. In the north, Tang forces brought Manchuria under imperial authority and forced the Silla kingdom in Korea to acknowledge the Tang emperor as overlord. To the south, Tang armies conquered the northern part of Vietnam. To the west they extended Tang

Barges make their way through a portion of the Grand Canal near the city of Wuxi in southern China. Built during the Sui dynasty, the waterways of the Grand Canal fostered the economic integration of northern and southern China.
Dean Conger/Corbis Documentary/Getty Images

authority almost as far as the Aral Sea and brought a portion of the high plateau of Tibet under Tang control. Territorially, the Tang empire ranks among the largest in Chinese history.

**Tang Foreign Relations** In an effort to fashion a stable diplomatic order, the Tang emperors revived the Han dynasty's practice of maintaining tributary relationships between China and neighboring lands. According to Chinese political theory, China was the Middle Kingdom, a powerful realm with the responsibility to bring order to subordinate lands through a system of tributary relationships. Neighboring lands and peoples would recognize Chinese emperors as their overlords. As tokens of their subordinate status, envoys from those states would regularly deliver gifts to the court of the Middle Kingdom and would perform the kowtow—a ritual prostration in which subordinates knelt before the emperor and touched their foreheads to the ground. In return, tributary states received confirmation of their authority as well as lavish gifts. Because Chinese authorities often had little real influence in these supposedly subordinate lands, there was always something of a fictional quality to the system. Nevertheless, it was extremely important throughout east Asia and central Asia because it institutionalized relations between China and neighboring lands, fostering trade and cultural exchanges as well as diplomatic contacts.

**Tang Decline** Under able rulers such as Taizong, the Tang dynasty flourished. During the mid-eighth century, however, casual and careless leadership brought the dynasty to a crisis from which it never fully recovered. In 755, while the emperor neglected public affairs in favor of music and his favorite concubine, one of the dynasty's foremost military commanders, An Lushan, mounted a rebellion and captured the capital at Chang'an, as well as the secondary capital at Luoyang. His revolt was short-lived: in 757 a soldier murdered An Lushan, and by 763 Tang forces had suppressed his army and recovered their capitals. But the rebellion left the dynasty in a gravely weakened state. Tang commanders were unable to defeat rebellious forces by themselves, so they invited a nomadic Turkic people, the **Uighurs,** to bring an army into China. In return for their services, the Uighurs demanded the right to sack Chang'an and Luoyang after the expulsion of the rebels.

The Tang imperial house never regained control of affairs after this crisis. The equal-field system deteriorated, and dwindling tax receipts failed to meet dynastic needs. Imperial armies were unable to resist the encroachments of Turkic peoples in the late eighth century. During the ninth century a series of rebellions devastated the Chinese countryside. One uprising, led by the military commander Huang Chao, embroiled much of eastern China for almost a decade, from 875 to 884. Huang Chao's revolt reflected and fueled popular discontent: he routinely pillaged the wealthy and distributed a portion of his plunder among the poor. In an effort to control the rebels, the Tang emperors granted progressively greater power and authority to regional military commanders, who gradually became the

**Uighurs** (WEE-goors)

In this wall painting from the tomb of a Tang prince, three Chinese officials (at left) receive envoys from foreign lands who pay their respects to representatives of the Middle Kingdom. The envoys probably come from the Byzantine empire and Korea.
What features of their personal appearance and dress provide clues to the envoys' lands of origin?
Henry Westheim Photography/Alamy Stock Photo

effective rulers of China. In 907 the last Tang emperor abdicated his throne, and the dynasty came to an end.

## The Song Dynasty

Following the Tang collapse, warlords ruled China until the Song dynasty reimposed centralized imperial rule in the late tenth century. Though it survived for more than three centuries, the **Song dynasty** (960–1279 C.E.) never built a very powerful state. Song rulers mistrusted military leaders, and they placed much more emphasis on civil administration, industry, education, and the arts than on military affairs.

**Song Taizu** The first Song emperor, **Song Taizu** (reigned 960–976 C.E.), inaugurated this policy. Song Taizu began his career as a junior military officer serving one of the most powerful warlords in northern China. He had a reputation for honesty and effectiveness, and in 960 his troops proclaimed him emperor. During the next several years, he and his army subjected the warlords to their authority and consolidated Song control throughout China. He then persuaded his generals to retire honorably to a life of leisure so that they would not seek to displace him, and he set about organizing a centralized administration that placed military forces under tight supervision.

Song Taizu regarded all state officials, even minor functionaries in distant provinces, as servants of the imperial government. In exchange for their loyalty, Song rulers rewarded these officials handsomely. They vastly expanded the bureaucracy based on merit by creating more opportunities for individuals to seek a Confucian education and take civil service examinations. They accepted many more candidates into the bureaucracy than their Sui and Tang predecessors, and they provided generous salaries for those who qualified for government appointments. They even placed civil bureaucrats in charge of military forces.

**Song Weaknesses** The Song approach to administration resulted in a more centralized imperial government than earlier Chinese dynasties had enjoyed. But it caused two big problems that weakened the dynasty and eventually brought about its fall. The first problem was financial: the enormous Song bureaucracy devoured China's surplus production. As the number of bureaucrats and the size of their rewards grew, the imperial treasury came under tremendous pressure. Efforts to raise taxes aggravated the peasants, who mounted two major rebellions in the early twelfth century. By that time, however, bureaucrats dominated the Song administration to the point that it was impossible to reform the system.

The second problem was military. Scholar-bureaucrats generally had little military education and little talent for military affairs, yet they led Song armies in the field and made military decisions. It was no coincidence that nomadic peoples flourished along China's northern border throughout the Song dynasty. From the early tenth through the early twelfth century, the Khitan, a seminomadic people from Manchuria,

**Song Taizu** (sawng tahy-zoo)

# SOURCES FROM THE PAST

## The Poet Du Fu on Tang Dynasty Wars

*The eighth century was a golden age of Chinese poetry. Among the foremost writers of the era was Du Fu (712–770 c.e.), often considered one of China's two greatest poets. Born into a prominent Confucian family, Du Fu wrote in his early years about the beauty of the natural world. After the rebellion of An Lushan, however, he fell into poverty and experienced difficulties. Not surprisingly, poetry of his later years lamented the chaos of the late eighth century. In the three following poems, Du Fu offered a bitter perspective on the wars that plagued China in the 750s and 760s.*

**The Recruiting Officers at the Village of the Stone Moat**

I sought a lodging for the night, at sunset, in the Stone Moat village.
Recruiting officers, who seize people by night, were there.
A venerable old man climbed over the wall and fled.
An old woman came out of the door and peered.
What rage in the shouts of the Recruiting Officers.
What bitterness in the weeping of the old woman.
I heard the words of the woman as she pled her cause before them:

'My three sons are with the frontier guard at Yeh Cheng,
From one son I have received a letter.
A little while ago two sons died in battle.
He who remains has stolen a temporary lease of life;
The dead are finished forever.
In the house there is still no grown man;
Only my grandson at the breast.
The mother of my grandson has not gone;
Going out, coming in, she has not a single whole skirt.
I am an old, old woman, and my strength is failing,
But I beg to go with the Recruiting Officers when they return this night.
I will eagerly agree to act as a servant at Ho Yang;
I am still able to prepare the early morning meal.'
The sound of words ceased in the long night,
It was as though I heard the darkness choke with tears.
At daybreak I went on my way.
Only the venerable old man was left.

Why is the old woman offering to go with the recruiting officers as a servant?

**Crossing the Frontier I**

When bows are bent, they should be bent strongly;
When arrows are used, they should be long.
The bowmen should first shoot the horses.
In taking the enemy prisoner, the leader should be taken first.
There should be no limit to the killing of men.
In making a country, there should naturally be a border.
If it were possible to regulate rebellion,
Would so many be killed and wounded?

What does the author mean by "regulate rebellion"?

**Crossing the Frontier II**

At dawn, the conscripted soldiers enter the camp outside the Eastern Gate.
At sunset they cross the bridge at Ho Yang.
The setting sunlight is reflected on the great flags.
Horses neigh. The wind whines—whines

*(Continued)*

Ten thousand tents are spread across the level sand.
Officers instruct their companies.
The bright moon hangs in the middle of the sky.
The written orders are strict that the night shall be still and empty.
Sadness everywhere. A few sounds from the nomad flute fill the air.
The strong soldiers are no longer proud, they quiver with sadness.
May one ask who is their general?
Perhaps it is Ho Piao Yao.

### For Further Reflection

- In Poem 1, what has been the impact of ongoing wars on the family of the old woman and the village in general?
- In Poem 2, is the poet offering military strategic advice or making some larger point about warfare?
- In Poem 3, why are the newly conscripted soldiers so sad?
- From your reading of these poems, what was the impact of the Tang wars on the poet Du Fu personally, and on Chinese society in general?

*Source:* Lowell, Amy. Fir-flower Tablets: Poems Translated from the Chinese. Massachusetts: Houghton Mifflin Harcourt, 1921, 109.

ruled a vast empire stretching from northern Korea to Mongolia. During the first half of the Song dynasty, the Khitan demanded and received large tribute payments of silk and silver from the Song state to the south. In the early twelfth century, the nomadic Jurchen conquered the Khitan, overran northern China, captured the Song capital at Kaifeng, and proclaimed establishment of the Jin empire. Thereafter the Song dynasty moved its capital to the prosperous port city of **Hangzhou** and survived only in southern China, so that the latter part of the dynasty is commonly known as the Southern Song. This truncated Southern Song shared a border with the Jin empire about midway between the Yellow River and the Yangzi River until 1279, when Mongol forces ended the dynasty and incorporated southern China into their empire.

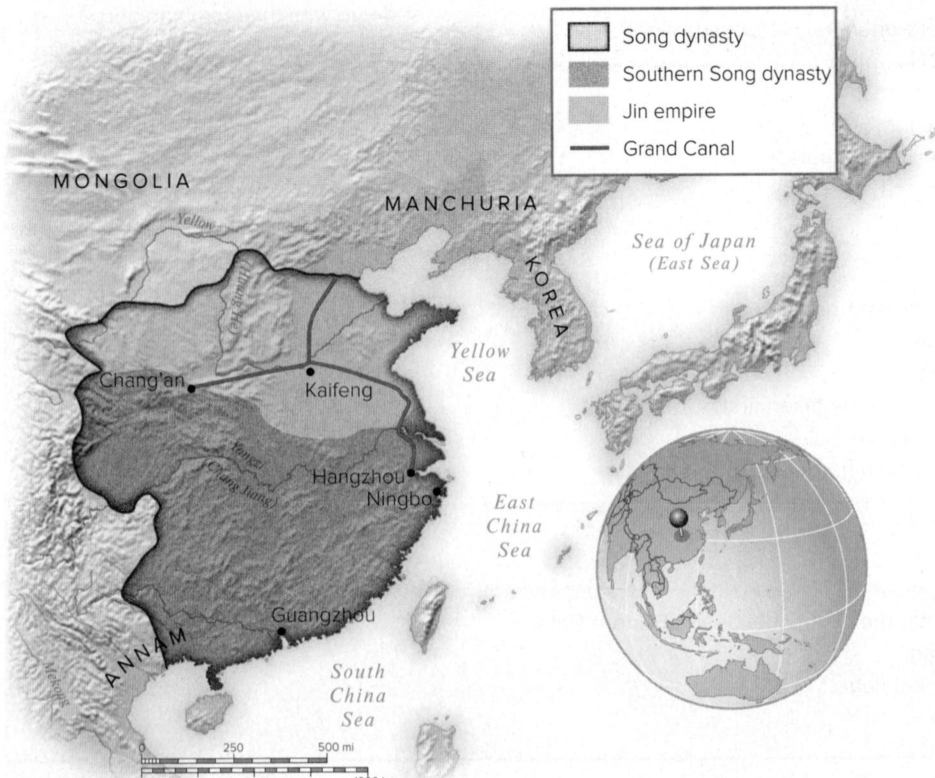


**MAP 1.2 The Song dynasty, 960–1279 C.E.**

After the establishment of the Jin empire, the Song dynasty moved its capital from Kaifeng to Hangzhou.

***Why would Song rulers have chosen Hangzhou as their new capital? What advantages did it offer? In what ways does the map demonstrate Song vulnerability to Mongol invasion?***

# THE ECONOMIC DEVELOPMENT OF TANG AND SONG CHINA

Although the Song dynasty did not develop a particularly strong military capacity, it benefited from a remarkable series of agricultural, technological, industrial, and commercial developments that transformed China into the economic powerhouse of Eurasia. This economic development originated in the Tang dynasty, but its results became most clear during the Song, which presided over a land of enormous prosperity. The economic surge of Tang and Song times had implications that went well beyond China because it stimulated trade and production throughout much of the eastern hemisphere for more than half a millennium, from about 600 to 1300 C.E.

## Agricultural Development

**Fast-Ripening Rice** The foundation of economic development in Tang and Song China was a surge in agricultural production. Sui and Tang armies prepared the way for increased agricultural productivity when they imposed their control over southern China and ventured into Vietnam. In Vietnam they encountered strains of fast-ripening rice that enabled cultivators to harvest two crops per year. When introduced to the fertile fields of southern China, fast-ripening rice quickly resulted in an expanded supply of food. Like the *dar al-Islam,* Tang and Song China benefited enormously from the introduction of new food crops.

**New Agricultural Techniques** Chinese cultivators also increased their productivity by adopting improved agricultural techniques. They made increased use of heavy iron plows, and they harnessed oxen (in the north) and water buffaloes (in the south) to help prepare land for cultivation. They enriched the soil with manure and composted organic matter. They also organized extensive irrigation systems. These included not only reservoirs, dikes, dams, and canals but also pumps and waterwheels, powered by both animals and humans, that moved water into irrigation systems. Artificial irrigation made it possible to extend cultivation to difficult terrain, including terraced mountainsides—a development that vastly expanded China's agricultural potential.

**Population Growth** Increased agricultural production had dramatic results. One was a rapid expansion of the Chinese population. After the fall of the Han dynasty, the population of China probably reached a low point, about 45 million in 600 C.E. By 800 it had rebounded to 50 million, and two centuries later to 60 million. By 1127, when the Jurchen conquered the northern half of the Song state, the Chinese population had passed 100 million, and by 1200 it stood at about 115 million. This rapid population growth reflected both the productivity of the agricultural economy and the well-organized distribution of food through transportation networks built during Sui and Tang times.

**Urbanization** Increased food supplies encouraged the growth of cities. During the Tang dynasty the imperial capital

A Northern Song Dynasty (960–1127) era Chinese painting of a water-powered mill for grain, with surrounding river transport.
The Picture Art Collection/ Alamy Stock Photo

of Chang'an was the world's most populous city, with perhaps as many as two million residents. During the Song dynasty, China was the most urbanized land in the world. In the late thirteenth century, Hangzhou, capital of the Southern Song dynasty, had more than one million residents. These cities supported hundreds of restaurants; noodle shops; taverns; teahouses; brothels; music halls; theaters; clubhouses; gardens; markets; craft shops; and specialty stores dealing in silk, gems, porcelain, lacquerware, and other goods. Hangzhou residents, like those in most cities, observed peculiar local customs. Taverns often had several stories, for example, and patrons gravitated to higher or lower stories according to their plans: those desiring only a cup or two of wine sat at street level, whereas those planning an extended evening of revelry sought tables on the higher stories, much like the situation in restaurants in Chinese cities today.

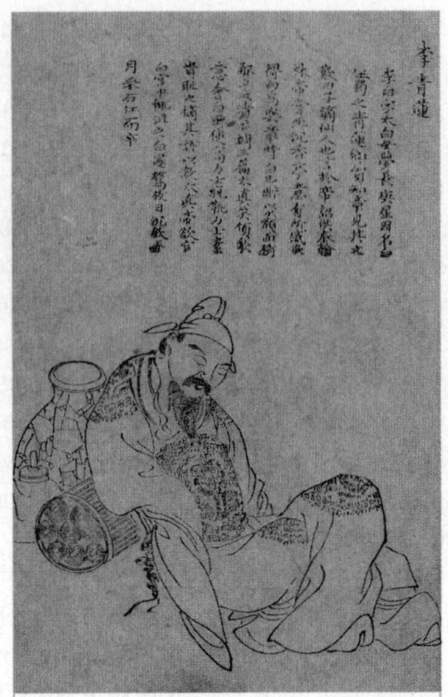

The great Tang dynasty poet Li Bai by Ming dynasty artist Jin Guilang.
The Picture Art Collection/Alamy Stock Photo

Although the capital Hangzhou was an exceptionally large city, it wasn't the only one with a large number of people. During the Tang and Song eras, scores of Chinese cities boasted populations of one hundred thousand or more. **Li Bai** (701–761 C.E.), who was perhaps the most popular poet of the Tang era, took the social life of these Chinese cities as one of his principal themes. Li Bai mostly wrote light, pleasing verse celebrating life, friendship, and especially wine. (Tradition holds that the drunken poet died by drowning when he fell out of a boat while attempting to embrace the moon's reflection in the water.) The annual spring festival was an occasion dear to the heart of urban residents, who flocked to the streets to shop for new products, have their fortunes told, and eat tasty snacks from food vendors.

Another result of increased food production was the emergence of a commercialized agricultural economy. Because fast-ripening rice yielded bountiful harvests, many cultivators could purchase inexpensive rice and raise vegetables and fruits for sale on the commercial market. Cultivators specialized in crops that grew well in their regions, and they often exported their harvests to distant regions. By the twelfth century, for example, the wealthy southern province of Fujian imported rice and devoted its land to the production of lychees, oranges, and sugarcane, which fetched high prices in northern markets. Indeed, market-oriented cultivation went so far that authorities tried—with only limited success—to require Fujianese to grow rice so as to avoid excessive dependence on imports.

**Patriarchal Social Structures** With increasing wealth and agricultural productivity, Tang and especially Song China experienced a tightening of patriarchal social structures, which perhaps reflected a concern to preserve family fortunes through enhanced family solidarity. During the Song dynasty the veneration of family ancestors became much more elaborate. Instead of simply remembering ancestors and invoking their aid in rituals performed at home, descendants diligently sought the graves of their earliest traceable forefathers and then arranged elaborate graveside rituals in their honor. Whole extended families often traveled great distances to attend annual rituals venerating their ancestors—a practice that strengthened the sense of family identity and cohesiveness.

**Foot Binding** Strengthened patriarchal authority also helps to explain the popularity of foot binding, which spread widely during the Song era. **Foot binding** involved the tight wrapping of young girls' feet with strips of cloth that prevented natural growth of the bones and resulted in tiny, malformed, curved feet. Women with bound feet could not walk easily or naturally. Usually, they needed canes to walk by themselves, and sometimes they depended on servants to carry them around in litters. Foot binding never became universal in China, but many wealthy families and sometimes also peasant families bound the feet of their daughters to enhance their attractiveness and gain increased control over the girls' behavior. Foot binding thus placed women under tight supervision of their husbands or other male guardians, who then managed the women's affairs in the interests of the larger family.

**Wu Zhao: The Lady Emperor** Ironically, this era of strong patriarchal authority produced a rare female ruler. **Wu Zhao** (626–706 C.E.), also known as Wu Zetian, was the daughter of a scholar-official. At the age of thirteen, she became a concubine at the court of Tang Taizong, where she attracted notice because of her intelligence, wit, and beauty. After Taizong's death, Wu Zhao became the concubine and later the wife of his successor. In 660 the emperor suffered a debilitating stroke, and Wu Zhao seized the opportunity to direct affairs as administrator of the court. In 690 she went further and claimed the imperial title for herself.

Confucian principles held that political leadership was a man's duty and that women should obey their fathers, husbands, and sons. Thus it was not surprising that factions emerged to oppose Wu Zhao's rule. The emperor, however, was resourceful in garnering support. She organized a secret police force to monitor dissident factions, and she ordered brutal punishment for those who stood in her way. She strengthened the civil service system as a way of undercutting aristocratic families that might attempt to displace her. She also generously patronized Buddhists, who returned the favor by composing treatises seeking to legitimize her rule. Although

## What's Left Out?

At several places in this chapter we refer to concubines, who were personal and often sexual partners of powerful men, including many Chinese emperors. The practice continued for thousands of years in China, from the most ancient dynasties through to the twentieth century, when it was banned by the Communist government. Historians have tried to understand the practice of concubinage through various lenses—in particular, those of gender and family relations, legal and social status, filial piety, and political influence. The practice seems to have emerged as a result of early social norms in China that made it illegal and socially disreputable for a man to have more than one wife. As a way of getting around this, however, these same norms determined that it was perfectly fine for a man to have as many concubines as he could afford. During the Later Han Dynasty, the number of concubines was restricted by law, although men of high rank could still possess as many as they could afford.

The manner in which a concubine was treated in society varied enormously and was influenced by the social status of the men involved. Yet the situation of concubines was always very different to that of legal wives, who had brought a dowry to the relationship. Once a concubine had entered a relationship with a man—and even if the concubine later ended the relationship—it was impossible for her to marry or even to return to her parents' home. The position of a concubine was thus always inferior to that of a wife, and this affected even the rules of filial piety. For example, although children and grandchildren would continue to offer rites to deceased legal mothers for generations, after the death of a concubine, only her sons were expected to make an offering—but not her grandsons nor any other descendants.

By the era of Qing Dynasty (1644–1911), the laws had changed, and it became easier for a man to marry a concubine, but only if his legitimate wife had died. During both the Ming and Qing Dynasties, imperial concubines were housed in luxury in the Forbidden City in Beijing, usually guarded by eunuchs to make sure no other man could have sexual relations with the concubines, ensuring that the only offspring they would produce would be those of the emperor. The Ming introduced an official selection system. Potential concubines had to be aged between fourteen and sixteen, and the criteria for selection included virtue, behavior, and facial and body appearance.

Concubines have been treated sympathetically in many works of Chinese literature, including the classic novel *Dream of the Red Chamber,* and also in many modern novels and television dramas. These tend to focus on the lives of those extraordinary women who rose out of concubinage to become politically powerful, including Empress Dowager Cixi of the Qing Dynasty—arguably the most powerful member of the imperial family in the last decade of the Qing—and, of course, Empress Wu Zhao (Zetian), who rose from her early status as teenage concubine of Tang Emperor Taizong to become the only empress ever to rule China!

### Thinking Critically About Sources

1. In what ways were concubines similar to modern sex workers?
2. In what ways were they considerably different?
3. To what extent to the experiences of the Empress Dowager Cixi and Empress Wu Zhou complicate our understanding of Chinese patriarchy?

Confucian scholars reviled her, Wu Zhao was an energetic and effective ruler. She quashed rebellions, organized military campaigns, and opened the imperial administration to talented commoners who rose through the civil service system. She held on to her rule until age eighty, when opponents were finally able to force an ailing Wu Zhao to abdicate in favor of her son. She was unique as a woman who publicly and officially wielded power in a rigidly patriarchal society. Other women exercised influence indirectly or even "ruled from behind a screen," but Wu Zhao was the only woman in Chinese history to claim the imperial title and rule as emperor.

## Technological and Industrial Development

**Porcelain** Abundant supplies of food enabled many people to pursue technological and industrial interests. During the Tang and Song dynasties, Chinese crafts workers generated a remarkable range of technological innovations. During Tang times they discovered techniques of producing high-quality **porcelain,** which was lighter, thinner, and adaptable to more uses than earlier pottery. When fired with glazes, porcelain could also become an aesthetically appealing utensil and even a work of art. Porcelain technology gradually diffused to other societies, and Abbasid crafts workers in particular produced porcelain in large quantities. Yet demand for Chinese porcelain remained strong, and the Chinese exported vast quantities of porcelain during the Tang and Song dynasties. Archaeologists have turned up Tang and Song porcelain at sites all along the trade networks of the later first millennium. Chinese porcelain graced the tables of wealthy and refined households in southeast Asia, India, Persia, and the port cities of east Africa. Tang and Song products gained such a reputation that fine porcelain has come to be known generally as *chinaware.*

**Metallurgy** Tang and Song craftsmen also improved metallurgical technologies. Production of iron and steel surged during this era, partly because of techniques that resulted in stronger and more useful metals. Chinese craftsmen discovered that they could use coke instead of coal in their furnaces and produce superior grades of metal. Between the early ninth and the early twelfth centuries, iron production increased almost tenfold according to official records, which understate total production. Most of the increased supply of iron and steel went into weaponry and agricultural tools: during the early Song dynasty, imperial armaments manufacturers produced 16.5 million iron arrowheads per year. Iron and steel also went into construction projects involving large structures such as bridges and pagodas. As in the case of porcelain technology, metallurgical techniques soon diffused to lands beyond China. Indeed, Song military difficulties stemmed partly from the fact that nomadic peoples quickly learned Chinese techniques and fashioned their own iron weapons for use in campaigns against China.

**Gunpowder** Quite apart from improving existing technologies, Tang and Song craftsmen invented entirely new products, tools, and techniques, most notably **gunpowder,** printing, and naval technologies. Daoist alchemists discovered how to make gunpowder during the Tang dynasty, as they tested the properties of various experimental concoctions while seeking elixirs to prolong life. They soon learned that it was unwise to mix charcoal, saltpeter, sulphur, and arsenic because the volatile compound often resulted in singed beards and even destroyed buildings. Military officials, however, recognized opportunity in the explosive mixture. By the mid-tenth century, they were using gunpowder in bamboo "fire lances," a kind of flamethrower, and by the eleventh century they had fashioned primitive bombs.

The earliest gunpowder weapons had limited military effectiveness: they probably caused more confusion because of noise and smoke than damage because of their destructive potential. Over time, however, refinements enhanced their effectiveness. Knowledge of gunpowder chemistry quickly diffused through Eurasia, and by the late thirteenth century peoples of southwest Asia and Europe were experimenting with metal-barreled cannons.

**Printing** The precise origins of printing lie obscured in the mists of time. Although some form of printing may have predated the Sui dynasty, only during the Tang era did printing become common. The earliest printers employed block-printing techniques: they carved a reverse image of an entire page into a wooden block, inked the block, and then pressed a sheet of paper on top. By the mid-eleventh century, printers had begun to experiment with reusable, movable type: instead of carving images into blocks, they fashioned dies in the shape of ideographs, arranged them in a frame, inked them, and pressed the frame over paper sheets. Because formal writing in the Chinese language involved as many as forty thousand characters, printers often found movable type to be unwieldy and inconvenient, so they continued to print from wooden blocks long after movable type became available.

Printing made it possible to produce texts quickly, cheaply, and in huge quantities. By the late ninth century, printed copies of Buddhist texts, Confucian works, calendars, agricultural treatises, and popular works appeared in large quantities, particularly in southwestern China (modern Sichuan province). Song dynasty officials broadly disseminated printed works by visiting the countryside with pamphlets that outlined effective agricultural techniques.

**Naval Technology** Chinese inventiveness extended also to naval technology. Before Tang times, Chinese mariners did not venture far from land. They traveled the sea lanes to Korea, Japan, and the Ryukyu Islands but relied on Persian, Arab,

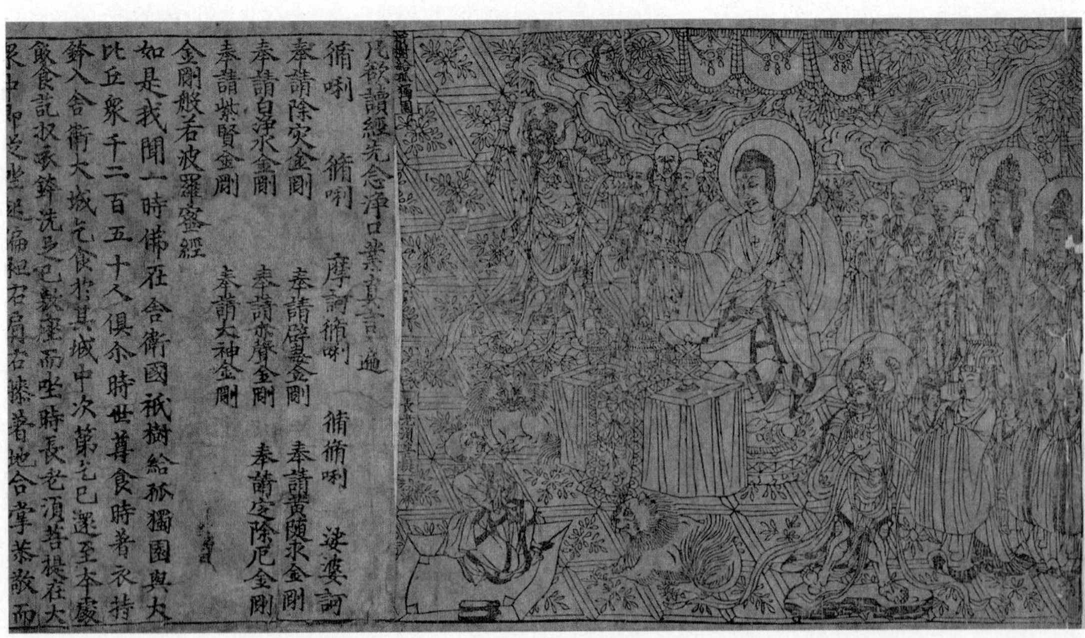


A printed book from the twelfth century presents a Chinese translation of a Buddhist text along with a block-printed illustration of the Buddha addressing his followers. PBL Collection/Alamy Stock Photo

## INTERPRETING IMAGES

A detail from a Song-era painting on silk depicts two sturdy, broad-bottomed junks, the workhorses of the Chinese merchant fleet.

**Analyze** *What are the benefits and drawbacks of the use of paper money?* Werner Forman Archive/Shutterstock

Indian, and Malay mariners for long-distance maritime trade. During the Tang dynasty, however, Chinese consumers developed a taste for the spices and exotic products of southeast Asian islands, and Chinese mariners increasingly visited those lands in their own ships. By the time of the Song dynasty, Chinese seafarers sailed ships fastened with iron nails, waterproofed with oils, furnished with watertight bulkheads, driven by canvas and bamboo sails, steered by rudders, and navigated with the aid of the "south-pointing needle"–the magnetic compass. Larger ships sometimes even had small rockets powered by gunpowder. Chinese ships mostly plied the waters between Japan and the Malay peninsula, but some ventured into the Indian Ocean and called at ports in India, Ceylon, Persia, and east Africa. Those long-distance travels helped to diffuse elements of Chinese naval technology, particularly the compass, which soon became the common property of mariners throughout the Indian Ocean basin.

An example of the world's oldest paper money, known as Jiaozi, first printed during the Southern Song dynasty. What economic conditions during the Southern Song demanded the introduction of paper money?

The Picture Art Collection/Alamy Stock Photo

## The Emergence of a Market Economy

Increased agricultural production, improved transportation systems, population growth, urbanization, and industrial production combined to stimulate the Chinese economy. China's various regions increasingly specialized in the cultivation of particular food crops or the production of particular manufactured goods, trading their products for imports from other regions. The market was not the only influence on the Chinese economy: government bureaucracies played a large role in the distribution of staple foods such as rice, wheat, and millet, and dynastic authorities closely watched militarily sensitive enterprises such as the iron industry. Nevertheless, millions of cultivators produced fruits and vegetables for sale on the open market, and manufacturers of silk, porcelain, and other goods supplied both domestic and foreign markets. The Chinese economy became more tightly integrated than ever before, and foreign demand for Chinese products fueled rapid economic expansion.

**Financial Instruments** Indeed, trade grew so rapidly during Tang and Song times that China experienced a shortage of the copper coins that served as money for most transactions. To alleviate the shortage, Chinese merchants developed alternatives to cash that resulted in even more economic growth. Letters of credit came into common use during the early Tang dynasty. Known as "flying cash," they enabled merchants to deposit goods or cash at one location and draw the equivalent in cash or goods elsewhere in China. Later developments included the use of promissory notes, which pledged payment of a given sum of money at a later date, and checks, which entitled the bearer to draw funds against cash deposited with bankers.

**Paper Money** The search for alternatives to cash eventually led to the invention of paper money. Wealthy merchants pioneered the use of printed paper money during the late ninth century. In return for cash deposits from their clients, they issued printed notes that the clients could redeem for

# SOURCES FROM THE PAST

## The Arab Merchant Suleiman on Business Practices in Tang China

*The Arab merchant Suleiman made several commercial ventures by ship to South Asia and China during the early ninth century* c.e. *In 851 an Arab geographer wrote an account of Suleiman's travels, describing the lands he visited for Muslim readers in southwest Asia. His report throws particularly interesting light on the economic conditions and business practices of Tang China.*

**The Chinese are dressed in silk** both winter and summer; and this kind of dress is common to the prince, the soldier, and to every other person, though of the lowest degree. In winter they wear drawers of a particular make, which fall down to their feet. Of these they put on two, three, four, five or more if they can, one over another, and are very careful to be covered quite down to their feet, because of the damp which is very great and much dreaded by them. In summer they only wear a single garment of silk or some such dress, but have no turbans . . . (p. 13)

In China commerce is carried out with the assistance of copper coins. They coin a great deal of copper money, like what the Arabs know by the name of Falus. They have treasuries like other kings, but no others have this sort of small money, and no other is current all over the country. For though they have gold, silver, pearls, silk, and rich stuffs in great abundance, they consider these only as merchandise, and copper pieces are the only current coin. From foreign parts [the Chinese] import ivory, incense, copper, the shells of turtles, and the horn of rhinoceros, from which they make ornaments . . . (p. 62)

When merchants enter China by sea the government agents seize on their cargo and convey it to warehouses, and so put a stop to their business for six months, and till the last merchantman has arrived. Then they take three in ten, or thirty percent of each commodity, and return the rest to the merchant. If the emperor wants any particular thing, his officers have a right to take it preferable to any other persons whatsoever; and paying for it at the utmost penny it is valued at, they dispatch this business immediately and without the least injustice. (p. 63)

Why would the Tang government so strictly regulate commerce in their ports?

[The Chinese] administer justice with great strictness and equity in all their tribunals. When any person enters into a business transaction with another, he (the lender) sets down his claim in writing and the defendant (the borrower) writes down his understanding, which he signs and affixes the imprint of two of his fingers. These two writings are delivered together, and after being examined . . . the parties each have his paper returned to him.

When one party denies what the other affirms, he is ordered to return his writing. And if the defendant thinks he may do it safely, he accordingly delivers in his paper again. They also call for that of the plaintif, and then they say to him who denies what the other seems to have reason to maintain, exhibit a writing whereby they make it appear that your antagonist has no right to demand of you what is in debate. But if it clearly betrays the truth of what you deny, you shall undergo twenty strokes of the bamboo upon the back side, and pay a fine of 20 Fakuges, which is about two hundred dinars [Arab currency of the time]. Now this punishment is such that the criminal could not survive. It is so grievous that no person in all of China may, of his own authority, inflict it upon another upon pain of death and confiscation of goods. And so . . . justice is well administered and very exactly distributed to everyone. (pp. 67–68)

### For Further Reflection

- Given the Chinese clothing the author describes, what class of Chinese did Suleiman most likely deal with?
- What is the economic value to the Chinese of treating gold and silver as commodities and only minting coins from copper?
- What effect would the various business practices the author describes have on the conduct of trade among Chinese merchants during the Tang Dynasty?

*Source:* Sirafi, Abu Zayd Hasan ibn Yazid, and Sulayman al-Tajir. Ancient accounts of India and China. Trans. by Eusebius Renaudot. London: Boston Public Library, 1733.

merchandise. In a society short of cash, these notes greatly facilitated commercial transactions. Occasionally, however, because of temporary economic reverses or poor management, merchants were not able to honor their notes. The resulting discontent among creditors often led to disorder and sometimes even to riots.

By the eleventh century, however, the Chinese economy had become so dependent on alternatives to cash that it was impractical to banish paper money altogether. To preserve its convenience while forestalling public disorder, government authorities forbade private parties to issue paper money and reserved that right for the state. The first paper money printed under government auspices appeared in 1024 in Sichuan province, the most active center of early printing. By the end of the century, government authorities throughout most of China issued printed paper money—complete with serial numbers and dire warnings against the printing of counterfeit notes. Rulers of nomadic peoples in central Asia soon began to adopt the practice in their states.

Printed paper money caused serious problems for several centuries after its appearance. Quite apart from contamination of the money supply by counterfeit notes, government authorities frequently printed currency representing more value than they actually possessed in cash reserves—a practice not unknown in more recent times. The result was a partial loss of public confidence in paper money. By the late eleventh century, some notes of paper money would fetch only 95 percent of their face value in cash. Not until the **Qing** dynasty (1644–1911 C.E.) did Chinese authorities place the issuance of printed money under tight fiscal controls. In spite of abuses, however, printed paper money provided a powerful stimulus to the Chinese economy.

**A Cosmopolitan Society** Trade and urbanization transformed Tang and Song China into a prosperous, cosmopolitan society. Trade came to China both by land and by sea. Muslim merchants from the Abbasid empire and central Asia helped to revive the Silk Roads network and flocked to large Chinese trading centers. Even subjects of the Byzantine empire made their way across the Silk Roads to China. Residents of large Chinese cities such as Chang'an and Luoyang became quite accustomed to merchants from foreign lands. Indeed, musicians and dancers from Persia became popular entertainers in the vibrant cities of the Tang dynasty. Meanwhile, Arab, Persian, Indian, and Malay mariners arriving by way of the Indian Ocean and South China Sea established sizable merchant communities in the bustling southern Chinese port cities of Guangzhou and Quanzhou. Contemporary reports said that the rebel general Huang Chao massacred 120,000 foreigners when he sacked Guangzhou and subjected it to a reign of terror in 879.

**China and the Hemispheric Economy** Indeed, high productivity and trade brought the Tang and Song economy a dynamism that China's borders could not restrain. Chinese consumers developed a taste for foreign goods that stimulated trade throughout much of the eastern hemisphere. Spices from the islands of southeast Asia made their way to China, along with products as diverse as kingfisher feathers and tortoise shell from Vietnam, pearls and incense from South Asia, and horses and melons from central Asia. Those items became symbols of a refined, elegant lifestyle—in many cases because of attractive qualities inherent in the commodities themselves but sometimes simply because of their scarcity and distant provenance. In exchange for such coveted items, Chinese sent abroad vast quantities of silk, porcelain, and lacquerware. In central Asia, southeast Asia, India, Persia, and the port cities of east Africa, wealthy merchants and rulers wore Chinese silk and set their tables with Chinese porcelain. China's economic surge during the Tang and Song dynasties thus promoted trade and economic growth throughout much of the eastern hemisphere.

## CULTURAL CHANGE IN TANG AND SONG CHINA

Interactions with peoples of other societies encouraged cultural change in China during the Tang and Song Dynasties. The Confucian and Daoist traditions did not disappear. But they made way for a foreign religion—**Mahayana Buddhism**—and they developed along new lines that reflected the conditions of Tang and Song society.

### The Establishment of Buddhism

Buddhist merchants traveling the ancient Silk Roads visited China as early as the second century B.C.E. During the Han dynasty their faith attracted little interest there: Confucianism, Daoism, and faiths that honored family ancestors were the most popular cultural alternatives. After the fall of the Han, however, the Confucian tradition suffered a loss of credibility. The purpose and rationale of **Confucianism** was to maintain public order and provide honest, effective government. But in an age of warlords and nomadic invasions, it seemed that the Confucian tradition had simply failed. Confucian educational and civil service systems went into decline, and rulers sometimes openly scorned Confucian values.

**Foreign Religions in China** During the unsettled centuries following the fall of the Han dynasty, several foreign religions established communities in China. Nestorian Christians and Manichaeans settled in China, followed later by Zoroastrians fleeing the Islamic conquerors of Persia. When the Nestorian Christians established communities in China by the late sixth century, the emperor Tang Taizong issued a proclamation praising their doctrine, and he allowed them to open monasteries in Chang'an and other cities. By the mid-seventh century, Arab and Persian merchants had also established Muslim communities in the port cities of south China. Indeed, legend holds that an uncle of Muhammad built a small red mosque in the port city of Guangzhou. These religions of salvation mostly served the needs of foreign merchants trading in China and converts from nomadic societies. Sophisticated residents of Chinese cities appreciated foreign music and dance as well as foreign foods and trade goods, but most foreign religious traditions attracted little interest.

**Dunhuang** Yet Mahayana Buddhism gradually found a popular following in Tang and Song China. **Buddhism** came to China over the Silk Roads. Residents of oasis cities in central Asia had converted to Buddhism during the last two centuries before the Common Era, and the oases became sites of Bud-

**Qing** (ching)

# How the Past Shapes the Future

## The Spread of Religious Traditions

**One of the defining characteristics of the late first and early second millennia C.E. was that the religions of Buddhism, Islam, Hinduism, and Christianity each won large numbers of converts far beyond their regions of origin. As a result, the values and doctrines of each religion profoundly shaped the societies where it won converts. At the same time, individual societies also shaped the beliefs and practices of each religion, so that Buddhism, Islam, Hinduism, and Christianity were all at least partially modified in the image of the new societies that adopted them. The consequences of these processes—which in most cases occurred gradually as a result of revived trade networks and the work of missionaries—had deep and long-lasting consequences that can still be seen in the religious distribution of the world's peoples today.**

### New Homes for Religious Traditions

In this chapter we have already seen how Buddhism—which originated in South Asia but had already spread along the Silk Roads in Central Asia—began to attract large numbers of converts in China from the seventh to the tenth centuries. Chinese influence, in turn, encouraged the spread of Buddhism to Korea, Vietnam, and Japan. By 1000 C.E., in fact, Buddhism had become a minority religion in its region of origin but continues to thrive in its adopted region of east Asia up to the present. But Buddhism was only one of several religious traditions to win converts in distant lands in this period. Indeed, from the seventh to the sixteenth centuries, Islam spread far from its origins in the Arabian peninsula, attracting converts in central and southwest Asia, north Africa, Iberia, India, and southeast Asia (chapters 14 and 15). Even as Islam was attracting converts in parts of the Indian subcontinent, traders and religious figures from the subcontinent encouraged a variety of states and kingdoms in southeast Asia to adopt either Buddhism or Hinduism between the sixth and fifteenth centuries (chapter 15). Orthodox Christianity, meanwhile, was adopted by Slavic peoples in eastern Europe on a massive scale during the ninth and tenth centuries, largely due to the political influence of Byzantium and the self-conscious efforts of Byzantine missionaries to proselytize among the Slavs (chapter 16). Over the course of the post-classical period, then, the spread of Buddhism, Islam, Hinduism, and Christianity from their regions of origin resulted in dramatic changes in the religious faith of millions of people.

### The Influence of Religious Traditions on Culture and Society

The spread of these religious traditions deeply influenced social, cultural, and political developments in the lands where they were adopted. For example, in China the concerns of Mahayana Buddhism with logical thought and the nature of the soul were so influential on Confucian thought that the two blended to become a new tradition known as neo-Confucianism—which itself influenced societies in east Asia for more than a millennium. In lands where Islam was widely adopted, shared beliefs in the values expressed by the Quran, the system of Islamic law (*sharia*), and the circulation of judges (*quadis*) and legal scholars (*ulama*) qualified to interpret such law contributed to a shared sense of cultural unity across many parts of Eurasia (chapter 14). In southeast Asia, rulers of a variety of states borrowed Hindu notions of political authority by assuming the title of *raja*, adopted the South Asian epic story of the *Ramayana* as their own, and built monumental architecture closely modeled on South Asian styles (chapter 15). And in eastern Europe, the Cyrillic alphabet devised by Byzantine monks in the ninth century to represent the Slavic language in translations of Christian literature became the primary vehicle for printed works and continues to be used in Russia and other states of the former Soviet Union in the present (chapter 16).

### The Influence of Societies on Religious Traditions

At the same time, the societies into which new religious traditions spread also had an impact on the beliefs and practices of the religions themselves. For example, as Islam spread, it was also deeply influenced by Persian literary traditions, South Asian scientific and mathematic traditions, Greek philosophy, and patriarchal traditions from the eastern Mediterranean (chapter 14). When Islam spread to southeast Asia, its expression was modified both by Hindu elements that had already shaped the region and by indigenous mystical traditions (chapter 15). Additionally, when Buddhism was adopted on a large scale by Chinese adherents, it was modified in ways that appealed to Chinese Daoist beliefs about spiritual life and in ways that complemented the primacy of the family in Chinese tradition. As a result of their adoption in lands far from their regions of origin, then, each of these major religions took on new forms of expression that remained influential for many centuries and, in some cases, to the present day.

These are only a small sampling of the historical reverberations of the spread of religious traditions in the late first and early second millennia. When reading subsequent chapters, try to identify additional short- and long-term consequences that resulted from these momentous processes.

dhist missionary efforts. By the fourth century C.E., a sizable Buddhist community had emerged at **Dunhuang** in western China (modern Gansu province). Between about 600 and 1000 C.E., Buddhists built hundreds of cave temples in the vicinity of Dunhuang and decorated them with murals depicting events in the lives of the Buddha and the bodhisattvas who played prominent roles in Mahayana Buddhism. They also assembled libraries of religious literature and operated scriptoria (a room in a monastery where manuscripts were stored and copied) to produce Buddhist texts. Missions supported by establishments such as those at Dunhuang helped Buddhism to establish a foothold in China.

**Buddhism in China** Buddhism attracted Chinese interest partly because of its high standards of morality, its intellectual sophistication, and its promise of salvation. Practical concerns also help to account for its appeal. Buddhists established monastic communities in China and accumulated sizable estates donated by wealthy converts. They cultivated those lands intensively and stored a portion of their harvests for distribution among local residents during times of drought, famine, or other hardship. Some monasteries engaged in banking or money-lending activities, and many others maintained schools that provided a basic education for local populations. Buddhist monasteries thus became important elements in the local economies of Chinese communities. Buddhism even had implications for everyday life in China. Buddhist monks introduced chairs into China: originally a piece of monastic furniture, the chair quickly became popular in secular society and found a place in domestic interiors throughout the land. Buddhist monks also introduced refined sugar into China and thus influenced both diet and cuisine.

In some ways, Buddhism posed a challenge to Chinese cultural and social traditions. Buddhist theologians typically took written texts as points of departure for elaborate, speculative investigations into metaphysical themes such as the nature of the soul. Among Chinese intellectuals, however, only the Confucians placed great emphasis on written texts, and they devoted their energies mostly to practical rather than metaphysical issues. Meanwhile, Daoists had limited interest in written texts of any kind. Buddhist morality called for individuals to strive for perfection by observing an ascetic ideal, and it encouraged serious Buddhists to follow a celibate, monastic lifestyle. In contrast, traditional Chinese morality centered on the family unit and the obligations of filial piety, and it strongly encouraged procreation so that generations of offspring would be available to venerate family ancestors. Some Chinese held that Buddhist monasteries were economically harmful because they paid no taxes, whereas others scorned Buddhism as an inferior creed because of its foreign origins.

Mural commemorating the victory of General Zhang Yichai and Chinese military forces over the forces of the Tibetan Empire. Mogao Caves 156, near Dunhuang, Late Tang Dynasty.

The History Collection/Alamy Stock Photo

**Buddhism and Daoism** Because of those differences and concerns, Buddhist missionaries sought to tailor their message to Chinese audiences. They explained Buddhist concepts in vocabulary borrowed from Chinese cultural traditions, particularly **Daoism.** They translated the Indian term *dharma* (the basic Buddhist doctrine) as *dao* ("the way" in the Daoist sense of the term), and they translated the Indian term ***nirvana*** (personal salvation that comes after an individual soul escapes from the cycle of incarnation) as ***wuwei*** (the Daoist ethic of noncompetition). While encouraging the establishment of monasteries and the observance of celibacy, they also recognized the validity of family life and offered Buddhism as a religion that would benefit the extended Chinese family: one son in the monastery, they taught, would bring salvation for ten generations of his kin.

**Pilgrimage to South Asia** Monks and pilgrims helped popularize Buddhism in China. The monk **Xuanzang** (602–664 C.E.), who we first met at the start of this chapter, was only one among hundreds of Chinese pilgrims who made the dangerous and difficult journey to the Indian subcontinent to visit holy sites and learn about Buddhism in its homeland. Xuanzang and other pilgrims returned to China with copies of treatises that deepened the understanding of Buddhism, and they were able to relate the teachings of South Asian Buddhist masters to Chinese disciples.

**Schools of Buddhism** Over the years, monks and scholars organized several distinctive schools of Buddhism that appealed to Chinese tastes and interests. Buddhists of the Chan school (also known by its Japanese name, Zen) placed little emphasis on written texts but held intuition and sudden flashes of insight in high regard. Thus Chan Buddhists made a place for Daoist values in Chinese Buddhism. Even more popular than **Chan Buddhism** was the Pure Land school, which held out the prospect of personal salvation for those who devoted themselves to the Buddha. The emperor Wu Zhao herself followed Pure Land teachings, and she enthusiastically promoted the school—especially after friendly monks circulated a treatise predicting reincarnation of the Buddha as a female ruler. Wu Zhao eventually proclaimed herself the universal ruler and protector of Buddhism, and she sponsored the construction of monasteries and stupas (a domed building constructed to house relics of the Buddha) throughout China.

**Hostility to Buddhism** In spite of its popularity, Buddhism met determined resistance from Daoists and Confucians. Daoists resented the popular following that Buddhists attracted, which resulted in diminished resources available for their tradition. Confucians despised Buddhists' exaltation of celibacy, and they denounced its teachings as alien superstition. They also condemned Buddhist monasteries as wasteful, unproductive burdens on society.

**Persecution** During the late Tang dynasty, Daoist and Confucian critics of Buddhism found allies in the imperial court. Beginning in the 840s the Tang emperors ordered the closure of monasteries and the expulsion of Buddhists as well as Zoroastrians, Nestorian Christians, and Manichaeans. Motivated largely by a desire to seize property belonging to foreign religious establishments, the Tang rulers did not implement their policy in a thorough way. Although it discouraged further expansion, Tang policy did not eradicate foreign faiths from China. Buddhism in particular enjoyed popular support that enabled it to survive. Indeed, it even influenced the development of the Confucian tradition during the Song dynasty.

## INTERPRETING IMAGES

This scroll painting depicts the return of the monk Xuanzang to China. His baggage included 657 books, mostly Buddhist treatises but also a few works on grammar and logic, as well as hundreds of relics and images.

**Analyze** *Buddhism often spread along trade routes. Why would Xuanzang's travels, books, and scholarship have had such a major impact as well? How would trade contribute to the development of neo-Confucianism?*

Ivy Close Images/Age Fotostock

## Neo-Confucianism

The Song emperors did not persecute Buddhists, but they actively supported traditional Chinese cultural traditions in hopes of limiting the influence of foreign religions. They contributed particularly generously to the Confucian tradition. They sponsored the studies of Confucian scholars, for example, and subsidized the printing and dissemination of Confucian writings.

**Confucians and Buddhism** Yet the Confucian tradition of the Song dynasty differed from that of earlier times. The earliest Confucians had concentrated resolutely on practical issues of politics and morality because they took the organization of a stable social order as their principal concern.

Artist's impression of Japanese Buddhist monk Ippen Shonen arriving at a town in rural Japan. Ippen Shonen popularized a Buddhist ceremonial practice that combined prayer with dance.
Burstein Collection/Getty Images

Confucians of the Song dynasty studied the classic works of their tradition, but they also became familiar with the writings of Buddhists. They found much to admire in Buddhist thought. Buddhism not only offered a tradition of logical thought and argumentation but also dealt with issues, such as the nature of the soul and the individual's relationship with the cosmos, not systematically explored by Confucian thinkers. Thus Confucians of the Song dynasty drew a great deal of inspiration from Buddhism. Because their thought reflected the influence of Buddhism as well as original Confucian values, it has come to be known as **neo-Confucianism.**

**Zhu Xi** The most important representative of Song neo-Confucianism was the philosopher **Zhu Xi** (1130–1200 C.E.). A prolific writer, Zhu Xi maintained a deep commitment to Confucian values emphasizing proper personal behavior and social harmony. Among his writings was an influential treatise titled *Family Rituals* that provided detailed instructions for weddings, funerals, veneration of ancestors, and other family ceremonies. As a good Confucian, Zhu Xi considered it a matter of the highest importance that individuals play their proper roles both in their family and in the larger society.

Yet Zhu Xi became fascinated with the philosophical and speculative features of Buddhist thought. He argued in good Confucian fashion for the observance of high moral standards, and he believed that academic and philosophical investigations were important for practical affairs. But he concentrated his efforts on abstract and abstruse issues of more theoretical than practical significance. He wrote extensively on metaphysical themes such as the nature of reality. He argued in a manner reminiscent of Plato that two elements accounted for all physical being: *li,* a principle somewhat similar to Plato's Forms or Ideas that defines the essence of the being, and *qi,* its material form.

**Neo-Confucian Influence** Neo-Confucianism ranks as an important cultural development for two reasons. First, it illustrates the deep influence of Buddhism in Chinese society. Even though the neo-Confucians rejected Buddhist religious teachings, their writings adapted Buddhist themes and reasoning to Confucian interests and values. Second, neo-Confucianism influenced east Asian thought over a very long term. In China, neo-Confucianism enjoyed the status of an officially recognized creed from the Song dynasty until the early twentieth century, and in lands that fell within China's cultural orbit—particularly Korea, Vietnam, and Japan—neo-Confucianism shaped philosophical, political, and moral thought for half a millennium and more.

## DEVELOPMENT OF COMPLEX SOCIETIES IN KOREA, VIETNAM,AND JAPAN

Like the *dar al-Islam,* Chinese society influenced the development of neighboring lands during the Tang and Song dynasties. Chinese armies periodically invaded Korea and Vietnam, and Chinese merchants established commercial relations with

**Zhu Xi** (ZHOO SHEE)

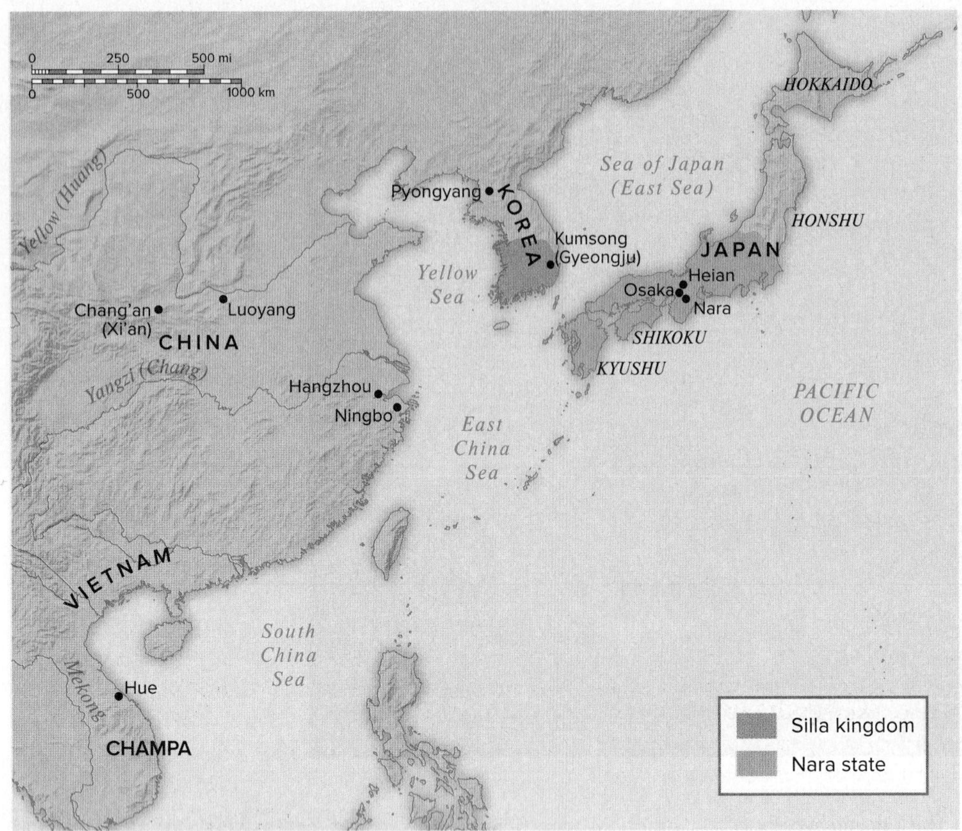


**MAP 1.3 Borderlands of China in the first millennium C.E.: Korea, Vietnam, and Japan.**

Note the geographic relationship of Korea, Vietnam, and Japan to China.

***What geographic conditions help to account for the varying degrees of Chinese influence in Korea, Vietnam, and Japan?***

Japan as well as with Korea and Vietnam. Chinese techniques of government and administration helped shape public life in Korea, Vietnam, and Japan, and Chinese values and cultural traditions won a prominent place alongside native traditions. By no means did those lands become absorbed into China: all maintained distinctive identities and cultural traditions. Yet they also drew deep inspiration from Chinese examples and built societies that reflected their participation in a larger east Asian society revolving around China.

## Korea and Vietnam

Chinese armies ventured into Korea and Vietnam on campaigns of imperial expansion as early as the Qin and Han dynasties. As the Han dynasty weakened, however, local aristocrats organized movements that ousted Chinese forces from both lands. Only during the powerful Tang dynasty did Chinese resources once again enable military authorities to mount large-scale campaigns. Although the two lands responded differently to Chinese imperial expansion, both borrowed Chinese political and cultural traditions and used them in their societies.

**The Silla Dynasty** During the seventh century, Tang armies conquered much of Korea before the native **Silla dynasty** rallied to prevent Chinese domination of the peninsula. Both Tang and Silla authorities preferred to avoid a long and costly conflict, so they agreed to a political compromise: Chinese forces withdrew from Korea, and the Silla rulers recognized the Tang emperor as their overlord. In theory, Korea was a vassal state in a vast Chinese empire. In practice, however, Korea was in most respects an independent kingdom, although the ruling dynasty prudently maintained cordial relations with its powerful neighbor.

Thus Korea entered into a tributary relationship with China. Envoys of the Silla rulers regularly delivered gifts to Chinese emperors, but those concessions brought considerable benefits to the Koreans. Moreover, the tributary relationship opened the doors for Korean merchants to trade, and students to study, in China.

**Chinese Influence in Korea** Meanwhile, the tributary relationship facilitated the spread of Chinese political and cultural influences to Korea. Embassies delivering tribute to China included Korean royal officials who observed the workings of the Chinese court and bureaucracy and then organized the Korean court on similar lines. The Silla monarchs (one of the most important of whom was a woman, Queen Seondeok) built a lavish new capital at their ancestral town of Kumsong (modern-day Kyongju in southeastern Korea), taking the Tang capital at Chang'an as their model. Silla rulers developed Kumsong from a small walled town with a few hundred families into a major capital with 179,000 households and nearly one million people. Their embassies to China included not only royal officials but also scholars who studied Chinese thought and literature and who took copies of Chinese writings back to Korea. Their efforts helped to build Korean interest in the Confucian tradition, particularly among educated aristocrats. While Korean elite classes turned to Confucius, Chinese schools of Buddhism attracted widespread popular interest. Chan Buddhism, which promised individual salvation, won the allegiance of peasants and commoners.

China and Korea differed in many respects. Most notably, perhaps, aristocrats and royal houses dominated Korean society much more than was the case in China. Although the Korean monarchy sponsored Chinese schools and a Confucian examination system, Korea never established a bureaucracy based on merit such as that of Tang and Song China. Political initiative remained firmly in the hands of the ruling classes. Nevertheless, extensive dealings with its powerful neighbor ensured that Korea reflected the influence of Chinese political and cultural traditions.

**China and Vietnam** Chinese relations with Vietnam were far more tense than with Korea. When Tang armies ventured into the land that Chinese called **Nam Viet,** they encountered spirited resistance on the part of the Viet people, who had settled in the region around the Red River. Tang forces soon won control of Viet towns and cities, and they launched efforts to absorb the Viets into Chinese society, just as their predecessors had absorbed the indigenous peoples of the Yangzi River valley. The Viets readily adopted Chinese agricultural methods and irrigation systems as well as Chinese schools and administrative techniques. Like their Korean counterparts, Viet elites studied Confucian texts and took examinations based on a Chinese-style education, and Viet traders marketed their wares in China. Vietnamese authorities even entered into tributary relationships with the Chinese court. Yet the Viets resented Chinese efforts to dominate the southern land, and they mounted a series of revolts against Tang authorities. When the Tang dynasty fell during the early tenth century, the Viets won their independence and successfully resisted later Chinese efforts at imperial expansion to the south.

Like Korea, Vietnam differed from China in many ways. Many Vietnamese retained their indigenous religions in preference to Chinese cultural traditions. Women played a much more prominent role in Vietnamese society and economy than did their counterparts in China. Southeast Asian women had dominated local and regional markets for centuries, and they participated actively in business ventures closed to women in the more rigidly patriarchal society of China.

Tang dynasty pottery figure of a Vietnamese dancer. Commercial and tributary relationships introduced southeast Asian performers to China, where sophisticated urban communities appreciated their exotic entertainment.
Heritage Image Partnership Ltd/ Alamy Stock Photo

**Chinese Influence in Vietnam** Nevertheless, Chinese traditions found a place in the southern land. Vietnamese authorities established an administrative system and bureaucracy modeled on that of China, and Viet ruling classes prepared for their careers by pursuing a Confucian education. Furthermore, Buddhism mostly came to Vietnam from China and won a large popular following. Thus, like Korea, Vietnam absorbed political and cultural influence from China and reflected the development of a larger east Asian society centered on China.

## Early Japan

Chinese armies never invaded Japan, but Chinese traditions deeply influenced early Japanese political and cultural development. The earliest inhabitants of Japan were nomadic peoples from northeast Asia who migrated to Japan about thirty-five thousand years ago. Their language, material culture, and religion derived from their parent society in northeast Asia. Later migrants, who arrived in several waves from the Korean peninsula, introduced cultivation of rice, bronze and iron metallurgy, and horses into Japan. As the population of the Japanese islands grew and built a settled agricultural society, small states dominated by aristocratic clans emerged. By the middle of the first millennium C.E., several dozen states ruled small regions.

**Nara Japan** The establishment of the powerful Sui and Tang dynasties in China had repercussions in Japan, where they demonstrated the value of centralized imperial government. One of the aristocratic clans in Japan, the Soga, insisted on its precedence over the others, although in fact it had never wielded effective authority outside its territory in central Japan. Inspired by the Tang example, this clan claimed imperial authority and introduced a series of reforms designed to centralize Japanese politics. The imperial house established a court modeled on that of the Tang, instituted a Chinese-style bureaucracy, implemented an equal-field system, provided official support for Confucianism and Buddhism, and in the year 710 moved to a new capital city at Nara (near modern Kyoto) that was a replica of the Tang capital at Chang'an. Never was Chinese influence more prominent in Japan than during the **Nara** period (710–794 C.E.).

Yet Japan did not lose its distinctive characteristics or become simply a smaller model of Chinese society. While adopting Confucian and Buddhist traditions from China, for example, the Japanese continued to observe the rites of **Shinto,** their indigenous religion, which revolved around the veneration of ancestors and a host of nature spirits and deities. Japanese society reflected the influence of Chinese traditions but still developed along its own lines.

The experiences of the Heian, Kamakura, and Muromachi periods clearly illustrate this point. In 794 the emperor of Japan transferred his court from Nara to a newly constructed capital at nearby Heian (modern Kyoto). During the next four centuries, Heian became the seat of a refined and sophisticated society that drew inspiration from China but also developed distinctively Japanese political and cultural traditions.

**Heian Japan** During the **Heian** period (794–1185 c.e.), local rulers on the island of Honshu mostly recognized the emperor as Japan's supreme political authority. Unlike their Chinese counterparts, however, Japanese emperors rarely ruled but, rather, served as ceremonial figureheads and symbols of authority. Effective power lay in the hands of the Fujiwara family, an aristocratic clan that controlled affairs from behind the throne through its influence over the imperial house and manipulation of its members.

After the ninth century the Japanese political order almost continuously featured a split between a publicly recognized imperial authority and a separate agent of effective rule. This pattern helps to account for the remarkable longevity of the Japanese imperial house. Because emperors have not ruled, they have not been subject to deposition during times of turmoil: ruling parties and factions have come and gone, but the imperial house has survived.

The cultural development of Heian Japan also reflected both the influence of Chinese traditions and the elaboration of peculiarly Japanese ways. Most literature imitated Chinese models and indeed was written in the Chinese language. Boys and young men who received a formal education in Heian Japan learned Chinese, read the classic works of China, and wrote in the foreign tongue. Officials at court conducted business and kept records in Chinese, and literary figures wrote histories and treatises in the style popular in China. Even Japanese writing reflected Chinese influence because scholars borrowed many Chinese characters and used them to represent Japanese words. They also adapted some Chinese characters into a Japanese syllabic script, in which symbols represent whole syllables rather than a single sound, as in an alphabetic script.

***The Tale of Genji*** Because Japanese women rarely received a formal Chinese-style education, in Heian times aristocratic women made the most notable contributions to literature in the Japanese language. Of the many literary works that have survived from that era, none reflects Heian court life better than

**Heian** (HAY-ahn)

## INTERPRETING IMAGES

The armor and weaponry of the samurai bespeak the militarism of the Kamakura era.

**Analyze** *Compare and contrast Chinese militarism with militarism in the Kamakura era of Japan. What kinds of long-term effects might develop from each approach?*

Library of Congress, Prints & Photographs Division [LC-DIG-jpd-01046]

***The Tale of Genji.*** Composed by Murasaki Shikibu, a lady-in-waiting at the Heian court who wrote in Japanese syllabic script rather than Chinese characters, this sophisticated work relates the experiences of a fictitious imperial prince named Genji. Living amid gardens and palaces, Genji and his friends devoted themselves to the cultivation of an ultrarefined lifestyle, and they became adept at mixing subtle perfumes, composing splendid verses in fine calligraphic hand, and wooing elegant women.

*The Tale of Genji* also offers a meditation on the passing of time and the sorrows that time brings to sensitive humans. As Genji and his friends age, they reflect on past joys and relationships no longer recoverable. Their thoughts suffuse *The Tale of Genji* with a melancholy spirit that presents a subtle contrast to the elegant atmosphere of their surroundings at the Heian court. Because of her limited command of Chinese, Lady Murasaki created one of the most remarkable literary works in the Japanese language.

**Decline of Heian Japan** As the charmed circle of aristocrats and courtiers led elegant lives at the imperial capital, the Japanese countryside underwent fundamental changes that brought an end to the Heian court and its refined society. The equal-field system gradually fell into disuse in Japan as it had in China, and aristocratic clans accumulated most of the islands' lands into vast estates. By the late eleventh century, two clans in particular—the Taira and the Minamoto—overshadowed the others. During the mid-twelfth century the two engaged in outright war, and in 1185 the Minamoto emerged victorious. The Minamoto did not seek to abolish imperial authority in Japan but, rather, claimed to rule the land in the name of the emperor. They installed the clan leader as ***shogun***—a military governor who ruled in place of the emperor—and established the seat of their government at Kamakura, near modern Tokyo, while the imperial court remained at Kyoto. For most of the next four centuries, one branch or another of the Minamoto clan dominated political life in Japan.

## Medieval Japan

Historians refer to the Kamakura and Muromachi periods as Japan's medieval period—a middle era falling between the age of Chinese influence and court domination of political life in Japan, as represented by the Nara and Heian periods, and the modern age, inaugurated by the Tokugawa dynasty in the sixteenth century, when a centralized government unified and ruled all of Japan. During this middle era, Japanese society and culture took on increasingly distinctive characteristics.

**Political Decentralization** In the Kamakura (1185–1333 C.E.) and Muromachi (1336–1573 C.E.) periods, Japan developed a decentralized political order in which provincial lords wielded effective power and authority in local regions where they controlled land and economic affairs. As these lords and their clans vied for power and authority in the countryside, they found little use for the Chinese-style bureaucracy that Nara and Heian rulers had instituted in Japan and still less use for the elaborate protocol and refined conduct that prevailed at the courts. In place of etiquette and courtesy, they valued military talent and discipline. The mounted warrior, the *samurai,* thus played the most distinctive role in Japanese political and military affairs.

**The Samurai** The **samurai** were professional warriors, specialists in the use of force and the arts of fighting. They served the provincial lords of Japan, who relied on the samurai both to enforce their authority in their own territories and to extend their claims to other lands. In return for those police and military services, the lords supported the samurai from the agricultural surplus and labor services of peasants working under their jurisdiction. Freed of obligations to feed, clothe, and house themselves and their families, samurai devoted themselves to hunting, riding, archery, and martial arts.

**Japan and East Asia** Thus, although it had taken its original inspiration from the Tang empire in China, the Japanese political order developed along lines different from those of the Middle Kingdom. Yet Japan clearly had a place in the larger east Asian society centered on China. Japan borrowed from China, among other things, Confucian values, Buddhist religion, a system of writing, and the ideal of centralized imperial rule. Though somewhat suppressed during the Kamakura and Muromachi periods, those elements of Chinese society not only survived in Japan but also decisively influenced Japanese development during later periods.

## CONCLUSION

The revival of centralized imperial rule in China had profound implications for all of east Asia and indeed for most of the eastern hemisphere. When the Sui and Tang dynasties imposed their authority throughout China, they established a powerful state that guided political affairs throughout east Asia. Tang armies extended Chinese influence to Korea, Vietnam, and central Asia. They did not invade Japan, but the impressive political organization of China prompted the islands' rulers to imitate Tang examples. Moreover, the Sui and Tang dynasties laid a strong political foundation for rapid economic development. Chinese society prospered throughout the later first and early second millenia C.E., partly because of technological and industrial innovation. Tang and Song prosperity touched all of China's neighbors because it encouraged surging commerce in east Asia. Chinese silk, porcelain, and lacquerware were prized commodities among trading peoples from southeast Asia to east Africa. Chinese inventions such as paper, printing, gunpowder, and the magnetic compass found a place in societies throughout the eastern hemisphere as they diffused across the Silk Roads and the sea lanes. It was also an age of religious as well as commercial and technological exchanges: Nestorian Christians, Zoroastrians, Manichaeans, and Muslims all maintained communities in Tang China, and Buddhism became the most popular religious tradition in all of east Asia. Finally, Chinese traditions of social organization and economic dynamism helped to sustain encounters between the peoples of the eastern hemisphere on an unprecedented scale.

## STUDY TERMS

Buddhism (46)
Chan Buddhism (56)
Confucianism (53)
Daoism (56)
Dunhuang (55)
equal-field system (42)
foot binding (48)
Grand Canal (41)
gunpowder (50)
Hangzhou (46)
Heian (60)
Li Bai (48)
Mahayana Buddhism (53)
Nam Viet (59)
Nara (59)
neo-Confucianism (56)
nirvana (56)
porcelain (49)
Qing dynasty (46)
samurai (61)
Shinto (60)
shogun (60)
Silla dynasty (58)
Song dynasty (44)
Song Taizu (44)
Sui dynasty (41)
Sui Yangdi (41)
*The Tale of Genji* (60)
Tang dynasty (41)
Tang Taizong (41)
Uighurs (43)
wuwei (56)
Wu Zhao (48)
Xuanzang (56)
Yang Jian (40)
Zhu Xi (56)

## FOR FURTHER READING

Robert Finlay. *The Pilgrim Art: The Culture of Porcelain in World History.* Berkeley, 2010. Brilliant study outlining the Chinese invention of porcelain and the product's appeal in the larger world.

Karl Friday. *Samurai, Warfare and the State in Early Medieval Japan.* New York, 2004. A lively analysis with apt comparisons to medieval Europe.

John Kieschnick. *The Impact of Buddhism on Chinese Material Culture.* Princeton, 2003. Fascinating scholarly study exploring the social effects of Buddhism in China.

Dieter Kuhn. *The Age of Confucian Rule: The Song Transformation of China.* Cambridge, Mass., 2009. Emphasizes social and economic developments.

Mark Edward Lewis. *China's Cosmopolitan Empire: The Tang Dynasty.* Cambridge, Mass., 2009. Perhaps the best single volume on Tang China.

Victor Mair, ed. T*he Columbia Anthology of Traditional Chinese Literature.* New York, 1994. A comprehensive collection of the classics of Chinese literature, including the superb poetry of the Tang dynasty.

Murasaki Shikibu. *The Tale of Genji.* New York, 2019. trans. by Dennis Washburn. Fresh translation of Genji that communicates with the modern author with immediacy and energy.

H. Paul Varley. *Japanese Culture.* 4th ed. Honolulu, 2000. An authoritative analysis of Japanese cultural development from early times to the present.

Roderick Whitfield, Susan Whitfield, and Neville Agnew. *Mogao: Art and History on the Silk Road.* Los Angeles, 2000. Excellent brief discussion of the cave temples and archaeological remains from Dunhuang.

Sally Hovey Wriggins. *The Silk Road Journey with Xuanzang.* Boulder, 2004. A fascinating and well-illustrated account of Xuanzang's journey to India and his influence on the development of Buddhism in China.

# CHAPTER 1 AP EXAM PRACTICE

Questions assume cumulative knowledge from this chapter and previous chapters.

## Section I

## Multiple Choice Questions

Use the image below and your knowledge of world history to answer questions 1 - 3.

A Northern Song Dynasty (960-1127) era Chinese painting of a water-powered mill for grain, with surrounding river transport.

The Picture Art Collection/Alamy Stock Photo

1. Historians could use this image of a water-powered mill to demonstrate
   (A) that the Chinese lacked the technology to build windmills.
   (B) the importance of waterways to the expansion of Chinese agriculture.
   (C) the Chinese importing fast growing rice from Vietnam.
   (D) how the Song emperors increased production to feed their armies.
2. The increase in wealth caused by innovations in agricultural production during the Song dynasty contributed to
   (A) Chinese merchants importing luxury items like silk and porcelain.
   (B) the spread of Buddhism to the middle class.
   (C) fewer elaborate rituals honoring the family ancestors.
   (D) an expanding population and urbanization.
3. A possible reason the artist chose to include this scene in his painting was to
   (A) show daily activities in a prosperous agricultural economy.
   (B) show the dominance of the patriarchal social structures.
   (C) honor the peaceful rule of the Song Dynasty.
   (D) give instructions for how to build a water-powered mill.

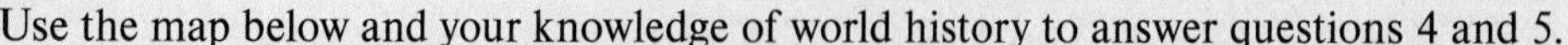

Use the map below and your knowledge of world history to answer questions 4 and 5.

Borderlands of China in the first millennium C.E.: Korea, Vietnam, and Japan.
McGraw Hill

4. Based on this map and your knowledge of world history, which of the following best describes the relationship between China and the Silla (Korean) kingdom?
   (A) The influence of Confucianism prevented the Koreans from accepting the rule of a female monarch.
   (B) The Silla monarchs accepted the tributary system and welcomed Chinese cultural influences in exchange for closer economic ties.
   (C) Because Korea was so close to China and could see the stability of Chinese government, they eliminated their aristocratic culture and replaced it with the Confucian examination system.
   (D) Koreans abandoned Buddhism in favor of Confucianism and Daoism.

5. Close ties between the Nara state (Japan) and China inspired
   (A) revolts against Chinese merchants.
   (B) Chinese attempts to invade Japan.
   (C) the creation of a centralized imperial government.
   (D) a decline in Shinto practices.

## Short Answer

6. Use this map below and your knowledge of world history to answer parts A, B, and C.

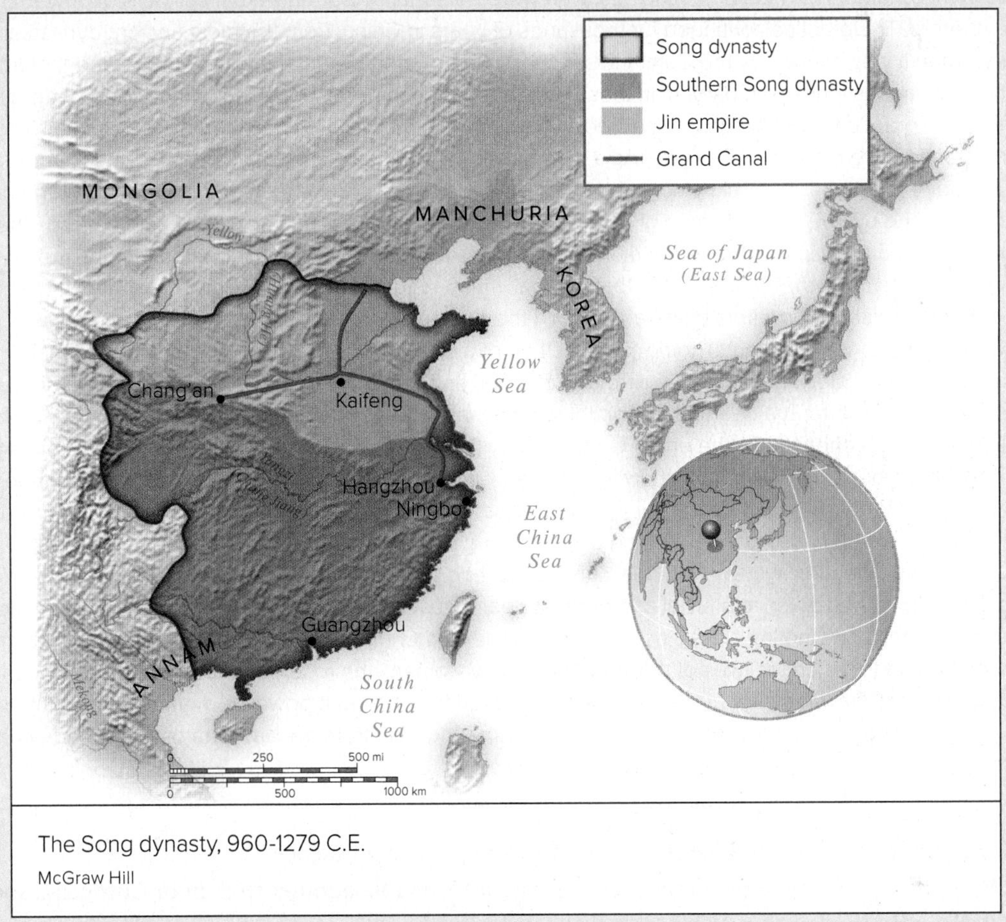


The Song dynasty, 960-1279 C.E.

McGraw Hill

(A) Identify ONE feature on this map that contributed to the Chinese economy during the Song Dynasty

(B) Explain ONE way that this map illustrates a change in the Song economy.

(C) Explain ONE continuity in Chinese economics in the Jin and Southern Song states.

7. Use this text selection and your knowledge of world history to answer parts A, B, and C.

> At several places in this chapter we refer to concubines, who were personal and often sexual partners of powerful men, including many Chinese emperors. The practice continued for thousands of years in China, from the most ancient dynasties through to the twentieth century, when it was banned by the Communist government. Historians have tried to understand the practice of con-cubinage through various lenses—in particular, those of gender and family relations, legal and social status, filial piety, and polit-ical influence. The practice seems to have emerged as a result of early social norms in China that made it illegal and socially disreputable for a man to have more than one wife. As a way of getting around this, however, these same norms determined that it was perfectly fine for a man to have as many concubines as he could afford. During the Later Han Dynasty, the number of con-cubines was restricted by law, although men of high rank could still possess as many as they could afford. The manner in which a concubine was treated in society varied enormously and was influenced by the social status of the men involved. Yet the situation of concubines was always very different to that of legal wives, who had brought a dowry to the relationship. Once a concubine had entered a relationship with a man—and even if the concubine later ended the relationship— it was impossible for her to marry or even to return to her parents' home. The position of a concubine was thus always inferior to that of a wife, and this affected even the rules of filial piety. For example, although children and grandchildren would continue to offer rites to deceased legal mothers for generations, after the death of a concubine, only her sons were expected to make an offering—but not her grandsons nor any other descendants. By the era of Qing Dynasty (1644–1911), the laws had changed, and it became easier for a man to marry a concubine, but only if his legitimate wife had died. During both the Ming and Qing Dynasties, imperial concubines were housed in luxury in the For-bidden City in Beijing, usually guarded by eunuchs to make sure no other man could have sexual relations with the concubines, ensuring that the only offspring they would produce would be those of the emperor. The Ming introduced an official selection system. Potential concubines had to be aged between fourteen and sixteen, and the criteria for selection included virtue, behav-ior, and facial and body appearance. Concubines have been treated sympathetically in many works of Chinese literature, including the classic novel *Dream of the Red Chamber,* and also in many modern novels and televi-sion dramas. These tend to focus on the lives of those extraordinary women who rose out of concubinage to become politically powerful, including Empress Dowager Cixi of the Qing Dynasty—arguably the most powerful member of the imperial family in the last decade of the Qing—and, of course, Empress Wu Zhao (Zetian), who rose from her early status as teenage concubine of Tang Emperor Taizong to become the only empress ever to rule China!

(A) Identify ONE way that women in East Asian societies had political influence.
(B) Explain ONE difference between the role of concubines and the role of other women in Confucian societies
(C) Explain ONE similarity shared by concubines and legal wives in China.

8. Use your understanding of world history to answer parts A, B, and C.
(A) Identify ONE historical context that contributes to the development of the literature and philosophy in Tang and Song China.
(B) Explain ONE way that Chinese literature and philosophy influenced other East Asian countries.
(C) Explain ONE way that indigenous traditions in Korea, Japan, or Vietnam were not replaced with a Chinese cultural tradition.

# Section II

## Document-Based Question

Based on the following documents and your knowledge of world history, analyze the influence of Confucian philosophy on Tang and Song government.

In your response you should do the following:

- Respond to the prompt with a historically defensible thesis or claim that establishes a line of reasoning.
- Describe a broader historical context relevant to the prompt.
- Support an argument in response to the prompt using all documents.
- Use at least one additional piece of specific historical evidence (beyond that found in the documents) relevant to an argument about the prompt.
- Explain how or why the document's point of view, purpose, historical situation, and /or audience is relevant to an argument.
- Use evidence to corroborate, qualify, or modify an argument that addresses the prompt.

## Document 1

Wall painting from a Tang dynasty tomb featuring three Chinese officials receiving foreign envoys.

Henry Westheim Photography/Alamy Stock Photo

## Document 2

When merchants enter China by sea the government agents seize on their cargo and convey it to warehouses, and so put a stop to their business for six months, and till the last merchantman has arrived. Then they take three in ten, or thirty percent of each commodity, and return the rest to the merchant. If the emperor wants any particular thing, his officers have a right to take it preferable to any other persons whatsoever; and paying for it at the utmost penny is valued at, they dispatch this business immediately and without the least injustice.

"The Arab Merchant Suleiman on Business Practices in Tang China, 851 C.E."

## Document 3

Song Taizu regarded all state officials, even minor functionaries in distant provinces, as servants of the imperial government. In exchange for their loyalty, Song rulers rewarded these officials handsomely. They vastly expanded the bureaucracy based on merit by creating more opportunities for individuals to seek a Confucian education and take civil service examinations. They accepted many more candidates into the bureaucracy than their Sui and Tang predecessors, and they provided generous salaries for those who qualified for government appointments. They even placed civil bureaucrats in charge of military forces.

Bentley & Ziegler, *Traditions and Encounters: A Global Perspective on the Past*, pg. 253.

## Long Essay

Develop a thoughtful and thorough historical argument that answers the question below. Begin your essay with a thesis statement and support it with relevant historical evidence.

Evaluate the extent to which Buddhism affected China during the Tang and Song eras.

Chapter 2

# The Expansive Realm of Islam

**A Prophet and His World**
- Muhammad and His Message
- Muhammad's Migration to Medina
- The Establishment of Islam in Arabia

**The Expansion of Islam**
- The Early Caliphs and the Umayyad Dynasty
- The Abbasid Dynasty

**Economy and Society of the Early Islamic World**
- New Crops, Agricultural Experimentation, and Urban Growth
- The Formation of a Hemispheric Trading Zone
- The Changing Status of Women

**Islamic Values and Cultural Exchanges**
- The Formation of an Islamic Cultural Tradition
- Islam and the Cultural Traditions of Persia, India, and Greece

## ZOOMING IN ON TRADITIONS

### Season of the Mecca Pilgrimage

In 632 C.E. the prophet Muhammad visited his native city of Mecca from his home in exile at Medina, and in doing so he set an example that devout Muslims have sought to emulate ever since. Today the ***hajj***—the holy pilgrimage to Mecca—draws Muslims by the hundreds of thousands from all parts of the world to Saudi Arabia. Each year Muslims travel to Mecca by land, sea, and air to make the pilgrimage and visit the holy sites of Islam.

In centuries past the numbers of pilgrims were smaller, but their observance of the hajj was no less conscientious. By the ninth century, pilgrimage had become so popular that Muslim rulers went to some lengths to meet the needs of travelers passing through their lands. With the approach of the pilgrimage season—the last month of the Islamic lunar calendar—crowds gathered at major trading centers such as Baghdad, Damascus, and Cairo. There they lived in tent cities, surviving on food and water provided by government officials, until they could join caravans bound for Mecca. Muslim rulers invested considerable sums in the maintenance of roads, wells, cisterns, and lodgings that accommodated pilgrims—as well as castles and police forces that protected travelers—on their journeys to Mecca and back.

A sixteenth-century Turkish manuscript depicts pilgrims praying at Mecca in the mosque surrounding the Ka'ba.
Leemage/Getty Images

The hajj was not only solemn observance but also an occasion for joy and celebration. Muslim rulers and wealthy pilgrims often made lavish gifts to caravan companions andothers they met en route to Mecca. During her famous hajj of 976–977, for example, the Mesopotamian princess Jamila bint Nasir al-Dawla provided food and fresh green vegetables for her fellow pilgrims and furnished five hundred camels for handicapped travelers. She also purchased freedom for five hundred slaves and distributed fifty thousand fine robes among the common people of Mecca.

Most pilgrims did not have the resources to match Jamila's generosity, but for common travelers, too, the hajj became a special occasion. Merchants and craftsmen made acquaintances and arranged business deals with pilgrims from other lands. Students and scholars exchanged ideas during their weeks of traveling together. For all pilgrims, participation in ritual activities lent new meaning and significance to their faith.

# CHAPTER FOCUS

- United by their new Islamic faith, Arab tribes banded together and launched stunningly successful wars of conquest. The Umayyad caliphs, based in the great trade city of Damascus, ruled as iron-fisted conquerors and were overthrown within 100 years. The Abbasids, like the Tang in China, reaped the benefits of peace and prosperity.
- As always, with conquest and expansion came increased trade and a diffusion of goods, ideas, and influences that created great opportunities for cultural synthesis. Note the extent to which conquered peoples converted to Islam. Merchants and rulers saw direct benefits in allying with the powerful and rich Muslim conquerors and were often the first to convert. Merchants then helped spread Islam among nonconquered countries.
- This vast and rapidly expanding realm of Islam developed commercial agriculture, relying on specific regions to produce specialty goods and then ship those goods to far-away markets. And like all urban-based societies in this period, the caliphates' social structures were hierarchical and patriarchal.

## Historical Developments

- Islam, Judaism, Christianity and the core beliefs and practices of these religions continued to shape societies in Africa and Asia.
- As the Abbasid Caliphate fragmented, new Islamic political entities emerged, most of which were dominated by Turkic peoples. These states demonstrated continuity, innovation, and diversity.
- Muslim rule continued to expand to many parts of Afro-Eurasia due to military expansion, and Islam subsequently expanded through the activities of merchants, missionaries, and Sufis.
- Muslim states and empires encouraged significant intellectual innovations and transfers.

## Reasoning Processes

- **Developments and Processes** Explain how early Islamic states fostered commerce and trade.
- **Sourcing and Situation** Identify the purpose and historical situation of Sufi Islam through primary source writings and images.
- **Source Claims and Evidence** Explain how various images support the notion that Islamic states were experiencing demographic and economic growth.
- **Contextualization** Identify and explain the historical context for the emergence of an Islamic cultural tradition.
- **Making Connections** Identify connections between Islamic communities and the cultural traditions of Greece, India and Persia.
- **Argumentation** Support the argument that there was a close relationship between the spread of religion and the spread of crops and agricultural practices to new lands.

## Historical Thinking Skills

- **Causation** Describe the effects of the spread of Islam throughout Afro-Eurasia.
- **Continuity and Change** Explain patterns of cultural continuity and change within Islamic states.

# CHAPTER OVERVIEW

The word ***Islam*** means "submission," signifying obedience to the rule and will of Allah, the only deity recognized in the strictly monotheistic Islamic religion. An individual who accepts the Islamic faith is a ***Muslim,*** meaning "one who has submitted." Though it began as one man's expression of unqualified faith in Allah, Islam quickly attracted followers and took on political and social as well as religious significance. During its first century, Islam reached far beyond its Arabian homeland, bringing Sasanian Persia and parts of the Byzantine Empire into its orbit. By the eighth century the realm of Islam and the Byzantine Empire stood as political and economic anchors of much of western and central Afro-Eurasia.

Early Islamic religious beliefs reflected the deep influence of Jewish and Christian traditions, while early Muslim society reflected the nomadic and mercantile Arabian society from which Islam arose. Over time, Muslims also drew inspiration from other societies and other cultural traditions. After toppling the Sasanians, Muslim conquerors adopted Persian techniques of government and finance to administer their lands. Persian literature, science, and religious values also found a place in Islamic society. During later centuries Muslims drew inspiration from Greek and Indian traditions as well. Thus Muslims did not invent a new Islamic society but, rather, fashioned it by blending elements from Arab, Persian, Greek, and Indian societies.

While drawing influence from other societies, however, Islam thoroughly transformed the cultural traditions that it absorbed. The expansive realm of Islam eventually provided a political framework for trade and diplomacy over a vast portion of the eastern hemisphere, from west Africa to the islands of southeast Asia. Many lands of varied cultural background thus became part of a larger society often called the ***dar al-Islam***—an Arabic term that means the "house of Islam" and that refers to lands under Islamic rule.

| CHRONOLOGY | |
|---|---|
| 570–632 | Life of Muhammad |
| 622 | The *hijra* |
| 632 | Muhammad's hajj |
| 650s | Compilation of the Quran |
| 661–750 | Umayyad dynasty |
| 750–1258 | Abbasid dynasty |
| 786–809 | Reign of Harun al-Rashid |
| 1050s | Establishment of Seljuq control over the Abbasid dynasty |
| 1058–1111 | Life of al-Ghazali |
| 1126–1198 | Life of Ibn Rushd |

# A PROPHET AND HIS WORLD

Islam arose in the Arabian peninsula, and the new religion faithfully reflected the social and cultural conditions of its homeland. Desert covers most of the peninsula, and agriculture is possible only in the well-watered area of Yemen in the south and in a few other places, such as the city of Medina, where oases provide water. Yet human communities have occupied Arabia for millennia. Nomadic peoples known as **bedouin** kept herds of sheep, goats, and camels, migrating through the deserts to find grass and water for their animals. The bedouin organized themselves in family and clan groups. Individuals and their immediate families depended heavily on their larger kinship networks for support in times of need. In an environment as harsh and unforgiving as the Arabian desert, cooperation with kin often made the difference between death and survival. Bedouin peoples developed a strong sense of loyalty to their clans and guarded their common interests with determination. Clan identities and loyalties survived for centuries after the appearance of Islam.

Arabia also figured prominently in the long-distance trade networks of the first millennium of the Common Era. Commodities arrived at ports on the Persian Gulf (near modern Bahrain), the Arabian Sea (near modern Aden), and the Red Sea (near Mecca) and then traveled overland by camel caravan to Palmyra or Damascus, which offered access to the Mediterranean basin. After the third century C.E., Arabia became an increasingly important link in trade between China and India in the east and Persia and Byzantium in the west. With the weakening of classical empires, trade routes across central Asia had become insecure. Merchants abandoned the overland routes in favor of sea lanes connecting with land routes in the Arabian peninsula. Trade passing across the peninsula was especially important for the city of Mecca, which became an important site of fairs and a stopping point for caravan traffic.

## Muhammad and His Message

**Muhammad's Early Life** The prophet **Muhammad** came into this world of bedouin herders and worldly merchants. Born about 570 C.E. into a reputable family of merchants in

**bedouin** (BEHD-oh-ihn)
**Muhammad** (muh-HAHM-mahd)

## INTERPRETING IMAGES

Some northern Arabs went to great lengths to demonstrate their devotion to Christianity. This structure, carved out of sheer rock along the wall of a ravine at Petra in modern-day Jordan, served as a monastery.

**Analyze** *How does the Arab Christian architecture at Petra compare to the Arab Muslim architecture you see later in this chapter? What differences do you see in how Arab Christians and Muslims express devotion to their faith in this period?*

Salail Wadhavkar/National Geographic Stock

Mecca, Muhammad ibn (a term than means son of) Abdullah lost both of his parents by the time he was six years old. His grandfather and uncle cared for him and provided him with an education, but Muhammad's early life was difficult. As a young man, he worked for a woman named Khadija, a wealthy widow whom he married about 595 C.E. Through this marriage he gained a position of some prominence in Meccan society, although he did not by any means enter the ranks of the elite.

By age thirty Muhammad had established himself as a merchant. He made a comfortable life for himself in Arabian society, where peoples of different religious and cultural traditions regularly dealt with one another. Most Arabs recognized many gods, goddesses, demons, and nature spirits whose favor they sought through prayers and sacrifices. Large communities of Jewish merchants also worked throughout Arabia, and, especially in the north, many Arabs had converted to Christianity by Muhammad's time. Although he was not deeply knowledgeable about Judaism or Christianity, Muhammad had a basic understanding of both traditions. He may even have traveled by caravan to Syria, where he would certainly have dealt with Jewish and Christian merchants.

**Muhammad's Spiritual Transformation** About 610 C.E., as he approached age forty, Muhammad underwent a profound spiritual experience that transformed his life and left a deep mark on world history. His experience left him with the convictions that in all the world there was only one true deity; **Allah** ("God"); that he ruled the universe; that idolatry and the recognition of other gods amounted to wickedness; and that Allah would soon bring his judgment on the world, rewarding the righteous and punishing the wicked. Muhammad experienced visions, which he understood as messages or revelations from Allah, delivered through the archangel Gabriel (also recognized by Jews and Christians as a special messenger of God), instructing him to explain his views to others. He did not set out to construct a new religion by combining elements of Arab, Jewish, and Christian beliefs. In light of his cultural context, however, it is not surprising that he shared numerous specific beliefs with Jews and Christians—and indeed also with Zoroastrians, whose views had profoundly influenced the development of both Judaism and Christianity. In any case, in accordance with instructions transmitted to him by Gabriel, Muhammad began to expound his beliefs to his family and close friends. Gradually, others showed interest in his message, and by about 620 C.E. an enthusiastic and expanding minority of Mecca's citizenry had joined his circle.

**The Quran** Muhammad originally presented oral recitations of the revelations he received during his visions. As the Islamic community grew, his followers prepared written texts of his teachings. During the early 650s devout Muslims compiled these written versions of Muhammad's revelations and issued them as the **Quran** ("recitation"), the holy book of Islam. A work of magnificent poetry, the Quran communicates in powerful and moving terms Muhammad's understanding of Allah and his relation to the world, and it serves as

**Quran** (koo-RAHN)

Current Islamic doctrine forbids artistic representations of Muhammad and Allah to prevent the worship of their images as idols. Although artists of previous centuries occasionally produced paintings of Muhammad, Islamic art has emphasized geometric design and calligraphy. This handsome page from a Quran written on vellum dates from the ninth or early tenth century.

Purchase, Friends of Islamic Art Gifts, 2004/Metropolitan Museum of Art

## What's Left Out?

Before the advent of Muhammad and Islam, the Ka'ba in the city of Mecca was just one of many religious sanctuaries recognized by the Arabs. As pilgrims traveled to these sacred sites, they naturally engaged in trade in the towns that surrounded them, and commercial fairs were established that coincided with the season of the pilgrimage. However, the question of just how extensive trade in Mecca was has led to considerable disagreement among historians. The standard argument has been that Mecca was the hub of extensive transregional trade routes that connected the ports of Yemen with the Byzantine and Sasanian empires, facilitating commerce in gold, silver, and spices in particular. But, more recently, scholars have pushed back against this theory, pointing out that the only sources that make this claim are Arabic and that not a single non-Arabic source has yet been discovered that supports this idea of Mecca as a hub of extensive transregional trade. They also point out that Mecca is not actually located on any trade routes and visiting it would have required a considerable and costly detour away from the main trading routes of the Arabian Peninsula. Some of these scholars go so far as to reject these Arabic source depictions of pre-Islamic Mecca as propaganda and myth.

There is no doubt that Mecca was out of the way, located in a barren valley and with nothing in particular to encourage a merchant caravan to visit. But Mecca did have one undeniable attraction—and that was the Ka'ba itself. There were many other sanctuaries in Arabia that were important to pilgrims, but none was as important as the Ka'ba. All the other sanctuaries were dedicated to a specific local deity, but the Ka'ba was a universal shrine that was believed to house all the deities of pre-Islamic Arabia. This undoubtedly meant that despite the long detour it required, all the merchants of Arabia would have felt a serious spiritual obligation to visit Mecca. This probably also means that even if the Arabic sources exaggerate the level of *transregional* trade that was being carried on in Mecca, considerable *regional* trade was undoubtedly occurring, and all of it was wholly dependent on the Ka'ba. This helps explain why Muhammad, on his triumphal return to Mecca from Medina in 630, retained the pre-Islamic sanctuary of the Ka'ba for both spiritual and commercial reasons and established the hajj as one of the Five Pillars of Islam. This decision has ensured Mecca's centrality to the Islamic faith ever since and also meant that the city has continued to depend on economic activity that is, still to this day, almost totally generated by the annual pilgrimage of the hajj.

*Source:* Reza Aslan. *No God but God.* New York, 2005.

### Thinking Critically About Sources

1. What arguments do scholars posit to undermine the thesis that the pilgrimage to Mecca promoted interregional trade?
2. What arguments do scholars present to support the thesis that the pilgrimage to Mecca promoted transregional and regional trade?

the definitive authority for Islamic religious doctrine and social organization.

Apart from the Quran, several other sources have provided moral and religious guidance for the Islamic community. Most important after the Quran are traditions known as ***hadith,*** which include sayings attributed to Muhammad and accounts of the prophet's deeds. Several collections of *hadith* written by leading Islamic intellectuals appeared between the ninth and eleventh centuries C.E., and Muslim scholars have often taken them as guides for interpretation of the Quran. Regarded as less authoritative than the Quran and the *hadith,* but still important as inspirations for Islamic thought, were various additional early works describing social and legal customs, biographies of Muhammad, and pious commentaries on the Quran.

## Muhammad's Migration to Medina

**Conflict at Mecca** The growing popularity of Muhammad's preaching brought him into conflict with the ruling elites at **Mecca.** Conflict centered on religious issues. Muhammad's insistence that Allah was the only divine power in the universe struck many polytheistic Arabs as offensive and dangerous as well because it disparaged long-recognized deities and spirits thought to wield influence over human affairs. The tensions also had a personal dimension. Mecca's ruling elites, who were also the city's wealthiest merchants, took it as a personal affront and a threat to their position when Muhammad denounced greed as moral wickedness that Allah would punish.

Muhammad's attack on idolatry also represented an economic threat to those who owned and profited from the many shrines to deities that attracted merchants and pilgrims to Mecca. The best known of those shrines was a large black rock long considered to be the dwelling of a powerful deity. Housed in a cube-shaped building known as the **Ka'ba,** it drew worshipers from all over Arabia and brought considerable wealth to Mecca. As Muhammad relentlessly condemned the idolatry officially promoted at the Ka'ba and other shrines, the ruling elites of Mecca began to persecute the prophet and his followers.

**The Hijra** The pressure became so great that some of Muhammad's followers fled to Abyssinia (modern Ethiopia). Muhammad himself remained in Mecca until 622 C.E., when he too fled and joined a group of his followers in Yathrib, a rival trading city 345 kilometers (214 miles) north of Mecca. Muslims called their new home **Medina** ("the city," meaning "the city of the prophet"). Known as the ***hijra*** ("migration"), Muhammad's move to Medina serves as the starting point of the official Islamic calendar.

**The Umma** In Mecca, Muhammad had lived within the established political framework and concentrated on the moral and religious dimensions of his faith. In Medina he found himself at the head of a small but growing society in exile that needed guidance in practical as well as spiritual affairs. He organized his followers into a cohesive community called the ***umma*** ("community of the faithful") and provided it with a comprehensive legal and social code. He led this community both in daily prayers to Allah and in battle with enemies at Medina, Mecca, and other places. He looked after the economic welfare of the *umma*—sometimes by organizing commercial ventures and sometimes by launching raids against caravans from Mecca. Remembering the difficult days of his youth, he provided relief for widows, orphans, and the poor, and he made almsgiving a prime moral virtue.

**The "Seal of the Prophets"** Muhammad's understanding of his religious mission expanded during his years at Medina. He began to refer to himself as a prophet, indeed as the "seal of the prophets"—the final prophet through whom Allah would reveal his message to humankind. Muhammad accepted the authority of earlier Jewish and Christian prophets, including Abraham, Moses, and Jesus, and he held the Hebrew scriptures and the Christian New Testament in high esteem. He also accepted his predecessors' monotheism: Allah was the same omnipotent, omniscient, omnipresent, and exclusive deity as the Jews' Yahweh and the Christians' God. Muhammad taught, however, that the message entrusted to him offered a more complete revelation of Allah and his will than Judaism and Christianity had made available. Thus, while at Medina, Muhammad came to see himself consciously as Allah's final prophet: not simply as a devout man who explained his spiritual insights to a small circle of family and friends, but as the messenger who communicated Allah's wishes and his plan for the world to all humankind.

## The Establishment of Islam in Arabia

**Muhammad's Return to Mecca** Throughout their sojourn at Medina, Muhammad and his followers planned ultimately to return to Mecca, which was both their home and the leading city of Arabia. In 629 C.E. they arranged with the authorities to participate in the annual pilgrimage to the Ka'ba, but they were not content with a short visit. In 630 they attacked Mecca and conquered the city. They forced the elites to adopt Muhammad's faith, and they imposed a government dedicated to Allah. They also destroyed the pagan shrines and replaced them with mosques, buildings that sought to instill a sense of sacredness and community where Muslims gathered for prayers. Only the Ka'ba escaped their efforts to cleanse Mecca of pagan monuments.

Muhammad and his followers denied that the Ka'ba was the home of a deity, but they preserved the black rock and its housing as a symbol of Mecca's greatness. They allowed only the faithful to approach the shrine, and in 632 Muhammad himself led the first Islamic pilgrimage to the Ka'ba, thus

**Ka'ba** (KAH-buh)

# SOURCES FROM THE PAST

## The Quran on Allah and His Expectations of Humankind

*The foundation of the Islamic faith is the understanding of Allah, his nature, and his plan for the world as outlined in the Quran. Through his visions Muhammad came to understand Allah as the one and only god, the creator and sustainer of the world in the manner of the Jews' Yahweh and the Christians' God. Those who rejected Allah and his message would suffer eternal punishment, but those who recognized and obeyed him would receive his mercy and secure his blessings.*

In the name of Allah, most benevolent, ever-merciful.
All praise be to Allah,
Lord of all the worlds,
Most beneficent, ever-merciful,
King of the Day of Judgement.
You alone we worship, and to You
alone turn for help.
Guide us (O Lord) to the path that is straight,
The path of those You have blessed,
Not of those who have earned Your anger,
nor those who have gone astray. . . .

Verily men and women who have come to submission,
men and women who are believers,
men and women who are devout,
truthful men and women,
men and women with endurance,
men and women who are modest,
men and women who give alms,
men and women who observe fasting,
men and women who guard their private parts,
and those men and women who remember God a great deal,
for them God has forgiveness and a great reward.
No believing men and women have any choice in a matter
after God and His Apostle [i.e., Muhammad] have decided it.
Whoever disobeys God and His Apostle
has clearly lost the way and gone astray. . . .
O you who believe, remember God a great deal,
And sing His praises morning and evening.
It is He who sends His blessings on you,
as (do) His angels, that He may lead you out of darkness into light,
for He is benevolent to the believers. . . .

How many of the Five Pillars of Islam do you see references to up to this point in the passage?

I call to witness
the early hours of the morning,
And the night when dark and still,
Your Lord has neither left you,
nor despises you.
What is to come is better for you
than what has gone before;
For your Lord will certainly give you,
and you will be content.
Did He not find you an orphan

*(Continued)*

and take care of you?
Did He not find you poor
and enrich you?
So do not oppress the orphan,
And do not drive
the beggar away,
And keep recounting the favours of your Lord. . . .

Say: "He is God
the one the most unique,
God the immanently indispensable.
He has begotten no one,
and is begotten of none.
There is no one comparable to Him."

### For Further Reflection

- What similarities and differences do you see between the teachings contained in the Quran and those of other leaders we have considered in previous chapters including Zoroaster, the Buddha and Jesus?
- Do you see any gender distinctions in these passages? That is, does Allah seem to have different expectations for men and women, or similar?
- Based on these passages, what kind of god is Allah for his believers? Is he an angry or a caring god?
- Based on this passage, would Allah promote "conversion by the sword"? Why or why not?

*Source: Al-Qur'an: A Contemporary Translation.* Trans. by Ahmed Ali. Princeton: Princeton University Press, 1984, pp. 11, 358, 359, 540, 559.

establishing the hajj as an example for all devout Muslims. Building on the conquest of Mecca, Muhammad and his followers launched campaigns against other towns and bedouin clans, and by the time of the prophet's death in 632, shortly after his hajj, they had brought most of Arabia under their control.

**The Five Pillars of Islam** Muhammad's personal leadership decisively shaped the values and the development of the Islamic community. The foundation of Islam as elaborated by Muhammad consists of obligations known as the **Five Pillars of Islam:** (1) Muslims must acknowledge Allah as the only god and Muhammad as his prophet. (2) They must pray to Allah daily while facing Mecca. (3) They must observe a fast during the daylight hours of the month of Ramadan. (4) They must contribute alms for the relief of the weak and poor. (5) And, in honor of Muhammad's visits to Mecca in 629 and 632, those who are physically and financially able must undertake the hajj and make at least one pilgrimage to Mecca. During the centuries since its appearance, Islam has generated many schools and sects, each with its own particular legal, social, and doctrinal features. The Five Pillars of Islam, however, constitute a simple but powerful framework that has bound the *umma* into a cohesive community.

**Jihad** Some Muslims, though by no means all, have taken jihad as an additional obligation. The term ***jihad*** literally means "struggle," and Muslims have understood its imperatives in various ways. In one sense, jihad imposes spiritual and moral obligations on Muslims by requiring them to combat vice and evil. In another sense, jihad calls on Muslims to struggle against ignorance and unbelief by spreading the word of Islam and seeking converts to the faith. In some circumstances, jihad also involves physical struggle, obliging Muslims to take up the sword and wage war against unbelievers who threaten Islam.

**Islamic Law: The Sharia** Beyond the general obligations prescribed by the Five Pillars, Islamic holy law, known as the ***sharia,*** emerged during the centuries after Muhammad and offered detailed guidance on proper behavior in almost every aspect of life. Elaborated by jurists and legal scholars, the sharia drew its inspiration especially from the Quran and the early historical accounts of Muhammad's life and teachings. It offered precise guidance on matters as diverse as marriage and family life, inheritance, slavery, business and commercial relationships, political authority in the *dar al-Islam,* and crime. Like many law codes in history, the sharia tended to be interpreted differently by different Islamic societies, but in all cases, the sharia evolved to become something more than a religious doctrine: it developed into a way of life complete with social and ethical values derived from Islamic religious principles.

---

**sharia** (shah-REE-ah)

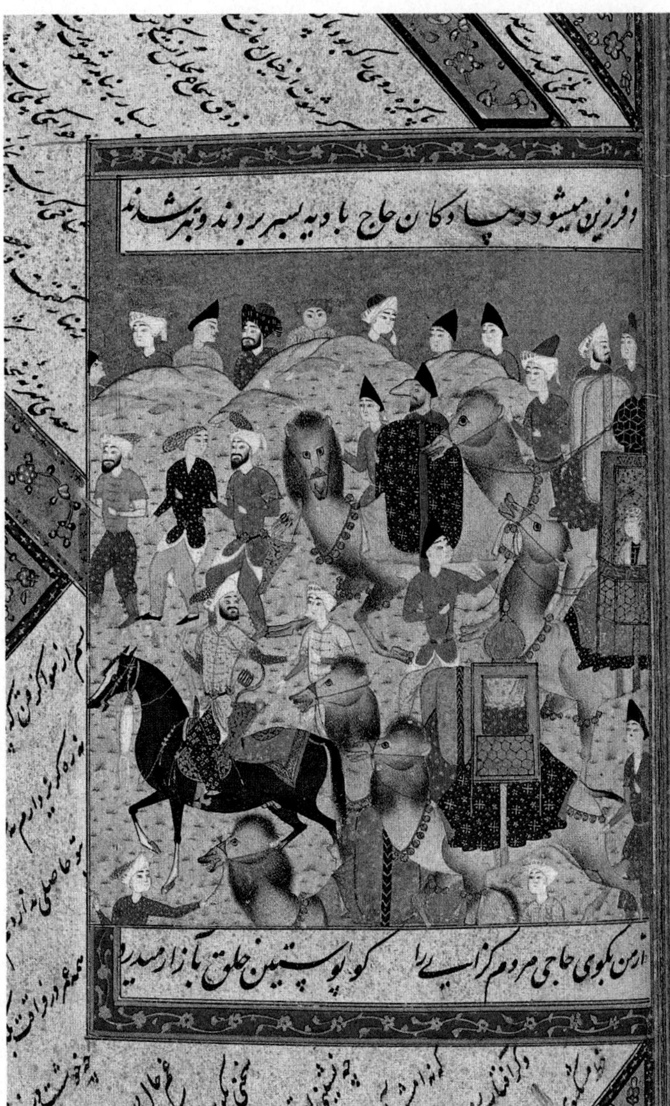

A watercolor painting from sixteenth-century Iran depicts a caravan of pilgrims traveling to Mecca while making the hajj. In what ways did the hajj facilitate social and business relationships?

Album/Alamy Stock Photo

## THE EXPANSION OF ISLAM

After Muhammad's death the Islamic community might well have unraveled and disappeared. Muhammad had made no provision for a successor, and there was serious division within the *umma* concerning the selection of a new leader. Many of the towns and bedouin clans that had recently accepted Islam took the opportunity of Muhammad's death to renounce the fledgling religion, reassert their independence, and break free from Mecca's control. Within a short time, however, the many different cultural and political groups that came to constitute the Islamic community throughout Afro-Eurasia had embarked on a stunningly successful round of military expansion that extended its political and cultural influence far beyond the boundaries of Arabia. Those conquests laid the foundation for the rapid growth of Islamic society.

### The Early Caliphs and the Umayyad Dynasty

**The Caliph** Because Muhammad was the "seal of the prophets," it was inconceivable that another prophet should succeed him. Shortly after Muhammad's death his advisers selected **Abu Bakr,** a genial man who was one of the prophet's closest friends and most devoted disciples, to serve as ***caliph*** ("deputy"). Thus Abu Bakr and later caliphs led the *umma* not as prophets but as lieutenants or substitutes for Muhammad. Abu Bakr became head of state for the Islamic community as well as chief judge, religious leader, and military commander. Under the caliph's leadership, the *umma* went on the offensive against the towns and bedouin clans that had renounced Islam after Muhammad's death, and within a year it had compelled them to recognize Islam and the rule of the caliph.

**The Shia** Immediately after the death of Muhammad the umma faced a crisis over who would succeed the prophet. These disagreements led to the emergence of the **Shia** sect, the most important and enduring of all the alternatives to the form of Islam observed by the majority of Muslims, known as **Sunni** Islam. The Shia sect originated as a party supporting the appointment of Ali and his descendants as caliphs. A cousin and son-in-law of Muhammad, Ali was a candidate for caliph when the prophet died, but support for Abu Bakr was stronger. Ali served briefly as the fourth caliph (656–661 C.E.), but his enemies assassinated him while he was praying in a mosque, killed many of his relatives, and imposed their own candidate as caliph. Partisans of Ali then organized the Shia ("party"), furiously resisted the victorious faction, and struggled to return the caliphate to the line of Ali. Although persecuted, the Shia survived and strengthened its identity by adopting doctrines and rituals distinct from those of the Sunnis ("traditionalists"), who accepted the legitimacy of the early caliphs. Shia partisans, for example, observed holy days in honor of their leaders and martyrs to their cause, and they taught that descendants of Ali were infallible, sinless, and divinely appointed to rule the Islamic community. Shia Muslims also advanced interpretations of the Quran that support the party's views, and the Shia itself has often served as a source of support for those who oppose the policies of Sunni leaders.

**Abu Bakr** (ah-BOO BAHK-uhr)
**caliph** (KHA-leef)
**Shia** (SHEE-ah)
**Sunni** (SOON-nee)

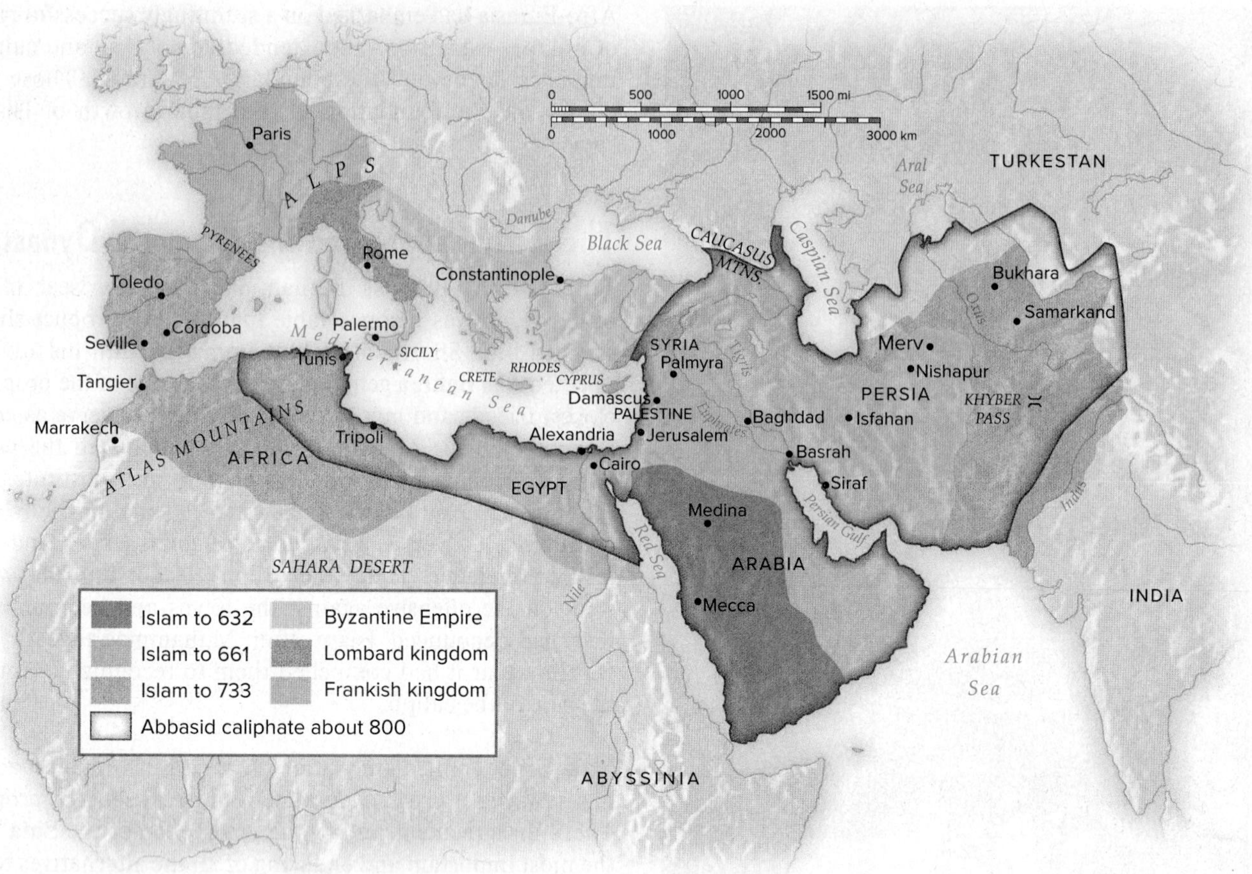


## MAP 2.1 The expansion of Islam, 632–733 C.E.

During the seventh and eighth centuries, the new faith of Islam expanded rapidly and dramatically beyond its Arabian homeland.

***What environmental, political, and social circumstances facilitated the rapid spread of the new faith? What were the cultural and political effects of the expansion of Islam?***

**The Expansion of Islam** During the century after Muhammad's death, Islamic armies ranged well beyond the boundaries of Arabia, carrying their religion and their authority to Byzantine and Sasanian territories and beyond. Although much less powerful than either the Byzantine Empire or the Sasanian empire, Muslim armies fought with particular effectiveness because their leaders had forged previously competing tribal groups into a powerful state unified by their allegiance to Islam. Moreover, the well-organized and superbly led Muslim armies attacked at a moment when the Byzantine and Sasanian empires were exhausted from perennial conflicts with each other and when they also faced internal uprisings by overtaxed peasants and oppressed ethnic or religious minorities. Between 633 and 637 C.E., taking advantage of those difficulties, Muslim forces seized Byzantine Syria and Palestine and took most of Mesopotamia from the Sasanians. During the 640s they conquered Byzantine Egypt and north Africa. In 651 they toppled the Sasanian dynasty and incorporated Persia into their expanding empire. In 711 they conquered the Hindu kingdom of Sind in northwestern India. Between 711 and 718 they extended their authority to northwest Africa and crossed the Strait of Gibraltar, conquering most of the Iberian peninsula and threatening the Frankish kingdom in Gaul. By the mid-eighth century an immense Islamic Empire ruled lands from India and the central Asian steppe lands in the east to northwest Africa and Iberia in the west.

During this rapid expansion the empire's rulers encountered difficult problems of governance and administration. One problem had to do with the selection of caliphs. During the early decades after Muhammad's death, leaders of the most powerful Arab clans negotiated among themselves and appointed the first four caliphs. Political ambitions, personal differences, and clan loyalties complicated their deliberations, however, and disputes soon led to the rise of factions and parties within the Islamic community.

**The Umayyad Dynasty** After the assassination of Ali, the establishment of the **Umayyad dynasty** (661–750 C.E.) solved the problem of succession, at least temporarily. The Umayyads

**Umayyad** (oo-MEYE-ahd)

The early expansion of Islam was achieved largely through warfare. This illustration from an Arabic manuscript of the thirteenth century depicts a battle between Muhammad's cousin Ali and his adversaries.
Iberfoto/SuperStock

ranked among the most prominent of the Meccan merchant clans, and their reputation and network of alliances helped them bring stability to the Islamic community. Despite their association with Mecca, the Umayyads established their capital at Damascus, a thriving commercial city in Syria, whose central location enabled them to maintain better communication with the vast and still-expanding Islamic Empire.

Although the Umayyads' dynasty solved the problem of succession, their tightly centralized rule and the favor they showed to their fellow Arabs generated an administrative problem. The Umayyads ruled the *dar al-Islam* as conquerors, and their policies reflected the interests of the Arab military aristocracy. The Umayyads appointed members of this elite as governors and administrators of conquered lands, and they distributed the wealth that they extracted among this privileged class.

**Policy toward Conquered Peoples** This policy contributed to high morale among Arab conquerors, but it caused severe discontent among the scores of ethnic and religious groups conquered by the Umayyad empire. Apart from Muslims, the empire included Christians, Jews, Zoroastrians, and Buddhists. In addition to Arabs and bedouin, it included Indians, Persians, Mesopotamians, Greeks, Egyptians, and nomadic Berbers in north Africa. The Arabs mostly allowed conquered peoples to observe their own religions—particularly Christians and Jews—but they levied a special head tax, called the ***jizya,*** on those who did not convert to Islam. Even those who converted did not enjoy access to wealth and positions of authority, which the Umayyads reserved almost exclusively for members of the Arab military aristocracy. This caused deep resentment among conquered peoples and led to restiveness against Umayyad rule.

**Umayyad Decline** Beginning in the early eighth century, the Umayyad caliphs became alienated even from other Arabs. They devoted themselves increasingly to luxurious living rather than to competent leadership of the *umma,* and they scandalized devout Muslims by their casual attitudes toward Islamic doctrine and morality. By midcentury the Umayyad caliphs faced not only the resistance of the Shia, whose members continued to promote descendants of Ali for caliph, but also the discontent of conquered peoples throughout their empire and even the disillusionment of Muslim Arab military leaders.

## The Abbasid Dynasty

**Abu al-Abbas** Rebellion in Persia brought the Umayyad dynasty to an end. The chief leader of the rebellion was Abu al-Abbas, a descendant of Muhammad's uncle. Although he was a Sunni Arab, Abu al-Abbas allied readily with Shias and with Muslims who were not Arabs, such as converts to Islam from southwest Asia. Particularly prominent among his supporters were Persian converts who resented the preference shown by the Umayyads to Arab Muslims. During the 740s Abu al-Abbas's party rejected Umayyad authority and seized control of Persia and Mesopotamia. In 750 his army shattered Umayyad forces in a huge battle. Afterward, Abu al-Abbas invited the remaining members of the Umayyad clan to a banquet under the pretext of reconciling their differences. During the festivities his troops arrested the Umayyads and slaughtered them, effectively bringing to an end the caliphate. Abu al-Abbas then founded the **Abbasid** dynasty, which was the principal source of authority in the *dar al-Islam* until the Mongols toppled it in 1258 C.E.

**Abbasid** (ah-BAH-sihd)

**The Abbasid Dynasty** The Abbasid dynasty differed considerably from the Umayyad. For one thing, the Abbasid state was far more cosmopolitan than its predecessor. Even though they sprang from the ranks of conquering Arabs, Abbasid rulers did not show special favor to the Arab military aristocracy. Arabs continued to play a large role in government, but Persians, Egyptians, Mesopotamians, and others also rose to positions of wealth and power.

The Abbasid dynasty differed from the Umayyad also in that it was not a conquering dynasty. The Abbasids sparred intermittently with the Byzantine Empire, they clashed frequently with nomadic peoples from central Asia, and in 751 they defeated a Chinese army at Talas River near Samarkand. The battle of Talas River was exceptionally important: it ended the expansion of China's Tang dynasty into central Asia (discussed in chapter 13), and it opened the door for the spread of Islam among Turkish peoples. Only marginally, however, did the Abbasids expand their empire by conquest. The *dar al-Islam* as a whole continued to grow during the Abbasid era, but the caliphs had little to do with the expansion. During the ninth and early tenth centuries, for example, largely autonomous Islamic forces from distant Tunisia mounted naval expeditions throughout the Mediterranean, conquering Crete, Sicily, and the Balearic Islands while seizing territories also in Cyprus, Rhodes, Sardinia, Corsica, southern Italy, and southern France. Meanwhile, Muslim merchants introduced Islam to southern India and sub-Saharan Africa (see chapter 18).

**Abbasid Administration** Instead of conquering new lands, the Abbasids largely contented themselves with administering the empire they inherited. Fashioning a government that could administer a sprawling realm with scores of linguistic, ethnic, and cultural groups was a considerable challenge. Before Muhammad, Arabs had no governments larger than city-states, nor did the Quran offer guidance for the administration of a huge empire. The Umayyad practice of allowing the Arab aristocracy to exploit subject lands and peoples had proven to be a failure. Thus Abu al-Abbas and his successors turned to long-standing Mesopotamian and Persian techniques of administration whereby rulers devised policies, built capital cities to oversee affairs, and organized their territories through regional governors and bureaucracies.

**Baghdad** Central authority emanated from the Abbasid court at Baghdad (capital of modern Iraq), a magnificent new city that the early Abbasid caliphs constructed near the Sasanid capital of Ctesiphon. By building this new center of government to replace the Umayyad capital at Damascus, the Abbasids associated themselves with the cosmopolitan environment of Mesopotamia. Baghdad was a round city protected by three round walls. At the heart of the city was the caliph's green-domed palace, from which instructions flowed to the distant reaches of the Abbasid realm. In the provinces, governors represented the caliph and implemented his political and financial policies.

Learned officials known as ***ulama*** ("people with religious knowledge") and ***qadis*** ("judges") set moral standards in local communities and resolved disputes. *Ulama* and *qadis* were not priests—Islam does not recognize priests as a distinct class of religious specialists—but they had a formal education that emphasized study of the Quran and the sharia. *Ulama* were pious scholars who sought to develop public policy in accordance with the Quran and sharia. *Qadis* heard cases at law and rendered decisions based on the Quran and sharia. Because of their moral authority, *ulama* and *qadis* became extremely influential officials who helped to ensure widespread observance of Islamic values. Apart from provincial governors, *ulama,* and *qadis,* the Abbasid caliphs kept a standing army, and they established bureaucratic ministries in charge of taxation, finance, coinage, and postal services. They also maintained the magnificent network of roads that the Islamic Empire inherited from the Sasanids.

**Harun al-Rashid** The high point of the Abbasid dynasty came during the reign of the caliph **Harun al-Rashid** (786–809 C.E.). By the late eighth century, Abbasid authority had lost some of its force in provinces distant from Baghdad, but it remained strong enough to bring reliable tax revenues from most parts of the empire. Flush with wealth, Baghdad became a center of banking, commerce, crafts, and industrial production, a metropolis with a population of several hundred thousand people. According to stories from his time, Harun al-Rashid provided liberal support for artists and writers, bestowed lavish and luxurious gifts on his favorites, and distributed money to the poor and the common classes by tossing coins into the streets of Baghdad. Once, he sent an elephant and a collection of rich presents as gifts to his contemporary Charlemagne, who ruled the Carolingian empire of western Europe.

Harun al-Rashid receiving a delegation sent by Charlemagne at his court in Baghdad. 1864 painting by Julius Köckert.

Historic Collection/Alamy Stock Photo

**Abbasid Decline** Soon after Harun al-Rashid's reign, the Abbasid empire entered a period of decline. Civil war between Harun's sons seriously damaged Abbasid authority, and disputes over succession rights became a recurring problem for the dynasty. Provincial governors took advantage of disorder in the ruling house by acting independently of the caliphs: instead of implementing imperial policies and delivering taxes to Baghdad, they built up local bases of power and in some cases actually seceded from the Abbasid empire. Meanwhile, popular uprisings and peasant rebellions, which often enjoyed the support of dissenting sects and heretical movements, further weakened the empire.

As a result of those difficulties, the Abbasid caliphs became mere figureheads long before the Mongols extinguished the dynasty in 1258. In 945, members of a Persian noble family seized control of Baghdad and established their clan as the power behind the Abbasid throne. Later, imperial authorities in Baghdad fell under the control of the Seljuq Turks, a nomadic people from central Asia who also invaded the Byzantine Empire. In response to rebellions mounted by peasants and provincial governors, authorities in Baghdad allied with the Seljuqs, who began to enter the Abbasid realm and convert to Islam about the mid-tenth century. By the mid-eleventh century the Seljuqs effectively controlled the Abbasid empire. During the 1050s they took possession of Baghdad, and during the following decades they extended their authority to Syria, Palestine, and Anatolia. They retained Abbasid caliphs as nominal sovereigns, but for two centuries, until the arrival of the Mongols, the Seljuq *sultan* ("chieftain" or "ruler") was the true source of power in the Abbasid empire.

In a thirteenth-century manuscript illustration, a fictional Muslim traveler passes a lively agricultural village. Sheep, goats, chickens, and date palms figure prominently in the local economy.

DEA/J.E. Bulloz/Getty Images

## ECONOMY AND SOCIETY OF THE EARLY ISLAMIC WORLD

In the *dar al-Islam,* as in other agricultural societies, peasants tilled the land as their ancestors had done for centuries before them, while manufacturers and merchants supported a thriving urban economy. Here, as in other lands, the creation of large empires had dramatic economic implications. The Umayyad and Abbasid empires created a zone of trade, exchange, and communication stretching from India to Iberia. Commerce throughout this zone served as a vigorous economic stimulus for both the countryside and the cities of the early Islamic world.

### New Crops, Agricultural Experimentation, and Urban Growth

**The Spread of Food and Industrial Crops** As soldiers, administrators, diplomats, and merchants traveled throughout the *dar al-Islam,* they encountered plants, animals, and agricultural techniques peculiar to the empire's various regions. They often introduced particularly useful crops to other regions. The most important of the transplants traveled west from India to Persia; southwest Asia; Arabia; Egypt; north Africa; Spain; and the Mediterranean islands of Cyprus, Crete, Sicily, and Sardinia. They included staple crops such as sugarcane, rice, and new varieties of sorghum and wheat; vegetables such as spinach, artichokes, and eggplants; fruits such as oranges, lemons, limes, bananas, coconuts, watermelons, and mangoes; and industrial crops such as cotton, indigo, and henna.

**Effects of New Crops** The introduction of these crops into the western regions of the Islamic world had wide-ranging effects. New food crops led to a richer and more varied diet. They also increased quantities of food available because they enabled cultivators to extend the growing season. In much of the Islamic world, summers are so hot and dry that cultivators traditionally left their fields fallow during that season. Most of the transplanted crops grew well in high heat, however, so cultivators in southwest Asia, north Africa, and other hot zones could till their lands year-round. The result was a dramatic increase in food supplies.

Some new crops had industrial uses. The most important of these was cotton, which became the basis for a thriving textile industry throughout much of the Islamic world. Indigo and henna yielded dyes that textile manufacturers used in large quantities.

**Agricultural Experimentation** Travel and communication in the *dar al-Islam* also encouraged experimentation with agricultural methods. Cultivators paid close attention to methods of irrigation, fertilization, crop rotation, and the like, and they outlined their findings in hundreds of agricultural manuals. Copies of these works survive in numerous manuscripts that circulated widely throughout the Islamic world. The combined effect of new crops and improved techniques was a far more productive agricultural economy, which in turn supported vigorous economic growth throughout the *dar al-Islam.*

**Urban Growth** Increased agricultural production contributed to the rapid growth of cities in all parts of the Islamic world from India to Spain. Delhi, Samarkand, Bukhara, Merv, Nishapur, Isfahan, Basra, Baghdad, Damascus, Jerusalem, Cairo, Alexandria, Palermo, Tunis, Tangier, Córdoba, and Toledo were all bustling cities, some with populations of several hundred thousand people. All these cities had flourishing markets supporting thousands of artisans, craftsmen, and merchants. Most of them were also important centers of industrial production, particularly of textiles, pottery, glassware, leather, iron, and steel.

One new industry appeared in Islamic cities during the Abbasid era: paper manufacture. Chinese craftsmen had made paper since the first century C.E., but their technology did not spread far beyond China until the eighth century. Paper was cheaper and easier to use than writing materials such as vellum sheets made from calfskin, and it soon became popular throughout the Islamic world. Paper facilitated the keeping of administrative and commercial records, and it made possible the dissemination of books and treatises in larger quantities than ever before. By the tenth century, mills produced paper in Persia, Mesopotamia, Arabia, Egypt, and Spain, and the industry soon spread to western Europe.

## The Formation of a Hemispheric Trading Zone

From its earliest days Islamic society drew much of its prosperity from commerce. Muhammad himself was a merchant, and he held merchants in high esteem. According to early accounts of his life, Muhammad once said that honest merchants would stand alongside martyrs to the faith on the day of judgment. By the time of the Abbasid caliphate, elaborate trade networks linked all the regions of the Islamic world and joined it to a larger, hemispheric economy.

**Overland Trade** When they overran the Sasanian empire, Muslim conquerors brought the prosperous trading cities of central Asia under control of the expanding *dar al-Islam.* Merv,

An artist's impression of a caravanserai, which is a Persian compound word meaning a place of shelter for travelers. Caravanserais were large, single-building structures, generally without roofs but with many places to house and feed merchants and their animals. What would the atmosphere have been like inside these caravanserais, where so many intense conversations took place between merchants and pilgrims of so many cultures and faiths?

DEA/G. Dagli Orti/Age Fotostock

Nishapur, Bukhara, and Samarkand were long-established commercial centers, and they made it possible for Muslim merchants to trade over a revived Silk Roads network extending from China in the east to the Mediterranean in the west. Thus Muslim merchants were able to take advantage of the extensive road networks originally built during the ancient era by imperial authorities in India, Persia, and the Mediterranean basin. Umayyad and Abbasid rulers maintained the roads that they inherited because they provided splendid routes for military forces and administrative officials traveling through the *dar al-Islam*. But those same roads also made excellent highways for merchants as well as missionaries and pilgrims. Travel along the roads could be remarkably speedy and efficient. After the tenth century, for example, the Muslim rulers of Egypt regularly imported ice from the mountains of Syria to their palace in Cairo. Even during the summer months, they received five camel loads of ice weekly to cool their food and drink.

**Camels and Caravans** Overland trade traveled mostly by camel caravan. Although they can be difficult to manage, camels endure the rigors of desert travel much better than oxen, horses, or donkeys. Moreover, when fitted with a well-designed saddle, camels can carry heavy loads. During the early centuries C.E., the manufacture of camel saddles spread throughout Arabia, north Africa, southwest Asia, and central Asia, and camels became the favored beasts of burden in deserts and other dry regions. As camel transport became more common, the major cities of the Islamic world and central Asia built and maintained caravanserais—inns offering lodging for caravan merchants as well as food, water, and care for their animals.

**Maritime Trade** Meanwhile, innovations in nautical technology contributed to a steadily increasing volume of maritime trade in the Red Sea, Persian Gulf, Arabian Sea, and Indian Ocean. Arab and Persian mariners borrowed the compass from its Chinese inventors and used it to guide them on the high seas. From southeast Asian and Indian mariners, they borrowed the lateen sail, a triangular sail that increased a ship's maneuverability. From the Hellenistic Mediterranean they borrowed the astrolabe, an instrument that enabled them to calculate latitude.

Thus equipped, Arab and Persian mariners ventured throughout the Indian Ocean basin, calling at ports from southern China to southeast Asia, Ceylon, India, Persia, Arabia, and the eastern coast of Africa. The twelfth-century Persian merchant Ramisht of Siraf (a flourishing port city on the Persian Gulf) amassed a huge fortune from long-distance trading ventures. One of Ramisht's clerks once returned to Siraf from a commercial voyage to China with a cargo worth half a million dinars—gold coins that were the standard currency in the Islamic world. Ramisht himself was one of the wealthiest men of his age, and he spent much of his fortune on pious causes. He outfitted the Ka'ba with a Chinese silk cover that reportedly cost him eighteen thousand dinars, and he also founded a hospital and a religious sanctuary in Mecca.

## INTERPRETING IMAGES

A map produced in the eleventh century by the Arab geographer al-Idrisi shows the lands known and reported by Muslim merchants and travelers. Note that, in accordance with Muslim cartographic convention, this map places south at the top and north at the bottom.

**Analyze** *Why did Muslim cartographers place the south at the top of the map and the north at the bottom? How might this understanding affect the ways that Muslim thinkers perceived the world they traveled and lived in?*

World History Archive/Alamy Stock Photo

**Banks** Banking also stimulated the commercial economy of the Islamic world. Banks had operated since antiquity, but Islamic banks of the Abbasid period conducted business on a much larger scale and provided a more extensive range of services than did their predecessors. They not only lent money to entrepreneurs but also served as brokers for investments and exchanged different currencies. They established multiple branches that honored letters of credit known as ***sakk***—the root of the modern word *check*—drawn on the parent bank. Thus merchants could draw letters of credit in one city and cash them in another, and they could settle accounts with distant business partners without having to deal in cash.

**The Organization of Trade** Trade benefited also from techniques of business organization. Like banking, these techniques had precedents in ancient Mediterranean society,

## INTERPRETING IMAGES

In this thirteenth-century manuscript illustration, merchants at a slave market in southern Arabia deal in black slaves captured in sub-Saharan Africa. Slaves traded in Islamic markets also came from Russia and eastern Europe.

**Analyze** *What were the central characteristics of the Arab Slave Trade? How would you describe this depiction of the Arab slave trade?*

akg-images/Newscom

but increasing volumes of trade enabled entrepreneurs to refine their methods of organization. Furthermore, Islamic law provided security for entrepreneurs by explicitly recognizing certain forms of business organization. Usually, Islamic businessmen preferred not to embark on solo ventures because an individual could face financial ruin if an entire cargo of commodities fell prey to pirates or went down with a ship that sank in a storm. Instead, like their counterparts in other contemporary societies, Abbasid entrepreneurs often pooled their resources in group investments. If several individuals invested in several cargoes, they could distribute their risks and more easily absorb losses. Furthermore, if several groups of investors rented cargo space on several different ships, they spread their risks even more. Entrepreneurs entered into a variety of legally recognized joint endeavors during the Abbasid caliphate. Some involved simply the investment of money in an enterprise, whereas others called for some or all of the partners to play active roles in their business ventures.

As a result of improved transportation, expanded banking services, and refined techniques of business organization, long-distance trade surged in the early Islamic world. Muslim merchants dealt in silk and ceramics from China, spices and aromatics from India and southeast Asia, and jewelry and fine textiles from the Byzantine Empire. Merchants also ventured beyond settled societies in China, India, and the Mediterranean basin to distant lands that previously had not engaged systematically in long-distance trade. They crossed the Sahara desert by camel caravan to trade salt, steel, copper, and glass for gold and slaves from the kingdoms of west Africa. They visited the coastal regions of east Africa, where they obtained slaves and exotic local commodities such as animal skins. They engaged in trade with Russia and Scandinavia by way of the Dnieper and Volga rivers and obtained high-value commodities such as animal skins, furs, honey, amber, and slaves as well as bulk goods such as timber and livestock. The vigorous economy of the Abbasid empire thus helped to establish networks of communication and exchange throughout much of the eastern hemisphere.

**Al-Andalus** The prosperity of Islamic Spain, known as **al-Andalus,** illustrates the far-reaching effects of long-distance trade during the Abbasid era. Most of the Iberian peninsula had fallen into the hands of Muslim Berber conquerors from north Africa during the early eighth century. The governors of al-Andalus were Umayyads who refused to recognize the Abbasid dynasty, and beginning in the tenth century they styled themselves caliphs in their own right rather than governors subject to Abbasid authority. Despite political and diplomatic tensions, al-Andalus participated actively in the commercial life of the larger Islamic world. The merchant-scholar al-Marwani of Córdoba, for example, made his hajj in 908 and then traveled to Iraq and India on commercial ventures. His profits amounted to thirty thousand dinars—all of which he lost in a shipwreck during his return home.

Imported crops increased the supply of food and enriched the diet of al-Andalus, enabling merchants and manufacturers to conduct thriving businesses in cities such as Córdoba, Toledo, and Seville. Ceramics, painted tiles, lead crystal, and gold jewelry from al-Andalus enjoyed a reputation for excellence and helped pay for imported goods and the building of a magnificent capital city at Córdoba. During the tenth century, Córdoba had more than 16 kilometers (10 miles) of lighted public roads as well as free Islamic schools, a gargantuan mosque, and a splendid library with four hundred thousand volumes.

**al-Andalus** (ahl ahn-duh-LUHS)

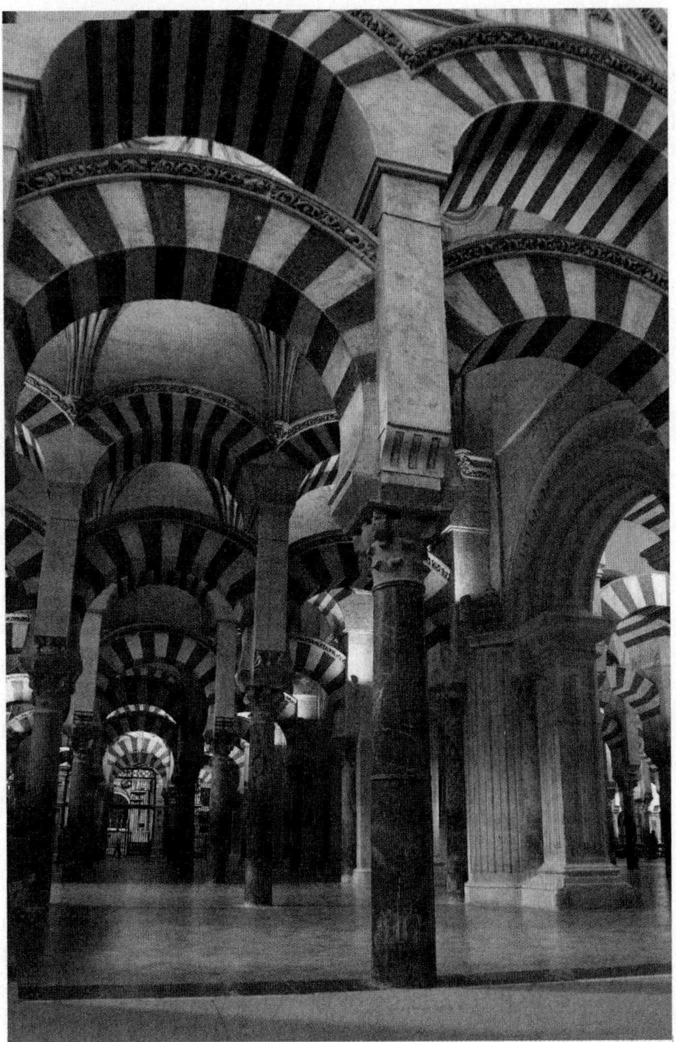

Interior of the mosque at Córdoba, originally built in the late eighth century and enlarged during the ninth and tenth centuries. One of the largest structures in the *dar al-Islam*, the mosque rests on 850 columns and features nineteen aisles.
Fernando Fernandez/age fotostock

## The Changing Status of Women

A patriarchal society had emerged in Arabia long before Muhammad's time, but Arab women enjoyed rights not accorded to women in many other lands. They could legally inherit property, divorce husbands on their own initiative, and engage in business ventures. Khadija, the first of Muhammad's wives, managed a successful commercial business.

In some respects the Quran enhanced the security of women in Arabian society. It outlawed female infanticide, and it provided that dowries went directly to brides rather than to their husbands and male guardians. It portrayed women not as the property of male guardians but as honorable individuals, equal to men before Allah, with their own rights and needs. Muhammad's kindness and generosity toward his wives, as related in early accounts of the prophet's life, also served as an example that may have improved the lives of Muslim women.

**The Quran and Women** For the most part, however, the Quran—and later the sharia as well—reinforced male dominance. The Quran and Islamic holy law recognized descent through the male line, and to guarantee proper inheritance, they placed a high premium on genealogical purity. To ensure the legitimacy of heirs, they subjected the social and sexual lives of women to the strict control of male guardians—fathers, brothers, and husbands. Though teaching that men should treat women with sensitivity and respect, the Quran and the sharia permitted men to take up to four wives, whereas women could have only one husband. The Quran and the sharia thus provided a religious and legal foundation for a decisively patriarchal society.

**Veiling of Women** When Islam expanded into the Byzantine and Sasanian empires, it encountered strong patriarchal traditions, and Muslims readily adopted long-standing customs such as the veiling of women. Social and family pressures had induced upper-class urban women to veil themselves in Mesopotamia as early as the thirteenth century B.C.E., and long before Muhammad the practice of veiling had spread to Persia and the eastern Mediterranean. As a sign of modesty, upper-class urban women covered their faces and ventured outside their homes only in the company of servants or chaperones so as to discourage the attention of men. When Muslim Arabs conquered Mesopotamia, Persia, and eastern Mediterranean lands, they adopted the veiling of women.

The Quran served as the preeminent source of authority in the world of Islam, and it provided specific rights for Muslim women. Over the centuries, however, jurists and legal scholars interpreted the Quran in ways that progressively limited those rights and placed women increasingly under the control of male guardians. To a large extent the increased emphasis on male authority in Islamic law reflected the influence of the strongly hierarchical and patriarchal societies of Mesopotamia, Persia, and eastern Mediterranean lands as Islam developed from a local faith to a large-scale complex society.

# ISLAMIC VALUES AND CULTURAL EXCHANGES

Since the seventh century C.E., the Quran has served as the cornerstone of Islamic society. Arising from a rich tradition of bedouin poetry and song, the Quran established Arabic as a flexible and powerful medium of communication. Even today Muslims regard the Arabic text of the Quran as the only definitive and reliable scripture: translations do not possess the power and authority of the original. When carrying their faith to new lands during the era of Islamic expansion, Muslim missionaries spread the message of Allah and provided instruction in the

In this manuscript illustration a Muslim teacher (the figure with the open book) instructs students in a library near Baghdad in the fine points of Islamic law.

DEA Picture Library/Getty Images

Quran's teachings, although usually they also permitted continued observance of pre-Islamic traditions. Muslim intellectuals drew freely from the long-established cultural traditions of Persia, India, and Greece, which they became acquainted with during the Umayyad and Abbasid eras.

## The Formation of an Islamic Cultural Tradition

Muslim theologians and jurists looked to the Quran, stories about Muhammad's life, and other sources of Islamic doctrine in their efforts to formulate moral guidelines appropriate for their society. The body of civil and criminal law embodied in the sharia provided a measure of cultural unity for the vastly different lands of the Islamic world. Islamic law did not by any means erase the differences, but it established a common cultural foundation that facilitated dealings between peoples of various Islamic lands and that lent substance to the concept of the *dar al-Islam.*

**Promotion of Islamic Values** On a more popular level, *ulama, qadis,* missionaries, and Muslim traders helped to bridge differences in cultural traditions and to spread Islamic values throughout the *dar al-Islam. Ulama* and *qadis* held positions at all Islamic courts, and they were prominent in the public life of all cities in the Islamic world. By resolving disputes according to Islamic law and ordering public observance of Islamic social and moral standards, they brought the values of the Quran and the sharia into the lives of peoples living far from the birthplace of Islam.

Formal educational institutions also promoted Islamic values. Many mosques maintained schools that provided an elementary education and religious instruction, for both girls and boys, and wealthy Muslims sometimes established schools and provided endowments for their support. By the tenth century institutions of higher education known as ***madrasas*** had begun to appear, and by the twelfth century they had become established in the major cities of the Islamic world. Muslim rulers often supported the madrasas in the interests of recruiting literate and learned students with an advanced education in Islamic theology and law for administrative positions. Inexpensive paper enhanced scholars' ability to instruct students and disseminate their views.

**Sufis** Among the most effective Islamic missionaries were mystics known as Sufis, a community that included both men and women. The term ***Sufi*** probably came from the patched woolen garments favored by the mystics. Sufis did not deny Islamic doctrine, and indeed many of them had an advanced education in Islamic theology and law. But they also did not find formal religious teachings to be especially meaningful. Thus, instead of concerning themselves with fine points of doctrine, Sufis worked to deepen their spiritual awareness. Most Sufis led pious and ascetic lives. Some devoted themselves to helping the poor. A few gave up their possessions and lived as mendicant beggars. Many sought a mystical, ecstatic union with Allah, relying on rousing sermons, passionate singing, or spirited dancing to bring them to a state of high emotion. Muslim theologians sometimes mistrusted Sufis, fearing that in their lack of concern for doctrine they would adopt erroneous beliefs. Nevertheless, after the ninth century Sufis became increasingly popular in Muslim societies because of their piety, devotion, and eagerness to minister to the needs of their fellow human beings.

**Al-Ghazali** Most important of the early Sufis was the Persian theologian al-Ghazali (1058–1111), who argued that human reason was too frail to understand the nature of Allah and hence could not explain the mysteries of the world. Only through devotion and guidance from the Quran could human beings begin to appreciate the uniqueness and power of Allah. Indeed, al-Ghazali held that philosophy and human reasoning were vain

**madrasas** (MAH-drahs-uhs)
**Sufi** (SOO-fee)

pursuits that would inevitably lead to confusion rather than understanding.

**Sufi Missionaries** Sufis were especially effective as missionaries because they emphasized devotion to Allah above mastery of doctrine. They sometimes encouraged individuals to revere Allah in their own ways, even if those ways did not have a basis in the Quran. They tolerated the continued observance of pre-Islamic customs, for example, as well as the association of Allah with deities recognized and revered in other faiths. The Sufis themselves led ascetic and holy lives, which won them the respect of the peoples to whom they preached. Because of their kindness, holiness, tolerance, and charismatic appeal, Sufis attracted numerous converts particularly in lands such as Persia and India, where long-established religious faiths such as Zoroastrianism, Christianity, Buddhism, and Hinduism had enjoyed a mass following for centuries.

## How the Past Shapes the Future 

### The Spread of Religious Traditions

As we saw in chapter 1, the first millennium of the Common Era was marked by the spread of religious traditions—including Islam—well beyond their regions of origin. In the case of Islam, people (including *qadis* and *ulama* who were trained in interpreting sharia law), institutions (including madrasas and mosques), and the Arabic languages (as expressed in the Quran) provided multiple avenues for the diffusion of Islamic values to areas distant from its birthplace in the Arabian peninsula. Consider the long-term legacies of this common religious foundation—even in the absence of a unified Islamic state—across the *dar al-Islam*. How might this common religious foundation have affected political relationships, cultural developments, or the movement of products and people within the *dar al-Islam* over the long term? How might it have affected relationships between Islamic regions and non-Islamic regions? And to what extent does the early expansion of Islam throughout large regions of Afro-Eurasia continue to affect politics and culture in the world of the twenty-first century?

**Hajj** The symbol of Islamic cultural unity was the Ka'ba at Mecca, which from an early date attracted pilgrims from all parts of the Islamic world. The Abbasid caliphs especially encouraged observance of the hajj: they saw themselves as supreme leaders of a cohesive Islamic community, and as a matter of policy they sought to enhance the cultural unity of their realm. They built inns along the main roads to Mecca for the convenience of travelers, policed the routes to ensure the safety of pilgrims, and made lavish gifts to shrines and sites of pilgrimage. Individuals from far-flung regions of the Abbasid empire made their way to Mecca, visited the holy sites, and learned firsthand the traditions of Islam. Over the centuries those pilgrims spread Islamic beliefs and values to all parts of the Islamic world, and with the work of *ulama, qadis,* and Sufi missionaries, their efforts helped to make the *dar al-Islam* not just a name but also a reality.

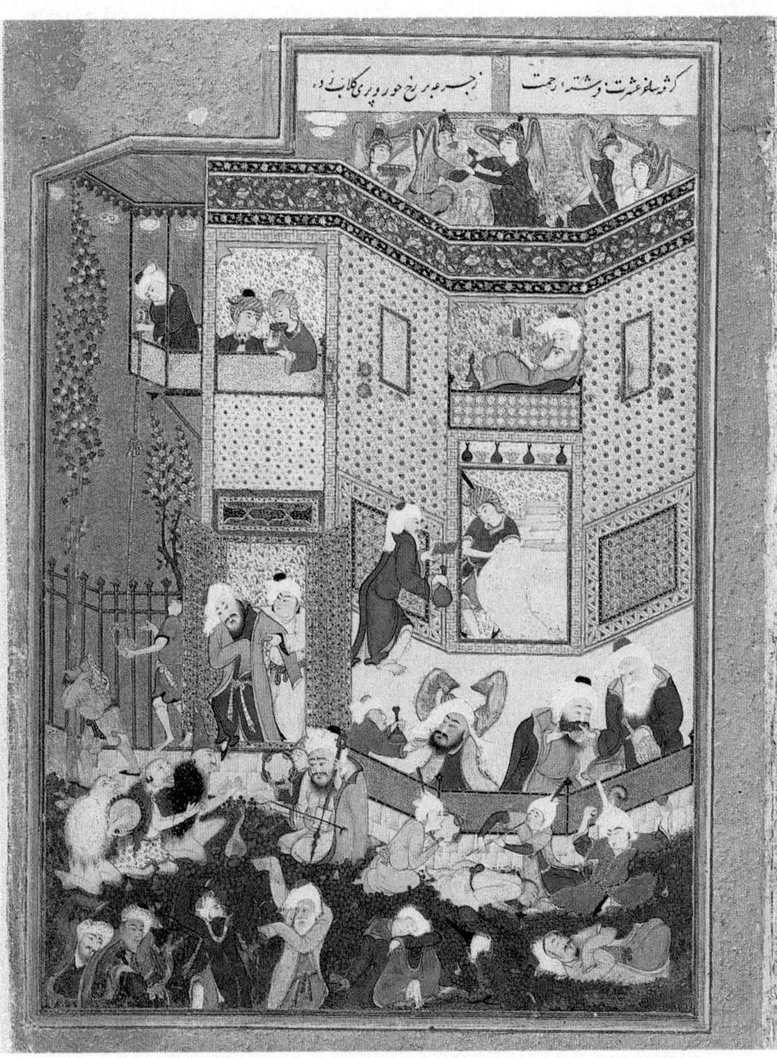

Through song, dance, and ecstatic experiences, sometimes enhanced by wine, Persian Sufis expressed their devotion to Allah, as in this sixteenth-century painting. How did Sufis facilitate the spread of Islam beyond Arabia?
Harvard Art Museums, Arthur M. Sackler Museum, promised Gift of Mr. and Mrs. Stuart Cary Welch, jr. Partially owned by the Metropolitan Museum of Art and the Arthur M. Sackler Museum, Harvard University, 1998. In honor of the students of Harvard University and Radcliffe college, 1988.460.3. Photo: Allan Macintyre. ©President and Fellows of Harvard College

# CONNECTING THE SOURCES

## Sufi mysticism and the appeal of Islam

**The problem** Although Muslim armies conquered vast territories in central and southwest Asia, north Africa, and Iberia in the century after Muhammad's death in 632 C.E., conquest alone cannot explain why so many people in the *dar al-Islam* made sincere and lasting conversions to Islam. Many individuals converted to Islam because of its profound spiritual appeal, made especially popular by Sufi mystics who often served as missionaries. While all Muslims believed that individuals would become close to God in the afterlife, Sufi mystics preached that it was possible to grow close to God while one was still alive if only individuals would surrender themselves, in love, to God. For Sufis, the key to surrendering to and loving God was learning to gain control over one's own ego, which they termed the "greater jihad," or *al-jihad al-akbar* (as opposed to the "lesser jihad," or *al-jihad al-asghar*, of fighting oppressors or injustice). Sufis taught, in short, that the path to God was a path of love, and that this path was open to all who wished to follow.

Below are two excerpts from texts written by well-known and influential Sufi mystics: Rabi'a al-'Addawiyya, a woman from Basra (modern Iraq) who lived from about 717 to 801 C.E., and Abu Hamid al-Ghazali, a man from Khorasan (modern Iran) who lived from 1058 to 1128 C.E. As you read the documents, think about the reasons their writings might have appealed to contemporaries and to generations who came after them.

**The documents** Read the documents below, and consider carefully the questions that follow.

### Document 1:

*Rabi'a al-'Adawiyya was an early Sufi saint and is the best-known woman Sufi mystic in Islamic history. She was sold into slavery as a child, but was reportedly freed later in life because of her religious devotion. She was known for her celibate and ascetic lifestyle and for her passionate devotion to the love of God. Rabi'a herself did not publish any of her poetry or writings, but they were later collected and printed by Faridu d'Din Attar in the thirteenth century. The following is one of the poems attributed to her.*

*O Lord,*
*If tomorrow on Judgment Day*
*You send me to Hell,*
*I will tell such a secret*
*That Hell will race from me*
*Until it is a thousand years away.*

Depiction of Rabi'a grinding grain.
The History Collection/Alamy Stock Photo

*O Lord,*
*Whatever share of this world*
*You could give to me,*
*Give it to Your enemies;*
*Whatever share of the next world*
*You want to give to me,*
*Give it to Your friends.*
*You are enough for me.*

*O Lord,*
*If I worship You*
*From fear of Hell, burn me in Hell.*

*O Lord,*
*If I worship You*
*From hope of Paradise, bar me from its gates.*

*But if I worship You for Yourself alone*
*Then grace me forever the splendor of Your Face.*

How does Rabi'ai's understanding of Allah compare to Christian conceptions of their God?

## Document 2:

*Abu Hamid al-Ghazali was one of the most important Sufi philosophers and Muslim theologians. As a young man he became a professor at Nizamiyah University in Baghdad, but spiritual transformation caused him to give up the academic life for a life of asceticism, reflection, and writing. He wrote numerous important works seeking to balance the rationalism of Greek philosophy with spiritualism derived from Sufi mysticism. The following selection is taken from his Alchemy of Happiness, originally published in the early twelfth century.*

***On the Love of God***

*O traveller on the way and seeker after the love of God! know that the love of God is a sure and perfect method for the believer to attain the object of his desires. It is a highly exalted station of rest, during the journey of the celestial traveler. It is the consummation of the desires and longings of those who seek divine truth. It is the foundation of the vision of the beauty of the Lord.*

*The love of God is of the most binding obligation upon every one. It is indeed the spirit of the body, and the light of the eye.*

*The prophet of God declares that the faith of the believer is not complete, unless he loves God and his prophet more than all the world besides. The prophet was once asked, what is faith? He replied, "It is to love God and his prophet more than wife, children and property." And the prophet was continually in the habit of praying, "O my God! I ask for thy love, I ask that I may love whomsoever loves thee, and that I may perform whatsoever thy love makes incumbent upon me."*

*On the resurrection day all sects will be addressed by the name of the prophet whom each followed, "O people of Moses! O people of Jesus! O people of Mohammed!" even to all the beloved servants of God, and it will be proclaimed to them, "O Friends and beloved of God, come to the blessed union and society of God! Come to Paradise and partake of the grace of your beloved!" When they hear this proclamation, their hearts will leap out of their places, and they will almost lose their reason. Yahya ben Moa'z says, "It is better to have as much love of God, even if only as much as a grain of mustard seed, than seventy years of devotion and obedience without love." Hassan of Basra says, "Whoever knows God, will certainly love him, and whoever knows the world, will shun it."*

What does the author mean by stating that whoever knows the world will shun it?

. . .

*O! seeker of divine love, that which renders man favorably inclined to persons of virtuous character, is the fact that God has created man after his own character; as it has come to us in the tradition that, "verily God created man after his own image." Hence whenever man sees or hears of a quality belonging to his own race and kind, as justice, generosity, forgiveness or patience, he will certainly have a sympathy with that quality and exercise love to its possessor. If we hear for instance that in a certain country there is a just sovereign or a just vizier, we heartily love that king or vizier, and we are always praising his excellence and worth, although there is not the least probability of any advantage accruing to us from his justice. If we hear of a generous man, although he may be in a foreign country, and we have no hope of any advantage from him or of any token of his generosity to ourselves, yet still from necessity we will love him, and whenever his name is mentioned we will invoke blessings upon him and praise him. It is thus with Hatem Tai whose name, though he was an infidel, is upon every tongue, because he was a generous and benevolent man, and all hearts are irresistibly led to love him. . . .*

*(Continued)*

*We see then that the love we bear to persons endowed with the virtuous qualities of man, is not bestowed by us for the sake of any fancied advantage from them or any hope of gain, but that on the contrary it is because the spirits of men are created in correspondence with the character of God, and when we see a trace or mark of a quality or affection of a kind like our own, we cannot help being attracted towards it, and must necessarily love it.*

### Questions

1. What can these sources definitively tell you about the lives of the people who produced them? Are there any actual biographical details contained in these sources?
2. In Document 1, how does the fact that Rabi'a was a woman complicate our understanding of the role of women in Islam in the century after Muhammad's death?
3. In Document 2, how does al-Ghazali's view of loving other people, even non-Moslems (or infidels), compare with common contemporary visions of Islam as a "religion of the sword"?
4. For both documents, how might these exhortations about loving God have appealed to individuals coming into contact with them for the first time?
5. To what extent can sources such as these help historians understand the spiritual dimensions of conversion to Islam, especially when read in conjunction with other textual and material evidence?

*Source Websites:* **Document 1:** Perfume of the Desert: Inspirations from Sufi Wisdom. Translated by Andrew Harvey and Eryk Hanut. Illinois: Quest Books, 1999. This material was reproduced by permission of Quest Books, the imprint of the Theosophical Publishing House(www.questbook.net). **Document 2:** Ghazali, Al. The Alchemy of Happiness. Translated by Henry Augustus Homes. New York: J. Munsell, 1873.

## Islam and the Cultural Traditions of Persia, India, and Greece

As the Islamic community expanded, Muslims of Arab ancestry interacted regularly with peoples from other cultural traditions, especially those of Persia, India, and Greece. In some cases, particularly in lands ruled by the Umayyad and Abbasid dynasties, large numbers of conquered peoples converted to Islam, and they brought elements of their inherited cultural traditions into Islamic society. In other cases, particularly in lands beyond the authority of Islamic rulers, Muslims became acquainted with the literary, artistic, philosophical, and scientific traditions of peoples who chose not to convert. Nevertheless, their traditions often held considerable interest for Muslims, who adapted them for their own purposes.

**Translators and Travelers** Muslims learned about different cultural traditions in several ways. The Abbasid dynasty officially supported the effort to acquire knowledge from other societies by inviting foreign scholars to the court at Baghdad and sponsoring translations of literary and scientific works from Greek, Latin, and Sanskrit into Arabic and Persian languages. By the tenth century Muslim as well as Jewish, Christian, and Zoroastrian translators had made a massive library of foreign knowledge available to Muslims. Meanwhile, Muslim merchants, missionaries, and other travelers compiled the most comprehensive body of geographic information ever assembled before European mariners made their way to all parts of the world after 1492. Drawing on Greek and Roman geographic knowledge as well as contemporary travelers' reports, Muslim geographers and cartographers produced maps, atlases, sea charts, and general descriptions of the world known to them, which included much of the eastern hemisphere. Particularly during its early centuries, the world of Islam was remarkably open to knowledge and ideas from other societies.

Arab physicians made note of medicines used in Persian, Indian, and Greek societies and added more of their own. In this manuscript illustration, a physician instructs a pharmacist in the preparation of medicines.
myLAM/Alamy Stock Photo

# INTERPRETING IMAGES

An illustration from a thirteenth-century Arabic-language manuscript depicts the Greek philosopher Aristotle teaching three students about the astrolabe, an instrument that enabled the user to determine latitude.

**Analyze** *Consider this image as well as the one on the previous page. In what ways did Persia, India, and Greece influence the culture and technology of the Arab world?*

DEA/G. Dagli Orti/Getty Images

**Persian Influences on Islam** Persian traditions quickly found a place in Islamic society because the culturally rich land of Persia fell under Islamic rule at an early date. Especially after the establishment of the Abbasid dynasty and the founding of its capital at Baghdad, Persian traditions deeply influenced Islamic political and cultural leaders. Persian administrative techniques, which Muslim conquerors borrowed from the Sasanid empire, were crucial for the organization of the imperial structure through which Umayyad and Abbasid rulers governed their vast empire. Meanwhile, Persian ideas of kingship profoundly influenced Islamic political thought. Muslim caliphs and regional governors drew readily on Persian views of kings as wise and benevolent but nonetheless absolute rulers.

Persian influence was also noticeable in literary works from the Abbasid dynasty. Although Arabic served as the language of religion, theology, philosophy, and law, Persian was the principal language of literature, poetry, history, and political reflection. The verses of Omar Khayyam titled the ***Rubaiyat*** ("quatrains") are widely known to western audiences because of a popular English translation by the Victorian poet Edward Fitzgerald, but many other writers composed works that in Persian display even greater literary elegance and originality. The marvelous collection of stories known as *The Arabian Nights,* or *The Thousand and One Nights,* for example, presented popular tales of adventure and romance set in the Abbasid empire and the court of Harun al-Rashid.

**Indian Influences on Islam** Indian mathematics, science, and medicine captured the attention of Arab and Persian Muslims who established Islamic states in northern India. The sophisticated mathematical tradition of Gupta India was attractive to Muslims both as a field of scholarship and for the practical purposes of reckoning and keeping accounts. Muslims readily adopted what they called "Hindi" numerals, which European peoples later called "Arabic" numerals, because they learned about them through Arab Muslims. Hindi numerals enabled Muslim scholars to develop an impressive tradition of advanced mathematics, concentrating on algebra (an Arabic word) as well as trigonometry and geometry. From a more practical point of view, Indian numerals vastly simplified bookkeeping for Muslim merchants working in the lively commercial economy of the Abbasid dynasty.

Muslims also found much to appreciate in the scientific and medical thought they encountered in India. With the aid of their powerful and flexible mathematics, Indian scholars were able to carry out precise astronomical calculations, which helped inspire the development of Muslim astronomy. Similarly, Indian medicine appealed to Muslims because of its treatments for specific ailments and its use of antidotes for poisons. Muslim visitors often railed against Indian religious beliefs—both Hindu and Buddhist—but they uniformly praised Indian mathematical, scientific, and medical thought, which they avidly adopted for their own uses and purposes.

**Greek Influences on Islam** Muslims also admired the philosophical, scientific, and medical writings of classical Greece. They became especially interested in Plato and Aristotle, whose works they translated and interpreted in commentaries. During the tenth and eleventh centuries, some Muslim philosophers sought to synthesize Greek and Muslim

Fourteenth-century illustration of an imaginary debate between Averroes and third-century philosopher Porphyry, by Monfredo de Monte Imperiali Liber de herbis, 14th century
FLHC 90/Alamy Stock Photo

thought by harmonizing Plato with the teachings of Islam. They encountered resistance among conservative theologians such as the Sufi al-Ghazali, who considered Greek philosophy a completely unreliable guide to ultimate truth because it relied on frail human reason rather than on the revelation of the Quran.

Partly in response to al-Ghazali's attacks, twelfth-century Muslim philosophers turned their attention more to Aristotle than to Plato. The most notable figure in this development was **Ibn Rushd** (1126–1198), *qadi* of Seville in the caliphate of Córdoba, who followed Aristotle in seeking to articulate a purely rational understanding of the world. Ibn Rushd's work not only helped to shape Islamic philosophy but also found its way to the schools and universities of western Europe, where Christian scholars knew Ibn Rushd as Averroes. During the thirteenth century his work profoundly influenced the development of scholasticism, the effort of medieval European philosophers to harmonize Christianity with Aristotelian thought.

Ibn Rushd's reliance on natural reason went too far for many Muslims, who placed more value on the revelations of the Quran than on the fruits of human logic. After the thirteenth century, Muslim philosophers and theologians who dominated the madrasas drew inspiration more from Islamic sources than from Greek philosophy. Platonic and Aristotelian influences did not disappear, but they lost favor in official seats of learning and fell increasingly under the shadow of teachings from the Quran and Sufi mystics. As they did with political and cultural traditions from Persia and India, Muslim thinkers absorbed Greek philosophy, reconsidered it, and used it to advance the interests of their society.

Quite apart from philosophy, Greek mathematics, science, and medicine appealed strongly to Muslims. Like their Indian counterparts, scholars in classical Greek and Hellenistic societies had developed elaborate traditions of scientific thought. Greek mathematics did not make use of Indian numerals, but it offered a solid body of powerful reasoning, particularly when dealing with calculations in algebra and geometry. Greek mathematics supported the development of astronomical and geographical scholarship, and studies of anatomy and physiology served as foundations for medical thought. Muslim scholars quickly absorbed those Greek traditions, combined them with influences from India, and used them all as points of departure for their studies. The result was a brilliant flowering of mathematical, scientific, and medical scholarship that provided Muslim societies with powerful tools for understanding the natural world.

**Ibn Rushd** (IB-uhn RUSHED)

## CONCLUSION

The prophet Muhammad did not intend to found a new religion. Instead, his intention was to express his convictions about Allah and perfect the teachings of earlier Jewish and Christian prophets by announcing a revelation more comprehensive than those Allah had entrusted to his predecessors. His message soon attracted a circle of devout and committed disciples, and by the time of his death most of Arabia had accepted Islam. During the two centuries following the prophet's death, Arab conquerors and missionaries spread Islam throughout southwest Asia and north Africa and introduced their faith to central Asia, India, the Mediterranean islands, and Iberia. This rapid expansion of Islam encouraged the development of an extensive trade and communication network: merchants, diplomats, and other travelers moved easily throughout the Islamic world exchanging goods and introducing agricultural crops to new lands. Rapid expansion also led to encounters between Islam and long-established religious and cultural traditions such as Hinduism, Judaism, Zoroastrianism, Christianity, Persian literature and political thought, and classical Greek philosophy and science. Muslim thinkers readily adapted those earlier traditions to their needs. As a result of its expansion, its extensive trade and communication networks, and its engagement with other religious and cultural traditions, the *dar al-Islam* became one of the most prosperous and cosmopolitan societies of Afro-Eurasia during the first millennium and a half of the common era.

## STUDY TERMS

Abbasid dynasty (79)
Abu Bakr (77)
al-Andalus (84)
Allah (82)
bedouin (71)
caliph (77)
*dar al-Islam* (71)
Five Pillars of Islam (76)
*hadith* (74)
hajj (69)
Harun al-Rashid (80)
*hijra* (74)
Ibn Rushd (92)
Islam (71)
jihad (76)
jizya (79)
Ka'ba (74)
madrasas (86)
Mecca (74)
Medina (74)
Muhammad (71)
Muslim (71)
*qadis* (80)
Quran (74)
*Rubaiyat* (91)
sakk (83)
sharia (76)
Shia (77)
Sufi (86)
Sunni (77)
*ulama* (80)
*umma* (74)
Umayyad dynasty (78)

## FOR FURTHER READING

Muhammad Manazir Ahsan. *Social Life under the Abbasids.* New York, 1979. Draws on a wide range of sources in discussing dress, food, drink, housing, and daily life during the Abbasid era.

Reza Aslan. *No God but God. The Origins, Evolution and Future of Islam.* New York, 2005. Offers a vivid and realistic account of the social and religious environment in which the Prophet Muhammad forged his message.

Jonathan P. Berkey. *The Formation of Islam: Religion and Society in the Near East, 600–1800.* Cambridge, 2003. Views the development of Islamic society in the context of relations among Muslims, Jews, and Christians.

John Esposito. *Islam: The Straight Path.* 3rd ed. New York, 2005. The best brief introduction to Islam.

Richard C. Foltz. *Spirituality in the Land of the Noble: How Iran Shaped the World's Religions.* Oxford, 2004. Includes an accessible discussion of Persian influences on the Islamic faith.

Ira M. Lapidus. *A History of Islamic Societies.* Cambridge, 1988. Authoritative survey of Islamic history, concentrating on social and cultural issues.

Ilse Lichtenstadter. *Introduction to Classical Arabic Literature.* New York, 1974. A brief overview, accompanied by an extensive selection of texts in English translation.

M. Lombard. *The Golden Age of Islam.* Princeton, 2004. Concentrates on the social and economic history of the Abbasid period.

*Al Qur'an: A Contemporary Translation.* Trans. by Ahmed Ali. Princeton, 1984. A sensitive translation of the holy book of Islam.

Francis Robinson, ed. *The Cambridge Illustrated History of the Islamic World.* Cambridge, 1996. An excellent and lavishly illustrated introduction to Islam and the Muslim world.

Michael Wolfe, ed. *One Thousand Roads to Mecca: Ten Centuries of Travelers Writing about the Muslim Pilgrimage.* New York, 1997. Presents selections from twenty-three accounts describing travelers' hajj experiences.

# CHAPTER 2 AP EXAM PRACTICE

Questions assume cumulative knowledge from this chapter and previous chapters.

## Section I

## Multiple Choice Questions

Use the image below and your knowledge of world history to answer questions 1 – 3.

A sixteenth-century Turkish manuscript depicts pilgrims praying at Mecca in the mosque surrounding the Ka'aba.
Leemage/Getty Images

1. Historians could use this image of Muslim pilgrims to
   (A) identify the individuals who went on pilgrimage to Mecca the year it was made.
   (B) show that wealthy pilgrims distributed charity while traveling to Mecca.
   (C) show that both men and women were obliged to practice the Five Pillars of Islam.
   (D) prove that only Turks were allowed to surround the Ka'ba during the pilgrimage.

2. What claims can be made based on the existence of a 16th century Turkish manuscript depicting the *hajj*?
   (A) The concept of the *dar-al-Islam* could expand to cultures beyond the Arab peninsula.
   (B) Only people who lived near Mecca went on pilgrimage.
   (C) Abbasid and Turkish rulers were in conflict over who controlled Mecca.
   (D) Turks were more accepting of women going on pilgrimage than Abbasid rulers had been.

3. What statement below describes the experience of going on pilgrimage?
   (A) It was a great burden on the poor who were required to go to Mecca when they could not afford it.
   (B) There was no specific season for pilgrimage. Pilgrims went to Mecca throughout the year.
   (C) Rulers did not want pilgrims in their cities.
   (D) While it was an act of devotion, it was also a time of great joy and festivities.

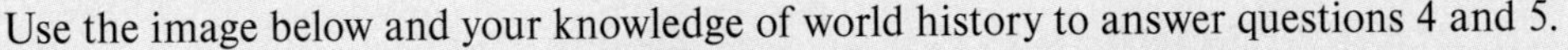

Use the image below and your knowledge of world history to answer questions 4 and 5.

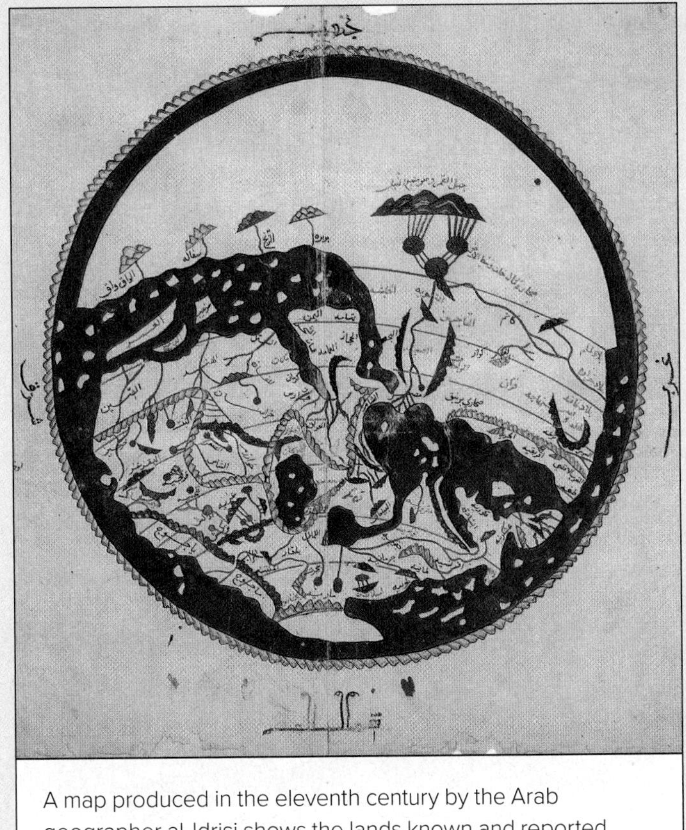

A map produced in the eleventh century by the Arab geographer al-Idrisi shows the lands known and reported by Muslim merchants and travelers.

World History Archive/Alamy Stock Photo

4. What does the existence of this map indicate about Islamic society?
   (A) Islamic books were printed upside down.
   (B) Muslim banks were had not yet developed letters of credit and could not fund exploration to sub-Saharan Africa.
   (C) Muslim cartographers defied Muhammed's rules against trade outside of the Arab peninsula.
   (D) The study of geography and cartography could be used to promote trade.

5. Based on this map and your knowledge of world history, what claims can be made about science and technology in the Islamic World?
   (A) Abbasid rulers shared new maps with Hindu and Confucian rulers in order to promote trade.
   (B) Nautical innovations improved transportation and made maritime trade more profitable.
   (C) South is at the top of the map because Islamic technology was primitive.
   (D) Al-Andalus (Islamic Spain) is small on this map because Muslim cartographers knew that things that are farther away appear smaller.

## Short Answer

6. Use the image below and your knowledge of world history to answer parts A, B, and C.

The early expansion of Islam was achieved largely through warfare. This illustration from an Arabic manuscript of the thirteenth century depicts a battle between Muhammad's cousin Ali and his adversaries.

Iberfoto/SuperStock

(A) Identify ONE religious belief or practice that makes Shia Islam different from Sunni Islam.
(B) Explain ONE political consequence of the death of Muhammad.
(C) Explain ONE way that the Ummayyad dynasty used religion to rule their empire.

7. Use this text selection and your knowledge of world history to answer parts A, B, and C.

> Verily men and women who have come to submission,
> Men and women who are believers,
> Men and women who are devout,
> Truthful men and women,
> Men and women with endurance,
> Men and women who are modest,
> Men and women who give alms,
> Men and women who observe fasting,
> Men and women who guard their private parts,
> And those men and women who remember God a great deal,
> For them God has forgiveness and a great reward
>
> **Source:** *Al-Qur'an: A Contemporary Translation.* Trans. by Ahmed Ali. Princeton: Princeton University Press, 1984, pp. 11, 358, 359, 540, 559.

(A) Identify ONE difference between the roles of men and women in Islamic society.
(B) Identify ONE similarity for men and women in Islam.
(C) Explain ONE reason why Islam might have appealed to women in the early centuries of Islamic history.

8. Use your understanding of world history to answer parts A, B, and C.
(A) Identify ONE way that the Islamic cultural traditions developed during the Abbasid caliphate.
(B) Explain ONE way that merchants contributed to cultural exchanges between the Islamic community and other peoples.
(C) Explain ONE reason why Islamic rulers supported trade with other countries.

# Section II

## Document-Based Question

Based on the following documents and your knowledge of world history, explain the role religion played in the development of the Abbasid state to 1258 C.E.

In your response you should do the following:

- Respond to the prompt with a historically defensible thesis or claim that establishes a line of reasoning.
- Describe a broader historical context relevant to the prompt.
- Support an argument in response to the prompt using all documents.
- Use at least one additional piece of specific historical evidence (beyond that found in the documents) relevant to an argument about the prompt.
- Explain how or why the document's point of view, purpose, historical situation, and /or audience is relevant to an argument.
- Use evidence to corroborate, qualify, or modify an argument that addresses the prompt.

### Document 1

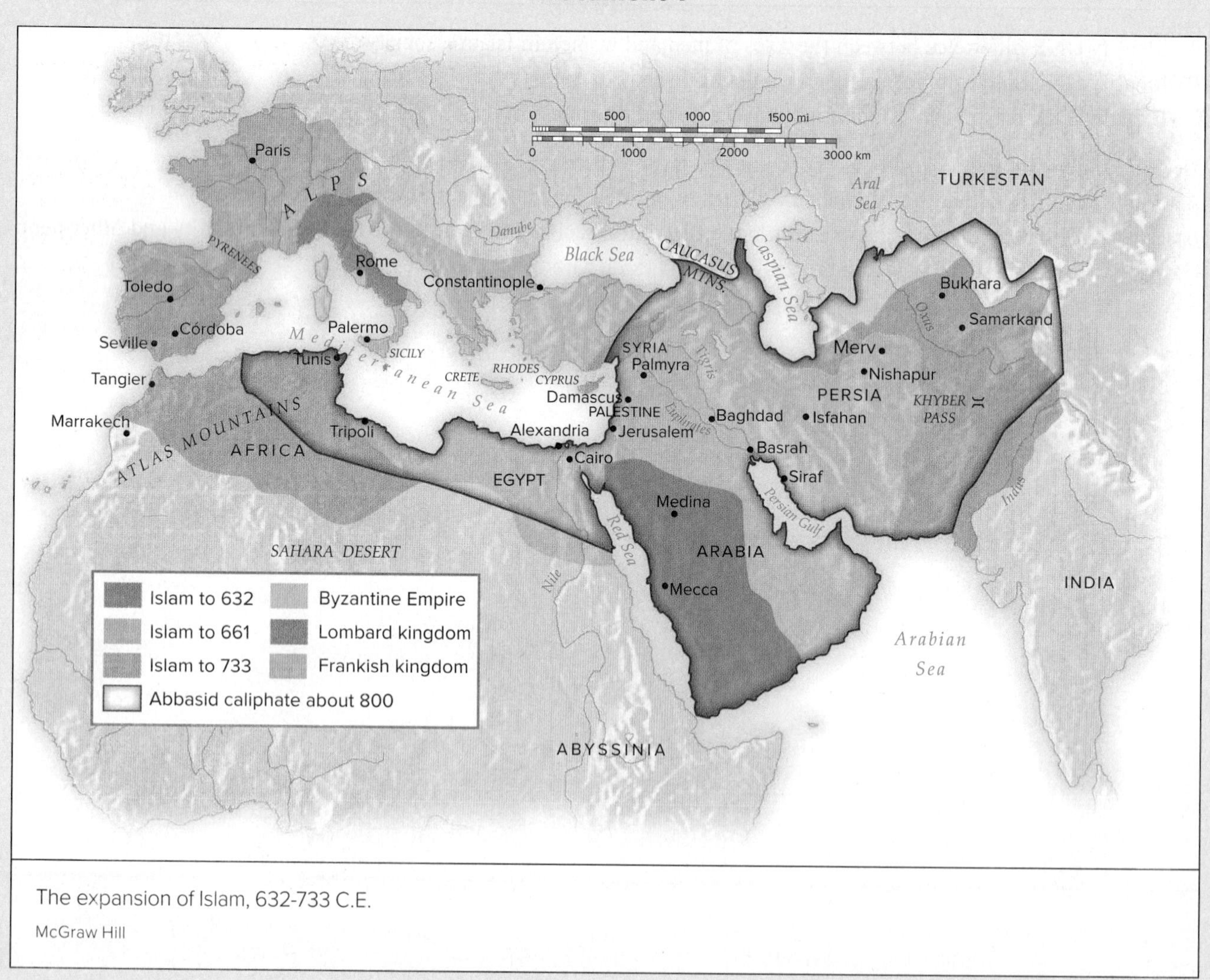


The expansion of Islam, 632-733 C.E.

McGraw Hill

## Document 2

The first millennium of the Common Era was marked by the spread of religious traditions—including Islam—well beyond their regions of origin. In the case of Islam, people (including *qadis* and *ulama* who were trained in interpreting sharia law), institutions (including madrasas and mosques), and the Arabic languages (as expressed in the Quran) provided multiple avenues for the diffusion of Islamic values to areas distant from its birthplace in the Arabian peninsula.

Bentley & Ziegler, *Traditions and Encounters: A Global Perspective on the Past*, pg. 289

## Document 3

On the resurrection day all sects will be addressed by the name of the prophet whom each followed, "O people of Moses! O people of Jesus! O people of Mohammed!" even to all the beloved servants of God, and it will be proclaimed to them, "O Friends and beloved of God, come to the blessed union and society of God! Come to Paradise and partake of the grace of your beloved!" When they hear this proclamation, their hearts will leap out of their places, and they will almost lose their reason.

Hamid al-Ghazali, *On the Love of God*

**Source:** Ghazali, Al. The Alchemy of Happiness. Translated by Henry Augustus Homes. New York: J. Munsell, 1873.

## Long Essay

Develop a thoughtful and thorough historical argument that answers the question below. Begin your essay with a thesis statement and support it with relevant historical evidence.

Using specific examples, write an essay that evaluates how the expansion of Islam during the Abbasid Caliphate (751-1258 C.E.) encouraged cultural and intellectual transfers.

Chapter 3

# India and the Indian Ocean Basin



## ZOOMING IN ON ENCOUNTERS

### Buzurg Sets His Sights on the Seven Seas

Buzurg ibn Shahriyar was a tenth-century shipmaster from Siraf, a prosperous and bustling port city on the Persian Gulf coast. He probably sailed frequently to Arabia and India, and he may have ventured also to Malaya, the islands of southeast Asia, China, and east Africa. Like all sailors, he heard stories about the distant lands that mariners had visited, the different customs they observed, and the adventures that befell them during their travels. About 953 C.E. he compiled 136 such stories in his *Book of the Wonders of India.*

Buzurg's collection included a generous proportion of tall tales. He told of a giant lobster that seized a ship's anchor and dragged the vessel through the water, of mermaids and sea dragons, of creatures born from human fathers and fish mothers who lived in human society but had flippers that enabled them to swim through the water like fish, of serpents that ate cattle and elephants, of birds so large that they crushed houses, of a monkey that seduced a sailor, and of a talking lizard. Yet alongside the tall tales, many of Buzurg's stories accurately reflected the conditions of his time. One recounted the story of a king from northern India who converted to Islam and requested translations of Islamic law. Others reported on Hindu customs, shipwrecks, encounters with pirates, and slave trading.

Several of Buzurg's stories tempted readers with visions of vast wealth attainable through maritime trade. Buzurg mentioned fine diamonds from Kashmir, pearls from Ceylon, and a merchant

An oceangoing dhow (commercial ship favored by Indian, Persian, and Arab sailors) off the coast of Zanzibar, Indian Ocean. Although this is a modern photograph, the design and sailing technique of dhows have changed little over the centuries.
Charles O. Cecil/Alamy Stock Photo

who left Persia penniless and returned from India and China with a shipload of priceless merchandise. Despite their embellishments and exaggerations, his stories faithfully reflected the trade networks that linked the lands surrounding the Indian Ocean in the tenth century. Although Buzurg clearly thought of India as a distinct land with its own customs, he also recognized a larger world of trade and communication that extended from east Africa to southeast Asia and beyond to China.

# CHAPTER FOCUS

- India had been without a centralized imperial state for a thousand years.
- Both Buddhism and Jainism originated in south Asia, but had since lost most of their support in the region.
- Hinduism remained the dominant religion in south Asia. It and the caste system were the only major continuities from south Asia's distant past.
- Significant similarities existed, however, between south Asia and both China and the Islamic caliphates in this period: increased agricultural production, population growth, increased urbanization, and enormous interregional trade.
- The subcontinent was centrally located in the Indian Ocean basin, and almost all the goods (and people) shipped from China to east Africa or the Mediterranean passed through a south Asian port.
- Some parts of the southeast Asia region were in China's tributary circle.
- Independent kingdoms' wealth was based on Indian Ocean trade networks. They were suppliers of luxury goods, or they collected taxes from passing merchant ships. When the monsoon winds were not blowing in the desired direction for sailing, these merchants set up what historians call diaspora communities—homes away from home—to wait for the winds and currents to change. They built Hindu temples and Islamic mosques, some married local women, and cultural syncretism began.

## Historical Developments

- Hinduism, Islam, and Buddhism, and their core beliefs and practices, continued to shape societies in South and Southeast Asia.
- State formation and development demonstrated continuity, innovation, and diversity, including the new Hindu and Buddhist states that emerged in South and Southeast Asia.

## Reasoning Processes

- **Comparison** Explain relevant similarities and/or differences in the spread of religions in India and in southeast Asia.
- **Continuity and Change** Explain the patterns of continuity and/or change facilitated by monsoon trade.

## Historical Thinking Skills

- **Developments and Processes** Explain the development of new kingdoms in India.
- **Source Claims and Evidence** Identify the evidence supporting the claim that India was well positioned as a center of trade and cross-cultural exchange in the Indian Ocean Basin.
- **Contextualization** Identify and describe the context of Islam's spread into the Indian Ocean Basin.
- **Making Connections** Explain the connection between monsoon trade networks and the spread of Islam and Hinduism in the Indian Ocean Basin and Southeast Asia.
- **Argumentation** Support the argument that "Indian Ocean Basin" is a better organizing principle than the separate geographic regions of south and southeast Asia.

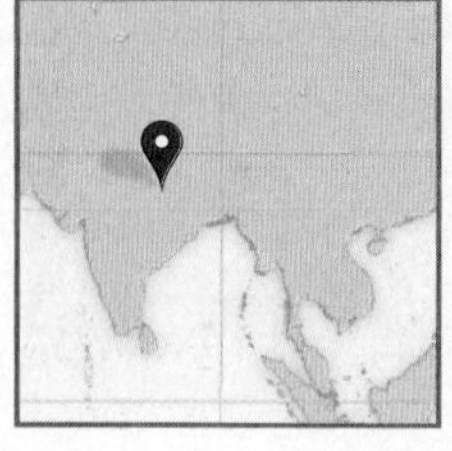

## CHAPTER OVERVIEW

Just as China served as the principal inspiration of a larger east Asian society in the first millennium of the Common Era, India influenced the development of a larger cultural zone in south and southeast Asia. Yet China and India played different roles in their respective spheres of influence. In east Asia, China was the dominant power, even if it did not always exercise authority directly over its neighbors. In south and southeast Asia, however, there emerged no centralized imperial authority like the Tang dynasty in China. Indeed, although several states organized large regional kingdoms, no single state was able to extend its authority to all parts of the Indian subcontinent, much less to the mainland and islands of southeast Asia.

Though politically disunited, India remained a coherent and distinct society as a result of powerful social and cultural traditions: the caste system and the Hindu religion shaped human experiences and values throughout the subcontinent during the first millennium C.E. Beginning in the seventh century Islam also began to attract a popular following in India, and by the eleventh century, had also become a powerful influence on Indian culture and society.

Beyond the subcontinent, Indian traditions helped to shape a larger cultural zone extending to the mainland and islands of southeast Asia. Throughout most of the region, ruling classes adopted Indian forms of political organization and Indian techniques of statecraft. Indian merchants took their Hindu and Buddhist faiths to southeast Asia, where they attracted the interest first of political elites and then of the popular masses. Somewhat later, Indian merchants also helped to introduce Islam to southeast Asia.

While Indian traditions influenced the political and cultural development of southeast Asia, the entire Indian Ocean basin began to move toward economic integration during this era, as Buzurg ibn Shahriyar's stories suggest. Lands on the rim of the Indian Ocean retained distinctive political and cultural traditions inherited from times past. Yet innovations in maritime technology, development of a well-articulated network of sea lanes, and the building of port cities enabled peoples living around the Indian Ocean to trade and communicate more actively than ever before. As a result, peoples from east Africa to southeast Asia and China increasingly participated in the larger economic, commercial, and cultural life of the Indian Ocean basin.

| CHRONOLOGY | |
|---|---|
| 1st to 6th century | Kingdom of Funan |
| 606–648 | Reign of Harsha |
| 670–1025 | Kingdom of Srivijaya |
| 711 | Conquest of Sind by Umayyad forces |
| early 9th century | Life of Shankara |
| 850–1267 | Chola kingdom |
| 889–1431 | Kingdom of Angkor |
| 1001–1027 | Raids on India by Mahmud of Ghazni |
| 11th to 12th century | Life of Ramanuja |
| 12th century | Beginning of the bhakti movement |
| 1206–1526 | Sultanate of Delhi |
| 1336–1565 | Kingdom of Vijayanagar |
| 1440–1518 | Life of guru Kabir |

## ISLAMIC AND HINDU KINGDOMS

Like the Han and Roman empires, the Gupta dynasty came under severe threat from nomadic invaders. From the mid-fourth to the mid-fifth century C.E., Gupta rulers resisted the pressures and preserved order throughout much of the Indian subcontinent. Beginning in 451 C.E., however, White Huns from central Asia also known as Hephthalites, invaded India and disrupted the Gupta administration. By the mid-sixth century, the Gupta state had collapsed, and effective political authority quickly devolved to invaders, local allies of the Guptas, and independent regional power brokers. From the end of the Gupta dynasty until the sixteenth century, when a Turkic-Mongol people known as the Mughals extended their authority and their empire to most of the subcontinent, India remained a politically divided land.

## The Quest for Centralized Imperial Rule

Northern and southern India followed different political trajectories after the fall of the Gupta empire. In the north, politics became turbulent and almost chaotic. Local states contested for power and territory, and northern India became a region of continuous tension and intermittent war. Nomadic Turkish-speaking peoples from central Asia frequently took advantage of that unsettled state of affairs to cross the Khyber Pass and force their way into India. They eventually found niches for themselves in the **caste system** and became completely absorbed into Indian society. However, this process of social absorption took a long time and came only after the arrival of nomadic peoples caused a long period of disruption in northern India.

**Harsha** Even after the collapse of the Gupta dynasty, the ideal of centralized imperial rule did not entirely disappear. During the first half of the seventh century, King **Harsha** (reigned 606–648 C.E.) temporarily restored unified rule in most of northern India and sought to revive imperial authority. Harsha came to the throne of his kingdom in the lower Ganges valley at the age of sixteen. Full of energy and ambition, he led his army throughout northern India. His forces included twenty thousand cavalry, fifty thousand infantry, and five thousand war elephants, and by about 612 he had subdued those who refused to recognize his authority. He also made his presence felt beyond India. He extended his influence to several Himalayan states, and he exchanged a series of embassies with his contemporary, Emperor Tang Taizong of China.

Harsha enjoyed a reputation for piety, tolerance, and scholarship. He was a Buddhist, but he looked kindly on other faiths. He built hospitals and provided free medical care for his subjects. The Chinese pilgrim Xuanzang visited northern India during his reign and reported that Harsha liberally distributed wealth to his subjects. On one occasion, Xuanzang said, the king and his aides doled out resources continuously for seventy-five days, making gifts to half a million people. Harsha also generously patronized scholars and reportedly even wrote three plays himself.

**Collapse of Harsha's Kingdom** Despite his energy and his favorable reputation, Harsha was unable to restore permanent centralized rule. Since the fall of the Gupta dynasty, local rulers had established their authority too securely in India's regions for Harsha to overcome them. Harsha spent much of his reign on horseback traveling throughout his realm to solidify alliances with local rulers, who were virtually kings in their own lands. He managed to hold his loose empire together mainly by the force of his personality and his constant attention to political affairs. Ultimately, however, he fell victim to an assassin and left no heir to maintain his realm. His Empire immediately disintegrated, and local rulers once again turned northern India into a contested region as they sought to enlarge their realms at the expense of their neighbors.

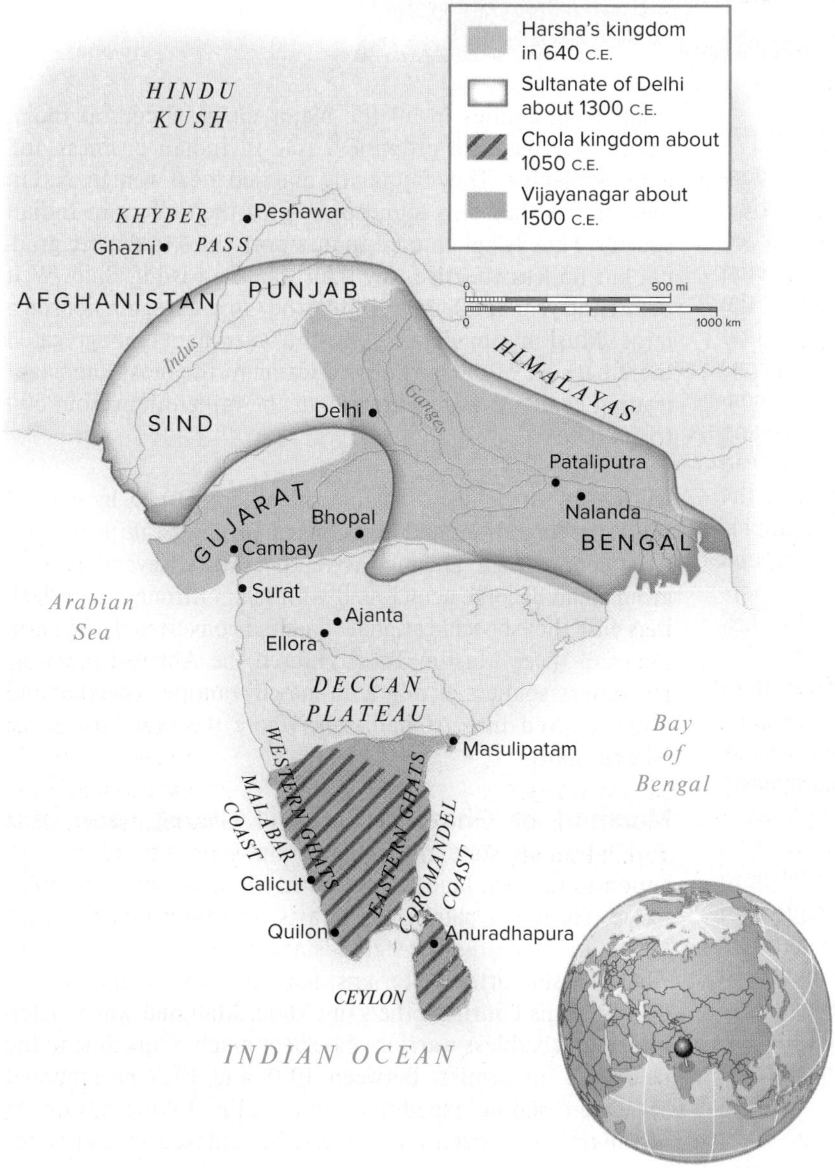

**MAP 3.1 Major states of India, 600–1600 C.E.**

Several large rivers and river valleys offered opportunities for inhabitants of northern India.

***What geographical and economic factors helped the peoples of southern India organize themselvs into flourishing states?***

Painting by an unknown Medieval artist depicting Mahmud of Ghazni and his court.
UtCon Collection/Alamy Stock Photo

## The Introduction of Islam to Northern India

**The Conquest of Sind** Amid nomadic incursions and contests for power, northern India also experienced the arrival of Islam and the establishment of Islamic states. Islam reached India by several routes. One was military: Arab forces entered India as early as the mid-seventh century, even before the establishment of the Umayyad caliphate, although their first expeditions were exploratory ventures rather than campaigns of conquest. In 711, however, a well-organized expedition conquered Sind, the Indus River valley in northwestern India, and incorporated it as a province of the expanding Umayyad empire. At mid-century, along with most of the rest of the *dar al-Islam,* Sind passed into the hands of the Abbasid caliphs.

Sind stood on the fringe of the Islamic world, well beyond the effective authority of the Abbasid caliphs. Much of its population remained Hindu, Buddhist, or Parsee, and it also sheltered a series of unorthodox Islamic movements. Infighting between Arab administrators eventually offered opportunities for local political elites to reassert Hindu authority over much of Sind. Yet the region remained nominally under the jurisdiction of the caliphs until the collapse of the Abbasid dynasty in 1258.

**Merchants and Islam** While conquerors brought Islam to Sind, Muslim merchants took their faith to coastal regions in both northern and southern India. Arab and Persian mariners had visited Indian ports for centuries before Muhammad, and their Muslim descendants dominated trade and transportation networks between India and western lands from the seventh through the fifteenth century. Muslim merchants formed small communities in all the major cities of coastal India, where they played a prominent role in Indian business and commercial life. They frequently married local women, and in many cases they also found places for themselves in Indian society. Thus Islam entered India's port cities in a more gradual but no less effective way than was the case in Sind. Well before the year 1000, for example, the Gujarat region housed a large Muslim population. Muslim merchants congregated there because of the port city of Cambay, the most important trading center in India throughout the millennium from 500 to 1500 C.E.

**Migrants and Islam** Islam also entered India by a third route: the migrations and invasions of Turkic-speaking peoples from central Asia. During the tenth century, several Turkish groups had become acquainted with Islam through their dealings with the Abbasid caliphate and had converted to the faith. Some of these Muslim Turks entered the Abbasid realm as mercenary soldiers or migrated into Byzantine Anatolia, and others moved into Afghanistan, where they established an Islamic state.

**Mahmud of Ghazni** **Mahmud of Ghazni,** leader of a Turkic-Iranian state in Afghanistan, soon turned his attention to the rich land to the south. Mahmud was a complex figure. He was a patron of the arts who built Ghazni (near Kabul in modern-day Afghanistan) into a refined capital, where he supported historians, mathematicians, and literary figures at his court. At the same time, Mahmud was a determined and ruthless warrior who spent much of his time in the field with his armies. Between 1001 and 1027 he mounted seventeen raiding expeditions into India. Taking advantage of infighting between local rulers, he annexed several states

**Mahmud of Ghazni** (mah-muhd of gahz-nee)

in northwestern India and the Punjab. For the most part, however, Mahmud had less interest in conquering and ruling India than in plundering the wealth stored in its many well-endowed temples. Mahmud and his forces demolished hundreds of sites associated with Hindu or Buddhist faiths, and their campaigns hastened the decline of Buddhism in the land of its birth. In 1025 Mahmud infamously destroyed the great Somnath Hindu Temple of Gujarat, killing more than fifty thousand people who tried to defend it, and taking away a booty of some 20 million dinars. Not surprisingly, Mahmud's raids did not encourage Indians to turn to Islam.

**The Sultanate of Delhi** During the late twelfth century, Mahmud's successors mounted a more systematic campaign to conquer northern India and place it under Islamic rule. By the early thirteenth century, they had conquered most of the Hindu kingdoms in northern India and established an Islamic state known as the **sultanate of Delhi.** The sultans established their capital at Delhi, a strategic site controlling access from the Punjab to the Ganges valley, and they ruled northern India, at least in name, for more than three centuries, from 1206 to 1526.

During the fourteenth century the sultans of Delhi commanded an army of three hundred thousand, and their state ranked among the most prominent in the Islamic world. They built mosques, shrines, and fortresses throughout their realm, and, like Mahmud of Ghazni, they were generous patrons of the arts and literature. Yet for the most part, the authority of the sultans did not extend far beyond Delhi. They often conducted raids in the Deccan region of southern India, but they never overcame Hindu resistance there. They had no permanent bureaucracy or administrative

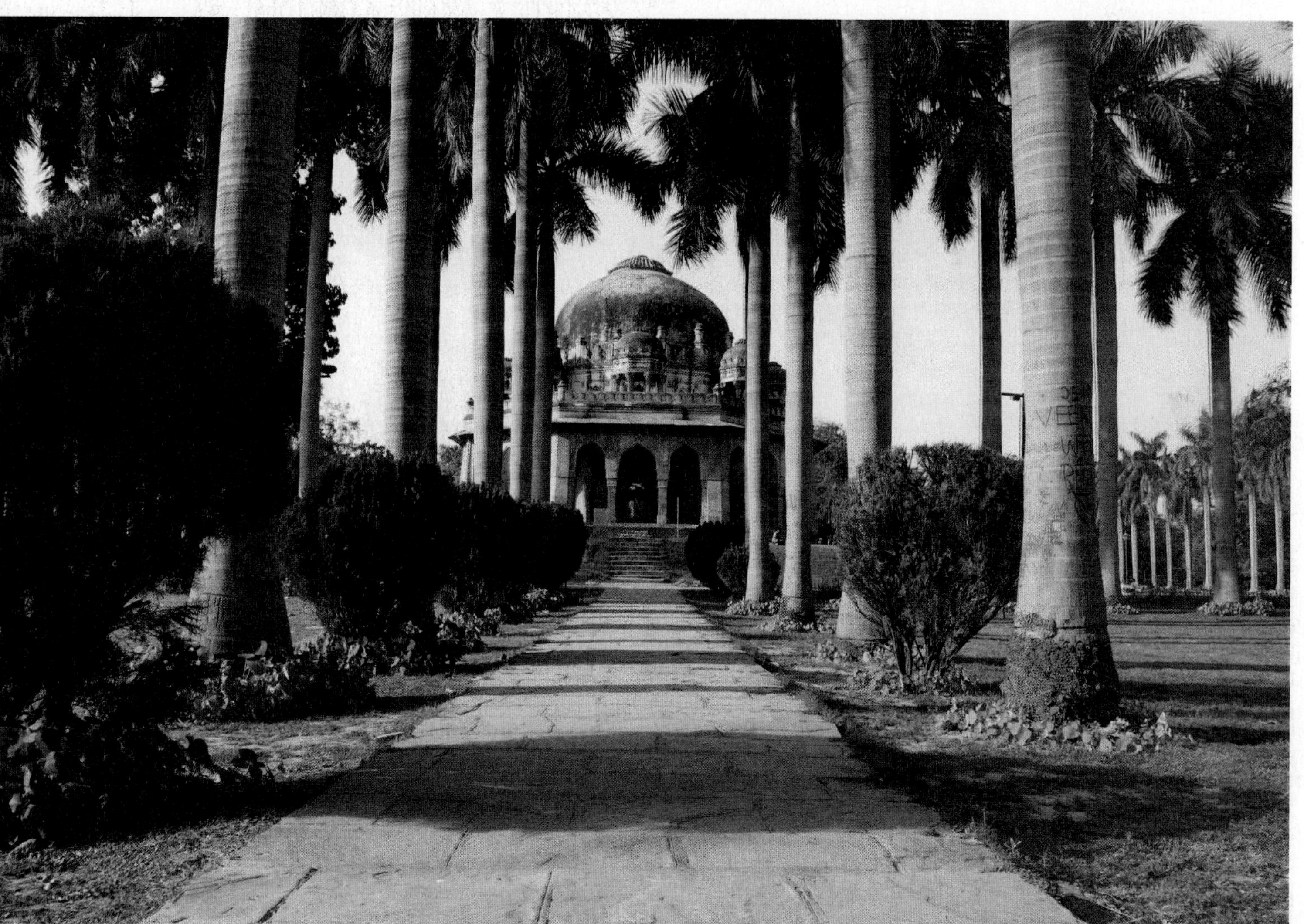

Lodi Gardens near Delhi is the cemetery of the Lodi sultans, the last dynasty to rule the sultanate of Delhi. Here a tomb reflects the introduction of Islamic architecture into India.
GeoMuse/Alamy Stock Photo

apparatus. Even in northern India, they imposed a thin veneer of Islamic political and military authority on a land populated mostly by Hindus, and they depended on the goodwill of Hindu kings to carry out their policies and advance their interests in local regions. Indeed, they did not even enjoy comfortable control of their own court: of the thirty-five sultans of Delhi, nineteen perished at the hands of assassins. Nevertheless, the sultans prominently sponsored Islam and played a large role especially in the establishment of Islam in the Bengal region.

## The Hindu Kingdoms of Southern India

Although it too remained politically divided, the southern part of the Indian subcontinent largely escaped the invasions, chronic war, and turmoil that troubled the north. Most Hindu rulers in the south presided over small, loosely administered states. Competition between states sometimes resulted in regional wars, but southern conflicts were less frequent, less intense, and less damaging than those that plagued the north.

**Coromandel** (kawr-uh-MAN-dul)

**The Chola Kingdom** Although many regional states organized affairs in local jurisdictions, two kingdoms expanded enough to exercise at least nominal rule over much of southern India. The first was the **Chola kingdom,** situated in the deep south, which ruled the Coromandel coast for more than four centuries, from 850 to 1267 C.E. At its high point, during the eleventh century, Chola forces conquered Ceylon and parts of southeast Asia. Financed by the profits of trade, the Chola navy dominated the waters from the South China Sea to the Arabian Sea.

Chola rulers did not build a tightly centralized state: they allowed considerable autonomy for local and village institutions as long as they maintained order and delivered tax revenues on time. Chola rulers had less interest in building a powerful

The Virupaksha Temple complex was built by Vijayanagar rulers in the capital of their empire, Hampi, located today in the modern state of Karnataka, India.
Dinodia Photos/Alamy Stock Photo

state than in realizing profits that came from their domination of trade in the Indian Ocean basin. Indeed, partly because of its loose institutional structure, the Chola state was in decline by the twelfth century. Native Sinhalese forces expelled Chola officials from Ceylon, and revolts erupted within southern India. The Chola realm did not entirely collapse, but by the early thirteenth century, much reduced in size and power, it had reverted to the status of one regional kingdom among many in southern India.

**The Kingdom of Vijayanagar** The second state that dominated much of southern India was the **Vijayanagar kingdom,** based in the northern Deccan. The kingdom owed its origin to efforts by the sultans of Delhi to extend their authority to southern India. Exploratory forays by Turkish forces provoked a defensive reaction in the south. Officials in Delhi dispatched two brothers, Harihara and Bukka, to represent the sultan and implement court policies in the south. Although they had converted from their native Hinduism to Islam, Harihara and Bukka recognized an opportunity to establish themselves as independent rulers. In 1336 they renounced Islam, returned to their original Hindu faith, and proclaimed the establishment of an independent empire of Vijayanagar (meaning "city of victory"). Their unusual coup did not lead to hostilities between Muslims and Hindus: Muslim merchants continued to trade unmolested in the ports of southern India, as they had for more than half a millennium. But the Hindu kingdom of Vijayanagar was the dominant state in southern India from the mid-fourteenth century until 1565, when it fell to an alliance of Muslim kingdoms.

As in northern India, then, political division and conflict between states characterized southern India's political history in postclassical times. India did not generate the sort of large-scale, centralized, imperial state that guided the fortunes of complex societies in the eastern Mediterranean, southwest Asia, or China. States such as the sultanate of Delhi in northern India and the kingdoms of Chola and Vijayanagar in the south were not powerful enough to organize political life throughout the subcontinent. Nevertheless, on the basis of trade, common social structures, and inherited cultural traditions, a coherent and distinctive society flourished in India during the first millennium and a half of the Common Era.

## PRODUCTION AND TRADE IN THE INDIAN OCEAN BASIN

As in the Mediterranean, southwest Asia, and China, agricultural yields increased significantly in postclassical India, enabling large numbers of people to devote themselves to trade and manufacturing rather than the production of food. Trade forged links between the various regions of the subcontinent and fostered economic development in southern India. Trade also created links between India and distant lands, as merchants and manufacturers transformed the Indian Ocean basin into a vast zone of communication and exchange. The increasing prominence of trade and industry brought change to Indian society, as merchant and artisan guilds became stronger and more influential than before. Yet caste identities and loyalties also remained strong, and the caste system continued to serve as the most powerful organizing feature of Indian society.

### Agriculture in the Monsoon World

**The Monsoons** Because of the rhythms of the **monsoons,** irrigation was essential for the maintenance of a large, densely populated, agricultural society. Because of cyclical changes in atmospheric pressure, during the spring and summer, warm, moisture-laden winds from the southwest bring most of India's rainfall. During the autumn and winter, cool and very dry winds blow from the northeast. To achieve their agricultural potential, Indian lands required a good watering by the southern monsoon, supplemented by irrigation during the dry months. Light rain during the spring and summer months or short supplies of water for irrigation commonly led to drought, reduced harvests, and widespread famine.

**Irrigation Systems** In northern India, irrigation had been a fixture of the countryside since the era of the Indus Civilization, when cultivators tapped the waters of the Indus River. Later, as Indo-Aryans migrated into the Ganges River valley, they found plentiful surface water and abundant opportunities to build irrigation systems. For the most part, however, southern India is an arid land without rivers like the Indus or the Ganges that can serve as sources for large-scale irrigation. Thus, as southern India became more densely populated, irrigation systems became crucial, and a great deal of energy and effort went into the construction of waterworks. Dams, reservoirs, canals, wells, and tunnels appeared in large numbers. Particularly impressive were monumental reservoirs lined with brick or stone that captured the rains of the spring and summer months and held them until the dry season, when canals carried them to thirsty fields. One such reservoir—actually an artificial lake constructed near Bhopal during the eleventh century—covered some 650 square kilometers (250 square miles). Projects of that size required enormous investments of human energy, both for their original construction and for continuing maintenance, but they led to significant increases in agricultural productivity.

**Population Growth** As a result of that increased productivity, India's population grew steadily throughout the first millennium and a half of the Common Era. In 600 C.E., shortly after the fall of the Gupta dynasty, the subcontinent's population stood at about 53 million. By 800 it had increased almost

**Vijayanagar** (vee-juh-yah-NAH-gahr)

20 percent to 64 million, and by 1000 it had grown by almost an additional 25 percent to 79 million. During the following centuries the rate of growth slowed, as Indian numbers increased by 4 to 5 million individuals per century. Toward 1500, however, the rate of growth increased again, and by 1500 the subcontinent's population had reached 105 million.

**Urbanization** This demographic surge encouraged the concentration of people in cities. During the fourteenth century, the high point of the sultanate of Delhi, the capital city had a population of about four hundred thousand, which made it second only to Cairo among Muslim cities. Many other cities—particularly ports and trading centers, such as Cambay, Surat, Calicut, Quilon, and Masulipatam—had populations well over one hundred thousand. Cities in southern India grew especially fast, partly as a result of increasing agricultural productivity in the region.

## Trade and the Economic Development of Southern India

Political fragmentation of the subcontinent did not prevent robust trade between the different states and regions of India. As the population grew, opportunities for specialized work became more numerous. Increased trade was a natural result of that process.

**Internal Trade** Most regions of the Indian subcontinent were self-sufficient in staple foods such as rice, wheat, barley, and millet. The case was different, however, with iron, copper, salt, pepper, spices, condiments, and specialized crops that grew well only in certain regions. Iron came mostly from the Ganges River valley near Bengal, copper mostly from the Deccan Plateau, salt mostly from coastal regions, and pepper from southern India. Those and other commodities sometimes traveled long distances to consumers in remote parts of the subcontinent. Pepper, saffron, and sugar were popular commodities in subcontinental trade, and even rice sometimes traveled as a trade item to northern and mountainous regions where it did not grow well.

Southern India and Ceylon benefited especially well from this trade. As invasions and conflicts disrupted northern India, southern regions experienced rapid economic development. The Chola kingdom provided relative stability in the south, and Chola expansion in southeast Asia opened markets for Indian merchants and producers. Coastal towns such as Calicut and Quilon flourished, and they attracted increasing numbers of residents.

**Temples and Society** The Chola rulers allowed considerable autonomy to their subjects, and the towns and villages of southern India largely organized their own affairs. Public life revolved around Hindu temples that served as economic and social centers. Southern Indians used their growing wealth to build hundreds of elaborate Hindu temples, which organized agricultural activities, coordinated work on irrigation systems, and maintained reserves of surplus production for use in times of need. These temples also provided basic schooling for boys in the community, and larger temples offered advanced instruction as well. Temples often possessed large tracts of agricultural land, and they sometimes employed hundreds of people, including brahmins, attendants, musicians, servants, and slaves. To meet their financial obligations to employees, temple administrators collected a portion of the agricultural yield from lands subject to temple authority. Administrators were also responsible for keeping order in their communities and delivering tax receipts to the Cholas and other political authorities.

Temple authorities also served as bankers, made loans, and invested in commercial and business ventures. As a result, temples promoted the economic development of southern India by encouraging production and trade. Temple authorities cooperated closely with the leaders of merchant guilds in seeking commercial opportunities to exploit. The guilds often made gifts of land or money to temples by way of consolidating their relationship with the powerful economic institutions. Temples thus grew prosperous and became crucial to the economic health of southern India.

## Cross-Cultural Trade in the Indian Ocean Basin

Indian prosperity sprang partly from the productivity of Indian society, but it depended also on the vast wealth that circulated in the commercial world of the Indian Ocean basin. Trade in the Indian Ocean Basin was not new in the first millennium of the Common Era. Indian merchants had been engaged in trans-regional maritime trade since the First Silk Roads Era, when they had regularly engaged with Roman merchants in search of pepper and other South Asian spices. During the first millennium C.E., however, larger ships and improved commercial organization supported a dramatic surge in the volume and value of trade in the Indian Ocean basin.

**Dhows and Junks** The earliest voyaging in the Indian Ocean followed the coastlines, but during the First Silk Roads Era mariners had recognized the rhythms of the monsoons. Over time they built larger ships, which enabled them to leave the coasts behind and ply the blue waters of the Indian Ocean: the **dhows** favored by Indian, Persian, and Arab sailors averaged about one hundred tons burden in 1000 and four hundred tons in 1500. After the naval and commercial expansion of the Song dynasty, large Chinese and southeast Asian **junks** also sailed the Indian Ocean: some of them could carry one thousand tons of cargo.

As large, stable ships came into use, mariners increasingly entrusted their crafts and cargoes to the reasonably predictable monsoons and sailed directly across the Arabian Sea and the

During the eighth century C.E., workers carved a massive temple out of sheer rock at Ellora in central India. Temple communities such as the one that grew up at Ellora controlled enormous resources in India during the first millennium C.E. How did temple communities become such wealthy institutions?
Mazur Travel/Shutterstock

Bay of Bengal. In the age of sail, it was impossible to make a round trip across the entire Indian Ocean without spending months at distant ports waiting for the winds to change, so merchants usually conducted their trade in stages.

**Emporia** Because India stood in the middle of the Indian Ocean basin, it was a natural site for **emporia** (commercial centers) and warehouses. Merchants coming from east Africa or Persia exchanged their cargoes at Cambay, Calicut, or Quilon for goods to take back west with the winter monsoon. Mariners from China or southeast Asia called at Indian ports and traded their cargoes for goods to ship east with the summer monsoon. Merchants also built emporia outside India: the storytelling mariner Buzurg ibn Shahriyar, who we met at the start of this chapter, came from the emporium of Siraf on the Persian Gulf, a port city surrounded by desert that nevertheless enjoyed fabulous wealth because of its trade with China, India, and east Africa. Because of their central location, however, Indian ports became the principal clearinghouses of trade in the Indian Ocean basin, and they became remarkably cosmopolitan centers. Hindus, Buddhists, Muslims, Jews, and others who inhabited the Indian port cities did business with counterparts from all over the eastern hemisphere and swapped stories like those recounted by Buzurg ibn Shahriyar. In combination, the sea lanes and emporia of the Indian Ocean basin made up a network of maritime Silk Roads—a web of transportation, communication, and exchange that complemented the land-based Silk Roads and promoted interaction between peoples throughout much of Afro-Eurasia.

Particularly after the establishment of the Umayyad and Abbasid dynasties in southwest Asia and the Tang and Song dynasties in China, trade in the Indian Ocean surged. Indian merchants and mariners sometimes traveled to distant lands in search of marketable goods, but the carrying trade between India and points west fell mostly into Arab and Persian hands. During the Tang and Song dynasties, Chinese vessels also

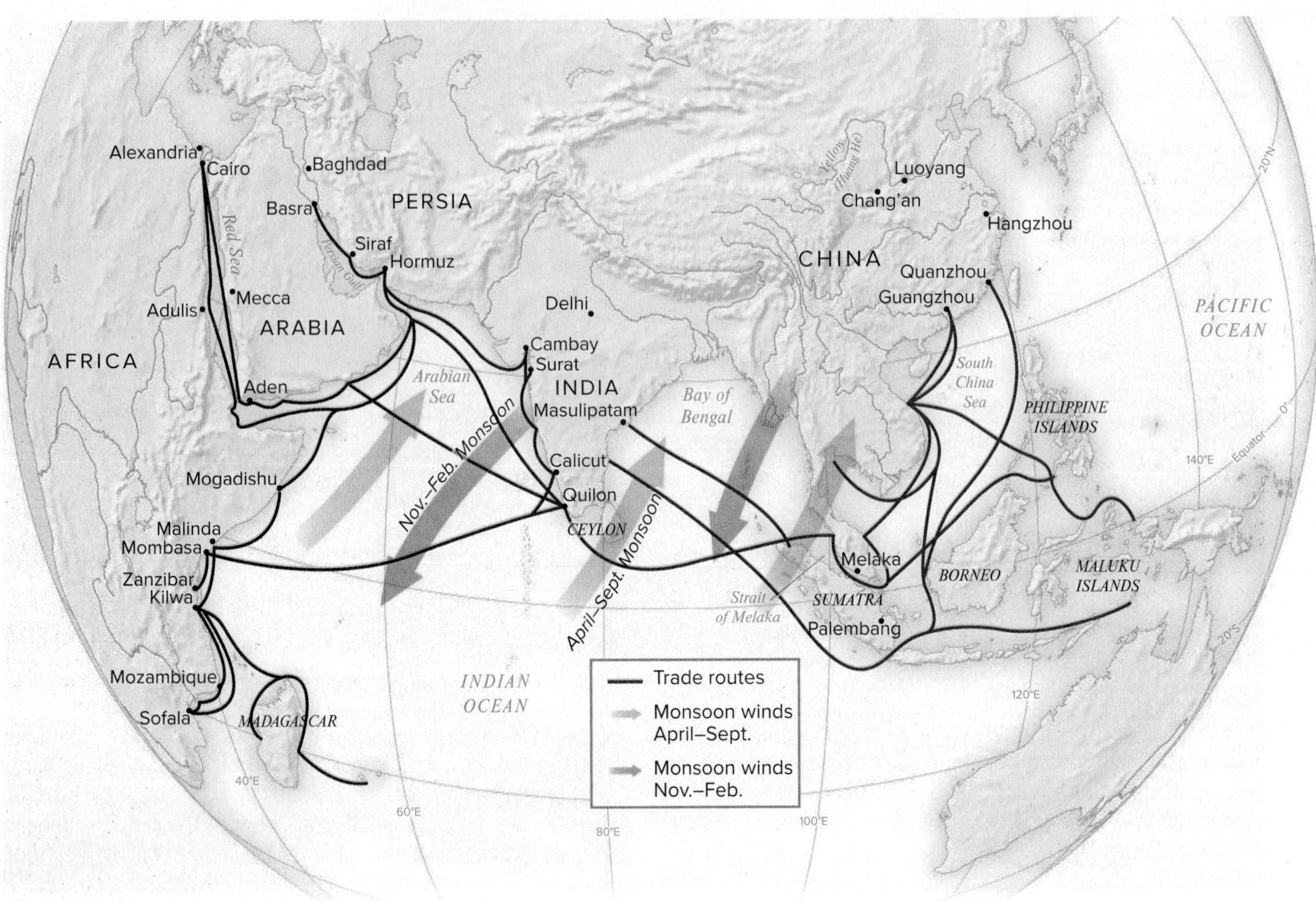


## MAP 3.2 The trading world of the Indian Ocean basin, 600–1600 C.E.

Note the directions of seasonal winds in the Indian Ocean basin.

***What impact would the monsoon winds have had on the direction and schedule of maritime trade during the era?***

***How do the trade routes indicated on the map undermine the generalization that 15th century European exploration introduced trade to the region?***

***To what extent would you expect to find Islam incorporated into the trading cities on the map?***

ventured into the western Indian Ocean and called at ports as far away as east Africa. In the Bay of Bengal and the China seas, Malay and Chinese vessels were most prominent.

**Specialized Production** As the volume of trade in the Indian Ocean basin increased, lands around the ocean began to engage in specialized production of commodities for the commercial market. For centuries Indian artisans had enjoyed a reputation for the manufacture of fine cotton textiles, which they produced in small quantities for wealthy consumers. During the first millennium their wares came into high demand throughout the trading world of the Indian Ocean basin. In response to that demand, Indian artisans built thriving local industries around the production of high-quality cotton textiles. These industries influenced the structure of the Indian economy: they created a demand for specific agricultural products, provided a livelihood for thousands of artisans, and enabled consumers to import goods from regions that specialized in the production of other commodities.

Alongside textiles, other specialized industries that emerged in postclassical India included sugar refining, leather tanning, stone carving, and carpet weaving. Iron and steel production also emerged as prominent industries. Indian artisans became well known especially for the pro-duction of high-carbon steel, which held a lethal cutting edge and consequently came into high demand for use in knives and swords. Other lands concentrated on the production of different manufactured goods and agricultural commodities: China produced silk, porcelain, and lacquerware; southeast Asian lands provided fine spices; incense, horses, and dates came from southwest Asia; and east Africa contributed gold, ivory, and slaves. Thus trade encouraged specialized production and

One of many stelae (elaborately carved obelisks) in the city of Axum in modern-day Ethiopia. The stelae were royal grave markers that were probably erected during the fourth century C.E.
Dave Bartruff/Corbis Documentary/Getty Images

economic development in all lands participating in the trade networks of the Indian Ocean basin: Because of all these developments, trans-regional trade during the era significantly shaped the economic, political, and social structures of states and cultures throughout much of Afro-Eurasia.

**The Kingdom of Axum** The experience of the kingdom of **Axum** (sometimes spelled Aksum) illustrates the potential of trade to support political as well as economic development throughout the Indian Ocean basin. Founded in the highlands of northern Ethiopia about the first century C.E., Axum was originally a small kingdom whose merchants traded from the port of Adulis on the Red Sea. Axum soon displaced Kush as Egypt's principal link to southern lands and sent the Nubian kingdom into economic and political decline: about 360 C.E. Axumite forces even invaded Kush and destroyed the capital city of Meroë. During the fourth and fifth centuries, Axumites adopted Christianity and established a distinctive church that maintained relations with Christian communities in Egypt and the Mediterranean basin. During the sixth century Axum embarked on a round of territorial expansion, building an empire that included most of modern-day Ethiopia as well as Yemen in southern Arabia. Indeed, an Axumite army and elephant corps campaigned as far north as Mecca in the year 571 C.E., birth year of the prophet Muhammad.

During the seventh and eighth centuries, Arab conquerors sought to bring Axum into the expanding realm of Islam, but the kingdom maintained its independence and its Christian religion. Because neighboring lands mostly adopted Islam, Axum fell out of communication with other Christian societies. Nevertheless, Axumite merchants not only maintained commercial ties with distant lands, as ships from Adulis routinely sailed for India and the islands of southeast Asia, but also traded regularly with Muslim merchants in neighboring lands. From the sixth to the ninth century C.E., Adulis was perhaps the most prominent port in east Africa, funneling gold, ivory, and slaves from

Mealtime for a Persian merchant and his two companions served by three women attendants in this ceiling decoration from the Ajanta caves in central India.
Shreekant Jadhav/ephotocorp/Alamy Stock Photo

sub-Saharan Africa to Egypt, the eastern Mediterranean region, and the Indian Ocean basin. Thus, even though challenged by Muslim forces, Axum was able to maintain its independence and prosperity, largely because of its participation in trading networks of the Indian Ocean and Mediterranean Sea.

## Caste and Society

The political, economic, and social changes of the postclassical era brought a series of challenges for India's caste system. Migrations, the growing prominence of Islam, economic development, and urbanization all placed pressures on the caste system as it had developed during the Vedic and classical eras. But the caste system has never been a rigid, unchanging structure. Rather, individuals and groups have continuously adjusted it and adapted it to new circumstances. Adjustments and adaptations of the postclassical era resulted in a caste system that was more complex than in earlier ages and that also extended its geographic reach deeper into southern India than ever before. In the absence of strong central governments, the caste system helped to maintain order in local communities by providing guidance on individuals' roles in society and their relationships with others.

**Caste and Migration** The caste system closely reflected changes in Indian society. It adapted to the arrival of migrants, for example, and helped to integrate them into Indian society. As Turkish peoples or Muslim merchants pursued opportunities in India, they gained recognition as distinct groups under the umbrella of the caste system. They established codes of conduct both for the regulation of behavior within their own groups and for guidance in dealing with members of other castes. Within a few generations their descendants had become absorbed into Indian society.

**Caste and Social Change** The caste system also accommodated the social changes brought about by trade and economic development. Indeed, the caste system influenced the lives of most people by helping to order their work and their relationships with other workers. The castes that individuals most closely identified with were the subcastes (*jati*), which often took the form of workers' guilds. As merchants and manufacturers became increasingly important in the larger economy, they organized powerful guilds to represent their interests. Merchant guilds in particular wielded political and economic influence because their members enjoyed access to considerable wealth and contributed in large measure to the economic health of their states. Guild members forged group identities by working within the caste system. Merchants specializing in particular types of commerce, such as the silk, cotton, or spice trade, established themselves as distinct subcastes, as did artisans working in particular industries, such as the iron, steel, or leather business.

**Expansion of the Caste System** Besides becoming more complex, the caste system also extended its geographic reach. Caste distinctions first became prominent in northern India following Aryan migrations into the subcontinent. During the postclassical era, the caste system became securely established in southern India as well. Economic development aided that process by encouraging commercial relationships between southern merchants and their caste-conscious counterparts in the north. The emergence of merchant and craft guilds in southern regions strengthened the caste system because guild members usually organized as a subcaste. Powerful temples also fostered caste distinctions. Caste-conscious brahmins who supervised the temples were particularly effective promoters of the system because temples provided the only formal education available in most regions and also served as centers of local social life. By about the eleventh century C.E., caste had become the principal basis of social organization in southern India.

## SOURCES FROM THE PAST

### Three Sources on Chinese Trade with Ports and Regions of the Indian Ocean Basin

*China was located at the eastern edge of the Indian Ocean Basin trading network, but it was absolutely fundamental to the vigor and success of that vast commercial enterprise for most of the first and early second millennia of the Common Era. The following three sources provide eyewitness accounts of the wealth being generated in China and elsewhere between the eighth and thirteenth centuries.*

**Source 1: The Superintendent of the Shipping Trade** Trade between various Southeast Asian ports and Tang China was so intense by the early eighth century that the government created a new official position to help regulate it: the Superintendent of the Shipping Trade. An official Chinese report created a century later comments on the regulation of trade between Southeast Asian countries and ports along the southern Chinese coast and the work of the Superintendent. During the Tang Dynasty, the Chinese referred to this as the *Nanhai* trade:

When [the laden Nanhai ships] arrive, a report is sent to the Court and announcements are made to the cities. The [chief merchants] who commanded them are made to register with Superintendent of the Shipping Trade their names and their cargo [or submit their manifest]. [The Superintendent collects the duties on the goods and sees that there are no prohibited precious and rare goods [of which the government had a monopoly]. There were some foreign merchants who were imprisoned for trying to deceive him.

What crime had the foreign merchants been imprisoned for?

*Source:* Wang Gungwu, *The Nanhai Trade: Early Chinese Trade in the South Chinese Sea* (Singapore: Eastern Universities Press, 2003), p. 94.

**Source 2: Chinese Report on the Wealth of a Javanese Commercial Kingdom** By the thirteenth century trade between China and other regions of the Indian Ocean Basin had generated enormous wealth for the various Southeast Asian states that functioned as commercial intermediaries. In this report a Chinese official, who is probably basing his information on reports received from Chinese merchants who regularly traveled to the Indonesian island of Java, comments on the political and commercial status of a wealthy West Javan kingdom:

The king wears his hair in a knot, on his head is a golden bell; he wears a silken robe and leather shoes. His throne is a square seat and his officers at their daily audience bow three times when withdrawing. When he goes forth he rides an elephant, or is carried in a chair followed by a company of some 500 to 700 armed soldiers. When any one of the people see the king, he squats down until [the king] has passed by . . . The [government does] not inflict corporal punishment and imprisonment on criminals; they are fined an amount in gold varying according to the gravity of the crime . . . [The country] produces rice, hemp, millet, beans, but no wheat. Ploughing is done with buffaloes. They also pay attention to the raising of silkworms and the weaving of the silk; they have various colored brocaded silks, cotton, and damasked cotton gauzes. They cast coins in an alloy of copper, silver, white copper and tin. Foreign merchants use gold and silver in trading. There is a vast store of pepper and the [Chinese] merchant ships, in view of the profit they derive from that trade, are in the habit of smuggling out of China copper cash for bartering purposes.

Why would the government fine criminals rather than physically punish or imprison them? Which would be the greater deterrent in a wealthy commercial state?

*Source:* Frederick Hurth and W. W. Rockhill, *Chau Ju-kua: His Work on the Chinese and Arab Trade in the Twelfth and Thirteenth Centuries, entitled Chu-fan-chi*, reprint edition (Taipei: Literature House, 1965), pp. 76–78.

**Source 3: Marco Polo of the Wealth of the Chinese Port City of Quanzhou** Venetian merchant Marco Polo visited China when it was under the control of the Mongol Yuan Dynasty (1271–1368), events discussed in chapter 17. From the account he later compiled, it appears as though the Yuan had further strengthened commercial connections between the southern Chinese ports and the thriving Indian Ocean commercial network. Marco Polo vividly describes the port city of Quanzhou, which he refers to as Zaiton, located in modern Fujian Province:

The splendid city of Zaiton . . . is the port for all the ships that arrive from India laden with costly wares and precious stones of great price and pearls of great quality . . . It is also the port for the merchandise of Manzi [Fujian], that is of all the surrounding territory, so that the total amount of traffic in gems and other merchandise entering and leaving the port is a marvel to behold. From this city and its port goods are exported to the whole province of Manzi. And I assure you that for one spice ship that goes to Alexandria or elsewhere to pick up pepper for export to Christendom, Zaiton is visited by a hundred. For you must know that it is one of the two ports in the world with the biggest flow of commerce.

Which other global ports in the fourteenth century might Marco Polo have been thinking of as candidates for having a flow of commerce equal to that of Zaiton?

*Source:* Ronald Latham, trans. and ed., *The Travels of Marco Polo* (London: Penguin, 1958), p. 237.

## For Further Reflection

- Collectively, what do these sources tell us about the evolution of Indian Ocean Basin trade between the eighth and fourteenth centuries?
- What role were governments playing in the regulation of transregional trade across the Indian Ocean?
- What financial and cultural impact was extensive trade having not only on the key commercial ports involved but on wider society?

## RELIGIOUS DEVELOPMENTS IN SOUTH ASIA

The Indian cultural landscape underwent a thorough transformation during the first millennium and a half of the Common Era. Jainism and Buddhism lost much of their popular following. Neither belief completely disappeared from India, and indeed, a small community continues to observe each faith there even today. After 1000 C.E., however, Hindu and Islamic traditions increasingly dominated the cultural and religious life of India.

Hinduism and Islam differed profoundly as religious traditions. The Hindu pantheon made places for numerous gods and spirits, for example, whereas Islamic theology stood on a firm foundation of monotheism. Yet both religions attracted large popular followings throughout the subcontinent, with Hinduism predominating in southern India and Islam in the north.

### The Increasing Popularity of Hinduism

Toward the end of the first millennium C.E., Buddhism flourished in east Asia, central Asia, and parts of southeast Asia but came under great pressure in India. Like Mahayana Buddhism, both Hinduism and Islam promised salvation to devout individuals, and they gradually attracted Buddhists to their own communities. Invasions of India by Turkish peoples hastened the decline of Buddhism because the invaders looted and destroyed Buddhist stupas and shrines. In 1196 Muslim forces overran the city of Nalanda and ravaged the schools where centuries earlier, Xuanzang and other foreign pilgrims had studied with the world's leading Buddhist philosophers and theologians. The conquerors torched Buddhist libraries and either killed or exiled thousands of monks living at Nalanda. Buddhism soon became a minor faith in the land of its birth.

**Vishnu and Shiva** Hinduism benefited from the decline of Buddhism. One reason for the increasing popularity of Hinduism was the remarkable growth of devotional communities, particularly those dedicated to **Vishnu** and **Shiva**, two of the most important deities in the Hindu pantheon. Vishnu was the preserver of the world, a god who observed the universe from the heavens and who occasionally entered the world in human form to resist evil or communicate his teachings. In contrast, Shiva was both a god of fertility and a destructive deity: he brought life but also took it away when its season had passed. Hindus recognized many other gods and goddesses associated with Vishnu and Shiva, but these two powerful deities were by far the most popular and important deities of veneration.

**Devotional Cults** The veneration of Vishnu and Shiva became especially popular in southern India, where individuals or family groups went to great lengths to honor their chosen deities. Often, new avenues of worship opened up when individuals identified Vishnu or Shiva with a local spirit or deity associated with a particular region or a prominent geographic feature. The worship of Shiva as lord of the dancers arose, for example, about the fifth or sixth century C.E. when devotees identified a stone long venerated locally in a southern Indian village as a symbol of Shiva. In the tenth century Chola kings took the dancing Shiva as their family god and spread the idea throughout southern India. By venerating images of Vishnu or Shiva, offering them food and drink, and meditating on the deities and their qualities, Hindus hoped to achieve a mystic union with the gods that would bring grace and salvation. As these spiritual approaches proliferated, temples and shrines dotted the landscape of southern India. Veneration of Vishnu and Shiva gradually became popular among Hindus in northern as well as southern India.

**Shankara** The significance of Hinduism extended well beyond popular religion: it also influenced philosophy. Just as Buddhism, Christianity, and Islam influenced moral thought and philosophy in other lands, devotional Hinduism guided

#### INTERPRETING IMAGES

Southern Indian artists often portrayed Shiva in bronze sculptures as a four-armed lord of dancers. In this figure from the Chola dynasty, Shiva crushes with his foot a dwarf demon symbolizing ignorance. One hand holds a bell to awaken his devotees, another bears the fire used by Shiva as creator and destroyer of the world, and a third gestures Shiva's benevolence toward his followers.

**Analyze** *In what ways does the statue of Shiva reflect Hindu religious beliefs?*

Kate S. Buckingham Fund/Art Institute of Chicago

the efforts of the most prominent philosophers in postclassical India. Brahmin philosophers such as Shankara and Ramanuja took the Upanishads as a point of departure for subtle reasoning and sophisticated metaphysics. **Shankara,** a southern Indian devotee of Shiva who was active during the early ninth century C.E., took it upon himself to digest all sacred Hindu writings and harmonize their sometimes contradictory teachings into a single, consistent system of thought. In a manner reminiscent of Plato, Shankara held that the physical world was illusion—a figment of the imagination—and that ultimate reality lay beyond the physical senses. Although he was a worshiper of Shiva, Shankara mistrusted emotional services and ceremonies, insisting that only by disciplined logical reasoning could human beings understand the ultimate reality of Brahman, the impersonal world-soul of the Upanishads. Only then could they appreciate the fundamental unity of the world, which Shankara considered a perfectly understandable expression of ultimate reality, even though to human physical senses that same world appears chaotic and incomprehensible.

An elaborate open-air rock carving at Mamallapuram, south of modern Madras, celebrates the Ganges River as a gift from Shiva and other gods.
Maciej Dakowicz/Alamy Stock Photo

**Ramanuja** **Ramanuja,** a devotee of Vishnu who was active during the eleventh and early twelfth centuries C.E., challenged Shankara's uncompromising insistence on logic. Also a brahmin philosopher from southern India, Ramanuja's thought reflected the deep influence of devotional cults. According to Ramanuja, intellectual understanding of ultimate reality was less important than personal union with the deity. Ramanuja granted that intellectual efforts could lead to comprehension of reality, but he held that genuine bliss came from salvation and identification of individuals with their gods. He followed the *Bhagavad Gita* in recommending intense devotion to Vishnu, and he taught that by placing themselves in the hands of Vishnu, devotees would win the god's grace and live forever in his presence. Thus, in contrast to Shankara's consistent, intellectual system of thought, Ramanuja's philosophy pointed toward a Hindu theology of salvation. Indeed, his thought inspired the development of new avenues of devotion throughout India, and it serves even today as a philosophical foundation for Hindu popular religion.

## How the Past Shapes the Future

### The Spread of Religious Traditions

As religious traditions spread from their regions of origin during the first millennium C.E., the Indian subcontinent became a region to which Islam spread from central Asia and also a region that exported its own religion of Hinduism to many parts of southeast Asia. By the tenth century, Indian merchants were also bringing knowledge of Islam to southeast Asia. Consider the long-term effects of the meeting of Islam and Hinduism in India. What were the effects of the popularity of these two religions on Jainism and Buddhism, which had also developed in India? Consider also the long-term effects of the Indianization of southeast Asia through the spread of both Hinduism and Islam. How did Indianization influence social organization, cultural expression, and political life in southeast Asia? And to what extent are these religious developments still affecting South and Southeast Asia today?

## Islam and Its Appeal

The Islamic faith did not attract much immediate interest among Indians when it arrived in the subcontinent. It won gradual acceptance in merchant communities where foreign Muslim traders took local spouses and found a place in Indian society. Elsewhere, however, circumstances did not favor its adoption because it was often brought to the region by conquering peoples. Muslim conquerors generally reserved important political and military positions for their Arab, Persian, and Turkish companions. Only rarely did they allow Indians—even those who had converted to Islam—to hold sensitive posts. Thus, quite apart from the fact that they introduced a foreign religion radically different from those of the subcontinent, conquerors offered little incentive for Indians to convert to Islam.

**Conversion to Islam** Gradually, however, many Indians did convert to Islam. By 1500 C.E. Indian Muslims numbered perhaps twenty-five million—about one-quarter of the subcontinent's population. Some Indians adopted Islam in hopes of improving their positions in society: Hindus of lower castes, for example, hoped to escape discrimination by converting to a faith that recognized the equality of all believers. In fact, Hindus rarely improved their social standing by conversion. Often, members of an entire caste or subcaste adopted Islam en masse, and after conversion they continued to play the same social and economic roles that they had before.

**Sufis** In India as elsewhere, the most effective agents of conversion to Islam were Sufi mystics. **Sufis** encouraged a personal, emotional, devotional approach to Islam. They did not insist on fine points of doctrine, and they sometimes even permitted their followers to observe rituals or venerate spirits not recognized by the Islamic faith. Because of their piety and sincerity, however, Sufi missionaries attracted individuals searching for a faith that could provide comfort and meaning for their personal lives. Thus, like Hinduism, Indian Islam emphasized piety and devotion. Even though Hinduism and Islam were profoundly different religions, they encouraged the cultivation of similar spiritual values that transcended the social and cultural boundary lines of postclassical India.

**The Bhakti Movement** In some ways, the gap between Hinduism and Islam narrowed in India during the early second millennium because both religions drew on long-established and long-observed cultural traditions. Sufis, for example, often attracted schools of followers in the manner of Indian gurus, spiritual leaders who taught Hindu values to disciples who congregated around them. Even more important was the development of the ***bhakti* movement,** a spiritual movement of love and devotion that ultimately sought to erase the distinction between Hinduism and Islam. The bhakti movement emerged in southern India during the twelfth century, and it originally encouraged a traditional piety and devotion to Hindu values. As the movement spread to the north, bhakti leaders increasingly encountered Muslims and became deeply attracted to certain Islamic values, especially monotheism and the notion of spiritual equality of all believers.

**Guru Kabir** The bhakti movement gradually rejected the exclusive features of both Hinduism and Islam. Thus **guru Kabir** (1440–1518), a blind weaver who was one of the most famous bhakti teachers, went so far as to teach that Shiva, Vishnu, and Allah were all manifestations of a single, universal deity, whom all devout believers could find within their own hearts. The bhakti movement did not succeed in harmonizing Hinduism and Islam. Nevertheless, like the Sufis, bhakti teachers promoted values that helped to build bridges between India's social and cultural communities.

In India as in other lands, Sufi mystics were the most effective Muslim missionaries. This seventeenth-century painting depicts the legendary Sufi master Khwaja Khidr, beloved in Muslim communities throughout northern India as one associated with springtime, fertility, water, and happiness. Why would Sufis believe that showing respect for more traditional beliefs and spirits was the best way to encourage their followers to develop a personal relationship with the Islamic faith?
The History Collection/Alamy Stock Photo

## INDIAN SOCIAL AND POLITICAL INFLUENCE IN SOUTHEAST ASIA

Just as China stood at the center of a larger east Asian society, India served as the principal source of political and cultural traditions widely observed throughout south and southeast Asia. For a millennium and more, southeast Asian peoples adapted Indian political structures and religions to local needs and interests. Although Indian armed forces rarely ventured into the region, southeast Asian lands reflected the influence of Indian society, as merchants introduced Hinduism, Buddhism, Sanskrit writings, and Indian forms of political organization. Beginning about the twelfth century, Islam also found solid footing in southeast Asia, as Muslim merchants, many of them Indians, established trading communities in the important

**MAP 3.3 Early states of southeast Asia: Funan and Srivijaya, 100–1025 C.E.**

Both Funan and Srivijaya relied heavily on maritime trade.

***What impact did the trans-regional maritime trade illustrated in Map 15.2 have on the development of states in Southeast Asia?***

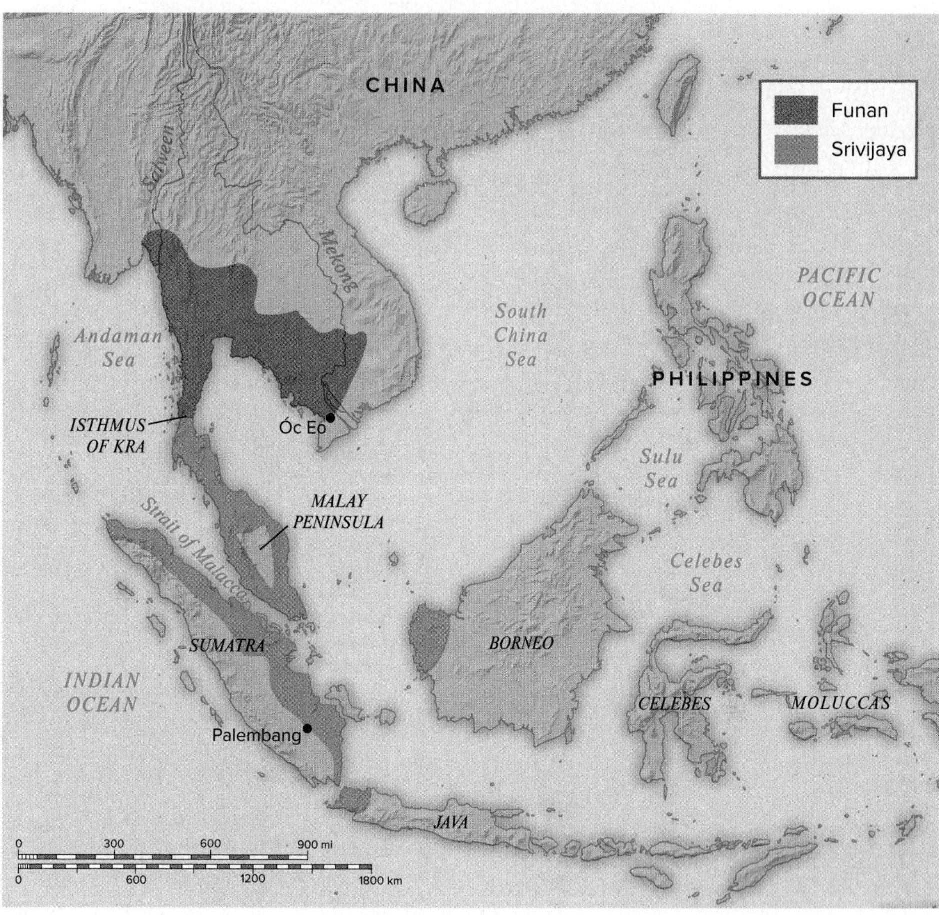


port cities of the region. During the next five hundred years, Islam attracted a sizable following and became a permanent feature in much of southeast Asia.

## The States of Southeast Asia

**Indian Influence in Southeast Asia** Indian merchants visited the islands and mainland of southeast Asia from an early date, perhaps as early as 500 B.C.E. By the early centuries C.E., they had become familiar figures throughout southeast Asia, and their presence brought opportunities for the native ruling elites of the region. In exchange for spices and exotic products such as pearls, aromatics, and animal skins, Indian merchants brought textiles, beads, gold, silver, manufactured metal goods, and objects used in political or religious rituals. Southeast Asian rulers used the profits from that trade to consolidate their political control.

Meanwhile, southeast Asian ruling elites became acquainted with Indian political and cultural traditions. Without necessarily giving up their own traditions, they borrowed Indian forms of political organization and accepted Indian religious faiths. On the model of Indian states, for example, they adopted kingship as the principal form of political authority. Regional kings in southeast Asia surrounded themselves with courts featuring administrators and rituals similar to those found in India.

Ruling elites also sponsored the introduction of Hinduism or Buddhism—sometimes both—into their courts. They embraced Indian literature such as the *Ramayana* and the *Mahabharata,* which promoted Hindu values, as well as treatises that explained Buddhist views on the world. They did not adopt the Indian caste system and continued to acknowledge the deities and nature spirits that southeast Asian peoples had venerated for centuries. But ruling elites readily adopted Hinduism and Buddhism, which they found attractive because the Indian faiths reinforced the principle of monarchical rule.

**Funan** The first state known to have reflected Indian influence in this fashion was **Funan,** which dominated the lower reaches of the Mekong River (including parts of modern Cambodia and Vietnam) between the first and the sixth centuries C.E. The rulers of Funan consolidated their grip on the Mekong Valley and built a capital city at the port of Oc Eo. Funan grew wealthy because it dominated the Isthmus of Kra, the narrow portion of the Malay peninsula across which merchants transported trade goods between China and India. (Directly crossing this small width of land enabled them to avoid a long voyage around the Malay peninsula.) The rulers of Funan drew enormous wealth by controlling trade between

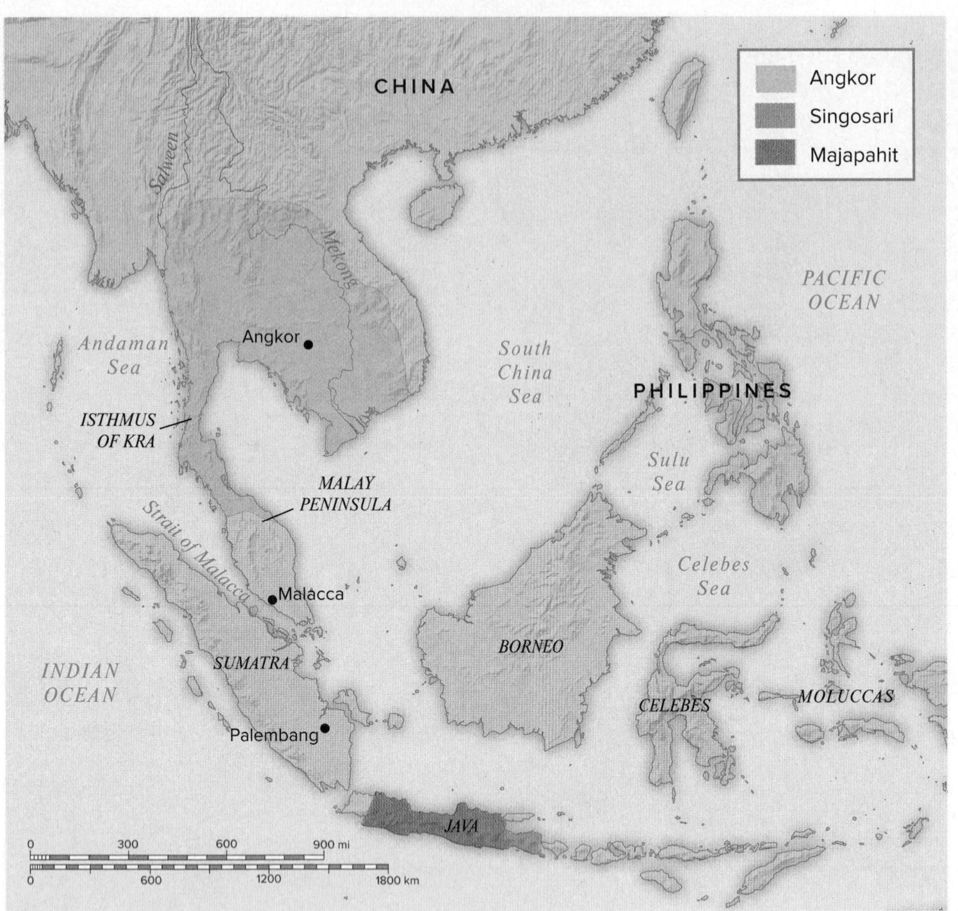


**MAP 3.4 Later states of southeast Asia: Angkor, Singosari, and Majapahit, 889–1520 C.E.**

Angkor was a largely agricultural society, whereas Singosari and Majapahit were more active in maritime trade.

***To what extent did these three states owe their success to continuing trans-regional trade between East and South Asia?***

East and South Asia. They used their profits to construct an elaborate system of water storage and irrigation—so extensive that aerial photography still reveals its lines—that served a productive agricultural economy in the Mekong delta.

As trade with India became an increasingly important part of Funan's economy, the ruling classes adopted Indian political, cultural, and religious traditions. They took the Sanskrit term *raja* ("king") for themselves and claimed divine sanction for their rule in the manner of Hindu rulers in India. They established positions for administrators and bureaucrats such as those found at Indian courts and conducted official business in Sanskrit. They introduced Indian ceremonies and rituals and worshiped Vishnu, Shiva, and other Hindu deities. They continued to honor local deities, particularly water spirits venerated widely throughout southeast Asia, but they eagerly welcomed Hinduism, which offered additional recognition and divine legitimacy for their rule. At first, Indian cultural and religious traditions were most prominent and most often observed at ruling courts. Over the longer term, however, those traditions extended well beyond ruling elites and won a secure place in southeast Asian society.

During the sixth century C.E., a bitter power struggle weakened Funan internally. Peoples from the north took advantage of that weakness, migrated to the lower Mekong Valley in large numbers, and overwhelmed Funan. Chams settled in the southern portion of modern Vietnam, and Khmers dominated in the region occupied by modern Cambodia. By the late sixth century, Funan's intricate irrigation system had fallen into ruin, and Funan itself soon passed into oblivion.

**Srivijaya** After the fall of Funan, political leadership in southeast Asia passed to the kingdom of **Srivijaya** (670–1025 C.E.) based on the island of Sumatra. The kings of Srivijaya built a powerful navy and controlled commerce in southeast Asian waters. They compelled port cities in southeast Asia to recognize their authority, and they financed their navy and bureaucracy from taxes levied on ships passing through the region. They maintained an all-sea trade route between China and India, eliminating the need for the portage of trade goods across the Isthmus of Kra. As the volume of shipping increased in the second half of the first millennium, the Srivijaya kingdom prospered until the expansive Chola kingdom of southern India eclipsed it in the eleventh century.

With the decline of Srivijaya, the kingdoms of **Angkor** (889–1431 C.E.), **Singosari** (1222–1292 C.E.), and **Majapahit** (1293–1520 C.E.) dominated affairs in southeast Asia. Many differences characterized these states. Funan had its base of operations in the Mekong Valley, Srivijaya at Palembang in southern Sumatra, Angkor in Cambodia, and Singosari and Majapahit on the island of Java. Funan and Angkor were

**Srivijaya** (sree-vih-JUH-yuh)
**Angkor** (AHN-kor)

## What's Left Out?

To the extent that we can generalize, it is fair to say that women in Southeast Asian societies enjoyed greater equality and a more prominent public role than women in other South and East Asian societies at this time. This is demonstrated by the life of Queen Pwa Saw of the wealthy state of Pagan, which ruled much of modern Myanmar (Burma) at the same time the Khmer people were ruling the kingdom of Angkor in modern Cambodia. Women in both kingdoms played significant public roles as village leaders, merchants, scribes, bankers, scholars, and advisers to the ruling kings. According to a chronicle that was written in the nineteenth century, one of the most influential rulers of Pagan was Queen Pwa Saw. However, because the chronicle was produced six hundred years after the events it discusses, historians are divided over how much of the story is fact and how much is myth.

According to the chronicle, young Pwa Saw entered the Pagan royal palace as one of many wives of King Uzana, although she quickly became the most powerful. Following the death of the king in 1256 from a hunting accident, Pwa Saw and her advisers influenced the succession so that one of Uzana's sons, Narathihapade, was crowned king, and Pwa Saw became his chief queen. As Narathihapade's reign progressed, however, he became increasingly paranoid, and only Pwa Saw was able to moderate his destructive behaviors. The king eventually went mad, executed many of his rivals, and refused the Mongols' offer of a tribute relationship to avoid an invasion, which led to the Mongol devastation of Pagan and a decline in the kingdom's fortunes. Even in the midst of this chaos, Pwa Saw arranged for Buddhist monasteries to be supported by her estate, and after mad King Narathihapade was murdered in 1287, the queen was able to facilitate a second smooth succession of the throne, this time to Kyawswar, another of the slain king's sons.

However, according to the chronicles, Pwa Saw was disappointed in Kyawswar's ineffective rule, and she plotted with former Pagan military commanders to overthrow the king and appoint a fourteen-year-old prince to the throne. Somehow Pwa Saw managed to survive decades of court intrigue, Mongol invasions, and royal madness, and live to the ripe old age of seventy-three. She was posthumously given the name Pwa Saw, which means "Queen Grandmother," and is remembered in Burma today as a wise, funny, beautiful, and powerful woman who was effectively the real power behind the Pagan throne for more than forty years.

*Source:* Craig A. Lockard, *Southeast Asia in World History* (Oxford: Oxford University Press, 2009), chap. 3.

### Thinking Critically About Sources

1. What strategies did Pwa Sam employ to gain and maintain power in 13th century Myanmar?
2. Compare and contrast her rule and legacy to any other female ruler you have studied.

land-based states that derived most of their wealth from productive agricultural economies, whereas Srivijaya, Singosari, and Majapahit were island-based states that prospered because they controlled maritime trade. Funan and Majapahit were largely Hindu states, but the kings of Srivijaya and Angkor made deep commitments to Buddhism. Native southeast Asian traditions survived in all these states, and at the court of Singosari, religious authorities fashioned a cultural blend of Hindu, Buddhist, and indigenous values. Sculptures at the Singosari court depicted Hindu and Buddhist personalities, for example, but used them to honor local deities and natural spirits rather than Indian deities.

**Angkor** The magnificent monuments of Angkor testify eloquently to the influence of Indian traditions in southeast Asia. Beginning in the ninth century, the kings of the Khmers began to build a capital city at Angkor Thom. With the aid of brahmin advisers from India, the kings designed the city as a microcosmic reflection of the Hindu world order. At the center, they built a temple representing the Himalayan Mount Meru, the sacred abode of Shiva, and surrounded it with numerous smaller temples representing other parts of the Hindu universe.

As the Khmers turned to Buddhism during the twelfth and thirteenth centuries, they added Buddhist temples to the complex, though without removing the earlier structures inspired by Hinduism. The entire complex formed a square with sides of about three kilometers (two miles), surrounded by a moat filled from the nearby Tonle Sap River. During the twelfth century the Khmer kings constructed a smaller but even more elaborate temple center at Angkor Wat, about one kilometer (just over half a mile) from Angkor Thom.

The Khmers abandoned Angkor in 1431 after Thai peoples invaded the capital and left much of it in ruins. Soon the jungle reclaimed both Angkor Thom and Angkor Wat, which remained largely forgotten until French missionaries and explorers rediscovered the sites in the mid-nineteenth century. Rescued from the jungle, the temple complexes of Angkor stand today as vivid reminders of the influence of Indian political, cultural, and religious traditions in southeast Asia and of the wealth generated in the region by trade between East and South Asia.

## The Arrival of Islam

Muslim merchants had ventured into southeast Asia by the eighth century, but only during the tenth century did they become prominent in the region. Some came from southern Arabia or Persia, but many were Indians from Gujarat or the port cities of southern India. Thus Indian influence helped to establish Islam as well as Hinduism and Buddhism in southeast Asia.

Maritime trade flourished in southeast Asia during postclassical times. This ninth-century relief carving from the Buddhist temple at Borobodur in Java depicts a typical southeast Asian merchant's ship.
Werner Forman/Universal Images Group/Getty Images

**Conversion to Islam** For several centuries Islam maintained a quiet presence in southeast Asia. Small communities of foreign merchants observed their faith in the port cities of the region but attracted little interest on the part of the native inhabitants. Gradually, however, ruling elites, traders, and others who had regular dealings with foreign Muslims became interested in the faith. During the late thirteenth century, the Venetian traveler Marco Polo visited the island of Sumatra and noted that many residents of the towns and cities had converted to Islam, whereas those living in the countryside and the hills retained their inherited traditions.

Like Hinduism and Buddhism, Islam did not enter southeast Asia as an exclusive faith. Ruling elites who converted to Islam often continued to honor Hindu, Buddhist, or native southeast Asian traditions. They adopted Islam less as an exclusive and absolute creed than as a faith that facilitated their dealings with foreign Muslims and provided additional divine sanction for their rule. Rarely did they push their subjects to convert to Islam, although they allowed Sufi mystics to preach their faith before popular audiences. As in India, Sufis in southeast Asia appealed to a large public because of their reputation for sincerity and holiness. They allowed converts to retain inherited customs while adapting the message of Islam to local needs and interests.

**Melaka** During the fifteenth century the spread of Islam gained momentum in southeast Asia, largely because the powerful state of **Melaka** sponsored the faith throughout the region. Founded during the late fourteenth century by Paramesvara, a rebellious prince from Sumatra, Melaka took advantage of its strategic location in the Strait of Melaka, near modern Singapore, and soon became prominent in the trading world of southeast Asia. During its earliest days Melaka was more a lair of pirates than a legitimate state. By the mid-fifteenth century, however, Melaka had built a substantial navy that patrolled the waters of southeast Asia and protected the region's sea lanes. Melakan fleets compelled ships to call at the port of Melaka, where ruling authorities levied taxes on the value of their cargoes. Thus, like southeast Asian states of earlier centuries, Melaka became a powerful state through the control of maritime trade.

In one respect, though, Melaka differed significantly from the earlier states. Although it began as a Hindu state, Melaka soon became predominantly Islamic. About the mid-fifteenth century the Melakan ruling class converted to Islam. It welcomed theologians, Sufis, and other Islamic authorities to Melaka and sponsored missionary campaigns to spread Islam

**Melaka** (muh-LAHK-kah)

## INTERPRETING IMAGES

General view of the temple complex dedicated to Vishnu at Angkor Wat. These temples reflect the deep influence of Indian political, cultural, and religious traditions in southeast Asia.

**Analyze** *Other than the fact that it is the largest religious structure in the world, what is the political, economic, and religious significance of Angkor Wat?*

Alain Evrard/Science Source

throughout southeast Asia. By the end of the fifteenth century, mosques had begun to define the urban landscapes of Java, Sumatra, and the Malay peninsula, and Islam had made its first appearance in the spice-bearing islands of Maluku and in the southern islands of the Philippine archipelago.

Thus, within several centuries of its arrival, Islam was a prominent feature in the cultural landscape of southeast Asia. Along with Hinduism and Buddhism, Islam helped link southeast Asian lands to the larger cultural world of India and to the larger commercial world of the Indian Ocean basin.

## CONCLUSION

Unlike the political situation in China, southwest and central Asia, and the eastern Mediterranean during the first millennium C.E., India did not experience a return of centralized imperial rule such as that provided by the Tang and Song dynasties, the Umayyad and Abbasid dynasties, and the Byzantine Empire. In other respects, however, India's development was similar to that experienced in these other regions. Increased agricultural production fueled population growth and urbanization, and trade encouraged specialized industrial production and rapid economic growth. The vigorous and voluminous commerce of the Indian Ocean basin influenced the structure of economies and societies from east Asia to east Africa. It brought prosperity especially to India, which not only contributed cotton, pepper, sugar, iron, steel, and other products to the larger hemispheric economy but also served as a major clearinghouse of trade. Like contemporary societies, India also experienced cultural change, and Indian traditions deeply influenced the cultural development of other lands. Hinduism and Islam emerged as the two most popular religious faiths within the subcontinent, and Indian merchants helped to establish Hinduism, Buddhism, and Islam in southeast Asian lands. Throughout the first and early second millennia C.E., India participated fully in the larger hemispheric zone of cross-cultural communication and exchange.

## STUDY TERMS

Angkor (118)
Axum (111)
bhakti movement (116)
caste system (103)
Chola kingdom (106)
dhows (108)
emporia (109)
Funan (117)
guru Kabir (116)
Harsha (103)
junks (108)
Mahmud of Ghazni (104)
Majapahit (118)
Melaka (120)
monsoons (107)
Ramanuja (115)
Shankara (115)
Shiva (114)
Singosari (118)
Srivijaya (118)
Sufis (116)
sultanate of Delhi (105)
Vijayanagar kingdom (107)
Vishnu (114)

## FOR FURTHER READING

Al-Biruni. *Alberuni's India.* 2 vols. Trans. by E. Sachau. London, 1910. English translation of al-Biruni's eleventh-century description of Indian customs, religion, philosophy, geography, and astronomy.

Edward Alpers. *The Indian Ocean in World History*. Oxford, 2014. A sweeping overview of the relationship between trade, politics and culture in the Indian Ocean world zone from ancient to modern times.

K. N. Chaudhuri. *Asia before Europe: Economy and Civilisation of the Indian Ocean from the Rise of Islam to 1750.* Cambridge, 1990. Controversial and penetrating analysis of economic, social, and cultural structures shaping societies of the Indian Ocean basin.

Ainslie T. Embree and Stephen Hay, eds. *Sources of Indian Tradition.* 2 vols. 2nd ed. New York, 1988. An important collection of primary sources in English translation.

Charles Higham. *The Civilization of Angkor.* London, 2001. Draws usefully on archaeological research in placing Angkor in historical context.

Michel Jacq-Hergoualc'h. *The Malay Peninsula: Crossroads of the Maritime Silk Road (100 B.C.-1300 A.D.).* Leiden, 2002. Scholarly study emphasizing the significance of maritime trade for southeast Asian societies.

Craig Lockard. *Southeast Asia in World History*. Oxford, 2009. Explores the history of Southeast Asia from ancient times to the present, with a strong focus on what the author terms the Golden Age between 800 and 1400 C.E.

Patricia Risso. *Merchants and Faith: Muslim Commerce and Culture in the Indian Ocean.* Boulder, 1995. Surveys the activities of Muslim merchants in the Indian Ocean basin from the seventh to the nineteenth century.

Tansen Sen. *Buddhism, Diplomacy, and Trade: The Realignment of Sino-Indian Relations, 600-1400.* Honolulu, 2003. A pathbreaking study exploring trade, diplomacy, and cultural exchanges between postclassical India and China.

Burton Stein. *Vijayanagara.* Cambridge, 1989. A study of the southern Hindu kingdom concentrating on political and economic history.

Romila Thapar. *Early India: From the Origins to A.D. 1300.* Berkeley, 2003. A scholarly analysis by one of the leading scholars of early Indian history.

# CHAPTER 3 AP EXAM PRACTICE

Questions assume cumulative knowledge from this chapter and previous chapters.

## Section I

## Multiple Choice Questions

Use the image below and your knowledge of world history to answer questions 1-3.

This seventeenth-century painting depicts the legendary Sufi master Khwaja Khidr, beloved in Muslim communities throughout northern India as one associated with springtime, fertility, water, and happiness.
The History Collection/Alamy Stock Photo

1. Which historical development is best exemplified by this image?
   (A) The development of the caste system
   (B) The spread of Hinduism to South Asia.
   (C) Decentralized government in India.
   (D) The spread of Islam to South Asia.

2. Historians could use this image of a Sufi mystic to show that
   (A) Sufi mystics adapted their teachings to appeal to other cultures.
   (B) eating fish was not allowed in Sufi dietary laws.
   (C) Islam, which developed out of a desert culture, associated the ocean with evil spirits.
   (D) Muhammed traveled to India to spread Islam.

3. What statement below describes the bhakti movement?
   (A) The bhakti movement emerged in the kingdom of Axum.
   (B) Bhakti teachings emphasized knowledge of Sanskrit and the ancient Indian philosophical tradition.
   (C) Bhakti leaders Hindus and Muslims to stay separate from each other.
   (D) The bhakti tradition emphasized practices that were common to both Hindus and Muslims.

Use the passage below and your knowledge of world history to answer questions 4 and 5.

Trade between various Southeast Asian ports and Tang China was so intense by the early eighth century that the government created a new official position to help regulate it: the Superintendent of the Shipping Trade. An official Chinese report created a century later comments on the regulation of trade between Southeast Asian countries and ports along the southern Chinese coast and the work of the Superintendent. During the Tang Dynasty, the Chinese referred to this as the *Nanhai* trade.

When [the laden Nanhai ships] arrive, a report is sent to the Court and announcements are made to the cities. The [chief merchants] who commanded them are made to register with Superintendent of the Shipping Trade their names and their cargo [or submit their manifest]. [The Superintendent collects the duties on the goods and sees that there are no prohibited precious and rare goods [of which the government had a monopoly]. There were some foreign merchants who were imprisoned for trying to deceive him.

*Source:* Wang Gungwu, *The Nanhai Trade: Early Chinese Trade in the South Chinese Sea.* (Singapore: Eastern Universities Press, 2003), p. 94.

4. Based on this primary source, what concerns did states have about trade in port cities?
   (A) Local bureaucrats preferred foreign ships, damaging local merchants.
   (B) The Superintendents of the Shipping Trade were easily bribed.
   (C) Governments wanted to prevent smuggling and protect certain monopolies.
   (D) Captains refused to trade in port cities that registered their cargo.

5. How could historians use this primary source to make a point about trade in Asia?
   (A) Tang Dynasty rulers wanted to prevent trade with Southeast Asia because it increased crime in port cities.
   (B) Smuggling was not a problem in trade with Southeast Asia.
   (C) Centralized states like the Tang Dynasty were able to create bureaucratic institutions that allowed overseas trade while protecting the Chinese economy.
   (D) Southeast Asian ships traveled to China so rarely that they were invited to court and other cities.

## Short Answer

6. Use the image below and your knowledge of world history to answer parts A, B, and C.

General view of the temple complex dedicated to Vishnu at Angkor Wat. These temples reflect the deep influence of Indian political, cultural, and religious traditions in southeast Asia.
Alain Evrard/Science Source

(A) Identify ONE similarity between Hinduism and Buddhism.
(B) Explain ONE way that Indian politics and culture influenced Southeast Asia.
(C) Explain ONE way that the cultures of Southeast Asia maintained their own traditions instead of adopting Indian ones.

7. Use the map below and your knowledge of world history to answer parts A, B, and C.

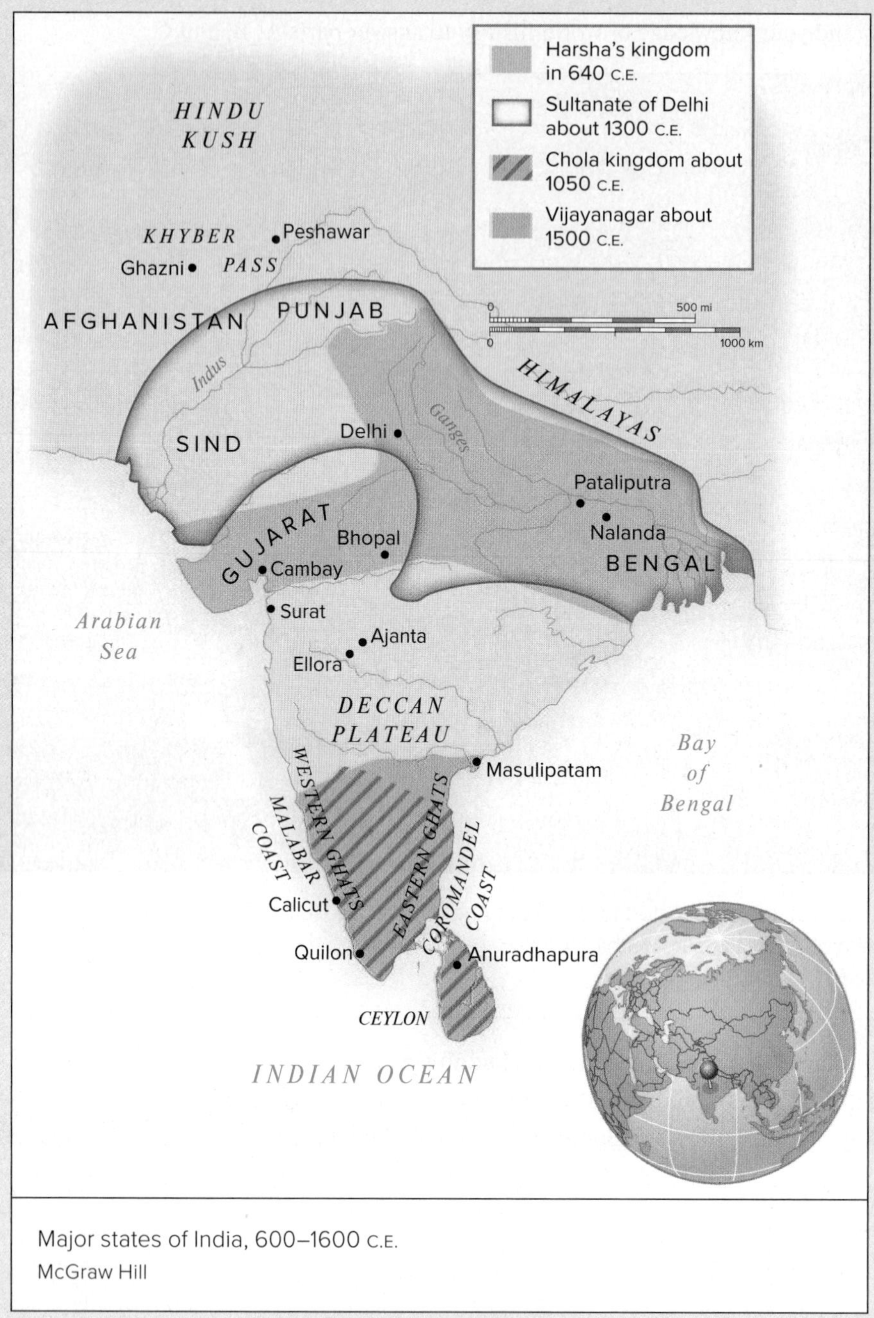


Major states of India, 600–1600 C.E.
McGraw Hill

(A) Identify ONE way that trade in India benefited from its location.
(B) Explain ONE difference between Northern and Southern Indian states.
(C) Explain ONE reason that India was unified in spite of the lack of a centralized state.

8. Use your understanding of world history to answer parts A, B, and C.
(A) Identify ONE important aspect of agricultural production in South and Southeast Asia.
(B) Explain ONE way that technology benefited Indian Ocean trade.
(C) Explain ONE way that Indian Ocean trade encouraged religious exchanges.

# Section II

## Document-Based Question

Based on the following documents and your knowledge of world history, explain how states in South and Southeast Asia created stable forms of government from 600–1600 C.E.

In your response you should do the following:

- Respond to the prompt with a historically defensible thesis or claim that establishes a line of reasoning.
- Describe a broader historical context relevant to the prompt.
- Support an argument in response to the prompt using all documents.
- Use at least one additional piece of specific historical evidence (beyond that found in the documents) relevant to an argument about the prompt.
- Explain how or why the document's point of view, purpose, historical situation, and /or audience is relevant to an argument.
- Use evidence to corroborate, qualify, or modify an argument that addresses the prompt.

### Document 1

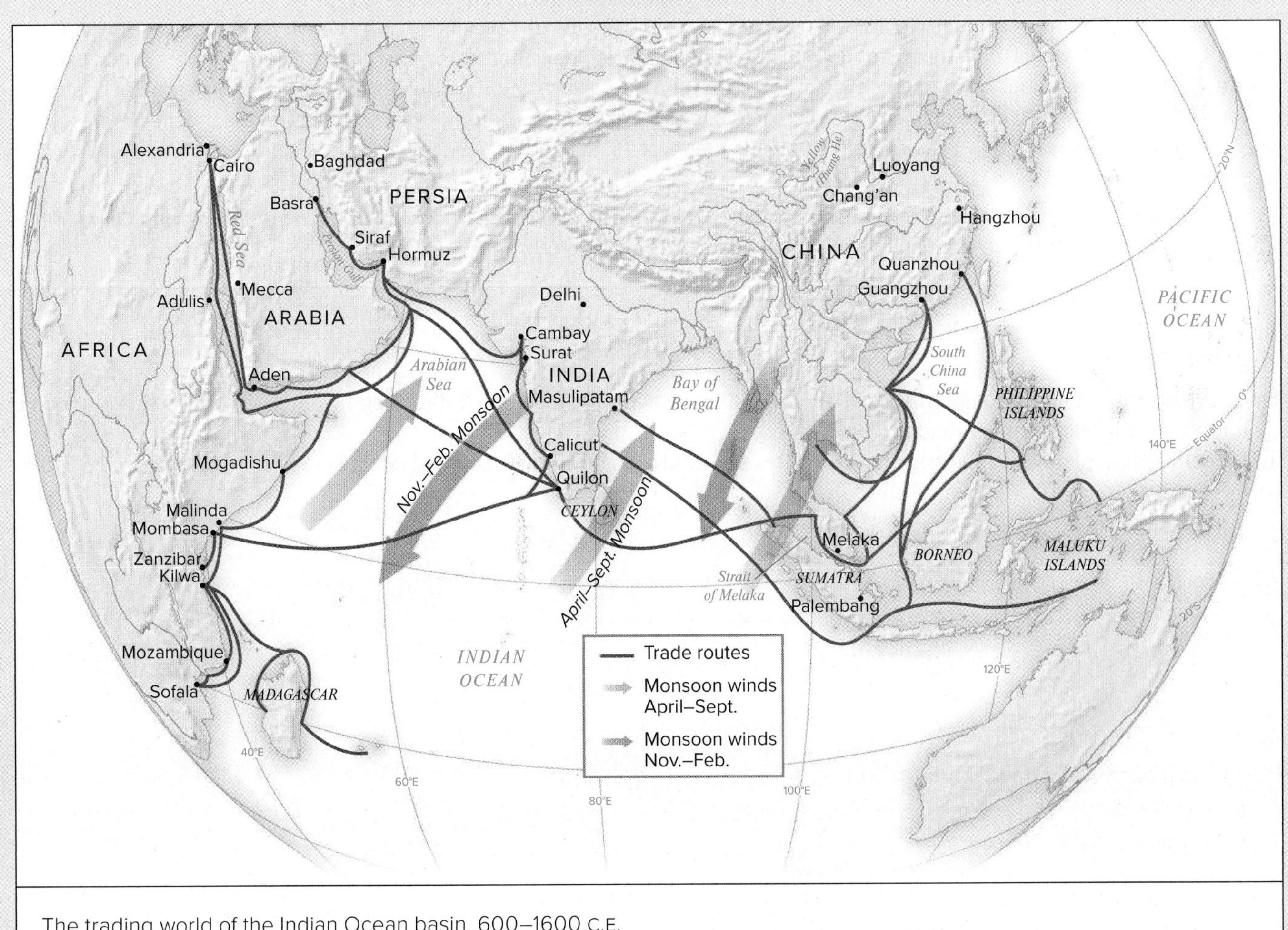


The trading world of the Indian Ocean basin, 600–1600 C.E.

McGraw Hill

## Document 2

Harsha enjoyed a reputation for piety, tolerance, and scholarship. He was a Buddhist, but he looked kindly on other faiths. He built hospitals and provided free medical care for his subjects. The Chinese pilgrim Xuanzang visited northern India during his reign and reported that Harsha liberally distributed wealth to his subjects. On one occasion, Xuanzang said, the king and his aides doled out resources continuously for seventy-five days, making gifts to half a million people. Harsha also generously patronized scholars and reportedly even wrote three plays himself.

*Source:* Bentley and Ziegler, *Traditions & Encounters: A Global Perspective on the Past*

## Document 3

The king wears his hair in a knot, on his head is a golden bell; he wears a silken robe and leather shoes. His throne is a square seat and his officers at their daily audience bow three times when withdrawing. When he goes forth he rides an elephant, or is carried in a chair followed by a company of some 500 to 700 armed soldiers. When any one of the people see the king, he squats down until [the king] has passed by . . . The [government does] not inflict corporal punishment and imprisonment on criminals; they are fined an amount in gold varying according to the gravity of the crime . . . [The country] produces rice, hemp, millet, beans, but no wheat. Ploughing is done with buffaloes. They also pay attention to the raising of silkworms and the weaving of the silk; they have various colored brocaded silks, cotton, and damasked cotton gauzes. They cast coins in an alloy of copper, silver, white copper and tin. Foreign merchants use gold and silver in trading. There is a vast store of pepper and the [Chinese] merchant ships, in view of the profit they derive from that trade, are in the habit of smuggling out of China copper cash for bartering purposes.

*Source:* Frederick Hurth and W. W. Rockhill, *Chau Ju-kua: His Work on the Chinese and Arab Trade in the Twelfth and Thirteenth Centuries, entitled Chu-fan-chi,* reprint edition (Taipei: Literature House, 1965), pp. 76–78.

## Long Essay

Develop a thoughtful and thorough historical argument that answers the question below. Begin your essay with a thesis statement and support it with relevant historical evidence.

Using specific exam ples, write an essay that compares and contrasts how Hinduism and Islam spread across South and Southeast Asia.

# Chapter 4 Eastern and Western Europe in the Early Medieval Period



## ZOOMING IN ON ENCOUNTERS

### Emperor Charlemagne and His Elephant

In the year 802 C.E., an unusual traveler arrived at Aachen (in modern Germany), capital of the western European empire ruled by Charlemagne. The traveler was a rare albino elephant, a diplomatic gift from the Abbasid caliph Harun al-Rashid to Charlemagne. The elephant—whom Harun named Abu al-Abbas, in honor of the Abbasid dynasty's founder—was born in India and went to Baghdad with his trainer in about 798. From Baghdad the animal accompanied an embassy overland through Syria and Egypt to a port on the Tunisian coast, then sailed across the Mediterranean to Portovenere (near Genoa in northern Italy), and finally trekked across the Alps and overland to Charlemagne's court. Abu al-Abbas must have shivered through the cold, damp winters of Europe. Yet he enjoyed swimming in the Rhine River, and until his death in 810, he amazed and delighted all who beheld him.

The church of Hagia Sophia ("Holy Wisdom") rises above the modern city of Istanbul. Originally a Christian church, the building then became an Islamic mosque, and finally a museum.
Catherine Leblanc/Corbis Documentary/Getty Images

Despite his enjoyment in receiving such an unusual gift from the Muslim court of Harun al-Rashid, Charlemagne was not a friend of Islam. At the battle of Tours (732 C.E.), his grandfather, Charles Martel, had defeated a Muslim army that ventured into Frankish territory after Muslim forces had conquered most of the Iberian peninsula. Charlemagne himself fought Muslims in an unsuccessful effort to restore Christian rule in northern Spain. One of the battles from his campaign provided the raw material for a popular poetic work called the *Song of Roland.* Nevertheless, in spite of his personal religious preferences, Charlemagne found it both necessary and convenient to have diplomatic dealings with Harun al-Rashid.

Charlemagne dispatched at least three embassies to Baghdad and received three in return. The embassies dealt with several issues: the safety of Christian pilgrims and merchants traveling in Abbasid-controlled Syria and Palestine, Charlemagne's relations with Muslim neighbors, and policy toward the Byzantine Empire, which stood between western Europe and the Abbasid caliphate. Charlemagne's realm was weak and poor compared with the Abbasid empire, but for about half a century, it seemed that Charlemagne and his successors might be able to reestablish a centralized imperial state in western Europe. His dealings with Harun al-Rashid—and the unusual odyssey of the elephant Abu al-Abbas—reflected a general recognition that Charlemagne had the potential to establish a western European empire similar to the Byzantine and Abbasid realms.

# CHAPTER FOCUS

- While the western half of the Roman empire collapsed entirely, the eastern Roman empire's government was able to defend itself much better.
- While the two former half of the Roman Empire were both predominantly Christian, they developed very different political, economic, and religious cultures during this postclassical period.
- Western Europe dissolved into small kingdoms that had little contact with other regions. New crises in early medieval Europe led to labor adaptation, and serfdom was a significant change.
- The Eastern Roman Empire continued for another 1,000 years as the Byzantine Empire based on Constantinople's earlier Greek name—Byzantium.
- The Vikings became important new players both in the west and the Byzantine Empire. They founded the new trading city of Novgorod, and traveled, traded, conquered, and looted from North America to Constantinople.

## Historical Developments

- Christianity, Judaism, Islam and the core beliefs and practices of these religions continued to shape societies in Europe.
- Europe was politically fragmented and characterized by decentralized monarchies, feudalism, and the manorial system.
- Europe was largely an agricultural society dependent on free and coerced labor, including serfdom.

## Reasoning Processes

- **Comparison** Describe similarities and/or differences between the eastern and western branches of Christianity.

## Historical Thinking Skills

- **Sourcing and Situation** Explain the significance of the Papacy's point of view on the peasantry of Europe using primary source accounts.
- **Contextualization** Identify and explain the role the Vikings played in the larger economic development of Western Europe and the Byzantine empire.
- **Argumentation** Make a historically defensible claim as to why the Byzantine empire and western Europe developed such different understandings of Christianity.

## CHAPTER OVERVIEW

Some historians refer to the period from about 500 to 1500 C.E. as the medieval period of European history—the "middle ages" falling between ancient and modern times. During the early medieval period, from about 500 to 1000 C.E., European peoples recovered from the many problems that plagued the later Roman Empire—epidemic disease, declining population, economic contraction, political turmoil, social unrest, and invasions by Germanic peoples. In doing so, they laid the foundations of subsequent European civilization.

The two very different halves of medieval Europe were the **Byzantine Empire** in the eastern half of the Mediterranean basin and the Germanic states that succeeded the Western Roman Empire after its collapse in the fifth century C.E. The Byzantine Empire was in fact a direct continuation of the Roman Empire in the east. It did not extend its authority to the entire Mediterranean basin, but it inherited the most prosperous and productive regions of the Roman Empire. Even after Muslim conquerors seized the wealthy provinces of Egypt and Syria in the seventh century, the Byzantine Empire remained a political and economic powerhouse throughout the first millennium of the Common Era. As a centralized imperial state like the Abbasid empire in southwest Asia or the Tang and Song dynasties in China, the Byzantine Empire dominated the eastern Mediterranean and Black Sea regions. As an urbanized center of manufacturing, the Byzantine Empire was also a highly productive society that both supported and benefited from trade throughout the eastern hemisphere.

Meanwhile, lands to the west of the Byzantine Empire fell under the sway of invading peoples who dismantled the western part of the Roman Empire and established a series of Germanic successor states. Charlemagne made extraordinary efforts to unify much of western Europe and establish a western counterpart to the Byzantine Empire, but internal tensions and new rounds of invasions brought an early end to his own imperial creation. Thus, during the era 500 to 1000 C.E., western Europe resembled the political situation in India at this time, where a restoration of imperial unity also turned out to be a fleeting experience. When Charlemagne's empire dissolved, western European peoples fashioned alternatives to imperial rule by creating new decentralized forms of government that vested public authority mostly in local or regional rulers. At the same time, they also began a process of economic recovery by dramatically boosting agricultural production.

Both the Byzantine Empire and the European states to the west inherited Christianity from the Roman Empire, and rulers in both regions promoted Christianity as a cultural and moral foundation for their rule. After the eighth century C.E., however, political and religious tensions increasingly complicated relations between the two halves of the former Roman Empire. Byzantine rulers bristled at the claims to empire made by Charlemagne and other western Christian rulers, and theologians in the two regions developed differing views on proper religious doctrine and practice. By the mid-eleventh century, the Byzantine and Roman churches had publicly and formally condemned each other. Byzantine missionaries promoted their brand of Christianity in Russia and other Slavic lands, while western Christians following the leadership of the popes in Rome spread their own views from the British Isles to Scandinavia and eastern Europe. Just as Abbasid leaders helped consolidate Islam as the principal cultural influence in the Muslim world, Byzantine and western Christians expanded the religious and moral authority of Christianity throughout Europe. In doing so, they created two culturally distinctive regions of Europe, a situation that to a certain extent has continued through to today.

| CHRONOLOGY | |
|---|---|
| 313–337 | Reign of Constantine |
| 329–379 | Life of St. Basil of Caesarea |
| 476 | Collapse of the Western Roman Empire |
| 480–547 | Life of St. Benedict of Nursia |
| 482–543 | Life of St. Scholastica |
| 527–565 | Reign of Justinian |
| 590–604 | Reign of Pope Gregory I |
| 717–741 | Reign of Leo III |
| 726–843 | Iconoclastic controversy |
| 732 | Battle of Tours |
| 751–843 | Carolingian kingdom |
| 768–814 | Reign of Charlemagne |
| 800 | Coronation of Charlemagne as emperor |
| 9th century | Missions of St. Cyril and St. Methodius to the Slavs |
| 989 | Conversion of Prince Vladimir of Kiev to Christianity |
| 1054 | Schism between Eastern Orthodox and Roman Catholic churches |

## THE QUEST FOR POLITICAL ORDER

During the fourth and fifth centuries, the eastern half of the Roman Empire suffered from invasions by Germanic peoples, but it did not collapse. The political challenge for rulers in this region—direct successors of the Roman emperors—was to restore order following the invasions. In the sixth century Byzantine rulers even tried to reestablish Roman authority throughout the Mediterranean basin. Their efforts fell short of that goal, and they soon lost

**Byzantine** (BIHZ-uhn-teen)

considerable territories to expansive Muslim forces, but they nevertheless presided over a powerful society in the eastern Mediterranean region.

Political challenges were greater in lands to the west. Germanic invaders mostly passed through the Eastern Roman Empire, but they mostly settled in western regions. Throughout Roman Europe and north Africa, Germanic invaders disrupted Roman authority, deposed Roman officials, and imposed new states of their own making. After two centuries of fighting, it looked as though one group of Germanic invaders, the Franks, might reestablish imperial authority in much of Roman Europe. If they had succeeded, they might have played a role similar to that of the Sui and Tang dynasties in China by reviving centralized imperial rule after a hiatus of several centuries. By the late ninth century, however, the Frankish empire had fallen victim to internal power struggles and a fresh series of devastating invasions. Political authority in western Europe then devolved to local and regional jurisdictions, whose leaders fashioned a decentralized political order.

## The Early Byzantine Empire

The Byzantine Empire takes its name from Byzantion—latinized as Byzantium—a modest market town and fishing village that occupied a site of enormous strategic significance. Situated on a defensible peninsula and blessed with a magnificent natural harbor known as the Golden Horn, Byzantion had the potential to control the Bosporus, the strait of water leading from the Black Sea to the Sea of Marmara and beyond to the Dardanelles, the **Aegean Sea,** and the Mediterranean. Apart from its maritime significance, Byzantion offered convenient access to the rich lands of Anatolia, southwestern Asia, and southeastern Europe. Sea lanes linked the city to ports throughout the Mediterranean basin.

### The City of Constantine

Recognizing its strategic value, the Roman emperor Constantine designated Byzantion the site of a new imperial capital, which he named **Constantinople** ("city of Constantine"). He built the new capital partly because the eastern Mediterranean was the wealthiest and most productive region of the Roman Empire and partly because relocation enabled him to maintain close watch over both the Sasanian empire in Persia and the Germanic peoples who lived along the lower stretches of the Danube River. The imperial government moved to Constantinople after 330 C.E., and the new capital rapidly reached metropolitan dimensions. Constantine filled the city with libraries, museums, and artistic treasures, and he constructed magnificent marble palaces, churches, baths, and public buildings—all in an effort to create a new Rome fit for the ruler of a mighty empire. The city kept the name Constantinople until it fell to the Ottoman Turks (1453 C.E.), who renamed it Istanbul. By convention, however, historians refer to the realm governed from Constantinople between the fifth and fifteenth centuries C.E. as the Byzantine Empire, or simply Byzantium, in honor of the original settlement.

### Caesaropapism

Constantine and his successors reinforced their rule with the aura of divinity and awesome splendor. As a Christian, Constantine could not claim the divine status that some of the earlier Roman emperors had appropriated for themselves. As the first Christian emperor, however, he claimed divine favor and sanction for his rule. He intervened in theological disputes and used his political position to support the views he considered orthodox while condemning those he deemed heretical. He initiated the policy of **"caesaropapism,"** whereby the emperor not only ruled as secular lord but also played an active and prominent role in ecclesiastical affairs.

Following Constantine's example, Byzantine emperors presented themselves as exalted, absolute rulers. Even dress and court etiquette testified to their lofty status. The emperors wore bejeweled crowns and dressed in magnificent silk robes dyed a dark, rich purple—a color reserved for imperial use and strictly forbidden to those not associated with the ruling house. High officials presented themselves to the emperor as slaves. When approaching the imperial majesty, they prostrated themselves three times and then ceremoniously kissed the imperial hands and feet before raising matters of business. By the tenth century, engineers had contrived a series of mechanical devices that worked dazzling effects and impressed foreign envoys at the Byzantine court: imitation birds sang as ambassadors approached the emperor while mechanical lions roared and swished their tails. During an audience the imperial throne itself sometimes moved up and down to emphasize the awesome splendor of the emperor.

### Justinian and Theodora

The most important of the early Byzantine emperors was **Justinian** (reigned 527–565 C.E.), an energetic worker known to his subjects as "the sleepless emperor," who ruled with the aid of his wife, **Theodora.** The couple came from obscure origins: Justinian was born into a Macedonian peasant family, and Theodora, the daughter of a bear keeper in the circus, worked as a striptease artist before meeting the future emperor. Yet both Justinian and Theodora were smart, strong-willed, and disciplined. Thanks to those qualities, Justinian received an education, found a position in the imperial bureaucracy, and mastered the intricacies of Byzantine finance. Theodora proved to be a sagacious adviser and a determined supporter of her emperor husband.

Like Constantine, Justinian lavished resources on the imperial capital. His most notable construction project was the church of **Hagia Sophia** ("Holy Wisdom"), a magnificent domed structure—later turned into a mosque by Ottoman conquerors—that ranks as one of the world's most important examples of Christian architecture. Visitors marveled at the

---

**Aegean** (ih-JEE-uhn)
**Hagia Sofia** (HAH-yah soh-FEE-uh)

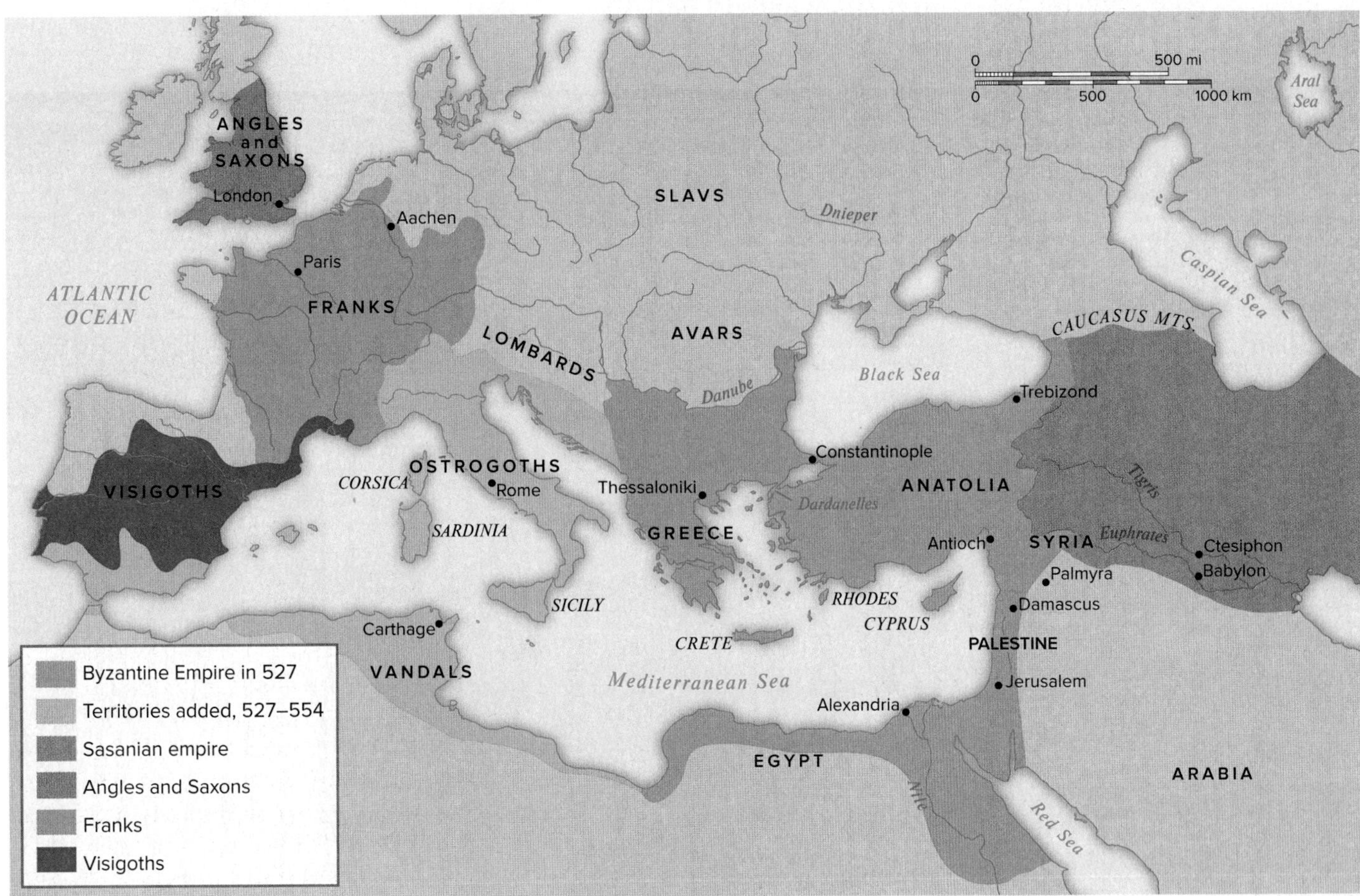


**MAP 4.1 Successor states to the Roman Empire, ca. 600 c.e.**

*What political, cultural, and environmental factors might explain the different outcomes in eastern and western Europe following the fragmentation of the Roman Empire?*

church's enormous dome, which they likened to the heavens encircling the earth, and at the gold, silver, gems, and thousands of lamps that decorated and illuminated Hagia Sophia.

**Justinian's Code** Justinian's most significant political contribution was his codification of Roman law. The origins of Roman law went back more than a thousand years to the times of the kings of Rome, and even though earlier scholars worked to codify the law, it had become a confusing mass of sometimes conflicting injunctions. Justinian ordered a systematic review of Roman law and issued the ***Corpus iuris civilis*** (*Body of the Civil Law*), which immediately won recognition as the definitive codification of Roman law. Updated by later emperors, Justinian's code has influenced civil law codes in most of Europe, in Japan, and in parts of the United States.

**Byzantine Conquests** Justinian's most ambitious venture was his effort to reconquer the Western Roman Empire from Germanic peoples and reestablish Roman authority throughout the Mediterranean basin. Between 533 and 565, Byzantine forces under General Belisarius gained control over Italy, Sicily, much of northwestern Africa, and southern Spain. Yet Byzantium did not possess the resources to sustain a long-term occupation and consolidate those conquests. Shortly after Justinian's death, Byzantine forces abandoned Rome, leaving the city of Ravenna on Italy's Adriatic coast as the headquarters of Byzantine authority in the western Mediterranean. As a result, Ravenna possesses magnificent examples of Byzantine art and architecture, but Justinian's dream of reconstituting the old Roman Empire soon faded into oblivion.

## Muslim Conquests and Byzantine Revival

Justinian's efforts showed that the ancient Roman Empire was beyond recovery. While the emperor devoted his efforts to the western Mediterranean, the Sasanians threatened Byzantium from the east and Slavic peoples approached from the north. Later Byzantine emperors had no choice but to redeploy their resources to meet other threats.

***Corpus iuris civilis*** (KOR-poos EW-rees sih-VEE-lees)

## INTERPRETING IMAGES

Byzantine emperor Justinian wears imperial purple robes (which have faded to brown over the centuries) in this mosaic, from the church of San Vitale in Ravenna, which depicts him in the company of ecclesiastical, military, and court officials.

**Analyze** *Why would the Ravenna mosaic depict the emperor surrounded by ecclesiastical, military, and court officials?*

Leemage/Universal Images Group/Getty Images

**Muslim Conquests** After the seventh century C.E., the expansion of Islam (discussed in chapter 14) posed even more serious challenges to Byzantium. Shortly after Muhammad's death, Arab warriors conquered the Sasanian empire in Persia and overran large portions of the Byzantine Empire as well. By the mid-seventh century, Byzantine Syria, Palestine, Egypt, and north Africa had fallen under Muslim rule. Muslim forces later subjected Constantinople itself to two prolonged sieges (in 674–678 and again in 717–718).

Byzantium resisted this northward thrust of Islam partly because of advanced military technology. Byzantine forces used a weapon known as **"Greek fire"**—a highly effective incendiary weapon whose ingredients were a state secret that has since been lost—which they launched at both the fleets and the ground forces of the invaders. Greek fire burned even when floating on water and thus created a hazard when deployed around wooden ships. On land it caused panic among enemy forces because it was extremely difficult to extinguish and often burned troops to death. As a result of this defensive

## INTERPRETING IMAGES

The interior of the church of Hagia Sophia ("Holy Wisdom"), built by Justinian and transformed into a mosque in the fifteenth century. The dome rises almost 60 meters (197 feet) above the floor, and its windows allow abundant light to enter the massive structure.

**Analyze** *Why does the transformation of the Hagia Sophia from cathedral to mosque after 1453 represent such a significant turning point in world history?*

mediacolor's/Alamy Stock Photo

effort, the Byzantine Empire retained its hold on Anatolia, Greece, and the Balkan region.

**The *Theme* System** Although diminished by Muslim conquests, the Byzantine Empire was more manageable after the eighth century than was the far-flung realm of Justinian. Byzantine rulers responded to the threat of Islam with political and social adjustments that strengthened their reduced empire. Their most important innovation was the reorganization of Byzantine society under the ***theme* system.** They placed an imperial province called a *theme* under the authority of a general, who assumed responsibility for both its military defense and its civil administration. Generals received their appointments from the emperor, who closely monitored their activities to prevent decentralization of power and authority. Generals recruited armies from the ranks of free peasants, who received allotments of land for their military service.

Armies raised under the *theme* system were effective fighting forces, and they enabled Byzantium to expand its influence between the ninth and the twelfth centuries. During the tenth century Byzantine forces reconquered Syria and pushed their authority west into the Balkan region. By the mid-eleventh century, the Byzantine Empire encompassed lands from Syria and Armenia in the east to southern Italy in the west, from the Danube River in the north to the islands of Cyprus and Crete in the south. Once again, Byzantium dominated the eastern Mediterranean region.

## The Rise of the Franks

In the year 476 C.E., the Germanic general **Odoacer** deposed the last of the western Roman emperors. He did not claim the imperial title for himself, however, nor did he appoint anyone else as a replacement. The emperor's post simply remained vacant. Roman administrators and armies continued to function, temporarily, but urban populations declined as continuing invasions and power struggles disrupted trade and manufacturing. Deprived of legitimacy and resources supplied from Rome and other major cities, imperial institutions progressively weakened.

**Germanic Kingdoms** Gradually, a series of Germanic kingdoms emerged as successor states to the Roman empire. Visigoths, Ostrogoths, Lombards, Franks, and other Germanic peoples occupied imperial provinces, displacing Roman authorities and institutions. As they built successor states, Germanic peoples absorbed a great deal of Roman influence. Many of them converted to Christianity, for example, and others adapted Roman law to the needs of their own societies.

**The Franks** Most successful and most influential of the Germanic peoples were the **Franks.** By the early sixth century, the Franks had conquered most of Roman Gaul and emerged as the preeminent military and political power in western

A manuscript illustration depicts Byzantine naval forces using Greek fire on their Arab enemies. Photo Researchers/ Science History Images/ Alamy Stock Photo

Europe. They also gained popular support when they abandoned their inherited polytheistic religion and converted to Christianity—a move that brought them the allegiance of the Christian population of the former Roman Empire as well as support from the pope and the western Christian church.

In the eighth century the aristocratic clan of the Carolingians dramatically extended Frankish power. The **Carolingian dynasty** takes its name from its founder, Charles (*Carolus* in Latin)—known as Charles Martel ("Charles the Hammer") because of his military prowess. In 732 at the battle of Tours (in central France), he turned back a Muslim army that had ventured north from recently conquered Spain. His victory helped persuade Muslim rulers of Spain that it was not worthwhile for them to seek further conquests in western Europe.

**Charlemagne** The Frankish realm reached its high point under Charles Martel's grandson **Charlemagne** ("Charles the Great"), who reigned from 768 to 814. Like King Harsha in India, Charlemagne temporarily reestablished centralized imperial rule in a society disrupted by invasion and contests for power between ambitious local rulers. Like Harsha again, Charlemagne possessed enormous energy, and the building of the Carolingian Empire was in large measure his personal accomplishment. Although barely literate, Charlemagne was intelligent. He spoke Latin, understood some Greek, and regularly conversed with learned men. He maintained diplomatic relations with the Byzantine Empire and the Abbasid caliphate. The gift of the albino elephant Abu al-Abbas, discussed earlier in the chapter, symbolized relations between the Carolingian and Abbasid empires, and until its death in 810, the animal accompanied Charlemagne on many of his travels.

When Charlemagne inherited the Frankish throne, his realm included most of modern France as well as the lands that now form Belgium, the Netherlands, and southwestern Germany. By the time of his death in 814, Charlemagne had extended his authority to northeastern Spain, Bavaria, and Italy as far south as Rome. He campaigned for thirty-two years to impose his rule on the Saxons of northern Germany and to repress their rebellions. Beyond the Carolingian Empire proper, rulers in eastern Europe and southern Italy paid tribute to Charlemagne as imperial overlord.

**Charlemagne's Administration** Charlemagne built a court and capital at Aachen (in modern Germany), but like Harsha in India, he spent most of his reign on horseback, traveling throughout his realm to maintain authority. Constant travel was necessary because Charlemagne did not have the financial resources to maintain an elaborate bureaucracy or an administrative apparatus that could enforce his policies. Instead, he relied on aristocratic deputies, known as counts, who held political, military, and legal authority in local jurisdictions. In an effort to keep the counts under control, Charlemagne instituted a group of imperial officials called the ***missi dominici*** ("envoys of the lord ruler"), who traveled annually to all jurisdictions and reviewed the accounts of local authorities.

Thus Charlemagne built the Frankish kingdom into an empire on the basis of military expeditions, and he began to outfit it with some centralized institutions. Yet he hesitated to call himself emperor because an imperial claim would constitute a direct challenge to the authority of the Byzantine

***missi dominici*** (MISS-ee doh-MIN-ih-chee)

Pope Leo III, crowning Charlemagne from Chroniques de France ou de Saint Denis, vol. 1; France, second quarter of 14th century.
Historic Images/Alamy Stock Photo

emperors, who regarded themselves as the only legitimate successors of the Roman emperors.

**Charlemagne as Emperor** Only in the year 800 did Charlemagne accept the title of emperor. While campaigning in Italy, Charlemagne attended religious services conducted by Pope Leo III on Christmas Day. During the services, the pope proclaimed Charlemagne emperor and placed an imperial crown on his head. It is not certain, but it is possible that Charlemagne did not know of the pope's plan and that Leo surprised him with an impromptu coronation. Charlemagne had no desire for strained relations with the Byzantine emperors, who deeply resented his imperial title, which they saw as a pretentious affront to their own dignity. In any case, Charlemagne had already built an imperial state, and his coronation constituted public recognition of his accomplishments.

## The End of the Carolingian Empire

If Charlemagne's empire had endured, Carolingian rulers might well have built a bureaucracy, used the *missi dominici* to enhance the authority of the central government, and reestablished imperial rule in western Europe. As it happened, however, internal disunity and external invasions brought the Carolingian Empire to an early end.

Charlemagne's only surviving son, **Louis the Pious** (reigned 814–840), succeeded his father and attempted to hold the empire together. Lacking Charlemagne's strong will and military skills, however, Louis lost control of local authorities, who increasingly pursued their own interests. Moreover, Louis's three sons disputed the inheritance of the empire and waged bitter wars against one another. In 843 they divided the empire into three roughly equal portions and ruled as three kings. Thus, less than a century after its creation, the Carolingian Empire dissolved.

## The Age of the Vikings

Even if internal divisions had not dismembered the Carolingian Empire, external pressures might well have brought it down. Beginning in the late eighth century, three groups of invaders pillaged the Frankish realm in search of wealth stored in towns and monasteries. From the south came Muslims, sometimes called Saracens by medieval historians, who raided towns, villages, churches, and monasteries in Mediterranean Europe. Muslim invaders also conquered the island of Sicily and seized territories in southern Italy and southern France. From the east came the **Magyars,** descendants of nomadic peoples who had settled in Hungary. Expert horsemen, the Magyars raided settlements in Germany, Italy, and southern France. From the north came the Vikings, most feared of all the invaders, who began mounting raids in northern France even during Charlemagne's lifetime.

The Viking invasions were part of a much larger process of expansion by the Nordic peoples of Scandinavia. One cause of Norse expansion was probably population growth fueled by increased agricultural production in Scandinavia. The main cause, however, was the quest for wealth through trading and

**Magyars** (MAH-jahrs)

## MAP 4.2 The Carolingian Empire, 814 C.E.

Notice the location of Charlemagne's capital at Aachen and also the extent of his empire.

***What geographic and political challenges did he face in his efforts to hold his empire together?***

raiding in European lands to the south of Scandinavia. Norse expansion depended on a remarkable set of shipbuilding techniques and seafaring skills that Scandinavian mariners developed during the seventh and eighth centuries. They built rugged, shallow-draft boats outfitted both with sails, which enabled them to travel through the open ocean, and with oars, which enabled them to navigate rivers.

**Vikings** Many Norse seafarers were merchants seeking commercial opportunities or migrants seeking lands to settle and cultivate. However, some of them, known as the **Vikings,** turned their maritime skills more toward raiding and plundering than trading or raising crops. The term *Viking* originally referred to a group that raided the British Isles from their home at Vik in southern Norway. Over time, however, the term came to refer more generally to Norse mariners who mounted invasions and plundered settlements from Russia and eastern Europe to Mediterranean lands. With their shallow-draft boats, the Vikings were able to make their way up the many rivers offering access to interior regions of Europe. Vikings coordinated their ships' movements and timed their attacks to take advantage of the tides. Fleets of Viking boats with ferocious dragon heads mounted on their prows could sail up a river, surprise a village or a monastery far from the sea, and spill out crews of warriors who conducted lightning raids on unprepared victims.

The first Viking invaders began to attack unprotected monasteries in the 790s. Learning from experience, Viking forces mounted increasingly daring raids. In 844 C.E., more than 150 Viking ships sailed up the Garonne River in southern France, plundering settlements along the way. Sometimes Viking fleets attacked sizable cities: in 845, some 800 vessels appeared without warning before the city of Hamburg in northern Germany; in 885, a Viking force consisting of at least 700 ships sailed up the Seine River and besieged Paris; and in 994, an armada of about 100 ships sailed swiftly up the Thames River and raided London. Some Vikings bypassed relatively close targets and ventured into the Mediterranean, where they plundered sites in the Balearic Islands, Sicily, and southern Italy. By following the Russian rivers to the Black Sea, other Vikings made their way to Constantinople, which they raided at least three times during the ninth and tenth centuries.

**Devolution of Political Authority** The Carolingians had no navy, no means to protect vulnerable sites, and no way to predict the movements of Viking raiders. Defense against the Magyars and the Muslims as well as the Vikings rested principally with local forces that could respond rapidly to invasions. Because imperial authorities were unable to defend their territories, the Carolingian Empire became the chief casualty of the invasions. After the ninth century, political and military initiative in western Europe increasingly devolved to regional and local authorities.

The Osenberg ship, the best-preserved Viking vessel from the early middle ages, was built in about 800 C.E. Using ships like these, the Vikings undertook extraordinary voyages across a vast region stretching from North America to central Asia.
World History Archive/Alamy Stock Photo

Danish Vikings prepare to invade England in this manuscript illustration produced at an English monastery from about 1130. Although renowned for their raiding, many Vikings later turned to trade and used their maritime skills to help connect western Europe, the Byzantine Empire, and the Islamic caliphate in a vigorous transregional trading network.
Album/Alamy Stock Photo

The devolution of political authority took different forms in different lands. In England and Germany, regional kingdoms emerged and successfully defended territories more compact than the sprawling Carolingian Empire. In France, the counts and other Carolingian subordinates usurped royal rights and prerogatives for themselves. The Vikings themselves established settlements in northern France and southern Italy, where they carved out small, independent states.

Following a century of internal conflict and external invasion, the emergence of regional kingdoms and local authorities made it increasingly unlikely that imperial rule would return to western Europe. Like India in the first millennium C.E., but unlike the situation in China, southwest Asia, and the eastern Mediterranean region, western Europe became a society of competing regional states. By putting an end to the ninth-century invasions and establishing a stable political order, these states laid a foundation for social, economic, and cultural development in later centuries.

## ECONOMY AND SOCIETY IN EARLY MEDIEVAL EUROPE

Economic and social development in eastern and western Europe reflected the different political structures that emerged in each region. Byzantium was an economic powerhouse in

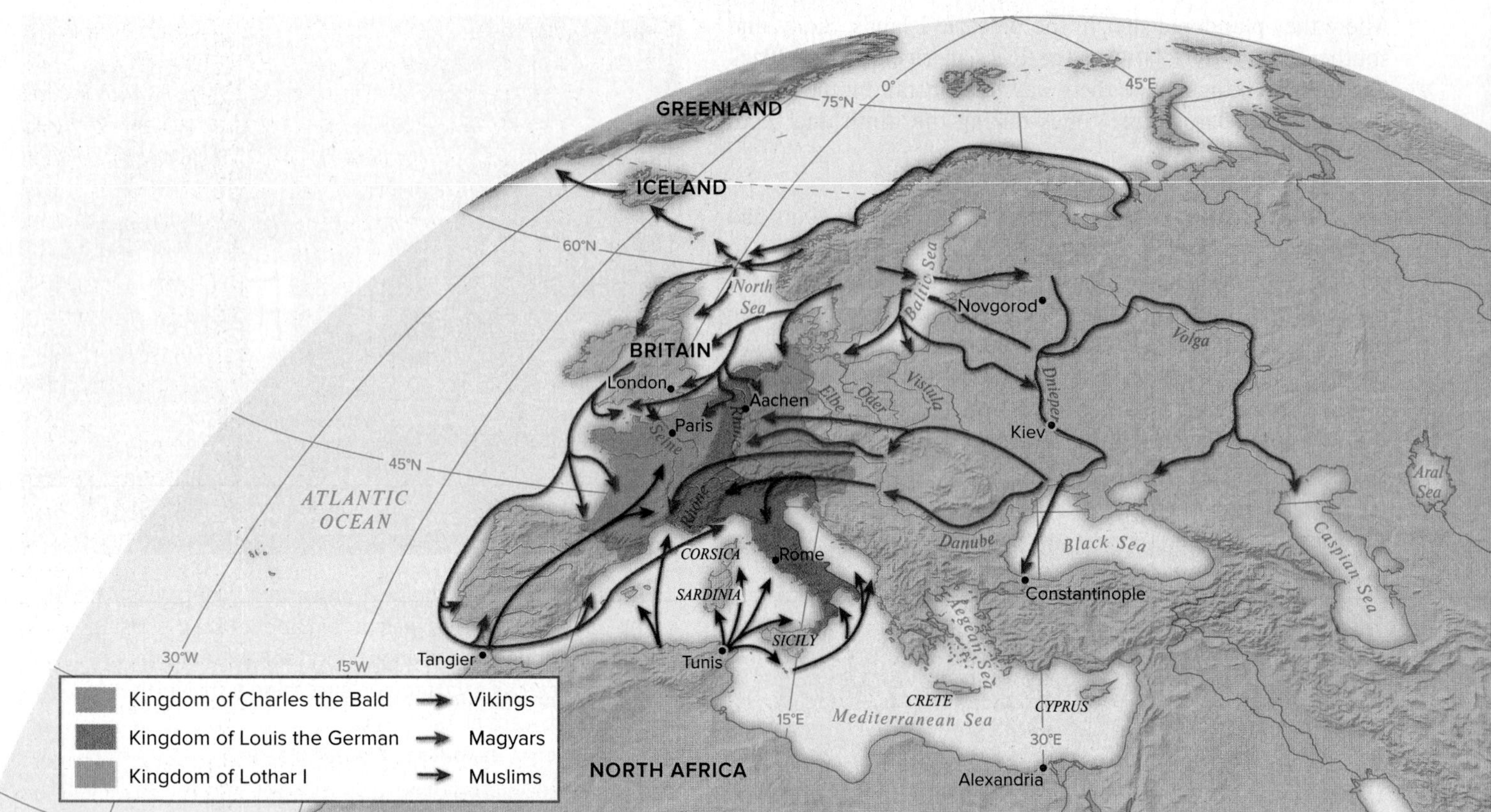


**MAP 4.3 The dissolution of the Carolingian Empire (843 C.E.) and the invasions of early medieval Europe in the ninth and tenth centuries.**

The various invaders of early medieval Europe took many routes and attacked both coastal and interior regions.

***What were some of the political, economic, and cultural effects of the Viking invasions?***

the eastern Mediterranean region. The Byzantine countryside produced abundant agricultural surpluses, which supported large urban populations and fueled the work of manufacturers. Byzantine merchants participated in long-distance commercial networks that linked lands throughout the eastern hemisphere. The small states and kingdoms of western Europe, by contrast, experienced both a decline of agricultural production and a weakening of cities as repeated invasions disrupted economic and social as well as political affairs. By the tenth century, however, a measure of political stability had been restored that served as a foundation for economic recovery, and western European peoples began to participate more actively in the larger trading world of the eastern hemisphere.

## The Two Economies of Early Medieval Europe

**Economy of the Byzantine Empire** Byzantium was strongest when its large class of free peasants had the freedom to cultivate land to the extent of their abilities as farmers. This was enhanced after the adoption of the *theme* system in the eighth century, which meant that soldiers received allotments of land when they mustered out of the army. This arrangement supported a large and prosperous class of free peasants, who cultivated their land intensively in hopes of improving their families' fortunes. The free peasantry entered an era of gradual decline after the eleventh century as wealthy cultivators managed to accumulate large estates. For as long as it flourished, however, the free peasantry provided agricultural surpluses that served as the foundation for general prosperity in the Byzantine Empire.

**Manufacturing** Agricultural surpluses supported manufacturing in Byzantium's cities, especially Constantinople, which was already a manufacturing megalopolis during Roman imperial times. The city was home to throngs of artisans and crafts workers, not to mention thousands of imperial officials and bureaucrats. Byzantine crafts workers enjoyed a reputation especially for their glassware, linen and woolen textiles, gems, jewelry, and fine work in gold and silver.

**Silk** In the sixth century, crafts workers added high-quality silk textiles to the list of products manufactured in the Byzantine Empire. The Byzantine historian Procopius reported that two Christian monks from Persia traveled to China, where they observed the techniques of silk production, which at that time were unknown outside China. According to Procopius, the monks hollowed out their walking staffs and filled them with silkworm eggs, which they smuggled out of China, through their native land of Persia, and into the Byzantine Empire. It is likely that Procopius simplified a more complex story by focusing attention on the monks, who by themselves could hardly have introduced a full-blown silk industry to Byzantium. The production of fine, Chinese-style silks required more than a few silkworm eggs. It called also for the mastery of sophisticated technologies and elaborate procedures that probably reached Byzantium by several routes.

In any case, silk textiles soon made major contributions to the Byzantine economy. By the late sixth century, Byzantine silks matched the quality of Chinese textiles, and Byzantium had become the principal supplier of the fashionable fabric to lands in the Mediterranean basin. The silk industry was so important to the Byzantine economy that the government closely supervised every step in its production and sale. Regulations allowed individuals to participate in only one activity—such as weaving, dyeing, or sales—to prevent the creation of a monopoly by a few wealthy or powerful entrepreneurs.

**Byzantine Trade** The Byzantine economy also benefited from trade. Sitting astride routes going east and west as well as north and south, Constantinople served as the main clearinghouse for trade in the western part of Eurasia. The merchants of Constantinople maintained commercial links with manufacturers and merchants in central Asia, Russia, Scandinavia, northern Europe, and the lands of the Black Sea and the Mediterranean basin. Even after the early Islamic conquests, Byzantine merchants traded regularly with their Muslim counterparts in Persia, Syria, Palestine, and Egypt except during periods of outright war between Byzantium and Muslim states. Indeed, Byzantium was so dominant in trade that the Byzantine gold coin, the *bezant,* served as the standard currency of the Mediterranean basin for more than half a millennium, from the sixth through the twelfth century.

Byzantium drew enormous wealth simply by controlling trade and levying customs duties on merchandise that passed through its lands. Moreover, Byzantium served as the western anchor of the Eurasian trading network during revivals of the ancient Silk Roads network. Silk and porcelain came to Constantinople from China, spices from India and southeast Asia. Carpets arrived from Persia and woolen textiles from western Europe, while timber, furs, honey, amber, and slaves came from Russia and Scandinavia. Byzantine subjects consumed some commodities from distant lands, but they redistributed most products, often after adding to their value by further processing—by fashioning jewelry out of gems imported from India, for example, or by dyeing raw woolen cloth imported from western Europe.

Peasants—probably sharecroppers—receive seeds and tend to vineyards in this painting from a Byzantine manuscript. What does this illustration suggest about the relationship between the two landowners or overseers (left, in the top register) and the five laborers?
The History Collection/Alamy Stock Photo

**Economy of Western Europe** As Byzantium prospered, western Europe struggled to find its economic footing in an era of intermittent invasion and political turmoil, which disrupted both agricultural production and large-scale manufacturing. While dealing with political and military challenges, though, western Europeans also adopted a series of innovations that yielded increased agricultural production.

**Heavy Plows** One innovation was a new kind of heavy plow that gradually replaced the light Mediterranean plows that had made their way north at the time of the Roman Empire. In light, well-drained Mediterranean soils, cultivators used small wooden plows that broke the surface of the soil, created a furrow, and uprooted weeds. This type of plow made little headway in the dense, moist soils of the north. After the eighth century a more serviceable plow came into use: a heavy tool equipped with iron tips and a mould-board that turned the soil so as to aerate it thoroughly and break up the root networks of weeds. The heavy plow was a more expensive piece of equipment than the light Mediterranean plow, and it required cultivators to harness more energy to pull it through damp northern soils. Once hitched to oxen or draft horses, however, the heavy plow contributed to greater agricultural production.

As the heavy plow spread throughout western Europe, cultivators took several additional steps that increased agricultural production. They cleared new lands for cultivation and built ponds for fish. They constructed water mills, which enabled them to take advantage of a ready and renewable source of inanimate energy, thus freeing human and animal energy for other work. They employed a special horse collar, which allowed them to rely less on slow-moving oxen and more on speedier horses to pull their heavy plows. They increased

# SOURCES FROM THE PAST

## The Wealth and Commerce of Constantinople

*The Spanish rabbi Benjamin of Tudela traveled throughout Europe, north Africa, and southwest Asia between 1165 and 1173 C.E. He may have ventured as far as India, and he mentioned both India and China in his travel account. His main purpose was to record the conditions of Jewish communities, but he also described the many lands and about three hundred cities that he visited. His travels took place during an era of political decline for the Byzantine Empire, yet he still found Constantinople a flourishing and prosperous city.*

**The circumference of the city** of Constantinople is eighteen miles; half of it is surrounded by the sea, and half by land, and it is situated upon two arms of the sea, one coming from the sea of Russia [the Black Sea], and one from the sea of Sepharad [the Mediterranean].

All sorts of merchants come here from the land of Babylon, from the land of Shinar [Mesopotamia], from Persia, Media [western Iran], and all the sovereignty of the land of Egypt, from the land of Canaan [Palestine], and the empire of Russia, from Hungary, Patzinakia [Ukraine], Khazaria [southern Russia], and the land of Lombardy [northern Italy] and Sepharad [Spain].

Constantinople is a busy city, and merchants come to it from every country by sea or land, and there is none like it in the world except Baghdad, the great city of Islam. In Constantinople is the church of Hagia Sophia, and the seat of the pope of the Greeks, since Greeks do not obey the pope of Rome. There are also as many churches as there are days of the year. . . . And in this church [Hagia Sophia] there are pillars of gold and silver, and lamps of silver and gold more than a man can count.

> Why is it that the Greeks do not obey the pope of Rome?

Close to the walls of the palace is also a place of amusement belonging to the emperor, which is called the Hippodrome, and every year on the anniversary of the birth of Jesus the emperor gives a great entertainment there. And in that place men from all the races of the world come before the emperor and empress with jugglery and without jugglery, and they introduce lions, leopards, bears, and wild asses, and they engage them in combat with one another; and the same thing is done with birds. No entertainment like this is to be found in any other land. . . .

> What Roman imperial form of entertainment does this description remind you of?

From every part of the Byzantine empire tribute is brought here every year, and they fill strongholds with garments of silk, purple, and gold. Like unto these storehouses and this wealth there is nothing in the whole world to be found. It is said that the tribute of the city amounts every year to 20,000 gold pieces, derived both from the rents of shops and markets and from the tribute of merchants who enter by sea or land.

The Greek inhabitants are very rich in gold and precious stones, and they go clothed in garments of silk and gold embroidery, and they ride horses and look like princes. Indeed, the land is very rich in all cloth stuffs and in bread, meat, and wine.

Wealth like that of Constantinople is not to be found in the whole world. Here also are men learned in all the books of the Greeks, and they eat and drink, every man under his vine and his fig-tree.

### For Further Reflection

- What role did the geographical location of Constantinople play in making it such a successful commercial center?
- In what ways does this passage support the idea that the Byzantine Empire was an extension of the Roman Empire?
- As well as information about the economy, what does the passage tell us about political organization in the Byzantine Empire?

*Source:* Benjamin of Tudela. *The Itinerary of Benjamin of Tudela.* Trans. by M. N. Adler. London: H. Frowde, 1907. (Translation slightly modified.)

In this twelfth-century manuscript illustration, a peasant guides a heavy, wheeled plow while his wife prods the oxen that pull the plow.
Album/Oronoz/Newscom

cultivation of beans and other legumes, which enriched diets throughout western Europe. Thus western Europeans made numerous small adaptations that created a foundation for rural prosperity after 1000 C.E.

**Trade in Western Europe** By no means did trade disappear from western Europe. Local markets and fairs offered opportunities for small-scale exchange, and itinerant peddlers shopped their wares from one settlement to another. Maritime trade flourished in the Mediterranean despite Muslim conquests in the region. Christian merchants from Italy and Spain regularly traded across religious boundary lines with Muslims of Sicily, Spain, and north Africa, who linked Europe indirectly with a larger world of communication and exchange.

**Norse Merchant-Mariners** Maritime trade flourished also in the North Sea and the Baltic Sea. Most active among the early medieval merchants in the northern seas were Norse seafarers, kinsmen of the Vikings. Norse traders followed the same routes as Viking raiders, and many individual mariners no doubt turned from commerce to plunder and back again as opportunities arose. Norse merchants called at ports from Russia to Ireland, carrying cargoes of fish and furs from Scandinavia, honey from Poland, wheat from England, wine from France, beer from the Low Countries, and swords from Germany. By traveling down the Russian rivers to the Black Sea, they were able to trade actively in both the Byzantine and the Abbasid empires. Thus, like Mediterranean merchants, but by different routes, Norse mariners linked western Europe with the world of Islam. Indeed, the Carolingian Empire depended heavily on this connection: Norse merchants took Scandinavian products to the Abbasid empire and exchanged them for silver, which they traded at Carolingian ports for wine, jugs, glassware, and other products. The silver transported from the Abbasid empire by Norse merchants was a principal source of bullion used for minting coins in early medieval Europe and hence a crucially important element of the western European economy. Thus, even if western European merchants were not as numerous or prominent as their Byzantine counterparts, they nevertheless participated in the trading networks of the larger Afro-Eurasian region.

## Social Development in Early Medieval Europe

**Byzantium: An Urban Society** The Byzantine Empire was rich in large, prosperous, cosmopolitan cities, including Alexandria, Antioch, and Damascus, to mention only a few. Indeed, until the Muslim conquests of the late seventh and eighth centuries, Byzantium was probably the world's most urbanized society, and residents of its cities enjoyed the benefits and observed urban traditions inherited from the classical Mediterranean world. Yet Constantinople had no rival among Byzantine cities. Subjects of the Byzantine Empire referred to it simply as "the City." The heart of the City was the imperial palace, which employed twenty thousand workers as palace staff. Peacocks strutted through gardens filled with sculptures and fountains. Most famous of them was a gold fountain that spouted wine for imperial guests.

**City Life** Aristocrats maintained enormous palaces that included courtyards, reception halls, libraries, chapels, and quarters for members of the extended family as well as servants and enslaved people. In the fifth century Constantinople boasted 4,388 mansions, as well as fourteen imperial and princely palaces. Women lived in separate apartments and did not receive male visitors from outside the household. Nor did they participate in banquets and parties, especially when

## What's Left Out?

This chapter offers several comparisons between the political, economic, social and religious structures of Eastern and Western Europe during the millennium following the fragmentation of the Roman Empire. In keeping with the theme of many of the What's Left Out features in other chapters, another way of comparing these two European regions is by looking at their attitudes towards women. We have seen that in the Byzantine Empire some women did rise to positions of power, notably the Empress Theodora. In fact, several Byzantine empresses are known to history, most of whom managed to play significant political and social roles by exerting influence on their imperial husbands. Yet these women were the exceptions; in general elite Byzantine women played virtually no part in their husband's public lives. Women lived in separate sections of the residences, were forbidden from receiving male visitors, and were not allowed to attend parties or banquets. The only public role acceptable for most elite women in Byzantium was to visit relatives, and even this had to be done in the company of male chaperones. Girls were married in their early teens, through contracts arranged by parents to improve a family's social standing. Education was limited to reading and writing, although some Byzantine women did excel as physicians, composers, and historians.

An exception to the norm was the Byzantine historian Anna Comnena (1083–1153). She was born into one of the most powerful families in Constantinople, and as the daughter of Emperor Alexis I received an excellent education; indeed she may have been one of the most educated European women who had lived to that point in history. She was groomed for leadership and had strong claims upon the throne, but in the end she was bypassed in succession by her younger brother John II. Bitterly disappointed and still with a burning ambition for power, she became involved in a plot against John which, when discovered, resulted in her forfeiting her property and status as a member of the imperial family. Sent in exile to a monastery, Anna dedicated herself to learning instead, particularly to the study of history and philosophy. She wrote her own study of the history of her time, the *Alexiad*, and because of this many regard Anna Comnena as the first female historian of Europe.

The *Alexiad*, which is focused on the reign of her father, was actually started by her husband, but upon his death Anna took up her pen at the age of 55. Using the works of Thucydides and Polybius as her model, Anna produced an insightful analysis of the political and military affairs of the Byzantines, particularly their conflicts with Western European states. Much of her analysis of the First Crusade was based on eye-witness accounts, and her description of the erratic often brutal behavior of the Crusaders, and the alarm this caused in Constantinople, provides a very different perspective on these 'Christian soldiers' to that offered by contemporary western historians. Although the *Alexiad* is somewhat biased because of Anna's attempts to praise her father and ridicule his successors, it is chronologically sound, highly analytical, and still useful to historians today.

Another exceptional woman emerges from the pages of Western European history at more or less the same time, Hildegard of Bingen (1098-1179), a near contemporary of Anna Comnena. She came from a long line of distinguished members of religious orders, and took her vows to become a Nun in her teens. Entering a nunnery was one of the few avenues available to elite western European women who wanted to receive a decent education. Hildegard rose to the position of abbess at Disibodenberg, but at age 49 after experiencing a number of visions, she left the abbey to found her own convent near Bingen. Here she worked with her nuns to explain her visions in a series of illuminated books, beginning with *Know the Ways of the Lord*, followed by *Book of Divine Works*. In the latter she articulated a unified vision of the history of humanity from Adam to the Apocalypse, and argued for the harmonious interaction of humans with the cosmos. Hildegard also wrote books on natural science and medicine. In the *Book of Medicine Carefully Arranged* she discussed dozens of different diseases, their causes and possible herbal and other cures, and also described the development of the human female reproductive system. Hildegard was highly regarded and even sought out by powerful men of both the secular and religious worlds, but this did not stop here from condemning rulers and Church authorities for corruption.

As remarkable as the lives of these two women were, most historians agree that they are the exceptions who very much prove the rule. Because we can find very few such examples of women who managed to rise to positions of influence and prestige in their male-dominated societies, it is clear that for most women in both Eastern and Western Europe during the Early Medieval Period, avenues to power, or even to anything approaching equality of opportunity, were so limited as to be almost non-existent.

See Bonnie Anderson and Judith Zinsser point out in their important 1988 book *A History of their Own: Women in Europe from Prehistory to the Present*, 1988, Vol 1, 190.

### Thinking Critically About Sources

1. Compare and contrast Anna Comnena and Hildegard of Bingen in terms of their education, writing, and legacy.
2. Why were they exceptions in history?

Women workers were prominent in Byzantine textile production. A manuscript illustration depicts one Byzantine woman weaving cloth (left) while another spins thread (right). Both women veil their hair for modesty.
The Picture Art Collection/ Alamy Stock Photo

wine flowed freely or when the affairs were likely to become so boisterous that they could compromise a woman's reputation. In Constantinople as well as other cities, upper-class women generally wore veils, like their Mediterranean ancestors from centuries past, to discourage the attention of men outside their own families.

Dwellings of less privileged classes were not so splendid. Artisans and crafts workers commonly lived in rooms above their shops, while clerks and government officials occupied multistory apartment buildings. Workers and the poor lived in rickety tenements where they shared kitchens and sanitary facilities with their neighbors.

**Attractions of Constantinople** Even for the poor, however, the City had its attractions. As the heir of Rome, Constantinople was a city of baths, which were sites of relaxation and exercise as well as hygienic bathing. Taverns and restaurants offered settings for social gatherings—checkers, chess, and dice games were especially popular activities at taverns—and theaters provided entertainment in the form of song, dance, and striptease. Mass entertainment took place in the Hippodrome, a large stadium adjacent to the imperial palace, where Byzantine subjects watched chariot races; athletic matches; contests between wild animals; and circuses featuring acts by clowns, jugglers, acrobats, and dwarfs.

**Western Europe: A Rural Society** Cities to the west had once offered similar pleasures, but they largely disappeared in the wake of Germanic invasions and the collapse of the Western Roman Empire in the late fifth century. The agricultural surplus of western Europe was sufficient to sustain local political elites but not substantial enough to support large, urban populations of artisans, crafts workers, merchants, and professionals. Towns survived, but they served more as economic hubs of surrounding regions than as vibrant centers integrating the economic activities of distant lands.

**The Question of Feudalism** How did the peoples of western Christendom reorganize their society after the collapse of the Western Roman Empire? Historians once routinely used the term *feudalism* to characterize the political and social order of medieval Europe. They spoke of a "feudal system" involving a hierarchy of lords and vassals, who collectively took charge of political and military affairs on the basis of personal relationships. Lords supposedly provided grants of land to their retainers in exchange for loyalty and military service. Over the years, scholarship has somewhat undermined that view of medieval society, and some historians have abandoned the concept of feudalism as a model that tends to oversimplify a more complex society. They argue that it is more accurate to view early medieval Europe as a society in which local political and military elites worked in various ad hoc ways to organize their territories and maintain social order. The arrangements they adopted had deep implications for the lives of political and military elites themselves and also for their relationships with commoners.

In the absence of an effective central authority such as an emperor, local notables or lords mobilized small private armies composed of armed supporters and mercenaries. Some of these lords were descendants of Carolingian or other

# SOURCES FROM THE PAST

## Pope Gregory the Great on Peasant Taxation on the Papal Estates, ca. 600

*Some useful insights into the lives and experiences of peasants can be found in this letter written by Pope Gregory I in about 600 C.E. The pope demonstrates concern for the excessive tax burden tenant farmers working in papal estates are being forced to pay. Despite papal concern, the document reminds us just how harsh the lives of peasant farmers in early medieval Europe were.*

**We have also learned** that in some of the holdings of the Church a most unjust exaction is made, so that three half measures out of seventy—it is shameful to say it—are solicited from the tenants; and furthermore, even this does not suffice, but they are said to be asked for something more, over and above this, by reason of a long-standing custom. This practice we absolutely detest, and we wish it to be absolutely eradicated from our patrimony. But let your experience guide you, whether it be a case of receiving a pound more, or whether it be a case of taking more than rightful measure from the serfs; and let everything count towards the sum total of the rent; and insofar as the serfs can bear it, let them pay full rent reckoned at two parts out of seventy by weight. Nor should the market tax be collected at more than a just pound weight, neither an excessive pound weight, nor other burdens greater than a pound; but by your calculation, so far as you are able to do it, let it be reckoned against the sum total of the rent, and so let filthy exaction never occur.

> What problems with the pound weight is the pope concerned with here?

But in order that these very burdens, imposed unjustly, which we have caused to be reckoned as part of the rent, may not in some way be increased after our death, and the rent be thus increased, and the serfs again be compelled to pay the burdens of superadding, we desire you to make out schedules of security about the rents, inscribing therein the amount of rent which each ought to pay, including the market tax, the grain tax, and other payments. But as for what has been taken for the use of the overseer from these little excrescences, we desire this to be taken from the sum total of the rent and applied to your own use.

Above all we wish you to attend to this carefully, that unjust weights be not used in collecting the rents. If you should find such, destroy them, and introduce new and just ones. For my son, the servant of God, the Deacon, has already found such as displeased him, but he did not have the authority to change them. Except in the case of inferior and cheap provisions, we want nothing over and above just weights to be demanded of the coloni of the Church.

We have further learned that if any one of the serfs has done wrong, punishment is not inflicted upon the man himself, but payment is levied on his property. Concerning this we ordain that whoever commits wrong shall, as is fitting, be punished; but let there be no acceptance of any payment whatever from him, except, perchance, a small sum which may defray the expenses of the bailiff sent to him.

> Why would punishments have evolved so that they were inflicted on the property of the perpetrator rather than on the person?

We have further learned that as often as a tenant has taken anything from a colonus it has not been returned, though repayment was demanded of the tenant; therefore we order that whatever has been taken with violence from any of the serfs be restored to him from whom it was taken and not put to our use, lest we ourselves seem to be the authors of violence. Further, we wish, that when you send outside the patrimony, those who are engaged in your service, small payments be received from them. Yet so that it turn out to their advantage, because we do not desire that the purse of the Church be disgraced by filthy lucre. We also order you carefully to prevent the placing of tenants on the holdings of the Church for payments, lest, through payments being sought, tenants be frequently changed, from which changing what else takes place but that the estates of the Church are never cultivated? Even the payments from charter lands should be reduced according to the sum total of the rent. On the score of filling the barns and collecting their contents we desire you to receive from the holdings of the Church only what is customary; what we have ordered you to buy should be bought from strangers.

Have that part of my letter which relates to the serfs read throughout all our holdings, that they may know wherein they might protect themselves from violence with our authority, and let there be given to them either an authentic document or a copy of the same.

### For Further Reflection

- On the basis of the letter from Pope Gregory I, what were some of the ways in which peasants and their labor were being exploited on papal estates at the end of the fifth century?
- What are the major practices in the relationship between the Church and the tenant farmers that the pope is concerned with in this letter?
- What might the pope's intentions be in demanding an end to some of these exploitative practices?
- To what extent could historians use this letter as evidence of the lives of feudal tenant farmers more generally in Early Medieval western Europe?

*Source:* J. P. Migne, *Patrologiae Cursus Completus*, Vol. LXXVII p. 498 (Paris, 1849), reprinted in Roy C. Cave and Herbert H. Coulson, eds., *A Source Book for Medieval Economic History* (Milwaukee: The Bruce Publishing Co., 1936; reprint ed., New York: Biblo & Tannen, 1965), pp. 41–43. (Translation slightly modified.)

ruling houses, and others were ambitious strongmen—essentially local warlords. Both the lords and their retainers were warriors with horses, weapons, and military expertise. Lords sometimes rewarded their retainers with grants of land or some other valuable, such as the right to income generated by a mill, the right to receive rents or payments from a village, or even a payment of money. In other cases, lords supported their retainers by maintaining them in their own households, where they provided equipment and training in military affairs. After the year 1000, lords increasingly hired their retainers, paying them for services on the basis of need. By one mechanism or another, lords and retainers constituted themselves as privileged political and military elites who dominated local regions.

**Peasants** Lords and retainers supported themselves and their families principally on the basis of the surplus agricultural production that they commandeered from a subject peasantry. Political and military elites obliged local peasants to provide labor services and payments of rents in kind, such as a portion of the harvest, a chicken, or a dozen eggs. Male peasants typically worked three days a week for their lords while also providing additional labor services during planting and harvesting season. Women peasants churned butter, made cheese, brewed beer, spun thread, wove cloth, or sewed clothes for their lords as well as for their own families. Some peasants also kept sheep or cattle, and their obligations to lords included products from their herds. Because lords provided peasants with land to cultivate and often with tools and animals as well, peasants had little opportunity to move to different lands. Indeed, they were commonly able to do so only with permission from their lords. They even had to pay fees for the right to marry a peasant who worked for a different lord.

**Population** During the fifth and sixth centuries, epidemic disease and political turmoil took a demographic toll in both Byzantium and western Europe. From a high point of about thirty-six million at the time of the Roman Empire in 200 C.E., population fell to about twenty-six million in the year 600—nineteen million in Byzantium and seven million in western Europe. Population fluctuated dramatically over the next two centuries, as Byzantium lost territories to Muslims, and western Europeans suffered repeated invasions. After the eighth century, however, both Byzantium and western Europe entered an era of demographic recovery. Political stability created a foundation for a more productive agricultural economy just as new food crops made their way from the Muslim world to Byzantium and Mediterranean Europe. Hard durum wheat, rice, spinach, artichokes, eggplant, lemons, limes, oranges, and melons brought increased calories and dietetic variety that supported increasing populations. By the year 800 eastern and western Europe had a combined population of about twenty-nine million, which rose to about thirty-two million in 900 and thirty-six million in 1000—the level of the Roman Empire's population some eight centuries earlier. Thus by the year 1000, both Byzantium and western Europe had built productive agricultural economies that sustained sizable and increasing populations.

## RELIGIOUS DEVELOPMENTS IN BYZANTIUM AND WESTERN EUROPE

As heirs of the Roman Empire, Byzantium and western Europe were both Christian societies. In the cases of political, social, and economic affairs, though, the two regions created distinctive and ultimately competing forms of their common religious inheritance. In both Byzantium and western Europe, Christianity served as the principal source of religious, moral, and cultural authority. Both lands supported ecclesiastical hierarchies with networks of monasteries. Both societies also worked to extend the reach of Christianity by sending missionaries to seek converts in northerly territories from Russia and Slavic lands to Scandinavia and the British Isles. By the year 1000 the twin heirs of Roman Christianity had laid the foundations for a large Christian cultural zone in the western part of the Eurasian continent that paralleled the Buddhist and Islamic cultural zones farther east. Yet even as they were promoting Christianity in their own societies and beyond, church authorities in Byzantium and western Europe fell into deep disagreement on matters of doctrine, ritual, and church authority. By the mid-eleventh century, their differences had become so great that church leaders formally denounced one another and established two rival communities: the Eastern Orthodox church in Byzantium and the Roman Catholic church in western Europe.

### Popes and Patriarchs

Christianity had a more hierarchical organizational structure than any other major religious tradition. For example, there was no pope of Buddhism, no patriarch in the Islamic world. Christianity inherited its strong organizational structure from the time of the late Roman Empire. In the early middle ages, the two most important Christian authorities were the bishop of Rome, known as the pope, and the patriarch of Constantinople.

**The Papacy** When the Western Roman Empire collapsed, the **papacy** survived and claimed continuing spiritual authority over all the lands formerly embraced by the Roman Empire. At first the popes cooperated closely with the Byzantine emperors, who seemed to be the natural heirs of the emperors of Rome. Beginning in the late sixth century, however, the popes acted more independently and devoted their efforts to strengthening the western Christian church based at Rome and clearly distinguishing it from the eastern Christian church based at Constantinople.

## INTERPRETING IMAGES

A twelfth century illustration depicting Pope Gregory I.
**Analyze** *In what ways does the illustration of Gregory I indicate the new roles popes would play during the next thousand years?*

Bettmann/Getty Images

**Pope Gregory I** The individual most responsible for charting an independent course for the Roman church was **Pope Gregory I** (590–604 C.E.). As pope, Gregory faced an array of challenges. During the late sixth century, the Germanic Lombards campaigned in Italy, menacing Rome and the church in the process. Gregory mobilized local resources and organized the defense of Rome, thus saving both the city and the church. He also faced difficulties within the church because bishops frequently acted as though they were supreme ecclesiastical authorities within their own dioceses. To regain the initiative, Gregory reasserted claims to papal primacy—the notion that the bishop of Rome was the ultimate authority for all the Christian church. Gregory also made contributions as a theologian. He emphasized the sacrament of penance, which required individuals to confess their sins to their priests and atone for them by penitential acts—a practice that enhanced the influence of the Roman church in the lives of individuals.

**The Patriarchs** The **patriarchs** of Constantinople were powerful officials, but they did not enjoy the independence of their brethren to the west. Following the tradition of caesaropapism inaugurated by the emperor Constantine in the fourth century, Byzantine emperors treated the church as a department of state. They appointed the patriarchs, and they instructed patriarchs, bishops, and priests to deliver sermons that supported imperial policy and encouraged obedience to imperial authorities. This caesaropapism was a source of tension between imperial and ecclesiastical authorities, and it also had the potential to provoke popular dissent when imperial views clashed with those of the larger society.

**Iconoclasm** The most divisive ecclesiastical policy implemented by Byzantine emperors was **iconoclasm,** inaugurated by Emperor Leo III (reigned 717–741 C.E.). Byzantium had a long tradition of producing icons—paintings of Jesus, saints, and other religious figures—many of which were splendid works of art. Most theologians took these icons as visual stimulations that inspired reverence for holy personages. Leo, however, became convinced that the veneration of images was sinful, tantamount to the worship of idols. In 726 C.E., he embarked on a policy of iconoclasm (which literally means "breaking of icons"), destroying religious images and prohibiting their use in churches. The policy immediately sparked protests and even riots throughout the empire because icons were extremely popular among the people. Debates about iconoclasm raged for more than a century. Only in 843 did Leo's followers abandon the policy of iconoclasm.

## Monks and Missionaries

Consumed with matters of theology, ritual, and church politics, popes and patriarchs rarely dealt directly with the lay population of their churches. For personal religious instruction and inspiration, lay Christians looked less to the church hierarchy than to local monasteries.

**Asceticism** Christian **monasticism** grew out of the efforts of devout individuals to lead especially holy lives. Early Christian ascetics in Egypt, Mesopotamia, and Persia adopted extreme regimes of self-denial in order to focus all their attention on religious matters. Some lived alone as hermits. Others formed communes where they devoted themselves to the pursuit of holiness rather than worldly success. Many dedicated themselves to celibacy, fasting, and prayer.

---

**iconoclasm** (eye-KAHN-oh-klazm)

## INTERPRETING IMAGES

This illustration from a psalter prepared about 900 C.E. depicts an iconoclast whitewashing an image of Jesus painted on a wall.

**Analyze** *Why was the policy of iconoclasm so divisive amongst Christians in Europe? Compare and contrast Gregory I's leadership to that of Renaissance popes in the 15th and 16th centuries. Compare and contrast the religious hierarchy of Christianity with leadership in Islam and Buddhism, especially in how leadership was represented in art.*

Art Collection 3/Alamy Stock Photo

A fourteenth-century manuscript illustration shows St. Benedict with his crosier, the staff carried by abbots to symbolize their position (left), and meeting with two monks beside a fishpond at their monastery (right). What does the fishpond suggest about the economic significance of monasteries?

Darling Archive/Alamy Stock Photo; Ann Ronan Pictures/Print Collector/Getty Images

Drawn by their reputation for piety, disciples gathered around these ascetics and established communities of men and women determined to follow their example. These communities became the earliest monasteries. During the early days of monasticism, each community developed its own rules, procedures, and priorities. The result was wild inconsistency: some monasteries imposed harsh and austere regimes of self-denial, and others offered little or no guidance.

**St. Basil and St. Benedict** Monasteries became much more influential when reformers provided them with discipline and a sense of purpose. The two most important reformers were the patriarch **St. Basil** of Caesarea (329–379 C.E.) in Byzantium and **St. Benedict** of Nursia (480–547 C.E.) in Italy. Both men prepared regulations for monasteries that provided for mild but not debilitating **asceticism** combined with meditation and work on behalf of the church. In both Basilian and Benedictine monasteries, individuals gave up their personal possessions and lived communal, celibate lives under the direction of the abbots who supervised the communities. Poverty, chastity, and obedience became the prime virtues for Basilian and Benedictine monks. At certain hours monks came together for religious services and prayers, dividing the remainder of the day into periods for study, reflection, and labor.

**St. Scholastica** Monasteries throughout Byzantium adopted the Basilian rule for their own use, while their counterparts in western Europe largely followed the rule of St. Benedict. Through the influence of St. Benedict's sister, the nun **St. Scholastica** (482–543 C.E.), an adaptation of the Benedictine rule soon provided guidance for the religious life of women living in convents.

**Monasticism and Society** Like Buddhist monasteries in Asian lands and charitable religious foundations in Muslim lands, Christian monasteries provided a variety of social services that enabled them to build close relations with local communities. Monks and nuns offered spiritual counsel to local laity, and they organized relief efforts by supplying food and medical attention at times of natural or other calamities. Monasteries and convents served both as orphanages and as inns

**asceticism** (uh-SET-uh-siz-uhm)

for travelers. Sometimes they also provided rudimentary educational services for local communities.

Because of the various roles they played in the larger society, monasteries were particularly effective agents in the spread of Christianity. While providing social services, monks also preached Christianity and tended to the spiritual needs of rural populations. For many people, a local neighboring monastery was the only source of instruction in Christian doctrine, and a local monastic church offered the only practical opportunity for them to take part in religious services. Thus, over decades and centuries, monks and nuns helped spread Christian teachings to countless generations of European peasants.

**Missionaries** Some monks went beyond the bounds of their own society and sought to spread Christianity in the larger world. Indeed, one of the remarkable developments of the early middle ages was the creation of a large Christian cultural zone in the western part of the Eurasian continent.

Christianity was already well established in the Mediterranean region, but pagan Germanic and Slavic peoples occupied the more northerly parts of Europe. In the late sixth century, Pope Gregory I sent **missionaries** to England and targeted the pagan Germanic kings who ruled various parts of the island, hoping that their conversion would induce their subjects to adopt Christianity. This tactic largely succeeded: by the early seventh century Christianity enjoyed a stable foothold, and by 800 England was securely within the fold of the Roman church. The Franks and Charlemagne later sponsored efforts to extend Christianity to northern Germany and Scandinavia. They met spirited resistance from Germanic peoples, who had no desire to abandon their inherited gods or pagan beliefs, but by the year 1000 Christianity had won a sizable and growing following.

Meanwhile, Byzantine authorities sent missionaries to Balkan and Slavic lands. The most famous of the missionaries to the Slavs were Saints Cyril and Methodius, two brothers from Thessaloniki in Greece. During the mid-ninth century, Cyril and Methodius conducted missions in Bulgaria and Moravia (which included much of the modern Czech, Slovakian, and Hungarian territories). There they devised an alphabet, known as the Cyrillic alphabet, for the previously illiterate Slavic peoples. Although adapted from written Greek, the Cyrillic alphabet represented the sounds of Slavic languages more precisely than did the Greek, and it remained in use in much of eastern Europe until supplanted by the Roman alphabet in the twentieth century. In Russia and many other parts of the former Soviet Union, the Cyrillic alphabet survives to the present day.

North of Bulgaria another Slavic people began to organize large states: the Russians. About 989, at the urging of Byzantine missionaries, Prince Vladimir of Kiev converted to Christianity and ordered his subjects to follow his example. Vladimir was no paragon of virtue: he lauded drunkenness and reportedly maintained a harem of eight hundred young women. After his conversion, however, Byzantine influences flowed rapidly into Russia. Cyrillic writing, literacy, and Christian missions all spread quickly throughout Russia. Byzantine teachers traveled north to establish schools, and Byzantine priests conducted services for Russian converts. Thus Kiev served as a conduit for the spread of Byzantine cultural and religious influence in Russia.

## INTERPRETING IMAGES

Monasteries were the principal centers of literacy in western Europe during the early middle ages. In this manuscript illustration, one monk copies a manuscript, another makes geometric calculations, a third cuts parchment, two work on the building, and one more rings the bells that call monks and members of the surrounding community to religious services.

**Analyze** *Why were monasteries the center of learning during the medival period? Why weren't secular schools established?*

Album/Alamy Stock Photo

## Two Churches

Although they professed the same basic Christian doctrine, the churches of Constantinople and Rome experienced increasing friction after the sixth century. Tensions mirrored political strains, such as deep resentment in Byzantium after Charlemagne accepted the title of emperor from the pope in Rome. Yet church authorities in Constantinople and Rome also harbored different views on religious and theological issues. The iconoclastic movement of the eighth and ninth centuries was one focus of difference. Western theologians regarded religious images as perfectly appropriate aids to devotion and resented Byzantine claims to the contrary, whereas the iconoclasts took offense at the efforts of their Roman counterparts to have images restored in Byzantium.

### How the Past Shapes the Future

#### The Spread of Religious Traditions

Between the late sixth century and 1000 C.E., missionaries from both the Roman and Byzantine churches moved north and west in quests to bring Christianity to nonbelievers. While the Roman missionaries were successful in the British Isles, in Scandinavia, and among Germanic peoples, the Byzantine missionaries had their greatest successes in the Balkans and in Slavic lands. Consider the long-term impact that the spread of these different traditions had in the lands where they won converts in terms of art, literature, and culture. In what ways are these legacies still visible in western and eastern Europe today?

**Religious Rivalry** Over time the Christian churches based in Constantinople and Rome disagreed on many other points. Some ritual and doctrinal differences concerned forms of worship and the precise wording of theological teachings—relatively minor issues that in and of themselves need not have caused deep division in the larger Christian community. Byzantine theologians objected, for example, to the fact that western priests shaved their beards and used unleavened rather than leavened bread when saying Mass. Other differences concerned more substantive theological matters, such as the precise relationship between God, Jesus, and the Holy Spirit—all regarded as manifestations of God by most Christian theologians of the day.

**Schism** Alongside ritual and doctrinal differences, the Byzantine patriarchs and the Roman popes disputed their respective rights and powers. Patriarchs argued for the autonomy of all major Christian jurisdictions, including that of Constantinople, whereas popes asserted the primacy of Rome as the sole seat of authority for all Christendom. Ultimately, relations became so strained that the eastern and western churches went separate ways. In 1054 the patriarch and pope mutually excommunicated each other, each refusing to recognize the other's church as properly Christian. This decision had profound historical consequences because, despite efforts at reconciliation, the **schism** between eastern and western churches has persisted to the present day. In light of the schism, historians refer to the eastern Christian church after 1054 as the Eastern Orthodox church and its western counterpart as the Roman Catholic church.

## CONCLUSION

After the collapse of the Western Roman Empire, the two halves of Europe followed very different historical paths. Byzantium inherited a thriving economy, a set of governing institutions, an imperial bureaucracy, an established church, and a rich cultural tradition from ancient Mediterranean society and the Roman Empire. Even after the loss of territories to Muslim conquerors, Byzantium remained a powerful and productive society in the eastern Mediterranean region. By contrast, western Europe experienced turmoil in the face of repeated invasion, which thoroughly disrupted social and economic as well as political affairs. Only after the ninth century did western Europeans gradually manage to achieve political stability and lay the foundations for a more predictable and prosperous society. For all their differences, though, the eastern and western European states both advanced the construction of a large Christian cultural zone that paralleled the lands of Islamic and Buddhist influence to the east. This Christian cultural zone harbored different and competing versions of a common religion—like the Islamic cultural zone with both Sunni and Shia advocates or the Buddhist cultural zone with Mahayana as well as Theravada adherents—but Byzantium and western Europe both relied on religion as a foundation for cultural unity and made Christianity the most important source of cultural and moral authority throughout Europe.

## STUDY TERMS

Aegean Sea (132)
asceticism (150)
Byzantine Empire (131)
Carolingian dynasty (136)
caesaropapism (132)
Charlemagne (136)
Constantinople (132)
*Corpus iuris civilis* (133)
Franks (135)
Greek fire (134)

Hagia Sofia (132)
iconoclasm (148)
Justinian (132)
Louis the Pious (136)
Magyars (136)
*missi dominici* (136)
missionaries (151)
monasticism (148)
Odoacer (135)
papacy (147)
patriarchs (148)
Pope Gregory I (148)
schism (152)
St. Basil (150)
St. Benedict (150)
St. Scholastica (150)
*theme* system (135)
Theodora (132)
Vikings (138)

## FOR FURTHER READING

Peter Brown. *The Rise of Western Christendom: Triumph and Diversity, A.D. 200–1000.* 2nd ed. Oxford, 2003. A landmark analysis of early Christian history.

Einhard and Notker the Stammerer. *Two Lives of Charlemagne.* Trans. by Lewis Thorpe. New York, 1969. Translations of two early biographies of Charlemagne.

Patrick J. Geary. *Before France and Germany: The Creation and Transformation of the Merovingian World.* 2nd ed. New York, 1997. Insightful study of Germanic societies in early medieval Europe.

Judith Herrin. *Byzantium: The Surprising Life of a Medieval Empire.* Princeton, 2009. A judicious survey of Byzantine history.

Anthony Kaldellis. *The Byzantine Empire. People and Power in New Rome.* Cambridge, Mass., 2015. Connects Byzantine politics and social structures with their Roman roots and argues that during its early centuries at least, the Byzantine Empire functioned similarly to the Roman republic.

Michael McCormick. *Origins of the European Economy: Communications and Commerce, A.D. 300–900.* Cambridge, Mass., 2001. A comprehensive analysis that emphasizes the participation of early medieval Europe in a larger Mediterranean economy.

Procopius. *History of the Wars, Secret History, and Buildings.* Trans. by A. Cameron. New York, 1967. Translations of writings by the most important historian in the time of Justinian.

Susan Reynolds. *Fiefs and Vassals: The Medieval Evidence Reinterpreted.* Oxford, 1994. A densely written but important book offering a powerful scholarly critique of the concept of feudalism.

Julian D. Richards. *The Vikings. A Very Short Introduction.* Oxford, 2005. A brief but surprisingly detailed and up-to-date survey of the significance of the Vikings.

John M. Riddle. *A History of the Middle Ages 300–1500.* Lanham, Md., 2008. A comprehensive and lively account of the history and culture of western Europe and the Byzantine Empire from the late classical era to the late medieval period.

# CHAPTER 4 AP EXAM PRACTICE

Questions assume cumulative knowledge from this chapter and previous chapters.

## Section I

## Multiple Choice Questions

Use the map below and your knowledge of world history to answer questions 1 – 3.

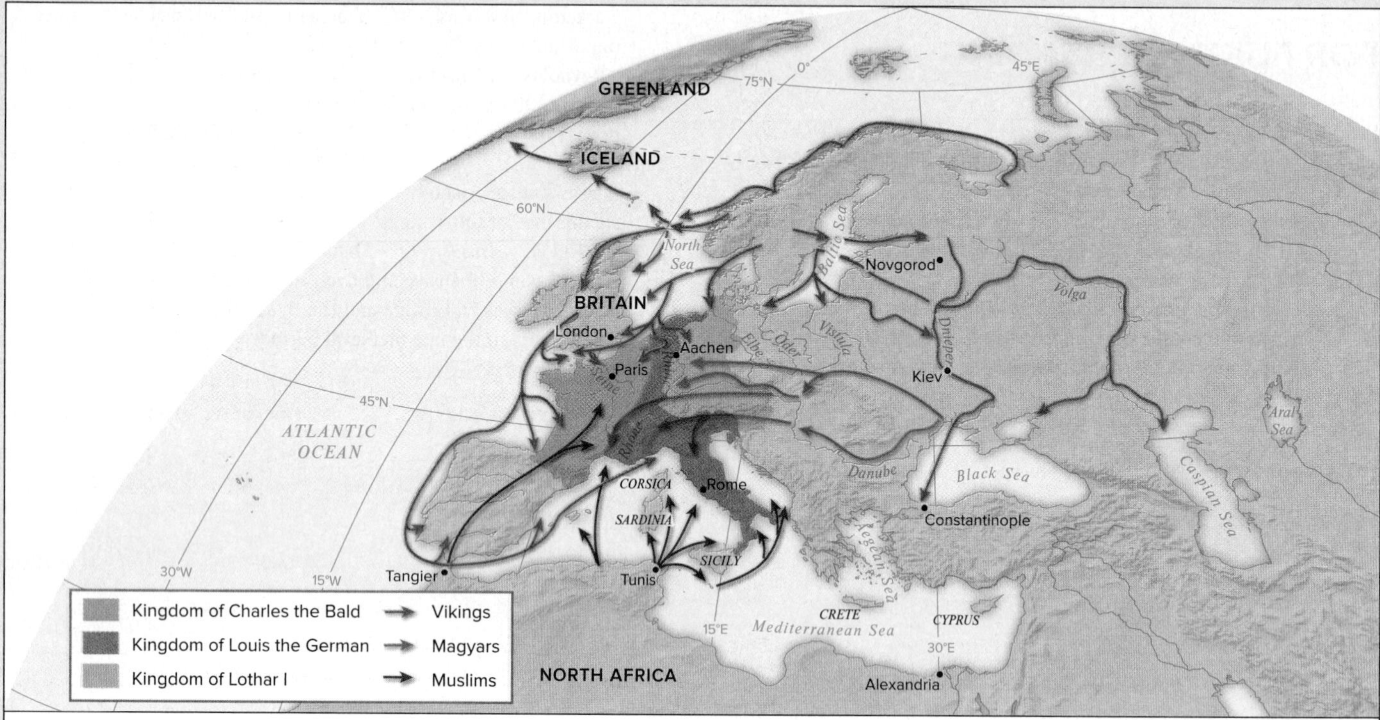


The dissolution of the Carolingian Empire (843 C.E.) and the invasions of early medieval Europe in the nineth and tenth centuries
McGraw Hill

1. What historical development can be seen in this map?
   (A) The spread of the Russian Empire into eastern Europe.
   (B) The Viking invasions contributed to the devolution of political authority in western Europe.
   (C) The expansion of the Byzantine navy and the use of Greek fire to control the Mediterranean.
   (D) The expansion of Christian lands loyal to the papacy in Rome.
2. Some routes shown on this map were made possible by
   (A) The increased sized of dhows able to carry more goods for longer distances during the monsoon season.
   (B) Improved storage for food and fresh water on ships.
   (C) The use of shallow-draft boats that could sail along coasts and navigate rivers.
   (D) Detailed maps of the European coastlines and port cities.
3. What statement below best describes the Scandinavians during the Middle Ages?
   (A) They were in an alliance with the Magyars and the Muslims to take over western Europe.
   (B) Their expansion into western Europe was caused by a decline in their agricultural production.
   (C) They never attacked monasteries because monks were poor.
   (D) They created a trading network that linked western Europe, the Byzantine Empire, and the Abbasid Caliphate.

Use the image below and your knowledge of world history to answer questions 4 and 5.

Women workers were prominent in Byzantine textile production. A manuscript illustration depicts one Byzantine woman weaving cloth (left) while another spins thread (right). Both women veil their hair for modesty.
The Granger Collection, New York

4. Based on this image, what could a historian argue about labor in the Byzantine Empire?
   (A) Because textile production was an insignificant part of the Byzantine economy, women worked in textile production instead of men.
   (B) Agricultural surpluses made it possible for workers to specialize in different aspects of textile manufacturing.
   (C) In the Byzantine Empire, women made small quantities of silk at home to supplement their husband's income.
   (D) Byzantine emperors allowed women to have a monopoly on silk production.

5. Which statement describes a historical context in the image?
   (A) Towns were regional economic hubs, but they did not engage in long distance trade.
   (B) Socializing in Constantinople took place in taverns, baths, and theaters.
   (C) Upper class women were expected to avoid the attention of men from outside their families.
   (D) Byzantine women held important roles in politics and public life.

## Short Answer

6. Use the image below and your knowledge of world history to answer parts A, B, and C.

Monasteries were the principal centers of literacy in western Europe during the early middle ages. In this manuscript illustration, one monk copies a manuscript, another makes geometric calculations, a third cuts parchment, two work on the building, and one more rings the bells that call monks and members of the surrounding community to religious services.
Album/Alamy Stock Photo

(A) Identify ONE role that monasteries played in medieval society
(B) Explain ONE change in the development of medieval European Christianity.
(C) Explain ONE continuity in the history of medieval European Christianity.

7. Use this text selection and your knowledge of world history to answer parts A, B, and C.

Peasants—probably sharecroppers—receive seeds and tend to vineyards in this painting from a Byzantine manuscript.

The History Collection/Alamy Stock Photo

(A) Identify ONE way that government influenced medieval agricultural production.
(B) Explain ONE difference between eastern and western European agricultural production.
(C) Explain ONE similarity between eastern and western European agricultural production.

8. Use your understanding of world history to answer parts A, B, and C.
(A) Explain ONE way that women in Europe had political influence.
(B) Explain ONE way that European women had religious authority.
(C) Explain ONE way that medieval women had economic roles in Europe.

# Section II

## Document-Based Question

Based on the following documents and your knowledge of world history, evaluate the role of religions in the Byzantine Empire. In your response you should do the following:

- Respond to the prompt with a historically defensible thesis or claim that establishes a line of reasoning.
- Describe a broader historical context relevant to the prompt.
- Support an argument in response to the prompt using all documents.
- Use at least one additional piece of specific historical evidence (beyond that found in the documents) relevant to an argument about the prompt.
- Explain how or why the document's point of view, purpose, historical situation, and /or audience is relevant to an argument.
- Use evidence to corroborate, qualify, or modify an argument that addresses the prompt.

### Document 1

Byzantine emperor Justinian wears imperial purple robes (which have faded to brown over the centuries) in this mosaic, from the church of San Vitale in Ravenna, which depicts him in the company of ecclesiastical, military, and court officials.
Leemage/Universal Images Group/Getty Images

## Document 2

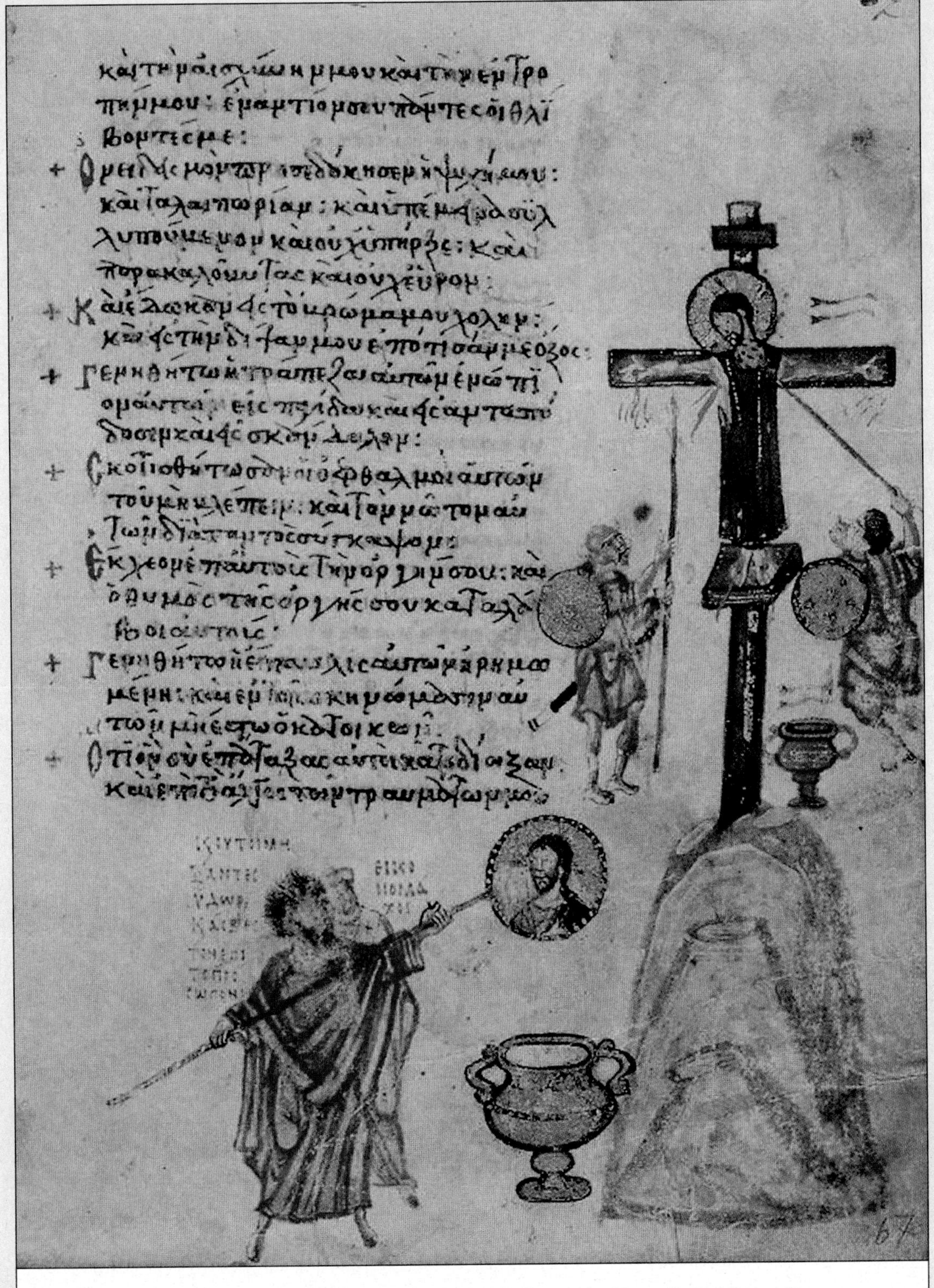

This illustration from a psalter prepared about 900 C.E. depicts an iconoclast whitewashing an image of Jesus painted on a wall.
Art Collection 3/Alamy Stock Photo

## Document 3

All sorts of merchants come here from the land of Babylon, from the land of Shinar [Mesopotamia], from Persia, Media [western Iran], and all the sovereignty of the land of Egypt, from the land of Canaan [Palestine], and the empire of Russia, from Hungary, Patzinakia [Ukraine], Khazaria [southern Russia], and the land of Lombardy [northern Italy] and Sepharad [Spain].

Constantinople is a busy city, and merchants come to it from every country by sea or land, and there is none like it in the world except Baghdad, the great city of Islam. In Constantinople is the church of Hagia Sophia, and the seat of the pope of the Greeks, since Greeks do not obey the pope of Rome. There are also as many churches as there are days of the year. . . . And in this church [Hagia Sophia] there are pillars of gold and silver, and lamps of silver and gold more than a man can count.

Close to the walls of the palace is also a place of amusement belonging to the emperor, which is called the Hippodrome, and every year on the anniversary of the birth of Jesus the emperor gives a great entertainment there. And in that place men from all the races of the world come before the emperor and empress with jugglery and without jugglery, and they introduce lions, leopards, bears, and wild asses, and they engage them in combat with one another; and the same thing is done with birds. No entertainment like this is to be found in any other land. . . .

*Source:* Benjamin of Tudela. *The Itinerary of Benjamin of Tudela.* Trans. by M. N. Adler. London: H. Frowde, 1907. (Translation slightly modified.)

## Long Essay

Develop a thoughtful and thorough historical argument that answers the question below. Begin your essay with a thesis statement and support it with relevant historical evidence.

Using specific examples, explain how the lives of peasants changed over time in Western Europe during the Middle Ages. What aspects of their lives did not change during this time?

Chapter 5

# Nomadic Empires and Eurasian Integration



## ZOOMING IN ON ENCOUNTERS

### The Goldsmith of the Mongolian Steppe

Guillaume Boucher was a goldsmith who lived during the early and middle decades of the thirteenth century. In the 1230s, he left his native Paris and went to Budapest. His new city, then part of the kingdom of Hungary, was in the midst of invasion by Mongol warriors. Mongols were known for their fearsome and destructive skills in battle, and we can only imagine the chaos that Boucher must have witnessed or the fear he may have felt. Yet Boucher survived and went on to become a valuable part of the Mongol enterprise. Noticing Boucher's metalworking skills, the Mongols took him captive. When they left Hungary in 1242, they took him back to their Central Asian homeland.

For at least the next fifteen years, Boucher lived at the Mongol capital at **Karakorum**. Though technically a slave, he enjoyed some prestige and the freedom to marry a fellow Frenchwoman. He supervised fifty assistants in a workshop that produced decorative objects of gold and silver for the Mongol court. Boucher also produced gold and silver statues in built carriages, designed buildings, and even sewed ritual garments for Roman Catholic priests conducting services for Christians living at Karakorum.

A thirteenth-century painting from an illustrated Persian history text depicts Mongol mounted warriors pursuing their fleeing enemies. Note the superb discipline and coordination of the Mongols, who used their superior military skills and organization to regularly defeat armies from a wide range of cultures and states.

DEA/A.DAGLI ORTI/De Agostini/Getty Images

**Karakorum** (kahr-uh-KOR-uhm)

Boucher was by no means the only European living at the Mongol court. In fact, the Mongols had a deliberate policy of resettling people who were skilled in specialized crafts and occupations. When they conquered an area, Mongols separated out those they considered "useful"—including soldiers, textile workers, secretaries, carpenters, and jewelsmiths like Boucher himself—and then sent them to areas where their talents were needed. Indeed, visitors to the Mongol court at Karakorum around the time Boucher lived encountered Germans, Slavs, and Hungarians as well as Chinese, Koreans, Turks, Persians, and Armenians, among others. This policy of resettlement encouraged Eurasian integration by fostering, often forcibly, increased exchanges between peoples of very different traditions.

## CHAPTER FOCUS

- From the eleventh through fifteenth centuries, nomac conquerors established empires in Eurasia.
- Nomadic warfare had advantages against the weaknesses of settled societies, yet the Mongol khanates, Delhi sultanate, and Tamerlane ultimately failed to maintain their power.
- While the conquest of these nomadic empires was violent and destructive, historians also use the phrase "Pax Mongolica" to describe the period of relative peace and stability that followed. Governments ensured that merchants and trade routes across much of Eurasia were protected, resulting in the peaceful transfer of technology and culture.
- Mongol khans, especially in China, continued the imperial strategy of hiring foreigners as administrators. Foreigners had no allegiance to anything except the rule who hired them. This enabled the Venetian Marco Polo to travel through Yuan (Mongol) China.
- Earlier nomadic societies were family- or clan-based and relatively egalitarian. Postclassical nomadic peoples who conquered settled societies brought these structures with them. This was especially noticeable in the state of women, who had to ride, hunt, and survive in the same rough environment as men. Mongol rules of China valued their wives' advice as much as that of male advisors.
- Several rulers retailed other nomadic traditions. The khanate of the Golden Horde, for example, set up yurts on the steppes outside Moscow and collected tribute but did not interfere with governance.

### Historical Thinking Skills

- **Continuity and Change** Explain the significance of the Mongol Empire in larger patterns of continuity and change across Afro-Eurasia.

### Reasoning Processes

- **Developments and Processes** Identify and explain the role of the Mongols in facilitating long-distance exchange and technological development across Afro-Eurasia.
- **Source Claims and Evidence** Explain how the natural environment shaped nomadic pastoralist society and culture using images and written primary accounts.
- **Contextualization** Explain how the nomadic migrations and conquests in this chapter fit into a longer historical pattern of relationships between nomadic and settled societies.
- **Making Connections** Identify the connections between nomadic pastoralist society and the manner in which the Turks and Mongols acted as conquerors and rulers.
- **Argumentation** Support the argument that the brief rule of the Mongols in Eurasia has long-term historical significance.

### Historical Developments

- Empires collapsed in different regions of the world, and in some areas were replaced by new imperial states, including the Mongol khanates.
- The expansion of empires—including the Mongols—facilitated Afro-Eurasian trade and communication as new people were drawn into their conquerors' economies and trade networks.
- Interregional contacts and conflicts between states and empires, including the Mongols, encouraged significant technological and cultural transfers.

# CHAPTER OVERVIEW

Between the eleventh and the fifteenth centuries, nomadic peoples became more prominent than ever before in Eurasian affairs. Turkish groups migrated to Persia, Anatolia, and India, where they overcame existing authorities and established new states. During the thirteenth and fourteenth centuries, the Mongols established themselves as the most powerful people of the central Asian steppes and then turned on settled societies in China, Persia, Russia, and eastern Europe. By the early fourteenth century, the Mongols had built the largest empire the world has ever seen, stretching from Korea and China in the east to Russia and Hungary in the west.

Most of the Mongol states collapsed during the late fourteenth and fifteenth centuries, but the decline of the Mongols did not signal the end of nomadic peoples' influence on Eurasian affairs. Although a native Chinese dynasty replaced the Mongol state in China, the possibility of a Mongol revival forced the new dynasty to focus attention and resources on its central Asian frontier. Moreover, from the fourteenth through the seventeenth century, Turkish peoples embarked on new campaigns of expansion that eventually brought most of India, much of central Asia, all of Anatolia, and a good portion of eastern Europe under their domination.

The military campaigns of nomadic peoples were exceedingly destructive. Nomadic warriors often demolished cities, slaughtered urban populations, and ravaged surrounding agricultural lands. Yet those same forces also encouraged systematic peaceful interaction between peoples of different societies. Between the eleventh and the fifteenth centuries, Turkish and Mongol peoples forged closer links than ever before between peoples of neighboring lands. By fostering cross-cultural communication and exchange on an unprecedented scale, the nomadic empires encouraged encounters between peoples from many different traditions. In so doing, they helped to integrate societies throughout much of the eastern hemisphere.

| CHRONOLOGY | |
|---|---|
| 1055 | Tughril Beg named sultan |
| 1071 | Battle of Manzikert |
| 1206–1227 | Reign of Chinggis Khan |
| 1211–1234 | Mongol conquest of northern China |
| 1219–1221 | Mongol conquest of Persia |
| 1237–1241 | Mongol conquest of Russia |
| 1258 | Mongol capture of Baghdad |
| 1264–1279 | Mongol conquest of southern China |
| 1264–1294 | Reign of Khubilai Khan |
| 1279–1368 | Yuan dynasty |
| 1295 | Conversion of Ilkhan Ghazan to Islam |
| 1336–1405 | Life of Tamerlane |
| 1453 | Ottoman capture of Constantinople |

# TURKISH MIGRATIONS AND IMPERIAL EXPANSION

Turkish peoples never formed a single, homogeneous group but instead organized themselves into clans and tribes that often fought bitterly with one another. All Turkish peoples spoke related languages, and all were nomads or descendants of nomads. From modest beginnings they expanded their influence until they dominated not only the steppes of central Asia but also settled societies in Persia, Anatolia, and India.

## Economy and Society of Nomadic Pastoralism

**Nomadic Pastoralists and Their Animals** Nomadic peoples of central Asia built societies by adapting to the ecological conditions of the arid lands they lived on. They were pastoralists who kept herds of animals—horses, sheep, goats, cattle, and camels. Central Asia does not receive enough rain to support large-scale agriculture, but grasses and shrubs flourish on the steppe lands. Maintenance of flocks required pastoral peoples of central Asia to move frequently. They drove their animals to lands with abundant grass and then moved them along as the animals thinned the vegetation. They did not wander aimlessly through the steppes but, rather, followed migratory cycles that accounted for the seasons and local climatic conditions. They lived mostly off the meat, milk, and hides of their animals. They used animal bones for tools and animal dung as fuel for fires. They made shoes and clothes out of wool from their sheep and skins from their other animals. Wool was also the source of the felt that they used to fashion large tents called **yurts** in which they lived. They even prepared an alcoholic drink from animal products by fermenting mare's milk into a potent concoction known as ***kumiss***.

The arid climate and the nomadic lifestyle limited the size of human societies in central Asia. Agriculture is necessary for dense populations to congregate, and that was only possible at oases, which were few and far between. Most settlements were few and small—and often temporary as well because nomads carried their collapsible felt yurts with them as they drove their herds. Nomads often engaged in small-scale cultivation of millet or vegetables when they found sources of water, but the

## INTERPRETING IMAGES

A painting from the late fourteenth century by the central Asian artist Mehmed Siyah Qalem suggests the physical hardships of nomadic life. In this scene from a nomadic camp, two men wash clothes (upper left), while another blows on a fire, and a companion tends to a saddle. Bows, arrows, and other weapons are readily available (top right).

**Analyze** *To what extent did the rigors of nomadic life enhance efforts to expand an empire?*

The Picture Art Collection/Alamy Stock Photo

harvests were sufficient only to supplement animal products, not to sustain whole societies. Nomads also produced limited amounts of pottery, leather goods, iron weapons, and tools. However, given their migratory habits, intensive agriculture and large-scale craft production were not possible.

**Nomadic and Settled Peoples** As a result, nomads avidly sought opportunities to trade with settled peoples, and as early as the classical era brisk trade linked nomadic and settled societies. Much of that commerce took place on a small scale as nomads sought agricultural products and manufactured goods to satisfy their immediate needs. But nomads also did participate in long-distance trade networks. Because of their mobility and their familiarity with large regions of central Asia, nomadic peoples were ideally suited to organize and lead the caravans that crossed central Asia and linked settled societies from China to the Mediterranean basin. During the postclassical era and later, Turkish peoples were especially prominent on the caravan routes of central Asia.

**Nomadic Society** Nomadic society typically had two social classes: elites and commoners. Elite charismatic leaders acquired the prestige needed to organize clans and tribes into alliances. Normally, these elite leaders did little governing because clans and tribes looked after their own affairs and resented interference. During times of war, however, elite rulers wielded absolute authority over their forces, and they immediately executed those who did not obey orders.

This nomadic "nobility" was a fluid class. Leaders passed elite status along to their heirs, but the heirs could lose their status if they did not continue to provide appropriate leadership for their clans and tribes. Over the course of a few generations, elites could return to the status of commoners who tended their own herds and followed new leaders. Meanwhile, commoners could become elites by their conduct, particularly by courageous behavior during war. Then, if they were clever diplomats, they could arrange alliances between clans and tribes and gain enough support to displace established leaders.

## SOURCES FROM THE PAST

### William of Rubruck on Gender Roles among the Mongols

*Mongol attacks on Hungary and Poland in 1241 deeply alarmed the pope in Rome. In 1245 he called a council to determine how best to respond to the threat Mongols seemed to pose for Europe. The council decided to send two Franciscan missionaries to the Mongol court as emissaries. William of Rubruck was the second missionary to make the journey, and from 1253 to 1255 he traveled extensively in the recently established Mongol Empire. During his travels he met all the leading Mongol figures of the day, including the Great Khan Möngke. After his return to France, William composed a long account of his journey with descriptions of life on the steppes. One of the things that intrigued him greatly about the Mongols was their gender roles.*

**A matron makes for themselves** the most beautiful wagons. A single rich Tartar has quite one hundred or two hundred such wagons. Baatu [a prominent Mongol general and grandson of Chinggis Khan] has twenty-six wives, each of which has a dwelling, exclusive of the other little ones which they set up after the big one, and which are like closets, in which the sewing girls live, and to each of these large dwellings are attached quite two hundred wagons. And when they set up their houses, the first wife places her dwelling on the extreme west side. and after her the others according to their rank, so that the last wife will be in the extreme east; and there will be the distance of a stone's throw between the yurt of one wife and that of another . . .

Why do you think William of Rubruck thought this was worth mentioning to his European readers?

It is the duty of the women to drive the wagons, get the dwellings on and off them, milk the cows, make butter and *grut* [a kind of cheese], and to dress and sew skins, which they do with a thread made of tendons. They divide the tendons into fine shreds, and then twist them into one long thread. They also sew the boots, the socks, and the clothing. They never wash clothes, for they say that God would be angered thereat, and that it would thunder if they hung them up to dry. Thunder they fear extraordinarily; and when it thunders they will turn out of their dwellings all strangers, wrap themselves in black felt, and thus hide themselves till it has passed away. Furthermore, they never wash their bowls, but when the meat is cooked they rinse out the dish in which they are about to put it with some of the boiling broth from the kettle, which they pour back into it. They also make the felt and cover the houses.

How might the practices described here have been different in a settled society?

The men make bows and arrows, manufacture stirrups and bits, make saddles, do the carpentering on their dwellings and the carts; they take care of the horses, milk the mares, churn the *cosmos* or mare's milk, make the skins in which it is put; they also look after the camels and load them. Both sexes look after the sheep and goats, sometimes the men, other times the women, milking them.

#### For Further Reflection

- Why did women play such prominent social and economic roles in nomadic pastoral societies?

*Source: The Journey of William of Rubruck to the Eastern Parts of the World, 1253–55,* as Narrated by Himself. Trans. William Woodville Rockhill. London: The Haklyut Society, 1800.

**Gender Relations** Adult males dominated nomadic pastoral societies, but women enjoyed much higher status than women in settled agricultural societies. In most nomadic pastoral societies, able-bodied men were frequently away from their herds on hunting expeditions or military campaigns. Thus women were primarily responsible for tending to the animals. Nomadic women were skilled horse riders and archers, and they sometimes fought alongside men in war. Because of their crucial economic roles, women wielded considerable influence—sometimes as advisers with strong voices in family or clan matters and occasionally as regents or rulers in their own right.

**Nomadic Religion** The earliest religion of the Turkish peoples revolved around **shamans**—religious specialists believed to be able to communicate with the gods and nature spirits, ask for divine help on behalf of their communities, and inform their companions of their gods' will. Yet many Turkish peoples became attracted to the religious and cultural traditions they encountered when trading with peoples of settled societies. They did not abandon their inherited beliefs or their shamans, but by the sixth century C.E. many Turks had converted to Buddhism, Nestorian Christianity, or **Manichaeism**. Partly because of their newly adopted religious and cultural traditions and partly because of their prominence in Eurasian trade networks, Turkish peoples also developed a written script.

**Turkish Conversion to Islam** Over the longer term, most Turks converted to Islam as a result of their continual encounters with Muslim peoples. The earliest converts were Turkish nomads captured in border raids by forces of the **Abbasid** caliphate in the early ninth century and integrated into the caliphate's armies as slave soldiers. The first large-scale conversion came in the late tenth century, when a Turkish ruling clan known as the Seljuqs converted to Islam. Although historians cannot be sure of the motivation behind this conversion, the fact that the Seljuqs then migrated to Persia suggests it may have been an attempt to improve their fortunes through alliance with Abbasid authorities. Between the tenth and the fourteenth centuries, most Turkish clans on the steppes of central Asia also adopted Islam, and they carried the new religion with them when they expanded their political and military influence to new regions.

**Military Organization** That expansion took place when nomadic leaders organized vast confederations of peoples all subject, at least nominally, to a **khan** ("ruler"). In fact, khans rarely ruled directly but, rather, through the leaders of allied tribes. Yet when organized on a large scale, nomadic peoples wielded enormous military power, mostly because of their outstanding cavalry forces. Nomadic warriors learned to ride horses as children, and they had excellent equestrian skills. Their arrows flew with deadly accuracy even when launched from the backs of galloping horses. Moreover, units of warriors coordinated their movements to outmaneuver and overwhelm their opponents.

Few armies were able to resist the mobility and discipline of well-organized nomadic warriors. When they found themselves at a disadvantage, they often were able to beat a hasty retreat and escape from their less speedy adversaries. Because of their military skills, several groups of Turkish nomads began in the tenth century C.E. to seize the wealth of settled societies and build imperial states in the regions surrounding central Asia.

## Turkish Empires in Persia, Anatolia, and India

**Seljuq Turks and the Abbasid Empire** Turkish peoples entered Persia, Anatolia, and India at different times and for different purposes. They approached Abbasid Persia much as Germanic peoples had earlier approached the Roman Empire. From about the mid-eighth to the mid-tenth century, Turkish peoples lived mostly on the borders of the Abbasid realm, which offered abundant opportunities for trade. By the mid- to late tenth century, large numbers of **Seljuq Turks** served in Abbasid armies and lived in the Abbasid realm itself. By the mid-eleventh century the Seljuqs overshadowed the Abbasid caliphs. Indeed, in 1055 the caliph recognized the Seljuq leader Tughril Beg as **sultan** ("chieftain" or "ruler"). Tughril first consolidated his hold on the Abbasid capital at Baghdad, then he and his successors extended Turkish rule to Syria, Palestine, and other parts of the realm. For the last two centuries of the Abbasid state, the caliphs served as figureheads of authority while actual governance lay in the hands of the Turkish sultans.

**Seljuq Turks and the Byzantine Empire** While some Turkish peoples established themselves in Abbasid Persia, others turned their attention to the rich land of Anatolia, breadbasket of the Byzantine Empire. Led by the Seljuqs, Turkish peoples began migrating into Anatolia in large numbers in the early eleventh century. In 1071, Seljuq forces inflicted a devastating defeat on the Byzantine army at Manzikert in eastern Anatolia and even took the Byzantine emperor captive. Following that victory, Seljuqs and other Turkish groups entered Anatolia almost at will. The peasants of Anatolia, who mostly resented their Byzantine overlords, often looked upon the Seljuqs as liberators rather than conquerors.

The migrants thoroughly transformed Anatolia. Turkish groups displaced Byzantine authorities and set up their own political and social institutions. They levied taxes on the Byzantine church, restricted its activities, and sometimes confiscated church property. Meanwhile, they welcomed converts to Islam and made political, social, and economic opportunities available to them. By 1453, when Ottoman Turks captured the Byzantine capital at Constantinople, Byzantine and Christian Anatolia had become largely a Turkish and Islamic land.

**Ghaznavid Turks and the Sultanate of Delhi** While the Seljuqs spearheaded Turkish migrations in Abbasid Persia and Byzantine Anatolia, Mahmud of Ghazni led the **Ghaznavid Turks** of Afghanistan in raids on lucrative sites in northern India. When the Ghaznavids began their campaigns in the early eleventh century, their principal goal was plunder. Gradually, though, they became more interested in permanent rule. They asserted their authority first over the Punjab and then over Gujarat and Bengal. By the thirteenth century, the Turkish **sultanate of Delhi** claimed authority over all of northern India. Several of the Delhi sultans conceived plans to conquer southern India and extend Muslim rule there, but none was able to realize those ambitions. The sultans faced constant challenges from Hindu princes in neighboring lands, and they periodically had to defend their northern frontiers from new Turkish or Mongol invaders. They maintained an enormous army with a large elephant corps, but those forces only enabled them to hold on to their territories rather than to expand their empire.

---

**Manichaeism** (MAN-ih-kee-izm)
**Seljuq** (sahl-JYOOK)

Mahmud of Ghazni on his throne.
Album/Alamy Stock Photo

Turkish rule had great social and cultural implications in India, as it did in Anatolia. Mahmud of Ghazni was a zealous foe of Buddhism and Hinduism alike, and he launched frequent raids on shrines, temples, and monasteries. His forces stripped Buddhist and Hindu establishments of their wealth, destroyed their buildings, and often slaughtered their residents and attendants as well. As Turkish invaders repressed Buddhism and Hinduism, they encouraged conversion to Islam and enabled their faith to establish a secure presence in northern India.

Though undertaken by different groups, for different reasons, and by different means, the Turkish conquests of Persia, Anatolia, and India represented part of a larger expansive movement by nomadic peoples. In all three cases, the formidable military prowess of Turkish peoples enabled them to move beyond the steppe lands of central Asia and dominate settled societies. By the thirteenth century, the influence of nomadic peoples was greater than ever before in Eurasian history. Yet the Turkish conquests represented only a prelude to an astonishing round of empire building launched by the Mongols during the thirteenth and fourteenth centuries.

# THE MONGOL EMPIRES

For most of their history the nomadic **Mongols** lived on the high steppe lands of eastern central Asia. Like other nomadic peoples, they displayed deep loyalty to kin groups organized into families, clans, and tribes. They frequently allied with Turkish peoples who built empires on the steppes, but they rarely played a leading role in the organization of states before the thirteenth century. Strong loyalties to kinship groups made it difficult for the Mongols to organize a stable society on a large scale. During the early thirteenth century, however, **Chinggis Khan** (sometimes spelled "Genghis Khan") forged the various Mongol tribes into a powerful alliance that built the largest empire the world has ever seen. Although the vast Mongol realm soon dissolved into a series of smaller empires—most of which disappeared within a century—the Mongols' imperial venture brought the societies of Eurasia into closer contact than ever before.

## Chinggis Khan and the Making of the Mongol Empire

The unifier of the Mongols was **Temüjin**, born about 1167 into a noble family. His father was a prominent warrior who forged an alliance between several Mongol clans and seemed likely to become a powerful leader. When Temüjin was about ten years old, however, rivals poisoned his father and destroyed the alliance. Abandoned by his father's allies, Temüjin led a precarious existence for some years. He lived in poverty because rivals seized the family's animals, and several times he eluded enemies seeking to eliminate him as a potential threat to their own ambitions. A rival once captured him and imprisoned him in a wooden cage, but Temüjin made a daring midnight escape and regained his freedom.

**Chinggis Khan's Rise to Power** During the late twelfth century, Temüjin made an alliance with a prominent Mongol clan leader. He also mastered the art of steppe diplomacy, which called for displays of personal courage in battle, combined with intense loyalty to allies—as well as a willingness to betray allies or superiors to improve one's position—and the ability to entice previously unaffiliated tribes into cooperative relationships. Temüjin gradually strengthened his position, sometimes by forging useful alliances, often by conquering rival contenders for power, and occasionally by turning suddenly against a troublesome ally. He eventually brought all the Mongol tribes into a single confederation, and in 1206 an assembly of Mongol leaders recognized Temüjin's supremacy by proclaiming him Chinggis Khan ("universal ruler").

**Chinggis Khan** (CHIHN-gihs Kahn)
**Temüjin** (TEM-oo-chin)

## INTERPRETING IMAGES

This painting by a Chinese artist depicts Chinggis Khan at about age sixty. Though most of his conquests were behind him, Chinggis Khan's focus and determination are readily apparent in this portrait.

**Analyze** *To what extent does the portrait, indicating the focus and determination of Chinggis Khan, explain his success as a leader? What other factors contributed?*

GL Archive/Alamy

**Mongol Political Organization** Chinggis Khan's policies greatly strengthened the Mongol people. Earlier nomadic state builders had ruled largely through the leaders of allied tribes. Because of his personal experiences, however, Chinggis Khan mistrusted the Mongols' tribal organization. He broke up the tribes and forced men of fighting age to join new military units with no tribal affiliations. He chose high military and political officials not on the basis of kinship or tribal status but, rather, because of their talents or their loyalty to him. Chinggis Khan spent most of his life on horseback and did not establish a proper capital, but his successors built a sumptuous capital at **Karakorum**—present-day Har Horin, located about 300 kilometers (186 miles) west of the modern Mongolian capital of Ulaanbaatar. As command center of a growing empire, Karakorum symbolized a source of Mongol authority superior to the clan or the tribe.

The most important institution of the Mongol state was the army, which magnified the power of the small population. In the thirteenth century the Mongol population stood at about one million people—less than 1 percent of China's numbers. During Chinggis Khan's life, his army numbered only 100,000 to 125,000 Mongols, although allied peoples also contributed forces. How was it possible for so few people to conquer the better part of Eurasia?

**Mongol Arms** Like earlier nomadic armies, Mongol forces relied on outstanding equestrian skills. Mongols grew up riding horses, and they honed their skills by hunting and playing competitive games on horseback. Their bows, short enough for archers to use while riding, were also stiff, firing arrows that could fell enemies at 200 meters (656 feet). Mongol horsemen were among the most mobile forces of the premodern world, sometimes traveling more than 100 kilometers (62 miles) per day to surprise an enemy. Furthermore, the Mongols understood the psychological dimensions of warfare and used them to their advantage. If enemies surrendered without resistance, the Mongols usually spared their lives, and they provided generous treatment for artisans, crafts workers, and those with military skills. In the event of resistance, however, the Mongols ruthlessly slaughtered whole populations, sparing only a few, whom they sometimes drove before their armies as human shields during future conflicts.

Once he had united the Mongols, Chinggis Khan turned his army and his attention to other parts of central Asia and particularly to nearby settled societies. He attacked the various Turkish peoples ruling in Tibet, northern China, Persia, and the central Asian steppes. His conquests in central Asia were important because they protected him against the possibility that other nomadic leaders might challenge his rule. But the Mongol campaigns in China and Persia had especially far-reaching consequences.

**Mongol Conquest of Northern China** Chinggis Khan himself extended Mongol rule to northern China, dominated since 1127 C.E. by the nomadic **Jurchen** people, while the Song dynasty continued to rule in southern China. The conquest of China began in 1211 C.E. when Mongol raiding parties invaded the Jurchen realm. Raids quickly became more frequent and intense, and soon they developed into a campaign of conquest. By 1215 the Mongols had captured the Jurchen capital near modern Beijing, which under the new name of **Khanbaliq** ("city of the khan") served also as the Mongol capital in China. Fighting between Mongols and Jurchen continued until 1234, but by 1220 the Mongols had largely established control over northern China.

**Mongol Conquest of Persia** While part of his army consolidated the Mongol hold on northern China, Chinggis Khan led another force to Afghanistan and Persia, ruled at that time by a successor to the Seljuqs known as the **Khwarazm shah**. In 1218 Chinggis Khan sought to open trade and diplomatic relations with the Khwarazm shah. The shah despised the

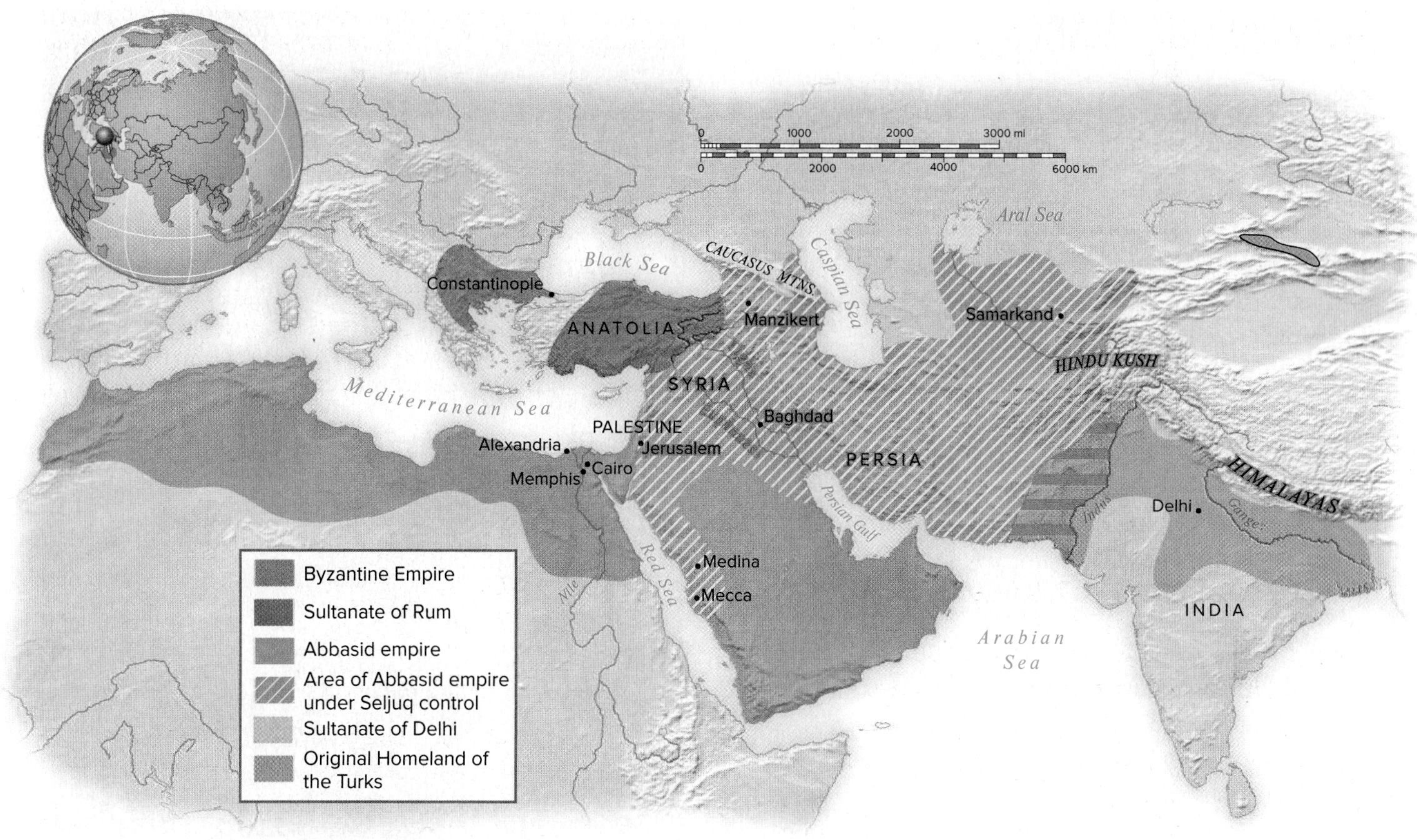


**MAP 5.1 Turkish empires and their neighbors, ca. 1210**

After about 1000 C.E., nomadic Turkish peoples conquered and ruled settled agricultural societies in several regions of Eurasia and north Africa.

***What motivated Turkish people to expand so far from their original homeland, and why were they so successful in creating new states? Compare and contrast the Turkish and Mongol expansion and maintenance of their empire.***

Mongols, however, and he ordered his officials to murder Chinggis Khan's envoys and the merchants accompanying them. The following year Chinggis Khan took his army west to seek revenge. Mongol forces pursued the Khwarazm shah to an island in the Caspian Sea where he died. Meanwhile, they shattered the shah's army and seized control of his realm.

To forestall any possibility that the shah's state might survive and constitute a challenge to his own empire, Chinggis Khan wreaked utter destruction on the conquered land. The Mongols ravaged one city after another, demolishing buildings and massacring hundreds of thousands of people. Some cities never recovered. The Mongols also destroyed the delicate *qanat* irrigation systems that sustained agriculture in the arid region, resulting in severely reduced agricultural production. For centuries after the Mongol conquest, Persian chroniclers cursed the invaders and the devastation they visited upon the land.

By the time of his death in 1227, Chinggis Khan had laid the foundation of a vast and mighty empire. He had united the Mongols, established Mongol supremacy in central Asia, and extended Mongol control to northern China in the east and Persia in the west. Chinggis Khan was a conqueror, however, not an administrator. He ruled the Mongols themselves through his control over the army, but he did not establish a central government for the lands that he conquered. Instead, he assigned Mongol overlords to supervise local administrators and to extract a generous tribute for the Mongols' own uses. Chinggis Khan's heirs continued his conquests, but they also undertook the task of designing a more permanent administration to guide the fortunes of the Mongol Empire.

## The Mongol Empires after Chinggis Khan

Chinggis Khan's death touched off a struggle for power among his sons and grandsons, several of whom had ambitions to succeed the great khan. Eventually, his heirs divided Chinggis Khan's vast realm into four regional empires. The great khans ruled China, the wealthiest of Mongol lands. Descendants of Chaghatai, one of Chinggis Khan's sons, ruled the **khanate of Chaghatai** in central Asia. Persia fell under the authority of rulers known as the ilkhans, and the **khans of the Golden Horde** dominated Russia. The great khans were nominally

## INTERPRETING IMAGES

Mongol soldiers firing their arrows from horseback, from a thirteenth-century illustrated history produced by Persian historian Rashid al-Din.

**Analyze** *To what extent did technology contribute to the success of Mongol expansion? What were additional contributing factors?*

akg-images/Newscom

superior to the others, but they were rarely able to enforce their claims to authority. In fact, for as long as the Mongol Empires survived, ambition fueled constant tension and occasional conflict among the four khans.

**Khubilai Khan** The consolidation of Mongol rule in China came during the reign of **Khubilai Khan** (sometimes spelled Qubilai), one of Chinggis Khan's grandsons. Khubilai was perhaps the most talented of the great conqueror's descendants. He unleashed ruthless attacks against his enemies, but he also took an interest in cultural matters and worked to improve the welfare of his subjects. He actively promoted Buddhism, and he provided support also for Daoists, Muslims, and Christians in his realm. The famous Venetian traveler Marco Polo, who lived almost two decades at Khubilai's court, praised him for his generosity toward the poor and his efforts to build roads. Though named great khan in 1260, Khubilai spent four years fighting off contenders. From 1264 until his death in 1294, Khubilai Khan presided over the Mongol Empire at its height.

**Khubilai** (KOO-bih-lie)
**Yuan** (yoo-AHN)

Depiction of Khubilai Khan on the hunt. Khubilai sits on the dark horse near the center.

Attributed to Liu Kuan-tao/Getty Images

**Mongol Conquest of Southern China** Khubilai extended Mongol rule to all of China. From his base at Khanbaliq, he relentlessly attacked the Song dynasty in southern China. The Song capital at Hangzhou fell to Mongol forces in 1276, and within three years Khubilai had eliminated resistance throughout China. In 1279 he proclaimed himself emperor and established the **Yuan dynasty**, which ruled China until its collapse in 1368.

# SOURCES FROM THE PAST

## Marco Polo on Mongol Military Tactics

*The Venetian Marco Polo is one of the best-known Europeans who traveled through Mongol territories in the late thirteenth century. His book of travel writings is an especially valuable source of information about the Mongol age because the Mongols left very little in the way of a written record. Among other things, he described the Mongol way of making war.*

**Their arms are bows and** arrows, sword and mace; but above all the bow, for they are capital archers, indeed the best that are known. . . .

When a Mongol prince goes forth to war, he takes with him, say, 100,000 men. Well, he appoints an officer to every ten men, one to every hundred, one to every thousand, and one to every ten thousand, so that his own orders have to be given to ten persons only, and each of these ten persons has to pass the orders only to another ten, and so on, no one having to give orders to more than ten. And every one in turn is responsible only to the officer immediately over him; and the discipline and order that comes of this method is marvellous, for they are a people very obedient to their chiefs. . . .

When they are going on a distant expedition they take no gear with them except two leather bottles for milk, a little earthenware pot to cook their meat in, and a little tent to shelter them from rain. And in case of great urgency they will ride ten days on end without lighting a fire or taking a meal. On such an occasion they will sustain themselves on the blood of their horses, opening a vein and letting the blood jet into their mouths, drinking till they have had enough, and then staunching it. . . .

What kind of reaction might this detail have produced among Marco Polo's European audience?

When they come to an engagement with the enemy, they will gain the victory in this fashion. They never let themselves get into a regular medley, but keep perpetually riding round and shooting into the enemy. And as they do not count it any shame to run away in battle, they will sometimes pretend to do so, and in running away they turn in the saddle and shoot hard and strong at the foe, and in this way make great havoc. Their horses are trained so perfectly that they will double hither and thither, just like a dog, in a way that is quite astonishing. Thus they fight to as good purpose in running away as if they stood and faced the enemy because of the vast volleys of arrows that they shoot in this way, turning round upon their pursuers, who are fancying that they have won the battle. But when the Mongols see that they have killed and wounded a good many horses and men, they wheel round bodily and return to the charge in perfect order and with loud cries, and in a very short time the enemy are routed. In truth they are stout and valiant soldiers, and inured to war. And you perceive that it is just when the enemy sees them run, and imagines that he has gained the battle, that he has in reality lost it, for the Mongols wheel round in a moment when they judge the right time has come. And after this fashion they have won many a fight.

Does it seem that Marco Polo admires the Mongol warriors? What language indicates how he feels about their tactics?

### For Further Reflection

- In what ways do the military practices described by Marco Polo reflect the influence of the steppe environment on the Mongols?
- Why would Marco Polo be so impressed by the military of the Mongols?

*Source*: Marco Polo. *The Book of Ser Marco Polo,* 3rd ed. Trans. and ed. by Henry Yule and Henri Cordier. London: John Murray, 1921, pp. 260–63. (Translation slightly modified.)

Beyond China, Khubilai had little success as a conqueror. During the 1270s and 1280s, he launched several invasions of Vietnam, Cambodia, and Burma as well as a naval expedition against Java involving between five hundred to one thousand ships and twenty thousand troops. But Mongol forces did not adapt well to the humid, tropical jungles of southeast Asia. Pasturelands were inadequate for their horses, and the fearsome Mongol horsemen were unable to cope with the guerrilla tactics employed by the defenders. In 1274 and again in 1281, Khubilai also attempted seaborne invasions of Japan, but on both occasions typhoons thwarted his plans. The storm of 1281 was especially vicious: it destroyed about 4,500 Mongol vessels carrying more than one hundred thousand armed troops—the largest seaborne expedition before World War II.

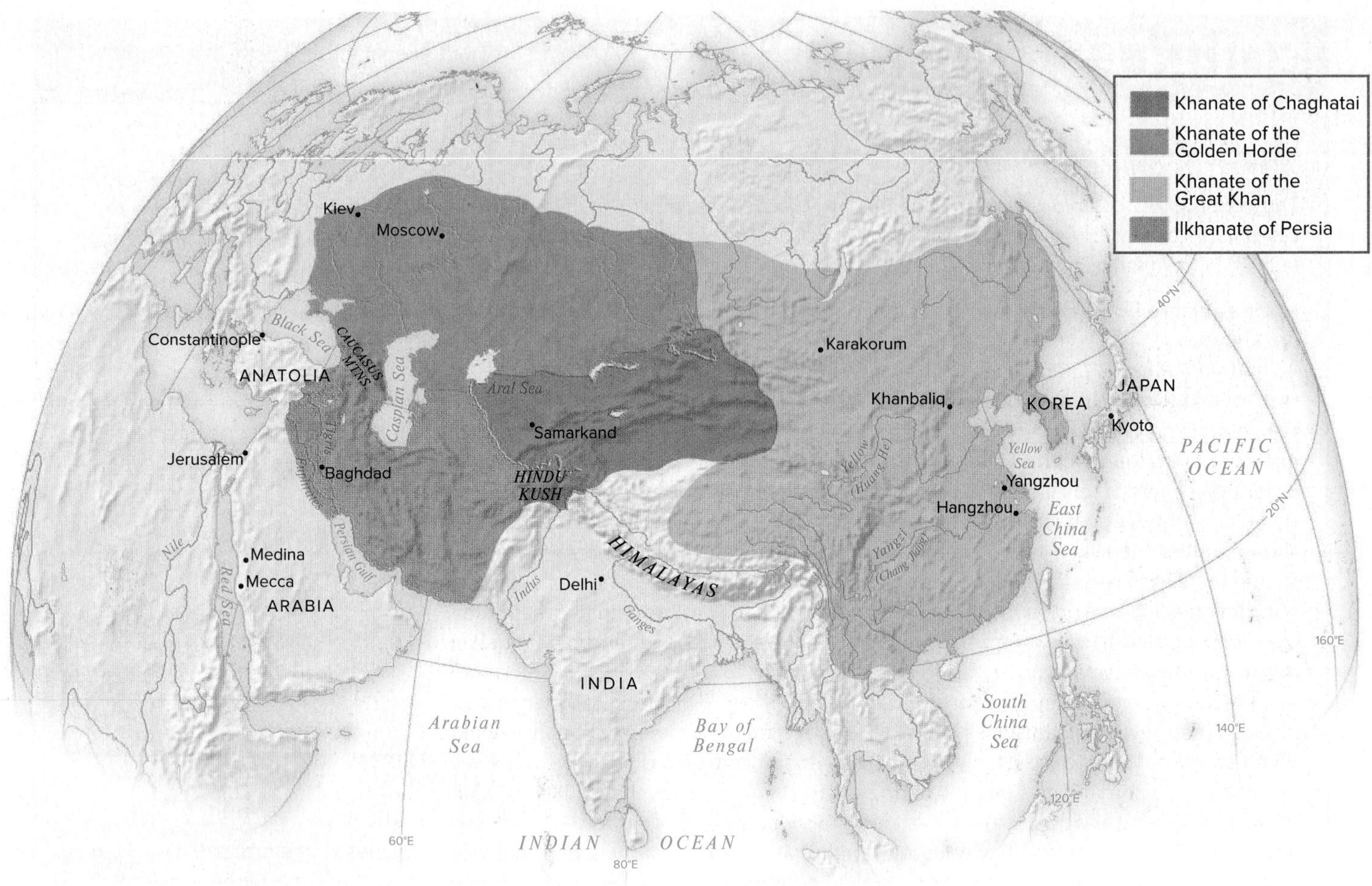


## MAP 5.2 The Mongol Empires, ca. 1300

The Mongol Empires stretched from Manchuria and China to Russia and eastern Europe.

***In what ways did Mongol Empires and Mongol policies facilitate trade, travel, and communication throughout Eurasia?***

Japanese defenders attributed their continued independence to the *kamikaze* ("divine winds").

**The Golden Horde** As Khubilai consolidated his hold on east Asia, his cousins and brothers tightened Mongol control on lands to the west. Mongols of the group known as the Golden Horde overran Russia between 1237 and 1241 and then mounted exploratory expeditions into Poland, Hungary, and eastern Germany in 1241 and 1242. Mongols of the Golden Horde prized the steppes north of the Black Sea as prime pastureland for their horses. They maintained a large army on the steppes from which they mounted raids into Russia. They did not occupy Russia, which they regarded as an unattractive land of forests, but they extracted tribute from the Russian cities and agricultural provinces. The Golden Horde maintained its hegemony in Russia until the mid-fifteenth century, when the princes of Moscow rejected its authority while building a powerful Russian state. By the mid-sixteenth century, Russian conquerors had extended their control to the steppes, but Mongol khans descended from the Golden Horde continued to rule the Crimea until the late eighteenth century.

**The Ilkhanate of Persia** While the Golden Horde established its authority in Russia, Khubilai's brother Hülegü toppled the Abbasid empire and established the Mongol **ilkhanate of Persia.** In 1258 he captured the Abbasid capital of Baghdad after a brief siege. His troops looted the city, executed the caliph, and massacred more than two hundred thousand residents by Hülegü's own estimate. From Persia, Hülegü's army ventured into Syria, but Muslim forces from Egypt soon expelled them and placed a limit on Mongol expansion to the southwest.

When the Mongols crushed ruling regimes in large settled societies, particularly in China and Persia, they discovered that they needed to become governors as well as conquerors. The Mongols had no experience administering complex societies, where successful governance required talents beyond the equestrian and military skills esteemed on the steppes. They had a

**ilkhanate** (EEL-kahn-ate)

## INTERPRETING IMAGES

The siege of Baghdad in 1258: a Persian manuscript illustration depicts Mongol forces camped outside the city walls while residents huddle within.

**Analyze** *What role did catapults (at bottom left and center right) play in sieges like this? In what ways did the Mongol siege of Baghdad impact the political vitality of Islam in the region?*

DEA/J. E. BULLOZ/De Agostini/Getty Images

difficult time adjusting to their role as administrators. Indeed, they never became entirely comfortable in the role, and most of their conquests fell out of their hands within a century.

**Mongol Rule in Persia** The Mongols adopted different tactics in the different lands that they ruled. In Persia they made important concessions to local interests. Although Mongols and their allies occupied the highest administrative positions, Persians served as ministers, provincial governors, and state officials at all lower levels. The Mongols basically allowed the Persians to administer the ilkhanate as long as they delivered tax receipts and maintained order.

Over time, the Mongols even assimilated to Persian cultural traditions. The early Mongol rulers of Persia mostly observed their native shamanism, but they tolerated all religions—including Islam, Nestorian Christianity, Buddhism, and Judaism—and they ended the privileges given Muslims during the Abbasid caliphate. Gradually, however, the Mongols themselves gravitated toward Islam. In 1295 Ilkhan Ghazan publicly converted to Islam, and most of the Mongols in Persia followed his example. Ghazan's conversion sparked large-scale massacres of Christians and Jews, and it signaled the return of Islam to a privileged position in Persian society. It also indicated the absorption of the Mongols into Muslim Persian society.

**Mongol Rule in China** In China, by contrast, the Mongol overlords stood aloof from their subjects, whom they scorned as mere cultivators. They outlawed intermarriage between Mongols and Chinese and forbade the Chinese from learning the Mongol language. Soon after their conquest some of the victors went so far as to suggest that the Mongols exterminate the Chinese people and convert China itself into pastureland for their horses. Cooler heads eventually prevailed, and the Mongols decided simply to extract as much revenue as possible from their Chinese subjects. In doing so, however, they did not make as much use of native administrative talent as did their counterparts in Persia. Instead, they brought foreign administrators into China and placed them in charge. Along with their nomadic allies, the Mongols' administrative staff included Arabs, Persians, and perhaps even Europeans: Marco Polo may have served as an administrator in the city of Yangzhou during the reign of Khubilai Khan.

The Mongols also resisted assimilation to Chinese cultural traditions. They ended the privileges enjoyed by the Confucian scholars, and they dismantled the Confucian educational and examination system, which had produced untold generations of civil servants for the Chinese bureaucracy. They did not persecute Confucians, but they allowed the Confucian tradition to wither in the absence of official support. Meanwhile, to remain on good terms with subjects of different faiths, the Mongols allowed the construction of churches, temples, and shrines, and they even subsidized some religious establishments. They tolerated all cultural and religious traditions in China, including Confucianism, Daoism, Buddhism, and Christianity. Of Khubilai Khan's four wives, his favorite was Chabi, a Nestorian Christian.

**The Mongols and Buddhism** For their part the Mongols mostly continued to follow their native shamanist traditions, although many of the ruling elite became enchanted with the Lamaist school of Buddhism that developed in Tibet. Lamaist Buddhism held several attractions for the Mongols. It made a prominent place for magic and supernatural powers, and in that respect it resembled the Mongols' shamanism. Moreover, Lamaist Buddhist leaders officially recognized the Mongols as legitimate rulers and went out of their way to court the Mongols' favor. They numbered the Mongols in the ranks of universal Buddhist rulers and even recognized the Mongol khans as incarnations of the Buddha. It is therefore not surprising that the Mongol ruling elites would find Lamaist Buddhism attractive.

Chabi, a Nestorian Christian and the favorite wife of Khubilai Khan, wearing the distinctive headgear reserved for Mongol women of the ruling class.
History and Art Collection/Alamy Stock Photo

## The Mongols and Eurasian Integration

In building their vast empire, the Mongols brought tremendous destruction to lands throughout much of the Eurasian landmass. While the human cost of such destruction should not be minimized, the Mongols also sponsored interaction and encounters among peoples of different societies and linked Eurasian lands more directly than ever before. Indeed, Mongol rulers positively encouraged travel and communication over long distances. Recognizing the value of regular communications for their vast empire, Chinggis Khan and his successors maintained a courier network that rapidly relayed news, information, and government orders. The network included relay stations with fresh horses and riders so that messages could travel almost nonstop throughout Mongol territories. The Mongols' encouragement of travel and communication facilitated trade, diplomatic travel, missionary efforts, and movements of peoples to new lands.

## What's Left Out?

The Mongols ruled such a vast array of territories that major textual sources documenting their rule exist in at least twelve languages. Many of these sources have not been translated from their original languages, which means that our historical knowledge of Mongol rule has tended to be partial and regional. Additionally, some khanates—such as those in China and Persia—produced many more contemporary sources than the khanates of Chagatai or the Golden Horde. Complicating the matter is that the Mongols left very few written sources of their own, which means that most of the sources we have were written by contemporary observers rather than by Mongols themselves. Given the fragmented nature of the sources, both by language and region, the ability of historians to tell a comprehensive and balanced story of the Mongols has been limited. How might the unbalanced nature of these sources affect the story of the Mongols presented in this chapter?

*Source:* There are few general surveys of the Mongols, but David Morgan, *The Mongols*, 2nd edition (2007), serves as one of the most respected.

### Thinking Critically About Sources

1. What would motivate contemporary observers of the Mongols to cast a positive light on their legacy?
2. What would motivate contemporary observers of the Mongols to cast a negative light on their legacy?

**The Mongols and Trade** As a nomadic people dependent on commerce with settled agricultural societies, the Mongols worked to secure trade routes and ensure the safety of merchants passing through their territories. The Mongol khans frequently fought among themselves, but they maintained reasonably good order within their realms and allowed merchants to travel unmolested through their empires. As a result, long-distance travel and trade became much less risky than in earlier times. Merchants increased their commercial investments, and the volume of long-distance trade across central Asia dwarfed that of earlier eras. Lands as distant as China and western Europe became directly linked for the first time because of the ability of individuals to travel across the entire Eurasian landmass.

**Diplomatic Missions** Like trade, diplomatic communication was essential to the Mongols, and their protection of roads and travelers benefited ambassadors as well as merchants. Chinggis Khan destroyed the Khwarazm shah in Persia because the shah unwisely murdered the Mongol envoys Chinggis Khan dispatched in hopes of opening diplomatic and commercial relations. Throughout the Mongol era the great khans in China, the ilkhans in Persia, and the other khans maintained close communications by means of diplomatic embassies. They also had diplomatic dealings with rulers in Korea, Vietnam, India, western Europe, and other lands as well. Some diplomatic travelers crossed the entire Eurasian landmass. Several European ambassadors traveled to Mongolia and China to deliver messages from authorities seeking to ally with the Mongols against Muslim states in southwest Asia. Diplomats also traveled west: Rabban Sauma, a Nestorian Christian monk born in Khanbaliq, visited Italy and France as a representative of the Persian ilkhan.

**Missionary Efforts** Like the Silk Roads in earlier times, Eurasian routes during the era of the Mongol Empires served as highways for missionaries as well as merchants and diplomats. Sufi missionaries helped popularize Islam among Turkish peoples in central Asia, while Lamaist Buddhism from Tibet attracted considerable interest among the Mongols. Nestorian Christians, who had long been prominent in oasis communities throughout central Asia, found new opportunities to win converts when they went to China to serve as administrators for Mongol rulers there. Roman Catholic Christians also mounted missionary campaigns in China. (See chapter 21 for further discussion of travel during the Mongol era.)

**Resettlement** Another Mongol policy that encouraged Eurasian integration was the practice of resettling peoples in new lands. As a nomadic people, the Mongols had limited numbers of skilled artisans and educated individuals, but the more their empire expanded, the more they needed the services of specialized crafts workers and literate administrators. Mongol overlords recruited the talent they needed largely from the ranks of their allies and the peoples they conquered, and they often moved people far from their homelands to sites where they could best make use of their services. Among the most important of the Mongols' allies were the Uighur Turks, who lived mostly in oasis cities along the Silk Roads. The **Uighurs** were literate and often highly educated, and they provided not only many of the clerks, secretaries, and administrators who ran the Mongol Empires but also units of soldiers who bolstered Mongol garrisons. Arab and Persian Muslims were also prominent among those who administered the Mongols' affairs far from their homelands.

Conquered peoples also supplied the Mongols with talent. When they overcame a city, Mongol forces routinely surveyed the captured population, separated out those with specialized skills, and sent them to the capital at Karakorum or some other place where there was demand for their services. From the ranks of conquered peoples came soldiers, bodyguards, administrators, secretaries, translators, physicians, armor makers, metalsmiths, miners, carpenters, masons, textile workers, musicians, and jewelers. After the 1230s the Mongols often took censuses of lands they conquered, partly to levy taxes and conscript military forces and partly to locate talented individuals. The Parisian goldsmith Guillaume Boucher, who we met at the beginning of this chapter, was only one among thousands of foreign-born individuals who became permanent residents of the Mongol capital at Karakorum because of their special talents. Like their protection of trade and diplomacy, the Mongols' policy of resettling allies and conquered peoples promoted Eurasian integration by increasing communication and exchange between peoples of different societies and traditions.

## Decline of the Mongols in Persia and China

**Collapse of the Ilkhanate** Soon after the long and prosperous reign of Khubilai Khan, the Mongols encountered serious difficulties governing Persia and China. In Persia excessive spending strained the treasury, and overexploitation of the peasantry led to reduced revenues. In the early 1290s the ilkhan tried to resolve his financial difficulties by introducing paper money and ordering all subjects to accept it for payment of all debts. The purpose of that measure was to drive precious metals into the hands of the government, but the policy was a miserable failure: rather than accept paper that they regarded as worthless, merchants simply closed their shops. Commerce ground to a halt until the ilkhan rescinded his order. Meanwhile, factional struggles plagued the Mongol leadership. The regime went into steep decline after the death of Ilkhan Ghazan in 1304. When the last of the Mongol rulers died without an heir in 1335, the ilkhanate itself simply collapsed. Government in Persia devolved to local levels until late in the fourteenth

# How the Past Shapes the Future

## The Diffusion of Technologies

**Between about 1000 and 1500 C.E., increased intercultural encounters—especially across and between Eurasia and Africa—led to a spectacular diffusion of technologies that would have an impact on the world's history for centuries to come. Technologies include tools and techniques that humans use to adapt the natural environment to their needs, and thus can range from items like plows and horseshoes to irrigation systems or ideas about which crops to plant. Of course, both the existence of technologies and their diffusion were hardly unique to the period between 1000 and 1500 C.E.—indeed, we have already seen numerous examples of technological diffusion (such as the spread of horse-drawn chariots and iron smelting, among many others) in chapters 1–16. But one of the reasons for the increased pace of interactions across Eurasia and Africa was because of the spread of the *dar-al-Islam* after the eighth century, which we read about in chapter 14, and especially because of the Muslim merchants who established stable trade routes within and beyond its bounds. Another reason was the huge conquests made by nomadic Turkic and Mongolian peoples from the eleventh to the thirteenth centuries. In the thirteenth century, Mongol conquests alone provided stable trade routes that connected Eurasia all the way from China to eastern Europe. Each of these developments provided the pathways not only for the introduction of new trade items and spiritual beliefs but also for the diffusion of technologies from distant regions. Here, we discuss two types of technologies that were widely diffused in this period: technologies of warfare and technologies of transportation.**

### Technologies of Warfare

When the Mongols were trying to conquer China, they learned about gunpowder for the first time. Gunpowder, of course, was not new to the Chinese: as we saw in chapter 13, Chinese alchemists discovered the compound during the Han dynasty, and by the eighth century Chinese strategists were using it for military purposes. But when Mongol invaders were introduced to gunpowder, they quickly incorporated its destructive powers into their arsenal of weapons: as early as 1214, for example, Chinggis Khan's armies included an artillery unit. Faced with the power of gunpowder—especially its usefulness in breaking sieges—societies all over Eurasia quickly sought to acquire the technology. Since the Mongols used gunpowder weapons to conquer Persia and other parts of southwest Asia in the mid-thirteenth century, Muslim armies were inspired to incorporate the technology quickly in order to defend themselves. By the mid-thirteenth century gunpowder technology had also reached Europe, and by the early fourteenth century armies across Eurasia possessed cannons. Although early cannons were not particularly accurate, the diffusion of gunpowder technologies permanently altered the nature of warfare. Indeed, over the eight centuries since Mongol armies began to use it, the use of gunpowder technologies has affected every part of the globe in profound ways.

### Technologies of Transportation

The period from around 1000 to 1500 C.E. also witnessed the widespread diffusion of technologies that improved both animal and maritime transportation—technologies that, in turn, allowed for both greater economic integration across long distances as well as greater economic growth. For example, Islamic merchants from north Africa utilized camels to cross the Sahara by the late eighth century C.E. (chapter 18). The diffusion of camels across the Sahara led to significant and long-term changes in a variety of sub-Saharan African societies, which included both the introduction of Islam as well as growing wealth resulting from being incorporated into much larger Eurasian markets. In Europe, meanwhile, the diffusion of the horse collar—most likely from both central Asia and north Africa—during the High Middle Ages helped to fuel European economic growth by allowing horses to pull much heavier loads without choking (chapter 19). The result was that Europeans could use horses for plowing and for transporting heavy loads rather than much slower oxen, which increased the amount of land that could be plowed as well as the rapidity with which goods could be brought to market.

Maritime technologies also diffused widely in this period. For example, the magnetic compass was invented by the Chinese during the Tang or Song dynasty, but by the mid-eleventh century it was being used by mariners throughout the Indian Ocean basin. By the mid-twelfth century, Europeans were also using compasses in the Mediterranean and Atlantic—devices that helped Portuguese mariners find their way into the Indian Ocean in the fifteenth century (chapter 21). In subsequent centuries, European mariners adopted many other maritime technologies from distant cultures—including the astrolabe—which were eventually used to cross the Atlantic to the Americas. Maritime technologies were not only important in Eurasia, however: during the twelfth and thirteenth centuries, voyages using sophisticated maritime techniques between the Hawaiian Islands and Tahiti allowed for the transfer of improved fishhook technologies to Hawaii (chapter 20).

When reading subsequent chapters, consider the effects that the diffusion of technologies have had on societies around the world over the very long term.

Siege of a north African town, fourteenth century.
Album/Alamy Stock Photo

century when Turkish peoples reintroduced effective central government.

**Decline of the Yuan Dynasty** Mongol decline in China was a more complicated affair. As in Persia, it had an economic dimension. The Mongols continued to use the paper money that the Chinese had introduced during the Tang and Song dynasties, but they did not maintain adequate reserves of the bullion that backed up paper notes. The general population soon lost confidence in paper money, and prices rose sharply as a reflection of its diminished value. As in Persia, too, factions and infighting hastened Mongol decline in China. As the richest of the Mongol Empires, China attracted the attention of ambitious warriors. Beginning in the 1320s power struggles, imperial assassinations, and civil war convulsed the Mongol regime in China.

**Bubonic Plague** Apart from financial difficulties and factional divisions, the Mongol rulers of China also faced an onslaught of epidemic disease. By facilitating trade and communications throughout Eurasia, the Mongols unwittingly expedited the spread of bubonic plague (discussed in chapter 21). During the 1330s plague erupted in southwestern China. From there it spread throughout China and central Asia, and by the late 1340s it had reached southwest Asia and Europe, where it became known as the Black Death. Bubonic plague sometimes killed half or more of an exposed population, particularly during the furious initial years of the epidemic, and it seriously disrupted economies and societies throughout much of Eurasia. In China depopulation and labor shortages that followed on the heels of epidemic plague weakened the Mongol regime. (Plague would also have caused serious problems for the Mongol rulers of Persia had the ilkhanate not collapsed before its arrival.)

The Mongols also faced a rebellious subject population in China. The Mongols stood apart from their Chinese subjects, who returned the contempt of their conquerors. Beginning in the 1340s southern China became a hotbed of peasant

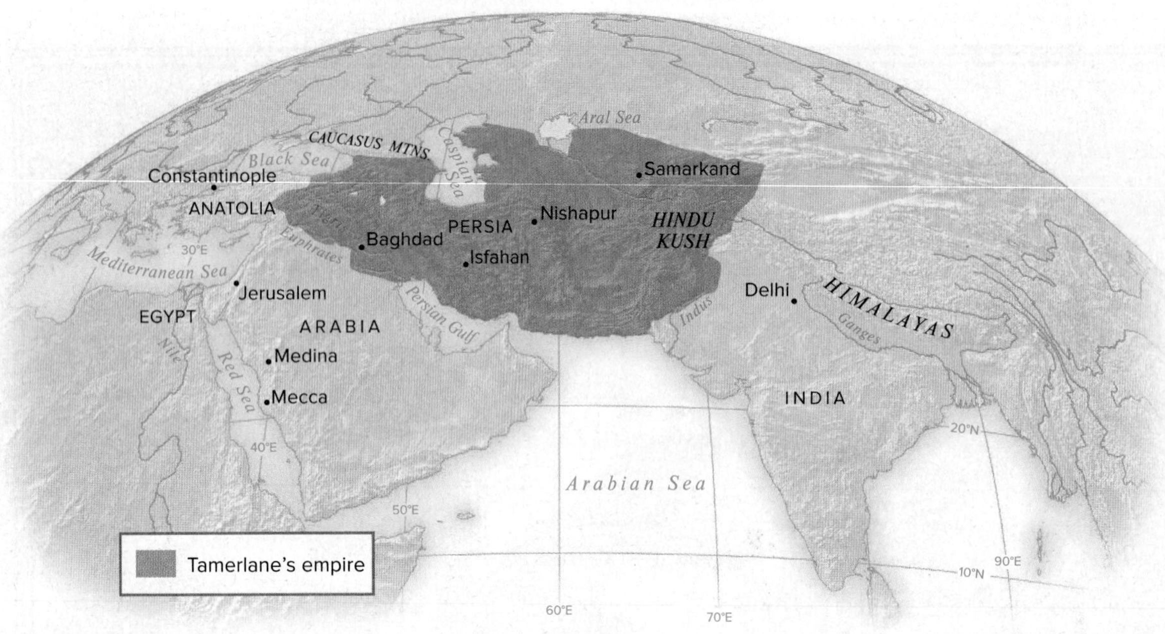


**MAP 5.3 Tamerlane's empire, ca. 1405**

Notice the similarity between Tamerlane's empire and the ilkhanate of Persia outlined in Map 5.2.

***To what extent do you think the cities and the administrative infrastructure of the region both helped and hindered Tamerlane's efforts to control his empire? Compare and contrast the rules of Chinggis Khan and Tamerlane.***

rebellion and banditry, which the Mongols could not control. In 1368 rebel forces captured Khanbaliq, and the Mongols departed China en masse and returned to the steppes.

**Surviving Mongol Khanates** Despite the collapse of the Mongol regimes in Persia and China, Mongol states did not completely disappear. The khanate of Chaghatai continued to prevail in central Asia, and Mongols posed a threat to the northwestern borders of China until the eighteenth century. Meanwhile, the khanate of the Golden Horde continued to dominate the Caucasus and the steppe lands north of the Black Sea and the Caspian Sea until the mid-sixteenth century when a resurgent Russian state brought the Golden Horde down. Like Mongols in China, however, Mongols in Russia continued to threaten until the eighteenth century, and Mongols who had settled in the Crimean peninsula retained their identity until Josef Stalin forcibly moved them to other parts of the Soviet Union in the mid-twentieth century.

## AFTER THE MONGOLS

By no means did the decline of the Mongols signal the end of nomadic peoples' influence in Eurasia. As Mongol strength waned, Turkish peoples resumed the expansive campaigns that the Mongols had interrupted. During the late fourteenth and early fifteenth centuries, the Turkic-Mongol conqueror **Tamerlane** built a central Asian empire rivaling that of Chinggis Khan himself. Although Tamerlane's empire foundered soon after his death, it deeply influenced three surviving Turkish Muslim states—the Mughal empire in India, the Safavid empire in Persia, and the **Ottoman Empire** based in Anatolia—and also embraced much of southwest Asia, southeastern Europe, and north Africa.

### Tamerlane and the Timurids

**The Lame Conqueror** The rapid collapse of the Mongol states left gaping power vacuums in China and Persia. While the native Ming dynasty filled the vacuum in China, a self-made Turkic-Mongol conqueror named Timur moved on Persia. Because he walked with a limp, contemporaries referred to him as Timur-i lang—"Timur the Lame," an appellation that made its way into English as Tamerlane.

Born about 1336 near Samarkand, Tamerlane took Chinggis Khan as his model. Like Chinggis Khan, Tamerlane came from a family of minor Mongol and Turkish elites, and had to make his own way to power. Like Chinggis Khan, too, he was a charismatic leader and a courageous warrior, and he attracted a band of loyal followers. During the 1360s he eliminated rivals to power, either by persuading them to join him as allies or by defeating their armies on the battlefield, and he won recognition as leader of his own tribe. By 1370 he had extended his authority throughout the khanate of Chaghatai and begun to build a magnificent imperial capital in Samarkand.

**Tamerlane** (TAM-er-lane)

Spoils from Tamerlane's campaigns and raids enriched the conqueror's capital at Samarkand. They financed, among other buildings, the magnificent tomb where Tamerlane's remains still rest.
silverfox999/Shutterstock

Although besieged by Ottoman forces, Constantinople received supplies from the sea for almost two months before Ottomans destroyed the city walls and completed their conquest of the Byzantine Empire.
Christophel Fine Art/Universal Images Group/Getty Images

**Tamerlane's Conquests** For the rest of his life, Tamerlane led his armies on campaigns of conquest. He turned first to the region between Persia and Afghanistan, and he took special care to establish his authority in the rich cities of the region so that he could levy taxes on trade and agricultural production. Next he attacked the Golden Horde in the Caucasus region and Russia, and by the mid-1390s he had severely weakened it. During the last years of the century, he invaded India and brutally conquered Delhi: contemporary chroniclers reported, with some exaggeration, that for a period of two months after the attack not even birds visited the devastated city. Later, Tamerlane campaigned along the Ganges, although he never attempted to incorporate India into his empire. He opened the new century with campaigns in southwest Asia and Anatolia. In 1404 he began preparations for an invasion of China, and he was leading his army east when he fell ill and died in 1405.

Like his model Chinggis Khan, Tamerlane was a conqueror, not a governor. He spent almost his entire adult life planning and fighting military campaigns: he even had himself carried around on a litter during his final illness, as he prepared to invade China. He did not create an imperial administration but, rather, ruled through tribal leaders who were his allies. He appointed overlords in the territories he conquered, but they relied on existing bureaucratic structures and simply received taxes and tributes on his behalf.

**Tamerlane's Heirs** Given its loose organization, it is not surprising that Tamerlane's Timurid empire experienced stresses and strains after the conqueror's death. Tamerlane's sons and grandsons engaged in a long series of bitter conflicts that resulted in the contraction of the Timurid empire and its division into four main regions. For a century after Tamerlane's death, however, they maintained control over the region from Persia to Afghanistan. When the last vestiges of Tamerlane's imperial creation disappeared, in the early sixteenth century, the Mughal, **Safavid,** and Ottoman empires that replaced it all clearly reflected the Turkish, Mongol, and Muslim legacy of the lame conqueror.

**Safavid** (SAH-fah-vihd)

## The Foundation of the Ottoman Empire

Chapter 15 will discuss the Mughal empire in India and the Safavid empire in Persia, both of which emerged during the early sixteenth century as Tamerlane's empire finally dissolved. The early stages of Ottoman expansion predated Tamerlane, however, and the foundation of the influential Ottoman Empire throws additional light on the influence of nomadic peoples during the period 1000 to 1500 C.E.

**Osman** After the Mongol conquest of Persia, large numbers of nomadic Turks migrated from central Asia to the ilkhanate and beyond to the territories in Anatolia that the Seljuq Turks had seized from the Byzantine Empire. There they followed charismatic leaders who organized further campaigns of conquest. Among those leaders was **Osman**, who during the late thirteenth and early fourteenth centuries carved a small state for himself in northwestern Anatolia. In 1299 Osman declared independence from the Seljuq sultan and launched a campaign to build a state at the expense of the Byzantine Empire. After every successful operation, Osman attracted more and more followers, who came to be known as Osmanlis or Ottomans.

**Ottoman Conquests** During the 1350s the Ottomans gained a considerable advantage over their Turkish rivals when they established a foothold across the Dardanelles at Gallipoli on the Balkan peninsula. The Ottomans quickly moved to expand the boundaries of their Balkan holdings. Byzantine forces resisted Ottoman incursions, but because of political fragmentation, ineffective government, and exploitation of the peasantry, the Ottomans found abundant local support. By the 1380s the Ottomans had become by far the most powerful people on the Balkan peninsula, and by the end of the century they were poised to capture Constantinople and take over the Byzantine Empire.

Tamerlane temporarily delayed Ottoman expansion in the Byzantine realm. In 1402 Tamerlane's forces crushed the Ottoman army, captured the sultan, and subjected the Ottoman state to the conqueror's authority. After Tamerlane's death, Ottoman leaders had to reestablish their rule in their own realm. This undertaking involved both the repression of ambitious local princes who sought to build power bases at Ottoman expense and the defense of Ottoman territories against Byzantine, Venetian, and other Christian forces that sought to turn back the advance of the Turkish Muslims. By the 1440s the Ottomans had recovered their balance and began again to expand in the Byzantine Empire.

**The Capture of Constantinople** The campaign culminated in 1453 when Sultan Mehmed II captured the city of Constantinople, thus bringing to an end more than a thousand years of Byzantine rule. After subjecting it to a sack, he made the city his own capital under the Turkish name of Istanbul. With Istanbul as a base, the Ottomans quickly absorbed the remainder of the Byzantine Empire. By 1480 they controlled all of Greece and the Balkan region. They continued to expand throughout most of the sixteenth century as well, extending their rule to southwest Asia, southeastern Europe, Egypt, and north Africa. Once again, then, a nomadic people asserted control over a long-settled society and quickly built a vast empire.

**Osman** (os-MAHN)

## CONCLUSION

This chapter has demonstrated that during the half millennium from 1000 to 1500 C.E., nomadic peoples of central Asia played a larger role than ever before in world history. In this period, they dominated affairs in most of Eurasia through their conquests and their construction of vast transregional empires. Turkish peoples built the most durable of the nomadic empires, but the spectacular conquests of the Mongols most clearly demonstrated the potential of nomadic peoples to project their formidable military power to settled agricultural societies. By establishing connections that spanned the Eurasian landmass, the nomadic empires laid the foundation for increasing encounters and exchanges among peoples of different societies and traditions, thereby fostering the integration of the eastern hemisphere. As the example of Guillaume Boucher at the start of this chapter illustrates, beginning in the mid-thirteenth century, merchants, artisans, diplomats, and missionaries traveled frequently between lands as far removed as France and Central Asia. This rich interchange between social and cultural traditions on the one hand and dynamic encounters on the other allows us to speak, for the first time, about a truly Eurasian history. The age of nomadic empires from 1000 to 1500 C.E. thus foreshadowed the integrated world of modern times.

## STUDY TERMS

Abbasid (166)
Chinggis Khan (167)
Ghaznavid Turks (166)
ilkhanate of Persia (172)
Jurchen (168)
Karakorum (168)
khan (166)
khanate of Chaghatai (169)
Khanbaliq (168)
khans of the Golden Horde (169)
Khubilai Khan (170)
Khwarazm shah (168)
*kumiss* (163)
Manichaeism (166)
Mongols (167)
Osman (180)
Ottoman Empire (178)
Safavid (179)
Seljuq Turks (166)
shamans (165)
sultan (166)
sultanate of Delhi (166)
Tamerlane (178)
Temüjin (167)
Uighurs (173)
Yuan dynasty (170)
yurts (163)

## FOR FURTHER READING


Thomas T. Allsen. *Culture and Conquest in Mongol Eurasia.* Cambridge, 2001. Carefully studies the cultural exchanges sponsored by Mongol rulers, particularly those passing between China and Iran.

Thomas J. Barfield. *The Nomadic Alternative.* Englewood Cliffs, N.J., 1993. A sensitive study of nomadic societies in Africa and Eurasia by a leading anthropologist.

Carter Vaughn Findley. *The Turks in World History.* New York, 2005. A welcome volume that lucidly outlines the history of Turkish peoples and discusses relations between Turks and neighboring peoples.

Peter Jackson. *The Mongols and the West, 1221–1410.* London, 2005. Offers a comprehensive review of military, diplomatic, commercial, and cultural relations between Mongol and European societies.

Paul Kahn, ed. *The Secret History of the Mongols: The Origin of Chingis Khan.* Adapted from the translation of F. W. Cleaves. San Francisco, 1984. A translation of the Mongols' history of their own society, adapted for modern readers.

Adam T. Kessler. *Empires beyond the Great Wall: The Heritage of Genghis Khan.* Los Angeles, 1993. Well-illustrated survey of nomadic states in central Asia from the Xiongnu to the Mongols.

George Lane. *Daily Life in the Mongol Empire.* London, 2006. Explores the lives of ordinary people under the reign of Chinggis Khan, including dwellings, health, food, law, and culture.

Beatrice Forbes Manz. *The Rise and Rule of Tamerlane.* Cambridge, 1989. Scholarly analysis of Tamerlane's career and his empire.

David Morgan. *The Mongols.* 2nd ed. Oxford, 2007. Lucid and witty, this remains one of the best short works on the Mongols.

Morris Rossabi. *Khubilai Khan: His Life and Times.* Berkeley, 1988. Excellent scholarly study of the greatest of the great khans.

# CHAPTER 5 AP EXAM PRACTICE

Questions assume cumulative knowledge from this chapter and previous chapters.

## Section I

## Multiple Choice Questions

Use the image below and your knowledge of world history to answer questions 1 - 3.

Chabi, a Nestorian Christian and the favorite wife of Khubilai Khan, wearing the distinctive headgear reserved for Mongol women of the ruling class.
History and Art Collection/Alamy Stock Photo

1. What historical context can be seen in this image?
   (A) The Mongols were tolerant of many of the religions in their empire, which created more opportunities for religious minorities.
   (B) Confucian scholars maintained their position of privilege in the Yuan Dynasty.
   (C) Nomadic peoples excelled at conquest but lacked bureaucratic institutions for ruling empires.
   (D) The Mongols allowed intermarriage to integrate Mongol and Chinese peoples.

2. In what way did the Mongols contribute to the spread of religions?
   (A) Mongol missionaries spread their shamanic traditions to the Persians and the Chinese.
   (B) Sufi missionaries introduced Lamaist Buddhism to Tibet.
   (C) Women who married Mongols were forced to become Nestorians.
   (D) Nestorian Christians sent missionaries along with administrators to China.

3. What argument might a historian make about the resettlement of peoples under the Mongols?
   (A) The Uighur Turks were moved to China so that they could take the Confucian exams and work in the Yuan bureaucracy.
   (B) The Mongols recruited agricultural workers to increase agricultural production in Karakorum.
   (C) Because they were nomads, Mongols lacked skilled artisans and scholars. They recruited people with those talents and moved them to places where they could best use them.
   (D) The Mongols kept the resettled peoples separate from each other, so little cultural exchanges took place.

Use the image below and your knowledge of world history to answer questions 4 and 5.

The siege of Baghdad in 1258: a Persian manuscript illustration depicts Mongol forces camped outside the city walls while residents huddle within.
Bibliotheque Nationale, Paris, France/Bridgeman Images

4. A historian would most likely use this image to illustrate which of the following?
   (A) Nomads were at a technological disadvantage when they laid siege to Baghdad. Their catapults were too weak against the high walls of the city.
   (B) The Mongol conquest swept aside traditional religious and political authorities, like the Abbasid caliph, and replaced them with Mongol leaders who ruled through control of the army.
   (C) The Abbasid caliph agreed to surrender if the Mongol leader agreed to convert to Islam. The caliph would be a religious figurehead and Mongol leader would be the sultan.
   (D) Tamerlane so thoroughly destroyed Baghdad that it is said even birds refused to visit the place for centuries after its fall.

5. The siege of Baghdad is an example that supports which statement about the Mongols?
   (A) Mongol forces did not adapt well to humid, tropical jungles.
   (B) Buddhist leaders officially recognized the Mongols as legitimate rulers and went out of their way to court the Mongols' favor.
   (C) Nomadic warriors often demolished cities, slaughtered urban populations, and ravaged surrounding agricultural lands. Yet those same forces also encouraged systematic peaceful interaction between peoples of different societies.
   (D) Chinggis Khan destroyed the Khwarazm shah in Persia because the shah unwisely murdered the Mongol envoys Chinggis Khan dispatched in hopes of opening diplomatic and commercial relations.

## Short Answer

6. Use the image below and your knowledge of world history to answer parts A, B, and C.

The siege of Mahdia, Tunisia, 1390. French and English forces encamped outside the castle town attack it with cannon and crossbow.
Album/Alamy Stock Photo

(A) Identify ONE technological transfer that took place from 1000 to 1450 C.E.

(B) Explain ONE cultural change brought about by the nomadic empires between 1000 and 1450 C.E.

(C) Explain ONE cultural continuity in the history of the Mongol and Turkish empires, 1000–1450 C.E.

7. Use this text selection and your knowledge of world history to answer parts A, B, and C.

> Their arms are bows and arrows, sword and mace; but above all the bow, for they are capital archers, indeed the best that are known. . . .
>
> When a Mongol prince goes forth to war, he takes with him, say, 100,000 men. Well, he appoints an officer to every ten men, one to every hundred, one to every thousand, and one to every ten thousand, so that his own orders have to be given to ten persons only, and each of these ten persons has to pass the orders only to another ten, and so on, no one having to give orders to more than ten. And every one in turn is responsible only to the officer immediately over him; and the discipline and order that comes of this method is marvellous, for they are a people very obedient to their chiefs. . . .
>
> *Source*: Marco Polo. *The Book of Ser Marco Polo*, 3rd ed. Trans. and ed. by Henry Yule and Henri Cordier. London: John Murray, 1921, pp. 260–63. (Translation slightly modified.)

(A) Identify ONE way that Chinggis Khan restructured Mongol society.
(B) Identify ONE factor that allowed the Mongols to conquer and govern their empire.
(C) Explain ONE way that Mongol religious policy benefited their empire.

8. Use your understanding of world history to answer parts A, B, and C.
(A) Identify ONE way that trade networks benefited in Mongol or Turkish empires.
(B) Explain ONE way these new empires affected the Afro-Eurasian economy, 1200-1450 C.E.
(C) Explain ONE difference between Mongol and Chinese women.

# Section II

## Document-Based Question

Based on the documents below and your knowledge of world history, evaluate how empires built by nomadic peoples from 1100-1450 C.E. affected the Afro-Eurasian economy.

In your response you should do the following:

- Respond to the prompt with a historically defensible thesis or claim that establishes a line of reasoning.
- Describe a broader historical context relevant to the prompt.
- Support an argument in response to the prompt using all documents.
- Use at least one additional piece of specific historical evidence (beyond that found in the documents) relevant to an argument about the prompt.
- Explain how or why the document's point of view, purpose, historical situation, and /or audience is relevant to an argument.
- Use evidence to corroborate, qualify, or modify an argument that addresses the prompt.

### Document 1

The period from around 1000 to 1500 C.E. also witnessed the widespread diffusion of technologies that improved both animal and maritime transportation—technologies that, in turn, allowed for both greater economic integration across long distances as well as greater economic growth. For example, Islamic merchants from north Africa utilized camels to cross the Sahara by the late eighth century C.E. (chapter 18). The diffusion of camels across the Sahara led to significant and long-term changes in a variety of sub-Saharan African societies, which included both the introduction of Islam as well as growing wealth resulting from being incorporated into much larger Eurasian markets. In Europe, meanwhile, the diffusion of the horse collar—most likely from both central Asia and north Africa—during the High Middle Ages helped to fuel European economic growth by allowing horses to pull much heavier loads without choking (chapter 19). The result was that Europeans could use horses for plowing and for transporting heavy loads rather than much slower oxen, which increased the amount of land that could be plowed as well as the rapidity with which goods could be brought to market.

*Source*: Bentley and Ziegler, *Traditions & Encounters: A Global Perspective on the Past*

## Document 2

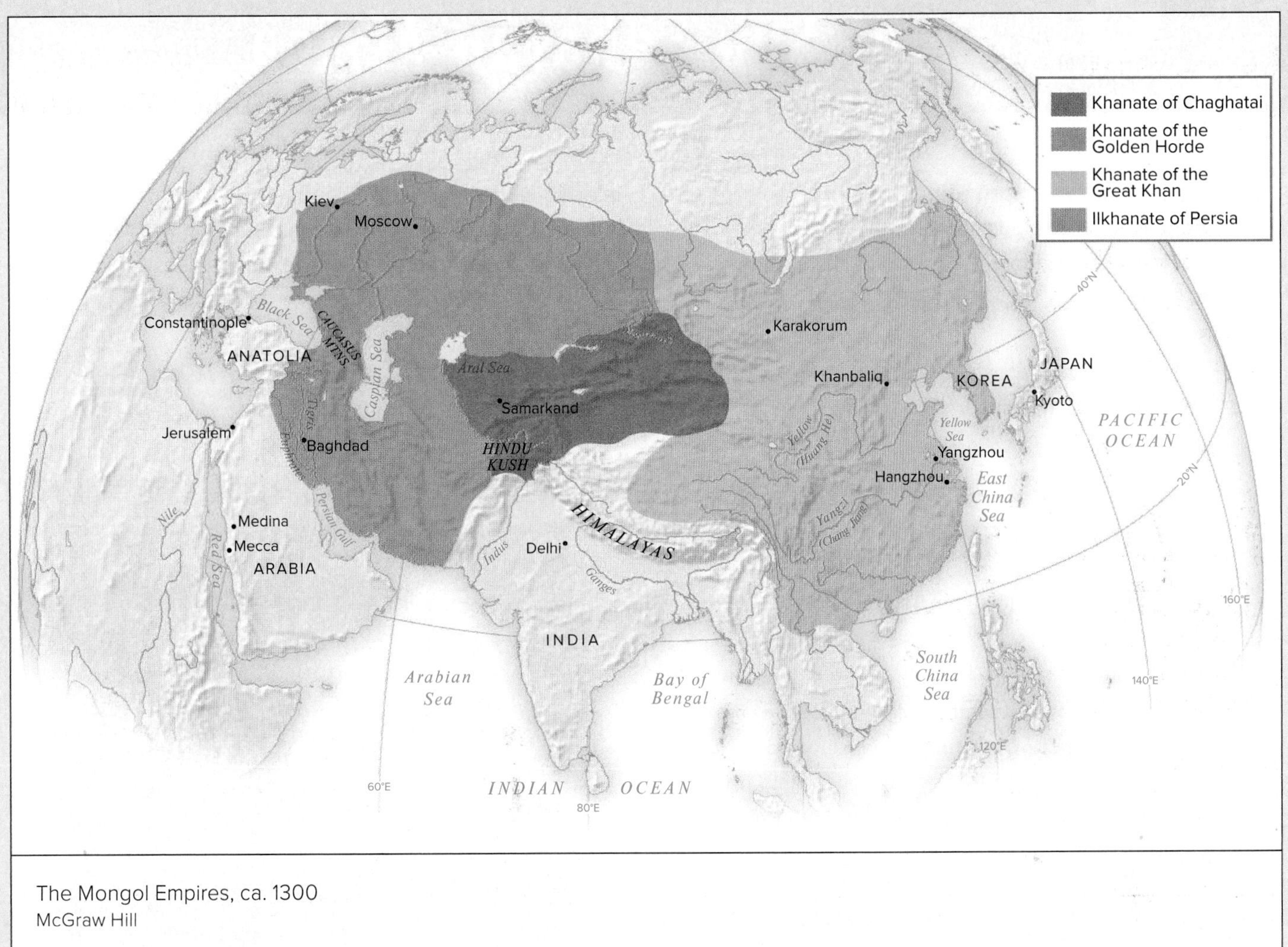


The Mongol Empires, ca. 1300
McGraw Hill

## Document 3

For at least the next fifteen years, Boucher lived at the Mongol capital at *Karakorum*. Though technically a slave, he enjoyed some prestige and the freedom to marry a fellow Frenchwoman. He supervised fifty assistants in a workshop that produced decorative objects of gold and silver for the Mongol court. Boucher also produced gold and silver statues in built carriages, designed buildings, and even sewed ritual garments for Roman Catholic priests conducting services for Christians living at Karakorum.

*Source*: Bentley and Ziegler, *Traditions & Encounters: A Global perspective on the Past*

## Long Essay

Develop a thoughtful and thorough historical argument that answers the question below. Begin your essay with a thesis statement and support it with relevant historical evidence.

Using specific examples and your knowledge of world history, compare and contrast Mongol rule over China and Persia.

# Chapter 6 States and Societies of Sub-Saharan Africa



## ZOOMING IN ON TRADITIONS

### The Lion Prince of Mali

A remarkable oral tradition preserves the story of the lion prince **Sundiata,** thirteenth-century founder of the Mali Empire in west Africa. Oral traditions include folk stories, factual histories, genealogies, and other accounts transmitted by professional singers and storytellers known in west Africa as **griots.** Until scholars began to write down and publish west African oral traditions about the middle of the twentieth century, the story of Sundiata was available only when a griot recited it.

According to the oral tradition, Sundiata's father ruled a small kingdom in what is now the nation of Guinea in west Africa. Despite his royal parentage, Sundiata had a difficult childhood because a congenitally defective leg left him unable to walk well. When the old king died, his enemies invaded the kingdom and killed the royal offspring, sparing Sundiata only because they thought he was too weak to be a threat to them. But Sundiata overcame his disability, learned to use the bow and arrow, and mastered the arts of hunting and warfare. As Sundiata grew stronger, his enemies began to fear him, and they forced him into exile. While in exile, Sundiata distinguished himself as a warrior and leader and assembled a powerful cavalry force.

The magnificent mosque at Jenne, constructed in the fourteenth century, served as a principal center of Islamic education and scholarship in the Mali Empire.
Explorer/Science Source

**Sundiata** (soon-JAH-tuh)
**griots** (GREE-oh)

About 1235 Sundiata returned to his homeland to claim the throne. His cavalry slashed through the countryside and defeated his enemies. Within a few years he had established the Mali Empire and consolidated his rule throughout a large portion of the valley of the Niger River. Although he respected traditional religious beliefs and magical powers, Sundiata was a Muslim and he welcomed Muslim merchants from north Africa into his realm. He built a capital city at Niani, which soon became a thriving commercial center. Indeed, as a result of its control of the trans-Saharan gold trade—and the political stability provided by Sundiata—the Mali Empire became one of the wealthiest lands in the world. For two centuries after Sundiata's death about 1260, the lion prince's legacy shaped the lives of west African peoples and linked west Africa with north Africa and the Mediterranean basin.

# CHAPTER FOCUS

- African societies were as diverse as those of Eurasia in this postclassical period. Political organizations ranged from empires to farming communities. There were more than 800 languages spoken on the continent.
- Centuries earlier Bantu migrations from west Africa spread agricultural and metallurgical techniques as well as languages. This chapter continues that story as sub-Saharan, Bantu-based populations grew due to farming, including the adoption of the banana from Madagascar via the Indian Ocean basin trade network.
- The west African kingdoms of Ghana and Mali flourished in the Niger River region, and were linked with the trans-Saharan trade routes. Trade and religious *hajjs* increased traffic on the trans-Saharan routes and brought Islamic culture and education to west Africa as well as exported gold, ivory, and slaves to the Middle East. European merchants also traveled south to the trading city of Timbuktu looking for the same goods.
- The east African coast saw the rise of trade-based citystates, like those of the Mediterranean or Indian Ocean basin. Merchants on the Indian Ocean coast traded with Arabs for so long that a new language of Swahili, a blend of Arabic and Bantu, was created. Swahili merchants navigated monsoon winds and currents to trade as far away as southeast Asia, and goods from as far away as China reached them in return. African merchants brought luxury goods (exotic animals, skins, ivory, slaves, and gold) from the south and central African interior to the Swahili coast
- Expect to see questions about the impact of the Bantu migrations on the AP exam: the spread of new foods and technologies along the trade routes; how and to what extent Islam and Christianity spread; and the significance of the travelers' reports for historians.

## Historical Developments

- In Africa, as in Eurasia and the Americas, state systems demonstrated continuity, innovation, and diversity, and expanded in scope and reach.
- The growth of interregional trade was encouraged by innovations in existing transportation technologies.
- The expansion of empires—including Mali in West Africa—facilitated Afro-Eurasian trade and communication as new people were drawn into the economies and trade networks.

## Reasoning Processes

- **Developments and Processes** Identify the process of state building and network exchanges in sub-Saharan Africa.
- **Sourcing and Situation** Explain the significance and historical situation of Ibn Battuta's travel writings on Islamic culture in Africa.
- **Source Claims and Evidence** Explain how various written accounts, images and archaeological remains support the claim that sub-Saharan Africa was connected to distant societies and cultures throughout Eurasia and the Indian Ocean basin.
- **Making Connections** Explain how the impact of Muslim traders operating in west African states relates to the impact of Indian Ocean traders operating within the Swahili states.
- **Argumentation** Use specific evidence to support the argument that religion and commerce were both factors in trans-Saharan trade.

## Historical Thinking Skills

- **Causation** Describe the causes and effects of the spread of Christianity and Islam throughout Sub-Saharan Africa.
- **Continuity and Change** Describe patterns of continuity and/or change over time following the introduction of Islam and Christianity in sub-Saharan Africa.

# CHAPTER OVERVIEW

From the ancient era (500 B.C.E.-500 C.E.) forward, people from east Asia to the Mediterranean to the west African Savannah basin established extensive networks of trade and communication. Africans living south of the Sahara participated in the larger economy of Afro-Eurasia, though not so fully as their counterparts in north Africa. Geographic conditions help to explain why trade and communication networks did not embrace sub-Saharan Africa as readily as they did other regions: the Sahara poses a formidable challenge to overland travelers from the north, the African coastlines offer few good natural harbors, and cataracts complicate travel up some of the continent's major rivers.

Nevertheless, like their Eurasian and north African counterparts, peoples of sub-Saharan Africa built powerful states and participated in large-scale networks of communication, encounter, and exchange. Internal African processes drove much of that development. Between 1000 and 1500 C.E., in the wake of the Bantu and other migrations (discussed in chapter 3), peoples of sub-Saharan Africa continued to expand the amount of territory under cultivation and to establish agricultural societies. Furthermore, as their population increased, they organized states, developed centers of economic specialization, and carried on interregional trade. Alongside these internal processes, relations with other peoples of Afro-Eurasia also profoundly influenced the development of African societies. From the early centuries C.E. to 1500 and later as well, trade with lands of the Mediterranean and the Indian Ocean basin encouraged African peoples to organize their societies to produce commodities desired by consumers throughout much of Afro-Eurasia. This trade promoted urban development, the organization of large states and empires, and the introduction of new food crops and new religious beliefs into sub-Saharan Africa.

| CHRONOLOGY | |
|---|---|
| 4th century C.E. | Introduction of bananas to Africa |
| 11th to 13th century | Kingdom of Ghana |
| 11th to 15th century | Swahili cities |
| 12th to 15th century | Kingdom of Great Zimbabwe |
| 12th to 16th century | Christian kingdom of Axum |
| 13th to 15th century | Mali Empire |
| 1230–1255 | Reign of Sundiata |
| 14th to 17th century | Kingdom of Kongo |
| 1312–1337 | Reign of Mansa Musa |
| 1324–1325 | Mansa Musa's pilgrimage to Mecca |

# EFFECTS OF EARLY AFRICAN MIGRATIONS

By 1000 C.E. Bantu-speaking peoples (originally from central Africa) had settled in most parts of Africa south of the equator, and Kushite, Sudanese, Mande, and other peoples had also established communities in lands far from their original homes. For the next several centuries, African people built societies on the foundation of small communities that the Bantu and other migrations had generated.

## Agriculture and Population Growth

The principal early result of the Bantu and other migrations was to spread agriculture and herding to almost all parts of Africa except deserts and dense, equatorial rain forests. As they established agricultural societies, cultivators and herders displaced many of the hunting, gathering, and fishing peoples who previously inhabited sub-Saharan Africa and absorbed them into their societies. By about 500 B.C.E. most Bantu-speaking peoples had mastered the techniques of iron metallurgy, which enabled them to fashion iron tools like axes and hoes that facilitated further clearing of lands and extension of agriculture. By the early centuries C.E., cultivation and herding had reached the southernmost parts of Africa. Yams, sorghum, and millet were the dietary staples of many peoples in south Africa, and the indigenous Khoi people had adopted cattle raising even before Bantu-speaking people and Kushite herders moved into the region. Those developments resulted in increased agricultural production, rising population, and competition for fertile lands between different groups.

**Bananas** First domesticated in southeast Asia, bananas probably entered Africa by way of sea lanes across the Indian Ocean. During the late centuries B.C.E., Malay seafarers from the islands that make up modern Indonesia sailed west beyond India, and by the early centuries C.E. they were exploring the east African coasts. Between about 300 and 500 C.E., they colonized the island of Madagascar and established banana cultivation there. (Apart from bananas, they brought Asian yams, taro, chickens, and southeast Asian cultural traditions. Malagasy, the language spoken on Madagascar even today, belongs to the Austronesian family of languages.) From Madagascar, bananas easily made the jump to the east African mainland. By 500 C.E. several varieties of bananas had become well established in Africa. They provided a nutritious supplement to Bantu diets and enabled the Bantu to expand into heavily forested regions where yams and millet did not grow well. Thus cultivation of bananas increased the supply of food available to the Bantu, enriched their diets, and allowed them to expand more rapidly than before.

**Population Growth** The population history of sub-Saharan Africa clearly reflects the significance of iron metallurgy and bananas. In 400 B.C.E., before iron working had deeply influenced the continent's societies, the population of sub-Saharan Africa stood at about 3.5 million. By the turn of the millennium, human numbers exceeded 11 million. By 800 C.E., after banana cultivation had spread throughout the continent, the sub-Saharan population had climbed to 17 million. And by 1000, when the Bantu migrations had introduced agriculture and iron metallurgy to most regions of sub-Saharan Africa, the population had passed 22 million.

**Bantu and Forest Peoples** The continuing **Bantu** migrations, the expansion of Bantu population, and the establishment of new Bantu communities contributed to changes in relationships between Bantu and foraging peoples such as the forest dwellers of central Africa (the peoples once referred to by the disparaging term "pygmies"). In earlier times, Bantu speakers had often regarded the forest peoples as useful guides to environments that were unfamiliar to them, and oral traditions suggest that they relied on foragers' expert knowledge to learn about the possibilities that new environments offered. As Bantu-speaking populations surged, however, it became increasingly difficult for foragers to flourish. Some forest peoples joined the cultivators and integrated into Bantu-speaking societies. Others retreated into the forests, where they were able to sustain small-scale societies by providing forest products such as animal skins in exchange for iron tools produced by neighboring Bantu communities.

## Political Organizations

By 1000 C.E., after more than two millennia of migrations, Bantu-speaking people had approached the limits of their expansion. Because agricultural peoples already occupied most of the continent, migrating into new territories and forming new settlements was much more difficult than in previous centuries. Instead of migrating in search of new lands to cultivate, then, sub-Saharan African peoples developed increasingly complex forms of government that enabled them to organize their existing societies on larger scales.

**Kin-Based Societies** Early Bantu-speaking societies did not depend on an elaborate hierarchy of officials or a bureaucratic apparatus to administer their affairs. Rather, Bantu-speaking peoples governed themselves mostly through family and kinship groups. Bantu-speaking peoples usually settled in villages with populations averaging about one hundred people. Older male heads of families constituted a village's ruling council, which decided the public affairs for the entire group. The most prominent of the family heads presided over the village as a chief and represented the settlement when it dealt with neighboring peoples. A group of villages might be linked by political and kinship ties, which became the principal individual focus of loyalties. Usually, there was no chief or larger government for the larger region. Instead, village chiefs negotiated on matters concerning two or more villages. Meanwhile, within individual villages, family and kinship groups disciplined their own members as necessary.

This type of organization lends itself particularly well to small-scale communities, but **kin-based societies** often grew to large proportions. Some networks of villages and districts organized the public affairs of several hundred thousand people. By the nineteenth century, for example, the Tiv people of Nigeria, numbering almost one million, conducted their affairs in a kin-based society built on a foundation of family and clan groups.

**Early Cities: Jenne-jeno** Meanwhile, speakers of Niger-Congo languages also established a vibrant urban society in the middle stretches of the Niger River, where low-lying lands forced the river into an inland delta. Equipped with iron tools, settlers arrived in the region during the late centuries B.C.E., and by 400 C.E. the settlement of **Jenne-jeno** ("Ancient Jenne," located just south of the modern city of Jenne in Mali) was emerging as a center of iron production and trade as well as manufactured textiles. Merchants of Jenne-jeno handled iron products as well as the region's abundant supplies of rice, fish, and domesticated animals, including cattle, sheep, and goats. They participated in an extensive trade network that reached from north Africa and the Mediterranean to the savannas and forests of central Africa. By the eighth century C.E., Jenne-jeno had become the principal commercial crossroads of west Africa. Although the city declined as west African kingdoms and empires arose in later centuries, it left a legacy of urban development in the region by inspiring the foundation of Timbuktu and other cities.

**Chiefdoms** After about 1000 C.E., many kin-based societies faced challenges as they sought control over human labor or valuable trade routes. Conflicts between villages and regions became more frequent and more intense. Increased conflict encouraged many African communities to organize military forces for both offensive and defensive purposes, and military organization in turn encouraged the development of more formal structures of government. Many districts fell under the leadership of powerful chiefs, who imposed their own authority on their territories. Some of these chiefs conquered their neighbors and consolidated their lands into small kingdoms. These kingdoms emerged in several regions of sub-Saharan

Seated figure, Mali, Inland Niger Delta region, Djenné peoples, 13th century.
The Metropolitan Museum of Art, New York, Purchase, Buckeye Trust and Mr. and Mrs. Milton F. Rosenthal Gifts, Joseph Pulitzer Be.

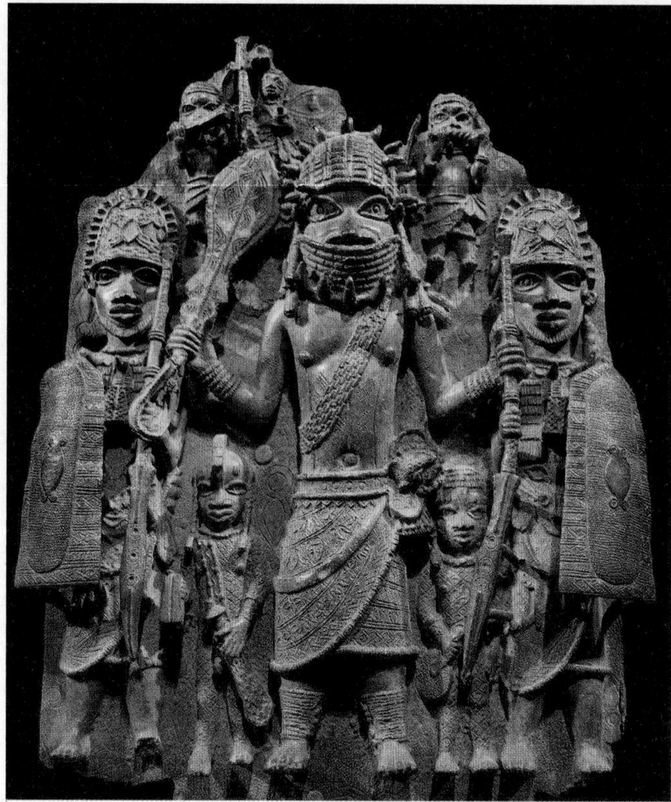

A bronze plaque from the kingdom of Benin depicts a local chief flanked by warriors and attendants.
Peter Horree/Alamy Stock Photo

Africa after about 1000 C.E. The kingdoms of **Ife** and **Benin,** for example, arose in the forested regions of west Africa. Both realms were city-states in which the court and urban residents controlled the surrounding countryside through family relationships and political alliances. Both Ife and Benin also produced magnificent sculptures that put human faces and figures to the early history of sub-Saharan Africa. Small kingdoms appeared also in southern Africa and central Africa.

**Kingdom of Kongo** One of the most active areas of political development was the basin of the Congo River (previously known as the Zaire River), a region where brisk economic development supported the emergence of large as well as small kingdoms. After about 1000 C.E., economic and military challenges encouraged kin-based societies in the Congo region to form small states embracing a few villages each. By 1200 conflict between these small states had resulted in the organization of larger, regional principalities that could resist political and military pressures better than small kingdoms could. One of the more prosperous of the Congolese states was the **kingdom of Kongo,** which participated actively in trade networks involving copper, raffia cloth, and nzimbu shells from the Atlantic Ocean. During the fourteenth century the kingdom of Kongo comprised much of the modern-day Republic of the Congo and Angola.

The central government of Kongo included the king and officials who oversaw military, judicial, and financial affairs. Beneath the central government were six provinces administered by governors, each of whom supervised several districts administered by subordinate officials. Within regions, villages ruled by chiefs provided local government. Though not the only kingdom in sub-Saharan Africa, Kongo was perhaps the most tightly centralized of the early Bantu kingdoms. In most cases the king or other central administrators could appoint or replace local officials at will, and the central government maintained a royal currency system based on seashells that came from the Indian Ocean. The kingdom of Kongo provided effective organization from the fourteenth until the mid-seventeenth century, when Portuguese slave traders undermined the authority of the kings and the central government.

Kin-based societies did not disappear with the emergence of formal states. On the contrary, they survived into the nineteenth century in much of sub-Saharan Africa. Yet regional states and large kingdoms became increasingly prominent

**Ife** (EE-fehy)
**Benin** (beh-NEEN)

during the centuries after 1000 C.E. as African people responded to competition for control over scarce labor or trade networks.

## AFRICAN SOCIETIES AND CULTURAL DEVELOPMENT

By the eleventh century C.E., there was enormous variation in the size and scale of African societies. The peoples of sub-Saharan Africa spoke some eight hundred different languages, and the continent supported a wide variety of societies and economies: mobile bands of hunting and gathering peoples, fishing peoples who lived alongside the continent's lakes and coasts, nomadic herders, subsistence farmers who migrated periodically to fresh lands, settled cultivators, and city-based societies that drew their livelihoods from mining, manufacturing, and trade. Although this diversity makes it difficult to speak of African society and cultural development in general terms, certain social forms and cultural patterns appeared widely throughout sub-Saharan Africa.

### Social Classes

In kingdoms, empires, and city-states, such as Kongo, Mali, and Kilwa, respectively, African peoples developed complex societies with clearly defined classes: ruling elites, military nobles, administrative officials, religious authorities, wealthy merchants, artisans, business entrepreneurs, common people, peasants, and slaves. These societies resembled those found in other settled, agricultural lands of Eurasia organized by powerful states.

In the small states and kin-based societies of sub-Saharan Africa, however, social structures were different. Small states often generated an aristocratic or ruling elite, and they always recognized a class of religious authorities. Outside the larger states and empires, however, kinship, sex and gender expectations, and age groupings were the principal considerations that determined social position in sub-Saharan Africa.

**Kinship Groups** Extended families and clans served as the main foundation of social and economic organization in small-scale agricultural and foraging societies. Unlike their counterparts in north Africa and Eurasia, sub-Saharan African peoples mostly did not recognize the private ownership of land. Instead, communities claimed rights to land and used it in common. The villages of sub-Saharan Africa, where most of the population lived, generally consisted of several extended family groups. Male heads of families jointly governed the village and organized the work of their own groups. They allocated portions of the communal lands for their relatives to cultivate and were responsible for distributing harvests equitably among all members of their groups. Thus most villagers functioned in society first as members of a family or a lineage.

**The Division of Labor** Sex and gender relations also influenced the roles individuals played in society. Sex largely

An illustration from a seventeenth-century missionary account shows an African blacksmith (seated at right) working at his forge while an attendant (seated at left) uses a bellows to pump air into the furnace.
Fotosearch/Stringer/Getty Images

determined work roles. Indeed, men dominated some of the most prestigious trades. Leather tanning, for example, was the work of men who carefully guarded knowledge of their techniques and tanning compounds, which they passed down to their heirs. Men also dominated iron working, which was a highly valued skill in many African societies because blacksmiths knew the secrets of turning ores into useful objects such as knives, hoes, spearheads, and swords. Blacksmiths often served as community leaders, and like leather tanners, they passed knowledge of their craft down to their heirs. Women in blacksmith families often served as potters for their communities. They too enjoyed special prestige because of their ability to transform ingredients from the earth into useful pottery vessels. When it came to agricultural and family life, men usually undertook the heavy labor of clearing land and preparing it for cultivation. Women contributed most of the labor for the planting and harvesting of crops and also took primary responsibility for domestic chores and child rearing.

**Women's Roles** As in other societies, men largely monopolized public authority. Yet women in sub-Saharan Africa generally had more opportunities open to them than did their counterparts in other lands. Women enjoyed high honor as the sources of life. On at least a few occasions, women made their way to positions of power, and aristocratic women often influenced public affairs by virtue of their prominence within their families. Women merchants commonly traded at markets, and they participated actively in both local and long-distance trade in Africa. Sometimes women even engaged in combat and organized all-female military units.

**Age Grades** Apart from kinship and expectations based on sex and gender roles, African societies made a place for age groups that included all individuals within a given community born within a few years of one another. Historical linguistic analysis suggests that the recognition of those age grades, or age sets, arose in the early days of agricultural society in the Sudan, and it is clear that in many African societies the practice of grouping individuals into **age grades** has continued into recent times. Members of age grades performed tasks appropriate for their level of development, and they often bonded with one another to form tight circles of friends and political allies. Members of an age grade might provide labor for community projects, for example, or take joint responsibility for looking after village elders. They aided members who experienced adversities and helped one another at crucial junctures, such as marriage and the building of a new household. Thus age grades had the effect of establishing social ties that crossed the lines of family and kinship.

**Slavery** One class of individuals stood apart from the other social groups: slaves. As in other lands, the institution of slavery had a place in Africa since remote antiquity, and slave holding and slave trading were prominent features of sub-Saharan African society. Most enslaved people were captives of war. Others came from the ranks of debtors and criminals. Within Africa most enslaved people probably worked as domestic laborers, although many also worked as construction laborers, miners, or porters.

Slave ownership was a major form of personal wealth in sub-Saharan Africa. Since there was little if any private ownership of land, it was impossible for individuals to become wealthy through the accumulation of landholdings. On the basis of their slaves' labor, however, slaveholders were able to build wealth through increased agricultural production. Slaves also brought enhanced social status for their owners.

**Slave Trading** After about the ninth century C.E., the expansion of the trans-Saharan and Indian Ocean trade networks stimulated increased traffic in African slaves. Muslim merchants provided access to markets in India, Persia, southwest Asia, and the Mediterranean basin, where the demand for slaves outstripped the supply available from eastern Europe, previously the main source of slaves. As a result, merchants from northern lands traded in sub-Saharan Africa not only for gold, ivory, and exotic local products but also for slaves.

In response to that demand, rulers of large-scale states and empires began to make war on smaller states and kin-based societies in search of captives destined for northern slave markets. In some years, ten thousand to twenty thousand Africans were forced from their homes and sold into slavery. During the mid-fourteenth century, the Moroccan traveler Ibn Battuta crossed the Sahara in a caravan that included six hundred slaves bound for north Africa and the Mediterranean basin. King Mansa Musa of Mali set out on his pilgrimage to Mecca with five hundred slaves, many of whom he distributed along the way as gifts to his hosts. Other slaves were taken from the coastal cities of east Africa for destinations in Persia and India.

**The Zanj Revolt** Records of this slave trade are scarce, but a lengthy uprising known as the **Zanj revolt** throws light on the nature of African slavery. The term *Zanj* referred to black slaves from the Swahili coast. At least by the seventh century C.E., many Zanj slaves labored under extremely difficult conditions in southern Mesopotamia, where they worked on sugarcane plantations or cleared land of salt deposits to prepare it for cultivation. On several occasions they mounted revolts, which Muslim authorities promptly snuffed. Following a series of riots, in about 869 an enslaved man named Ali bin Muhammad organized about fifteen thousand Zanj slaves into an immense force that captured Basra, the most important city of southern Mesopotamia, and even established a rebel state in the region. Distracted by other threats, the Abbasid rulers of Mesopotamia turned their full attention to the rebellion only

---

**Zanj** (zahn-jee)

in 879, a full decade after it had begun. By 883 they had crushed the revolt, killed Ali bin Muhammad, and executed the other rebel leaders. Despite its ultimate collapse, the fourteen-year Zanj revolt clearly demonstrated both the determination of enslaved people to escape their brutal circumstances as well as the extreme desire of slaveholders to maintain the status quo.

Though smaller than the Atlantic slave trade of modern times, the **Islamic slave trade** was a sizable affair: between 750 and 1500 C.E., the number of African slaves transported to foreign lands may have exceeded ten million. The high demand led to the creation of networks within Africa for the purpose of capturing people and selling them as slaves. This economic system has the dubious distinction of serving as a foundation for the Atlantic slave trade in later centuries.

## African Religions

Peoples of sub-Saharan Africa developed a wide range of languages, societies, and cultural traditions. Religious beliefs and practices in particular took many forms. The continent's peoples referred to their deities by different names, told different stories about them, and honored them with different rituals. Yet certain features were common to many religions of sub-Saharan Africa. In combination, those features offer considerable insight into the cultural and religious climate of sub-Saharan Africa in premodern times.

**Creator God** Many African peoples had recognized a single, dominant creator god from the early days of Sudanic agriculture. Through the centuries, their beliefs underwent considerable development as individual peoples learned about deities honored in other societies or as they sought their own improved understandings of the gods and their roles in the world. Nevertheless, many peoples recognized a single divine force or male god as the agent responsible for setting the world in motion and providing it with order. Some peoples believed that this god also sustained the world, intervening indirectly, through spirits, to influence the course of human affairs. Some considered this deity to be all-powerful, others regarded him as all-knowing, and many considered him both omnipotent and omniscient.

**Lesser Deities and Spirits** Apart from the superior creator god, Africans recognized many lesser deities and spirits often associated with the sun, wind, rain, trees, rivers, and other natural features. Unlike the creator god, these lesser deities participated actively in the workings of the world. They could confer or withhold benefits and bring favor or injury to humans. Similarly, many Africans believed that the souls of departed ancestors had the power to intervene in the lives and experiences of their descendants: the departed could shape events to the advantage of descendants who behaved properly and honored their ancestors, and could bring misfortune as punishment for evil behavior and neglect of their ancestors' memory. Much of the ritual of African religions focused on honoring deities, spirits, or ancestors' souls to win their favor or regain their goodwill. The rituals included prayers, animal sacrifices, and ceremonies marking important stages of life—such as birth, circumcision, marriage, and death.

**Diviners** Like other peoples of the world, Africans recognized classes of religious specialists—individuals who by virtue of their innate abilities or extensive training had the power to mediate between humans and supernatural beings. Often referred to as diviners, they were usually men, although they were sometimes women who understood clearly the networks of political, social, economic, and psychological relationships within their communities. When afflicted by illness, sterility, crop failure, or some other disaster, individuals or groups consulted diviners to learn the cause of their misfortune. Diviners then consulted oracles; identified the causes of the trouble; and

Masks such as this one from Congo were essential to the proper observance of religious rituals, which often involved communicating with natural or animal spirits. In what ways do the features of this mask associate the diviner with powers not accessible to normal humans?
De Agostini Picture Library/Getty Images

prescribed medicine, rituals, or sacrifices designed to eliminate the problem and bring about a return to normality.

For the most part, African religions were concerned not with matters of theology but, rather, with the more practical business of explaining, predicting, and controlling the experiences of individuals and groups in the world. Thus African religions strongly emphasized morality and proper behavior as essential to the maintenance of an orderly world. Failure to observe high moral standards would lead to disorder, which would displease deities, spirits, and departed ancestors and ensure that misfortune befell the negligent parties. Because proper moral behavior was so important to their fortunes, family and kinship groups took responsibility for policing their members and disciplining those who fell short of expected standards.

## The Arrival of Christianity

Alongside religions that concentrated on the practical matter of maintaining an orderly world, two religions of salvation won converts in sub-Saharan Africa—Christianity and Islam. Both arrived in Africa as foreign faiths introduced by outsiders, though in time sub-Saharan adherents adapted both faiths to the needs and interests of their societies.

**Early Christianity in North Africa** Christianity reached Egypt and north Africa during the first century C.E., soon after its appearance. Alexandria in Egypt became one of the most prominent centers of early Christian thought, and north Africa was the home of St. Augustine, among many other leaders of the fledgling church. Yet for several centuries Christianity remained a Mediterranean tradition whose appeal did not reach sub-Saharan Africa.

**The Christian Kingdom of Axum** About the middle of the fourth century C.E., Christianity established a foothold in the kingdom of **Axum,** located in the highlands of modern Ethiopia. The first Axumite converts were probably local merchants who traded with Mediterranean Christians calling at the port of Adulis on the Red Sea. As missionaries visited Ethiopia, the kings of Axum also converted to Christianity, possibly in hopes of improving relations with their powerful neighbors to the north in Egypt. Indeed, the kings of Axum were some of the first royal converts to Christianity, which they adopted shortly after the Roman emperor Constantine himself. Missionaries later established monasteries, translated the Bible into the Ethiopian language, and worked to popularize Christianity throughout the kingdom.

In the late seventh century C.E., the ruling house of Axum fell into decline, and during the next several centuries the expansion of Islam left an isolated island of Christianity in the Ethiopian highlands. During the twelfth century, however, a new ruling dynasty undertook a centralizing campaign and enthusiastically promoted Christianity as a foundation of cultural unity for the land. From the twelfth through the sixteenth century, Christianity enjoyed particular favor in Ethiopia. During the twelfth century, the Ethiopian kings ordered the carving of eleven massive churches out of solid rock—a monumental work of construction that required enormous resources and untold hours of labor. During the

**Axum** (AHK-soom)

## What's Left Out?

Perhaps more than any other region of the world, the history of sub-Saharan Africa has been stereotyped as static, unchanging, and primitive. Why? In part it is because the discipline of history was itself being formed in the West just as Europeans—with their deeply racist assumptions about the primitive nature of people with darker skins—were in the process of conquering large portions of the region in the late nineteenth century. In part it is because sub-Saharan African history had largely been preserved in oral histories instead of textual archives, which were not valued by the Europeans who encountered them. As a result, Europeans were unable to access the rich and evolving histories of sub-Saharan Africans and assumed they did not exist. But the growth of African Studies in the twentieth century, practiced in many cases by people born in Africa, has demonstrated that such stereotypes are as false for sub-Saharan Africa as they are for anywhere else. At the same time, more recent academic comprehension of oral history as a complex and sophisticated means of recording the past has allowed historians to gain a much greater understanding of sub-Saharan African histories. Consider how much history remains untold when historians value only textual sources, in pre-modern sub-Saharan Africa or elsewhere.

*Source:* Jonathan Reynolds. "History and the Study of Africa." Oxford University African Bibliographies. Fall 2013.

### Thinking Critically About Sources

1. What are some of the common stereotypes about Africa?
2. According to the reading, what erroneous assumptions have Westerners made about Africans and their history?
3 What surprised you about the history you just read?

## INTERPRETING IMAGES

The church of St. George at Lalibela, Ethiopia, (built in the 12th or 13th century) is a massive structure in the form of a cross. Workers excavated the surrounding earth and then carved the church itself out of a rock.

**Analyze** *Compare and contrast the Ethiopian Church with a Greek Orthodox church from the same period. What makes this image distinctively Ethiopian? According to the Pew Research Center (2017), Ethiopia has the largest Orthodox Christian population outside Europe. In what ways does Ethiopia's early Christian history explain the current strength of its religion?*

Gavin Hellier/robertharding/Getty images

thirteenth century, rulers of Ethiopia's Solomonic dynasty claimed descent from the Israelite kings David and Solomon in an effort to lend additional biblical luster to their authority. The fictional work *Kebra Negast* (*The Glory of Kings*), which undertook to trace that lineage, in fact became popular in the twentieth century among Rastafarians and fans of reggae music in Ethiopia, Jamaica, and other places. Meanwhile, Christianity retained its privileged status in Ethiopia until it fell out of favor following the socialist revolution of 1974.

**Ethiopian Christianity** For centuries after the introduction of Christianity to Ethiopia, Ethiopian Christians had little contact with Christians in other lands. As a result, although Ethiopian Christianity retained basic Christian theology and rituals, it increasingly reflected the interests of its African devotees. For example, Ethiopian Christians believed that a large host of evil spirits populated the world, and they carried amulets or charms for protection against these menacing spirits. The twelfth-century carved-rock churches themselves harked back to pre-Christian values because rock shrines had been a prominent feature in Ethiopian religion from the second or perhaps even third millennium B.C.E. The rock churches absorbed that tradition into Ethiopian Christianity. Not until the sixteenth century, when Portuguese mariners began to visit Ethiopia en route to India, did Ethiopians reestablish relations with Christians from other lands.

***Kebra Negast*** (kee-brah NAH-gahst)

# ISLAMIC KINGDOMS AND EMPIRES

In the seventh and eighth centuries, merchants from north Africa and southwest Asia introduced Islam to sub-Saharan Africa. Islam arrived in sub-Saharan Africa by two routes: it went to west Africa overland by trans-Saharan camel caravans, and it traveled to coastal east Africa over the sea lanes of the Indian Ocean in the vessels of merchant-mariners. After the eighth century C.E., Islam profoundly influenced the political, social, and economic development of both Saharan and sub-Saharan Africa as well as its cultural and religious development. At the same time, Africans in both west and east Africa adapted Islam to their own cultures, giving African Islam distinctly African characteristics.

## Trans-Saharan Trade and Islamic States in West Africa

The Sahara has never served as an absolute barrier to communication between human societies. Small numbers of nomadic peoples have lived in the desert ever since the Sahara's formation about 5000 B.C.E. Those nomads migrated around the desert and had dealings with other peoples settled on its fringes. Even in ancient and classical times, merchants occasionally organized commercial expeditions across the desert, although the value and volume of trade was much smaller than in the Mediterranean and Red Sea basins.

**Camels** The arrival of the camel was instrumental to improving communication and transportation across the Sahara. **Camels** came to north Africa from Arabia, by way of Egypt and the Sudan, sometime in the first millennium B.C.E. and perhaps earlier. During the late centuries B.C.E., a special camel saddle, which took advantage of the animals' distinctive physical structure, also made its way to north Africa. Because a caravan took seventy to ninety days to cross the Sahara and because camels could travel long distances before needing water, they proved to be useful beasts of burden in an arid region. After about 300 C.E., camels increasingly replaced horses and donkeys as the preferred transport animals throughout the Sahara as well as in the deserts of central Asia.

When Arab conquerors introduced Islam into north Africa during the seventh and eighth centuries, they also integrated the region into a larger network of commerce and communication. Thus it was natural for Muslims in north Africa to explore the potential of trade across the Sahara. By the late eighth century, Islamic merchants in search of gold had trekked across the desert and established commercial relations with societies in sub-Saharan west Africa. There they found not only gold but a series of long-established trading centers such as Gao, a terminus of caravan routes across the Sahara that offered access to the Niger River valley, which was a flourishing market for copper, ironware, cotton textiles, salt, grains, and carnelian beads.

**The Kingdom of Ghana** The principal state of west Africa at the time of the Muslims' arrival there was the **kingdom of Ghana** (not related to the modern state of Ghana), situated between the Senegal and Niger rivers in a region straddling the border between the modern states of Mali and Mauritania.

**Gold Trade** As trade and traffic across the desert increased, Ghana underwent a dramatic transformation. It became the

**Ghana** (GAH-nuh)

Early-twentieth-century photograph of dromedary camels and their handlers in the Sahara. Note the special camel saddle and rigging that are specifically adapted to the animals' unique physical structure. Michael Maslan/Corbis Historical/Getty Images

## How the Past Shapes the Future

### The Diffusion of Technologies

Camels had been used for centuries by traders in Arabia and North Africa—thanks especially to the camel saddle invented in about 200 C.E.—before Muslim traders made their way across the Sahara to West Africa in the seventh and eighth centuries. Camels, although living beings, can be considered a technology because their use helped humans adapt the natural environment to their needs, making it possible to reliably and repeatedly traverse the vast Sahara. Think about the variety of ways that the diffusion of camels to sub-Saharan Africa—in terms of trade, urban growth, the accumulation of wealth, and the slave trade—affected the region over the very long term.

most important commercial site in west Africa because it controlled the trade in **gold** that was mined and smelted nearby. Muslim merchants flocked to camel caravans traveling across the Sahara to Ghana in search of gold for consumers in the Mediterranean basin and elsewhere in the Islamic world. Ghana itself did not produce gold, but the kings procured nuggets from lands to the south—probably from the region around the headwaters of the Niger, Gambia, and Senegal rivers, which enjoyed the world's largest supply of gold available at the time. By controlling and taxing trade in the precious metal, the kings both enriched and strengthened their realm. Apart from gold, merchants from Ghana provided ivory and slaves for traders from north Africa. In exchange, they received horses, cloth, small manufactured wares, and salt—a crucial commodity but one that local sources could not supply in large quantities.

This west African terra-cotta sculpture from the thirteenth or fourteenth century depicts a helmeted and armored warrior astride a horse with elaborate harness and head protection. Heritage Image Partnership Ltd/Alamy Stock Photo

**Koumbi-Saleh** Integration into **trans-Saharan trade** networks brought enormous wealth and considerable power to Ghana. The kingdom's capital and principal trading site stood at **Koumbi-Saleh,** a small town today but a thriving commercial center with a population of some fifteen thousand to twenty thousand people when the kingdom was at its height, from the ninth to the twelfth century. Al-Bakri, a Spanish Muslim traveler of the mid-eleventh century, described Koumbi-Saleh as a flourishing settlement with buildings of stone and more than a dozen mosques. Koumbi-Saleh's wealth also supported a large number of *qadis* and Muslim scholars. From taxes levied on trade passing through Ghana, the kings financed a large army—al-Bakri reported that they could field two hundred thousand warriors—that protected the sources of gold, maintained order in the kingdom, kept allied and tributary states in line, and defended Ghana against nomadic incursions from the Sahara.

**Islam in West Africa** By about the tenth century, the kings of Ghana had converted to Islam. Their conversion led to improved relations with Muslim merchants from north Africa as well as Muslim nomads from the desert who transported trade goods across the Sahara. It also brought them recognition and support from Muslim states in north Africa. The kings of Ghana made no attempt to impose Islam forcibly on their society nor did they accept Islam exclusively even for their own purposes. Instead, they continued to observe traditional religious customs: al-Bakri mentioned, for example, that native religious specialists practiced what he believed to be magic and kept idols in the woods surrounding the royal palace at Koumbi-Saleh. Even in the absence of efforts to impose Islam on Ghana, however, the faith attracted converts, particularly among those engaged in trade with Muslim merchants from the north.

As the kingdom expanded to the north, it became vulnerable to attacks by nomadic peoples from the Sahara who sought to seize some of the kingdom's wealth. During the early thirteenth century, raids from the desert weakened the kingdom, and it soon collapsed. Several successor states took over portions of Ghana's territory, but political leadership in west Africa fell to the powerful **Mali Empire,** which emerged just as the kingdom of Ghana dissolved.

**Sundiata** As we saw in the introduction to this chapter, the lion prince Sundiata (reigned 1230–1255) built the Mali Empire during the first half of the thirteenth century after his return from exile. While away from home, he made astute alliances with local rulers, gained a reputation for courage in battle, and assembled a large army dominated by cavalry. By about 1235 he had consolidated his hold on the Mali Empire, which expanded to include Ghana as well as other neighboring kingdoms in the regions surrounding the Senegal and Niger rivers. The empire included most of the modern state of Mali and extended also to lands now known as Mauritania, Senegal, Gambia, Guinea-Bissau, Guinea, and Sierra Leone.

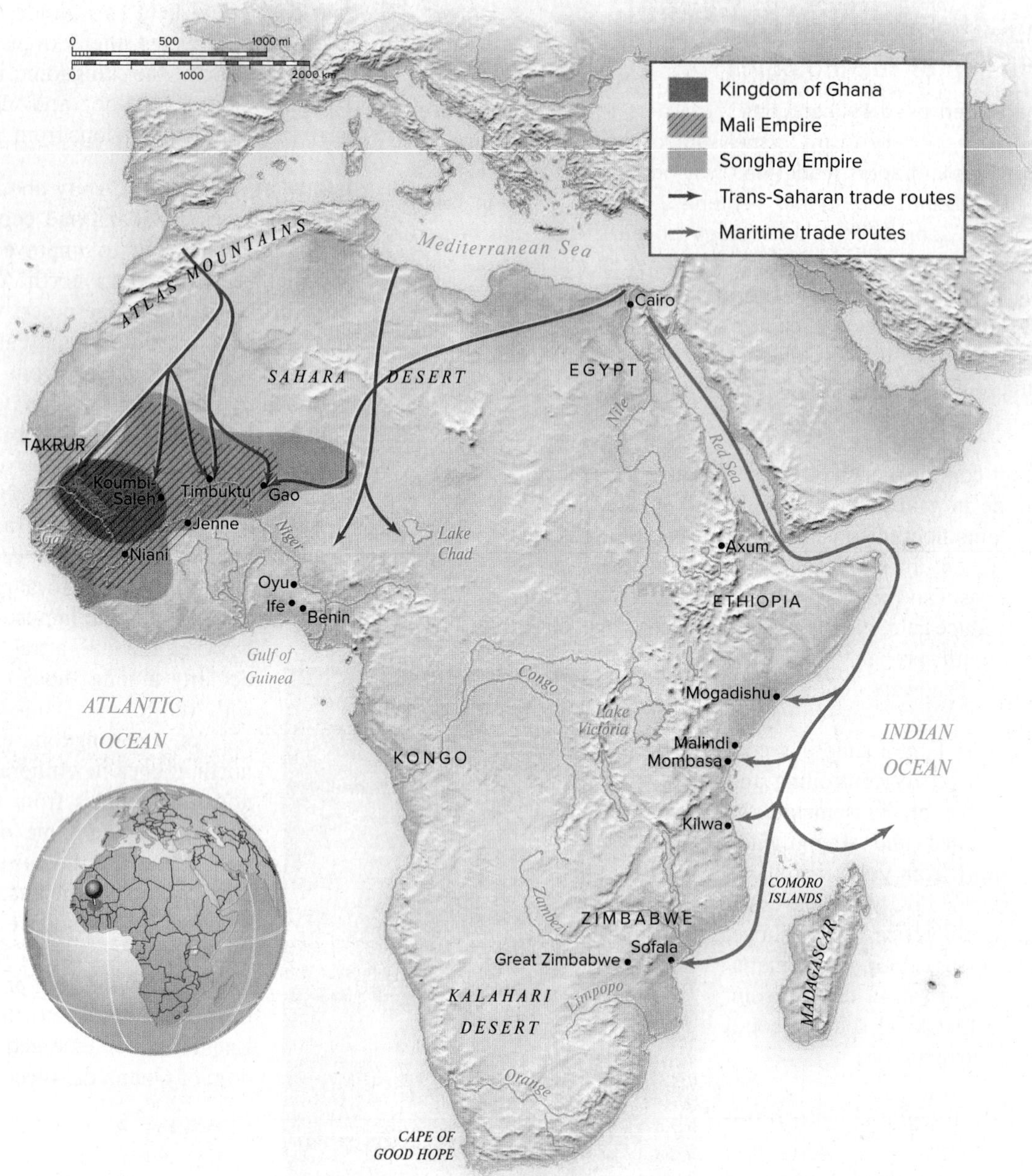


## MAP 6.1 Kingdoms, empires, and city-states of sub-Saharan Africa, 800–1500 C.E.

After the emergence of Islam, trans-Saharan overland routes linked sub-Saharan west Africa with the Mediterranean region, and maritime trade routes linked sub-Saharan east Africa to the Indian Ocean basin.

***How critical was the role of trade in the emergence of cities and states in sub-Saharan Africa?***

***Why did both overland and maritime trade expand after the emergence of Islam?***

***Why didn't trade increase in the interior?***

***What products could be added to the map to illustrate the motives for trade?***

**The Mali Empire and Trade** Mali benefited from trans-Saharan trade on an even larger scale than Ghana did. From the thirteenth until the late fifteenth century, Mali controlled and taxed almost all trade passing through west Africa. Enormous caravans with as many as twenty-five thousand camels linked Mali to north Africa. The capital city of Niani attracted merchants seeking to enter the gold trade, and market cities on the caravan routes such as **Timbuktu,** Gao, and Jenne became prosperous centers featuring buildings of brick and stone. Like the earlier kings of Ghana, the rulers of Mali converted to Islam and provided protection, lodging, and comforts for Muslim merchants from the north. Although they did not force Islam on their realm, they encouraged its spread on a voluntary basis.

Mansa Musa, emperor of Mali, enjoyed a widespread reputation as the wealthiest king in the world. On this map, prepared in 1375 by a cartographer from the Mediterranean island of Majorca, Mansa Musa holds a gold nugget about the size of a grapefruit. What does this illustration reveal about the image of west Africa in the Mediterranean world?
Abraham Cresques/Getty Images

**Mansa Musa** The significance of trade and Islam for west Africa became clearest during the reign of Sundiata's grand-nephew **Mansa Musa,** who ruled Mali from 1312 to 1337, during the high point of the empire. Mansa Musa observed Islamic tradition by making his pilgrimage to Mecca in 1324–1325. His party formed a gargantuan caravan that included thousands of soldiers, attendants, subjects, and slaves as well as a hundred camels carrying satchels of gold. Mansa Musa bestowed lavish gifts on those who hosted him along the way, and during his three-month visit to Cairo, he distributed so much gold that the metal's value declined by as much as 25 percent on local markets.

**Mansa Musa and Islam** Mansa Musa drew great inspiration from his pilgrimage to Mecca, and upon return to Mali he took his religion even more seriously than before. He built mosques, particularly in the trading cities frequented by Muslim merchants, and he sent promising students to study with distinguished Islamic scholars in north Africa. He also established religious schools and brought in Arabian and north African teachers, including four descendants of Muhammad himself, to make Islam better known in Mali.

Yet within a century of Mansa Musa's reign, Mali was in serious decline: factions crippled the central government, provinces seceded from the empire, and military pressures came both from neighboring kingdoms and from desert nomads. By the late fifteenth century, the Songhay Empire had completely overcome Mali. Yet Mansa Musa and other Mali rulers had established a tradition of centralized government that the Songhay realm itself would continue, and they had ensured that Islam would have a prominent place in west African society over the long term.

## Indian Ocean Trade and Islamic States in East Africa

While trans-Saharan caravan traffic linked west Africa to the larger trading world of the eastern hemisphere, merchant-mariners sailing the sea lanes of the Indian Ocean performed a similar service for coastal east Africa. Indian and Persian sailors had visited the east African coasts after about 500 B.C.E., and Hellenistic and Roman mariners sailed through the Red Sea en route to the same coasts. After the late centuries B.C.E., Malay seafarers also ventured into the western Indian Ocean from their island homelands in southeast Asia, and by the fourth and fifth centuries C.E. they had established colonies on the island of Madagascar.

**Timbuktu** (tim-buhk-TOO)
**Gao** (gou)
**Jenne** (jehn-neh)
**Mansa Musa** (MAHN-suh MOO-suh)

By the second century C.E., Bantu-speaking peoples had populated much of east Africa. They introduced agriculture, cattle herding, and iron metallurgy to the region, and here, as elsewhere in sub-Saharan Africa, they founded complex societies governed by small, local states. As their population increased and merged with indigenous inhabitants, they founded settlements on the coasts and offshore islands as well as the interior regions of east Africa. Those coast dwellers supplemented their agricultural production with ocean fishing and maritime trade. They were the founders of **Swahili** society.

This Chinese vase was brought to East Africa as part of the Indian Ocean trade.
Heritage Image Partnership Ltd/Alamy Stock Photo

**The Swahili** *Swahili* is an Arabic term meaning "coasters," referring to those who engaged in trade along the east African coast. The Swahili dominated the east African coast from Mogadishu in the north to Kilwa, the Comoro Islands, and Sofala in the south. They spoke Swahili, a Bantu language supplemented with words and ideas borrowed from Arabic. Swahili peoples developed different dialects, but they

**Swahili** (swah-HEE-lee)

Gerezani Fortress on the east African coast at Kilwa, a testament to the wealth and military power of this major Swahili city on the Indian Ocean.
Ulrich Doering/Alamy Stock Photo

## SOURCES FROM THE PAST

### Ibn Battuta on Muslim Society at Mogadishu

*During the fourteenth century the Muslim Moroccan jurist Ibn Battuta traveled throughout much of the eastern hemisphere. Twice he visited sub-Saharan Africa: in 1331, when he traveled along the Swahili coast, and in 1351–1352, when he visited the Mali Empire. His account of his visit to the Swahili city of Mogadishu offers insight into the mercantile and social customs of the city as well as the hospitality accorded to distinguished visitors.*

**[Mogadishu]** is an exceedingly large city. The custom here is, that whenever any ships approach, the young men of the city come out, and each one addressing himself to a merchant, becomes his host. If there be a theologian or a noble on board, he takes up his residence with the Qadi [magistrate of shari'a law]. When it was heard that I was there, the Qadi came with his students to the beach: and I took up my abode with him. He then took me to the Sultan, whom they style Sheikh. Their custom is, that a noble or a theologian, must be presented to the Sultan, before he takes up his abode in the city. When, therefore, the Qadi came to the palace, one of the King's servants met him. . . . The servant then went to the Sultan, and informed him: but soon returned to us with a basket of vegetables, and some fawfel [areca] nut. These he divided among us, and then presented us with rose-water; which is the greatest honour done among them to anyone. He then said: It is the command of the King, that this person should reside in the student's house. The Qadi then took me by the hand, and conducted me to it. It was near the palace, was spread with carpets, and prepared for a feast. The servants then brought meats from the palace.

> Why did Ibn Battuta's hosts treat him with such special care?

Their meat is generally rice roasted with oil, and placed in a large wooden dish. Over this they place a large dish of elkushan, which consists of flesh, fish, fowl, and vegetables. They also roast the fruit of the plantain, and afterwards boil it in new milk: they then put it on a dish, and the curdled milk on another. They also put on dishes, some of preserved lemon, bunches of preserved pepper-pods salted and pickled, as also grapes, which are not unlike apples, except that they have stones. These, when boiled, become sweet like fruit in general, but are crude before this: they are preserved by being salted and pickled. In the same manner they use the green ginger. When, therefore, they eat the rice, they eat after it these salts and pickles. The people of [Mogadishu] are very corpulent: they are enormous eaters, one of them eating as much as a congregation ought to do.

> Why do travelers so frequently comment on the food and eating habits of other people?

The Sultan then sent for me and for each of my companions a [suitable] dress; after which I was presented to him. . . I remained some days the King's guest, and then set out for the country of the Zanuj [it is not clear what place he refers to here], proceeding along the sea-shore.

#### For Further Reflection

- From Ibn Battuta's report, how could you characterize the role of hospitality on the Swahili coast?
- What evidence do you find that the Swahili city of Mogadishu was wealthy?

Source: Ibn Battuta, 1304–1377, and Samuel Lee. The Travels of Ibn Battuta. London: Printed for the Oriental translation committee, sold by J. Murray [etc.], 1829, 56–57.

communicated readily among themselves because individuals frequently visited other Swahili communities in their oceangoing crafts. Indeed, all along the east African coast, Swahili society underwent similar patterns of development with respect to language, religion, architecture, and technology.

By the tenth century, Swahili people increasingly adopted Islam and also interacted with Muslim traders from other places. From the interior regions of east Africa, the Swahili traded for gold, slaves, ivory, and local products such as tortoise shells and leopard skins, which they traded for pottery, glass, and textiles that Muslim merchants brought from Persia, India, and China. The rapidly increasing volume and value of trade had large repercussions for Swahili states and societies, just as the expansion of the trans-Saharan trade had for west African societies.

**The Swahili City-States** By the eleventh and twelfth centuries, coastal East Africans had grown wealthy through their trading activities. By controlling and taxing trade within their jurisdictions, local chiefs strengthened their own authority and increased the influence of their communities. Gradually, trade concentrated at several coastal and island port cities that enjoyed sheltered or especially convenient locations: Mogadishu, Lamu, Malindi, Mombasa, Zanzibar, Kilwa, Mozambique, and Sofala. Each of those sites developed into a powerful city-state governed by kings who supervised trade and organized public life in the region.

The cities themselves underwent an impressive transformation. Villages in the interior regions of east Africa had buildings made of wood and dried mud, the principal materials used even for prominent structures such as mosques. By about the twelfth century, however, Swahili peoples began to construct much larger buildings of coral, and by the fifteenth century the main Swahili towns boasted handsome stone mosques and public buildings. Meanwhile, the ruling elites and wealthy merchants of Swahili trading cities dressed in silk and fine cotton clothes, and they set their tables with porcelain imported from China.

**Kilwa** Travelers' reports and recent archaeological discoveries have thrown especially clear light on the development of **Kilwa**, one of the busiest city-states on the east African coast. The earliest Bantu inhabitants of Kilwa relied mostly on fishing and engaged in a limited amount of trade between about 800 and 1000 C.E. During the next two centuries, they imported pottery and stoneware from other regions in east Africa and began to rely more on agriculture to support their growing numbers. By the early thirteenth century, Kilwans were prosperous enough to erect multistory stone buildings, and they used copper coins to facilitate economic transactions. Between 1300 and 1505, Kilwa enjoyed tremendous prosperity. The Moroccan traveler Ibn Battuta visited the city in 1331 and

**Kilwa** (KIHL-wah)

The massive stone complex of Great Zimbabwe, which featured very fine construction techniques, required the services of numerous expert masons and other crafts workers.
Georg Gerster/Science Source

reported that Muslim scholars from Arabia and Persia lived at Kilwa and consulted regularly with the local ruler.

With a population of about twelve thousand, Kilwa was a thriving city that had many stone buildings and mosques. Residents imported cotton and silk textiles as well as perfumes and pearls from India, and archaeologists have unearthed a staggering amount of Chinese porcelain. Merchants of Kilwa imported those products in exchange for gold, slaves, and ivory obtained from interior regions. By the late fifteenth century, Kilwa exported about a ton of gold per year. Participation in Indian Ocean trade networks brought similar experiences to the other major Swahili cities.

In fact, the influence of long-distance trade passed well beyond the coasts to the interior regions of east Africa. Villagers in the interior did not enjoy the cosmopolitan lifestyles of the Swahili elites, but trade and the wealth that it brought underwrote the establishment of large and powerful kingdoms in east and central Africa.

**Zimbabwe** The best known of these kingdoms was **Zimbabwe**. The term *zimbabwe* refers simply to the dwelling of a chief. As early as the fifth and sixth centuries C.E., the region occupied by the modern states of Zimbabwe and Mozambique featured many wooden residences known throughout the land as *zimbabwe*. By the ninth century, chiefs had begun to build their *zimbabwe* of stone—indicating an increasingly complex society that could invest resources in expensive construction projects. About the early thirteenth century, a magnificent stone complex known as Great Zimbabwe began to arise near Nyanda in the modern state of Zimbabwe. Within stone walls 5 meters (16 feet) thick and 10 meters (32 feet) tall, **Great Zimbabwe** was a city of stone towers, palaces, and public buildings that served as the capital of a large kingdom situated between the Zambesi and Limpopo rivers. At the time of its greatest extent, during the late fifteenth century, up to eighteen thousand people may have lived in the vicinity of the stone complex at Great Zimbabwe, and the kingdom stretched from the outskirts of the Swahili city of Sofala deep into the interior of south-central Africa.

Kings residing at Great Zimbabwe controlled and taxed the trade between the interior and coastal regions. They organized the flow of gold, ivory, slaves, and regional products from sources of supply to the coast. Their control over those products enabled them to forge alliances with local leaders and to profit handsomely from commercial transactions. Just as the trans-Saharan trade encouraged the building of states and empires in west Africa, the Indian Ocean trade generated wealth that financed the organization of city-states on the coast and large kingdoms in the interior regions of east and central Africa.

**Islam in East Africa** In east Africa, again as in west Africa, trade brought cultural as well as political changes. Like their counterparts in west Africa, the ruling elites and the wealthy merchants of east Africa converted to the Islamic faith. They did not necessarily give up their religious and cultural traditions but, rather, continued to observe them for purposes of providing cultural leadership in their societies. By adopting Islam, however, they laid a cultural foundation for close cooperation with Muslim merchants trading in the Indian Ocean basin. Moreover, Islam served as a fresh source of legitimacy for their rule because they gained recognition from Islamic states in southwest Asia, and their conversion opened the door to political alliances with Muslim rulers in other lands. Even though the conversion of elite classes did not bring about the immediate spread of Islam throughout their societies, it enabled Islam to establish a presence in east Africa under the sponsorship of some particularly influential patrons. The faith eventually attracted interest in larger circles and became one of the principal cultural and religious traditions of east Africa.

**Zimbabwe** (zihm-BAHB-way)

## CONCLUSION

States and societies of sub-Saharan Africa shared similarities with and also differed from societies in other parts of the eastern hemisphere. The foundations of most sub-Saharan societies were the traditions of agricultural economy and iron-working skills that spread throughout most of the African continent. As these peoples migrated to new regions and established new communities, at first they based their societies on kin groups. When different societies came into conflict with one another, however, they increasingly established formal political authorities to guide their affairs. African peoples organized states of various sizes, some very small and others quite large. When they entered into commercial relationships with Muslim peoples in southwest Asia and north Africa, they also built formidable imperial states in west Africa and bustling city-states in coastal east Africa. These states had far-reaching implications for sub-Saharan societies because they depended on a regular and reliable flow of trade goods—particularly gold, ivory, and slaves. Trade and the regular encounters it entailed also had cultural implications because it facilitated the introduction of Islam, which together with native African traditions profoundly influenced the development of sub-Saharan societies. After the eighth century, many ruling elites in both west Africa and coastal east Africa—like Sundiata, King of Mali, who we encountered at the beginning of the chapter—accepted Islam and strengthened its position in their societies by building mosques, consulting Muslim advisers, and supporting Islamic schools. By 1500 C.E. African traditions and Islamic influences had combined to fashion a series of powerful, productive, and distinctive societies in sub-Saharan Africa that were increasingly integrated into wider networks of exchange and encounter in North Africa and Eurasia.

## STUDY TERMS

age grades (194)
Axum (196)
Bantu (191)
Benin (192)
camels (198)
gold (199)
Great Zimbabwe (205)
griots (188)
Ife (192)
Islamic slave trade (195)
Jenne-jeno (191)
Kebra Negast (197)
Kilwa (204)
kin-based societies (191)
kingdom of Ghana (198)
kingdom of Kongo (192)
Koumbi-Saleh (199)
Mali Empire (199)
Mansa Musa (201)
Sundiata (188)
Swahili (202)
Timbuktu (201)
trans-Saharan trade (199)
Zanj revolt (194)
Zimbabwe (205)

## FOR FURTHER READING

Ibn Battuta. *Ibn Battuta in Black Africa.* Ed. and trans. by Said Hamdun and Noel King. Princeton, 1998. Translations of travel accounts of visits to coastal east Africa and the empire of Mali by a famous fourteenth-century Moroccan traveler.

Christopher Ehret. *The Civilizations of Africa: A History to 1800.* Charlottesville, Va., 2002. An important contribution that views Africa in the context of world history.

Mary Anne Fitzgerald and Phillip Marsden, *Ethiopia: The Living Churches of an Ancient Kingdom.* Cairo, 2017. Beautifully illustrated volume that traces the history of the ancient churches of Ethiopia.

Bernd Heine and Derek Nurse. *African Languages: An Introduction.* Cambridge, 2000. A sophisticated treatment of the historical complexity of African languages by expert linguists.

J. F. P. Hopkins and N. Levtzion, eds. *Corpus of Early Arabic Sources for West African History.* Princeton, 2000. Translations of numerous important accounts by Muslim merchants and geographers who reported on conditions in west Africa before modern times.

Mark Horton and John Middleton. *The Swahili: The Social Landscape of a Mercantile Society.* Oxford, 2000. Useful survey that draws on both archaeological and written evidence.

John S. Mbiti. *African Religions and Philosophy.* 2nd ed. London, 1990. A thorough and systematic study of traditional African religions in their cultural context.

Roderick James McIntosh. *The Peoples of the Middle Niger: The Island of Gold.* Oxford, 1998. Fascinating volume emphasizing the environmental context of west African history.

D. T. Niane, ed. *Sundiata: An Epic of Old Mali.* 2nd ed. Trans. by G. D. Pickett. London, 2006. Translation of the story of Sundiata, founder of the Mali Empire, as preserved in African oral tradition.

Jan Vansina. *Paths in the Rainforests: Toward a History of Political Tradition in Equatorial Africa.* Madison, 1990. A brilliant synthesis of early African history by one of the world's foremost historians of Africa.

# CHAPTER 6 AP EXAM PRACTICE

Questions assume cumulative knowledge from this chapter and previous chapters.

## Section I

## Multiple Choice Questions

Use the image below and your knowledge of world history to answer questions 1 – 3.

17th century illustration from a missionary account showing African iron-making.
Fotosearch/Stringer/Getty Images

1. The inclusion of this image in the missionary's account of sub-Saharan Africa in the 1800s was most probably intended to
   (A) feature subsistence agriculture and the use of slave labor.
   (B) showcase the use of technological skills and division of labor.
   (C) highlight pagan practices and the need for Christian intervention.
   (D) reinforce a European stereotype of African primitiveness and savagery.

2. An historian could use this image to illustrate how texts of the time tended to feature
   (A) gender specific roles with emphasis on women's contributions.
   (B) religious beliefs based on European Christianity and early Islam.
   (C) family and kinship relationships as central to social organization.
   (D) male dominance in the economic and social structures.

3. The illustrator has signaled support of the claim that gender expectations were principal considerations of social position by
   (A) placing individuals singularly, regardless of gender.
   (B) placing genders in one horizontal plane.
   (C) creating foreground and background gender groupings.
   (D) mixing of the genders heterogeneously.

Use the image below and your knowledge of world history to answer questions 4 and 5.

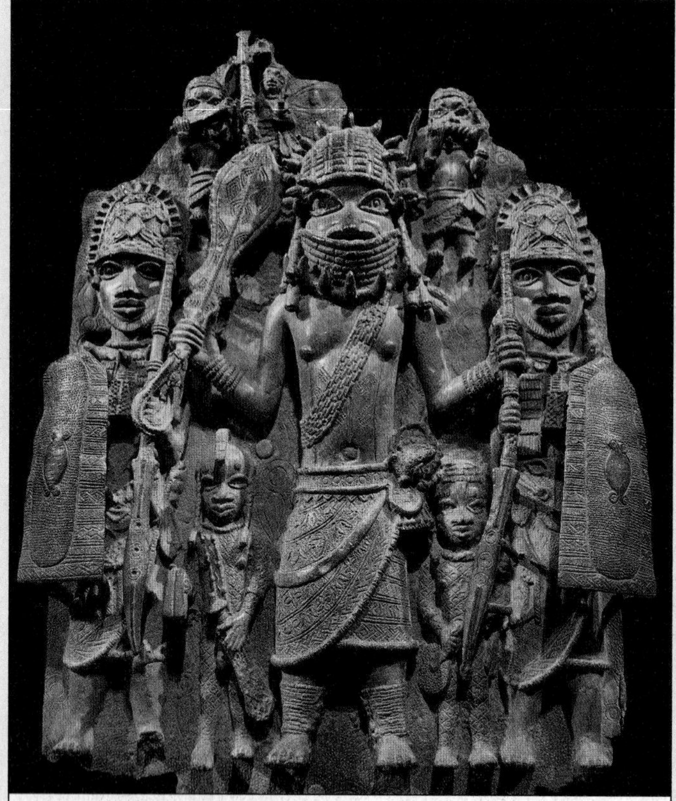

Bronze plaque from the kingdom of Benin depicting a chief flanked by warriors and attendants.
Peter Horree/Alamy Stock Photo

4. The main purpose in commissioning this bronze plaque was most likely to
   (A) indicate the important role of diviners in political decisions.
   (B) showcase gender equity in both economic and social spheres.
   (C) demonstrate the military and political force of the city-state.
   (D) herald the stateless kin-based society built on family and clan groups.
5. Which of the following was most responsible for the development of the political structure featured in the bronze plaque?
   (A) A decrease in population that led to a labor shortage.
   (B) A decrease in tensions among Bantu communities.
   (C) An increase in migration opportunities.
   (D) An increase in rivalry for diminishing resources.

## Short Answer

6. Use the passage below and your knowledge of world history to answer parts A, B, and C.

> Perhaps more than any other region of the world, the history of sub-Saharan Africa has been stereotyped as static, unchanging, and primitive. Why? In part it is because the discipline of history was itself being formed in the West just as Europeans—with their deeply racist assumptions about the primitive nature of people with darker skins—were in the process of conquering large portions of the region in the late nineteenth century. In part it is because sub-Saharan African history had largely been preserved in oral histories instead of textual archives, which were not valued by the Europeans who encountered them. As a result, Europeans were unable to access the rich and evolving histories of sub-Saharan Africans and assumed they did not exist. But the growth of African Studies in the twentieth century, practiced in many cases by people born in Africa, has demonstrated that such stereotypes are as false for sub-Saharan Africa as they are for anywhere else. At the same time, more recent academic comprehension of oral history as a complex and sophisticated means of recording the past has allowed historians to gain a much greater understanding of sub-Saharan African histories. Consider how much history remains untold when historians value only textual sources, in pre-modern sub-Saharan Africa or elsewhere.
>
> *Source:* Jonathan Reynolds. "History and the Study of Africa." *Oxford University African Bibliographies*. Fall 2013.

(A) Explain ONE basis on which, according to Reynolds, Europeans constructed their view of African culture.

(B) Explain ONE recent development in historiography that, according to the excerpt, has led to revisionist views of the cultures of sub-Saharan Africa prior to the arrival of the Europeans.

(C) Identify ONE other example of cultural bias outside of sub-Saharan Africa and explain its effects of a particular culture or region.

7. Use the image below and your knowledge of world history to answer parts A, B, and C.

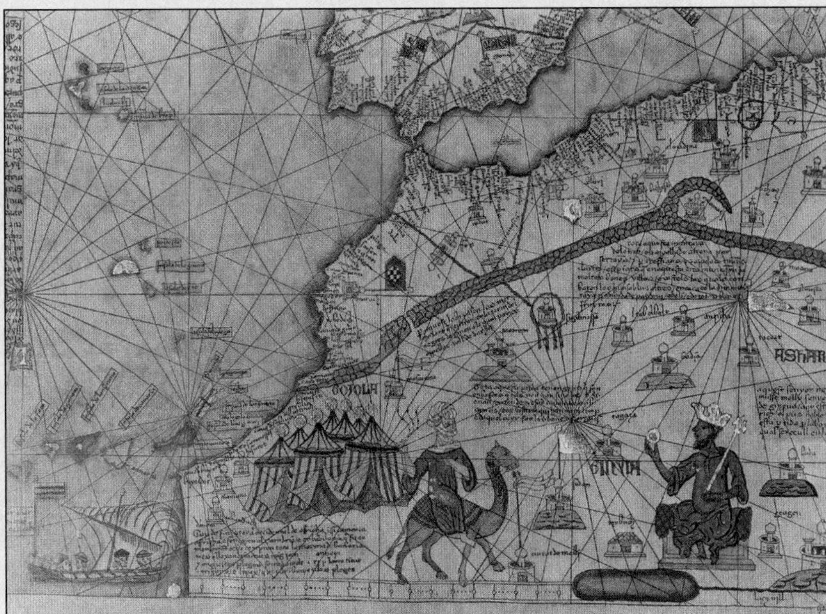

Mansa Musa, emperor of Mali, enjoyed a widespread reputation as the wealthiest king in the world. On this map, prepared in 1375 by a cartographer from the Mediterranean island of Majorca, Mansa Musa holds a gold nugget about the size of a grapefruit.
Abraham Cresques/Getty Images

(A) Identify ONE way the cartographer portrayed Mansa Musa's power.

(B) Explain ONE historical development in Europe during the 14th century that mirrored the depiction of Mansa Musa shown on the map.

(C) Identify ONE non-European area with similar political and/or economic circumstances during this time period.

8. Use your understanding of world history to answer parts A, B, and C.

(A) Explain and give ONE example of how the movement of people affected linguistic developments.

(B) Identify ONE negative consequence of African encounter with other cultures before 1400 and its effects.

(C) Identify ONE positive consequence of African encounter with other cultures before 1400 and its effects.

# Section II

## Document-Based Question

Evaluate the extent to which the architecture of sub-Saharan Africa prior to 1500 reflected the political, economic, and/or cultural forces of that time and place.

In your response you should do the following:

- Respond to the prompt with a historically defensible thesis or claim that establishes a line of reasoning.
- Describe a broader historical context relevant to the prompt.
- Support an argument in response to the prompt using all documents.
- Use at least one additional piece of specific historical evidence (beyond that found in the documents) relevant to an argument about the prompt.
- Explain how or why the document's point of view, purpose, historical situation, and /or audience is relevant to an argument.
- Use evidence to corroborate, qualify, or modify an argument that addresses the prompt.

### Document 1

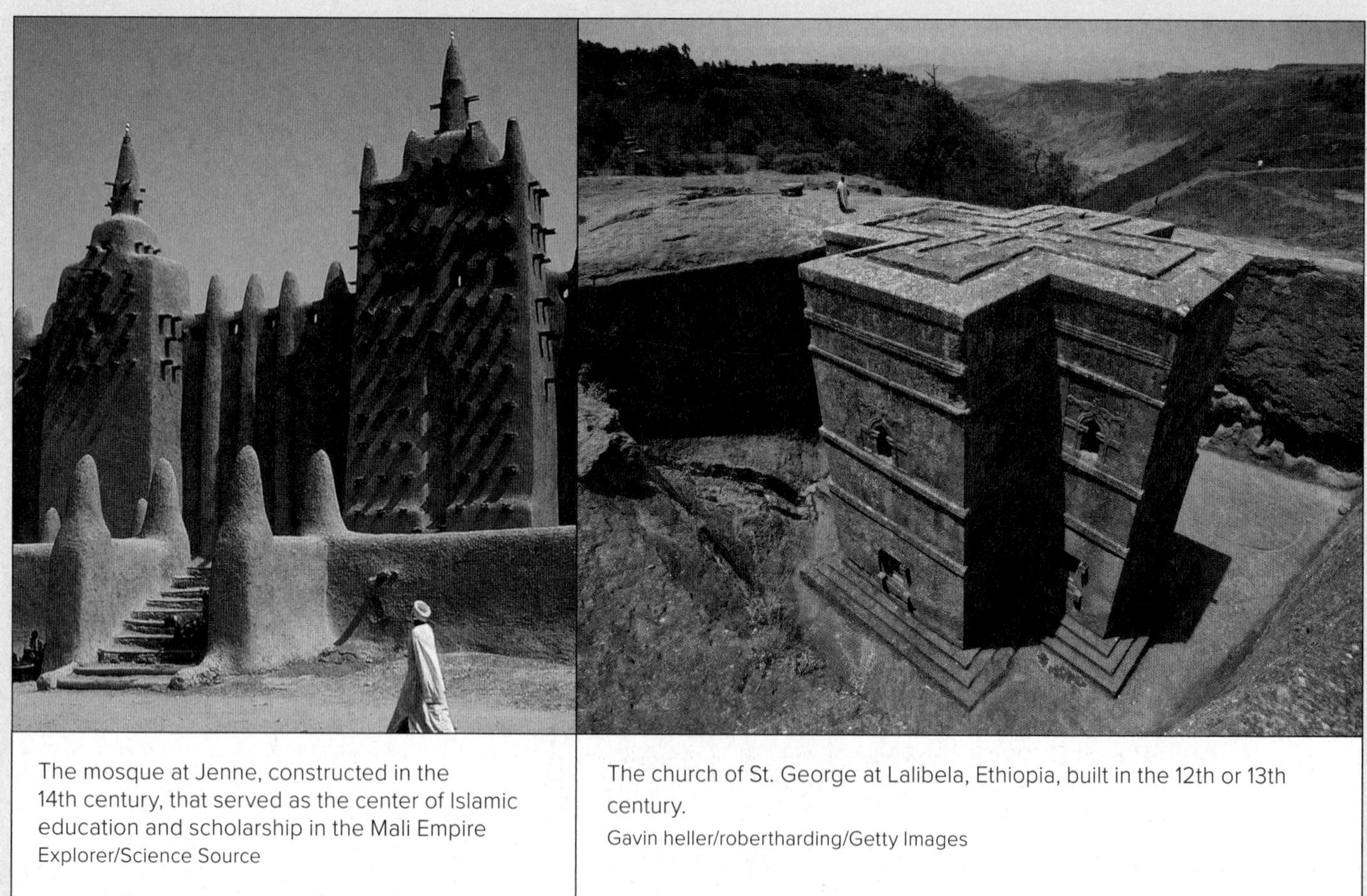

The mosque at Jenne, constructed in the 14th century, that served as the center of Islamic education and scholarship in the Mali Empire
Explorer/Science Source

The church of St. George at Lalibela, Ethiopia, built in the 12th or 13th century.
Gavin heller/robertharding/Getty Images

## Document 2

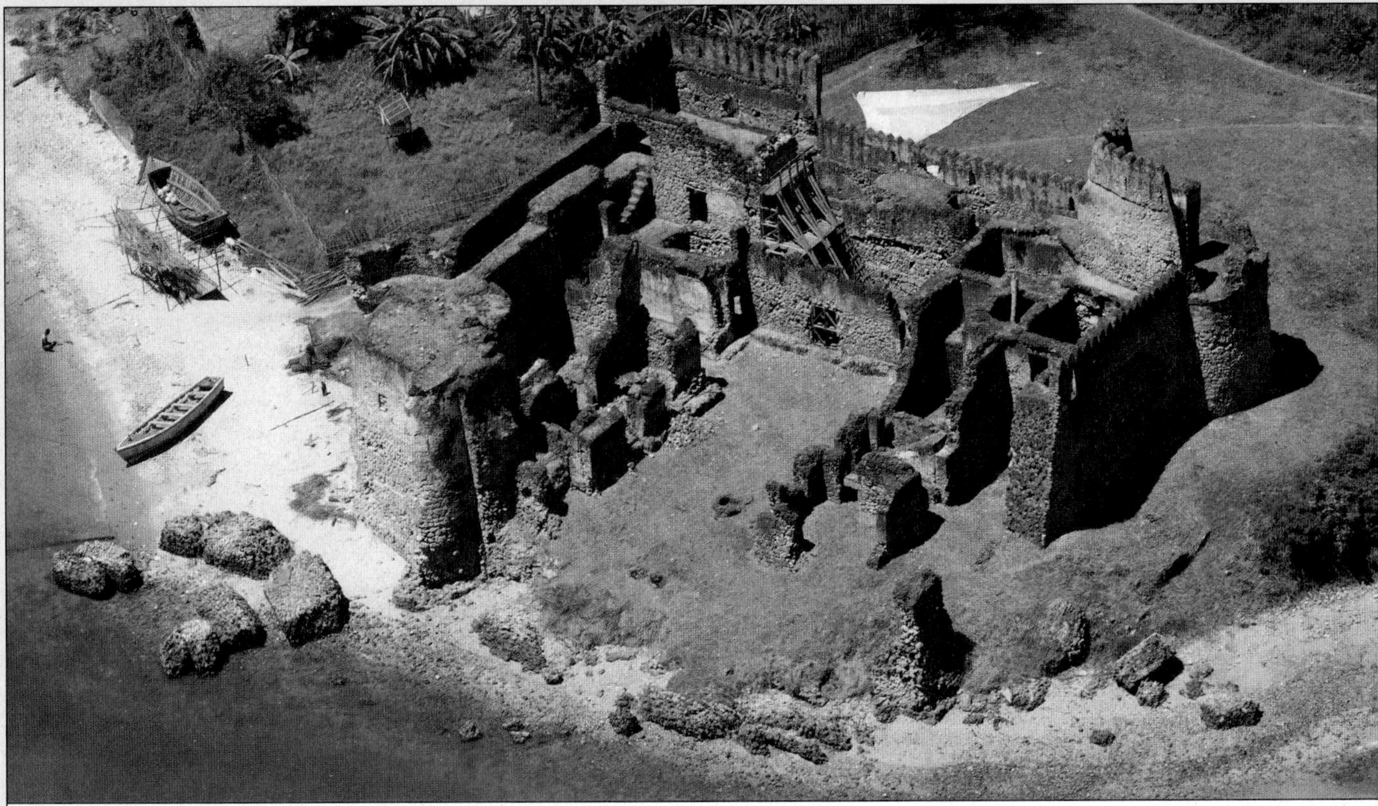

Gerezani Fortress on the east African coast at Kilwa
Ulrich Doering/Alamy Stock Photo

## Document 3

The best known of these kingdoms was **Zimbabwe**. The term *zimbabwe* refers simply to the dwelling of a chief. As early as the fifth and sixth centuries C.E., the region occupied by the modern states of Zimbabwe and Mozambique featured many wooden residences known throughout the land as *zimbabwe*. By the ninth century, chiefs had begun to build their *zimbabwe* of stone—indicating an increasingly complex society that could invest re- sources in expensive construction projects. About the early thirteenth century, a magnificent stone complex known as **Great Zimbabwe** began to arise near Nyanda in the modern state of Zimbabwe. Within stone walls 5 meters (16 feet) thick and 10 meters (32 feet) tall, Great Zimbabwe was a city of stone towers, palaces, and public buildings that served as the capital of a large kingdom situated between the Zambesi and Limpopo rivers. At the time of its greatest extent, during the late fifteenth century, up to eighteen thousand people may have lived in the vicinity of the stone complex at Great Zimbabwe, and the kingdom stretched from the outskirts of the Swahili city of Sofala deep into the interior of south-central Africa.

*Source:* Bentley and Ziegler, *Traditions & Encounters: A Global perspective on the Past*

## Long Essay

Develop a thoughtful and thorough historical argument that answers the question below. Begin your essay with a thesis statement and support it with relevant historical evidence.

Develop an argument that evaluates the extent to which religious conversion to Islam and Christianity affected sub-Saharan Africa prior to 1500.

Chapter

# 7 The Increasing Integration of Europe with the Wider World



## ZOOMING IN ON TRADITIONS AND ENCOUNTERS

### From Venice to China and Back

In 1260 C.E. two brothers, Niccolò and Maffeo Polo, traveled from their native Venice to Constantinople. The Polo brothers were jewel merchants, and while in Constantinople, they decided to pursue opportunities farther east. They made their way to the great central Asian trading city of Bokhara, where they spent three years and received an invitation to join a diplomatic embassy going to the court of Khubilai Khan. They readily agreed and traveled by caravan to the Mongol court in China, where the great khan received them and inquired about their land, rulers, and religion.

Khubilai was especially interested in learning more about Roman Catholic Christianity so he asked the Polo brothers to return to Europe and request the pope to send learned priests who could serve as authoritative sources of information on Christian doctrine. They accepted the mission and returned to Italy in 1269 as envoys of the great khan.

Venice, home of Marco Polo and a legion of merchants, drew enormous prosperity from trade. This image depicts Marco Polo leaving Venice on his eastward journey.
Timewatch Images/Alamy Stock Photo

As it turned out, the Polo brothers were not able to satisfy the great khan's desire for expertise in Christian doctrine even though the pope had been willing to send priests to accompany them back to China. In fact, the pope designated two missionaries to accompany the Polos, and the party set out in 1271, together with Niccolò's seventeen-year-old son, **Marco Polo.** Soon, however, the missionaries became alarmed at fighting along the route, and they decided to abandon the embassy and return to Europe. Thus only the Polos completed the difficult and sometimes dangerous journey, arriving at the Mongol court of Shangdu three and a half years later, in 1274. Although they instead presented Khubilai with letters and presents from the pope—including a sample of lamp oil from the church of the Holy Sepulchre in Jerusalem—they did not bring the requested missionaries. The great khan nevertheless received the Polos warmly and welcomed them to his court. In fact, they remained in China in the service of the great khan for the next seventeen years. Their mission gave rise to Marco Polo's celebrated account of his travels, and it signaled the reintegration of Europe into the political and economic affairs of the larger eastern hemisphere.

## CHAPTER FOCUS

- Around the year 1000, the anarchy and violence that characterized the early medieval states in west Europe settled into a calmer and more prosperous pattern of political and economic stability.
- Although the Byzantine empire remained far more economically vibrant and politically unified, it began to have internal problems and external invasions. Nomadic Turkic-speaking peoples from the steppes of central Asia, who had converted to Islam in the aftermath of the Arab invasions in the eighth century, began invading the weak spots of the Byzantine empire, specifically the Balkan peninsula and the Middle Eastern regions. By 1453 they succeeded in collapsing the empire.
- You will need to know why the Catholic Church in Rome launched the crusades, and how they were religious failures, but economic and cultural bonanzas for western Europeans.
- New crops collected from *dar al-Islam* and new technologies—like the horse collar—spurred agricultural productivity, a demographic boom, more specialized labor, and the repopulation of older cities and the creation of new ones.
- New technologies like gunpowder weapons, wood-pulp paper, and news of the moveable-type printing press came home with the crusaders.
- The city-state of Venice became a Mediterranean super power, and as other port cities did more trade with the sophisticated Byzantine, Muslim, and by extension Silk Road merchants, western European urban populations were reintroduced to Greek culture and eastern luxury goods. These were the roots of the Renaissance, or rebirth of Greco-Roman culture in the west.

### Historical Developments

Increased cross-cultural interactions resulted in the diffusion of literary, artistic, and cultural traditions, as well as scientific and technological innovations.

- The fate of cities varied greatly, with periods of significant decline and periods of increased urbanization, buoyed by rising productivity and expanding networks.
- The growth of interregional trade in luxury goods was encouraged by innovations in previously existing transportation and commercial technologies, including the caravanserai, forms of credit, and the development of money economies

### Reasoning Processes

- **Sourcing and Situation** Explain the purpose and historical situation of trade privileges granted to the Hanse of Cologne.
- **Source Claims and Evidence** Identify text-based and non-text based evidence used throughout the chapter to support the claim that trade and finance were thriving in Europe in the middle ages.
- **Contextualization** Explain how the Christian "Reconquista" of Spain and the Crusades were part of a larger medieval expansion of Europe.
- **Making Connections** Explain how the Crusades relate to the spread of culture and technology.

### Historical Thinking Skills

- **Causation** Explain the ways governments in medieval western Europe were products of cultural syncretism.
- **Continuity and Change** Describe patterns of continuity and/or change from early medieval Europe (Chapter 4) to the high middle ages of Europe (Chapter 7).

## CHAPTER OVERVIEW

As a result of the turmoil and disarray that plagued Europe during the half millennium from 500 to 1000 C.E., western Europeans practiced their own traditions and played little role in the development of a hemispheric economy during the era dominated by the Tang, Song, Abbasid, and Byzantine empires. But during the early middle ages, Europeans laid the foundations of a more dynamic and stable society. Regional states became the basis for a more enduring political order. New tools and technologies led to increased agricultural production and economic growth. The missionary efforts of the western Christian church brought cultural and religious unity to most of Europe. During the "high middle ages" of European history—the period from about 1000 to 1300 C.E.—European peoples built a vibrant society on the political, economic, and cultural foundations laid during the early middle ages.

Although the idea of empire continued to fascinate political thinkers and leaders, empire builders of the high middle ages did not manage to bring all of Europe under their control. Instead, local rulers organized strong regional states. Increased agricultural production fueled rapid population growth. Economic expansion led to increased long-distance trade, enriched cities, and supported the establishment of new towns. Cultural and religious affairs also reflected the dynamism of the high middle ages, as European philosophers and theologians reconsidered traditional doctrines in light of fresh knowledge.

Political organization, demographic increase, and economic growth pushed Europeans once again into encounters with the larger world. European merchants began to participate directly in the commercial economy of the eastern hemisphere, sometimes traveling as far as China—as we saw in the case of the Polo family—in search of luxury goods. Ambitious military and political leaders expanded the boundaries of Christendom by seizing Muslim-held territories in Spain and the Mediterranean islands, in the process expanding their encounters with new peoples and ideas. European forces even mounted a series of military crusades that sought to bring Islamic lands of the eastern Mediterranean basin under Christian control. While the Crusades ultimately failed, they clearly demonstrated that Europeans were beginning to play a much larger role in the world than they had for the previous half millennium.

| CHRONOLOGY | |
|---|---|
| 962 | Coronation of Otto I as Holy Roman emperor |
| 1056–1106 | Reign of Emperor Henry IV |
| 1066 | Norman invasion of England |
| 1073–1085 | Reign of Pope Gregory VII |
| 1096–1099 | First crusade |
| 1122–1204 | Life of Eleanor of Aquitaine |
| 1152–1190 | Reign of Emperor Frederick Barbarossa |
| 1170–1221 | Life of St. Dominic |
| 1182–1226 | Life of St. Francis |
| 1187 | Recapture of Jerusalem by Saladin |
| 1202–1204 | Fourth crusade |
| 1225–1274 | Life of St. Thomas Aquinas |
| 1271–1295 | Marco Polo's trip to China |
| 1453 | Fall of Constantinople to Ottoman Turks |

## THE REGIONAL STATES OF MEDIEVAL EUROPE

Long after its collapse, the Roman Empire inspired European philosophers, theologians, and rulers, who dreamed of a centralized political structure embracing all of Christian Europe. The Byzantine Empire survived as the dominant power in the eastern Mediterranean region, where it flourished through the early eleventh century. By 1100 C.E., however, Byzantium experienced domestic social and economic difficulties as well as foreign pressure from both east and west. Even as Byzantium influenced the emergence of new states in Russia and eastern Europe, the empire itself gradually declined and in 1453 fell to Muslim Turkish invaders. As Byzantium weakened, western Europe underwent an impressive round of state building. Beginning in the late tenth century, German princes formed the so-called **Holy Roman Empire,** which they viewed as a Christian revival of the earlier Roman Empire. Meanwhile, independent monarchies emerged in France and England, and other authorities ruled in the various regions of Italy and Spain. Thus medieval Europe became a political mosaic of independent and competing regional states.

### The Late Byzantine Empire

**Social and Economic Problems** For about three centuries, the ***theme* system**—which granted farm land to men who served as soldiers—served the Byzantine Empire well by supporting both a powerful army and a prosperous independent peasantry. About the eleventh century, however, wealthy landowners increasingly undermined the *theme* system by acquiring the properties of independent peasants and accumulating them into large estates. That development transformed formerly free peasants into a class of dependent agricultural laborers while reducing incentives for individuals to serve in Byzantine military forces. It also led to diminished tax receipts for the central government.

**Challenges from the West** As domestic problems mounted, Byzantium also faced fresh foreign challenges. From the west came representatives of an increasingly dynamic western Europe, where rapid economic development supported a round of military and political expansion. During the early eleventh century, Norman adventurers—descendants of Vikings who had settled on the Norman peninsula in northern France—carved out a regional state in southern Italy and expelled the last Byzantine authorities there. During the twelfth and thirteenth centuries, the Normans and other western European peoples mounted a series of crusades—vast military campaigns intended to recapture Jerusalem and other sites holy to Christians from Muslim rule—and took the opportunity to plunder the Byzantine Empire. Venetian merchants even managed to hijack the fourth crusade (1202–1204 C.E.) from its original mission in the eastern Mediterranean and targeted Constantinople instead. Venetians had become prominent in the commercial life of the eastern Mediterranean, and they viewed the fourth crusade as an opportunity to strengthen their position against Byzantine competition. In 1204 the crusaders conquered Constantinople, looted its art and treasure, and destroyed parts of the city. Byzantine forces recaptured the city in 1261, but the humiliating destruction of the imperial capital dealt the empire a blow from which it never completely recovered.

## MAP 7.1 The regional states of medieval Europe, 1000–1300

Note the large number of states and the different kinds of states that claimed sovereignty in medieval Europe.

***To what extent did the invasions of the ninth and tenth centuries (depicted in Map 16.3) influence the political development of medieval Europe?***

***The map of medieval Europe displays very large empires. Given the history of 1000-1300, why might the map be misleading? What events contributed to weakness in these regional states?***

During the sack of Constantinople in 1204, crusading forces seized and carted away Byzantine treasures of all sorts—including the great bronze horses that now reside in St. Mark's basilica in Venice.

**Analyze** *What does this image demonstrate about the mixed motives of the Crusades? Why would crusading forces take items from other Christians in Byzantium if their enemy was Muslims?*

Leemage/Universal Images Group/Getty Images

**Challenges from the East** As Europeans advanced from the west, nomadic Turkish peoples invaded from the east. Most important among them were the Muslim Seljuqs, who, beginning in the eleventh century, sent waves of invaders into Anatolia, the agricultural heartland of the Byzantine Empire. Given the military and financial problems of Byzantium, the Seljuqs found Anatolia ripe for plunder. In 1071 they handed the Byzantine army a demoralizing defeat at the **battle of Manzikert.** Byzantine forces then turned on each other in civil war, allowing the Seljuqs almost free rein in Anatolia. By the late twelfth century, the Seljuqs had seized much of Anatolia, while crusaders from western Europe held most of the remainder.

The loss of Anatolia sealed the fate of the Byzantine Empire. A territorially truncated Byzantium survived until the mid-fifteenth century, but it enjoyed little autonomy and faced a series of challenges from Italian merchants, western European adventurers, and Turkish invaders. In 1453, following a long era of decline, the Byzantine Empire came to an end when Ottoman Turks, under the dynamic leadership of twenty-one-year-old Sultan Mehmed II, captured Constantinople and absorbed Byzantium's last remaining territories into their expanding realm.

## The Holy Roman Empire

**Otto I** As the Carolingian Empire—which ruled over much of western Europe from 800–888—faded at the end of the ninth century, counts, dukes, and other local authorities took responsibility for providing order in their own regions. Gradually, some of them extended their influence beyond their own jurisdictions and built larger states. **Otto I** of Saxony was particularly aggressive. By the mid-tenth century, he had

## INTERPRETING IMAGES

Fourteenth-century illustration of Pope Gregory VII receiving Henry IV at his fort at Canossa, after Henry showed his penitence by kneeling in the snow for three days.

**Analyze** *What does the illustration reveal about the power of the Catholic Church?*

Album/Alamy Stock Photo

established himself as king in what is now northern Germany. He campaigned east of the Elbe River in lands populated by Slavic peoples (in what is now eastern Germany, western Poland, and the Czech Republic), and twice he ventured into Italy to quell political disturbances and protect the pope. In appreciation for his aid in protecting the papal states during a rebellion, Pope John XII proclaimed Otto Emperor of the Romans in 962 C.E., thus reviving the idea of the Holy Roman Empire born during the time of Charlemagne (r. 800–814).

The imperial title had considerable cachet, and on several occasions energetic emperors almost transformed the Holy Roman Empire into a hegemonic state that might have reintroduced imperial unity to Europe. Conflict with the papacy, however, prevented the emperors from building a strong and dynamic state. Although the popes crowned the medieval emperors, their relations were usually tense because both popes and emperors made large claims to authority in Christian Europe. Relations became especially strained when emperors sought to influence the selection of church officials, which the popes regarded as their own prerogative, or when emperors sought to extend their authority into Italy, where the popes had long provided political leadership.

**Investiture Contest** Neither the popes nor the emperors were strong enough to dominate the other, but the popes were able to prevent the emperors from building a powerful imperial state that would threaten the papacy as Europe's principal spiritual authority. The capacity of the papacy to weaken the empire became apparent during the **Investiture Contest,** a controversy over the appointment of church officials in the late eleventh and early twelfth centuries. From the earliest days of the Holy Roman Empire, imperial authorities had named important church officials to their positions because the higher clergy provided political as well as religious services. In an effort to regain control of the clergy and ensure that church officials met appropriate spiritual criteria, Pope Gregory VII (1073–1085 C.E.) ordered an end to the practice of lay investiture–the selection and installation of church officials by nonchurch rulers such as emperors. When Emperor Henry IV (1056–1106 C.E.) challenged the pope's policy, Gregory excommunicated him and released his subjects from their duty to obey him. The German princes then took the opportunity to rebel against the emperor. Henry eventually regained control of the empire but only after beseeching Gregory's mercy while standing barefoot in the snow. Because of the pope's intervention in imperial affairs, however, the German princes won concessions that enhanced their independence and diminished the emperor's authority.

**Frederick Barbarossa** Popes and emperors clashed over their conflicting interests in Italy as well as over the appointment of church officials. Among the most vigorous of the medieval emperors was Frederick I, known as **Frederick Barbarossa**—"the red beard"—a strong opponent of papal power who reigned from 1152 to 1190 C.E. Working from his ancestral lands in southern Germany, Barbarossa sought to absorb the wealthy and increasingly urban region of Lombardy in northern Italy. Integration of Lombardy with his German holdings might have provided Barbarossa with the resources to control the German princes, build a powerful state, and dominate much of Europe. That prospect did not appeal to the popes, who marshaled support from other European states on behalf of the Italian cities. By the end of Barbarossa's reign, the papal coalition had forced the emperor to relinquish his rights in Lombardy. Once again, papal policies forestalled the transformation of the Holy Roman Empire into a powerful state.

Voltaire, the eighteenth-century French writer, once quipped that the Holy Roman Empire was "neither holy, nor Roman, nor an empire." Indeed, the Holy Roman Empire was an empire principally in name. In reality, it was a regional state ruling Germany, though it also wielded influence intermittently in eastern Europe and Italy. In no sense, however, did the Holy Roman Empire restore imperial unity to western Europe.

## Regional Monarchies in France and England

In the absence of an effective imperial power, regional states emerged throughout medieval Europe. In France and England, princes established regional monarchies on the basis of relationships between lords and their retainers (subjects or followers).

**Capetian France** The French monarchy grew slowly from humble beginnings. When the last of the Carolingians died, in 987 C.E., the lords of France elected a minor noble named Hugh Capet to serve as king. Capet held only a small territory around Paris, and he was in no position to challenge his retainers, some of whom were far more powerful than the king himself. During the next three centuries, however, his descendants, known as the **Capetian** kings, gradually added to their fortunes and expanded their political influence. Relying on relationships between lords and retainers, they absorbed the territories of retainers who died without heirs and established the right to administer justice throughout the realm. By the early fourteenth century, the Capetian kings had gradually centralized power and authority in France.

**The Normans** The English monarchy developed quite differently. Its founders were the **Normans** of what is now modern France. Though nominally subject to Carolingian and later to Capetian rulers, the dukes of Normandy in fact pursued their own interests with little regard for their lords. Within Normandy the dukes built a tightly centralized state in which all authority stemmed from the dukes themselves. The dukes also retained title to all land in Normandy, and in an effort to forestall conflicts of interest they strictly limited the right of their retainers to grant land to others. By the late tenth century, Norman lords had built a series of castles from which disciplined armies dominated their territories, and in the eleventh century they emerged as prominent political and military leaders throughout Europe and much of the Mediterranean basin as well.

**Norman England** In 1066 Duke William of Normandy assembled a fleet of ships carrying seven thousand men and two thousand horses, and sailed across the English Channel to invade England. At the time England was ruled by descendants of the Angles, the Saxons, and other Germanic peoples who had migrated there during the fifth and sixth centuries. The Duke, who became known as **William the Conqueror,** won a speedy military victory and quickly began to introduce Norman principles of government and land tenure to England. While retaining many institutions of their Anglo-Saxon predecessors, the Norman kings of England ruled over a much more tightly centralized realm than did the Capetian kings of France.

Both the Capetians and the Normans faced challenges from retainers seeking to pursue independent policies or enlarge their powers at the expense of the monarchs. Both dynasties also faced external challenges: indeed, they often battled each other because the Normans periodically sought to expand their possessions in France. On the basis of relationships between lords and retainers, however, both the Capetians and the Normans managed to organize regional monarchies that maintained order and provided reasonably effective government.

## Regional States in Italy and Iberia

**Church Influence in Italy** Regional states emerged also in other lands of medieval Europe, though not on such a large scale as the monarchies of France and England. In Italy, for example, no single regime controlled the entire peninsula. Rather, a series of ecclesiastical (run by the church) states, city-states, and principalities competed for power and position. In central Italy the popes had provided political

---
**Capet** (KAHP-ay)

## INTERPRETING IMAGES

The Bayeux tapestry, a magnificent mural of woven linen about 70 meters (230 feet) long, depicts the Norman invasion and conquest of England in 1066, led by William the Conqueror. In this section Norman warriors sail across the English Channel and disembark in southern England.

**Analyze** *The Bayeux tapestry is one of the most valuable artifacts in Europe due to the significance of William the Conqueror's victory. Why was this so significant for European and world history?*

Hulton Archive/Getty Images

leadership since the Carolingian era. Indeed, although the papacy was a spiritual rather than a political post, the popes ruled a good-sized territory in central Italy known as the Papal State. In northern Italy, too, the church influenced political affairs because bishops of the major cities took much of the initiative in organizing public life in their regions. During the high middle ages, however, as the cities grew wealthy from trade and manufacturing, lay classes challenged the bishops and eventually displaced them as ruling authorities.

**Italian States** By about the twelfth century, a series of prosperous city-states—including Florence, Bologna, Genoa, Milan, and Venice—dominated not only their own urban districts but also the surrounding rural areas. Meanwhile, in southern Italy, Norman mercenaries—cousins of those who conquered Anglo-Saxon England—invaded territories still claimed by the Byzantine Empire and various Muslim states. Normans first intervened in Italian affairs in the year 999, when a group of Norman pilgrims aided the people of Salerno as they fought off an attack by a Muslim army. Other Normans later aided the city of Bari in its struggle for independence from Byzantine authority (1017–1018). When they learned that opportunities might be available for ambitious adventurers in an unstable region, Norman mercenaries soon made their way to southern Italy in large numbers. With papal approval and support, they overcame Byzantine and Muslim authorities, brought southern Italy into the orbit of Roman Catholic Christianity, and laid the foundations for the emergence of the powerful kingdom of Naples.

**Christian and Muslim States in Iberia** As in Italy, a series of regional states competed for power in the Iberian

The Italian city-state of Florence grew rapidly during the high middle ages. This portrait of the city concentrates on the space enclosed by walls completed in the early fourteenth century.
DEA PICTURE LIBRARY/DeAgostini/Getty Images

peninsula. From the eighth to the eleventh century, a series of Muslim states ruled most of the peninsula. Only in northern Spain did small Christian states hold sway, mostly in mountainous regions. Beginning in the mid-eleventh century, though, Christians from those states began to attack Muslim territories and enlarge their own domains. As in southern Italy, political and military instability attracted the attention of Norman mercenaries, many of whom traveled to Spain and joined the armies of the Christian kingdoms as soldiers of fortune. By the late thirteenth century, the Christian kingdoms of Castile, Aragon, and Portugal controlled most of the Iberian peninsula, leaving only the small kingdom of Granada in Muslim hands.

With its Byzantine Empire, Holy Roman Empire, regional monarchies, ecclesiastical principalities, city-states, and new states founded on conquest, medieval Europe might seem to present a chaotic and confusing political spectacle, particularly when compared with a land such as China, which by this time had been reunified by centralized imperial rule. Moreover, European rulers rarely sought to maintain the current state of affairs but, rather, campaigned constantly to enlarge their holdings at the expense of their neighbors. As a result, the political history of medieval Europe was a complicated affair. Yet the regional states of the high middle ages effectively tended to public affairs in limited regions. In doing so, they fashioned alternatives to large, centralized empires as a form of political organization.

# ECONOMIC GROWTH AND SOCIAL DEVELOPMENT

As regional states provided increasingly effective political organization, medieval Europe experienced dramatic economic growth and social development. The economic revival closely resembled the processes that in an earlier era had strengthened China, India, and the Islamic world. Increased agricultural production, urbanization, manufacturing, and trade transformed Europe into a powerful society and drew it once again into commercial relationships with distant lands, as the example of the Polo family's travel attests.

## Growth of the Agricultural Economy

As in China, India, and the Islamic world during the early postclassical era, a dramatic increase in agricultural yields was the foundation of economic growth and social development in medieval Europe. Several developments help to account for this increased agricultural production: the opening of new lands to cultivation, improved agricultural techniques, the use of new tools and technologies, and the introduction of new crops.

**Expansion of Arable Land** Beginning in the late tenth century, as local lords pacified their territories and put an end to invasions, Europe began to experience population pressure.

In this painting from the late fifteenth century, the lord of the manor (in robes) watches his laborers harvest hay and cut wood.
Photo 12/Archives Snark/Alamy Stock Photo

In response serfs and monks cleared forests, drained swamps, and increased the amount of land devoted to agriculture. At first, some lords opposed those efforts because they reduced the amount of land available for game preserves, where nobles enjoyed hunting wild animals. Gradually, however, the lords realized that expanding agricultural production would yield higher taxes and increase their own wealth. By the early twelfth century, lords were encouraging the expansion of cultivation, and the process gathered momentum.

**Improved Agricultural Techniques** Meanwhile, reliance on improved methods of cultivation and better agricultural technology led to significantly higher productivity. During the high middle ages, European cultivators refined and improved their techniques in the interests of larger yields. They experimented with new crops and with different cycles of crop rotation to ensure the most abundant harvests possible without compromising the fertility of the soil. They increased cultivation especially of beans, which not only provided dietary protein but also enriched the land because of their property of fixing nitrogen in the soils where they grow. They kept more domestic animals, which not only performed crucial farm labor such as plowing the fields but also served as sources of food and enriched fields with their droppings. They dug ponds in which they raised fish, which provided yet another dietary supplement. By the thirteenth century, observation and experimentation with new crops and new techniques had vastly increased understanding of agricultural affairs. News of those discoveries circulated widely throughout Europe in books and treatises on household economics and agricultural methods. Written in vernacular languages for lay readers, these works helped to publicize innovations, which in turn led to increased agricultural productivity.

**New Tools and Technologies** During the high middle ages, European peoples expanded their use of water mills and heavy plows, which had appeared during the early middle ages, and also introduced new tools and technologies. Two items in particular—the horseshoe and the horse collar—made it possible to increase sharply the amount of land that cultivators could work. Horseshoes helped to prevent softened and split hooves on horses that tramped through moist European soils. Horse collars—which had been in use in China since the third century—placed the burden of a heavy load on an animal's chest and shoulders rather than its neck and enabled horses to pull heavy plows without choking. Thus Europeans could hitch their plows to horses rather than to slower oxen and bring more land under the plow.

**New Crops** Expansion of land under cultivation, improved methods of cultivation, and the use of new tools and technologies combined to increase both the quantity and the quality of food supplies. During the early middle ages, the European diet consisted almost entirely of grains and grain products such as gruel and bread. During the centuries from 1000 to 1300, meat, dairy products, fish, vegetables, and legumes such as beans and peas became much more prominent in the European

## How the Past Shapes the Future

### The Diffusion of Technologies

Scholars believe that the emergence of the horse collar in Europe was a complex phenomenon, with the collar itself coming to northern Europe via central Asia, and the breast strap arriving from north Africa via Islamic Iberia. The horse collar was key to the increased agricultural productivity of Europeans by the thirteenth century. Because we know that agricultural productivity was an important factor in allowing Europeans to engage more consistently with regions outside Europe, consider the role of technological innovations in shaping the long-term future of regions around the world.

Increasing specialization of labor and an expansion of urban centers led to a dramatic increase in the production of wool and other textiles. This illustration shows merchants cutting and sewing woolen fabrics while customers shop for goods. What was the impact of the increased trade in woolen products on economic development throughout Europe during this period?
DEA /A. VILLANI/DeAgostini/Getty Images

diet, though without displacing grains as staple foods. Spain, Italy, and other Mediterranean lands benefited also from widespread cultivation of crops that had earlier been disseminated through the Islamic world: hard durum wheat, rice, spinach, artichokes, eggplant, lemons, limes, oranges, and melons all became prominent items in Mediterranean diets during the high middle ages.

**Population Growth** As in other lands, increased agricultural productivity supported rapid population growth in medieval Europe. In 800 C.E., during the Carolingian era, European population stood at about twenty-nine million. By 1000, when regional states had ended invasions and restored order, it had edged up to thirty-six million. During the next few centuries, as the agricultural economy expanded, population surged. By 1100 it had reached forty-four million; by 1200 it had risen to fifty-eight million, an increase of more than 30 percent within one century; and by 1300 it had grown an additional 36 percent, to seventy-nine million. During the fourteenth century, epidemic plague severely reduced populations and disrupted economies in Europe as well as Asia and north Africa—a development discussed in chapter 21. Between 1000 and 1300, however, rapid demographic growth helped stimulate a vigorous revival of towns and trade in medieval Europe.

## The Revival of Towns and Trade

**Urbanization** With abundant supplies of food, European society was able to support large numbers of urban residents—artisans, crafts workers, merchants, and professionals. Attracted by urban opportunities, peasants and serfs from the countryside flocked to established cities and founded new towns at strategically located sites. Cities founded during Roman times, such as Paris, London, and Toledo, again became thriving centers of government and business, and new urban centers emerged from Venice in northern Italy to Bergen on the west coast of Norway. Northern Italy and Flanders (the northwestern part of modern Belgium) experienced especially strong urbanization. For the first time since the fall of the Western Roman Empire, cities began to play a major role in European economic and social development.

**Textile Production** The growth of towns and cities brought about increasing specialization of labor, which in turn resulted in a dramatic expansion of manufacturing and trade. Manufacturing concentrated especially on the production of wool textiles. The cities of Italy and Flanders in particular became lively centers for the spinning, weaving, and dyeing of wool. Trade in wool products helped to fuel economic development throughout Europe. By the twelfth century the counts of Champagne in northern France sponsored fairs that operated almost year-round and that served as vast marketplaces where merchants from all parts of Europe compared and exchanged goods.

**Mediterranean Trade** The revival of urban society was most pronounced in Italy, which was geographically well

Genoese bankers change money and check the accounts of their clients in this fourteenth-century manuscript illustration. Album/Alamy Stock Photo

situated to participate in the trade networks of the Mediterranean basin. During the tenth century the cities of Amalfi and Venice served as ports for merchants engaged in trade with Byzantine and Muslim partners in the eastern Mediterranean. During the next century the commercial networks of the Mediterranean widened to embrace Genoa, Pisa, Naples, and other Italian cities. Italian merchants exchanged salt, olive oil, wine, wool fabrics, leather products, and glass for luxury goods such as gems, spices, silk, and other goods from India, southeast Asia, and China that Muslim merchants brought to eastern Mediterranean markets.

As trade expanded, Italian merchants established colonies in the major ports and commercial centers of the Mediterranean and the Black Sea. By the thirteenth century, Venetian and Genoese merchants maintained large communities in Constantinople, Alexandria, Cairo, Damascus, and the Black Sea ports of Tana, Caffa, and Trebizond. Caffa was in fact the first destination of the Venetian brothers Niccolò and Maffeo Polo when they embarked on their commercial venture of 1260. Those trading posts enabled them to deal with Muslim merchants engaged in the Indian Ocean and overland trade with India, southeast Asia, and China. By the mid-thirteenth century the Polos and a few other Italian merchants were beginning to venture beyond the eastern Mediterranean region to central Asia, India, and China in search of commercial opportunities.

**The Hanseatic League** Although medieval trade was most active in the Mediterranean basin, a lively commerce grew up also in the northern seas. The Baltic Sea and the North Sea were sites of a particularly well-developed trade network known as the **Hanseatic League**, or more simply as the Hansa—an association of trading cities stretching from Novgorod in Russia to London and embracing all the significant commercial centers of Poland, northern Germany, and Scandinavia. The Hansa dominated trade in grain, fish, furs, timber, and pitch from northern Europe. The fairs of Champagne and the Rhine, the Danube, and other major European rivers linked the Hansa trade network with that of the Mediterranean.

**Improved Business Techniques** As in postclassical China and the Islamic world, a rapidly increasing volume of trade encouraged the development of credit, banking, and new forms of business organization in Europe. Bankers issued letters of credit to merchants traveling to distant markets, thus freeing them from the risk and inconvenience of carrying cash or bullion. Having arrived at their destinations, merchants exchanged their letters of credit for merchandise or cash in the local currency. In the absence of credit and banking networks, it would have been impossible for merchants to trade on a large scale.

Meanwhile, merchants devised new ways of spreading and pooling the risks of commercial investments. They entered into partnerships with other merchants, and they limited the liability of partners to the extent of their individual investments. The limitation on individual liability encouraged the formation of commercial partnerships, thus further stimulating the European economy.

## Social Change

**The Three Estates** Medieval social commentators frequently held that European society embraced **three estates** or classes: "those who pray, those who fight, and those who work." Those who prayed were clergy of the Roman Catholic

**Hanseatic** (han-see-AT-ik)

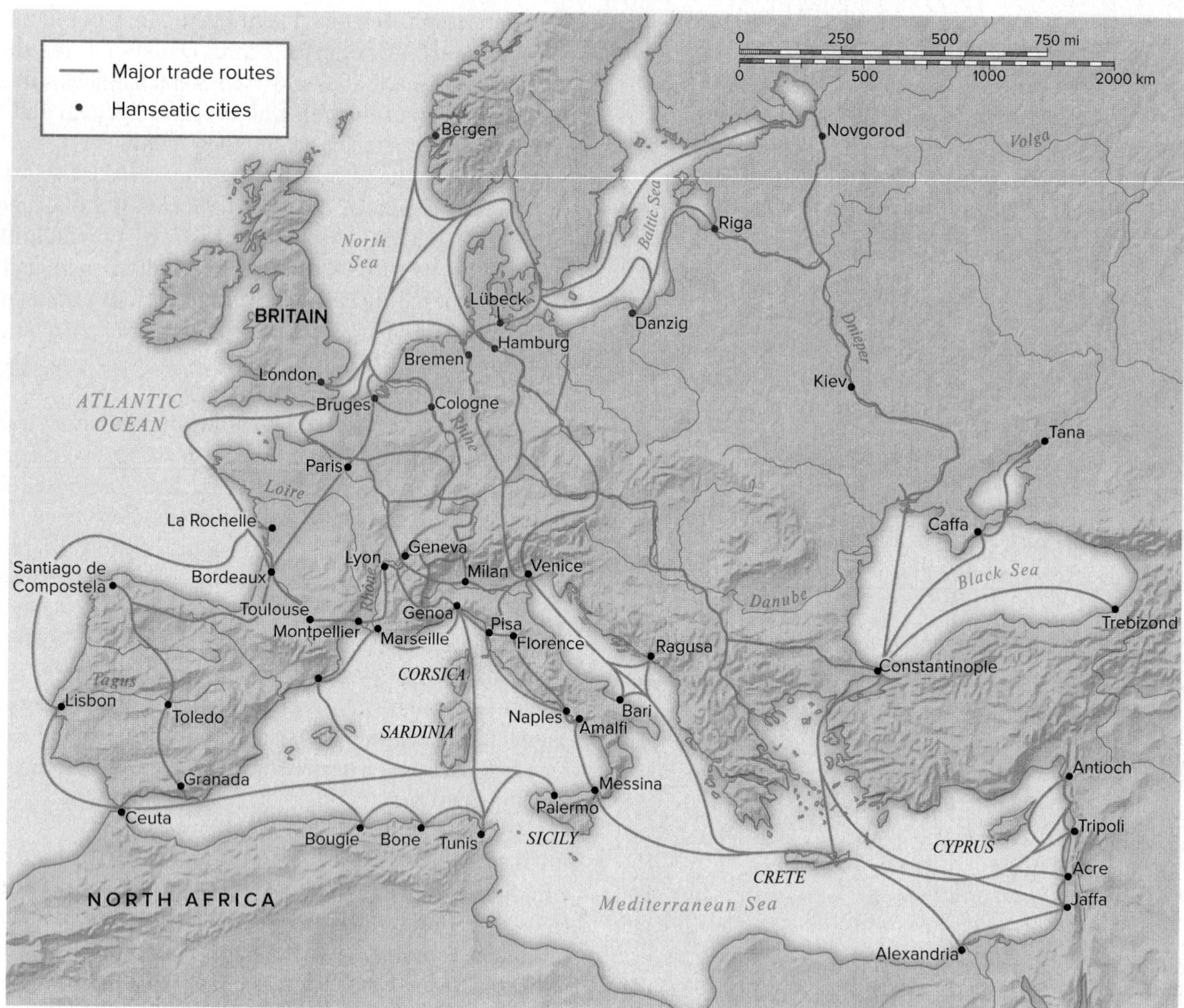


## MAP 7.2 Major trade routes of medieval Europe.

By the eleventh century, overland, river, and maritime trade routes created a commercial network that linked all parts of Europe. These routes also facilitated trade between European Christians and Muslims in the Mediterranean basin and southwest Asia.

***What does the proliferation of trading routes and cities suggest about the state of the medieval European economy?***

church. From humble parish priests to bishops, cardinals, and popes, the clergy constituted a spiritual estate owing its loyalty to the church rather than secular rulers. The fighters came from the ranks of nobles. They inherited their positions in society and received an education that concentrated on equestrian skills and military arts. Finally, there were those who worked—the vast majority of the population—who mostly cultivated land as peasants dependent for protection on lords, those who fought.

The formula dividing society neatly into three classes, though a simplification, captures some important truths about medieval Europe. It clearly reflects a society marked by political, social, and economic inequality: although they did not necessarily lead lives of luxury, those who prayed and those who fought enjoyed rights and honors denied to those who worked. Though bound by secular law, for example, clerics were members of an international spiritual society before they were subjects of a lord, and if they became involved in legal difficulties, they normally faced courts of law administered by the church rather than secular rulers. For their part the nobles mostly lived off the surplus production of dependent peasants and serfs, and lived in much greater comfort than "those who worked."

**Chivalry** Again though expressing some truths, the formula overlooks processes that brought considerable change to medieval European society. Within the ranks of the nobles, **chivalry** was an informal but widely recognized code of ethics and behavior considered appropriate for nobles. Church officials originally promoted the chivalric code in an effort to curb

## What's Left Out?

One of the things usually left out of surveys of most pre-modern histories is what life was like on a day-to-day basis for the majority of people. In the case of Europe during the Middle Ages (and in much of the rest of the world, too), by far the largest number of people were peasants and village-dwellers. Their lives were often difficult; full of hard work; and dependent on unpredictable things like the seasons, the weather, and the harvest. Because they were generally not literate, most left no records of their own. Historians can therefore only catch glimpses of them through sources like church records, which tell us when people were born, when they died, when they married, and when they had children. But some sources, such as coroner's records, can give us a taste of some of the everyday hazards of life in the Middle Ages. Coroners in England, for example, were required to investigate all unexpected deaths. A sample of coroners' records from one English county in the thirteenth century included multiple instances of accidental drowning in wells or rivers, lethal scalding after falling into vats of boiling water for laundry, and deaths when cooking fires caused houses to burn down. While these records do not tell us what people were thinking, they do allow us to get a sense for both the effort and the danger involved in performing even the simplest tasks—such as drinking, washing, and cooking—during the Middle Ages. Consider how much of the human experience is left out when we focus mainly on sources kept by the tiny minority of European people in the Middle Ages who were from literate, noble, or elite backgrounds.

*Source:* Emilie Amt, Women's Lives in Medieval Europe: A Sourcebook (Routledge, 2010).

### Thinking Critically About Sources

1. In addition to indicating various "hazards of life," what would be the importance of statistics gleaned from church and court records?
2. Given the number of dangers during the medieval period, what can you infer about attitudes toward life and death?
3. Why would the church play an important role in the lives of peasants?

fighting within Christendom. By the twelfth century the ritual by which a young man became initiated into the nobility as a knight commonly called for the candidate to place his sword upon a church altar and pledge his service to God. Thus, rather than seeking wealth and power, the noble who observed the chivalric code was supposed to devote himself to the causes of order, piety, and the Christian faith.

**Troubadours** Aristocratic women found the chivalric code much to their liking. Instead of emphasizing the code's religious dimensions, however, they promoted refined behavior and tender, respectful relations between the sexes. Reflections of their interests survive in the songs and poems of the **troubadours,** a class of traveling poets, minstrels, and entertainers whom aristocratic women enthusiastically patronized. The troubadours, who were most active in southern France and northern Italy, drew inspiration from a long tradition of love poetry produced in nearby Muslim Spain. Many troubadours visited the expanding Christian kingdoms of Spain, where they heard love poems and songs from servants, slaves, and musicians of Muslim ancestry. Enchanted by that refined literature, they began to produce similar verses for their own aristocratic patrons.

**Eleanor of Aquitaine** During the late twelfth and thirteenth centuries, troubadours traveled from one aristocratic court to another, where noblewomen rewarded them for singing songs and reciting verses that celebrated passionate love between a man and a woman. Troubadours flocked especially to Poitiers, where **Eleanor of Aquitaine** (1122–1204) liberally supported romantic poets and entertainers. Eleanor was the wealthiest and most powerful woman of her day, at different times the wife of two kings and the mother of three more. She used her influence to encourage the cultivation of good manners, refinement, and romantic love. The troubadours' performances did not instantly transform rough warriors into polished courtiers. Over the long term, however, the code of chivalry and the romantic poetry and song presented at aristocratic courts gradually softened the rough manners of the nobility.

**Independent Cities** Social change also touched those who worked. By the twelfth century the ranks of workers included not only peasants but also increasing numbers of merchants, artisans, crafts workers, and professionals such as physicians and lawyers, who filled the growing towns of medieval Europe. The expansion of the urban working population promoted the development of towns and cities as jurisdictions that fit awkwardly in the framework of the medieval political order. Because of their military power, lords could dominate small towns and tax their wealth. As towns grew larger, however, urban populations were increasingly able to resist the demands of nobles and guide their own affairs. By the late eleventh century, inhabitants of prosperous towns were demanding that local lords grant them charters of incorporation that exempted them from political regulation, allowed them to manage their own affairs, and abolished taxes and tolls on commerce within the urban district. Sometimes groups of cities organized

Eleanor of Aquitaine on horseback, from a thirteenth-century fresco in the Chapel of St. Radegund, France.
De Agostini Picture Library/Getty Images

leagues to advance their commercial interests, as in the case of the Hansa, or to protect themselves against the encroachments of political authorities.

**Guilds** The cities of medieval Europe were by no means egalitarian societies: cities attracted noble migrants as well as peasants and serfs, and urban nobles often dominated city affairs. Yet medieval towns and cities also reflected the interests and contributions of the working people. Merchants and workers in all the arts, crafts, and trades organized **guilds** that regulated the production and sale of goods within their jurisdictions. By the thirteenth century the guilds had come to control much of the urban economy of medieval Europe. They established standards of quality for manufactured goods, sometimes even requiring members to adopt specific techniques of production, and they determined the prices at which members had to sell their products. In an effort to maintain a balance between supply and demand—and to protect their members' interests—they also regulated the entry of new workers into their groups.

Guilds had social as well as economic significance. They provided a focus for friendship and mutual support in addition to work. Guild members regularly socialized with one another, and prosperous guilds often built large halls where members held meetings, banquets, and sometimes boisterous drinking parties. Guilds came to the aid of members and their families by providing financial and moral support for those who fell ill. They also arranged funeral services for their deceased and provided support for survivors. Quite apart from regulating work, then, guilds constituted a kind of social infrastructure that made it possible for medieval cities to function while also enhancing the welfare of their members.

**Urban Women** Women who lived in the countryside continued to perform the same kinds of tasks that their ancestors tended to in the early middle ages: household duties, weaving, and the care of domestic animals. But medieval towns and cities offered fresh opportunities for women as well as for men. In the patriarchal society of medieval Europe, few routes to public authority were open to women, but in the larger towns and cities women worked alongside men as butchers, brewers, bakers, candle makers, fishmongers, shoemakers, gemsmiths, innkeepers, launderers, money changers, merchants, and occasionally physicians and pharmacists. Women dominated some occupations, particularly those involving textiles and decorative arts, such as sewing, spinning, weaving, and the making of hats, wigs, and fur garments.

Most guilds admitted women into their ranks, and some guilds had exclusively female memberships. In thirteenth-century Paris, for example, there were approximately one hundred guilds. Six of them admitted only women, but eighty others included women as well as men among their members. Despite the persistence of patriarchal social structures, the increasing prominence of women in European society illustrates the significance of towns and cities as agents of social change in medieval Europe.

## EUROPEAN CHRISTIANITY DURING THE HIGH MIDDLE AGES

Throughout the middle ages, Christianity guided European thought on religious, moral, and ethical matters—Eastern Orthodox Christianity in the Byzantine Empire and Roman Catholic Christianity in western Europe. Representatives of the Orthodox and Roman Catholic churches administered the

This painting from 1568 depicts a woman fishmonger working alongside her husband.
Peter Horree/Alamy Stock Photo

rituals associated with birth, marriage, and death. Most of the art, literature, and music of the high middle ages drew inspiration from Christian doctrines and stories. Just as mosques and minarets defined the skylines of Muslim cities, the spires of churches and cathedrals dominated the landscape of medieval Europe, testifying visually to the importance of religion and the pervasive presence of the Eastern Orthodox and Roman Catholic churches.

## Schools, Universities, and Scholastic Theology

During the early middle ages, European society was not stable and wealthy enough to support institutions of advanced education. Monasteries sometimes maintained schools that provided a rudimentary education, and political leaders occasionally supported scholars who lived at their courts, but very few schools offered formal education beyond an elementary level. In the absence of a widely observed curriculum or course of study, early medieval scholars drew their inspiration from the Bible and from major spokesmen of the early Christian church such as St. Augustine of Hippo.

**Cathedral Schools** During the high middle ages, economic development sharply increased the wealth of Europe and made more resources available for education. Meanwhile, an increasingly complex society created a demand for educated individuals who could deal with complicated political, legal, and theological issues. Beginning in the early eleventh century, bishops and archbishops in France and northern Italy organized schools in their cathedrals and invited well-known scholars to serve as master teachers. Schools in the cathedrals of Paris, Chartres, and Bologna in particular attracted students from all parts of Europe.

By the twelfth century the **cathedral schools** had established formal curricula based on writings in Latin, the official language of the Roman Catholic church. Instruction concentrated on the liberal arts, especially literature and philosophy. Students read the Bible and the writings of the church fathers, such as St. Augustine, St. Jerome, and St. Ambrose, as well as classical Latin literature and the few works of Plato and Aristotle that were available in Latin translation. Some cathedral schools also offered advanced instruction in law, medicine, and theology.

**Universities** About the mid-twelfth century, students and teachers organized academic guilds and persuaded political authorities to grant charters guaranteeing their rights. Student guilds demanded fair treatment for students from townspeople, who sometimes charged excessive rates for room and board, and called on their teachers to provide rigorous, high-quality instruction. Faculty guilds sought to vest teachers with the right to bestow academic degrees, which served as licenses to teach in other cities, and to control the curriculum in their institutions. These guilds had the effect of transforming cathedral schools into universities. The first universities were those of Bologna, Paris, and Salerno—noted for instruction in law, theology, and medicine, respectively—but by the late thirteenth century, universities had appeared also in Rome, Naples, Seville, Salamanca, Oxford, Cambridge, and other cities throughout Europe.

**The Influence of Aristotle** The evolution of the university coincided with the rediscovery of the works of Aristotle. Western European scholars of the early middle ages knew only a few of Aristotle's minor works that were available in Latin translation. Byzantine scholars knew Aristotle in the original Greek, but they rarely had any dealings with their Roman Catholic counterparts. During the high middle ages, as commerce and communication increased between Byzantine Orthodox and Roman Catholic Christians, western Europeans learned about Aristotle's thought and obtained Latin translations from Byzantine philosophers. Western European scholars also learned about Aristotle through Muslim philosophers who appreciated the power of his thought and had most of his works translated into Arabic. Christian and Jewish scholars in Sicily and Spain became aware of those Arabic translations, which they retranslated into Latin. Although the resulting works had their flaws—they filtered Aristotle's original Greek through both Arabic and Latin—they made Aristotle's thought accessible to Western European scholars.

**Scholasticism: St. Thomas Aquinas** During the thirteenth century, understanding of Aristotle's thought and Latin translations of his works spread throughout Europe, and they profoundly influenced almost all branches of thought. The most notable result was the emergence of **scholasticism,** which sought to synthesize the beliefs and values of Christianity with the logical rigor of Greek philosophy. The most famous of the scholastic theologians was **St. Thomas Aquinas** (1225–1274), who spent most of his career teaching at the University of Paris. While holding fervently to his Christian convictions, St. Thomas believed that Aristotle had understood and explained the workings of the world better than any other thinker of any era. St. Thomas saw no contradiction between Aristotle and Christian revelation but, rather, viewed them as complementary authorities: Aristotle provided the most powerful analysis of the world according to human reason, and Christianity explained the world and human life as the results of a divine plan. By combining Aristotle's rational power with the teachings of Christianity, St. Thomas expected to formulate the most truthful and persuasive system of thought possible.

In St. Thomas's view, for example, belief in the existence of God did not depend exclusively on an individual's faith. By drawing on Aristotle, St. Thomas believed, it was possible to prove rationally that God exists. Aristotle himself never recognized a personal deity such as the Jewish and Christian God,

**Aquinas** (uh-KWIY-nuhs)

but he argued that a conscious agent had set the world in motion. St. Thomas borrowed Aristotle's arguments and identified the conscious agent with the Jewish and Christian God, who outlined his plan for the world in the Hebrew scriptures and the Christian New Testament. Thus, as expressed in the thought of St. Thomas Aquinas, scholastic theology represented the harmonization of Aristotle with Christianity and the synthesis of reason and faith. Like the neo-Confucianism of Zhu Xi or the Islamic philosophy of Ibn Rushd, scholastic theology reinterpreted inherited beliefs in light of the most advanced knowledge of the time.

A manuscript illustration depicts a professor, at top left, lecturing in a medieval German university. About half the students listen and take notes diligently, while the others catch up on their sleep or chat with friends.
Album/Oronoz/Newscom

## Popular Religion

St. Thomas and the other scholastic theologians addressed a sophisticated, intellectual elite, not the common people of medieval Europe. The popular masses neither knew nor cared much about Aristotle. For their purposes, Christianity was important primarily as a set of beliefs and rituals that gave meaning to individual lives and that bound them together into coherent communities. Thus formal doctrine and theology did not appeal to popular audiences as much as the ceremonies and observances that involved individuals in the life of a larger community—and that also brought benefits in the form of supernatural aid or protection for an individual's crops or family.

**Sacraments** Popular piety generally entailed observance of the sacraments and devotion to the saints recognized by the Roman Catholic church. Sacraments are holy rituals that bring spiritual blessings on the observants. The church recognized seven sacraments, including baptism, matrimony, penance, and the Eucharist. Most important was the Eucharist, during which priests offered a ritual meal commemorating Jesus' last meal with his disciples before his trial and execution by Roman authorities. In addition to preparing individuals for salvation and symbolizing their membership in a holy community, the Eucharist had mundane uses: popular beliefs held that the sacrament would protect individuals from sudden death and advance their worldly interests.

**Devotion to Saints** Popular religion also took the form of devotion to the saints. According to church teachings, saints were human beings who had led such exemplary lives that God held them in special esteem. As a result, they enjoyed special influence with heavenly authorities and were able to intervene on behalf of individuals living in the world. Medieval Europeans constantly prayed for saints to look after their spiritual interests and to ensure their admission to heaven. Often, they also invoked the aid of saints who had reputations for helping living people as well as souls of the dead. Tradition held that certain saints could cure diseases, relieve toothaches, or guide sailors through storms to a port.

**The Virgin Mary** During the high middle ages, the most popular saint was always the Virgin Mary, mother of Jesus, who personified the Christian ideal of womanhood, love, and sympathy, and who reportedly lavished aid on her devotees. According to a widely circulated story, the Virgin once even spared a criminal from hanging when he called upon her name. During the twelfth and thirteenth centuries, Europeans dedicated hundreds of churches and cathedrals to the Virgin, among them the splendid cathedral of Notre Dame ("Our Lady") of Paris.

**Saints' Relics** Medieval Europeans went to great lengths to express their adoration of the Virgin and other saints through veneration of their **relics** and physical remains, widely believed to retain the powers associated with those holy individuals. Churches assembled vast collections of relics, such as clothes, locks of hair, teeth, and bones of famous saints. Especially esteemed were relics associated with Jesus or the Virgin, such as the crown of thorns that Jesus reportedly wore during his crucifixion or drops of the Virgin's milk miraculously preserved in a vial. The practice of assembling relics clearly opened the door to fraud, but medieval Europeans avidly continued to admire and venerate saints' relics.

**Pilgrimage** Some collections of relics became famous well beyond their own regions. Like Muslims making the hajj, pilgrims trekked long distances to honor the saints the relics represented. Throughout the high middle ages, streams of pilgrims visited two European cities in particular—Rome in Italy and Compostela in Spain—and some ventured even farther to Jerusalem and the holy land of Christian origins. Rome was the spiritual center of western Christian society: apart from the popes and the central administration of the Roman Catholic church, the relics of St. Peter and St. Paul, the two

# SOURCES FROM THE PAST

## Margery Kempe's Pilgrimage to Jerusalem

*Margery Kempe (1373–1438) was the daughter of a five-time mayor of the bustling city of Bishop's (now King's) Lynn in Norfolk, England. She was not a noble, but a member of the growing urban elite of the time. She married John Kempe in 1393 and had fourteen children. Jesus Christ began to appear to her in visions shortly after the birth of her first child, and she continued to experience visions for much of her adult life. In 1414, she began the first of her many long-distance pilgrimages to Christian religious sites, visiting both Rome and Jerusalem over the course of a year. Although she was not literate, she wanted her story to be preserved and dictated her story to a priest before she died. Her Book of Margery Kempe may be the first known autobiography in English. Below, Margery describes reaching the holy city of Jerusalem.*

**And so they went forth** into the Holy Land till they might see Jerusalem. And when this creature [Kempe] saw Jerusalem, riding on an ass, she thanked God with all her heart, praying him for his mercy that like as he had brought her to see this earthly city Jerusalem, he would grant her grace to see the blissful city Jerusalem above, the city of Heaven. . . .

> Note that Kempe is asking God to receive her in heaven after her death. What might this tell us about the concerns people in the Middle Ages might have had about mortality?

Then they went to the Temple in Jerusalem, and they were let in that one day at evensong time [the time of evening prayers for Christians] and they abide there till the next day at evensong time. Then the friars lifted up a cross and led the pilgrims about from one place to another where our Lord had suffered his pains and his passions, every man and woman bearing a wax candle in their hand. And the friars always as they went about told them what our Lord suffered in every place. And the foresaid creature [Kempe] wept and sobbed so plentivously [sic] as though she had seen our Lord with her bodily eye suffering his Passion at that time. Before her in her soul she saw him verily by contemplation, and that caused her to have compassion. And when they came up onto the Mount of Calvary she fell down that she might not stand nor kneel but wallowed and wrested with her body, spreading her arms abroad, and cried with a loud voice as though her heart should 'a burst asunder, for in the city of her soul she saw verily and freshly how our Lord was crucified. Before her face she heard and saw in her ghostly sight the mourning of our Lady, of St. John and of Mary Magdalene, and of many other that loved our Lord. And she had so great compassion and so great pain to see our Lord's pain that she might not keep herself from crying and roaring. . .

> Why did the friars' actions have such an effect on Kempe? What do you think she might have been trying to convey about her faith here?

> While it was not unusual for mystics to receive visions of god and the saints, Kempe was unusual in her loud prostrations. What might her companions have thought of her response?

### For Further Reflection

- Margery Kempe was one of a number of Christian mystical women in the Middle Ages who were neither nobles nor nuns. What does her experience as a traveler from England all the way to Jerusalem in 1414–1415 tell us about the increasing integration of Europeans with the wider world? What kinds of things can it tell us about European women in the Middle Ages?
- Why do you think Margery Kempe's autobiography is not well known?
- What are the contributions and cautions about using autobiography as a historical source?

*Source:* Joel Fredell, editor. The Book of Margery Kempe, folio 33. http://english.selu.edu/humanitiesonline/kempe/legal.php. Translated into modern English from the original.

most prominent apostles of early Christianity, rested in the churches of Rome. Compostela stood on the very periphery of Christian society, in a remote corner of northwestern Spain. Yet the relics of St. James preserved in the cathedral of Santiago de Compostela exercised a powerful attraction for the pious, who made Compostela the second-most popular **pilgrimage** destination of medieval Europe. Some devoted pilgrims also visited Jerusalem and the sites associated with the origins of Christianity: spiritual as well as commercial interests called Europeans into the larger world.

The making of pilgrimages became so common during the high middle ages that a travel industry emerged to serve the needs of pilgrims. Inns dotted the routes leading to popular churches and shrines, and guides shepherded groups of

The cathedral of Notre Dame de Paris ("Our Lady of Paris"), viewed from the south. Built in the second half of the twelfth century, the cathedral is one of the triumphs of the Gothic style of architecture that became popular in western Europe during the medieval period. The cathedral suffered serious damage in a fire that broke out in April 2019.
Catherine Ursillo/Science Source

pilgrims to religious sites and explained their significance. There were even guidebooks that pointed out the major attractions along pilgrims' routes and warned them of difficult terrain and unscrupulous scoundrels who took advantage of visitors. Geoffrey Chaucer's well-known *Canterbury Tales* is, in fact, a collection of stories about a group of pilgrims traveling together to the English town of Canterbury during the fourteenth century.

## Reform Movements and Popular Heresies

Although veneration of the saints and the making of pilgrimages indicated a deep reservoir of piety, popular religion also reflected the social and economic development of medieval Europe. Particularly in western Europe, as wealth increased, several groups of particularly devout individuals feared that European society was becoming excessively materialistic. Even the Roman Catholic church seemed tainted by materialism. Benedictine monasteries, in which monks originally observed the virtues of poverty, chastity, and obedience, had in many cases become comfortable retreats where privileged individuals led leisurely lives. Meanwhile, the central administration of the Roman church expanded dramatically as lawyers and bureaucrats ran the church's affairs and sought ways to swell its treasury.

**Dominicans and Franciscans** The devout responded to this state of affairs in several ways. Working within the Roman church, some individuals organized movements designed to champion spiritual over materialistic values. Most prominent of them were St. Dominic (1170–1221) and St. Francis (1182–1226). During the thirteenth century St. Dominic and St. Francis founded orders of mendicants (beggars), known as the Dominican and Franciscan friars, who would have no personal possessions and would have to beg for their food and other needs from audiences to whom they preached. Mendicants were especially active in towns and cities, where they addressed throngs of recently arrived migrants whose numbers were so large that existing urban churches and clergy could not serve them well. The **Dominicans** and the **Franciscans** also worked zealously to combat heretical (nonconforming) movements and to persuade heretics to return to the Roman Catholic church.

**Popular Heresy** Whereas the Dominicans and the Franciscans worked within the church, others rejected the Roman Catholic church altogether and organized alternative religious movements. During the twelfth and thirteenth centuries in particular, several popular movements protested the increasing materialism of European society. The Waldensians, who were most active in southern France and northern Italy, despised the Roman Catholic clergy as immoral and corrupt, and they advocated modest and simple lives. They asserted the right of the laity to preach and administer sacraments—functions that the church reserved exclusively for priests—and they did not hesitate to criticize the church on the basis of biblical teachings. Although church authorities declared them heretical, the Waldensians continued to attract enthusiastic participants: a few Waldensians survive even today.

**Bogomils and Cathars** Some popular heresies flourished in both the Byzantine Empire and western Europe. As long-distance trade networks linked Mediterranean lands, alternative religious ideas spread readily throughout the region. Reviving the dualistic views of the ancient Manichaeans, the **Bogomils** of Bulgaria and Byzantium viewed the world as a site of unrelenting, cosmic struggle between the forces of good and evil. In a quest for purity and spiritual perfection, they despised the material world and adopted an ascetic regime,

St. Francis of Assisi was the son of a wealthy merchant in central Italy, but he abandoned the comforts that he inherited and pledged himself to a life of poverty and preaching. Stories represented in this fresco from the basilica of St. Francis at Assisi report that he preached to the birds and encouraged them to sing in praise of God.
The Print Collector/Heritage Images/Alamy Stock Photo

renouncing wealth, marriage, and material pleasures. Their movement grew rapidly in the late tenth century, and in the eleventh century the **Cathars** (sometimes called Albigensians) were promoting similar views in southern France and northern Italy. Bogomils and Cathars rejected official churches, which they considered hopelessly corrupt, along with their priests and sacraments.

Both in Byzantium and in western Europe, established authorities took a dim view of these popular movements, which they regarded as threats to cultural stability and religious orthodoxy. Beginning in the late eleventh century, government and church officials teamed up and mounted ruthless campaigns to destroy the Bogomils and the Cathars. By the fourteenth century, Bogomils and Cathars survived in only a few remote regions of Europe.

# THE MEDIEVAL EXPANSION OF EUROPE

During the high middle ages, the relationship between western European peoples and their neighbors underwent dramatic change. Powerful regional states, economic expansion, and demographic growth all strengthened European society, and church officials encouraged the colonization of pagan and Muslim lands as a way to extend the influence of Roman Catholic Christianity. Beginning about the mid-eleventh century, Europeans embarked on expansive ventures on several fronts: Atlantic, Baltic, and Mediterranean. Scandinavian seafarers ventured into the Atlantic Ocean, establishing colonies in Iceland, Greenland, and even for a short time North America. In the Baltic region, Europeans conquered and introduced Christianity to Prussia, Livonia, Lithuania, and Finland. In the Mediterranean basin, Europeans recaptured Spain and the Mediterranean islands that Muslims had conquered between the eighth and the tenth centuries. Finally, knights from all over Europe mounted enormous campaigns designed to seize the holy land of Palestine from Muslims and place it under Christian authority. As military ventures, the crusades—as they were known—achieved limited success because they brought the holy land into Christian hands only temporarily. Nevertheless, the crusades signaled clearly that Europeans were beginning to play a larger role in the affairs of the eastern hemisphere than they had during the early middle ages.

## Atlantic and Baltic Colonization

**Vinland** When regional states began to emerge and protect western Europe from Viking raids during the ninth and tenth centuries, Scandinavian seafarers turned their attention to the islands of the North Atlantic Ocean. They occupied Iceland beginning in the late ninth century, and at the end of the tenth century a party led by Eric the Red discovered Greenland and established a small colony there. About 1000 C.E. his son Leif Ericsson led another exploratory party south and west of Greenland, arriving eventually at modern Newfoundland in Canada. There the party found plentiful supplies of fish and timber. Because of the wild grapes growing in the region, Leif called it Vinland ("Wine Land"). During the years following Leif's voyage, Greenlanders made several efforts to establish permanent colonies in Vinland.

Since the 1960s, archaeologists in northern Newfoundland have uncovered Scandinavian tools and building foundations dating to the early eleventh century. From this evidence and the stories of maritime ventures preserved in Scandinavian sagas, it is clear that the Greenlanders founded a colony in Newfoundland and maintained it for several decades. Ultimately, they left Vinland—or died there—since they did not have the resources to sustain a settlement over the stormy seas of the North Atlantic Ocean. Nonetheless, the establishment of even a short-lived colony indicated a growing capacity of Europeans to venture into the larger world.

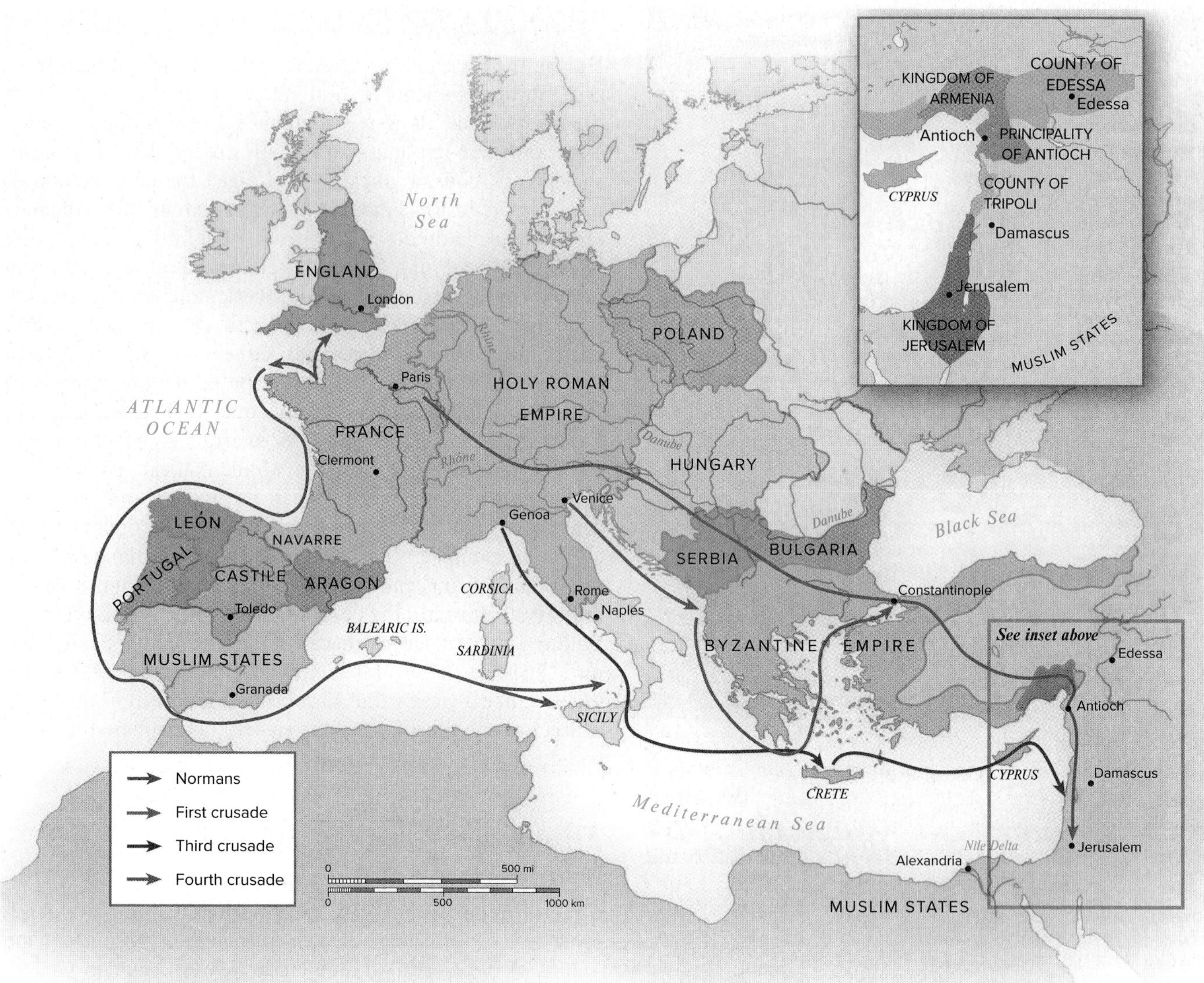


## MAP 7.3 The medieval expansion of Europe, 1000–1250

Compare Map 19.3 with Map 16.3. How can you explain the differences between these two maps?

***What does Map 19.3 suggest about the military and organizational capabilities, strategies, and aims of medieval Europe?***

**Christianity in Scandinavia** While Scandinavians explored the North Atlantic, the Roman Catholic church drew Scandinavia itself into the community of Christian Europe. The kings of Denmark and Norway converted to Christianity in the tenth century. Conversion of their subjects came gradually and with considerable resistance because most held tightly to their inherited traditions. Yet royal support for the Roman Catholic church ensured that Christianity would have a place in Danish and Norwegian societies. In 999 or 1000 the Norwegian colony in Iceland also formally adopted Christianity. Between the twelfth and the fourteenth centuries, Sweden and Finland followed their neighbors into the Christian faith.

**Crusading Orders and Baltic Expansion** In the Baltic lands of Prussia, Livonia, and Lithuania, Christian authority arrived in the wake of military conquest. During the era of crusades, zealous Christians formed a series of hybrid, military-religious orders. The most prominent were the Templars, Hospitallers, and Teutonic Knights, who not only took religious vows but also pledged to devote their lives and efforts to the struggle against Muslims and pagans. The Teutonic Knights were most active in the Baltic region, where they waged military campaigns against the pagan Slavic peoples during the twelfth and thirteenth centuries. Aided by German missionaries, the Knights founded churches and monasteries in the territories they subdued. By the late thirteenth century, the Roman Catholic church had established its presence throughout the Baltic region, which progressively became absorbed into the larger society of Christian Europe.

## The Reconquest of Sicily and Spain

The boundaries of Christian Europe also expanded in the Mediterranean basin. There, Europeans came into conflict with Muslims, whose ancestors had conquered the major Mediterranean islands and most of the Iberian peninsula between the eighth and the tenth centuries. As their society became stronger, Europeans undertook to reconquer those territories and reintegrate them into Christian society.

The crusades involved brutal conflict and atrocities from all sides. In this twelfth-century manuscript illustration, crusaders lob severed enemy heads at Muslims defending a fortress.

The Picture Art Collection/Alamy Stock Photo

**The Reconquest of Sicily** Most important of the islands was Sicily, which Muslims had conquered in the ninth century. During the eleventh century, Norman warriors returned Sicily to Christian hands. The Norman adventurer Robert Guiscard carved out a state for himself in southern Italy while his brother Roger undertook the conquest of Sicily. By 1090, after almost twenty years of conflict, Roger had established his authority throughout the island. Missionaries and clergy soon appeared and reintroduced Roman Catholic Christianity to Sicily. Islam did not disappear immediately: Muslims continued to practice their faith privately, and Muslim scholars in Sicily introduced their Christian counterparts to the Arabic translations of Aristotle that inspired the scholastic philosophers. Over the longer term, however, as Muslims either left Sicily or converted to Christianity, Islam gradually disappeared from the island.

**The Reconquista of Spain** The reconquest of Spain—known as the ***reconquista***—took a much longer time than did the recapture of Sicily. Following the Muslim invasion and conquest of the early eighth century, the caliphate of Córdoba ruled almost all of the Iberian peninsula. A small Christian state survived in Catalonia in the far northeast, and the kingdom of León resisted Muslim advances in the far northwest. The process of *reconquista* began in the 1060s from those Christian toeholds. By 1085 Christian forces had pushed as far south as Toledo, and by 1150 they had recaptured Lisbon and established their authority over half of the peninsula. Their successes lured reinforcements from France and England, and in the first half of the thirteenth century a new round of campaigns brought most of Iberia as well as the Balearic Islands (off the coast of eastern Spain) into Christian hands. Only the kingdom of Granada in the far south of the peninsula remained Muslim. It survived as an outpost of Islam until 1492, when Christian forces mounted a campaign that conquered Granada and completed the *reconquista.*

The political, economic, and demographic strength of Christian Europe helps to explain the reconquests of Sicily and Spain as military ventures. Especially in the case of Spain, however, it is clear that religious concerns also helped to drive the *reconquista.* The popes and other leading clergy of the Roman Catholic church regarded Islam as a threat to Christianity, and they enthusiastically encouraged campaigns against the Muslims. When reconquered territories fell into Christian hands, church officials immediately established bishoprics and asserted Christian authority. They also organized campaigns to convert local populations. Dominican friars were especially active in Spain. They appealed to learned audiences by explaining Christianity in the terms of scholastic theology and arguments derived from Aristotle, whom Muslim intellectuals held in high esteem. When addressing popular audiences, they simply outlined the basic teachings of Christianity and urged their listeners to convert. With the establishment of Christian rule, the Roman Catholic church gradually began to displace Islam in conquered Spain.

***reconquista*** (ray-kohn-KEE-stah)

## The Crusades

The term *crusade* refers to a holy war. It derives from the Latin word *crux,* meaning "cross," the device on which Roman authorities had executed Jesus. When a pope declared a crusade, warriors would "take up the cross" as a symbol of their faith, sew strips of cloth in the form of a cross on the backs of their garments, and venture forth to fight on behalf of Christianity. The wars that Christians fought against pagans in the Baltic and Muslims in the Mediterranean were crusades in this sense of the term, as was the campaign waged by Roman Catholic Christians against Cathar heretics in southern France. In popular usage, though, *crusades* generally refers to the huge expeditions that Roman Catholic Christians mounted in an effort to recapture Palestine, the land of Christian origins, and the holy city of Jerusalem from Muslim authorities.

**Urban II** **Pope Urban II** launched the crusades in 1095. Speaking at the Council of Clermont (in central France), Urban warned church leaders that Muslim Turks were threatening the eastern borders of Christendom. Indeed, the pope had recently received an urgent appeal from the Byzantine emperor, who requested military forces from western Europe to reinforce his own armies as Turkish invaders advanced toward Constantinople. Urban urged European princes to stabilize Christendom's borders and then go further to recapture Jerusalem and restore Christian rule to the holy land. He added emphasis to his appeal with the assertion that "Deus vult"—"God wills it!"

**The First Crusade** Shortly after Pope Urban announced the crusade, French and Norman nobles began to organize a military expedition to the holy land. In late 1096 the crusading armies began the long trek to Palestine. In 1097 and 1098 they captured Edessa, Antioch, and other strategic sites. In 1099 Jerusalem fell to the crusaders, who then proceeded to extend their conquests and carve conquered territories into Christian states.

Although the crusaders did not realize it, hindsight shows that their quick victories came largely because of division and disarray in the ranks of their Muslim foes. The crusaders' successes, however, encouraged Turks, Egyptians, and other Muslims to settle their differences, at least temporarily, in the interests of expelling European Christians from the eastern Mediterranean. By the mid-twelfth century, the crusader communities had come under tremendous pressure. The crusader state of Edessa fell to Turks in 1144, and during the third crusade the Muslim leader Salah al-Din, known to Europeans as **Saladin**, recaptured Jerusalem in 1187. Crusaders maintained several of their enclaves for another century, but Saladin's victories sealed the fate of Christian forces in the eastern Mediterranean.

A fourteenth-century manuscript illustration depicts Muslims burning captured crusaders at the stake.
Album/Alamy Stock Photo

**Later Crusades** Europeans did not immediately concede Palestine to the Muslims. By the mid-thirteenth century, they had launched five major crusades, but none of the later ventures succeeded in reestablishing a Christian presence in Palestine. The fourth crusade (1202–1204) was a particularly demoralizing affair, as crusaders ravaged Constantinople, the seat of Eastern Orthodox Christianity. Nevertheless, even though the later crusades failed in their principal objective, the crusading idea inspired European dreams of conquest in the eastern Mediterranean until the late sixteenth century.

**Consequences of the Crusades** As holy wars intended to reestablish Roman Catholic Christianity in the eastern Mediterranean basin, the crusades were wars of military and political expansion. Yet in the long run, the crusades were much more important for their social, economic, commercial, and cultural consequences. Even as European armies built crusader states in Palestine and Syria, European scholars and missionaries encountered Muslim philosophers and theologians, and European merchants traded eagerly with their Muslim counterparts. The result was a large-scale exchange of ideas, technologies, and trade goods that profoundly influenced European development. Through their sojourns in

**Saladin** (SAHL-uh-din)

Palestine and their regular dealings with Muslims throughout the Mediterranean basin, European Christians became acquainted with the works of Aristotle, Islamic science and astronomy, "Arabic" numerals (which Muslims had borrowed from India), and techniques of paper production (which Muslims had learned from the Chinese). They also learned to appreciate new food and agricultural products such as spices, granulated sugar, coffee, and dates as well as trade goods such as silk products, cotton textiles, carpets, and tapestries.

In the early days of the crusades, Europeans had little to exchange for those products other than rough wool textiles, furs, and timber. During the crusading era, however, demand for the new commodities increased throughout western Europe as large numbers of people developed a taste for goods previously available only to wealthy elites. Seeking to meet the rising demand for luxury goods, Italian merchants developed new products and marketed them in commercial centers and port cities such as Constantinople, Alexandria, Cairo, Damascus, Tana, Caffa, and Trebizond. Thus Niccolò, Maffeo, and Marco Polo traded in gems and jewelry, and other merchants marketed fine woolen textiles or glassware. By the thirteenth century, large numbers of Italian merchants had begun to travel well beyond Egypt, Palestine, and Syria to avoid Muslim intermediaries and to deal directly with the producers of silks and spices in India, China, and southeast Asia. Thus, although the crusades largely failed as military ventures, they encouraged the reintegration of western Europe into the larger economy of the eastern hemisphere.

## CONCLUSION

From 1000 to 1300, Europe underwent thorough political and economic reorganization. Building on foundations laid during the early middle ages, political leaders founded a series of independent regional states. But despite the establishment of the Holy Roman Empire, they did not revive central imperial authority in western Europe. Regional states maintained good order and fostered rapid economic growth, which fostered the development of regional traditions. Beginning in the tenth century, Agricultural improvements brought increased food supplies, which encouraged urbanization, manufacturing, and trade. By the thirteenth century, European peoples traded actively throughout the Mediterranean, Baltic, and North Sea regions encountering new people and ideas. As we saw in the case of Marco Polo and his family, a few plucky merchants even ventured as far away as China in search of commercial opportunities. In the high middle ages, as in the early middle ages, Christianity was the cultural foundation of European society. The church prospered during the high middle ages, and advanced educational institutions such as cathedral schools and universities reinforced the influence of Christianity throughout Europe. Christianity even played a role in European political and military expansion because church officials encouraged crusaders to conquer pagan and Muslim peoples in Baltic and Mediterranean lands. Thus between 1000 and 1300, western European peoples strengthened the traditions of their own society and began in various ways to have regular encounters with their counterparts in other regions of the eastern hemisphere. After a long period of relative isolation, by the end of the high middle ages Europe had become far more integrated with the wider world than in centuries past.

## STUDY TERMS

battle of Manzikert (216)
Bogomils (230)
Capetian (218)
Cathars (231)
cathedral schools (227)
chivalry (224)
*crusades* (234)
Dominicans (230)
Eleanor of Aquitaine (225)
Franciscans (230)
Frederick Barbarossa (218)
guilds (226)
Hanseatic League (223)
Holy Roman Empire (214)
Investiture Contest (217)
Marco Polo (213)
Normans (218)
Otto I (216)
pilgrimage (229)
Pope Urban II (234)
relics (228)
reconquista (233)
Saladin (234)
scholasticism (227)
St. Thomas Aquinas (227)
three estates (223)
theme system (214)
William the Conqueror (218)

## FOR FURTHER READING

Thomas Asbridge. *The Crusades.* New York, 2010. A breezy narrative history of the early crusades.

Robert Bartlett. *The Making of Europe: Conquest, Colonization, and Cultural Change, 950–1350.* Princeton, 1993. A well-documented examination of European expansion from a cultural point of view.

Judith Bennett. *Medieval Europe: A Short History*. New York, 2010. An engaging survey of medieval Europe written by a pioneer in the field.

Rosalind Brooke and Christopher Brooke. *Popular Religion in the Middle Ages: Western Europe, 1000–1300.* London, 1984. Well-illustrated essays on the faith of the masses.

Caroline Walker Bynum. *Holy Feast and Holy Fast: The Religious Significance of Food to Medieval Women.* Berkeley, 1998. A pathbreaking book about the ways women shaped their relationships to religion in the medieval period.

J. R. S. Phillips. *The Medieval Expansion of Europe.* Oxford, 1988. Excellent survey of European ventures in the larger world during the high and late middle ages.

Daniel Power, ed. *The Central Middle Ages.* Oxford, 2006. Seven leading scholars discuss aspects of medieval European history.

Christopher Tyerman. *God's War: A New History of the Crusades.* Cambridge, Mass., 2006. A comprehensive review of crusades throughout Europe and the larger Mediterranean basin.

Elisabeth van Houts, ed. *The Normans in Europe.* Manchester, 2000. Presents English translations of sources illuminating Norman roles in medieval Europe.

Jeffrey Wigelsworth. *Science and Technology in Medieval European Life*. Westport, Conn, 2006. An introductory survey of medieval European technology and scientific thought that also explores the relationship between science and religion.

# CHAPTER 7 AP EXAM PRACTICE

Questions assume cumulative knowledge from this chapter and previous chapters.

## Section I

## Multiple Choice Questions

Use the image below and your knowledge of world history to answer questions 1 – 3.

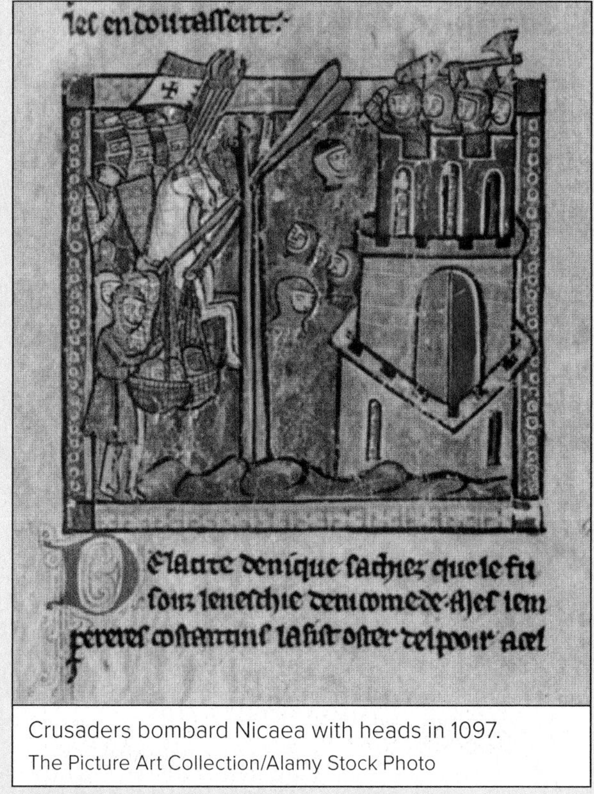

Crusaders bombard Nicaea with heads in 1097.
The Picture Art Collection/Alamy Stock Photo

1. This image is best understood in context of which historical event?
   (A) The division of the Roman Empire
   (B) The Mongol Conquest.
   (C) European expansion and colonization.
   (D) Missionaries spreading religion along the Silk Road.

2. Which of the following was a long-term consequence of events like that shown in this image?
   (A) The bubonic plague was spread to Muslim cities.
   (B) Ideas, goods, and technologies were exchanged between Europeans and Muslims.
   (C) Sicily remained an independent Muslim state.
   (D) Europe was cut off from the economy of the eastern hemisphere.

3. In what other location might a scene like the one in this image have taken place?
   (A) The Iberian peninsula
   (B) The Hindu Kush
   (C) Aquitaine
   (D) Northern Italy

Use the image below and your knowledge of world history to answer questions 4 and 5.

Marco Polo leaving Venice on this eastward journey, 1338.
Timewatch/Alamy Stock Photo

4. This image best reflects which historical development?
   (A) Western European challenges to the Byzantine Empire.
   (B) Increased integration of Europe into the Afro-Eurasian economy.
   (C) The growth of universities in the cities.
   (D) The development of guilds.

5. The purpose behind this depiction of the city might have been to?
   (A) emphasize the importance of shipping and knowledge of overseas routes to the Venetian economy.
   (B) show Marco Polo's missionary zeal.
   (C) show how Venice dominated the surrounding rural areas.
   (D) encourage western Europeans to go on crusade against Constantinople.

## Short Answer

6. Use the map below and your knowledge of world history to answer parts A, B, and C.

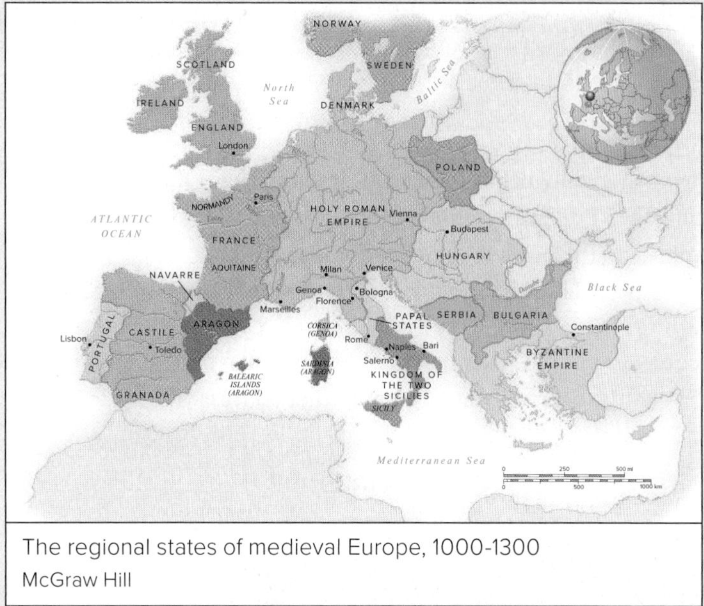

The regional states of medieval Europe, 1000-1300
McGraw Hill

(A) Identify ONE way in which Europe's political development was different from that of other Afro-Eurasian regions from c. 1100 to c. 1300.

(B) Explain ONE change that happened in the late Byzantine Empire, c. 1100–1300 C.E.

(C) Explain ONE way in which western European states effectively developed their forms of political organization.

7. Use the image below and your knowledge of world history to answer parts A, B, and C.

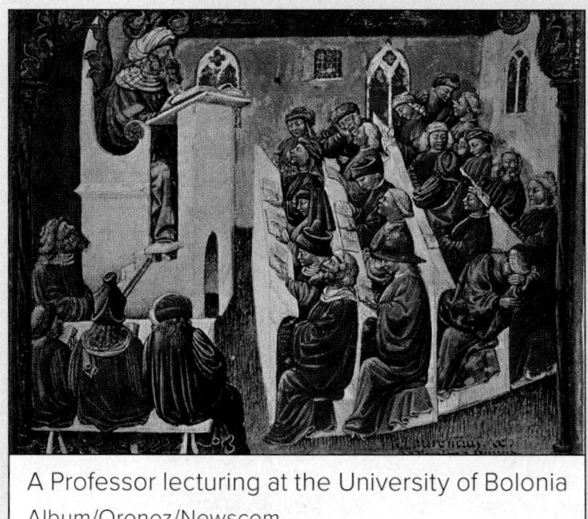
A Professor lecturing at the University of Bolonia
Album/Oronoz/Newscom

(A) Identify ONE development in European Christianity in the High Middle Ages.

(B) Identify ONE similarity *or* difference between popular Christianity and the Christianity of the elite schools and universities.

(C) Explain ONE way that Christians tried to reform the church of the high Middle Ages, c. 1100-1450 C.E.

8. Use your understanding of world history to answer parts A, B, and C.

(A) Identify ONE change in European society that took place in the cities of the High Middle Ages.

(B) Explain ONE change in European arts and literature during the High Middle Ages.

(C) Explain ONE continuity between the Early and High Middle Ages in European society.

# Section II

## Document-Based Question

Based on the documents below and your knowledge of world history, evaluate the effects that increased integration with Afro-Eurasia had on Europeans from c. 1100–1450.

In your response you should do the following:

- Respond to the prompt with a historically defensible thesis or claim that establishes a line of reasoning.
- Describe a broader historical context relevant to the prompt.
- Support an argument in response to the prompt using all documents.
- Use at least one additional piece of specific historical evidence (beyond that found in the documents) relevant to an argument about the prompt.
- Explain how or why the document's point of view, purpose, historical situation, and /or audience is relevant to an argument.
- Use evidence to corroborate, qualify, or modify an argument that addresses the prompt.

### Document 1

Genoese bankers change money and check the accounts of their clients in this fourteenth-century manuscript illustration.
Album/Alamy Stock Photo

## Document 2

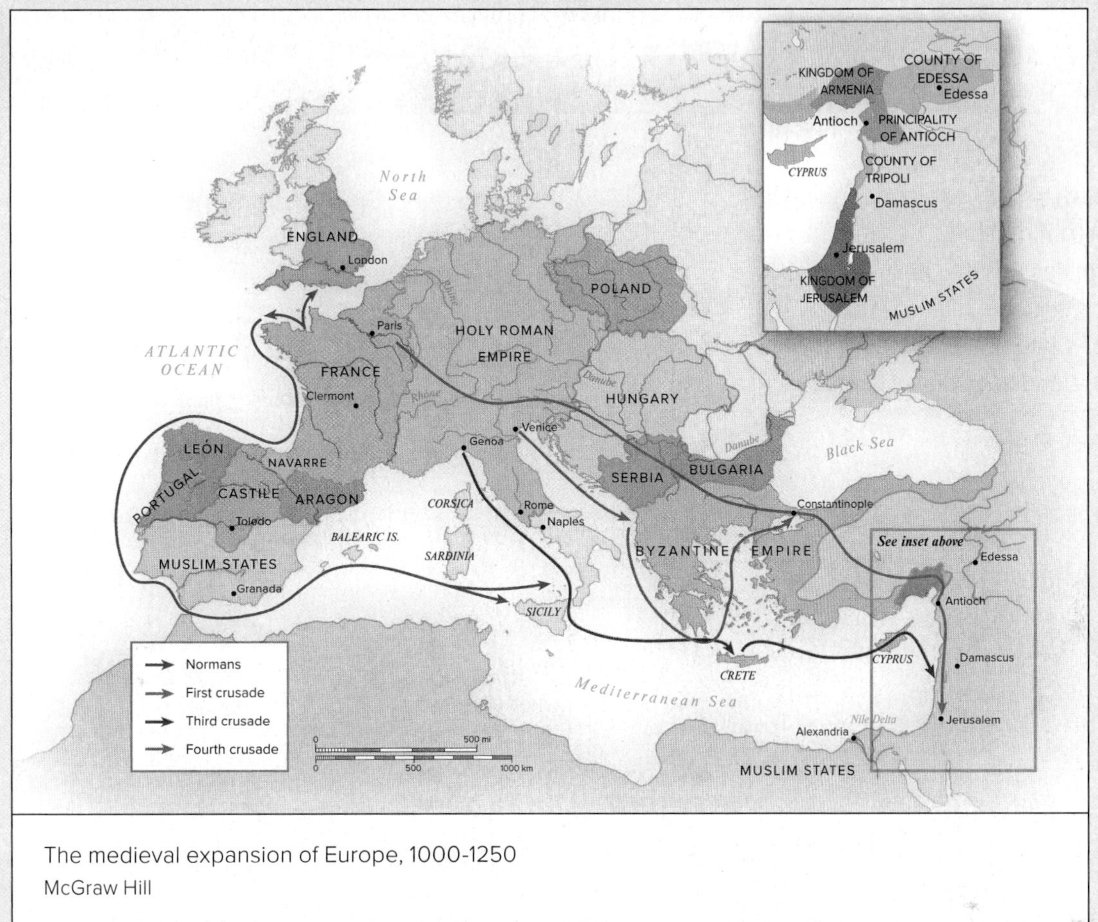


The medieval expansion of Europe, 1000-1250
McGraw Hill

## Document 3

**And so they went forth** into the Holy Land till they might see Jerusalem. And when this creature [Kempe] saw Jerusalem, riding on an ass, she thanked God with all her heart, praying him for his mercy that like as he had brought her to see this earthly city Jerusalem, he would grant her grace to see the blissful city Jerusalem above, the city of Heaven. . . .

Then they went to the Temple in Jerusalem, and they were let in that one day at evensong time [the time of evening prayers for Christians] and they abide there till the next day at evensong time. Then the friars lifted up a cross and led the pilgrims about from one place to another where our Lord had suffered his pains and his passions, every man and woman bearing a wax candle in their hand. And the friars always as they went about told them what our Lord suffered in every place. And the foresaid creature [Kempe] wept and sobbed so plentivously [sic] as though she had seen our Lord with her bodily eye suffering his Passion at that time.

*Soure*: Joel Fredell, editor. *The Book of Margery Kempe*, folio 33. http://english.selu.edu/humanitiesonline/kempe/legal.php. Translated into modern English from the original.

## Long Essay

Develop a thoughtful and thorough historical argument that answers the question below. Begin your essay with a thesis statement and support it with relevant historical evidence.

Using specific examples and your knowledge of world history, evaluate the extent to which cities led to European economic growth from c. 1100 to 1450.

Chapter 8

# Worlds Apart: The Americas and Oceania



## ZOOMING IN ON TRADITIONS

### The Aztec Capital at Its Height

In November 1519 a small Spanish army first encountered **Tenochtitlan,** capital city of the Aztec Empire. The Spanish forces came in search of gold, and they had heard many reports about the wealth of the Aztec Empire. Yet none of those reports prepared them adequately for what they saw.

Years later, Bernal Díaz del Castillo, a soldier in the invading Spanish army, described the city just before its conquest. Tenocthtitlan sat in the water of Lake Texcoco, connected to the surrounding land by three broad causeways, and as in Venice, canals allowed canoes to navigate to all parts of the city. Bernal Diaz recalled that the route to Tenochtitlan had been full of wonders even before reaching Tenochtitlan, confessing that he and his men "saw so many cities and villages built in the water and other great towns on dry land and that straight and level causeway going towards Mexico [Tenochtitlan], we were amazed . . . on account of the great towers and [temples] and buildings rising from the water, and all built of masonry." Once in Tenochtitlan, Bernal Diaz noted that the imperial palace included many large rooms and apartments while its armory was well stocked with swords, lances, knives, bows, arrows, slings, armor, and shields. The aviary of Tenochtitlan included eagles, hawks, parrots, and smaller birds, while jaguars, mountain lions, wolves, foxes, and rattlesnakes were noteworthy residents of the zoo.

Huitzilopochtli, the patron god of the Mexica people.
The History Collection/Alamy Stock Photo

To Bernal Díaz the two most impressive sights were the markets and the temples of Tenochtitlan. The markets aston-

**Tenochtitlan** (teh-NOCH-tee-tlahn)
**Texcoco** (TEHS-ko-ko)
**Tlatelolco** (tl-tay-LOL-ko)
**Huitzilopochtli** (we-tsee-loh-POCK-tlee)

ished him because of their size, the variety of goods they offered, and the order that prevailed there. In the principal market at Tlatelolco, a district of Tenochtitlan, Bernal Díaz found gold and silver jewelry, gems, feathers, embroidery, slaves, cotton, cacao, animal skins, maize, beans, vegetables, fruits, poultry, meat, fish, salt, paper, and tools. It would take more than two days, he said, to walk around the market and investigate all the goods offered for sale. His fellow soldiers compared the market of Tlatelolco favorably to those of Rome and Constantinople.

The temples also struck Bernal Díaz, though in a different way. Aztec temples were the principal sites of rituals involving human sacrifice. Bernal Díaz described climbing to the top of the main pyramidal temple in Tenochtitlan, where fresh blood lay pooled around the stone that served as a sacrificial altar. He described priests with hair entangled and matted with blood. Interior rooms of the temple were so encrusted with blood, Bernal Díaz reported, that their walls and floors had turned black, and the stench overcame even professional Spanish soldiers. Some of the interior rooms held the dismembered limbs of sacrificial victims, and others were resting places for thousands of human skulls and bones.

The contrast between Tenochtitlan's markets and its temples challenged Bernal Díaz and his fellow soldiers. In the markets they witnessed peaceful and orderly exchange of the kind that took place all over the world. In the temples, however, they saw signs of human sacrifice on a scale rarely matched, if ever, anywhere in the world. Yet by the cultural traditions of the Aztec Empire, there was no difficulty reconciling the commercial activity of the marketplaces with the human sacrifice of the temples. Both had a place in the maintenance of the world: trade enabled a complex society to function, while sacrificial rituals pleased the gods and persuaded them to keep the world going.

## CHAPTER FOCUS

- The Aztec absorbed the traditional Olmec, Mayan, and Toltec gods and calendar into their polytheistic religion and used preexisting languages, architectural styles, and writing systems.
- The Aztecs created an enormous tributary empire, extracting payments of goods and labor from conquered peoples.
- Tenochtitlan was the center of the empire, and by 1500 was one of the largest cities in the world. It was also the center of a vast trade network in Mesoamerica and the Caribbean, and probably connected to North American trade routes as well.
- Local rulers had autonomy as long as they sent regular tribute to the emperor.
- The Inca empire was also a tributary empire, demanding goods and workers from its conquered peoples, and kidnapping or resettling rebellious peoples.
- Inca rulers created a vast road network with granaries placed at strategic crossroads for their military and to provide grain in times of famine.
- Andean farmers used communal organizations that allowed a great degree of self-sufficiency, which resulted in little need for foreign trade, making the Inca economy very different from other postclassical economies.
- Historians are still learning about the North American city of Cahokia, which was unearthed in the early 1960s. Historians haven't found a written language for this society, but its location east of the Mississippi River in Illinois made it a hub of river-based trade routes, with goods obtained at least as far away as Lake Superior. In 1250, Cahokia was bigger than the city of London.
- Off the west coast of the Americas, Polynesians were making extraordinary voyages across the eastern Pacific, settling people, plants, animals, languages, and technologies throughout distant islands. These maritime nomads would make a good comparison with the Bantu.

### Historical Developments

- In the Americas, as in Afro-Eurasia, state systems demonstrated continuity, innovation, and diversity, and expanded in scope and reach.
- Rulers continued to use religious ideas, art, and monumental architecture to legitimize their rule.
- Rulers used tribute collection, tax farming, and innovative tax collection systems to generate revenue, in order to forward state power and expansion.

## Reasoning Processes

- **Sourcing and Situation** Explain the historical situation of oral history accounts depicting the colonization of Hawaii.
- **Source Claims and Evidence** Identify the evidence to support the claim that religion was of central importance in Mexica society.
- **Contextualization** Explain how the development of the powerful Aztec and Incan states were within the broader context of the environment of Mesoamerica and the Andes.
- **Making Connections** Identify patterns among or connections between the development of states in Mesoamerica, South America, and North America.
- **Argumentation** Make a historically defensible claim that explains why the Mexica engaged in ritual bloodletting and human sacrifice.

## Historical Thinking Skills

- **Continuity and Change** Explain how and why states in the Americas developed and changed over time.

## CHAPTER OVERVIEW

Although the peoples of Africa, Asia, and Europe interacted regularly before modern times, the indigenous peoples of the Americas had only sporadic dealings with their contemporaries across the oceans. Scandinavian seafarers established a short-lived colony in Newfoundland, and occasional ships from Europe and west Africa may have made their way to the western hemisphere. Before 1492, however, interaction between peoples of the eastern and western hemispheres was fleeting and random rather than a sustained and regular affair. During the period from 1000 to 1500 C.E., however, the peoples of North and South America, like their counterparts in the eastern hemisphere, organized large empires with distinctive cultural and religious traditions, and they created elaborate trade networks touching most regions of the American continents.

As in the Americas, the indigenous peoples of Australia and the Pacific islands had irregular and sporadic dealings with peoples outside Oceania. Asian trade networks extended to the Philippines, the islands of Indonesia, and New Guinea. They even touched a few regions of northern Australia and the Mariana Islands, including Guam, but they did not extend to the more distant island societies of the Pacific Ocean. Pacific islanders themselves often sailed over the open ocean, creating and sustaining links between the societies of various island groups. They also had some dealings with the inhabitants of Asian and American lands bordering the Pacific Ocean. But like their counterparts in the western hemisphere, the indigenous peoples of Australia and the Pacific islands built self-sufficient societies and developed unique traditions distinct from those in Afro-Eurasia. Even though they had extremely limited amounts of land and other natural resources to work with, by the thirteenth century C.E. they had established well-organized agricultural societies and chiefly states throughout the Pacific islands. Until the fifteenth century for the Americas and the eighteenth century for Oceania, the world's oceans ensured that these two regions were truly worlds apart from the more interconnected regions of Africa, Asia, and Europe.

### CHRONOLOGY

| AMERICAS | |
|---|---|
| 950–1150 | High point of the Toltec empire |
| 1175 | Collapse of the Toltec empire |
| 1250 | Inca settlement near Cuzco |
| 1345 | Foundation of Tenochtitlan by the Mexica |
| 1400 | Emergence of the five Iroquois nations |
| 1428–1440 | Reign of the Aztec ruler Itzcóatl |
| 1438–1471 | Reign of the Inca ruler Pachacuti |
| 1440–1469 | Reign of the Aztec ruler Motecuzoma I |
| 1502–1520 | Reign of the Aztec ruler Motecuzoma II |
| 1519 | Arrival of Spanish conquerors in Mexico |
| **OCEANIA** | |
| 11th century | Beginning of population growth in Pacific islands |
| 12th century | Beginning of two-way voyages between Hawai`i and Tahiti and the Marquesas islands |
| 13th century | Emergence of distinct social classes and chiefly states |
| 14th century | Construction of fishponds in Hawai`i |

## STATES AND EMPIRES IN MESOAMERICA AND NORTH AMERICA

Mesoamerica entered an era of war and conquest in the eighth century C.E. Great stores of wealth had accumulated in **Teotihuacan,** the largest early city in Mesoamerica (discussed in chapter 6). When Teotihuacan declined, it became a target for less-prosperous but well-organized forces from the countryside and northern Mexico. Attacks on Teotihuacan opened a long era of militarization and empire building in Mesoamerica that lasted until Spanish forces conquered the region in the sixteenth century. Most prominent of the peoples contesting for power in Mesoamerica were the Toltecs and the **Mexica,** the architects of the Aztec Empire.

### The Toltecs and the Mexica

During the ninth and early tenth centuries, after the collapse of Teotihuacan, several regional states dominated portions of the high central valley of Mexico, the area surrounding Mexico City where agricultural societies had flourished since the late centuries B.C.E. Although these successor states and their societies shared the religious and cultural traditions of Teotihuacan, they fought relentlessly among themselves. Their capital cities all stood on well-defended hill sites, and warriors figured prominently in their works of art.

**Toltecs** With the emergence of the **Toltecs** and later the Mexica, much of central Mexico again came under unified rule. The Toltecs began to migrate into the area about the eighth century. They came from the arid land of northwestern Mexico, and they settled mostly at **Tula,** about 50 kilometers (31 miles) northwest of modern Mexico City. Though situated in a corner of the valley of Mexico that possesses thin soil and receives little rainfall, the Toltecs tapped the waters of the nearby River Tula to irrigate crops of maize, beans, peppers, tomatoes, chiles, and cotton. At its high point, from about 950 to 1150 C.E., Tula supported an urban population that might have reached sixty thousand people. Another sixty thousand lived in the surrounding region.

The Toltecs maintained a large and powerful army that campaigned periodically throughout central Mexico. They built a compact regional empire and maintained fortresses far to the northwest to protect their state from invasion by nomadic peoples. From the mid-tenth through the mid-twelfth century, they exacted tribute from subject peoples and transformed their capital into a wealthy city. Residents lived in spacious houses made of stone, adobe, or mud and sometimes covered their packed-earth floors with plaster.

**Tula** The city of Tula became an important center of weaving, pottery, and obsidian work, and residents imported large quantities of jade, turquoise, animal skins, exotic bird feathers, and other luxury goods from elsewhere in Mesoamerica. The Toltecs maintained close relations with societies on the Gulf coast as well as with the Maya of Yucatan. Indeed, Tula shared numerous architectural designs and art motifs with the Maya city of Chichén Itzá (discussed in chapter 6) some 1,500 kilometers (932 miles) to the east.

Beginning about 1125 C.E. the Toltec empire faced serious difficulties as conflicts between different ethnic groups living at Tula led to civil strife. By the mid-twelfth century, large numbers of migrants–mostly nomadic peoples from northwestern Mexico–had entered Tula and settled in the surrounding area. By 1175 conflicts between the various groups, old and new, had destroyed the Toltec state. Archaeological evidence suggests that fire destroyed much of Tula about the same time. Large numbers of people continued to inhabit the region around Tula, but by the end of the twelfth century the Toltecs no longer dominated Mesoamerica.

**The Mexica** Among the migrants drawn to central Mexico from northwestern regions were people who called themselves the Mexica, often referred to as Aztecs because they dominated the alliance that built the **Aztec Empire** in the fifteenth century. (The term *Aztec* derives from *Aztlán,* "the place of the seven legendary caves," which the Mexica remembered as the home of their ancestors.) The Mexica arrived in central Mexico about the middle of the thirteenth century. They had a reputation for causing conflicts by kidnapping women from nearby communities and seizing land already cultivated by others. They were often expelled by the communities they encountered. For a century they migrated around central Mexico, jostling and fighting with other peoples and sometimes surviving only by eating fly eggs and snakes.

**Tenochtitlan** About 1345 the Mexica settled on an island in a marshy region of Lake Texcoco and founded the city that would become their capital–Tenochtitlan, on top of which Spanish conquerors later built Mexico City. Though inconvenient at first, the site offered several advantages. The lake harbored plentiful supplies of fish, frogs, and waterfowl. Moreover, the lake enabled the Mexica to develop the ***chinampa*** system of agriculture. The Mexica dredged a rich and fertile muck from the lake's bottom and built it up into small plots of land known as *chinampas.* During the dry season, cultivators tapped water from canals leading from the lake to their plots, and in the temperate climate they grew crops of maize, beans, squashes, tomatoes, peppers, and chiles year-round. *Chinampas* were so fertile and productive that cultivators were sometimes able to harvest seven crops per year from their gardens. Finally, the lake served as a natural defense: waters protected Tenochtitlan on all sides, and Mexica warriors patrolled the three causeways that eventually linked their capital to the surrounding mainland.

**Teotihuacan** (teh-o-tee-WAH-kahn)
**Mexica** (MEHK-si-kah)

## MAP 8.1 The Toltec and Aztec empires, 950–1520 C.E.

The Aztec Empire stretched from the Gulf of Mexico to the Pacific Ocean.

***What political and cultural methods did Aztec rulers use to control these diverse territories and peoples?***

**The Aztec Empire** By the early fifteenth century, the Mexica were powerful enough to overcome their immediate neighbors and demand tribute from their new subjects. During the middle decades of the century, prodded by the military elite that ruled Tenochtitlan, the Mexica launched ambitious campaigns of imperial expansion. Under the rule of "the Obsidian Serpent" **Itzcóatl** (1428–1440) and **Motecuzoma I** (1440–1469), also known as Moctezuma or Montezuma, they advanced first against Oaxaca in southwestern Mexico. After conquering the city and slaying many of its inhabitants, they populated Oaxaca with colonists, and the city became a bulwark for the emerging Mexica empire.

The Mexica next turned their attention to the Gulf coast, whose tropical products made welcome tribute items in Tenochtitlan. Finally, they conquered the cities of the high plateaus between Tenochtitlan and the Gulf coast. About the mid-fifteenth century, the Mexica joined forces with two neighboring cities, Texcoco and Tlacopan (modern Tacuba), to create a triple alliance that guided the Aztec Empire. Dominated by the Mexica and Tenochtitlan, the allies imposed their rule on about twelve million people and most of Mesoamerica, excluding only the arid northern and western regions and a few small pockets where independent states resisted the expanding empire.

**Tribute and Trade** The main objective of the triple alliance was to exact tribute from subject peoples. From nearby peoples the Mexica and their allies received food crops and manufactured items such as textiles, rabbit-fur blankets, embroidered clothes, jewelry, and obsidian knives. Tribute obligations were sometimes very oppressive for subject peoples. The annual tribute owed by the state of Tochtepec on the Gulf coast, for example, included 9,600 cloaks, 1,600 women's garments, 200 loads of cacao, and 16,000 rubber balls, among other items. Ruling elites entrusted some of these tribute items to officially recognized merchants, who took them to distant lands and exchanged them for local products. These included luxury items such as translucent jade, emeralds, tortoise shells, jaguar skins, parrot feathers, seashells, and game animals. The tropical lowlands also supplied vanilla beans and cacao—the source of cocoa and chocolate—from which Mexica elites prepared tasty beverages. Unlike imperial states in the eastern hemisphere, the Aztec Empire had no elaborate bureaucracy or administration. The Mexica and their allies simply conquered their subjects and

**Itzcóatl** (tsee-ko-atl)
**Motecuzoma** (mo-tek-oo-ZO-mah)
**Oaxaca** (wah-HAH-kah)

assessed tribute, leaving local governance and the collection of tribute in the hands of the conquered peoples. The allies did not even maintain military garrisons throughout their empire. Nor did they keep a permanent, standing army. They simply assembled forces as needed when they launched campaigns of expansion or mounted punitive expeditions against insubordinate subjects. Nevertheless, the Mexica in particular had a reputation for military prowess, and fear of reprisal tended to keep most subject peoples in line.

At the high point of the Aztec Empire in the early sixteenth century, tribute from 489 subject territories flowed into Tenochtitlan, which as a result was an enormously wealthy city. The Mexica capital had a population of about two hundred thousand people, and three hundred thousand others lived in nearby towns and suburban areas. The principal market even had separate sections for merchants dealing in gold, silver, slaves, henequen and cotton cloth, shoes, animal skins, turkeys, dogs, wild game, maize, beans, peppers, cacao, and fruits.

An artist's depiction of *chinampas* agriculture, made by staking out and framing "fields" in shallow lake beds, then building them up until they were above the level of the lake. What made this technique worth the intensive work required to establish growing areas in the first place?
Alfredo Dagli Orti/Shutterstock

## Mexica Society

Mexica society was rigidly hierarchical and stratified between nobles and non-nobles. The Mexica looked upon all males as potential warriors, and public honors and rewardswere reserved mostly for the military elite. Although individuals of common birth could distinguish themselves on the battlefield and thereby improve their social standing, for the most part, the military elite came from the Mexica aristocracy. Men of noble birth received the most careful instruction and intense training in military affairs, and they enjoyed the best opportunities to display their talents on the battlefield.

## What's Left Out?

More contemporary source material survives about the Mexica and their subjects than any other peoples of the pre-Columbian Americas. However, nearly all of the sources that survive are problematic in some way. For example, while there are some books written by the Mexica in their own language (Nahuatl), scholars do not agree about when these books were produced. Furthermore, many Mexica documents appear to have been destroyed either by Mexica kings prior to the Spanish arrival or by the Spanish who sought to eradicate Mexica beliefs after the conquest. Some Spanish conquistadores wrote letters and accounts of their initial contact with the Mexica, but these obviously tell the story from their point of view rather than from the Mexica point of view. In addition, some of these sources—including the one written by Bernal Diaz del Castillo that introduces this chapter—were only written decades after the conquest. Still others, such as the famous *Florentine Codex* from which the "Sources of the Past" for this chapter was taken, were the result of lengthy interviews in Nahuatl conducted by Spanish missionaries with Mexica priests, elders, and other leaders a few decades after the conquest. But even though sources like the *Florentine Codex* seem to be told from the point of view of the Mexica, scholars argue that it is unclear how free the Mexica were to tell their version of their past given the power differences between the Spanish and the Mexica. Not only that, the original manuscript (completed in 1555) did not survive, and thus we are left with summaries that have been revised and translated many times since the sixteenth century. Yet in spite of multiple problems with the existing sources, nearly all histories written about the Mexica to date have been based on them. Consider how different the histories we are able to tell might be if we had access to more pre-conquest Mexica sources. How might these alter our perceptions of the Mexica people and their culture?

*Sources:* Fray Bernardino de Sahagún. *Historia general de las cosas de Nueva España.* Known as the *Florentine Codex.* Edited by Francisco del Paso y Troncoso. 4 vols. Madrid: *Fototipia de Hauser y Menet,* 1905. English translation: Fray Bernardino de Sahagún. *General History of the Things of New Spain.* 2nd. ed., rev. 4 vols. Santa Fe, New Mexico: School of American Research, 1900.

### Thinking Critically About Sources

1. Speculate about the depiction of Mexica from the point of view of those who lived there at the time, rather than Spanish interpretations, or "problematic" sources written later. Why is it so important to consider the Mexican point of view?

**Warriors** The Mexica showered wealth and privileges on the military elite. Accomplished warriors received extensive land grants as well as tribute from commoners for their support. The most successful warriors formed a council whose members selected the ruler, discussed public issues, and filled government positions. They ate the best foods—turkey, pheasant, duck, deer, boar, and rabbit—and they consumed most of the luxury items such as vanilla and cacao that came into Mexica society by way of trade or tribute. Even dress reflected social status in Mexica society. Sumptuary laws (laws that regulate consumption and dress) required commoners to wear coarse, burlaplike garments made of henequen (fibers made from the agave plant) but permitted aristocrats to drape themselves in cotton. Warriors enjoyed the right to don brightly colored capes and adorn themselves with lip plugs and eagle feathers after they captured enemies on the battlefield and brought them back to Tenochtitlan.

**Mexica Women** Women played almost no role in the political affairs of a society so dominated by military values, but they wielded influence within their families and enjoyed high honor as mothers of warriors. Mexica women did not inherit property or hold official positions, and the law subjected them to the strict authority of their fathers or husbands. Women were prominent in the marketplaces, as well as in crafts involving embroidery and needlework. Yet Mexica society prodded them toward motherhood and homemaking.

With the exception of a few who dedicated themselves to the service of a temple, nearly all Mexica women married. Mexica traditions taught that the principal function of women was to bear children, especially males who might become distinguished warriors. In fact, society recognized the bearing of children as equal to a warrior's capture of enemy in battle, and women who died in childbirth won the same fame as warriors who died valiantly on the battlefield. Even among the elite classes, Mexica women had the responsibilities of raising young children and preparing food for their families.

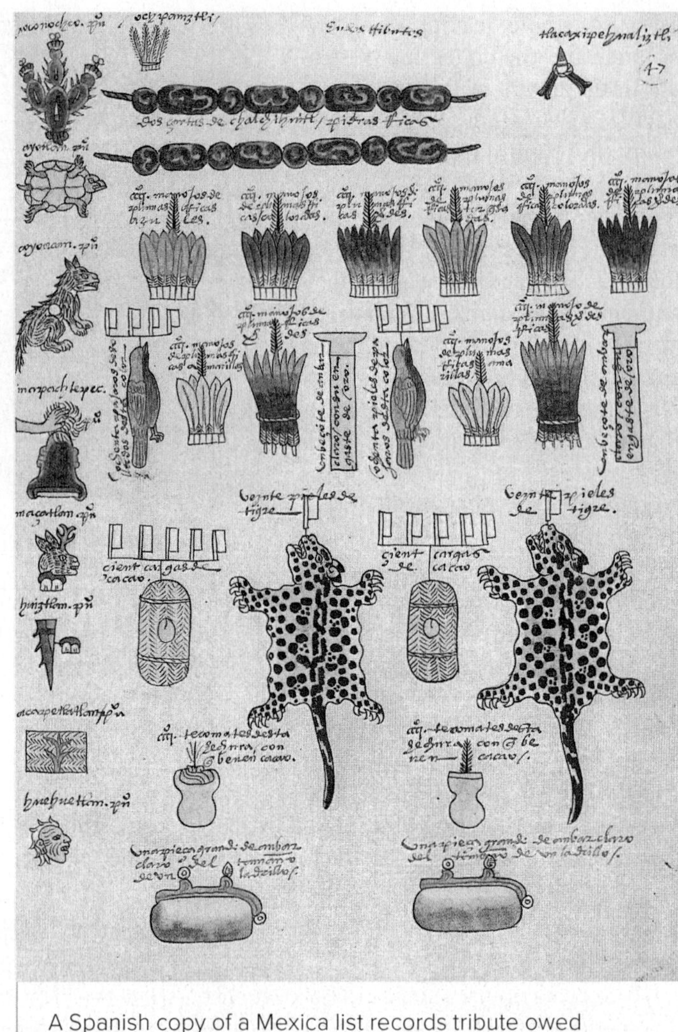

A Spanish copy of a Mexica list records tribute owed by conquered people to the Aztec ruler, which included animal skins, bird feathers, grains of various kinds, and jewelry.

Universal History Archive/Shutterstock

**Priests** In addition to the military aristocracy, a priestly class also ranked among the Mexica elite. Priests received a special education in calendrical and ritual lore, and they presided over religious ceremonies that the Mexica viewed as crucial to the continuation of the world. Priests read omens and explained the forces that drove the world, thereby wielding considerable influence as advisers to Mexica rulers. On a few occasions, priests even became supreme rulers of the Aztec Empire: the ill-fated Motecuzoma II (reigned 1502–1520), ruler of the Aztec empire when Spanish invaders appeared in 1519, was a priest of the most popular Mexica cult.

**Cultivators and Slaves** The vast majority of the Mexica population consisted of commoners who lived in hamlets cultivating *chinampas* and fields allocated to their families by community groups known as ***calpulli.*** Originally, *calpulli* were clans or groups of families claiming descent from common ancestors. With the passage of time, ancestry became less important to the nature of the *calpulli* than the fact that groups of families lived together in communities, organized their own affairs, and allocated community property to individual families. Apart from cultivating plots assigned by their *calpulli,* Mexica commoners worked on lands awarded to aristocrats or prominent warriors and contributed labor services to public works projects involving the construction of palaces, temples, roads, and irrigation systems. Cultivators delivered periodic tribute payments to state agents, who distributed a portion of what they collected to

***calpulli*** (kal-po-lee)

# SOURCES FROM THE PAST

## Mexica Expectations of Boys and Girls

*Bernardino de Sahagún was a Franciscan missionary who worked to convert the native peoples of Mesoamerica to Christianity in the mid-sixteenth century. He interviewed Mexica elders and assembled a vast amount of information about what their society was like before the arrival of Europeans in what became known as the* Florentine Codex. *Although not unproblematic as sources (see the* What's Left Out *feature in this chapter), his records include the speeches made by midwives as they delivered infants to aristocratic families. The speeches indicate clearly the roles men and women were expected to play in Mexica society.*

**[To a newborn boy the** midwife said:] "Heed, hearken: thy home is not here, for thou art an eagle, thou art an ocelot; thou art a roseate spoonbill, thou art a troupial [a bird like an oriole]. Thou art the serpent, the bird of the lord of the near, of the nigh. Here is only the place of thy nest. Thou hast only been hatched here; thou hast only come, arrived. Thou art only come forth on earth here. Here dost thou bud, blossom, germinate. Here thou becomest the chip, the fragment [of thy mother]. Here are only the cradle, thy cradle blanket, the resting place of thy head: only thy place of arrival. Thou belongest out there; out there thou hast been consecrated. Thou hast been sent into warfare. War is thy desert, thy task. Thou shalt give drink, nourishment, food to the sun, the lord of the earth. Thy real home, thy property, thy lot is the home of the sun there in the heavens. . . . Perhaps thou wilt receive the gift, perhaps thou wilt merit death [in battle] by the obsidian knife, the flowered death by the obsidian knife. . . ."

> What do the types of animals named here suggest about the expected nature of boys' lives?

And if it were a female, the midwife said to her when she cut her umbilical cord: "My beloved maiden, my beloved noblewoman, thou has endured fatigue! Our lord, the lord of the near, of the nigh, hath sent thee. Thou hast come to arrive at a place of weariness, a place of anguish, a place of fatigue where there is cold, there is wind. . . . Thou wilt be in the heart of the home, thou wilt go nowhere, thou wilt nowhere become a wanderer, thou becomest the banked fire, the hearth stones. Here our lord planteth thee, burieth thee. And thou wilt become fatigued, thou wilt become tired; thou art to provide water, to grind maize, to drudge; thou art to sweat by the ashes, by the hearth."

> Compared with the animals meant to represent boys, why are girls likened to banked fires and hearth stones? What do these images imply about expectations for their lives?

Then the midwife buried the umbilical cord of the noblewoman by the hearth. It was said that by this she signified that the little woman would nowhere wander. Her dwelling place was only within the house; her home was only within the house; it was not necessary for her to go anywhere. And it meant that her very duty was drink, food. She was to prepare drink, to prepare food, to grind, to spin, to weave.

### For Further Reflection

- How did gender roles and expectations of Mexica society compare with those of other settled, agricultural societies, such as China, India, the Islamic world, sub-Saharan Africa, and Europe?
- The source presents speeches by midwives. What information would you seek in the Florentine Codes either to corroborate or qualify the depiction of gender roles described by the midwives?

*Source:* Bernardino de Sahagún. *Florentine Codex: General History of the Things of New Spain,* 13 vols. Trans. by Charles E. Dibble and Arthur J. O. Anderson. Salt Lake City: University of Utah Press, 1950–82, 171–73 (book 6, chapter 31).

the elite classes and stored the remainder in state granaries and warehouses. In addition to these cultivators of common birth, Mexica society included slaves, who usually worked as domestic servants. Most enslaved people were not foreigners, but Mexica. Families sometimes sold younger members into servitude out of financial distress, and other Mexica were forced into slavery because of criminal behavior.

**Artisans and Merchants** Skilled artisans, particularly those who worked with gold, silver, cotton textiles, tropical bird feathers, and other items destined for consumption by the elite, enjoyed considerable prestige in Mexica society. Merchants specializing in long-distance trade occupied an important but somewhat insecure position in Mexica society. Merchants supplied the exotic products such as gems, animal skins, and tropical bird feathers consumed by the elites and provided political and military intelligence about the lands they visited. Yet they often fell under suspicion as greedy profiteers, and aristocratic warriors sometimes blatantly seized their wealth and goods because they knew most merchants did not have powerful protectors.

## Mexica Culture

When they migrated to central Mexico, the Mexica already spoke the Nahuatl language, which had been the prevalent tongue in the region since the time of the Toltecs. The Mexica soon adopted other cultural and religious traditions, some of which dated from the time of the Olmecs (discussed in chapter 6), shared by all the peoples of Mesoamerica. Most Mesoamerican peoples played a ball game in formal courts, for example, and maintained a complicated calendar based on a solar year of 365 days and a ritual year of 260 days. The Mexica enthusiastically adopted the ball game, and they kept a sophisticated calendar, although it was not as elaborate as the Maya calendar.

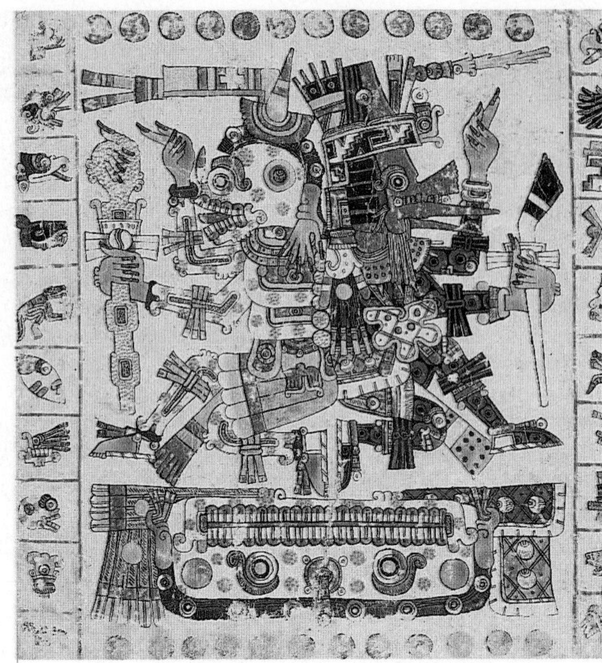

A Mexica manuscript known as the *Codex Borgia* depicts Quetzalcóatl (left) as the lord of life and Tezcatlipoca (right) as the god of death.
Biblioteca Apostolica Vaticana/Index S.A.S.

**Mexica Gods** The Mexica also absorbed the religious beliefs common to Mesoamerica. Two of their principal gods—**Tezcatlipoca,** "the Smoking Mirror," and **Quetzalcóatl,** "the Feathered Serpent"—had figured in Mesoamerican pantheons at least since the time of Teotihuacan, although different peoples knew them by various names. Tezcatlipoca was a powerful figure, the giver and taker of life and the patron deity of warriors, whereas Quetzalcóatl had a reputation for supporting arts, crafts, and agriculture.

**Ritual Bloodletting** Like their predecessors, the Mexica believed that their gods had set the world in motion through acts of individual sacrifice. By letting their blood flow, the gods had given the earth the moisture it needed to bear maize and other crops. To propitiate the gods and ensure the continuation of the world, the Mexica honored their deities through sacrificial bloodletting. Mexica priests regularly performed acts of self-sacrifice, piercing their earlobes or penises with cactus spines in honor of the primeval acts of their gods. The religious beliefs and bloodletting rituals clearly reflected the desire of the Mexica to keep their agricultural society going.

**Huitzilopochtli** Mexica priests also presided over the sacrificial killing of human victims. From the time of the Olmecs, and possibly even earlier, Mesoamerican peoples had regarded the ritual sacrifice of human beings as essential to the world's survival. The Mexica, however, placed much more emphasis on human sacrifice than their predecessors had. To a large extent the Mexica enthusiasm for human sacrifice followed from their devotion to the god **Huitzilopochtli.** Mexica warriors took Huitzilopochtli as their patron deity in the early years of the fourteenth century as they subjected neighboring peoples to their rule. Military success persuaded them that Huitzilopochtli especially favored the Mexica, and as military successes mounted, the priests of Huitzilopochtli's cult demanded sacrificial victims to keep the war god appeased.

Some of the victims were Mexica criminals, but others came as tribute from neighboring peoples or from the ranks of warriors captured on the battlefield during the many conflicts between the Mexica and their neighbors. In all cases, the Mexica viewed human sacrifice not as a gruesome form of entertainment but, rather, as a ritual essential to the world's survival. They believed that the blood of sacrificial victims sustained the sun and secured a continuing supply of moisture for the earth, thus ensuring that human communities would be able to cultivate their crops and perpetuate their societies.

## Peoples and Societies of North America

Beyond Mexico the peoples of North America developed a rich variety of political, social, and cultural traditions. Many North American peoples depended on hunting, fishing, and collecting edible plants. In the arctic and subarctic regions, for example, diets included sea mammals such as whale, seal, and walrus supplemented by land mammals such as moose and caribou. Peoples in coastal regions consumed fish, but in interior regions (the North American plains, for example), they hunted large animals such as bison and deer. Throughout the continent nuts, berries, roots, and grasses such as wild rice supplemented

**Tezcatlipoca** (tehs-cah-tlee-poh-cah)
**Quetzalcóatl** (keh-tzahl-koh-AHTL)

In this manuscript illustration an aide stretches a victim over a sacrificial altar while a priest opens his chest, removes the still-beating heart, and offers it to Huitzilopochtli. At the bottom of the structure, attendants remove the body of an earlier victim. Library of Congress, Prints and Photographs Division [LC-USZC4-743].

the meat provided by hunters and fishers. Like their counterparts elsewhere, hunting, fishing, and foraging peoples of North America built societies on a relatively small scale because food resources in the wild would not support dense populations.

**Pueblo and Navajo Societies** In several regions of North America, agricultural economies enabled peoples to maintain settled societies with large populations. In what is now the American southwest, for example, **Pueblo** and **Navajo** peoples tapped river waters to irrigate crops of maize, which constituted as much as 80 percent of their diets. They also cultivated beans, squashes, and sunflowers, and they supplemented their crops with wild plants and small game such as rabbit. The hot and dry environment periodically brought drought and famine. Nevertheless, by about 700 C.E. the Pueblo and the Navajo began to construct permanent stone and adobe buildings. Archaeologists have discovered about 125 sites where agricultural peoples built village communities.

**Iroquois Peoples** Large-scale agricultural societies emerged also in the woodlands east of the Mississippi River. Woodlands peoples began to cultivate maize and beans during the early centuries C.E., and after about 800 these cultivated foods made up the bulk of their diets. They lived in settled communities, and they often surrounded their larger settlements with wooden palisades, which served as defensive walls. By 1000, for example, the Owasco people had established a distinct society in what is now upstate New York, and by about 1400 the five **Iroquois** nations (Mohawk, Oneida, Onondaga, Cayuga, and Seneca) had emerged from Owasco society. Women were in charge of

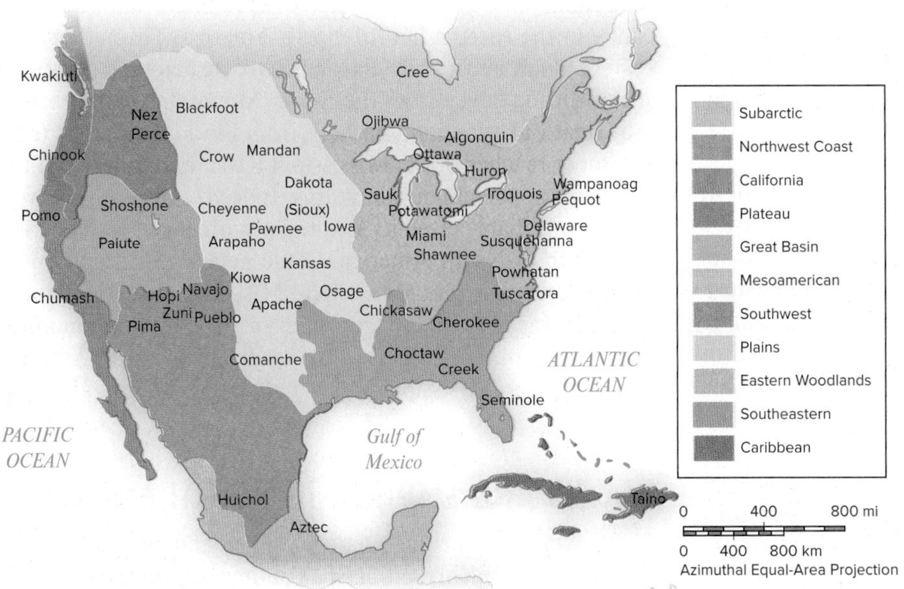


## MAP 8.2 North American cultural groups, CA. 1600

Selected cultural groups of North America around 1600. Note the great diversity of groups in every region from west to east.

In what ways does the map indicating tribes demonstrate the correlation between geography and culture?

**Navajo** (NAH-vah-ho)

Originally constructed about 1000 C.E., the Great Serpent Mound sits atop a ridge in modern Ohio. The serpent's coiled tail is visible at the left, while its open mouth holds an egg on the right. What purposes might a ridgetop mound like this have served?
Georg Gerster/Science Source

Iroquois villages and longhouses, in which several related families lived together, and supervised cultivation of fields surrounding their settlements. Men took responsibility for affairs beyond the village—hunting, fishing, and war.

**Mound-Building Peoples** The most impressive structures of the woodlands were the enormous earthen mounds that dotted the countryside throughout the eastern half of North America. Woodlands peoples used those mounds sometimes as stages for ceremonies and rituals, often as platforms for dwellings, and occasionally as burial sites. Modern agriculture, road building, and real estate development have destroyed most of the mounds, but several surviving examples demonstrate that they sometimes reached gigantic proportions.

**Cahokia** The largest surviving structure is a mound at **Cahokia** near East St. Louis, Illinois. More than 30 meters (100 feet) high, 300 meters (1,000 feet) long, and 200 meters (650 feet) wide, it was the third-largest structure in the western hemisphere before the arrival of Europeans. Only the temple of the sun in Teotihuacan and the temple of Quetzalcóatl in Cholula were larger. When the Cahokia society was at its height, from approximately 900 to 1250 C.E., more than one hundred smaller mounds stood within a few kilometers of the highest and most massive mound. Scholars have estimated that during the twelfth century, fifteen thousand to thirty-eight thousand people lived in the vicinity of the Cahokia mounds.

**Iroquois** (EAR-uh-kwoi)
**Cahokia** (kuh-HOH-kee-uh)

**Trade** Because peoples north of Mexico had no writing, information about their societies comes almost exclusively from archaeological discoveries. Burial sites reveal that mound-building peoples recognized various social classes because they bestowed grave goods of differing quality and quantities on their departed kin. Archaeologists have shown, too, that trade linked widely separated regions and peoples of North America. An elaborate network of rivers—notably the Mississippi, Missouri, Ohio, and Tennessee rivers, along with their many tributaries—facilitated encounters and trade by canoe in the eastern half of North America. Throughout the eastern woodlands, archaeologists have turned up stones with sharp cutting edges from the Rocky Mountains, copper from the Great Lakes region, seashells from Florida, minerals from the upper reaches of the Mississippi River, and mica from the southern Appalachian mountains. Indeed, the community at Cahokia probably owed its size and prominence to its location at the hub of North American trade networks. Situated near the confluence of the Mississippi, Missouri, and Ohio rivers, Cahokia was most likely the center of trade and communication networks linking the eastern woodlands of North America with the lower Mississippi Valley and lands bordering the Gulf of Mexico.

## STATES AND EMPIRES IN SOUTH AMERICA

South American peoples had no script and no tradition of writing before the arrival of Spanish invaders in the early sixteenth century. As a result, the experiences of early South American societies are much more difficult to recover than those of Mesoamerica, where writing had been in use since the fifth century B.C.E. Yet, from archaeological evidence and information recorded by Spanish conquerors, it is possible to reconstruct much of the historical experience of Andean South America, which had been the site of complex societies since the first millennium B.C.E. As in Mesoamerica, cities and secular government in South America began to overshadow ceremonial centers and priestly regimes during the centuries from 1000 to 1500 C.E. Toward the end of the period, like the Mexica in Mesoamerica, the Incas built a powerful state, extended their authority over a vast region, and established the largest empire South America had ever seen.

## The Coming of the Incas

After the disappearance of the Chavín and Moche societies (discussed in chapter 6), a series of autonomous regional states organized public affairs in Andean South America. The states frequently clashed, but rarely did one of them gain a long-term advantage over the others. For the most part they controlled areas either in the mountainous highlands or in the valleys and coastal plains.

**Chucuito** After the twelfth century, for example, the kingdom of **Chucuito** dominated the highlands region around Lake Titicaca, which straddles the border between modern Peru and Bolivia at about 4,000 meters (13,000 feet) of elevation. Chucuito depended on the cultivation of potatoes and the herding of llamas and alpacas—camel-like beasts that were the only large domesticated animals anywhere in the Americas before the sixteenth century. In elaborately terraced fields built with stone retaining walls, cultivators harvested potatoes of many colors, sizes, and tastes. Like maize in Mesoamerica, potatoes served as the staple of the highlanders' diet, which revolved around a potato-based stew enlivened by maize, tomatoes, green vegetables, peppers, chiles, and meat from llamas, alpacas, or tender, domesticated guinea pigs.

Apart from meat, llamas and alpacas provided the highlanders with wool, hides, and dung, widely used as fuel in a land with few trees. In exchange for potatoes and woolen textiles, the highlanders obtained maize and coca leaves from societies in lower valleys. They used maize to enhance their diet and to brew a beerlike beverage, and they chewed the coca leaves, which worked as a mild stimulant and enhanced stamina in the thin air of the high Andes. (When processed, coca leaves yield a much more powerful stimulant with addictive properties—cocaine.)

**Chimu** In the lowlands the powerful kingdom of **Chimu** (sometimes referred to as Chimor) emerged in the tenth century and expanded to dominate some 900 kilometers (560 miles) of the Peruvian coast for about a century before the arrival of the Incas in the mid-fifteenth century. Chimu governed a large and thriving society. Irrigation networks tapped

**MAP 8.3 The Inca Empire, 1471–1532**

The Incas built the largest empire in the pre-Columbian Americas.

***How were they able to maintain control over their extensive realm?***

the rivers and streams flowing from the Andes mountains, watered fields in the lowlands, and helped to generate abundant yields of maize and sweet potatoes. Judging from goods excavated at grave sites, Chimu society enjoyed considerable wealth and recognized clear distinctions between social classes.

Chimu's capital city, Chanchan, whose ruins lie close to the modern city of Trujillo, had a population that exceeded fifty thousand and may have approached one hundred thousand. Chanchan featured massive brick buildings, which indicated a capacity for mobilizing large numbers of people and resources for public purposes. The city's geography reflected a well-defined social order: each block belonged to an individual clan that supervised the affairs of its members and coordinated their efforts with those of other clans.

---

**Chucuito** (CHEW-keeto)

For several centuries, regional states such as Chucuito and Chimu maintained order in Andean South America. Yet, within a period of about thirty years, these and other regional states fell under the domination of the dynamic and expansive society of the Incas. The word *Inca* originally was the title of the rulers of a small kingdom in the valley of Cuzco, but in modern usage the term refers more broadly to those who spoke the Incas' **Quechua** language, or even to all subjects of the Inca Empire.

*Quipu* threads were different lengths and colors (though the colors in this example are faded). These designated the different items recorded: population, animals, textiles, weapons, and perhaps even rulers and notable events of their reigns. People needed an advanced education to record and "read" information by *quipu*.
Brendan Smialowski/AFP/Getty Images

**The Inca Empire** After a long period of migration in the highlands, the Incas settled in the region around Lake Titicaca about the mid-thirteenth century. At first, they lived as one among many peoples inhabiting the region. About 1438, however, the Inca ruler Pachacuti (reigned 1438–1471) launched a series of military campaigns that vastly expanded the Incas' authority. Pachacuti ("Earthshaker") was a fierce warrior. According to Inca legends, he fought so furiously in one early battle that he inspired the stones in the field to stand up and combat his enemies. The campaigns of the Earthshaker were long and brutal. Pachacuti first extended Inca control over the southern and northern highlands and then turned his forces on the coastal kingdom of Chimu. Though well defended, Chimu had to submit to the Incas when Pachacuti gained control of the waters that supplied Chimu's irrigation system.

By the late fifteenth century, the Incas had built a huge empire stretching more than 4,000 kilometers (2,500 miles) from modern Quito to Santiago. It embraced almost all of modern Peru, most of Ecuador, much of Bolivia, and parts of Chile and Argentina as well. Only the tropical rain forests of the Amazon and other river valleys set a limit to Inca expansion to the east, and the Pacific Ocean defined its western boundary. With a population of about 11.5 million, the **Inca Empire** easily ranked as the largest state ever built in South America.

The Incas ruled as a military and administrative elite. They led armies composed mostly of conquered peoples, and staffed the bureaucracy that managed the empire's political affairs. But the Incas were not numerous enough to overwhelm their subjects. They routinely sought to encourage obedience among subject peoples by taking hostages from their ruling classes and forcing them to live at the Inca capital. When conquered peoples became restive or uncooperative, the Incas sent loyal subjects as colonists, provided them with choice land and economic benefits, and established them in garrisons to maintain order. When conquered peoples rebelled, Inca armies forced them to leave their homes and resettle in distant parts of the empire.

**Inca Administration** The vast Inca realm presented a serious administrative challenge to its rulers. The Inca administrative system was the invention of Pachacuti himself—the same Earthshaker who conquered the territories that made up the Inca Empire. Toward the end of his reign, about 1463, Pachacuti entrusted military affairs to his son and settled in the highland village of Cuzco, where he designed a system of government to consolidate his conquests. He implemented taxes to support Inca rulers and administrators, and he organized a system of state-owned storehouses to stock agricultural surpluses and craft products such as textiles. He also began construction on an extensive network of roads that enabled Inca military forces and administrators to travel quickly to all parts of the empire.

**Quipu** In the absence of any script or system of writing, Inca bureaucrats and administrators relied on a mnemonic aid (memory device) known as ***quipu*** to keep track of their responsibilities. *Quipu* consisted of an array of small cords of various colors and lengths, all suspended from one large, thick cord. Experts tied a series of knots in the small cords, which sometimes numbered a hundred or more, to help them remember certain kinds of information. Most *quipu* recorded statistical information having to do with population, state property, taxes, and labor services that communities owed to the central government. Occasionally, though, *quipu* also helped experts to remember historical information having to do with the establishment of the Inca Empire, the Inca rulers, and their deeds. Although much more unwieldy and less flexible than writing, *quipu* enabled Inca bureaucrats to keep track of information well enough to run an orderly empire.

**Cuzco** **Cuzco** served as the administrative, religious, and ceremonial center of the Inca Empire. When Pachacuti retired there, Cuzco was a modest village, but the conqueror soon transformed it into a magnificent capital that Incas considered "the navel of the universe." At the center was a huge plaza filled with glistening white sand transported from Pacific

**Quechua** (keh-CHUA)
***quipu*** (KEE-poo)

beaches to the high Andean city. Surrounding the plaza were handsome buildings constructed of red stone cut so precisely by expert masons that no mortar was necessary to hold them together. The most important buildings sported gold facings, which threw off dazzling reflections when rays of the Andean sun fell on them.

Since Cuzco was primarily a capital and a ceremonial center, the city's permanent population was sizable but not enormous—perhaps forty thousand—but some two hundred thousand Inca subjects lived in the immediate vicinity. Apart from high-ranking imperial administrators, the most prominent permanent residents of Cuzco proper included the Inca rulers and high nobility, the high priests of the various religious cults, and the hostages of conquered peoples who lived with their families under the watchful eyes of Inca guardians.

**Inca Roads** A magnificent and extensive road system enabled the central government at Cuzco to communicate with all parts of the far-flung Inca Empire and to dispatch large military forces rapidly to distant trouble spots. Two roads linked the Inca realm from north to south—one passing through the mountains, the other running along the coast. Scholars have estimated the combined length of those trunk routes at 16,000 kilometers (almost 10,000 miles). The combined length of the entire network of all Inca roads, including lesser thoroughfares as well as the major trunk routes, may have amounted to 40,000 kilometers (almost 25,000 miles).

Inca roads were among the best ever constructed before modern times. During the early sixteenth century, Spanish conquerors marveled at the roads—paved with stone, shaded by trees, and wide enough to accommodate eight horsemen riding abreast. A corps of official runners carried messages along the roads so that news and information could travel between Cuzco and the most distant parts of the empire within a few days. When the Inca rulers desired a meal of fresh fish, they dispatched runners from Cuzco to the coast, more than 320 kilometers (200 miles) away, and had their catch within two days. Like roads in empires in other parts of the world, the Incas' roads favored their efforts at centralization. Their roads even facilitated the spread of the Quechua language and their religious cult focusing on the sun, both of which became established throughout their empire.

## INTERPRETING IMAGES

Part of the Inca coastal road, here shown at Pachacamac Sanctuary.

**Analyze** *The Roman empire was also known for its reads. Compare and contrast the political, economic, social and religious characteristics Incan Empire and the Roman empire.*

Electra Kay-Smith/Alamy Stock Photo

## Inca Society

**Trade** Despite those splendid roads, Inca society did not generate large classes of merchants and skilled artisans. On the local level the Incas and their subjects bartered surplus agricultural production and handcrafted goods among themselves. Long-distance trade, however, fell under the supervision of the central government. Administrators organized exchanges of agricultural products, textiles, pottery, jewelry, and craft goods, but the Inca state did not permit individuals to become independent merchants. In the absence of a market economy, there was no opportunity for a large class of professional, skilled artisans to emerge. Many individuals produced pottery, textiles, and tools for local consumption, and a few produced especially fine goods for the ruling, priestly, and aristocratic classes. But skilled crafts workers were much less prominent among the Incas than among the Mexica and the peoples of the eastern hemisphere.

**Ruling Elites** The main classes in Inca society were the rulers, the aristocrats, the priests, and the peasant cultivators of common birth. The Incas considered their chief ruler a god descended from the sun. In theory, this god-king owned all land, livestock, and property in the Inca realm, which he governed as an absolute and infallible ruler. Inca rulers retained their prestige even after death. Their descendants mummified the royal remains and regarded departed kings as intermediaries with the gods. Succeeding rulers often deliberated state policy in the presence of royal mummies so as to benefit from their counsel. Indeed, on the occasion of certain festivals, rulers brought out the mummified remains of their ancestors, dressed them in fine clothes, adorned them with gold and silver jewelry, honored them, and presented them with offerings of food and drink to maintain cordial relations with former rulers. Meanwhile, by way of tending to the needs of their living subjects, the Inca god-kings supervised a class of bureaucrats, mostly aristocrats, who allocated plots of land for commoners to cultivate on behalf of the state.

**Aristocrats and Priests** Like the ruling elites, Inca aristocrats and priests led privileged lives. Aristocrats consumed fine foods and dressed in embroidered clothes provided by common subjects. Aristocrats also had the right to wear large ear spools that distended their lobes so much that Spanish conquerors referred to them as "big ears." Priests often came from royal and aristocratic families. They led celibate and ascetic lives, but they deeply influenced Inca society because of their education and their responsibility for overseeing religious rituals. The major temples supported hundreds of priests, along with attendants and virgin women devoted to divine service who prepared ceremonial meals and wove fine ritual garments for the priestly staff.

**Peasants** The cultivators were mostly peasants of common birth who lived in communities known as ***ayllu,*** similar to the Mexicas' *calpulli,* which were the basic units of rural society. Ranging in size from small villages to larger towns, *ayllus* consisted of several families who lived together, sharing land, tools, animals, crops, and work. Peasants supported themselves by working on lands allocated to individual families by their *ayllu.* Instead of paying taxes or tribute, peasants also worked on state lands administered by aristocrats. Much of the production from these state lands went to support the ruling, aristocratic, and priestly classes. The rest went into state storehouses for public relief in times of famine and for the support of widows, orphans, and others unable to cultivate land for themselves. Apart from agricultural work, peasants also owed compulsory labor services to the Inca state. Men provided the heavy labor required for the construction, maintenance, and repair of roads, buildings, and irrigation systems. Women delivered tribute in the form of textiles, pottery, and jewelry. With the aid of *quipu,* Inca bureaucrats kept track of the labor service and tribute owed by local communities.

**Inti** (ihn-tee)
**Viracocha** (veer-rah-coh-chah)

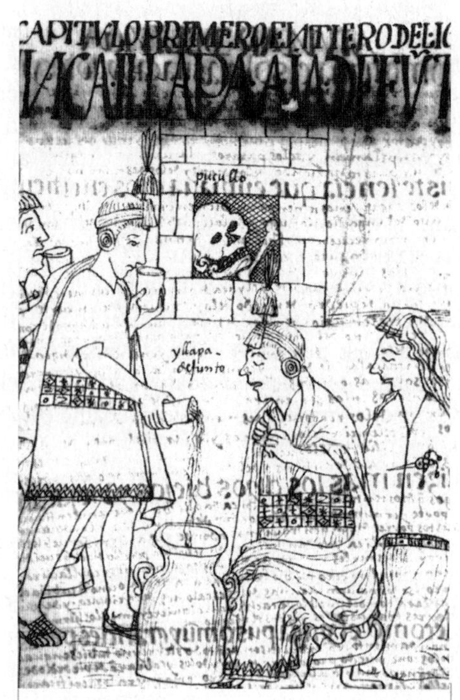
Descendants prepare a ritual meal for a mummified Inca ruler (depicted in the background).
Det Kongelige Bibliotek, Copenhagen.

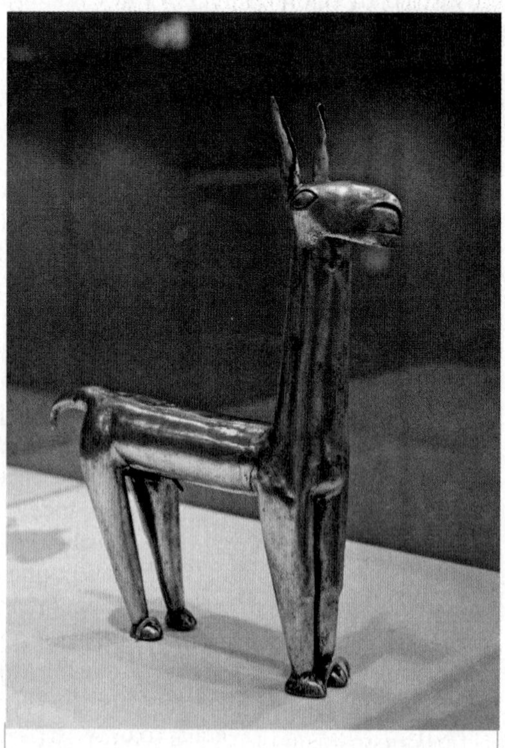
A handsome llama fashioned from silver from Inca Peru.
Mark Dunn/Alamy Stock Photo

**Inca Religion** Members of the Inca ruling class venerated the sun as a god and as their major deity, whom they called **Inti.** They also recognized the moon, stars, planets, rain, and other natural forces as divine. Some Incas, including the energetic ruler Pachacuti, also showed special favor to the god **Viracocha,** creator of the world, humankind, and all else in the universe. The cult of the sun, however, outshone all the others. In Cuzco alone some four thousand priests, attendants, and virgin devotees served Inti, whose temple attracted pilgrims from all parts of the Inca Empire. The first Spanish visitors to Cuzco reported that it took four hundred paces for them to walk around the temple complex, and they expressed amazement at its lavish decoration, including a golden sculpture of the sun encrusted with gems. Particularly astonishing to the visitors was an imitation garden in which grains of gold represented a field, which was planted with stalks of maize fabricated from gold and surrounded by twenty golden llamas with their attendants, also sculpted in gold. Priests of Inti and those serving other cults honored their deities with sacrifices, which in Inca society usually took the form of agricultural produce or animals such as llamas and guinea pigs rather than humans.

**Moral Thought** In addition to sacrifices and ritual ceremonies, Inca religion had a strong moral dimension. The Incas taught a concept of sin as a violation of the established social or natural order, and they believed in a life beyond death, during which individuals would receive rewards or punishments based on the quality of their earthly lives. Sin, they believed, would bring divine disaster both for individuals and for their larger communities. The Incas also observed rituals of confession and penance by which priests absolved individuals of their sins and returned them to the good graces of the gods.

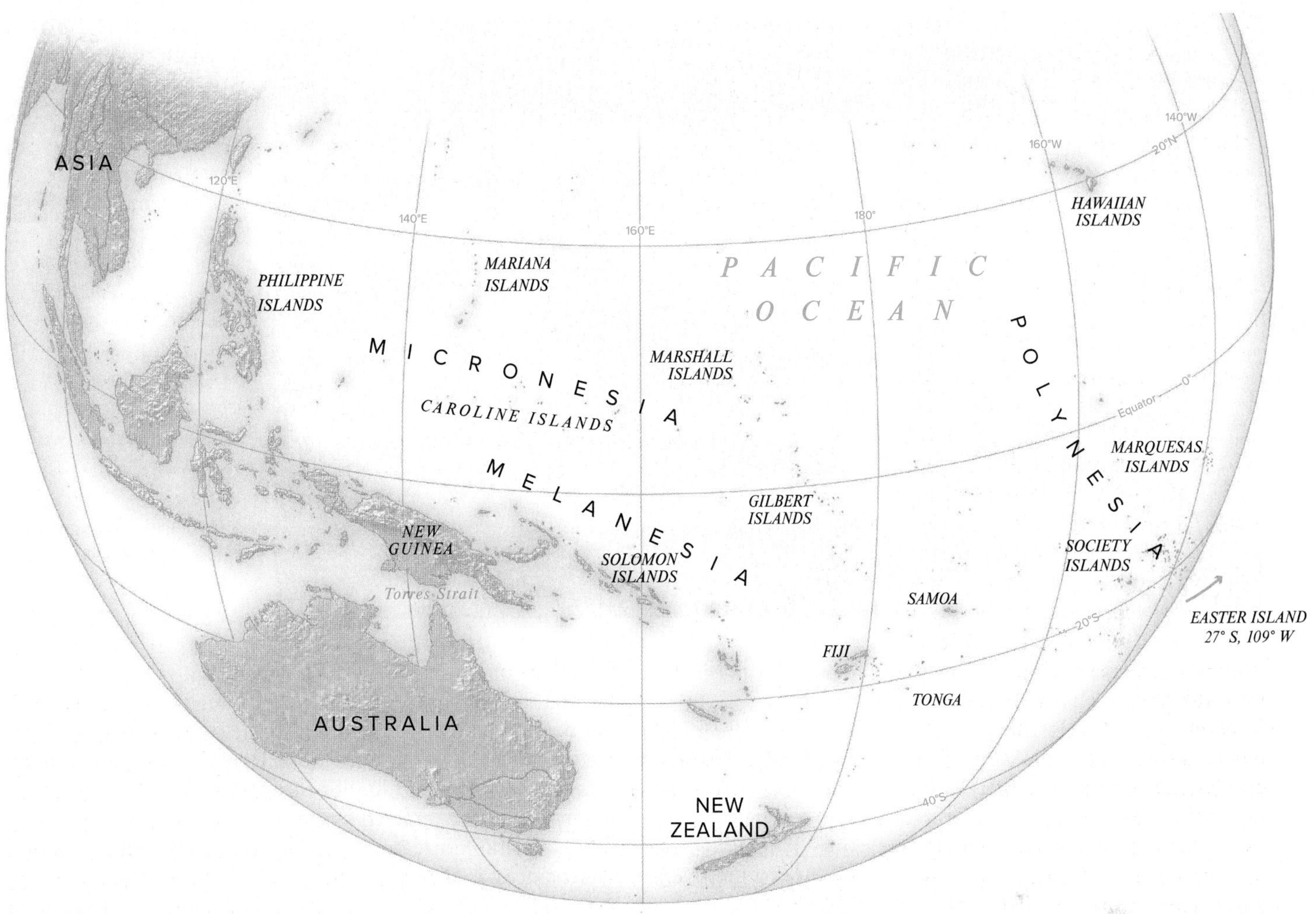


## MAP 8.4 Oceania

Islands are much more numerous and much closer together in the western Pacific than in the eastern Pacific.

***In what ways did proximity to or distance from other islands influence the development of Pacific island societies?***

# THE SOCIETIES OF OCEANIA

Inhabitants of Oceania did not interact with peoples of different societies as frequently or systematically as did their counterparts in the eastern hemisphere, but they built and maintained flourishing traditions and societies of their own. The **aboriginal peoples** of Australia ventured over vast stretches of their continent and created networks of trade and exchange between hunting and gathering societies. Only in the far north, however, did they encounter peoples beyond Australia as they traded sporadically with merchants from New Guinea and the islands of southeast Asia. Meanwhile, throughout the Pacific Ocean, islanders built complex agricultural societies. By the time European mariners sailed into the Pacific Ocean in the sixteenth century, the larger island groups had sizable populations, hierarchical social orders, and hereditary chiefly rulers. In the central and western Pacific, mariners sailed regularly between island groups and established elaborate trade networks. Islanders living toward the eastern and western edges of the Pacific Ocean also had occasional dealings with American and Asian peoples, sometimes with significant consequences for the Pacific island societies.

## The Nomadic Foragers of Australia

After the aboriginal peoples of Australia learned how to exploit the resources of the continent's varied regions, they led lives that in some ways changed little over the centuries. Unlike their neighbors to the north, they did not turn to agriculture. The inhabitants of New Guinea began to herd swine and cultivate root crops about 5000 B.C.E., and the inhabitants of islands in the Torres Strait (which separates Australia from New Guinea) took up gardening soon thereafter. Although aboriginal peoples of northern Australia must have known about foods cultivated in neighboring lands, they maintained nomadic, foraging societies until European peoples migrated to Australia in large numbers during the nineteenth and twentieth centuries.

A late-eighteenth-century sketch of priests traveling across Kealakekua Bay in Hawai'i wearing helmets made from gourds and foliage. Note the construction of the canoes. Using oceangoing vessels such as these, Polynesian peoples discovered and populated all the inhabitable islands of the vast Pacific Ocean.
Historical Picture Archive/Corbis Historical/Getty Images

**Trade** As a result of their mobile and nomadic way of life, aboriginal Australians frequently encountered people from neighboring societies. Because Australia is a continent of enormous climatic and ecological diversity, different peoples enjoyed access to food and other resources unknown to others they encountered during their seasonal migrations. Even though as nomads they did not accumulate large quantities of material goods, groups regularly exchanged surplus food and small items when they met.

That sort of small-scale exchange eventually enabled trade goods to spread throughout most of Australia. Individuals did not travel along all the trade routes. Instead, trade goods passed from one aboriginal community to another until they came to rest in regions often distant from their origins. Baler and oyster pearl shells were among the most popular trade items. Archaeologists have turned up many of these shells fashioned into jewelry more than 1,600 kilometers (1,000 miles) from the waters where the oysters bred. From interior regions came stone axe heads, spears, boomerangs, furs, skins, and fibers.

Aboriginal peoples occasionally traded foodstuffs, but with the exception of some root vegetables, those items were generally too perishable for exchange. Peoples on the north coast also engaged in a limited amount of trade with mariners from New Guinea and the islands of southeast Asia. Australian spears and highly prized pearly shells went north in exchange for exotic items such as the striking flowers of the bird-of-paradise plant, stone clubs, decorative trinkets—and occasionally iron axes, much coveted by aboriginal peoples who had no tradition of metallurgy.

**Cultural and Religious Traditions** In spite of seasonal migrations, frequent encounters with peoples from other aboriginal societies, and trade over long distances, the cultural traditions of Australian peoples mostly did not diffuse much beyond the regions inhabited by individual societies. Aboriginal peoples paid close attention to the prominent geographic features of the lands around them. Rocks, mountains, forests, mineral deposits, and bodies of water were crucial for their survival, and they related stories and myths about those and other geographic features. Often, they conducted religious observances designed to ensure continuing supplies of animals, plant life, and water. Given the intense concern of aboriginal peoples with their immediate environments, their cultural and religious traditions focused on local matters and did not appeal to peoples from other regions.

## The Development of Pacific Island Societies

By the early centuries C.E., humans had established agricultural societies in almost all the island groups of the Pacific Ocean. About the middle of the first millennium C.E., they ventured to the large islands of New Zealand—the last large, habitable region of the earth to receive members of the human species. After 1000 C.E., **Polynesians** inhabiting the larger Pacific islands grew especially numerous, and their surging population prompted remarkable social and political development.

**Trade between Island Groups** In the central and western regions of the Pacific, where several clusters of islands are relatively close to one another, mariners linked island societies. Regional trade networks facilitated exchanges of useful goods such as axes and pottery, exotic items such as shells and decorative ornaments, and sometimes even foodstuffs such as yams. Regional trade within individual island groups served social and political as well as economic functions because it

## How the Past Shapes the Future

### The Diffusion of Technologies

Although the Polynesian islands were remote from other landmasses and from one another, between 1000 and 1500 C.E. Polynesian peoples nevertheless managed to diffuse technologies even to islands thousands of miles away. In the twelfth and thirteenth centuries, Tahitians who sailed to the Hawaiian islands introduced new ways of organizing society, new linguistic terms, and new technologies for constructing fishhooks—all of which were adopted by Hawaiian peoples. Given the importance of fish in the Hawaiian diet, how might new technologies for catching fish have impacted Hawaiian health and population over the long term? In the context of Polynesian societies, consider whether or not the diffusion of technologies that improved fishing techniques could be seen as being as important as the spread of gunpowder technologies or as the horse collar in Eurasia.

helped ruling elites establish and maintain harmonious relations with one another. In some cases, trade crossed longer distances and linked different island groups. Inhabitants of the Tonga, Samoa, and Fiji islands traded mats and canoes, for example, and also intermarried, thus creating political and social relationships.

**Long-Distance Voyaging** Elsewhere in Polynesia, vast stretches of deep blue water made it much more complicated to travel between different island groups and societies. As a result, regular trade networks did not emerge in the eastern Pacific Ocean. Nevertheless, mariners undertook lengthy voyages on an intermittent basis, sometimes with momentous results. After the original settlement of Easter Island about 300 C.E., for example, Polynesian mariners probably ventured to the western coast of South America, where they learned about the cultivation of sweet potatoes. Between about 400 and 700 C.E., mariners spread sweet potatoes throughout Polynesia and beyond to New Caledonia and Vanuatu. The new crop quickly became a prominent source of food in all the islands it reached. Sweet potatoes were especially important for the **Maori** population of New Zealand because the staple crops of the tropical Pacific did not flourish in the temperate climes of New Zealand. Thus long-distance voyages were responsible for the dissemination of sweet potatoes to remote islands situated thousands of kilometers from the nearest inhabited lands.

Another case of long-distance voyaging prompted social changes in the Hawaiian Islands. For centuries after the voyages that brought the original settlers to the islands in the early centuries C.E., there was little travel or communication between Hawai`i and other Polynesian societies. During the twelfth and thirteenth centuries, however, a series of two-way voyages linked Hawai`i with Tahiti and the Marquesas Islands. Memories of those voyages survive in oral traditions that relate the introduction into Hawai`i of new chiefly and priestly lines from Tahiti. Evidence for the voyages comes also from Hawaiian adoption of fishhook styles from Tahiti and words from the Tahitian language.

**Population Growth** While undertaking regular or intermittent voyages over long distances, islanders throughout the Pacific Ocean also built productive agricultural and fishing societies. They cultivated taro, yams, sweet potatoes, bananas, breadfruit, and coconuts, and they kept domesticated chickens, pigs, and dogs. They also fed on abundant supplies of fish, which they caught by spear, net, and hook. After about the fourteenth century, as their population increased, the inhabitants of Hawai`i built ingenious fishponds that allowed small fry to swim from the ocean through narrow gates into rock-enclosed spaces but prevented larger fish from escaping. Fishponds enabled Hawaiians to harvest large quantities of mature fish with relative ease and thus contributed to the islanders' food supplies. The establishment of agricultural and fishing societies led to rapid population growth in all the larger Pacific island groups—Samoa, Tonga, the Society Islands (including Tahiti), and Hawai`i. In Hawai`i, the most heavily populated of the Polynesian island groups, the human population may have exceeded five hundred thousand when European mariners arrived in the late eighteenth century.

**Nan Madol** In other lands, dense populations promoted social organization on a scale never before seen in Oceania. On

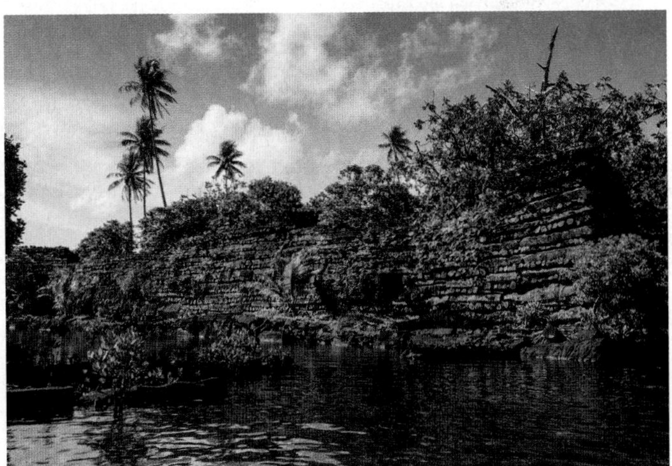

A massive wall constructed of basalt rock protects a burial site at Nan Madol in Pohnpei.

Michael Runkel/Robert Harding World Imagery/Getty Images

**Maori** (MAU-ree)

# SOURCES FROM THE PAST

## Mo`ikeha's Migration from Tahiti to Hawai`i

*A group of Polynesian oral traditions preserves memories of numerous two-way voyages between Tahiti and Hawai`i in the twelfth and thirteenth centuries. One of them has to do with Mo`ikeha, a high chief who left Tahiti because of domestic difficulties and migrated to Hawai`i, where he founded a new chiefly line. The legend recounts several voyages between Tahiti and Hawai`i. The following excerpts deal with Mo`ikeha's establishment as a chief in Hawai`i and the later arrival of his Tahitian son La`amaikahiki, who is credited with the introduction of Tahitian religious and cultural traditions to Hawai`i.*

**It was dark by the** time they arrived [at the Hawaiian island of Kaua`i], so they did not land, instead, mooring their canoe offshore. Early the next morning the people saw this double-hulled canoe floating offshore with the kapu sticks of a chief aboard. The canoe was brought ashore and the travellers got off. Meanwhile the locals were gathering in a crowd to go surf-riding. . . . Among them were the two daughters of the ali`i nui [chief] of Kaua`i, Ho`oipoikamalanai and Hinauu.

> Does Mo`ikeha's reception on Kaua'i indicate that the people on the island saw him as an outsider or as a member of a common culture?

Mo`ikeha and his companions saw the crowd and followed along to take part in the morning exercise. Mo`ikeha was a handsome man with dark reddish hair and a tall, commanding figure.

When Ho`oipoikamalanai and her sister saw Mo`ikeha, they immediately fell in love with him, and they decided to take him for their husband. Mo`ikeha in the meantime was also struck with the beauty and grace of the two sisters, and he, too, fell in love with them and decided to take one of them to be his wife. After enjoying the surf for a time, Ho`oipoikamalanai and her sister returned home and told their father about the new arrival and said: "We wish to take that young chief as a husband for one of us." The father approved.

Orders were issued that Mo`ikeha be brought to the house of the two ali`i women. Mo`ikeha and his company were sent for and brought in the presence of the king [the ali`i nui of Kaua`i]. The love of these young people being mutual, Ho`oipoikamalanai and Hinauu took Mo`ikeha to be their husband. Mo`ikeha became ali`i nui of Kaua`i after the death of his father-in-law. . . .

Mo`ikeha worked to make his two wives and five children happy, giving his undivided attention to the bringing up of his boys. He thought no more of Lu`ukia [his lover in Tahiti], but after a while, he began to feel a yearning desire to see his son La`amaikahiki, his child by his first wife Kapo. So he called his five sons together and said to them: "I'm thinking of sending one of you boys to bring your elder brother to Hawai`i." . . .

> What might the fact that the two daughters of the chief were able to take the same man as their husband, and the fact that Mo'ikeha could take two more wives in addition to his first, say about marriage laws in Polynesia?

[After Mo`ikeha's son Kila sailed to Tahiti and found his elder half-brother] La`amaikahiki immediately prepared to accompany his brother to Hawai`i, as Mo`ikeha wished. La`amaikahiki took his priests and his god Lonoika`ouali`i, and set sail for Hawai`i with the men who had come with Kila. When they were approaching Kaua`i, La`amaikahiki began beating his drum. Mo`ikeha heard his drum and ordered everything, the land as well as the house, to be made ready for the reception of the chief La`amaikahiki. Upon the arrival of La`amaikahiki and Kila, the high priest of Kaua`i, Poloahilani, took La`amaikahiki and his god Lonoila`ouali`i ("Lono at the Chiefly Supremacy") to the heiau [temple]. It is said that La`amaikahiki was the first person to bring a god (akua) to Hawai`i. . . .

[After returning to Tahiti, then sailing again to Hawai`i, La`amaikahiki] set sail again, going up the Kona coast [of Hawai`i Island]. . . . It was on this visit that La`amaikahiki introduced hula dancing, accompanied by the drum, to Hawai`i. . . .

La`amaikahiki stayed a long time on Kaua`i teaching the people the art of dancing. From Kaua`i La`amaikahiki visited all the other islands of this group and thus the drum dance (hula ka`eke) spread to the other islands.

### For Further Reflection

- How would you characterize the political, social, and cultural significance of two-way voyaging between Tahiti and Hawai`i?
- Often "outsiders" are greeted with suspicion and/or animosity. To what do you attribute the congenial exchange between the Tahiti and Hawaii?

*Source:* Teuira Henry and others. *Voyaging Chiefs of Havai`i.* Ed. by Dennis Kawaharada. Honolulu: Kalamaku Press, 1995, pp. 138–39, 144–46.

Pohnpei in the Caroline Islands, for example, the Sandeleur dynasty built a powerful state and organized construction of a massive stone palace and administrative center at **Nan Madol.** Built mostly during the period from 1200 to 1600, the complex included ninety-three artificial islets protected by seawalls and breakwaters on three sides.

**Development of Social Classes** Beginning about the thirteenth century, expanding populations prompted residents of many Pacific islands to develop increasingly complex social and political structures. Especially on the larger islands, workers became more specialized: some concentrated on cultivating certain crops, and others devoted their efforts to fishing; producing axes; or constructing large, seagoing canoes. Distinct classes emerged as aristocratic and ruling elites decided the course of public affairs in their societies and extracted surplus agricultural production from those of common birth. The islands of Tonga, Tahiti, and Hawai`i had especially stratified societies with sharp distinctions between various classes of high chiefs, lesser chiefs, and commoners. Hawaiian society also recognized distinct classes of priests and skilled artisans, such as adze (a cutting tool similar to an axe) makers and canoe builders, ranking between the chiefly and common classes.

**The Formation of Chiefly States** In addition to distinct social classes, island societies generated strong political leadership. Ruling chiefs generally oversaw public affairs in portions of an island, sometimes in an entire island, and occasionally in several islands situated close to one another. In Tonga and Hawai`i, high chiefs frequently launched campaigns to bring additional islands under their control and create large centralized states. Rarely, however, were these militant chiefs able to overcome geographic and logistic difficulties and realize their expansionist ambitions before the nineteenth century.

Nevertheless, high chiefs guided the affairs of complex societies throughout Polynesia. They allocated lands to families, mobilized labor for construction projects, and organized men into military forces. They commanded enormous respect within their societies. In Hawai`i, for example, the classes of high chiefs known as ***ali`i nui*** intermarried, ate the best fish and other foods that were ***kapu*** ("taboo") to commoners, and had the right to wear magnificent cloaks adorned with thousands of bright red and yellow bird feathers. Indeed, a *kapu* forbade commoners to approach or even cast a shadow on the *ali`i nui.*

**Polynesian Religion** High chiefs often claimed that their power descended directly from the gods. They also worked closely with priests, who served as intermediaries between human communities and the gods. Gods of war and agriculture were common throughout the Pacific islands, but individual islands and island groups recognized deities particular to their own regions and interests. The most distinctive architecture of early Pacific societies was the ceremonial precinct and temple structure known as ***marae*** (or *heiau* in Hawaiian). *Marae* often had several terraced floors with a rock or coral wall designating the boundaries of the sacred space. In Tonga and Samoa, temples made of timber and thatched roofs served as places of worship, sacrifice, and communication between priests and the gods, whereas in eastern Polynesia religious ceremonies took place on platforms in open-air courtyards. The largest of those structures, the *marae* Mahaiatea on Tahiti, took the form of a step pyramid about 15 meters (49 feet) high with a base measuring 81 by 22 meters (266 by 72 feet).

Pacific island societies did not have access to the range of technologies developed by continental peoples until the sixteenth and later centuries. Yet Pacific islanders cleverly exploited their environments; established productive agricultural economies; built elaborate, well-organized traditions and societies; and reached out when possible to engage in trade with their neighbors. Their achievements testify anew to the human impulses toward densely populated communities and interaction with other societies.

## CONCLUSION

The original inhabitants of the Americas and Oceania lived in societies that were considerably smaller than those of the eastern hemisphere. They did not possess the metallurgical technologies that enabled their counterparts to exploit more fully the natural environment, nor did they possess the transportation technologies based on wheeled vehicles and domesticated animals that facilitated trade and communication among peoples of the eastern hemisphere. Nevertheless, long before they entered into sustained encounters with European and other peoples, they built complex societies and developed sophisticated cultural and religious traditions. Indigenous peoples established foraging, fishing, and agricultural societies throughout the Americas, and they fashioned tools from wood, stone, and bone that enabled them to produce enough food to support sizable communities. In Mesoamerica and Andean South America, they also built imperial states that organized public affairs on a large scale. The cultural and religious traditions of these imperial societies reflected their concern for agricultural production and the maintenance of complex social structures.

The original inhabitants of Australia and the Pacific islands built societies on a smaller scale than did the peoples of the Americas, but they too devised effective means of exploiting the natural environment, developing strong traditions, and organizing flourishing communities. Australia was a continent of foraging nomadic peoples, whereas the Pacific islands supported densely populated agricultural societies. Although they had limited communication with peoples of the Americas or the eastern hemisphere, the peoples of Oceania had regular encounters with their neighbors, and inhabitants of the Pacific islands sometimes undertook lengthy voyages to trade with distant island groups. Although the peoples of the Americas and of Oceania were a world apart from their counterparts in Africa, Asia, and Europe, they built vigorous traditions and engaged in long-distance encounters within their own regions.

## STUDY TERMS

aboriginal peoples (257)
*ali`i nui* (261)
*ayllu* (417)
Aztec Empire (256)
Cahokia (252)
*calpulli* (256)
*chinampa* (245)
Chimu (253)
Chucuito (253)
Cuzco (254)
Huitzilopochtli (242)
Inca Empire (254)
Inti (256)
Iroquois (251)
Itzcóatl (246)
*kapu* (261)
Maori (259)
*marae* (261)
Mexica (245)
Motecuzoma I (246)
Nan Madol (261)
Navajo (251)
Polynesians (258)
Pueblo (251)
Quechua (254)
Quetzalcóatl (250)
*quipu* (254)
Tenochtitlan (242)
Teotihuacan (245)
Tezcatlipoca (250)
Toltecs (245)
Tula (245)
Viracocha (256)

## FOR FURTHER READING

Inga Clendinnen. *Aztecs: An Interpretation.* Cambridge, 1991. A brilliant re-creation of the Mexica world, concentrating on cultural and social themes.

George A. Collier, Renato I. Rosaldo, and John D. Wirth, eds. *The Inca and Aztec States, 1400–1800: Anthropology and History.* New York, 1982. Seventeen well-focused essays represent approaches that scholars have taken to the Inca and Aztec empires.

Ross Hassig. *Aztec Warfare: Imperial Expansion and Political Control.* Norman, Okla., 1988. A solid scholarly study of Mexica military affairs and their role in the building of the Aztec Empire.

Peter Hiscock. *Archaeology of Ancient Australia,* London, 2008. Comprehensive overview of the current state of archaeological investigation into aboriginal culture and history.

Patrick V. Kirch. *On the Road of the Winds: An Archaeological History of the Pacific Islands before European Contact.* Berkeley, 2000. A valuable synthesis of recent scholarship by the foremost contemporary archaeologist of the Pacific islands.

Charles C. Mann. *1491: New Revelations of the Americas before Columbus.* New York, 2006. Summarizes a great deal of archaeological research on the pre-Columbian Americas.

Gordon McEwan. *The Incas: New Perspectives.* New York, 2008. Offers recent interpretations of Inca culture, politics, economics, and daily life.

Michael E. Moseley. *The Incas and Their Ancestors: The Archaeology of Peru.* Rev. ed. London, 2001. A comprehensive survey of Andean history through the era of the Incas.

Christina Thompson. *Sea People: The Puzzle of Polynesia.* New York, 2019. Engaging and fresh account about who settled Polynesia and how they got there.

Camilla Townsend. *Fifth Sun: A New History of the Aztecs.* Oxford, 2019. Revisionist history of the Aztec conquest told solely through documents produced by Mexica peoples themselves.

# CHAPTER 8 AP EXAM PRACTICE

Questions assume cumulative knowledge from this chapter and previous chapters.

## Section I

## Multiple Choice Questions

Use the image below and your knowledge of world history to answer questions 1 – 3.

An artist depiction of *chinampas* agriculture.
Alfredo Dagli Orti/Shutterstock

1. Which of the following was NOT a reason why Lake Texcoco was important to the Aztec Empire?
   (A) The lake provided a water supply.
   (B) The lake connected to river systems that led to the Pacific coast.
   (C) The causeways across the lake were roads for bringing goods into Tenochtitlan.
   (D) The Aztecs used the lake to provide food through chinampa agriculture.

2. This image illustrates what historical development?
   (A) Large rafts were used to travel between islands in Lake Texcoco.
   (B) Mexica society was divided into an aristocratic warrior class and a working peasant class.
   (C) The Mexica learned how to make canoes from the Polynesians.
   (D) The Mexica grew orchards in the lake to provide a fuel supply for the city.

3. What problems do historians have with sources for Aztec history?
   (A) Archaeologists have not been able to study Mexica cities because they were all flooded by the lake.
   (B) Nahuatl, the language of the Mexica, has not been translated so scholars are not able to read the sources from that time.
   (C) Most of the existing written sources about the Aztecs were written by the Spanish or by Mexica working under Spanish authority.
   (D) Archives do not allow scholars to study Mexica documents.

Use the map below and your knowledge of world history to answer questions 4 and 5.

The Inca Empire, 1471-1532

McGraw Hill

4. Renaissance humanists, architects, and artists drew inspiration from ancient Rome and what other source?
   (A) The naturalistic style of Daoist art.
   (B) Admiration for the way the Russians defied Mongol influence.
   (C) A desire to memorialize the lives lost during the Black Death.
   (D) The wealth and products that were imported from across Afro-Eurasia.

5. Italian Renaissance cities were important trading hubs. Which of the following characterized major trading centers across Afro-Eurasia?
   (A) Strategic locations, order, and low custom fees
   (B) Hilltop locations, defensive walls, and good roads
   (C) Large cathedrals, beautiful architecture, and scenic views
   (D) Good climate, local artists, and universities

## Short Answer

6. Use the image below and your knowledge of world history to answer parts A, B, and C.

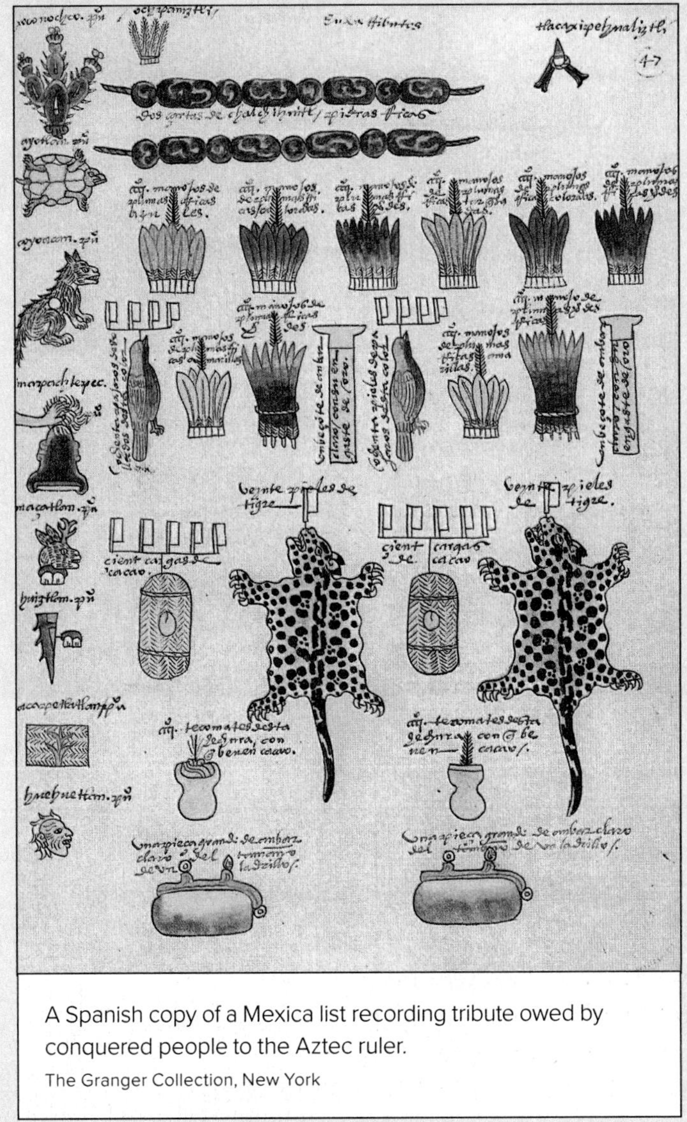

A Spanish copy of a Mexica list recording tribute owed by conquered people to the Aztec ruler.

The Granger Collection, New York

(A) Identify ONE way, other than tribute, that the Aztecs controlled subject peoples.
(B) Explain ONE way the Aztec Empire benefited from the tribute system.
(C) Explain ONE difference between the tribute systems in the Aztec and Incan Empires.

7. Use the image below and your knowledge of world history to answer parts A, B, and C.

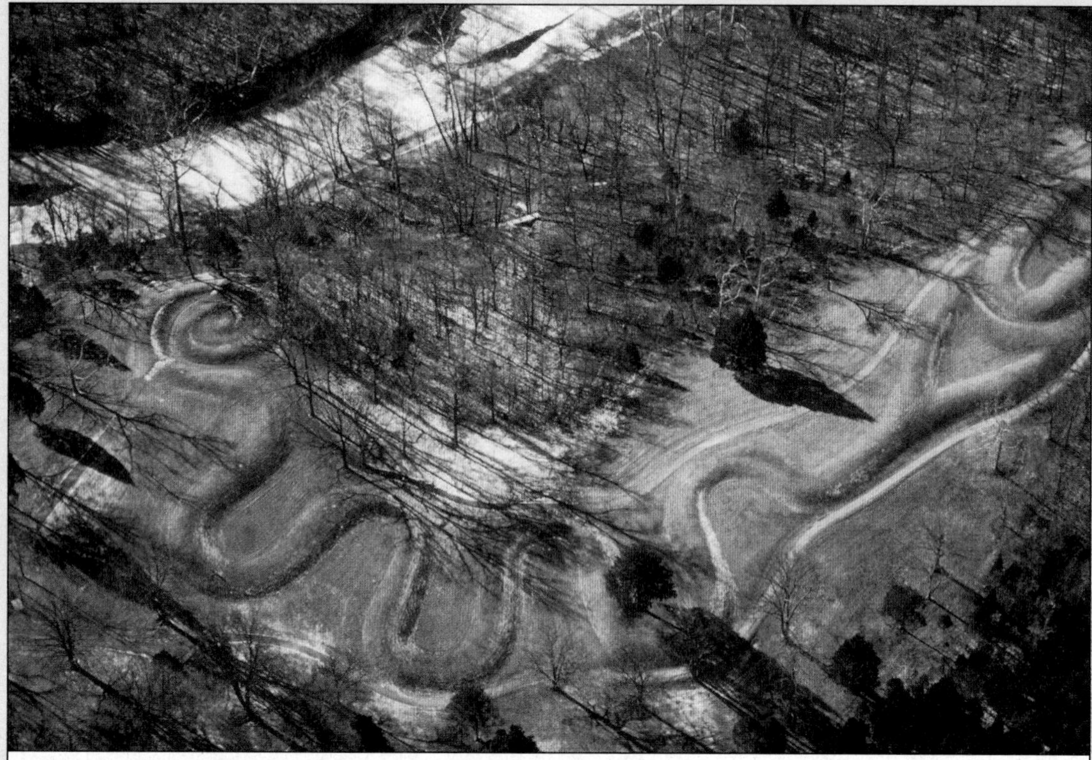

Great Serpent Mound in modern day Ohio, constructed around 1000 C.E.
Georg Gerster/Science Source

(A) Identify ONE source that historians use to understand the history of North America before 1492, C.E.
(B) Identify ONE reason why some North American cultures used the mound structures.
(C) Explain ONE way that the environment influences the development of states in North America before 1492 C.E.

8. Use your understanding of world history to answer parts A, B, and C.
(A) Explain ONE technology helped Polynesians manage a growing population.
(B) Explain ONE way that social classes developed in Polynesia.
(C) Identify ONE difference between Polynesian and Australian society.

# Section II

## Document-Based Question

Based on the documents below and your knowledge of world history, evaluate how the Aztec Empire continued the traditions of the Mexica region while also introducing their own political and religious innovations

In your response you should do the following:

- Respond to the prompt with a historically defensible thesis or claim that establishes a line of reasoning.
- Describe a broader historical context relevant to the prompt.
- Support an argument in response to the prompt using all documents.
- Use at least one additional piece of specific historical evidence (beyond that found in the documents) relevant to an argument about the prompt.
- Explain how or why the document's point of view, purpose, historical situation, and /or audience is relevant to an argument.
- Use evidence to corroborate, qualify, or modify an argument that addresses the prompt.

### Document 1

[**To a newborn boy the** midwife said:] "Heed, hearken: thy home is not here, for thou art an eagle, thou art an ocelot; thou art a roseate spoonbill, thou art a troupial [a bird like an oriole]. Thou art the serpent, the bird of the lord of the near, of the nigh. Here is only the place of thy nest. Thou hast only been hatched here; thou hast only come, arrived. Thou art only come forth on earth here. Here dost thou bud, blossom, germinate. Here thou becomest the chip, the fragment [of thy mother]. Here are only the cradle, thy cradle blanket, the resting place of thy head: only thy place of arrival. Thou belongest out there; out there thou hast been consecrated. Thou hast been sent into warfare. War is thy desert, thy task. Thou shalt give drink, nourishment, food to the sun, the lord of the earth. Thy real home, thy property, thy lot is the home of the sun there in the heavens. . . . Perhaps thou wilt receive the gift, perhaps thou wilt merit death [in battle] by the obsidian knife, the flowered death by the obsidian knife. . . ."

*Source:* Bernardino de Sahagún. *Florentine Codex: General History of the Things of New Spain*, 13 vols. Trans. by Charles E. Dibble and Arthur J. O. Anderson. Salt Lake City: University of Utah Press, 1950–82, 171–73 (book 6, chapter 31).

### Document 2

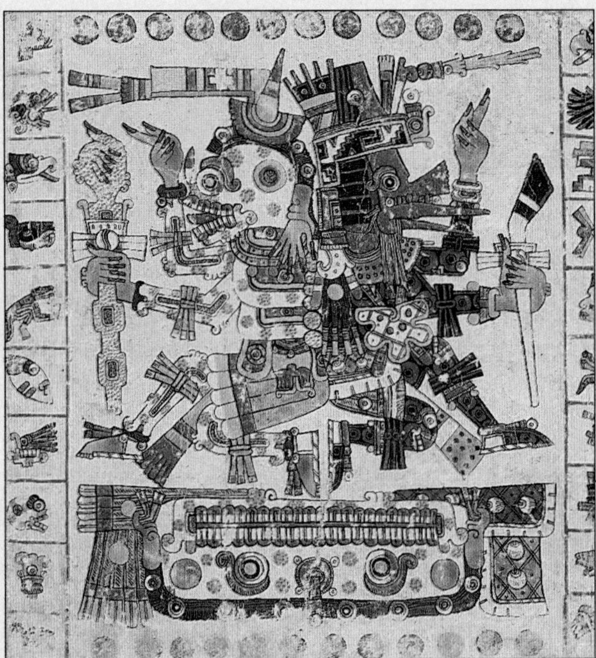

A Mexica manuscript known as the Codex Borgia depicts Quetzalcóatl (left) as the lord of life and Tezcatlipoca (right)as the god of death.

Biblioteca Apostolica Vaticana/Index S.A.S.

## Document 3

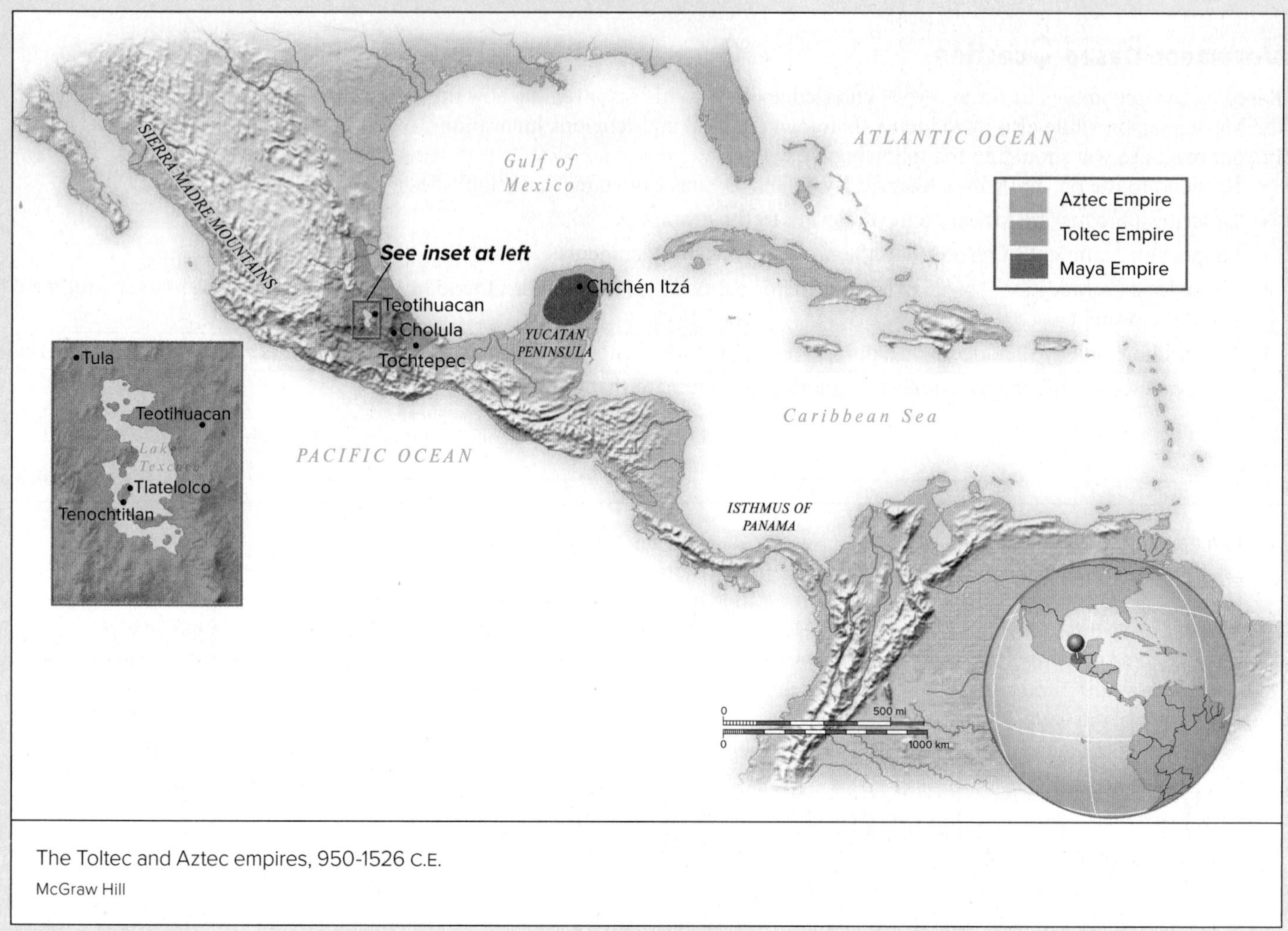


The Toltec and Aztec empires, 950-1526 C.E.

McGraw Hill

## Long Essay

Develop a thoughtful and thorough historical argument that answers the question below. Begin your essay with a thesis statement and support it with relevant historical evidence.

Using specific examples and your knowledge of world history, evaluate the role of religion and society in the Inca state.

# Part 1 A Global Tapestry c. 1200–c. 1450

It should be clear from reading the preceding chapters that the reasons for and consequences of increasing trade, contact, and wealth are a critical part of understanding this era of world history. It's also important not to forget the people. As you reflect on these post-classical "Global Tapestry" chapters, think about what sort of people functioned in which roles:

- Who were the merchants, the workers, the bankers, the soldiers and sailors, the enslaved?
- Where did these people and their work "fit" into society?
- How was one's position on the social ladder determined?
- How did women fare in these postclassical societies?
- What was considered "women's work," and how much influence did women of different classes or castes have on "men's work"?
- Did newly introduced religious beliefs improve or suppress the influence of women in a society?

Think especially about the pastoralist peoples—the Mongols, the Bantu, the Arabs, and Berbers: their roles in trade, cultural exchange, and conquest will continue to impact the development of societies and the global system.

More written documents have survived from the postclassical era than from earlier periods, and those highlighted in AP World History tend be travelers' writings. Why? Because travelers in foreign lands commented on the people and their social practices, telling us how much or how little intercultural knowledge and understanding existed. When you think back on the travel accounts you read in Part 1, what kinds of things stood out to you? What did the writers notice about the societies they encountered? What elements are common between these accounts? In contrast, what differs between the accounts? What do those differences tell us about the cultures that produced these travelers?

Another significant pattern highlighted in this period—and critical to your understanding of AP World History and its themes—is the continuing importance of cities and their enormous growth.

- Why did they rise and fall? Did religious leaders in a region locate themselves in cities, and, if so, why?
- Who ruled the cities, and were the cities important because they were political centers (capitals), or commercial or religious centers?
- Who lived in the cities, and where did they come from? Were the cities centers of learning and the arts?

You will want to be able to explain the religious, commercial (trade), governmental, and cultural functions of at least two major cities in this period, as this will help you prepare for questions that might arise on the AP exam.

As you review what you have learned, consider how the AP World History themes were demonstrated through these chapters.

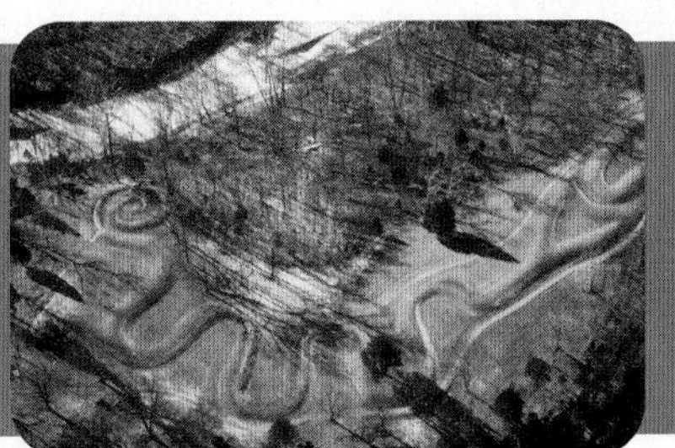

## THEME 1: HUMANS AND THE ENVIRONMENT (ENV)

The environment shapes human societies, and as populations grow and change, these populations in turn shape their environments. (This also includes geography. The history of India would be much different had there not been the Khyber Pass.)

## THEME 2: CULTURAL DEVELOPMENTS AND INTERACTIONS (CDI)

The development of ideas, beliefs, and religions illustrates how groups in society view themselves, and the interactions of societies and their beliefs often have political. social, and cultural implications.

## THEME 3: GOVERNANCE (GOV)

A variety of internal and external factors contribute to state formation, expansion, and decline. Governments maintain order through a variety of administrative institutions, policies, and procedures, and governments obtain, retain, and exercise power in different ways and for different purposes. (Pay attention to the reasons for the rise and fall of governments/dynasties/empires.)

## THEME 4: ECONOMIC SYSTEMS (ECN)

As societies develop, they affect and are affected by the ways that they produce, exchange, and consume goods and services. (The major focus of this theme before 1750 is going to be trade, which is a constant item on the AP exam.)

## THEME 5: SOCIAL INTERACTIONS AND ORGANIZATION (SIO)

The process by which societies group their members and the norms that govern the interactions between these groups and between individuals influence political, economic, and cultural institutions and organization.

## THEME 6: TECHNOLOGY AND INNOVATION (TEC)

Human adaptation and innovation have resulted in increased efficiency, comfort. and security, and technological advances have shaped human development and interactions with both intended and unintended consequences. (Quick definition: technology is anything that helps human beings manipulate their environment. The use of fire, for example, was one of the first technological advances.)

(This also a point at which to remember the cross-over between the themes. Large parts of Theme 1 and Theme 4 have to do with changes in technology.)

Explorer/Science Source, Georg Gerster/Science Source, Album/Alamy Stock Photo

# PART 1 AP EXAM PRACTICE

Questions assume cumulative knowledge from this Part.

## Section I

## Multiple Choice Questions

Using the passage below and your knowledge of world history, answer questions 1-3.

> "For even the high lifted and chivalric Crusaders of old times were not content to traverse two thousand miles of land to fight for their holy sepulchre, without committing burglaries, picking pockets, and gaining other pious perquisites by the way. Had they been strictly held to their one final and romantic object—that final and romantic object, too many would have turned from in disgust."
>
> **– Herman Melville, *Moby Dick***
>
> *Source:* Melville, Herman. *Moby Dick; or, The Whale*. Project Gutenberg, 2001.

1. One proof of Melville's thoughts about the crusades would be:
   (A) The Crusades signaled Europe's larger involvement in the affairs of the Middle East.
   (B) The Order of the Knights of Saint John of the Hospital
   (C) The sacking of the Christian city of Constantinople.
   (D) The bringing Muslim technology back to Europe by the crusaders.

2. Another example which would help to prove Melville's thesis would be
   (A) Mahmud of Ghazni pillaging and destroying Hindu temples and putting mosques in their place.
   (B) Chinggis Khan not moving into Europe because he saw nothing worth taking.
   (C) One of the Tang emperors lowering the tax rate to a very low 2.5 percent.
   (D) Mohammed conquering Mecca and not letting his followers pillage the city.

3. An argument against Melville's thesis would be
   (A) The founding of mendicant orders of knights.
   (B) The conquest of Mexico by Hernan Cortez.
   (C) The siege of Kilwa by the Portuguese.
   (D) Henry VIII's seizure of Catholic monasteries.

4. The shift from the Tang to the Song Dynasty demonstrates which principle of Chinese political philosophy?
   (A) The Neo-Confucian edict of "Shifting rule."
   (B) The "Mandate of Heaven."
   (C) The idea of "Divine Right Monarchy."
   (D) The Confucian idea of filial piety.

5. The Five Pillars of Islam are:
   (A) The Profession of Faith, Prayer, Missionary work, Charity, the Hajj.
   (B) The Profession of Faith, Missionary work, Fasting during Ramadan, Charity, the Hajj.
   (C) The Profession of Faith, Prayer, Fasting during Ramadan, Charity, the Hajj.
   (D) Missionary work, Prayer, Fasting during Ramadan, Charity, the Hajj.

Using the image below and your knowledge of world history, answer questions 6-8.

A scene from the Bayeux Tapestry, depicting the Norman Invasion of 1066. William the Conqueror's troops land at Pevensey and make their way to Hastings, where they prepare food. The tapestry is housed in the town of Bayeux in Normandy.
Hulton Archive/Getty Images

6. The ships shown in the Bayeux Tapestry make reference to
   (A) the Normans Mediterranean trade network
   (B) the Normans Viking heritage
   (C) the Normans copying Indian Ocean dhows.
   (D) the Normans having prototype caravels

7. The tapestry commemorates
   (A) the Moors invasion of the Iberian Peninsula
   (B) the Norman's retaking of Sicily from the Muslims
   (C) the Vikings pillaging of the Lindisfarne monastery in Ireland
   (D) William the Conqueror's invasion of England

8. The date is approximately
   (A) the middle 1000s
   (B) the early 1000s
   (C) the early 1100s
   (D) the middle 1100s

Using the image below and your knowledge of world history, answer questions 9-11.

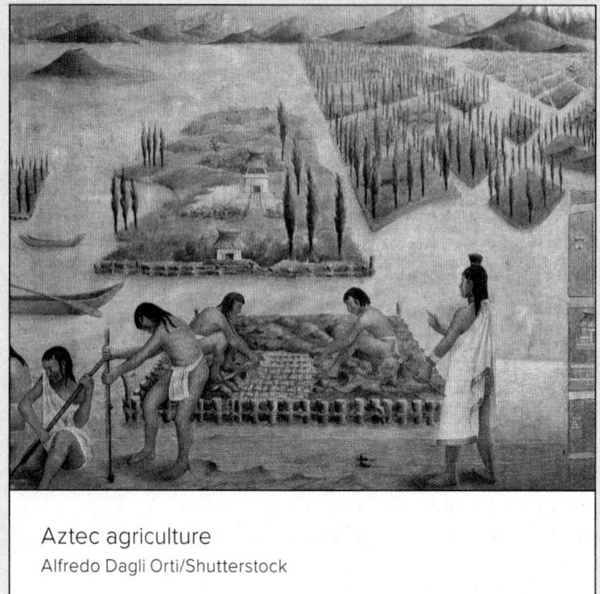

Aztec agriculture
Alfredo Dagli Orti/Shutterstock

9. The picture above shows the Aztec method of cultivation known as
   (A) quipu
   (B) calpulli
   (C) chinampa
   (D) heiau

10. This method allowed the Aztecs to produce large amounts of surplus food which brought about changes in life style not unlike the
   (A) the Chinese acquiring fast-ripening rice from Vietnam
   (B) the Mongol use of iron plows
   (C) the bringing of potatoes to South Asia
   (D) the introduction of wheat into Mali by Mansa Musa when he returns from the Hajj

11. The advantage of this technique appears to be
   (A) the ability to grow large citrus trees
   (B) to use the islands as fish hatcheries
   (C) constant irrigation, even in the dry season
   (D) the ability to move the islands away from the shore and thus escape paying taxes.

12. The Zanj Revolt refers to the
   (A) Christian revolt in Ethiopia
   (B) Swahili revolt against the Portuguese in the city of Kilwa
   (C) revolt by African slaves in southern Mesopotamia
   (D) revolt by Africans against the slave trade in the Kongo Kingdom

Using the passage below and your knowledge of world history, answer questions 13-15.

> You nobles, you sons of my chiefs, you superfine dandies, you have trusted to your birth and your possessions and have set at naught my orders to your own advancement; you have neglected the pursuit of learning and you have given yourselves over to luxury and sport, to idleness and profitless pastimes. By the King of Heaven, I take no account of your noble birth and your fine looks, though others may admire you for them. Know this for certain, that unless you make up for your former sloth by vigourous study, you will never get any favour from Charles.
>
> — Charlemagne- To noble-born students whose work was poor while lesser-born children had worked hard to write well; as related by Notker the Stammerer in De Carolo Magno.
>
> *Source:* Halsall, Paul. *Early Lives of Charlemagne by Eginhard and the Monk of St. Gall,1926.* New York: Fordham University, 1998.

13. Which of Charlemagne's policies are in line with his thinking as expressed in the quotation?
    (A) His reliance on aristocrats to help him manage his empire.
    (B) His use of the church leaders as members of the *missi dominici.*
    (C) His acceptance of the hereditary crown to become king of the Franks.
    (D) His use of non-noble officers at the Battle of Tours.

14. Another leader who followed a similar policy was
    (A) Charles Martel
    (B) Emperor Yang Jian
    (C) Chinggis Khan
    (D) King Harsha

15. Another reflection of this idea is the
    (A) the choosing of the Shi'i sultan
    (B) the divine right of kings
    (C) the Bureaucracy of Merit
    (D) the selection of the Japanese emperor.

## Short Answer

Use the passage below to answer all parts of the questions that follow.

6. Using the passage below and your knowledge of world history, answer parts A, B, and C.
   (A) Identify ONE Chinese emperor who appeared to have followed Confucian principles.
   (B) Identify ONE Chinese emperor who appeared to not have followed Confucian principles.
   (C) Explain ONE example of the Japanese following the principles set forth in the Analects.

7. Using the image below and your knowledge of world history, answer parts A, B, and C.
   (A) Give ONE reason why this image seems to match with the principles of the Hajj.
   (B) Give ONE reason why this image does not seem to match with principles of the Hajj.
   (C) Give ONE reason (either historical or religious) why Muhammed is not pictured.

Turkish epic of the life of Mohammed written by Mustafa, son of Yusef of Erzurum; original completed in c.1388; illustrated during reign of Murad III and completed in 1595
Bildarchiv Steffens/Bridgeman Images

8. Using your knowledge of world history, answer parts A, B, and C.
   (A) Give ONE reason for a religious similarity between the Byzantine and western Christian Churches
   (B) Give ONE reason for a religious difference between the Byzantine and western Christian Churches
   (C) Give ONE example of how the similarity/difference contributed to the economies of either the Byzantine Empire or western Europe.

## Document-Based Question

Suggested reading and writing time: 1 hour
It is suggested that you spend 15 minutes reading the documents and 45 minutes writing your response.

Note: You may begin writing your response before the reading period is over.
The documents have been edited for the purpose of this exercise.

Evaluate the extent to which the various views of Chinggis (Genghis) Khan compare with your own from your knowledge of history.

In your response you should do the following.

- Respond to the prompt with a historically defensible thesis or claim that establishes a line of reasoning.
- Describe a broader historical context relevant to the prompt.
- Support an argument in response to the prompt using at least six documents.
- Use at least one additional piece of specific historical evidence (beyond that found in the documents) relevant to an argument about the prompt.
- For at least three documents, explain how or why the document's point of view, purpose, historical situation, and/or audience is relevant to an argument.
- Use evidence to corroborate, qualify, or modify an argument that addresses the prompt.

Note: The map below is provided as a reference. The map is NOT one of the seven documents. The documents begin below the map.

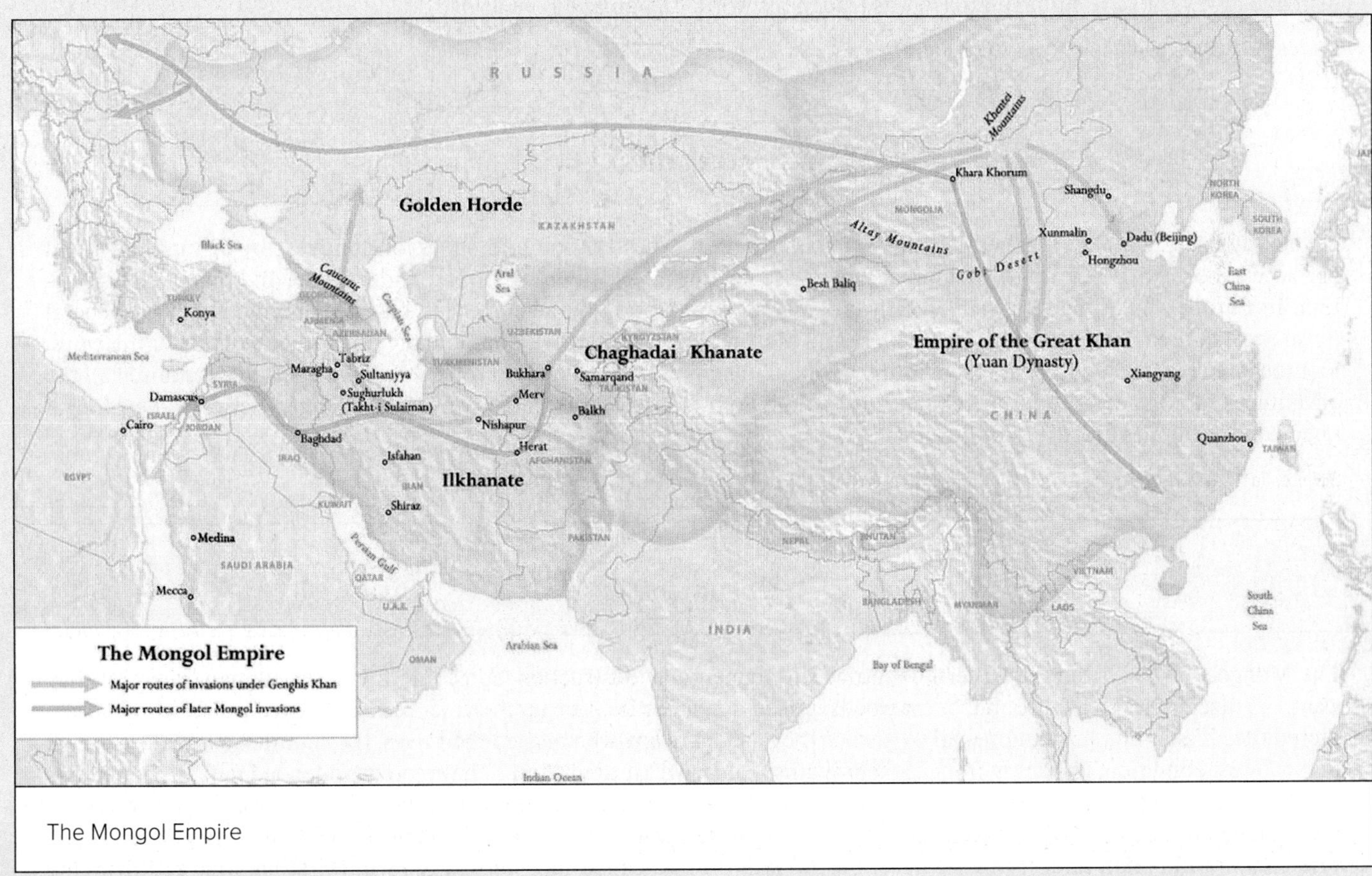


The Mongol Empire

## Document 1

The Master said, "If the people be led by laws, and uniformity sought to be given them by punishments, they will try to avoid the punishment, but have no sense of shame.
"If they be led by virtue, and uniformity sought to be given them by the rules of propriety, they will have the sense of shame, and moreover will become good."
Confucius, *The Analects*
For even Antichrist will spare such as follow him, though he destroy those who oppose him, but these Tatars spared none, slaying women and men and children, ripping open pregnant women and killing unborn babes. ... the hurt was universal; and which passed over the lands like clouds driven by the wind.
Ibn al-Athir, Muslim historian, On The Tatars [Mongols], 1220-1221 C.E.

*Source:* Edward G. Browne, *A Literary History of Persia*, (Cambridge: Cambridge University Press, 1902), Vol. II, pp. 427–431.

## Document 2

'At Sarray in the country of Tartars there lived a king who waged war on Russia, through which many a brave man died. This noble king was called Genghis Khan. He was of such great fame in his time that there was nowhere in any region so excellent a king in everything. He lacked nothing that was proper for a king. As for the religion to which he was born, he was faithful to its law (teaching), to which he was sworn. And moreover, he was robust, wise, and rich. He was kindhearted, just, and always alike (evenhanded). He was true to his word, benign and honourable.

*Source:* 'The Canterbury Tales', Wordsworth Poetry Library edition, 1995.

## Document 3

"In nearly every country touched by the Mongols, the initial destruction and shock of conquest by an unknown and barbaric tribe yielded quickly to an unprecedented rise in cultural communication, expanded trade, and improved civilization. In Europe, the Mongols slaughtered the aristocratic knighthood of the continent, but, disappointed with the general poverty of the area compared with the Chinese and Muslim countries, turned away and did not bother to conquer the cities, loot the countries, or incorporate them into the expanding empire. In the end, Europe suffered the least yet acquired all the advantages of contact through merchants such as the Polo family of Venice and envoys exchanged between the Mongol khans and the popes and kings of Europe.

*Source:* Jack Weatherford, historian, *Genghis Khan and the Making of the Modern World*, 2004.

## Document 4

The Mongols . . . "ravaged the eastern countries with lamentable destruction, spreading fire and slaughter wherever they went. . . . razed cities to the ground, burnt woods, pulled down castles, tore up the vine-trees, destroyed gardens, and massacred the citizens and husbandmen; if by chance they did spare any who begged their lives, they compelled them, as slaves of the lowest condition, to fight in front of them against their own kindred. And if they merely pretended to fight, or perhaps warned their countrymen to flee, the Tartars following in their rear, slew them; and if they fought bravely and conquered, they gained no thanks by way of recompense, and thus these savages ill-treated their captives as though they were horses. The men are inhuman and of the nature of beasts, rather to be called monsters than men, thirsting after and drinking blood, and tearing and devouring the flesh of dogs and human beings."

*Source:* Paris, Matthew and William Rishanger. Trans. By J.A. Giles. *Matthew Paris's English History: From the Year 1235 to 1273, vol. 1.* United Kingdom: H.G. Bohn, 1852.

## Document 5

Genghis Khan seated on his throne with his wife
Gainew Gallery/Alamy Stock Photo

## Document 6

Sayings attributed to Chinggis Khan
"Conquering the world on horseback is easy; it is dismounting and governing that is hard."
"An action committed in anger is an action doomed to failure."
"There is no good in anything until it is finished."
"A man's greatest joy is crushing his enemies."

*Source:* Khan, Genghis. "Genghis Khan Quotes." Goodreads, Inc., 2021.

## Document 7

Elbegdorj Tsahkia, Mongolian prime minister, interview, 2005
"Genghis Khan wasn't really a bad guy. He just had bad press."

*Source:* Pocha, Jehangir P. "Mongolia sees Genghis Khan's good side." *The New York Times,* May 2005.

# Long Essay

1. Evaluate the extent to which the following comment paints an accurate picture of the Indian Ocean as discussed in Part 1.
   "Whoever controls the Indian Ocean will dominate Asia... This ocean is the key to the seven seas in the twenty-first century, the destiny of the world will be decided in these waters."
   -Rear Admiral Alfred Thayer Mahan, USN (Ret.) Writing in 1918.
2. Evaluate the extent to which the environment shaped the various native peoples of North America.
3. Evaluate the extent to which technology changed western Europe in the period from 1000 C.E. to 1450 C.E.

In your response you should do the following:

- Respond to the prompt with a historically defensible thesis or claim that establishes a line of reasoning.
- Describe a broader historical context relevant to the prompt.
- Support an argument in response to the prompt using specific and relevant examples of evidence.
- Use historical reasoning (e.g. comparison, causation, continuity or change) to frame or structure an argument that addresses the prompt.
- Use evidence to corroborate, qualify, or modify an argument that addresses the prompt.

# Part 2 Land-Based Empires and Transoceanic Empires (1450–1750)

Historical Picture Archive/Corbis/Getty Images



## LEARNING OBJECTIVES

As you study Part 2 you will:

- Analyze the deepening and widening of networks of human interaction within and across regions.
- Explain how knowledge, scientific learning, and technology from the Classical, Islamic, and Asian worlds spread.
- Explain how political, religious, and economic rivalries caused European states to establish new maritime empires.
- Identify reasons why the growth of the plantation economy increased the demand for slaves in the Americas, leading to significant demographic, social, and cultural changes.
- Analyze how imperial conquests and widening global economic opportunities contributed to the formation of new political and economic elites.
- Examine the causes and consequences of the increased use of gunpowder, cannons, and armed trade to establish large empires in both hemispheres.

The enormous change that drives the study of AP World History in Part 2 is the permanent interconnection of the eastern and western hemispheres. Even though the Columbian voyages from ca. 1450 to ca. 1750 and their consequences were huge, the empires and states of east Asia, south Asia, and southwest Asia remained powerful and wealthy. Remember that western Europeans wanted to go east to gain access to those luxury goods. One of your tasks in this section is to recognize how the goods and peoples of the Americas were integrated into the trade routes and peoples of Afro-Eurasia, and vice versa. Look for new developments as well as continuities or themes from previous periods.

The next seven chapters develop many of the AP World History: Modern themes. As you read them, keep in mind the changes and continuities in governance, social organization, relationship to the environment, cultural developments, and the creation of new technologies. Consider how more frequent, intense, and truly global interactions caused new developments in these themes.

The over-land and maritime trade routes in Asia and the Indian Ocean were still active and the source of luxury goods—and the tax revenue this trade could provide. The western European joint-stock companies were new, minor players in this trade. They borrowed maritime technologies from classical, Islamic, and Asian civilizations and used them to sail into the Indian, Atlantic, and Pacific oceans. Consider how wealth and resources from the Americas made it possible for Europeans to expand their role in the older Afro-Eurasian trade systems.

Even though trade seems to have dominated the economy in this period, the world's economic and productive systems were still heavily agricultural. New crops, larger populations, emerging markets, and new business practices transformed traditional peasant-farmer agriculture, increased the demand for labor, and fueled the global need for raw materials and finished products. AP students may be asked to compare labor sources and practices, especially forced or coerced labor. You will need to ask and

answer questions such as: Who wanted the labor? How did they pay for it and who was paid for it? Who worked, and who decided who worked? Who profited from the labor?

It was mostly men who traveled and profited from these global trade routes, but women were also key players. Study the roles women played in the new global landscape: they were mothers of mixed-ethnicity children in the Americas; they were the main merchants in southeast Asia; they helped run family businesses; and they took over important ruling functions when men disappeared, such as in west Africa. In the AP World History: Modern course, we use the terms "new social and political elites" and the "restructuring of racial and gender hierarchies" to describe this profound rearrangement of social, racial, and gender positions.

Around the world, rulers of empires and states pursued strategies of centralization. Kings and emperors tried to take the power to make laws, war, and taxes away from nobles and give it to government officials (bureaucrats) appointed by the rulers themselves. Because they were appointed, bureaucrats were loyal to the ruler. Rulers used religion and the arts to legitimize their quests for power. They used tax money to pay for many of these symbols of power. And of course, there were wars within and between these powerful empires because of the desire for power and wealth. Global conquests and new money-making opportunities resulted in newly wealthy individuals who wanted power and influence in their societies. Their newfound wealth and position shifted the traditional social and economic structures, and they tended to challenge the established land-based elites. Astute rulers took advantage of this conflict and played one group off the other. Be prepared to explain and compare the techniques rulers used to centralize their power.

Exploration, trade, and conquest required money. Rulers came up with different ways to collect taxes and generate revenue so that they could continue to expand and consolidate their own power over their large states. In AP World History: Modern, you'll be asked how some rulers managed to massively expand their empires and what the consequences of these expansions were for the conquerors and the conquered. Be ready to compare the strategies of those who acquired huge land-based empires (China, India, Ottomans, Russians) and those who established maritime empires (European states). And of course, all the competition over land and trade routes caused wars, revolts, and significant resistance to state power. As of ca. 1750, world history was much more modern, more global, and more complex.

## PART 2 BIG QUESTIONS:

- What were the global economic processes of the early modern era and how did they affect peoples all over the world?
- What were the causes and consequences of the expansion of land-based and maritime empires?
- How did the integration of the Americas with Afro-Eurasia contribute to cultural, technological, and biological diffusion?

Universal History Archive/Getty Images, The Picture Art Collection/Alamy Stock Photo, DEA/G. Dagli Orti/De Agostini/Getty Images, BL/Robana/age footstock, Index/Heritage Images/Heritage Image Partnership Ltd/Alamy Stock Photo

Chapter 9

# Expanding Horizons of Cross-Cultural Interaction



## ZOOMING IN ON ENCOUNTERS

### On the Road with Ibn Battuta

One of the great world travelers of all time was the Moroccan legal scholar **Ibn Battuta.** Born in 1304 at Tangier, Ibn Battuta followed family tradition and studied Islamic law. In 1325 he left Morocco to make a pilgrimage to Mecca [also called the hajj]. He traveled by caravan across north Africa and through Egypt, Palestine, and Syria, arriving at Mecca in 1326. After completing his hajj, Ibn Battuta spent a year visiting Mesopotamia and Persia, then traveled by ship through the Red Sea and down the east African coast as far south as Kilwa. By 1330 he had returned to Mecca, but then soon set off for India when he learned that the Muslim sultan of Delhi offered handsome rewards to foreign legal scholars. In 1333 he arrived in Delhi after following a long and circuitous land route that took him through Egypt, Syria, Anatolia, Constantinople, the Black Sea, and the great trading cities of central Asia—Bokhara and Samarkand.

For the next eight years, Ibn Battuta remained in India, serving mostly as a ***qadi*** (judge) in the government of the sultan of Delhi. In 1341 Ibn Battuta began his travels again, this time making his way around southern India, Ceylon, and the Maldive Islands before continuing to China about 1345. He

A giraffe from east Africa sent as a present by wealthy Swahili traders to China in 1414 and painted by a Chinese artist at a zoo in Ming dynasty China.
Barney Burstein/Corbis/VCG/Getty Images

**Ibn Battuta** (ih-bun BAH-too-tah)
***qadi*** (KAH-dee)

defeated his enemies. Within a few years he had established the Mali Empire and consolidated his rule throughout a large portion of the valley of the Niger River. Although he respected traditional religious beliefs and magical powers, Sundiata was a Muslim and he welcomed Muslim merchants from north Africa into his realm. He built a capital city at Niani, which soon became a thriving commercial center. Indeed, as a result of its control of the trans-Saharan gold trade—and the political stability provided by Sundiata—the Mali Empire became one of the wealthiest lands in the world. For two centuries after Sundiata's death about 1260, the lion prince's legacy shaped the lives of west African peoples and linked west Africa with north Africa and the Mediterranean basin.

# CHAPTER FOCUS

- This chapter presents the end of the postclassical era in western Europe. From the fall of the western Roman empire to Marco Polo's voyages to China and back, western Europeans slowly rebuilt their agricultural productivity and urban-based societies, and significantly reengaged with Afro-Eurasian trade after the debacle of the crusades. Both the cultural flowering of the Renaissance and the maritime explorations were based on the prosperity, ideas, and technologies generated from interacting with east Asia and *dar al-Islam* and the network of trade routes in between.
- After the Mongol Yuan dynasty was deposed in China, the Ming ("brilliant") dynasty took over. This is the last postclassical imperial reconstruction, so note what the rulers did to assert their Chinese ethnicity and culture after almost a century of foreign rule. The voyages of Zheng He demonstrated that the Chinese had a history of maritime trade and diplomacy which the Mongols, a land-based culture, did not.
- Other "travelers" on the trade routes had significant roles: the plague reappeared; sugarcane, cotton, rice, citrus fruits moved westward from the Indian Ocean basin trade into *dar al-Islam* and from there to western European luxury shops; the Mongols took gunpowder weapons from China across Eurasia. Europeans eventually used hand-held gunpowder weapons on their maritime explorations and conquests. Iberian plantation owners ultimately chose to invest in slave labor rather than pay high wages to free laborers, thereby linking west African slave markets to the developing Atlantic trade routes.

## Historical Developments

- As exchange networks intensified, an increased number of travelers within Afro-Eurasia wrote about their travels.
- There was continued diffusion of crops and pathogens, with epidemic diseases, the bubonic plague, along trade routes.
- A deepening and widening of networks of human interaction within and across regions contributed to cultural, technological, and biological diffusion within and between various societies.
- Improved commercial practices led to an increased volume of trade and expanded the geographical range of existing trade routes—including the Silk Roads—promoting the growth of powerful new trading cities.

## Reasoning Processes

- **Developments and Processes** Explain the various impacts long-distance exchanges had on Afro-Eurasian societies.
- **Source Claims and Evidence** Identify and describe the ways in which travel accounts reveal the extent of trade and travel across Afro-Eurasia.
- **Contextualization** Identify and describe Byzantine and Islamic influences on the western European Renaissance.
- **Making Connections** Identify connections between long distance exchanges and the spread of bubonic plague.

## Historical Thinking Skills

- **Causation** Describe the effects of long-distance exchange networks on Afro-Eurasian societies.

# CHAPTER OVERVIEW

Between 1000 and 1500 C.E., the peoples of the Eastern Hemisphere traveled, traded, communicated, and interacted more regularly and intensively than ever before. The large empires of the Mongols (discussed in chapter 17) and other nomadic peoples provided a political foundation for this cross-cultural interaction. When they conquered and pacified vast regions, nomadic peoples provided safe roads for merchants, diplomats, missionaries, and other travelers. Quite apart from the nomadic empires, improvements in maritime technology led to increased traffic in the sea lanes of the Indian Ocean and the South China Sea. As a result, long-distance travel became much more common than in earlier eras, which enabled individual travelers like Ibn Battuta and Marco Polo to venture throughout much of the Eastern Hemisphere.

Merchants and travelers exchanged more than trade goods. They diffused technologies and spread religious faiths. They also exchanged diseases that caused widespread and deadly epidemics. During the middle decades of the fourteenth century, bubonic plague traveled the trade routes from western China to central Asia, southwest Asia, north Africa, and Europe. During its initial, furious onslaught, bubonic plague caused death and destruction on a huge scale and interrupted long-distance trade networks.

By the early fifteenth century, however, societies had begun to revover from the plague. Chinese and western European peoples in particular restabilized their societies and had begun to renew cross-cultural encounters. In Europe, that effort had profound consequences for modern world history. As European mariners sought entry to the markets of Asia, they not only established direct connections with African and Asian peoples but also sailed to the Western Hemisphere and the Pacific Ocean. Their voyages brought the peoples of the Eastern Hemisphere, the Western Hemisphere, and Oceania into permanent and sustained interaction. Thus cross-cultural interactions of the period 1000 to 1500 had already laid the groundwork for global interdependence, a principal characteristic of modern world history.

| CHRONOLOGY | |
|---|---|
| 1214 | Creation of a Mongol artillery unit |
| 1253–1324 | Life of Marco Polo |
| 1287–1288 | Rabban Sauma's embassy to Europe |
| 1291–1328 | John of Montecorvino's mission to China |
| 1304–1369 | Life of Ibn Battuta |
| 1304–1374 | Life of Francesco Petrarca |
| 1330s | First outbreaks of bubonic plague in China |
| 1337–1453 | Hundred Years' War |
| 1347 | Arrival of bubonic plague in the Mediterranean basin |
| 1368–1644 | Ming dynasty |
| 1405–1433 | Zheng He's expeditions in the Indian Ocean |
| 1466–1536 | Life of Desiderius Erasmus of Rotterdam |
| 1488 | Bartolomeu Dias's voyage around Africa |
| 1492 | Christopher Columbus's first voyage to the Western Hemisphere |
| 1497–1498 | Vasco da Gama's voyage to India |

# LONG-DISTANCE TRADE AND TRAVEL

Travelers embarked on long-distance journeys for a variety of reasons. Nomadic peoples ranged widely in the course of migrations and campaigns of conquest. East European and African slaves were forced to travel to the Mediterranean basin, southwest Asia, India, and sometimes even southern China. Buddhist, Christian, and Muslim pilgrims undertook extraordinary journeys to visit holy shrines. Three of the more important motives for long-distance travel between 1000 and 1500 C.E. were trade, diplomacy, and missionary activity. The cross-cultural interactions that resulted helped spread technological innovations throughout the Eastern Hemisphere.

## Patterns of Long-Distance Trade

Merchants engaged in long-distance trade relied on two principal networks of trade routes. Luxury goods of high value relative to their weight, such as silk textiles and precious stones, often traveled overland on the Silk Roads used since classical times. Bulkier commodities, such as steel, stone, coral, and building materials, traveled the sea lanes of the Indian Ocean because it would have been unprofitable to transport them overland. The Silk Roads linked all of the Eurasian landmass, and trans-Saharan caravan routes drew west Africa into the larger economy of the Eastern Hemisphere. The sea lanes of the Indian Ocean served ports in southeast Asia, India, Arabia, and east Africa while also offering access

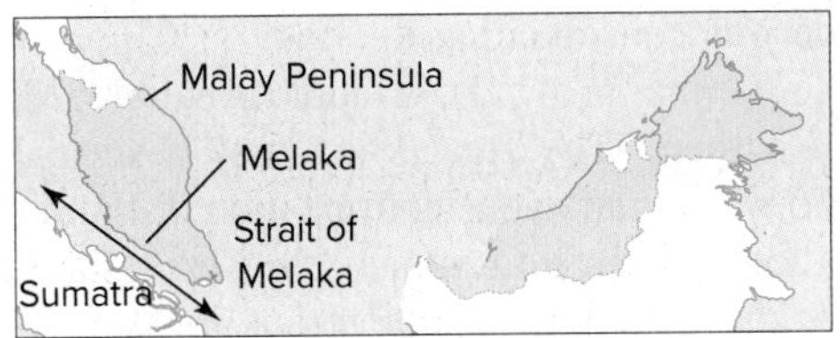


**MAP 9.1 Melaka and the Melaka Strait.**

*Look at the position of Melaka relative to the strait. Why would the city have been such a strategic location for any power that ruled it?*

via the South China Sea to ports in China, Japan, Korea, and the spice-bearing islands of southeast Asia. Thus, in combination, land and sea routes touched almost every corner of the Eastern Hemisphere.

**Trading Cities** As the volume of trade increased, the major trading cities and ports grew rapidly, attracting buyers, sellers, brokers, and bankers from parts near and far. Khanbaliq (modern Beijing), Hangzhou, Quanzhou, Melaka, Cambay, Samarkand, Hormuz, Baghdad, Caffa, Cairo, Alexandria, Kilwa, Constantinople, Venice, Timbuktu, and many other cities had large quarters occupied by communities of foreign merchants. When a trading or port city enjoyed a strategic location, maintained good order, and resisted the temptation to levy excessive customs fees, it had the potential to become a major emporium serving long-distance trade networks. A case in point is **Melaka** (in modern Malaysia). Founded in the 1390s, within a few decades Melaka became the principal clearinghouse of trade in the eastern Indian Ocean. The city's authorities policed the strategic Strait of Melaka and maintained a safe market that welcomed all merchants and levied reasonable fees on goods exchanged there. By the end of the fifteenth century, Melaka had a population of some fifty thousand people, and in the early sixteenth century the Portuguese merchant Tomé Pires reported that more than eighty languages could be heard in the city's streets.

During the early and middle decades of the thirteenth century, the Mongols' campaigns caused economic disruption throughout much of Eurasia—particularly in China and southwest Asia, where Mongol forces toppled the Song and Abbasid dynasties (discussed in chapter 17). Mongol conquests inaugurated a long period of economic decline in southwest Asia where the conquerors destroyed cities and allowed irrigation systems to fall into disrepair. As the Mongols consolidated their hold on conquered lands, however, they laid the political foundation for a surge in long-distance trade along the Silk Roads.

An illustration from a fourteenth-century French manuscript depicts Marco Polo tasting pepper as nearby laborers harvest it in southern India. Note that Polo is fully dressed and seems relaxed, while the laborers are clearly toiling in the sun.
DEA/J. E. Bulloz/Getty Images

Merchants traveling the Silk Roads faced less risk of banditry or political turbulence than in previous times. Meanwhile, strong economies in China, India, and western Europe fueled demand for foreign commodities. Many merchants traveled the whole distance from Europe to China in pursuit of profit.

**Marco Polo** The best-known long-distance traveler of Mongol times was the Venetian **Marco Polo** (1253–1324). Marco's father, Niccolò, and uncle Maffeo were among the first European merchants to visit China. Between 1260 and 1269 they traveled and traded throughout Mongol lands, and they met Khubilai Khan as he was consolidating his hold on China. When they returned to China in 1271, seventeen-year-old Marco Polo accompanied them. The great khan took a special liking to Marco, who was a marvelous conversationalist and storyteller. Khubilai allowed Marco to pursue his mercantile interests in China and also sent him on numerous diplomatic missions, partly because Marco regaled him with stories about the distant parts of his realm. After seventeen years in China, the Polos decided to return to Venice, and Khubilai granted them permission to leave. They went back on the sea route by way of Sumatra, Ceylon, India, and Arabia, arriving in Venice in 1295.

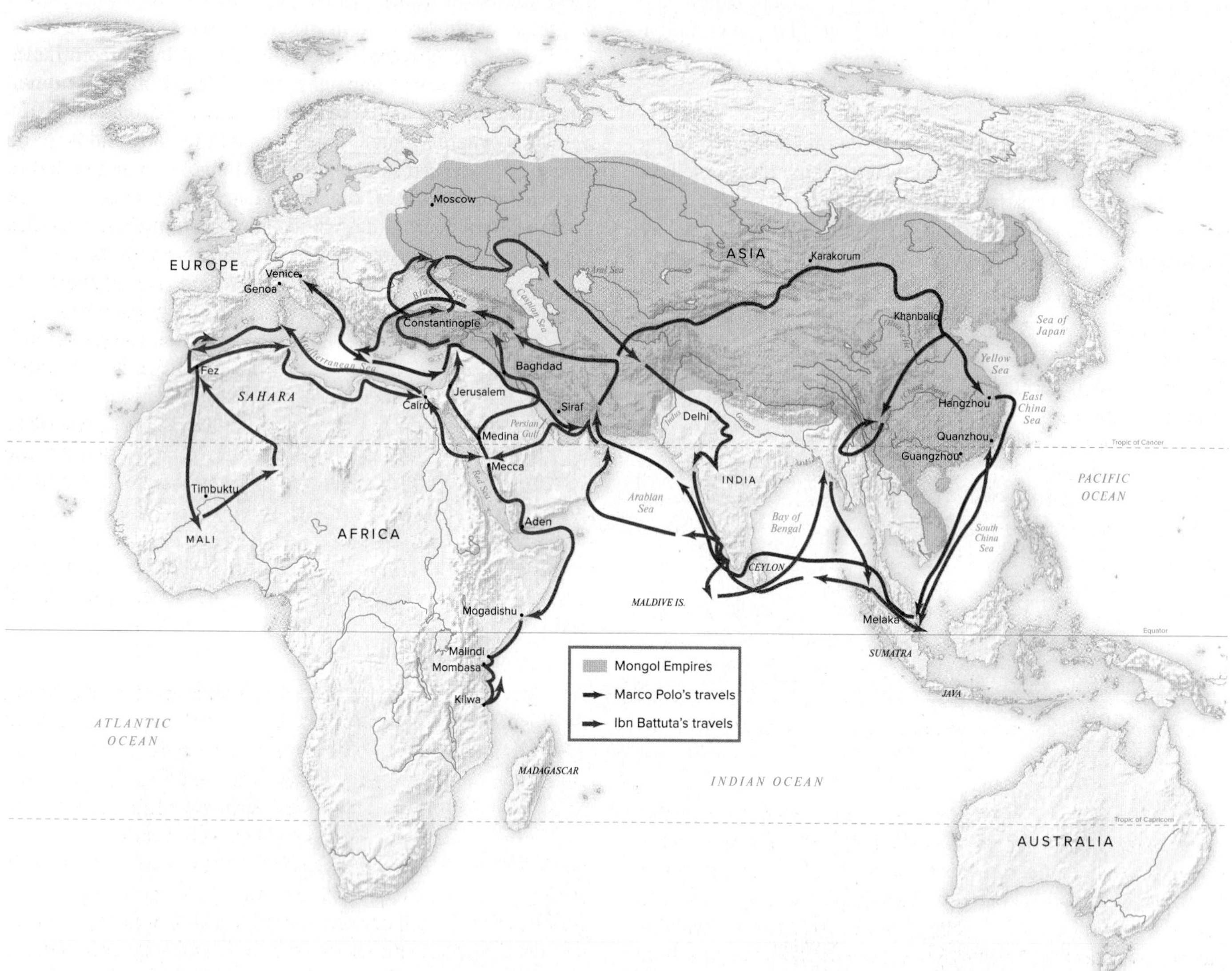


**MAP 9.2 Travels of Marco Polo and Ibn Battuta.**

Between them, Marco Polo and Ibn Battuta traveled across much of the Eurasian landmass, as well as parts of Africa and southeast Asia.

***Compare the routes taken by Marco Polo and Ibn Battuta during their travels. How did the two men choose where to travel? What conditions made it possible for them to travel so far from their homes?***

***What motivated both Marco Polo and Ibn Battuta to travel such a distance and overcome the challenges of geography and climate?***

A historical accident has preserved the story of Marco Polo's travels. After his return from China, Marco was captured and made a prisoner of war during a conflict between his native Venice and its commercial rival, Genoa. While imprisoned, Marco related tales of his travels to his fellow prisoners. One of them was a writer of romances, and he compiled the stories into a large volume that circulated rapidly throughout Europe.

In spite of occasional exaggerations and tall tales, Marco's stories deeply influenced European readers. Marco always mentioned the textiles, spices, gems, and other goods he observed during his travels, and European merchants took note, eager to participate in the lucrative trade networks of Eurasia. The Polos were among the first Europeans to visit China, but they were far from the last. Hundreds of others, mostly Italians, quickly followed the Polos. In most cases, their stories do not survive, but their travels helped to increase European participation in the larger economy of the Eastern Hemisphere.

## Political and Diplomatic Travel

Marco Polo came from a family of merchants, and merchants were among the most avid readers of his stories. Marco himself most likely collaborated closely with Italian merchants during his years in China. Yet his experiences also throw light on long-distance travel undertaken for political and diplomatic purposes. Khubilai Khan and the other Mongol rulers of China did not entirely trust their Chinese subjects and regularly appointed foreigners to administrative posts. In his account of his travels, Marco reported that Khubilai appointed him governor of the large trading city of Yangzhou. There is no independent evidence to confirm that claim, but Marco may well have filled some sort of administrative position. In addition, he represented Khubilai Khan's interests on diplomatic missions. To support himself in China, then, Marco supplemented his mercantile ventures with various official duties assigned to him by his patron, the great khan.

**Mongol-Christian Diplomacy** The emergence of elaborate trading networks and the establishment of vast imperial states created great demand for political and diplomatic representation during the centuries after 1000 C.E. The thirteenth century was a time of especially active diplomacy involving parties as distant as the Mongols and western Europeans, both of whom considered a military alliance against their common Muslim foes. As European Christians sought to revive the crusading movement and recapture Jerusalem from Muslim forces, the Mongols were attacking the Abbasid empire from the east. During the 1240s and 1250s, Pope Innocent IV dispatched a series of envoys who invited the Mongol khans to convert to Christianity and join Europeans in an alliance against the Muslims. The khans declined the invitation, proposing in reply that the pope and European Christians submit to Mongol rule or face destruction.

**Rabban Sauma** Although the early round of Mongol-European diplomacy offered little promise of cooperation, the Mongols later initiated another effort. In 1287 the Mongol ilkhan of Persia planned to invade the Muslim-held lands of southwest Asia, capture Jerusalem, and crush Islam as a political force in the region. In hopes of attracting support for the project, he dispatched **Rabban Sauma,** a Nestorian Christian priest born in the Mongol capital of Khanbaliq but of Turkish ancestry, as an envoy to the pope and European political leaders.

Rabban Sauma met with the kings of France and England, the pope, and other high officials of the Roman Catholic church. He enjoyed a fine reception, but he did not succeed in attracting European support for the ilkhan. Only a few years later, in 1295, Ghazan, the new ilkhan of Persia, converted to Islam, thus precluding any further possibility of an alliance between the Mongols of Persia and European Christians. Nevertheless, the flurry of diplomatic activity illustrates the complexity of political affairs in the Eastern Hemisphere and the need for diplomatic consultation over long distances.

The expansion of Islamic influence in the Eastern Hemisphere encouraged a different kind of politically motivated travel. Legal scholars and judges played a crucial role in Islamic societies because the **sharia** (Islamic law) prescribed religious observances and social relationships based on the Quran. Conversions to Islam and the establishment of Islamic states in India, southeast Asia, and sub-Saharan Africa created a demand for Muslims educated in Islamic law. After about the eleventh century, educated Muslims from southwest Asia and north Africa regularly traveled to recently converted lands to help instill Islamic values.

**Ibn Battuta** As we saw in the introduction to this chapter, the best known of the Muslim travelers was Ibn Battuta (1304–1369). Islamic rulers governed most of the lands Ibn Battuta visited—including India, the Maldive Islands, the Swahili city-states of east Africa, and the Mali Empire—but very few Muslims educated in the law were available in those lands. With his legal credentials Ibn Battuta had littledifficulty finding government positions. As *qadi* and adviser to the sultan of Delhi, he supervised the affairs of a wealthy mosque and heard cases at law, which he strictly enforced according to Islamic standards of justice. On one occasion Ibn Buttuta sentenced a man to receive eighty lashes because he had drunk wine eight years earlier.

After leaving northern India, Ibn Battuta obtained a post as *qadi* in the Maldive Islands. There he heard cases at law and worked zealously to promote proper observance of Islam. He ordered lashings for men who did not attend Friday prayers,

# SOURCES FROM THE PAST

## Ibn Battuta on Customs in the Mali Empire

*Long-distance travelers often encountered unfamiliar customs in foreign societies. The Moroccan traveler Ibn Battuta—who is featured in the introduction to this chapter—approved heartily when staying with hosts who appeared to honor the values of his own Muslim society, but he had little tolerance for those whose practices differed from what he thought was acceptable behavior for Muslims. Here he describes his impressions of the Muslim-ruled Mali Empire (West Africa) when he visited the court of the sultan in the mid-fourteenth century.*

**Of all people,** the blacks debase themselves most in presence of their king: for when any one of them is called upon to appear before him, he will immediately put off his usual clothing, and put on a worn-out dress, with a dirty cap; he will then enter the presence like a beggar, with his clothes lifted up to the middle of his legs; he will then beat the ground with both his elbows, and remain in the attitude of a person performing a prostration. When the Sultan addresses one of them, he will take up the garment off his back, and throw dust upon his head; and, as long as the Sultan speaks, everyone present will remain with his turban taken off. One of the best things in these parts is, the regard they pay to justice; for, in this respect the Sultan regards neither little nor much. The safety, too, is very great; so that a traveler may proceed alone among them, without the least fear of a thief or robber. Another of their good properties is, that when a merchant happens to die among them, they will make no effort to get possession of his property: but will allow the lawful successors to it to take it. Another is, their constant custom of attending prayers with the congregation; for, unless one makes haste, he will find no place left to say his prayers in. Another is, their insisting on the Koran's being committed to memory: for if a man finds his son defective in this, he will confine him till he is quite perfect, nor will he allow him his liberty until he is so. As to their bad practices, they will exhibit their little daughters, as well as their male and female slaves, quite naked. In the same manner will the women enter into the presence of the King, which his own daughters will also do. Nor do the free women ever clothe themselves till after marriage.

Are there clues in Ibn Battuta's language that indicate whether or not he thought these practices of subservience to the sultan were positive or negative features of their customs?

Thinking back to chapter 14 (The Expansive Realm of Islam), what was it about the teachings of Islam that made women's public nudity seem offensive to Ibn Battuta?

### For Further Reflection

- Think about the various ways in which Islamic influences and established local customs came together in the Mali Empire, and why this might have produced different results in Mali as compared to other places.
- In what ways do Muslims in various countries exhibit different customs today?

*Source:* Batuta, Ibn, 1304–1377, and translated by Samuel Lee. *The Travels of Ibn Batūta.* London: Printed for the Oriental translation committee, sold by J. Murray [etc.], 1829, 263–264.

and he once sentenced a thief to lose his right hand in accordance with punishment prescribed by the *sharia.* He also attempted, unsuccessfully, to persuade island women to meet the standards of modesty observed in other Islamic lands by covering their breasts. In both east and west Africa, Ibn Battuta consulted with Muslim rulers and offered advice about government, women's dress, and proper relationships between the sexes. Like many legal scholars whose stories went unrecorded, Ibn Battuta provided guidance in the ways of Islam in societies recently converted to the faith.

## Missionary Campaigns

**Sufi Missionaries** Islamic values spread not only through the efforts of legal scholars but also through the missionary activities of Sufi mystics. As in the early days of Islam, **Sufis** in the period from 1000 to 1500 ventured to recently conquered or converted lands and sought to win a popular following for the faith in India, southeast Asia, and sub-Saharan Africa. Sufis did not insist on a strict, doctrinally literal understanding of Islam but, rather, emphasized piety and devotion to Allah.

They even tolerated continuing reverence of traditional deities, whom the Sufis treated as manifestations of Allah and his powers. By taking a flexible approach to their missions, the Sufis spread Islamic values without facing the resistance that unyielding campaigns would likely have provoked.

**Christian Missionaries** Meanwhile, Roman Catholic missionaries also traveled long distances in the interests of spreading Christianity. Missionaries accompanied the crusaders and other forces to all the lands where Europeans extended their influence after the year 1000. In lands where European conquerors maintained a long-term presence—such as the Baltic lands, the Balkan region, Sicily, and Spain—missionaries attracted converts in large numbers, and Roman Catholic Christianity became securely established. In the eastern Mediterranean region, however, where crusaders were unable to hold their conquests permanently, Christianity remained a minority faith.

Woodcut of John of Montecorvino (1246–1328).
Picture from History/Newscom.

The most ambitious missions sought to convert Mongols and Chinese to Roman Catholic Christianity. Until the arrival of European merchants and diplomats in the thirteenth century, probably no Roman Catholic Christian had ever ventured as far east as China, although Nestorian Christians from central Asia had maintained communities there since the seventh century. As more Europeans traveled to China, their emigrant communities created a demand for Roman Catholic services. Many of the Roman Catholic priests who traveled to China probably intended to serve the needs of those communities, but some of them also sought to attract converts.

**John of Montecorvino** Most active of the Roman Catholic missionaries in China was **John of Montecorvino,** an Italian Franciscan who went to China in 1291, became the first archbishop of Khanbaliq in 1307, and died there in 1328. While serving the community of Roman Catholic Europeans in China, John worked energetically to establish Christianity in larger Chinese society. He translated the New Testament and the book of Psalms into Turkish, a language commonly used at the Mongol court, and he built several churches in China. He took in young boys from Mongol and Chinese families, baptized them, and taught them Latin and Roman Catholic rituals. He claimed to have baptized six thousand individuals by 1305, and he invited the great khan himself to convert to Christianity. Although popular and widely respected among Europeans, Chinese, and Mongols alike, John attracted few Asian peoples to Christianity.

Roman Catholic authorities in Europe dispatched many other priests and missionaries to China during the early fourteenth century, but like John of Montecorvino, they won few converts. Missions successfully established Christian communities in Scandinavia, eastern Europe, Spain, and the Mediterranean islands that European armies recaptured from Muslims during the centuries after 1000 C.E., but east Asia was too distant for the resources available to the Roman Catholic church. Moreover, east Asian peoples already possessed sophisticated religious and cultural traditions, so Christianity had little appeal. Nevertheless, Christian missions to China continued until the mid-fourteenth century, when the collapse of the Mongols' Yuan dynasty and the eruption of epidemic disease temporarily disrupted long-distance travel across Eurasia.

## Long-Distance Travel and Cross-Cultural Exchanges

**Cultural Exchanges** Long-distance travel of all kinds, whether for commercial, political, diplomatic, or missionary purposes, encouraged cultural exchanges between peoples of different societies. Songs, stories, religious ideas, philosophical views, and scientific knowledge all passed readily among travelers who ventured into the larger world during the era from 1000 to 1500 C.E. The troubadours of western Europe, for example, drew on the poetry, music, and love songs of Muslim performers when developing the literature of courtly love. Similarly, European scientists avidly consulted their Muslim and Jewish counterparts in Sicily and Spain to expand their understanding of the natural world.

Large numbers of travelers also facilitated agricultural and technological diffusion during the period from 1000 to 1500. Indeed, technological diffusion sometimes facilitated long-distance travel. The magnetic compass, for example, invented in China during the Tang or the Song dynasty, spread throughout the Indian Ocean basin during the eleventh century, and by the mid-twelfth century European mariners used compasses in the Mediterranean and the Atlantic Ocean. Diffusion of the compass was a boon to maritime trade because it allowed mariners to sail over long stretches of deep water with confidence in their ability to find their destinations and return home safely.

## SOURCES FROM THE PAST

### John of Montecorvino on His Mission in China

*The Franciscan John of Montecorvino (1247–1328) served as a Roman Catholic missionary in Armenia, Persia, and India before going to China in 1291. There he served as priest to expatriate European Christians, and he sought to attract converts to Christianity from the Mongol and Chinese communities. In a letter of 8 January 1305 asking for support from his fellow Franciscans in Italy, John outlined some of his activities during the previous thirteen years.*

**[After spending thirteen months in India]** I proceeded on my further journey and made my way to China, the realm of the emperor of the Mongols who is called the great khan. To him I presented the letter of our lord the pope and invited him to adopt the Catholic faith of our Lord Jesus Christ, but he had grown too old in idolatry. However, he bestows many kindnesses upon the Christians, and these two years past I have gotten along well with him. . . .

I have built a church in the city of Khanbaliq, in which the king has his chief residence. This I completed six years ago; and I have built a bell tower to it and put three bells in it. I have baptized there, as well as I can estimate, up to this time some 6,000 persons. . . . And I am often still engaged in baptizing.

Also I have gradually bought one hundred and fifty boys, the children of pagan parents and of ages varying from seven to eleven, who had never learned any religion. These boys I have baptized, and I have taught them Greek and Latin after our manner. Also I have written out Psalters for them, with thirty hymnals and breviaries [prayer books]. By help of these, eleven of the boys already know our service and form a choir and take their weekly turn of duty as they do in convents, whether I am there or not. Many of the boys are also employed in writing out Psalters and other suitable things. His Majesty the Emperor moreover delights much to hear them chanting. I have the bells rung at all the canonical hours, and with my congregation of babes and sucklings I perform divine service, and the chanting we do by ear because I have no service book with the notes. . . .

> Since John of Montecorvino purchased these boys, how free do you think they would have been to choose their own religion?

Indeed if I had but two or three comrades to aid me, it is possible that the emperor khan himself would have been baptized by this time! I ask then for such brethren to come, if any are willing to come, such I mean as will make it their great business to lead exemplary lives. . . .

> According to John of Montecorvino, what has been his main limitation in converting Chinese people to Christianity?

I have myself grown old and grey, more with toil and trouble than with years, for I am not more than fifty-eight. I have got a competent knowledge of the language and script which is most generally used by the Tartars. And I have already translated into that language and script the New Testament and the Psalter and have caused them to be written out in the fairest penmanship they have, and so by writing, reading, and preaching, I bear open and public testimony to the law of Christ.

#### For Further Reflection

- How did John of Montecorvino seem to regard the khan and his Chinese subjects? Does his tone sound hopeful about the eventual success of his Christian mission in China? Why or why not?
- John of Montecorvino describes building a church and 6,000 attendees. Other than the 150 boys he bought, what attracted the converts to his church?

*Source:* Yule, Henry and Henri Cordier, eds. *Cathay and the Way Thither,* 4 vols. London: Printed for the Hakluyt Society, 1866, 3:45–50. (Translation slightly modified.)

**Spread of Crops** Long-distance journeys enabled Muslim travelers to introduce new food and commercial crops to sub-Saharan Africa. These crops included citrus fruits and Asian strains of rice, which enriched diets in west Africa after the eleventh century. Muslims also introduced cotton to west Africa, and by 1100, cotton fabrics had become popular with the ruling elites and wealthy merchants of the west African kingdoms. Cotton grew well in the savannas, and by 1500 it was the principal textile produced in sub-Saharan Africa.

**Sugarcane** Muslims were also instrumental in the continuing diffusion of sugarcane. Muslim merchants and other travelers had begun large-scale cultivation of sugarcane in southwest Asia and north Africa during the Abbasid caliphate (750–1258 C.E.). They experimented with the plant in west Africa but had limited success because of adverse environmental conditions.

After the twelfth century, however, Muslims facilitated the westward spread of sugarcane by acquainting European crusaders with crystallized sugar refined from cane. Up to that

## INTERPRETING IMAGES

An illustration from a manuscript of 1282 depicts a Christian (left) playing chess with a Muslim (right). Chess was one of many cultural elements that passed from Muslim to Christian societies during the crusading era.

**Analyze** *In addition to the illustration showing a Muslim and Christian playing chess together, what were other indications that the two religions coexisted peacefully and exchanged ideas?*

Index/Heritage Images/Heritage Image Partnership Ltd /Alamy Stock Photo

time Europeans had little access to refined sugar, and they relied on honey and fruits as sweeteners. They immediately appreciated the convenience of refined sugar. Italian entrepreneurs began to organize sugarcane plantations on Mediterranean islands such as Sicily, Cyprus, Crete, and Rhodes. Rapidly increasing demand for refined sugar encouraged investors to seek suitable locations throughout the Mediterranean basin. The cultivation of sugarcane had deep social and economic implications. Besides influencing local economic development in lands where it spread, it touched distant societies. Like their Muslim predecessors, European sugar producers often used slave labor on their plantations, and the growth of plantations fueled an increasing demand for Muslim war captives and black Africans who could be forced into slavery.

**Gunpowder Technologies** Although Muslim merchants and travelers were especially prominent agents of diffusion, Mongols also contributed to the process, notably by helping to spread gunpowder technologies west from China. Mongol invaders learned about gunpowder from Chinese military engineers in the early thirteenth century and soon incorporated gunpowder-based weapons into their arsenal: as early as 1214 Chinggis Khan's armies included an artillery unit. During the 1250s, as they campaigned in Persia and southwest Asia, the Mongols used catapults and trebuchets to lob gunpowder bombs into cities under siege. Muslim armies soon developed similar weapons in response.

By the mid-thirteenth century, gunpowder had reached Europe—possibly by way of Mongol-ruled Russia—and Europeans had begun to experiment with gunpowder-fueled rockets. By the early fourteenth century, armies from China to Europe possessed primitive cannons. Although not especially accurate, the weapons were powerful enough to blow holes in the defensive walls of cities under siege. Thus, with the assistance of Mongol warriors, gunpowder technology rapidly spread from its homeland in China across the entire Eurasian landmass.

Agricultural and technological diffusions of the era 1000 to 1500 C.E. were by no means unique processes in world history. For millennia, agricultural crops and technological skills had spread widely whenever peoples of different societies interacted with one another. Because of the particularly intense interactions of the period from 1000 to 1500 C.E., however, agricultural and technological diffusion profoundly influenced the lives of peoples throughout the Eastern Hemisphere. The spread of food crops enriched diets and supported increasing populations, and the spread of industrial crops such as cotton promoted economic development. The diffusion of the magnetic compass enabled mariners to sail the seas more safely and effectively, and the spread of gunpowder technology forever changed the nature of war.

## CRISIS AND RECOVERY

As Eurasian peoples traveled over long distances, they not only exchanged trade goods, agricultural crops, and technological expertise but also unwittingly helped disease pathogens to spread. When diseases broke out among previously unexposed populations, they often caused deadly epidemics that severely disrupted whole societies. During the fourteenth century, **bubonic plague** erupted in epidemics that ravaged societies throughout most of Asia, Europe, and north Africa. Epidemic plague struck intermittently until the seventeenth century, but by the fifteenth century Chinese and European societies had begun to recover from its effects and wield their influence in the larger world.

### Bubonic Plague

**Climate Changes** About 1300 C.E. a process of global climate change caused temperatures to decline significantly and abruptly throughout much of the world. For more than five hundred years, the earth experienced a **"little ice age,"** when temperatures were much cooler than in the era from 1000 to 1300 C.E. With markedly cooler temperatures and shorter growing seasons, agricultural production declined in many lands, leading to famine and sometimes even starvation. In some northerly lands, agriculture ceased to be a practical possibility: after the onset of the little ice age, Norse settlers abandoned the colonies they had occupied in Greenland since the tenth century.

**Origins of Epidemic Bubonic Plague** As they struggled to cope with the cooling climate, peoples in much of the Eastern Hemisphere suddenly encountered a new challenge in the form of devastating epidemic disease. Bubonic plague spread from the Yunnan region of southwestern China, where it probably had been endemic for centuries. The plague bacillus infects rodents such as rats, squirrels, and prairie dogs, and fleas transmit the pathogen from one rodent to another. If rodent populations decline, fleas seek other hosts and sometimes spread the disease to human victims. In the early fourteenth century, Mongol military campaigns helped spread plague from Yunnan to China's interior: an epidemic in 1331 reportedly killed 90 percent of the population in Hebei province in northeastern China, near modern Beijing. During the 1350s epidemics broke out in widely scattered regions of China, and contemporaries reported that plague carried away two-thirds of the population in some afflicted areas.

**Spread of Plague** During the 1340s Mongols, merchants, and other travelers spread the disease along trade routes to

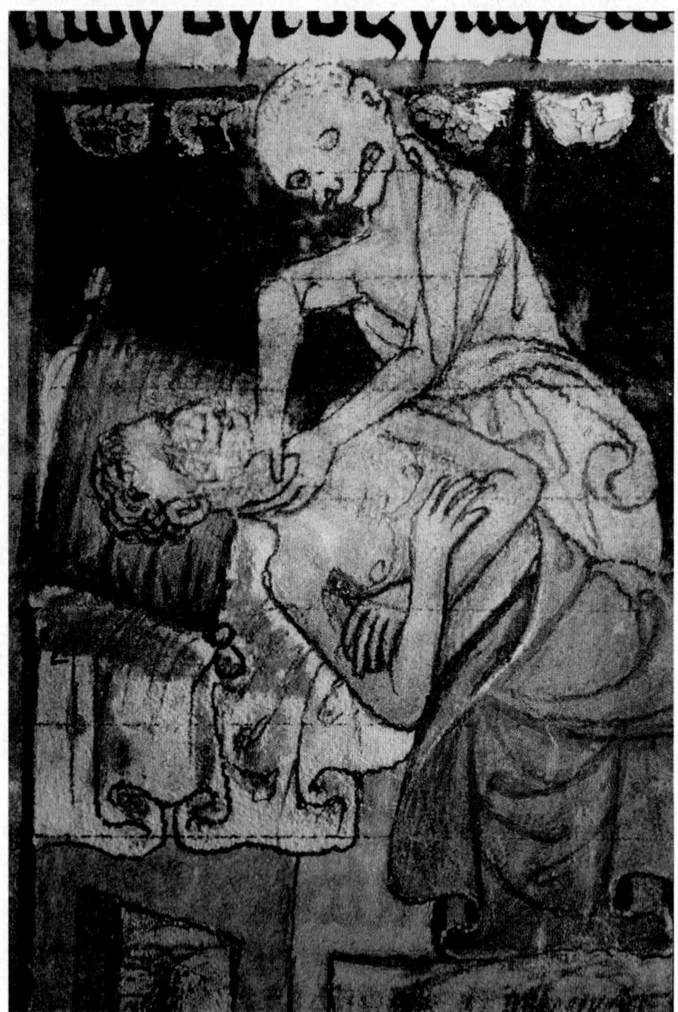

A painting from 1376 graphically communicates the horror felt by medieval Europeans when bubonic plague struck their communities. Here, death strangles a victim of the Black Death plague.
Werner Forman/Universal Images Group/Getty Images

points west of China. It thrived in the oases and trading cities of central Asia, where domestic animals and rodents provided abundant breeding grounds for fleas and the plague bacillus. By 1346 it had reached the Black Sea ports of Caffa and Tana. In 1347, Italian merchants fled plague-infected Black Sea ports and unwittingly spread the disease throughout the Mediterranean basin. By 1348, following the trade routes, plague had sparked epidemics in most of western Europe.

Wherever it appeared, bubonic plague struck with frightful effects. Victims developed inflamed lymph nodes, particularly in the neck, armpit, and groin areas, and most died within a few days after the onset of symptoms. Internal hemorrhaging often discolored the inflammations known as buboes—which gave rise to the term *bubonic*—and because of the black or purple swellings, Europeans referred to the plague as the "Black Death." Bubonic plague typically killed 60 to 70 percent of its human victims and had the potential to ravage a society within a few months. In some small villages and towns, disease wiped out the entire population. A spate of new births generally followed outbreaks of plague as societies tried to replenish their numbers, but plague also returned and claimed new victims. In Europe plague erupted intermittently from the 1340s until the late seventeenth century.

Some parts of the Eastern Hemisphere did not suffer directly from plague epidemics. The long, cold winters of Scandinavia discouraged the proliferation of plague-bearing rodents and fleas, so the northernmost parts of Europe escaped the plague's worst effects. For reasons that are still poorly understood, India also seems to have avoided serious difficulties. In fact, the Indian population grew from 91 million in the year 1300 to 97 million a century later and 105 million in 1500. Epidemics also largely bypassed sub-Saharan Africa, even though plague had long been endemic in the Great Lakes region of east Africa.

## INTERPRETING IMAGES

Ming artisans won worldwide fame for their blue-and-white porcelain, which inspired the founders of the Delft porcelain factory in the Netherlands. This porcelain bottle dates from the seventeenth century.

**Analyze** *Silk and spices were obvious attractions for European traders. Why was Ming porcelain such a significant luxury item? What does it suggest about the level of Chinese technology in contrast to that of Europeans during the 1300s?*

Gift of Martin A. Ryerson/Art Institute of Chicago.

### Population Decline

In lands hard hit by plague, however, it took a century and more to begin recovery from the demographic consequences of epidemic disease. In 1300 China's population, already reduced by conflicts with the Mongols since the early thirteenth century, stood at eighty-five million. In 1400, after about seventy years of epidemic plague, Chinese numbers amounted to only seventy-five million. A century later demographic recovery was under way, and China's population rebounded to one hundred million.

European society also reeled from the effects of bubonic plague. From seventy-nine million in 1300, Europe's population dropped by almost 25 percent to sixty million in 1400. As in China, demographic recovery in Europe was under way in 1500 when the European population climbed to eighty-one million. Islamic societies in southwest Asia, Egypt, and north Africa also suffered devastating population losses, and demographic recovery took much longer there than in China and Europe. In Egypt human population probably did not reach preplague levels until the nineteenth century.

### Social and Economic Effects

Because of the heavy demographic toll that it levied, bubonic plague disrupted societies and economies throughout Eurasia and north Africa. Epidemics killed the young, the weak, and the old in especially high numbers, but they spared no group. Peasants and laborers, artisans and crafts workers, merchants and bankers, priests and nuns, rulers and bureaucrats all fell before the plague's onslaught. The disease caused severe labor shortages, which in turn generated social unrest.

In western Europe, for example, urban workers demanded higher wages, and many left their homes in search of better conditions. Political authorities responded by freezing wages and forbidding workers to leave their homes. For their part, peasants in the countryside also sought to improve their circumstances by moving to regions where landlords offered better terms. Landlords responded to that challenge by restricting the freedom of peasants to move and by reimposing labor requirements: in effect, the lords sought to reinstate conditions of serfdom (in which peasants are tied to the land) that they had allowed to lapse before the arrival of plague. As a result of sharply conflicting interests, disgruntled workers and peasants mounted a series of rebellions that rocked both the towns and the countryside of western Europe. Authorities eventually extinguished the revolts but only after considerable social disruption and loss of life.

By the seventeenth century the plague had lost much of its ferocity. Epidemics occurred more sporadically, and they did not seriously diminish human populations. Since the 1940s, antibiotic drugs have brought the disease largely under control among human populations, although it survives in rodent communities throughout much of the world.

## What's Left Out?

Royal and imperial states utilized the services of eunuchs to administer their realms since antiquity. In China, we know the Ming emperors believed eunuchs were less likely than other men to threaten their rule because they were unable to build their own dynasties. As a result, the imperial family employed several thousand eunuchs at any given time. But few histories explore the reasons men chose to become eunuchs, not to mention the difficulties and dangers of the procedure itself. In fact, although some males in imperial China were castrated as a means of punishment, most eunuchs voluntarily chose to undergo castration as adults. Motivations varied but included poverty, the desire for a more comfortable life, or the desire to gain access to the imperial court and to serve the imperial family. The rewards could be significant as some eunuchs gained considerable power and influence at the imperial court. But the costs were high: Ming medical manuals indicated that complications from the procedure included infection, hemorrhage, and even death; that the healing time was about 100 days; and that eunuchs could suffer negative health effects for the remainder of their lives. Does the enormous personal sacrifice involved in becoming a eunuch help explain the trust Ming emperors placed in them?

*Source:* Shih-shan Henry Tsai, *The Eunuchs in the Ming Dynasty* (New York: SUNY Press, 1995).

### Thinking Critically About Sources

The passage describes the motives and dangers of becoming a eunuch during the Ming dynasty.

1. What additional information and insight could be added to our understanding through a primary source by a eunuch?

## Recovery in China: The Ming Dynasty

By the mid-fourteenth century, the Mongols' Yuan dynasty was experiencing very difficult times. Financial mismanagement led to serious economic difficulties, and political conflicts led to assassinations and factional fighting among the Mongols. In 1368, with bubonic plague raging, the Chinese forces toppled the Yuan dynasty, and the Mongols departed China en masse and returned to the steppes, leaving China in a state of both demographic and political turmoil. An increasing birthrate soon helped to replenish human numbers. Political recovery accompanied the demographic rebound.

**Hongwu** When the Yuan dynasty fell, the governance of China returned to Chinese hands. The new emperor came from a family so poor that he spent much of his youth as a beggar. Orphaned, he entered a Buddhist monastery to assure himself of food, clothing, and shelter. Because of his size and strength, he came to the notice of military commanders, and he made his way through the ranks to lead the rebellious forces that toppled the Yuan dynasty. In 1368 he became Emperor **Hongwu,** and he proclaimed the establishment of the **Ming** ("brilliant") **dynasty,** which lasted until 1644.

**Ming Centralization** Hongwu immediately set about eliminating all traces of Mongol rule and establishing a government on the model of traditional Chinese dynasties. Like the founders of several earlier Chinese dynasties (discussed in chapter 8), Hongwu had little interest in scholarly matters, but he reestablished the Confucian educational and civil service systems to ensure a supply of talented officials and bureaucrats. At the same time, he moved to centralize authority more tightly than ever before in Chinese history. In 1380, when he suspected his chief minister of involvement in a treasonous plot, Hongwu executed the minister and his bureaucratic allies and also abolished the minister's position altogether. From that time forward the Ming emperors ruled directly, without the aid of chief ministers, and they closely supervised imperial affairs.

**Mandarins and Eunuchs** The Ming emperors insisted on absolute obedience to the policies and initiatives of the central government. They relied heavily on the **mandarins,** a special class of powerful officials sent out as emissaries of the central government to ensure that local officials implemented imperial policy. The Ming emperors also turned to **eunuchs** (castrated males) for governmental services. Earlier Chinese emperors, as well as rulers of other lands, had long relied on eunuchs because they could not generate families and build power bases that might challenge ruling houses. In keeping with their centralizing policy, however, the Ming emperors employed eunuchs much more extensively than any of their predecessors, in the expectation that servants whose fortunes depended exclusively on the emperors' favor would work especially diligently to advance the emperors' interests.

The employment of mandarins and eunuchs enhanced the authority of the central government. The tightly centralized administration instituted by the early Ming emperors lasted more than five hundred years. Although the dynasty fell in 1644 to Manchu invaders, who founded the **Qing dynasty,** the Manchus retained the administrative framework of the Ming state, which largely survived until the collapse of the Qing dynasty in 1911.

**Economic Recovery** While building a centralized administration, the Ming emperors also worked toward economic recovery from nomadic rule and epidemic disease. The new rulers conscripted laborers to rebuild irrigation systems that had fallen into disrepair during the previous century, and agricultural

**eunuchs** (YOO-nihks)
**Qing** (ching)

# Connecting the Sources

## Individual experiences of the bubonic plague

**The problem** The rapid spread of bubonic plague from China to most of Eurasia in the fourteenth century was a disaster that had profound and lasting effects on historical developments in China, central and southwest Asia, north Africa, and Europe, from massive population decline to economic disruption to social and political unrest. Although historians and scientists continue to dispute exact mortality rates, it is clear that the plague killed many millions of people, reducing populations wherever it struck by at least 25 percent, and sometimes much more. When exploring the history of disasters like the plague, it can be easy to forget that each individual who lived through the event—or died from it—had his or her own story, feelings, and family. In world history, while it is important to understand the "big picture," it is also important to remember that the "big picture" is always composed of millions of individual stories. These individual stories remind us that experiencing terrible events was not easier for individuals just because many suffered similar fates or because they occurred a long time ago.

The following documents are only two examples—one from Italy and the other from Syria—of how individuals experienced the plague as it tore through Europe and southwest Asia in 1348.

**The documents** Read the documents below, and consider carefully the questions that follow.

### Document 1:

*Francesco Petrarca (1304–1374) was an Italian scholar and early humanist who lived through the plague that struck Italy in 1348. Scholars believe he wrote the following letter, known as the Metrica, to himself in about 1348.*

> *O what has come over me? Where are the violent fates pushing me back to? I see passing by, in headlong flight, time which makes the world a fleeting place. I observe about me dying throngs of both young and old, and nowhere is there a refuge. No haven beckons in any part of the globe, nor can any hope of longed for salvation be seen. Wherever I turn my frightened eyes, their gaze is troubled by continual funerals: the churches groan encumbered with biers, and, without last respects, the corpses of the noble and the commoner lie in confusion alongside each other. The last hour of life comes to mind, and, obliged to recollect my misfortunes, I recall the flocks of dear ones who have departed, and the conversations of friends, the sweet faces which suddenly vanished, and the hallowed ground now insufficient for repeated burials. This is what the people of Italy bemoan, weakened by so many deaths; this is what France laments, exhausted and stripped of inhabitants; the same goes for other peoples, under whatever skies they reside. Either it is the wrath of God, for certainly I would think that our misdeeds deserve it, or it is just the harsh assault of the stars in their perpetually changing conjunctions. . . . Dense shadows have covered me with fear. For whosoever thinks they can recall death and look upon the moment of their passing with fearless face is either mistaken or mad, or, if he is fully aware, then he is very courageous.*

What must it have been like for Petrarca to see so many friends, neighbors, and fellow city dwellers die in such great numbers from the plague?

### Document 2:

*Ibn al-Wardi (ca. 1290–1349) was a Muslim writer who lived and worked in Aleppo (modern Syria). He wrote the following "Essay on the Report of the Pestilence" after the plague struck his region in the spring of 1348. The next year, in March 1349, al-Wardi himself died of the plague.*

*Continued*

*This plague is for the Muslims a martyrdom and a reward, and for the disbelievers a punishment and a rebuke. . . . I take refuge in God from the yoke of the plague. Its high explosion has burst into all countries and was an examiner of astonishing things. Its sudden attacks perplex the people. The plague chases the screaming without pity and does not accept a treasure for ransom. Its engine is far-reaching. The plague enters into the house and swears it will not leave except with all of its inhabitants. . . . Among the benefits of this . . . is the removal of one's hopes and the improvement of his earthly works. It awakens men from their indifference for the provisioning of their final journey. . . . Come then, seek the aid of God Almighty for raising the plague, for He is the best helper. Oh God, we call You better than anyone did before. We call You to raise from us the pestilence and plague. . . . We plead with You, by the most honored of the advocates, Muhammad, the Prophet of mercy, that You take away from us this distress. Protect us from the evil and the torture and preserve us.*

What role did God play in the outbreak of the plague, according to al-Wardi?

This 1411 illustration of plague-infected people is taken from the Toggenburg Bible.
Fine Art/Corbis Historical/Getty Images

## Questions

1. What can these sources definitively tell you about the lives of the people who produced them? What **facts** can be gleaned from these sources?
2. In Document 1, what is Petrarca's state of mind? How does he describe the effects of the plague on himself and his loved ones? Do you think his reaction to the plague would have been shared by others in Italy, or might others have reacted differently?
3. In Document 2, what is the cause of the plague, according to al-Wardi? How does he describe the effects of the plague on those around him? What kinds of advantages does he argue that the plague has brought?
4. For both documents, how do each of the men view God's role in the plague? What are the similarities between the two excerpts? What are the differences? Finally, do you think their experience of the plague is representative, given that both were highly educated men? Why or why not? How useful are individual stories in interpreting and understanding world historical events?

*Source Citations:* **Document 1:** Petrarca, Francesco: Ad Seipsum (To Himself) (Epistola Metrica I, 14: lines 1–55). Translate by Jonathan Usher. Scotland: University of Edinburgh, 1384. **Document 2:** Aberth, John. *The First Horseman: Disease in Human History* (Upper Saddle River, N.J.: Pearson Prentice Hall, 2007), pp. 42–43.

English forces besiege a French citadel during the Hundred Years' War (1337–1453). Note that the besiegers on the left side of this manuscript illustration employ small firearms that launch gunpowder bombs. Although essentially a dynastic conflict between two European ruling houses, the series of conflicts that constituted the Hundred Years' War had a significant impact on military technology and strategy and were a major influence on developing notions of French and English patriotism.
Album/Alamy Stock Photo

production surged as a result. At the same time, they promoted the manufacture of porcelain, lacquerware, and fine silk and cotton textiles. Ming rulers did not actively promote trade with other lands, but private Chinese merchants eagerly sought commercial opportunities and conducted a thriving business marketing Chinese products in ports and trading cities from Japan to the islands of southeast Asia. Meanwhile, domestic trade surged within China, reflecting increasing productivity and prosperity.

**Cultural Revival** In addition to political and economic recovery, the Ming dynasty sponsored a kind of cultural revival in China. Emperor Hongwu tried to eradicate all signs of the recent nomadic occupation by discouraging the use of Mongol names and the wearing of Mongol dress. Ming emperors actively promoted Chinese cultural traditions, particularly the Confucian and neo-Confucian schools. Hongwu's successor, **Yongle,** organized the preparation of a vast encyclopedia that compiled all significant works of Chinese history, philosophy, and literature. This ***Yongle Encyclopedia*** ran to almost twenty-three thousand manuscript rolls, each equivalent to a medium-size book. The government originally planned to issue a printed edition of the encyclopedia but abandoned the project because of its enormous expense. Nevertheless, the *Yongle Encyclopedia* was a remarkable anthology, and it signaled the Ming rulers' interest in supporting native Chinese cultural traditions.

## Recovery in Europe: State Building

Demographic recovery strengthened states in Europe as it did in China. In Europe, however, political authority rested with a

**Yongle** (YAWNG-leh)

Portrait of the first Hongwu emperor (r. 1368–1398).
Pictures from History/Newscom.

series of regional states rather than a centralized empire. By the late fifteenth century, states in Italy, Spain, France, England, and Russia had devised techniques of government that vastly enhanced their power.

During the later middle ages (1300-1500), internal problems as well as bubonic plague complicated European political affairs. The Holy Roman Empire survived in name, but after the mid-thirteenth century effective authority lay with the German princes and the Italian city-states rather than the emperor. In Spain descendants of Muslim conquerors held the kingdom of Granada in the southern portion of the Iberian peninsula. The kings of France and England sparred constantly over lands claimed by both. Their hostilities eventually resulted in the **Hundred Years' War** (1337-1453), a protracted series of intermittent campaigns in which the warring factions sought control of lands in France. Russia had even more difficult problems. In the late 1230s Mongol armies conquered the flourishing commercial center of Kiev, and descendants of Chinggis Khan extracted tribute from Russia for almost 250 years thereafter. In the fifteenth century, however, the Mongol states fell into disorder, giving rise to a vast power vacuum in Russia.

**Taxes and Armies** By the late fifteenth century, however, regional states in western Europe had greatly strengthened their societies, and some had also laid the foundations for the emergence of powerful monarchies. The state-building efforts of the later middle ages involved two especially important elements. The first was the development of fresh sources of finance, usually through new taxes levied directly on citizens and subjects, which supplemented the income that rulers received from their subordinates. The second was the maintenance of large standing armies, which, particularly since the Hundred Years' War, were often composed of mercenary forces and equipped with gunpowder weapons, supported by state funds.

**Italian States** The state-building process began in Italy, where profits from industrial production and trade enriched the major cities. The principal Italian states—the city-states of Milan, Venice, and Florence, the papal state based in Rome, and the kingdom of Naples—needed large numbers of officials to administer their complex affairs. They also needed ready access to military forces that could protect their interests. Beginning as early as the thirteenth century, the Italian city-states financed those needs by levying direct taxes and issuing long-term bonds that they repaid from treasury receipts. With fresh sources of finance, the principal Italian states strengthened their authority within their own boundaries and between them controlled public affairs in most of the Italian peninsula.

**France and England** During the fourteenth and fifteenth centuries, Italian administrative methods made their way beyond the Alps. Partly because of the enormous expenses they incurred during the Hundred Years' War, the kings of France and England began to levy direct taxes and assemble powerful armies. The French kings taxed sales, hearths, and salt; their English counterparts instituted annual taxes on hearths (the number of fireplaces within each home), individuals, and plow teams. Rulers in both lands asserted the authority of the central government over the nobility. The English kings did not establish a standing army, but they were able to raise powerful forces when rebellion threatened public order. In France, however, King Louis XI (reigned 1461-1483) maintained a permanent army of about fifteen thousand troops, many of them professional mercenary soldiers equipped with firearms. Because the high expense of maintaining such forces was beyond the means of the nobility, Louis and his successors enjoyed a decisive edge over ambitious subordinates seeking to challenge royal authority or build local power bases.

**Spain** The process of state building was most dramatic in Spain, where the marriage in 1469 of Fernando of Aragon and Isabel of Castile united the two wealthiest and most important Iberian realms. Receipts from the sales tax, the primary source of royal income, supported a powerful standing army. Under Fernando and Isabel, popularly known as the Catholic Kings, Christian forces completed the *reconquista* (the reconquering of the Iberian peninsula from Muslim kingdoms) by conquering the kingdom of Granada and absorbing it into their state in 1492. The Catholic Kings also projected their authority beyond Iberia. When a French army threatened the kingdom of Naples in 1494, they seized southern Italy, and by 1559 Spanish forces had established their hegemony throughout most of the Italian peninsula. Fernando and Isabel also sought to make a place for Spain in the markets of Asia by sponsoring Christopher Columbus's quest for a western route to China.

**Russia** State building took place in Russia as well as in western Europe. After the fourteenth century, as Mongol power waned, Russian princes sought to expand their territories. Most successful among them were the grand princes of Moscow. As early as the mid-fourteenth century, the princes began the process of "gathering the Russian land" by acquiring territories surrounding their strategically located commercial town of Moscow on the Volga River. In 1480 Grand Prince Ivan III (reigned 1462–1505), later known as Ivan the Great, stopped paying tribute to the Mongol khan. By refusing to acknowledge the khan's supremacy, Ivan in effect declared Russian independence from Mongol rule. He then made Moscow the center of a large and powerful state. His territorial annexations were impressive: Muscovy, the principality ruled from Moscow, almost tripled in size as he brought Russian-speaking peoples into his realm. The most important addition to his possessions came with the acquisition of the prosperous trading city of Novgorod. A hub of the lucrative fur trade and a member of the Hanseatic League of Baltic commercial cities, Novgorod was an autonomous city-state that governed its affairs through a town council. The city's merchants had strong ties to Poland and Lithuania to the west, and Ivan wanted to make sure that Novgorod's prosperity did not benefit neighboring states. Thus he demanded that the city acknowledge his authority. After crushing a futile uprising organized by Novgorod's merchants, he ended the city's independence in 1478 and absorbed it into the expansive Muscovite state. With the aid of Novgorod's wealth, Ivan was then able to build a strong centralized government modeled on the Byzantine Empire. Indeed, Ivan went so far as to call himself ***tsar*** (sometimes spelled *czar*)—a Russianized form of the term *caesar,* which Byzantine rulers had borrowed from the classical Roman Empire to signify their imperial status.

Competition between European states intensified as they tightened their authority in their territories. This competition led to frequent small-scale wars between European states, and it encouraged the rapid development of military and naval technology. As states sought technological advantages over their neighbors, they encouraged the refinement and improvement of weapons, ships, and sails. When one state acquired powerful weapons—such as personal firearms or ships equipped with cannons—neighboring states sought more advanced devices in the interests of security. Thus technological innovations vastly strengthened European armies just as they began to venture again into the larger world.

## Recovery in Europe: The Renaissance

Demographic recovery and state-building efforts in Europe coincided with a remarkable cultural flowering known as the **Renaissance.** The French word *renaissance* means "rebirth," and it refers to a period of artistic and intellectual creativity that took place from the fourteenth to the sixteenth century and that reflected the continuing development of a sophisticated urban society, particularly in western Europe. Painters, sculptors, and architects of the Renaissance era drew inspiration from classical Greek and Roman artists rather than from their medieval predecessors. They admired the convincing realism of classical sculpture and the stately simplicity of classical architecture. In their efforts to revive classical aesthetic standards, they transformed European art. Meanwhile, Renaissance scholars known as humanists looked to classical rather than medieval literary models, and they sought to update medieval moral thought and adapt it to the needs of a bustling urban society.

Brunelleschi's magnificent dome on the cathedral of Florence dominates the city's skyline even today.
Adam Sylvester/Science Source

**Italian Renaissance Art** Just as they pioneered new techniques of statecraft, the Italian city-states also sponsored Renaissance innovations in art and architecture. In search of realistic depictions, Italian artists studied the human form and represented the emotions of their subjects. Italian painters such as Masaccio (1401–1428) and **Leonardo da Vinci** (1452–1519) relied on the technique of linear perspective to represent the three dimensions of real life on flat, two-dimensional surfaces. Sculptors such as Donatello (1386–1466) and **Michelangelo Buonarotti** (1475–1564) sought to depict their subjects in natural poses that reflected the actual workings of human muscles rather than in the awkward and rigid postures often found in earlier sculptures.

**Renaissance** (ren-uh-SAHNS)
**Leonardo da Vinci** (lee-uh-NAHR-doh duh-VIHN-chee)
**Michelangelo Buonarotti** (mik-uhl AN-juh-low baw-nahr-RAW-tee)

A painting by Venetian artists Gentile and Giovanni Bellini reflects Renaissance interests in the Muslim world. The painting depicts St. Mark (standing in the pulpit, left) preaching in Alexandria, Egypt. The audience includes Egyptians, Berbers, Turks, Persians, Ethiopians, and Mongols. Note also the technique of linear perspective to depict figures in realistic relationship to one another and their surroundings. How does linear perspective lend a sense of depth to this scene?
Alinari Archives/Getty Images

**Renaissance Architecture** Renaissance architects designed buildings in the simple, elegant style preferred by their classical Greek and Roman predecessors. Their most impressive achievement was the construction of domed buildings—awesome structures that enclosed large spaces but kept them open and airy under massive domes. Roman architects had built domes, but their technology and engineering did not survive the collapse of the Roman Empire. Inspired by the Pantheon, a handsome Roman temple constructed in the second century C.E., the Florentine architect Filippo Brunelleschi (1377–1446) reinvented equipment and designs for a large dome. During the 1420s and 1430s, he oversaw the construction of a magnificent dome on the cathedral of Florence. Residents of Florence took Brunelleschi's dome as a symbol of the city's wealth and its leadership in artistic and cultural affairs.

**The Humanists** Like Renaissance artists and architects, scholars and literary figures known as humanists also drew inspiration from classical models. The term ***humanist*** referred to scholars interested in the humanities—literature, history, and moral philosophy. They had little to do with the secular and often antireligious interests of movements that go under the name humanism today: on the contrary, Renaissance humanists were deeply committed to Christianity. Several humanists worked diligently to prepare accurate texts and translations of the New Testament and other Christian writings. Most notable of them was **Desiderius Erasmus** of Rotterdam (1466–1536), who in 1516 published the first edition of the Greek New Testament along with a revised Latin translation and copious annotations. Other humanists drew inspiration from the intense spirituality and high moral standards of early Christianity and promoted those values in their society.

Humanists scorned the dense and often convoluted writing style of the scholastic theologians (discussed in chapter 19). Instead, they preferred the elegant and polished language of classical Greek and Roman authors and the early church fathers, whose works they considered more engaging and more persuasive than the weighty tomes of medieval philosophers and theologians. Thus humanists such as the Florentine **Francesco Petrarca,** also known in English as Petrarch (1304–1374), traveled throughout Europe searching for manuscripts of classical works. In the monastic libraries of Italy, Switzerland, and southern France, they found hundreds of Latin writings that medieval scholars had overlooked. During the fifteenth century, Italian humanists became acquainted with Byzantine scholars and enlarged the body of classical Greek as well as Latin works available to scholars.

**Desiderius Erasmus** (des-i-DEER-ee-uhs ih-raz-muhs)
**Francesco Petrarca** (frahn-CHES-koh PEE-trahrk-a)

**Humanist Moral Thought** Classical Greek and Latin values encouraged the humanists to reconsider medieval ethical teachings. Medieval moral philosophers had taught that the most honorable calling was that of monks and nuns who withdrew from the world and dedicated their lives to prayer, contemplation, and the glorification of God, but the humanists drew inspiration from classical authors such as Cicero, who demonstrated that it was possible to lead a morally virtuous life while participating actively in the affairs of the world. Renaissance humanists argued that it was perfectly honorable for Christians to enter into marriage, business relationships, and public affairs, and they offered a spirited defense for those who rejected the cloister in favor of an active life in society. Humanist moral thought thus represented an effort to reconcile Christian values and ethics with the increasingly urban and commercial society of Renaissance Europe.

**Renaissance Europe and the Larger World** Quite apart from their conscious effort to draw inspiration from classical antiquity, Renaissance art and thought also reflected increasing European participation in the affairs of the Eastern Hemisphere. As merchants linked Europe to the larger hemispheric economy, European peoples experienced increased prosperity that enabled them to invest resources in artistic production and support for scholarship. Renaissance painters filled their canvases with images of silk garments, ceramic vessels, lacquered wood, spice jars, foreign peoples, and exotic animals that had recently come to European attention. Princes and wealthy patrons commissioned hundreds of these paintings that brought a cosmopolitan look to their palaces, residences, and places of business.

This enchantment with the larger world extended also into the realm of ideas. The Italian humanist Giovanni **Pico della Mirandola** (1463–1494) perhaps best reflected the enthusiasm of Renaissance scholars to comprehend the world beyond western Europe. In his exuberant *Oration on the Dignity of Man* (1486), Pico made a spirited effort to harmonize the divergent teachings of Plato, Aristotle, Judaism, Christianity, and Islam, not to mention Zoroastrianism and various occult and mystical traditions. His ambitious endeavor was ultimately unsuccessful: Pico had limited information about several of the traditions he sought to reconcile, and he sometimes offered superficial interpretations of doctrines that he imperfectly understood. Nevertheless, his *Oration* gave eloquent voice to the burning desire of many European scholars to understand the larger world. It is not surprising that just as Pico and other Renaissance humanists were undertaking that effort, European mariners were organizing expeditions to explore the lands and seas beyond Christendom.

## EXPLORATION AND COLONIZATION

As peoples of the Eastern Hemisphere recovered from demographic collapse and restored order to their societies, they also sought to revive the networks of long-distance trade and communication that epidemic plague had disrupted. Most active in that effort were China and western Europe—the two societies that recovered most rapidly from the disasters of the fourteenth century. During the early Ming dynasty, Chinese ports accommodated foreign traders, and mariners mounted a series of enormous naval expeditions that visited almost all parts of the Indian Ocean basin. Meanwhile, Europeans ventured from the Mediterranean into the Atlantic Ocean, which served as a highway to sub-Saharan Africa and the Indian Ocean basin. By the end of the fifteenth century, Europeans not only had established sea lanes to India but also had made several return voyages to the American continents, thus inaugurating a process that brought all the world's peoples into permanent and sustained interaction.

### The Chinese Reconnaissance of the Indian Ocean Basin

Having ousted the Mongols, the early Ming emperors were not eager to have large numbers of foreigners residing in China. Yet the emperors permitted foreign merchants to trade in the closely supervised ports of Quanzhou and Guangzhou, where they obtained Chinese silk, porcelain, and manufactured goods in exchange for pearls, gems, spices, cotton fabrics, and exotic products such as tortoise shells and animal skins. The early Ming emperors also refurbished the large Chinese navy built during the Song dynasty, and they allowed Chinese merchants to participate in overseas trading ventures in Japan and southeast Asia.

**Zheng He's Expeditions** Moreover, for almost thirty years, the Ming government sponsored a series of seven ambitious naval expeditions designed to establish a Chinese presence in the Indian Ocean basin. Emperor Yongle organized the expeditions for two main purposes: to impose imperial control over foreign trade with China and to impress foreign peoples with the power and might that the Ming dynasty had restored to China. Indeed, he might well have hoped to extend the tributary system, by which Chinese dynasties traditionally recognized foreign peoples, to lands in the Indian Ocean basin.

The expeditions took place between 1405 and 1433. Leading them was the eunuch admiral **Zheng He,** a Muslim from Yunnan in southwestern China who rose through the ranks of eunuch administrators to become a trusted adviser of Yongle. Zheng He embarked on each voyage with an awesome fleet of vessels complemented by armed forces large enough to overcome resistance at any port where the expedition called. On the first voyage, for example, Zheng He's fleet consisted of 317 ships accompanied by almost twenty-eight thousand armed troops. Many of these vessels were mammoth,

**Zheng He** (jung ha)

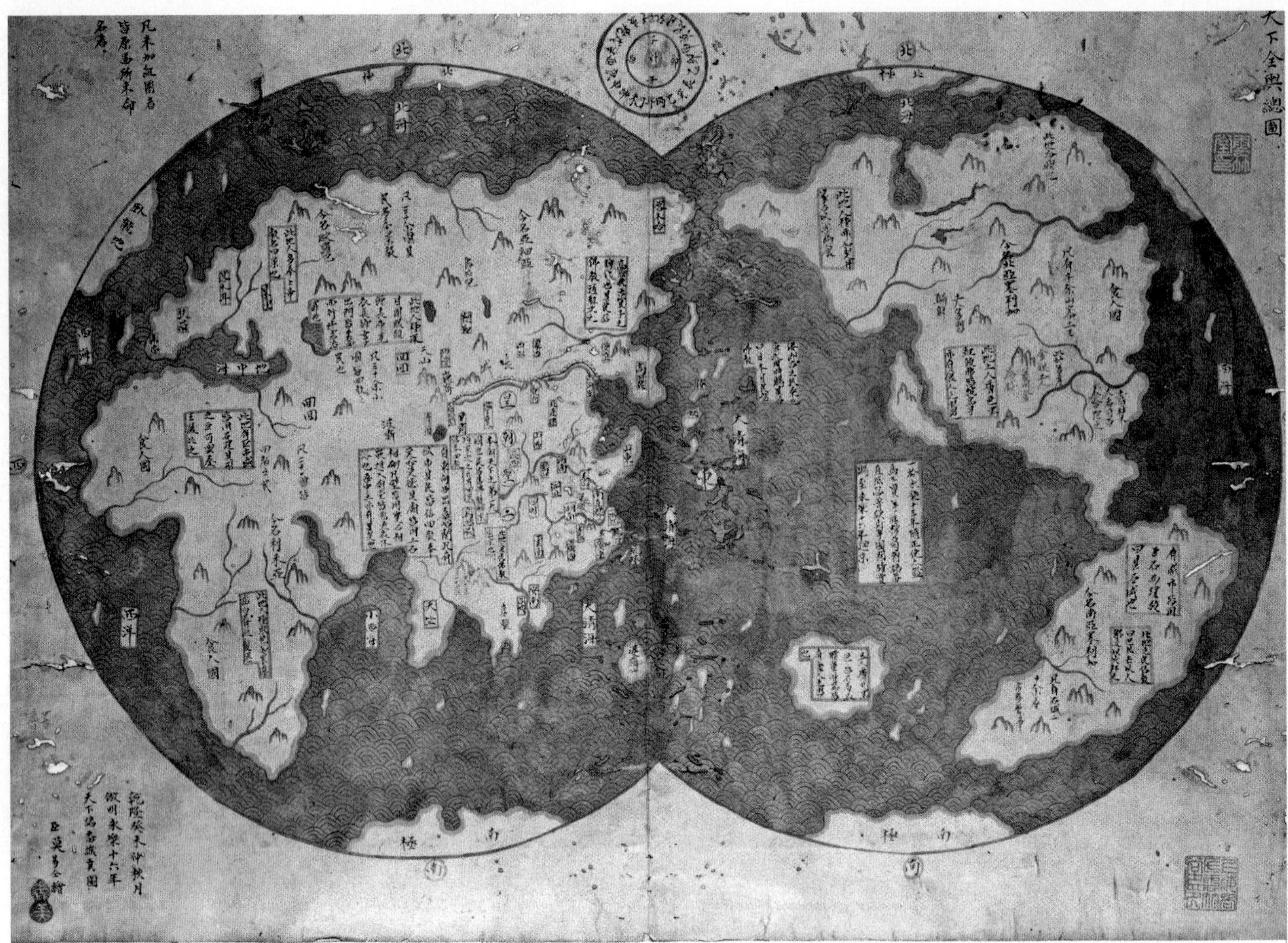


The Kangnido Map (1470) is one of the few surviving large-scale maps from east Asia before modern times. Produced in Korea, it draws on Chinese and Muslim sources, while exaggerating the size of the Korean peninsula.
Universal History Archive/Universal Images Group/Getty Images

nine-masted "treasure ships" with four decks capable of accommodating five hundred or more passengers, as well as huge stores of cargo. Measuring up to 124 meters (408 feet) long and 51 meters (166 feet) wide, these treasure ships were by far the largest marine craft the world had ever seen.

On the first three voyages, Zheng He took his fleet to southeast Asia, India, and Ceylon. The fourth expedition went to the Persian Gulf and Arabia, and later expeditions ventured down the east African coast, calling at ports as far south as Malindi in modern Kenya. Throughout his travels, Zheng He liberally dispensed gifts of Chinese silk, porcelain, and other goods. In return he received rich and unusual presents from his hosts, including African zebras and giraffes, which ended their days in the Ming imperial zoo. Zheng He and his companions paid respect to the local deities and customs they encountered, and in Ceylon they erected a monument honoring Buddha, Allah, and Vishnu.

**Chinese Naval Power** Zheng He generally sought to attain his goals through diplomacy. For the most part, his large contingents of armed troops overawed his hosts, and he had little need to engage in hostilities. But a contemporary reported that Zheng He walked like a tiger, and he did not shrink from violence when he considered it necessary to impress foreign peoples with China's military might. He ruthlessly suppressed pirates who had long plagued Chinese and southeast Asian waters. He also intervened in a civil disturbance to establish his authority in Ceylon, and he made displays of military force when local officials threatened his fleet in Arabia and east Africa. The seven expeditions established a Chinese presence and reputation in the Indian Ocean basin. Returning from his fourth voyage, Zheng He brought envoys from thirty states who traveled to China and paid their respects at the Ming court.

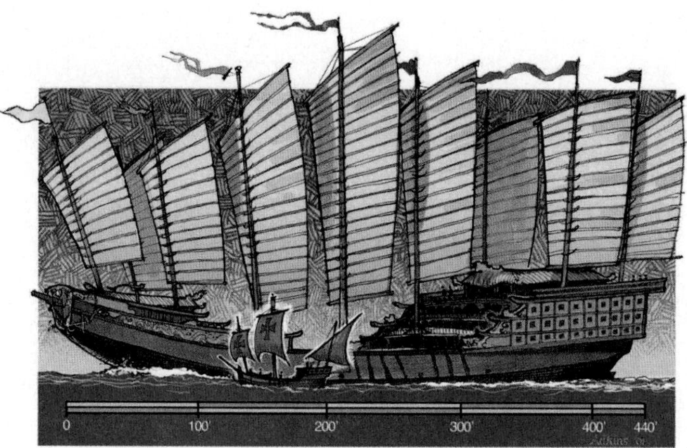


An artist's impression of the comparative size of one of the great treasure ships of Ming dynasty admiral Zheng He and one of the much smaller ships in the fleet in which Columbus sailed from Europe to the Americas.
Jan Adkins.

**End of the Voyages** Yet suddenly, in the mid-1430s, the Ming emperors decided to end the expeditions. Confucian ministers, who mistrusted Zheng He and the eunuchs who supported the voyages, argued that resources committed to the expensive expeditions would go to better uses if devoted to agriculture. Moreover, during the 1420s and 1430s the Mongols mounted a new military threat from the northwest, and land forces urgently needed financial support.

Thus in 1433, after Zheng He's seventh voyage, the expeditions ended. Chinese merchants continued to trade in Japan and southeast Asia, but imperial officials destroyed most of the nautical charts that Zheng He had carefully prepared and gave up any plans to maintain a Chinese presence in the Indian Ocean. The decommissioned treasure ships sat in harbors until they rotted away, and Chinese craftsmen forgot the technology of building such large vessels. Yet Zheng He's voyages demonstrated clearly that China could exercise military, political, and economic influence throughout the Indian Ocean basin.

## European Exploration in the Atlantic and Indian Oceans

As Chinese fleets reconnoitered the Indian Ocean, European mariners were preparing to enter both the Atlantic and the Indian Ocean basins. Unlike Zheng He and his companions, Europeans did not venture onto the seas in the interests of diplomacy or in hopes of establishing a political and military reputation in foreign lands. Instead, they acted on two different but complementary motives: the desire to expand the boundaries of Roman Catholic Christianity and the desire to profit from commercial opportunities.

**Portuguese Exploration** The experience of Portugal illustrates that mixture of motives. Though Portuguese merchants were not especially prominent in trading circles, Portuguese fishermen had a long tradition of seafaring in the stormy Atlantic Ocean. Building on that experience, Portuguese mariners emerged as the early leaders in both Atlantic exploration and the search for a sea route to Asian markets through the Indian Ocean. During the fifteenth century Prince Henrique of Portugal, often called **Prince Henry the Navigator,** embarked on an ambitious campaign to spread Christianity and increase Portuguese influence on the seas. In 1415 he watched as Portuguese forces seized the Moroccan city of **Ceuta,** which guarded the Strait of Gibraltar from the south. He regarded his victory both as a blow against Islam and as a strategic move enabling Christian vessels to move freely between the Mediterranean and the Atlantic.

**Colonization of the Atlantic Islands** Following the capture of Ceuta, Henrique encouraged Portuguese mariners to venture into the Atlantic. During their voyages they discovered the Madeiras and Azores Islands, all uninhabited, which they soon colonized. They also made an unsuccessful effort to occupy the Canary Islands, inhabited by indigenous peoples but claimed since the early fifteenth century by the kingdom of Castile. Later discoveries included the Cape Verde islands, Fernando Po, São Tomé, and Principe off the west African coast. Because these Atlantic islands enjoyed fertile soils and a Mediterranean climate, Portuguese entrepreneurs soon began to cultivate sugarcane there, often in collaboration with Italian investors. Italians had financed sugar plantations in the Mediterranean islands since the twelfth century, and their commercial networks provided a ready means to distribute sugar to Europeans, who were rapidly developing a taste for sweets.

**Slave Trade** During the middle decades of the fifteenth century, a series of Portuguese fleets also explored the west African coast, each expedition proceeding a bit farther than its predecessor. Originally, the Portuguese traded guns, textiles, and other manufactured items for African gold and slaves. Portuguese traders took full advantage of the long- established African commerce in slaves, but they also changed the nature of the **slave trade** by dramatically increasing its volume and by sending slaves to new destinations. By the mid-fifteenth century, the Portuguese forced thousands of slaves annually to their forts on islands off the African coast. They sent most of their human cargo to recently founded sugar plantations in the Atlantic islands, where enslaved people worked as laborers, although some worked as domestic servants in Europe. The use of African slaves to perform heavy labor on commercial plantations soon became common practice, and it fueled the development of a huge, Atlantic-wide trade that would eventually deliver as many as twelve million enslaved Africans to destinations in North America, South America, and the Caribbean region.

**Ceuta (SYOO-tuh)**

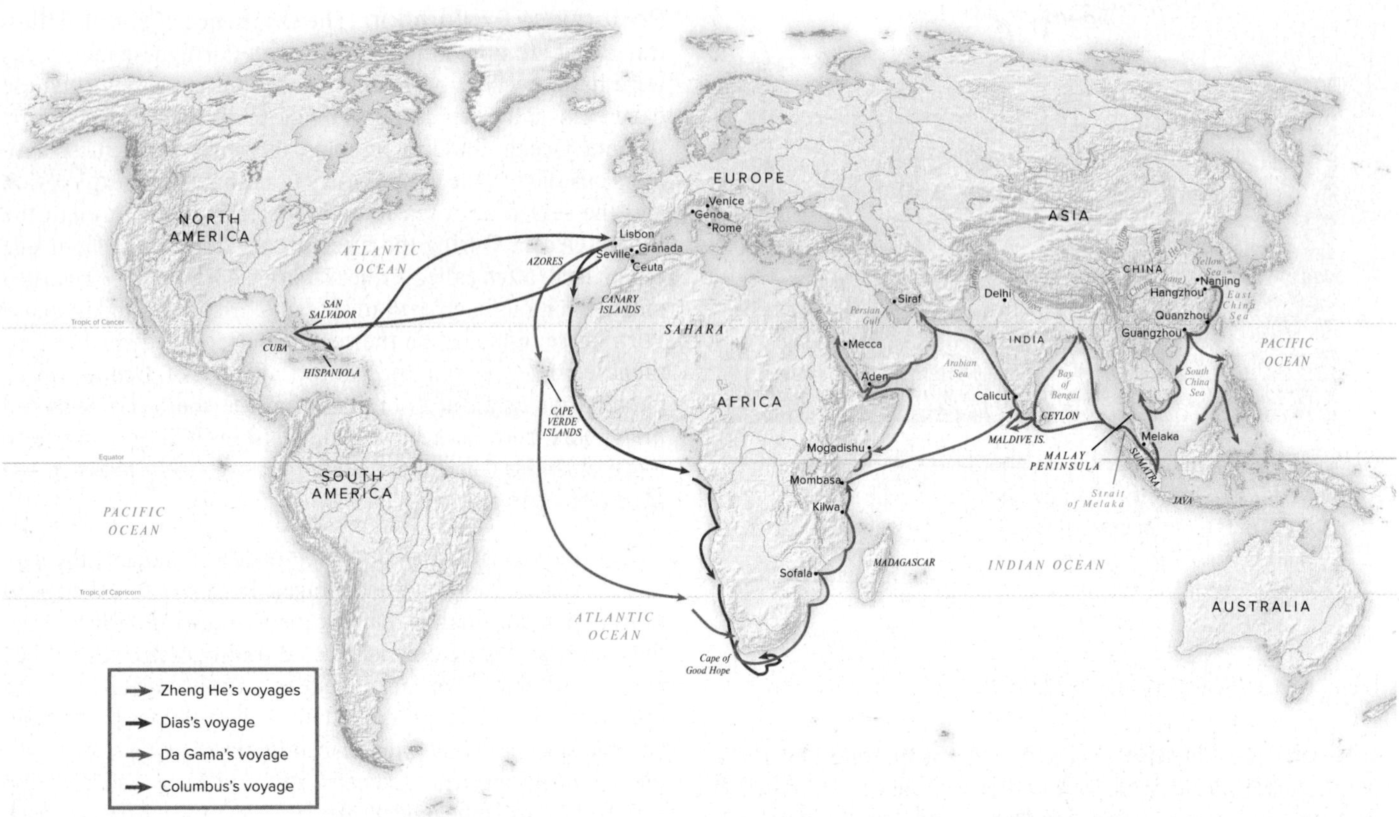


## MAP 9.3 Chinese and European voyages of exploration, 1405–1498.

Although they followed different routes, all the voyagers represented on this map were seeking destinations in the Indian Ocean basin.

***Why did Chinese and Iberian mariners want to establish a presence in the Indian Ocean during the fifteenth century? What made the Indian Ocean basin so desirable?***

**Indian Ocean Trade** While some Portuguese mariners traded profitably in west Africa, others sought to enter the lucrative trade in Asian silk and spices. A sea route to Asian markets would enable Portuguese merchants to avoid Muslim and Italian intermediaries in the Mediterranean and over land. Almost all Asian luxury goods reached European markets through such intermediaries, which prevented the Portuguese (and others) from participating directly in the flourishing commercial world of the Indian Ocean basin. Toward the end of the fifteenth century, Portuguese mariners began to search seriously for a sea lane from Europe around Africa and into the Indian Ocean. By 1488 **Bartolomeu Dias** had sailed around the Cape of Good Hope and entered the Indian Ocean. Restless because of the long journey and distance from home, the crew forced Dias to return immediately to Portugal, but his voyage proved that it was possible to sail from Europe to the Indian Ocean. In 1497 Vasco da Gama departed Portugal with the intention of sailing to India. After rounding the Cape of Good Hope, he cruised up the east African coast and found a Muslim pilot who showed him how to take advantage of the seasonal monsoon winds to sail across the Arabian Sea to India. In 1498 he arrived at Calicut, and by 1499 he had returned to Lisbon with a hugely profitable cargo of pepper and spices.

During the following century, Portuguese merchants and mariners dominated trade between Europe and Asia. Indeed, they attempted to control all shipping in the Indian Ocean. Their ships, armed with cannons, were able to overpower the vessels of Arabs, Persians, Indians, southeast Asians, and others who sailed the Indian Ocean. They did not have enough ships to police the entire Indian Ocean, however, so most merchants easily evaded their efforts to control the region's commerce. Nevertheless, the entry of Portuguese mariners into the Indian Ocean signaled the beginning of European attempts to dominate commerce in Asia.

**Christopher Columbus** While Portuguese seafarers sought a sea route around Africa to India, the Genoese mariner Cristoforo Colombo, known in English as **Christopher Columbus,** conceived the idea of sailing west to reach Asian markets. Because geographers in the Eastern Hemisphere knew nothing of the Americas, Columbus's notion made a certain amount of sense, although many doubted that his plan could lead to profitable trade because of the long distances involved. After the king of Portugal declined to sponsor an expedition to test Columbus's plan, the Catholic Kings, Fernando and Isabel of Spain, agreed to underwrite a voyage.

# INTERPRETING IMAGES

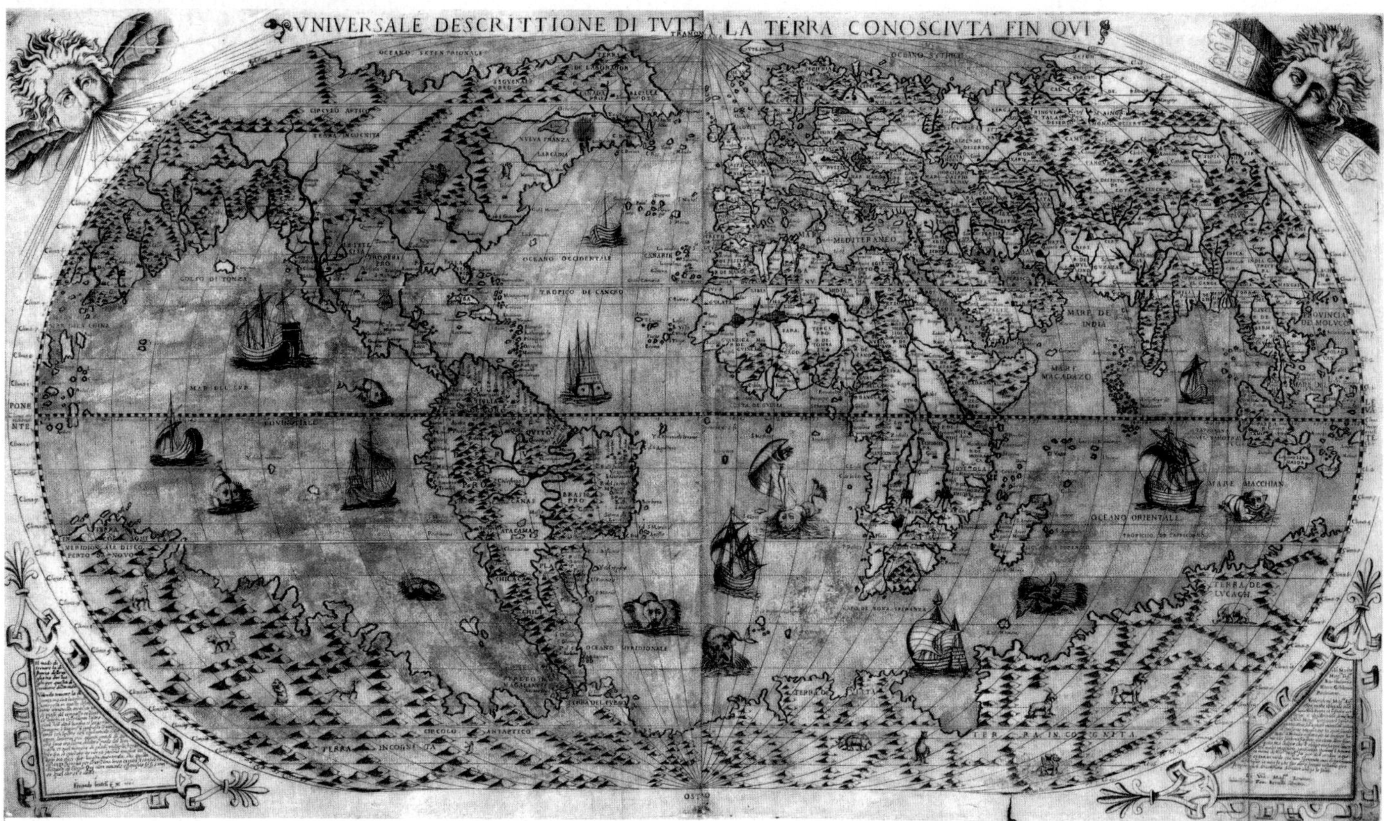


Although Christopher Columbus believed that he had sailed into Asian waters, later mariners soon realized that the Americas were continents unknown to geographers of the eastern hemisphere. This map, prepared in 1565 by Paulo Forlani, shows that by the mid-sixteenth century, European geographers had acquired a rough but accurate understanding of South America and the Atlantic coastline of North America.

**Analyze** *How would a map produced in China at the time be different?*

Everett Collection Historical/Alamy Stock Photo

## How the Past Shapes the Future

### The Diffusion of Technologies

When European mariners set out to spread Christianity and explore commercial possibilities in the Atlantic and Indian ocean basins, they employed a combination of technologies that had been diffused over the centuries from east and southwest Asia. One particularly effective combination was the use of technologies of transportation such as the compass (and later the astrolabe) along with technologies of warfare—especially cannons mounted on the sides of their ships. These diffused technologies allowed Europeans the ability to travel effectively by sea and to compel—using deadly force—vessels from other regions to comply with their desire to dominate trade. While Europeans were not able to dominate maritime trade completely, consider how important their use and adaptation of a variety of diffused technologies to suit their own goals were in their ability to explore the world's oceans between the fifteenth and the eighteenth centuries and how much these innovations changed the world once Europeans made contact with the Americas in the late fifteenth century.

In 1492 Columbus set sail. After a stop in the Canary Islands to take on supplies and make repairs, his fleet of three ships crossed the Atlantic Ocean, reaching land at San Salvador (Watling Island) in the Bahamas.

Columbus returned to Spain without the gold, silk, and spices that he had expected to find, but he persistently argued that he had reached islands near the Asian mainland and the markets of China and Japan. Although he made three more voyages to the Caribbean region, Columbus never acknowledged that his expeditions had not reached Asia. News of his voyages spread rapidly, however, and by the end of the fifteenth century other mariners had explored the Caribbean and the American continents enough to realize that the Western Hemisphere constituted a world apart from Europe, Asia, and Africa.

# CONCLUSION

For millennia, peoples of different societies had traded, communicated, and interacted. But between 1000 and 1500 C.E., the intensity of these interactions increased dramatically as technologies of transportation improved. By 1500 the Indian Ocean served as a highway linking peoples from China to east Africa, and overland traffic kept the Silk Roads busy from China to the Mediterranean Sea, allowing people like Ibn Battuta and Zheng He to travel many thousands of miles. Trade goods, diplomatic missions, religious faiths, technological skills, agricultural crops, and—unfortunately for many—disease pathogens all moved readily over the sea lanes and the Silk Roads, and they profoundly influenced the development of societies throughout the Eastern Hemisphere.

By the year 1500, the world stood on the brink of a new era in the experience of humankind. As a result of European oceanic voyages across the Atlantic, peoples of the world's three major geographic zones—the the Eastern Hemisphere, the Western Hemisphere, and Oceania—were poised to enter into permanent and sustained interaction. The results of their engagements were profitable and beneficial for some peoples but difficult and even disastrous for others. The formation and reconfiguration of global networks of power, communication, and exchange that followed from those interactions rank among the most prominent themes of modern world history, and it is impossible to comprehend them except in context of the acceleration of cross-cultural interaction in the era 1000 to 1500.

# STUDY TERMS

Bartolomeu Dias (304)
bubonic plague (292)
Ceuta (303)
Christopher Columbus (304)
Desiderius Erasmus (300)
eunuch (294)
Francesco Petrarca (300)
Hongwu (294)
humanist (300)
Hundred Years' War (298)
Ibn Battuta (282)
John of Montecorvino (289)
Leonardo da Vinci (299)
little ice age (292)
mandarin (294)
Marco Polo (286)
Melaka (285)
Michelangelo Buonarotti (299)
Ming dynasty (294)
*qadi* (282)
Qing dynasty (294)
Pico della Mirandola (301)
Prince Henry the Navigator (303)
Rabban Sauma (287)
Renaissance (299)
sharia (287)
slave trade (303)
Sufis (288)
*tsar* (299)
Yongle (297)
*Yongle Encyclopedia* (297)
Zheng He (301)

# FOR FURTHER READING

John Aberth. *The First Horseman: Disease in Human History.* London, 2006. Global exploration of the dramatic effects disease has had on human communities over time.

Janet L. Abu-Lughod. *Before European Hegemony: The World System, a.d. 1250–1350.* New York, 1989. An important study of long-distance trade networks during the Mongol era.

Jerry H. Bentley. *Old World Encounters: Cross-Cultural Contacts and Exchanges in Pre-Modern Times.* New York, 1993. Studies cultural and religious exchanges in the Eastern Hemisphere before 1500 C.E.

Timothy Brook. *The Troubled Empire: China in the Yuan and Ming Dynasties.* Cambridge, MA, 2010. Well-written overview of the values, ecology, and interstate connections of China in this period.

Jerry Brotton. *The Renaissance Bazaar: From the Silk Road to Michelangelo.* Oxford, 2002. A provocative and well-illustrated study arguing that encounters in the larger world deeply influenced Renaissance cultural development in Europe.

K. N. Chaudhuri. *Asia before Europe: Economy and Civilisation of the Indian Ocean from the Rise of Islam to 1750.* Cambridge, 1990. Controversial and penetrating analysis of economic, social, and cultural structures shaping societies of the Indian Ocean basin.

Ross E. Dunn. *The Adventures of Ibn Battuta: A Muslim Traveler of the 14th Century: With a New Preface.* Berkeley, 2012. Fascinating reconstruction of Ibn Battuta's travels and experiences.

Brian Fagan. *The Little Ice Age: How Climate Made History, 1300–1850.* New York, 2000. Popular account of the little ice age, with emphasis on its effects in Europe and North America.

Monica Green, ed. *Pandemic Disease in the Medieval World: Rethinking the Black Death.* Amsterdam, 2015. Series of essays written by historians and scientists on the history and significance of the Black Death in global perspective.

John Larner. *Marco Polo and the Discovery of the World.* New Haven, Conn., 1999. Excellent study of Marco Polo and his significance, based on a thorough review of both textual evidence and recent scholarship.

Louise L. Levathes. *When China Ruled the Seas: The Treasure Fleet of the Dragon Throne, 1405–1433.* New York, 1994. Excellent popular account of Zheng He's voyages.

Karen Raber. *A Cultural History of Women in the Renaissance.* London, 2015. Explores the way the social and scientific changes of the Renaissance affected ideologies of gender and the lived experiences of women.

# CHAPTER 9 AP EXAM PRACTICE

Questions assume cumulative knowledge from this chapter and previous chapters.

## Section I

## Multiple Choice Questions

Use the image below and your knowledge of world history to answer questions 1-3.

An illustration from a manuscript of 1282 depicts a Christian (left) playing chess with a Muslim (right).

Index/Heritage Images/Heritage Image Partnership Ltd /Alamy Stock Photo

1. Which of the following was a way cultural exchange between Christians and Muslims took place from 1000 to 1500 C. E.?
   (A) Muslim legal scholars traveled to India, Asia, and Africa to teach sharia law.
   (B) (Troubadours borrowed Muslim literary styles for courtly love literature.
   (C) Marco Polo was given an administrative appointment by Kublai Khan
   (D) Ibn Battuta advised Mali rulers on modest clothing.

2. Which of these is an item that Europeans learned to produce through contact with Muslims?
   (A) Gunpowder weapons
   (B) Swords
   (C) Tents
   (D) Refined sugar

3. A historian could use this image to make which possible historical point?
   (A) Chess was a critical aspect of world diplomacy, and a required skill for all ambassadors during the crusading era.
   (B) Marco Polo introduced the travel-sized chess set to the Silk Road trade route.
   (C) Long-distance travel for any purpose (trade, diplomacy, missions, etc.) facilitated cross-cultural exchanges.
   (D) The Black Death was spread by Mongols and merchants traveling on trade routes.

Use the image below and your knowledge of world history to answer questions 4 and 5.

Brunelleschi's dome on the cathedral of Florence.
Adam Sylvester/Science Sources

4. Renaissance humanists, architects, and artists drew inspiration from ancient Rome and what other source?
   (A) The naturalistic style of Daoist art.
   (B) Admiration for the way the Russians defied Mongol influence.
   (C) A desire to memorialize the lives lost during the Black Death.
   (D) The wealth and products that were imported from across Afro-Eurasia.

5. Italian Renaissance cities were important trading hubs. Which of the following characterized major trading centers across Afro-Eurasia?
   (A) Strategic locations, order, and low custom fees
   (B) Hilltop locations, defensive walls, and good roads
   (C) Large cathedrals, beautiful architecture, and scenic views
   (D) Good climate, local artists, and universities

## Short Answer

6. Use the image below and your knowledge of world history to answer parts A, B, and C.

Harvesting pepper, from the Livre des merveilles du monde (Book of the Wonders of the World) by Marco Polo and Rustichello. France, 15th century.
DEA/J. E. Bulloz/Getty Images

(A) Identify ONE reason why Marco Polo was able to travel to China.
(B) Explain ONE way religion played a role in Mongol diplomacy.
(C) Explain ONE way that the story of Marco Polo influenced Europeans.

7. Use the image below and your knowledge of world history to answer parts A, B, and C.

Death strangling a victim of the Black Death plague, from a codex called the Clementinum Collection by Thomas of Stitny. Czech Republic. 1376 C.E.
Werner Forman/Universal Images Group/Getty Images

(A) Identify ONE reason why the Black Death was able to spread across Asia and Europe.
(B) Explain ONE economic effect of the Black Death on Europe.
(C) Explain ONE effect of the Black Death on Christians or Muslims.

8. Use your understanding of world history to answer parts A, B, and C.
(A) Identify ONE way that the Ming Emperors built a centralized government.
(B) Explain ONE reason why Ming Emperors relied on eunuchs.
(C) Explain ONE way that Chinese culture was revived during the Ming Dynasty.

# Section II

## Document-Based Question

Based on the documents below and your knowledge of world history, evaluate the extent to which long distance travel contributed to cultural diffusion in Afro-Eurasia between 1000 and 1500 C.E.

In your response you should do the following:

- Respond to the prompt with a historically defensible thesis or claim that establishes a line of reasoning.
- Describe a broader historical context relevant to the prompt.
- Support an argument in response to the prompt using all documents.
- Use at least one additional piece of specific historical evidence (beyond that found in the documents) relevant to an argument about the prompt.
- Explain how or why the document's point of view, purpose, historical situation, and /or audience is relevant to an argument.
- Use evidence to corroborate, qualify, or modify an argument that addresses the prompt.

### Document 1

**[After spending thirteen months in India]** I proceeded on my further journey and made my way to China, the realm of the emperor of the Mongols who is called the great khan. To him I presented the letter of our lord the pope and invited him to adopt the Catholic faith of our Lord Jesus Christ, but he had grown too old in idolatry. However, he bestows many kindnesses upon the Christians, and these two years past I have gotten along well with him. . . . I have built a church in the city of Khanbaliq, in which the king has his chief residence. This I completed six years ago; and I have built a bell tower to it and put three bells in it. I have baptized there, as well as I can estimate, up to this time some 6,000 persons. . . . And I am often still engaged in baptizing.

*Source:* Yule, Henry and Henri Cordier, eds. *Cathay and the Way Thither,* 4 vols. London: Hakluyt Society, 1866, 3:45–50. (Translation slightly modified.)

### Document 2

Another of their good properties is, that when a merchant happens to die among them, they will make no effort to get possession of his property: but will allow the lawful successors to it to take it. Another is, their constant custom of attending prayers with the congregation; for, unless one makes haste, he will find no place left to say his prayers in. Another is, their insisting on the Koran's being committed to memory: for if a man finds his son defective in this, he will confine him till he is quite perfect, nor will he allow him his liberty until he is so. As to their bad practices, they will exhibit their little daughters, as well as their male and female slaves, quite naked. In the same manner will the women enter into the presence of the King, which his own daughters will also do. Nor do the free women ever clothe themselves till after marriage.

*Source:* Batuta, Ibn, 1304–1377, and translated by Samuel Lee. *The Travels of Ibn Batūta.* London: Printed for the Oriental translation committee, sold by J. Murray [etc.], 1829, 263–264.

## Document 3

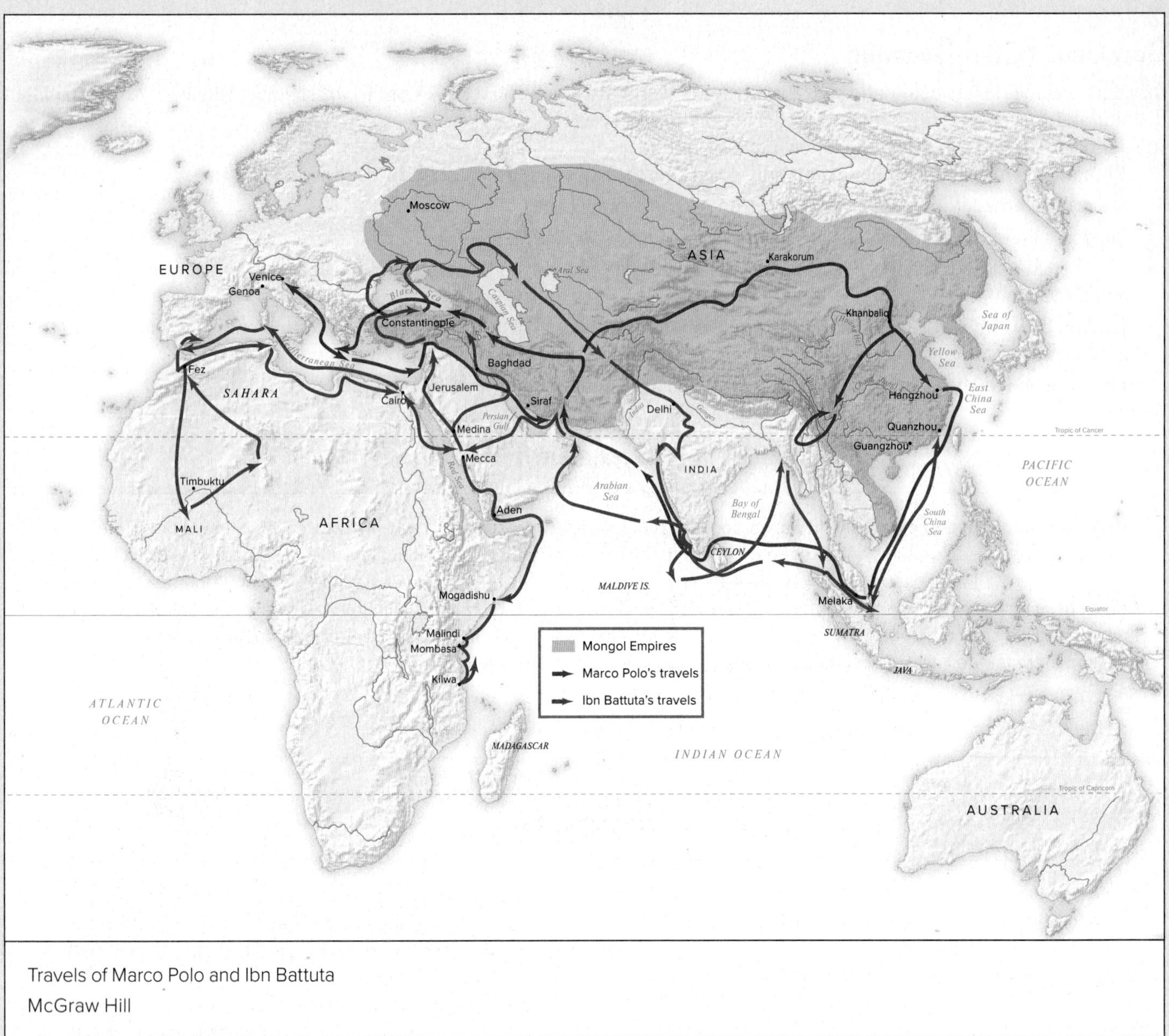


Travels of Marco Polo and Ibn Battuta
McGraw Hill

## Long Essay

Develop a thoughtful and thorough historical argument that answers the question below. Begin your essay with a thesis statement and support it with relevant historical evidence.

Using specific examples and your knowledge of world history, compare and contrast how maritime trade contributed to state building in China and Europe from 1350 to 1500 C.E.

Chapter 10

# Transoceanic Encounters and Global Connections



## ZOOMING IN ON ENCOUNTERS

### Vasco da Gama's Search for Spices

On 8 July 1497 the Portuguese mariner **Vasco da Gama** led a small fleet of four armed merchant vessels with 170 crewmen out of the harbor at Lisbon. His destination was India, which he planned to reach by sailing around the continent of Africa and through the Indian Ocean, and his goal was to enter the highly lucrative trade in spices dominated in Europe by the merchants of Venice. He carried letters of introduction from the king of Portugal as well as cargoes of gold, pearls, wool textiles, bronzeware, iron tools, and other goods that he hoped to exchange for spices in India.

Before there would be an opportunity to trade, however, da Gama and his crew had a prolonged voyage through two oceans. They sailed south from Portugal to the Cape Verde Islands off the west coast of Africa, where they took on water and fresh provisions. On 3 August they headed south into the Atlantic Ocean to take advantage of the prevailing winds. For the next ninety-five days, the fleet saw no land as it sailed through some six thousand nautical miles of open ocean. By October, da Gama came across westerly winds in the southern Atlantic, which helped propel him around the Cape of Good Hope and into the Indian Ocean. The fleet slowly worked its

Vasco da Gama's flagship on the journey to India in 1497, the *San Rafael*.
Photo Researchers/Science History Images/Alamy Stock Photo

**Vasco da Gama** (VAHS-koh duh GAHM-uh)

way up the east coast of Africa, engaging in hostilities with local authorities at Mozambique and Mombasa, as far as Malindi, where da Gama secured the services of an Indian Muslim pilot to guide his ships across the Arabian Sea. On 20 May 1498—more than ten months after its departure from Lisbon—the fleet anchored at Calicut in southern India.

In India the Portuguese fleet encountered a wealthy, cosmopolitan society. Upon their arrival local authorities in Calicut dispatched a pair of Tunisian merchants who spoke Spanish and Italian to serve as translators for the newly arrived party. The markets of Calicut offered not only pepper, ginger, cinnamon, and other spices sought so eagerly by da Gama, but also rubies, emeralds, gold jewelry, and fine cotton textiles. But apart from gold and some striped cloth, the merchants at Calicut thought the goods that da Gama had brought to trade were worthless and showed no interest in them. Nevertheless, da Gama managed to exchange gold for a cargo of pepper and cinnamon that turned a handsome profit when the fleet returned to Portugal in August 1499. Da Gama's expedition opened the door to direct maritime trade between European and Asian peoples and helped to establish permanent links between the world's various regions.

# CHAPTER FOCUS

- Globalization begins in 1492.
- Maritime technologies from Asia and *Dar al-Islam* enabled western European exploration and increasing integration.
- Portuguese, Dutch, English, and French explorers sailed around Africa and into the Indian Ocean basin, setting up coastal trading posts financed by joint-stock companies.
- Columbus sailed west to reach the "East Indies," and ended up in the Caribbean instead. This new connection had massive environmental and demographic effects—the first *global* exchange of people, animals, plants, and diseases, known as the Columbian Exchange.
- Magellan, first to circumnavigate the global, claimed all "unknown" lands for the Spanish King Philip II, including the newly named Philippine Islands, which gave Spanish merchants a critical base to trade with the Chinese.
- Pay particular attention to how historical narratives shifted. What is "known" and "unknown," and whose knowledge takes precedence? How does that affect our historical understanding even today?

## Historical Developments

- Knowledge, scientific learning, and technology from the Classical, Islamic, and Asian worlds spread, facilitating European technological developments and innovation.
- The developments included the production of new tools, innovations in ship designs, and an improved understanding of regional wind and currents patterns—all of which made transoceanic travel and trade possible.
- Portuguese development of maritime technology and navigational skills led to increased travel to and trade with Africa and Asia and resulted in the construction of a global trading-post empire.
- Northern Atlantic crossings were undertaken under English, French, and Dutch sponsorship, often with the goal of finding alternative sailing routes to Asia.
- The new connections between the Eastern and Western Hemispheres resulted in the exchange of new plants, animals, and diseases, known as the Columbian Exchange.
- Populations in Afro-Eurasia benefited nutritionally from the increased diversity of American food crops.
- Empires achieved increased scope and influence around the world, shaping and being shaped by the diverse populations they incorporated.

## Reasoning Processes

- **Developments and Processes** Explain the Columbian Exchange and its consequences in the Americas and Afro-Eurasia.
- **Source Claims and Evidence** Identify the evidence used to support the claim that the voyages of Christopher Columbus and Vasco da Gama were motivated by commerce.
- **Contextualization** Identify the historical context of the Seven Years' War.
- **Making Connections** Identify patterns among or connections between the Spanish, English, Dutch, Portuguese, and Russian empires in Asia.
- **Argumentation** Make a historically defensible claim that explains the motives of Spanish and Portuguese voyages of exploration.

## Historical Thinking Skills

- **Causation** Describe the causes and effects of the Columbian Exchange.
- **Continuity and Change** Explain patterns of continuity and change in European economic systems from the fifteenth to the eighteenth century.

## CHAPTER OVERVIEW

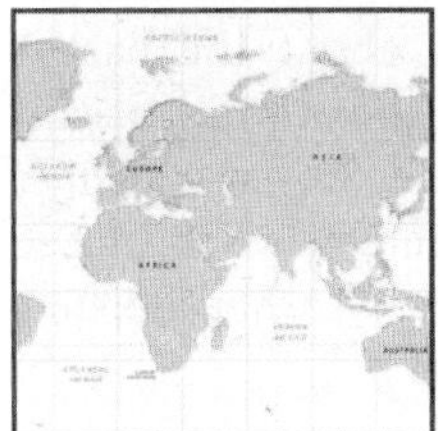

Cross-cultural interactions and encounters have been a persistent feature of historical development. Even in ancient times mass migration, campaigns of imperial expansion, and long-distance trade deeply influenced societies throughout the world. But after 1500 c.e., cross-cultural interactions took place on a much larger geographic scale, and encounters thus affected greater numbers of people than in earlier centuries. Equipped with a variety of technologies and a powerful military arsenal, western European peoples began to cross the world's oceans in large numbers during the early modern era (ca. 1500–ca. 1800). At the same time, Russian adventurers built an enormous Eurasian empire and ventured into the Pacific Ocean.

Europeans were not the only peoples who actively explored the larger world during the early modern era. In the early fifteenth century the Ming emperors of China sponsored a series of seven massive maritime expeditions that visited all parts of the Indian Ocean basin. Although state-sponsored expeditions came to an end after 1435, Chinese merchants and mariners were prominent figures in east Asian and southeast Asian lands throughout the early modern era. In the sixteenth century Ottoman mariners also ventured into the Indian Ocean. Following the Ottoman conquest of Egypt in 1517, both merchant and military vessels established an Ottoman presence throughout the Indian Ocean basin. Ottoman explorers traveled as far as China, but they were most active in Muslim lands from east Africa and Arabia to India and southeast Asia, where they enjoyed especially warm receptions.

Although other peoples also made their way into the larger world, it was Europeans who, initially by chance, linked the lands and peoples of the Eastern Hemisphere, the Western Hemisphere and Oceania. Because they began to travel regularly between the world's major geographic regions, in this period European peoples benefited from unparalleled opportunities to increase their power, wealth, and influence. By 1800, the projection of European influence brought about a decisive shift in the global balance of power. During the millennium 500 to 1500 c.e., the world's most powerful societies had been those organized by imperial states such as the Tang dynasty of China, the Abbasid dynasty in southwest Asia, the Byzantine Empire in the eastern Mediterranean region, and the Mongol Empires that embraced much of Eurasia. After 1500, however, European peoples became more prominent than before in the larger world, and they began to establish vast empires that by the nineteenth century dominated much of the world.

The expansion of European influence also resulted in the establishment of truly global networks of transportation, communication, and exchange. A worldwide diffusion of plants, animals, diseases, and human communities followed European ventures across the oceans, and intricate trade networks eventually gave birth to a global economy. The consequences to the peoples of the Americas and Oceania were disastrous, as epidemic diseases killed millions of people. Over much of the rest of the world, however, the spread of food crops and domesticated animals contributed to a dramatic surge in global population. The establishment of global trade networks established in this period ensured that interactions between the world's peoples would continue and intensify.

| CHRONOLOGY | |
|---|---|
| 1394–1460 | Life of Prince Henry the Navigator of Portugal |
| 1488 | Bartolomeu Dias's voyage around the Cape of Good Hope into the Indian Ocean |
| 1492 | Christopher Columbus's first voyage to the Western Hemisphere |
| 1497–1499 | Vasco da Gama's first voyage to India |
| 1500 | Establishment of Portuguese trading post in Calicut, India |
| 1519–1522 | Ferdinand Magellan's circumnavigation of the world |
| 1565–1575 | Spanish conquest of the Philippines |
| 1619 | Establishment of Batavia by the Dutch on the island of Java |
| 1756–1763 | Seven Years' War |
| 1768–1780 | Captain James Cook's voyages in the Pacific Ocean |

## THE EXPLORATION OF THE WORLD'S OCEANS

Between 1400 and 1800, European mariners launched a remarkable series of exploratory voyages that took them to all the earth's waters, with the exception of those in extreme polar regions. These voyages were very expensive and required the latest technologies for their success. Yet private investors and government authorities had strong motives to underwrite the expeditions and outfit them with advanced nautical technology. The voyages of exploration paid large dividends: they enabled European mariners to chart the world's ocean basins and develop an accurate understanding of world geography. On the basis of that knowledge, European merchants and mariners established global networks of communication, transportation, and exchange that had dramatic consequences for the whole world.

## The Technology of Exploration

Without advanced nautical technology and navigational skills, European mariners would not have been able to explore the world's oceans. Embarking on voyages that would keep them out of the sight of land for weeks at a time, mariners needed sturdy ships, navigational equipment, and sailing techniques that would permit them to make their way across the seas and back again. They inherited much of their nautical technology from Mediterranean and northern European maritime traditions and combined it imaginatively with elements of Chinese and Arabic origin.

**Ships and Sails** From their experiences in the coastal waters of the Atlantic, European sailors learned to construct ships strong enough to survive most adverse conditions. Beginning about the twelfth century, they increased the maneuverability of their craft by building a rudder onto the stern. (The sternpost rudder was a Chinese invention that had diffused across the Indian Ocean and probably became known to Europeans through Arab ships in the Mediterranean.) They outfitted their vessels with two main types of sail, both of which Mediterranean mariners had used since classical times. Square sails enabled them to take full advantage of a following wind (a wind blowing from behind), although these sails did not work well in crosswinds. Triangular lateen sails, on the other hand, were very maneuverable and could catch winds from the side as well as from behind. With a combination of square and lateen sails, European ships were able to use whatever winds arose. Their ability to tack–to advance against the wind by sailing across it–was crucial for the exploration of regions with uncooperative winds.

**Navigational Instruments** The most important navigational equipment on board these vessels were **magnetic compasses** and **astrolabes** (soon replaced by **cross staffs** and **back staffs**). The compass was a Chinese invention of the Tang or Song dynasty that had diffused throughout the Indian Ocean basin in the eleventh century. By the mid-twelfth century, European mariners used compasses to determine their heading in Mediterranean and Atlantic waters. The astrolabe was a simplified version of an instrument used by Greek and Persian astronomers to determine latitude by measuring the angle of the sun or the pole star (or North Star) above the horizon. Portuguese mariners visiting the Indian Ocean in the late fifteenth century encountered Arab sailors using simpler and more serviceable instruments for determining latitude, which the Portuguese then used as models for the construction of cross staffs and back staffs.

European mariners' ability to determine direction and latitude based on these many borrowed technologies enabled them to assemble a vast body of data about the earth's geography and to find their way around the world's oceans with reasonable accuracy and efficiency. (The measurement of longitude requires the ability to measure time precisely and so had to wait until the late eighteenth century, when dependable, spring-driven clocks became available.)

**Knowledge of Winds and Currents** Equipped with the latest technological hardware, European mariners ventured into the oceans and gradually compiled a body of practical knowledge about the winds and currents that determined navigational possibilities in the age of sail. In both the Atlantic and the Pacific Oceans, strong winds blow regularly to create giant "wind wheels" both north and south of the equator, and ocean currents follow a similar pattern. Between about five and twenty-five degrees of latitude north and south of the equator, winds (called "trade winds" by Europeans) blow from the east. Between about thirty and sixty degrees north and south, westerly winds prevail. Winds and currents in the Indian Ocean follow a different, but still regular and reliable, pattern. During the summer months, generally between April and October, monsoon winds blow from the southwest throughout the Indian Ocean basin, whereas during the winter they blow from the northeast. Once mariners understood these patterns, they were able to take advantage of prevailing winds and currents to sail to almost any part of the earth.

**The *volta do mar*** Prevailing winds and currents often forced mariners to take indirect routes to their destinations.

By using cross staffs to measure the angle of the sun or the pole star above the horizon, mariners could determine latitude.

European vessels sailed easily from the Mediterranean to the Canary Islands, for example, because regular trade winds blew from the northeast. But those same trade winds complicated the return trip. By the mid-fifteenth century, Portuguese mariners had developed a strategy called the ***volta do mar*** ("return through the sea") that enabled them to sail from the Canaries to Portugal. Instead of trying to force their way against the trade winds–a slow and perilous business–they sailed northwest into the open ocean until they found westerly winds and then turned east for the last leg of the homeward journey.

Although the *volta do mar* took mariners well out of their way, experience soon taught that sailing around contrary winds was much faster, safer, and more reliable than butting up against them. Portuguese and other European mariners began to rely on the principle of the *volta do mar* in sailing to destinations other than the Canary Islands. When Vasco da Gama departed for India, for example, he sailed south to the Cape Verde Islands and then allowed the trade winds to carry him southwest into the Atlantic Ocean until he approached the coast of Brazil. There da Gama caught the prevailing westerlies that enabled him to sail east, round the Cape of Good Hope, and enter the Indian Ocean. As they became familiar with the wind systems of the world's oceans, European mariners developed variations on the *volta do mar* that enabled them to travel reliably to coastlines around the world.

## Motives for Exploration

A complex combination of motives prompted Europeans to explore the world's oceans. Most important of these motives were the search for basic resources and lands suitable for the cultivation of cash crops, the desire to establish new trade routes to Asian markets, and the aspiration to expand the influence of Christianity.

**Portuguese Exploration** Mariners from the relatively poor kingdom of Portugal were initially the most prominent in the search for fresh resources to exploit and lands to cultivate. Beginning in the thirteenth century, Portuguese seamen ventured away from the coasts and into the open Atlantic Ocean. They originally sought fish, seals, whales, timber, and lands where they could grow wheat to supplement the meager resources of Portugal. By the early fourteenth century, they had discovered the uninhabited Azores and Madeiras Islands. They also traveled frequently to the Canary Islands, inhabited by the indigenous Guanche people, which Italian and

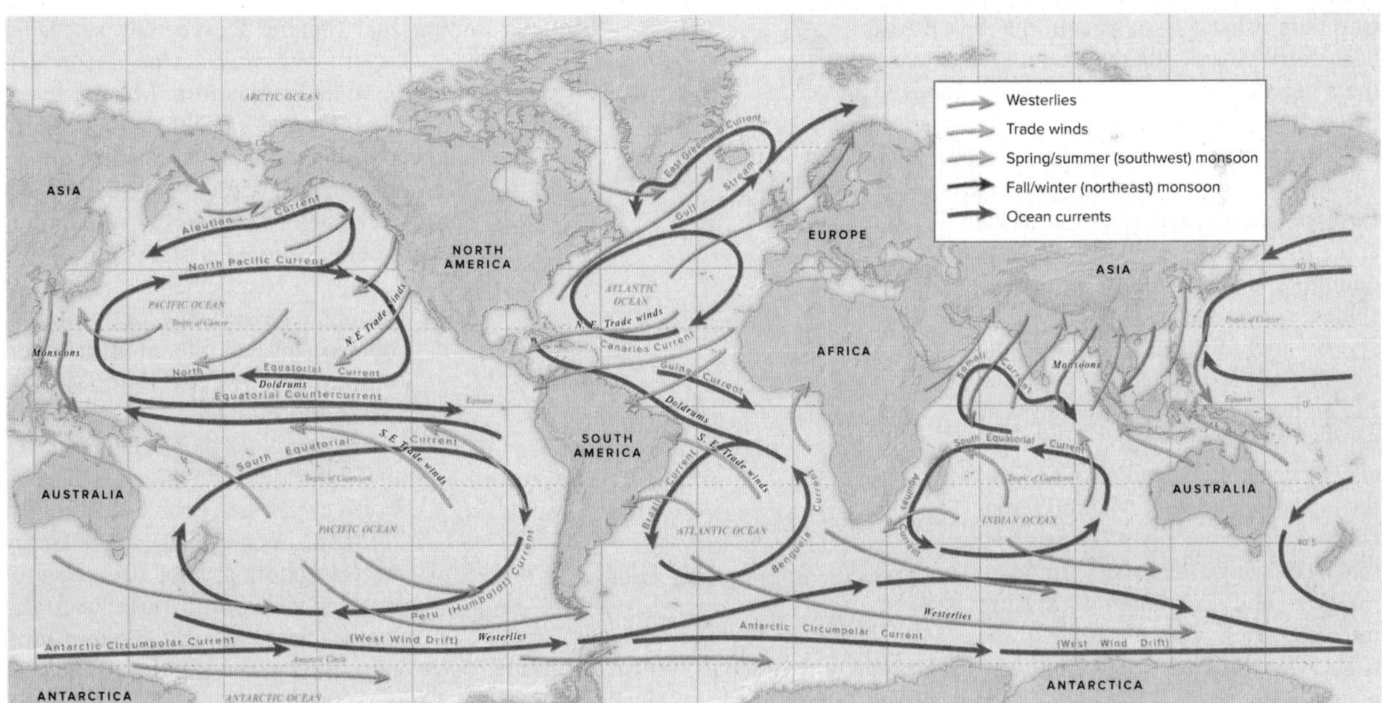


## MAP 10.1 Wind and current patterns in the world's oceans.

Note how the winds of the Atlantic and Pacific resemble wind wheels, revolving clockwise north of the equator and counterclockwise south of the equator.

***How crucial was an understanding of the world's wind patterns to the success of European overseas expansion?***

Iberian mariners had visited since the early fourteenth century. Because European demand for sugar was strong and increasing, the prospect of establishing sugar plantations on the Atlantic islands was very tempting. Italian entrepreneurs had organized sugar plantations in Palestine and the Mediterranean islands since the twelfth century, and in the fifteenth century Italian investors worked with Portuguese mariners to establish plantations in the Atlantic islands using slave labor (discussed more fully in chapter 25). Continuing Portuguese voyages also led to the establishment of plantations on more southerly Atlantic islands, including the Cape Verde Islands, São Tomé, Principe, and Fernando Po.

**Trade** Even more important than the exploitation of fresh lands and resources was the goal of establishing maritime trade routes to the markets of Asia. During the era of the Mongol Empires, European merchants often traveled overland as far as China to trade in silk, spices, porcelain, and other Asian goods. In the fourteenth century, however, with the collapse of the Mongol Empires and the spread of bubonic plague, travel on what we now call the Silk Roads became much less safe than before. Arab mariners continued to bring Asian goods through the Indian Ocean and the Red Sea to Cairo, where Italian merchants purchased them for distribution in western Europe. But prices at Cairo were high, and Europeans sought ever-larger quantities of Asian goods, particularly spices.

By the fourteenth century the wealthy classes of Europe regarded Indian pepper and Chinese ginger as expensive necessities, and they especially prized cloves and nutmeg from the spice islands of Maluku. Merchants and monarchs alike realized that by offering direct access to Asian markets and eliminating Muslim intermediaries, new maritime trade routes would increase the quantities of spices and other Asian goods available in Europe—and would also yield enormous profits. This was, indeed, the motive behind Vasco da Gama's voyage to India in 1497 that we read about in the introduction to this chapter.

Europeans were also interested in African trade. Since the twelfth century, camel caravans had delivered west African gold, ivory, and enslaved people to north African ports, where Europeans—along with many others—took part in their trade (for more on the trans-Saharan trade, see chapter 25). Gold was an especially important commodity because the precious metal from west Africa was Europeans' principal form of payment for Asian luxury goods. As in the case of Asian trade, European merchants were interested in maritime routes that eliminated Muslim intermediaries and offered more direct access to African markets.

The earliest surviving world globe, produced in 1492 by the German cartographer Martin Behaim, depicts the Eastern Hemisphere quite accurately but shows almost no land west of Iberia except for east Asia.
DEA Picture Library/Getty Images

**Missionary Efforts** Alongside material incentives, the goal of expanding the boundaries of Christianity also drove Europeans into the larger world. Like Buddhism and Islam, Christianity is a missionary religion. The New Testament specifically urged Christians to spread their faith throughout the world. Efforts to spread the faith often took peaceful forms. During the era of the Mongol Empires, Franciscan and Dominican missionaries had traveled as far as India, central Asia, and China in search of converts. Yet the expansion of Christianity was by no means always a peaceful affair. Beginning in the eleventh century, western Europeans had launched a series of crusades and holy wars against Muslims in Palestine, the Mediterranean islands, and Iberia. Crusading zeal remained especially strong in Iberia, where the *reconquista* (the "reconquering" of Spain and Iberia from Muslim rulers who had been there for 800 years) came to an end in 1492: the Muslim kingdom of Granada fell to Spanish Christian forces just weeks before Christopher Columbus set sail on his famous first voyage to the Western Hemisphere. Whether through persuasion or violence, overseas voyages offered fresh opportunities for western Europeans to spread their faith.

In practice, the various motives for exploration combined and reinforced each other. Prince Henrique of Portugal, often called **Prince Henry the Navigator,** promoted voyages of exploration in west Africa specifically to enter the gold trade, discover profitable new trade routes, gain intelligence about the extent of Muslim power, win converts to Christianity, and make alliances against the Muslims with any Christian rulers he might find. When the Portuguese mariner Vasco da Gama reached the Indian port of Calicut in 1498, local authorities asked him what he wanted there. His reply: "Christians and spices." The goal of spreading Christianity thus became a powerful justification and reinforcement for the more material motives for the voyages of exploration.

A depiction of the Indian port of Calicut in 1572, when Portugal dominated the pepper trade.
FLHC A20/Alamy Stock Photo

## European Voyages of Exploration: From the Mediterranean to the Atlantic

In 1291 the Vivaldi brothers departed from Genoa in two ships with the intention of sailing around Africa to India. They did not succeed, but the idea of exploring the Atlantic and establishing a maritime trade route from the Mediterranean to India persisted. During the fourteenth century Genoese, Portuguese, and Spanish mariners sailed frequently into the Atlantic Ocean and rediscovered the Canary Islands. The Guanche people had settled the Canaries from their original home in Morocco, in around the fifth century B.C.E. but there had been no contact between the Guanches and other peoples since the time of the Roman Empire.

## What's Left Out?

In Europe during the late Middle Ages, spices like pepper, cloves, nutmeg, cinnamon, and ginger were extremely expensive, costing approximately one to three English shillings per pound. Compare this to a whole cow, which cost between six and ten shillings, or a pig, which cost two. An ordinary soldier's wages, by comparison, were about a shilling a day, while a kitchen servant's wages were between 2 and 4 shillings for a whole year. What was it about the spices we now take for granted that made people want to pay such high prices for them and for others to risk their lives and all their material possessions to trade them? Spices were used to enhance the taste and smell of many foods and drinks, to mask bad odors, and as medicines. Pepper, ginger, and cinnamon, for example, were used to treat a myriad of ailments, including headache, insomnia, and digestive problems. But scholars now believe it was the very rarity of spices, and the mythology associated with their mysterious and distant origins, that was the real source of their value. Precisely because they came from so far away and were thus so expensive, spices were viewed as the ultimate status symbols. In addition, many Europeans believed fantastic stories about the way spices were procured. Pepper, for example, was thought to come from trees guarded by serpents who would poison anyone attempting to harvest the peppercorns that grew on them. Stories such as these added to the allure of spices, which in turn helped to explain the very high prices Europeans were willing to pay for them.

*Source:* John Keay, *The Spice Route: A History* (Berkeley: University of California Press, 2006).

### Thinking Critically About Sources

The passage clearly demonstrates the value of Indian spices.

1. Can you suggest reasons Portugal did not economically rival other European countries during the 16th and 17th centuries?

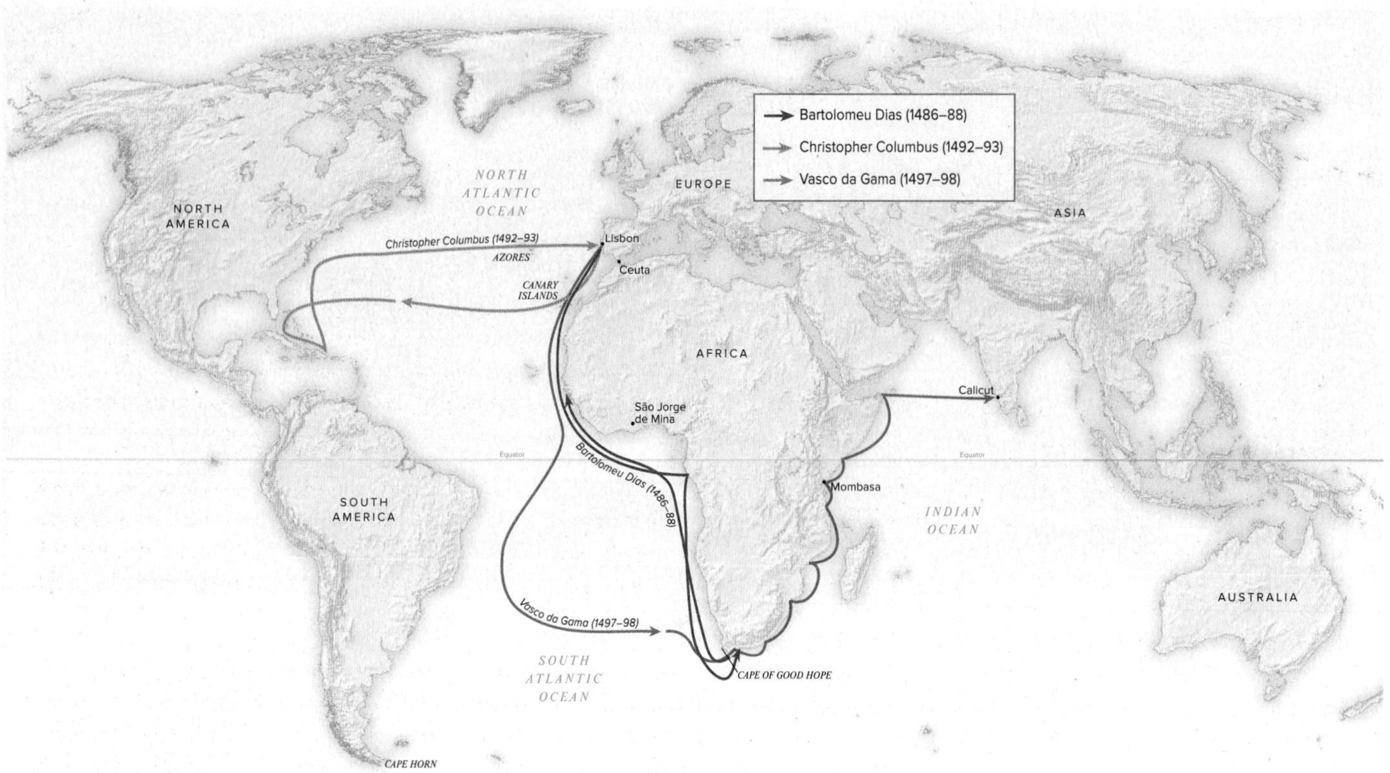


## MAP 10.2 European exploration in the Atlantic Ocean, 1486–1498.

Observe the difference between Bartolomeu Dias's journey and Vasco da Gama's journey around the Cape of Good Hope.

***Why did da Gama go so far out into the Atlantic before rounding the Cape?***

Iberian mariners began to visit the Canaries regularly, and in the fifteenth century—after a long and brutal war in which the Guanche put up fierce resistance—Castilian forces conquered the islands and made them an outpost for further exploration.

**Prince Henry of Portugal** The pace of European exploration quickened after 1415 when Prince Henry of Portugal (1394–1460) conquered the Moroccan port of **Ceuta** and sponsored a series of voyages down the west African coast. Portuguese merchants soon established fortified trading posts at **São Jorge da Mina** (in modern Ghana) and other strategic locations. There they exchanged European horses, leather, textiles, and metalwares for gold and, increasingly, enslaved people (for an in-depth discussion of the emerging Atlantic slave trade, see chapter 25). Portuguese explorations continued after Henry's death, and in 1488 **Bartolomeu Dias** rounded the Cape of Good Hope and entered the Indian Ocean. He did not proceed farther because of storms and a restless crew, but the route to India, China, and the spice-bearing islands of southeast Asia lay open. The sea route to the Indian Ocean offered European merchants the opportunity to buy silk, spices, and pepper at the source, rather than through Muslim intermediaries, and to take part in the flourishing trade of Asia described by Marco Polo.

**Vasco da Gama** Portuguese mariners did not immediately follow up Dias's voyage because domestic and foreign problems distracted royal attention from voyages to Asia. In 1497, however, Vasco da Gama departed Lisbon with a fleet of four armed merchant ships bound for India. As we saw in the introduction, his experience—and the experiences of his crew—was not pleasant. His fleet went more than three months without seeing land, and his cargoes excited little interest in Indian markets. His return voyage was especially difficult, and more than half of his crew died slow and painful deaths from scurvy (vitamin C deficiency) before making it back to Portugal. Yet his cargo of pepper and cinnamon was hugely profitable, and Portuguese merchants began immediately to organize further expeditions. By 1500 they had built a trading post at Calicut, the site of da Gama's original landing, and Portuguese mariners soon called at ports throughout India and the Indian Ocean basin. By the late sixteenth century, English and Dutch mariners had followed the Portuguese into the Indian Ocean basin.

**Ceuta** (SYOO-tuh)
**São Jorge da Mina** (sou hor-hay dah meena)
**Bartolomeu Dias** (bahr-tol-uh-MEY-oh dee-as)

# SOURCES FROM THE PAST

## Christopher Columbus's First Impressions of American Peoples

*Christopher Columbus kept journals of his experiences during his voyages to the Western Hemisphere. These journals were not meant to be private, but instead were to be shared with his benefactors, Ferdinand and Isabella of Spain, and also to record his accomplishments for posterity. The journal of his first voyage survives mostly in summary, but it clearly communicates Columbus's first impressions of the people he met in the Caribbean islands. The following excerpts show that Columbus, like other European mariners, had both Christianity and commerce in mind when exploring distant lands. Keep in mind that Columbus treated the indigenous Taíno with brutality even from the first day of his arrival, when he had six people seized as servants. Look for places in the text in which Columbus uses dehumanizing language, or suggests how the Taíno could be useful to Europeans.*

**Thursday, 11 October [1492]. . . .**

I . . . in order that they would be friendly to us—because I recognized that they were people who would be better freed [from error] and converted to our Holy Faith by love than by force—to some of them I gave red caps, and glass beads which they put on their chests, and many other things of small value, in which they took so much pleasure and became so much our friends that it was a marvel. Later they came swimming to the ships' launches where we were and brought us parrots and cotton thread in balls and javelins and many other things, and they traded them to us for other things which we gave them, such as small glass beads and bells. In sum, they took everything and gave of what they had willingly.

But it seemed to me that they were a people very poor in everything. All of them go as naked as their mothers bore them; and the women also, although I did not see more than one quite young girl. And all those that I saw were young people, for none did I see of more than 30 years of age. They are very well formed, with handsome bodies and good faces. Their hair [is] coarse—almost like the tail of a horse—and short. They wear their hair down over their eyebrows except for a little in the back which they wear long and never cut. . . .

They do not carry arms nor are they acquainted with them, because I showed them swords and they took them by the edge and through ignorance cut themselves. They have no iron. Their javelins are shafts without iron and some of them have at the end a fish tooth and others of other things. All of them alike are of good-sized stature and carry themselves well. I saw some who had marks of wounds on their bodies and I made signs to them asking what they were; and they showed me how people from other islands nearby came there and tried to take them, and how they defended themselves and I believed and believe that they come here from *tierra firme* [the continent] to take them captive. They should be good and intelligent servants, for I see that they say very quickly everything that is said to them; and I believe that they would become Christians very easily, for it seemed to me that they had no religion. . . .

> On what basis might Christopher Columbus have been making such an observation about religious faith? What might he have been missing?

**Monday, 12 November. . . .**

They are very gentle and do not know what evil is; nor do they kill others, nor steal; and they are without weapons and so timid that a hundred of them flee from one of our men even if our men are teasing them. And they are credulous and aware that there is a God in heaven and convinced that we come from the heavens; and they say very quickly any prayer that we tell them to say, and they make the sign of the cross. So that Your Highnesses ought to resolve to make them Christians: for I believe that if you begin, in a short time you will end up having converted to our Holy Faith a multitude of peoples and acquiring large dominions and great riches and all of their peoples for Spain. Because without doubt there is in these lands a very great quantity of gold; for not without cause do these Indians that I bring with me say that there are in these islands places where they dig gold and wear it on their chests, on their ears, and on their arms, and on their legs; and they are very thick bracelets. And also there are stones, and there are precious pearls and infinite spicery. . . . And also here there is probably a great quantity of cotton; and I think that it would sell very well here without taking it to Spain but to the big cities belonging to the Grand [Mongol] Khan.

> Does this statement contradict Columbus' earlier assertion that the people he encountered "had no religion"?

### For Further Reflection

- On the basis of Columbus's account, what inferences can you draw about his plans for American lands and peoples? Based on this small excerpt, is it possible to surmise how contemporary Taíno people might have described Columbus and his men?
- What indications do you find that Columbus' descriptions were meant for Ferdinand and Isabella of Spain?
- Why is the description "predictable," given Columbus' original goal?

*Source:* Columbus, Christopher. *The Diario of Christopher Columbus's First Voyage to America.* Trans. by Oliver Dunn and James E. Kelley Jr. Norman: University of Oklahoma Press, 1989, pp. 65–69, 143–45.

**Christopher Columbus** While Portuguese navigators plied the sea route to India, the Genoese mariner Cristoforo Colombo, known in English as **Christopher Columbus** (1451–1506), proposed sailing to the markets of Asia by a western route. On the basis of wide reading of literature on geography, Columbus believed that the Eurasian landmass covered 270 degrees of longitude and that the earth was a relatively small sphere with a circumference of about 17,000 nautical miles. (In fact, the Eurasian landmass from Portugal to Korea covers only 140 degrees of longitude, and the earth's circumference is almost 25,000 nautical miles.) By Columbus's calculations, Japan should be less than 2,500 nautical miles west of the Canary Islands. (The actual distance between the Canaries and Japan is more than 10,000 nautical miles.) This geography suggested that sailing west from Europe to Asian markets would be profitable, and Columbus sought royal sponsorship for a voyage to prove his ideas. The Portuguese court declined his proposal, partly out of skepticism about his geography and partly because Dias's voyage of 1488 already pointed the way toward India.

Fernando and Isabel of Spain eventually agreed to sponsor Columbus's expedition, but it was Italian bankers who actually financed the voyage. In August 1492 his fleet of three ships departed Palos in southern Spain. He sailed south to the Canaries, picked up supplies, and then turned west with the trade winds. On the morning of 12 October 1492, he made landfall at an island in the Bahamas that the native **Taíno** inhabitants called **Guanahaní** and that Columbus rechristened San Salvador (also known as Watling Island). Thinking that he had arrived in the spice islands known familiarly as the Indies, Columbus called the Taíno "Indians." He sailed around the Caribbean for almost three months searching for gold, and at the large island of Cuba he sent a delegation to seek the court of the emperor of China. When Columbus returned to Spain, he reported to his royal sponsors that he had reached islands just off the coast of Asia.

**Hemispheric Links** In spite of what he believed, Columbus never reached the riches of Asia. Moreover, although he made three additional voyages across the Atlantic Ocean, he obtained very little gold in the Caribbean. Yet news of his voyage spread rapidly throughout Europe, and hundreds of Spanish, English, French, and Dutch mariners soon followed in his wake. Particularly in the early sixteenth century, many of them continued to seek the passage to Asian waters that Columbus himself had pursued. Over the longer term, however, it became clear that the American continents and the Caribbean islands themselves held abundant opportunities for entrepreneurs. Thus Columbus's voyages to the Western Hemisphere had unintended but profound consequences because they established links between the eastern and Western Hemisphere and paved the way for the conquest, settlement, and exploitation of the Americas by European peoples.

## European Voyages of Exploration: From the Atlantic to the Pacific

While some Europeans sought opportunities in the Americas, others continued to seek a western route to Asian markets. The Spanish military commander Vasco Nuñez de Balboa sighted the Pacific Ocean in 1513 while searching for gold in Panama, but in the early sixteenth century no one knew how much ocean lay between the Americas and Asia. Indeed, no one even suspected the vast size of the Pacific Ocean, which covers one-third of the earth's surface.

**Ferdinand Magellan** The initial exploration of the Pacific Ocean basin began with the Portuguese navigator Fernão de Magalhães (1480–1521), better known as **Ferdinand Magellan.** While sailing in the service of Portugal, Magellan had visited ports throughout the Indian Ocean basin and had traveled east as far as the spice islands of Maluku. He believed that the spice islands and Asian markets lay fairly close to the western coast of the Americas, and he decided to pursue Christopher Columbus's goal of establishing a western route to Asian waters. Because Portuguese mariners had already reached Asian markets through the Indian Ocean, they had little interest in Magellan's proposed western route. Thus, on his Pacific expedition Magellan sailed in the service of Spain.

**The Circumnavigation** Magellan's voyage was an exercise in endurance. He left Spain in September 1519, and then began probing the eastern coast of South America in search of a strait leading to the Pacific. Eventually, he found and sailed through the tricky and treacherous strait, later to bear his name, near the southern tip of South America. After exiting the strait, his fleet sailed almost four months before taking on fresh provisions at Guam. During that period crewmen survived on worm-ridden biscuits only and water gone foul. Ship's rats that were unfortunate enough to fall into the hands of famished sailors quickly became the centerpiece of a meal. A survivor reported in his account of the voyage that crewmen even ate ox hides, which they softened by dragging them through the sea for four or five days and then grilled on coals. Lacking fresh fruits and vegetables in their diet, many of the crew fell victim to the dreaded disease of scurvy, which caused painful rotting of the gums, loss of teeth, abscesses, hemorrhaging, weakness, loss of spirit, and in most cases death. Scurvy killed twenty-nine members of Magellan's crew during the Pacific crossing.

---

**Taíno** (TEYE-noh)

**Guanahaní** (Gwah-nah-nee)

**Ferdinand Magellan** (FUR-dih-nand muh-JEHL-uhn)

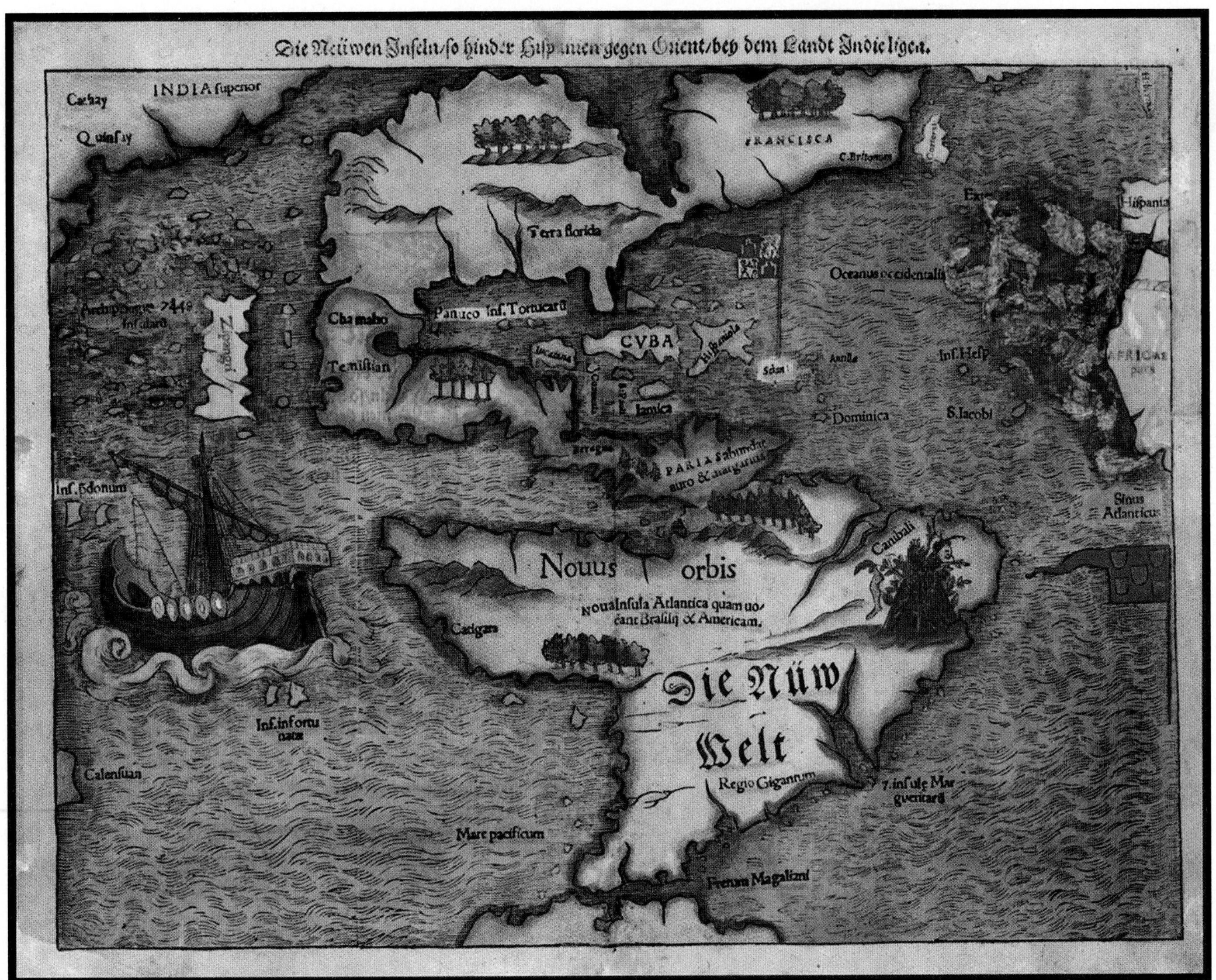


This 1561 map shows Ferdinand Magellan's name for the Pacific (Mare Pacificum) and the Strait of Magellan (Frenum Magaliani).
The History Collection/Alamy Stock Photo

Conditions improved after the fleet arrived in Guam in March 1521, but its ordeal had not come to an end. From Guam, Magellan proceeded to the Philippine Islands, where he became involved in a local political dispute that took the lives of Magellan himself and 40 of his crew A local chief had asked for Magellan's help in a dispute with a rival tribe, and in the fighting that ensued, Magellan was hit by a poisoned arrow and left to die by his crewmen. The survivors continued on to the spice islands of Maluku, where they took on a cargo of cloves. Rather than brave the Pacific Ocean once again, they sailed home through the familiar waters of the Indian Ocean—and thus completed the first circumnavigation of the world—returning to Spain after a voyage of almost exactly three years. Of Magellan's five ships and 280 men, only a single spice-laden ship with 18 of the original crew returned.

**Exploration of the Pacific** The Pacific Ocean is so vast that it took European explorers almost three centuries to chart its features. Spanish merchants built on information gleaned from Magellan's expedition and established a trade route between the Philippines and Mexico, but they did not continue to explore the ocean basin itself. English navigators, however, ventured into the Pacific in search of an elusive northwest passage from Europe to Asia. In fact, a northwest passage exists, but most of its route lies within the Arctic Circle. It is so far north that ice clogs its waters for much of the year, and it was only in the twentieth century that the

# SOURCES FROM THE PAST

## Captain Cook's Journal from Tahiti

*James Cook (1728–1779) was an English explorer from a small village in Yorkshire. He joined the Royal Navy in 1755 and served in North America, where he learned to chart and survey coastal territories. In 1768, the Royal Society and the British Admiralty chose Cook to captain an expedition to find the as-yet-undisovered "southern continent." Between 1768 and 1771, Cook and his crew sailed the Pacific, landing in Tahiti in 1769 and then making contact with (and claiming) what is now New Zealand. He made two more Pacific voyages before he was killed in hostilities with Hawaiians in a visit there in 1779. Below, he describes in his journal one of the first interactions of his crew with the people of Tahiti in 1769.*

**Tahiti, Saturday [April] 15th, 1769** . . . This morning several of the Chiefs we had seen Yesterday came on board, and brought with them Hogs, Bread fruit, etc., and for these we gave them Hatchets, Linnen, and such things as they valued. Having not met with yesterday a more Convenient situation for every purpose we wanted than the place we now are, I therefore, without delay, resolved to pitch upon some spot upon the North-East point of the Bay . . . and there to throw up a small fort for our defence. Accordingly I went ashore with a party of men, accompanied by Mr. Banks, Dr. Solander, and Mr. Green. We took along with us one of Mr. Banks's Tents, and after we had fix'd upon a place fit for our purpose we set up the Tent and marked out the ground we intended to Occupy. By this time a number of the Natives had got collected together about us, seemingly only to look on, as not one of them had any weapon, either Offensive or defensive. I would suffer none to come within the lines I had marked out, excepting one who appeared to be a chief . . . we endeavour'd to explain, as well as we could, that we wanted that ground to Sleep upon such a number of nights and then we should go away. Whether they understood us or no is uncertain, but no one appeared the least displeased at what we was about; indeed the Ground we had fixed upon was of no use to them, being part of the sandy Beach upon the shore of the Bay, and not near to any of their Habitations. It being too late in the day to do anything more, a party with a petty officer was left to guard the Tent, while we with another party took a Walk into the woods, and with us most of the natives. We had but just crossed the River when Mr. Banks shott three Ducks at one shott, which surprised them so much that most of them fell down as though they had been shott likewise. I was in hopes this would have had some good effect, but the event did not prove it, for we had not been long from the Tent before the natives again began to gather about, and one of them more daring than the rest pushed one of the Centinels [sic] down, snatched the Musket out of his hand and made a push at him, and then made off, and with him all the rest. Immediately upon this the Officer ordered the party to fire, and the Man who took the musket was shot Dead before he had got far from the Tent, but the musquet was carried quite off when this hapned [sic]. I and Mr. Banks with the other party was about half a Mile off, returning out of the woods, upon hearing the firing of Muskets, and the Natives leaving us at the same time, we Suspected that something was the matter and hastened our march, but before we arrived the whole was over, and every one of the Natives fled except old Owhaa, who stuck by us the whole time . . . [Soon after, Owhaa helped convince some of the Tahitians] to come to the Tent and there sit down with us, and Endeavour'd by every means in our power to Convince them that the Man was kill'd for taking away the Musket, and that we still would be friends with them. At sunset they left us seemingly satisfied, and we struck our Tent and went on board.

> What does Captain Cook's resolve to set up a defensive fort imply about his feelings of entitlement to the land in Tahiti?

> Why might the Tahitians present at the time have been so surprised by Mr. Banks's musket shot? What kind of "good effect" was Captain Cook hoping for here?

### For Further Reflection

- What does this event tell us about the attitudes of Captain Cook and his men toward the indigenous people of Tahiti? Does Cook's language suggest that he and his men saw Tahitians as equals or inferiors, threatening or nonthreatening? Which specific turns of phrase suggest these attitudes?
- What alternative attitudes and approaches could Captain Cook and other Europeans have taken to ensure more positive long-term effects of their presence in Tahiti?

*Source:* Cook, Captain James. *Captain Cook's Journal During His First Voyage Round the World, Made in H.M. Bark "Endeavor," 1768–1771* (London, 1893).

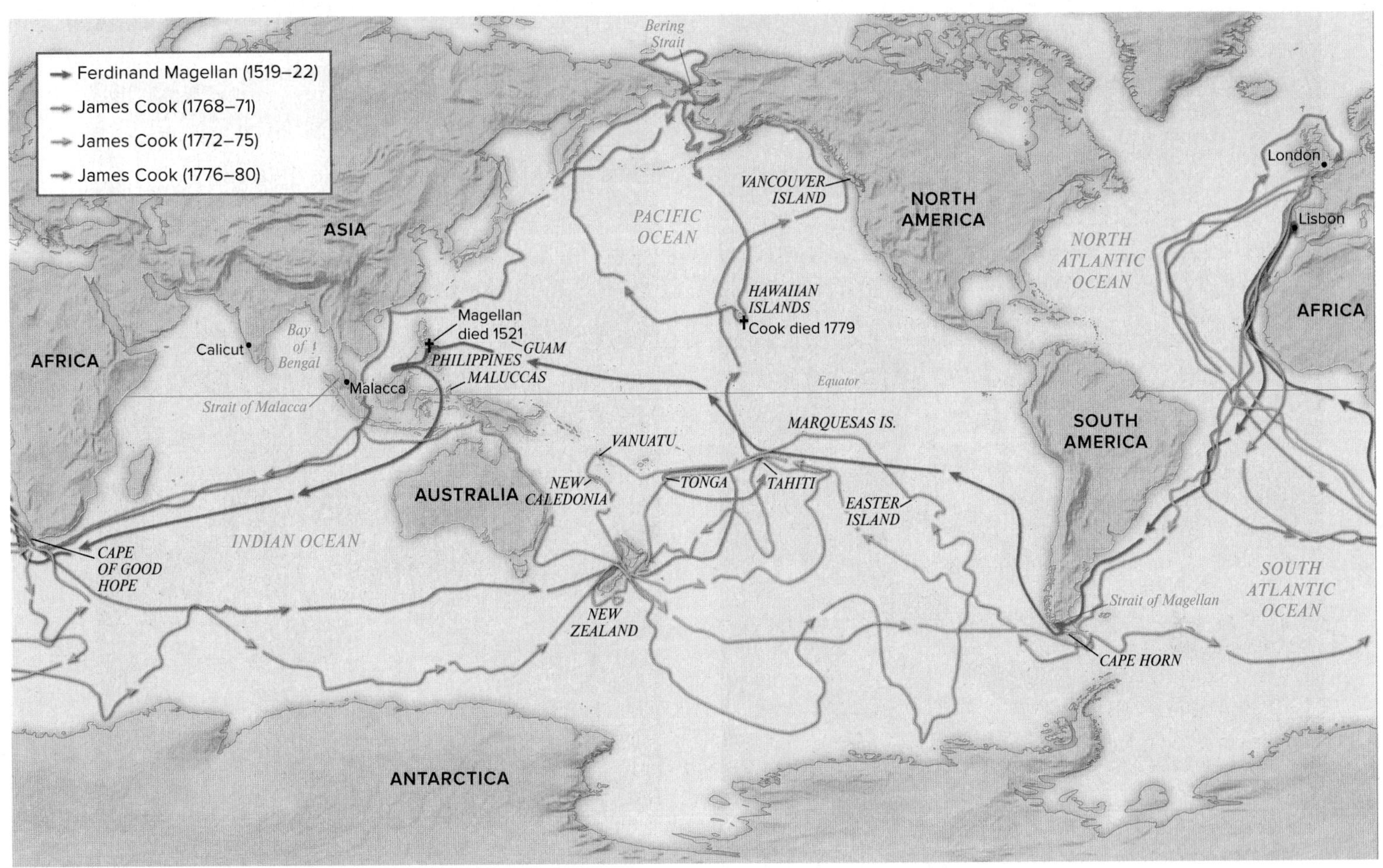


**MAP 10.3 Pacific voyages of Magellan and Cook, 1519–1780.**

*What made exploration of the Pacific Ocean so daunting? What fate befell both Magellan and Cook?*

Norwegian explorer Roald Amundsen traveled from the Atlantic to the Pacific by way of the northwest passage. Nevertheless, while searching for a passage, English mariners established many of the details of Pacific geography. In the sixteenth century, for example, Sir Francis Drake scouted the west coast of North America as far north as Vancouver Island. By the mid-eighteenth century, French mariners had joined English seafarers in exploring the Pacific Ocean in search of a northwest passage.

Russian expansion was mostly a land-based affair in early modern times, but by the eighteenth century Russians also explored the Pacific Ocean. Russian officials commissioned the Danish navigator **Vitus Bering** to undertake two maritime expeditions (1725–1730 and 1733–1742) in search of a northeast passage to Asian ports. Bering sailed through the icy Arctic Ocean and the Bering Strait, which separates Siberia from Alaska, and reconnoitered northern Asia as far as the Kamchatka peninsula. Other Russian explorers made their way from Alaska down the western Canadian coast to northern California. By 1800, Russian mariners were scouting the Pacific Ocean as far south as the Hawaiian Islands. Indeed, they built a small fort on the island of Kaua`i and engaged in trade there for a few years in the early nineteenth century.

### Captain James Cook

Along with the Russian explorers and Magellan, one of the most important of the Pacific explorers was **Captain James Cook** (1728–1779), who led three expeditions to the Pacific and died in a scuffle with the indigenous people of Hawai`i. Cook charted eastern Australia and New Zealand, and he added New Caledonia, Vanuatu, and Hawai`i to European maps of the Pacific. He probed the frigid waters of the Arctic Ocean and spent months at a time in the tropical islands of Tahiti, Tonga, and Hawai`i, where he showed deep interest in the manners, customs, and languages of Polynesian peoples. By the time Cook's voyages had come to an end, European geographers had compiled a reasonably accurate understanding of the world's ocean basins, their lands, and their peoples.

A portrait of Captain James Cook painted by William Hodges about 1775 depicts a serious and determined man.
Ian Dagnall/Alamy Stock Photo

This European drawing from Captain James Cook's first voyage focuses on the facial tattoos of a Maori chief's son, which would have seemed unusual to Europeans.
BL/Robana/age fotostock

## ECOLOGICAL EXCHANGES

European explorers and those who followed them established links between all the lands and peoples of the world. Interaction between peoples in turn resulted in an unprecedented volume of exchange across the boundary lines of societies and cultural regions. Some of that exchange involved biological species: plants, food crops, animals, human populations, and disease pathogens all spread to new regions. These biological exchanges had differing and dramatic effects on human populations, destroying some of them through epidemic diseases while enlarging others through increased food supplies and richer diets. Commercial exchange also flourished in the wake of the voyages of exploration as European merchants traveled to ports throughout the world in search of trade. By the late sixteenth century, they had built fortified trading posts at strategic sites in the Indian, Atlantic, and Pacific Ocean basins. By the mid-eighteenth century, they had established global networks of trade and communication.

### The Columbian Exchange

Processes of biological exchange were prominent features of world history well before modern times. The early expansion of Islam, for example, had facilitated the diffusion of plants and food crops throughout much of the Eastern Hemisphere during the period from about 700 to 1100 C.E., and transplanted species helped spark demographic and economic growth in all the lands where they took root. And during the fourteenth century the spread of bubonic plague caused drastic demographic losses when epidemic disease struck Eurasian and north African lands.

**Biological Exchanges** Yet the **Columbian exchange**—the global diffusion of plants, food crops, animals, human populations, and disease pathogens that took place after voyages of exploration by Christopher Columbus and other European

# How the Past Shapes the Future

## Short-Term and Long-Term Effects of the Columbian Exchange

**Some events or processes in the global past are so momentous that they produce social, political, economic, or environmental changes for centuries—even in places thousands of miles from their points of origin. In other words, we can see the effects of these events or processes in multiple places and in multiple timelines long after they occur, even up to the present. Understanding the spectrum of consequences spurred by such momentous events and processes can help us trace the historical connections between the world's people and places, even when such connections may not have been obvious to people living at the time.**

Although the European mariners who first came into contact with the people, plants, and animals of the Americas could not have understood it at the time, their encounters set in motion a process that permanently transformed not just the Americas but the entire world in ways that are still relevant today. Two facets of the exchange demonstrate how this was so: disease and the transfer of flora and fauna.

### Disease

In this chapter we have already seen the devastating effect of disease on populations indigenous to the Americas, with scholars estimating between 50 and 90 percent mortality across the entire region. Such high mortality was a key factor in allowing European invaders to conquer, settle, and expand throughout the Americas—a process discussed in chapter 24. In other words, if disease had not ravaged indigenous populations, it seems likely that Europeans would not have been able to use American lands for their own purposes on such a large scale, and also that the population of the present-day Americas would be composed of many more peoples whose ancestors were native to the area. A longer-term consequence of disease during the Columbian exchange was that there were simply not enough laborers in large parts of the Americas to carry out the work required by large-scale agricultural enterprises developed by Europeans after conquest. As a result, first the Portuguese and then many other Europeans began to import enslaved African laborers to the Americas, a process discussed in chapter 25. The Atlantic slave trade, in turn, had profound effects on enslaved individuals, the African states involved, and the eventual composition of populations in the Americas.

### Flora and Fauna

In this chapter we have seen that the Columbian exchange involved extensive movement of plants and animals between Eurasia and the Americas. Over the long term, these exchanges transformed landscapes around the world by introducing plant and animal species that became invasive in their new environments (such as dandelions in the Americas or pigs on the island of Barbados). Some introductions to the Americas, like the horse, brought about fundamental cultural changes. For example, Plains Indians adopted horses in order to hunt wild game more effectively, resulting in dramatic changes in gender ideologies and lifestyle. Products that originated in the Americas also had a profound impact on other parts of the world. For example, nutritional foods native to the Americas—including potatoes, corn, and sweet potatoes—helped spur population growth in places like China that were not involved in the initial process of exchange at all. Nonfood crops were important to the Columbian exchange as well: tobacco, introduced from the Americas, was widely and quickly integrated into the cultures of both Europe and the Islamic empires. In fact, in just a little more than one hundred years after being introduced to tobacco for the first time, Europeans had introduced tobacco to Europe, Asia, west Africa, and the Near East. In the present, approximately 1.1 billion of the world's people are smokers, and about 25 percent of smokers die from smoke-related causes.

These are only a small sampling of the historical consequences of the Columbian exchange, both through time and across space. When reading subsequent chapters, try to identify additional developments that may have their origins in this truly momentous process.

Tobacco was long used for religious and spiritual purposes in the Americas. After their arrival in the Americas, Europeans quickly popularized tobacco as a trade item and as a recreational drug to be smoked, snuffed, or chewed.
Historical Picture Archive/Corbis Historical/Getty Images

mariners—had consequences much more profound than any of the earlier rounds of biological exchange. Unlike the earlier processes, the Columbian exchange involved lands with radically different flora, fauna, and diseases. For thousands of years the various species of the Eastern Hemisphere, the Western Hemisphere, and Oceania had evolved along separate lines. By creating links between these biological zones, the European voyages of exploration set off a round of biological exchange that permanently altered the world's human geography and natural environment.

Beginning in the early sixteenth century, infectious and contagious diseases brought devastating demographic losses to indigenous peoples of the Americas and the Pacific islands. The most virulent disease was smallpox, but measles, diphtheria, whooping cough, and influenza also took heavy tolls. Before the voyages of exploration, none of these maladies had reached the Western Hemisphere or Oceania, and the peoples of those regions consequently had no inherited or acquired immunities to those pathogens. In the Eastern Hemisphere, these diseases had mostly become endemic: they claimed a certain number of victims from the ranks of infants and small children, but survivors gained immunity to the diseases through exposure at an early age. In some areas of Europe, for example, smallpox was responsible for 10 to 15 percent of deaths, but most victims were younger than age ten. Although its effects were tragic for individual families and communities, smallpox did not pose a threat to European society as a whole because it did not carry away adults, who were mostly responsible for economic production and social organization.

## INTERPRETING IMAGES

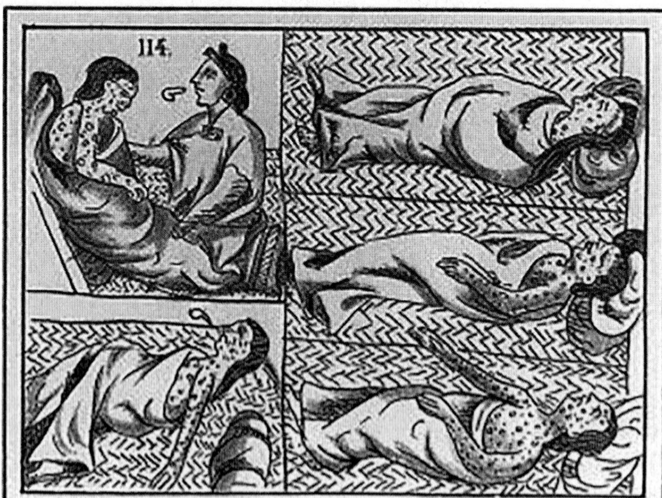


Smallpox victims in the Aztec Empire. The disease killed most of those it infected and left disfiguring scars on survivors.

**Analyze** *"All told, disease epidemics sparked by the Columbian Exchange probably caused the worst demographic calamity in all of world history." Why do you think smallpox was more devastating to the Aztec empire than the Bubonic plague was in Europe?*

Peabody Museum, Harvard University (2004.24.29636).

**Epidemic Diseases and Population Decline** When infectious and contagious diseases traveled to previously unexposed populations, however, they touched off ferocious epidemics that sometimes destroyed entire societies. Beginning in 1519, epidemic smallpox ravaged the Aztec Empire, often in combination with other diseases, and within a century the indigenous population of Mexico had declined by as much as 90 percent, from about 17 million to 1.3 million. By that time Spanish conquerors had imposed their rule on Mexico, and the political, social, and cultural traditions of the indigenous peoples had either disappeared or fallen under Spanish domination.

Imported diseases took their worst tolls in densely populated areas such as the Aztec and Inca empires, but they did not spare other regions. Smallpox and other diseases were so easily transmissible that they raced to remote areas of North and South America and sparked epidemics even before the first European explorers arrived in those regions. By the 1530s smallpox may have spread as far from Mexico as the Great Lakes in the north and the pampas of Argentina in the south.

When introduced to the Pacific islands, infectious and contagious diseases struck vulnerable populations with the same horrifying effects as in the Americas, albeit on a smaller scale. All told, disease epidemics sparked by the Columbian exchange probably caused the worst demographic calamity in all of world history. Between 1500 and 1800, upwards of 100 million people may have died of diseases imported by Europeans into the Americas and the Pacific islands.

**Food Crops and Animals** Over the long term, however, the Columbian exchange increased rather than diminished human population because of the global spread of food crops and animals that it sponsored. In the long term, a better-nourished world was an important contributing factor in the growth of the world's population, which began in the eighteenth century and continues in the present. Out of Eurasia to the Western Hemisphere traveled wheat, rice, sugar, bananas, apples, cherries, peaches, peas, and citrus fruits. Wheat in particular grew well on the plains of North America and on the pampas of Argentina, regions either too dry or too cold for the cultivation of maize (corn). Africa contributed yams, okra, collard greens, and coffee. Dairy and meat-yielding animals—horses, cattle, pigs, sheep, goats, and chickens—went from Europe to the Americas, where they sharply increased supplies of food and animal energy.

**American Crops** Food crops native to the Americas also played prominent roles in the Columbian exchange. American crops that took root in Africa, Asia, and Europe include maize, potatoes, beans, tomatoes, peppers, peanuts, manioc, papayas, guavas, avocados, pineapples, and cacao, to name some of the most important. (A less nutritious transplant was tobacco.) Residents of the Eastern Hemisphere only gradually developed a taste for American crops, but by the eighteenth century maize and potatoes in particular had contributed to a sharply increased number of calories in Eurasian diets. Maize became especially important in China because it grew in eco-niches unsuitable for rice and millet production. With the exception of Bengal (India), Asian lands proved less welcoming to the potato. But in northern Europe, the potato eventually became a staple crop, from Ireland to Russia, because of its impressive nutritional qualities. American bean varieties added protein to diets around the world, and tomatoes and peppers provided vitamins and zesty flavors in lands from western Europe to China. Peanuts and manioc flourished in tropical southeast Asian and west African soils that otherwise would not produce large yields or support large populations. The Americas also supplied medicinal plants. Derived from the bark of the Peruvian cinchona tree, bitter-tasting quinine was the first effective treatment for malaria and proved vital to Europeans trying to survive in tropical areas inhabited by the mosquitoes that spread the disease.

**Population Growth** The Columbian exchange of plants and animals fueled a surge in world population. In 1500, as Eurasian peoples were recovering from epidemic bubonic plague, world population stood at about 425 million. By 1600 it had increased more than 25 percent to 545 million. Human numbers increased less rapidly during the next century, reaching 610 million in 1700. But thereafter they increased at a faster rate than ever before in world history. By 1750 human population stood at 720 million, and by 1800 it had surged to 900 million, having grown by almost 50 percent during the previous century. Much of the rise was due to the increased nutritional value of diets enriched by the global exchange of food crops and animals.

**Migration** Alongside disease pathogens and plant and animal species, the Columbian exchange also involved the spread of human populations through transoceanic migration, both voluntary and forced. During the period from 1500 to 1800, the largest contingent of migrants consisted of enslaved Africans transported against their will to South American, North American, and Caribbean destinations. A smaller but still sizable migration involved Europeans who traveled to the Americas as settlers. In some cases, they settled on lands that had previously been depopulated by infectious and contagious diseases, while in others they forced out existing populations through violence and forced relocation. During the nineteenth century, European peoples traveled in massive numbers mostly to the Western Hemisphere but also to south Africa, Australia, and Pacific islands where diseases had diminished indigenous populations, while equal numbers of Asian peoples migrated to tropical and subtropical destinations throughout much of the world. In combination, those migrations have profoundly influenced modern world history.

## The Origins of Global Trade

Besides stimulating commerce in the Eastern Hemisphere, the voyages of European merchant mariners encouraged the emergence of a genuinely global trading system. European manufactured goods traveled west across the Atlantic in exchange for silver from Mexican and Peruvian mines and agricultural products such as sugar and tobacco, both of which were in high demand among European consumers. Trade in human beings also figured in Atlantic commerce. European textiles, guns, and other manufactured goods went south to west Africa, where merchants exchanged them for African slaves, who then were forcibly transported to the tropical and subtropical regions of the Western Hemisphere to work on plantations.

**The Manila Galleons** The experience of the **Manila galleons** illustrates the early workings of the global economy in the Pacific Ocean basin. For 250 years, from 1565 to 1815, Spanish galleons–sleek, fast, heavily armed ships capable of carrying large cargoes–regularly plied the waters of the Pacific Ocean between Manila in the Philippines and Acapulco on the west coast of Mexico. From Manila they took Asian luxury goods to Mexico and exchanged them for silver. Most of the precious metal made its way to China, where a thriving domestic economy demanded increasing quantities of silver, the basis of Chinese currency. In fact, the demand for silver was so high in China that European merchants exchanged it for Chinese gold, which they later traded profitably for more silver as well as luxury goods in Japan. Meanwhile, some of the Asian luxury goods from Manila remained in Mexico or went to Peru, where they contributed to a comfortable way of life for Spanish ruling elites. Most, however, went overland across Mexico and then traveled by ship across the Atlantic to Spain and European markets.

**Environmental Effects of Global Trade** As the demand for silver fueled growing volumes of global trade, pressures fell on several animal species that had the misfortune to become prominent commodities on the world market. Fur-bearing animals came under particularly intense pressure, as hunters sought their pelts for sale to consumers in China, Europe, and North America. During the seventeenth century, an estimated two hundred to three hundred thousand sable pelts flowed annually from Siberia to the global market, and

This is an artist's rendering of a Spanish galleon. Galleons were large, multidecked, highly stable and maneuverable sailing ships used by Europeans for war or commerce. The Spanish and the Portuguese built the largest types for their profitable overseas trade.
Bettmann/Getty Images

during the eighteenth century, more than sixteen million North American beaver pelts fed consumers' demands for fur hats and cloaks. Wanton hunting of fur-bearing animals soon drove many species into extinction or near-extinction, permanently altering the environments they had formerly inhabited. In addition to fur-bearing animals, early modern hunters harvested enormous numbers of deer, codfish, whales, walruses, seals, and other species as merchants sought to supply skins, food, oil, ivory, and other animal products to global consumers.

By the late sixteenth century, conditions favored the relentless human exploitation of the world's natural and agricultural resources, as European mariners had permanently linked the world's port cities and created global trading networks. During the next two centuries, the volume of global trade expanded, as English, Dutch, French, and other merchants contributed to the development of global markets. During the seventeenth century, for example, Dutch merchants imported, among other commodities, wheat from south Africa, cowry shells from India, and sugar from Brazil. The wheat fed domestic consumers, who increasingly worked as merchants, bankers, or manufacturers rather than as cultivators. English, Dutch, and other merchants eagerly purchased the cowry shells—which served as currency in much of sub-Saharan Africa—and exchanged them for slaves destined for plantations in the Western Hemisphere. The sugar went on the market at Amsterdam and found its way to consumers throughout Europe. During the eighteenth century, world trade became even more intricate as mass markets emerged for commodities such as coffee, tea, sugar, and tobacco. By 1750 all parts of the world except Australia participated in global networks of commercial relations in which European merchant mariners played prominent roles.

## TRADE AND CONFLICT IN EARLY MODERN ASIA

The voyages of exploration taught European mariners how to sail to almost any coastline in the world and return safely. Once they arrived at their destinations, they sought commercial opportunities. In the Eastern Hemisphere they built a series of fortified trading posts that offered footholds in regions where established commercial networks had held sway for centuries. They even attempted to control the spice trade in the Indian Ocean but with limited success. They mostly did not have the human numbers or military power to impose their rule in the Eastern Hemisphere, although Spanish and Dutch forces established small island empires in the Philippines and Indonesia, respectively. In a parallel effort involving expansion across land rather than the sea, Russian explorers and adventurers established a presence in central Asian regions formerly ruled by the Mongols and in the tundra and forests of Siberia, thus laying the foundations for a vast Eurasian empire. Commercial and political competition in both the Eastern and Western Hemispheres led to conflict between European peoples, and by the end of the Seven Years' War in 1763, English military and merchant forces had gained an initiative over their rivals that enabled them to dominate world trade and build the vast British empire of the nineteenth century.

## Trading-Post Empires

**Portuguese Trading Posts** Portuguese mariners built the earliest trading-post empire. Their goal was not to conquer territories but, rather, to control trade routes by forcing merchant vessels to call at fortified trading sites and pay duties there. Vasco da Gama obtained permission from local authorities to establish a trading post at Calicut when he arrived there in 1498. By the mid-sixteenth century, Portuguese merchants had built more than fifty trading posts between west Africa and east Asia. At São Jorge da Mina, they traded in west African slaves, and at Mozambique they attempted to control the south African gold trade. From Hormuz they controlled access to the Persian Gulf, and from Goa they organized trade in Indian pepper. At Melaka they oversaw shipping between the South China Sea and the Indian Ocean, and they channeled trade in cloves and nutmeg through Ternate in the spice islands of Maluku. Posts at Macau and Nagasaki offered access to the markets of China and Japan.

**Afonso d'Alboquerque** Equipped with heavy artillery, Portuguese vessels were able to overpower most other craft that they encountered, and they sometimes effectively bombarded coastal communities with their cannons. The architect of their aggressive policy was **Afonso d'Alboquerque,** commander of Portuguese forces in the Indian Ocean during the early sixteenth century. Alboquerque's fleets seized Hormuz in 1508, Goa in 1510, and Melaka in 1511. From these strategic sites, Alboquerque sought to control Indian Ocean trade by forcing merchant ships to purchase safe-conduct passes and present them at Portuguese trading posts. Ships without passes were subject to confiscation, along with their cargoes. Alboquerque's forces punished violators of his policy by executing them or cutting off their hands. Alboquerque was confident of Portuguese naval superiority and its ability to control trade in the Indian Ocean. After taking Melaka, he boasted that the arrival of Portuguese ships sent other vessels scurrying and that even the birds left the skies and sought cover.

Alboquerque's boast was an exaggeration. Although heavily armed, Portuguese forces did not have enough vessels to enforce the commander's orders. Arab, Indian, and Malay merchants continued to play prominent roles in Indian Ocean commerce, usually without taking the precaution of securing a safe-conduct pass. Portuguese ships transported perhaps half the pepper and spices that Europeans consumed during the early and middle decades of the sixteenth century, but Arab vessels delivered shipments through the Red Sea, which Portuguese forces never managed to control, to Cairo and Mediterranean trade routes.

By the late sixteenth century, Portuguese influence in the Indian Ocean weakened. Portugal was a small country with a small population—about one million in 1500—and was unable to sustain a large seaborne trading empire for long. The crews of Portuguese ships often included Spanish, English, and Dutch sailors, who became familiar with Asian waters while in Portuguese service. By the late sixteenth century, investors in other lands began to organize their own expeditions to Asian markets. Most prominent of those who followed the Portuguese into the Indian Ocean were English and Dutch mariners.

**English and Dutch Trading Posts** Like their predecessors, English and Dutch merchants built trading posts on Asian coasts and sought to channel trade through them, but they did not attempt to control shipping on the high seas. They occasionally seized Portuguese sites, most notably when a Dutch fleet conquered Melaka in 1641. Yet Portuguese authorities held many of their trading posts into the twentieth century: Goa remained the official capital of Portuguese colonies in Asia until independent India reclaimed it in 1961. Meanwhile, English and Dutch entrepreneurs established parallel networks. English merchants concentrated on India and built trading posts at Bombay, Madras, and Calcutta, while the Dutch operated more broadly from Cape Town, Colombo, and Batavia (modern Jakarta on the island of Java).

English and Dutch merchants enjoyed two main advantages over their Portuguese predecessors. They sailed faster, cheaper, and more powerful ships, which offered both an economic and a military edge over their competitors. Furthermore, they conducted trade through an efficient form of commercial organization—the **joint-stock company**—which enabled investors to realize handsome profits while limiting the risk to their investments.

**The Trading Companies** English and Dutch merchants formed two especially powerful joint-stock companies: the English **East India Company,** founded in 1600, and its Dutch counterpart, the United East India Company, known from its initials as the **VOC** (Vereenigde Oost-Indische Compagnie), established in 1602. Private merchants advanced funds to launch these companies, outfit them with ships and crews, and provide them with commodities and money to trade. Although they enjoyed government support, the companies were privately owned enterprises. Unhampered by political oversight, company agents concentrated strictly on profitable trade. Their charters granted them the right to buy, sell, and build trading posts, and even make war in the companies' interests.

The English and Dutch companies experienced immediate financial success. In 1601, for example, five English ships set sail from London with cargoes mostly of gold and silver

---

**Afonso d'Alboquerque** (al-FAWN-soo d'AL-buh-kur-kee)

coins valued at thirty thousand pounds sterling. When they returned in 1603, the spices that they carried were worth more than one million pounds sterling. The first Dutch expedition did not realize such fantastic profits, but it more than doubled the investments of its underwriters. Because of their advanced nautical technology, powerful military arsenal, efficient organization, and relentless pursuit of profit, the English East India Company and the VOC contributed to the early formation of a global network of trade.

## European Conquests in Southeast Asia

Following voyages of exploration to the Western Hemisphere, the massive demographic catastrophe caused by the introduction of contagious diseases to indigenous peoples meant that Europeans were able to build territorial empires and establish colonies settled by European migrants. In the Eastern Hemisphere, however, they were mostly unable to force their will on large Asian populations and powerful centralized states. With

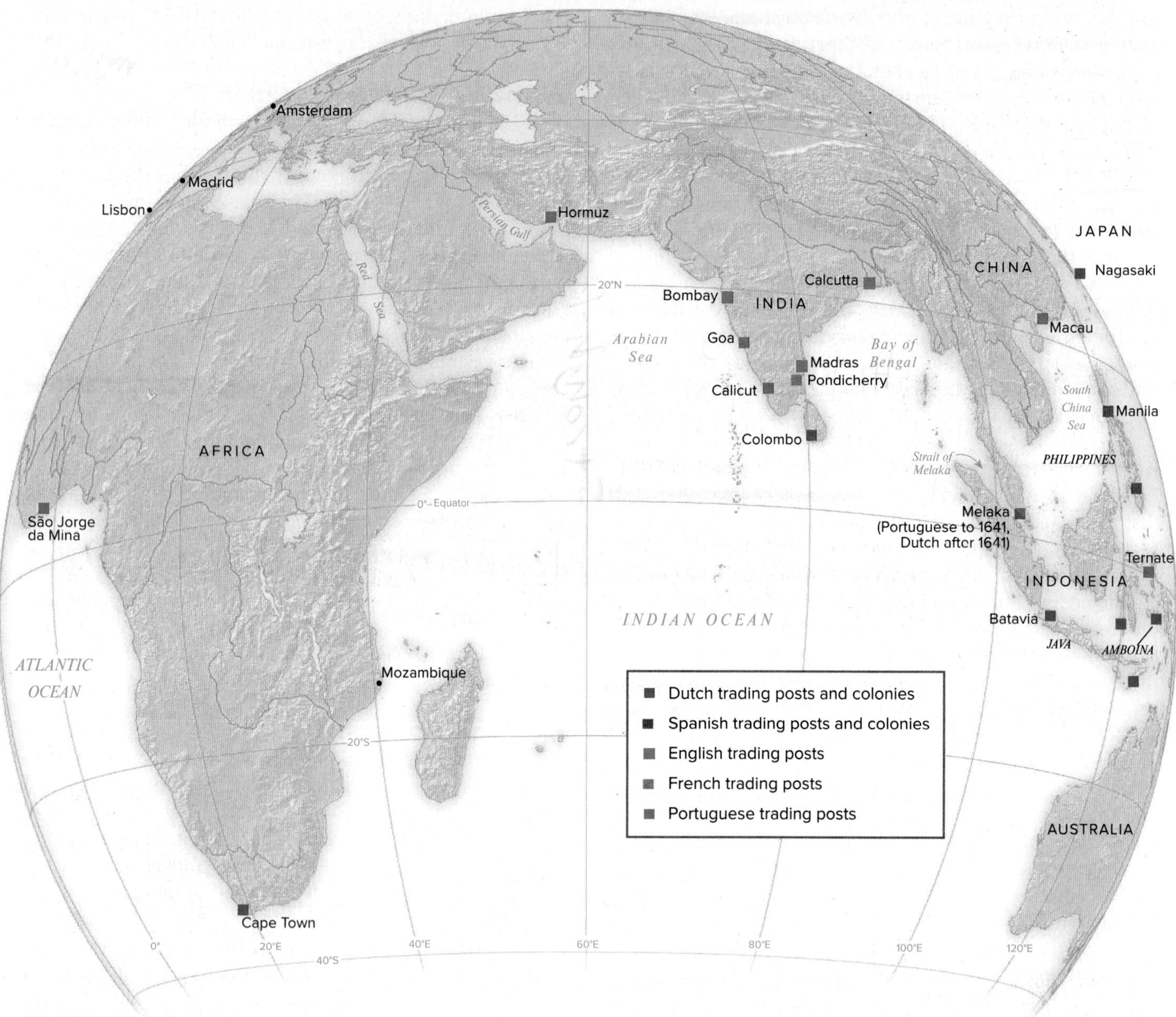


**MAP 10.4 European trading posts in Africa and Asia, about 1700.**

Note how many more trading posts there were in Asia than in Africa.

***Despite the exploration of the African coast and the establishment of trading posts there, as well as the development of the slave trade, why did Europeans continue to focus on trade with Asia rather than explore potential valuables in the interior of Africa?***

The Tijgersgracht Canal in the Dutch VOC settlement at Batavia (modern Jakarta, Indonesia) during the seventeenth century.
ART Collection/Alamy Stock Photo

the decline of the Portuguese effort to control shipping in the Indian Ocean, Europeans mostly traded peacefully in Asian waters alongside Arab, Indian, Malay, and Chinese merchants.

Yet in two island regions of southeast Asia—the Philippines and Indonesia—Europeans were able to make limited conquests during the early modern period. Though densely populated, neither the Philippines nor Indonesia were ruled by a single powerful state when Europeans arrived there in the sixteenth century. Nor did imperial authorities in China or India lay claim to the island regions. Heavily armed ships enabled Europeans to use violence to establish imperial regimes that favored the interests of European merchants.

**Conquest of the Philippines** Spanish forces approached the Philippines in 1565 under the command of **Miguel López de Legazpi,** who named the islands after King Philip II of Spain. Legazpi overcame local authorities in Cebu and Manila in almost bloodless contests. Because the Philippines had no central government, there was no organized resistance to the intrusion. The resistance the Spanish forces faced were from a series of small, disunited chiefdoms, who were not able to fend off Spanish ships and guns. By 1575 Spanish forces controlled the coastal regions of the central and northern islands, and during the seventeenth century they extended their authority to most parts of the archipelago. The main region outside their control was the southern island of Mindanao, where a large Muslim community stoutly resisted Spanish expansion.

**Miguel López de Lagazpi** (mee-GEHL LOH-pess day la-GAHS-pee)

**Manila** Spanish policy in the Philippines revolved around trade and Christianity. **Manila** soon emerged as a bustling, multicultural entrepôt—a port city for trade, particularly in silk—and it quickly became the hub of Spanish commercial activity in Asia. Chinese merchants were especially prominent in Manila. They occupied a specially designated commercial district of the city, and they accounted for about one-quarter of Manila's forty-two thousand residents in the mid-seventeenth century. They supplied the silk goods that Spanish traders shipped to Mexico in the so-called Manila galleons. Their commercial success brought suspicion on their community, and resentful Spanish and Filipino residents massacred Chinese merchants by the thousands in at least six major eruptions of violence in 1603, 1639, 1662, 1686, 1762, and 1819. Nevertheless, Spanish authorities continued to rely heavily on the wealth that Chinese merchants brought to Manila.

Apart from promoting trade, Spanish authorities in the Philippines also sought to spread Roman Catholicism throughout the archipelago. Spanish rulers and missionaries pressured prominent Filipinos to convert to Christianity in hopes of persuading others to follow their example. They opened schools to teach the fundamentals of Christian doctrine, along with basic literacy, in densely populated regions throughout the islands. The missionaries encountered stiff resistance in highland regions, where Spanish authority was not as strong as on the coasts, and resistance drew support from opponents of Spanish domination as well as from resentment of the newly arrived faith. Over the long term, however, Filipinos turned increasingly to Christianity, and by the nineteenth century the Philippines had become one of the most fervent Roman Catholic lands in the world.

**Conquest of Java** Dutch mariners, who imposed their rule on the islands of Indonesia, did not worry about seeking converts to Christianity but concentrated instead on the trade in spices, particularly cloves, nutmeg, and mace. The architect of Dutch policy was **Jan Pieterszoon Coen,** who in 1619 founded Batavia on the island of **Java** to serve as an entrepôt for the VOC. Batavia occupied a strategic site near the Sunda Strait, and its market attracted both Chinese and Malay vessels. Coen's plan was to establish a VOC monopoly over spice production and trade, thus enabling Dutch merchants to reap enormous profits in European markets. Coen brought his naval power to bear on the small Indonesian spice-growing islands and forced them to deliver spices only to VOC merchants. On larger islands such as Java, he took advantage of tensions between local princes and authorities and extracted concessions from many in return for providing them with aid against the others. By the late seventeenth century, the VOC controlled all the ports of Java as well as most of the important spice-bearing islands throughout the Indonesian archipelago.

Dutch numbers were too few for them to rule directly over their whole southeast Asian empire. They made alliances with local authorities to maintain order in most regions, reserving for direct Dutch rule only Batavia and the most important spice-bearing islands such as clove-producing Amboina and the Banda Islands. They sought less to rule than to control the production of spices. The Dutch did not embark on campaigns of conquest for purposes of adding to their holdings, but they uprooted spice-bearing plants on islands they did not control and mercilessly attacked peoples who sold their spices to merchants not associated with the VOC. In some cases, such as on the island of Banda in 1621, Dutch traders murdered most of the population and burned their villages when they resisted Dutch attempts to monopolize the spice trade on the island. Eventually, monopoly profits from the spice trade not only enriched the VOC but also made the Netherlands the most prosperous land in Europe throughout most of the seventeenth century.

## Foundations of the Russian Empire in Asia

While western European peoples were building maritime empires, Russians were laying the foundations for a vast land empire that embraced most of northern Eurasia. This round of expansion began in the mid-sixteenth century, as Russian forces took over several Mongol khanates in central Asia. These acquisitions resulted in Russian control over the Volga River and offered opportunities for trade with the Ottoman empire, Iran, and even India through the Caspian Sea. Because of its strategic location on the Volga delta where the river flows into the Caspian Sea, the city of Astrakhan became a bustling

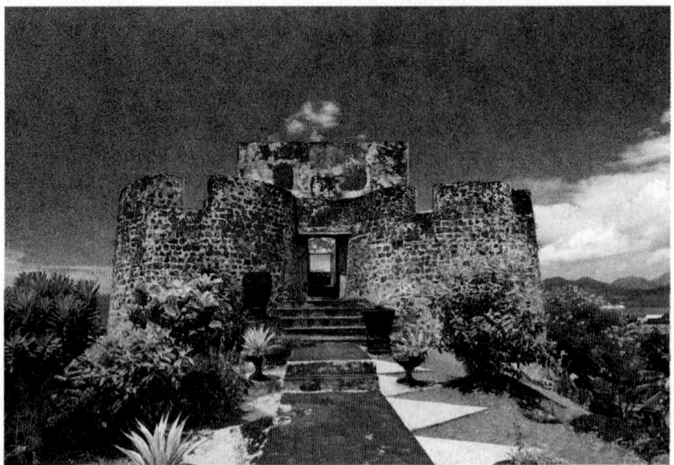

Modern image of Fort Tolukko, a trading fortification originally built by the Portuguese on the spice island of Ternate. The Dutch occupied it in the early seventeenth century.
Ali Trisno Pranoto/Getty Images

**Jan Pieterszoon Coen** (yahn PEE-tuhr-sohn KOH-uhn)

commercial center, home to a community of several hundred foreign merchants from as far away as northern India. During the seventeenth and eighteenth centuries, some of the Indian merchants regularly made their way up the Volga River to trade in Moscow and the Russian interior, while others devised plans (which they never realized) to extend their activities to the Baltic Sea and take their business to western Europe. In the eighteenth century, Russian forces extended their presence in the Caspian Sea region by absorbing much of the Caucasus, a multiethnic region embracing the modern-day states of Georgia, Armenia, and Azerbaijan.

**Encounters in Siberia** Far more extensive were Russian acquisitions in northeastern Eurasia. The frozen tundras and dense forests of **Siberia** posed formidable challenges, but explorers and merchants made their way into the region in a quest for fur. Throughout the early modern era, fur was a lucrative commodity that encouraged Russians to look eastward, just as North American fur attracted the interest of English, French, and Dutch merchants. Russian expansion in northeastern Eurasia began in 1581 when the wealthy Stroganov family hired an adventurer named Yermak to capture the khanate of Sibir in the Ural Mountains. In the following decades, Russian explorers pushed into the interior regions of Siberia by way of the region's great rivers. By 1639 they had made their way across the Eurasian landmass and reached the Pacific Ocean.

**Indigenous Peoples of Siberia** Siberia was home to about twenty-six major ethnic groups that lived by hunting, trapping, fishing, or herding reindeer. These indigenous peoples varied widely in language and religion, and they responded in different ways to the arrival of Russian adventurers who sought to exact tribute from them by coercing them to supply pelts on a regular basis. Some groups readily accepted iron tools, woven cloth, flour, tea, and liquor for the skins of fur-bearing animals such as otter, lynx, marten, arctic fox, and especially the sleek sable. Others resented the ever-increasing demands for tribute and resisted Russian encroachment on their lands. Russian forces then resorted to punishing raids and hostage taking to induce Siberian peoples to deliver furs. The Yakut people of the Lena and Aldan River valleys in central Siberia mounted a revolt against Russian oppression in 1642 and experienced a brutal retribution that continued for forty years, forcing many Yakut out of their settlements and reducing their population by an estimated 70 percent. Quite apart from military violence, like people in the Americas and Oceania, the peoples of Siberia also reeled from epidemic diseases that reduced many populations by more than half.

As violence and disease sharply diminished the delivery of furs, the Russian government recognized that its interests lay in protection of the "small peoples," as state officials called the indigenous inhabitants of Siberia. Government-sponsored missionaries sought to convert Siberian peoples to Orthodox Christianity and bring them into Russian society, but they had little success. Few Siberians expressed an interest in Christianity, and those few came mostly from the ranks of criminals, abandoned hostages, slaves, and others who had little status in their own societies. Furthermore, once indigenous peoples converted to Christianity, they

This is an engraving of an indigenous Siberian hunter, wearing the fur he helped to collect. He grasps his weapons in one hand while the other holds two fur-pelted animal carcasses. Science & Society Picture Library/ Getty Images

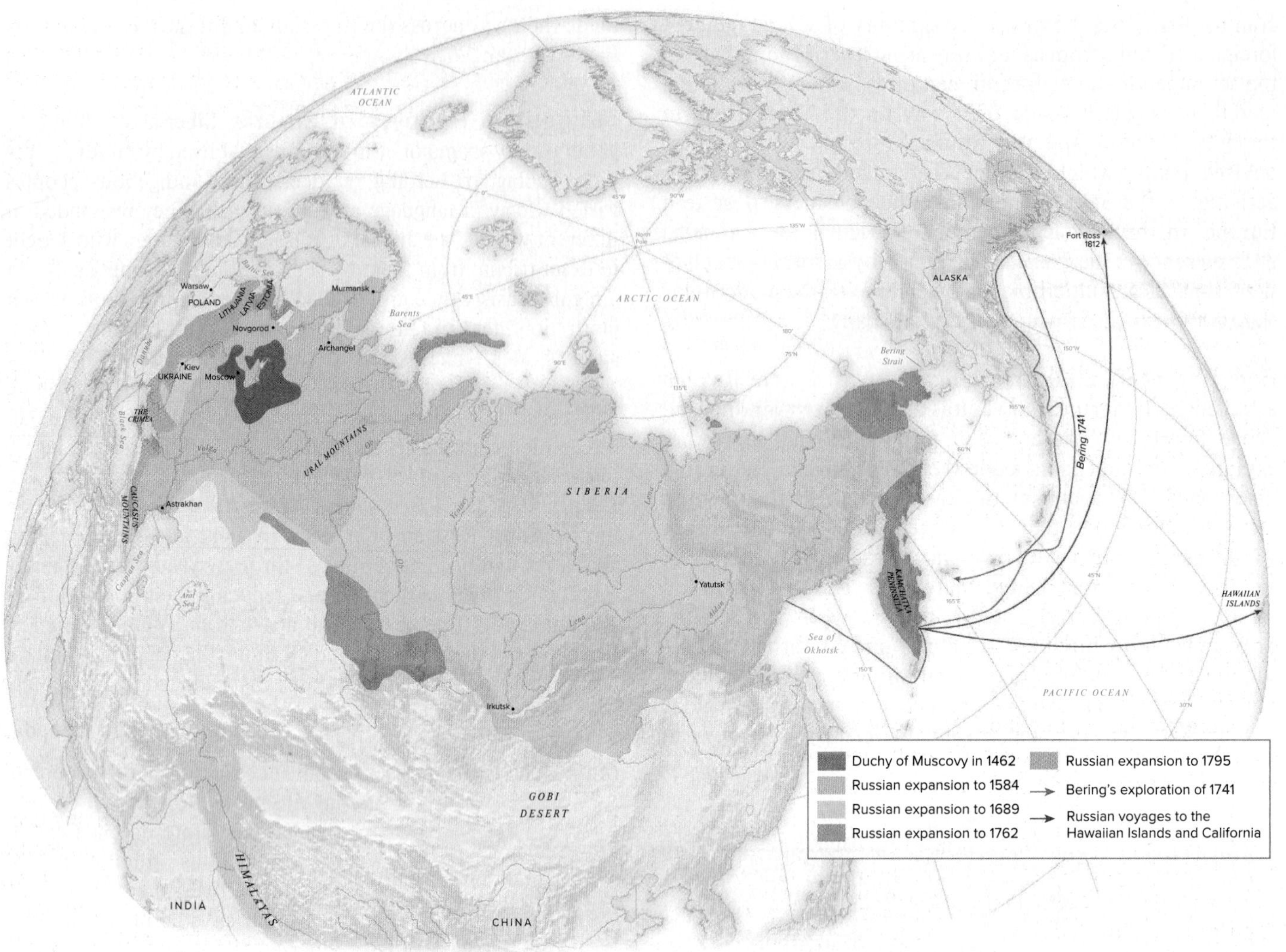


## MAP 10.5 Russian expansion, 1462–1795.

Observe how vast the empire became after it added the territory of Siberia.

***How did Russians exert their control over such a huge and unforgiving territory?***

were exempt from obligations to provide fur tributes, so the Russian government demonstrated less zeal in its religious mission than did the Spanish monarchs, who made the spread of Roman Catholic Christianity a prime goal of imperial expansion. Although they managed to attract a few Siberian converts, Orthodox missionaries mostly served the needs of Russian merchants, adventurers, and explorers in Siberia. For their part, the indigenous peoples of Siberia continued to practice their inherited religions guided by shamans.

**The Russian Occupation of Siberia** The settlers who established a Russian presence in Siberia included adventurers, convicted criminals, and even prisoners of war. Despite the region's harsh terrain, Russian migrants gradually filtered into Siberia and thoroughly altered its demographic complexion. Small agricultural settlements grew up near many trading posts, particularly in the fertile Amur River valley. Siberian landowners offered working conditions that were much lighter than those of Russia proper, so disgruntled peasants sometimes fled to settlements east of the Ural Mountains. Over time, Siberian trading posts with their garrisons developed into Russian towns with Russian-speaking populations attending Russian Orthodox churches. By 1763 some 420,000 Russians lived in Siberia, nearly double the number of indigenous inhabitants. In the nineteenth century, large numbers of additional migrants moved east to mine Siberian gold, silver, copper, and iron. By this time, the Russian state was well on the way toward consolidating its control over the region.

## Commercial Rivalries and the Seven Years' War

Exploration and imperial expansion led to conflicts not only between Europeans and Asians but also among Europeans themselves. Mariners competed vigorously for trade in Asia and the Americas, and their efforts to establish markets—and sometimes monopolies as well—led frequently to clashes with their counterparts from different lands.

**Competition and Conflict** Indeed, throughout the seventeenth and early eighteenth centuries, commercial and political rivalries led to running wars between ships representing different states. Dutch vessels were most numerous in the Indian Ocean, and they enabled the VOC to dominate the spice trade. Dutch forces expelled most Portuguese merchants from southeast Asia and prevented English mariners from establishing secure footholds there. By the early eighteenth century, trade in Indian cotton and tea from Ceylon had begun to overshadow the spice trade, and English and French merchants working from trading posts in India became the dominant carriers in the Indian Ocean. Fierce competition again generated violence: in 1746 French forces seized the English trading post at Madras, one of the three principal centers of British operations in India.

Commercial competition led to conflict also in the Caribbean and the Americas. English pirates and privateers preyed on Spanish shipping from Mexico, often seizing vessels carrying cargoes of silver. English and French forces constantly skirmished and fought over sugar islands in the Caribbean while also contesting territorial claims in North America. Almost all conflicts between European states in the eighteenth century spilled over into the Caribbean and the Americas.

**The Seven Years' War** Commercial rivalries combined with political differences and came to a head in the **Seven Years' War** (1756–1763). The Seven Years' War was a global conflict in that it took place in several distinct geographic theaters—Europe, India, the Caribbean, and North America—and involved Asian and indigenous American peoples as well as Europeans. Sometimes called "the great war for empire," the Seven Years' War had deep implications for global affairs because it laid the foundation for 150 years of British imperial hegemony in the world.

In Europe the war pitted Britain and Prussia against France, Austria, and Russia. In India, British and French forces each allied with local rulers and engaged in a contest for dominance in the Indian Ocean. In the Caribbean, Spanish forces joined with the French in an effort to limit British expansion in the Western Hemisphere. In North America—where the Seven Years' War merged with a conflict already under way known as the French and Indian War (1754–1763)—British and French armies made separate alliances with indigenous peoples in an effort to outmaneuver each other.

**British Dominance** British forces fought little in Europe, where their Prussian allies held off massive armies seeking to surround and crush the expansive Prussian state. Elsewhere, however, British armies and navies fought often and handily overcame their enemies. They ousted French merchants from India and took control of French colonies in Canada, although they allowed French authorities to retain most of their Caribbean possessions. They allowed Spanish forces to retain Cuba but took Florida from the Spanish empire. Despite these victories, Britain couldn't rest easy; powerful states continuously challenged British ambitions. Yet victory in the Seven Years' War placed Britain in a position to dominate world trade for the foreseeable future, and "the great war for empire" paved the way for the establishment of the British empire in the nineteenth century. The war also suggested how close together earlier global exchanges had brought the peoples of the world.

## CONCLUSION

Global commercial and biological exchanges and encounters arose from the efforts of European mariners to explore the world's waters and establish sea lanes that would support long-distance trade. Their search for sea routes to Asia accidentally led them to the Western Hemisphere and the vast expanse of the Pacific Ocean. The geographic knowledge that they accumulated enabled them to link the world's regions into an ever more finely articulated network of trade. But commercial exchange was not the only result of this global network. Food crops, animal stocks, disease pathogens, and human migrants also traveled the sea lanes and dramatically influenced societies throughout the world. In the Americas, the Pacific Islands, and (to a lesser extent) Siberia, epidemics sparked by unfamiliar disease pathogens ravaged indigenous populations, while massive migrations of human communities transformed the social and cultural landscape of the Americas. At the same time, in most of the Eastern Hemisphere, transplanted crops and animal species led to improved nutrition and marked population growth. Europeans did not achieve global dominance in early modern times. However, their voyages of exploration and consequent development of transoceanic trading networks meant that European peoples now played a more prominent role in world affairs than any of their ancestors. In addition, their efforts helped foster the development of an increasingly interdependent world.

## STUDY TERMS

Afonso d'Alboquerque (331)
astrolabe (316)
back staffs (316)
Bartolomeu Dias (320)
Captain James Cook (325)
Ceuta (320)
Christopher Columbus (322)
Columbian Exchange (326)
cross staffs (316)
East India Company (331)
Ferdinand Magellan (322)
Guanahaní (322)
Jan Pieterszoon Coen (334)
Java (334)
joint-stock company (331)
magnetic compass (316)
Manila (334)
Manila galleons (329)
Miguel López de Legazpi (333)
Prince Henry the Navigator (318)
São Jorge da Mina (320)
Seven Years' War (337)
Siberia (335)
Taíno (322)
Vasco da Gama (313)
Vitus Bering (325)
VOC (331)
*volta do mar* (317)

## FOR FURTHER READING

Rene J. Barendse. *The Arabian Seas.* Eastgate, N.Y., 2002. A pathbreaking and complex work that emphasizes the long predominance of Asia in the world economy.

Jerry Brotton. *A History of the World in 12 Maps.* New York, 2013. A cross-cultural sampling of maps, both ancient and current, and the ideas and beliefs that shaped them.

Christopher Columbus. *The* Diario *of Christopher Columbus's First Voyage to America.* Trans. by Oliver Dunn and James E. Kelley Jr. Norman, Okla., 1989. A careful translation.

Dorothy Crawford. *Deadly Companions: How Microbes Shaped Our History.* Oxford, 2007. Explores how microbes and humans evolved together from earliest humanity to the present.

Alfred W. Crosby. *The Columbian Exchange: Biological and Cultural Consequences of 1492.* Westport, Conn., 1972. Focuses on early exchanges of plants, animals, and diseases between Europe and America.

Charles C. Mann. *1493: Uncovering the New World Christopher Columbus Created.* New York, 2011. A thorough account of the ways the ecological and economic exchanges fundamentally transformed societies in the Americas, Europe, East Asia, and Africa.

Lincoln Paine. *The Sea and Civilization: A Maritime History of the World.* New York, 2013. An accessible, enjoyable, and refreshing maritime history of the world.

John F. Richards. *The Unending Frontier: An Environmental History of the Early Modern World.* Berkeley, 2003. Thoroughly explores the environmental effects of the global historical processes that shaped the early modern world.

Yuri Slezkine. *Arctic Mirrors: Russia and the Small Peoples of the North.* Ithaca, N.Y., 1994. Thoughtful analysis of Russian relations with the hunting, fishing, and herding peoples of Siberia.

Heather Streets-Salter and Trevor Getz. *Empires and Colonies in the Modern World.* New York, 2015. A globally focused exploration of imperialism and colonialism from the fourteenth century to the present.

# CHAPTER 10 AP EXAM PRACTICE

Questions assume cumulative knowledge from this chapter and previous chapters.

## Section I

## Multiple Choice Questions

Use the image below and your knowledge of world history to answer questions 1 – 3.

Vasco da Gama's flagship on the journey to India in 1497, the *San Rafael.*
ART Collection/Alamy Stock Photo

1. Which of the following statements describes da Gama's 1497 voyage?
   (A) Da Gama had 30 ships and 1000 sailors on this journey.
   (B) Merchants in India were overwhelmed by the wide variety of high-quality European products that da Gama brought to sell.
   (C) The journey to India was quick and easy.
   (D) Da Gama made a profit from buying pepper and cinnamon in India and selling it in Europe.

2. Which of these statements is a likely reason why the painter depicted da Gama's voyage this way?
   (A) The gods sent terrible storms to destroy da Gama's ships.
   (B) The use of crosses on the sails and the heavens above shows that the painter thinks da Gama's journey was blessed by God.
   (C) The calm waters show that the painter thought the voyage was relatively easy.
   (D) The painter wanted to show how to sail with the volta do mar technique.

3. This image best illustrates which historical development?
   (A) Portuguese development of maritime technology and navigational skills led to increased travel to and trade with Africa and Asia and resulted in the construction of a global trading-post empire.
   (B) The new connections between the Eastern and Western Hemispheres resulted in the exchange of new plants, animals, and diseases, known as the Columbian Exchange.
   (C) Northern Atlantic crossings were undertaken under English, French, and Dutch sponsorship, often with the goal of finding alternative sailing routes to Asia.
   (D) Populations in Afro-Eurasia benefitted nutritionally from the increased diversity of American food crops.

Use the image below and your knowledge of world history to answer questions 4 and 5.

View of the Tijgersgracht on Batavia
Photo Researchers/Science History Images/Alamy Stock Photo

4. Which of the following statements is NOT true about the Dutch in Indonesia?
   (A) The Dutch were interested in acquiring spices.
   (B) The Dutch took advantage of rivalries between local Indonesian authorities.
   (C) Dutch colonists moved to Indonesia and became a large segment of the population.
   (D) Dutch imperial policy included specific plans to convert the Indonesians to Christianity.

5. How was the European presence in the Philippines and Indonesia different from their activities in other parts of the Indian Ocean?
   (A) Europeans generally traded peacefully with the Arabs, Indians, Malaysians, and Chinese, but the Dutch and the Spanish used violence in Indonesia and the Philippines.
   (B) Indonesia and the Philippines provided no valuable products that Europeans wanted, so there was no reason for Europeans to conquer those islands.
   (C) Both Indonesia and the Philippines were already Christian cultures, so the Europeans generally left them alone.
   (D) Strong, centralized governments in Indonesia and the Philippines limited Europeans to trading in only one city.

## Short Answer

6. Use the map below and your knowledge of world history to answer parts A, B, and C.

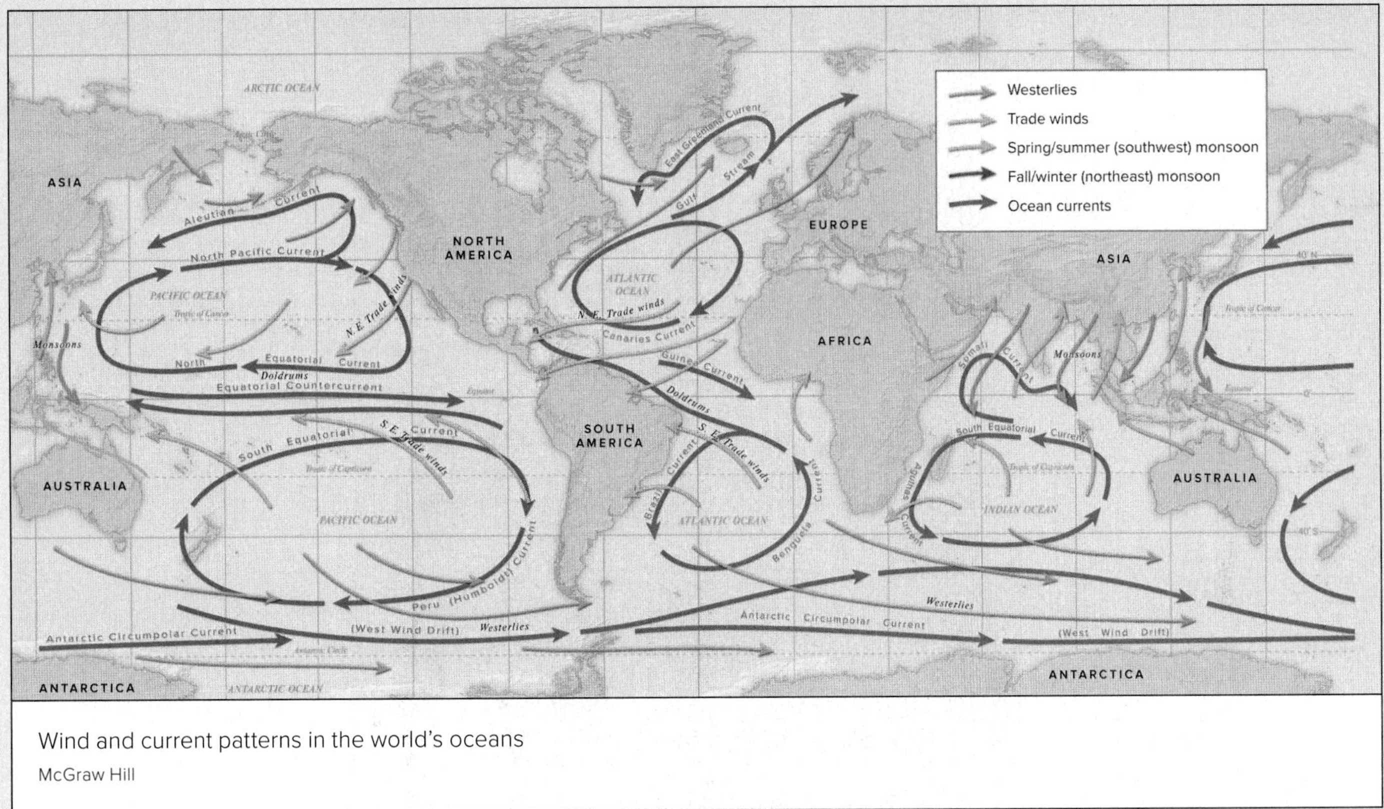


Wind and current patterns in the world's oceans
McGraw Hill

(A) Identify ONE technology that helped mariners understand wind or current patterns.

(B) Explain ONE way that Europeans were able to use knowledge of wind patterns to expand overseas.

(C) Explain ONE difference between European voyages in the Atlantic and the Pacific.

7. Use the image below and your knowledge of world history to answer parts A, B, and C.

*Tabacum Latifolium* by Basil Besler
Historical Picture Archive/Corbis Historical/Getty Images

(A) Explain the significance of importing ONE native American plant or animal to Afro-Eurasia in the Columbian Exchange.
(B) Explain the significance of importing ONE Afro-Eurasian plant or animal to the Americas during the Columbian Exchange.
(C) Identify ONE way that the Columbian Exchange contributed to the migration of peoples.

8. Use your understanding of world history to answer parts A, B, and C.
(A) Explain ONE way that the Portuguese used trading posts to create their empire.
(B) Explain ONE advantage English and Dutch trading networks had over the Portuguese.
(C) Identify ONE reason why Portugal lost its influence in the Indian Ocean by the end of the 16th century.

# Section II

## Document-Based Question

Based on the documents below and your knowledge of world history, analyze the similarities and differences in the way that Europeans interacted with indigenous peoples.

In your response you should do the following:

- Respond to the prompt with a historically defensible thesis or claim that establishes a line of reasoning.
- Describe a broader historical context relevant to the prompt.
- Support an argument in response to the prompt using all documents.
- Use at least one additional piece of specific historical evidence (beyond that found in the documents) relevant to an argument about the prompt.
- Explain how or why the document's point of view, purpose, historical situation, and /or audience is relevant to an argument.
- Use evidence to corroborate, qualify, or modify an argument that addresses the prompt.

### Document 1

Engraving of a fur-clad indigenous hunter, possibly from Siberia, holding a bow and trident in one hand, and two dead mink or ermine in the other.

Science & Society Picture Library/Getty Images

## Document 2

They are very gentle and do not know what evil is; nor do they kill others, nor steal; and they are without weapons and so timid that a hundred of them flee from one of our men even if our men are teasing them. And they are credulous and aware that there is a God in heaven and convinced that we come from the heavens; and they say very quickly any prayer that we tell them to say, and they make the sign of the cross. So that Your Highnesses ought to resolve to make them Christians: for I believe that if you begin, in a short time you will end up having converted to our Holy Faith a multitude of peoples and acquiring large dominions and great riches and all of their peoples for Spain. Because without doubt there is in these lands a very great quantity of gold; for not without cause do these Indians that I bring with me say that there are in these islands places where they dig gold and wear it on their chests, on their ears, and on their arms, and on their legs; and they are very thick bracelets. And also there are stones, and there are precious pearls and infinite spicery. . . . And also here there is probably a great quantity of cotton; and I think that it would sell very well here without taking it to Spain but to the big cities belonging to the Grand [Mongol] Khan.

*Source:* Columbus, Christopher. *The* Diario *of Christopher Columbus's First Voyage to America.* Trans. by Oliver Dunn and James E. Kelley Jr. Norman: University of Oklahoma Press, 1989, pp. 65–69, 143–45.

## Document 3

We took along with us one of Mr. Banks's Tents, and after we had fix'd upon a place fit for our purpose we set up the Tent and marked out the ground we intended to Occupy. By this time a number of the Natives had got collected together about us, seemingly only to look on, as not one of them had any weapon, either Offensive or defensive. I would suffer none to come within the lines I had marked out, excepting one who appeared to be a chief . . . we endeavour'd to explain, as well as we could, that we wanted that ground to Sleep upon such a number of nights and then we should go away. Whether they understood us or no is uncertain, but no one appeared the least displeased at what we was about; indeed the Ground we had fixed upon was of no use to them, being part of the sandy Beach upon the shore of the Bay, and not near to any of their Habitations. It being too late in the day to do anything more, a party with a petty officer was left to guard the Tent, while we with another party took a Walk into the woods, and with us most of the natives. We had but just crossed the River when Mr. Banks shott three Ducks at one shott, which surprised them so much that most of them fell down as though they had been shott likewise. I was in hopes this would have had some good effect, but the event did not prove it, for we had not been long from the Tent before the natives again began to gather about, and one of them more daring than the rest pushed one of the Centinels [sic] down, snatched the Musket out of his hand and made a push at him, and then made off, and with him all the rest. Immediately upon this the Officer ordered the party to fire, and the Man who took the musket was shot Dead before he had got far from the Tent, but the musquet was carried quite off when this hapned [sic].

*Source:* Cook, Captain James. *Captain Cook's Journal During His First Voyage Round the World, Made in H.M. Bark "Endeavor," 1768–1771* (London, 1893).

## Long Essay

**Develop a thoughtful and thorough historical argument that answers the question below. Begin your essay with a thesis statement and support it with relevant historical evidence.**

**Using specific examples and your knowledge of world history, describe similarities and differences in how disease affected Asia, the Americas, and the Pacific from 1450 to 1750 C.E.**

# Chapter 11 The Transformation of Europe



## ZOOMING IN ON TRADITIONS

### Martin Luther Challenges the Church

In 1517 an obscure German monk posed a challenge to the Roman Catholic church. Martin Luther of Wittenberg denounced the church's sale of indulgences, a type of pardon that excused individuals from doing penance for their sins, making it easier for their souls to go to heaven when they died. Indulgences had been available since the eleventh century, but to raise funds for the reconstruction of St. Peter's basilica in Rome, church authorities began to sell indulgences aggressively in the early sixteenth century. From their point of view, indulgences were splendid devices: they encouraged individuals to reflect piously on their behavior while also bringing large sums of money into the church's treasury.

To Martin Luther, however, indulgences were signs of greed, hypocrisy, and moral rot in the Roman Catholic church. Luther despised what he saw as the pretentiousness of church authorities who claimed powers that belonged only to God: Luther believed that no human being had the power to absolve individuals of their sins and grant them admission to heaven, so for him the sale of indulgences was a huge moral and religious fraud. In October 1517, following academic custom of theday,

This detail from a sixteenth-century painting by François Dubois depicts the brutal murder of French Protestants in Paris during the St. Bartholomew's Day Massacre on August 23, 1572.
Alfredo Dagli Orti/Shutterstock

he offered to debate publicly with anyone who wished to dispute his views, and he denounced the sale of indulgences in a document called the ***Ninety-Five Theses.***

Contrary to popular legend, Luther did not nail his work to the church door in Wittenberg. Nevertheless, news of the *Ninety-Five Theses* spread rapidly: within a few weeks, printed copies were available throughout Europe. Luther's challenge galvanized opinion among many who resented the power of the Roman church. It also drew severe criticism from religious and political authorities seeking to maintain the established order. Church officials subjected Luther's views to examination and judged them erroneous, and in 1520 Pope Leo X excommunicated the unrepentant monk. In 1521 the Holy Roman emperor Charles V, a devout Roman Catholic, summoned Luther to an assembly of imperial authorities and demanded that he publicly renounce his views. Luther's response: "I cannot and will not recant anything, for it is neither safe nor right to act against one's conscience. Here I stand. I can do no other. God help me. Amen."

Martin Luther's challenge held enormous religious and political implications. Though expelled from the church, Luther still considered himself Christian—indeed, he considered his own faith true Christianity—and he held religious services for a community of devoted followers. Wittenberg became a center of religious dissent, which by the late 1520s had spread through much of Germany and Switzerland. During the 1530s these dissenters—who became known as Protestants because of their protest against the established church—organized movements in France, England, the Low Countries, and even Italy and Spain. By midcentury Luther's act of individual rebellion had mushroomed into the Protestant Reformation, which shattered the religious unity of western European Christendom.

# CHAPTER FOCUS

- From 1450–1750, western European governments became increasingly centralized while religious and scientific beliefs changed, and capitalism became stronger throughout the region. These developments mark the shift from medieval to early modern.
- The Thirty Years' War began as a Catholic vs. Lutheran conflict within the Holy Roman Empire, but Catholic France joined on the side of the Lutherans, hoping to defeat the Catholic Holy Roman emperor.
- The Treaty of Westphalia in 1648 settled the Thirty Years' War, compromised the kingdoms and faiths, and kept international peace in Europe for over 150 years. It is also widely understood as the beginning of the nation-state in Europe.
- Focus on how various rulers weakened the traditional power of local nobles during the process of state centralization.
- Many European monarchs used the divine right theory of rule, magnificent palaces, and patronage of the arts to impress their subjects—think about how this might compare to how rulers consolidated power in other regions.
- Merchants were happy to support a government that helped finance international businesses, yet in England and the Netherlands, constitutions created by nobles and bourgeoisie limited rulers' powers somewhat. Note the class position of those writing the constitutions—they were still a relatively small proportion of society, not an express of mass constitutional democracy.
- Global commerce brought new and inexpensive foods to Europe, causing populations to explode due to better nutrition and lower infant and maternal mortality. More people moved to cities, but rural folks were also pulled into the modern economy through participating in cottage industries.

## Historical Developments

- State expansion and centralization led to resistance from an array of social, political, and economic groups on a local level.
- The Protestant Reformation marked a break with existing Christian traditions and both the Protestant and Catholic Reformations contributed to the growth of Christianity.
- American foods became staple crops in various parts of Europe, Asia, and Africa. Cash crops were grown primarily on plantations with coerced labor and were exported mostly to Europe and the Middle East.
- Europeans established new trading posts in Africa and Asia, which proved profitable for the rulers and merchants involved in new global trade networks. Some Asian states sought to limit the disruptive economic and cultural effects of European dominated long-distance trade by adopting restrictive or isolationist trade policies.
- Peasant and artisan labor continued and intensified in many regions as the demand for food and consumer goods increased.

## Reasoning Processes

- **Developments and Processes** Explain the religious fragmentation of Christian Europe and why it is important for world history more broadly.
- **Source Claims and Evidence** Identify the point of view and historical situation of Galileo's claims about the cosmos.
- **Contextualization** Identify and describe the historical context of the Thirty Years' War.
- **Making Connections** Identify patterns among systems of rule in absolute monarchies and constitutional states.
- **Argumentation** Using specific evidence, support the argument that European rulers used art to enhance their power.

## Historical Thinking Skills

- **Causation** Describe the causes of the Protestant Reformation and the Thirty Years' War.
- **Continuity and Change** Describe patterns of continuity and change in European understandings of the natural world.

## CHAPTER OVERVIEW

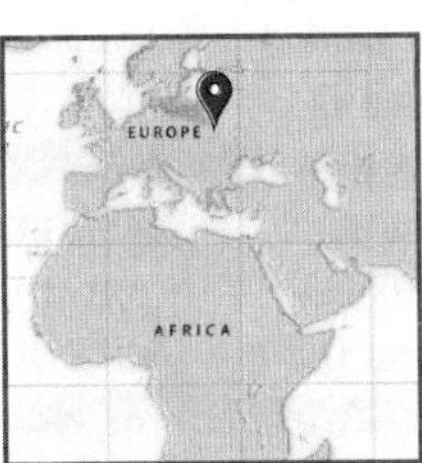


For all its unsettling effects, the Protestant Reformation was only one of several powerful movements that transformed European society during the early modern era. Another was the consolidation of strong centralized states, which took shape partly because of the Reformation. Between the sixteenth and the eighteenth centuries, monarchs in western Europe took advantage of religious quarrels to tighten control over their societies. By the mid-eighteenth century, some rulers had concentrated so much power in their own hands that historians refer to them as absolute monarchs.

Alongside religious conflict and the building of powerful states, capitalism and early modern science also profoundly influenced western European society in early modern times. Early capitalism—an economic system based on free market conditions and private ownership of goods and services—pushed European merchants and manufacturers into competition with one another and encouraged them to reorganize their businesses in search of maximum efficiency. Early modern science challenged traditional ways of understanding the world and the universe and prompted European intellectuals to seek an entirely rational understanding of the natural world.

As a result of these phenomena, between 1500 and 1800 western Europe underwent a thorough transformation. Although the combination of religious, political, social, economic, intellectual, and cultural change was unsettling and disruptive, it ultimately strengthened European society. The states of early modern Europe competed vigorously and mobilized their human and natural resources in order to do so effectively. By 1800 several of them had become especially powerful, wealthy, and dynamic. They stood poised to play major roles in world affairs during the nineteenth and twentieth centuries.

| CHRONOLOGY | |
|---|---|
| 1473–1543 | Life of Nicolaus Copernicus |
| 1478 | Foundation of the Spanish Inquisition |
| 1483–1546 | Life of Martin Luther |
| 1491–1556 | Life of Ignatius Loyola |
| 1509–1547 | Reign of King Henry VIII |
| 1509–1564 | Life of John Calvin |
| 1517 | Publication of the *Ninety-Five Theses* |
| 1519–1556 | Reign of Emperor Charles V |
| 1540 | Foundation of the Society of Jesus |
| 1545–1563 | Council of Trent |
| 1556–1598 | Reign of King Philip II |
| 1564–1642 | Life of Galileo Galilei |
| 1571–1630 | Life of Johannes Kepler |
| 1588 | Spanish Armada |
| 1618–1648 | Thirty Years' War |
| 1642–1727 | Life of Isaac Newton |
| 1643–1715 | Reign of King Louis XIV |
| 1648 | Peace of Westphalia |
| 1706–1749 | Life of Émilie du Châtelet |

## THE FRAGMENTATION OF WESTERN EUROPEAN CHRISTENDOM

Although the peoples of western Europe spoke different languages, ate different foods, and observed different customs, the church of Rome provided them with a common religious and cultural heritage. During the sixteenth and seventeenth centuries, however, revolts against the Roman Catholic church shattered the religious unity of western Europe. Followers of **Martin Luther** and other Protestant reformers established a series of churches independent of Rome, and Roman Catholic leaders strengthened their own church against the challengers. Throughout early modern times, religious controversies fueled social tensions.

### The Protestant Reformation

**Roots of Reform** The **Protestant Reformation** dates from the early sixteenth century, but many of the underlying conditions that prompted reformers to challenge the authority of the Roman Catholic church had existed for hundreds of years. Over the course of centuries, the church and its top officials had become deeply involved in the political affairs of western Europe. But political intrigues, combined with the church's growing wealth and power, also fostered greed and corruption, which undermined the church's spiritual authority and made it vulnerable to criticism. The blatant pursuit of pleasure and crass materialism of church officials—including, in some cases, living in luxury and taking mistresses—only further emphasized the perceived betrayal of Christian ideals. Although the church continued to enjoy the loyalty of most Christians, it faced a disapproval of its abuses that became increasingly strident in the decades before 1517. Alongside such criticism came a growing demand for a more personal involvement with God. Efforts by church authorities to eliminate pre-Christian traditions and alternative kinds of spirituality only intensified the desire among laypeople for forms of devotion that would connect them more directly with God than the church allowed.

**Martin Luther** Martin Luther coalesced these expressions of religious discontent into a powerful revolt against the church. Martin Luther (1483–1546) attacked the sale of indulgences as an individual, but he soon attracted enthusiastic support from others who resented the policies of the Roman church. Luther was a prolific and talented writer, and he published numerous works condemning the Roman church. His cause benefited enormously from the printing press, which had first appeared in Europe in the mid-fifteenth century.

**Johannes Gutenberg** (ca. 1395–1468) introduced printing to Europe and his invention of mechanical movable type printing, around 1439, started a printing revolution. From Gutenberg's hometown of Mainz, Germany, printing soon spread to more than two hundred European cities. Luther's translation of the Bible into German stimulated the production and distribution of religious books and pamphlets and proved to be a decisive factor in the spread of literacy. A growing literate public eagerly consumed printed works on both religious and nonreligious themes, as both supporters and critics of Martin Luther took their own works to the printers. Religious controversies kept the presses busy churning out millions of pamphlets and treatises for a century and more.

In his publications, writings, and speeches, Luther attacked the Roman church for a wide range of abuses and called for thorough reform of Christendom. He advocated the closure of monasteries; translation of the Bible from Latin into regional languages; and an end to priestly authority, including the authority of the pope himself. Most important, Luther believed that salvation and the entry to heaven could never be earned through good works or through the prayers of others. Instead, he argued, humans could be saved only through faith in the promises of God as revealed in the Bible. This idea of "justification by faith alone" became the core of Protestant beliefs. When opponents pointed out that his reform program ran counter to church policy, Luther rejected the authority of the church hierarchy and proclaimed that the Bible was the only source of Christian religious authority.

Luther's works drew an enthusiastic popular response, and in Germany they fueled a movement to reform the church along the lines of Luther's teachings. Ordinary Christians flocked to hear Luther preach in Wittenberg, and several princes of the Holy Roman Empire warmed to Luther's views—partly because of personal conviction but partly because religious controversy offered opportunities for them to build their own power bases. During the 1520s and 1530s, many of the most important German cities—Strasbourg, Nuremberg, and Augsburg, among others—passed laws prohibiting Roman Catholic observances and requiring all religious services to follow Lutheran doctrine and procedures.

By the mid-sixteenth century, about half the German population had adopted Lutheran Christianity, and reformers had launched Protestant movements and established alternative churches in other lands as well. By the late 1520s, the prosperous cities of Switzerland—Zurich, Basel, and Geneva—had fledgling Protestant churches. The heavily urbanized Low Countries also responded enthusiastically to Protestant appeals. Protestants appeared even in Italy and Spain, although authorities in those lands handily suppressed their challenge to the Roman church.

**John Calvin** Meanwhile, an even more influential Reformation was taking shape in France and the French-speaking parts of Switzerland. The initiator was a French lawyer, John Calvin (1509–1564), who in the 1530s converted to Protestant Christianity. Because the French monarchy sought to suppress Protestants, Calvin slipped across the border to French-speaking Geneva in Switzerland. There he organized a Protestant community and worked with local officials to impose a strict code of morality and discipline on the city. Calvin also composed an influential treatise, *Institutes of the Christian Religion* (1536), that codified Protestant teachings and presented them as a coherent and organized package.

Although Calvin believed in the basic elements of Luther's Protestant teachings, his ideas differed from those of Luther in important ways. Most fundamentally, Calvin emphasized the awesome power of God more than Luther did. Indeed, he believed not only that humans could never earn salvation through prayers and good works but also that God had in fact already determined which individuals would be saved from damnation even before they were born. These individuals, known as "the elect," were predestined for salvation regardless of their deeds on earth. This doctrine of "predestination" grew increasingly important to the Calvinist church in the generations after Calvin's death.

Calvin's Geneva was bound by a strict code of morality and discipline. **Calvinists** were expected to dress simply, to study the Bible regularly, and to refrain from activities such as dancing or playing cards. It was, in effect, a Protestant model community. Geneva also became an important missionary center from which Calvinist doctrine spread to other parts of Europe. Calvinist missionaries were most active in France, where they attracted strong interest in the cities, but they ventured also to Germany, the Low Countries, England, Scotland, and even distant Hungary. They established churches in all these lands and worked for reform along Protestant lines. They were most successful in the Netherlands and Scotland.

**The English Reformation** In England a Reformation took place for political as well as religious reasons. Lutherans and other Protestants worked to build a following in England from the 1520s, but they faced significant government resistance until King Henry VIII (reigned 1509–1547) came into conflict with the pope. Henry wanted to divorce his wife, who had not given birth to a male heir, but the pope refused to allow him to do so. Henry's response was to cut off relations with the Roman church and make himself Supreme Head of the Anglican church—in essence, an English pope. While Henry reigned, the theology of the English church changed little, but under pressure of reformers, his successors replaced Roman Catholic with Protestant doctrines and rituals. By 1560 England had permanently left the Roman Catholic community. Indeed, by the late sixteenth century, Lutherans, **Anglicans,** and Calvinists together had built communities large enough that a return to religious unity in western Europe was inconceivable.

Inspired by the Catholic Reformation, many devout individuals sought mystic union with God. One of the most famous of the mystics was St. Teresa of Avila (in Spain), who founded a strict order of nuns and often experienced religious visions. A famous sculpture by the Italian artist Gianlorenzo Bernini depicts St. Teresa in an ecstatic trance accompanied by an angel.
Stefano Valeri/Shutterstock

## The Catholic Reformation

Partly in response to the Protestant Reformation, Roman Catholic authorities undertook an enormous reform effort within their own church in the sixteenth century. To some extent their efforts represented a reaction to Protestant success. Yet Roman Catholic authorities also sought to define points of doctrine and thus clarify differences between Roman and Protestant churches, to persuade Protestants to return to the Roman church, and to deepen the sense of spirituality and religious commitment in their own community. Taken together, their efforts constituted the **Catholic Reformation.**

**The Council of Trent** Two institutions were especially important for defining the Catholic Reformation and advancing its goals—the Council of Trent and the Society of Jesus. The **Council of Trent** was an assembly of bishops, cardinals, and other high church officials who met intermittently between 1545 and 1563 to address matters of doctrine and reform. Drawing heavily on the works of the thirteenth-century scholastic theologian St. Thomas Aquinas (discussed in chapter 19), the council defined the elements of Roman Catholic theology in detail. The council acknowledged that abuses had alienated many people from the Roman church, and it took steps to reform the church. The council demanded that church authorities observe strict standards of morality, and it required them to establish schools and seminaries in their districts to prepare priests properly for their roles.

**St. Ignatius Loyola** While the Council of Trent dealt with doctrine and reform, the **Society of Jesus** went on the offensive and sought to extend the boundaries of the reformed Roman church. The society's founder was **St. Ignatius Loyola** (1491–1556), a Basque nobleman and soldier who in 1521 suffered a devastating leg wound that ended his military career. While recuperating he read spiritual works and popular accounts of saints' lives, and he resolved to put his energy into religious work. In 1540, together with a small band of disciples, he founded the Society of Jesus.

**The Society of Jesus** Ignatius required that members of the society, known as Jesuits, complete a rigorous and advanced education. They received instruction not only in theology and philosophy but also in classical languages, literature, history, and science. As a result of that preparation—and their unswerving dedication to the Roman Catholic church—the Jesuits made extraordinarily effective missionaries. They were able to outargue most of their opponents and acquired a reputation for discipline and determination. They often served as counselors to kings and rulers and used their influence to promote policies that benefited the Roman church. They also were the most prominent of the early Christian missionaries outside Europe: in the wake of the European reconnaissance of the world's oceans, Jesuits attracted converts in India, China, Japan, the Philippines, and the Americas, thus making Christianity a genuinely global religion.

## Witch-Hunts and Religious Wars

Religion was central to the lives of most Europeans in the sixteenth century, and religious divisions helped to fuel social and political conflict. Apart from wars, the most destructive violence that afflicted early modern Europe was the hunt for witches, which was especially prominent in regions such as the Rhineland (in modern Germany) where tensions between Protestants and Roman Catholics ran high.

The Burning of Three Witches (1585), by Johann Jakob Wick. This illustration depicts the execution by burning of three accused "witches" in Baden, Switzerland on November 4, 1585.
The History Collection/Alamy Stock Photo

Like many other peoples, Europeans had long believed that certain individuals possessed unusual powers to influence human affairs or discover secret information such as the identity of a thief. During the late fifteenth century, theologians developed a theory that witches derived their powers from the devil. According to that theory, witches made agreements to worship the devil in exchange for supernatural powers, including the ability to fly through the night on brooms, pitchforks, or animals. Theorists believed that the witches regularly flew off to distant places to attend the "witches' sabbath," a gathering that featured devil worship, lewd behavior, and the concoction of secret potions, culminating in sexual relations with the devil himself.

**Witch-Hunting** Although the witches' sabbath was sheer fantasy, fears that individuals were making alliances with the devil sparked an intensive hunt for witches beginning in the sixteenth century. Witchcraft became a convenient explanation for any unpleasant turn of events, including failure of a crop, outbreak of a fire, an unexpected death, or inability to conceive a child. About 110,000 individuals underwent trial as suspected witches during the sixteenth and seventeenth centuries, and about 45,000 of them were executed, either by hanging or by burning at the stake. As a rule, church courts tried large numbers of witches, but they usually imposed nonlethal penalties such as excommunication or imprisonment. It was secular courts that condemned and executed the vast majority of witches.

**Witches and Gender** Gender played an important role in the **witch-hunts.** Although men were among the victims, most convicted witches were women. Indeed, women may have accounted for 85 percent or more of the condemned. Many of the women were poor, old, single, or widowed—individuals who lived on the margins of their societies and were easy targets for accusers because they had few protectors.

By 1700 the fear of witches had largely diminished. Accusations, trials, and executions occurred only sporadically thereafter. The last legal execution for witchcraft in Europe took place in Switzerland in 1782. For the better part of two centuries, however, the intermittent pursuit of witches clearly revealed the stresses and strains that afflicted European society during early modern times and also the ways women were made to serve as scapegoats for them.

**Religious Wars** Religious tensions even led to outright war between Protestant and Roman Catholic communities. Religious wars racked France for thirty-six years (1562–1598), for example, and they also complicated relations between Protestant and Roman Catholic states. In 1588 King Philip II of Spain (reigned 1556–1598) attempted to force England to return to the Roman Catholic church by sending the Spanish Armada—a huge flotilla consisting of 130 ships and 30,000 men—to dethrone the Protestant Queen Elizabeth. The effort collapsed, however, when English forces disrupted the Spanish fleet by sending blazing, unmanned ships into its midst. Then a ferocious gale scattered Spanish vessels throughout the North Sea.

Religious convictions also aggravated relations between the Netherlands and Spain by fueling the revolt of the Dutch provinces from their overlord, the king of Spain. In 1567 Philip sent an army to tighten his control over the provinces and to suppress the Calvinist movement there. Resistance escalated into a full-scale rebellion. By 1610 the seven northern provinces (the modern Netherlands) had won their independence and formed a republic known as the United Provinces, leaving ten southern provinces (modern Belgium) under Spanish and later Austrian rule until the late eighteenth century.

**The Thirty Years' War** The religious wars culminated in a massive continental conflict known as the **Thirty Years' War** (1618–1648). The war opened after the Holy Roman emperor attempted to force his Bohemian (in modern Czechoslovakia) subjects to return to the Roman Catholic church, though the main battleground was the emperor's territory in Germany. Other parties soon entered the fray, however, and by the time the war ended, Spanish, French, Dutch, German, Swedish, Danish, Polish, Bohemian, and Russian forces had taken part in the conflict.

## INTERPRETING IMAGES

Israel ex. Cum Priuil. Reg.
A la fin ces Voleurs infames et perdus,
Comme fruits malheureux a cet arbre pendus
Monstrent bien que le crime (horrible et noire engeance)
Est luy mesme instrument de honte et de vengeance,
Et que cest le Destin des hommes vicieux
Desprouuer tost ou tard la iustice des Cieux. 11


The Thirty Years' War offered abundant opportunity for undisciplined mercenary soldiers to prey on civilian populations. Only rarely, as in the mass hanging depicted in this engraving of 1633, did soldiers receive punishment for their criminal acts.

**Analyze** *Why did mercenary soldiers prey on civilians? What is the difference between mercenaries and a professional, standing military?*

Anne S.K. Brown Military Collection, Brown University Library.

## What's Left Out?

Chroniclers and historians of the Thirty Years' War have pointed out the brutalities and suffering it caused since the end of the conflict itself. Most textbooks, including this one, rightly point out that the Thirty Years' War was the most destructive European conflict until the even more brutal World Wars of the twentieth century. But the need to be brief and to cover many topics often means that textbooks cannot delve into the details of what such a claim might have meant for the ordinary people who lived through the war. In German territories alone, nearly a quarter of the population died as a result of the war, and in some places the toll was closer to 50 percent. The incredible destruction of the war was due to a number of reasons that had little to do with religion or loyalties. Among the most important was the lack of separation between battle fronts and home fronts, which meant that civilians often found themselves directly in the path of invading or defending armies. In addition, both invading and defending armies required food, clothing, and shelter, and these frequently were taken from civilians by both friendly and enemy troops. Moreover, when civilians had to endure the destruction of their lands, their crops, their homes, their food stores, and the infrastructure of their towns and cities, famines and food shortages became a grim reality. Weakened individuals then died from sickness and disease on a vast scale. People like Hans Heberle—a cobbler from what is now southern Germany—endured staggering losses during the war. He and his wife and children were driven from their home and lost all their possessions. They were then forced to take refuge in forests, in neighboring towns, and in a fortress to protect themselves from invading armies. Heberle watched as those around him were reduced to famine conditions, eating grass and weeds as well as dogs, cats, mice, and horses. In 1635, just one year in the war, fifteen thousand people died from famine and disease in his hometown of Ulm. Over the course of the war, approximately eight million soldiers and civilians died, each of whom could have told an equally horrific story of fear, loss, and brutality.

*Source:* Hans Medick and Benjamin Marschke, *Experiencing the Thirty Years War: A Brief History with Documents* (Bedford St. Martin's, 2013).

### Thinking Critically About Sources

1. The passage offers details about the impact of the Thirty Years' War on the lives of ordinary people and the suffering they endured. Other than space limitations in books, why are the non-elite so frequently ignored in historical narratives?

The motives that prompted these states to enter the war were sometimes political or economic, but religious differences complicated the other issues and made them more difficult to resolve. Regardless of the motives, the Thirty Years' War was the most destructive European conflict before the twentieth century. Quite apart from violence and brutalities committed by undisciplined soldiers, the war damaged economies and societies throughout Europe and led to the deaths of about one-third of the German population. The destructiveness of the Thirty Years' War raised questions about the viability of Europe as a region of strong, independent, well-armed, and intensely competitive states.

## THE CONSOLIDATION OF SOVEREIGN STATES

Although fundamentally a religious movement, the Reformation had strong political implications, and centralizing monarchs readily made use of religious issues in their efforts to strengthen their states and enhance their authority. Ruling elites had their own religious preferences, and they often promoted a Protestant or Roman Catholic cause out of personal conviction. Religious controversies also offered splendid opportunities for ambitious subordinates who built power bases by appealing to particular religious communities. Over the long run, centralizing monarchs profited most from religious controversy generated by the Reformation. While the Holy Roman Empire fell into disarray because of political and religious quarrels, monarchs in other lands augmented their revenues, enhanced their authority, and created powerful sovereign states. After the devastation of the Thirty Years' War, rulers of these states devised a diplomatic system that sought to maintain order among the many independent and competitive European states.

### The Attempted Revival of Empire

After the dissolution of the **Carolingian** empire in the ninth century C.E., (discussed in chapter 16) there was no effective imperial government in western Europe. The so-called Holy Roman Empire emerged in the tenth century, but its authority extended only to Germany and northern Italy, and even there the emperors encountered stiff opposition from powerful princes and thriving cities. During the early sixteenth century, it seemed that Emperor Charles V (reigned 1519–1556) might establish the Holy Roman Empire as the preeminent political authority in Europe, but by midcentury it was clear that there would be no revival of empire. Thus, unlike China, India, and Ottoman lands in southwest Asia and north Africa, early modern Europe developed as a region of independent states.

**Charles V** After 1438 the Habsburg family, with extensive dynastic holdings in Austria, dominated the Holy Roman

**Carolingian** (kar-uh-LIHN-jee-uhn)

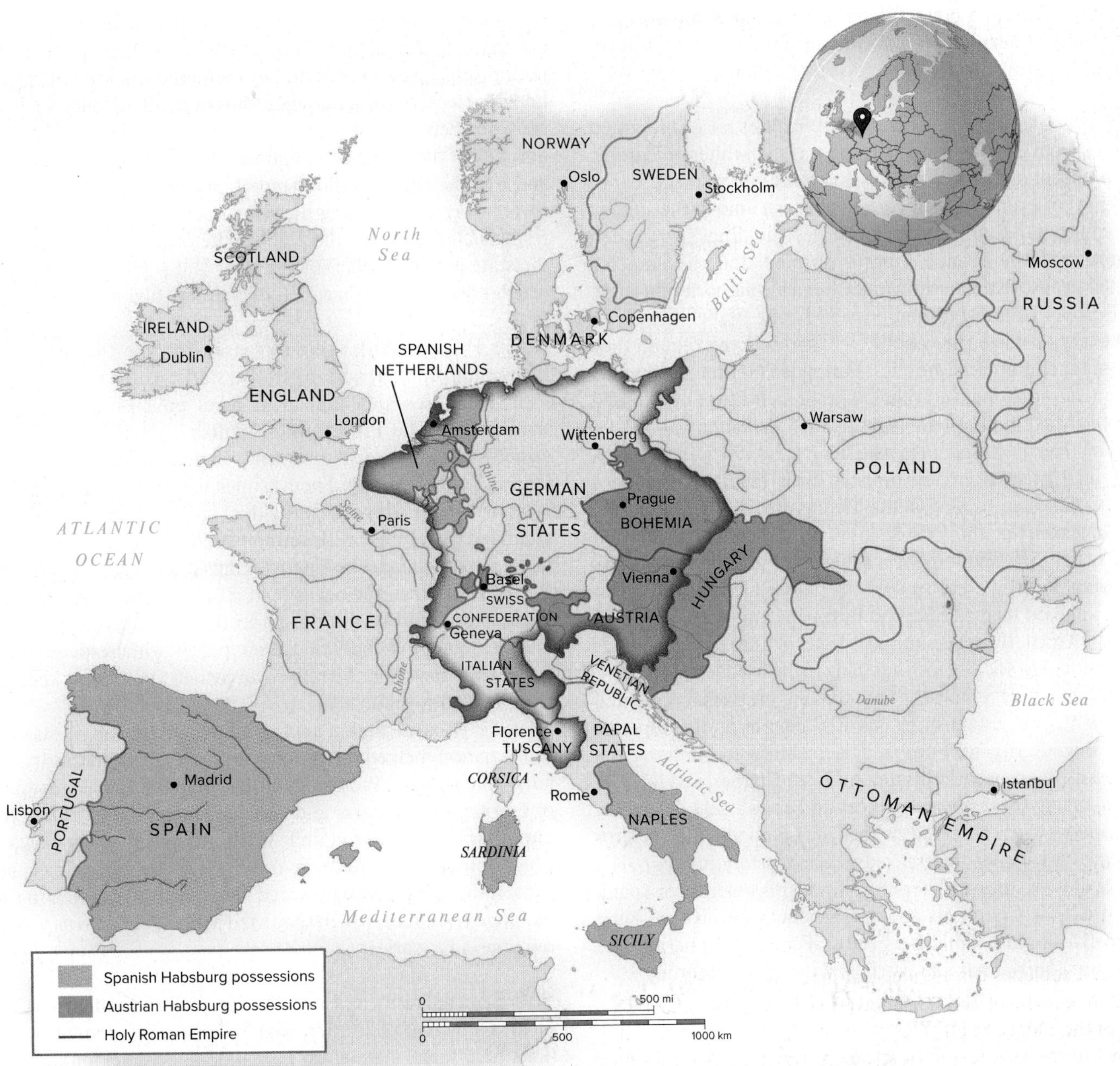


**MAP 11.1 Sixteenth-century Europe.**

Note the extent of Habsburg territories and the wide boundaries of the Holy Roman Empire.

***With such powerful territories, what prevented the Habsburgs from imposing imperial rule on most of Europe?***

Empire. Through marriage alliances with princely and royal families, the **Habsburgs** accumulated rights and titles to lands throughout Europe and beyond. **Charles V** inherited authority over the Habsburgs' Austrian domains as well as the duchy of Burgundy (including the wealthy provinces of the Low Countries) and the kingdom of Spain (including its possessions in Italy and the Americas). When he became emperor in 1519, he acquired authority over Germany, Bohemia, Switzerland, and parts of northern Italy. His empire stretched from Vienna in Austria to Cuzco in Peru.

**Imperial Fragmentation** In spite of his far-flung holdings, Charles did not extend his authority throughout Europe or even establish a lasting imperial legacy. Throughout his reign Charles had to devote much of his attention and energy to the Lutheran movement and to imperial princes who took advantage of religious controversy to assert their independence. Moreover, Charles did not build an administrative structure for his empire but, instead, ruled each of his lands according to its own laws and customs. He was able to draw on the financial resources of wealthy lands such as the Low Countries and

Spain to maintain a powerful army. Yet Charles did not have the ambition to extend his authority by military force. Instead, he used his army mostly to put down rebellions.

**Foreign Challenges** Foreign difficulties also prevented Charles from establishing his empire as the arbiter of Europe. The prospect of a powerful Holy Roman Empire struck fear in the kings of France, and it caused concern among the sultans of the Ottoman Empire as well. Charles's holdings surrounded France, and the French kings suspected that the emperor wanted to absorb their realm and extend his authority throughout Europe. To forestall that possibility, the French kings created every obstacle they could for Charles. Even though they were staunch Roman Catholics, they aided German Lutherans and encouraged them to rebel. The French kings even allied with the Muslim Ottoman Turks against the emperor.

For their part, the Ottoman sultans did not want to see a powerful Christian empire threaten their holdings in eastern Europe and their position in the Mediterranean basin. With the encouragement of the French king, Turkish forces conquered Hungary in 1526, and three years later they even laid siege briefly to Vienna. Moreover, during the early sixteenth century Ottoman forces imposed their rule beyond Egypt and embraced almost all of north Africa. By midcentury, Turkish holdings posed a serious threat to Italian and Spanish shipping in the Mediterranean.

All of these domestic and foreign problems prevented Charles V from establishing his vast empire as the supreme political authority in Europe. His inability to suppress the Lutherans was especially disappointing to Charles, and in 1556, after agreeing that imperial princes and cities could determine the religious faith observed in their jurisdictions, the emperor abdicated his throne and retired to a monastery in Spain. His empire did not survive. Charles bestowed his holdings in Spain, Italy, the Low Countries, and the Americas on his son, King Philip II of Spain, while his brother Ferdinand inherited the Habsburg family lands in Austria and the imperial throne.

## The New Monarchs

In the absence of effective imperial power, guidance of public affairs fell to the various regional states that had emerged during the middle ages. The city-states of Italy were prominent because of their economic power: since the eleventh century they had been Europe's most important centers of trade, manufacturing, and finance. The most powerful European states, however, were the kingdoms of England, France, and Spain. During the late fifteenth and sixteenth centuries, rulers of these lands, known as the "new monarchs," marshaled their resources, curbed the nobility, and built strong centralized regimes.

**Finance** The new monarchs included Henry VIII of England, Louis XI and Francis I of France, and Fernando and Isabel of Spain. All the new monarchs sought to increase their wealth by developing new sources of revenue. The French kings levied direct taxes on sales, households, and the salt trade. A new sales tax dramatically boosted Spanish royal income in the sixteenth century. For fear of provoking rebellion, the English kings did not introduce new taxes, but they increased revenues by raising fines and fees for royal services. Moreover, after Henry VIII severed ties between the English and Roman churches, he shut down all of the monasteries and took possession of all their land and wealth. This financial windfall enabled Henry to enhance royal power by increasing the size of the state and adding to its responsibilities. After the English Reformation, for example, the state provided relief for the poor and support for orphans, which previously had been left to churches and monasteries.

**State Power** With their increased income the new monarchs enlarged their administrative staffs, which enabled them to collect taxes and implement royal policies more reliably than before. The French and Spanish monarchs also maintained standing armies that vastly increased their power with respect to the nobility. Their armies with thousands of infantrymen were too large for individual nobles to match, and they equipped their forces with cannons that were too expensive for nobles to purchase. The English kings did not need a standing army to put down the occasional rebellion that flared in their island realm and so did not go to the expense of supporting one. Yet they too increased their power with respect to the nobles by subjecting them to royal justice and forcing them to comply with royal policy.

The debates and disputes launched by the Protestant Reformation helped monarchs increase their authority. In lands that adopted Protestant faiths—including England, much of Germany, Denmark, and Sweden—rulers expropriated the monasteries and used church wealth to expand their powers. That option was not open to Roman Catholic kings, but Protestant movements provided them with a justification to mobilize resources, which they used against political as well as religious adversaries.

**The Spanish Inquisition** The **Spanish Inquisition** was the most distinctive institution that relied on religious justifications to advance state ends. Fernando and Isabel founded the Spanish Inquisition in 1478, and they obtained the approval of the pope to operate the institution as a royal agency. Its original task was to ferret out those who secretly practiced Judaism or Islam, but Charles also charged it with detecting Protestant heresy (beliefs contrary to the doctrines of the Roman church) in Spain. Throughout the late fifteenth and sixteenth centuries, the Spanish Inquisition served political as well as religious purposes. Moreover, its reach extended well beyond the Iberian peninsula. Just as the fear of witchcraft crossed the Atlantic Ocean and inspired witch-hunts in England's North American colonies, concerns about heresy also made their way to the Western Hemisphere, where inquisitors worked to protect Spanish colonies from heretical teachings.

Inquisitors had broad powers to investigate suspected cases of heresy. Popular legends have created an erroneous impression of the Spanish Inquisition as an institution running amok,

## INTERPRETING IMAGES

This engraving, *Judgment Scene at Spanish Inquisition,* depicts an *auto-da-fé,* or "act of faith," involving the execution of Jews by burning at the stake. An *auto-da-fé* more specifically was the ritual of public penance and punishment of condemned heretics. In 1492, the Catholic monarchy of Spain ordered the expulsion of Jews from Spain.

**Analyze** *What is the relationship between political and religious power depicted in this image? What is the significance of the expulsion of Jews from Spain in 1492 for other aspects of European and world history?*
Bettmann/Getty Images

framing innocent victims and routinely subjecting them to torture. In fact, inquisitors usually observed rules of evidence, and they released many suspects after investigations turned up no sign of heresy. Yet, when they detected the scent of heresy, inquisitors could be ruthless. They sentenced hundreds of victims to hang from the gallows or burn at the stake and imprisoned many others in dank cells for extended periods of time. Fear of the inquisition intimidated many into silence, and a strict Roman Catholic orthodoxy prevailed in Spain. The inquisition deterred nobles from adopting Protestant views out of political ambition, and it used its influence on behalf of the Spanish monarchy. From 1559 to 1576, for example, inquisitors imprisoned the archbishop of Toledo—the highest Roman Catholic church official in all of Spain—because of his political independence.

## Constitutional States

During the seventeenth and eighteenth centuries, as they sought to restore order after the Thirty Years' War, European states developed along two lines. Rulers in England and the Netherlands shared authority with representative institutions and created constitutional states, whereas monarchs in France, Spain, Austria, Prussia, and Russia concentrated power in their own hands and created a form of state known as absolute monarchy.

### Constitutional States

The island kingdom of England and the maritime Dutch republic did not have written constitutions specifying the powers of the state, but during the seventeenth century they evolved governments that claimed limited powers and recognized rights pertaining to individuals and representative institutions. Their **constitutional states** took different forms: in England a constitutional monarchy emerged, whereas the Netherlands produced a republic based on representative government. In neither land did constitutional government come easily into being: in England it followed a civil war, and in the Netherlands it emerged after a long struggle for independence. In both lands, however, constitutional government strengthened the state and provided a political framework that enabled merchants to flourish as never before in European experience.

### The English Civil War

Constitutional government came to England after political and religious disputes led to the **English Civil War** (1642–1649). From the early seventeenth century, the English kings had tried to institute new taxes without approval of the parliament, which for more than three centuries had traditionally approved new levies. While royal financial policies generated political tensions, religious disagreements aggravated matters further. As Anglicans, the kings supported a church with relatively ornate ceremonies and a hierarchy of bishops working under authority of the monarchs themselves. Meanwhile, however, many of the boldest and most insistent voices within parliament belonged to zealous Calvinists known as Puritans because they sought to purify the English church of any lingering elements, such as ornate ceremonies and a hierarchy of bishops, suggestive of Roman Catholic Christianity. By 1641, King Charles I and parliament were in dispute, unable to cooperate or even communicate effectively with each other. Both sides raised armies. In the conflicts that followed, parliamentary forces under the leadership of Oliver Cromwell (1599–1658) captured Charles, tried him for tyranny, and in an act that shocked all of Europe, marched him up on a platform and beheaded him in 1649.

In this contemporary painting, the executioner holds up the just-severed head of King Charles I of England. The spectacle of a royal execution overcomes one woman, who faints (at bottom). How does the image of a beheaded king reflect the ongoing political changes in Europe?
Art Collection 2/Alamy Stock Photo

**The Glorious Revolution** In the absence of a king, Cromwell's Puritan regime took power but soon degenerated into a disagreeable dictatorship, prompting parliament to restore the monarchy in 1660 by installing Charles II (the son of the last king). The monarchy and parliament, however, soon resumed their conflicts. The issue came to a head a few decades later in a bloodless change of power known to some as the **Glorious Revolution** (1688–1689), when parliament deposed King James II and invited his daughter Mary and her Dutch husband, William of Orange, to assume the throne. The resulting arrangement provided that kings would rule in cooperation with parliament, thus guaranteeing that nobles, merchants, and other constituencies would enjoy representation in government affairs.

**The Dutch Republic** As in England, a potent combination of political and religious tensions led to conflict from which constitutional government emerged in the Netherlands. In the mid-sixteenth century, authority over the Low Countries, including modern-day Belgium as well as the Netherlands, rested with King Philip II of Spain. In 1567 Philip, a devout Roman Catholic, moved to suppress an increasingly popular Calvinist movement in the Netherlands—a measure that provoked large-scale rebellion against Spanish rule. In 1579 a group of Dutch provinces formed an anti-Spanish alliance, and in 1581 they proclaimed themselves the independent United Provinces. Representative assemblies organized local affairs in each of the provinces, and on this foundation political leaders built a Dutch republic. Spain did not officially recognize the independence of the United Provinces until the end of the Thirty Years' War in 1648, but the Dutch republic was effectively organizing affairs in the northern Low Countries by the early seventeenth century.

In many ways, the constitutional governments of England and the Dutch republic represented historical experiments. Apart from the Roman republic in classical times and a few Italian city-states of the medieval and Renaissance eras, European peoples had little experience with representative government. In their responses to political crises, popular leaders in both England and the Netherlands found it possible to mobilize support by appealing to the political and religious interests of broad constituencies and making a place for them in the government. The result was a pair of states that effectively harnessed popular support and used it to magnify state power.

In both England and the Dutch republic, merchants were especially prominent in political affairs, and state policy in both lands favored maritime trade and the building of commercial empires overseas. The constitutional states allowed entrepreneurs to pursue their economic interests with minimal

Although best known as Louis XIII's "first minister," Cardinal Richelieu also gained fame for his patronage of the arts. Most notably, he founded the Académie Française, the learned society responsible for matters pertaining to the French language.
Alfredo Dagli Orti/Shutterstock

interference from public authorities, and during the late seventeenth and eighteenth centuries, both states experienced extraordinary prosperity as a result of those policies. Indeed, in many ways the English and Dutch states represented an alliance between merchants and rulers that worked to the benefit of both. Merchants supported the state with the wealth that they generated through trade—especially overseas trade—while rulers followed policies that looked after the interests of their merchants.

## Absolute Monarchies

Whereas constitutional states devised ways to share power and authority, absolute monarchies found other ways to increase state power. **Absolutism** stood on a theoretical foundation known as the divine right of kings. This theory held that kings derived their authority from God and served as "God's lieutenants upon earth." There was no role in divine-right theory for common subjects or even nobles in public affairs: the monarch made law and determined policy. Noncompliance or disobedience merited punishment, and rebellion was a despicable act tantamount to blasphemy. In practice, absolute monarchs always relied on support from nobles and other social groups, but the claims of divine-right theory clearly reflected efforts at royal centralization.

The most conspicuous absolutist state was the French monarchy. The architect of French absolutism was a prominent church official, Cardinal **Richelieu,** who served as chief minister to King Louis XIII from 1624 to 1642. Richelieu worked systematically to undermine the power of the nobility and enhance the authority of the king. He destroyed nobles' castles and ruthlessly crushed aristocratic conspiracies. As a counterweight to the nobility, Richelieu built a large bureaucracy staffed by commoners loyal to the king. He also appointed officials to supervise the implementation of royal policy in the provinces. Finally, Richelieu attacked French Calvinists, who often allied with independent nobles, and destroyed their political and military power, although he allowed them to continue observing their faith. By midcentury France was under control of a tightly centralized absolute monarchy.

**The Sun King** The ruler who best epitomized royal absolutism was King **Louis XIV** (reigned 1643–1715), who once reportedly declared that he was himself the state: *"l'état, c'est moi."* Known as *le roi soleil* ("the sun king"), Louis surrounded himself with splendor befitting one who ruled by divine right. During the 1670s he built a magnificent residence at **Versailles,** a royal hunting lodge near Paris, and in the 1680s he moved his court there. Louis's palace at Versailles was the largest building in Europe, with 230 acres of formal gardens and 1,400 fountains. Because Louis did not want to wait years for saplings to grow, he ordered laborers to dig up 25,000 fully grown trees and haul them to Versailles for transplanting.

The sun king was the center of attention at Versailles. Court officials hovered around him and tended to his every need. All prominent nobles established residences at Versailles for their families and entourages. Louis strongly encouraged them to live at court, where he and his staff could keep an eye on them, and ambitious nobles gravitated there anyway in hopes of winning influence with the king. Louis himself was the arbiter of taste and style at Versailles, where he lavishly patronized painters, sculptors, architects, and writers whose creations met with his approval.

While nobles living at Versailles mastered the intricacies of court ritual and attended banquets, concerts, operas, balls, and theatrical performances, Louis and his ministers ran the state. In effect, Louis provided the nobility with luxurious accommodations and endless entertainment in exchange for absolute rule. From Versailles, Louis and his advisers promulgated laws and controlled a large standing army that kept order throughout the land. They also promoted economic development by supporting the establishment of new industries, building roads and canals, abolishing internal tariffs,

**Richelieu** (RISH-uh-loo)
**Versailles** (vehr-SEYE)

## INTERPRETING IMAGES

The French painter Hyacinthe Rigaud, renowned for his portrait paintings of the royalty and nobility of Europe, created this vision of Louis XIV. Louis' reign, from 1643 to his death in 1715, lasted seventy-two years, three months, and eighteen days, and is the longest documented reign of any European monarch.

**Analyze** *Consider this portrait in contrast to the illustration of Peter the Great on the next page. How do these depictions indicate the contrast between the status of France and Russia in the 17th and early 18th centuries?*

SuperStock/Getty Images

and encouraging exports. Finally, they waged a series of wars designed to enlarge French boundaries and establish France as the preeminent power in Europe.

**Absolutism in Russia** Louis XIV was not the only absolute monarch of early modern Europe: Spanish, Austrian, and Prussian rulers embraced similar policies. The potential of absolutism to increase state power was particularly conspicuous in the case of Russia, where tsars of the Romanov dynasty (1613–1917) tightly centralized government functions. (*Tsar,* sometimes spelled *czar,* is a Russianized form of the term *caesar,* which Russian rulers borrowed from Byzantine emperors, who in turn had borrowed it from the classical Roman Empire to signify their imperial status.) The **Romanovs** inherited a state that had rapidly expanded its boundaries since the mid-fourteenth century. Building on the foundation of a small principality around the trading city of Moscow, by 1600 Russia had become a vast empire extending from the Arctic seas in the north to the Caspian Sea in the south, with an increasing presence in the tundra and forests of Siberia as well.

**Peter I** Most important of the Romanov tsars was Peter I (reigned 1682–1725), widely known as **Peter the Great,** who inaugurated a thoroughgoing process of state transformation. Peter had a burning desire to make Russia, a huge but underpopulated land, into a great military power like those that had recently emerged in western Europe. In pursuit of that goal, he worked to transform Russia on the model of western European lands. In 1697–1698 he led a large party of Russian observers on a tour of Germany, the Netherlands, and England to learn about western European administrative methods and military technology. His traveling companions often behaved crudely by western European standards: they consumed beer, wine, and brandy in quantities that astonished their hosts, and King William III sent Peter a bill for damages done by his entourage at the country house where they lodged in England. (Among other things, Peter had ruined the gardens by having his men march through them in military formation.)

Upon returning to Moscow, Peter set Russia spinning. He reformed the army by offering better pay and drafting peasants who served for life as professional soldiers. He provided his forces with extensive training and equipped them with modern weapons. He ordered aristocrats to study mathematics and geometry so that they could calculate how to aim cannons accurately, and he began the construction of a navy with an eye toward domination of the Baltic and other northern seas. He also overhauled the government bureaucracy to facilitate tax collection and improve administrative efficiency. His transformation of Russia even involved a cosmetic makeover, as he commanded his aristocratic subjects to wear western European fashions and ordered men to shave their traditional beards. These measures, which were extremely unpopular among conservative Russians, provoked spirited protest among those who resented the influence of western European ways. Yet Peter insisted on observance of his policies—to the point that he reportedly went into the streets and personally hacked the beards off recalcitrants' faces. Perhaps the best symbol of his policies was St. Petersburg, a newly built seaport that Peter opened in 1703 to serve as a magnificent capital city and haven for Russia's fledgling navy.

**Catherine II and the Limits of Reform** The most able of Peter's successors was Catherine II (reigned 1762–1796), also known as **Catherine the Great.** Like Peter, Catherine sought to make Russia a great power. She worked to improve governmental efficiency by dividing her vast empire into fifty administrative provinces, and she promoted economic development in Russia's towns. For a while, she even worked to improve the conditions of Russia's oppressed peasantry by restricting the punishments that noble landowners could inflict on the serfs who worked their lands. She sought to eliminate common penalties such as torture, beating, and the mutilation of individuals by cutting off their noses, ears, or tongues.

Yet her interest in social reform cooled rapidly when it seemed to inspire challenges to her rule. She faced a particularly unsettling rebellion in 1773 and 1774, when a disgruntled former soldier named **Yemelian Pugachev** mounted an uprising in the steppe lands north of the Caspian Sea. Pugachev raised a motley army of adventurers, exiles, peasants, and serfs who killed thousands of noble landowners and government officials before imperial forces crushed the uprising. Government authorities took the captured Pugachev to Moscow in chains, beheaded him, quartered his body, and displayed its parts throughout the city as a warning against rebellion. Thereafter, Catherine's first concern was the preservation of autocratic rule rather than the transformation of Russia according to western European models.

Thus, in Russia as in other European lands, absolutist policies resulted in tight centralization and considerable strengthening of the state. The enhanced power that flowed from absolutism became dramatically clear in the period 1772 to 1797, when Austria, Prussia, and Catherine II's Russia picked the weak kingdom of Poland apart. In a series of three "partitions," the predatory absolutist states seized Polish territory and absorbed it into their own realms, ultimately wiping Poland entirely off the map. The lesson of the partitions was clear: any European state that hoped to survive needed to construct an effective government that could respond promptly to challenges and opportunities.

Tsar Peter the Great, with a pair of shears, readies himself to remove the beard of a conservative noble. Peter had traveled widely in Europe, and he wanted to impose newer European customs on his subjects. That included being more cleanly shaved. Nobles wishing to keep their beloved beards had to pay a yearly tax to do so.
akg-images/Newscom

## INTERPRETING IMAGES

Russian portrait of the German-born empress of Russia, Catherine II. Although admired by many Russians as a source of national pride, she is also remembered as a ruthless ruler who affirmed absolutism and extended serfdom on a large scale.

**Analyze** *How is Catherine the Great depicted as a monarch in this image? Why is she described a "ruthless" when her predecessor Peter the Great is not?*

DEA/A. Dagli Orti/De Agostini/Getty Images

## The European States System

Whether they relied on absolutist or constitutional principles, European governments of early modern times built states much more powerful than those of their medieval predecessors. This round of state development led to difficulties within Europe because conflicting interests fueled interstate competition and war. In the absence of an imperial authority capable of

**Yemelian Pugachev** (yehm-eel-ian puh-gah-chehf)

imposing and maintaining order in Europe, sovereign states had to find other ways to resolve conflicts.

**The Peace of Westphalia** The Thirty Years' War demonstrated the chaos and devastation that conflict could bring. In an effort to avoid tearing their society apart, European states ended the Thirty Years' War with the **Peace of Westphalia** (1648), which laid the foundations for a system of independent, competing states. Almost all the European states participated in drafting the Peace of Westphalia, and by the treaty's terms they regarded one another as sovereign and equal. They also mutually recognized their rights to organize their own domestic affairs, including religious affairs. Rather than envisioning imperial or papal or some other sort of supreme authority, the Peace of Westphalia entrusted political and diplomatic affairs to states acting in their own interests. European religious unity had disappeared, and the era of the sovereign state had arrived.

The Peace of Westphalia did not bring an end to war. Indeed, war was almost constant in early modern Europe. Most conflicts were minor affairs inaugurated by monarchs seeking to extend their authority to new lands or to reclaim territories seized by others, but they nevertheless disrupted local economies and drained resources. A few wars, however,

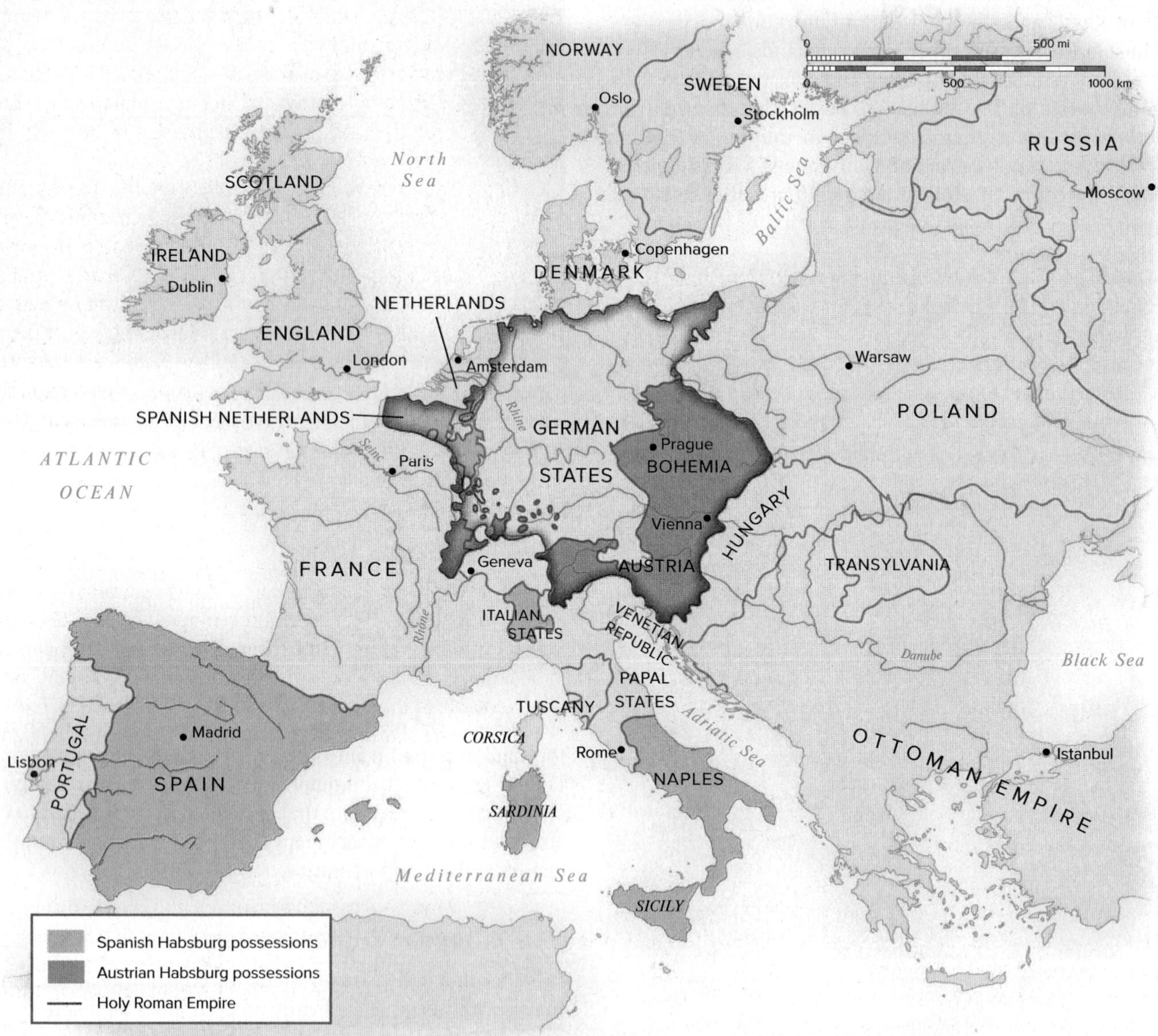


**MAP 11.2 Europe after the Peace of Westphalia, 1648.**

Compare this map with Map 23.1.

***How have the boundaries of the Holy Roman Empire changed, and why?***

grew to sizable proportions. Most notable among them were the wars of Louis XIV and the Seven Years' War. Between 1668 and 1713, the sun king sought to expand his borders east into Germany and to absorb Spain and the Spanish Netherlands into his kingdom. That prospect prompted England, the United Provinces, and Austria to mount a coalition against Louis. Later, the Seven Years' War (1756–1763) pitted France, Austria, and Russia against Britain and Prussia, and it merged with conflicts between France and Britain in India and North America to become a global war for imperial supremacy.

**The Balance of Power** These shifting alliances illustrate the principal foundation of European diplomacy in early modern times—the balance of power. No ruler wanted to see another state dominate all the others. Thus, when any particular state began to grow too strong, others formed coalitions against it. Balance-of-power diplomacy was risky business: it was always possible that a coalition might repress one strong state only to open the door for another. Yet, in playing balance-of-power politics, statesmen prevented the building of empires and ensured that Europe would be a land of independent, sovereign, competing states.

**Military Development** Frequent wars and balance-of-power diplomacy drained the resources of individual states but strengthened European society as a whole. European states competed vigorously and sought to develop the most expert military leadership and the most effective weapons for their arsenals. States organized military academies where officers received advanced education in strategy and tactics and learned how to maintain disciplined forces. Demand for powerful weapons stimulated the development of a sophisticated armaments industry that turned out ever more lethal products. Gun foundries manufactured cannons of increasing size, range, power, and accuracy as well as small arms that allowed infantry to unleash withering volleys against their enemies.

In China, India, and Islamic lands, imperial states had little or no incentive to encourage similar technological innovation in the armaments industry. These states possessed the forces and weapons they needed to maintain order within their boundaries, and they rarely encountered foreign threats backed up with superior armaments. In Europe, however, failure to keep up with the latest improvements in arms technology could lead to defeat on the battlefield and decline in state power. Thus Europeans continuously sought to improve their military arsenals, and as a result, by the eighteenth century European armaments outperformed all others.

## EARLY CAPITALIST SOCIETY

While the Protestant Reformation and the emergence of sovereign states brought religious and political change, a rapidly expanding population and economy encouraged the development of capitalism, which in turn led to a restructuring of European economy and society. Technologies of communication and transportation enabled businessmen to profit from distant markets, and merchants and manufacturers increasingly organized their affairs with the market rather than local communities in mind.

Capitalism generated considerable wealth, but its effects were uneven and sometimes unsettling. Economic development and increasing prosperity were noticeable in western Europe, particularly England, France, Germany, and the Netherlands. Yet eastern Europe experienced much less economic growth, as Poland and Russia increasingly became suppliers of grain and raw materials rather than centers of trade or production. Even in western Europe, early capitalism encouraged social change that sometimes required painful adjustments to new conditions.

### Population Growth and Urbanization

**American Food Crops** The foundation of European economic expansion in early modern times was a rapidly growing population, which reflected improved nutrition and decreasing mortality. The Columbian exchange enriched European diets by introducing new food crops to European fields and tables. Most notable of the introductions was the potato, which during the sixteenth and seventeenth centuries enjoyed the reputation of being an aphrodisiac. Although potatoes probably did not inspire much romantic ardor, they provided a welcome source of carbohydrates for peasants and laborers who were having trouble keeping up with the rising price of bread. From Ireland to Russia and from Scandinavia to the Mediterranean, cultivators planted potatoes and harvested crops that added calories to European diets. American maize also made its way to Europe. Maize, however, served mostly as feed for livestock rather than as food for human consumption, although peasants sometimes used cornmeal to make bread or porridges like polenta. Other American crops, such as tomatoes and peppers, added vitamins and tangy flavor to European diets.

**How the Past Shapes the Future**

**The Columbian Exchange**

As discussed in chapter 22, the Columbian exchange introduced new food crops that provided vital nutrition to ordinary people in Europe, which in turn helped fuel an impressive round of population growth across the region at precisely the same time indigenous American societies were devastated by European diseases. Yet European reliance on certain American food crops—especially the potato—would, over time, result in a dangerous dependency that led to famine when the crop failed, as it did in Ireland in 1845. Consider the ways that the exchange of items as seemingly mundane as new food crops can help shape historical developments over the long term, in both positive and negative ways.

While recently introduced American crops improved European diets, old diseases lost some of their ferocity. Smallpox continued to carry off about 10 percent of Europe's infants, and dysentery, influenza, tuberculosis, and typhus claimed victims among young and old, rich and poor alike. Yet better-nourished populations were better able to resist those maladies. Bubonic plague, a virulent epidemic killer during the fourteenth and fifteenth centuries, receded from European society. After its initial onslaught in the mid-fourteenth century, plague made periodic appearances throughout the early modern era. After the mid-seventeenth century, however, epidemics were rare and isolated events. The last major outbreaks of plague in Europe occurred in London in 1660 and Marseilles in 1720. By the mid-seventeenth century, epidemic disease was almost negligible as an influence on European population.

**Population Growth** Although European birthrates did not rise dramatically in early modern times, decreasing mortality resulted in rapid population growth. In 1500 the population of Europe, including Russia, was about 81 million. During the sixteenth century, as Europe recovered from epidemic plague, the population rose to 100 million. The Thirty Years' War—along with the famine and disease that the war touched off—led to population decline from about 1620 to 1650, but by 1700 European population had rallied and risen to 120 million. During the next century it grew by an additional 50 percent to 180 million.

**Urbanization** Rapid population growth drove a process of equally rapid urbanization. Some cities grew because rulers chose them as sites of government. Madrid, for example, was a minor town with a few thousand inhabitants until 1561 when King Philip II decided to locate his capital there. By 1600 the population of Madrid had risen to 65,000, and by 1630 it had reached 170,000. Other cities were commercial and industrial as well as government centers, and their numbers expanded along with the European economy. In the mid-sixteenth century, for example, the population of Paris was about 130,000, and London had about 60,000 inhabitants. A century later the population of both cities had risen to 500,000. Other European cities also experienced growth, even if it was not so dramatic as in Madrid, Paris, and London: Amsterdam, Berlin, Copenhagen, Dublin, Stockholm, Vienna, and others became prominent European cities during the early modern era.

## Early Capitalism and Protoindustrialization

**The Nature of Capitalism** Population growth and rapid urbanization helped spur a round of remarkable economic development. This economic growth coincided with the emergence of **capitalism**—an economic system in which private parties make their goods and services available on a free market and seek to take advantage of market conditions to profit from their activities. Whether they are single individuals or large companies, private parties own the land, machinery, tools, equipment, buildings, workshops, and raw materials needed for production. Private parties pursuing their own economic interests hire workers and decide for themselves what to produce: economic decisions are the prerogative of capitalist businessmen, not governments or social superiors. The center of a capitalist system is the market in which business owners compete with one another, and the forces of supply and demand determine the prices received for goods and services. If business owners organize their affairs efficiently, they realize handsome profits when they place their goods and services on the market. Otherwise, they incur losses and perhaps even lose their businesses.

The desire to accumulate wealth and realize profits was by no means new. Ever since the introduction of agriculture and the production of surplus crops, some individuals and groups had accumulated great wealth. Indeed, for several thousand years before the early modern era, merchants in China, southeast Asia, India, southwest Asia, the Mediterranean basin, and sub-Saharan Africa had pursued commercial ventures in hopes of realizing profits. Banks, investors, and insurance underwriters had supported privately organized commercial ventures throughout much of the Eastern Hemisphere since the postclassical era (500–1500 C.E.).

**Supply and Demand** During early modern times, however, European merchants and entrepreneurs transformed their society in a way that none of their predecessors had done. The capitalist economic order developed as individuals learned to take advantage of market conditions by building efficient networks of transportation and communication. Dutch merchants might purchase cheap grain from Baltic lands such as Poland or Russia, for example; store it in Amsterdam until they learned about a famine in the Mediterranean; and then transport it and sell it in southern France or Spain. Their enormous profits fueled suspicions that they took advantage of those in difficulty, but their activities also supplied hungry communities with the necessities of life, even if the price was high.

Private parties organized an array of institutions and services to support early capitalism. Banks, for example, appeared in all the major commercial cities of Europe: they held funds on account for safekeeping and granted loans to merchants or entrepreneurs launching new business ventures. Banks also published business newsletters—forerunners of the *Wall Street Journal* and *Fortune* magazine—that provided readers with reports on prices, information about demand for commodities in distant markets, and political news that could have an impact on business. Insurance companies mitigated financial losses from risky undertakings such as transoceanic voyages. Stock exchanges arose in the major European cities and provided markets where investors could buy and sell shares in joint-stock companies and trade in other commodities as well.

**Joint-Stock Companies** **Joint-stock companies** were especially important institutions in early capitalist society. Large trading companies such as the English East India Company and its Dutch counterpart, the Vereenigde Oost-Indische

The Old Stock Exchange of Amsterdam, depicted here in a painting of the mid-seventeenth century, attracted merchants, investors, entrepreneurs, and businessmen from all over Europe. There they bought and sold shares in joint-stock companies such as the VOC and dealt in all manner of commodities traded in Amsterdam.
Amsterdam Historisch Museum (INV.NR.SA3025)

Compagnie (VOC), spread the risks attached to expensive business enterprises and also took advantage of extensive communications and transportation networks. The trading companies organized commercial ventures on a larger scale than ever before. They were the principal foundations of the global economy that emerged in early modern times, and they were the direct ancestors of contemporary multinational corporations.

**Politics and Empire** Capitalism did not develop in a political vacuum. To the contrary, it emerged with the active support of government authorities who saw a capitalist order as the one best suited to their individual and collective interests. Merchants were especially influential in the affairs of the English and Dutch states, so it is not surprising that these lands adopted policies that were most favorable to capitalist enterprises throughout the early modern era. The English and Dutch states recognized individuals' rights to possess private property, enforced their contracts, protected their financial interests, and settled disputes between parties to business transactions. They also chartered joint-stock companies and authorized some of them to explore, conquer, and colonize distant lands in search of commercial opportunities. Thus early capitalism developed in the context of imperialism, as European peoples established fortified trading posts in Asia and colonial regimes in both southeast Asia and the Americas. Indeed, imperial expansion and colonial rule were crucial

An anonymous engraver depicts activity in a Dutch shipyard where workers build a massive, oceangoing sailing ship. In the seventeenth century, Dutch ships were inexpensive to operate, yet they accommodated abundant cargoes. What kinds of cargoes were Dutch ships likely to carry in this period?
North Wind Picture Archives/Alamy Stock Photo

for the development of capitalism because they enabled European merchants to gain access to the natural resources and commodities that they distributed so effectively through their transportation networks.

Quite apart from its influence on trade and the distribution of goods, capitalism encouraged European entrepreneurs to organize new ways to manufacture goods. For centuries, craft guilds had monopolized the production of goods such as textiles and metalwares in European towns and cities. Guilds fixed prices and wages, and they regulated standards of quality. They did not seek to realize profits so much as to protect markets and preserve their members' places in society. As a result, they actively discouraged competition and sometimes resisted technological innovation.

**Putting-out System** Capitalist entrepreneurs seeking profits found the guilds cumbersome and inflexible, so they sidestepped them and moved production into the countryside. Instead of relying on urban artisans to produce cloth, for example, they organized a "putting-out system" by which they delivered unfinished materials such as raw wool to rural households. Men and women in the countryside would then spin the wool into yarn, weave the yarn into cloth, cut the cloth according to patterns, and assemble the pieces into garments. The entrepreneur paid workers for their services, picked up the finished goods, and sold them on the market. During the seventeenth and eighteenth centuries, entrepreneurs moved the production of cloth, nails, pins, pots, and many other goods into the countryside through the putting-out system.

Because rural labor was usually plentiful, entrepreneurs spent relatively little on wages and realized handsome profits on their ventures. The putting-out system represented an early effort to organize efficient industrial production. Indeed, some historians refer to the seventeenth and eighteenth centuries as an age of **protoindustrialization.** The putting-out system remained a prominent feature of European society until the rise of industrial factories in the nineteenth century.

## Social Change in Early Modern Europe

Capitalist economic development brought significant change to European lands. The putting-out system, for example, introduced considerable sums of money into the countryside. Increased wealth brought material benefits, but it also undermined long-established patterns of rural life. The material standards of rural life rose dramatically: peasant households acquired more cabinets, furnishings, and tableware, and rural residents wore better clothes, ate better food, and drank better wine. Individuals suddenly acquired incomes that enabled them to pursue their own economic interests and to become financially independent of their families and neighbors. When young adults and women began to earn their own incomes, however, many feared that they might slip out of the control of their families and abandon their kin who continued to work at agricultural tasks.

The putting-out system did not become a prominent feature of production in eastern Europe, but early capitalism prompted deep social change there as well as in lands to the west. Eastern Europe had few cities in early modern times, so in expansive agrarian states such as Poland, Bohemia, and Russia, most people had no alternative to working in the countryside. Landlords took advantage of this situation by forcing peasants to work under extremely harsh conditions.

**Serfdom in Russia** Russia in particular was a vast but sparsely populated empire with little trade or manufacturing. Out of a concern to retain the allegiance of the powerful nobles who owned most of Russia's land, the Romanov tsars restricted the freedoms of most Russian peasants and tied them to the land as serfs. The institution of **serfdom** had emerged in the early middle ages as a labor system that required peasants to provide labor services for landowners and prevented them from marrying or moving away without their landlords' permission. After the fifteenth century, serfdom gradually came to an end in western Europe. In eastern Europe, however, landowners and rulers tightened restrictions on peasants during the sixteenth century, and in Russia the institution of serfdom survived until the nineteenth century. In effect, the Romanovs won the support of the Russian nobles by ensuring that laborers would be available to work their estates, which otherwise would have been worthless. In 1649 the government enacted a law code that provided for tight state control over the Russian labor force by establishing a rigid, castelike social order that sharply restricted both occupational and geographic mobility. The law of 1649 did not legally turn serfs into chattel slaves, but in fact the line between the two was extremely blurred: for example, during the late seventeenth and eighteenth centuries landlords commonly sold serfs to one another as if they were indeed private property. Under those conditions, landlords operated estates with inexpensive labor and derived enormous incomes from the sale of agricultural products on the market.

These arrangements played crucial roles in the emergence of capitalism. In the larger economy of early modern Europe, eastern European lands relied on serfs to cultivate grains and provide raw materials such as timber for export to western Europe, where merchants and manufacturers were able to employ free wage labor in building a capitalist economy. Already by the early sixteenth century, consumers in the Netherlands depended for their survival on grains imported from Poland and Russia through the Baltic Sea. Thus it was possible for capitalism to flourish in western Europe only because the peasants and semifree serfs of eastern Europe provided inexpensive foods and raw materials that fueled economic development. From its earliest days, capitalist economic organization had implications for peoples and lands far removed from the centers of capitalism itself.

**Profits and Ethics** Capitalism also posed moral challenges. Medieval theologians had regarded profit-making activity as morally dangerous because profiteers looked to their own advantage rather than the welfare of the larger community. Church officials even attempted to forbid the collection of interest on loans because they considered interest an unearned and immoral profit. But profit was the lifeblood of capitalism, and bankers were not willing to risk large sums of money on business ventures without realizing returns on their investments in the form of interest. Even as it transformed the European economy, capitalism found advocates who sought to explain its principles and portray it as a socially beneficial form of economic organization. Most important of the early apostles of capitalism was the Scottish philosopher Adam Smith (1723–1790), who argued that society would prosper when individuals pursued their own economic interests.

Nevertheless, the transition to capitalist society was long and painful. When individuals abandoned the practices of their ancestors and declined to help those who had fallen on hard times, their neighbors readily interpreted their actions as expressions of selfishness rather than economic prudence. Thus capitalist economic practices generated deep social strains, which often manifested themselves in violence. Bandits plagued the countryside of early modern Europe, and muggers turned whole sections of large cities into danger zones. Some historians believe that witch-hunting activities reflected social tensions generated by early capitalism and that accusations of witchcraft represented hostility toward women who were becoming economically independent of their husbands and families.

**The Nuclear Family** In some ways, capitalism favored the nuclear family as the principal unit of society. For centuries European couples had mostly married late—in their mid-twenties—and set up independent households. Early capitalism offered opportunities for these independent families to increase their wealth by cultivating agricultural crops or producing goods for sale on the market. As nuclear families became more important economically, they also became more socially and emotionally independent. Love between a man and a woman became a more important consideration in the making of marriages than the interests of the larger extended families, and affection between parents and their children became a more important ingredient of family life. Capitalism did not necessarily cause these changes in family life, but it may have encouraged developments that helped to define the nature and role of the family in modern European society.

## TRANSFORMATIONS IN SCIENTIFIC THINKING

While experiencing religious, political, economic, and social change, western Europe also underwent intellectual and cultural transformation. Astronomers and physicists rejected classical Greek and Roman authorities, whose theories had dominated scientific thought during the middle ages, and based their understanding of the natural world on direct observation and mathematical reasoning. During the seventeenth and eighteenth centuries, they elaborated a new vision of the earth and the larger universe. Scholars relied on observation and mathematics to transform the natural sciences in a process known as the scientific revolution. The results of early modern science were so powerful that some European intellectuals sought to overhaul moral, social, and political thought by adapting scientific methods and relying on reason rather than traditional cultural authorities. Over time, their efforts weakened the influence of churches in western Europe and encouraged the development of secular values.

# SOURCES FROM THE PAST

## Adam Smith on the Capitalist Market

*Adam Smith (1723–1790) was a Scottish economist, philosopher, and author who devoted special thought to the nature of early capitalist society and the principles that made it work. In 1776 he published a lengthy book titled* An Inquiry into the Nature and Causes of the Wealth of Nations, *a vastly influential work that championed free, unregulated markets and capitalist enterprise as the principal ingredients of prosperity. Smith's optimism about capitalism sprang from his conviction that society as a whole benefits when individuals pursue their own economic interests and trade on a free market.*

**Every individual is continually exerting** himself to find out the most advantageous employment for whatever capital he can command. It is his own advantage, indeed, and not that of the society, which he has in view. . . .

As every individual, therefore, endeavours as much as he can both to employ his capital in the support of domestic industry, and so to direct that industry that its produce may be of the greatest value, every individual necessarily labours to render the annual revenue of the society as great as he can. He generally, indeed, neither intends to promote the public interest, nor knows how much he is promoting it. By preferring the support of domestic to that of foreign industry, he intends only his own security; and by directing that industry in such a manner as its produce may be of the greatest value, he intends only his own gain, and he is in this, as in many other cases, led by an invisible hand to promote an end which was no part of his intention. Nor is it always the worse for the society that it was no part of it. By pursuing his own interest he frequently promotes that of the society more effectually than when he really intends to promote it. I have never known much good done by those who affected to trade for the public good. It is an affectation, indeed, not very common among merchants, and very few words need be employed in dissuading them from it.

> Smith's notion of an "invisible hand" operating on the economy is famous. What do you think Smith meant by this?

What is the species of domestic industry which his capital can employ, and of which the produce is likely to be of the greatest value, every individual, it is evident, can, in his local situation, judge much better than any statesman or lawgiver can do for him. The statesman, who should attempt to direct private people in what manner they ought to employ their capitals, would not only load himself with a most unnecessary attention, but assume an authority which could safely be trusted, not only to no single person, but to no council or senate whatever, and which would nowhere be so dangerous as in the hands of a man who had folly and presumption enough to fancy himself fit to exercise it.

> Why, according to Smith, are individuals better able to judge how to spend their money than representatives of the state?

To give the monopoly of the home market to the produce of domestic industry, in any particular art or manufacture, is in some measure to direct private people in what manner they ought to employ their capitals, and must, in almost all cases, be either a useless or a hurtful regulation. If the produce of domestic industry can be brought there as cheap as that of foreign industry, the regulation is evidently useless. If it cannot, it must generally be hurtful. It is the maxim of every prudent master of a family, never to attempt to make at home what it will cost him more to make than to buy. The tailor does not attempt to make his own shoes, but buys them of the shoemaker. The shoemaker does not attempt to make his own clothes, but employs a tailor. The farmer attempts to make neither the one nor the other, but employs those different artificers. All of them find it for their interest to employ their whole industry in a way in which they have some advantage over their neighbours, and to purchase with a part of its produce, or, what is the same thing, with the price of a part of it, whatever else they have occasion for.

### For Further Reflection

- To what extent do you think Adam Smith's analysis reflected the experiences of his own times, and to what extent did they represent universally valid observations?
- What rationale does Smith provide for emphasizing the worth and goals of the individual over the "public good," "public interest," or "society"?
- What arguments might you lodge to counter his thesis?

*Source:* Adam Smith. *An Inquiry into the Nature and Causes of the Wealth of Nations.* Edinburgh: 1863, pp. 198–200.

## The Reconception of the Universe

**The Ptolemaic Universe** Until the seventeenth century, European astronomers based their understanding of the universe on the work of the Greek scholar Claudius Ptolemy of Alexandria. About the middle of the second century C.E., Ptolemy composed a work known as the *Almagest* that synthesized theories about the universe. Ptolemy envisioned a motionless earth surrounded by a series of nine hollow, concentric spheres that revolved around it. Each of the first seven spheres had one of the observable heavenly bodies—the sun, the moon, Mercury, Venus, Mars, Jupiter, and Saturn—embedded in its shell. The eighth sphere held the stars, and an empty ninth sphere surrounded the whole cosmos and provided the spin that kept all the others moving. Beyond the spheres Christian astronomers located heaven, the realm of God.

Following Ptolemy, astronomers believed that the heavens consisted of matter unlike any found on earth. Glowing like perfect jewels in the night skies, heavenly bodies were composed of a pure substance that did not experience change or corruption, and they were not subject to the physical laws that governed the world below the moon. They followed perfect circular paths in making their revolutions around the earth.

**Planetary Movement** Although theoretically attractive, this earth-centered, or geocentric, cosmology did not mesh readily with the erratic movements of the planets—a term that comes from the Greek word *planetes,* meaning "wanderer." From the vantage point of the earth, the planets often followed regular courses through the skies, but they sometimes slowed down, stopped, or even turned back on their courses—motions that would be difficult to explain if the planetary spheres revolved regularly around the earth. Astronomers went to great lengths to explain planetary behavior as the result of perfect circular movements. The result was an awkward series of adjustments known as epicycles—small circular revolutions that planets made around a point in their spheres, even while the spheres themselves revolved around the earth.

**The Copernican Universe** As astronomers accumulated data on planetary movements, most of them sought to reconcile their observations with Ptolemaic theory by adding increasing numbers of epicycles to their cosmic maps. In 1543, however, the Polish astronomer **Nicolaus Copernicus** published a treatise, *On the Revolutions of the Heavenly Spheres,* that broke with Ptolemaic theory and pointed European science in a new direction. Copernicus argued that the sun rather than the earth stood at the center of the universe and that the planets, including the earth, revolved around the sun.

Compared with Ptolemy's earth-centered universe, this new sun-centered, or heliocentric, theory harmonized much better with observational data, but it did not receive a warm welcome. Copernicus's ideas not only challenged prevailing scientific theories but also threatened cherished religious beliefs. His theory implied that the earth was just another planet and that humans did not occupy the central position in the universe. To some it also suggested the unsettling possibility that there might be other populated worlds in the universe—a notion that would be difficult to reconcile with Christian teachings, which held that the earth and humanity were unique creations of God.

## The Scientific Revolution

Although it was unpopular in many quarters, Copernicus's theory inspired some astronomers to examine the heavens in fresh ways. As evidence accumulated, it became clear that the **Ptolemaic universe** simply did not correspond with reality. Astronomers based their theories on increasingly precise observational data, and they relied on mathematical reasoning to organize the data. Gradually, they abandoned the Ptolemaic in favor of the Copernican model of the universe. Moreover, some of them began to apply their analytical methods to mechanics—the branch of science that deals with moving bodies—and by the mid-seventeenth century accurate observation and mathematical reasoning dominated both mechanics and astronomy. Indeed, reliance on observation and mathematics transformed the study of the natural world and brought about the process we now call the **scientific revolution.**

**Galileo Galilei** The works of two scientists—**Johannes Kepler** of Germany and **Galileo Galilei** of Italy—rang the death knell for the Ptolemaic universe. Kepler (1571–1630) demonstrated that planetary orbits are elliptical, not circular as in Ptolemaic theory. Galileo (1564–1642) showed that the heavens were not the perfect, unblemished realm that Ptolemaic astronomers assumed but, rather, a world of constant change. Galileo took a recently invented instrument—the telescope—turned it skyward, and reported observations that astonished his contemporaries. With his telescope he could see spots on the sun and mountains on the moon—observations that discredited the notion that heavenly bodies were smooth, immaculate, unchanging, and perfectly spherical. He also noticed four of the moons that orbit the planet Jupiter—bodies that no human being had ever before observed—and he caught sight of previously unknown distant stars, which implied that the universe was much larger than anyone had previously suspected.

In addition to his astronomical discoveries, Galileo contributed to the understanding of terrestrial motion. He designed ingenious experiments to show that the velocity of falling bodies depends not on their weight but, rather, on the height from which they fall. This claim brought him scorn from scientists who subscribed to scientific beliefs deriving from Aristotle. But it offered a better explanation of how moving bodies behave under the influence of the earth's gravitational pull. Galileo also anticipated the modern law of

---

**Ptolemaic** (TAWL-oh-may-ihk)

In this seventeenth-century engraving, Galileo Galilei faces the Inquisition, a Roman Catholic institution that prosecuted individuals accused of a wide variety of crimes related to heresy. At a trial in 1633, the Inquisition found Galileo "vehemently suspect of heresy," forced him to recant Copernicanism, and placed him under house arrest for the remainder of his life.
Stefano Bianchetti/Corbis Historical/Getty Images

inertia, which holds that a moving body will continue to move in a straight line until some force intervenes to check or alter its motion.

**Isaac Newton** The new approach to science culminated in the work of the English mathematician **Isaac Newton** (1642–1727), who depended on accurate observation and mathematical reasoning to construct a powerful synthesis of astronomy and mechanics. Newton outlined his views on the natural world in an epoch-making volume of 1687 titled *Mathematical Principles of Natural Philosophy.* Newton's work united the heavens and the earth in a vast, cosmic system. He argued that a law of universal gravitation regulates the motions of bodies throughout the universe, and he offered precise mathematical explanations of the laws that govern movements of bodies on the earth. Newton's laws of universal gravitation and motion enabled him to synthesize the sciences of astronomy and mechanics. They also allowed him to explain a vast range of seemingly unrelated phenomena, such as the ebb and flow of the tides, which move according to the gravitational pull of the moon, and the eccentric orbits of planets and comets, which reflect the gravitational influence of the sun, the earth, and other heavenly bodies. Until the twentieth century, Newton's universe served as the unquestioned framework for the physical sciences.

Newton's work symbolized the scientific revolution, but it by no means marked the end of the process by which observation and mathematical reasoning transformed European science. Inspired by the dramatic discoveries of astronomers and physicists, other scientists began to turn away from classical authorities and to construct fresh approaches to the understanding of the natural world. During the seventeenth and eighteenth centuries, anatomy, physiology, microbiology, chemistry, and botany underwent a thorough overhaul, as

# SOURCES FROM THE PAST

## Galileo Galilei, Letter to the Grand Duchess Christina

*The Italian physicist and astronomer Galileo Galilei (1564–1642) was one of the most important European scientists in the early 1600s. His staunch defense of Nicolaus Copernicus's theory of a sun-centered universe threatened Catholic clergy, who were worried that such a theory threatened the authority of both the Bible and the Church. In 1615 Galileo, himself a devout Catholic, defended his scientific beliefs and argued why they should not be condemned by the church in a published letter to Christina, the grand duchess of Tuscany. Although the Church forced Galileo to publicly renounce his scientific beliefs in 1632, over the long term his writings contributed greatly to the reconception of the universe using the new scientific methodology.*

**I am inclined to believe,** that the intention of the sacred Scriptures is to give to mankind the information necessary for their salvation, and which, surpassing all human knowledge can by no other means be accredited than by the mouth of the Holy Spirit. But I do not hold it necessary to believe, that the same God who has endowed us with senses, with speech, and intellect, intended that we should neglect the use of these, and seek by other means for knowledge which they are sufficient to procure us; especially in a science like astronomy, of which so little notice is taken in the Scriptures, that none of the planets, except the sun and moon, and, once or twice only, Venus under the name of Lucifer, are so much as named there. This therefore being granted, methinks that in the discussion of natural problems we ought not to begin at the authority of texts of Scripture, but at sensible experiments, and necessary demonstrations: for, from the divine word, the sacred Scripture and nature did both alike proceed, and I conceive that, concerning natural effects, that which either sensible experience sets before our eyes, or necessary demonstrations do prove unto us, ought not upon any account to be called into question, much less condemned, upon the testimony of Scriptural texts. . . Again, to command the very professors of astronomy that they of themselves see to the confuting of their own observations and demonstrations, is to enjoin a thing beyond all possibility of doing; for it is not only to command them not to see that which they do see, and not to understand that which they do understand, but it is to order them to seek for and to find the contrary of that which they happen to meet with. I would entreat these wise and prudent fathers, that they would with all diligence consider the difference that is between opinionative and demonstrative doctrines; . . . that it is not in the power of the professors of demonstrative sciences to change their opinions at pleasure, and adopt first one side and then another; and that there is a great difference between commanding a mathematician or a philosopher, and the disposing of a lawyer or a merchant; and that the demonstrated conclusions touching the things of nature and of the heavens cannot be changed with the same facility as the opinions are touching what is lawful or not in a contract, bargain, or bill of exchange. Therefore, first let these men apply themselves to examine the arguments of Copernicus and others, and leave the condemning of them as erroneous and heretical to whom it belongeth. . .

By what process does Galileo argue that people should explain natural phenomena?

What argument is Galileo using to demonstrate that the Bible, and religious figures, should not be used as an authority on matters of astronomy?

### For Further Reflection

- Why might religious authorities have found Galileo's astronomical observations threatening?
- Although Galileo appeared to renounce his scientific stance, he hid his work, which was published later. How does his argument here, as well as his preserved research, advance the cause of science beyond astronomy?

Source: *Life of Galileo: With Illustrations of the Advancement of Experimental Philosophy* (Boston, William Hyde and Company, 1832), 143–145. Bethune, Drinkwater, John Elliot. before Life of Galileo (full credit: Bethune, John Elliot Drinkwater. Life of Galileo Galilei: With Illustrations of the Advancement of Experimental Philosophy. Boston: William Hyde and Company, 1832), 143–145.

A portrait of Sir Isaac Newton (1642–1727) by Sir Godfrey Kneller (1646–1723), the leading portrait painter in England during the late seventeenth and early eighteenth centuries. Although commonly hailed as one of the most influential scientists of all time, Newton was more humble when judging his own achievements, writing to a fellow scientist: "If I have seen further it is by standing on the shoulders of giants."
Imagno/Hulton Fine Art Collection/Getty Images

scientists tested their theories against direct observation of natural phenomena and explained them in rigorous mathematical terms.

## Women and Science

In the sixteenth and seventeenth centuries, Europe's learned men challenged some of the most hallowed traditions concerning the nature of the physical universe and supplanted them with new scientific principles. Yet, when male scientists studied female anatomy, female physiology, and women's reproductive organs, they were commonly guided not by scientific observation but by tradition, prejudice, and fanciful imagination. William Harvey (1578–1657), the English physician who discovered the principles of the circulation of human blood, also applied his considerable talents to the study of human reproduction. After careful dissection and observation of female deer, chickens, and roosters, he hypothesized that women, like hens, served as mere receptacles for the "vivifying" male fluid. According to him, it was the male semen—endowed with generative powers so potent that it did not even have to reach the uterus to work its magic—from which the unfertilized egg received life and form. Anatomy, physiology, and limited reproductive function seemed to confirm the innate inferiority of women, adding a "scientific" veneer to the traditionally limited images, roles, and functions of women. With the arrival of printing, men were able to disseminate more widely those negative conclusions about women.

**Émilie du Châtelet** Despite prevailing critical attitudes, some women found themselves drawn to the new intellectual currents of the time. **Émilie du Châtelet** (1706–1749) established her reputation as a scientist with her three-volume work on the German mathematician Gottfried Leibniz (1646–1716)

Émilie du Châtelet was perhaps the most exceptional female scientist of the eighteenth century. Although she had to contend with the conventional demands on women, she remained committed to her study of Newton and science.
DEA/G. Dagli Orti/De Agostini/Getty Images

in 1740. Her crowning achievement, however, was her translation of Isaac Newton's monumental work *Principia Mathematica,* which has remained the standard French translation of the work. She did not simply render Newton's words into another language, however; rather, she explained his complex mathematics in graceful prose, transformed his geometry into calculus, and assessed the current state of Newtonian physics. She finished her work in the year of her death, at age forty-three, six days after giving birth to a child. Underscoring the difficulty of reconciling a woman's reproductive duties with her intellectual aspirations was her lover Voltaire's commentary. He declared in a letter to his friend Frederick II, King of Prussia (reigned 1740–1786), that du Châtelet was "a great man whose only fault was being a woman."

## CONCLUSION

During the early modern era, European society experienced a series of profound and sometimes painful changes. The Protestant Reformation ended the religious unity of western Europe, and intermittent religious conflict disrupted European society for a century and more. Centralizing monarchs strengthened their realms and built a society of sovereign, autonomous, and intensely competitive states with distinctive traditions. Capitalist entrepreneurs reorganized the production and distribution of manufactured goods, and although their methods led to increased wealth, their quest for efficiency and profits clashed with traditional values. Modern science based on direct observation and mathematical explanations emerged as a powerful tool for the investigation of, and encounters with, the natural world. At just the time that European merchants, colonists, and adventurers were seeking new opportunities and encounters in the larger world, European society was becoming more powerful, more experimental, and more competitive than ever before. Given that Europeans now possessed the latest armaments and were willing to use them to achieve political and economic goals, this combination would have profound effects for many regions of the world in the future.

## STUDY TERMS

absolutism (357)
Anglicans (349)
Calvinists (349)
capitalism (362)
Carolingian (352)
Catherine the Great (358)
Catholic Reformation (349)
Charles V (353)
constitutional states (355)
Council of Trent (349)
Émilie du Châtelet (370)
English Civil War (355)
Galileo Galilei (367)
Glorious Revolution (356)
Habsburgs (353)
Isaac Newton (368)
Johannes Gutenberg (348)
Johannes Kepler (367)
joint-stock companies (362)
Louis XIV (357)
Martin Luther (348)
Nicolaus Copernicus (367)
*Ninety-Five Theses* (346)
Peace of Westphalia (360)
Peter the Great (358)
Protestant Reformation (348)
protoindustrialization (364)
Ptolemaic universe (367)
Richelieu (357)
Romanov (358)
scientific revolution (367)
serfdom (365)
Society of Jesus (350)
Spanish Inquisition (354)
St. Ignatius Loyola (350)
Thirty Years' War (351)
Versailles (357)
witch-hunts (351)
Yemelian Pugachev (359)

## FOR FURTHER READING

Paul Dukes. *The Making of Russian Absolutism, 1613–1801.* 2nd ed. London, 2015. A succinct study of two disparate centuries, the seventeenth and eighteenth, and two influential tsars, Peter and Catherine.

Patricia Fara. *Pandora's Breeches: Women, Science, and Power in the Enlightenment.* London, 2004. An engaging account of the contributions women made to science in the seventeenth and eighteenth centuries.

Philip S. Gorski. *The Disciplinary Revolution: Calvinism and the Rise of the Early Modern State.* Chicago, 2003. Argues that the formation of strong European states was a result of religious and social control policies initiated by the Protestant Reformation.

Thomas S. Kuhn. *The Structure of Scientific Revolutions.* 3rd ed. Chicago, 1997. An influential theoretical work that views scientific thought in larger social and cultural contexts.

Brian P. Levack. *The Witch-Hunt in Early Modern Europe.* New York, 2006. A compact but comprehensive survey of European witchcraft beliefs and pursuit of witches in the sixteenth and seventeenth centuries.

Jerry Z. Muller. *The Mind and the Market: Capitalism in Modern European Thought.* New York, 2002. Broad history of the development of capitalism through the eyes of major European thinkers, including Adam Smith, Joseph Schumpeter, and Karl Marx.

Andrew Pettegree. *Reformation and the Culture of Persuasion.* Cambridge, 2005. Investigates why people chose to support the Reformation in an era before mass literacy.

Paolo Rossi. *The Birth of Modern Science.* Malden, Mass., 2001. Explores specific seventeenth-century value systems and traditions that were central to the rise of modern science.

Merry Wiesner-Hanks. *Women and Gender in Early Modern Europe,* 4th ed. Cambridge, 2019. Comprehensive overview of women's lives and of ideas about gender in the early modern period, with attention to race, migration, and global issues.

Peter Wilson. *The Thirty Years' War: Europe's Tragedy.* Cambridge, Mass., 2011. Comprehensive study of the destructiveness of the war and its social, political, and economic causes as well as its religious causes.

# CHAPTER 11 AP EXAM PRACTICE

Questions assume cumulative knowledge from this chapter and previous chapters.

## Section I

## Multiple Choice Questions

Use the passage below and your knowledge of world history to answer questions 1 - 3.

> Like many other peoples, Europeans had long believed that certain individuals possessed unusual powers to influence human affairs or discover secret information such as the identity of a thief. During the late fifteenth century, theologians developed a theory that witches derived their powers from the devil. According to that theory, witches made agreements to worship the devil in exchange for supernatural powers, including the ability to fly through the night on brooms, pitchforks, or animals. Theorists believed that the witches regularly flew off to distant places to attend the "witches' sabbath," a gathering that featured devil worship, lewd behavior, and the concoction of secret potions, culminating in sexual relations with the devil himself.
>
> *Source:* Bentley and Ziegler, *Traditions & Encounters: A Global Perspective on the Past*

1. Which of the following statements describes beliefs about witchcraft in sixteenth and seventeenth century Europe?
   (A) Only women could practice witchcraft.
   (B) Witches only existed in stories.
   (C) The fear that witches were in league with the devil was a recent theory.
   (D) There were several schools across Europe that taught magic and witchcraft.

2. Which of these statements about witch-hunting is NOT true?
   (A) Approximately 85% of the people convicted of witchcraft were women.
   (B) Secular courts were more likely to impose severe punishments while church courts usually gave lighter sentences.
   (C) Witches were thought to be responsible for crop failures, deaths, and infertility.
   (D) The majority of convicted witches were burned at the stake.

3. Which of these is a reasonable claim a historian could make about witch-hunting?
   (A) New ideas about witchcraft and the increase in witch trials may have been caused by social tensions from the rise of capitalism, religious wars, and expansion of state power.
   (B) German speaking countries were more likely to prosecute witches because the Habsburgs wanted to exert absolute power over the Holy Roman Empire.
   (C) As an alternative to executions, convicted witches were allowed to join merchant ships to Asia, Africa, and the Americas in the hope that they could control the weather.
   (D) Witch-hunting benefitted Europe because the witches were no longer about to destroy crops. This led to the population increases and urbanization.

Use the map below and your knowledge of world history to answer questions 4 and 5.

Sixteenth-century Europe
McGraw Hill

4. How were the Habsburgs able to gain control over so much of European territory?
   (A) Charles V inherited these lands because of a series of marriage alliances.
   (B) Charles V conquered Spain and Naples with a German army.
   (C) The Ottoman Empire gave Hungary and Austria to the Habsburgs to form a buffer state between their empires.
   (D) The desire to reform the Carolingian empire inspired rulers to make Charles V their heir.

5. Which of the following is NOT a reason Charles V was unable to become an absolutist monarch?
   (A) Charles was distracted by too many foreign and domestic problems.
   (B) There was no bureaucratic structure for the whole empire.
   (C) The Ottomans and the French worked together to prevent the Holy Roman Empire from becoming too strong.
   (D) Charles was only emperor for a few years before he retired in 1556 to join a monastery.

## Short Answer

6. Use the image below and your knowledge of world history to answer parts A, B, and C.

Tsar Peter the Great, with a pair of shears, readies himself to remove the beard of a conservative noble. Peter had traveled widely in Europe, and he wanted to impose newer European customs on his subjects. That included being more cleanly shaved. Nobles wishing to keep their beloved beards had to pay a yearly tax to do so.
akg-images/Newscom

(A) Describe ONE way that absolutist monarchs attempted to control the nobility.
(B) Explain ONE way that new monarchs built centralized regimes in Europe.
(C) Explain ONE reason the Protestant Reformation contributed to the founding of constitutionalist states.

7. Use the image below and your knowledge of world history to answer parts A, B, and C.

*The Ecstasy of Saint Teresa in the Church of Santa Maria della Vittoria in Rome, Italy.*
Stefano Valeri/Shutterstock

(A) Identify ONE similarity between the Protestant and Catholic reformations.
(B) Identify ONE difference between the Protestant and Catholic reformations.
(C) Explain ONE reason why the Protestant reformers were more successful spreading their ideas than earlier critics of the church had been.

8. Use your understanding of world history to answer parts A, B, and C.
(A) Explain ONE effect that religious changes had on ordinary people.
(B) Explain ONE effect that the growth of sovereign states had on ordinary people.
(C) Identify ONE effect that the transformation of Europe from 1450 to 1750 C.E.

# Section II

## Document-Based Question

Based on the documents below and your knowledge of world history, analyze the extent to which the era of the Scientific Revolution marks a change or a continuity between medieval and modern Europe.

In your response you should do the following:

- Respond to the prompt with a historically defensible thesis or claim that establishes a line of reasoning.
- Describe a broader historical context relevant to the prompt.
- Support an argument in response to the prompt using all documents.
- Use at least one additional piece of specific historical evidence (beyond that found in the documents) relevant to an argument about the prompt.
- Explain how or why the document's point of view, purpose, historical situation, and /or audience is relevant to an argument.
- Use evidence to corroborate, qualify, or modify an argument that addresses the prompt.

### Document 1

The Burning of Three Witches (1585), by Johann Jakob Wick. This illustration depicts the execution by burning of three accused "witches" in Baden, Switzerland on November 4, 1585.
The History Collection/Alamy Stock Photo

## Document 2

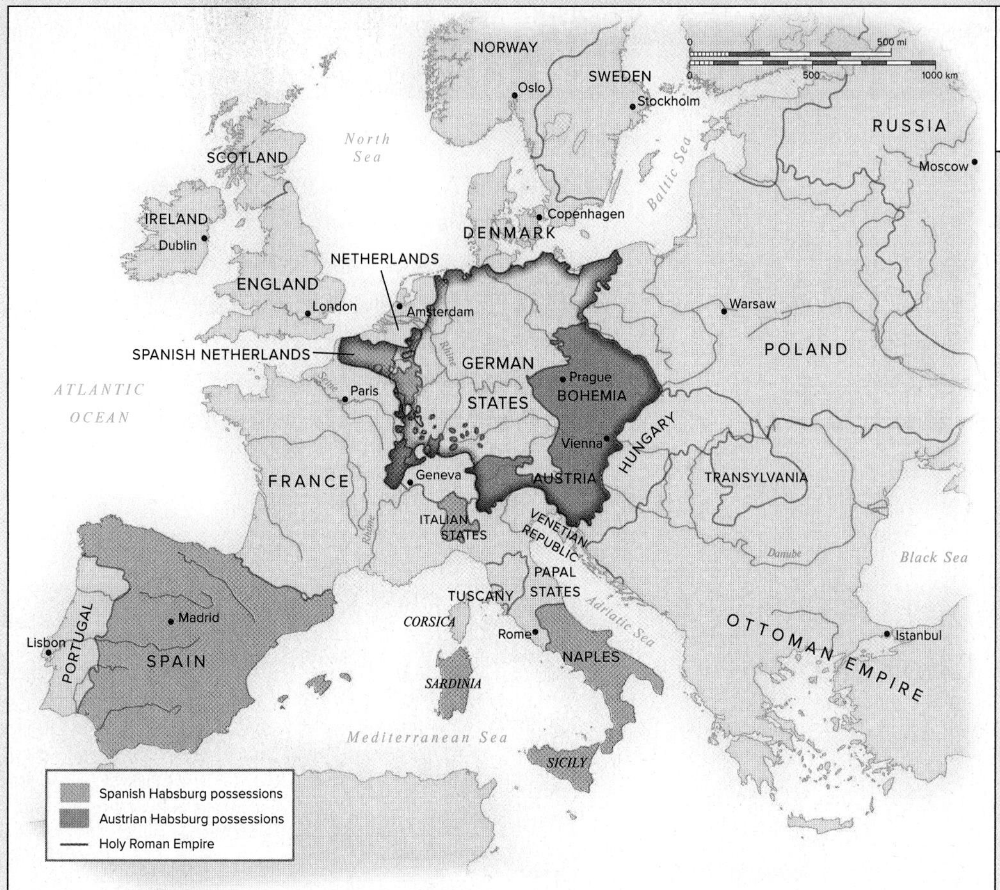


Europe after the Peace of Westphalia, 1648
McGraw Hill

## Document 3

But I do not hold it necessary to believe, that the same God who has endowed us with senses, with speech, and intellect, intended that we should neglect the use of these, and seek by other means for knowledge which they are sufficient to procure us; especially in a science like astronomy, of which so little notice is taken in the Scriptures, that none of the planets, except the sun and moon, and, once or twice only, Venus under the name of Lucifer, are so much as named there. This therefore being granted, methinks that in the discussion of natural problems we ought not to begin at the authority of texts of Scripture, but at sensible experiments, and necessary demonstrations: for, from the divine word, the sacred Scripture and nature did both alike proceed, and I conceive that, concerning natural effects, that which either sensible experience sets before our eyes, or necessary demonstrations do prove unto us, ought not upon any account to be called into question, much less condemned, upon the testimony of Scriptural texts. . .

*Source: Life of Galileo: With Illustrations of the Advancement of Experimental Philosophy* (Boston, William Hyde and Company, 1832), 143–145. Bethune, Drinkwater, John Elliot. before Life of Galileo (full credit: Bethune, John Elliot Drinkwater. Life of Galileo Galilei: With Illustrations of the Advancement of Experimental Philosophy. Boston: William Hyde and Company, 1832), 143–145.

## Long Essay

Develop a thoughtful and thorough historical argument that answers the question below. Begin your essay with a thesis statement and support it with relevant historical evidence.

Using specific examples and your knowledge of world history, evaluate the extent to which capitalism caused social changes in Europe from 1450 to 1750 C.E.

Chapter

# 12 The Integration of the Americas and Oceania with the Wider World



## ZOOMING IN ON ENCOUNTERS

### The Complicated Choices of Doña Marina

A remarkable young woman played a pivotal role in the Spanish conquest of Mexico. Sometimes called **Malintzin,** over the years she has come to be better known as **Doña Marina,** the name bestowed on her by Spanish forces. Doña Marina was born about 1500 in central Mexico. Her mother tongue was **Nahuatl,** the principal language of the Aztec Empire. When she was a girl, Doña Marina's family sent her to the Mexican coast as a slave, and later, her slaveholders sent her to their neighbors in the Yucatan peninsula. On her journey, she became fluent in Maya as well as her native Nahuatl language.

When **Hernán Cortés** arrived on the Mexican coast in 1519, his small army included a Spanish soldier who had learned the Maya language during a period of captivity in the Yucatan. But he had no way to communicate with the Nahuatl-speaking peoples of central Mexico until a Maya chieftain presented him with twelve young women, including Doña Marina, when he entered into an alliance with Cortes against the Aztecs. Doña Marina's linguistic abilities enabled Cortés to communicate

A contemporary mural by Tlaxala artist Desiderio Hernández Xochitiotzin—which is based on a sixteenth-century indigenous painting—suggests the central place of Doña Marina in facilitating encounters between Hernán Cortés (on the right) and the indigenous peoples of Mexico.
Benson Latin American Collection, General Libraries, University of Texas at Austin.

**Malintzin** (mal-een-tzeen)
**Nahuatl** (na-watl)
**Hernán Cortés** (er-NAHN kor-TEZ)

through an improbable chain of languages—from Spanish to Maya to Nahuatl and then back again—while making his way to the Aztec capital of **Tenochtitlan.** Before long, Doña Marina learned Spanish and thus eliminated the Maya link in the linguistic chain.

Doña Marina provided Cortés with information and diplomatic services as well. On several occasions she learned of plans by indigenous peoples to destroy the tiny Spanish army, and she alerted Cortés in time for him to prevent an attack. Once, she was able to report the precise details of a planned ambush because she played along with an effort by Cortes' enemies to bring her into the scheme. She also helped Cortés negotiate with emissaries from Tenochtitlan and other major cities of central Mexico. In fact, without Doña Marina's help, it is difficult to see how Cortés's small band could have survived to see the Aztec capital.

Precisely because of her pivotal role in aiding Cortés in his invasion of the Aztec Empire, Doña Marina earned another name commonly bestowed on her in Mexican history: La Malinche, or the traitor. The belief that she betrayed her people by collaborating with the Spanish underscores the complicated choices Doña Marina was faced with in their encounters with Europeans. Mesoamerican societies were not monolithic, and many people chose to ally themselves with the Spanish because of their disaffection from Aztec imperial rule. In Doña Marina's specific case, it is also important to remember her lack of power as a slave woman. After being given to Cortes, she may have felt the need to protect her new membership in his group by making herself valuable. Using her linguistic and diplomatic talents to aid Cortes may well have been a means of survival. Whatever her motives, it is clear that Doña Marina's aid was crucial to the success of Cortes' small group.

In addition to facilitating the Spanish conquest of the Aztec Empire, Doña Marina played a role in the formation of a new society in Mexico. In 1522, one year after the fall of Tenochtitlan, she gave birth to a son fathered by Cortés, and in 1526 she bore a daughter to a Spanish captain whom she had married. Given her status as a slave, historians have no way of knowing whether Doña Marina conceived her children willingly or not. Nevertheless, although her offspring were not the first children born in the Western Hemisphere of indigenous and Spanish parentage, they symbolize the early emergence of a mestizo population in Mexico. Doña Marina died soon after the birth of her daughter, probably in 1527, but during her short life she contributed to the thorough transformation of Mexican society.

**Tenochtitlan** (teh-noch-tee-TLAHN)

## CHAPTER FOCUS

- Historians use the term *Atlantic World* to discuss the interconnections of western Europe, west Africa, and the Americas.
- Initial exploration and exploitation of the Americas was all about silver and sugar.
- Silver was the engine of the world's economies in the seventeenth century. After the Spanish conquered the Aztec and Inca empires, the Spanish extracted so much silver from the Inca Potosi mine that it wreaked inflationary havoc on the western European economy throughout the 1600s. The Pacific also became part of the globalizing trade networks when the Spanish claimed lands and sent enormous amounts of silver across the ocean to buy luxury goods from China.
- Sugar, metaphorically and literally, was the frosting on the economic cake. The wealthy in Europe paid dearly for it, and families in Africa were decimated because of it. Spanish, Portuguese, French, and British sugar planters transported enslaved Africans to work on the sugar plantations in the Caribbean and coastal tropical areas.
- Historians identify two patterns of European settlement in the Americas: non-settler colonies and settler colonies.
- In the Americas, new social classes were created as people from three continents lived together for the first time. Children of these encounters became the foundation of mixed ethnicity in Central and South American populations.
- Religions commingled through conversion and evangelization.
- Indigenous peoples and enslaved Africans retained their traditional beliefs and practices while outwardly acknowledging the conquerors' Christian religion.

## Historical Developments

- Driven largely by political, religious, and economic rivalries, European states established new maritime empires, including the Portuguese, Spanish, Dutch, French, and British.
- Newly developed colonial economies in the Americas largely depended on agriculture, utilized existing labor systems, including the Incan *mit'a* and introduced new labor systems, including chattel slavery, indentured servitude, *encomienda*, and *hacienda* systems.

- State expansion and centralization led to resistance from an array of social, political, and economic groups on a local level.
- Slave resistance challenged existing authorities in the Americas.

## Reasoning Processes

- **Developments and Processes** Explain the conquest and transformation of Native American societies following the arrival of Europeans.
- **Sourcing and Situation** Identify the point of view and historical situation of Captain James Cook's account of Native Hawaiians.
- **Source Claims and Evidence** Identify and describe the claims made by Spanish accounts of Native Americans
- **Contextualization** Identify and describe the context of the silver and sugar trades.

## Historical Thinking Skills

- **Comparison** Describe similarities and/or differences between settler colonies and non-settler colonies.
- **Continuity and Change** Describe patterns of continuity and change over time within Native American society and culture.

## CHAPTER OVERVIEW

Until 1492 the peoples of the Eastern and Western Hemispheres had few dealings with one another. After 1492, however, the voyages of European mariners led to permanent and sustained contact between the peoples of the Eastern Hemisphere, the Western Hemisphere, and Oceania. The resulting encounters brought profound and violent change to both American and Pacific lands. European peoples possessed powerful military weapons, horses, and sailing ships that provided them with technological advantages over the peoples they encountered in the Americas and the Pacific Islands. Moreover, most Europeans also enjoyed complete or partial immunity to diseases that caused demographic disasters when introduced to the Western Hemisphere and Oceania. Because of their technological advantages and the wholesale depopulation that followed from epidemic diseases, European peoples were able to establish a strong presence throughout the Americas and much of the Pacific Ocean basin.

In Australia and the Pacific Islands, the European presence laid a foundation for dramatic and often traumatic change in the nineteenth and twentieth centuries. In the Western Hemisphere, however, large numbers of European migrants helped to bring about a profound transformation of American societies in early modern times. In Mexico and Peru, Spanish conquerors established territorial empires that were ruled from Spain. In Brazil, Portuguese entrepreneurs founded sugar plantations and imported African slaves to perform the heavy labor required for their

| CHRONOLOGY | |
|---|---|
| 1492 | First voyage of Christopher Columbus to the Western Hemisphere |
| 1494 | Treaty of Tordesillas |
| 1500 | Brazil claimed for Portugal by Pedro Alvares de Cabral |
| 1500–1527 | Life of Doña Marina |
| 1502–1520 | Reign of Motecuzoma |
| 1518 | Smallpox epidemic in the Caribbean |
| 1519–1521 | Spanish conquest of Mexico |
| 1525 | Execution of Cuauhtémoc |
| 1531 | Juan Diego's vision of the Virgin of Guadalupe |
| 1532–1540 | Spanish conquest of Peru |
| 1545 | Spanish discovery of silver near Potosí |
| 1604 | Foundation of Port Royal (Nova Scotia) |
| 1607 | Foundation of Jamestown |
| 1608 | Foundation of Quebec |
| 1619 | First enslaved Africans brought to Virginia |
| 1623 | Foundation of New Amsterdam |
| ca. 1642–1698 | French and Iroquois Wars |
| 1630 | Foundation of the Massachusetts Bay Colony |
| 1688 | Smallpox epidemic on Guam |
| 1754–1763 | French and Indian war in North America |
| 1763 | Transfer of French Canadian possessions to British rule |
| 1768–1779 | Captain James Cook's exploration of the Pacific Ocean |
| 1788 | Establishment of first European colony in Australia |

operation. In North America, French, English, and Dutch fur traders allied with indigenous peoples who provided them with animal skins, and their more sedentary compatriots founded settler societies concentrating on the production of cash crops for export. Throughout the Western Hemisphere, peoples of European, African, and American ancestry interacted to fashion altogether new societies.

## COLLIDING WORLDS

When European peoples first sought to establish their presence in the Americas, they brought a range of technology unavailable to the peoples they encountered in the Western Hemisphere. Even more important than technology, however, was the combination of devastating epidemic disease Europeans brought with them and European willingness to exploit existing divisions between indigenous peoples. With the help of technology, disease, and ruthless political maneuvering, Spanish conquerors toppled the Aztec and Inca empires and imposed their own rule in Mexico and Peru. In later decades Portuguese planters built sugar plantations on the Brazilian coastline. French, English, and Dutch migrants displaced indigenous peoples in North America and established settler colonies under the rule of European peoples.

### The Spanish Caribbean

**The Taíno** When Spanish mariners arrived in the Caribbean, the **Taíno** (also known as Arawaks) were the most prominent people in the region. During the late centuries B.C.E., the ancestors of the Taíno sailed in canoes from the Orinoco River valley in South America to the Caribbean islands, and by about 900 C.E. they had settled throughout the region. The Taíno cultivated manioc and other crops, and they lived in small villages under the authority of chiefs who allocated land to families and supervised community affairs. They showed interest in the glass, beads, and metal tools that Spanish mariners brought as trade goods because these were new to them. Meanwhile, the Spanish showed great interest in trading for the gold jewelry worn by the Taíno. Although at first the Taíno received the Spanish warmly, within a few months relations between the Taíno and the Spanish turned sour when it became clear that the Spanish were not satisfied with the amount of gold they were getting through trade alone.

**Spanish Arrival** Christopher Columbus and his immediate followers made the island of Hispaniola (which embraces modern Haiti and the Dominican Republic) the base of Spanish operations in the Caribbean. There, Spanish settlers established the fort of Santo Domingo, and the city, officially founded in 1498, became the capital of the Spanish Caribbean. Columbus's original plan was to build forts and trading posts where merchants could trade with local peoples for products desired by European consumers. Within a few years of Spanish arrival, however, it became clear that the Caribbean region offered no silks or spices for the European market. If Spanish settlers wanted to maintain their presence in the Caribbean, they would need to find some way to make a living.

The settlers first attempted to support their society by mining gold. Spanish settlers were too few in number to mine gold—and in any case they were not inclined to perform heavy physical labor—so the miners came largely from the ranks of the Taíno. Recruitment of labor came through an institution known as the ***encomienda,*** which involved Spanish *encomenderos* ("settlers") forcing the Taíno to work in their mines or fields. In return for labor, *encomenderos* were supposed to look after their workers' health and welfare and to encourage their conversion to Christianity.

Conscription of Taíno labor was a brutal business that, in practice, functioned like a system of slavery. *Encomenderos* worked their charges hard and punished them severely when they did not deliver the expected quantities of gold or work sufficiently hard in the fields. The Taíno occasionally organized rebellions, but their bows, arrows, and slings had little effect against horse-mounted Spanish forces wielding steel swords and firearms. By about 1515, enslavement and physical abuse had brought dramatic decline to Taíno populations on the large Caribbean islands of Hispaniola, Jamaica, Puerto Rico, and Cuba. On the island of Hispaniola alone, by 1514 the Taíno population had declined to about 32,000 from a pre-contact population of several hundred thousand.

**Smallpox** Another serious demographic decline then set in after 1518, when **smallpox** reached the Caribbean region and touched off devastating epidemics among the peoples of the Western Hemisphere. To replace laborers lost to disease, *encomenderos* launched raiding parties to kidnap and enslave Taíno and other peoples. This tactic exposed additional victims to introduced diseases and hastened the decline of indigenous populations.

Under pressure of **epidemic disease,** the indigenous population of the Caribbean plummeted from about four million in 1492 to a few thousand in the 1540s. As a result, some indigenous societies passed almost completely out of existence. Only a few Taíno cultural elements survived: *canoe, hammock, hurricane, barbecue, maize,* and *tobacco* all derive from Taíno words, but the society that generated them had largely disappeared by the middle of the sixteenth century.

**From Mining to Plantation Agriculture** Deposits of gold were not plentiful in the Caribbean, but optimistic Spanish adventurers continued to seek treasure there for a century and more. After the mid-sixteenth century, however, when Spanish

**Taíno** (tah-EE-noh)
***encomienda*** (ehn-KOH-mee-ehn-dah)

One of the earliest European depictions of Native Americans was this engraving of 1505. The caption informed readers that American peoples lived in communal society, where men took several wives but none had private possessions, and that they routinely smoked and consumed the bodies of slain enemies. How might such representations have shaped European ideas about Native Americans?

North Wind Picture Archives/Alamy Stock Photo

explorers located exceptionally rich sources of silver in Mexico and Peru, the Caribbean became a much less important part of the Spanish Empire. English pirates lurked in Caribbean waters hoping to intercept imperial fleets carrying American silver to Spain, but the region was not a center of production. Then, in about the 1640s, French, English, and Dutch settlers began to flock to the Caribbean with the intention of establishing plantations. It became clear that even if the Caribbean islands lacked precious metals, they offered ideal conditions for the cultivation of cash crops, particularly sugar, which would fetch high prices in European markets. Later, tobacco also became a prime cash crop of the region. Meanwhile, because indigenous populations had been decimated, planters lacked the labor they needed to operate their estates. Based on earlier Spanish practices in the Azores and Canary Islands, Europeans solved the labor shortage by forcibly importing several million slaves from Africa. By 1700 Caribbean society consisted of a small class of European landowners and large numbers of enslaved Africans.

## Mexico and Peru at the Time of Contact

Spanish interest soon shifted from the Caribbean to the American mainland, where settlers hoped to find more resources to exploit. During the early sixteenth century, Spanish ***conquistadores*** ("conquerors") pressed beyond the Caribbean islands, moving west into Mexico and south into Panama and Peru. Aided especially by the spread of epidemic

***conquistadores*** (kon-kees-tah-DOH-rayz)

## How the Past Shapes the Future

### The Columbian Exchange

Recall that the spread of epidemic diseases like smallpox, measles, and influenza from Eurasia to the Americas was one of the key features of the Columbian exchange—a process that began almost immediately after contact between Europeans and indigenous Americans in the late fifteenth century. Since indigenous Americans had no immunity to Eurasian diseases, they took a staggering toll: in some cases, as in colonial Mexico, the mortality rate may have been as high as 90 percent. If epidemic disease had not caused such high mortality among indigenous Americans, in what ways might the history of the Americas in the sixteenth and seventeenth centuries have been different?

disease, between 1519 and 1521 Hernán Cortés and a small band of men brought down the Aztec Empire in Mexico, and between 1532 and 1533 **Francisco Pizarro** and his followers toppled the Inca Empire in Peru. Those conquests laid the foundations for colonial regimes that would transform the Americas.

In Mexico and Peru, Spanish explorers found societies quite different from those of the Caribbean islands. Both Mexico and Peru had been sites of agricultural societies, cities, and large states for more than a millennium. In the early fifteenth century, both lands fell under the sway of powerful imperial states: the Mexica people and their allies founded the Aztec Empire that expanded to embrace most of Mesoamerica, while the Incas imposed their rule on a vast realm extending from modern Ecuador in the north to modern Chile in the south—the largest state South America had ever seen. But neither the Inca nor the Aztec Empire could count on all its subjects to rally to its defense. In fact, the very success of Spanish military campaigns often rested on the support of indigenous allies, who were eager to shake off Aztec or Inca rule. As allies they played a crucial role in the conquest, supplying auxiliary troops, logistical support, and secure bases in friendly territory.

**Hernán Cortés** The conquest of Mexico began with an expedition to search for gold on the American mainland. In 1519 Cortés led about 450 soldiers to Mexico and made his way from Veracruz on the Gulf coast to the island city of Tenochtitlan, the large and vibrant Aztec capital situated in Lake Texcoco. They seized the emperor **Motecuzoma** II, who died in 1520 during a skirmish between Spanish forces and residents of Tenochtitlan. Fierce Aztec resistance soon drove the conquistadores from the capital, and Cuauhtémoc (ca. 1502–1525)—the nephew and son-in-law of Motecuzoma—emerged as the last Aztec emperor. Cortés built a small fleet of ships, placed Tenochtitlan under siege, and in 1521 starved the city into surrender. Cuauhtémoc withstood the torture Cortés inflicted upon him in an attempt to uncover the whereabouts of Aztec gold and treasures. However, he ultimately could not escape the execution ordered by Cortés in 1525.

Steel swords, muskets, cannons, and horses offered Cortés and his soldiers some advantage over the forces they met and help to account for the Spanish conquest of the Aztec Empire. Yet weaponry alone clearly would not enable Cortés's tiny force to overcome a large, densely populated society. Quite apart from military technology, Cortés's expedition forged alliances with peoples who resented domination by the Mexica, the leaders of the Aztec Empire, and who reinforced the small Spanish army with thousands of veteran warriors. Indigenous allies also provided Spanish forces with logistical support and secure bases in friendly territory.

**Epidemic Disease** On the mainland, as in the Caribbean, epidemic disease aided Spanish efforts. During the siege of Tenochtitlan, smallpox raged through the city, killing inhabitants by the tens of thousands and fatally sapping the strength of defensive forces. Smallpox rapidly spread beyond the capital, raced through Mexico, and killed so many people that Aztec society was unable to function. Only in the context of this drastic depopulation is it possible to understand the Spanish conquest of Mexico.

**Francisco Pizarro** Francisco Pizarro experienced similar results when he led a Spanish expedition from Central America to Peru. Pizarro set out in 1530 with 180 soldiers, later joined by reinforcements to make a force of about 600. The conquistadores arrived in Peru just after a bitter dispute between Huascar (1503–1532) and **Atahualpa** (ca. 1502–1533), two brothers within the Inca ruling house, and Pizarro's forces exploited the differences between those factions. Already by 1533 they had taken the Inca capital at Cuzco. Under pretext of holding a conference, they called the Inca ruling elites together, seized them, and killed most of them. They spared the Inca ruler Atahualpa until he had delivered a large quantity of gold to Pizarro. Then they strangled him and decapitated his body. The search for treasure continued after the end of Inca rule. Pizarro and his conquistadores looted gold and silver plaques from Cuzco's temples and public buildings, melted down statuettes fashioned from precious metals, and even stole jewelry and ornaments from the embalmed bodies of deceased Inca rulers.

Several considerations help to explain how Pizarro's tiny force was able to topple the Inca Empire. Many subjects of the

**Motecuzoma** (mo-tek-oo-ZO-mah)
**Atahualpa** (ah-tah-WAHL-pah)

# SOURCES FROM THE PAST

## First Impressions of Spanish Forces

*As the Spanish army made its way to Tenochtitlan, Motecuzoma dispatched a series of emissaries to communicate with Cortés and learn his intentions. The following document, based on indigenous accounts but filtered through the Spanish sensibilities of Bernardino de Sahagun, suggested that Motecuzoma reacted with fright when presented with reports that were less than reassuring because they focused on fearsome weapons and animals of the Spanish. Given the vigorous resistance by the Aztecs to the Spanish invaders, it seems highly likely that the source exaggerated Motecuzoma's terror. At the same time, at the very least it suggests that Motecuzoma took the threat posed by the Spanish very seriously.*

**And when [Motecuzoma] had heard** what the messengers reported, he was terrified, he was astounded. . . .

Especially did it cause him to faint away when he heard how the gun, at [the Spaniards'] command, discharged [the shot]; how it resounded as if it thundered when it went off. It indeed bereft one of strength; it shut off one's ears. And when it discharged, something like a round pebble came forth from within. Fire went showering forth; sparks went blazing forth. And its smoke smelled very foul; it had a fetid odor which verily wounded the head. And when [the shot] struck a mountain, it was as if it were destroyed, dissolved. And a tree was pulverized; it was as if it vanished; it was as if someone blew it away.

> For someone who had never seen a firearm in action before, does this description seem to do an adequate job of relaying its effects?

All iron was their war array. In iron they clothed themselves. With iron they covered their heads. Iron were their swords. Iron were their crossbows. Iron were their shields. Iron were their lances.

And those which bore them upon their backs, their deer [that is, horses], were as tall as roof terraces.

And their bodies were everywhere covered; only their faces appeared. They were very white; they had chalky faces; they had yellow hair, though the hair of some was black. Long were their beards; they also were yellow. They were yellow-headed. [The black men's hair] was kinky, it was curly.

> Why might the Aztecs have paid particular attention to the Europeans with blond hair?

And their food was like fasting food—very large, white, not heavy like [tortillas]; like maize stalks, good-tasting as if of maize stalk flour; a little sweet, a little honeyed. It was honeyed to eat; it was sweet to eat.

And their dogs were very large. They had ears folded over; great dragging jowls. They had fiery eyes—blazing eyes; they had yellow eyes—fiery yellow eyes. They had thin flanks—flanks with ribs showing. They had gaunt stomachs. They were very tall. They were nervous; they went about panting, with tongues hanging out. They were spotted like ocelots; they were varicolored.

And when Motecuzoma heard all this, he was much terrified. It was as if he fainted away. His heart saddened; his heart failed him.

### For Further Reflection

- What did the Spanish and their indigenous allies hope to gain by presenting this image of Motecuzoma?
- Motecuzuma's description of his astonishment and fear of Spanish weapons and appearance are only part of the story. What other reasons account for the defeat of the Aztecs?

*Source:* Bernardino de Sahagún. *Florentine Codex: General History of the Things of New Spain,* 13 vols. Trans. by Arthur J. O. Anderson and Charles E. Dibble. Salt Lake City: University of Utah Press, 1950–82, 13:19–20. (Translation slightly modified.)

empire despised the Incas as overlords and tax collectors. Indeed, many allied with the Spanish invaders. Epidemic disease also discouraged resistance: smallpox had spread from Mexico and Central America to Peru in the 1520s, long before Pizarro's arrival, and had already significantly weakened Andean populations. Hence, by 1540 Spanish forces had established themselves securely in Peru.

## Spanish and Portuguese Empires in the Americas

During the early days after the conquests, Cortés and Pizarro allocated lands and labor rights to their troops on their own authority. Gradually, however, the Spanish monarchy extended its control over the growing American empire, and

Tlaxcalan allies of the Spanish on their way to the Aztec capital of Tenochtitlan. A Spanish warrior is at the front right of the drawing on his horse. Taken from the sixteenth-century Lienzo de Tlaxcala manuscript.
The Picture Art Collection/Alamy Stock Photo

by about 1570 the semiprivate regime of the conquistadores had given way to formal rule under the Spanish crown. Bureaucrats charged with the implementation of royal policy and the administration of royal justice replaced the soldiers of fortune who had conquered Mexico and Peru. The conquistadores did not welcome the arrival of the bureaucrats, but with the aid of Spanish lawyers, tax collectors, and military forces, royal officials had their way.

**Spanish Colonial Administration** Spanish administrators established two main centers of authority in the Americas—Mexico (which they called **New Spain**) and Peru (known as New Castile)—each governed by a viceroy who was responsible to the king of Spain. In Mexico they built a new capital, Mexico City, on top of Tenochtitlan. In Peru they originally hoped to rule from the Inca capital of Cuzco, but they considered the high altitude unpleasant and also found the Andean city too inaccessible for their purposes. In 1535 they founded Lima and transferred the government to the coast where it was accessible to Spanish shipping.

The viceroys were the king's representatives in the Americas, and they wielded considerable power. The kings of Spain, attempting to ensure that their viceroys would not build personal power bases and become independent, subjected them to the review of courts known as ***audiencias*** staffed by university-educated lawyers. The *audiencias* heard appeals

***audiencias*** (AW-dee-ehns-see-ahs)

against the viceroys' decisions and policies and had the right to address their concerns directly to the Spanish king. Furthermore, the *audiencias* conducted reviews of viceroys' performance at the end of their terms, and negative reviews could lead to severe punishment.

In spite of this structure, in many ways Spanish administration in the Americas was a ragged affair. Transportation and communication difficulties limited the ability of viceroys to supervise their territories. In many regions, local administration fell to *audiencias* or town councils. Meanwhile, the Spanish monarchy exercised even less influence on American affairs than the viceroys. It often took two years for the central government in Spain to respond to a query from Mexico or Peru, and many replies simply asked for further information rather than providing firm directives. When viceroys received clear orders that they did not like, they found ways to procrastinate: they often responded to the king that "I obey, but I do not enforce," implying that with additional information the king would alter his decision.

In this illustration from Peru native Felipe Guaman Poma de Ayala's letter of complaint to the Spanish king—a record of grievances against Spanish overlords—conquistadores decapitate Atahualpa after executing him by strangulation in 1533. DEA/G. DAGLI ORTI /De Agostini/Getty Images

**New Cities** Spanish rule in the Americas led to the rapid establishment of cities throughout the viceroyalties. Like their compatriots in Spain, colonists preferred to live in cities even when they derived their income from the agricultural production of their landed estates. As the numbers of migrants increased, they expanded the territory under Spanish imperial authority and built a dense network of bureaucratic control based in recently founded cities. The jurisdiction of the viceroyalty of New Spain reached from Mexico City as far as St. Augustine in Florida (founded in 1565). Administrators in Lima oversaw affairs from Panama (founded in 1519) to Concepción (founded in 1550) and Buenos Aires (founded in 1536).

**The Portuguese in Brazil** While Spanish conquistadores and administrators built a territorial empire in Mexico and Peru, Portuguese forces established an imperial presence in **Brazil.** The Portuguese presence came about by an odd twist of diplomatic convention. In 1494 Spain and Portugal signed the Treaty of Tordesillas, which divided the world along an imaginary north-south line 370 leagues west of the Azores and Cape Verde Islands. According to this agreement, Spain could claim any land west of that line, so long as it was not already under Christian rule, and Portugal gained the same rights for lands east of the line. Thus Portugal gained territory along the northeastern part of the South American continent, a region known as Brazil from the many brazilwood trees that grew along the coast, while the remainder of the Western Hemisphere fell under Spanish control. Of course, this treaty completely disregarded preexisting indigenous claims to any of these lands—an indication of the conceit of both the Spanish and the Portuguese.

The Portuguese mariner Pedro Alvares de Cabral stopped in Brazil briefly in 1500 while making a tack through the Atlantic Ocean en route to India. His compatriots did not display much immediate interest in the land. When French and Dutch mariners began to visit Brazilian shores, however, the Portuguese king decided to consolidate his claim to the land. He made vast land grants to Portuguese nobles in the expectation that they would develop and colonize their holdings, and later he dispatched a governor to oversee affairs and implement royal policy. Portuguese interest in Brazil rose dramatically after mid-century when entrepreneurs established profitable sugar plantations—based on slave labor—on the coast.

**Colonial American Society** The cities of the Spanish and Portuguese empires became centers of European-style society in the Americas: the spires of churches and cathedrals defined their skylines, and Spanish and Portuguese were the languages of government, business, and society. Beyond the urban districts, however, indigenous ways of life persisted. In the Amazon basin and Paraguay, for example, indigenous peoples produced little agricultural surplus, and there were no mineral deposits to attract European migrants. The few Spanish and Portuguese colonists who ventured to those regions learned to adapt to indigenous societies and customs: they ate bread made of manioc flour, made use of native hammocks and canoes, and communicated in the Guaraní and Tupí languages. Indeed, indigenous languages flourish even today throughout much of Latin America: among the more prominent are Nahuatl in Mexico; K′iché in Guatemala; Guaraní in Paraguay; and Quechua in the Andean highlands of Peru, Ecuador, and Bolivia.

Spanish and Portuguese peoples saw the Western Hemisphere more as a land to exploit and administer than as a place to settle and colonize. Nevertheless, sizable contingents of

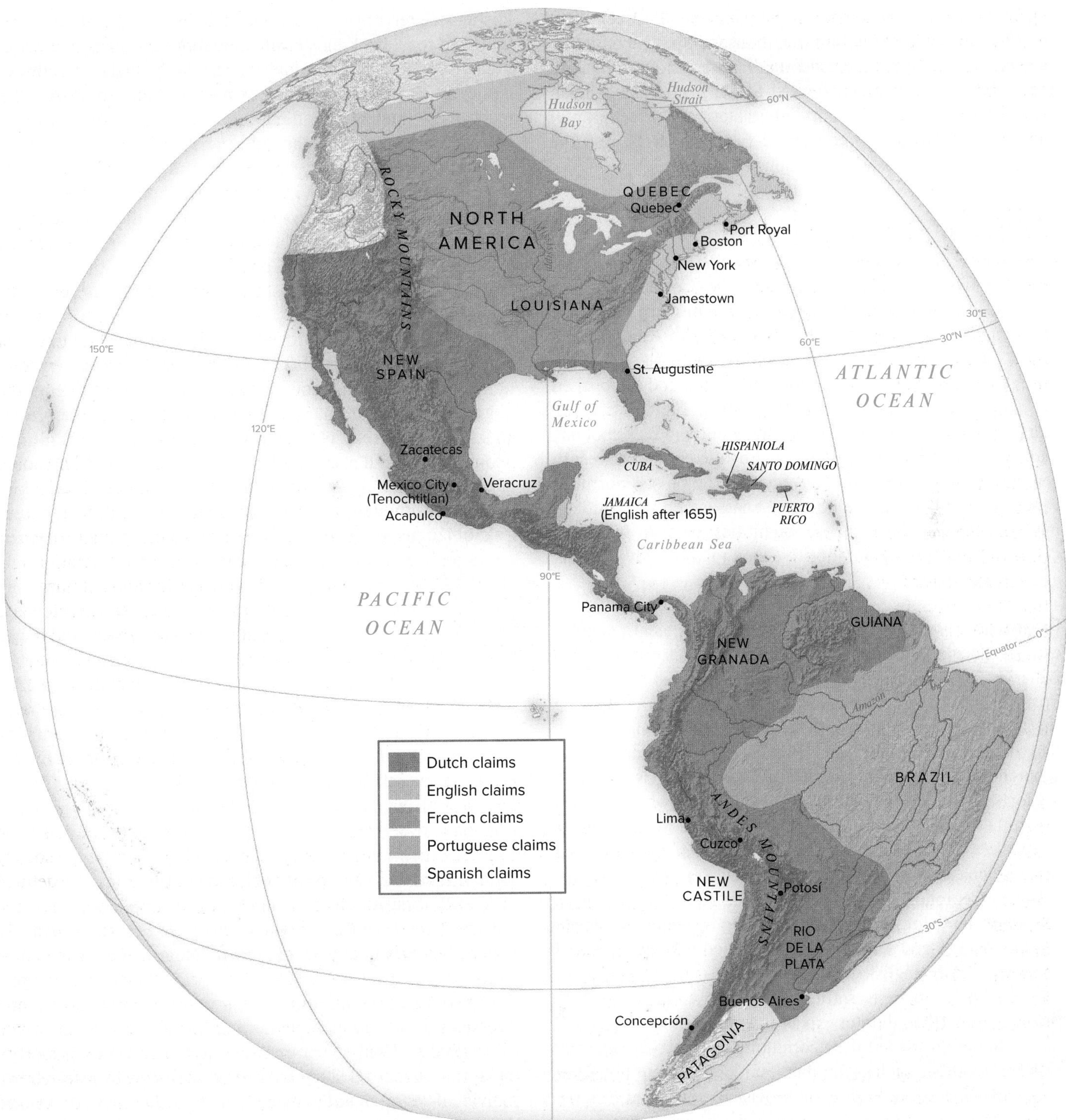


## MAP 12.1 European empires and colonies in the Americas about 1700.

Locate the major cities and settlements of each imperial power.

***What factors decided where settlements would be placed? Why are so few settlements in the interior of either North or South America?***

migrants settled permanently in the Americas. Between 1500 and 1800, upwards of five hundred thousand Spanish migrants crossed the Atlantic, alongside one hundred thousand Portuguese. Their presence contributed to the making of a much more globalized world—a world characterized by meaningful encounters between the peoples of Europe, Africa, and the Americas—in the Western Hemisphere.

## Settler Colonies in North America

Throughout the sixteenth century, Spanish explorers sought opportunities north of Mexico and the Caribbean. They established towns, forts, and missions from modern Florida as far north as Virginia on the east coast of North America, and they scouted shorelines off Maine and Newfoundland. On the west coast they ventured into modern Canada and established a fort on Vancouver Island. By mid-century, French, English, and Dutch mariners sailed the North Atlantic in search of fish and a northwest passage to Asia, and by the early seventeenth century they were dislodging Spanish colonists north of Florida. Their search for a northwest passage proved fruitless, but they harvested immense quantities of fish from the cod-filled banks off Labrador, Newfoundland, Nova Scotia, and New England.

**Foundation of Colonies** In the early seventeenth century explorers began to establish permanent colonies on the North American mainland. French settlers established colonies at Port Royal (Nova Scotia) in 1604 and Quebec in 1608. During the seventeenth and eighteenth centuries, French migrants settled in eastern Canada, and French explorers and traders scouted the St. Lawrence, Ohio, and Mississippi Rivers, building forts all the way to the Gulf of Mexico. Meanwhile, English migrants founded Jamestown in 1607 and the Massachusetts Bay Colony in 1630, and proceeded to establish colonies along the east coast of the present-day United States of America. Dutch entrepreneurs built a settlement at New Amsterdam in 1623, but the colony did not remain long in Dutch hands: an English fleet seized it in 1664, rechristened it New York, and absorbed it into English colonial holdings.

Life in those early settlements was extremely difficult. Most of the settlers did not expect to cultivate food crops but, rather, hoped to sustain their communities by producing valuable commodities such as fur, pitch, tar, or lumber, if not silver and gold. They relied heavily on provisions sent from Europe, and when supply ships did not arrive as expected, they sometimes avoided starvation only because indigenous peoples provided them with food. In Jamestown (located in present-day Virginia in the United States), food shortages and disease became so severe that only sixty of the colony's five hundred inhabitants survived the winter of 1609–1610.

**Colonial Government** The French and English colonies in North America differed in several ways from Spanish and Portuguese territories to the south. Whereas Iberian explorations had royal backing, private investors played larger roles in French and English colonial efforts. Individuals put up the money to finance expeditions to America, and they retained much more control over their colonies' affairs than did their Iberian counterparts. Although English colonies were always subject to royal authority, for example, they also maintained their own assemblies and influenced the choice of royal governors: there were no viceroys or *audiencias* in the North American colonies. At the conclusion of the Seven Years' War in 1763, the French colony in Canada fell under British control, and it, too, soon acquired institutions of self-government.

**Relations with Indigenous Peoples** French and English colonies differed from Iberian territories also in their relationships with indigenous peoples. French and English migrants did not find large, centralized states like the Aztec and Inca empires. Nor did they encounter agricultural peoples living in densely settled societies. Rather, the peoples of eastern North America had formed dozens of distinct societies, even though most spoke Algonquian, Iroquois, or Lakota languages. Many practiced agriculture, but most also relied on hunting and consequently moved their villages frequently in pursuit of game. They did not claim ownership of precisely bounded territories, but they regularly migrated between well-defined regions and utilized the resources of the land as they did so.

But when European settlers saw forested lands not bearing crops or supporting villages, they viewed them as "empty" and unclaimed. Even when lands had been in use by multiple Native American groups over many hundreds of years, Europeans believed they had the right to claim such lands. Thus, they staked out farms and excluded the indigenous peoples who had, over many centuries, used the lands during the course of their migrations. The availability of fertile farmland soon attracted large numbers of European migrants. Upwards of 150,000 English migrants moved to North America during the seventeenth century alone, and sizable French, German, Dutch, and Irish contingents joined them in the search for land.

European migrants took pains to justify their claims to American lands. English settlers in particular brought with them English legal structures such as treaties and property deeds that suggested land could be permanently transferred to individuals or groups. They fundamentally did not understand that the Native American way of life in the region depended on a very different way of using, and laying claim to, land. For Native American groups, using the land productively entailed keeping hunting grounds healthy, while for Europeans land could only be considered productive if under cultivation.

**Conflict** French and English settlers frequently clashed with indigenous peoples who resented intrusions on their hunting grounds and thus their means of survival, but the conflicts

This painting of the English settlement at Jamestown in the early seventeenth century illustrates the precarious position of European settlers trying to live in the midst of indigenous people. Note the heavy palisades surrounding the settlement.
MPI/Archive Photos/Getty Images

differed from the campaigns of conquest carried out by the conquistadores in Mexico and Peru. Although English settlers negotiated rights to American lands by treaty, native peoples did not accept that land should be used exclusively for one owner. When Europeans tried to insist on their exclusive use of land, Native Americans resisted by mounting raids on farms and villages. During an assault of 1622, for example, they killed almost one-third of the English settlers in the Chesapeake region. Attacks on European communities brought equally severe reprisals on Native American communities, including the ruthless destruction of entire towns and villages. Edward Waterhouse, who survived the raid of 1622, went so far as to advocate annihilation of the indigenous population: "Victorie may bee gained many waies: by force, by surprize, by [causing] famine [through] burning their Corne, by destroying and burning their Boats, Canoes, and Houses, by breaking their fishing Weares [nets], by assailing them in their huntings, whereby they get the greatest part of their sustenance in Winter, by pursuing and chasing them with our horses, and blood-Hounds to draw after them, and Mastives [mastiffs] to teare them."

Indeed, a combination of epidemic disease and violent conflict dramatically reduced the indigenous population of North America between the sixteenth and nineteenth centuries. In 1492 the native population of the territory now embraced by the United States was greater than five million, perhaps as high as ten million. By the mid-sixteenth century, however, smallpox and other diseases had begun to spread north from Mexico and ravage native societies in the plains and eastern woodlands of North America. Between 1600 and 1800 about one million English, French, German, Dutch, Irish, and Scottish migrants crossed the Atlantic and sought to displace indigenous peoples as they pursued economic opportunities in North America. By 1800, indigenous peoples in the territory of the present-day United States numbered only six hundred thousand, as against almost five million settlers of European ancestry and about one million enslaved people of African ancestry. As with the Iberian incursions in the South, the European settlement of North America fundamentally transformed the Western Hemisphere.

## COLONIAL SOCIETY IN THE AMERICAS

The European migrants who flooded into the Western Hemisphere interacted both with the indigenous inhabitants and with African peoples whom they forcibly imported as enslaved laborers. Throughout the Americas, relations between individuals of American, European, and African ancestry soon led to the emergence of what were known at the time as **mestizo** populations. Notwithstanding such intercultural mixing, European peoples and their Euro-American offspring increasingly dominated political and economic affairs in the Americas. Using enslaved labor and Native American knowledge, they mined precious metals, cultivated cash crops such as sugar and tobacco, and trapped fur-bearing animals to supply capitalist markets that met the voracious demands of European and Asian consumers. Over time they also established their Christian religion as the dominant faith of the Western Hemisphere.

## SOURCES FROM THE PAST

### Miantanamo's Call for Unity

*Miantanamo (ca. 1600–1643) was a chief of the Narragansett tribe, which claimed territories in what is now Rhode Island, Connecticut, and eastern Massachusetts. In 1637 Miantanamo and the Narragansetts (along with other tribes) allied with the English against the Pequot tribe in what became known as the Pequot War. English settlers in Massachusetts nevertheless suspected him of trying to plot against them, and in 1640 he was brought to Boston where he successfully defended himself against these charges. In 1643 he assembled a force to attack his enemy of the Mohegan tribe, Uncas, but was caught. Uncas turned Miantanamo over to the English authorities in Connecticut. There they recommended the death penalty but asked Uncas to carry it out on Mohegan land. Miantanamo was executed at the command of Uncas in 1643. The speech below was given sometime in 1642 or 1643.*

**Brothers, we must be as one** as the English are, or we shall all be destroyed. You know our fathers had plenty of deer and skins and our plains were full of game and turkeys, and our coves and rivers were full of fish.

But, brothers, since these Englishmen have seized our country, they have cut down the grass with scythes, and the trees with axes. Their cows and horses eat up the grass, and their hogs spoil our bed of clams; and finally we shall all starve to death; therefore, stand not in your own light, I ask you, but resolve to act like men. All the sachems both to the east and the west have joined with us, and we are resolved to fall upon them at a day appointed, and therefore I come secretly to you, cause you can persuade your Indians to do what you will.

What are Miantanamo's main complaints about the presence of the English?

#### For Further Reflection

- Given Miantanamo's complicated history of alliances with the English and against some other Native American tribes, is it possible to read Miantanamo's plea here at face value? How realistic was such a call to unity given this history of shifting alliances?
- Why do you think it was so difficult for the various Native American groups to create alliances against the Europeans?

*Source:* Sylvester, Herbert Milton. *Indian wars of New England by Sylvester.* Boston: W.B. Clarke Company, 1910, vol. I, p. 386.

## The Formation of Multicultural Societies

European migrants radically transformed the social order in the regions where they established imperial states or settler colonies, although it is important to remember that their influence only reached the American interior gradually. All European territories became multicultural societies where peoples of varied ancestry lived together under European or Euro-American dominance. Spanish and Portuguese territories soon became not only multicultural but ethnically mixed as well, largely because of migration patterns. Migrants to the Iberian colonies were overwhelmingly men: about 85 percent of the Spanish migrants were men, and the Portuguese migration was even more male-dominated than the Spanish. Because of the small numbers of European women, Spanish and Portuguese migrants tended to enter into relationships with indigenous women, which soon gave rise to an increasingly mixed ("mestizo") society.

## Mestizo Society

Most Spanish migrants went to Mexico, where there was soon a growing population of mestizos—those of Spanish and native parentage, like the children of Doña Marina. Women were more prominent among the migrants to Peru than to Mexico, and Spanish colonists there lived mostly in cities, where they maintained a more distinct community than did their counterparts in Mexico. In the colonial cities, Spanish migrants married among themselves and re-created a European-style society. In less settled regions, however, Spanish men associated with indigenous women and gave rise to mestizo society.

With few European women available in Brazil, Portuguese men readily entered into relations—some consensual and some forced—both with indigenous women and with enslaved African women. Brazil soon had large populations not only of mestizos but also of people known as mulattoes, who were born of Portuguese and African parents; those

## INTERPRETING IMAGES

Indigenous Zapotec painter Miguel Mateo Maldonado y Cabrera (1695–1768) created this domestic portrait of a multicultural family in the viceroyalty of New Spain, today's Mexico. A Spanish man gazes at his Mexican Indian wife and their mestizo daughter.

**Analyze** *How does the portrait reflect the social structure that evolved in Latin American after the Europeans polarized it? How and why did Latin American social structures differ from those of North America?*

Album/Alamy Stock Photo

known as ***zambos,*** who were born of indigenous and African parents; and other combinations arising from these groups. Indeed, marriages between members of different racial and ethnic communities became common in colonial Brazil and generated a society even more thoroughly mixed than that of Mexico.

**The Social Hierarchy** In both Spanish and Portuguese colonies, migrants born in the Iberian peninsula in Europe (known as ***peninsulares***) stood at the top of the social hierarchy. They were followed by ***criollos,*** or *creoles,* those born in the Americas of Iberian parents. In the early days of the colonies, mestizos lived on the fringes of society. As time went on, however, the numbers of mestizos grew, and they became essential contributors to their societies, especially in Mexico and Brazil. Meanwhile, mulattoes, *zambos,* and others of mixed parentage became prominent groups in Brazilian society, although they were usually subordinate to European migrants, Euro-American creoles, and even mestizos. In all the Iberian colonies, enslaved and conquered peoples stood at the bottom of the social hierarchy. Over time, this highly unequal social order became codified into a system of classification known as the *casta system*. Taken from the Spanish word that means 'lineage,' the casta system reflected Spanish understandings of themselves as superior to those of mixed (mestizo or mulatto), indigenous, or African heritage. Although the casta system was not fixed and grew to incorporate various combinations of peoples, it helped maintain Spanish superiority by placing 'pure' Spaniards at the top, followed by mestizos, indigenous peoples and, at the very bottom, those of African heritage. Casta paintings that survive from this period depict numerous combinations of what we would now call 'mixed race' people.

**Sexual Hierarchies** Race and ethnicity were crucial in shaping a person's position and role in colonial society. But the defining factor in both Spanish and Portuguese America was the existence of a clear sexual hierarchy that privileged men. Women lived in a patriarchal world, where men occupied positions of power and delineated the boundaries of acceptable female behavior. Although there were exceptions to the rule, women's power tended to be expressed informally through their influence on relationships and in domestic duties. Only when it came to punishing disobedient slaves did society ignore gender—both male and female slaves could count on the same harsh punishment, which usually took the form of flogging.

Gender alone, however, did not explain the diverse experiences of women in colonial society. Commonly, the ratio of men to women in a given community either enhanced or limited women's choices. Women's experiences also varied with the degree of prosperity and the nature of the local economy. As women moved from childhood through marriage and motherhood, to being widows or "spinsters," their experiences and roles in society likewise underwent change. Race and class usually figured as powerful forces shaping women's lives. Women of European descent, though under strict patriarchal control and under pressure to conform to the stereotype of female dependence and passivity, sometimes used their elite position to their advantage. By necessity, women of color and

***peninsulares*** (pehn-IHN-soo-LAH-rayz)
***criollos*** (kree-OH-lohs)

those from the low class became part of the colonial labor force, performing tasks closely tied to the commercialization of traditional female work such as food preparation, laundering, and weaving. Although poor, these women were freer to move about in public and to interact with others than were their elite counterparts. The most disadvantaged women were black, mulatta, and zamba slaves, who were required to perform hard physical tasks such as planting and cutting cane or working as laundresses. Since they had few powerful protectors, such women were also frequently the targets of forced sexual relationships with European men.

**North American Societies** The social structure of the French and English colonies in North America differed markedly from that of the Iberian colonies. Women were more numerous among the French and especially the English migrants than in Spanish and Portuguese communities, and settlers tended to marry within their own groups. Although French fur traders often associated with native women and generated ***métis*** (French for "mixed") in regions around forts and trading posts, in French colonial cities such as Port Royal and Quebec, liaisons between French and native peoples were less common.

Mingling between peoples of different ancestry was least common in the English colonies of North America. Colonists disdained the indigenous peoples they encountered and regarded them as heathens who did not recognize private property and did not exert themselves to cultivate the land. Later, they also scorned imported enslaved Africans as inferior beings. Those attitudes fueled a virulent racism, as English settlers attempted to maintain sharp boundaries between themselves and peoples of Native American and African ancestry.

Yet English settlers nevertheless interacted with American and African peoples, and they readily borrowed useful cultural elements from other communities. They learned about American plants and animals, for example, and they used indigenous terms to refer to unfamiliar animals such as raccoons and opossums or trees such as hickory and pecan. They adapted moccasins and deerskin clothes, and they gave up European military customs of marching in massed ranks and announcing their presence with drums and flying colors. From enslaved peoples they borrowed African food crops and techniques for the cultivation of rice. Yet, unlike their Iberian neighbors to the south, the English settlers discouraged relationships between individuals of different ancestry and sometimes refused to accept or even acknowledge offspring of mixed parentage.

## Mining and Agriculture in the Spanish Empire

From the Spanish perspective the greatest attractions of the Americas were precious metals, which drew thousands of migrants from all levels of Spanish society. The conquistadores thoroughly looted the easily accessible treasures of the Aztec and Inca empires. Ignoring the artistic or cultural value of artifacts, the conquerors simply melted down silver and gold treasures and fashioned them into ingots. Their followers opened mines to extract the mineral wealth of the Americas in more systematic fashion.

**Silver Mining** Gold was not the most abundant American treasure. Silver far outweighed gold in quantity and value, and much of Spain's American enterprise focused on its extraction. Silver production concentrated on two areas: the thinly populated Mexican north, particularly the region around **Zacatecas,** and the high, cold central Andes, particularly the stunningly rich mines of **Potosí** (present-day Bolivia). Both sites employed large numbers of indigenous laborers. Many laborers went to Zacatecas voluntarily as their home villages experienced the pressures of conquest and disease. Over time they became professional miners, spoke Spanish, and lost touch with the communities of their birth.

Meanwhile, Spanish prospectors discovered a large vein of silver near Potosí in 1545 and began large-scale mining there in the 1580s. By 1600 Potosí was a boomtown with a population of 150,000. Rapid growth created an explosive demand for labor. As in the Mexican mines, Spanish administrators relied mostly on voluntary labor, but they also adapted the Inca practice of requisitioning draft labor, known as the ***mita* system,** to recruit workers for particularly difficult and dangerous chores that free laborers would not accept. Under the *mita* system, Spanish authorities annually required each village to send one-seventh of its male population to work for four months in the mines at Potosí. Draft laborers received payment for their work, but wages were very low, and the conditions of work were extremely harsh. Some *mita* laborers hauled heavy baskets of silver ore up steep mine shafts, while others worked with toxic mercury, which miners used to separate the silver from its ore. Death rates of draft laborers were high, and many indigenous men sought to evade *mita* obligations by fleeing to cities or hiding in distant villages. Thus, even though at any given moment draft laborers represented only about 10 percent of the workforce at Potosí, the *mita* system touched a large portion of the indigenous population and influenced settlement patterns throughout the Andean region.

**The Global Significance of Silver** The mining industries of Mexico and Peru powered the Spanish economy in the Americas and even stimulated the world economy of early modern times. Silver produced profits for private investors and revenues for the crown. The Spanish government reserved a fifth of the silver production for itself. This share, known as the ***quinto,*** represented the principal revenue that the crown derived from its American possessions. American silver helped Spanish kings finance a powerful army and bureaucracy, but much of it also went well beyond Spain to lubricate the European and the larger world economies.

***métis*** (may-TEE)
**Zacatecas** (sah-kah-TEH-kahs)
**Potosí** (paw-taw-SEE)
***quinto*** (KEEN-toh)

Mining operations at Potosí in South America gave rise to a large settlement that housed miners and others who supplied food, made charcoal, fashioned tools, and supported the enterprise. In this illustration from the mid-1580s, llamas laden with silver ore descend the mountain (background) while laborers work in the foreground to crush the ore and extract pure silver from it.
Courtesy of the Hispanic Society of America, New York.

Most American silver made its way across the Atlantic to Spain and markets throughout Europe, and from there European merchants traded it for silk, spices, and porcelain in the markets of Asia. Some silver went from Acapulco on the west coast of Mexico across the Pacific to the Philippines in the **Manila galleons,** and from Manila it also made its way to Asian markets, especially China. No matter which direction it went or which oceans it crossed, American silver quickly traveled throughout the world and powerfully stimulated global trade.

**The Hacienda** Apart from mining, the principal occupations in Spanish America were farming, stock raising, and craft production. The organization of mining industries created opportunities for cultivators, herders, and artisans to provision mining towns with food, wine, textiles, tools, furniture, and craft items. By the seventeenth century the most prominent site of agricultural and craft production in Spanish America was the estate, or **hacienda,** which produced foodstuffs for its own use as well as for sale to local markets in nearby mining districts, towns, and cities. The products of the hacienda were mostly of European origin: wheat, grapes, and meat from pigs and cattle were the most prominent agricultural products. Bordering the large estates were smaller properties owned by Spanish migrants or creoles as well as sizable tracts of land held by indigenous peoples who lived in native villages and practiced subsistence agriculture.

**Labor Systems** The major source of labor for the haciendas was the indigenous population. Spanish conquerors first organized native workforces under the *encomienda* system. As originally developed in Spain during the era of the *reconquista* (see chapter 19), the *encomienda* system rewarded Spanish conquerors by allowing them to exact both labor and tribute from defeated Moorish populations, while in theory requiring the *encomenderos* to look after the physical and spiritual welfare of their workers. Later, Spanish conquerors transferred the system to the Caribbean, Mexico, Central America, and Andean South America. From the 1520s to the 1540s, the *encomienda* system led to rampant abuse of indigenous peoples, as Spanish landowners overworked their laborers and skimped on their maintenance. After mid-century, *encomenderos* in agriculturally productive regions increasingly required their subject populations to provide tribute but not labor. Populations living under indigenous leadership owned much of the land that they cultivated in villages. In some ways, their payments to Spanish colonists resembled the tributes their ancestors had provided to Aztec rulers.

As the *encomienda* system gradually went out of use, Spanish landowners resorted to a system of debt peonage to recruit labor for their haciendas. Under this system, landowners advanced loans to native peoples so that they could buy

**hacienda** (ah-SYEN-dah)

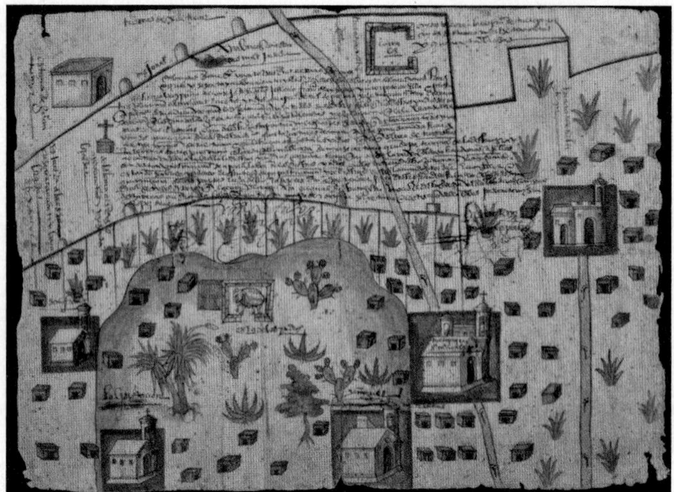

Map drawn in 1569 of Spanish settlement around the Hacienda de Santa Ines in New Spain. The map was intended to be a legal document between Spanish settlers and indigenous inhabitants of the area.
Newberry Library.

seeds, tools, and supplies. The debtors then repaid the loans with labor, but wages were so low that they were never able to pay off their debts. Because legal restrictions often prevented debtors from leaving their lands and escaping their obligations, landowners had in effect a captive labor force to work their estates. In effect, then, the line between debt peonage and slavery was not always clear, and indeed the system is sometimes referred to as "debt slavery."

**Resistance to Spanish Rule** The Spanish regimes in the Americas met considerable resistance from indigenous peoples. Resistance took various forms: rebellion, work slowdowns, and retreat into the mountains and forests where Spanish power did not reach. In 1680, for example, after experiencing nearly a century of forced labor on Spanish estates, several indigenous groups in northern Mexico (the modern-day American state of New Mexico) mounted a large uprising known as the Pueblo revolt. Led by an indigenous shaman named Popé, the rebels attacked missions, killed priests and colonists, and drove Spanish settlers out of the region for twelve years. Spanish forces in Peru faced an even larger rebellion in 1780, when a force of about sixty thousand native peoples revolted in the name of Túpac Amaru, the last of the Inca rulers, whom Spanish conquistadores had beheaded in 1572. This rebellion raged for almost two years before Spanish forces suppressed it and executed thousands of its participants.

On some occasions, indigenous peoples turned also to Spanish law and administrators in search of aid against oppressive colonists. In 1615, for example, Felipe Guaman Poma de Ayala, a native of Peru, fired off a 1,200-page letter—accompanied by some four hundred hand-drawn illustrations—to King Philip III of Spain asking for protection for indigenous peoples against greedy colonists. Although Guaman Poma's letter never made it to the king, it somehow made its way to Denmark, where it remained undiscovered in a library until 1908.

Nevertheless, Guaman Poma's complaint serves as a record of grievances against the Spanish. The author wrote passionately of men ruined by overtaxation and women driven to prostitution, of Spanish colonists who grabbed the lands of indigenous peoples and Spanish priests who preyed sexually upon the wives of indigenous men. Guaman Poma warned the king that the peoples of Peru were dying fast because of disease and abuse and that if Philip wanted anything to remain of his Andean empire, he should intervene and protect the indigenous peoples of the land.

## Sugar and Slavery in Brazil

Whereas the Spanish American empire concentrated on the extraction of silver, the Portuguese Empire in Brazil depended on the production and export of sugar. The different economic and social foundations of the Spanish and Portuguese empires led to different patterns of labor recruitment. Spanish conquistadores subjugated sedentary peoples with effective administrative systems and compelled them to provide labor in the mines and estates of Mexico and Peru. Portuguese nobles and entrepreneurs established sugar plantations in regions without the administrative machinery to recruit workers and relied instead on imported enslaved Africans as laborers. Indeed, Africans and their descendants became the majority of the population in Brazil, not simply an auxiliary labor force as in Spanish America.

**The Engenho** Colonial Brazilian life revolved around the sugar mill, or ***engenho.*** Strictly speaking, the term *engenho* (related to the English word *engine*) referred only to the mill itself, but it came to represent a complex of land, labor, buildings, animals, capital, and technical skills related to the production of sugar. Unlike other crops, sugarcane required extensive processing to yield molasses or refined sugar as a profitable export. Thus *engenhos* always combined agricultural and industrial enterprises. They depended both on heavy labor for the planting and harvesting of cane and on the specialized skills of individuals who understood the intricacies of the sugar-making process. As a result, *engenhos* were among the most complex business enterprises in the Americas.

In a colonial economy where sugar figured as the most important export, the Portuguese planters and owners of sugar mills were a privileged class, exercising political, social, and economic power. As long as they contributed to the government's revenues, they could usually count on strong royal support. The planters acted like landed nobility, but the nature of their enterprises required them to pay attention to affairs like businessmen. They operated on very small profit margins. Their exalted social position often disguised difficult financial predicaments, and turnover in the business was always high.

***engenho*** (en-GEHN-ho)

**The Search for Labor** Like their Spanish counterparts, Portuguese colonists first tried to enlist local populations as laborers. Unlike the inhabitants of Mexico and Peru, however, the peoples of Brazil were not sedentary cultivators. They resisted efforts to commandeer their labor, evaded Portuguese forces by retreating to interior lands, and took every opportunity to escape captors who managed to force them into servitude. In addition, as elsewhere in the Americas, epidemic diseases devastated indigenous populations in Brazil. During the 1560s, smallpox and measles ravaged the whole Brazilian coast, making it difficult for Portuguese settlers even to find potential laborers, let alone force them to work.

**Slavery** Faced with those difficulties, the colonists turned to another labor source: enslaved Africans. As we saw in chapter 22, Iberians had been using the labor of enslaved Africans on the Canary and Madeira islands since the late fifteenth century. Using this experience as their guide, Portuguese plantation managers in Brazil imported enslaved people as early as the 1530s, but they began to rely on African labor on a large scale only in the 1580s. The labor demands of cane cultivation and sugar production exacted a heavy toll from enslaved communities, who faced arduous working conditions, physical and sexual abuse, tropical heat, poor nutrition, and inadequate housing. These conditions resulted in high rates of disease and mortality for enslaved Africans in Brazil. In any given year, 5 to 10 percent of slaves on engenhos died from such conditions. In Brazil, as in most other plantation societies, the number of deaths in the slave population usually exceeded the number of births, so there was a constant demand for more slaves.

Although a few Portuguese criticized this brutal system, government officials mostly left matters of labor management to slaveholders. To them the balance sheet of sugar production dictated practices that paid scant heed to the preservation of the lives of enslaved people, as long as the owners realized profits. Indeed, if an enslaved person lived five to six years, the investment of the average slaveholder doubled and permitted him to purchase a new and healthy enslaved person without taking a monetary loss. As a result, slaveholders had little economic incentive to improve conditions for enslaved people or to increase their birthrates. Children required financial outlays for at least twelve years, which from the perspective of the slaveholder represented a financial loss. All told, the business of producing Brazilian sugar was so brutal that every ton of the sweet substance cost one human life.

An illustration from a nineteenth-century painting showing Native Americans trading pelts onboard Henry Hudson's ship, in Nova Scotia in 1609. Hudson (born ca. 1560s/1570s) was an English explorer and navigator, who repeatedly searched for a northwest passage to Asia.
Bettmann/Getty Images

## Fur Traders and Settlers in North America

**The Fur Trade** European mariners first frequented North American shores in search of fish. Although fishing was a profitable enterprise, trade in furs became far more lucrative. The North American **fur trade** began when fishermen bartered for fur with local peoples. After explorers found a convenient entrance to rich fur-producing regions through the Hudson Strait and Hudson Bay, they began the systematic exploitation of the northern lands. Royal agents, adventurers, businessmen, and settlers began to connect large parts of the North American interior by a chain of forts and trading posts. Indigenous peoples trapped animals for Europeans and exchanged the pelts for manufactured goods such as wool blankets, iron pots, firearms, and distilled spirits. The hides went mostly to Europe, where capitalist markets experienced burgeoning demand for beaver skin hats and fur clothing.

**Effects of the Fur Trade** The fur trade generated tremendous conflict in North America. American beaver populations, which were the chief targets of the trade, declined so rapidly that trappers constantly had to push farther inland in search of untapped beaver grounds. When hunting grounds became depleted, indigenous peoples poached or invaded others' territories, which sometimes led to war. Among the most brutal of those conflicts were the French and Iroquois Wars (also called the Beaver Wars) of the seventeenth century, which pitted Iroquois against Hurons and their French allies.

The Iroquois sought to expand their diminished hunting grounds into the territory of the Hurons (and others) to the north and thus maintain their livelihoods in the fur trade.

Competition between Native American groups over the fur trade was complicated by rivalries between European groups. During the French and Iroquois Wars, the Iroquois were allied with the Dutch, while the Huron were allied with the French. The Iroquois used firearms supplied by the Dutch in their campaign to control the fur trade in Huron territory, and in the process tried to eliminate their enemies. Hurons survived the war, although in greatly diminished numbers, but the Iroquois vastly increased their strength and destroyed Huron power.

This painting features the "first smoke" of Sir Walter Raleigh (1552–1618). He was an English aristocrat, writer, poet, soldier, courtier, spy, and explorer. He is also well known for popularizing tobacco in England.

The Picture Art Collection/Alamy Stock Photo

**Settler Society** European settler-cultivators posed an even more serious challenge to native ways of life than did the fur traders because they displaced indigenous peoples from the land and turned hunting grounds into plantations. The earliest colonists experienced difficult times because European crops such as wheat did not grow well in their settlements. Indeed, many of the early colonies would have perished except for maize, game, and fish supplied by indigenous peoples. Over time, however, French and especially English migrants stabilized their societies and distinguished them sharply from those of indigenous peoples.

**Tobacco and Other Cash Crops** As colonists' numbers increased, they sought to integrate their American holdings into the larger capitalist economy of the Atlantic Ocean basin by producing cash crops that they could market in Europe. In the English colonies of Virginia and Carolina, settlers concentrated on the cultivation of **tobacco,** a plant they learned about from Native American societies. Christopher Columbus had observed Taíno people smoking the leaves of a local plant through a pipe called a *tobago*—the origin of the word *tobacco.* Later, European visitors frequently observed tobacco consumption among indigenous peoples, who had been using the plant for two thousand years for ritual, medicinal, and social purposes. Maya worshipers blew tobacco smoke from their mouths as offerings to the gods. Priests of the Aztec Empire both smoked tobacco and took it in the form of snuff as an accompaniment to religious sacrifices.

## What's Left Out?

The history of slavery in North America has, until recently, focused mainly on enslaved Africans in what became the American South. Although many textbooks acknowledge that the northern colonies also permitted slavery for a time, these colonies have nevertheless usually been depicted as less dependent on slave labor. Moreover, a large body of historical work once argued that Native Americans were unwilling or unable to tolerate slavery and thus were not commonly enslaved by Europeans. Recent scholarship, however, is revising these longstanding perceptions. Indeed, during the seventeenth and eighteenth centuries, New England colonists enslaved many thousands of Native Americans and depended on their labor to build new lives for themselves. During both the Pequot War (1630s) and King Philip's War (1670s), thousands of Native Americans were captured and sold into slavery. King Philip's War, in fact, had erupted in part because a Wampanoag-led coalition protested the use of forced Indian labor. But the war ended in defeat for the Wampanoags and did not end the practice of enslaving indigenous peoples. Instead, one study shows that after the war nearly 40 percent of Indians remaining in the southern portion of New England were serving as slaves or indentured servants in English households. In addition, European colonists in Virginia, North Carolina, and South Carolina similarly enslaved and traded indigenous peoples. These practices continued until the late eighteenth century, when large numbers of enslaved Africans began to displace indigenous slaves. In what ways can new information such as this add, nuance or even alter our perceptions about the early history of the United States?

*Source:* Margaret Ellen Newell, *Brethren by Nature: New England Indians, Colonists, and the Origins of American Slavery* (Ithaca: Cornell University Press, 2015).

### Thinking Critically About Sources

1. Why has the information about enslaved Native Americans been "left out of" or obscured in many many history books?
2. If Native Americans did not leave written accounts of these experiences, what resources could reveal these stories?

The widespread popularity of this plant was due to the addictive nature of nicotine, an oily, toxic substance present in tobacco leaves. The word "nicotine" comes from the French diplomat, Jean Nicot, who introduced tobacco use to Paris in 1560. Spanish and English promoters first touted the health benefits of tobacco to European consumers. Many physicians ascribed miraculous healing powers to tobacco, which they referred to as "the herb panacea," "divine tobacco," or the "holy herb nicotine." Merchants and mariners soon spread the use of tobacco throughout Europe and beyond to all parts of the world that European ships visited.

In 1612, English settlers cultivated the first commercial crop of tobacco in Virginia. By 1616, Virginia colonists exported 2,300 pounds of tobacco. European demand for the addictive weed resulted in skyrocketing exports amounting to 200,000 pounds in 1624 and three million pounds in 1638. By the late seventeenth century, most consumers used tobacco socially and for pleasure because tobacco's alleged health benefits never lived up to expectations. By the eighteenth century settlers in the southern colonies had established plantation complexes that produced rice and indigo as well as tobacco, and by the nineteenth century cotton also had become a prominent plantation crop.

**Indentured Labor** The plantations created high demand for inexpensive labor. Colonists in North America enslaved indigenous peoples in large numbers, but still the demand for labor grew. By the seventeenth century, colonists began to recruit indentured servants from Europe to increase the supply of labor. People who had little future in Europe—the chronically unemployed, orphans, political prisoners, and criminals—were often willing to sell a portion of their working lives in exchange for passage across the Atlantic and a new start in life. Throughout the seventeenth and eighteenth centuries, indentured servants came to the American colonies in hopes that after they had satisfied their obligation to provide four to seven years of labor they might become independent artisans or planters themselves. (The **indentured labor** trade in the Americas continued on a smaller scale even into the early twentieth century.) Some indentured servants went on to become prominent figures in colonial society, but many died of disease or overwork before completing their terms of labor, and others found only marginal employment.

**Slavery in North America** Most indentured servants eventually gained their freedom, but other laborers remained in bondage all their lives. Like Iberian colonists, English settlers also used the labor of enslaved Africans in their colonial territories. In 1619 a group of about twenty Africans was brought to Virginia. While it took some time to determine the legal status of Africans, in 1661 Virginia law recognized all Africans as slaves. After 1680, planters increasingly replaced indigenous slaves and indentured servants with enslaved Africans. By 1750 about 120,000 enslaved Africans tilled Chesapeake tobacco, and 180,000 more cultivated Carolina rice.

Plantation labor was not prominent in the agricultural production of the northern colonies, principally because the land and the climate were not suitable for the cultivation of labor-intensive cash crops. But European settlers in the northern colonies also exploited both indigenous and African slave labor until slavery was outlawed in the late eighteenth and early nineteenth centuries. In addition, the economies of these colonies also profited handsomely from slavery. Many New England merchants traded in enslaved people destined for the West Indies: by the mid-eighteenth century, half the merchant fleet of Newport carried human cargo. The economies of New York and Philadelphia benefited from the building and outfitting of slave vessels, and the seaports of New England became profitable centers for the distillation of rum. The chief ingredient of this rum was slave-produced sugar from the West Indies, and merchants traded much of the distilled spirits for enslaved people on the African coast. Thus, although the southern plantation societies became most directly identified with a system that exploited African labor, all the North American colonies participated in and profited from the slave trade.

## Christianity and Indigenous Religions in the Americas

Like Buddhists and Muslims in earlier centuries, Christian explorers, conquerors, merchants, and settlers took their religious traditions with them when they traveled overseas. Centuries of warfare against Muslims had convinced the Spanish monarchs that non-Christians should be converted to Christianity. In the aftermath of Christopher Columbus's voyages, Queen Isabella of Spain asserted that the indigenous peoples of the Western Hemisphere were her subjects, and as such had to be converted to Christianity. Thus, when Spanish conquistadores, colonists, and priests came to the Americas, they came both as conquerors as well as evangelists. In the long term, their conversion efforts succeeded, but in the process Catholicism evolved into a religion that integrated Christian concepts with aspects of indigenous beliefs and traditions.

**Spanish Missionaries** From the beginning of Spanish colonization in Mexico and Peru, Roman Catholic priests served as representatives of the crown and reinforced civil administrators. Franciscan, Dominican, Jesuit, and other missionaries campaigned to Christianize indigenous peoples. In Mexico, for example, a group of twelve Franciscan missionaries arrived in 1524. They founded a school in Tlatelolco, the bustling market district of the Aztec capital of Tenochtitlan, where they educated the sons of prominent noble families in Latin, Spanish, and Christian doctrine. The missionaries themselves learned native languages and sought to explain Christianity in terms their audiences could understand. They also compiled a vast amount of information about indigenous societies in hopes of learning how best to communicate their message. The work of the Franciscan Bernardino de Sahagún was especially important. Sahagún preserved volumes of information about the language, customs, beliefs, literature, and history of Mexico before the arrival of Spanish forces there (a tiny portion of which can be seen in the first "Sources of the Past"

## INTERPRETING IMAGES

An eighteenth-century engraving depicts work on a tobacco plantation: several enslaved Africans prepare flour and bread from manioc (left), while others hang tobacco leaves to dry in a shed (right). The illustration helps capture the labor intensity of plantation life for enslaved peoples.

**Analyze** *Consider this image and that of Sir Walter Raleigh on page 396. Compared to spices, gems, and even sugar, tobacco may be considered less desirable, and yet it became a major expert product. Why?*

Everett Collection/age fotostock

selection in this chapter). His work remained largely unstudied until the twentieth century, but in recent times it has shed enormous light both on Aztec society and on the methods of early missionaries in Mexico.

**Survival of Indigenous Religions** Christian missionaries encountered considerable resistance in the Americas. In both Mexico and Peru, indigenous peoples continued to observe their inherited faiths into the seventeenth century and beyond, even though Spanish authorities sponsored the Roman Catholic faith and tried to eliminate the worship of indigenous gods. In the face of Spanish persecution, indigenous peoples often continued their religious practices in locations inaccessible to Catholic priests.

Yet Christianity also won adherents in Spanish America. In the wake of conquest and epidemic disease, many indigenous leaders in Mexico concluded that their gods had abandoned them and looked to the missionaries for spiritual guidance. When indigenous peoples adopted Christianity, however, they blended their own interests and traditions with the faith taught by Spanish missionaries. When they learned about Roman Catholic saints, for example, they revered saints with qualities like those of their inherited gods or those whose feast days coincided with traditional celebrations.

**The Virgin of Guadalupe** In Mexico, Roman Catholicism became especially popular after the mid-seventeenth century. One reason for this was the **Virgin of Guadalupe,** who came to be worshipped almost as a national symbol. According to legends, the Virgin Mary appeared before the devout peasant Juan Diego on a hill near Mexico City in 1531. The site of the apparition soon became a popular local shrine visited mostly by Spanish settlers. By the 1640s the shrine attracted pilgrims from all parts of Mexico, and the Virgin of Guadalupe gained a reputation for working miracles on behalf of individuals who visited her shrine. The Virgin of Guadalupe, with her darker, indigenous complexion, came to symbolize a distinctly Mexican faith, and in later years she became transformed as a result into a powerful symbol of Mexican nationalism. The popularity of the Virgin of Guadalupe helped to ensure not only that Roman Catholic Christianity would dominate cultural and religious matters in Mexico but also that Mexican religious faith would retain strong indigenous influences.

**French and English Missions** French and English missionaries did not attract nearly as many converts to Christianity in North America as their Spanish counterparts did in Mexico and Peru. In part this was because French and English colonists did not rule over conquered populations of sedentary cultivators: it was much more difficult to conduct missions among peoples who frequently moved about the countryside than among those who lived permanently in villages, towns, or cities. English colonists, moreover, displayed little interest in converting indigenous peoples to Protestantism. The colonists did not discourage converts, but they made little effort to seek them, nor did they welcome converted indigenous people into their agricultural and commercial society. In contrast, Catholic French missionaries worked actively among native communities in the St. Lawrence, Mississippi, and Ohio River valleys

**Virgin of Guadalupe** (gwah-dah-LOO-pay)

Famed Mexican painter Miguel Cabrera crafted this eighteenth-century depiction of the Virgin of Guadalupe. Recognized as the greatest painter in New Spain, he featured in this work one of Mexico's most powerful religious icons.
Album/Alamy Stock Photo

Their efforts, however, were only modestly successful. Yet even though native peoples did not embrace Christianity, the burgeoning settlements of French and especially English colonists guaranteed that European religious traditions would figure prominently in North American society.

# EUROPEANS IN THE PACIFIC

Though geographically distant from the Americas, Australia and the Pacific Islands underwent experiences similar to those that transformed the Western Hemisphere in early modern times. Like their American counterparts, the peoples of Oceania had no inherited or acquired immunities to diseases that were common to peoples throughout the Eastern Hemisphere, and their numbers plunged when epidemic disease struck their populations. For the most part, however, the peoples of Australia and the Pacific Islands experienced epidemic disease and the arrival of European migrants later than did the peoples of the Americas. European mariners thoroughly explored the Pacific basin between the sixteenth and eighteenth centuries, but only in Guam and the Mariana Islands did they establish permanent settlements before the late eighteenth century. Nevertheless, their scouting of the region laid a foundation for much more intense interactions between European, Euro-American, Asian, and Oceanic peoples during the nineteenth and twentieth centuries.

## Australia and the Larger World

At least from the second century C.E., European geographers had speculated about ***terra australis incognita*** ("unknown southern land") that they thought must exist in the world's southern hemisphere to balance the huge landmasses north of the equator. As European mariners explored the Atlantic and Pacific Oceans during early modern times, they searched expectantly for a southern continent. Yet their principal interest was trade, and they rarely abandoned the pursuit of profit to sail out of their way in search of an unknown land.

**Dutch Exploration** Europeans first approached the Australian continent from the west in Southeast Asia. Portuguese mariners likely charted much of the western and northern coast of Australia as early as the 1520s, but Dutch sailors made the first recorded European sighting of the southern continent in 1606. The Dutch VOC (see chapter 22) authorized exploratory voyages, but mariners found little to encourage further efforts. In 1623, after surveying the dry landscapes of western Australia, the Dutch mariner Jan Carstenzs reported that his party had not seen "one fruit-bearing tree, nor anything that man could make use of: there are no mountains or even hills, so that it may be safely concluded that the land contains no metals, nor yields any precious woods." He went on to describe the land as "the most arid and barren region that could be found anywhere on earth."

Nevertheless, Dutch mariners continued to visit Australia. By the mid-seventeenth century, they had scouted the continent's northern, western, and southern coasts, and they had ascertained that New Guinea and Tasmania were islands separate from Australia itself. Dutch explorers were so active in the reconnaissance of Australia that Europeans referred to the southern continent as "New Holland" throughout the seventeenth century. Yet neither Dutch nor any other European seamen visited the eastern coast until **James Cook** approached

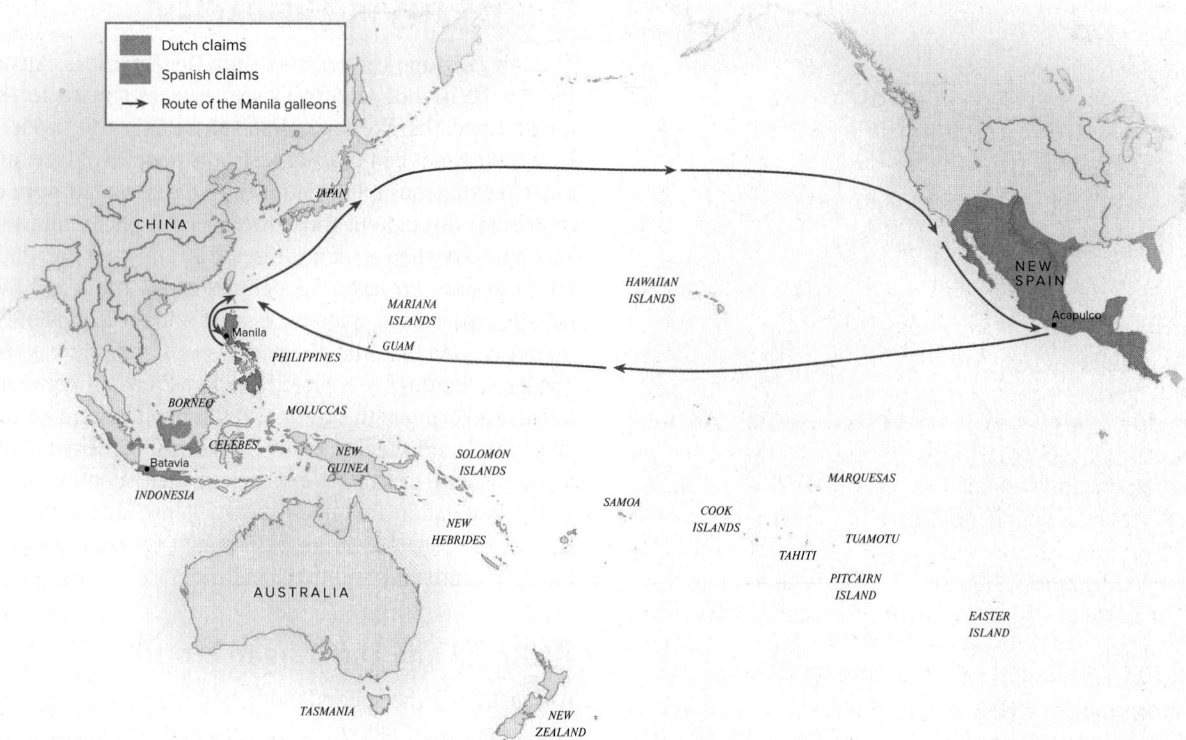


**MAP 12.2 Manila galleon route and the lands of Oceania, 1500–1800.**

Note the route taken by the Manila galleons in relation to the majority of the Pacific Islands.

***Why did Spanish mariners not explore the Hawaiian Islands and the more southerly Pacific Islands as they made their way to the Philippines?***

Australia from the southeast and charted the region in 1770, barely escaping destruction on the Great Barrier Reef.

Although European mariners explored Australian coastlines in the seventeenth and eighteenth centuries, they made only brief landfalls and had only fleeting encounters with indigenous peoples. The aboriginal peoples of Australia had formed many distinct foraging and fishing societies, but European visitors did not linger long enough to become familiar with either the peoples or their societies. Because they were nomadic foragers rather than sedentary cultivators, Europeans did not hold them in high regard. In the absence of tempting opportunities to trade, European mariners made no effort to establish permanent settlements in Australia.

**British Colonists** Only after Cook's charting of the eastern coast in 1770 did European peoples become seriously interested in Australia. Cook dropped anchor for a week at Botany Bay (near modern Sydney) and reported that the region was suitable for settlement. In 1788 a British fleet arrived at Sydney carrying about one thousand passengers, eight hundred of them convicts, who established the first European settlement in Australia as a penal colony. For half a century Europeans in Australia numbered only a few thousand, most of them convicts who herded sheep. Free settlers did not outnumber convicted criminals until the 1830s. Thus exploratory voyages of the seventeenth and eighteenth centuries led to fleeting encounters between European and aboriginal Australian peoples, but only in the nineteenth and twentieth centuries did a continuing stream of European settlers link Australia more directly to the larger world.

## The Pacific Islands and the Larger World

The entry of European mariners into the Pacific Ocean basin did not bring immediate change to most of the Pacific Islands. In these islands, as in Australia, European merchants and settlers did not arrive in large numbers until the late eighteenth century. Guam and the Mariana Islands underwent dramatic change already in the sixteenth century, however, and the ventures of European merchants and explorers in the Pacific basin set the stage for profound upheavals in other island societies during the nineteenth and twentieth centuries.

**Spanish Voyages in the Pacific** In 1521 Ferdinand Magellan and his crew became the first Europeans to cross the Pacific Ocean. Before reaching the Philippines, they encountered only one inhabited island group–the Marianas, dominated by Guam. In 1565 Spanish mariners inaugurated the Manila galleon trade between Manila and Acapulco. Because their primary goal was to link New Spain to Asian markets, they rarely went out of their way to explore the Pacific Ocean or to search for other islands. Spanish vessels visited the Marquesas, Tuamotu, Cook, Solomon, and New Hebrides islands in the sixteenth century, and it is likely that one or more stray ships accidentally ended up in Hawai'i. Yet Spanish mariners found little to interest them in most of the Pacific islands and did not establish regular communications with island peoples. They usually sailed before the trade winds from Acapulco to Manila on a route that took them south of Hawai'i and north of other Polynesian islands. On the return trip they sailed before the westerlies on a route that took them well north of all the Pacific Islands.

**Guam** The only Pacific Islands that attracted substantial Spanish interest in the sixteenth century were Guam and the northern Mariana Islands. Manila galleons called regularly at Guam, which lay directly on the route from Acapulco to Manila. For more than a century, they took on fresh provisions and engaged in mostly peaceful trade with the indigenous Chamorro people. During the 1670s and 1680s, Spanish authorities decided to consolidate their position in Guam and bring the Mariana Islands under the control of the viceroy of New Spain in Mexico. They dispatched military forces to the islands to impose Spanish rule and subject the Chamorro to the spiritual authority of the Roman Catholic church. The Chamorro strongly opposed those efforts, but a smallpox epidemic in 1688 severely reduced their numbers and crippled their resistance. By 1695 the Chamorro population had declined from about fifty thousand at mid-century to five thousand, partly because of Spanish campaigns but mostly because of smallpox. By the end of the seventeenth century, Spanish forces had established garrisons throughout the Mariana Islands and relocated surviving Chamorro into communities supervised by Spanish authorities.

**Visitors and Trade** Like the aboriginal peoples of Australia, the indigenous peoples of the Pacific Islands had mostly fleeting encounters with European visitors during early modern times. By the late eighteenth century, however, growing European and Euro-American interest in the Pacific Ocean basin led to sharply increased interactions between islanders and mariners. English and French mariners explored the Pacific basin in search of commercial opportunities and the elusive northwest passage from Europe to Asia. They frequently visited Tahiti after 1767, and they soon began to trade with the islanders, whose societies were complex and highly stratified by social class and by occupation (discussed in greater depth in chapter 20). European mariners received provisions and engaged in sexual relations with Tahitian women in exchange for nails, knives, iron tools, and textiles. Although trade was mostly peaceful, misunderstandings based on European ignorance about social practices often led to skirmishes and acts of violence, and European captains occasionally trained their cannons on fleets of war canoes or villages in the Pacific Islands.

**Captain Cook and Hawai'i** The experiences of Captain James Cook in Hawai'i illustrate a common pattern. In 1778, while sailing north from Tahiti in search of the northwest passage, Cook happened across the Hawaiian Islands. He immediately recognized Hawaiians as a people related to Tahitians and other Polynesians whose lands he had visited during his explorations of the Pacific Ocean since 1768, and he was able to communicate with Hawaiians on the basis of familiarity with Polynesian languages. Cook and his crew mostly got along well with Hawaiians, who readily traded pigs and provisions for ironwares. Sailors and island women avidly consorted with one another, resulting in the transmission of venereal diseases to Hawai'i, even though Cook had ordered infected crewmen to remain aboard ship. After a few weeks' stay in the islands, Cook resumed his northern course to seek the northwest passage. When he revisited Hawai'i late in 1779, he faced a very different climate, one in which islanders were

As depicted in 1816 by artist Ludwig Choris, the port of Honolulu in the Hawaiian Islands was home to European ships, horses, cattle, and warehouses as well as Hawaiians inhabiting traditional dwellings.
Honolulu Museum of Art, Gift of the Honolulu Art Society, 1944 (12,161).

less accommodating than before. Indeed, he lost his life when disputes over petty thefts escalated into a bitter conflict between his crew and islanders of Hawai'i.

Nevertheless, in the wake of Cook, whose reports soon became known throughout Europe, whalers began to venture into Pacific waters in large numbers, followed by missionaries, merchants, and planters. By the early nineteenth century, European and Euro-American peoples had become prominent figures in all the major Pacific Islands groups. During the nineteenth and twentieth centuries, interactions among islanders, visitors, and migrants brought rapid and often unsettling change to Pacific Islands societies.

## CONCLUSION

The Americas underwent thorough transformation in early modern times. Smallpox and other diseases sparked ferocious epidemics that devastated indigenous populations and undermined their societies. In the wake of severe depopulation, European peoples toppled imperial states, established mining and agricultural enterprises, imported enslaved African laborers, and founded colonies throughout much of the Western Hemisphere. Some indigenous peoples disappeared entirely as distinct groups. Others maintained their communities, identities, and cultural traditions but fell increasingly under the influence of European migrants and their Euro-American offspring. In Oceania only Guam and the Mariana Islands felt the full effects of epidemic disease and migration in the early modern era. By the late eighteenth century, however, European and Euro-American peoples with advanced technologies had thoroughly explored the Pacific Ocean basin, and epidemic diseases featured largely in their encounters with the peoples of Australia and the Pacific Islands. As a result, during the nineteenth and twentieth centuries, Oceania underwent a social transformation similar to the one experienced earlier by the Americas. These encounters in both regions profoundly shaped the course of their history into the modern era.

## STUDY TERMS

Atahualpa (383)
*audiencias* (385)
Brazil (386)
*conquistadores* (382)
*criollos* (390)
Doña Marina (378)
*encomienda* (381)
*engenho* (394)
epidemic disease (381)
Francisco Pizarro (383)
fur trade (395)
hacienda (393)
Hernán Cortés (378)
indentured labor (397)
James Cook (399)
Malintzin (378)
Manila galleons (393)
mestizo (389)
*métis* (392)
*mita system* (392)
Motecuzoma II (383)
Nahuatl (378)
New Spain (385)
*peninsulares* (391)
Potosí (392)
*quinto* (392)
smallpox (381)
Taíno (381)
Tenochtitlan (379)
*terra australis incognita* (399)
tobacco (396)
Virgin of Guadalupe (398)
Zacatecas (392)
*zambos* (391)

## FOR FURTHER READING


Rolena Adorno. *Guaman Poma: Writing and Resistance in Colonial Peru.* Austin, 2000. A native Andean, who came of age after the fall of the Inca Empire, tells Philip III of Spain of the evils of colonialism and the need for reform.

Colin G. Callaway. *New Worlds for All: Indians, Europeans, and the Remaking of Early America.*, 2nd ed. Baltimore, 2013. Scholarly synthesis examining interactions and cultural exchanges between European and indigenous American peoples.

William Cronon. *Changes in the Land: Indians, Colonists, and the Ecology of New England*, rev. ed. New York, 2003. New York, 1983. Brilliant study concentrating on the different ways English colonists and native peoples in colonial New England used the environment.

John H. Elliot. *Empires of the Atlantic World: Britain and Spain in America 1492-1830.* New Haven, 2006. Excellent comparative study of Spanish and English colonies in the Americas.

K. R. Howe. *Where the Waves Fall: A New South Sea Island History from First Settlement to Colonial Rule.* Honolulu, 1984. A thoughtful survey of Pacific Islands history emphasizing interactions between islanders and visitors.

John E. Kicza. *Resilient Cultures: America's Native Peoples Confront European Colonization, 1500-1800.* Upper Saddle River, N.J., 2002. A comprehensive comparative study assessing the impact of colonization on indigenous American peoples as well as native influences on American colonial history.

Karen Ordahl Kupperman. *Indians and English: Facing Off in Early America.* Ithaca, N.Y., 2000. Fascinating reconstruction of the early encounters between English and indigenous American peoples, drawing on sources from all parties to the encounters.

Kathleen Ann Meyers. *Neither Saints nor Sinners: Writing the Lives of Women in Spanish America.* New York, 2003. Examines female self-representation through the life writings of six seventeenth-century women in Latin America.

Matthew Restall, Lisa Sousa, and Kevin Terraciano, eds. *Mesoamerican Voices: Native Language Writings from Colonial Mexico, Yucatan, and Guatemala.* Cambridge, 2005. Composed between the sixteenth and eighteenth centuries, this collection of texts offers access to an important historical source.

Daniel Richter. *Facing East from Indian Country: A Native History of North America.* Cambridge, 2003. Explores the active ways Native American communities engaged with European colonization efforts into the interior of North America.

David J. Weber. *Bárbaros: Spaniards and Their Savages in the Age of Enlightenment.* New Haven, 2005. Pathbreaking and nuanced study of how Spanish administrators tried to forge a more enlightened policy toward native peoples.

Richard White. *The Middle Ground: Indians, Empires, and Republics in the Great Lakes Region, 1650-1815.* Cambridge, 1991. Insightful study of relations between French, English, and indigenous peoples in the Great Lakes region.

# CHAPTER 12 AP EXAM PRACTICE

Questions assume cumulative knowledge from this chapter and previous chapters.

## Section I

### Multiple Choice Questions

Use the image below and your knowledge of world history to answer questions 1–3.

European engraving of Native Americans from 1505
North Wind Picture Archives/Alamy Stock Photo

1. Which of these is a possible reason why the artist depicted Caribbean society?
   (A) He wanted to show the colors that people liked to wear.
   (B) He wanted the Taínos to welcome Spanish ships and Spanish colonial authority.
   (C) He wanted to show the Spanish that Native American society was different and could be conquered.
   (D) He wanted to show what products the Taínos could trade.

2. Which of the following is NOT true about life in the Spanish Caribbean?
   (A) Many Native Americans died from smallpox and other diseases.
   (B) The Spanish conscripted the Taínos for encomienda labor.
   (C) The Taínos never fought back against the Spanish.
   (D) Enslaved Africans were brought to the Caribbean as the Taíno population declined.

3. Which of these describes Caribbean society?
   (A) By 1700, there was a small European population and a much larger African population.
   (B) All Native American culture was gone by 1700.
   (C) By 1700, there was a large European population of gold miners.
   (D) Sugar could not grow in the Caribbean, so there were no cash crops.
   (E) As an alternative to executions, convicted witches were allowed to join merchant ships to Asia, Africa, and the Americas in the hope that they could control the weather.
   (F) Witch-hunting benefitted Europe because the witches were no longer about to destroy crops. This led to the population increases and urbanization.

Use the map below and your knowledge of world history to answer questions 4 and 5.

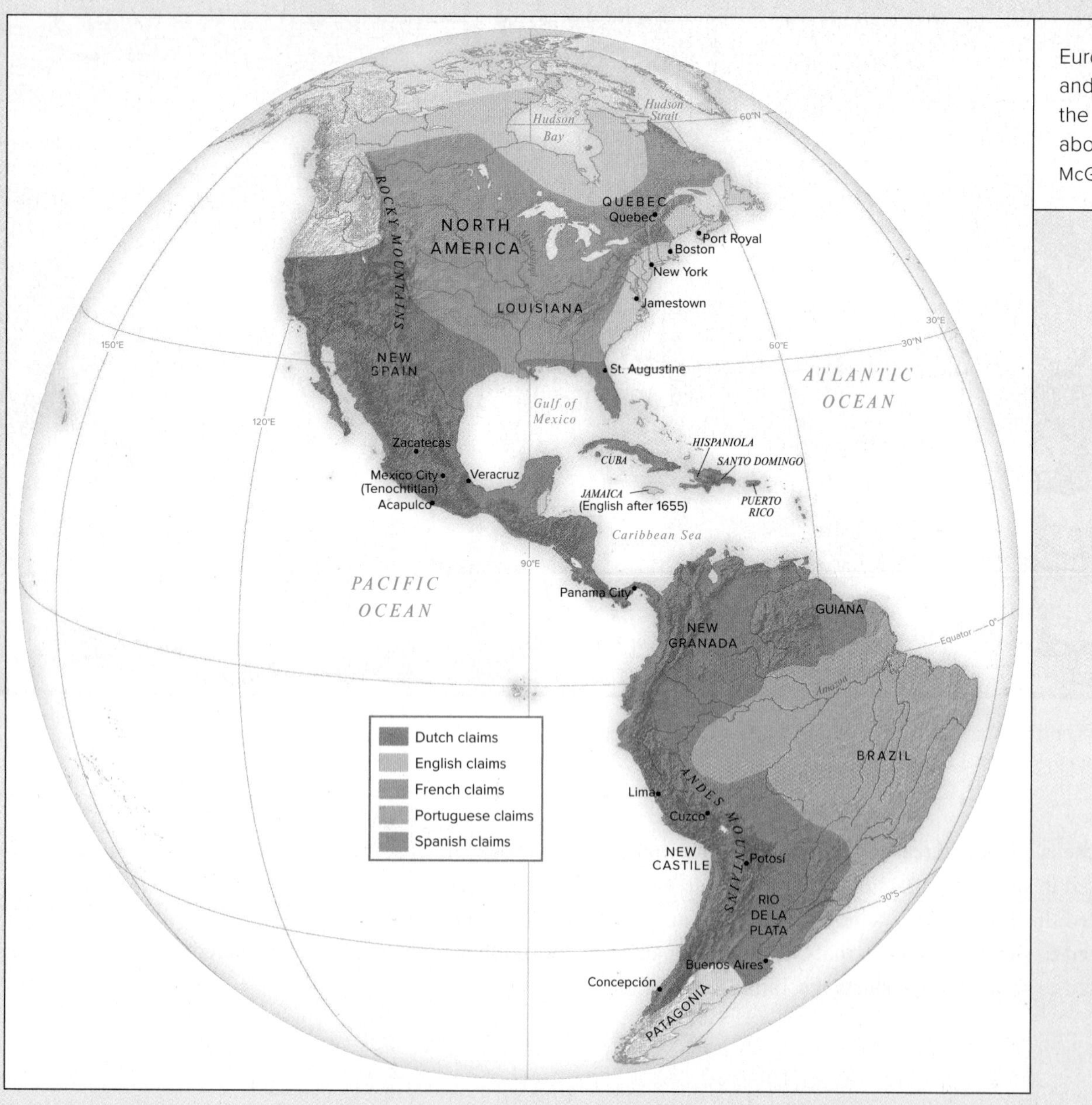


European empires and colonies in the Americas about 1700.
McGraw Hill

4. Which of the following claims about colonial cities can be made based on this map?
   (A) Many cities of the Spanish Empire were located where there was a large, sedentary population before the conquest.
   (B) Brazil's capital city was located in the interior of the colony.
   (C) The French territory had no cities.
   (D) Travel between Spanish cities was quick and easy.

5. What argument could a historian make about this map?
   (A) Portuguese sugar plantations in Brazil stretched from the coast to the Andes mountains.
   (B) The only colony in the Dutch maritime empire was Guiana.
   (C) The English colonies in the Caribbean were separated from their other North American colonies so they did not trade with each other.
   (D) The map shows the territory European powers claimed, but not how many Europeans were present or where they lived in the colonies.

## Short Answer

6. Use the image below and your knowledge of world history to answer parts A, B, and C.

Mining operations in Potosí in South America
Courtesy of the Hispanic Society of America, New York

(A) Identify ONE kind of labor system used in the Americas from 1450 to 1750.
(B) Explain ONE similarity in the lives of laborers in the mining and sugar industries.
(C) Explain ONE difference in the lives of laborers in the mining and sugar industries.

7. Use the image below and your knowledge of world history to answer parts A, B, and C.

*La Virgen de Guadalupe. Museum: MUSEO DE AMERICA MADRID*
Album/Alamy Stock Photo

(A) Explain ONE difference in missionary efforts in French, English, and Spanish colonies from 1450-1750.
(B) Explain ONE way that indigenous religions survived after 1492.
(C) Identify ONE aspect of the Virgin of Guadalupe that shows a blend of Catholic and indigenous traditions.

8. Use your understanding of world history to answer parts A, B, and C.
(A) Explain ONE reason why Australia was not colonized by Europeans until the eighteenth century.
(B) Explain ONE way that Europeans affected societies in the Pacific islands.
(C) Identify ONE reason why Europeans explored the Pacific.

# Section II

## Document-Based Question

Based on the documents below and your knowledge of world history, analyze how and why the indigenous peoples of the Americas responded to the presence of Europeans.

In your response you should do the following:

- Respond to the prompt with a historically defensible thesis or claim that establishes a line of reasoning.
- Describe a broader historical context relevant to the prompt.
- Support an argument in response to the prompt using all documents.
- Use at least one additional piece of specific historical evidence (beyond that found in the documents) relevant to an argument about the prompt.
- Explain how or why the document's point of view, purpose, historical situation, and /or audience is relevant to an argument.
- Use evidence to corroborate, qualify, or modify an argument that addresses the prompt.

### Document 1

But, brothers, since these Englishmen have seized our country, they have cut down the grass with scythes, and the trees with axes. Their cows and horses eat up the grass, and their hogs spoil our bed of clams; and finally we shall all starve to death; therefore, stand not in your own light, I ask you, but resolve to act like men. All the sachems both to the east and the west have joined with us, and we are resolved to fall upon them at a day appointed, and therefore I come secretly to you, cause you can persuade your Indians to do what you will.

*Source:* Sylvester, Herbert Milton, *Indian Wars of New England* (Cleveland, 1910), vol. I, p. 386.

### Document 2

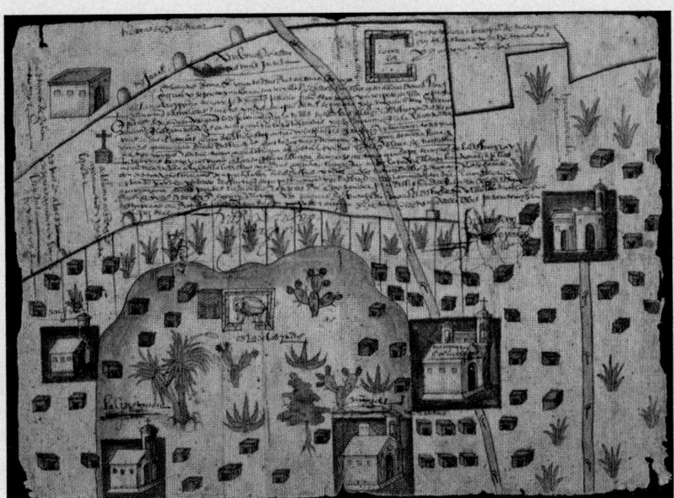

Map drawn in 1569 of Spanish settlement around the Hacienda de Santa lines in New Spain

Newberry Library.

## Document 3

The entrance to Chalco, on the way to the Aztec capital.

The Picture Art Collection/Alamy Stock Photo

## Long Essay

Develop a thoughtful and thorough historical argument that answers the question below. Begin your essay with a thesis statement and support it with relevant historical evidence.

Using specific examples and your knowledge of world history, evaluate the extent to which capitalism caused social changes in Europe from 1450 to 1750 C.E.

# Chapter 13 Africa and the Atlantic World

## ZOOMING IN ON TRADITIONS AND ENCOUNTERS

### An Enslaved Man's Long Trip Back to Africa

Between 1760 and 1792, a west African man named Thomas Peters crossed the Atlantic Ocean four times. In 1760, slave raiders captured Peters, whose original African name is unknown, marched him to the coast, and sold him to French slave merchants. He traveled in a slave ship to the French colony of Louisiana, where he probably worked on a sugar plantation. But Peters was not a docile servant. He attempted to escape at least three times, and his slaveholder punished him by beating him, branding him with a hot iron, and forcing him to wear shackles around his legs. During the 1760s his French slaveholder sold Peters to an English planter, and about 1770 a Scottish landowner in North Carolina bought him.

SLAVES PACKED BELOW AND ON DECK.

Young people held on board an illegal slave ship captured by the British in 1857.
Historia/Shutterstock

During the 1770s, as English colonists in North America prepared to rebel against the British government in the interests of "life, liberty, and the pursuit of happiness," enslaved people of African ancestry considered their own prospects and looked for ways to obtain freedom. Peters was among them. When war broke out in 1776, he made his way with his wife and daughter to British lines and joined the Black Pioneers, a company of people who had escaped slavery and who fought to maintain British rule in the colonies. When the colonists won the war, Peters escaped to Nova Scotia with his family and many other formerly enslaved people.

Slavery was illegal in Nova Scotia, but the white ruling elites forced people of African ancestry to till marginal lands and live in segregated villages. In hopes of improving their lot, some two hundred black families designated Peters as their spokesman and sent him to London to petition the government for better treatment or resettlement in a more favorable land. In 1790 Peters sailed to England, where he promoted the establishment of a colony for formerly enslaved people in Sierra Leone. His efforts succeeded, and the next year he returned to Nova Scotia to seek recruits for the colony. In 1792 he led 1,196 formerly enslaved people aboard a convoy of fifteen ships and began his fourth crossing of the Atlantic Ocean. The colonists arrived safely at Freetown, where Peters served as a leader of the new community. His time in Freetown was tense and short—the conditions Peters and his fellow colonists encountered fell far short of what they had been promised, and then only four months after arriving, Peters fell ill and died of malarial fever. Nevertheless, through his own life and experiences, Thomas Peters personified the links connecting the lands and peoples of the Atlantic Ocean basin and is remembered for his fight for black justice and self-determination in North America and West Africa.

# CHAPTER FOCUS

- Two main themes in the history of early modern Africa: the continuing involvement of African peoples and kingdoms in the trans-Saharan and Indian Ocean basin trade networks; and the increasing influence of Europeans and the Atlantic World on African societies.
- Examine how African rulers and merchants profited from the new Atlantic slave trade as well as the continuing Islamic, Mediterranean, and Indian Ocean basin slave trades, and consider how understandings of enslavement differed within these systems.
- Distinguish between the types of kingdoms and societies across the continent. The Swahili states' experiences were different from those of the west coast kingdom of Songhay; both differed from the experiences of Dahomey, Kongo, and Benin on the Atlantic coast.
- Consider the relationship between the consumer cultures of western Europe, the plantation societies of the Americas, and the Atlantic slave trade from the sixteenth to eighteenth centuries.
- Note the demographic complexities of early modern history—for example, despite millions of Africans enslaved and taken to the Americas, the population of the African continent increased in this period because of the Columbian exchange.
- Pay attention to the demographic effects of this increased trade in people: Angola, on the Atlantic coast, was two-thirds women at the height of the Atlantic slave trade; this was not true for Mogadishu on the east coast.
- The emotional and physical toll of enslavement cannot be adequately conveyed: the shock of displacement, loss of family and community on both sides of the Atlantic, harsh work, and language barriers. On plantations, where Africans outnumbered whites by as much as 90 percent, enslaved people developed syncretic (blended) languages, religions, musical styles, fictive kin relationships, and foods. These adaptations solidified into American cultural traditions in the modern eras.

## Historical Developments

- Afro-Eurasian fruit trees, grains, sugar, and domesticated animals were brought by Europeans to the Americas, while other foods were brought by enslaved Africans.
- Europeans established new trading posts in Africa and Asia which provide profitable for rulers and merchants involved in new global trade networks. Some Asian states sought to limit the disruptive economic and cultural effects of European dominated long-distance trade by adopting restrictive or isolationist trade policies.
- The expansion of maritime trading networks fostered the growth of states in Africa, including the Asante and the Kingdom of Kongo, whose participation in trading networks led to an increase in influence.
- The growth of the plantation economy increased the demand for enslaved labor in the Americas, leading to significant demographic, social, and cultural changes in both Africa and the Americas.

## Reasoning Processes

- **Developments and Processes** Explain the impact of the Atlantic slave trade on sub-Saharan African states and communities.
- **Contextualization** Identify and explain the historical context of the African diaspora.
- **Argumentation** Support the argument that African cultural traditions endured in the Americas in blended, or creole forms.

## Historical Thinking Skills

- **Continuity and Change** Describe the patterns of continuity and change over time among sub-Saharan African states and enslaved peoples.
- **Causation** Describe the causes and effects of the trans-Atlantic slave trade.

## CHAPTER OVERVIEW

The establishment of global trade networks in the early modern period brought deep change to sub-Saharan Africa. Commercial opportunities drew European vessels to the coast of west Africa, and maritime trade soon turned the attention of west African leaders to the Atlantic. Maritime commerce did not put an end to the trans-Saharan caravan trade that linked west Africa to the Mediterranean, but it helped promote the emergence of prosperous port cities and the establishment of powerful coastal kingdoms that traded through the ocean rather than the desert. In central and south Africa, European merchants brought the first substantial opportunities for long-distance trade because Muslim merchants had not ventured previously to those regions in large numbers.

Trade through the Atlantic profoundly affected African society because it included trade in human beings. Africans had made a place for slavery within their societies for centuries, and they had also supplied enslaved people to Muslim merchants who transported them to markets in the Mediterranean and the Indian Ocean basin. The Atlantic slave trade, however, operated on a vastly larger scale than the trans-Saharan slave trade, and it had more serious consequences for African society. Between the fifteenth and the nineteenth centuries, it not only siphoned millions of people from their societies but also provoked turmoil in large portions of sub-Saharan Africa because some peoples raided others' communities in search of captives for sale to slave traders.

The vast majority of Africans sold into the Atlantic slave trade went to destinations in the Caribbean or the Americas. Most worked on plantations cultivating cash crops for export, although some worked as domestic servants, miners, or laborers. Together they made up the largest forced migration in history before the nineteenth century and gave rise to an African diaspora in the Western Hemisphere. Under the restrictive conditions of slavery, they could not reconstitute African societies, but neither did people of European ancestry permit them to join Euro-American society. Instead, people of African ancestry preserved some African traditions and blended them with European and American traditions to create hybrid societies.

| CHRONOLOGY | |
|---|---|
| 1441 | Beginning of the Portuguese slave trade |
| 1464–1493 | Reign of Sunni Ali |
| 1464–1591 | Songhay Empire |
| 1506–1542 | Reign of King Afonso I of Kongo |
| 1623–1663 | Reign of Queen Nzinga of Ndongo |
| 1706 | Execution of Dona Beatriz |
| 1745–1797 | Life of Olaudah Equiano |
| 1793–1804 | Haitian revolution |
| 1807 | End of the British slave trade |
| 1865 | Abolition of slavery in the United States |

## AFRICAN POLITICS AND SOCIETY IN EARLY MODERN TIMES

For perhaps three millennia (2000 B.C.E. to 1000 C.E.), Bantu-speaking peoples migrated throughout sub-Saharan Africa. Many organized themselves into villages governed by kinship groups rather than formal states. As their numbers grew, they devised political structures and built a series of chiefdoms and regional kingdoms. After the eighth century increased transregional trade encouraged the formation of large kingdoms and empires in west Africa and thriving city-states in east Africa.

In the early modern era, the influence of maritime trade across the Atlantic and Indian Oceans changed patterns of state development. Regional kingdoms replaced the imperial states of west Africa as peoples organized their societies to take advantage of Atlantic as well as trans-Saharan commerce. The city-states of east Africa fell under the domination of Portuguese merchant-mariners seeking commercial opportunities in the Indian Ocean basin. The extension of trade networks also led to the formation of regional kingdoms in central Africa and south Africa. As the volume of long-distance trade grew, both Islam and Christianity became more prominent in sub-Saharan African societies.

### The States of West Africa and East Africa

Between the eighth and the sixteenth centuries, powerful kingdoms and imperial states ruled the savannas of west Africa. The earliest was the kingdom of **Ghana,** which originated perhaps as early as the fourth or fifth century and established its dominance in the region in the eighth century. By controlling and taxing the trans-Saharan trade in gold, the kings of Ghana gained the financial resources they needed to field a large

**Ghana** (GAH-nuh)

Timbuktu, the commercial and cultural center of the Mali and Songhay empires, as sketched by a French traveler in 1828. Though in decline by that time, the city's mosques, mud-brick dwellings, and crowds of people suggest the prosperous city of an earlier era.
Everett Historical/Shutterstock

army and influence affairs in much of west Africa. In the thirteenth century the **Mali Empire** replaced Ghana as the preeminent power in west Africa, but the Mali rulers continued the Ghana policy of controlling trans-Saharan trade.

**The Songhay Empire** By the fifteenth century the Mali Empire had begun to weaken, and the expansive state of Songhay emerged to take its place as the dominant power of the western grasslands. Based in the trading city of Gao, Songhay rulers built a flourishing city-state perhaps as early as the eighth century. In the early fifteenth century, they rejected Mali authority and mounted raids deep into Mali territory. In 1464 the Songhay ruler **Sunni Ali** (reigned 1464–1493) embarked on a campaign to conquer his neighbors and consolidated the **Songhay Empire** (1464–1591). He brought the important trading cities of **Timbuktu** and **Jenne** under his control and used their wealth to dominate the central Niger valley.

**Songhay Administration** Sunni Ali built an elaborate administrative and military apparatus to oversee affairs in his realm. He appointed governors to provinces and instituted a hierarchy of command that turned his army into an effective military force. He also created an imperial navy to patrol the Niger River, which was an important commercial highway in the Songhay Empire. Songhay military might enabled Sunni Ali's successors to extend their authority north into the Sahara, east toward Lake Chad, and west toward the upper reaches of the Niger River.

The Songhay emperors presided over a prosperous land. The capital city of Gao had about seventy-five thousand residents, many of whom participated in the lucrative trans-Saharan trade that brought salt, textiles, and metal goods south in exchange for gold and enslaved people. The emperors were Muslim: they supported mosques, built schools to teach the Quran, and maintained an Islamic university at Timbuktu. Like the rulers of Ghana and Mali, the Songhay emperors valued Islam as a cultural foundation for cooperation with Muslim merchants and Islamic states in north Africa. Nevertheless, the Songhay emperors did not abandon traditional religious practices: Sunni Ali himself often consulted non-Muslim African diviners and magicians.

**Fall of Songhay** The Songhay Empire dominated west Africa for most of the sixteenth century, but it was the last of the great imperial states of the grasslands. In 1591 a musket-bearing Moroccan army trekked across the Sahara and

**Songhay** (song-AHY)
**Sunni Ali** (soon-ee ah-lee)
**Jenne** (jehn-neh)

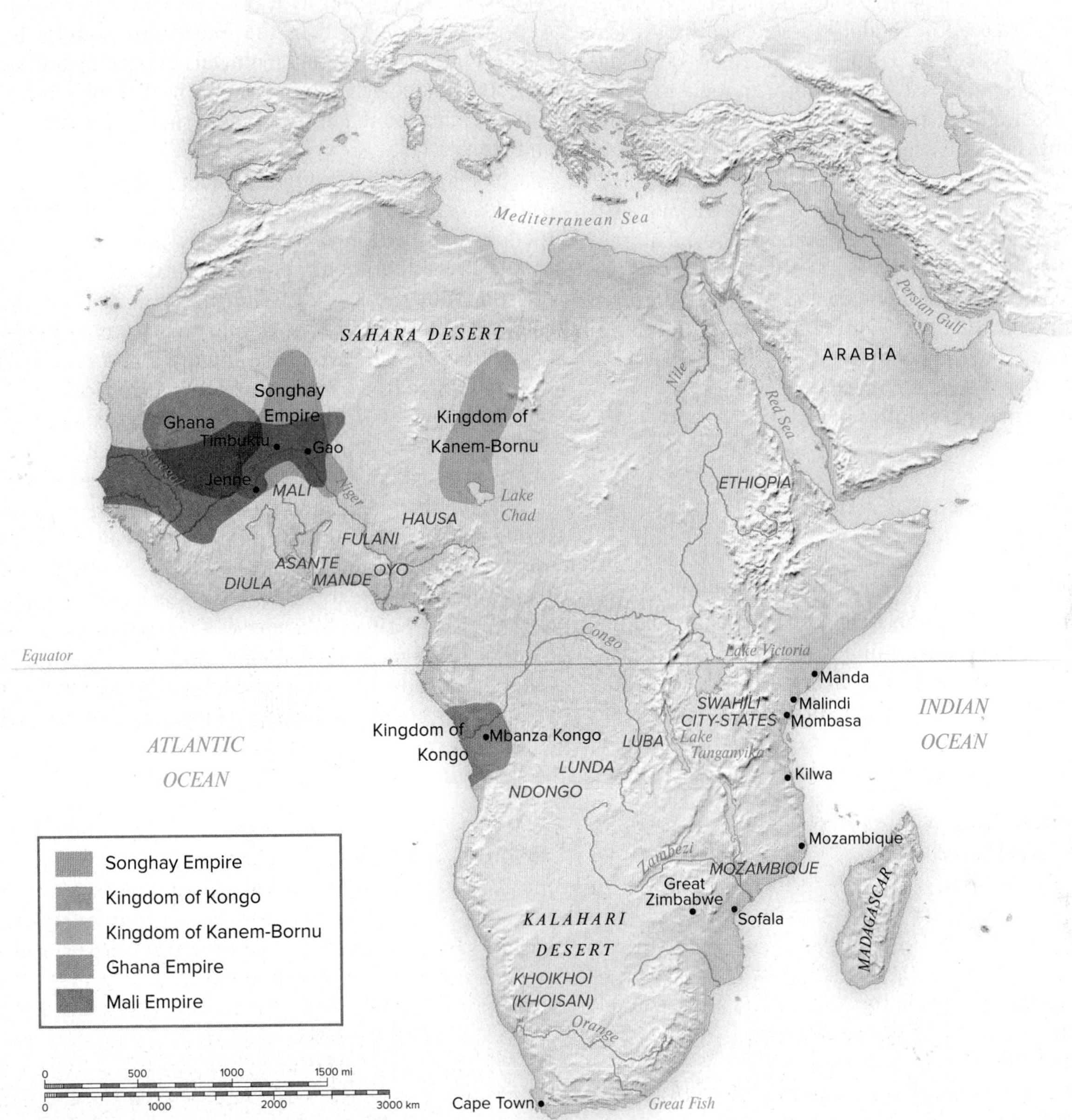


**MAP 13.1 African states, 1500–1650.**

Locate the three largest states of Songhay, Kongo, and Kanem-Bornu.

***What was it about their respective locations that favored the development of such large polities?***

***Why did such prosperous and extensive empires decline?***

attacked the previously invincible Songhay military machine. Songhay forces withered under the assault, and subject peoples took the opportunity to revolt against Songhay domination.

As the Songhay Empire crumbled, a series of small, regional kingdoms and city-states emerged in west Africa. The kingdom of Kanem-Bornu dominated the region around Lake Chad, and the Hausa people established thriving commercial city-states to the west. In the forests south of the grasslands, Oyo and **Asante** peoples built powerful regional kingdoms. On the coasts Diula, Mande, and other trading peoples established a series of states that entered into commercial relations with European merchant-mariners who called at west African ports after the fifteenth century. The increasing prominence of Atlantic trade in west African society worked against the interests of imperial states like Mali and Songhay, which had relied on control of trans-Saharan trade to finance their empires.

**Swahili Decline** While regional states displaced the Songhay Empire in west Africa, the **Swahili** city-states of east Africa fell on hard times. When the Portuguese mariner Vasco da Gama made his way up the east African coast en route to India in 1497 and 1498, he skirmished with local forces at Mozambique and Mombasa. On his second voyage to India in 1502, he forced the ruler of Kilwa to pay tribute, and his followers trained their cannons on Swahili ports all along the east African coast. In 1505 a massive Portuguese naval expedition subdued all the Swahili cities from Sofala to Mombasa. Portuguese forces built administrative centers at Mozambique and Malindi and constructed forts throughout the region in hopes of controlling trade in east Africa. They did not succeed in that effort, but they disrupted trade patterns enough to send the Swahili cities into a decline from which they never fully recovered.

## The Kingdoms of Central Africa and South Africa

**The Kingdom of Kongo** As trade networks multiplied and linked all regions of sub-Saharan Africa, an increasing volume of commerce encouraged state building in central Africa and south Africa. In central Africa the principal states were the kingdoms of Kongo, Ndongo, Luba, and Lunda in the basin of the Congo River (also known as the Zaire River). Best known of them was the kingdom of **Kongo** because abundant written records throw light on its experience in early modern times. The kingdom emerged in the fourteenth century. Its rulers built a centralized state with officials overseeing military, judicial, and financial affairs, and by the late fifteenth century Kongo embraced much of the modern-day Republic of Congo and Angola.

In 1483 a small Portuguese fleet mapped out the estuary of the Congo River and initiated commercial relations with the kingdom of Kongo. Within a few years, Portuguese merchants had established a close political and diplomatic relationship with the kings of Kongo. They supplied the kings with advisers; provided a military garrison to support the kings and protect Portuguese interests; and brought tailors, shoemakers, masons, miners, and priests to Kongo.

The kings of Kongo converted to Christianity and thus established closer commercial relations with Portuguese merchants and diplomatic relations with the Portuguese monarchy. The kings appreciated the fact that Christianity offered a strong endorsement of their monarchical rule. The new faith was appealing also because the saints of the Roman Catholic church were similar to spirits long recognized in Kongolese religion. **King Nzinga Mbemba** of Kongo, also known as King Afonso I (reigned 1506–1542), became a devout Roman Catholic and sought to convert all his subjects to Christianity. Portuguese priests in Kongo reported that he attended religious services daily and studied the Bible so zealously that he sometimes neglected to eat. The Kongo capital of

**Nzinga Mbemba** (N-zinga MEHM-bah)

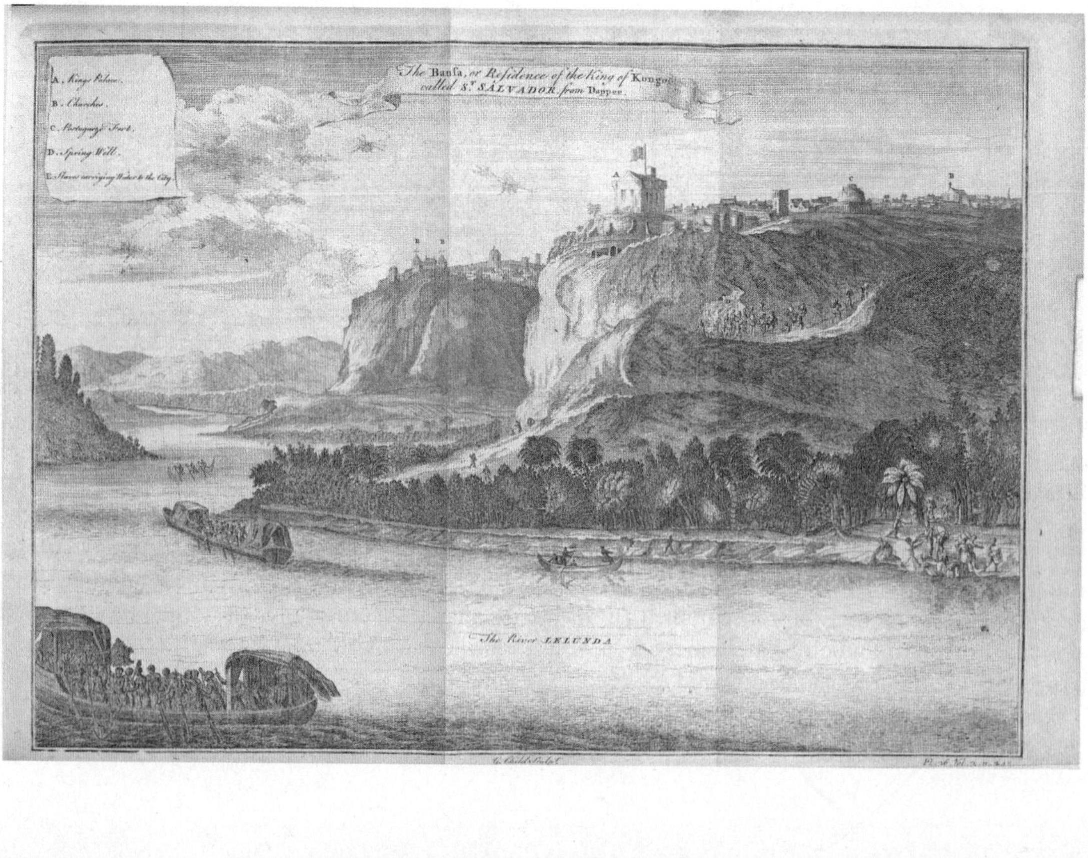

An engraving depicts São Salvador in Angola in the late seventeenth century. A flag flies over the royal palace while the Portuguese citadel (to the right of the palace) guards the city. Churches appear at the center and on the far right side of the engraving.
Rare Book Division/New York Public Library

## INTERPRETING IMAGES

Engraving from 1626 showing Queen Nzinga of Matamba, who is sitting on a prostrate man while having an audience with a group of Portuguese men.

**Analyze** *For forty years, Queen Nzinga (pictured here) led "spirited resistance" against the Portuguese. How was she able to succeed? Why did she ultimately fail?*

Fotosearch/Stringer/Getty Images

Mbanza—known to Europeans as São Salvador—had so many churches during the sixteenth century that contemporaries referred to it as "Kongo of the Bell."

**Slave Raiding in Kongo** Relations with Portugal brought wealth and foreign recognition to Kongo but led eventually to the destruction of the kingdom and the establishment of a Portuguese colony in Angola. In exchange for the textiles, weapons, advisers, and artisans that they brought to Kongo, Portuguese merchants sought high-value merchandise such as copper; ivory; and, most of all, enslaved people. They sometimes embarked on slaving expeditions themselves, but more often they made alliances with local authorities in interior regions and provided them with weapons in exchange for captured people. Some of their local allies were enemies of the kings of Kongo, while others were royal subordinates. In either case, Portuguese tactics undermined the authority of the kings, who appealed repeatedly but unsuccessfully for the Portuguese to cease or at least to limit their trade in slaves.

In spite of these problems, Kongo remained strong until the mid-seventeenth century. Portuguese forces aided Kongo in expelling invaders, but at the same time they continued to trade in slaves. Some Portuguese merchants settled in Kongo, took local wives, and henceforth looked more after the interests of their adoptive home than their native land. Over time, though, relations between Kongo and Portugal deteriorated, particularly after Portuguese agents began to pursue opportunities south of Kongo. By 1665 Portuguese colonists to the south even went to war with Kongo. Portuguese forces quickly defeated the Kongolese army and decapitated King Antonio I (also called Nvita a Nkanga) that same year. Soon thereafter, Portuguese merchants began to withdraw from Kongo in search of more profitable business in the kingdom of Ndongo to the south. By the eighteenth century the kingdom of Kongo had largely disintegrated.

**The Kingdom of Ndongo** Meanwhile, Portuguese explorers were developing a brisk slave trade to the south in the kingdom of **Ndongo,** which the Portuguese referred to as **Angola** from the title of the king, *ngola.* During the sixteenth century, Ndongo had grown from a small chiefdom subject to the kings of Kongo to a powerful regional kingdom in its own right, largely on the basis of the wealth it was able to attract by trading directly with Portuguese merchants rather than through Kongolese intermediaries. Portuguese merchants founded a small coastal colony in Ndongo as early as 1575. After 1611 they steadily increased their influence inland by allying with neighboring peoples who delivered increasing numbers of war captives to feed the growing slave trade. Over the next several decades, Portuguese forces

**Ndongo** (n'DAWN-goh)

campaigned in Ndongo in an effort to establish a colony that would support large-scale trading in slaves.

**Queen Nzinga** The conquest of Ndongo did not come easily. For forty years **Queen Nzinga** (reigned 1623–1663) led spirited resistance against Portuguese forces. Nzinga came from a long line of warrior kings. She dressed as a male warrior when leading troops in battle and insisted that her subjects refer to her as king rather than queen. She sometimes went so far in playing male roles as to travel with a group of "concubines"—young men dressed as women companions of the "king." She mobilized central African peoples against her Portuguese adversaries, and she also allied with Dutch mariners, who traded frequently on the African coast during the mid-seventeenth century. Her aim was to drive the Portuguese from her land, expel the Dutch, and then to create a vast central African empire embracing the entire lower Congo basin.

**The Portuguese Colony of Angola** Although she was a cunning strategist and an effective military leader, Nzinga was unable to oust Portuguese forces from Ndongo. She stymied Portuguese efforts to extend their influence, but with their powerful arms and considerable wealth, Portuguese forces were able to exploit the political divisions that perennially plagued central Africa. When Nzinga died in 1663, Portuguese forces faced less capable resistance, and they both extended and tightened their control over the region they now called Angola, the first European colony in sub-Saharan Africa.

**Regional Kingdoms in South Africa** Historical records do not shed as much light on the political structures of south Africa as they do on Kongo and Angola, but it is clear that in the south, as in central Africa, regional kingdoms dominated political affairs. Kingdoms had begun to emerge as early as the eleventh century, largely as a result of increasing trade. Merchants from the Swahili city-states of coastal east Africa sought gold, ivory, and people to enslave from the interior regions of south Africa. By controlling commerce, chieftains increased their wealth, enhanced their power, and extended their authority. By 1300 rulers of one such kingdom had built a massive, stone-fortified city known as **Great Zimbabwe,** near the city of Nyanda in modern Zimbabwe, and they dominated the gold-bearing plain between the Zambesi and Limpopo rivers until the late fifteenth century.

**European Arrival in South Africa** After the fifteenth century a series of smaller kingdoms displaced the rulers of Great Zimbabwe, and Portuguese and Dutch mariners began to play a role in south African affairs. In search of commercial opportunities, Europeans struck alliances with local peoples and intervened in disputes with the aim of supporting their allies and advancing their own interests. They became especially active after Dutch mariners built a trading post at Cape Town in 1652. There they encountered the hunting and gathering **Khoikhoi** people, whom they referred to pejoratively as Hottentots. With the aid of firearms, they claimed lands for themselves and commandeered Khoikhoi labor with relative ease. By 1700 large numbers of Dutch colonists had begun to arrive in south Africa, and by mid-century they had established settlements throughout the region bounded by the Orange and the Great Fish rivers. Their conquests laid the foundation for a series of Dutch and British colonies, which eventually became the most prosperous European possessions in sub-Saharan Africa.

A bronze plaque from Benin offers an early African view of Europeans: it depicts a Portuguese soldier armed with a musket and accompanied by a dog.
Werner Forman/Universal Images Group/Getty Images

## Islam and Christianity in Early Modern Africa

Indigenous religions remained influential throughout sub-Saharan Africa in early modern times. Although many Africans recognized a supreme, remote creator god, they also devoted attention to powerful spirits who were thought to intervene directly in human affairs. Many of these spirits were associated with prominent geographic features such as mountains, waters, or forests. Others were thought of as the "living dead"—spirits of ancestors who roamed the world, not only distributing rewards to descendants who led worthy lives and who honored the memories of departed kin but also meting out punishments to those who did not.

**Islam in Sub-Saharan Africa** Although most Africans continued to observe indigenous religions, both Islam and Christianity attracted increasing interest in sub-Saharan Africa. Islam was most widely adopted in the commercial centers of west Africa and the Swahili city-states of east

**Khoikhoi** (KOY-koy)

An illustration from the Dutch work called the *Description of Africa*, published in 1688, shows King Alvaro I of Kongo receiving Dutch ambassadors.
DEA/A. Dagli Orti/Getty Images

Africa. In the sixteenth century the trading city of Timbuktu had a prominent Islamic university and 180 schools that taught the Quran. Students flocked to Timbuktu by the thousands from all parts of west Africa.

African Muslims often blended Islam with indigenous beliefs and customs. The result was a syncretic style of Islam that not only made a place for African beliefs in spirits and magic but also permitted men and women to associate with each other on much more familiar terms than was common in north Africa, Arabia, and southwest Asia. Although it appealed to Africans, this syncretic Islam struck many devout Muslims as impure. Muslim merchants and travelers from north Africa and Arabia often commented on their shock at seeing women in tropical Africa who went out in public with bare breasts and socialized freely with men outside their own families.

**The Fulani and Islam** Some Muslims in sub-Saharan Africa also shared these concerns about the purity of Islam. Most important of them were the **Fulani,** originally a pastoral people who for centuries kept herds of cattle in the savannas of west Africa. By the late seventeenth century, many Fulani had settled in cities, where they observed a strict form of Islam like that practiced in north Africa and Arabia. Beginning about 1680 and continuing through the nineteenth century, the Fulani led a series of military campaigns to establish Islamic states and impose their own style of Islam in west Africa.

The Fulani did not by any means stamp out African religions, nor did they eliminate indigenous elements from the syncretic Islam practiced in west Africa. But they founded powerful states in what is now Guinea, Senegal, Mali, and northern Nigeria, and they promoted the spread of Islam beyond the cities to the countryside. They even established schools in remote towns and villages to teach the Quran and Islamic doctrine. Their campaigns strengthened Islam in sub-Saharan Africa and laid a foundation for new rounds of Islamic state building and conversion efforts in the nineteenth and twentieth centuries.

**Christianity in Sub-Saharan Africa** Like Islam, Christianity in sub-Saharan Africa was a syncretic blend of Christian doctrine and indigenous traditions and beliefs. The Portuguese community in Kongo and Angola supported priests and missionaries who introduced Roman Catholic Christianity to central Africa. They found strong interest among rulers such as King Afonso I of Kongo and his descendants, who eagerly adopted European-style Christianity. Beyond the ruling courts, however, Christian teachings frequently blended with African traditions. Some Africans wore crosses and other Christian symbols as amulets to ward off danger from angry spirits.

**The Antonian Movement** A particularly influential form of Christianity was the **Antonian movement** in Kongo, which flourished in the early eighteenth century, when the Kongolese monarchy faced challenges throughout the realm. The Antonian movement began in 1704 when an aristocratic woman named **Dona Beatriz** proclaimed that St. Anthony of Padua had possessed her and chosen her to communicate his messages. St. Anthony was a thirteenth-century Franciscan missionary and popular preacher. Born in Lisbon, St. Anthony died near Padua in Italy, where his followers built a large church in his honor. He was extremely popular among Portuguese Christians, who introduced his cult to Kongo. Dona Beatriz gained a reputation for working miracles and curing diseases, and she used her prominence to promote an African form of Christianity. She taught that Jesus Christ had been a black African man, that Kongo was the true holy land of Christianity, and that heaven was for Africans. She urged Kongolese to ignore European missionaries and heed her disciples instead, and she sought to harness the widespread popular interest in her teachings and use it to end the wars plaguing Kongo.

Dona Beatriz's movement was a serious challenge to Christian missionaries in Kongo. In 1706 they persuaded King Pedro IV of Kongo to arrest the charismatic prophetess on suspicion of heresy. Upon examining her, the missionaries satisfied themselves that Dona Beatriz was a false prophet and that she knowingly taught false doctrine. On their recommendation the royal government sentenced her to death and burned her at the stake. Yet the Antonian movement did not disappear: Dona Beatriz's disciples continued working to strengthen the monarchy and reconstruct Kongolese society. In 1708 an army of almost twenty thousand Antonians challenged King Pedro, whom they considered an unworthy ruler. Their efforts illustrate clearly the tendency of Kongolese Christians to fashion a faith that reflected their own needs and concerns.

## Social Change in Early Modern Africa

Despite increased state-building activity and political turmoil, African societies followed long-established patterns during the early modern era. Kinship groups, for example, continued to serve as the basis of social organization and sometimes political organization as well. Within agricultural villages throughout sub-Saharan Africa, clans under the leadership of prominent individuals organized the affairs of their kinship groups and disciplined those who violated community standards. In

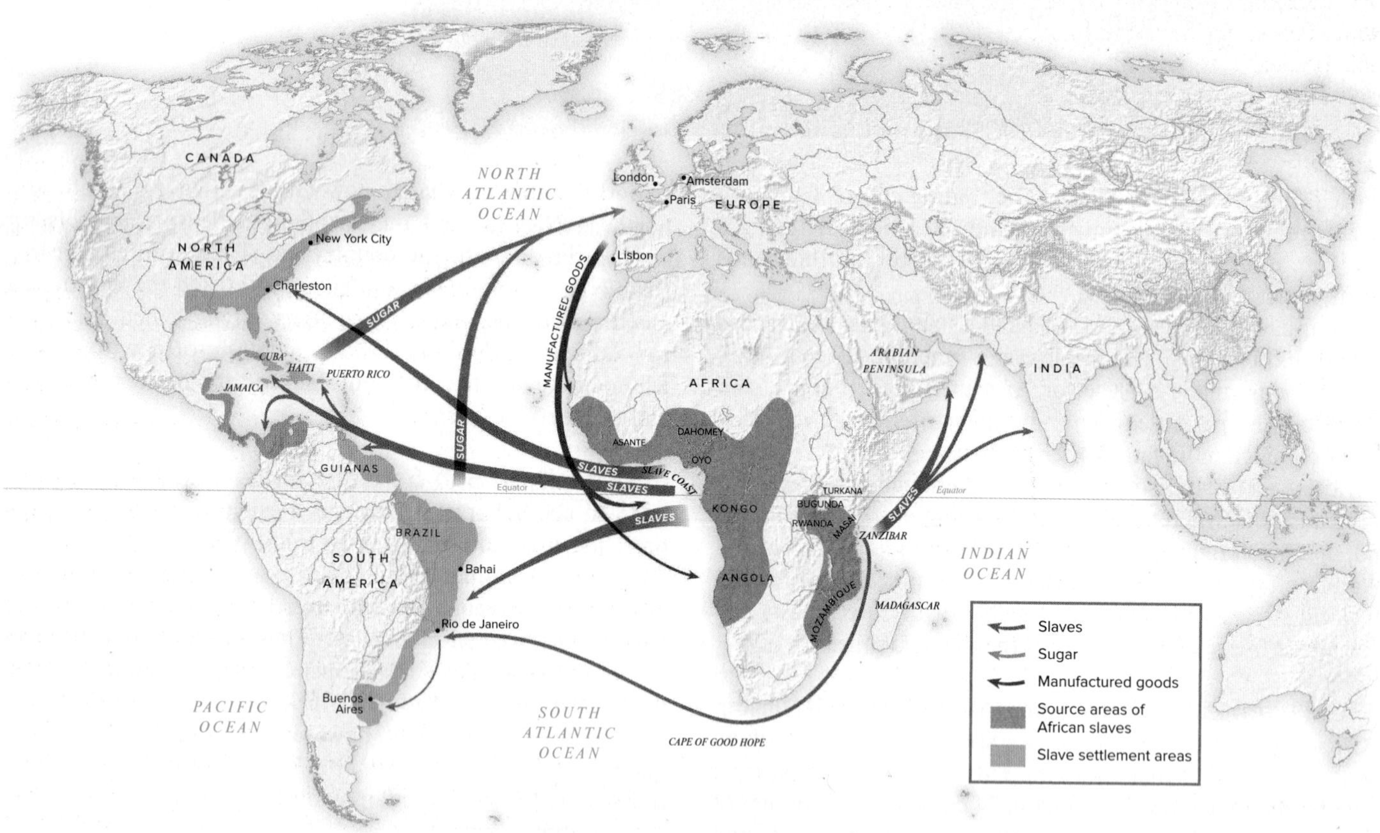


**MAP 13.2 The Atlantic slave trade, 1500–1800.**

Note the "triangular" pattern of the Atlantic trade routes between Europe, Africa, and the Americas.

***Why were most enslaved people in the Atlantic system taken from west and central Africa, and where were they taken?***

***What surprises you about the Atlantic slave trade?***

***It was lucrative for many reasons; what were they?***

regions where kingdoms and empires had not emerged, clan leaders consulted with one another and governed large regions. Indeed, even in lands ruled by formal states, clan leaders usually implemented state policy at the village level.

**American Food Crops in Sub-Saharan Africa** In the mid-sixteenth century, American crops such as manioc, maize, and peanuts arrived in Africa aboard Portuguese ships. These crops supplemented bananas, yams, rice, and millet, the principal staple foods of sub-Saharan Africa. The most important American crop was **manioc** because of its high yield and because it thrived in tropical soils not well suited to cultivation of the other crops.

**Population Growth** By the eighteenth century, bread made from manioc flour had become a staple food in much of west Africa and central Africa, where it helped provide a foundation for steady population growth. In 1500 C.E. the population of sub-Saharan Africa was about thirty-four million. By 1600 it had increased by almost one-third to forty-four million, and it continued climbing to fifty-two million in 1700 and sixty million in 1800. This strong demographic expansion is all the more remarkable because it took place precisely when millions of Africans underwent involuntary, forced migration to destinations in the Caribbean and the Americas. Even in spite of the loss of millions of people to the slave trade and the violence surrounding it, American food crops supported expanding populations in all regions of sub-Saharan Africa during early modern times.

## THE ATLANTIC SLAVE TRADE

Of all the processes that linked Africa to the larger Atlantic world in early modern times, the most momentous was the **Atlantic slave trade.** From the fifteenth to the nineteenth centuries millions of Africans were brutally enslaved and sent to the Americas to work on European-owned agricultural plantations. In exchange for providing enslaved people, African slave traders sought European manufactured products–most notably firearms, which they sometimes used to strengthen military forces that then sought to capture more people for the slave trade. Only in the early nineteenth century did the Atlantic slave trade come to an end. During the course of that century, most states abolished the institution of slavery itself.

### Foundations of the Slave Trade

**Slavery in Africa** The institution of slavery was already in existence in remote antiquity, and until the nineteenth century most settled agricultural societies in the world utilized slave labor in some form. Slavery was common throughout Africa after the Bantu-speaking people spread agriculture to all parts of the continent. As in other societies, most enslaved people in Africa came from the ranks of war captives, although criminals and individuals expelled from their clans also frequently fell into slavery. Once enslaved, an individual had no personal or civil rights. Owners could order enslaved people to perform any kind of work, punish them at will, and sell them as chattel (property). Enslaved Africans usually worked as cultivators in societies far from their homes, although some worked as administrators, soldiers, or even highly placed advisers. The Songhay emperors, for example, often employed enslaved people as administrators and soldiers because the rulers distrusted free nobles, whom they considered excessively ambitious. Agricultural plantations in the Songhay Empire often had hundreds of enslaved laborers, many of them working under the management of slave administrators.

Below decks on an illegal slave ship seized by a British antislavery patrol in 1846. Note the extremely cramped quarters in which captives were forced to spend most of their time. They were both deeply uncomfortable and contributed to dangerously unsanitary conditions.
The Art Archive/Shutterstock

Yet despite similarities with slavery in other places like Europe and Asia, African slavery was also distinct in some ways. African law did not recognize private property but, rather, vested ownership of land in communities. Thus wealth and power in Africa came not from the possession of land but from control over the human labor that made the land productive. Enslaved people were a form of private investment, a type of heritable property, and a means of measuring wealth. Those who controlled large numbers of enslaved people were able to harvest more crops and accumulate more wealth than others. Africans routinely purchased enslaved people to enlarge their families and enhance their power. Often, they assimilated them into their kinship groups, so that within a generation an enslaved person might obtain both freedom and an honorable position in a new family or clan.

**The Trans-Saharan Slave Trade** After the eighth century, Muslim merchants from north Africa, Arabia, and Persia sought slaves in sub-Saharan Africa for sale and distribution to destinations in the Mediterranean basin, southwest Asia, India, and even southeast Asia and China. When demand for enslaved people outstripped supply, merchants resorted to raiding villages, capturing innocent individuals, and forcing them into slavery. State officials sometimes allied with the merchants by providing cavalry forces to mount lightning raids on undefended communities. Merchants then transported the victims of these raids across the Sahara desert by camel caravan for distribution in the Mediterranean basin. Alternatively, they forced them to board ships at the Swahili port cities of east Africa for delivery to destinations across the Indian Ocean. During a millennium and more of the trans-Saharan slave trade, which lasted into the twentieth century, as many as ten million Africans may have been enslaved.

By the time Europeans ventured to sub-Saharan Africa in the fifteenth and sixteenth centuries, traffic in enslaved people was a well-established feature of African society, and a system for capturing, selling, and distributing enslaved people had functioned effectively for more than five hundred years. But when Europeans began to pursue commercial interests in Africa and the Americas, the slave trade expanded dramatically. After 1450, European peoples initially tapped existing networks and then greatly expanded commerce in enslaved Africans from the Mediterranean and the Indian Ocean to the Atlantic Ocean basin. This Atlantic slave trade brought about an enormous forced migration that influenced the development of societies throughout the Atlantic Ocean basin.

### How the Past Shapes the Future

#### The Columbian Exchange

Think back to the effects of Eurasian diseases on the original inhabitants of the Americas after 1492. In what ways was the massive death toll among indigenous Americans related to the origins of the Atlantic slave trade?

## Human Cargoes

The Atlantic slave trade began small, but it grew steadily and eventually reached enormous proportions. The earliest European slave traders were Portuguese explorers who navigated and mapped the west African coast in the mid-fifteenth century. In 1441 a raiding party seized twelve African men and took them to Portugal as slaves. Portuguese mariners encountered stiff resistance when they attempted to capture people into slavery as African warriors fired thousands of poison-tipped arrows at gangs of would-be slave raiders. Soon, however, the mariners learned that they could purchase enslaved people rather than capturing them, and by 1460 they were delivering five hundred enslaved people per year to Portugal and Spain. In Europe, enslaved Africans usually worked as miners, porters, or domestic servants because free peasants and serfs cultivated the land.

**The Early Slave Trade** Slave traders also delivered their human cargoes to Portuguese island colonies in the Atlantic. There was no supply of labor to work plantations in the Azores, Madeiras, Cape Verde Islands, and São Tomé, all of which were uninhabited when explorers discovered them in the fifteenth century. The Portuguese population was too small to provide large numbers of colonists, let alone laborers. Sugar planters on the island of São Tomé in particular called for slave labor to solve this labor shortage. By the 1520s some two thousand enslaved people per year went to São Tomé, which allowed sugar production on the island to soar. Soon thereafter Portuguese entrepreneurs extended the use of slave labor to South America. During the 1530s Portuguese planters imported enslaved people directly from Kongo and Angola to Brazil, which eventually became the wealthiest of the sugar-producing lands of the Western Hemisphere.

Meanwhile, Spanish explorers and conquerors also sought laborers to work lands in the Caribbean and the Americas. As imported diseases ravaged indigenous populations in the Western Hemisphere, the conquerors found themselves in possession of vast stretches of land but few laborers to work them. The Spanish attempted to harness the labor of those who survived the diseases, but their desire for labor exceeded the number of available indigenous people. Gradually, Spanish settlers began to rely on enslaved people from Africa as well. In 1518 the first shipment of enslaved Africans went directly from west Africa to the Caribbean, where they worked on recently established sugar plantations. During the 1520s Spanish authorities introduced enslaved Africans to Mexico, where they worked as cultivators and miners. By the early seventeenth century, English colonists had introduced enslaved Africans also to the North American mainland.

**Triangular Trade** The demand for labor in the Western Hemisphere stimulated a profitable commerce known as the **triangular trade** because European ships often undertook voyages of three legs. On the first leg they carried horses and European manufactured goods—mostly cloth and metalwares, especially firearms—that they exchanged in sub-Saharan Africa for enslaved people. The second leg took enslaved Africans to Caribbean and American destinations. Upon arrival merchants sold their human cargoes to plantation owners for two to three times what they had cost on the African coast. Sometimes they exchanged enslaved people for cash, but in sugar-producing regions they often bartered them for sugar or molasses. Then they filled their vessels' hulls with American products before embarking on their voyage back to Europe.

At every stage of the process, the slave trade was a brutal and inhumane business. The original capture of Africans into slavery was almost always a violent affair. As European demand for enslaved people grew, some African chieftains organized raiding parties to seize individuals from

# SOURCES FROM THE PAST

## Olaudah Equiano on the Middle Passage

*Olaudah Equiano (1745–1797) was a native of Benin in west Africa. When he was ten years old, slave raiders seized him and his sister at their home while their parents were tending the fields. He spent the next twenty-one years in slavery. Eventually, Equiano purchased his freedom and worked against the slave trade for the rest of his life. In his autobiography published in 1789, Equiano described the horrors of the middle passage.*

**The first object which saluted** my eyes when I arrived on the coast was the sea, and a slave ship which was then riding at anchor and waiting for its cargo. These filled me with astonishment, which was soon converted into terror when I was carried on board. I was immediately handled and tossed up to see if I were sound by some of the crew, and I was now persuaded that I had gotten into a world of bad spirits and that they were going to kill me. . . .

I was not long suffered to indulge my grief; I was soon put down under the decks, and there I received such a salutation in my nostrils as I had never experienced in my life: so that with the loathsomeness of the stench and crying together, I became so sick and low that I was not able to eat, nor had I the least desire to taste anything. I now wished for the last friend, death, to relieve me; but soon, to my grief, two of the white men offered me eatables, and on my refusing to eat, one of them held me fast by the hands and laid me across I think the windlass and tied my feet while the other flogged me severely. I had never experienced anything of this kind before, and although not being used to the water I naturally feared that element the first time I saw it, yet nevertheless if I could have gotten over the nettings I would have jumped over the side, but I could not; and besides, the crew used to watch very closely over those of us who were not chained down to the decks, lest we should leap into the water: and I have seen some of these poor African prisoners most severely cut for attempting to do so, and hourly whipped for not eating. This indeed was often the case with myself. . . .

> Why was it so important to the ship's crew that the Africans on board eat?

One day when we had a smooth sea and moderate wind, two of my wearied countrymen who were chained together (I was near them at the time), preferring death to such a life of misery, somehow made through the nettings and jumped into the sea: immediately another quite dejected fellow, who on account of his illness was suffered to be out of irons, also followed their example; and I believe many more would very soon have done the same if they had not been prevented by the ship's crew, who were instantly alarmed. Those of us that were the most active were in a moment put down under the deck, and there was such a noise and confusion amongst the people of the ship as I never heard before, to stop her and get the boat to go after the slaves. However, two of the wretches were drowned, but they got the other and afterwards flogged him unmercifully for thus attempting to prefer death to slavery. In this manner we continued to undergo more hardships than I can now relate, hardships which are inseparable from this accursed trade.

> Consider how terrible the conditions on board the ship must have been to encourage some of the Africans on board to choose death over survival.

### For Further Reflection

- On the basis of Equiano's account, what measures did the crews of slave ships take to ensure maximum profits from their business of transporting human cargoes?
- Equiano's account of the Middle Passage, published the same year as the U.S. Constitution is gripping and heart-wrenching. Although it was a "bestseller," why did relatively few people oppose slavery?

*Source:* Equiano, Olaudah. *The Interesting Narrative of the Life of Olaudah Equiano, or Gustavus Vassa, the African, Written by Himself.* 2 vols. London, 1789. (Translation slightly modified.)

neighboring societies. Others launched wars for the purpose of capturing victims for the slave trade. They often snatched individuals right out of their homes, fields, or villages: millions of lives changed instantly, as slave raiders grabbed their victims and then immediately spirited them away in captivity.

**The Middle Passage** Following capture, enslaved individuals underwent a forced march to the coast, where they lived in holding pens until a ship arrived to transport them to the Western Hemisphere. Then they embarked on the dreadful **middle passage,** the trans-Atlantic journey aboard filthy and crowded

# Connecting the Sources

## Using indirect sources to reconstruct the lives of slaves

**In order to write about the past, historians must find and interpret primary sources. Primary sources can include material objects, archaeological evidence, oral traditions, texts (including official documents, letters, accounts, newspapers), or images. They provide the evidence on which historical narratives rest. This exercise highlights some of the challenges of interpreting original primary sources by asking you to consider the kinds of contextual information you might need to interpret such documents accurately and by asking you to consider what individual documents can and cannot tell you.**

**The problem** Sometimes historians want to find out about the experiences of groups that may not have had much power in the past, such as women, peasants, or enslaved people. This can be difficult, however, because such groups frequently did not leave many textual records behind. In the case of Africans who became part of the Atlantic slave trade, it is difficult to find primary sources created by individual enslaved people themselves, particularly in the seventeenth and eighteenth centuries. Many enslaved people were not literate in European languages, and even when they were the documents they created may not have been saved for later inclusion in historical archives. Some voices—like Olaudah Equiano's—have survived from that period, as we see in this chapter. But to understand the varieties of experiences enslaved people might have had, historians must use many primary sources written by others, including those written by slave traders, slave owners, courts, and governments. Let us consider two such sources as a way of thinking about what indirect sources can and cannot tell us about the experience of slavery in the eighteenth century.

FL Historical 28/Alamy Stock Photo

**The documents** Read the documents below, and consider carefully the questions that follow.

### Document 1:

*This advertisement comes from the New London Summary (Connecticut) on March 30, 1764.*

*The text reads:*

*Ran away from me the subscriber, the 14th instant, a Molatto named Bilhah, a tall, thick-built well-proportioned Wench; had on a brown short stuff Gown, batt'd with Yellow, a blue camblet Quilt, and check'd linnen Apron, black silk Bonnet, a large pair flower'd silver Shoe-Buckles; may possibly pretend to be a Free Woman, or may Change her Apparel for Men's Cloathing. All Masters of Vessels are cautioned from carrying off said Molatto–Any Person who shall secure said Molatto Wench in any of His Majesty's Goals, shall have FOUR DOLLARS Reward, and necessary Charges paid by Jared Eliot. Killingworth, Mar. 21, 1764.*

## Document 2:

*This broadside advertisement was posted in Charlestown, South Carolina, in 1769.*

*The text reads:*

*CHARLESTOWN, April 27, 1769*
*TO BE SOLD,*
*On Wednesday the Tenth Day of*
*May next,*
*A CHOICE CARGO OF*
*Two Hundred & Fifty*
*NEGROES:*

*ARRIVED in the Ship*
*Countess of Sussex, Thomas Davies,*
*Master, directly from Gambia, by*
*JOHN CHAPMAN, & Co.*

*THIS is the Vessel that had the Small-Pox on Board at the Time of her Arrival the 31st of March last: Every necessary Precaution hath since been taken to cleanse both Ship and Cargo thoroughly, so that those who may be inclined to purchase need not be under the least Apprehension of Danger from Infliction.*

*The NEGROES are allowed to be the likeliest Parcel that have been imported this Season.*

## Questions

1. What can these advertisements definitively tell you about their respective situations? What facts can be gleaned from these brief sources?
2. In Document 1, what might this advertisement imply about the experience of slavery from Bilhah's point of view? For example, does it imply that Bilhah was unhappy with her status as a slave, or is it simply impossible to know?
3. Also in Document 1, what might this advertisement imply about Bilhah's treatment prior to her departure? Are there any clues that indicate how she lived under Jared Eliot's care?
4. In Document 2, what kinds of information can you glean about the possible experience of the enslaved people held aboard the *Countess of Sussex*? For example, what might it have been like to cross the Atlantic with smallpox aboard?
5. Taking both documents together, what kinds of contextual information would you need in order to understand these advertisements more fully? For example, would your conclusions about the meaning of Document 1 change if you knew that hundreds of slaves ran away every year or, alternatively, if Bilhah was a rare exception? Would your conclusions regarding Document 2 be different if you knew that the *Countess of Sussex* was one of many slave ships to arrive in port at Charlestown in 1769, or if you knew such a landing was a rare occurrence? What further information would you need in order to use these documents to interpret the experience of enslaved people in North America in the eighteenth century?
6. Sources such as these make up the building blocks on which historians base their interpretations of the past. In most cases, however, historians discover that they must use a variety of primary and secondary sources in order to make accurate interpretations.

*Source:* **Document 1:** Eliot, Jared. "Advertisement for Bilhah." *The New London Summary (Connecticut Gazette)*, March 30, 1764. **Document 2:** Davies, Thomas. "Broadside announcing the sale of slaves." *John Chapman & Co.* (Charlestown Newspaper), April 27, 1769.

slave ships. Enslaved passengers traveled below decks in hideously cramped quarters. Most ships provided enslaved people with enough room to sit upright, although not to stand, but some forced them to lie in chains on shelves with barely half a meter (twenty inches) of space between them. Conditions were so bad that many prisoners attempted to starve themselves to death or mounted revolts. Ship crews attempted to preserve the lives of enslaved people, intending to sell them for a profit at the end of the voyage, but they nevertheless treated the unwilling passengers with cruelty and contempt. Crew members used

| Numbers and Destinations of Enslaved People in the Transatlantic Slave Trade by Year. | | | | | | | | | | |
|---|---|---|---|---|---|---|---|---|---|---|
| | Europe | Mainland North America | British Caribbean | French Caribbean | Dutch Americas | Danish West Indies | Spanish Americas | Brazil | Africa | Totals |
| 1501–1600 | 903 | 0 | 0 | 0 | 0 | 0 | 241,917 | 34,686 | 0 | 277,506 |
| 1601–1700 | 3,639 | 19,956 | 405,117 | 50,356 | 145,980 | 22,610 | 313,301 | 910,361 | 4,312 | 1,875,631 |
| 1701–1800 | 6,256 | 358,845 | 2,139,819 | 1,178,518 | 339,559 | 81,801 | 175,438 | 2,210,931 | 3,451 | 6,494,619 |
| 1801–1866 | 0 | 93,581 | 218,475 | 99,549 | 28,654 | 25,455 | 860,589 | 2,376,141 | 171,137 | 3,873,580 |
| **Totals** | **10,798** | **472,381** | **2,763,411** | **1,328,422** | **514,192** | **129,867** | **1,591,245** | **5,532,118** | **178,901** | **12,521,336** |

Source: *The Trans-Atlantic Slave Trade Database. Emory University.*

tools to pry open the mouths of those who refused to eat and pitched sick individuals into the ocean rather than have them infect others or waste limited supplies of food.

In good sailing conditions, the journey to Caribbean and American destinations took four to six weeks, during which heat, cold, and disease levied a heavy toll on the enslaved people aboard the ships. During the early days of the slave trade on particularly cramped ships, mortality sometimes exceeded 50 percent. As the volume of the trade grew, slavers built larger ships, carried more water, and provided better nourishment and facilities for their cargoes, and mortality eventually declined to about 5 percent per voyage. Over the course of the Atlantic slave trade, however, approximately 25 percent of individuals enslaved in Africa died during the middle passage.

## The Impact of the Slave Trade in Africa

**Volume of the Slave Trade** Before 1600 the Atlantic slave trade operated on a modest scale. Figures varied considerably from one year to the next, but on average about two thousand enslaved people left Africa annually during the late fifteenth and sixteenth centuries. During the seventeenth century, the trade in humans from Africa rose dramatically to twenty thousand per year, as European peoples settled in the Western Hemisphere and sought African labor to cultivate their lands. The high point of the slave trade came in the eighteenth century, when the number of enslaved people brought to the Americas averaged fifty-five thousand per year. During the 1780s slave arrivals averaged eighty-eight thousand per year, and in some individual years they exceeded one hundred thousand. From beginning to end, the Atlantic slave trade brought about the forced migration of about twelve million Africans to the Western Hemisphere. An additional four million or more died resisting seizure or during captivity before arriving at their intended destination.

The impact of the slave trade varied over time and from one African society to another. The kingdoms of Rwanda and Bugunda on the great lakes and the herding societies of the Masai and Turkana of east Africa largely escaped the worst effects of the slave trade, partly because they resisted it and partly because their lands were distant from the major slave ports on the west African coast. Other societies flourished during early modern times and benefited economically from the slave trade. Those Africans who raided, took captives, and sold enslaved people to Europeans profited handsomely from the trade, as did the port cities and the states that coordinated trade with European merchants. Asante, Dahomey, and Oyo peoples, for example, took advantage of the slave trade to obtain firearms from European merchants and build powerful states in west Africa. In the nineteenth century, after the abolition of slavery, some African merchants complained bitterly about losing their livelihood and tried to undermine the efforts of the British navy to patrol Atlantic waters and put an end to slave trading.

**Social Effects of the Slave Trade** On the whole, however, sub-Saharan Africa suffered serious losses from the slave trade. The Atlantic slave trade alone deprived African societies of about sixteen million individuals, in addition to several million others forced into the continuing trans-Saharan slave trade during the early modern era. Although total African population rose during the early modern era, partly because American food crops enriched diets, several individual societies experienced severe losses because of the slave trade. West African societies between Senegal and Angola were especially vulnerable to slave raiding because of their proximity to the most active slave ports.

**Gender and Slavery** While diverting labor from sub-Saharan Africa to other lands, the slave trade also distorted sex ratios both in the Americas and in Africa. Approximately two-thirds of all Africans enslaved were young men between fourteen and thirty-five years of age. This reflected European preferences because men in their physical prime had the best potential to repay their buyers' investments by providing heavy labor over an extended period of time. It also coincided with the desire of African slavers to retain enslaved women for use in households. The resulting gender imbalance meant, at least initially, that enslaved African communities could not reproduce

Armed escorts march a group of captured Africans to the coast for sale on slave markets. Chained together are African men, women, and children. What motivated states and individuals in Africa to take part in capturing people to sell in the Atlantic slave trade?
North Wind Picture Archives

quickly enough through childbirth. When combined with the high mortality rate among enslaved Africans due to brutal conditions and hard physical work, the result was a continuous demand for new shipments of enslaved people from Africa. The need to replenish populations of enslaved men was especially acute on Caribbean sugar plantations, where death rates were especially high. The preference for men to enslave also had implications for sub-Saharan societies. By the late eighteenth century, for example, women made up more than two-thirds of the adult population of Angola, encouraging Angolans to embrace polygyny, the practice of having more than one wife at a time. In addition, women by necessity took on duties that earlier had been the responsibility of men.

**Political Effects of the Slave Trade** Apart from its demographic and social effects, the slave trade brought turmoil to African societies. While African groups fought a variety of wars that had little or nothing to do with the slave trade during the early modern period, the existence of the trade also encouraged people to participate in conflicts that might never have occurred in its absence.

Violence escalated especially after the late seventeenth century, when African states and kingdoms increasingly exchanged enslaved people for European firearms. When the kingdom of Dahomey obtained effective firearms, for example, its armies were able to capture people from unarmed neighboring societies and exchange them for more weapons. During the eighteenth century, Dahomey expanded rapidly and absorbed neighboring societies by increasing its arsenal of firearms and maintaining a constant flow of enslaved people to the coast. Indeed, the Dahomey army, which included a regiment of women soldiers, became largely a slave-raiding force. By no means did all African states take such advantage of the slave trade, but Dahomey's experience illustrates the potential of the slave trade to alter the patterns of African politics and society.

## THE AFRICAN DIASPORA

Some enslaved Africans worked as urban laborers or domestic servants, and in Mexico and Peru many worked also as miners. The vast majority, however, worked as agricultural laborers on plantations in the Caribbean or the Americas. There they cultivated cash crops that made their way into commercial arteries linking lands throughout the Atlantic Ocean basin. Although deprived of their freedom and frequently treated with brutality,

Enslaved men and women cutting sugar cane on the island of Antigua, 1823.
Chronicle of World History/Alamy Stock Photo

enslaved people often resisted their bondage, and they built hybrid cultural traditions compounded of African, European, and American elements. Most European and American states ended the slave trade and abolished slavery during the nineteenth century. By that time the **African diaspora**—the dispersal of African peoples and their descendants—had left a permanent mark throughout the Western Hemisphere.

## Plantation Societies

Most enslaved Africans went to plantations in the tropical and subtropical regions of the Western Hemisphere. When European peoples arrived in the Caribbean and the Americas, they envisioned taking the vast stretches of fertile land they found for themselves. Their goal was to establish profitable **plantations** that would produce agricultural commodities like tobacco and sugar for European and global markets. Spanish colonists established the first of these plantations in 1516 on the island of Hispaniola (which is now modern Haiti and the Dominican Republic) and soon extended them to Mexico as well. Beginning in the 1530s Portuguese entrepreneurs established plantations in Brazil, and by the early seventeenth century English, Dutch, and French settlers had also established plantations in the Caribbean and the Americas.

**Cash Crops** Many of these plantations produced sugar, which was one of the most lucrative cash crops of early modern times. But plantations produced other crops as well. During the seventeenth century, tobacco rivaled sugar as a profitable product. Rice also became a major plantation product, as did indigo (which was used as a dye). By the eighteenth century many plantations concentrated on the cultivation of cotton, and coffee had begun to emerge as a plantation cash crop.

Regardless of the crops they produced, Caribbean and American plantations had certain elements in common. All

**diaspora** (die-AS-per-uh)

of them specialized in the production of some agricultural crop in high demand. Plantations often maintained gardens that produced food for the local community, but their purpose was to profit from the production and export of commercial crops. These plantations relied almost exclusively on slave labor. Plantation communities often included a hundred or more enslaved individuals whose unpaid labor helped keep their agricultural products competitive. Plantations also featured a sharp racial division of labor. Small numbers of European or Euro-American supervisors governed plantation affairs, while large numbers of enslaved Africans or people of African-descent performed most of the community's physical labor.

**Regional Differences** In spite of their structural similarities, plantation societies differed considerably from one region to another. In the Caribbean and South America, slave populations usually were unable to sustain their numbers. Many enslaved people fell victim to tropical diseases such as malaria and yellow fever. On the plantations, they faced brutal working conditions and low standards of sanitation and nutrition. Moreover, enslaved people had low rates of reproduction because plantation owners mostly imported men and allowed only a few to establish families. Thus, in the Caribbean and South America, plantation owners imported continuing streams of enslaved Africans to maintain their workforces. Of all the people forced from Africa to the Western Hemisphere, about half went to the Caribbean, and about one-third went to Brazil. Smaller numbers went to other destinations in South America and Central America.

Only about 5 percent of enslaved Africans went to North American destinations. Diseases there were less threatening than in the Caribbean and Brazil, and in some ways conditions were less harsh than in the more southerly regions. North American planters imported larger numbers of enslaved women, and encouraged them to form families and bear children. Their support for natural reproduction was especially strong in the eighteenth century, when the prices of individual slaves from Africa rose dramatically.

**Resistance to Slavery** No matter where they lived, enslaved people did not meekly accept their servile status. Instead, like Thomas Peters—who we met in the introduction—they resisted it in numerous ways. Some forms of resistance were mild but costly to slave owners: individuals might purposefully work slowly for their masters but diligently in their own gardens, for example. Some enslaved people might also sabotage plantation equipment or work routines. A more serious form of resistance involved running away from the plantation community. Runaways known as *maroons* gathered in mountainous, forested, or swampy regions and built their own self-governing communities. Maroons often raided nearby plantations for arms, tools, provisions, and even other enslaved people to increase their own numbers or to provide labor for their communities. Many maroons had gained military experience in Africa, and they organized runaways into effective military forces. Maroon communities flourished throughout slave-holding regions of the Western Hemisphere, and some of them survived for centuries. In present-day Suriname, for example, the Saramaka people maintain an elaborate oral tradition that traces their descent from eighteenth-century maroons.

Enslaved people were vulnerable to cruel treatment that often provoked them to run away from their plantations or even mount revolts. A French visitor to Brazil in the early nineteenth century depicted a Portuguese overseer administering a brutal whipping to a bound man on a plantation near Rio de Janeiro.
Pictorial Press Ltd/Alamy Stock Photo

## What's Left Out?

While we know that both African men and women were forced into the Atlantic slave trade, we also know that there were differences in the ways enslaved women and enslaved men experienced slavery. In the case of enslaved women, European slave traders and settlers often wrongly believed that African women were hypersexual and that they were uninhibited about sexual encounters. These beliefs, combined with the power of ownership over enslaved women's bodies, contributed to a strong sense of entitlement over their reproductive capacities. Indeed, slave owners viewed enslaved women not only as laborers but as profitable vessels for producing additional slaves. Sexual violence by Europeans was a routine part of enslaved women's lives and resulted in many unwanted pregnancies. Even when enslaved women gave birth to children by partners of their own choosing, their children were subject to sale, and thus they could not control basic aspects of their futures. Enslaved women often resisted these practices, but the structure of slave societies meant that they could not turn to the law or to the larger society for assistance. It is important to remember that the practice of slavery in the Americas and the Caribbean involved control over labor as well as the most intimate aspects of daily life. For women, this involved significant loss of control over their bodies and their reproductive capacities.

*Source:* Jennifer Morgan, *Laboring Women: Reproduction and Gender in New World Slavery* (Philadelphia: University of Pennsylvania Press, 2004).

### Thinking Critically About Sources

1. How was the dehumanization of enslavement a gendered experience?
2. What legacy was left for both Black and white residents in areas where enslavement had been prevalent?

**Slave Revolts** The most dramatic form of resistance to slavery was organized revolt. Enslaved people far outnumbered others in most plantation societies, and they had the potential to organize and overwhelm slaveholders. Slave revolts brought stark fear to plantation owners and supervisors, and they often resulted in widespread death and destruction. Yet these revolts almost never brought slavery itself to an end because the European and Euro-American ruling elites had access to arms, horses, and military forces that extinguished most rebellions. Only in the French sugar colony of **Saint-Domingue** did a revolt abolish slavery as an institution (1793). Indeed, the enslaved Africans of Saint-Domingue declared independence from France, renamed the land **Haiti,** and established a self-governing republic (1804). The Haitian revolution terrified slaveholders and inspired enslaved people throughout the Western Hemisphere, but no other rebellion matched its accomplishments.

**Slavery and Economic Development** The physical labor of enslaved people made crucial contributions to the building of new societies in the Americas and also to the making of the early modern world as a whole. Enslaved people cultivated many of the crops and extracted many of the minerals that made their way around the world in the global trade networks of the early modern era. They themselves did not enjoy the fruits of their labors, which flowed disproportionately to European peoples and their Euro-American descendants. Had it not been for the labor of enslaved African peoples and their African descendants, however, it would have been impossible for prosperous new societies to emerge in the Americas during the early modern era.

## The Making of Hybrid Cultural Traditions

When Africans were forced into the Atlantic slave trade, they were not allowed to bring any of their material culture with them—including clothing, artwork, furniture, and tools. Once in the Americas and Caribbean, individuals found themselves enslaved with other Africans from many regions who spoke a wide variety of languages. As a result, it was difficult for enslaved Africans to maintain their cultural traditions in the Western Hemisphere. Instead, enslaved people adapted by constructing hybrid languages and religions based on many African traditions combined with new European and American elements. In adapting to new circumstances, enslaved people constructed distinctive hybrid cultural traditions.

**African and Creole Languages** European languages were dominant in the plantation societies of the Western Hemisphere, but African languages also influenced communication. Occasionally, enslaved Africans from a particular region were numerous enough to speak among themselves in their native tongues. More often, they spoke a **creole language** that drew on several African and European languages. In the low country of South Carolina and Georgia, for example, enslaved people made up about three-quarters of the population in the eighteenth century and regularly communicated in the creole languages **Gullah** and **Geechee,** respectively.

**African-Influenced Religions** Like their languages, religions of enslaved Africans also combined elements from

**Gullah** (GUHL-uh)

different societies. Some enslaved people brought from Africa were Muslims, some were Christians, and many others converted to Christianity after their arrival in the Western Hemisphere. Most Africans and African descendants did not practice European Christianity, however, but rather a syncretic faith that made considerable room for African interests and traditions. Because they developed mostly in plantation societies under conditions of slavery, these syncretic religions usually did not create an institutional structure or establish a hierarchy of priests and other church officials. Yet in several cases—most notably **Voudou** in Haiti, **Santeria** in Cuba, and **Candomblé** in Brazil—they became exceedingly popular among enslaved people.

All the syncretic religions with African elements drew inspiration from Christianity: they met in parish churches; sought personal salvation; and made use of European Christian paraphernalia such as holy water, candles, and statues. Yet they also preserved African traditions. They associated African deities with Christian saints and relied heavily on African rituals such as drumming, dancing, and sacrificing animals. Indeed, the core of these syncretic faiths was often participation in rituals like those observed in Africa. They also preserved beliefs in spirits and supernatural powers: magic, sorcery, witchcraft, and spirit possession all played prominent roles in the new hybrid religions.

An 1823 engraving of enslaved men practicing the martial art of Capoeira. Enslaved people often practiced this extremely physically demanding martial art to music, but its purpose was to teach enslaved people a method of self-defense. Capoeira originated in Angola, and was brought by enslaved people to Brazil. It is still practiced today.
The Picture Art Collection/Alamy Stock Photo

**Hybrid African Music** As in language and religion, enslaved people relied on African traditions in creating new, hybrid musical forms because they were not allowed to bring material items from their homelands. Music was one of the means by which enslaved Africans reminded themselves of their homes and communities. Once in the Americas, enslaved Africans adapted African musical traditions, including both rhythmic and lyrical elements, to their new environments. Under the brutal circumstances of slavery, music may have been one of the means by which enslaved people resisted their new lives and survived its brutal conditions. In the process, they created new musical forms that influenced not only enslaved communities but also the multicultural societies of the Caribbean and the Americas over the long term.

Enslaved people fashioned new identities in part by blending west African instruments and musical traditions with European languages, Christian religion, and the work routines of American plantations. Musicians played drums and stringed instruments such as banjos that closely resembled traditional African instruments. They adapted west African call-and-response patterns of singing to the rhythms of field work on plantations. The call-and-response format also found its way into the music of spirituals that blended Christian, European, and African influences.

Some slave owners sought to ban music out of fear that it harbored subversive potential. Slave owners in South Carolina recalled, for example, that enslaved people had used drums to signal one another to rise up during the Stono rebellion of 1739. Despite efforts to suppress African influences, the music of enslaved people and later of their free descendants survived and testified to the continuing relevance of music as a means of shaping community identity and resistance to oppression. From work songs and spirituals to the blues, jazz, and soul, African-inspired music evolved to mirror the difficult and often brutal circumstances of life in the Americas.

**African-Inspired Cultural Traditions** African traditions also made their effects felt throughout much of the Western Hemisphere. Enslaved people introduced African foods to Caribbean and American societies and helped give rise to distinctive hybrid cuisines. They combined African okra, for example, with European-style sautéed vegetables and American shellfish to produce magnificent gumbos, which found their way to Euro-American tables and the tables of Africans and their descendants. (*Okra* and *gumbo* are both African words.) Enslaved people introduced rice cultivation to tropical and subtropical regions, including South Carolina, Georgia, and Louisiana, and added variety to American diets. They also built houses, fashioned clay pots, and wove grass baskets in west African styles. In many ways, the African diaspora influenced the ways all people lived in plantation societies.

**Voudou** (voo-doo)
**Santeria** (sahn-tuh-REE-uh)
**Candomblé** (kan-duhm-BLEH)

## The End of the Slave Trade and the Abolition of Slavery

Almost as old as the Atlantic slave trade itself were voices calling for its abolition. The American and French revolutions stimulated the abolitionist cause. The American call for "life, liberty, and the pursuit of happiness" and the French appeal for "liberty, equality, and fraternity" suggested that there was a universal human right to freedom and equality.

Olaudah Equiano as depicted in the first edition of his autobiography (1789).
The British Library/Robana/Getty Images

**Olaudah Equiano** Africans also took up the struggle to abolish commerce in human beings. Frequent revolts in the eighteenth and nineteenth centuries made the institution of slavery an expensive and dangerous business. Some formerly enslaved people contributed to the abolitionist cause by writing books that exposed the brutality of institutional slavery. Most notable of them was the west African **Olaudah Equiano** (1745–1797), who in 1789 published an autobiography detailing his experiences as an enslaved and as a free man. Captured at age ten in his native Benin (in modern Nigeria), Equiano was enslaved in the West Indies, Virginia, and Pennsylvania. He accompanied one of his slaveholders on several campaigns of the Seven Years' War before purchasing his freedom in 1766. Equiano's book became a best-seller, and the author traveled throughout the British isles giving speeches and denouncing slavery as an evil institution. He lobbied government officials and members of Parliament, and his efforts strengthened the antislavery movement in England.

**The Economic Costs of Slavery** Quite apart from moral and political arguments, economic forces contributed to the end of slavery and the slave trade. Plantations, slavery, and the slave trade continued to flourish as long as they were profitable, notwithstanding the efforts of abolitionists. Yet it gradually became clear that slave labor did not come cheap. The possibility of rebellion forced plantation societies to maintain expensive military forces. Even in peaceful times enslaved people often worked unenthusiastically, but owners had to provide basic food and shelter for them throughout their lives no matter how hard they worked. Furthermore, in the late eighteenth century a rapid expansion of Caribbean sugar production led to declining prices. About the same time, African slave traders and European merchants sharply increased the prices they charged for individual enslaved people.

As the profitability of slavery declined, Europeans began to shift their investments from sugarcane and other agricultural products to newly emerging manufacturing industries. Investors soon found that wage labor in factories was less expensive than slave labor on plantations. As an additional benefit, free workers spent much of their income on manufactured goods. Meanwhile, European investors realized that leaving Africans in Africa where they could secure raw materials and buy manufactured goods in exchange was profitable. Thus European entrepreneurs began to look upon Africa less as a source of slave labor and more as a source of raw materials and as a market for manufactured goods.

**End of the Slave Trade** In 1803 Denmark abolished the slave trade, and other lands followed the Danish example: Great Britain in 1807, the United States in 1808, France in 1814, the Netherlands in 1817, and Spain in 1820. The end of the legal commerce in enslaved people did not abolish the institution of slavery itself, however, and as long as plantation slavery continued, a clandestine trade shipped enslaved people across the Atlantic. British naval squadrons sought to prevent this trade by patrolling the west coast of Africa and conducting search and seizure operations, so gradually the illegal slave trade ground to a halt. The last documented ship that carried enslaved people across the Atlantic arrived in Cuba in 1867.

**The Abolition of Slavery** The abolition of the institution of slavery itself was a long and drawn-out process: emancipation of all enslaved people came in 1833 in British colonies, 1848 in French colonies, 1865 in the United States, 1886 in Cuba, and 1888 in Brazil. Saudi Arabia and Angola abolished slavery in the 1960s. Officially, slavery no longer exists, but millions of people live in various forms of slavery even today.

---

**Olaudah Equiano** (oh-LAU-duh eh-kwee-AHN-oh)

# SOURCES FROM THE PAST

## A Cargo of Black Ivory, 1829

*In 1807, the British Parliament passed a bill prohibiting the slave trade in the British Empire. To enforce the law, a naval force, the West African Squadron, patrolled the west coast of Africa seizing slave ships, fining their captains, and freeing the enslaved people on board. In the following excerpt, from a piece entitled "A Cargo of Black Ivory," the outspoken abolitionist Reverend Robert Walsh in 1829 recounted the horrifying conditions found aboard a slaving ship bound for Brazil from Africa. His British vessel had stopped the ship on suspicion of piracy or illegal trafficking.*

**. . . Our boat was now hoisted out,** and I went on board with the officers. When we mounted her decks, we found her full of slaves. She was called the Veloz, commanded by Captain Jose Fiarbosa, bound to Bahia. She was a very broad-decked ship, with a mainmast, schooner-rigged, and behind her foremast was that large formidable gun, which turned on a broad circle of iron, on deck, and which enabled her to act as a pirate, if her slaving speculation had failed. She had taken in, on the coast of Africa, 336 males, and 226 females, making in all 562, and had been out seventeen days, during which she had thrown overboard fifty-five. The slaves were all enclosed under grated hatchways, between decks. The space was so low, that they sat between each other's legs, and stowed so close together, that there was no possibility of their lying down, or at all changing their position, by night or day. As they belonged to, and were shipped on account of different individuals, they were all branded, like sheep, with the owners' marks of different forms. . . These were impressed under their breasts, or on their arms, and as the mate informed me, with, perfect indifference. . . "burnt with the red-hot iron." Over the hatchway stood a ferocious looking fellow, with a scourge of many twisted thongs in his hand, who was the slave-driver of the ship, and whenever he heard the slightest noise below, he shook it over them, and seemed eager to exercise it. . . .

> Why were the enslaved individuals on board the ship branded with hot irons?

The heat of these horrid places was so great, and the odour so offensive, that it was quite impossible to enter them, even had there been room. They were measured as above when the slaves had left them. The officers insisted that the poor suffering creatures should he admitted on deck to get air and water. This was opposed by the mate of the slaver, who, from a feeling that they deserved it, declared they would murder them all. The officers, however, persisted, and the poor beings were all turned up together. It is impossible to conceive the effect of this eruption—517 fellow-creatures of all ages and sexes, some children, some adults, some old men and women, all in a state of total nudity, scrambling out together to taste the luxury of a little fresh air and water. They came swarming up, like bees from the aperture of a hive, till the whole deck was crowded to suffocation, from stem to stern; so that it was impossible to imagine where they could all have come from, or how they could have been stowed away. On looking into the places where they had been crammed, there were found some children next to the sides of the ship, in the places most remote from light and air; they were lying nearly in a torpid state, after the rest had turned out. The little creatures seemed indifferent as to life or death, and when they were carried on deck, many of them could not stand. . .

It was not surprising that they should have endured much sickness and loss of life, in their short passage. They had sailed from the coast of Africa on the 7th of May, and had been out but seventeen days, and they had thrown overboard no less than fifty-five, who had died of dysentery and other complaints, in that space of time, though they had left the coast in good health. Indeed, many of the survivors were seen lying about the decks in the last stage of emaciation, and in a state of filth and misery not to be looked at. Even-handed justice had visited the effects of this unholy traffic, on the crew who were engaged in it. Eight or nine had died, and at that moment six were in hammocks on board, in different stages of fever. This mortality did not arise from want of medicine. There was a large stock ostentatiously displayed in the cabin, with a manuscript book, containing directions as to the quantities; but the only medical man on board to prescribe it was a black, who was as ignorant as his patients.

> Why did the author think it was justice that so many of the ship's crew had become sick with fever?

While expressing my horror at what I saw, and exclaiming against the state of this vessel for conveying human beings, I was informed by my friends, who had passed so long a time on the coast of Africa, and visited so many ships, that this was one of the best they had seen. The height, sometimes, between decks, was only eighteen inches; so that the unfortunate beings could not turn round, or even on their sides, the elevation being less than the breadth of their shoulders; and here they are usually chained to the decks, by the neck and legs. . . .

### For Further Reflection

- The Reverend Walsh clearly expressed his horror and moral outrage at the conditions suffered by the slaves. What did this presumably precious "cargo" have to endure? What treatment did the reverend find especially offensive?
- Note the dates: the slave trade was abolished in 1807; this horrifying account was written in 1829. Why was it so difficult to eradicate the practice, even after it was declared illegal?
- The author, Reverend Robert Walsh, was among many Christian moralists who spoke out against slavery. Why was government action necessary?

*Source:* Walsh, Reverend Robert. "A Cargo of Black Ivory." As found in American History told by Contemporaries, vol. 3, 1783-1845. Edited by Albert Bushnell Hart. New York: Macmillan Company, 1908.

## INTERPRETING IMAGES

Enslaved people in chains on the island of Zanzibar (off the east coast of modern Tanzania) where slavery was abolished on 5 March 1873. Zanzibar had served as east Africa's principal port for the slave trade between Africa and Asia.

**Analyze** *This photo illustrates the ongoing tragedy of the slave trade. Why is it so difficult to "learn from history" and eradicate such injustice?*

Bojan Brecelj/Corbis Historical/Getty Images

According to the Anti-Slavery Society for the Protection of Human Rights, debt bondage, contract labor, sham adoptions, servile marriages, and other forms of forced servitude still oppress more than two hundred million people, mostly in Africa, south Asia, and Latin America. Meanwhile, the legacy of the Atlantic slave trade remains visible throughout much of the Western Hemisphere, where the African diaspora has given rise to distinctive communities as well as cultural traditions that have shaped societies as a whole throughout the Americas and Caribbean.

## CONCLUSION

During the early modern era, many sub-Saharan Africans continued the tradition of living in small kinship groups as they had for centuries. Others built states and traded with Muslim societies as they had since the eighth century C.E. Yet Africans also experienced dramatic changes as they participated in the formation of an integrated Atlantic Ocean basin. Among the agents of change were European merchant-mariners who sought commercial opportunities in sub-Saharan Africa. They brought European manufactured goods and introduced American food crops that fueled population growth throughout Africa. But they also encouraged a vast expansion of existing slave-trading networks as they sought unfree laborers for plantations in the Western Hemisphere. The Atlantic slave trade violently removed sixteen million or more individuals from their home societies and traditions, which led to political turmoil and social disruption throughout much of sub-Saharan Africa. Enslaved Africans and their descendants were mostly prohibited from building independent states in the Western Hemisphere. But they formed an African diaspora from multiple encounters between peoples from all over sub-Saharan Africa and, as a result, were able to maintain some African traditions and to build new ones inspired by African knowledge. The individuals who made up the African diaspora profoundly influenced the development of societies in all slave-holding regions of the Caribbean and the Americas as well as in Africa itself, like Thomas Peters from the introduction to this chapter, who brought former enslaved people back to Africa. Ultimately, Africans and African-descended people took action and collaborated with others to bring about an end to the slave trade and the abolition of slavery itself.

## STUDY TERMS

African diaspora (426)
Angola (415)
Antonian movement (417)
Asante (413)
Atlantic slave trade (419)
Candomblé (429)

creole language (428)
Dona Beatriz (417)
Fulani (417)
Geechee (428)
Ghana (411)
Great Zimbabwe (416)
Gullah (428)
Haiti (428)
Jenne (412)
Khoikhoi (416)
King Nzinga Mbemba (414)
Kongo (414)
Mali Empire (412)
manioc (419)
middle passage (421)
Ndongo (415)
Olaudah Equiano (430)
plantations (426)
Queen Nzinga (416)
Saint-Domingue (428)
Santeria (429)
Songhay Empire (412)
Sunni Ali (412)
Swahili (414)
Timbuktu (412)
triangular trade (420)
Voudou (429)

## FOR FURTHER READING


Vince Brown. *The Reaper's Garden: Death and Power in the World of Atlantic Slavery*. Cambridge, Mass., 2008. A fascinating exploration about the ways death shaped multiple aspects of life in Jamaica in the time of slavery.

Michael L. Conniff and Thomas J. Davis. *Africans in the Americas: A History of the Black Diaspora.* New York, 2002. A comprehensive survey of African-European relations, the slave trade, and the African diaspora.

Christopher Ehret. *The Civilizations of Africa: A History to 1800.* Charlottesville, Va., 2002. An important contribution that views Africa in the context of world history.

Olaudah Equiano and Vincent Carretta. *The Interesting Life of Olaudah Equiano*. Rev. ed. New York, 2003. Autobiography of an enslaved man who turned into an abolitionist, with an informative introduction and editorial comments.

Philip Gould. *Barbaric Traffic: Commerce and Antislavery in the Eighteenth-Century Atlantic World.* Cambridge, 2003. Compelling study of Anglo-American antislavery literature that suggests the discourse was less a debate over the morality of slavery than a concern with the commercial aspects of the slave trade.

Patrick Manning. *The African Diaspora: A History through Culture*. New York, 2010. A truly global exploration of the connections wrought between Africans as they interacted across the continents after 1400.

Stephanie Smallwood. *Saltwater Slavery: A Middle Passage from Africa to American Diaspora*. Cambridge, Mass., 2008. A harrowing look at the process of becoming enslaved from the perspective of enslaved people themselves.

James H. Sweet. *Recreating Africa: Culture, Kinship, and Religion in the African-Portuguese World, 1441–1770.* Chapel Hill, N.C., 2006. Engaging study of African slave culture in Portuguese Brazil and the process of creolization.

Dale W. Tomich. *Through the Prism of Slavery: Labor, Capital, and World Economy.* Lanham, Md., 2004. Brief overview of slavery's role in the development of global capitalism.

Jan Vansina. *Paths in the Rainforest: Toward a History of Political Tradition in Equatorial Africa.* Madison, 1990. A thoughtful analysis that considers both indigenous traditions and external influences on African history.

# CHAPTER 13 AP EXAM PRACTICE

Questions assume cumulative knowledge from this chapter and previous chapters.

## Section I

## Multiple Choice Questions

Use the image below and your knowledge of world history to answer questions 1 – 3.

Engraving from 1626 showing Queen Nzinga of Matamba, who is sitting on a prostrate man while having an audience with a group of Portuguese men.

Fotosearch/Stringer/Getty Images

1. What does this image indicate about gender in African society?
   (A) Muslim men and women socialized more in Africa.
   (B) Young women like Dona Beatriz could lead religious movements.
   (C) Women of African royal families could exercise political power.
   (D) African women made up two thirds of the population of Angola.

2. Why might the artist have depicted Queen Nzinga in this way?
   (A) The artist wanted to show the Angolan landscape.
   (B) Showing her seated on a man recalls her role as a king with male concubines who dressed as women.
   (C) The image was intended to show the kinds of products the Portuguese wanted to buy in Africa, including rugs.
   (D) The artist depicted Queen Nzinga toward the end of her reign, so that the Portuguese would know she was less able to fight them.

3. Which of these was a successful strategy used by Queen Nzinga?
   (A) She promoted the worship of St. Anthony of Padua to improve relations with the Portuguese.
   (B) She purchased muskets and invaded the Songhay empire.
   (C) She forced the Khoikhoi people into labor service.
   (D) She formed an alliance with the Dutch, Portugal's rival.

Use the map below and your knowledge of world history to answer questions 4 and 5.

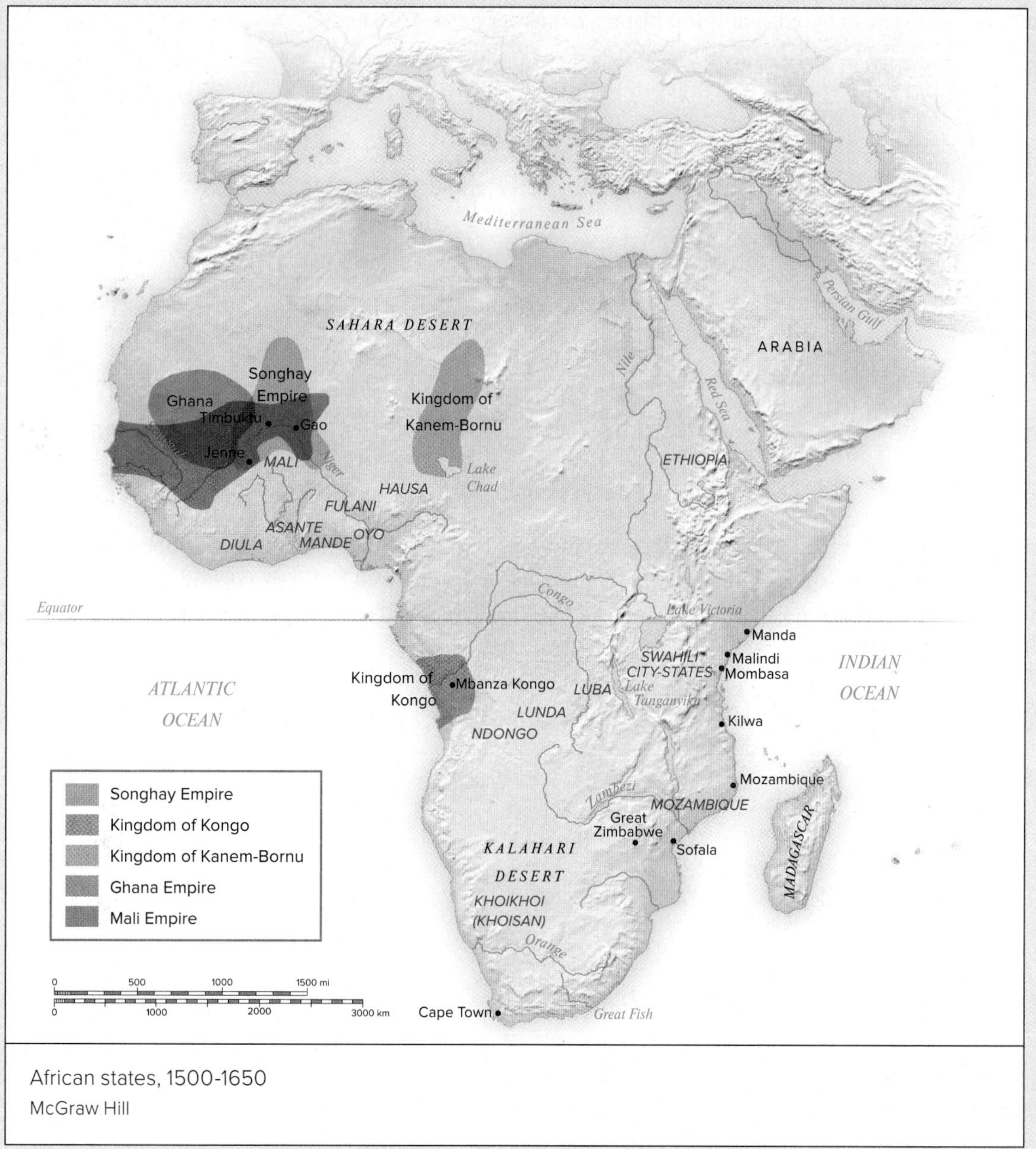


African states, 1500-1650
McGraw Hill

4. Why is it that large, centralized states were formed in the regions shown on the map?
   (A) These states were connected by trans-African railroads.
   (B) The states shown on the map benefited from access to the transatlantic, river system, or trans-Saharan trade routes.
   (C) The west African states were controlled by the east African coastal cities who taught them better forms of government.
   (D) The west African empires had navies with direct access to the Indian Ocean trading system, which brought great wealth to their states.

5. What historical development can be illustrated with this map?
   (A) Nutrition in the African diet improved because of new crops from the Americas.
   (B) Dutch and Portuguese merchants built cities on the African coast, and many intermarried with the local population,
   (C) The region around the Niger river provided resources sufficient to maintain a series of kingdoms and empires.
   (D) Islam blended with the African religious traditions of west Africa.

## Short Answer

6. Use the table below and your knowledge of world history to answer parts A, B, and C.

**Numbers and Destinations of Enslaved People in the Transatlantic Slave Trade by Year.**

| | Europe | Mainland North America | British Caribbean | French Caribbean | Dutch Americas | Danish West Indies | Spanish Americas | Brazil | Africa | Totals |
|---|---|---|---|---|---|---|---|---|---|---|
| 1501–1600 | 903 | 0 | 0 | 0 | 0 | 0 | 241,917 | 34,686 | 0 | 277,506 |
| 1601–1700 | 3,639 | 19,956 | 405,117 | 50,356 | 145,980 | 22,610 | 313,301 | 910,361 | 4,312 | 1,875,631 |
| 1701–1800 | 6,256 | 358,845 | 2,139,819 | 1,178,518 | 339,559 | 81,801 | 175,438 | 2,210,931 | 3,451 | 6,494,619 |
| 1801–1866 | 0 | 93,581 | 218,475 | 99,549 | 28,654 | 25,455 | 860,589 | 2,376,141 | 171,137 | 3,873,580 |
| **Totals** | **10,798** | **472,381** | **2,763,411** | **1,328,422** | **514,192** | **129,867** | **1,591,245** | **5,532,118** | **178,901** | **12,521,336** |

Source: *The Trans-Atlantic Slave Trade Database. Emory University.*

(A) Explain ONE reason that accounts for the difference in totals for Europe and the British Caribbean.
(B) Explain ONE reason why there is a difference in the number of the enslaved between 1701–1800 and 1801–1866.
(C) Identify ONE historical development that explains the increase in the total number of enslaved people from the sixteenth to the eighteenth century.

7. Use the image below and your knowledge of world history to answer parts A, B, and C.

King Alvaro I of Kongo receiving the Dutch ambassadors
DEA/A. Dagli Orti/Getty Images

(A) Identify ONE way that African rulers responded to Europeans in their states.
(B) Explain ONE aspect of Christianity that was unique to sub-Saharan Africa.
(C) Explain ONE aspect of Islam that was unique to sub-Saharan Africa.

8. Use your understanding of world history to answer parts A, B, and C.
(A) Explain ONE impact of the triangular trade system.
(B) Explain ONE way that Africans resisted the influence of Europeans.
(C) Identify ONE way that the transatlantic slave trade was different from the traditional forms of slavery that had been practiced in Africa.

# Section II

## Document-Based Question

Based on the documents below and your knowledge of world history, explain the way that enslaved Africans resisted the Atlantic slave trade.

In your response you should do the following:

- Respond to the prompt with a historically defensible thesis or claim that establishes a line of reasoning.
- Describe a broader historical context relevant to the prompt.
- Support an argument in response to the prompt using all documents.
- Use at least one additional piece of specific historical evidence (beyond that found in the documents) relevant to an argument about the prompt.
- Explain how or why the document's point of view, purpose, historical situation, and /or audience is relevant to an argument.
- Use evidence to corroborate, qualify, or modify an argument that addresses the prompt.

### Document 1

Olaudah Equiano as depicted in the first edition of his autobiography (1789)
The British Library/Robana/Getty Images

## Document 2

Ran away from me the subscriber, the 14th instant, a Molatto named Bilhah, a tall, thick-built well-proportioned Wench; had on a brown short stuff Gown, batt'd with Yellow, a blue camblet Quilt, and check'd linnen Apron, black silk Bonnet, a large pair flower'd silver Shoe-Buckles; may possibly pretend to be a Free Woman, or may Change her Apparel for Men's Cloathing.

*Source*: Eliot, Jared. "Advertisement for Bilhah." The New London Summary (Connecticut Gazette), March 30, 1764.

## Document 3

Only in the French sugar colony of Saint-Domingue did a revolt abolish slavery as an institution (1793). Indeed, the enslaved Africans of Saint-Domingue declared independence from France, renamed the land **Haiti,** and established a self-governing republic (1804). The Haitian revolution terrified slaveholders and inspired enslaved people throughout the Western Hemisphere, but no other rebellion matched its accomplishments.

Source: Bentley and Ziegler, *Traditions & Encounters: A Global Perspective on the Past*

## Long Essay

Develop a thoughtful and thorough historical argument that answers the question below. Begin your essay with a thesis statement and support it with relevant historical evidence.

Using specific examples and your knowledge of world history, analyze the extent to which African American culture before the Civil War was similar to or different from the culture enslaved Africans had experienced in Africa.

# Chapter 14 Tradition and Change in East Asia



## ZOOMING IN ON ENCOUNTERS

### Matteo Ricci and Chiming Clocks in China

In January 1601 a mechanical clock chimed the hours for the first time in the city of Beijing. In the early 1580s, devices that Chinese people called "self-ringing bells" had arrived at the port of Macau, where Portuguese merchants impressed local authorities with their chiming clocks. Reports of them soon spread throughout southern China and beyond to Beijing. The Roman Catholic missionary **Matteo Ricci** conceived the idea of capturing the emperor's attention with mechanical clocks and then persuading him and his subjects to convert to Christianity. From his post at Macau, Ricci let imperial authorities know that he could supply the emperor with a chiming clock. When the emperor **Wanli** (r. 1572–1620) granted him permission to travel to Beijing and establish a mission, Ricci took with him both a large mechanical clock intended for public display and a smaller, self-ringing bell for the emperor's personal use.

European-style buildings on the waterfront in eighteenth-century Guangzhou, where foreign merchants conducted their business.
The Picture Art Collection/Alamy Stock Photo

Emperor Wanli was enchanted by the chiming clocks, and they soon became the rage in elite society throughout China. Wealthy Chinese merchants paid handsome sums for the devices, and Europeans often found that their business in China went better if they presented gifts of self-ringing bells to the government officials they dealt with. By the eighteenth century the imperial court maintained a workshop to manufacture and repair mechanical clocks and watches. While most

**Matteo Ricci** (maht-TAY-oh REE-chee)
**Wanli** (wahn-LEE)

Chinese people could not afford to purchase mechanical clocks, commoners also had opportunities to encounter self-ringing bells. Outside their residence in Beijing, Matteo Ricci and his missionary colleagues installed a large mechanical clock that regularly attracted crowds of curious neighbors when it struck the hours.

But chiming clocks did not have the effect that Ricci desired. The emperor showed no interest in Christianity, and the missionaries attracted only small numbers of Chinese converts. Yet, by opening the doors of the imperial court to the missionaries, the self-ringing bells symbolized the increasing frequency of encounters between East Asian and European peoples.

# CHAPTER FOCUS

- The pursuit of an clearer route to East Asian markets was the primary motive of European explorers. The Spanish sent half their American-mined silver to their colonial city of Manila in the Philippines so Spanish merchants could buy Asian goods.
- The Ming rulers of China (1368–1644) solidified the government and economy after the Mongol/Yuan dynasty. The Ming brought back traditional Chinese practices, expanded the Great Wall, and built a colossal imperial complex—the Forbidden City—to impress and reflect their own legitimacy to rule.
- The subsequent Manchu/Qing dynasty continued these same policies. Like the Mongols, the Manchu adopted a dynasty name (Qing), appointed other Manchus as top advisors, and required Chinese men to wear their hair in queue to be instantly identifiable as subservient.
- Chinse merchants maintained businesses along well-established Afro=Eurasian trade routes. They received new crops from the Columbian exchange, and populations grew dramatically. Expanding cities incubated thriving cultures that included Buddhism and a syncretic of reinterpreted Confucianism, called neo-Confucianism.
- The Tokugawa family in Japan won a long civil war and took control as shoguns. They reduced the power of the daimyo (feudal nobility) and centralized their authority, as we see in other kingdoms in Eurasia.
- Chinese culture continued to hold considerable influence in Japanese culture.
- The late Ming and half of the Qing dynasty limited western European' presence in China.
- The Tokugawa and Korea's Chosun rulers passed more severe restrictions on western influence.
- The expulsion of Christian missionaries in east Asia and exclusion of Europeans was done based on the presumed inferiority of European religions, culture, and trade goods. For east Asians, these assumptions were not questioned for two centuries.

## Historical Developments

- In some cases, the increase and intensification of interactions between newly connected hemispheres expanded the reach and furthered development of existing religions, and contributed to religious conflicts and the development of syncretic belief systems and practices.
- Imperial conquests and widening global economic opportunities contributed to the formation of new political and economic elites, including in China where the transition to the Qing dynasty and in the Americas with the rise of the Casta System.
- Empires achieved increased scope and influence around the world, shaping and being shaped by the diverse populations they incorporated.
- Peasant and artisan labor continued and intensified in many regions as the demand for food and consumer goods increased.

## Reasoning Processes

- **Source Claims and Evidence** Identify the evidence used to support the claim that states in China and Japan carefully regulated their contacts with Europeans.
- **Contextualization** Identify and describe the historical context for the unification of Japan under the Tokugawa shogunate.

## Historical Thinking Skills

- **Comparison** Describe similarities and/or differences between Chinese and Japanese governance and social transformations.
- **Continuity and Change** Explain patterns of continuity and/or change in Chinese religions.

# CHAPTER OVERVIEW

By linking all the world's regions and peoples, the European voyages of exploration inaugurated a new era in world history. Yet transoceanic connections influenced different societies in very different ways. In contrast to sub-Saharan Africa, where the Atlantic slave trade bred instability and provoked turmoil, for the most part east Asian lands benefited from long-distance trade because it brought silver that stimulated their economies. East Asian societies benefited also from American plant crops that made their way across the seas as part of the Columbian exchange.

Unlike the Americas, where Europeans profoundly influenced historical development from the time of their arrival, east Asian societies controlled their own affairs until the nineteenth century. Europeans were active on the coastlines, but they had little influence on internal affairs in the region. Because of its political and cultural preeminence, China remained the dominant power in east Asia. Established during the Qin (221-206 B.C.E.) and Han (206 B.C.E.-220 C.E.) dynasties, long-standing political, social, and cultural traditions endowed Chinese society with a sense of stability and permanence. China was also a remarkably prosperous land. Indeed, with its huge population, enormous productive capacity, and strong demand for silver, China was a leading economic powerhouse driving world trade in early modern times. By the late eighteenth century, however, China experienced social and economic change that eventually caused problems both for state authorities and for Chinese society as a whole.

During the seventeenth and eighteenth centuries, Japan also underwent major transformations. The Tokugawa shoguns unified the Japanese islands for the first time and laid a foundation for long-term economic growth. While tightly restricting contacts and relations with the larger world, Tokugawa Japan generated a distinctive set of social and cultural traditions. Those developments helped fashion a Japan that would play a decisive role in global affairs by the twentieth century.

| CHRONOLOGY | |
|---|---|
| 1368–1644 | Ming dynasty (China) |
| 1368–1398 | Reign of Hongwu |
| 1403–1424 | Reign of Yongle |
| 1552–1610 | Life of Matteo Ricci |
| 1572–1620 | Reign of Emperor Wanli |
| 1600–1867 | Tokugawa shogunate (Japan) |
| 1616–1626 | Reign of Nurhaci |
| 1642–1693 | Life of Ihara Saikaku |
| 1644–1911 | Qing dynasty (China) |
| 1661–1722 | Reign of Kangxi |
| 1736–1795 | Reign of Qianlong |

# THE QUEST FOR POLITICAL STABILITY

During the thirteenth and fourteenth centuries, China experienced the trauma of rule by the Yuan dynasty (1279-1368) of nomadic Mongol warriors (discussed in chapter 17). Mongol overlords ignored Chinese political and cultural traditions, and they displaced Chinese bureaucrats in favor of Turkish, Persian, and other foreign administrators. When the Yuan dynasty came to an end, the Ming emperors who succeeded it sought to erase all signs of Mongol influence and restore traditional ways to China. Looking to the Tang and Song dynasties for inspiration, they built a powerful imperial state, revived the civil service staffed by Confucian scholars, and promoted Confucian thought. Rulers of the succeeding **Qing dynasty** were themselves Manchus of nomadic origin, but they too worked zealously to promote Chinese ways. Ming and Qing emperors alike were deeply conservative: their principal concern was to maintain stability in a large agrarian society, so they adopted policies that favored Chinese political and cultural traditions. The state they fashioned governed China for more than half a millennium.

## The Ming Dynasty

**Ming Government** When the Yuan dynasty collapsed, the **Ming dynasty** (1368-1644) restored Han Chinese rule to China. **Hongwu** (reigned 1368-1398), founder of the Ming ("brilliant") dynasty, drove the Mongols out of China and built a tightly centralized state. As emperor, Hongwu made extensive use of mandarins, imperial officials who traveled throughout the land and oversaw implementation of government policies. He also placed great trust in **eunuchs** based on

**Qing** (ching)
**eunuchs** (YOO-nihks)

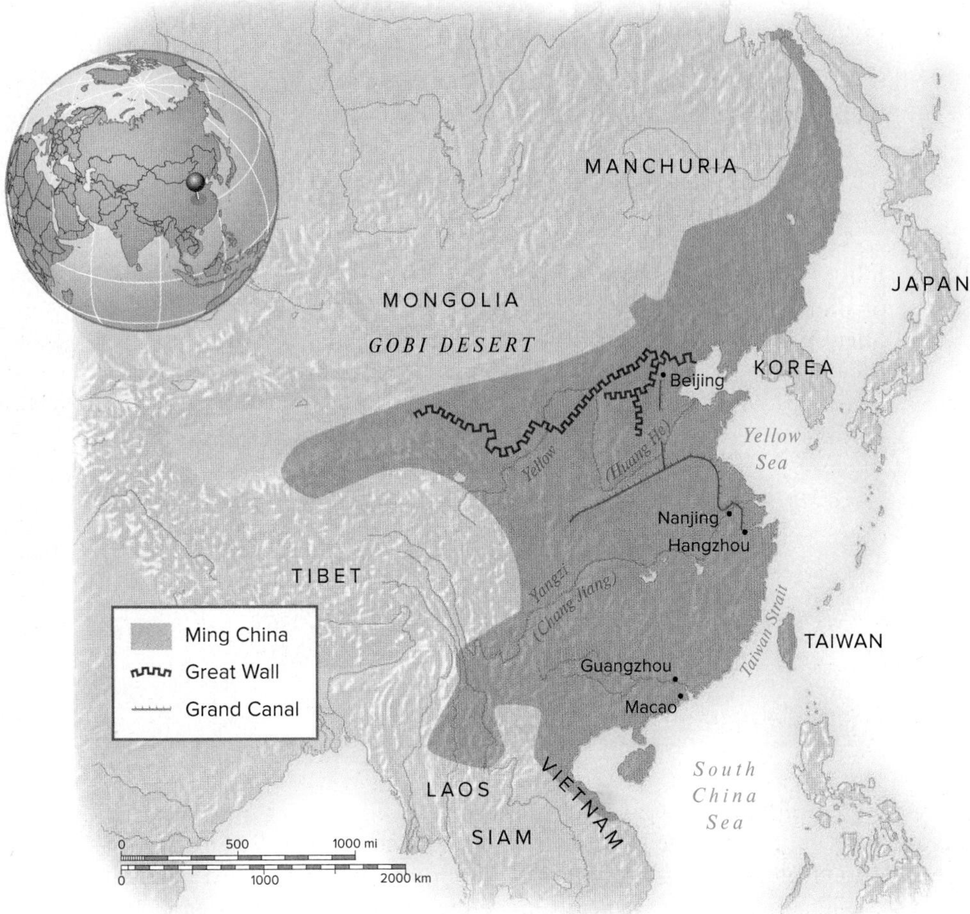


## MAP 14.1 Ming China, 1368–1644.

Locate the old Ming capital at Nanjing and the new Ming capital at Beijing.

***Why would the Ming emperors have wanted to move so far north?***

***The Ming dynasty followed the Yuan dynasty (Mongols). Why?***

***Why do you think there is ongoing friction between Mongolia and the People's Republic of China in the 21st century?***

the thinking that they could not generate families and hence would not build power bases that would challenge imperial authority. The emperor **Yongle** (reigned 1403–1424) launched a series of naval expeditions that sailed throughout the Indian Ocean basin and showed Chinese colors as far away as Malindi in east Africa (discussed in chapter 21). Yongle's successors discontinued the expensive maritime expeditions but maintained the tightly centralized state that Hongwu had established.

The Ming emperors were determined to prevent new invasions. In 1421 Yongle moved the capital from Nanjing in the south to Beijing to keep closer watch on the Mongols and other nomadic peoples in the north. The early Ming emperors commanded powerful armies that controlled the Mongols militarily, but by the mid-fifteenth century they had lost their effectiveness. Mongol forces massacred several Chinese armies in the 1440s, and in 1449 they captured the Ming emperor himself.

**The Great Wall** The later Ming emperors sought to protect their realm by building new fortifications, including the **Great Wall** of China, along the northern border. The Great Wall had precedents dating back to the fourth century B.C.E., and the first emperor of the Qin dynasty had ordered construction of a long defensive wall during the third century B.C.E. Those early walls had all fallen into ruin, however, and thus the Great Wall was a Ming dynasty project. Workers by the hundreds of thousands labored throughout the late fifteenth and sixteenth centuries to build a massive stone and brick barrier that ran some 2,500 kilometers (1,550 miles). The Great Wall was 10 to 15 meters (33 to 49 feet) high, and it featured watchtowers, signal towers, and accommodations for troops stationed at the border.

**Yongle** (YAWNG-leh)

A portion of the Great Wall in Jinshanlang, Hebei province.
Benjamin B/Shutterstock

The Ming emperors also set out to eradicate Mongol and other foreign influences and to create a stable society in the image of the Chinese past. With Ming encouragement, for example, individuals abandoned the Mongol names and dress that many had adopted during the Yuan dynasty. Respect for Chinese traditions facilitated the restoration of institutions that the Mongols had ignored or suppressed. The government sponsored study of Chinese cultural traditions, especially Confucianism (discussed in chapter 8), and provided financial support for imperial academies and regional colleges. Most important, the Ming state restored the system of civil service examinations that Mongol rulers had neglected.

**Ming Decline** The vigor of early Ming rule did not survive beyond the mid-sixteenth century, when a series of problems weakened the dynasty. From the 1520s to the 1560s, pirates and smugglers operated almost at will along the east coast of China. (Although Ming officials referred to the pirates as Japanese, in fact most of them were Chinese.) Both the Ming navy and coastal defenses proved ineffective, and conflicts with pirates often led to the disruption of coastal communities and sometimes even interior regions. In 1555, for example, a band of sixty-seven pirates went on a three-month rampage during which they looted a dozen cities in three provinces and killed more than four thousand people.

Suppression of pirates took more than forty years, partly because of serious problems in the imperial government. The later Ming emperors lived extravagantly in the Forbidden City, a vast complex in Beijing that was isolated from the outside world and only received news about what was happening in the rest of China from eunuch servants and administrators. The emperors sometimes ignored government affairs for decades while satisfying their various appetites. Throughout his long reign, for example, the emperor Wanli (1572–1620) refused to meet with government officials. Instead, while indulging his taste for wine, he conducted business through eunuch intermediaries. Powerful eunuchs won the favor of the later Ming emperors by procuring concubines for them and providing for their amusement. The eunuchs then used their power and position to enrich themselves and lead lives of luxury. Over time, corruption and inefficiency spread throughout the government and weakened the Ming state.

**Ming Collapse** When a series of famines struck China during the early seventeenth century, the government was unable to organize effective relief efforts. Peasants in stricken regions resorted to eating grass roots and tree bark. By the 1630s peasants organized revolts throughout China, and they gathered momentum as one city after another withdrew its loyalty from the Ming dynasty. To complicate matters further, **Manchu** forces invaded from the north in search of opportunities for expansion in China. In 1644, Chinese rebel forces captured the Ming capital at Beijing. Manchu invaders allied with an army loyal to the Ming, crushed the rebels, and recovered Beijing. The Manchus portrayed themselves as avengers who saved the capital from dangerous rebels, but instead of

## INTERPRETING IMAGES

Bird's-eye view of the Forbidden City, which was built by the Emperor Yongle (r. 1402–1424) as a vast, walled imperial retreat at the center of Beijing. Note the extent of the grounds.

**Analyze** *After such extraordinary success and wealth, why did the Ming dynasty yield to the Qing?*

Sovfoto/Getty Images

restoring Ming rule, they moved their own capital to Beijing and displaced the Ming dynasty.

## The Qing Dynasty

**The Manchus** When the Ming dynasty fell, Manchus poured into China from their homeland of Manchuria north of the Great Wall. The victors proclaimed a new dynasty, the Qing ("pure"), which ruled China until the early twentieth century (1644–1911).

The Manchus were primarily pastoral nomads, although many had turned to agriculture and settled in the rich farmlands of southern Manchuria. Their remote ancestors had traded with China since the Qin dynasty, and they had frequently clashed with their neighbors over land and resources in northern China and southern Manchuria. During the late sixteenth and early seventeenth centuries, an ambitious chieftain named **Nurhaci** (reigned 1616–1626) unified Manchu tribes into a centralized state, established a code of laws, and organized a powerful military force. During the 1620s and 1630s, the Manchu army expelled Ming garrisons in Manchuria, captured Korea and Mongolia, and launched small-scale invasions into China. After their seizure of Beijing in 1644, the Manchus moved to extend their authority throughout China. For almost forty years they waged campaigns against Ming loyalists and other rebels in southern China until by the early 1680s the Manchus had consolidated the Qing dynasty's hold throughout the land.

The establishment of the Qing dynasty was due partly to Manchu military might and partly to Chinese support for the Manchus. During the 1630s and 1640s, many Chinese generals deserted the Ming dynasty because of its corruption and inefficiency. Confucian scholar-bureaucrats also worked against the Ming because they despised the eunuchs who dominated the imperial court. The Manchu ruling elites were schooled in Chinese language and Confucian thought, and they were often more respected by Chinese scholar-bureaucrats than the emperor and high administrators of the Ming dynasty itself.

Yet the Manchus were also careful to preserve their own ethnic and cultural identity. They not only outlawed intermarriage between Manchus and Chinese but also forbade Chinese from traveling to Manchuria and from learning the Manchurian language. Qing authorities also forced Chinese men to shave the front of their heads and grow a Manchu-style queue (somewhat like a pony-tail) as a sign of submission to the dynasty.

**Nurhaci** (NOOR-hacheh)

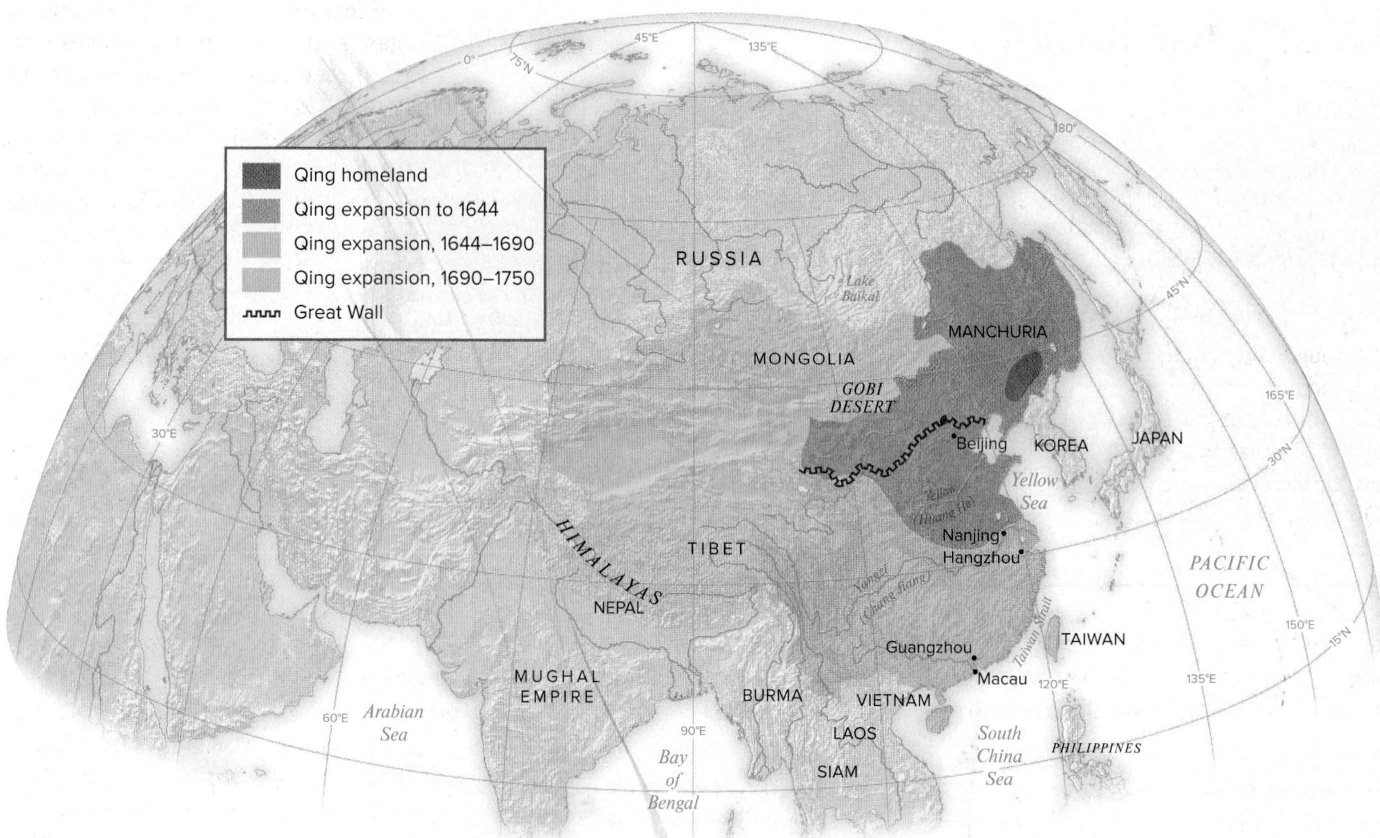


**MAP 14.2 The Qing empire, 1644–1911.**

Compare this map with Map 14.1.

***Why would the Qing emperors have wanted to incorporate such extensive territories in Mongolia and Tibet into their empire?***

**Kangxi and His Reign** Until the nineteenth century, strong imperial leadership muted tensions between Manchu rulers and Chinese subjects. The long reigns of two particularly effective emperors, **Kangxi** (1661–1722) and **Qianlong** (1736–1795), helped the Manchus consolidate their hold on China. Kangxi was a Confucian scholar as well as an enlightened ruler. He was a voracious reader and occasionally composed poems. He studied the Confucian classics and sought to apply their teachings through his policies. For example, he organized flood-control and irrigation projects in observance of the Confucian precept that rulers should look after the welfare of their subjects and promote agriculture. He also generously patronized Confucian schools and academies.

Kangxi was also a conqueror, and he oversaw the construction of a vast empire. He conquered the island of Taiwan, where Ming loyalists had retreated after being expelled from southern China, and absorbed it into his empire. Like his predecessors of the Han and Tang dynasties, Kangxi sought to forestall problems with nomadic peoples by projecting Chinese influence into central Asia. His conquests in Mongolia and central Asia extended almost to the Caspian Sea, and he imposed a Chinese protectorate over Tibet. Kangxi's grandson Qianlong continued this expansion of Chinese influence. Qianlong sought to consolidate Kangxi's conquests in central Asia by maintaining military garrisons in eastern Turkestan (the territory now known as Xinjiang province in western China) and encouraging merchants to settle there in hopes they would stabilize the region. Under Qianlong's reign, Vietnam, Burma, and Nepal became tributary states to China.

**Qianlong and His Reign** Qianlong's reign marked the height of the Qing dynasty. Like Kangxi, Qianlong was a sophisticated and learned man. He reportedly composed more than one hundred thousand poems, and he was a discriminating connoisseur of painting and calligraphy. During his long, stable, and prosperous reign, the imperial treasury collected so much wealth that on four occasions Qianlong cancelled tax collections. Toward the end of his reign, Qianlong paid less attention to imperial affairs and delegated many responsibilities to his favorite eunuchs. His successors continued that

---

**Kangxi** (kahng-shee)
**Qianlong** (chyahn-lawng)

practice, devoting themselves to hunting and court life, and by the nineteenth century the Qing dynasty faced serious difficulties. Throughout the reign of Qianlong, however, China remained a wealthy and well-organized land.

## The Son of Heaven and the Scholar-Bureaucrats

Although Qing rulers usually appointed Manchus to the highest political posts, they relied on the same governmental apparatus that the Ming emperors had established. Both the Ming and the Qing dynasties presided over a tightly centralized state, which they administered through a bureaucracy staffed by Confucian scholars. For more than five hundred years, the autocratic state created by the Ming emperor Hongwu governed China's fortunes.

Though painted in the nineteenth century, this portrait depicts Kangxi in his imperial regalia as he looked at about age fifty. Kangxi reigned for sixty-one years, making him the longest-ruling emperor in Chinese history.
Universal History Archive/Getty Images

**The Son of Heaven** Although the emperor of China during the Ming and Qing dynasties was not quite a god, he was more than a mere mortal. Chinese tradition held that he was the **"Son of Heaven,"** the human being designated by heavenly powers to maintain order on the earth. He led a privileged life within the walls of the Forbidden City. Hundreds of concubines resided in his harem, and thousands of eunuchs looked after his every need. His daily activities were carefully choreographed performances and included inspections, audiences, banquets, and other official duties. Everything about his person and the institution he represented conveyed a sense of awesome authority. The imperial wardrobe and personal effects bore designs no one else was allowed to wear, for instance, and it was forbidden throughout the realm to write the characters of the emperor's name. Individuals who had the rare privilege of a personal audience with the emperor had to perform the kowtow—three kneelings and nine head knockings. Those who gave even minor offense faced severe punishment. Even the highest official could have his bare buttocks flogged with bamboo canes, a punishment that sometimes brought victims to the point of death.

**The Scholar-Bureaucrats** Day-to-day governance of the empire fell to scholar-bureaucrats appointed by the emperor. With few exceptions these officials came from the class of well-educated and highly literate men known as the scholar-gentry. These men had earned academic degrees by passing rigorous civil service examinations, and they dominated China's political and social life.

Preparations for the examinations began at an early age. Sometimes they took place in local schools, which like the civil service examinations were open only to males. Wealthy families often engaged the services of tutors, who made formal education available also to girls. By the time students were eleven or twelve years old, they had memorized several thousand characters that were necessary to deal with the Confucian curriculum, including the ***Analects* of Confucius** and other standard works. They followed those studies with instruction in calligraphy, poetry, and essay composition. Diligent students also acquainted themselves with a large corpus of commentaries, histories, and literary works in preparing for **civil service examinations.**

**Civil Service Examinations** The examinations consisted of a battery of tests administered at the district, provincial, and metropolitan levels. Stiff official quotas restricted the number of successful candidates in each examination—only three hundred students could pass metropolitan examinations—and students frequently took the examinations several times before earning a degree.

Writing the examinations was a grueling ordeal. At the appointed hour, candidates presented themselves at the examination compound. Each candidate brought a water pitcher, a chamber pot, bedding, food, an inkstone, ink, and brushes. After guards had verified their identities and searched them for hidden printed materials, the new arrivals proceeded along narrow lanes to a honeycomb of small, cell-like rooms barely large enough to accommodate one man and his possessions. Aside from a bench, a makeshift bed, and boards that served as a desk, the rooms were empty. For three days and two nights, the cramped rooms were home to the candidates, who spent all their time writing "eight-legged essays"—literary compositions with eight distinct sections—on questions posed by the examiners. There were no interruptions, nor was there any communication between candidates. If someone died during the examination period, officials wrapped his body in a straw mat and tossed it over the high walls that ringed the compound.

**The Examination System and Chinese Society** The possibility of bureaucratic service—with prospects for rich social and financial rewards—ensured that competition for degrees was ferocious at all levels. Yet a degree did not ensure

Imperial civil-service examination hall in Suzhou, 1759. Note the tiny cells in which students took the exams.
The Picture Art Collection/ Alamy Stock Photo

government service. During the Qing dynasty the empire's one million degree holders competed for twenty thousand official civil service positions. Those who passed only the district exams had few opportunities for bureaucratic employment and usually spent their careers "plowing with the writing brush" by teaching in local schools or serving as family tutors. Those who passed the metropolitan examinations, however, could look forward to powerful positions in the imperial bureaucracy.

The examination system was a pivotal institution. By opening the door to honor, power, and rewards, the examinations encouraged serious pursuit of a formal education. Furthermore, since the system did not erect social barriers before its recruits, it provided an avenue for upward social mobility. Years of education and travel to examination sites were expensive, so candidates from wealthy families certainly enjoyed advantages over others, but the exams themselves were open to all males regardless of age or social class. Finally, in addition to selecting officials for government service, the education and examination system molded the personal values of those who managed day-to-day affairs in imperial China. By concentrating on Confucian classics and neo-Confucian commentaries, the examinations guaranteed that Confucianism would be at the heart of Chinese education and that Confucians would govern the state.

## ECONOMIC AND SOCIAL CHANGES

By modeling their governmental structure on the centralized imperial states of earlier Chinese dynasties, the Ming and Qing emperors succeeded in their goal of restoring and maintaining traditional ways in China. They also sought to preserve the traditional hierarchical and patriarchal social order. Yet, while the emperors promoted conservative political and social policies, China experienced economic and social changes, partly as a result of influences and encounters from abroad. Agricultural production increased dramatically—especially after the introduction of new food crops from the Americas—and fueled rapid population growth. Meanwhile, global trade brought China enormous wealth, which stimulated the domestic economy by encouraging increased trade, manufacturing, and urban growth. These developments deeply influenced Chinese society and partly undermined the stability that the Ming and Qing emperors sought to preserve.

### The Patriarchal Family

**Filial Piety** Moralists portrayed the Chinese people as one large family, and they extended family values to the larger society. **Filial piety,** for example, implied not only duties of children toward their parents but also loyalty of subjects toward the emperor. Like the imperial government, the Chinese family ideal was hierarchical, patriarchal, and authoritarian. The father was head of the household, and he passed leadership of the family to his eldest son. The veneration of ancestors, which the state promoted, strengthened the authority of the patriarchs by honoring the male line of descent in formal family rituals. Filial piety was the cornerstone of family values. Children had the duty to look after their parents' happiness and well-being, and a crucial obligation was to support parents in their old age. Young children heard stories of sons who went so far as to cut off parts of their bodies to ensure that their parents had enough to eat!

The Chinese family ideal extended into patrilineal (tracing descent through the male line) descent groups such as the clan. Sometimes numbering into the thousands, clan members came from all social classes, though members of the gentry usually dominated a given clan. Clans assumed responsibilities that exceeded the capacities of the nuclear family, such as the maintenance of local order, organization of local economies, and provision for welfare. Clan-supported education gave poor but promising relatives the opportunity to succeed in the civil service examinations. The principal motives behind such charity were self-interest as well as altruism. A government position brought prestige and prosperity to the entire clan, so educational support was a good investment. As a result of educating their members for a chance to take the civil service examinations, clans served as a means for the transmission of Confucian values from the gentry leaders to all social classes within the clan.

**Gender Relations** Within the family, Confucian principles subjected women to the authority of men. The subordination of females began at an early age. Chinese parents preferred boys over girls. Whereas a boy might have the opportunity to take the official examinations, become a government official, and thereby bring honor and financial reward to the entire clan, parents regarded a girl as a social and financial liability. After years of expensive upbringing, most girls would marry and become members of other households. Under those circumstances some people even resorted to female infanticide when a girl was born to them.

During the Ming and Qing dynasties, patriarchal authority over females probably became tighter than ever before in China. Since ancient times, relatives had discouraged widows from remarriage, but social pressures increased during the Ming dynasty. Friends and relatives not only encouraged widows to honor the memory of their departed husbands but also heaped honors on those who committed suicide and followed their spouses to the grave.

**Foot Binding** **Foot binding,** a custom that probably originated in the Song dynasty, became exceptionally popular during the late Ming and Qing dynasties. Because small and dainty feet were considered attractive and even erotic, some families bound the feet of girls with strips of linen to make their feet even smaller. Bound feet could not grow naturally and so would not support the weight of an adult woman. For this reason, the practice of foot binding became most widespread among the wealthy classes because it demonstrated an ability to support women who could not perform physical labor. Sometimes, however, commoners bound the feet of girls who they hoped could attract marriage prospects that would enhance the family's social standing.

Marriage itself was a contractual affair whose principal purpose was to continue the male line of descent. A bride became a member of the husband's family, and there was no ambiguity about her position in the household. On her wedding day, as soon as she arrived at her husband's home, the bride performed ritual acts demonstrating subservience to her husband and her new family. Women could not divorce their husbands, but men could divorce their wives in cases where there was no offspring or where the wife was guilty of adultery, theft, disobedience to her husband's family, or even being too talkative.

Thus custom and law combined to strengthen patriarchal authority in Chinese families during the Ming and Qing

## What's Left Out?

The practice of foot-binding in China was certainly painful for the (mostly elite) women who underwent the process. There is also no doubt that it permanently limited women's mobility, increasing their dependency on others around them. Westerners certainly saw the practice as a grotesque symbol of the oppression of women in Qing culture. But it is important to remember that foot-binding was only one example of many around the world in which women altered or deformed their bodies in the name of beauty. In fact, in the eighteenth and nineteenth centuries—the very same period westerners were pointing out the cruelties and pain associated with foot-binding—middle-class and elite western European women were wearing whale-bone corsets around their torsos to alter their shapes significantly. Like foot-binding, corseting was painful and could permanently deform women's bodies so that they assumed an ideal shape. Corseting also had significant adverse health effects for women, including breathing and lung disorders, prolapsed uteruses, digestive problems, an inability to move quickly or vigorously, and back pain. The point here is that it is important to remember that while ideals of female beauty differed from place to place, Chinese society during the Qing period was not distinctive for encouraging some women to alter their bodies to achieve a physical ideal. Moreover, many of the methods for attaining these ideals of female beauty, including foot-binding and corseting, also had secondary effects of limiting the mobility of women.

*Sources:* John Robert Shepherd, *Foot-Binding as Fashion: Ethnicity, Labor, and Status in Traditional China* (Seattle: University of Washington Press, 2019); Leigh Summers, *Bound to Please: A History of the Victorian Corset* (Oxford: Berg Publishers, 2001).

### Thinking Critically About Sources

1. The passage describes the grotesque and harmful effects of both Chinese foot binding and Western corseting. Why would so many men, especially the elite, deem these practices as signs of beauty?
2. Why are the practices a metaphor for underlying attitudes?

## INTERPRETING IMAGES

To encourage widows to remain unmarried, the Ming and Qing governments constructed arches in honor of those who did not marry again after the death of their husbands. These arches erected during the Qing dynasty still stand in Anhui province in the Yangzi River valley.

**Analyze** *Compare and contrast the Chinese arches depicted and the Indian pyres required of widows.*

Imagemore/age fotostock

dynasties. Yet, while family life continued to develop along traditional lines, the larger Chinese society underwent considerable change between the sixteenth and the eighteenth centuries.

## Population Growth and Economic Development

China was a predominantly agricultural society, a fact that meshed agreeably with the Confucian view that land was the source of everything praiseworthy. The emperor himself acknowledged the central importance of agriculture by plowing the first furrow of the season. Yet only a small fraction of China's land is suitable for planting: even today only about 11 percent is in cultivation. To feed the country's large population, China's farmers relied on intensive, garden-style agriculture that was highly productive. On its strong agrarian foundation, China supported a large population and built the most highly commercialized economy of the preindustrial world.

**American Food Crops** By intensively cultivating every available parcel of land, Chinese peasants increased their yields of traditional food crops—especially rice, wheat, and millet—until the seventeenth century. Beginning about the mid-seventeenth century, as peasants approached the upper limits of agricultural productivity, Spanish merchants coming by way of the Philippines introduced American food crops to China. American maize (corn), sweet potatoes, and peanuts permitted Chinese farmers to take advantage of soils that previously had gone uncultivated. The introduction of new crops increased the food supply and supported further population growth.

**Population Growth** In spite of recurring epidemic diseases such as plague, which claimed the lives of millions, China's population rose rapidly from 100 million in 1500 to 160 million in 1600. Partly because of rebellion and war during the transition between the Ming and Qing empires, it

### How the Past Shapes the Future

#### The Columbian Exchange

Prior to the sixteenth century, crops such as corn, sweet potatoes, and peanuts had only been known in the Americas. As a result of the Columbian exchange, however, food crops native to the Americas were brought not only to Europe but also to Asia and Africa. The introduction of such crops to China during the sixteenth century both changed Chinese cuisine and also allowed more land to be cultivated. The result was dramatic population growth, which had both positive and negative effects for Chinese people over the long term. In this case, consider the ways that events and processes that occurred in the Americas played an important but unforeseen role in shaping historical developments in east Asia.

## INTERPRETING IMAGES

A Ming-era vase painting depicts a woman weaving silk as an attendant pours tea. Silk and tea were among the exports China produced for global trade.

**Analyze** *To what extent was the decline of the Ming dynasty similar to the decline with the Yuan? How as it different? How did the roles of artists change?*

DeAgostini/Getty Images

fell to 140 million in the mid-seventeenth century, but returned to 160 million by 1700 and then surged to 225 million by 1750—an increase of more than 40 percent in just half a century. This rapid demographic growth set the stage for economic and social problems because agricultural production could not keep pace with population over the long term. Acute problems did not occur until the nineteenth century, but per capita income in China began to decline as early as the reign of Qianlong.

While an increasing population placed pressure on Chinese resources, the growing commercial market offered opportunities for entrepreneurs. Because of demographic expansion, entrepreneurs had access to a large, mobile labor force, and they were able to recruit workers readily at low cost. After the mid-sixteenth century, the Chinese economy benefited also from the influx of Japanese and American silver, which stimulated trade and financed further commercial expansion.

**Foreign Trade** Global trade brought prosperity to China, especially during the early Qing dynasty. Chinese workers produced vast quantities of silk, porcelain, lacquerware, and tea for consumers in the Indian Ocean basin, central Asia, and Europe. The silk industry was especially well organized: weavers worked in workshops for regular wages producing fine satins and brocades for export. Chinese imports were relatively few: they included spices from Maluku, exotic products such as birds and animal skins from tropical regions, and small quantities of woolen textiles from Europe. Payment for exports came most importantly in the form of silver bullion, which supported the silver-based Chinese economy and fueled manufacturing.

Economic growth and commercial expansion took place mostly in an atmosphere of tight government regulation. Although the emperor Yongle had sought to establish a Chinese presence in the Indian Ocean during the early fifteenth century through the expeditions of admiral **Zheng He,** after his reign the Ming government withdrew its support for expensive maritime expeditions and even tried to prevent Chinese subjects from dealing with foreign peoples. In its effort to pacify southern China during the later seventeenth century, the Qing government tried to end maritime activity altogether. An imperial edict of 1656 forbade "even a plank from drifting to the sea," and in 1661 the emperor Kangxi ordered evacuation of the southern coastal regions. Those policies had only a limited effect—small Chinese vessels continued to trade actively in Japan and southeast Asian ports—and when Qing forces pacified southern China in the 1680s, government authorities rescinded the strictest measures. Thereafter, however, Qing authorities closely supervised the activities of foreign merchants in China. They permitted Portuguese merchants to operate only at the port of Macau, and British agents had to deal exclusively with the official merchant guild in Guangzhou.

While limiting the activities of foreign merchants, government policies also discouraged the organization of large-scale commercial ventures by Chinese merchants. In the absence of government approval, it was impossible, for example, to maintain shipyards that could construct large sailing ships like the mammoth, nine-masted treasure ships that Zheng He had led throughout the Indian Ocean. Similarly, it was impossible to organize large trading firms like the English East India Company or the Dutch VOC.

**Trade and Migration to Southeast Asia** Nevertheless, thousands of Chinese merchants worked either individually or in partnerships, plying the waters of the China seas to link China with global trade networks. Chinese merchants were especially prominent in Manila (in the Philippines), where they exchanged silk and porcelain for American silver that came across the Pacific Ocean with the Manila galleons. They were

**Zheng He** (jehng huh)

# SOURCES FROM THE PAST

## Qianlong on Chinese Trade with England

*Qing administrators tightly restricted foreign trade. Foreign merchants had to deal with government-approved agents outside the city walls of Guangzhou and had to depart as soon as they had completed their business. In 1793 a British diplomat representing King George III of England bestowed gifts on the emperor Qianlong (r. 1735–1796) and petitioned for the right to trade at ports other than Guangzhou. In a letter to King George, Qianlong outlined his views on Chinese trade with England. His letter also clearly demonstrates the active role of the imperial government in the formation of commercial and economic policies.*

**You, O king, from afar** have yearned after the blessings of our civilization, and in your eagerness to come into touch with our influence have sent an embassy across the sea bearing a memorandum. I have already taken note of your respectful spirit of submission, have treated your mission with extreme favor and loaded it with gifts, besides issuing a mandate to you, O king, and honoring you with the bestowal of valuable presents. . . .

Yesterday your ambassador petitioned my ministers to memorialize me regarding your trade with China, but his proposal is not consistent with our dynastic usage and cannot be entertained. Hitherto, all European nations, including your own country's barbarian merchants, have carried on their trade with our Celestial Empire at Guangzhou. Such has been the procedure for many years, although our Celestial Empire possesses all things in prolific abundance and lacks no product within its own borders. There was therefore no need to import the manufactures of outside barbarians in exchange for our own produce. But as the tea, silk, and porcelain which the Celestial Empire produces are absolute necessities to European nations and to yourselves, we have permitted, as a signal mark of favor, that trading agents should be established at Guangzhou, so that your wants might be supplied and your country thus participate in our beneficence. But your ambassador has now put forward new requests which completely fail to recognize our throne's principle to "treat strangers from afar with indulgence," and to exercise a pacifying control over barbarian tribes the world over. . . . Your England is not the only nation trading at Guangzhou. If other nations, following your bad example, wrongfully importune my ear with further impossible requests, how will it be possible for me to treat them with easy indulgence? Nevertheless, I do not forget the lonely remoteness of your island, cut off from the world by intervening wastes of sea, nor do I overlook your excusable ignorance of the usages of our Celestial Empire. I have consequently commanded my ministers to enlighten your ambassador on the subject, and have ordered the departure of the mission. . . .

> Does the language of emperor Qianlong here signal an attitude of deference or an attitude of superiority to the English?

If, after the receipt of this explicit decree, you lightly give ear to the representations of your subordinates and allow your barbarian merchants to proceed to Zhejiang and Tianjin, with the object of landing and trading there, the ordinances of my Celestial Empire are strict in the extreme, and the local officials, both civil and military, are bound reverently to obey the law of the land. Should your vessels touch the shore, your merchants will assuredly never be permitted to land or to reside there, but will be subject to instant expulsion. In that event your barbarian merchants will have had a long journey for nothing. Do not say that you were not warned in due time! Tremblingly obey and show no negligence! A special mandate!

> What will the consequences be for English traders who try to trade outside Guangzhou in spite of the emperor's ban?

### For Further Reflection

- What considerations might have prompted the Chinese government to take such a restrictive approach to foreign trade?
- In what ways does Qianlong's attitude reflect the traditional Chinese concept of the "Middle Kingdom"?
- Other than superior products to trade, what was the basis of the Chinese perception of their superiority?

*Source:* J. O. P. Bland. *Annals and Memoirs of the Court of Peking.* Boston: Houghton Mifflin, 1914, pp. 325–31. (Translation slightly modified.)

also frequent visitors at the Dutch colonial capital of Batavia, where they supplied the VOC with silk and porcelain in exchange for silver and Indonesian spices. Entrepreneurial Chinese merchants ventured also to lands throughout southeast Asia—including Borneo, Sumatra, Malaya, Thailand, and elsewhere—in search of tropical products for Chinese consumers. Indeed, the early modern era was an age when merchants established a prominent Chinese presence throughout southeast Asia.

**Government and Technology** During the Tang and Song dynasties, Chinese engineers had produced a veritable flood of inventions, and China was the world's leader in

Chinese peasants plowing, ca. 1770.
Chronicle/Alamy Stock Photo

technology. Yet by early Ming times, technological innovation had slowed. Imperial armed forces adopted European cannons and advanced firearms for their own uses—thus borrowing forms of gunpowder technology that had originated in China and that Europeans had refined and improved—but little innovation in agricultural and industrial technologies occurred during the Ming and Qing dynasties.

Part of the explanation for the slowdown had to do with the role of the government in the formation of economic and social policies. During the Tang and Song dynasties, the imperial government had encouraged technological innovation as a foundation of military and economic strength. In contrast, the Ming and Qing regimes favored political and social stability over technological innovation, which they thought would lead to unsettling change. Alongside government policy, the abundance and availability of skilled workers also discouraged technological innovation. When employers wanted to increase production, they found that hiring additional workers was cost-effective, and thus there was little need for new technologies. In the short term this tactic maintained relative prosperity in China while keeping most of the population gainfully employed. Over the longer term, however, the fact that Europeans were investing in a variety of technological innovations by the late eighteenth century meant that there would be an imbalance in technological knowledge that would favor Europeans by the nineteenth century.

## Gentry, Commoners, Soldiers, and "Mean" People

**Privileged Classes** Aside from the emperor and his family, scholar-bureaucrats and people from the highest social classes occupied the most exalted positions in Chinese society. Because of their official positions, the scholar-bureaucrats ranked slightly above gentry. Nevertheless, scholar-bureaucrats had much in common with the gentry: they came largely from gentry ranks, and after leaving government service they usually rejoined gentry society. The scholar-bureaucrats and gentry functioned as intermediaries between the imperial government and local society. By organizing water control projects and public security measures, they played a crucial role in the management of local society.

Scholar-bureaucrats and gentry wore distinctive clothing—black gowns with blue borders adorned with various rank insignia—and commoners addressed them with honorific terms. They received favorable legal treatment that reflected their privileged status. As a rule, commoners could not call members of privileged classes to appear as witnesses in legal proceedings. They also enjoyed immunity from corporal punishment and exemption from labor service and taxes.

Most of the gentry owned land, which was their major source of income. As long as they did not have to perform physical labor, some gentry also supplemented their income by operating pawn and rice shops. Many of them were also silent business partners of merchants and entrepreneurs. Their principal source of income, however, came from the government service to which only they had access by virtue of their academic degrees. In contrast to landed elites elsewhere, who often lived on rural estates, China's gentry resided largely in cities and towns, where they tended to political, social, and financial affairs.

**Working Classes** Confucian tradition ranked three broad classes of commoners below the gentry: peasants, artisans or workers, and merchants. By far the biggest class consisted of peasants, a designation that covered everyone from day laborers to tenant farmers, to small landlords. Confucian principles regarded peasants as the most honorable of the three classes because they provided the food that supported the entire population.

The category of artisans and workers encompassed a wide spectrum of occupations. Despite their lower status, crafts workers, tailors, barbers, physicians, and workers in manufacturing plants generally enjoyed higher income than peasants. Artisans and workers were usually employees of the state or of gentry and merchant families, but they also pursued their occupations as self-employed persons.

**Merchants** Merchants, from street peddlers to individuals of enormous wealth and influence, ranked at the bottom level of the Confucian social hierarchy. Because moralists looked upon them as unscrupulous social parasites, merchants enjoyed little legal protection, and government policy was always critically important to their pursuits. Yet Chinese merchants often garnered official support for their enterprises, either through bribery of government bureaucrats or through profit-sharing arrangements with gentry families. Indeed, the participation of gentry families in commercial ventures such as warehousing, money lending, and pawnbroking blurred the distinction between gentry and merchants. Merchants blurred the distinction further by providing their sons with an education that prepared them for government examinations, which in turn could result in promotion to gentry status and appointment to civil service positions.

## INTERPRETING IMAGES

Portrait of Howqua (Wu Bingjian—1769–1843) in the early nineteenth century. His elegant clothing and surroundings suggest the great wealth of merchants in late Imperial China.

**Analyze** *Compare this portrait with that of Emperor Kangxi on page 447. They were painted in the same century. How are they different? Who is the audience for each portrait and what are they trying to convey about the subject?*

IanDagnall Computing/Alamy Stock Photo

Although Qing China was still a basically agricultural land, the increasing wealth of the merchant classes signaled that manufacturing and commerce had become much more economically important than in ancient times.

**Lower Classes** Beyond the Confucian social hierarchy were members of the military forces and the "mean" people. Confucian moralists regarded armed forces as a wretched but necessary evil and attempted to avoid military dominance of society by placing civilian bureaucrats in the highest command positions, even at the expense of military effectiveness. The "mean" people included enslaved people, indentured servants, entertainers, prostitutes, and other marginal groups such as the "beggars of Jiangsu" and the "boat people of Guangdong."

## THE CONFUCIAN TRADITION AND NEW CULTURAL INFLUENCES

The Ming and Qing emperors looked to Chinese traditions for guidance in framing their cultural as well as their political and social policies. They provided generous support for Confucianism, particularly in the form of neo-Confucianism articulated by the twelfth-century scholar **Zhu Xi,** and they ensured that formal education in China revolved around Confucian thought and values. Yet the Confucian tradition was not the only cultural alternative in Ming and Qing China. Demographic and urban growth encouraged the emergence of a vibrant popular culture in Chinese cities, and European missionaries reintroduced Roman Catholic Christianity to China and introduced Chinese intellectuals to European science and technology as well.

### Neo-Confucianism and Pulp Fiction

Imperial sponsorship of Chinese cultural traditions meant primarily support for the Confucian tradition, especially as systematized by the Song dynasty scholar Zhu Xi, the most prominent architect of neo-Confucianism. Zhu Xi combined the moral, ethical, and political values of Confucius with the logical rigor and speculative power of Buddhist philosophy. He emphasized the values of self-discipline, filial piety, and obedience to established rulers, all of which appealed to Ming and Qing emperors seeking to maintain stability in their vast realm. Cultural policies of the Ming and Qing dynasties made the neo-Confucian tradition the reigning imperial ideology from the fourteenth to the early twentieth century.

**Confucian Education** To promote Confucian values, the Ming and Qing emperors supported educational programs at several levels. They funded the Hanlin Academy, a research institute for Confucian scholars in Beijing, and maintained provincial schools throughout China where promising students could study for the civil service examinations. The exams themselves encouraged the cultivation of Confucian values because they focused largely on Confucian texts and neo-Confucian commentaries.

Ming and Qing courts also provided generous funding for other projects emphasizing Chinese cultural traditions. The Ming emperor Yongle sponsored the compilation of the ***Yongle Encyclopedia,*** a vast collection of Chinese philosophical, literary, and historical texts that filled almost twenty-three thousand scrolls. During the Qing dynasty both Kangxi and Qianlong organized similar projects. Kangxi's ***Collection of Books*** was smaller than the *Yongle Encyclopedia,* but it was more influential because the emperor had it printed and

**Zhu Xi** (JHOO SHEE)

distributed, whereas Yongle's compilation was available only in three manuscript copies. Qianlong's ***Complete Library of the Four Treasuries*** was too large to publish—it ran to 93,556 pamphlet-size volumes—but the emperor deposited manuscript copies in seven libraries throughout China.

**Popular Culture** While the imperial courts promoted Confucianism, a lively popular culture took shape in the cities of China. Most urban residents did not have an advanced education and knew little about Confucius, Zhu Xi, or other intellectual luminaries. Many of them were literate merchants, however, and they preferred intellectually engaging entertainment and diversion over the type typically found in local teahouses and wine shops. Popular novels met their needs.

**Popular Novels** Confucian scholars looked down on popular novels as crude fiction that had little to do with the realities of the world. Printing made it possible to produce books cheaply and in mass quantities, however, and urban residents eagerly consumed the fast-paced novels that flooded Chinese cities during the Ming and Qing eras. Many of the novels had little literary merit, but their tales of conflict, horror, wonder, excitement, and sometimes unconcealed pornography appealed to readers.

Yet many popular novels also offered thoughtful reflections on the world and human affairs. The historical novel ***The Romance of the Three Kingdoms,*** for example, explored the political intrigue that followed the collapse of the Han dynasty. ***The Dream of the Red Chamber*** told the story of cousins deeply in love who could not marry because of their families' wishes. Through the prism of a sentimental love story, the novel explored the complicated dynamics of wealthy scholar-gentry families. In a different vein, ***Journey to the West*** dealt with the seventh-century journey to India of the famous Buddhist monk Xuanzang. In the popular novel, Xuanzang's traveling companion was a monkey with magical powers who, among other things, could jump 10,000 kilometers (6,215 miles) in a single bound. While promoting Buddhist values, *Journey to the West* also made the trickster monkey a wildly popular and celebrated character in Chinese literature. As recently as 1987, Chinese-American novelist Maxine Hong Kingston adapted this character to modern times in her novel *Tripmaster Monkey.*

Italian Jesuit Matteo Ricci (left) with Xu Quangqi, his most famous Chinese disciple. Both men wear the distinctive Chinese gowns of educated, refined scholar-gentry. A distinguished scholar who held an appointment at the Hanlin Academy, Xu helped Ricci translate Euclid's geometrical works into Chinese.
Private Collection/AF Fotografie/Alamy Stock Photo

## The Return of Christianity to China

Nestorian Christians had established churches and monasteries in China as early as the seventh century C.E., and Roman Catholic communities were prominent in Chinese commercial centers during the Yuan dynasty. After the outbreak of epidemic plague and the collapse of the Yuan dynasty in the fourteenth century, however, Christianity disappeared from China. When Roman Catholic missionaries returned in the sixteenth century, they had to start from scratch in their efforts to win converts and establish a Christian community.

**Matteo Ricci** The most prominent of the missionaries were the **Jesuits,** who worked to strengthen Roman Catholic Christianity in Europe and also to spread their faith abroad. Founder of the mission to China was the Italian Jesuit Matteo Ricci (1552–1610), who had the ambitious goal of converting China to Christianity, beginning with the Ming emperor Wanli. Ricci was a brilliant and learned man as well as a polished diplomat, and he became a popular figure at the Ming court. Upon arrival at Macau in 1582, Ricci immersed himself in the study of the Chinese language and the Confucian classics. He had a talent for languages, and his phenomenal memory enabled him to master the thousands of characters used in literary Chinese writing. By the time he first traveled to Beijing and visited the imperial court in 1601, Ricci was able to write learned Chinese and converse fluently with Confucian scholars.

Ricci's mastery of Chinese language and literature opened doors for the Jesuits, who then impressed their hosts with European science and gadgetry. Ricci and his colleagues had an advanced education in mathematics and astronomy, and they were able to correct Chinese calendars that consistently miscalculated solar eclipses. The Jesuits also prepared maps of the world—with China placed diplomatically at the center—on the basis of geographic knowledge that Europeans had gained during their voyages through the world's seas. The Jesuits even supervised the casting of high-quality bronze cannons for Ming and early Qing armies.

**Confucianism and Christianity** The Jesuits piqued Chinese curiosity with mechanical devices. Finely ground glass prisms became popular because of their refraction of sunlight into its various colors. Harpsichords also drew attention, and Jesuits with musical talents often composed songs for their hosts. Most popular of all, as we saw in the introduction, were the devices that Chinese called "self-ringing bells"—spring-driven mechanical clocks that kept tolerably accurate time, chimed the hours, and sometimes even struck the quarter hours as well.

The Jesuits sought to capture Chinese interest with European science and technology, but their ultimate goal was always to win converts. They portrayed Christianity as a faith very similar to Chinese cultural traditions. Ricci, for example, wrote a treatise titled ***The True Meaning of the Lord of Heaven*** in which he argued that the doctrines of Confucius and Jesus were very similar, if not identical. Over the years, according to Ricci, neo-Confucian scholars had altered Confucius's own teachings, so adoption of Christianity by Chinese would represent a return to a more pure and original Confucianism. The Jesuits also held religious services in the Chinese language and allowed converts to continue the time-honored practice of venerating their ancestors.

In spite of their tolerance, flexibility, and genuine respect for their hosts, the Jesuits attracted few converts in China. By the mid-eighteenth century, Chinese Christians numbered about 200,000—a tiny proportion of the Chinese population of 225 million. Chinese people hesitated to adopt Christianity partly because of its exclusivity: for centuries, Chinese had honored Confucianism, Daoism, and Buddhism at the same time. Like Islam, though, Christianity claimed to be the only true religion, so conversion implied that Confucianism, Daoism, and Buddhism were inferior or even fallacious creeds—a proposition most Chinese people were unwilling to accept.

**End of the Jesuit Mission** Ultimately, the Roman Catholic mission in China came to an end because of squabbles between the Jesuits and members of the Franciscan and Dominican orders, who also sought converts in China. Jealous of the Jesuits' presence at the imperial court, the Franciscans and Dominicans complained to the pope about their rivals' tolerance of ancestor veneration and willingness to conduct Chinese-language services. The pope sided with the critics and in the early eighteenth century issued several proclamations ordering missionaries in China to suppress ancestor veneration and conduct services according to European standards. In response to that demand, the emperor Kangxi ordered an end to the preaching of Christianity in China. Although he did not strictly enforce the ban, the mission weakened, and by the mid-eighteenth century it had effectively come to an end.

The Roman Catholic mission to China did not attract large numbers of Chinese converts, but it nonetheless had important cultural effects. Besides making European science and technology known in China, the Jesuits made China known in Europe. In letters, reports, and other writings distributed widely throughout Europe, the Jesuits described China as an orderly and rational society. The Confucian civil service system attracted the attention of European rulers, who began to design their own civil service bureaucracies in the eighteenth century. The rational morality of Confucianism also appealed to European thinkers, who sought alternatives to Christianity as the foundation for ethics and morality. For the first time since Marco Polo, the Jesuits made firsthand observations of China available to Europeans and stimulated strong European interest in east Asian societies.

## THE UNIFICATION OF JAPAN

During the late sixteenth and early seventeenth centuries, the political unification of Japan ended an extended period of civil disorder. Like the Ming and Qing emperors in China, the **Tokugawa** shoguns sought to lay a foundation for long-term political and social stability, and they provided generous support for neo-Confucian studies in an effort to promote traditional values. Indeed, the shoguns went even further than their Chinese counterparts in promoting conservative values and tightly restricting foreign influence in Japan. As in China, however, demographic expansion and economic growth fostered social and cultural change in Japan, and merchants introduced Chinese and European influences into Japan.

### The Tokugawa Shogunate

From the twelfth through the sixteenth century, a ***shogun*** ("military governor") ruled Japan through retainers who received political rights and large estates in exchange for military services. Theoretically, the shogun ruled as a temporary stand-in for the Japanese emperor, the ultimate source of political authority. In fact, however, the emperor was nothing more than a figurehead, and the shogun sought to monopolize power. After the fourteenth century the conflicting ambitions of shoguns and retainers led to constant turmoil, and by the sixteenth century Japan was in a state of civil war. Japanese historians often refer to the sixteenth century as the era of ***sengoku***—"the country at war."

**Tokugawa Ieyasu** Toward the end of the sixteenth century, powerful states emerged in several regions of Japan, and a series of military leaders brought about the unification of the land. In 1600 the last of these chieftains, **Tokugawa Ieyasu** (reigned 1600–1616), established a military government known as the Tokugawa ***bakufu*** ("tent government" because it theoretically was only a temporary replacement for the emperor's rule). Ieyasu and his descendants ruled the *bakufu* as shoguns from 1600 until the end of the Tokugawa dynasty in 1867.

The principal aim of the Tokugawa shoguns was to stabilize their realm and prevent the return of civil war. Consequently, the shoguns needed to control the ***daimyo*** ("great names"), powerful territorial lords who ruled most of Japan from their vast, hereditary landholdings. The 260 or so daimyo

**Tokugawa** (TOH-koo-GAH-wah)
***daimyo*** (DEYEM-yoh)

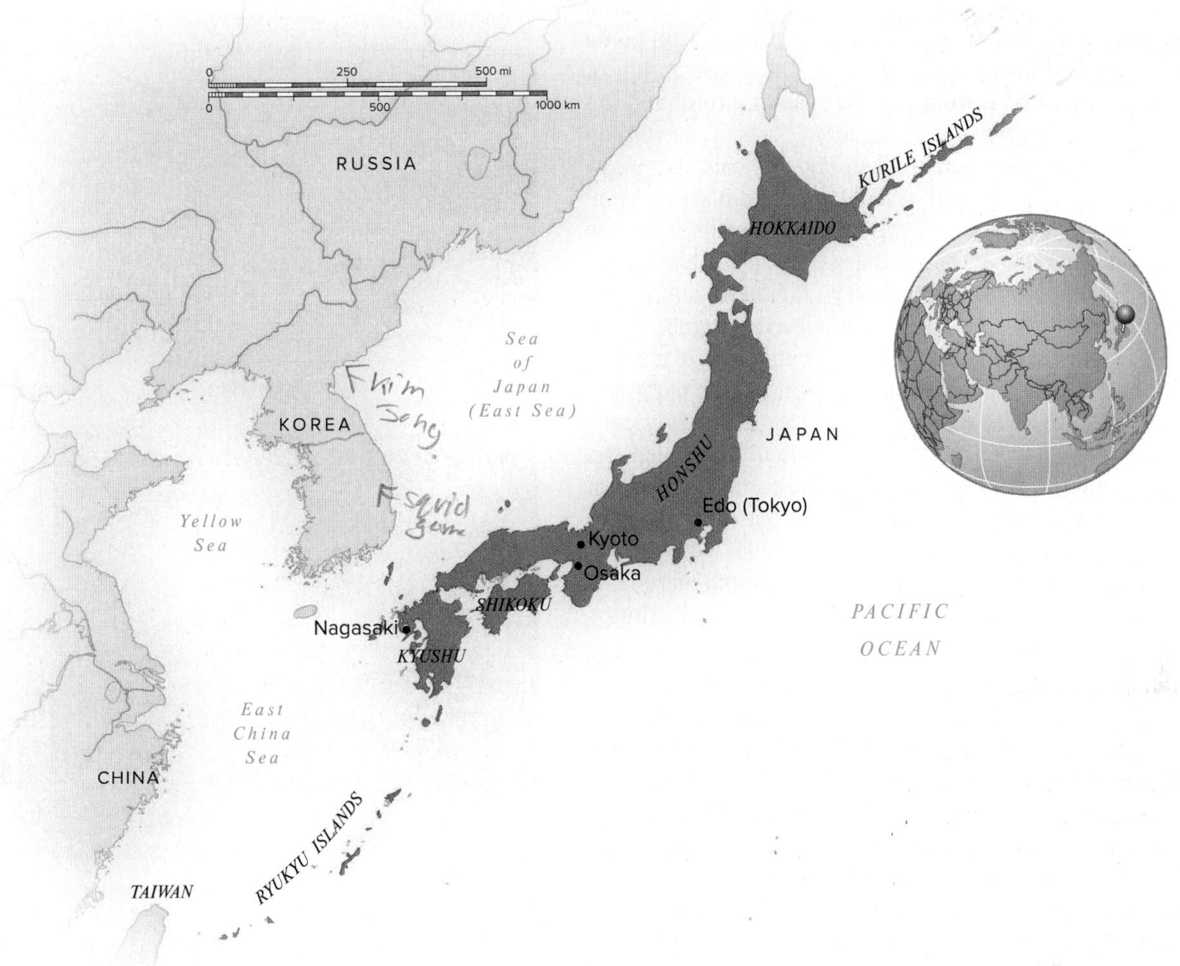


## MAP 14.3 Tokugawa Japan, 1600–1867.

Consider Japan's position with regard to China, Korea, and Russia.

***Would it have been easy or difficult to enforce the ban on foreign trade during most of the period?***

functioned as near-absolute rulers within their domains. Each maintained a government staffed by military subordinates, supported an independent judiciary, established schools, and circulated paper money. Moreover, after the mid-sixteenth century, many daimyo established relationships with European mariners, from whom they learned how to manufacture and use gunpowder weapons. During the last decades of the *sengoku* era, cannons and personal firearms played prominent roles in Japanese conflicts.

**Control of the Daimyo** From the castle town of Edo (modern Tokyo), the shogun governed his personal domain and sought to extend his control to the daimyo. The shoguns instituted the policy of "alternate attendance," which required daimyo to maintain their families at Edo and spend every other year at the Tokugawa court. This policy enabled the shoguns to keep an eye on the daimyo, and as a side benefit it encouraged daimyo to spend their money on lavish residences and comfortable lives in Edo rather than investing it in military forces that could challenge the *bakufu*. The shoguns also subjected marriage alliances between daimyo families to *bakufu* approval, discouraged the daimyo from visiting one another, and required daimyo to obtain permits for construction work on their castles. Even meetings between the daimyo and the emperor required the shogun's permission.

In an effort to prevent European influences from destabilizing the land, the Tokugawa shoguns closely controlled relations between Japan and the outside world. They knew that Spanish forces had conquered the Philippine Islands in the sixteenth century, and they feared that Europeans might jeopardize the security of the *bakufu* itself. Even if Europeans did not conquer Japan, they could cause serious problems by making alliances with daimyo and supplying them with weapons.

**Control of Foreign Relations** Thus during the 1630s the shoguns issued a series of edicts sharply restricting Japanese relations with other lands: these remained in effect for more than two centuries. The policies forbade Japanese from going abroad on pain of death and prohibited the construction of large ships. It expelled Europeans from Japan, prohibited foreign merchants from trading in Japanese ports, and even forbade the import of foreign books. The policies did allow carefully controlled trade with Asian lands, and it also permitted small numbers of Chinese and Dutch merchants to trade under tight restrictions at the southern port city of Nagasaki.

During the seventeenth century, Japanese authorities strictly enforced these policies. In 1640 a Portuguese merchant ship arrived at Nagasaki in hopes of engaging in trade in spite of the ban. Officials beheaded sixty-one of the party and spared thirteen others so that they could relate the experience to their compatriots. Yet authorities gradually loosened the restrictions, and the policy never led to the complete isolation of Japan from the outside world. Throughout the Tokugawa period, Japan carried on a flourishing trade with China, Korea, Taiwan, and the Ryukyu Islands, and Dutch merchants regularly brought news of European and larger world affairs.

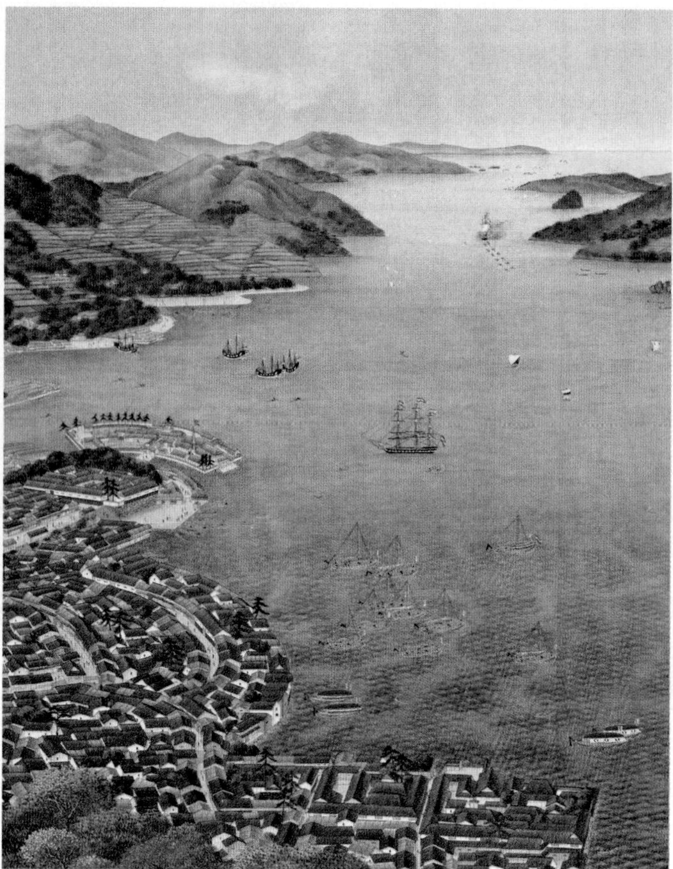

Dutch sailing ships and smaller Japanese vessels mingle in Nagasaki harbor, the only place the Japanese government allowed the Dutch to trade. Dutch merchants conducted their business on the artificial island of Deshima, at left.
CPA Media Pte Ltd/Alamy Stock Photo

## Economic and Social Change

By ending civil conflict and maintaining political stability, the Tokugawa shoguns set the stage for economic growth in Japan. Ironically, peace and a booming economy encouraged social change that undermined the order that the *bakufu* sought to preserve.

Economic growth had its roots in increased agricultural production. New crop strains, new methods of water control and irrigation, and the use of fertilizer brought increased yields of rice. Production of cotton, silk, indigo, and sake (rice wine) also increased dramatically. In many parts of Japan, villages moved away from subsistence farming in favor of production for the market. Between 1600 and 1700, agricultural production doubled.

**Population Growth** Increased agricultural production brought about rapid demographic growth: during the seventeenth century the Japanese population rose by almost one-third, from twenty-two million to twenty-nine million. Thereafter, however, Japan underwent a demographic transition, as many families practiced population control to maintain or raise their standard of living. Between 1700 and 1850 the Japanese population grew moderately, from twenty-nine million to thirty-two million. Contraception, late marriage, and abortion all played roles in limiting population growth, as did infanticide, euphemistically referred to as "thinning out the rice shoots." Japanese families resorted to those measures primarily because Japan was land poor. During the seventeenth century, populations in some areas strained resources, causing financial difficulties for local governments and distress for rural communities.

The Tokugawa era was an age of social as well as demographic change in Japan. Because of Chinese cultural influence, the Japanese social hierarchy followed Confucian precepts in ranking the ruling elites—including the shogun, daimyo, and samurai warriors—as the most prominent and privileged class of society. Beneath them were peasants and artisans. Merchants ranked at the bottom, as they did in China.

**Social Change** The extended period of peace ushered in by Tokugawa rule undermined the social position of the ruling elites. Since the twelfth century the administration of local affairs had fallen mostly to daimyo and samurai warriors. Once Japan was stable, however, the interest of Tokugawa authorities was to reduce the numbers of armed professional warriors, so they pushed daimyo and samurai to become bureaucrats and government functionaries. They even encouraged daimyo and samurai to turn their talents to scholarship, a pursuit that their martial ancestors would have utterly despised. As they lost their accustomed place in society, many of the ruling elite also fell into financial difficulty. Their principal income came in the form of rice collected from peasant cultivators of their lands. They readily converted rice into money through brokers, but the price of rice did not keep pace with other costs. Moreover,

This hanging scroll depicts the pleasure quarters or courtesan district of Kyoto in the late seventeenth century. Courtesans awaited clients behind the wooden grill.
Ashmolean Museum/Heritage Images/Getty Images

daimyo and samurai lived in expensive and sometimes ostentatious style—particularly daimyo who sought to impress others with their wealth while residing at Edo in alternate years. Many of them became indebted to rice brokers and gradually declined into genteel poverty.

Meanwhile, as in China, merchants in Japan became increasingly wealthy and prominent. Japanese cities flourished throughout the Tokugawa era—the population of Edo approached one million by 1700—and merchants prospered handsomely in the vibrant urban environment. Rice dealers, pawnbrokers, and sake merchants soon controlled more wealth than ruling elites. Those who became especially wealthy sometimes purchased elite ranks or contracted marriages with elite families in efforts to improve their social standing.

## Neo-Confucianism and Floating Worlds

Japan had been deeply influenced by Chinese culture in the past, and the influence of China continued throughout the Tokugawa era. Formal education began with study of Chinese language and literature. As late as the nineteenth century, many Japanese scholars wrote their philosophical, legal, and religious works in Chinese. The common people embraced Buddhism, which had come to Japan from China, and Confucianism was the most influential philosophical system.

**Neo-Confucianism in Japan** Like the Ming and Qing emperors in China, the Tokugawa shoguns promoted the **neo-Confucianism** of Zhu Xi. With its emphasis on filial piety and loyalty to superiors, neo-Confucianism provided a respectable ideological underpinning for the *bakufu.* The shoguns patronized scholars who advocated neo-Confucian views, which figured prominently in the educational curriculum. All those who had a formal education—including the sons of merchants as well as offspring of government officials—received constant exposure to neo-Confucian values. By the early eighteenth century, neo-Confucianism had become the official ideology of the Tokugawa *bakufu.*

A colored woodcut by Okumura Masanobu depicts the audience at a seventeenth-century kabuki theater. Enthusiastic actors often ran down wooden ramps and played their roles among the audience.
Universal History Archive/Getty Images

**Native Learning** Yet even with Tokugawa sponsorship, neo-Confucianism did not dominate intellectual life in Japan. Although most scholars recognized Japan's debt to Chinese intellectual traditions, some sought to establish a sense of Japanese identity that did not depend on cultural kinship with China. Particularly during the eighteenth century, scholars of "native learning" scorned neo-Confucianism and even Buddhism as alien cultural imports and emphasized instead the importance of folk traditions and the indigenous Shinto religion for Japanese identity. Many scholars of native learning viewed Japanese people as superior to all others and regarded foreign influence as dangerous. They urged the study of Japanese classics and glorified the supposed purity of Japanese society before its corruption by Chinese and other foreign influences.

While scholars of neo-Confucianism and native learning debated issues of philosophy and Japanese identity, the emergence of a prosperous merchant class encouraged the development of a vibrant popular culture. During the seventeenth and eighteenth centuries, an exuberant middle-class culture flourished in cities such as Kyoto, the imperial capital; Edo, Japan's largest city and home to bureaucrats and daimyo; and Osaka, the commercial hub of the islands. In those and other cities, Japan's finest creative talents catered to middle-class appetites.

**Floating Worlds** The centers of Tokugawa urban culture were the ***ukiyo*** **("floating worlds")**, entertainment and pleasure quarters where teahouses, theaters, brothels, and public baths offered escape from social responsibilities and the rigid rules of conduct that governed public behavior in Tokugawa society. In contrast to the solemn, serious proceedings of the imperial court and the *bakufu,* the popular culture of urban residents was secular and satirical. The main expressions of this lively culture were prose fiction and new forms of theater.

Ihara Saikaku (1642–1693), one of Japan's most prolific poets, helped create a new genre of prose literature, the "books of the floating world." Much of his fiction revolved around the

This fresco, entitled the "Twenty-six Martyrs of Japan," famously illustrates the crucifixion of Christians, mainly Japanese converts, ordered by Hideyoshi Toyotomi during the shogunate's repression of the religion.
Pontino/Alamy Stock Photo

themes of sex and love. In ***The Life of a Man Who Lived for Love,*** for example, Ihara chronicled the experiences of a townsman who devoted his life, beginning at the tender age of eight, to a quest for sexual pleasure. Ihara's treatment of love stressed the erotic, and the brief, episodic stories that made up his work appealed to literate urban residents who were not inclined to pore over dense neo-Confucian treatises.

Beginning in the early seventeenth century, two new forms of drama became popular in Japanese cities. One was ***kabuki*** theater, which usually featured several acts consisting of lively and sometimes bawdy skits where stylized acting combined with lyric singing, dancing, and spectacular staging. A crucial component of kabuki was the actor's ability to improvise and embellish the dialogue, for the text of plays served only as guides for the dramatic performance. The other new dramatic form was ***bunraku,*** the puppet theater. In bunraku, chanters accompanied by music told a story acted out by puppets. Manipulated by a team of three, each puppet could execute the subtlest and most intricate movements, such as brushing a tear from the eye with the sleeve of a kimono. Both kabuki and bunraku attracted enthusiastic audiences in search of entertainment and diversion.

## Christianity and Dutch Learning

**Christian Missions** Alongside neo-Confucianism, native learning, and middle-class popular culture, Christian missionaries and European merchants contributed their own distinctive threads to the cultural fabric of Tokugawa Japan. The Jesuit **Francis Xavier** traveled to Japan in 1549 and opened a mission to seek converts to Christianity. In the early decades of their mission, Jesuits experienced remarkable success in Japan. Several powerful daimyo adopted Christianity and ordered their subjects to do likewise. The principal interest of the daimyo was to establish trade and military alliances with Europeans, but many Japanese converts became enthusiastic Christians and worked to convert their compatriots to the new faith. By the 1580s about 150,000 Japanese had converted to Christianity, and by 1615 Japanese Christians numbered about 300,000.

Although Christians were only a tiny minority of the Japanese population, the popularity of Christianity generated a backlash among government officials and moralists seeking to preserve Japanese religious and cultural traditions. The Tokugawa shoguns restricted European access to Japan largely because of concerns that Christianity might serve as a cultural bridge for alliances between daimyo and European adventurers, which in turn could lead to destabilization of Japanese society and even threats to the *bakufu.* Meanwhile, Buddhist and Confucian scholars resented the Christian conviction that their faith was the only true doctrine. Some Japanese converts to Christianity themselves eventually rejected their adopted faith out of frustration because European missionaries refused to allow them to become priests or play leadership roles in the mission.

**Anti-Christian Campaign** Between 1587 and 1639, shoguns promulgated several decrees ordering a halt to Christian missions and commanding Japanese Christians to renounce their faith. In 1612 the shoguns began rigorous enforcement of those decrees. They tortured and executed European missionaries who refused to leave the islands as well as Japanese Christians who refused to abandon their faith. They often executed victims by crucifixion or burning at the stake, which Tokugawa authorities regarded as especially appropriate punishments for Christians. The campaign was so effective that even some European missionaries abandoned Christianity. Most notable of them was the Portuguese Jesuit **Christovão Ferreira,** head of the Jesuit mission in Japan, who

**Francis Xavier** (fran-sis ZEY-vee-er)
**Christovão Ferreira** (kris-TOH-vo feh-RAY-rah)

# SOURCES FROM THE PAST

## Fabian Fucan Rejects Christianity

*Fabian Fucan (ca. 1565–1621) was a Japanese Buddhist who converted to Christianity and entered the Jesuit order as a novice in 1586. In the early seventeenth century, however, his relations with the Jesuits soured, and he eventually left the order. In 1620 he composed a treatise titled* Deus Destroyed *that leveled a spirited attack at Christianity and its God ("Deus" in Latin). His work reveals deep concerns about European imperial expansion as well as Christian doctrine.*

**I joined this creed at** an early age; diligently, I studied its teachings and pursued its practices. Due to my stupidity, however, I was long unable to realize that this was a perverse and cursed faith. Thus fruitlessly I spent twenty years and more! Then one day—I clearly perceived that the words of the adherents of Deus were very clever and appeared very near reason—but in their teaching there was little truth. So I left their company. Some fifteen years have passed since: every morning I have lamented my desertion of the Great Holy True Law [of Buddhism]; every evening I have grieved over my adherence to the crooked path of the barbarians. All that effort to no effect! But I had a friend who remonstrated with me, saying: "'If you have made a mistake, do not be afraid of admitting the fact and amending your ways' [a Confucian precept]. Here, this is the Confucians' golden rule of life—act on it! Before, you learned all about the cursed faith of Deus; take pen in hand now, commit your knowledge to writing, and counter their teachings. Not only will you thereby gain the merit of destroying wickedness and demonstrating truth; you will also supply a guide toward new knowledge."

Does Fucan indicate what it was that caused him to turn away from Christianity?

All right. Though I am not a clever man, I shall by all means try to act on this advice. I shall gather the important points about the teachings of the Deus sect and shall skip what is not essential; my aim is to write concisely. Thus shall I mount my attack; and I shall call my volume DEUS DESTROYED. . . .

Japan is the Land of the Gods. The generations of our rulers have received the Imperial Dignity from [the gods] Amaterasu Omikami, through U-gaya-fuki-awsezu no Mikoto and his August Child Jimmu Tenno, who became the progenitor of our Hundred Kings. The Three Divine Regalia [symbols of rule received from the gods] became the protectors of the Empire, so that among all the customs of our land there is not one which depends not on the Way of the Gods. . . .

And this, the adherents of Deus plan to subvert! They bide their time with the intent to make all of Japan into their own sectarians, to destroy the Law of Buddha and the Way of the Gods. Because the Law of Buddha and the Way of the Gods are planted here, the Royal Sway also flourishes; and since the Royal Sway is established here the glory of the Buddhas and the gods does grow. And therefore the adherents of Deus have no recourse but to subvert the Royal Sway, overthrow the Buddhas and the gods, eliminate the customs of Japan, and then to import the customs of their own countries; thus only will advance the plot they have concocted to usurp the country themselves.

They have dispatched troops and usurped such countries as Luzon [the Philippines]—and Nova Hispania [Mexico], lands of barbarians with nature close to animal. But our land by far surpasses others in fierce bravery; and therefore the ambition to diffuse their faith in every quarter and thus to usurp the country, even if it take a thousand years, has penetrated down to the very marrow of their bones. Ah!—but what a gloomy prospect awaits them! For the sake of their faith they value their lives less than trash, than garbage. *Martyr,* they call this. When a wise sovereign rules the Empire good is promoted and evil is chastised. Rewards promote good and punishments chastise evil. There is no greater punishment than to take away life; but the adherents of Deus, without even fearing that their lives be cut, will not change their religion. How horrible, how awful it is!

According to Fucan, what makes Japan different than the Phillipines or Mexico in terms of conversion to Christianity?

### For Further Reflection

- Discuss the various religious, cultural, historical, political, and social aspects of Fabian Fucan's attack on Christianity.
- Fucan does not elaborate on the reasons he was drawn to Christianity or explicit objections to the faith. What can you infer about his objections, other than his attitudes of superiority?

*Source:* Elison, George. *Deus Destroyed: The Image of Christianity in Early Modern Japan, vol. 72.* Cambridge, Mass.: Harvard University Press, 1973, pp. 259–60, 283–84.

gave up Christianity under torture, adopted Buddhism, and interrogated many Europeans who fell into Japanese hands in the mid-seventeenth century. By the late seventeenth century, the anti-Christian campaign had claimed tens of thousands of lives, and Christianity survived as a secret, underground religion observed only in rural regions of southern Japan.

**Dutch Learning** Tokugawa policies ensured that Christianity would not soon reappear in Japan, but they did not entirely prevent contacts between Europeans and Japanese. After 1639, Dutch merchants trading at Nagasaki became Japan's principal source of information about Europe and the world beyond east Asia. A small number of Japanese scholars learned Dutch in order to communicate with the foreigners. Their studies, which they called **Dutch learning,** brought considerable knowledge of the outside world to Japan. After 1720, Tokugawa authorities lifted the ban on foreign books, and Dutch learning began to play a significant role in Japanese intellectual life.

European art influenced Japanese scholars interested in anatomy and botany because of its accurate representations of objects. Scholars translated Dutch medical and scientific treatises into Japanese and learned to draw according to the principles of linear perspective, which enabled them to prepare textbooks that were more accurate than the Chinese works they had previously used. European astronomy was also popular in Japan because it enabled scholars to improve calendars and issue accurate predictions of eclipses and other celestial events. By the mid-eighteenth century, the Tokugawa shoguns themselves had become enthusiastic proponents of Dutch learning, and schools of European medicine and Dutch studies flourished in several Japanese cities.

## CONCLUSION

Both China and Japan controlled their own affairs throughout the early modern era and avoided the turmoil that afflicted societies in the Americas and much of sub-Saharan Africa. After driving the Mongols to the steppe lands of central Asia, rulers of the Ming dynasty built a powerful centralized state in China. They worked diligently to eradicate all vestiges of Mongol rule and restore traditional ways by reviving Chinese political institutions and providing state sponsorship for neo-Confucianism. In the interest of stability, authorities also restricted encounters with foreigners by limiting foreign merchants' access to China and the activities of Christian missionaries. The succeeding Qing dynasty pursued similar policies. The Ming and Qing dynasties both brought political stability, but China experienced considerable social and economic change in early modern times. American food crops helped increase agricultural production, which fueled rapid population growth, and global trade stimulated the Chinese economy, which improved the position of merchants and artisans in society. The experience of the Tokugawa era in Japan was much like that of the Ming and Qing eras in China. The Tokugawa *bakufu* brought political order to the Japanese islands and closely controlled encounters with foreigners, but a vibrant economy promoted social change that enhanced the status of merchants and artisans.

## STUDY TERMS

*Analects* of Confucius (447)
*bakufu* (456)
*bunraku* (461)
Christovão Ferreira (461)
civil service examinations (447)
*Collection of Books* (454)
*Complete Library of the Four Treasuries* (455)
*daimyo* (456)
*The Dream of the Red Chamber* (455)
Dutch learning (463)
eunuch (442)
filial piety (448)
floating worlds (460)
foot binding (449)
Francis Xavier (461)
Great Wall (443)
Hongwu (442)
Jesuits (455)
*Journey to the West* (455)
*kabuki* (461)
Kangxi (446)
*The Life of a Man Who Lived for Love* (461)
Manchu (444)
Matteo Ricci (440)
Ming dynasty (442)
neo-Confucianism (459)
Nurhaci (445)
Qianlong (446)
Qing dynasty (442)
*The Romance of the Three Kingdoms* (455)
*sengoku* (456)
*shogun* (456)
Son of Heaven (447)
Tokugawa (456)
Tokugawa Ieyasu (456)
*The True Meaning of the Lord of Heaven* (456)
*ukiyo* (460)
Wanli (440)
Yongle (443)
*Yongle Encyclopedia* (454)
Zheng He (451)
Zhu Xi (454)

## FOR FURTHER READING

Timothy Brook. *The Confusions of Pleasure: Commerce and Culture in Ming China.* Berkeley, 1998. Fascinating social and cultural analysis of Ming China focusing on the role of commerce as an agent of social change.

______. *The Troubled Empire: China in the Yuan and Ming Dynasties.* Cambridge, Mass., 2010. A readable and intriguing account of the Yuan and Ming dynasties.

Adam Clulow. *The Company and the Shogun: The Dutch Encounter with Tokugawa Japan.* New York, 2013. Explores the Dutch East India Company's clashes with Tokugawa Japan over trade and diplomacy.

Mark C. Elliott. *The Manchu Way: The Eight Banners and Ethnic Identity in Late Imperial China.* Stanford, 2001. Important scholarly study focusing on relations between Manchus and Chinese during the Qing dynasty.

Benjamin A. Elman. *A Cultural History of Civil Examinations in Late Imperial China.* Berkeley, 2000. A meticulous study of one of the most important institutions in Chinese history.

Susan Mann and Yu-Ying Cheng, eds. *Under Confucian Eyes: Writings on Gender in Chinese History.* Berkeley, 2001. A rich anthology of primary texts documenting the lives of women in imperial China.

Kenneth Pomeranz. *The Great Divergence: China, Europe, and the Making of the Modern World Economy.* Princeton, 2000. Pathbreaking scholarly study that illuminates the economic history of the early modern world through comparison of economic development in Asian and European lands.

William T. Rowe. *China's Last Empire: The Great Qing.* Cambridge, Mass., 2009. Revisionist history that challenges ideas of the Qing Empire as inward-looking.

Ronald P. Toby. *State and Diplomacy in Early Modern Japan: Asia in the Development of the Tokugawa Bakufu.* Princeton, 1984. An important study dealing with Japanese trade and relations with other lands under Tokugawa rule.

H. Paul Varley. *Japanese Culture.* 4th ed. Honolulu, 2000. Places the cultural history of the Tokugawa era in its larger historical context.

# CHAPTER 14 AP EXAM PRACTICE

Questions assume cumulative knowledge from this chapter and previous chapters.

## Section I

## Multiple Choice Questions

Use the image below and your knowledge of world history to answer questions 1-3.

Tangyue Memorial Archways erected during the Qing dynasty in Anhui province in China's Yangzi River valley
Imagemore/agefotostock

1. Which of these statements illustrates the influence of the Confucian idea of filial piety?
   (A) Confucianism taught that the emperor was the Son of Heaven
   (B) The Confucian examination system determined who was eligible for a bureaucratic job.
   (C) Clans assumed responsibilities that exceeded the means of a nuclear family.
   (D) The Chinese family was hierarchical with authority passing from father to eldest son.

2. Why were widows honored for not remarrying during the Ming and Qing dynasties?
   (A) Marriage was a contract, and by remaining a widow a woman maintained her part of the contract and position in her husband's family.
   (B) Honoring widows with the arches created job opportunities for artisans.
   (C) Chinese families saved money for years to build monuments for the important women in the family.
   (D) The arches were designed to commemorate the process of foot binding.

3. These arches are an example of which historical development?
   (A) Neo-Confucianism created new moral and ethical values.
   (B) Custom and law strengthened patriarchal authority in the Ming and Qing eras.
   (C) Popular culture promoted new romance novels.
   (D) European science and mathematics were valued in Chinese society.

Use the image below and your knowledge of world history to answer questions 4 and 5.

Chinese peasants plowing, ca. 1770
Chronicle/Alamy Stock Photo

4. In Confucianism, which of the classes below was considered most honorable?
   (A) Merchants.
   (B) Peasants.
   (C) Artisans or workers.
   (D) Entertainers.

5. What claims might a historian make based on this image?
   (A) Chinese peasants plowed the fields by day and studied Confucianism at night.
   (B) Because peasants were honored in Confucianism, agricultural labor was easy and less intense in China.
   (C) Even though peasants were considered more honorable in Confucianism, other classes had more wealth and higher standards of living.
   (D) The Chinese nuclear family worked by themselves without support from larger kinship networks.

## Short Answer

6. Use the image below and your knowledge of world history to answer parts A, B, and C.

Imperial civil service examination hall in Suizhou, 1759
The Picture Art Collection/Alamy Stock Photo

(A) Identify ONE factor that allowed for the territorial expansion of the Manchus.
(B) Explain ONE policy implemented by the Qing that maintained their distinct Manchu identity.
(C) Explain ONE Qing policy that supported Chinese traditions.

7. Use the image below and your knowledge of world history to answer parts A, B, and C.

A Ming-era vase painting depicts a woman weaving silk as an attendant pours tea
DeAgostino/Getty Images

(A) Identify ONE wary this image indicates an economic continuity with earlier eras of Chinese history.
(B) Explain ONE way the Columbian exchange affected China.
(C) Explain ONE change in the Chinese economy started in the mid-sixteenth century.

8. Use your understanding of world history to answer parts A, B, and C.
(A) Identify ONE social change in Tokugawa Japan.
(B) Explain ONE way the Tokugawa shoguns pacified the daimyo.
(C) Identify ONE way Japanese culture changed in the Tokugawa era.

# Section II

## Document-Based Question

Based on the documents below and your knowledge of world history, analyze how and why Chinese and Japanese rulers restricted outsiders in their empires.

In your response you should do the following:

- Respond to the prompt with a historically defensible thesis or claim that establishes a line of reasoning.
- Describe a broader historical context relevant to the prompt.
- Support an argument in response to the prompt using all documents.
- Use at least one additional piece of specific historical evidence (beyond that found in the documents) relevant to an argument about the prompt.
- Explain how or why the document's point of view, purpose, historical situation, and /or audience is relevant to an argument.
- Use evidence to corroborate, qualify, or modify an argument that addresses the prompt.

### Document 1

But as the tea, silk, and porcelain which the Celestial Empire produces are absolute necessities to European nations and to yourselves, we have permitted, as a signal mark of favor, that trading agents should be established at Guangzhou, so that your wants might be supplied and your country thus participate in our beneficence. But your ambassador has now put forward new requests which completely fail to recognize our throne's principle to "treat strangers from afar with indulgence," and to exercise a pacifying control over barbarian tribes the world over. . . . Your England is not the only nation trading at Guangzhou. If other nations, following your bad example, wrongfully importune my ear with further impossible requests, how will it be possible for me to treat them with easy indulgence? Nevertheless, I do not forget the lonely remoteness of your island, cut off from the world by intervening wastes of sea, nor do I overlook your excusable ignorance of the usages of our Celestial Empire. I have consequently commanded my ministers to enlighten your ambassador on the subject, and have ordered the departure of the mission. . . .

*Source:* J. O. P. Bland. *Annals and Memoirs of the Court of Peking.* Boston: Houghton Mifflin, 1914, pp. 325–31. (Translation slightly modified.)

## Document 2

Dutch sailing ships and smaller Japanese vessels mingle in Nagasaki harbor, the only place the Japanese government allowed the Dutch to trade. Dutch merchants conducted their business on the artificial island of Deshima, at left.
CPA Media Pte Ltd/Alamy Stock Photo

## Document 3

A bird's-eye view of the Forbidden City Palace Museum, the Imperial Palace of the Ming and Qing Dynasties, in Beijing.
Sovfoto/Getty Images

## Long Essay

Develop a thoughtful and thorough historical argument that answers the question below. Begin your essay with a thesis statement and support it with relevant historical evidence.

Using specific examples and your knowledge of world history, compare and contrast the interactions of Christians with Ming and Qing China society to their position in Tokugawa Japan.

Chapter 15

# Empires in South and Southwest Asia



## ZOOMING IN ON TRADITIONS

### Shah Jahan's Monument to Love and Allah

In 1635 **Shah Jahan,** the emperor of Mughal India, took his seat on the Peacock Throne. Seven years in the making, the Peacock Throne is probably the most spectacular seat on which any human being has rested. Shah Jahan ordered the throne encrusted with ten million rupees' worth of diamonds, rubies, emeralds, and pearls. Atop the throne itself stood a magnificent, golden-bodied peacock with a huge ruby and a fifty-carat, pear-shaped pearl on its breast and a brilliant elevated tail fashioned of blue sapphires and other colored gems.

Yet, for all its splendor, the Peacock Throne ranks a distant second among the artistic projects Shah Jahan sponsored: pride of place goes to the Taj Mahal. Built over a period of eighteen years as a tomb for Shah Jahan's beloved wife, **Mumtaz Mahal,** who died during childbirth in 1631, the Taj Mahal is a graceful and elegant monument both to the departed empress and to Shah Jahan's Islamic faith. The emperor and his architects conceived the Taj Mahal as a vast allegory in stone symbolizing the day when Allah would cause the dead to rise and undergo judgment before his heavenly throne. Its gardens

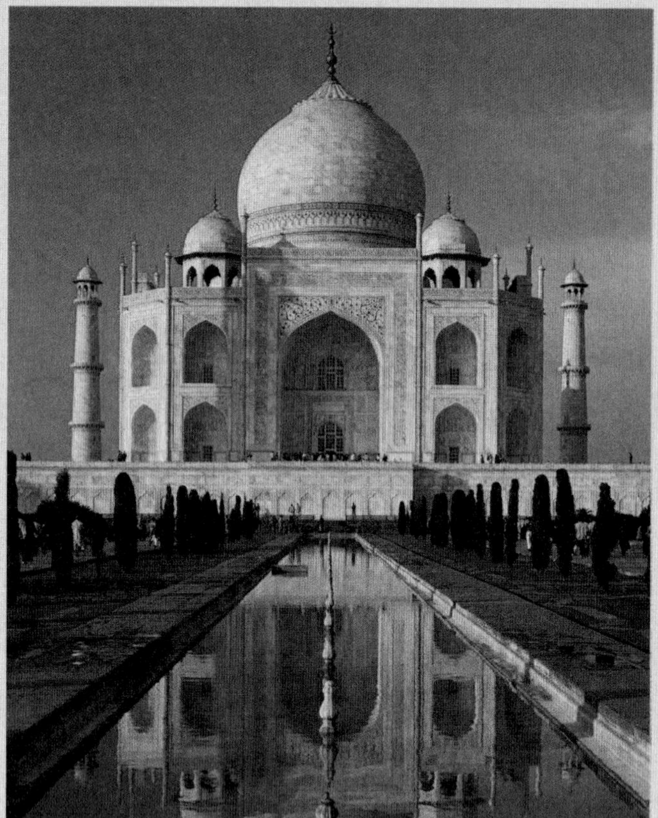

The Taj Mahal was a sumptuous mosque and tomb built between 1632 and 1649 by Shah Jahan in memory of his wife, Mumtaz Mahal.
Andrea Pistolesi/The Image Bank/Getty Images

**Shah Jahan** (shah jah-han)
**Mumtaz Mahal** (moom-tahz muh-HAHL)

represented the gardens of paradise, and the four water channels running through them symbolized the four rivers of the heavenly kingdom. The domed marble tomb of Mumtaz Mahal represented the throne of Allah, and the four minarets surrounding the structure served as legs supporting the divine throne. Craftsmen carved verses from the Quran throughout the Taj Mahal. The main gateway to the structure features the entire text of the chapter promising that on the day of judgment, Allah will punish the wicked and gather the faithful into his celestial paradise.

# CHAPTER FOCUS

- The Ottoman (Turkey), Mughal (Indian), and Safavid (Persia, today Iran) empires were founded by nomadic Turkic conquerors from the steppes of central Asia shared two important distinctions: all the rulers were Muslim, and they passed power to a male heir they deemed best—not necessarily the eldest son.
- This method of inheritance caused instability for large imperial states. All three empires had ethnically and religiously diverse populations, but all used Islam to create loyalty and to inspire imperial expansion.
- Safavid Persians were Shi'a Muslims while Ottomans were Sunni Muslims, and the two empires fought many wars.
- As conquest and merchants spread Islam, the religion was adapted to local customs.
- In the 1400s, rulers of the Turkish Ottoman empires, like other new emperors, looked to outsiders for bureaucratic loyalty. They created the *devshime* system, which brought poor Christian boys from the Balkan peninsula to be enslaved and trained as advisers to the sultan or to be part of his special forces, the Janissaries.
- The Safavids relied on a long tradition of Persian administrators.
- The Mughals used both Muslims and Hindus to help them rule.
- All three empires were located on established trade routes that continued to enrich their economies in the early modern period. Europeans sought their luxury goods, and joint-stock companies had offices in Istanbul, Ifsahan, and Indian port cities to facilitate trade.
- Just as silk production had increased in China, cotton cloth production increased in Mughal India in response to global demand.
- Trade in enslaved Africans also rose across the Mediterranean and Indian Ocean trade routes.

## Historical Developments

- Imperial expansion relied on the increased use of gunpowder, cannons, and armed trade to establish large empires in both hemispheres.
- Recruitment and use of bureaucratic elites, as well as the development of military professionals, became more common among rulers who wanted to maintain centralized control over their populations and resources.
- Rulers used tribute collection, tax farming, and innovative tax collection systems to generate revenue, in order to forward state power and expansion.
- Political rivalries between the Ottoman and Safavid empires intensified the split within Islam between Sunni and Shi'a.
- Sikhism developed in South Asia in a context of interactions between Hinduism and Islam.

## Reasoning Processes

- **Developments and Processes** Explain the formation and expansion of the Ottoman, Safavid, and Mughal empires.
- **Source Claims and Evidence** Identify the evidence used to support the claim that rulers of the Islamic empires used art and architecture to enhance and project their power.
- **Making Connections** Identify the connections between state power, religious beliefs, and cultural patronage in the Islamic empires.
- **Argumentation** Use a range of evidence to make a complex argument as to how the Islamic empires maintained harmony among such culturally and religiously diverse populations.

## Historical Thinking Skills

- **Comparison** Describe similarities and differences between the Ottoman, Safavid, and Mughal empires.

## CHAPTER OVERVIEW

The Peacock Throne and the Taj Mahal testify to the wealth of the Mughal empire, while the tomb of Mumtaz Mahal highlights the Islamic character of the ruling dynasty. But the Mughal empire, which ruled most of the Indian subcontinent for more than three hundred years, was not the only well-organized empire in south and southwest Asia during early modern times. The Ottoman Empire was a dynastic Muslim state centered in what is today Turkey. At the height of its power, it controlled a vast area from southeastern Europe to western Asia and North Africa. It was also the longest-lived of the empires in these two regions, as it remained intact until the early twentieth century. On the eastern borders of the Ottoman Empire lay the ancient lands of Persia, where yet another powerful empire emerged during the early sixteenth century. Ruled by the Safavid dynasty, this state never expanded far beyond its heartland of present-day Iran, but its Shiite rulers challenged the Sunni Ottomans for dominance in southwest Asia. The Safavid realm prospered from its place in trade networks linking China, India, Russia, southwest Asia, and the Mediterranean basin.

All three empires in this broad region had Turkish ruling dynasties. The Ottomans, Safavids, and Mughals came from nomadic, Turkish-speaking peoples of central Asia who conquered the settled agricultural lands of Anatolia, Persia, and India, respectively. All three dynasties retained political and cultural traditions that their ancestors had adopted while leading nomadic lives on the steppes, but they also adapted readily to the city-based agricultural societies that they conquered. The Ottoman dynasty made especially effective use of the gunpowder weapons that transformed early modern warfare, and the Safavids and the Mughals also incorporated gunpowder weapons into their arsenals. All three dynasties officially embraced Islam and drew cultural guidance from Islamic values.

During the sixteenth and early seventeenth centuries, the three empires presided over expansive and prosperous societies. About the mid-seventeenth century, however, they all began to weaken. Their waning fortunes reflected the fact that they had ceased to expand territorially and gain access to new sources of wealth. Instead, each empire waged long, costly wars that drained resources without bringing compensating benefits. The empires also faced domestic difficulties. Each of them was an ethnically and religiously diverse realm, and each experienced tensions when conservative Muslim leaders lobbied for strict observance of Islam while members of other communities sought greater freedom for themselves. All three empires—especially the Mughal and Ottoman—relied increasingly on trade with Europeans, who came to their lands with textiles, food items, and armaments. Although it could not have been predicted initially, such reliance eventually put the empires at both an economic and technological disadvantage to Europeans, who increasingly sought to dominate the world around them. By the mid-eighteenth century, the Safavid empire had collapsed, and the Ottoman and Mughal realms were rapidly falling under European influence.

| CHRONOLOGY | |
|---|---|
| 1289–1923 | Ottoman dynasty |
| 1451–1481 | Reign of Mehmed the Conqueror |
| 1453 | Ottoman conquest of Constantinople |
| 1501–1524 | Reign of Shah Ismail |
| 1501–1722 | Safavid dynasty |
| c. 1502–1558 | Life of Hürrem Sultan |
| 1514 | Battle of Chaldiran |
| 1520–1566 | Reign of Süleyman the Magnificent |
| 1526–1858 | Mughal dynasty |
| 1556 | Construction of Süleymaniye Mosque |
| 1556–1605 | Reign of Akbar |
| 1588–1629 | Reign of Shah Abbas the Great |
| ca. 1600 | Introduction of tobacco to the Ottoman Empire |
| 1632–1649 | Construction of the Taj Mahal |
| 1659–1707 | Reign of Aurangzeb |

## FORMATION OF THE EMPIRES OF SOUTH AND SOUTHWEST ASIA

By the sixteenth century, Turkish warriors had transformed much of south and southwest Asia into vast regional empires. These empires divided up the greater part of the Islamic world at the time: the **Ottoman Empire,** which was distinguished by its multiethnic character; the **Safavid empire** of Persia, which served as the center of Shiite Islam; and the **Mughal empire,** which had been imposed over a predominantly Hindu Indian subcontinent. The creation of these durable and powerful political entities attempted centralization throughout south and southwest Asia.

All three empires began as small warrior principalities in frontier areas. They expanded at varying rates and with

**Mughal** (MOO-guhl)

varying degrees of success at the expense of neighboring states. As they grew, they devised elaborate administrative and military institutions. Under the guidance of talented and energetic rulers, each empire organized an effective governmental apparatus and presided over a prosperous society.

## The Ottoman Empire

**Osman** The Ottoman Empire was an unusually successful frontier state. The term *Ottoman* derived from **Osman Bey,** founder of the dynasty that continued in unbroken succession from 1289 until the dissolution of the empire in 1923. Osman was *bey* (chief) of a band of seminomadic Turks who migrated to northwestern Anatolia in the thirteenth century. Osman and his followers sought above all to become ***ghazi,*** Muslim religious warriors, who fought in the name of Islam against non-Muslims.

**Ottoman Expansion** The Ottomans' location on the borders of the Byzantine Empire afforded them ample opportunity to wage war against non-Muslims. Their first great success came in 1326 with the capture of the Anatolian city of Bursa, which became the capital of the Ottoman principality. Around 1352 they established a foothold in Europe when they seized the fortress of Gallipoli while aiding a claimant to the Byzantine throne. Numerous *ghazi,* many of them recent converts to Islam, soon flocked to join the Ottomans. The city of Edirne (Adrianople) became a second Ottoman capital and served as a base for further expansion into the Balkans. As warriors settled in frontier districts and pushed their boundaries forward, they took spoils and gathered revenues that enriched both the *ghazi* and the central government. Bursa, for example, developed into a major commercial and intellectual center with inns, shops, schools, libraries, and mosques.

A formidable military machine drove Ottoman expansion. Ottoman military leaders initially organized *ghazi* recruits into two forces: a light cavalry and a volunteer infantry. As the Ottoman state became more firmly established, it added a professional cavalry force equipped with heavy armor and financed by land grants. After expanding into the Balkans,

***ghazi*** (GAH-zee)

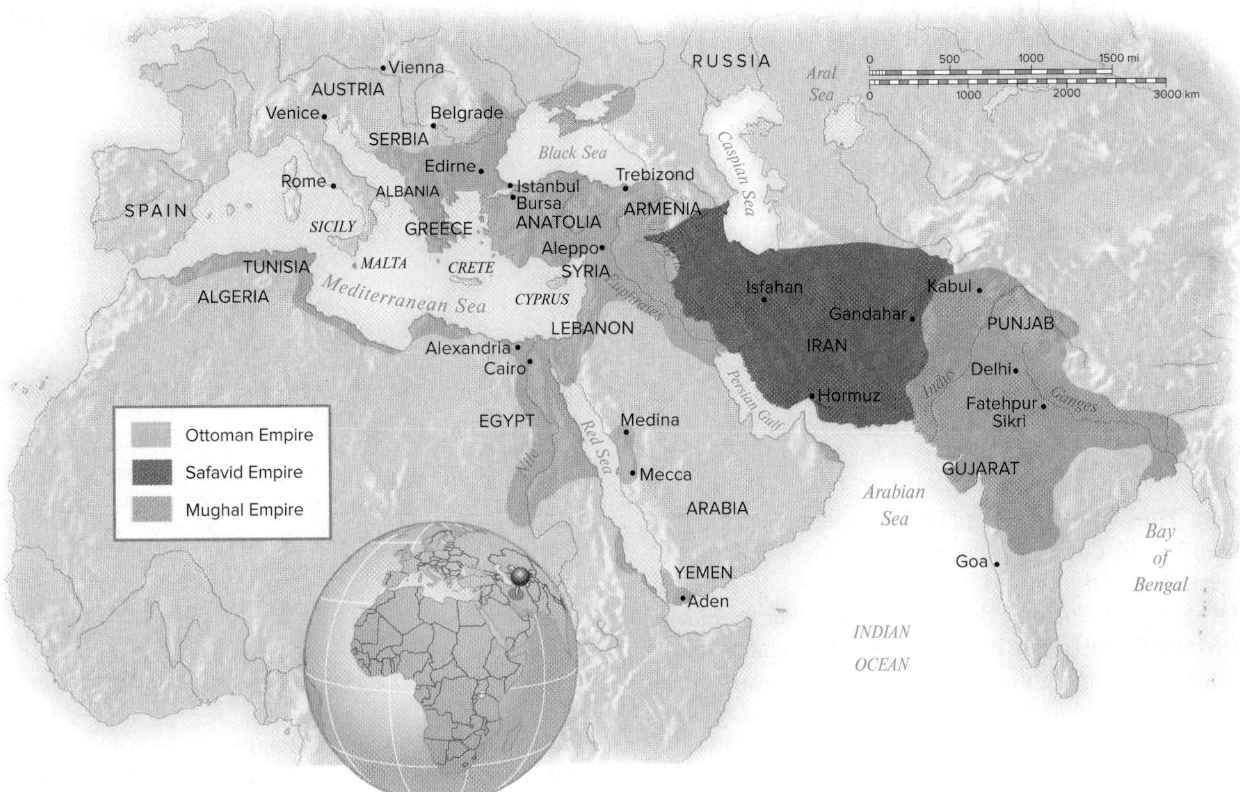


**MAP 15.1 The Empires of South and Southwest Asia.**

Locate the Ottoman capital of Istanbul, the Safavid capital of Isfahan, and the Mughal capital of Delhi.

***What strategic or commercial purposes did each of these capitals fulfill, and how would their locations have aided or hindered imperial administration? The massive "gunpowder empires" displayed here, with the architecture such as that on pgs. 577 and 585 represent a contrast to the state of Western Europe during this same period. How would you describe this contrast?***

the Ottomans created a powerful force composed of slave troops. Through an institution known as the ***devshirme,*** the Ottomans required the Christian population of the Balkans to contribute young boys to become slaves of the sultan. The boys received special training, learned Turkish, and converted to Islam. According to individual ability, they entered either the Ottoman civilian administration or the military. Those who became soldiers were known as **Janissaries,** from the Turkish *yeni cheri* ("new troops"). Despite the fact that they did not choose these roles for themselves, the Janissaries quickly gained a reputation for intense group pride, loyalty to the sultan, and readiness to employ new military technology. Besides building powerful military forces, the Ottomans outfitted their forces with gunpowder weapons and used them effectively in battles and sieges.

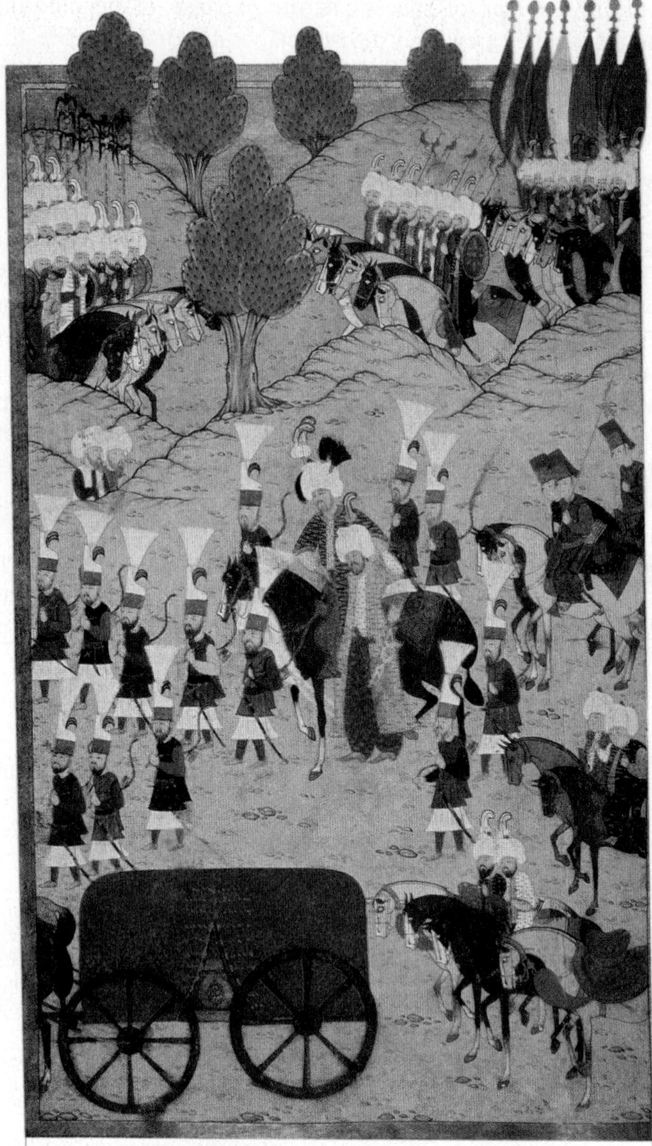

Sultan Süleyman (center, on horse) leads Ottoman forces as they march on Europe. How does this illustration promote the power and prominence of Süleyman and his Ottoman forces?
Leemage/Universal Images Group/Newscom

**Mehmed the Conqueror** The capture of Constantinople in 1453 by Mehmed II (reigned 1451–1481)—known as **Mehmed the Conqueror**—opened a new chapter in Ottoman expansion. With its superb location and illustrious heritage, Constantinople became the new Ottoman capital, subsequently known as Istanbul, and Mehmed worked energetically to stimulate its role as a commercial center. With the capture of the great city behind him, Mehmed presented himself not just as a warrior-sultan but also as a true emperor, ruler of the "two lands" (Europe and Asia) and the "two seas" (the Black Sea and the Mediterranean). He laid the foundations for a tightly centralized, absolute monarchy, and his army faced no serious rival. He completed the conquest of Serbia; moved into southern Greece and Albania; eliminated the last Byzantine outpost at Trebizond on the Black Sea; captured Genoese ports in the Crimea; initiated a naval war with Venice in the Mediterranean; and reportedly hoped to cross the Strait of Otranto, march on Rome, and capture the pope himself. Toward the end of his life, he launched an invasion of Italy and briefly occupied Otranto, but his successors abandoned Mehmed's plans for expansion in western Europe.

**Süleyman the Magnificent** The Ottomans continued their expansion in the early sixteenth century when sultan Selim the Grim (reigned 1512–1520) occupied Syria and Egypt. Ottoman expansion climaxed in the reign of **Süleyman the Magnificent** (reigned 1520–1566). Süleyman vigorously promoted Ottoman conquests both in southwest Asia and in Europe. In 1534 he conquered Baghdad and added the Tigris and Euphrates valleys to the Ottoman domain. In Europe he kept the rival Hapsburg Empire on the defensive throughout his reign. He captured Belgrade in 1521, defeated and killed the king of Hungary at the battle of Mohács in 1526, consolidated Ottoman power north of the Danube, and in 1529 subjected the Hapsburgs' prized city of Vienna to a brief siege.

Under Süleyman the Ottomans also became a major naval power. In addition to their own Aegean and Black Sea fleets, the Ottomans inherited the navy of the Mamluk rulers of Egypt. A Turkish corsair, Khayr al-Din Barbarossa Pasha, who had challenged Spanish forces in Tunisia and Algeria, placed his pirate fleet under the Ottoman flag and became Süleyman's leading admiral. Thus Süleyman was able to challenge Christian vessels throughout the Mediterranean as

**Süleyman** (SOO-lee-mahn)

# SOURCES FROM THE PAST

## Ghiselin de Busbecq's Concerns about the Ottoman Empire

*Ogier Ghiselin de Busbecq (1522–1592) was a diplomat who traveled to Istanbul in 1555 as a representative of Hapsburg King Ferdinand of Hungary and Bohemia to negotiate a border dispute between Ferdinand and Sultan Süleyman the Magnificent. In a series of four letters to a friend, Ghiselin commented on the Ottoman state, society, customs, and military forces. His observations left him deeply concerned about the prospects of Christian Europe in the event of conflict with the Ottoman realm.*

**The Sultan [Süleyman "the Lawgiver"] was seated** on a very low ottoman, not more than a foot from the ground, which was covered with a quantity of costly rugs and cushions of exquisite workmanship; near him lay his bow and arrows . . .; The Sultan then listened to what I had to say; but the language I used was not at all to his taste, for the demands of his Majesty breathed a spirit of independence and dignity, which was by no means acceptable to one who deemed that his wish was law; and so he made no answer beyond saying in an impatient way, "Giusel, giusel," that is, "well, well." After this we were dismissed to our quarters.

The Sultan's hall was crowded with people, among whom were several officers of high rank. Besides these, there were all the troopers of the Imperial guard, and a large force of Janissaries [the elite infantry corps], but there was not in all that great assembly a single man who owed his position to anything save his valor and his merit. No distinction is attached to birth among the Turks; the respect to be paid to a man is measured by the position he holds in the public service. There is no fighting for precedence; a man's place is marked out by the duties he discharges . . ., It is by merit that men rise in the service, a system which ensures that posts should only be assigned to the competent. Each man in Turkey carries in his own hand his ancestry and his position in life, which he may make or mar as he will. Those who receive the highest offices from the Sultan are for the most part the sons of shepherds or herdsmen, and so far from being ashamed of their parentage, they actually glory in it, and consider it a matter of boasting that they owe nothing to the accident of birth; for they do not believe that high qualities are either natural or hereditary, nor do they think, that they can be handed down from father to son, but that they are partly the gift of God, and partly the result of good training, great industry, and unwearied zeal; arguing that high qualities do not descend from a father to his son or heir, any more than a talent for music, mathematics or the like . . .; Among the Turks, therefore, honors, high posts, and judgeships are the rewards of great ability and good service. If a man is dishonest, or lazy, or careless, he remains at the bottom of the ladder, an object of contempt; for such qualities there are no honors in Turkey!

> Does de Busbecq seem surprised by the fact that merit is valued more highly than birth by the Ottomans? Why?

This is the reason that they are successful in their undertakings, that they lord it over others, and are daily extending the bounds of their empire. These are not our ideals, with us there is no opening left for merit; birth is the standard for everything; the prestige of birth is the sole key to advancement in public service.

It makes me shudder to think of what the result of a struggle between such different systems must be; one of us must prevail and the other be destroyed, at any rate we cannot both exist in safety. On their side is the vast wealth of their empire, unimpaired resources, experience and practice in arms, a veteran soldiery, an uninterrupted series of victories, readiness to endure hardships, union, order, discipline, thrift, and watchfulness. On ours are found an empty exchequer, luxurious habits, exhausted resources, broken spirits, a raw and insubordinate soldiery, and greedy generals; there is no regard for discipline, license runs riot, the men indulge in drunkenness and debauchery, and worst of all, the enemy are accustomed to victory, we, to defeat. Can we doubt what the result must be?

> What advantages, according to de Busbecq, does a system of rewarding merit have over a system of rewarding birth?

### For Further Reflection

- What was de Busbecq's purpose in writing this letter? Was he trying to prompt a reaction and, if so, from whom?

*Source:* Foster, C. T., and F. H. Blackburne Daniell. "Süleyman 'the Lawgiver.'" in *The Life and Letters of Ogier Ghiselin de Busbecq*. vol. 1. London: Hakluyt Society, 1881. pp. 152–156.

well as Portuguese fleets in the Red Sea and the Indian Ocean. The Ottomans seized the island of Rhodes from the Knights of St. John, besieged Malta, secured Yemen and Aden, and even dispatched a squadron to attack the Portuguese fleet at Diu in India.

## The Safavid Empire

In 1499 a twelve-year-old boy named **Ismail** left the swamps of Gilan near the Caspian Sea, where he had hidden from the enemies of his family for five years, to seek his revenge. Two years later he entered Tabriz (in modern Iran) at the head of an army and laid claim to the ancient Persian imperial title of shah. The young Shah Ismail (reigned 1501–1524) also proclaimed that the official religion of his realm would be **Twelver Shiism,** and he proceeded to impose it, by force when necessary, on the formerly **Sunni** population. Over the next decade he seized control of the Iranian plateau and launched expeditions into the Caucasus, Anatolia, Mesopotamia, and central Asia.

**The Safavids** For propaganda purposes, Shah Ismail and his successors carefully controlled accounts of their rise to power—and expediently changed the story when circumstances warranted. They traced their ancestry back to Safi al-Din (1252–1334), leader of a Sufi religious order in northwestern Persia. Sufism, a mystical belief and practice, formed an important Islamic tradition (discussed in chapter 14). The goal of a Sufi mystic, such as Safi al-Din, was to recover the lost intimacy between God and the human soul and to find the truth of divine knowledge and love through a direct personal experience of God. The famous tomb and shrine of Safi al-Din at Ardabil became the home of Shah Ismail's family (named "Safavids" after the holy man himself); the headquarters of his religious movement; and the center of a determined, deliberate campaign to win political power for his descendants. The Safavids changed their religious preferences several times in the hope of gaining popular support before settling on a form of **Shiism** that appealed to the nomadic Turkish tribes moving into the area in the post-Mongol era.

**Twelver Shiism** Twelver Shiism held that there had been twelve infallible imams (or religious leaders) after Muhammad, beginning with the prophet's cousin and son-in-law Ali. The twelfth, "hidden" imam had gone into hiding around 874 to escape persecution, but the Twelver Shiites believed he was still alive and would one day return to take power and spread his true religion. Ismail's father had instructed his Turkish followers to wear a distinctive red hat with twelve pleats in memory of the twelve Shiite imams, and they subsequently became known as the ***qizilbash*** ("red heads"). Safavid propaganda also suggested that Ismail was himself the hidden imam or even an incarnation of Allah. Although most Muslims, including most Shiites, would have regarded those claims as utterly blasphemous, the *qizilbash* enthusiastically accepted them because they resembled traditional Turkish conceptions of leadership that associated military leaders with divinity. The *qizilbash* believed that Ismail would make them invincible in battle, and they became extremely loyal to the Safavid cause.

**Battle of Chaldiran** Shah Ismail's curious blend of Shiism and Turkish traditions gave his regime a distinctive identity, particularly since he made conversion to Shiite Islam mandatory for the largely Sunni population. At the same time, it also created some powerful enemies. Foremost among them were the staunchly Sunni Ottomans, who believed that the first legitimate successor to Mohammed was Mohammed's father-in-law Abu Bakr, not Ali as the Safavids believed. The Ottoman Sunni detested the Shiite Safavids and feared not only Safavid territorial expansion but also the spread of Safavid propaganda among the nomadic Turks in their territory. As soon as Selim the Grim became sultan, he launched a persecution of Shiites in the Ottoman Empire and prepared for a full-scale invasion of Safavid territory.

At the critical battle of **(battle of) Chaldiran** (1514), the Ottomans deployed heavy artillery and thousands of Janissaries equipped with firearms behind a barrier of carts. Although the Safavids knew about gunpowder technology and had access to firearms, the Ottomans maintained a clear technological advantage. Trusting in the protective charisma of Shah Ismail, the *qizilbash* cavalry strenuously attacked the Ottoman line and suffered devastating casualties. Ismail had to slip away, and the Ottomans temporarily occupied his capital at Tabriz. The Ottomans badly damaged the Safavid state but lacked the resources to destroy it, and the two empires remained locked in intermittent conflict for the next two centuries.

Later Safavid rulers recovered from the disaster at Chaldiran. They relied more heavily than Ismail had on the Persian bureaucracy and its administrative talents. Ismail's successors abandoned the extreme Safavid ideology that associated the emperor with Allah in favor of more conventional Twelver Shiism, from which they still derived legitimacy as descendants and representatives of the imams. They also assigned land grants to the *qizilbash* officers to retain their loyalty and give them a stake in the survival of the regime.

**Shah Abbas the Great** **Shah Abbas the Great** (reigned 1588–1629) fully revitalized the Safavid empire. He moved the capital to the more central location of Isfahan, encouraged trade with other lands, and reformed the administrative and military institutions of the empire. He incorporated male slaves of the royal household into the army, increased the use of gunpowder weapons, and sought European assistance against the Ottomans and the Portuguese in the Persian Gulf. With newly strengthened military forces, Shah Abbas led the Safavids to numerous victories. He attacked and defeated the nomadic Uzbeks in central Asia, expelled the Portuguese from Hormuz, and engaged the Ottomans in a series of wars from 1603 to the end of his reign. His campaigns brought most of northwestern Iran, the Caucasus, and Mesopotamia under Safavid rule.

## The Mughal Empire

**Babur** In 1523 Zahir al-Din Muhammad, known as **Babur** ("the Tiger"), a Chaghatai Turk who claimed descent from both Chinggis Khan and Tamerlane (see chapter 17), suddenly appeared in northern India. Unlike the Ottomans, who sought to be renowned *ghazis,* or the Safavids, who acted as champions of Shiism, Babur made little pretense to be anything more

***qizilbash*** (gih-ZIHL-bahsh)

**Babur** (BAH-ber)

Shah Ismail and the *qizilbash*. This miniature painting from a Safavid manuscript depicts the shah and his *qizilbash* warriors wearing the distinctive red pleated cap that was their emblem of identity.
Album/Alamy Stock Photo

This colorful scene at a spring in Kabul highlights Babur (1483–1530), founder of the Mughal dynasty, who stands in a central position near the life-giving water.
Angelo Hornak/Corbis Historical/Getty Images

than an adventurer and soldier of fortune in the manner of his illustrious ancestors. His father had been the prince of Farghana (in modern Uzbekistan), and Babur's great ambition was to transform his inheritance into a glorious central Asian empire. Yet envious relatives and Uzbek enemies frustrated his ambitions.

Never able to extend his authority much beyond Kabul and Qandahar (both in modern Afghanistan) and reduced at times to hardship and a handful of followers, Babur turned his attention to India. With the aid of gunpowder weapons, including both artillery and firearms, Babur mounted invasions in 1523 and 1525, and successfully conquered Delhi in 1526. Ironically, Babur cared little for the land he had conquered. Many in his entourage wanted to take their spoils of war and leave the hot and humid Indian climate, which among other things ruined their finely crafted compound bows, but Babur elected to stay. He probably hoped to use the enormous wealth of India to build a vast central Asian empire like that of Tamerlane—an elusive dream that his successors would nonetheless continue to cherish. By the time of his death in 1530, Babur had built a loosely knit empire that stretched from Kabul through the Punjab to the borders of Bengal. He founded a dynasty called the *Mughal* (a Persian term for "Mongol"), which eventually embraced almost all the Indian subcontinent.

**Akbar** The real architect of the Mughal empire was Babur's grandson **Akbar** (reigned 1556–1605), a brilliant and charismatic ruler. Akbar gathered the reins of power in his own hands in 1561 following a violent argument with Adham Khan, a powerful figure at the imperial court and commander of the Mughal army. Akbar murdered Adham Khan during the argument and thereafter took personal control of the Mughal government and did not tolerate challenges to his rule. He created a centralized administrative structure with ministries regulating the various provinces of the empire. His military campaigns consolidated Mughal power in Gujarat to the west and Bengal to the east. He also began to absorb the recently defeated Hindu kingdom of Vijayanagar, thus laying the foundation for later Mughal expansion in southern India.

Akbar was a thoughtful, reflective man deeply interested in religion and philosophy. He pursued a policy of religious toleration that he hoped would reduce tensions between Hindu and Muslim communities in India. Although illiterate (probably due to dyslexia), he was extremely intelligent and had books read to him daily. Instead of imposing Islam on his subjects, he encouraged the elaboration of a syncretic religion called the "divine faith" that focused attention on the emperor as a ruler common to all the religious, ethnic, and social groups of India.

**Aurangzeb** The Mughal empire reached its greatest extent under **Aurangzeb** (reigned 1659–1707). During his long reign, Aurangzeb waged a relentless campaign to push Mughal authority deep into southern India. By the early eighteenth century, Mughals ruled the entire subcontinent except for a small region at the southern tip.

Although he greatly expanded Mughal boundaries, Aurangzeb presided over a troubled empire. He faced rebellions throughout his reign, and religious tensions generated conflicts between Hindus and Muslims. Aurangzeb was a devout Muslim, and he broke with Akbar's policy of religious toleration. He demolished several famous Hindu temples and replaced them with mosques. He also imposed a tax on Hindus in an effort to encourage conversion to Islam. His promotion of Islam appealed strongly to the Mughals themselves and other Indian Muslims, but it provoked deep hostility among Hindus and enabled local leaders to organize movements to resist or even rebel against Mughal authority.

## IMPERIAL SOCIETY

Despite their ethnically and religiously diverse populations, there were striking similarities in the development of Ottoman, Safavid, and Mughal societies. All relied on bureaucracies that drew inspiration from the steppe traditions of Turkish and Mongol peoples as well as from the heritage of Islam. They adopted similar economic policies and sought ways to maintain harmony in societies that embraced many different religious and ethnic groups. Rulers of all the empires also sought to enhance the legitimacy of their regimes by providing for public welfare and associating themselves with literary and artistic talent.

### INTERPRETING IMAGES

This manuscript illustration from about 1590 depicts Akbar (at top, shaded by attendants) inspecting construction of a new imperial capital at Fatehpur Sikri.

**Analyze** *Examine this illustration and those on the previous page depicting Shah Ismail and Babur. Describe indications of power and wealth in the Safavid and Mughal empires represented in these illustrations.*

Picturenow/Universal Images Group/Getty Images

### The Dynastic State

The Ottoman, Safavid, and Mughal empires were all military creations, regarded by their rulers as their personal possessions by right of conquest. The rulers exercised personal command of the armies, appointed and dismissed officials at will,

# SOURCES FROM THE PAST

## The *Ain I Akbari* on Akbar's Imperial Harem

*From 1590 until his death in 1602, Abu'l-Fazl—Akbar's court historian—wrote a history of Akbar's reign, which became known as the* Akbar Nama (Chronicle of Akbar). *Book three of this expansive, three-volume work is called the* Ain I Akbari (Institutes of Akbar) *and presents a detailed look at both Mughal institutions and Mughal India more generally. Abu'l-Fazl used vast quantities of imperial records in his work and set the standard for royal chronicles in the region for centuries. Throughout the* Akbar Nama, *Abu'l-Fazl presented Akbar as a semi-divine ruler who presided over a multiethnic and multireligious empire. Below, he describes Akbar's harem.*

**His majesty forms matrimonial alliances** with princes of Hindustan, and of other countries; and secures by these ties of harmony the peace of the world.

Why would marriage with women from princely Hindu families have secured "peace" in Akbar's realm?

As the sovereign, by the light of his wisdom, has raised fit persons from the dust of obscurity, and appointed them to various offices, so does he also elevate faithful persons to the several ranks in the service of the seraglio [women's apartments] . . . "The saying of the wise is true that the eye of the exalted is the elixir for producing goodness." Such also are the results flowing from the love of order of his majesty [Akbar], from his wisdom, insight, regard to rank, his respect for others, his activity, his patience. . . .

What is the author trying to say here about Akbar's ideas about merit versus birth?

His majesty has made a large enclosure with fine buildings inside, where he reposes. Though there are more than five thousand women, he has given to each a separate apartment. He has also divided them into sections, and keeps them attentive to their duties. Several chaste women have been appointed as *daroghas* [officials], and superintendents over each section, and one has been appointed as a writer [record-keeper] . . .

The inside of the Harem is guarded by sober and active women; the most trustworthy of them are placed about the apartments of his Majesty. Outside of the enclosure the eunuchs are placed; and at a proper distance, there is a guard of faithful *Rajputs* [soldiers from a Hindu military caste], beyond whom are the porters of the gates . . . Notwithstanding the great number of faithful guards, his Majesty does not dispense with his own vigilance, but keeps the whole in proper order.

### For Further Reflection

- Why was it so important to keep Akbar's harem under such heavy guard? Was he more concerned with keeping people out of the harem or keeping people in? Was there reason to be concerned about maintaining armed order inside the harem, given the many conflicts over succession in the Mughal empire?
- The author of the passage was the court historian. How does his role influence his perspective on Akbar?
- There is no consideration of the point of view of the 5,000 women in the Harem. Why not? Speculate about the variety of points of view that might be represented.

*Source:* Abū al-Faẕl ibn Mubārak. *The Ain i Akbari.* Trans. by Henry Blochmann. Printed for the Asiatic Society of Bengal, 1873, 44–45. HathiTrust Digital Library.

and adopted policies of their own making. In theory, the emperors owned all land and granted use of it to peasant families on a hereditary basis in return for the payment of fixed taxes. The emperors and their families derived revenues from crown lands, and revenues from other lands supported military and administrative officials.

**The Emperors and Islam** In the Ottoman, Safavid, and Mughal empires, the prestige and authority of the dynasty derived from the personal piety and the military prowess of the ruler and his ancestors. The Safavids were prominent leaders of a Sufi religious order, and the Ottomans and Mughals associated closely with famous **Sufis.** Devotion to Islam encouraged rulers to extend their faith to new lands. The *ghazi* ideal of spreading Islam by fighting non-believers or heretics meshed well with the traditions of Turkish and Mongolian peoples, which emphasized the glory of battle.

**Women and Politics** Even though Muslim theorists agreed that women should have no role in public affairs and decried the involvement of women in politics as a sure sign of decadence, in practice women played important roles in managing all three empires. Many Ottoman, Safavid, and Mughal emperors followed the example of Chinggis Khan, who bestowed special privileges and authority on his mother and his first, and favorite, wife. Ottoman courtiers often complained loudly

This romantic portrait of Shah Jahan (reigned 1628–1658) and his most beloved wife, Mumtaz Mahal (died 1631), suggested the strong bond between them that drove him to build a white marble mausoleum, the Taj Mahal.
Dinodia Photos/Alamy Stock Photo

A sixteenth century portrait of Hürrem Sultan (c. 1502–1588), born Aleksandra Lisowska and also known as Roxelana.
ART Collection/Alamy Stock Photo

about the "rule of women," thus offering eloquent testimony to the power that women could wield. Süleyman the Magnificent, for example, fell in love with Hürrem Sultan (also known as Roxelana), a concubine of Ukrainian origin who had been brought to the sultan's harem as a slave. Eventually, Süleyman elevated her to the status of a legal wife, consulted her on state policies, and deferred to her judgment on a variety of matters. It was rumored that Hürrem counseled Süleyman to have his son and heir by another wife executed. While it is not clear if this was the case, Süleyman did have his oldest son executed, and his son with Hürrem, Selim II, eventually became sultan. After Hürrem's unexpected death in 1558, a devastated Süleyman constructed a mausoleum for her next to his own in the courtyard of the great mosque in Istanbul.

Women also played prominent political roles in the Safavid and Mughal empires. In Safavid Persia, Khayr al-Nesa, better known as Mahd-e Olya and mother of the future Shah Abbas I, gained enormous influence over her husband. Her efforts to limit the power of the *qizilbash* so enraged them that in 1579 they murdered her. The aunt of another shah scolded the ruler for neglecting his duties and used her own money to raise an army to put down a revolt. The Mughal emperor **Jahangir** was content to let his wife Nur Jahan run the government, while Aurangzeb often followed his daughter's political advice.

**Steppe Traditions** The autocratic authority wielded by the rulers of all three empires reflected the steppe traditions of their origins. The early emperors largely did as they pleased, regardless of religious and social norms in the areas they conquered. The Ottoman sultans, for example, unilaterally issued numerous legal edicts. The greatest of these were the many ***kanun*** ("laws") issued by Süleyman–Europeans called him Süleyman the Magnificent, but the Ottomans referred to him as Süleyman Kanuni, "the Lawgiver." Safavid and Mughal rulers went even further than the Ottomans in asserting their spiritual authority. Shah Ismail did not hesitate to force his Shiite religion on his subjects. Akbar issued a decree in 1579 claiming broad authority in religious matters, and he promoted his own eclectic religion, which glorified the emperor as much as Islam.

Steppe practices also brought succession problems. In the steppe empires the ruler's relatives often managed components of the states, and succession to the throne became a hot contest between competing members of the family. Problems of succession were compounded by the fact that rulers of all three empires maintained large harems that could include many wives and concubines as well as their children, and thus rivalry for succession was deeply intertwined with the desire of different wives to maintain their position at court. The Mughal empire in particular became tied up in family controversies: conflicts among Mughal princes and rebellions of sons against fathers were recurrent features throughout the history of the empire. The Safavids also engaged in murderous struggles for the throne. Shah Abbas himself lived in fear that another member of the family would challenge him. He kept his sons confined to the palace and killed or blinded relatives he suspected, almost wiping out his family in the process.

The early Ottomans assigned provinces for the sultan's sons to administer but kept the empire as a whole tightly unified. After the fifteenth century, however, the sultans moved to protect their position by eliminating family rivals. Mehmed the Conqueror decreed that a ruler could legally kill off his brothers—many of whom would have been half-siblings by different mothers—after taking the throne. His successors observed that tradition until 1595, when the new sultan executed nineteen brothers, many of them infants, as well as fifteen expectant mothers. After that episode, sultans confined their sons in special quarters of the imperial harem and forbade them to go outside except to take the throne.

Ottoman coffeehouse. This nineteenth-century depiction of a coffeehouse in Istanbul demonstrates the centrality of tobacco smoking to the experience. Beginning in the seventeenth century, men in the Ottoman Empire socialized in coffeehouses while smoking from elaborate water pipes called hookahs.
Historical Picture Archive//Corbis/Getty Images

## Agriculture and Trade

**Food Crops** Productive agricultural economies were the foundations of all three empires. Each extracted surplus agricultural production and used it to finance armies and bureaucracies. For the most part, all three empires relied on crops of wheat and rice that had flourished for centuries in the lands they ruled. In addition, European merchants introduced maize, potatoes, tomatoes, and other crops from the Americas to each of the empires, and the new arrivals soon found a place in regional cuisines. Potatoes appeared in the curries of southern India, and tomatoes enlivened dishes in the Ottoman Empire as well as other Mediterranean lands. Maize did not win a place in the cuisine of the empires of south and southwest Asia, but it became popular as feed for animal stocks, especially in the Ottoman Empire.

## What's Left Out?

In textbook overviews such as this, women in the empires of south and southwest Asia tend to appear only briefly, usually in the context of imperial harems. There is a reason for this: Extensive records were kept about (and sometimes by) the elite women who inhabited these harems. But it would be a mistake to imagine that the lives of most women in the Ottoman, Mughal, and Safavid empires were similar to the lives of women in imperial harems. If we take the Ottoman Empire during the seventeenth century as an example, we would see that only a tiny proportion of Ottoman women lived in the secluded and isolated conditions of harems. Instead, Ottoman women were visible in multiple contexts, though their visibility depended upon their social class and geographical location. Elite women, as was the case in many parts of the world, were more constrained in their mobility than those from laboring classes but nevertheless could be seen moving through towns and cities with their bodies covered. Women of the farming and agricultural classes, in contrast, were integral to family labor and were visible in the fields driving horses and threshing grain. In cities and large towns, laboring women could be seen selling crafts on the streets. And in both rural and urban areas, slave women were constantly visible in public while they performed a wide variety of tasks for their owners. In the realm of law, Ottoman women were highly visible in the courts, where they frequently brought suits against others. Additionally, Ottoman law allowed women to own property in their own names and to dispose of it as they pleased. Thus, while it is important to remember that Ottoman women were not considered equal to men (such a status did not exist anywhere in the world at this time), they also were not the invisible, secluded, highly controlled creatures that images of the harem tend to suggest.

*Source:* Ebru Boyar and Kate Fleet, eds. *Ottoman Women in Public Space* (Leiden: Brill, 2016).

### Thinking Critically About Sources

1. The passage emphasizes that Ottoman, Mughal, and Safavid women were "highly visible." What examples are provided?
2. Is it only one class of women who were visible in these societies?
3. What were various roles these women performed, outside the home?

Global trade networks also strongly encouraged consumption of coffee and tobacco, especially in the Ottoman and Safavid empires. Although native to Ethiopia and cultivated in southern Arabia by the fifteenth century, coffee did not become popular in Islamic lands until the sixteenth century. Like sugar, coffee became a cash crop in the Americas, which then was sold for profit in markets around the world. By the eighteenth century, American producers and European merchants supplied Muslim markets with both coffee and sugar.

**Tobacco** According to the Ottoman historian Ibrahim Pechevi, English merchants introduced tobacco around 1600, claiming it was useful for medicinal purposes. Within a few decades it had spread throughout the Ottoman Empire. The increasing popularity of coffee drinking and pipe smoking encouraged entrepreneurs to establish coffeehouses where customers could indulge their appetites for caffeine and nicotine at the same time. The popularity of coffeehouses provoked protest from moralists who worried that these popular attractions were dens of iniquity that distracted patrons from their religious duties and encouraged idleness. Pechevi complained about the odor of tobacco, the messy ashes, and the danger that smoking could cause fires. Religious leaders claimed that coffee was an illegal beverage and that it was worse to frequent a coffeehouse than a tavern that served alcoholic beverages. Sultan Murad IV (r. 1623–1640) went so far as to outlaw coffee and tobacco and to execute those who continued to partake. That effort, however, was a losing battle. Both pastimes eventually won widespread acceptance, and the coffeehouse became a prominent social institution in all three empires.

**Population Growth** The population of India surged during early modern times, growing from 105 million in 1500 to 135 million in 1600, 165 million in 1700, and 190 million in 1800. This population growth resulted more from intensive agriculture along traditional lines than from any other factor. The Safavid population grew less rapidly, from 5 million in 1500 to 6 million in 1600, and to 8 million in 1800. Ottoman numbers grew from 9 million in 1500 to 28 million in 1600, as the empire enlarged its boundaries to include populous regions in the Balkans, Egypt, and southwest Asia. After 1600, however, the Ottoman population declined to about 24 million, where it remained until the late 1800s. The decline reflected loss of territory more than a shrinking population, but even in the heartland of Anatolia, Ottoman numbers did not expand nearly as dramatically as those of other lands in early modern times. From 6 million in 1500, the population of Anatolia rose to 7.5 million in 1600, 8 million in 1700, and 9 million in 1800.

**Trade** The Islamic empires ruled lands that had figured prominently in long-distance trade for centuries and participated actively in global trade networks in early modern times. In the Ottoman Empire, for example, the early capital at Bursa was also the terminus of a caravan route that brought raw silk from Persia to supply the Italian market. The Ottomans also granted special trading concessions to merchants from England and France to cement alliances against common enemies in Spain and central Europe. Aleppo became an emporium for foreign merchants engaged primarily in the spice trade and served as local headquarters for the operations of the English Levant Company.

In this anonymous painting produced about 1670, Dutch and English ships lie at anchor in the harbor of the busy port of Surat in northwestern India. Surat was the major port on the west coast of India, and it served as one of the chief commercial cities of the Mughal empire.
Rijksmuseum, Amsterdam

Shah Abbas promoted Isfahan as a commercial center, extending trading privileges to foreign merchants and even allowing Christian monastic orders to set up missions there to help create a favorable environment for trade. European merchants sought Safavid raw silk, carpets, ceramics, and high-quality craft items. The English East India Company, the French East India Company, and the Dutch VOC all traded actively with the Safavids. To curry favor with them, the English company sent military advisers to introduce gunpowder weapons to Safavid armed forces and provided a navy to help them retake Hormuz in the Persian Gulf from the Portuguese.

The Mughals did not pay as much attention to foreign trade as the Ottomans and the Safavids did, partly because of the enormous size and productivity of the domestic Indian economy and partly because the Mughal rulers concentrated on their land empire and had little interest in maritime affairs. Nevertheless, the Mughal treasury derived significant income from foreign trade. The Mughals allowed the creation of trading stations and merchant colonies by Portuguese, English, French, and Dutch merchants. Meanwhile, Indian merchants formed trading companies of their own, ventured overland as far as Russia, and sailed the waters of the Indian Ocean to port cities from Persia to Indonesia.

## INTERPRETING IMAGES

In a seventeenth-century painting, the emperor Akbar presides over discussions between representatives of various religious groups. Two Jesuits dressed in black robes kneel at the left.

**Analyze** *In what ways does Akbar's represent a contrast to rulers in European and Asia during the seventeenth century?*

DeAgostini/Getty Images

## Religious Affairs

**Religious Diversity** Each of the empires had populations that were religiously and ethnically diverse, and imperial rulers had the daunting challenge of maintaining harmony between different religious communities. The Ottoman Empire included large numbers of Christians and Jews in the Balkans, Armenia, Lebanon, and Egypt. The Safavid empire embraced sizable Zoroastrian and Jewish communities as well as many Christian subjects in the Caucasus. The Mughal empire was especially diverse. Most Mughal subjects were Hindus, but large numbers of Muslims lived alongside smaller communities of Jains, Zoroastrians, Christians, and Sikhs.

**Christian Mission in India** Portuguese Goa became the center of a Christian mission in India. Priests at Goa sought to attract converts to Christianity and established schools that provided religious instruction for Indian children. In 1580 several Portuguese Jesuits traveled to the Mughal court at Akbar's invitation. They had visions of converting the emperor to Christianity and then spreading their faith throughout India, but their hopes went unfulfilled. Akbar received the Jesuits cordially and welcomed their participation in religious and philosophical discussions at his court, but he was not interested in conversion.

**Akbar's Divine Faith** Indeed, Akbar was not fervent even about his own Islamic faith. In his efforts to find a religious synthesis that would serve as a cultural foundation for unity in his diverse empire, he supported the efforts of the early Sikhs, who combined elements of Hinduism and Islam in a new syncretic faith. He also attempted to elaborate his own "divine faith" that emphasized loyalty to the emperor while borrowing eclectically from different religious traditions. Akbar never explained his ideas systematically, but it is clear that they drew most heavily on

Topkapi Palace. View of the palace from the Bosphorus Sea.
Firdes Sayilan/Shutterstock

Islam. The divine faith was strictly monotheistic, and it reflected the influence of Shiite and Sufi teachings. But it also glorified the emperor: Akbar even referred to himself as the "lord of wisdom," who would guide his subjects to understanding of the world's creator god. The divine faith was tolerant of Hinduism, and it even drew inspiration from Zoroastrianism in its effort to bridge the gaps between Mughal India's many cultural and religious communities.

**Status of Religious Minorities** Each of the empires relied on a long-established model to deal with subjects who were not Muslims. They did not require conquered peoples to convert to Islam but extended to them the status of ***dhimmi*** ("protected people"). In return for their loyalty and payment of a special tax known as ***jizya,*** *dhimmi* communities retained their personal freedom, kept their property, practiced their religion, and handled their legal affairs. In the Ottoman Empire, for example, autonomous religious communities known as ***millet*** retained their civil laws, traditions, and languages. *Millet* communities usually also assumed social and administrative functions in matters concerning birth, marriage, death, health, and education.

The situation in the Mughal empire was different because its large number of religious communities made a *millet* system impractical. Mughal rulers reserved the most powerful military and administrative positions for Muslims, but in the day-to-day management of affairs, Muslims and Hindus cooperated closely. Some Mughal emperors sought to forge links between religious communities. Akbar in particular worked to integrate Muslim and Hindu elites. In an effort to foster communication and understanding among the different religious communities of his realm, he abolished the *jizya;* tolerated all faiths; and sponsored discussions and debates between Muslims, Hindus, Jains, Zoroastrians, and Christians.

**Promotion of Islam** Some Indian Muslims worried that policies of religious toleration would lead to the loss of their religious identity or that they might be absorbed into Hindu society as another caste. Some therefore insisted that Mughal rulers create and maintain an Islamic state based on Islamic law. When Aurangzeb reached the Mughal throne in 1659, these ideas gained strength. Aurangzeb reinstated the *jizya* and promoted Islam as the official faith of Mughal India. His policy satisfied zealous Muslims but at the cost of deep bitterness among his Hindu subjects. Tension between Hindu and Muslim communities in India persisted throughout the Mughal dynasty and beyond.

The massive Süleymaniye mosque built for Sultan Süleyman the Magnificent by the Ottoman architect Sinan Pasha in 1556.
Anadolu Agency/Getty Images

***dhimmi*** (DIHM-mee)
***jizya*** (JIHZ-yuh)

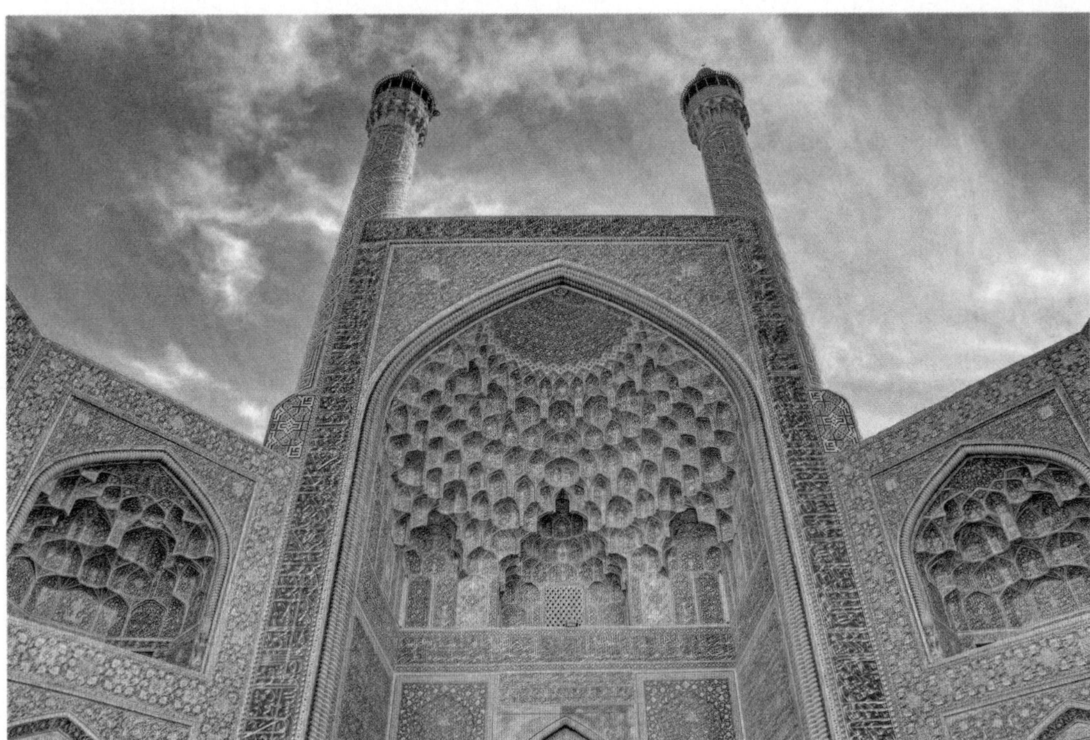

Isfahan Royal Mosque. The Royal Mosque of Isfahan, centerpiece of the city as rebuilt by Shah Abbas at the end of the sixteenth century. With its combination of an open space flanked by markets, the palace, and religious structures, Isfahan stands as a unique example of urban planning in Islamic lands.
DrRave/E+/Getty Images

stop here

## Cultural Patronage

As the empires matured, the rulers of all three empires sought to enhance their prestige through public works projects and patronage of scholars. They competed to attract outstanding religious scholars, poets, artists, and architects to their courts. They lavished resources on mosques, palaces, government buildings, bridges, fountains, schools, hospitals, and soup kitchens for the poor.

**Istanbul** Capital cities and royal palaces were the most visible expressions of imperial majesty. The Ottomans beautified both Bursa and Edirne, but they took particular pride in **Istanbul.** Dilapidated and deserted after the conquest, it quickly revived and became a bustling, prosperous city of more than a million people. At its heart was the great **Topkapi palace,** which housed government offices, such as the mint, and meeting places for imperial councils. At its core was the sultan's residence with its harem, gardens, pleasure pavilions, and a repository for the most sacred possessions of the empire, including the mantle of the prophet Muhammad. Sultan Süleyman the Magnificent was fortunate to be able to draw on the talents of the architectural genius **Sinan Pasha** (1489–1588) to create the most celebrated of all the monuments of Istanbul. Sinan built a vast religious complex called the **Süleymaniye,** which blended Islamic and Byzantine architectural elements. It combined tall, slender minarets with large domed buildings supported by half domes in the style of the Byzantine church Hagia Sofia (which the Ottomans converted into the mosque of Aya Sofya).

**Isfahan** Shah Abbas made his capital, **Isfahan,** into one of the leading Persian cities and the prime center of urban architectural development anywhere in the world: its inhabitants still boast that "Isfahan is half the world." Abbas concentrated markets, the palace, and the royal mosque around a vast polo field and public square. Broad, shaded avenues and magnificent bridges linked the central city to its suburbs. Safavid architects made use of monumental entryways; vast arcades; spacious courtyards; and intricate, colorful decoration. Unlike the sprawling Ottoman and Mughal palaces, the Safavid palaces in Isfahan were relatively small and emphasized natural settings with gardens and pools. They were also much more open than Topkapi, with its series of inner courts and gates. Ali Qapu, the palace on the square in Isfahan, had a striking balcony, and most of the palaces had large, open verandas. The point was not only to enable the shah to observe outside activities but also to emphasize his visibility and accessibility, qualities long esteemed in the Persian tradition of kingship.

**Fatehpur Sikri** To some extent, in accordance with steppe traditions, the early Mughals regarded the capital as wherever the ruler happened to camp. Yet they too came to sponsor urban development. Their work skillfully blended central Asian traditions with elements of Hindu architecture, and they built on a scale that left no doubt about their wealth and resources. They constructed scores of mosques, fortresses,

**Topkapi** (TOHP-kah-pih)
**Sinan Pasha** (sih-NAHN pah-cha)

Fatehpur Sikri, built by Akbar in the 1570s, commemorated the emperor's military conquests and housed the tomb of his religious guide. It included a palace, an audience hall where Akbar attended religious and philosophical debates, and a great mosque. Gavin Hellier/robertharding/Alamy Stock Photo

and palaces and sometimes created entire cities. The best example was **Fatehpur Sikri,** a city planned and constructed by Akbar that served as his capital from 1569 to 1585. It commemorated his conquest of the prosperous commercial province of Gujarat in a campaign that enabled Akbar to head off both Portuguese attacks and Ottoman intervention there. With its mint, records office, treasury, and audience hall, the new city demonstrated Akbar's strength and imperial ambitions. Fatehpur Sikri was also a private residence and retreat for the ruler, reproducing in stone a royal encampment with exquisite pleasure palaces where Akbar indulged his passions for music and conversation with scholars and poets. At yet another level, it was a dramatic display of Mughal piety and devotion, centered on the cathedral mosque and the mausoleum of Akbar's Sufi guru, **Shaykh Salim Chishti.** Despite their intensely Islamic character, many of the buildings consciously incorporated Indian elements such as verandas supported by columns and decorations of stone elephants. Even the tomb of Shaykh Chishti bore some resemblance to a Hindu shrine. Unfortunately, Akbar selected a poor site for the city and soon abandoned it because of its bad water supply.

**The Taj Mahal** The most famous of the Mughal monuments was the **Taj Mahal**, which we read about in the introduction to this chapter. Shah Jahan had twenty thousand workers toil for eighteen years to erect the exquisite white marble mosque and tomb. He originally planned to build a similar mausoleum out of black marble for himself, but his son Aurangzeb deposed him before he could carry out the project. Shah Jahan spent his last years confined to a small cell with a tiny window, and only with the aid of a mirror was he able to catch the sight of his beloved wife's final resting place.

**Fatehpur Sikri** (fah-teh-poor SIH-kree)
**Shaykh Salim Chishti** (sheyk sah-LEEM CHEESH-tee)

## THE EMPIRES IN TRANSITION

The empires of south and southwest Asia underwent dramatic change between the sixteenth and the eighteenth centuries. The Safavid empire disappeared entirely. In 1722 a band of Afghan tribesmen marched all the way to Isfahan, blockaded the city until its starving inhabitants resorted to cannibalism, forced the shah to abdicate, and executed thousands of Safavid officials as well as many members of the royal family. After the death of Aurangzeb in 1707, Mughal India experienced provincial rebellions and foreign invasions. By mid-century the subcontinent was falling under British imperial rule. By 1700 the Ottomans, too, were on the defensive: the sultans lost control over remote provinces such as Lebanon and Egypt, and throughout the eighteenth and nineteenth centuries European and Russian states placed political, military, and economic pressure on the shrinking Ottoman realm.

### Economic and Military Decline

In the sixteenth century, each of the empires had strong domestic economies and played prominent roles in global trade networks. By the eighteenth century, however, domestic economies were under great stress, and foreign trade had declined dramatically or had fallen under the control of European powers. The empires were well on their way to becoming dependent on goods produced elsewhere.

**Economic Difficulties** The high cost of maintaining an expensive military and administrative apparatus helped to bring about economic decline in each of the empires. As long as the empires were expanding, they were able to finance their armies and bureaucracies with fresh resources extracted from newly conquered lands. When expansion slowed, ceased, or reversed, however, they faced the problem of supporting their institutions with limited resources. The long, costly, and unproductive wars fought by the Ottomans with the Hapsburgs in central Europe, by the Safavids and the Ottomans in Mesopotamia, and by Aurangzeb in southern India exhausted the treasuries of the empires without making fresh resources available to them. As early as 1589 the Ottomans tried to pay the Janissaries in debased coinage and immediately provoked a mutiny. The next 150 years witnessed at least six additional military revolts.

As expansion slowed and the empires lost control over remote provinces, officials reacted to the loss of revenue by raising taxes, selling public offices, accepting bribes, or resorting to simple extortion. All those measures were counterproductive. Although they might provide immediate cash, they did long-term economic damage. Foreign trade initially seemed to provide a partial solution, as the goods they brought provided extra revenue for the state and helped satisfy consumer demands for things like textiles and tobacco. The Ottomans therefore expanded the privileges enjoyed by foreign merchants, while the Mughals encouraged the establishment of Dutch and English trading outposts and welcomed the expansion of their business in India. Imperial authorities were content to have foreign traders come to them. Only later did it become clear that welcoming European traders to their lands gave Europeans the leverage to become economically dominant and, in the case of India, conquerors.

**Military Decline** As they lost initiative to western European peoples in economic and commercial affairs, the empires of south and southwest Asia also experienced military decline. As early as the fifteenth century, the Ottomans had relied heavily on European technology in gunnery; indeed, the cannon that Mehmed the Conqueror used in 1453 to breach the defensive wall of Constantinople was the product of a Hungarian gun-founder. During the sixteenth and early seventeenth centuries, the Islamic empires were able to purchase European weapons in large numbers and attract European expertise that kept their armies supplied with powerful gunpowder weapons. In 1605, for example, the cargo of an English ship bound for Anatolia included seven hundred barrels of gunpowder, one thousand musket barrels, five hundred fully assembled muskets, and two thousand sword blades, alongside wool textiles and bullion.

Although each of the empires of south and southwest Asia continued to be able to purchase European weapons and expertise, this ready availability was one of the reasons none of them developed large armament industries of their own. When combined with financial difficulties within each of the empires, the result was an inability to buy the latest technologies. Over time, their equipment and arsenals became increasingly dated. By the late eighteenth century, the Ottoman navy, which had long influenced maritime affairs in the Mediterranean, Red Sea, Persian Gulf, and Arabian Sea, closed its own

Each of the empires in south and southwest Asia fought numerous wars, many of which exhausted resources without adding to the productive capacities of the empires. This illustration depicts Ottoman forces (right) clashing with heavily armored Austrian cavalry near Budapest in 1540.
Images & Stories/Alamy Stock Photo

ship-building operations. From then on, the Ottomans ordered all new military ships from European shipyards.

## The Deterioration of Imperial Leadership

Strong and effective central authority had long been essential to the empires of south and southwest Asia, and Muslim political theorists never tired of emphasizing the importance of rulers who were diligent, virtuous, and just. Weak, negligent, and corrupt rulers would allow institutions to become dysfunctional and social order to break down. The Ottomans were fortunate in having a series of talented sultans for three centuries, and the Safavids and Mughals produced their share of effective rulers as well.

**Dynastic Decline** Eventually, however, all three dynasties had rulers who were incompetent or more interested in spending vast sums of money on personal pleasures than in tending to affairs of state. Moreover, all three dynasties faced difficulties because of suspicion and fighting among competing members of their ruling houses. The Ottomans sought to limit problems by confining princes in the palace, but that measure had several negative consequences. The princes had no opportunity to gain experience in government, but they were frequently exposed to plots and intrigues of the various factions maneuvering to bring a favorable candidate to the throne. Notorious examples of problem rulers included Süleyman's successor Selim the Sot (reigned 1566–1574) and Ibrahim the Crazy (reigned 1640–1648), who taxed and spent to such excess that government officials deposed and murdered him. Several energetic rulers and talented ministers attempted to keep the government on track. Nonetheless, after the late seventeenth century, weak rule increasingly provoked mutinies in the army, provincial revolts, political corruption, economic oppression, and insecurity throughout the Ottoman realm.

**Religious Tensions** Political troubles often arose from religious tensions. Conservative Muslim clerics strongly objected to policies and practices that they considered affronts to Islam. Muslim leaders had considerable influence in each of the empires because of their monopoly of education and their deep involvement in the everyday lives and legal affairs of ordinary subjects. The clerics mistrusted the emperors' interests in unconventional forms of Islam such as Sufism, objected when women or subjects who were not Muslims played influential political roles, and protested any exercise of royal authority that contradicted Islamic law.

In the Ottoman Empire, disaffected religious students often joined the Janissaries in revolt. A particularly serious threat came from the **Wahhabi movement** in Arabia, which denounced the Ottomans as dangerous religious innovators who were unfit to rule. Conservative Muslims fiercely protested the construction of an astronomical observatory in Istanbul and forced the sultan to demolish it in 1580. In 1742 they also forced the closure of the Ottoman printing press, which they regarded as an impious technology.

The Safavids, who began their reign by crushing Sunni religious authorities, fell under the domination of the very Shiites they had supported. Shiite leaders pressured the shahs to persecute Sunnis, non-Muslims, and even the Sufis who had helped establish the dynasty. Religious tensions also afflicted Mughal India. Already in the seventeenth century, the conservative Shaykh Ahmad Sirhindi (1564–1624) fearlessly rebuked Akbar for his policy of religious tolerance and his interest in other faiths. In the mid-eighteenth century, as he struggled to claim the Mughal throne, Aurangzeb drew on Sirhindi's ideas when he required non-Muslims to pay the poll tax and ordered the destruction of Hindu temples. Those measures inflamed tensions between the various Sunni, Shiite, and Sufi branches of Islam and also fueled animosity among Hindus and other Mughal subjects who were not Muslims.

# CONCLUSION

Like China and Japan, the empires of south and southwest Asia remained strong and powerful throughout the early modern era. Ruling elites of the Ottoman, Safavid, and Mughal empires came from nomadic Turkish stock, and they all drew on steppe traditions in organizing their governments. But the rulers also adapted steppe traditions to the needs of settled agricultural societies they encountered and devised institutions that maintained order over the long term. During the sixteenth and seventeenth centuries, each of the empires enjoyed productive economies and participated actively in the global trade networks of early modern times. Their leaders sponsored magnificent architectural and artistic projects as well as campaigns for expansion, and their populations boomed. Each of the empires was religiously and ethnically diverse, and their leaders devised policies to accommodate non-Muslims. By the early eighteenth century, however, these same empires were experiencing difficulties that led to political and military decline. Extensive military campaigns eventually drained the imperial treasuries, while slowed territorial expansion decreased imperial revenues. The diversity that characterized each of the realms also led to religious tensions, and a series of weak rulers encouraged resistance and rebellion. By the late eighteenth century, the Safavid empire had collapsed, and economic difficulties and cultural insularity had severely weakened the Ottoman and Mughal empires and made them vulnerable to outside influences.

## STUDY TERMS

Akbar (479)
Aurangzeb (480)
Babur (577)
(battle of) Chaldiran (478)
*devshirme* (476)
*dhimmi* (486)
Fatehpur Sikri (488)
*ghazi* (475)
Isfahan (487)
Ismail (477)
Istanbul (487)
Jahangir (482)
Janissaries (476)
*jizya* (486)
kanun (482)
Mehmed the Conqueror (476)
*millet* (486)
Mughal Empire (474)
Mumtaz Mahal (472)
Osman Bey (475)
Ottoman Empire (474)
*qizilbash* (478)
Safavid empire (474)
Shah Abbas the Great (478)
Shah Jahan (472)
Shaykh Salim Chishti (488)
Shiism (478)
Sinan Pasha (487)
Sufis (481)
Süleyman the Magnificent (476)
Süleymaniye (487)
Sunni (478)
Taj Mahal (488)
Topkapi palace (487)
Twelver Shiism (478)
Wahhabi movement (490)

## FOR FURTHER READING


Giancarlo Casale. *The Ottoman Age of Exploration.* New York, 2010. This work argues convincingly that the Ottoman Turks were important players in the maritime explorations of the sixteenth century.

Stephen F. Dale. *The Muslim Empires of the Ottomans, Safavids, and Mughals.* Cambridge, 2010. This is a learned but approachable comparative study of three Islamic empires from 1300 to 1923.

Andrew de la Garza. *The Mughal Empire at War: Babur, Akbar and the Indian Military Revolution, 1500–1605.* London, 2016. Argues that the military innovations introduced in the early Mughal empire constituted a fundamental military revolution.

Carter Vaughn Findley. *The Turks in World History.* New York, 2005. A highly readable account that connects the two-thousand-year history of the Turkic peoples with larger global processes.

Douglas Howard. *A History of the Ottoman Empire.* Cambridge, 2017. Covers the entire social and political history of the Ottoman Empire from its origins to the twentieth century.

Kemal H. Karpat. *The Politicization of Islam: Reconstructing Identity, State, Faith, and Community in the Late Ottoman State.* New York, 2001. Scholarly study of the Ottoman state's role in constructing Muslim identity.

Moazzen Maryam. *Formation of a Religious Landscape: Shii Higher Learning in Safavid Iran.* Leiden, 2017. Explores the ways religious information was produced and transmitted during the second half of Safavid rule via institutions of higher learning.

Andrew J. Newman. *Safavid Iran: Rebirth of a Persian Empire.* London and New York, 2008. Based on meticulous scholarship, this is the definitive single volume work on the subject.

Leslie Pierce. *The Imperial Harem: Women and Sovereignty in the Ottoman Empire.* Oxford, 1993. Challenges many stereotypes about the role of women in the imperial Ottoman elite.

John F. Richards. *The Mughal Empire.* Cambridge, 1993. A concise and reliable overview of Mughal history, concentrating on political affairs.

# CHAPTER 15 AP EXAM PRACTICE

Questions assume cumulative knowledge from this chapter and previous chapters.

## Section I

## Multiple Choice Questions

Use the passage below and your knowledge of world history to answer questions 1-3.

> The Sultan's hall was crowded with people, among whom were several officers of high rank. Besides these, there were all the troopers of the Imperial guard, and a large force of Janissaries [the elite infantry corps], but there was not in all that great assembly a single man who owed his position to anything save his valor and his merit. No distinction is attached to birth among the Turks; the respect to be paid to a man is measured by the position he holds in the public service. There is no fighting for precedence; a man's place is marked out by the duties he discharges . . ., It is by merit that men rise in the service, a system which ensures that posts should only be assigned to the competent
>
> *Source:* Foster, C. T., and F. H. Blackburne Daniell. "Süleyman 'the Lawgiver.'" in The *Life and Letters of Ogier Ghiselin de Busbecq.* vol. 1. London: Hakluyt Society, 1881. pp. 152–156.

1. Where did the Janissaries come from?
   (A) They were mercenaries hired from across Asia.
   (B) The Ottoman empire required all men to register for the draft.
   (C) They were taken from the Balkans to be slaves of the emperor.
   (D) They were taken from the Safavid border to be slaves of the emperor.

2. Why was Ghiselin de Busbecq surprised at the role of merit at the Ottoman court?
   (A) He was unfamiliar with the civil service examination that trained bureaucrats in Islamic philosophy.
   (B) At European courts, those that served royalty were often born into noble status.
   (C) He assumed that emperors governed through eunuchs.
   (D) He thought all Turks were dishonest, lazy, and careless.

3. What argument could a historian make based on this passage?
   (A) One of the strengths of the Ottoman empire was that it incorporated its diverse population into government and the military.
   (B) The Turks had no concept of nobility.
   (C) Ottoman emperors use Islam to justify their rule.
   (D) One of the strengths of the Ottoman empire was that it allowed only Turks to serve in the government and military.

Use the image below and your knowledge of world history to answer questions 4 and 5.

This manuscript illustration from about 1590 depicts Akbar (at top, shaded by attendants) inspecting construction of a new imperial capital at Fatehpur Sikri.
Picturenow/Universal Images Group/Getty Images

4. What might the artist be communicating with the way he depicts Akbar in this image?
   (A) The emperor liked to ask artisans about their work.
   (B) The emperor like to tell artisans how to do their jobs.
   (C) The emperor was dissatisfied with the pace of construction.
   (D) The emperor was personally involved in the planning and construction of the new capital.

5. What was a result of Akbar's religious policies?
   (A) Twelver Shi'ism became the dominant religion of the empire.
   (B) Some Muslims were worried that they would lose their identity and be absorbed into Hinduism.
   (C) Some Hindus were worried that they would lose their identity and be absorbed into Islam.
   (D) Portuguese Jesuits were worried that Christianity would be replaced by Akbar's "Divine Faith."

## Short Answer

6. Use the image below and your knowledge of world history to answer parts A, B, and C.

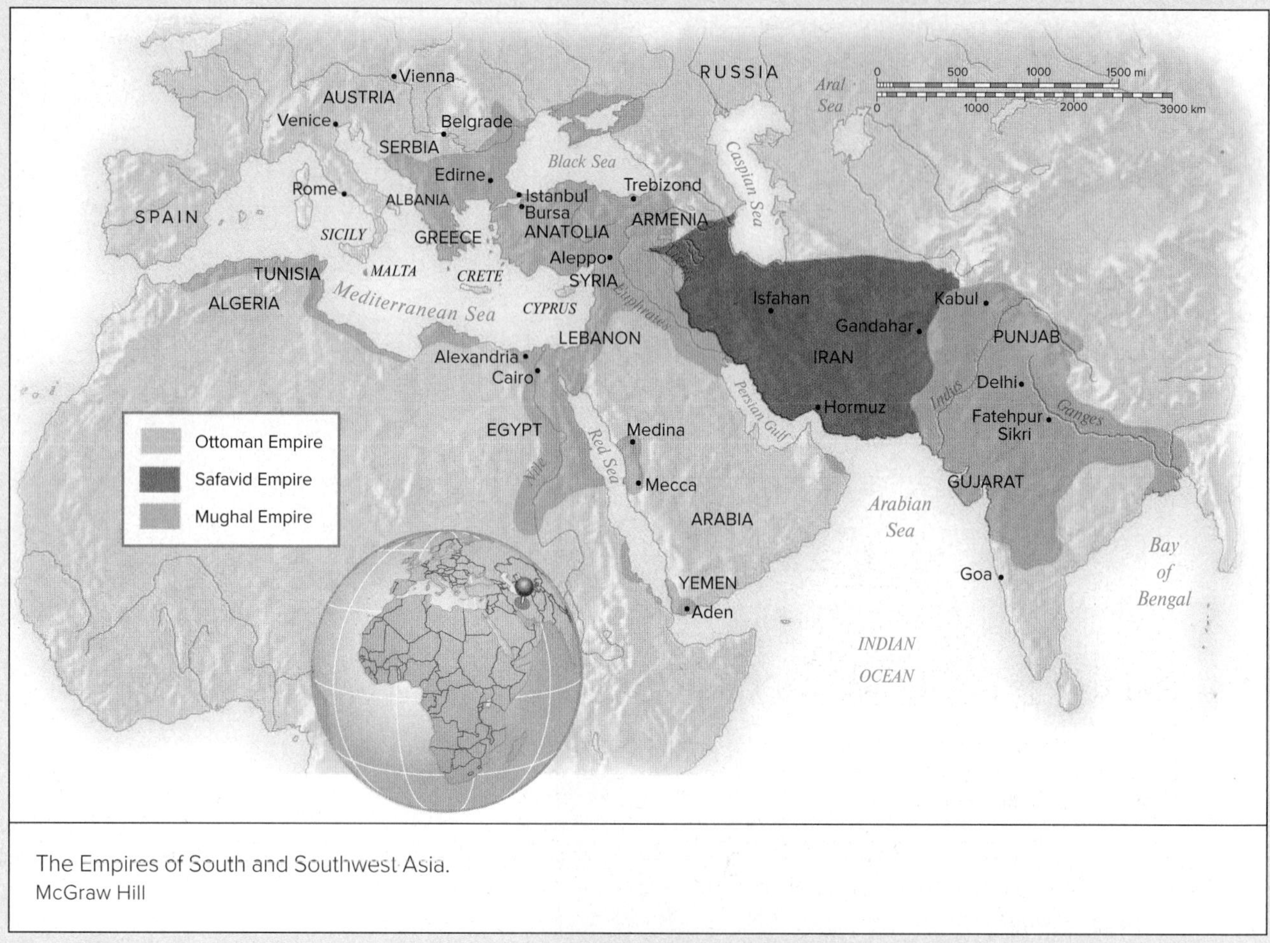


The Empires of South and Southwest Asia.
McGraw Hill

(A) Identify ONE way that gunpowder contributed to the expansion of these empires.
(B) Explain ONE way the Ottoman military was different from that of the Safavids and Mughals.
(C) Explain ONE way that military decline affected these empires.

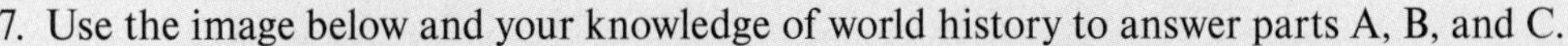

7. Use the image below and your knowledge of world history to answer parts A, B, and C.

Dutch painting from around 1670 depicting Dutch and English ships in the port of Surat in northwestern India.
Rijksmuseum, Amsterdam

(A) Identify ONE commodity traded in the three gunpowder empires as part of long-distance trade.
(B) Explain ONE way long-distance trade benefitted the early modern Islamic empires.
(C) Explain ONE reason why the gunpowder empires experienced economic and military decline.

8. Use your understanding of world history to answer parts A, B, and C.
(A) Explain ONE similarity in the way the gunpowder empires established an emperor's right to rule.
(B) Explain ONE difference in the way an Ottoman, Mughal, or Safavid emperor established his right to rule.
(C) Identify ONE example of an Ottoman, Safavid, or Mughal emperor using architecture to legitimize his rule.

# Section II

## Document-Based Question

Based on the documents below and your knowledge of world history, evaluate the extent to which steppe traditions offered women political power in the Ottoman, Safavid, and Mughal empires.

In your response you should do the following:

- Respond to the prompt with a historically defensible thesis or claim that establishes a line of reasoning.
- Describe a broader historical context relevant to the prompt.
- Support an argument in response to the prompt using all documents.
- Use at least one additional piece of specific historical evidence (beyond that found in the documents) relevant to an argument about the prompt.
- Explain how or why the document's point of view, purpose, historical situation, and /or audience is relevant to an argument.
- Use evidence to corroborate, qualify, or modify an argument that addresses the prompt.

### Document 1

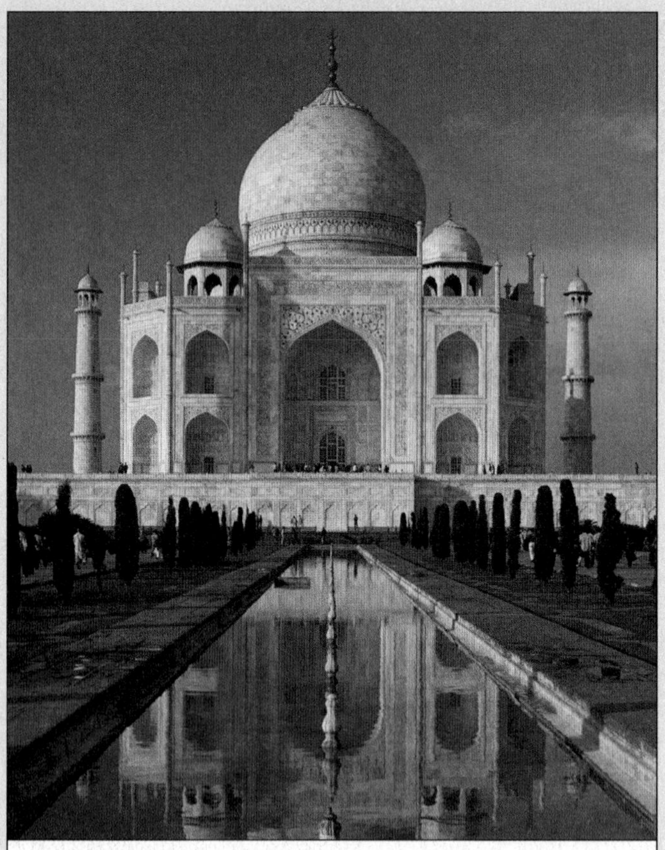

The Taj Mahal, a sumptuous mosque and tomb built between 1632 and 1649 by Shah Jahan in memory of his wife, Mumtaz Mahal.
Andrea Pistolesi/The Image Bank/Getty Images

## Document 2

A sixteenth century portrait of Hürrem Sultan (1510-1588), born Aleksandra Lisowska and also known as Roxelana.
ART Collection/Alamy Stock Photo

## Document 3

His majesty has made a large enclosure with fine buildings inside, where he reposes. Though there are more than five thousand women, he has given to each a separate apartment. He has also divided them into sections, and keeps them attentive to their duties. Several chaste women have been appointed as *daroghas* [officials], and superintendents over each section, and one has been appointed as a writer [record-keeper] . . .

The inside of the Harem is guarded by sober and active women; the most trustworthy of them are placed about the apartments of his Majesty. Outside of the enclosure the eunuchs are placed; and at a proper distance, there is a guard of faithful *Rajputs* [soldiers from a Hindu military caste], beyond whom are the porters of the gates . . . Notwithstanding the great number of faithful guards, his Majesty does not dispense with his own vigilance, but keeps the whole in proper order.

*Source:* Abū al-Faẕl ibn Mubārak. *The Ain i Akbari.* Trans. by Henry Blochmann. Printed for the Asiatic Society of Bengal, 1873, 44–45. HathiTrust Digital Library.

## Long Essay

Develop a thoughtful and thorough historical argument that answers the question below. Begin your essay with a thesis statement and support it with relevant historical evidence.

Using specific examples and your knowledge of world history, evaluate the different approaches Ottoman, Safavid, and Mughal rulers developed to manage religious minorities.

# Part 2 Land-Based Empires and Transoceanic Empires, 1450–1750

In the fifteenth century, the world's peoples were no strangers to long-distance travels and meetings, nor were cross-cultural interactions and exchanges foreign experiences for them. Peoples of the world's three major geographic zones—the eastern hemisphere, the western hemisphere, and Oceania—had been dealing for thousands of years with counterparts from different societies.

Even as they built their own distinctive political, social, economic, and cultural traditions, the inhabitants of these different geographic zones also engaged the larger world beyond their own societies. Their interactions were often hostile or unpleasant, taking the form of raids, wars, campaigns of imperial expansion, or transmissions of epidemic diseases. Yet their engagements also took more peaceful and beneficial forms, as trade, missionary activity, technological diffusion, and the spread of agricultural crops linked peoples of different societies.

Until 1492, however, long-distance travels and cross-cultural interactions took place mostly within the world's three broad regions. With rare and fleeting exceptions, peoples of the eastern hemisphere, the western hemisphere, and Oceania kept to their own parts of the world.

In the year 1500 the world stood on the brink of a new era in the experience of humankind. The peoples of the world were poised to enter into permanent and sustained interaction. The results of their engagements were profitable and beneficial for some peoples but difficult or disastrous for others.

Whether signaled by a young Mexican woman serving as an interpreter for Spanish conquerors or by the sounds of chiming clocks in China, novel cross-cultural experiences—on both an intimately human and a coldly technological level—symbolized the intense global transformations taking place in the early modern world. Mariners and voyagers from as far afield as east Asia, the Ottoman empire, and western Europe charted the vast expanses of the world's oceans and opened up new human vistas on a world where two previously isolated hemispheres coexisted in an ever-tightening web of global interaction.

Now that you have read these seven chapters, take a moment to consider the changes that a more globally connected world brought to the AP World History themes.

# THEME 1: HUMANS AND THE ENVIRONMENT (ENV)

The environment shapes human societies, and as populations grow and change, these populations in turn shape their environments.

# THEME 2: CULTURAL DEVELOPMENTS AND INTERACTIONS (CDI)

The development of ideas, beliefs, and religions illustrates how groups in society view themselves, and the interactions of societies and their beliefs often have political, social, and cultural implications.

# THEME 3: GOVERNANCE (GOV)

A variety of internal and external factors contribute to state formation, expansion, and decline. Governments maintain order through a variety of administrative institutions, policies, and procedures, and governments obtain, retain, and exercise power in different ways and for different purposes.

# THEME 4: ECONOMIC SYSTEMS (ECN)

As societies develop, they affect and are affected by the ways that they produce, exchange, and consume goods and services.

# THEME 5: SOCIAL INTERACTIONS AND ORGANIZATION (SIO)

The process by which societies group their members and the norms that govern the interactions between these groups and between individuals influence political, economic, and cultural institutions and organization.

# THEME 6: TECHNOLOGY AND INNOVATION (TEC)

Human adaptation and innovation have resulted in increased efficiency, comfort, and security, and technological advances have shaped human development and interactions with both intended and unintended consequences.

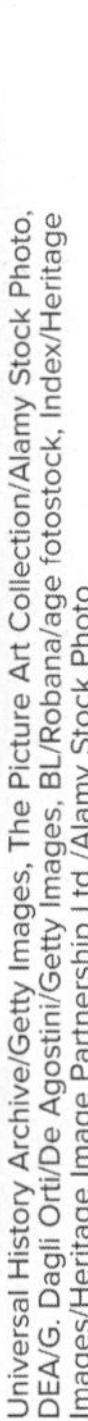

# PART 2 AP EXAM PRACTICE

Questions assume cumulative knowledge from this Part.

## Section I

## Multiple Choice Questions

Using the passage below and your knowledge of world history, answer questions 1–3.

Pedro Teixeira, *The Travels of Pedro Teixeira*, c. 1610, Chapter VI, "Concerning the City of Bagdad" p. 62.

"Amongst other public buildings, as I have said, is a coffee-house. Coffee is a vegetable of the size and appearance of little dry beans, brought from Arabia, prepared and sold in public houses built to that end; wherein all men who desire it meet to drink it, be they great or mean. They sit in order, and it is brought to them very hot, in porcelain cups holding four or five ounces each. Every man takes his own in his hand, cooling and sipping it. It is black and rather tasteless; and, although some good qualities are ascribed to it, none are proven."

*Source:* Teixeira, Pedro. The Travels of Pedro Teixeira: With His "Kings of Harmuz" and Extracts from His "Kings of Persia." London: The Hakluyt Society, 1902.

1. Which of the following, like coffee, was a cash crop that was grown in the Americas?
   (A) tobacco
   (B) rice
   (C) maize
   (D) potatoes

2. Based on Teixeira's observations, why were coffeehouses popular in the Ottoman and Safavid empires?
   (A) People in the coffeehouses were mean to each other.
   (B) They were good places to eat nutritious vegetables.
   (C) Men were treated to the same experience regardless of social standing.
   (D) Patrons were allowed to keep their own porcelain cups.

3. Why did some people pressure the Ottoman emperors to close the coffeehouses?
   (A) They thought coffee was worse than alcohol and encouraged idleness.
   (B) They wanted to end competition for the tea shops.
   (C) They thought coffee was bitter and had no good qualities.
   (D) They thought coffeehouses charged too much for four or five ounces.

Using the map below and your knowledge of world history, answer questions 4–6.

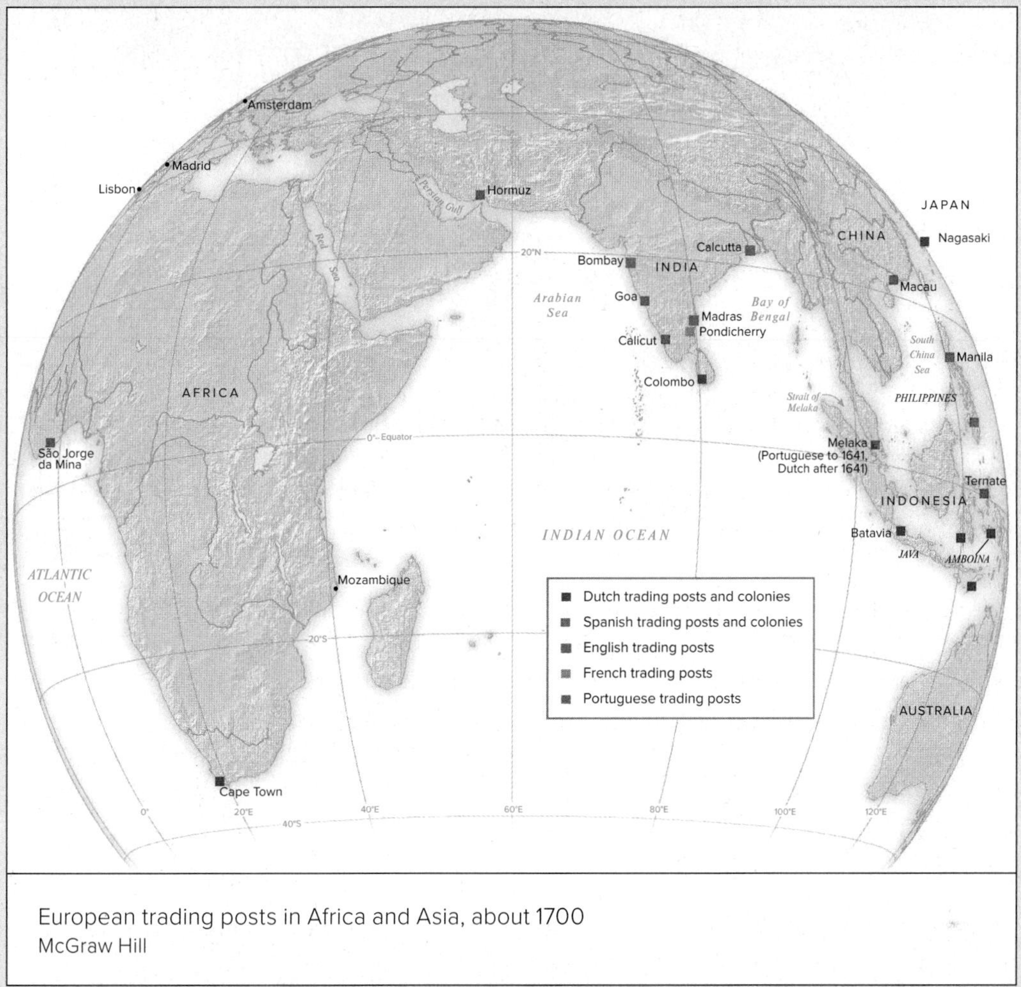


European trading posts in Africa and Asia, about 1700
McGraw Hill

4. What did the English East India Company and Dutch VOC have in common?
   (A) English and Dutch are both Indo-European languages.
   (B) They were both financial failures.
   (C) They were both joint-stock companies.
   (D) Afonso d'Alboquerque worked for both of them.

5. With the exception of the Philippines and Indonesia, European merchants set up trading posts instead of colonies in Asia and the Indian Ocean. Why?
   (A) The large populations and centralized governments of the region did not allow Europeans to build territorial empires.
   (B) Asia and the Indian Ocean lacked the products that would generate enough profit to justify the expense of colonies.
   (C) The Mongol navy had too much control of the Indian Ocean trade routes, preventing outsiders from conquering the region.
   (D) Admiral Zheng He had already colonized much of Asia and the Indian Ocean trade routes for China.

6. What was significant about the Dutch trading post at Nagasaki in 1700, the year depicted on the map?
   (A) Dutch ships from Indonesia gathered in Nagasaki before sailing to Europe.
   (B) The Japanese government had excluded all other European states from trading in Japan.
   (C) The Japanese government had excluded all other countries from trading in Japan.
   (D) The Japanese government wanted more European trading partners, but only the Dutch thought it was profitable.

Using the image below and your knowledge of world history, answer questions 7–9.

Iſrael ex. Cum Priuil. Reg.
A la fin ces Voleurs infames et perdus ,
Comme fruits malheureux a cet arbre pendus
Monſtrent bien que le crime (horrible et noire engeance)
Eſt luy meſme inſtrument de honte et de vengeance ,
Et que ceſt le Deſtin des hommes vicieux
Deſprouuer toſt ou tard la iuſtice des Cieux .


Pillaging mercenary soldiers from the Thirty Years' War hanged for their crimes, circa 1633.
Anne S.K. Brown Military Collection, Brown University Library

7. What agreement ended the Thirty Years' War?
   (A) The Peace of Paris
   (B) The Treaty of Versailles
   (C) The Peace of Westphalia
   (D) The Geneva Accords

8. Which of the following did ordinary Germans NOT experience during the war?
   (A) attacks from enemy armies
   (B) attacks from allied armies
   (C) natural disasters
   (D) famine

9. What claim could a historian make about the Thirty Years War based on this image?
   (A) soldiers' crimes were rarely punished because states were too weak to discipline their armies.
   (B) the executed soldiers did not receive fair trials.
   (C) diplomats insisted that criminals in the armies be punished before they signed the peace agreement.
   (D) only foreign soldiers were executed. The rest only had to pay a fine.

Using the image below and your knowledge of world history, answer questions 10–12.

Courtesan district of Kyoto in the seventeenth century.
Ashmolean Museum/Heritage Images/Getty Images

10. How did Japanese society change during the Tokugawa era?
    (A) Because the country was at peace, the daimyo and samurai became scholars.
    (B) Anime emerged as the dominant form of the graphic arts.
    (C) The was no need for the warrior classes, so Japan became a society of merchants and peasants.
    (D) The shoguns resigned their office and the country was ruled by the emperor.

11. Which of the following was not found in the floating worlds?
    (A) teahouses
    (B) brothels
    (C) cat cafes
    (D) public baths

12. Which of these was a theme in kabuki theater?
    (A) bawdy skits
    (B) Neo-Confucian philosophy
    (C) Christian martyrs
    (D) Puppet

Using the map below and your knowledge of world history, answer questions 13–15.

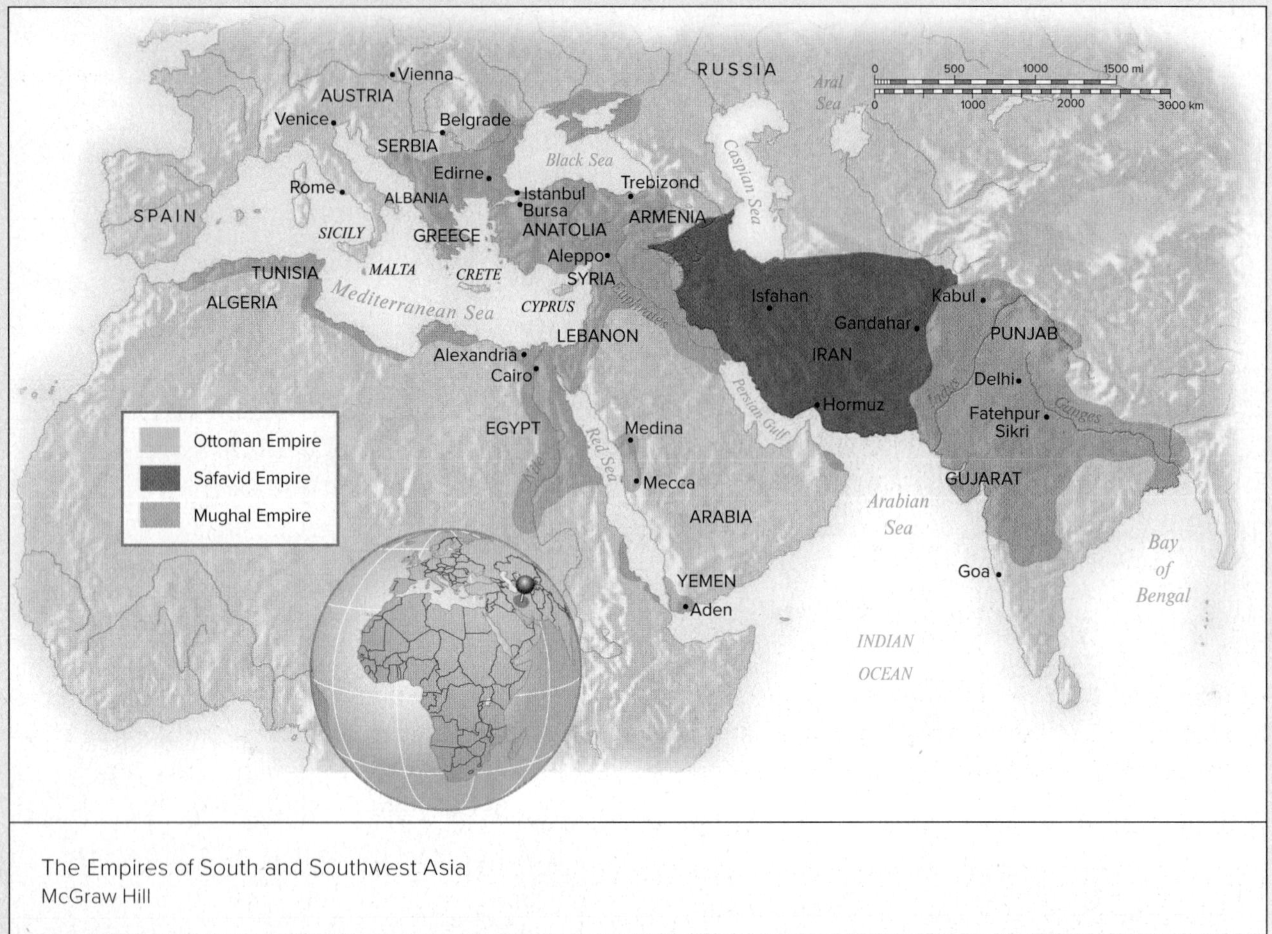


The Empires of South and Southwest Asia
McGraw Hill

13. How did the Mughal Empire resemble the sultanate of Delhi?
(A) The legal system of both empires used a strict interpretation of sharia law.
(B) Both empires tried to destroy Hinduism.
(C) Both empires refused to allow Europeans to trade in their cities.
(D) Their empires were centered in northern India, but they occasionally tried to conquer southern India.

14. How were the demographics of the Islamic empires similar?
(A) They all contained ethnically and religious diverse populations.
(B) The people of all three empires were Muslims.
(C) They were all ethnic Arabs.
(D) All three were warrior societies ruling over peasants without a merchant class.

15. What historic development might explain the decline of these empires?
(A) Barbarian nomads from the north overran their borders.
(B) There was a worldwide gunpowder shortage in the eighteenth century.
(C) Dependence on Europeans might have put them at an economic and technical disadvantage.
(D) The expansion of the Qing empire into Afghanistan and Central Asia threatened their borders.

## Short Answer

16. Use the map below and your knowledge of world history to answer parts A, B, and C.

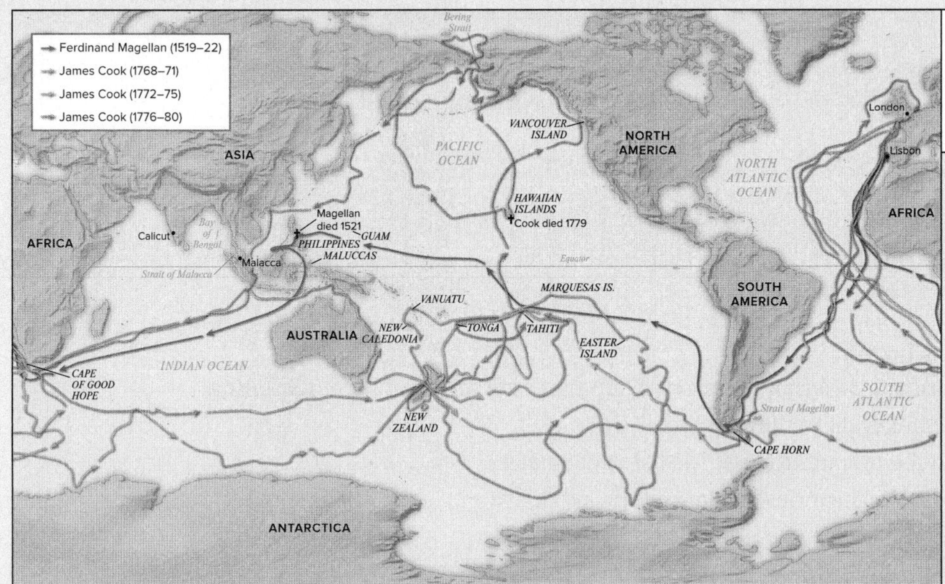


Pacific voyages of Magellan and Cook, 1519–1780
McGraw Hill

(A) Identify ONE technology that made it possible for European ships to explore the Pacific.
(B) Explain ONE reason why the Spanish were interested in sailing across the Pacific Ocean between 1450 and 1750.
(C) Explain ONE reason why Captain James Cook's voyages in the Pacific were significant.

17. Using the chart below and your knowledge of world history, answer parts A, B, and C.

Louis XIV Receiving the Persian Ambassador at Versailles
Granger

(A) Identify ONE form of labor used in the silver mines of Peru.
(B) Explain ONE European historical development that could explain high silver production from 1611-1701.
(C) Explain ONE way that Peru was affected by silver production.

18. Use your knowledge of history to answer all parts of the questions that follow.
(A) Explain ONE kind of tax and how it was used to expand state power between 1450 and 1750.
(B) Explain ONE contrast between how states in this period used taxes to manage their populations.
(C) Identify ONE specific way that taxes were avoided.

# Section II

## Document-Based Question

Suggested reading and writing time: 1 hour
It is suggested that you spend 15 minutes reading the documents and 45 minutes writing your response.

Note: You may begin writing your response before the reading period is over.
The documents have been edited for the purpose of this exercise.

Based on your analysis of the documents below, write an essay that explain how and why chiefs, kings, and emperors found ways to legitimate their rule in the period from 1450 to 1750.

In your response you should do the following.

- Respond to the prompt with a historically defensible thesis or claim that establishes a line of reasoning.
- Describe a broader historical context relevant to the prompt.
- Support an argument in response to the prompt using at least six documents.
- Use at least one additional piece of specific historical evidence (beyond that found in the documents) relevant to an argument about the prompt.
- For at least three documents, explain how or why the document's point of view, purpose, historical situation, and/or audience is relevant to an argument.
- Use evidence to corroborate, qualify, or modify an argument that addresses the prompt.

Note: The map below is provided as a reference. The map is NOT one of the seven documents. The documents begin below the map.

## Document 1

Born al-Hasan ibn Muhammed and raised in Fez, Morocco, Leo Africanus was on a diplomatic mission to Istanbul when he was enslaved by Spanish pirates and given to the pope. He was freed and converted to Christianity taking the name John Leo Africanus.

Of the kingdom of Timbuktu. There is a most stately temple to be seen, the walls wherof are made of stone and lime; and a princely palace also built by a most excellent workman of Granada. Here are many shops of artisans, and merchants, expecially of such as weave linen and cotton cloth. . . . All the women of this region except maid-servants go with their faces covered. . . . The rich king of Timbuktu has many plates and scepters of gold, some whereof weigh 1300 pounds, and he keeps a magnificent and well furnished court. When he travels anywhere he rides upon a camel, which is led by some of his noblemen, and so he does likewise when he goes to warfare, and all his soldiers ride upon horses.

*Source:* Leo Africanus, *A History and Description of Africa*, Vol. III, Book VII, c. 1526, p. 824.

## Document 2

Abu'l Fazl was the grand vizier of Emperor Akbar.

No dignity is higher in the eyes of God than royalty, and those who are wise drink from its auspicious fountain. A sufficient proof of this, for those who require one, is the fact that royalty is a remedy for the spirit of rebellion, and the reason why subjects obey. . . . If royalty did not exist, the storm of strife would never subside, nor selfish ambition disappear. Mankind, being under the burden of lawlessness and lust, would sink into the pit of destruction; this world, this great market place, would lose its prosperity, and the whole world become a barren waste. But by the light of imperial justice, some follow with cheerfulness the road of obedience, while others abstain from violence through fear of punishment; and out of necessity make choice of the path of rectitude. . . .

Royalty is a light emanating from God, and a ray from the sun, the illuminator of the universe, the argument of the book of perfection, the receptacle of all virtues. Modern language calls this light the divine light, and the tongue of antiquity called it the sublime halo. It is communicated by God to kings without the intermediate assistance of anyone, and men, in the presence of it, bend the forehead of praise toward the ground of submission.

*Source:* Abu'l Fazl, *The Ain I Akbari*, trans. H. Blochmann p ii-iii. Mughal Empire, sixteenth century.

## Document 3

Mo`ikeha's Migration from Tahiti to Hawai`i.

[After Mo`ikeha's son Kila sailed to Tahiti and found his elder half-brother] La`amaikahiki immediately prepared to accompany his brother to Hawai`i, as Mo`ikeha wished. La`amaikahiki took his priests and his god Lonoika`ouali`i, and set sail for Hawai`i with the men who had come with Kila. When they were approaching Kaua`i, La`amaikahiki began beating his drum. Mo`ikeha heard his drum and ordered everything, the land as well as the house, to be made ready for the reception of the chief La`amaikahiki. Upon the arrival of La`amaikahiki and Kila, the high priest of Kaua`i, Poloahilani, took La`amaikahiki and his god Lonoila`ouali`i ("Lono at the Chiefly Supremacy") to the heiau [temple]. It is said that La`amaikahiki was the first person to bring a god (akua) to Hawai`i. . . .

[After returning to Tahiti, then sailing again to Hawai`i, La`amaikahiki] set sail again, going up the Kona coast [of Hawai`i Island]. . . . It was on this visit that La`amaikahiki introduced hula dancing, accompanied by the drum, to Hawai`i. . . . La`amaikahiki stayed a long time on Kaua`i teaching the people the art of dancing. From Kaua`i La`amaikahiki visited all the other islands of this group and thus the drum dance (hula ka`eke) spread to the other islands.

*Source:* Teuira Henry and others. *Voyaging Chiefs of Havai`i.* Ed. by Dennis Kawaharada. Honolulu: Kalamaku Press, 1995, pp. 138–39, 144–46.

## Document 4

Emperor Kangxi's *Sacred Edicts* with commentary from his son, the emperor Yongzheng, c. 1724.

Illustrate the Principles of a Polite and Yielding Carriage in Order to Improve Manners.

Kung-tsze [Confucius] said, "To secure repose to superiors in the government of a people, there is nothing better than propriety." For propriety is the immoveable state of the heavens and the earth, the preface and conclusion of the myriads of things. Its nature is supremely great–its utility most extensive. Were reason, virtue, benevolence, and justice void of propriety, they could not be carried to perfection. Were honor and meanness, nobility and ignobility, without propriety, their distinctions would be undetermined."

*Source:* Legge, James. *The Analects of Confucius (from the Chinese Classics).* Illinois: Project Gutenberg, 2002.

## Document 5

Louis XIV Receiving the Persian Ambassador at Versailles, 1715. The Persian ambassador and his retinue approach Louis seated in his throne while the French nobles observe.
*Source:* https://www.britishmuseum.org/collection/object/P_1917-1208-3937
SuperStock/Getty Images

## Document 6

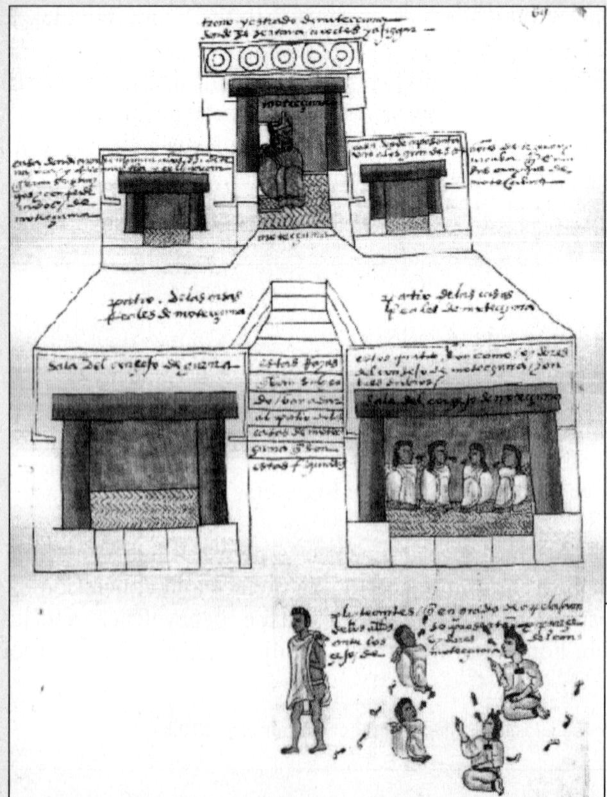

Anonymous, *The Codex Mendoza*, 1542. Image of the palace of emperor Motecuhzoma. The emperor is depicted at the top of the palace with court officials and guests in the rooms and courtyards below.
The Picture Art Collection/Alamy Stock Photo

## Document 7

Eksander Beg Monshi, *The History of Shah Abbas the Great*, Vol I, Book I, Discourse 1, c. 1629. Eksander Beg Monshi was a secretary at the Safavid court of Shah Abbas.

Shah Abbas was never remiss in seeking to approach God's throne; when he prayed, he was so absorbed in his devotions that he appeared to have left his material body. In all affairs of state, he would seek and augury from the Koran, and he would take no action in the realm of government without asking god's advice. If the text of the Koran expressly forbade something, he would respect God's wise counsel and refrain from taking that action, even though it was desirable in order to gain some material advantage.

*Source:* Monshi, Eskandar Beg. *History of Shah 'Abbas the Great, Vol. 1.* Trans. Roger M. Savory. (Boulder, CO: Westview Press, 1930).

## Long Essay

1. Compare and contrast demographic and environmental effects of the Columbian Exchange on the Americas in 1500 and 1750.
2. Evaluate changes and continuities in sub-Saharan African labor systems from 1450 to 1750.
3. From 1450 to 1750, different factors led to the emergence of new ideas in Christianity and Confucianism. Develop an argument that evaluates the factors that led to these changes during this time period.

In your response you should do the following:

- Respond to the prompt with a historically defensible thesis or claim that establishes a line of reasoning.
- Describe a broader historical context relevant to the prompt.
- Support an argument in response to the prompt using specific and relevant examples of evidence.
- Use historical reasoning (e.g. comparison, causation, continuity or change) to frame or structure an argument that addresses the prompt.
- Use evidence to corroborate, qualify, or modify an argument that addresses the prompt.

Part 3

# Revolutions and Consequences of Industrialization, 1750–1900

Heritage Images/Hulton Fine Art Collection/Getty Images



## LEARNING OBJECTIVES

As you study Part 3 you will:

- Analyze how the ideas of the eighteenth-century Enlightenment advocated relying on reason and experimentation, rather than tradition or religion.
- Explain why there were several successful political and social revolutions in the Atlantic World.
- Analyze how and why slavery was questioned and eventually abolished in the Americas.
- Identify reasons why suffrage was eventually extended to all men and all women.
- Identify the economic changes that came with the Industrial Revolution.

One of the fascinating aspects of history is that none of it occurs in a vacuum and no single element or event is isolated from another. AP World History calls your attention to themes and key topics, and your mission is to begin to see the interconnectedness in history. For example, the industrial revolution resulted in migration and changes in labor systems which, in turn, led to shifts in gender roles. As you continue to study these chapters, focus on the relationship that the themes have with each other, and reflect on earlier historical events to gain a better perspective on what led people to this new era.

The following chapters make up what is considered the first modern period in AP World History, spanning from roughly 1750 to 1914. As you will see, the ideas and actions from the intellectual, political, and economic revolutions of this time reoriented the way people interacted and formed the foundation of many of our modern world systems. Historians don't use the term revolution lightly. It implies a dramatic 180-degree change. With a shift this dramatic, historians pay very close attention, particularly when one revolution seems to trigger others.

The powerful divergence of intellectual ideas of this period is called the Enlightenment. Philosophers interested in government argued that all men were born equal, and therefore all men should have a say in governing themselves, rather than following the ideas of people born into certain families who claimed a divine right to rule. The globalization of these Atlantic world ideas about equality and human rights, structures of governments, and nationalism has held significant influence from the eighteenth century to the present day. Wealth and talent gradually replaced birth and land ownership as markers of success and power.

AP students will need to compare the political and social revolutions in the United States, France, Haiti, and Latin America in terms of their causes, participants, and outcomes. The industrial revolution was a huge shift in how people supported themselves. Northwest European countries and the United States, followed by Japan, were the first industrialized economies, and you will need to explain why that was.

You will be expected to know how and by whom goods were produced, transported, and financed. You will also have to understand the varying ways the industrial revolution in different parts of the world changed the lives of people in different social classes, ages, and gender. This is a huge topic, and one for which AP students are often asked to compare, or to trace changes and continuities over time.

The creation of industrialized economies had a ripple effect in international relations. Industrialized countries needed access to cheap raw materials, a low-wage labor force, and markets for their manufactured goods. Industrialized nations used their new technologies, such as rail roads, steam ships, telegraph lines, and machine guns, to accumulate colonies in Africa and Asia to better supply their needs.

This second round of acquiring colonies, often called nineteenth century imperialism, tightened the web that the Columbian voyages had begun almost four centuries before. Colonial people were not merely passive victims. They often fought overtly to the death trying to hold on to their independence. Some colonists were covert in their resistance, using techniques that would undermine the imperialists while appearing to be acquiescent.

AP students will be asked to evaluate how the lives, economies, governments, and environments of colonial peoples were changed by these colonial incursions, and how the colonists resisted.

Rulers of well-established empires such as the Ottoman, Qing China, Russia, and the Japanese Tokugawa shogunate had to decide whether or how much to industrialize in order to compete militarily or economically with the west. Some feared industrialization because of the foreign influences that would accompany it. Others wanted to embrace industrialization to be able to compete with and join western capitalist economies. The tension of all these forces often led to deep political, social, and economic divisions within these societies at the crossroads.

Industrialization, increasing global integration (globalization), and imperialism changed the patterns of human migration in this period. As family and community sizes expanded, and despite increased food production and improved medical conditions, there was often not enough land or work to accommodate the growing populations. Cities expanded, energy consumption skyrocketed, and industrial centers became heavily polluted. In these ways the industrial revolution marked a fundamentally new relationship between humans and the environment.

Migration occurred on a different scale than seen in earlier chapters as rural workers moved to urban areas to work in industrial economies. Migration also occurred on a transnational scale as workers chose to move or were forced to move—many in search of work. Often migration occurred within an imperial system when, for example, indentured servants from British India went to work in the British Cape Colony. Historians study why people migrated, and what happened to the lands they left and the lands to which they moved. We also look at how governments attempted to regulate migrants, and what happened when different cultures lived and worked together.

By about 1900, many human patterns and interactions are recognizably modern—we can see the roots of our own world in the revolutionary changes of the eighteenth and nineteenth centuries.

## PART 3 BIG QUESTIONS:

- Identify the factors that allowed Europeans to expand their empires between the late eighteenth and twentieth centuries.
- What did revolutions, industrialization, and imperialism mean for people in Africa, the Americas, and Asia?
- What was the global impact of migration on societies, economies, and governments?

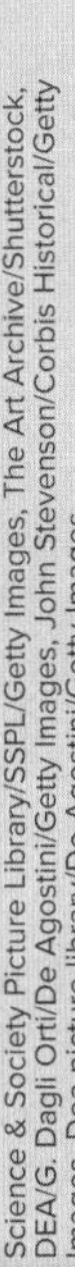

Science & Society Picture Library/SSPL/Getty Images, The Art Archive/Shutterstock,
DEA/G. Dagli Orti/De Agostini/Getty Images, John Stevenson/Corbis Historical/Getty
Images, Dea picture library/De Agostini/Getty Images

Chapter 16

# Revolutions and National States in the Atlantic World

**Revolutionary Ideas**
- The Enlightenment
- Popular Sovereignty

**Revolutions**
- The American Revolution
- The French Revolution
- The Reign of Napoleon
- The Haitian Revolution
- Wars of Independence in Latin America

**Consequences and Implications of the Revolutions**
- The Emergence of New Ideologies
- Testing the Limits of Revolutionary Ideals: Slavery
- Testing the Limits of Revolutionary Ideals: Women's Rights

**The New Nations and Nationalism in Europe**
- Nations and Nationalism
- The Emergence of National Communities
- The Unifications of Italy and Germany

## ZOOMING IN ON TRADITIONS

### Olympe de Gouges Declares the Rights of Women

Marie Gouze was a French butcher's daughter who educated herself by reading books before moving to Paris and marrying a junior army officer. Under the name **Olympe de Gouges,** she won fame as a journalist, actress, and playwright. Gouges was as flamboyant as she was talented, and news of her well-publicized love affairs scandalized Parisian society.

Gouges was also a revolutionary and a strong advocate of women's rights. She responded enthusiastically when the French revolution broke out in July 1789, and she applauded in August when revolutionary leaders proclaimed freedom and equality for all citizens in the Declaration of the Rights of Man and the Citizen. It soon became clear, however, that in the view of revolutionary leaders, freedom and equality pertained only to male citizens. They welcomed women's contributions to the revolution but withheld the right to vote and left women under the patriarchal authority of their fathers and husbands.

Gouges campaigned fervently to raise the standing of women in French society. She called for more education and demanded that women share equal rights in family property. She challenged

**Olympe de Gouges** (oh-LAHMP de gouj)

François Toussaint L'Ouverture (1743–1803) proclaims the constitution of the Republic of Haiti in the midst of the Haitian Revolution on July 1, 1801.
World History Archive/Alamy Stock Photo

traditions associated with patriarchal authority and appealed to Queen Marie Antoinette to use her influence to advance women's rights. In 1791 Gouges published a Declaration of the Rights of Woman and the Female Citizen, which claimed the same rights for women that revolutionary leaders had granted to men in August 1789. She asserted that freedom and equality were inalienable rights of women as well as men, and she insisted on the rights of women to vote, speak their minds freely, participate in the making of law, and hold public office.

Gouges's declaration attracted a great deal of attention but little support. Revolutionary leaders dismissed her appeal as a publicity stunt and refused to put women's rights on their political agenda. In 1793 they executed her because of her affection for Marie Antoinette and her persistent crusade for women's rights. Yet Gouges's campaign illustrated the power of the Enlightenment ideals of freedom and equality, which played an important role in inspiring all of the Atlantic revolutions. Indeed, once revolutionaries in France and elsewhere had proclaimed freedom and equality as universal human rights, they were unable to suppress demands to extend them to other groups—such as women, enslaved people, and people of color—who the revolutionaries often originally intended to exclude.

# CHAPTER FOCUS

- "No taxation without representation!" and "liberty, equality, and fraternity!" were goals of revolution, nationalism, and reform—movements you will learn about in this chapter.
- Understand and follow the powerful Enlightenment ideas that became part of the language of most of the revolutions. New radical concepts—such as "all men are created equal"; people have the right to decide their own government (popular sovereignty); and people can and should remove any government that does not fulfill its responsibilities (social contract)—contradicted all conventional European ideas of patriarchal, hierarchical, and divine-right-based governments and society.
- Economically, Scottish philosopher Adam Smith argued that the only way to make a nation wealthy was to let entrepreneurs compete with no rules or regulations.
- Amidst these radical ideas, the revolutions in the Americas were started by educated European males whose primary goal was independence for political and economic reasons.
- The French revolution, in all its complexity, was also started by educated middle-class men who wanted political power equivalent to their social standing and economic power in the Atlantic world.
- The Haitian revolution began as a slave revolt and stands out as very different from the other revolutions. Enslaved people did not need a philosopher to explain the evils of slavery.
- The process of fighting common enemies and winning, in combination with Enlightenment rhetoric and ideals, created the modern notion of a nation and nationalism.
- As an eighteenth and nineteenth century concept, a "nation" is made up of people with common ethnicity, religion, language, history, and culture. Perhaps most importantly, a "nation" should govern itself.
- The Industrial Revolution took place simultaneously to these political revolutions.

## Historical Developments

- The rise and diffusion of Enlightenment thought that questioned established traditions in all areas of life often preceded revolutions and rebellions against existing governments.
- Nationalism also became a major force shaping the historical development of states and empires.
- Enlightenment ideas, and religious ideals, influenced various reform movements. These reform movements contributed to the expansion of rights, as seen in expanded suffrage, the abolition of slavery, and the end of serfdom.
- People around the world developed a new sense of commonality based on language, religion, social customs and territory. This was sometimes harnessed by governments to foster a sense of unity.
- Discontent with monarchist and imperial rule encouraged the development of systems of government and various ideologies, including democracy and 19th-century liberalism.

## Reasoning Processes

- **Sourcing and Situation** Identify the purpose and historical situation of the *Declaration of the Rights of Man and the Citizen and the Declaration of the Rights of Woman and the Female Citizen.*
- **Contextualization** Identify and describe the historical context surrounding the rise of nations and nationalism.

## Historical Thinking Skills

- **Causation** Describe the effects of enlightenment philosophy on the political revolutions of the late 18th and early 19th centuries.
- **Continuity and Change** Describe patterns of continuity and change in Europe as absolute monarchies gave way to nations.

## CHAPTER OVERVIEW

Violence rocked lands throughout much of the Atlantic Ocean basin in the late eighteenth and early nineteenth centuries as a series of revolutions and wars of independence brought dramatic political and social change. People attempted to restructure their societies—if necessary by violent means—by abolishing traditional social and political institutions and replacing them with new ones. Politically active people now sought not only to participate in government but also actually viewed it as their inherent right to do so, and they rejected the idea that god had created a division between rulers and ruled. And while each revolution was different, they all shared several features. First, all were at least partially inspired by Enlightenment ideals. Second, wars fought between the major imperial powers created the conditions for each of the revolutions to erupt. Finally, the revolutions were deeply interlinked: in fact, beginning with the American revolution, each successive revolution helped to create the conditions for the next.

Revolution broke out first in the British colonies of North America, where colonists asserted their independence and founded a new republic. Partly as a result of the lavish spending of the French on helping the American revolutionaries, revolution broke out in France just a few years later. There, revolutionaries abolished the French monarchy and thoroughly reorganized French society. During the French revolution, enslaved people in the French sugar island of St. Domingue seized the opportunity to revolt against French rule and establish their independence. The Napoleonic wars (1799-1815) then created the conditions for the peoples of Latin America to seek independence from Spain and Portugal. By the 1830s, peoples had reorganized political and social structures throughout western Europe and the Americas.

The revolutions of the late eighteenth and early nineteenth centuries had two results of deep global significance. First, they helped to spread a cluster of Enlightenment ideas concerning freedom, equality, and popular sovereignty. Revolutionary leaders argued that political authority arose from the people and worked to establish states in the interests of the people rather than the rulers. In fact, early revolutionaries extended political rights to a privileged group of white men, but they justified their actions in general terms that invited excluded groups to seek the same rights. By the mid-twentieth century, nearly every state in the world formally recognized the freedom and equality of all its citizens—even if they did not always honor their official positions—and claimed authority to rule on the basis of popular sovereignty.

| CHRONOLOGY | |
|---|---|
| 1694–1778 | Life of Voltaire |
| 1712–1778 | Life of Jean-Jacques Rousseau |
| 1744–1803 | Life of Toussaint Louverture |
| 1748–1793 | Life of Olympe de Gouges |
| 1753–1811 | Life of Miguel Hidalgo y Costilla |
| 1756–1763 | Seven Years' War |
| 1769–1821 | Life of Napoleon Bonaparte |
| 1773–1859 | Life of Klemens von Metternich |
| 1774–1793 | Reign of King Louis XVI |
| 1775–1781 | American revolution |
| 1783–1830 | Life of Simón Bolívar |
| 1789–1799 | French revolution |
| 1791–1803 | Haitian revolution |
| 1799–1814 | Reign of Napoleon |
| 1805–1872 | Life of Giuseppe Mazzini |
| 1810–1825 | Wars of independence in Latin America |
| 1814–1815 | Congress of Vienna |
| 1815–1898 | Life of Otto von Bismarck |
| 1821–1827 | War of Greek independence |
| 1859–1870 | Unification of Italy |
| 1864–1871 | Unification of Germany |

Second, while promoting Enlightenment values, the revolutions of this period also encouraged the consolidation of national states as the principal form of political organization. As peoples defended their states from enemies and sometimes mounted attacks on foreign lands, they developed a powerful sense of identity with their compatriots, and nationalist convictions inspired them to work toward the foundation of states that would advance the interests of the national community. During the nineteenth century, strong national identities and movements to build national states profoundly influenced the political experiences of European states. During the late nineteenth and twentieth centuries, efforts to harness nationalist sentiments and form states based on national identity became one of the most powerful and dynamic movements in world history.

## REVOLUTIONARY IDEAS

Revolutionaries of the eighteenth and nineteenth centuries sought to fashion an equitable society by instituting governments that were responsive to the needs and interests of the peoples they governed. In justifying their policies, revolutionaries attacked monarchical and aristocratic regimes and argued for popular sovereignty—the idea that legitimate political authority resides not in kings but, rather, in the people who make up a society. In North America, colonists declared independence from British rule and instituted a new government founded on the principle of popular sovereignty. Soon thereafter, French revolutionaries abolished the monarchy and restructured the social order. French revolutionaries resented royal, noble, and clerical privileges and sought freedom of religion, liberty, and republicanism. Their goals resonated with many others in the Atlantic basin, including people in the Caribbean and Latin America, who fought their own revolutions in the name of liberty and freedom. Meanwhile, Napoleon Bonaparte's invasions of states in western Europe helped spread revolutionary ideas to much of the region.

### The Enlightenment

Isaac Newton's vision of the universe (discussed in chapter 23) was so powerful and persuasive that its influence extended well beyond science. His work suggested that rational analysis could lead to fresh insights about the human as well as the natural world. From Scotland to Sicily, and from Philadelphia to Moscow, European and Euro-American thinkers launched an ambitious project to transform human thought and to use reason to transform the world. Like the early modern scientists, they abandoned Aristotelian philosophy, Christian theology, and other traditionally recognized authorities, and they sought to subject the human world to purely rational analysis. The result of their work was a movement known as the **Enlightenment.**

**Science and Society** Enlightenment thinkers sought to discover natural laws that governed human society in the same way that Newton's laws of universal gravitation and motion regulated the universe. Their search took different forms. The English philosopher **John Locke** (1632–1704) worked to discover natural laws of politics. He attacked theories that promoted the idea that monarchs had a divine right to rule and, instead, advocated constitutional government on the grounds that sovereignty resides in the people rather than the state or its rulers. Indeed, he provided much of the theoretical justification for the Glorious Revolution of 1688 and the establishment of constitutional monarchy in England (discussed in chapter 23). The Scottish philosopher **Adam Smith** turned his attention to economic affairs and held that laws of supply and demand determine what happens in the marketplace. The French nobleman Charles Louis de Secondat, better known as the **Baron de Montesquieu** (1689–1755), sought to establish a science of politics and discover principles that would foster political liberty in a prosperous and stable state.

The center of Enlightenment thought was France, where prominent intellectuals known collectively as ***philosophes*** ("philosophers") advanced the cause of reason. The philosophes were not philosophers in the traditional sense of the term so much as public intellectuals. They addressed their works more to the educated public than to scholars: instead of formal philosophical treatises, they mostly composed histories, novels, dramas, satires, and pamphlets on religious, moral, and political issues.

**Voltaire** More than any other philosophe, François-Marie Arouet (1694–1778) epitomized the spirit of the Enlightenment. Writing under the pen name **Voltaire,** he published his first book at age seventeen. By the time of his death at age eighty-four, his published writings included some ten thousand letters and filled seventy volumes. With stinging wit and sometimes bitter irony, Voltaire championed individual freedom and attacked any institution sponsoring intolerant or oppressive policies. Targets of his caustic wit included the French monarchy and the Roman Catholic church. When the king of France sought to save money by reducing the number of horses kept in royal stables, for example, Voltaire suggested that it would be more effective to get rid of the asses who rode the horses. Voltaire also waged a long literary campaign against the Roman Catholic church, which he held responsible for fanaticism, intolerance, and incalculable human suffering. Voltaire's battle cry was *écrasez l'infame* ("crush the damned thing"), meaning the church that he considered an agent of oppression.

---

**Montesquieu** (MON-teh-skew)
***philosophes*** (fil-uh-sofs)
**Voltaire** (vohl-TAIR)

**Deism** Some philosophes were conventional Christians, while a few turned to atheism. Like Voltaire, however, most of them were **deists** who believed in the existence of a god but denied the supernatural teachings of Christianity, such as Jesus' virgin birth and his resurrection. To the deists the universe was an orderly realm. Deists held that a powerful god set the universe in motion and established natural laws that govern it, but did not take a personal interest in its development or intervene in its affairs. In a favorite simile of the deists, this god was like a watchmaker who did not need to interfere constantly in the workings of his creation because it operated by itself according to rational and natural laws.

**The Theory of Progress** Most philosophes were optimistic about the future of the world and humanity. They expected knowledge of human affairs to advance as fast as modern science, and they believed that rational understanding of human and natural affairs would bring about a new era of constant progress. In fact, progress became almost an ideology of the philosophes, who believed that natural science would lead to greater human control over the world while rational sciences of human affairs would lead to individual freedom and the construction of a prosperous, just, and equitable society.

The philosophes' fond wishes for progress, prosperity, and social harmony did not come to pass. Yet the Enlightenment helped to bring about a thorough cultural transformation of European society. It weakened the influence of organized religion, although it by no means destroyed institutional churches. Enlightenment thought encouraged the replacement of Christian values, which had guided European thought on religious and moral affairs for more than a millennium, with a new set of secular values. Furthermore, the Enlightenment encouraged political and cultural leaders to subject society to rational analysis and intervene actively in its affairs in the interests of promoting progress and prosperity.

## Popular Sovereignty

Since ancient times, kings or emperors ruled almost all settled agricultural societies. Small societies occasionally instituted democratic governments, in which all citizens participated in political affairs, or republican governments, in which delegates represented the interests of various constituencies. Some societies, especially those with weak central leadership, also relied on aristocratic governments, in which privileged elites supervised public affairs. But hierarchical rule flowing from a king or an emperor was by far the most common form of government in settled agricultural societies.

In justifying their rule, kings and emperors throughout the world often identified themselves with gods or claimed divine sanction for their authority. Some rulers were priests, although most cooperated closely with religious authorities. On the basis of their association with divine powers, kings and emperors claimed sovereignty—the authority to rule. In imperial China, for example, dynastic houses claimed to rule in accordance with the "mandate of heaven," and in early modern Europe monarchs often asserted a "divine right of kings" as the foundation of their authority.

During the seventeenth and eighteenth centuries, philosophes and other advocates of Enlightenment ideas began to question these long-standing notions of sovereignty. The philosophes rarely challenged monarchical rule but sought instead to make kings responsible to the people they governed. They commonly regarded government as the result of a contract between rulers and ruled. The English philosopher John Locke (1632–1704) formulated one of the most influential theories of contractual government. In his *Second Treatise of Civil Government,* published in 1690, Locke held that government arose in the remote past when people decided to work together, form civil society, and appoint rulers to protect and promote their common interests. Individuals granted political rights to their rulers but retained personal rights to life, liberty, and property. Any ruler who violated those rights was subject to being overthrown. Furthermore, according to Locke, because individuals voluntarily formed society and established government, rulers derived their authority from the consent of those whom they governed. If subjects withdrew their consent, they had the right to replace their rulers. In effect, Locke's political thought relocated sovereignty, removing it from rulers as divine agents and vesting it in the people of a society.

**Individual Freedom** Enlightenment thinkers addressed issues of freedom and equality as well as sovereignty. Philosophes such as Voltaire resented the persecution of religious minorities and censorship by royal officials, who had the power to prevent printers from publishing works that did not meet the approval of political and religious authorities. Philosophes called for religious toleration and freedom to express their views openly. When censors prohibited the publication of their writings in France, they often worked with French-speaking printers in Switzerland or the Netherlands who published their books and smuggled them across the border into France.

**Political and Legal Equality** Many Enlightenment thinkers also called for equality. They condemned the legal and social privileges enjoyed by aristocrats, who in the philosophes' view made no more contribution to the larger society than a peasant, an artisan, or a crafts worker. They recommended the creation of a society in which all individuals would be equal before the law. The most prominent advocate

**Jean-Jacques Rousseau** (zhahn-zhahk roo-soh)

Socially prominent women deeply influenced the development of Enlightenment thought by organizing and maintaining salons—gatherings where philosophes, scientists, and intellectuals discussed the leading ideas of the day. Although produced in 1814, this painting depicts the Parisian salon of Mme. Geoffrin (center left), a leading patron of the French philosophes, about 1775. In the background is a bust of Voltaire, who lived in Switzerland at the time.
The Picture Art Collection/Alamy Stock Photo

of political equality was the French-Swiss thinker **Jean-Jacques Rousseau** (1712–1778), who identified with simple working people and deeply resented the privileges enjoyed by elite classes. In his influential book ***The Social Contract*** (1762), Rousseau argued that members of a society were collectively the sovereign. In an ideal society all individuals would participate directly in the formulation of policy and the creation of laws. In the absence of royalty, aristocrats, or other privileged elites, the general will of the people would carry the day.

Enlightenment thought on freedom, equality, and popular sovereignty reflected the interests of educated and talented individuals who sought to increase their influence and enhance their status in society. Most Enlightenment thinkers were of common birth but comfortable means. Although seeking to limit the prerogatives of ruling and aristocratic classes, most did not envision a society in which they would share political rights with women, children, peasants, laborers, enslaved people, or people of color.

**Global Influence of Enlightenment Values** Enlightenment thought constituted a serious challenge to long-established notions of political and social order. Revolutionary leaders in Europe and the Americas readily adopted Enlightenment ideas when justifying their efforts to overhaul the political and social structures they inherited. Over time, Enlightenment political thought influenced the organization of states and societies throughout the world. In part, this was because reformers and revolutionaries around the Atlantic basin had access to a vibrant print culture that allowed people in distant places to read about—and be inspired by—ideologies and events happening elsewhere.

# REVOLUTIONS

## The American Revolution

In the mid-eighteenth century there were few signs that North America might become a center of revolution. Residents of the thirteen British colonies there regarded themselves as British subjects: they recognized British law, read English-language books, and often braved the stormy waters of the North Atlantic Ocean to visit friends and family in England. Trade brought prosperity to the colonies, and British military forces protected colonists' interests. From 1754 to 1763, for example, British forces waged an extremely expensive conflict in North America known as the French and Indian War. This conflict merged with a larger contest for imperial supremacy, the Seven Years' War (1756–1763), in which British and French forces battled each other in Europe and India as well as North America. Victory in the Seven Years' War ensured that Britain would dominate global trade and that British possessions, including the North American colonies, would prosper.

Engraved likeness of Deborah Sampson (1760–1827). During the American revolution, Sampson disguised herself as a man in order to serve as a soldier in the Continental army. She served as Robert Shirtliff for seventeen months, until she was discovered after being wounded in combat. She was honorably discharged in 1783.
FLHC 12/Alamy Stock Photo

**Tightened British Control of the Colonies** But the Seven Years' War also provided the circumstances in which American colonists became increasingly discontented with British rule. The war had been enormously expensive for the British government and had increased the tax burden of ordinary people living in Britain, so when it was over, the British government wanted the American colonists to help pay their fair share for the continuing maintenance and protection of the colonies. To achieve this, the British Parliament passed legislation to levy new taxes on goods and services in the colonies. But the American colonists had become accustomed to a degree of autonomy from the British government. Nearly every colony had an elective legislative assembly that controlled legislation affecting taxation and defense and that ultimately controlled the salaries paid to royal officials. They had also grown used to very lax enforcement of taxes and duties on imported goods. Thus, when the British attempted to increase its control in the colonies, the colonists resisted. Colonists especially resented the imposition of taxes on molasses by the Sugar Act (1764), on publications and legal documents by the Stamp Act (1765), on a wide variety of imported items by the Townshend Act (1767), and on tea by the Tea Act (1773). They objected to strict enforcement of navigation laws—some of them a century old, but widely disregarded—that required cargoes to travel in British ships and clear British customs. Colonists also took offense at the Quartering Act (1765), which required them to provide housing and accommodations for British troops.

In responding to British policies, the colonists argued that Parliament could not make policy for the colonies without the consent of the colonists themselves because they were protected by all the common-law rights of British citizens. The colonists in effect embraced legal traditions that were first demonstrated during the English civil war (1641–1651), establishing the constitutional precedent that an English monarch cannot govern without Parliament's consent. This concept was legally enshrined in the Bill of Rights (1689), which established, among other rights, that the consent of Parliament is required for the implementation of new taxes. Thus, the colonists responded to the imposition of new taxes by Parliament with the slogan "no taxation without representation." They boycotted British products; physically attacked British officials; and mounted protests such as the Boston Tea Party (1773), in which colonists dumped a cargo of tea into Boston harbor rather than pay duties under the Tea Act. They also organized the **Continental Congress** (1774), which coordinated the resistance to British policies across the thirteen colonies. By 1775 tensions were so high that British troops and a colonial militia skirmished at the village of Lexington, near Boston. The **American revolution** had begun.

**The Declaration of Independence** On 4 July 1776 the Continental Congress adopted a document titled "The unanimous Declaration of the thirteen united States of America." This **Declaration of Independence** drew deep inspiration from Enlightenment political thought in justifying the colonies' quest for independence. The document asserted "that all men are created equal, that they are endowed by their Creator with certain unalienable Rights, that among these are Life, Liberty, and the pursuit of Happiness." It echoed John Locke's contractual theory of government in arguing that individuals established governments to secure those rights and that governments derive their power and authority from "the consent of the governed." When any government infringes upon individuals' rights, the document continued, "it is the Right of the People to alter or abolish it, and to institute new Government." The Declaration of Independence presented a long list of specific abuses charged to the British crown and concluded by proclaiming the colonies "Free and Independent States" with "full Power to levy War, conclude Peace, contract Alliances, establish Commerce, and to do all other Acts and Things which Independent States may of right do."

**Divided Loyalties** It was one thing to declare independence, but a different matter altogether to make independence a reality. At the beginning of the war for independence, Britain enjoyed many advantages over the rebels: a strong government with clear lines of authority, the most powerful navy in the world, a competent army, a sizable population of loyalists in the colonies, and an overall colonial population with mixed sentiments about revolution and independence from Britain. In their political views and attitudes, the colonial population was far from homogeneous. Political loyalties varied between and within regions and communities and frequently shifted during the course of the revolution. Although "patriots," those who supported the revolution, were in the majority, not every colonist favored a violent confrontation with the British Empire. An estimated 20 percent of the white population of the colonies were "loyalists" or "Tories" who remained loyal to the British monarchy. A minority of people tried to stay neutral in the conflict, most notably the Religious Society of Friends of Pennsylvania, a religious movement better known as the Quakers. Native Americans were also divided in their loyalties. Tribes that depended on colonial trade usually threw

*Washington Crossing the Delaware* is an 1851 oil-on-canvas painting by German American artist Emanuel Leutze. It commemorates Washington's crossing of the Delaware on 25 December 1776, during the American revolutionary war. A copy of this painting hangs in the West Wing reception area of the White House The painting emphasizes the mythological qualities of Washington as hero.
The Metropolitan Museum of Art, New York, Gift of John Stewart Kennedy, 1897

their weight behind the patriots, but most Native Americans east of the Mississippi distrusted the colonists based on plentiful past experience and thus supported the British cause.

**MAP 16.1 The American revolution, 1781.**

Note both the location of the major towns and cities in the colonies and the location of the major battles that occurred during the revolution.

***Why were both situated so close to the eastern coast?***

**Colonial Advantages** In spite of Britain's many advantages, it nevertheless lost the war. This can be explained in part by the distance between Britain and the colonies because the British had to ship supplies and troops across the Atlantic in order to engage in combat. **George Washington** (1732–1799) also provided strong and imaginative military leadership for the colonial army while local militias employed guerrilla tactics effectively against British forces. Most important, however, was the eventual support rival European powers—especially France—gave to the American colonists. The French had reason to help the colonists because they wanted revenge against the British for their recent losses in the Seven Years' War. Once the Americans proved they could fight effectively by defeating a British army at Saratoga in 1777, the French entered into a formal alliance with them. By 1780, the French were providing the Americans with not only substantial sums of money but also naval support and a large force of trained soldiers and officers.

In fact, the French were critical in forcing the British to surrender at Yorktown in October 1781. An army of French and American soldiers had surrounded the British forces of Charles Cornwallis at Yorktown, Virginia, and laid siege to his encampment. Cornwallis had planned to escape via the sea but found his way blocked by a French naval force in the Chesapeake Bay and was forced to surrender. Although the war continued into 1782, Cornwallis' surrender ensured an eventual American victory. In September 1783 diplomats concluded the Peace of Paris, by which the British government formally recognized American independence, thanks in very large measure to French aid.

**Building an Independent State** The leaders of the fledgling republic organized a state that reflected Enlightenment principles. In 1787 a constitutional convention drafted the blueprint for a new system of government—the Constitution of the United States—which emphasized the rights of individuals. American leaders based the federal government on popular

A contemporary print depicts the storming of the Bastille in 1789. The deeds of common people working in crowds became a favorite theme of artists after the outbreak of the French revolution.
PRISMA ARCHIVO/Alamy Stock Photo

sovereignty, and they agreed to follow this written constitution that guaranteed individual liberties such as freedom of speech, of the press, and of religion. They did not, however, grant political and legal equality to all inhabitants of the newly independent land. They accorded full rights only to men of property, withholding them from landless men, women, enslaved people, and indigenous peoples. Over time, however, disenfranchised groups claimed and struggled for political and legal rights. Their campaigns involved considerable personal sacrifice and sometimes led to violence because those in possession of rights did not share them readily with others. Yet in spite of its imperfections, the early American republic served as an inspiration to others around the Atlantic basin, who similarly sought to create governments based on popular sovereignty.

## The French Revolution

Among those most inspired by the success of the American revolution were the French philosophes and their followers, who for decades had been arguing in favor of popular sovereignty and greater social and political equality. Although French Enlightenment thinkers drew inspiration from the American example, the **French revolution** that began in 1789 was a more radical affair than its American counterpart. American revolutionary leaders sought independence from British imperial rule, but they were content to retain British law and much of their British social and cultural heritage. In contrast, French revolutionary leaders repudiated existing society; often referred to as the ***ancien régime*** ("old order"); and sought to replace it with new political, social, and cultural structures.

**The Estates General** Serious fiscal problems within the French government provided the opportunity for French revolutionaries to put their ideas into practice. In the 1780s approximately half of the French royal government's revenue went to pay off war debts—nearly a quarter of which were amassed as a result of French support for colonists in the war of American independence. Combined with the need to maintain the French armed forces and the lavish spending of the French court, by 1789 the French government faced complete bankruptcy. King **Louis XVI** (reigned 1774–1793) was unable to raise more revenue from the overburdened peasantry, so he sought to increase taxes on the French nobility. The nobility, which had traditionally been exempt from taxation, protested. This then forced Louis to summon the **Estates General,** which was an assembly that represented the entire French population through groups known as estates, to get the money he needed. In the ancien

***ancien régime*** (ahn-syen REY-zheem)
**Louis** (LOO-ee)

régime there were three estates, or political classes. The first estate consisted of about one hundred thousand Roman Catholic clergy, and the second included some four hundred thousand nobles. The third estate embraced the rest of the population—about twenty-four million serfs; free peasants; and urban residents ranging from laborers, artisans, and shopkeepers to physicians, bankers, and attorneys. Though founded in 1303, the Estates General had not met since 1614. The third estate had as many delegates as the other two estates combined, but that numerical superiority offered no advantage when the assembly voted on issues because voting took place by estate—one vote for each—rather than by individuals.

In May 1789 King Louis called the Estates General into session at the royal palace of Versailles in hopes that it would authorize new taxes and save the kingdom from financial ruin. Louis never controlled the assembly. Representatives of the third estate arrived at Versailles demanding political and social reform based on Enlightenment thinking regarding popular sovereignty. Although some members of the lower clergy and a few prominent nobles supported such reforms, in general the first and second estates were far more socially and politically conservative than the third estate and actively thwarted efforts to push reforms through the Estates General.

**The National Assembly** On 17 June 1789, after several weeks of fruitless debate, representatives of the third estate took the dramatic step of seceding from the Estates General and proclaiming themselves to be the **National Assembly.** Three days later, meeting in an indoor tennis court, members of the new Assembly swore not to disband until they had provided France with a new constitution. On 14 July 1789 a Parisian crowd, fearing that the king sought to undo events of the previous weeks, stormed the Bastille, a royal jail and arsenal, in search of weapons. The military garrison protecting the Bastille surrendered to the crowd but only after killing many of the attackers. To vent their rage, members of the crowd hacked the defenders to death. One assailant used his pocketknife to sever the garrison commander's head, which the victorious crowd mounted on a pike and paraded around the streets of Paris. News of the event soon spread, sparking insurrections in cities throughout France.

Emboldened by popular support, the National Assembly undertook a broad program of political and social reform. The **Declaration of the Rights of Man and the Citizen,** which the National Assembly promulgated in August 1789, articulated its guiding principles. Reflecting the influence of American revolutionary ideas, the Declaration of the Rights of Man and the Citizen proclaimed the equality of all men; declared that sovereignty resided in the people; and asserted individual rights to liberty, property, and security.

**Liberty, Equality, and Fraternity** Between 1789 and 1791 the National Assembly reconfigured French society. Taking "liberty, equality, and fraternity" as its goals, the Assembly abolished the old social order along with the many fees and labor services that peasants owed to their landlords. It dramatically altered the role of the church in French society by seizing church lands, abolishing the first estate, defining clergy as civilians, and requiring clergy to take an oath of loyalty to the state. It also issued a constitution that made the king the chief executive official but deprived him of legislative authority. France became a constitutional monarchy in which men of property—about half the adult male population—had the right to vote in elections to choose legislators. In these ways, the French revolution represented an effort to put Enlightenment political thought into practice.

**The Convention** The revolution soon took a radical turn. The French nobility, who were not happy with their diminished status, sought to mobilize foreign powers in support of

The guillotine was an efficient killing machine during the French revolution. In this contemporary print the executioner displays the just-severed head of King Louis XVI to the crowd assembled to witness his execution.
adoc-photos/Corbis Historical/Getty Images

# SOURCES FROM THE PAST

## Declaration of the Rights of Man and the Citizen

*This declaration, which became part of the official revolutionary platform in France in August 1789, was written in close collaboration with Thomas Jefferson, the principal author of the American Declaration of Independence and the U.S. ambassador to France that year. Thus it is not surprising that the Declaration of the Rights of Man and the Citizen reflects the strong influence of American revolutionary ideas.*

**First Article. Men are born** and remain free and equal in rights. Social distinctions may be based only on common utility.

Article 2. The goal of every political association is the preservation of the natural and inalienable rights of man. These rights are liberty, property, security, and resistance to oppression.

Article 3. The principle of all sovereignty resides essentially in the nation. No body and no individual can exercise authority that does not flow directly from the nation.

> According to this statement, was it possible for kings to be sovereign?

Article 4. Liberty consists in the freedom to do anything that does not harm another. The exercise of natural rights of each man thus has no limits except those that assure other members of society their enjoyment of the same rights. These limits may be determined only by law . . .

Article 6. Law is the expression of the general will. All citizens have the right to participate either personally or through their representatives in the making of law. The law must be the same for all, whether it protects or punishes. Being equal in the eyes of the law, all citizens are equally eligible for all public honors, offices, and occupations, according to their abilities, without any distinction other than that of their virtues and talents.

Article 7. No person shall be accused, arrested, or imprisoned except in the cases and according to the forms prescribed by law. Any one soliciting, transmitting, executing, or causing to be executed, any arbitrary order, shall be punished. But any citizen summoned or arrested in virtue of the law shall submit without delay, as resistance constitutes an offense . . .

Article 9. As all persons are held innocent until they shall have been declared guilty, if arrest shall be deemed indispensable, all harshness not essential to the securing of the prisoner's person shall be severely repressed by law . . .

Article 11. The free communication of thoughts and opinions is one of the most precious rights of man: every citizen may thus speak, write, and publish freely, but will be responsible for abuse of this freedom in cases decided by the law . . .

> Is it possible to learn something of French society under the ancien régime by reading these articles?

Article 13. For the maintenance of public military force and for the expenses of administration, common taxation is necessary: it must be equally divided among all citizens according to their means . . .

Article 15. Society has the right to require from every public official an accounting of his administration.

Article 16. Any society in which guarantees of rights are not assured and separation of powers is not defined has no constitution at all.

Article 17. Property is an inviolable and sacred right. No one may be deprived of property except when public necessity, legally determined, clearly requires it, and on condition of just and prearranged compensation.

### For Further Reflection

- In what ways do the principles established in the Declaration reflect the political transformations taking place throughout the age of Atlantic revolutions?
- What Enlightenment ideals are evident in the Declaration?
- What is the difference between "equality" and "equal in rights"?
- Why is the word "inalienable" so power?
- Why is the context, described before the passage, so significant?

Source: *Déclaration des droits de l'homme et du citoyen (Declaration of the Rights of Man and the Citizen, 1789).* Translated by Jerry H. Bentley.

the king and to restore the ancien régime. This gave the Assembly the pretext to declare war against Austria and Prussia in April 1792. Adding to the military burden of France, revolutionary leaders declared war in the following year on Spain, Britain, and the Netherlands. Fearing military defeat and counterrevolution, revolutionary leaders created the Convention, a new legislative body elected by universal manhood suffrage, which abolished the monarchy and proclaimed

France a republic. The Convention rallied the French population by instituting the ***levée en masse*** ("mass levy"), or universal conscription that drafted people and resources for use in the war against invading forces. The Convention also rooted out enemies at home. It made frequent use of the guillotine, a recently invented machine that brought about supposedly humane executions by quickly severing a victim's head. In 1793 King Louis XVI and his wife, Queen Marie Antoinette, themselves were killed by guillotine when the Convention found them guilty of treason.

Revolutionary chaos reached its peak in 1793 and 1794 when Maximilien Robespierre (1758–1794) and the radical Jacobin party dominated the Convention. A lawyer by training, Robespierre had emerged during the revolution as a ruthless but popular radical known as "the Incorruptible," and he dominated the Committee of Public Safety, the executive authority of the Republic. The Jacobins believed passionately that France needed complete restructuring, and they unleashed a campaign of terror to promote their revolutionary agenda. They sought to eliminate the influence of Christianity in French society by closing churches and forcing priests to take wives. They promoted a new "cult of reason" as a secular alternative to Christianity. They reorganized the calendar, keeping months of thirty days but replacing seven-day weeks with ten-day units that recognized no day of religious observance. The Jacobins also proclaimed the inauguration of a new historical era with the Year I, which began with the declaration of the First Republic on 22 September 1792. They encouraged citizens to display their revolutionary zeal by wearing working-class clothes. They granted increased rights to women by permitting them to inherit property and divorce their husbands, although they did not allow women to vote or participate in political affairs. The Jacobins also made frequent use of the guillotine: between the summer of 1793 and the summer of 1794, they executed about forty thousand people and imprisoned three hundred thousand suspected enemies of the revolution. Even the feminist Olympe de Gouges (1748–1793)—to whom we were introduced in the introduction to this chapter—was a victim of the Jacobins, who did not appreciate her efforts to extend the rights of freedom and equality to women.

Jacques-Louis David's *Napoleon on Horseback at the St. Bernard Pass* (1800) presents a famously heroic image of Napoleon's attack on Italy in 1800. David's art clearly served the interests of Napoleon's political regime. The powerful and dynamic image was intended to convey Napoleon's greatness and his place in the history of conquering heroes.
Leemage/Corbis/Getty Images

**The Directory** Many victims of this **reign of terror** were fellow radicals who fell out of favor with Robespierre and the Jacobins. The instability of revolutionary leadership eventually undermined confidence in the regime itself. In July 1794 the Convention arrested Robespierre and his allies, convicted them of tyranny, and sent them to the guillotine. A group of conservative men of property then seized power and ruled France under a new institution known as the Directory (1795–1799). Though more pragmatic than previous revolutionary leaders, members of the Directory were unable to resolve the economic and military problems that plagued revolutionary France. In seeking a middle way between the ancien régime and radical revolution, they lurched from one policy to another and faced constant challenges to their authority. The Directory came to an end in November 1799 when a young general named Napoleon Bonaparte staged a coup d'état and seized power.

## The Reign of Napoleon

Born to a minor noble family of Corsica, a Mediterranean island annexed by France in 1768, **Napoleon Bonaparte** (1769–1821) studied at French military schools and became an officer in the army of King Louis XVI. A brilliant military leader, he became a general at age twenty-four. He was a fervent supporter of the revolution and defended the Directory against a popular uprising in 1795. In a campaign of 1796–1797, he drove the Austrian army from northern Italy and established French rule there. In 1798 he mounted an invasion of Egypt to gain access to the Red Sea and threaten British control of the sea route to India, but the campaign ended in a complete British victory. Politically ambitious, Napoleon returned to France in 1799; overthrew the Directory; and set

***levée en masse*** (le-VAY ahn mahs)
**Napoleon Bonaparte** (nuh-POH-lee-uhn BOH-nuh-pahrt)

up a new government, the Consulate. Although he ostensibly shared power with two other consuls, it was Napoleon who was henceforth the real master of France. Having established a dictatorship, he crowned himself emperor in 1804.

**Napoleonic France** Napoleon brought political stability to a land torn by revolution and war. He made peace with the Roman Catholic church and in 1801 concluded an agreement with the pope. The pact, known as the Concordat, provided that the French state would retain church lands seized during the revolution, but the state agreed to pay clerics' salaries, recognize Roman Catholic Christianity as the preferred faith of France, and extend freedom of religion to Protestant Christians and Jews. This measure won Napoleon a great deal of support from people who supported the political and social goals of the revolution but balked at radicals' efforts to replace Christianity with a cult of reason.

In 1804 Napoleon issued the **Civil Code,** a revised body of civil law, which also helped stabilize French society. The Civil Code affirmed the political and legal equality of all adult men and established a merit-based society in which individuals qualified for education and employment because of talent rather than birth or social standing. The code protected private property, and Napoleon allowed aristocratic opponents of the revolution to return to France and reclaim some of the property that had been taken from them. The Civil Code confirmed many of the moderate revolutionary policies of the National Assembly but retracted measures passed by the more radical Convention. For example, the code restored patriarchal authority in the family by making women and children subservient to male heads of households. And although he approved the Enlightenment ideal of equality, Napoleon was no champion of intellectual freedom or representative government. He limited free speech and routinely censored newspapers and other publications. He established a secret police force that relied heavily on spies and detained suspected political opponents by the thousands. He made systematic use of propaganda to manipulate public opinion. He ignored elective bodies and surrounded himself with loyal military officers who ensured that representative assemblies did not restrict his authority. When he crowned himself emperor, he founded a dynasty that set his family above and apart from the people in whose name they ruled.

**Napoleon's Empire** While working to stabilize France, Napoleon also sought to extend his authority throughout Europe. Napoleon's armies conquered Spain, Portugal, and Italy; occupied the Netherlands; and inflicted humiliating defeats on Austrian and Prussian forces. Napoleon sent his brothers and other relatives to rule the conquered and occupied lands, and he forced Austria, Prussia, and Russia to ally with him and respect French hegemony in Europe. But Napoleon's empire began to unravel in 1812, when he decided to invade Russia. Convinced that the tsar was conspiring with his British enemies, Napoleon led a Grand Army of six hundred thousand soldiers to Moscow. He captured the city, but the tsar withdrew and refused to surrender. Russians set Moscow ablaze, leaving Napoleon's massive army without adequate shelter or supplies. By the end of the campaign, more than 400,000 French soldiers had died.

**The Fall of Napoleon** Napoleon's disastrous Russian campaign emboldened his enemies. A coalition of British, Austrian, Prussian, and Russian armies converged on France and forced Napoleon to abdicate his throne in April 1814. The victors restored the French monarchy and exiled Napoleon to the tiny Mediterranean island of Elba, near Corsica. But Napoleon's adventure had not yet come to an end. In March 1815 he escaped from Elba, returned to France, and reconstituted his army. For a hundred days he ruled France again before a British army defeated him at **Waterloo** in Belgium. Unwilling to take further chances with the wily general, European powers banished Napoleon to the remote and isolated island of St. Helena in the South Atlantic Ocean, where he died of natural causes in 1821.

## The Haitian Revolution

The success of the American revolution appealed not only to French social reformers but also to enslaved people and free people of color in the Caribbean. But on the French portion of the island of Hispaniola it was the French revolution that provided the immediate inspiration and the opportunity for the revolution that broke out there in 1791.

Indeed, the only successful slave revolt in history took place on Hispaniola in the midst of the French revolution. By the eighteenth century, Hispaniola was a major center of sugar production with hundreds of prosperous plantations. The Spanish colony of Santo Domingo occupied the eastern part of the island (modern Dominican Republic), and the French colony of Saint-Domingue occupied the western part (modern Haiti). Saint-Domingue was one of the richest of all European colonies in the Caribbean: sugar, coffee, and cotton produced there accounted for almost one-third of France's foreign trade.

**Saint-Domingue Society** On the eve of the **Haitian revolution,** the population of Saint-Domingue was comprised of three major groups. There were about forty thousand white colonials, subdivided into several classes: European-born Frenchmen who monopolized colonial administrative posts; a class of plantation owners, chiefly minor aristocrats who hoped to return to France as soon as possible; and lower-class whites, who included artisans, shopkeepers, slave dealers, and day laborers. A second group comprised about twenty-eight thousand ***gens de couleur*** (French for "people of color"), most of whom were mixed race. Many of them were artisans, domestic servants, or overseers, but a small and influential proportion owned small plots of land and held enslaved people. The remainder of the population made up the third group, consisting of some five hundred thousand enslaved people, some of

***gens de couleur*** (zhen de coo-LEHR)

## MAP 16.2 Napoleon's empire in 1812.

Observe the number of states dependent on or allied with Napoleon in contrast to those who were at war with him.

***Were there geographic conditions that allowed some states to resist Napoleon's efforts at conquest better than others?***

whom were mixed-race and born in St. Domingue but most of whom were African-born.

Most of the colony's enslaved people toiled in fields under brutal conditions. Planters worked enslaved people so hard and provided them with so little care that mortality was very high. Not surprisingly, white planters and enslaved people frequently had violent conflicts. Aware that they were outnumbered by enslaved people by a factor of more than ten, plantation owners lived in constant fear of rebellion. Many enslaved people ran away into the mountains. By the late eighteenth century, Saint-Domingue had many large communities of maroons (enslaved people who had run away), who maintained their own societies and sometimes attacked plantations in search of food, weapons, tools, and additional recruits. As planters lost laborers as a result of death and escape, they imported new enslaved people from Africa and other Caribbean islands. This pattern continued throughout the eighteenth century, until prices of new slaves from Africa rose dramatically.

The American and French revolutions both inspired and helped to ignite violent political and social revolution in Saint-Domingue. Because the French government supported North American colonists against British rule, colonial governors in Saint-Domingue sent about five hundred *gens de couleur* to fight in the American war of independence. Having seen revolutionary ideals in practice, they returned to Saint-Domingue with the intention of reforming society there. Then, when the French revolution broke out a few years later in 1789, white settlers in Saint-Domingue sought the right to govern themselves, but they opposed proposals to grant political and legal equality to the *gens de couleur.* By May 1791 civil war had broken out between white settlers and *gens de couleur.*

Nineteenth-century mural of Jean-Jacques Dessalines (1758–1806), a leader of the Haitian Revolution and the first ruler of independent Haiti under the constitution of 1805. Historic Images/Alamy Stock Photo

**Slave Revolt** The conflict expanded dramatically when a charismatic Voudou priest named Boukman organized a slave revolt. In August 1791 some twelve thousand enslaved people began a campaign of killing white settlers, burning their homes, and destroying their plantations. Within a few weeks the rebels attracted almost one hundred thousand enslaved people into their ranks. Many enslaved people were battle-tested veterans of wars in Africa, and they drew on their military experience to organize large armies. Slave leaders also found recruits and reinforcements in Saint-Domingue's maroon communities. Foreign armies soon complicated the situation: French troops arrived in 1792 to restore order, and British and Spanish forces intervened in 1793 in hopes of benefiting from France's difficulties.

**Toussaint Louverture** Boukman died while fighting shortly after launching the revolt, but slave forces eventually overcame white settlers, *gens de couleur,* and foreign armies. Their successes were due largely to the leadership of François-Dominique **Toussaint** (1744-1803), who after 1791 called himself **Louverture**—from the French *l'ouverture,* meaning "the opening," to indicate the one who created an opening in enemy ranks. The son of enslaved parents, Toussaint learned to read and write from a Roman Catholic priest. Because of his education and intelligence, he rose to the position of livestock overseer on the plantation where he was enslaved. Later, he leased land for planting coffee, where he used "rented" slaves for labor. He was able to buy his freedom in 1776. When the slave revolt broke out in 1791, Toussaint helped his masters escape to a safe place, then left the plantation and joined the rebels.

Toussaint was a skilled organizer, and by 1793 he had taken a leadership role in the revolt and built a strong, disciplined army. He shrewdly played French, British, and Spanish forces against one another while also jockeying for power with

**Toussaint Louverture** (too-SAHNT loo-vehr-TOOR)

INTERPRETING IMAGES

A French depiction of the Battle of Crête à Pierrot (March 4–12, 1802) during the Haitian Revolution.

**Analyze** *Compare and contrast the Haitian Revolution with the French and American Revolutions. How are they depicted in the paintings here and on pages 519 and 521?*

Niday Picture Library/Alamy Stock Photo

other African and mixed-race generals. By 1797 he led an army of twenty thousand and controlled most of Saint-Domingue. In 1801 he issued a constitution that granted equality and citizenship to all residents of Saint-Domingue. He stopped short of declaring independence from France, however, because he did not want to provoke Napoleon—who had by that time seized power in France—into attacking the island.

**The Republic of Haiti** Toussaint's worries about Napoleon were well founded. In 1802 Napoleon dispatched forty thousand troops to restore French authority in Saint-Domingue. Toussaint attempted to negotiate a peaceful settlement, but the French commander arrested him and sent him to France, where he died in jail of maltreatment in 1803. By the time he died, however, yellow fever had ravaged the French army in Saint-Domingue, and the generals who took Toussaint's place had defeated the remaining troops and driven them out of the colony. Late in 1803 they declared independence, and on 1 January 1804 they proclaimed the establishment of Haiti, meaning "land of mountains," which became the second independent republic in the Western Hemisphere after the United States.

## Wars of Independence in Latin America

**Latin American Society** Revolutionary ideals also traveled to the Spanish and Portuguese colonies in the Americas. Though governed by ***peninsulares*** (colonial officials from Spain or Portugal), the Iberian colonies all had a large, wealthy, and powerful class of ***criollos*** (creoles), or people of European descent who had been born in the Americas. In 1800 the *peninsulares* numbered about 30,000, while the creole population was 3.5 million. The Iberian colonies also had a large population—about 10 million in all—of less privileged classes. Enslaved people formed a majority in Brazil, but elsewhere indigenous peoples and individuals of mixed European and African or European and indigenous ancestry were most numerous.

Creoles benefited greatly during the eighteenth century as they established plantations and ranches in the colonies and participated in rapidly expanding trade with Spain and Portugal. Yet the creoles also had grievances. Like British colonists in North America, the creoles resented administrative control and economic regulations imposed by the Iberian powers. They drew inspiration from Enlightenment political thought and occasionally took part in tax revolts and popular uprisings. The creoles desired neither social reform like that promoted by Robespierre nor the establishment of an egalitarian society like Haiti. Rather, they sought to displace the *peninsulares* but retain their privileged position in society: political independence on the model of the United States in North America struck them as an attractive alternative to colonial status. Their opportunity came as a result of the Napoleonic Wars in Europe because Napoleon invaded and conquered Portugal in 1807 and Spain in 1808. In the Spanish case, this effectively left Spanish settlers in the Americas to rule themselves until Napoleon was defeated and the Spanish king was restored in 1814. As a result of their experiences with self-rule, between 1810 and 1825 creoles led movements that brought independence to all Spanish colonies

***peninsulares*** (peh-neen-soo-LAH-rehs)
***criollos*** (kree-OH-yohs)

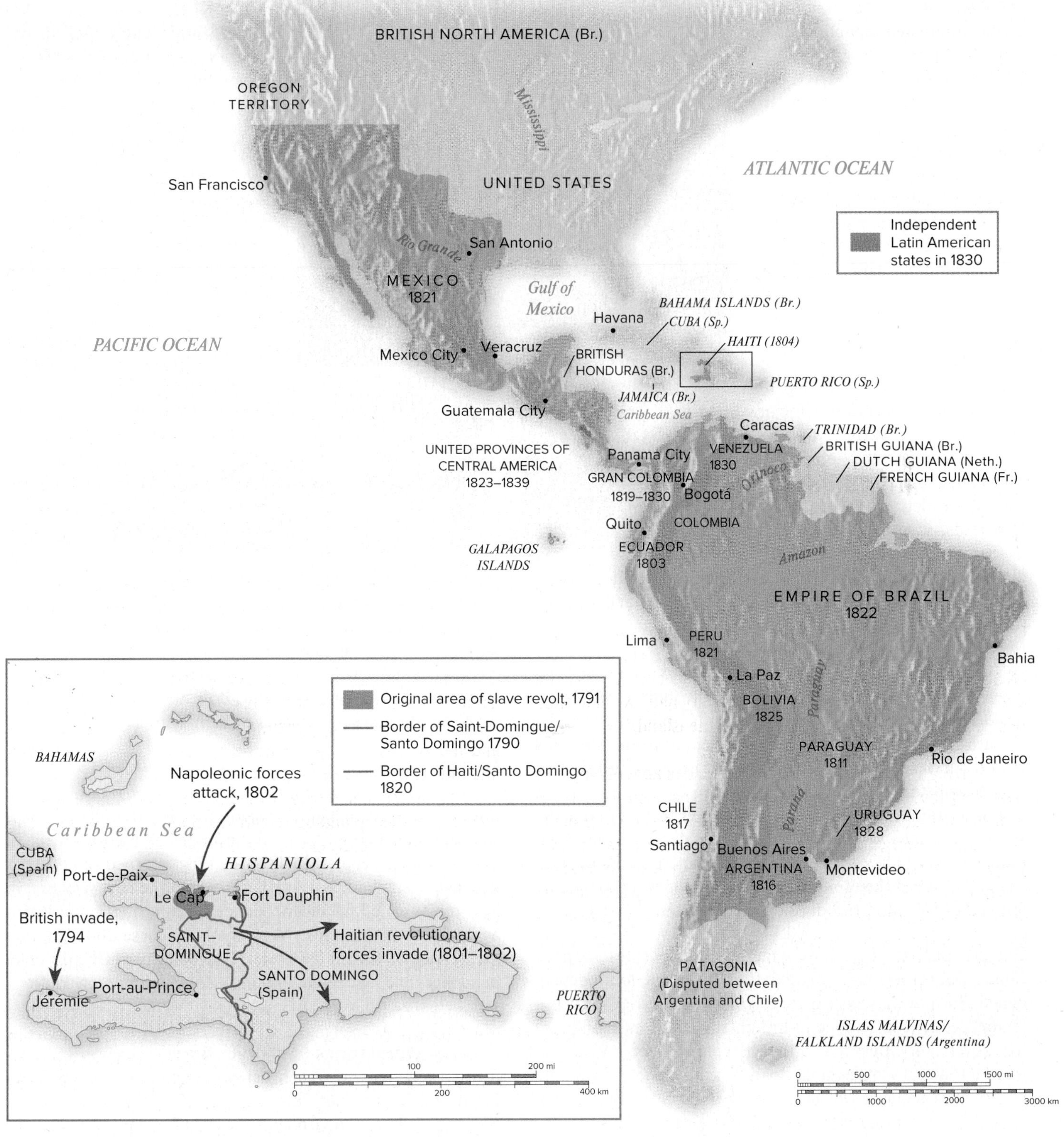


## MAP 16.3 Latin America in 1830.

Note the dates each state won its independence.

***Since most states became independent in very close succession, what conditions prevented Latin American states from joining together in a federation like that in the United States?***

***How did the Haitian, French, and American revolutions inspire the Latin American independence movements of the early nineteenth century?***

in the Americas—except Cuba and Puerto Rico—and established creole-dominated republics.

**Mexican Independence** By 1810, weakened royal authority in the Americas spurred revolts against Spanish rule in Argentina, Venezuela, and Mexico. The most serious was a peasant rebellion in Mexico led by a parish priest, **Miguel Hidalgo y Costilla** (1753–1811), who rallied indigenous peoples and mestizos—people of mixed European and indigenous descent—against colonial rule. Many contemporaries viewed Hidalgo's movement for independence from Spanish rule as social and economic warfare by the masses against the elites of Mexican society, particularly since he called for the death of Spaniards. Conservative creoles soon captured Hidalgo and executed him, but his rebellion continued to flare for three years after his death. Hidalgo became the symbol of Mexican independence, and the day on which he proclaimed his revolt—16 September 1810—is Mexico's principal national holiday.

Simón Bolívar, creole leader of the independence movement in Latin America, was a favorite subject of painters in the nineteenth century.
Photo Researchers/Science Source

Colonial rule in Mexico actually came to an end in 1821, when the creole general Augustín de Iturbide (1783–1824) declared independence from Spain. In the following year, he declared himself emperor of Mexico. Neither Iturbide nor his empire survived for long. Though an able general, Iturbide was an incompetent administrator, and in 1823 creole elites deposed him and established a republic. Two years later the southern regions of the Mexican empire declared their own independence. They formed a Central American Federation until 1838, when they split into the independent states of Guatemala, El Salvador, Honduras, Nicaragua, and Costa Rica.

**Simón Bolívar** In South America, creole elites such as **Simón Bolívar** (1783–1830) led the movement for independence. Born in Caracas (in modern Venezuela), Bolívar was a fervent republican steeped in Enlightenment ideas about popular sovereignty. Inspired by the example of George Washington, he took up arms against Spanish rule in 1811, during the period of weakened royal authority when the Spanish king had been deposed. In the early days of his struggle, Bolívar experienced many reversals and twice went into exile. In 1819, however, he assembled an army that surprised and crushed the Spanish army—sent by the Spanish King Ferdinand VII almost immediately after his restoration to power in 1814—in Colombia. Later, he campaigned in Venezuela, Ecuador, and Peru, coordinating his efforts with other creole leaders, such as José de San Martín (1778–1850) in Argentina and Bernardo O'Higgins (1778–1842) in Chile. By 1825 creole forces had overcome Spanish armies and deposed Spanish rulers throughout South America.

Bolívar's goal was to weld the former Spanish colonies of South America into a great confederation like the United States in North America. During the 1820s independent Venezuela, Colombia, and Ecuador formed a republic called **Gran Colombia,** and Bolívar attempted to bring Peru and Bolivia (named for Bolívar himself) into the confederation as well. By 1830, however, strong political and regional differences had undermined Gran Colombia. As the confederation disintegrated, a bitterly disappointed Bolívar pronounced South America "ungovernable" and lamented that "those who have served the revolution have plowed the sea." Shortly after the breakup of Gran Colombia, Bolívar died of tuberculosis while en route to self-imposed exile in Europe.

**Brazilian Independence** Independence came to Portuguese Brazil at the same time as to Spanish colonies, but by a different process. When Napoleon invaded Portugal in 1807, the royal court fled Lisbon and established a government in exile in Rio de Janeiro. In 1821 the king returned to Portugal, leaving his son Pedro in Brazil as regent. The next year Brazilian creoles called for independence from Portugal, and Pedro agreed to their demands. When the Portuguese *Cortes* (parliament) tried to curtail his power, Pedro declared Brazil's independence and accepted appointment as Emperor Pedro I (reigned 1822–1834).

**Creole Dominance** Although Brazil achieved independence as a monarchy rather than a republic, creole elites dominated Brazilian society just as they did in former Spanish colonies. Indeed, independence brought little social change in Latin America. The *peninsulares* returned to Europe, but Latin American society remained as rigidly stratified as it had been in 1800. The newly independent states granted military authority to local charismatic strongmen, known as ***caudillos,*** who allied with creole elites. The new states also permitted the continuation of slavery, confirmed the wealth and authority of the Roman

---

**Miguel Hidalgo y Costilla** (mee-GEL hee-DAHL-goh ee koh-STEE-ya)
**Simón Bolívar** (see-MOHN boh-LEE-vahr)
***caudillos*** (KAW-dee-ohs)

Catholic church, and repressed the poor. The principal beneficiaries of independence in Latin America were the creole elites.

# CONSEQUENCES AND IMPLICATIONS OF THE REVOLUTIONS

The ideals of the Atlantic revolutions resulted in the birth of new ideologies, including especially the ideologies of conservatism and liberalism. An ideology is a coherent vision of human nature, human society, and the larger world that proposes some particular form of political and social organization as ideal. Whereas conservatism sought to justify the current state of affairs, liberalism sharply criticized the status quo and argued for the need to improve society. The revolutions also encouraged social reformers to organize broader programs of liberation. Whereas the American, French, and Latin American revolutions guaranteed political and legal rights to white men, social reformers sought to extend those rights to women and slaves of African ancestry. During the nineteenth century all European and American states abolished slavery, but former slaves and their descendants remained an underprivileged and oppressed class in most of the Atlantic world. The quest for women's rights also proceeded slowly during the nineteenth century.

## The Emergence of New Ideologies

### Conservatism

The modern ideology of **conservatism** arose as political and social theorists responded to the challenges of the American and especially the French revolutions. Conservatives viewed society as an organism that changed slowly over the generations. The English political philosopher Edmund Burke (1729–1797) held, for example, that society was a compact between a people's ancestors, the present generation, and their descendants as yet unborn. While admitting the need for gradual change that came about by general consensus, Burke condemned radical or revolutionary change, which in his view could only lead to anarchy. Thus Burke approved of the American revolution, which he took as an example of natural change in keeping with the historical development of North American society, but he denounced the French revolution as a chaotic and irresponsible assault on society.

### Liberalism

In contrast to conservatives, liberals took change as normal and welcomed it as the agent of progress. They viewed conservatism as an effort to justify the status quo, maintain the privileges enjoyed by favored classes, and avoid dealing with injustice and inequality in society. For liberals the task of political and social theory was not to stifle change but, rather, to manage it in the best interests of society. Liberals championed the Enlightenment values of freedom and equality, which they believed would lead to higher standards of morality and increased prosperity for the whole society. They usually favored republican forms of government in which citizens elected representatives to legislative bodies, and they called for written constitutions that guaranteed freedom and equality for all citizens and that precisely defined the political structure and institutions of their societies.

The **liberalism** that emerged from the Atlantic revolutions was concerned with civil rights but was not as concerned with political and social rights. Most liberals, for example, held the view that voting was more of a privilege than a right and therefore was legitimately subject to certain qualifications. Limitations on voting were in fact characteristic of postrevolutionary societies, and citizens were routinely denied the vote on the basis of class, age, gender, and race, among other factors. But as the nineteenth century progressed liberalism changed its character. As general populations became more assertive, liberalism could not concern itself mainly with interests of the more privileged strata of society. Consequently, there was a shift from early classical liberalism to a more democratic variety. Equality before the law was supplemented by equality before the ballot box. Liberalism's traditional emphasis on minimizing the role and power of government was reversed, and by the end of the nineteenth century, liberals started to look to government to minimize or correct the problems that accompanied industrialization.

The most prominent exponent of early liberalism was John Stuart Mill (1806–1873), an English philosopher, economist, and social reformer. Mill tirelessly promoted the freedom of individuals to pursue economic and intellectual interests. He tried to ensure that powerful minorities, such as wealthy businessmen, would not curb the freedoms of the poorly organized majority, but he also argued that it was improper for the majority to impose its will on minorities with different interests and values. He advocated universal suffrage as the most effective way to advance individual freedom, and he called for taxation of business profits and high personal incomes to limit the power of the wealthiest classes. Mill went further than most liberals of his time in seeking to extend the rights of freedom and equality to women and working people as well as men of property.

### Voting Rights and Restrictions

As Mill recognized, the age of revolutions in the Atlantic world illustrated the centrality of suffrage in establishing a people's and a nation's sense of democratic legitimacy and political sovereignty. **Suffrage** refers to the right or the privilege to vote in order to elect public officials or to adopt laws. The concept of suffrage derived its revolutionary significance from Enlightenment notions about self-government and about governments deriving authority from the consent of the people. Voting rights and restrictions evolved into powerful political concerns both during and after the age of revolutions.

## Testing the Limits of Revolutionary Ideals: Slavery

The Enlightenment ideals of freedom and equality were watchwords of revolution in the Atlantic Ocean basin. Yet different revolutionaries understood the implications of freedom and equality in very different ways. In North America revolution led to political independence, a broad array of individual freedoms, and the legal equality of adult white men. In France it destroyed the hierarchical social order of the ancien régime and temporarily extended political and legal rights to all citizens, although Napoleon and later rulers effectively curbed some of those rights. In Haiti revolution brought independence from French rule and the end of slavery. In South America it led to independence from Iberian rule and societies dominated by creole elites. In the wake of the Atlantic revolutions, social activists in Europe and the Americas considered the possibility that the ideals of freedom and equality might have further implications as yet unexplored. They turned their attention especially to the issues of slavery and women's rights.

**Movements to End the Slave Trade** The campaign to end the slave trade and abolish slavery began in the eighteenth century. Formerly enslaved people such as Olaudah Equiano (1745–1797) were among the earliest critics of slavery. Beginning in the 1780s European Christian moralists also voiced opposition to slavery.

Only after the American, French, and Haitian revolutions, however, did the antislavery movement gain momentum. The leading spokesman of the movement was **William Wilberforce** (1759–1833), a prominent English philanthropist elected in 1780 to a seat in Parliament. There he tirelessly attacked slavery on moral and religious grounds. After the Haitian revolution he attracted supporters who feared that continued reliance on enslaved labor would result in more and larger slave revolts, and in 1807 Parliament passed Wilberforce's bill to end the slave trade. Under British pressure, other states also banned commerce in enslaved people: the United States in 1808, France in 1814, the Netherlands in 1817, and Spain in 1845. The British navy, which dominated the North Atlantic Ocean, patrolled the west coast of Africa to ensure compliance with the law. But the slave trade died slowly because illegal trade continued on a small scale: the last documented ship to carry slaves across the Atlantic Ocean arrived in Cuba in 1867.

**Movements to Abolish Slavery** The abolition of slavery itself was a much bigger challenge than ending the slave trade because owners had property rights in the people they enslaved. Planters and merchant elites strongly resisted efforts to alter the system that provided them with abundant supplies of inexpensive labor. Nevertheless, the end of the slave trade doomed the institution of slavery in the Americas. In Haiti the end of slavery came with the revolution. In much of South America, slavery ended with independence from Spanish rule, as Simón Bolívar freed enslaved people who joined his forces and provided constitutional guarantees of free status for all residents of Gran Colombia. In Mexico slavery was abolished in 1829, though not solely for humanitarian reasons. Rather, abolition in Mexico served as a mechanism to stop the influx of residents from the southern United States coming in with enslaved people to grow cotton.

Meanwhile, as they worked to ban traffic in human labor, Wilberforce and other moralists also launched a campaign to free enslaved people and abolish the institution of slavery itself. In 1833, one month after Wilberforce's death, Parliament provided twenty million pounds sterling as compensation to slave holders and abolished slavery throughout the British Empire. Other states followed the British example: France abolished slavery in 1848, the United States in 1865, Cuba in 1886, and Brazil in 1888.

**Freedom without Equality** Abolition brought legal freedom for African and African American people, but it did not bring political equality. In most lands other than Haiti, African American peoples had little influence in society. Property requirements, literacy tests, poll taxes, and campaigns of intimidation effectively prevented them from voting. Nor did emancipation bring social and economic improvements for former enslaved people and their descendants. White elites owned most of the property in the Americas, and they kept people of color subordinated by forcing them to accept low-paying work. A few African Americans owned small plots of land, but they could not challenge the economic and political power of creole elites.

## Testing the Limits of Revolutionary Ideals: Women's Rights

Women participated alongside men in the movement to abolish slavery, and their experience inspired some social reformers to seek equality with men. They argued that women suffered many of the same legal disabilities as enslaved people: they had little access to education, they could not enter professional occupations that required advanced education, and they were legally deprived of the right to vote. They drew on Enlightenment thought in making a case for women's rights, but in spite of support from prominent liberals such as John Stuart Mill, they had little success before the twentieth century.

**Enlightenment Ideals and Women** Enlightenment thought called for the restructuring of government and society, but the philosophes mostly held conservative views on women and their roles in family and society. Rousseau, for example, advised that girls' education should prepare them to become devoted wives and mothers. Yet social reformers found Enlightenment thought extremely useful in advocating for women's rights. Drawing on the political thought of John Locke, for example, the English writer Mary Astell (1666–1731) argued that absolute sovereignty was no more appropriate in a family than in a state. Astell also reflected Enlightenment influence in asking why, if all men were born free, all women were born slaves.

During the eighteenth century, advocates of women's rights were particularly active in Britain, France, and North America. Among the most prominent was the British writer **Mary Wollstonecraft** (1759–1797). Although she had little schooling, Wollstonecraft avidly read books at home and gained an informal self-education. In 1792 she published an influential essay titled *A Vindication of the Rights of Woman.*

Portrait of Mary Wollestonecraft (1759–1797) in 1790–1791, painted by John Opie.
Niday Picture Library/Alamy Stock Photo

Like Astell, Wollstonecraft argued that women possessed all the rights that Locke had granted to men. She insisted on the right of women to education: it would make them better mothers and wives, she said, and would enable them to contribute to society by preparing them for professional occupations and participation in political life.

**Women and Revolution** Women played crucial roles in the revolutions of the late eighteenth and early nineteenth centuries. Some women supported the efforts of men by sewing uniforms; rolling bandages; or managing farms, shops, and businesses. Others actively participated in revolutionary activities. In October 1789, for example, about six thousand Parisian women marched to Versailles to protest the high price of bread. Some of them forced their way into the royal apartments and demanded that the king and queen return with them to Paris—along with the palace's supply of flour. In the early 1790s, pistol-wielding members of the Republican Revolutionary Women patrolled the streets of Paris. The fate of Olympe de Gouges made it clear, however, that revolutionary women had little prospect of holding official positions or playing a formal role in public affairs.

Under the National Assembly and the Convention, the French revolution brought increased rights for women. The republican government provided free public education for girls as well as boys, granted wives a share of family property, and legalized divorce. Yet the French Revolution did not bring women the right to vote or to play major roles in public affairs. Under the Directory and Napoleon's rule, women lost even the rights that they had won in the early days of the revolution. In other places, women never gained as much as they did in

## What's Left Out?

In the eighteenth century, women were barred from serving in the military almost everywhere in the world. While some women defied this restriction in by disguising themselves as men and fighting alongside them, many more played active roles in military conflicts as spies. Female secret agents were particularly active during the American revolution and provided critical intelligence for both the American and British sides. Spying was dangerous work because the punishment for being caught was death. But women took advantage of the fact that they were seldom suspected of espionage: men on both sides of the conflict thought women were too busy with mundane household tasks or else were too delicate to pose a serious threat to either side. As a result, women were often able to carry out their work in plain sight, by hiding messages in their clothing, by posing as peddlers in army camps, and by serving food and drink to officers planning their next moves. One example of hiding in plain sight was Anna Smith Strong, whose main job was to let other agents know where to pick up secret messages and anti-British intelligence. Her system was simple: when information was ready to be picked up, she hung a black petticoat outside on her laundry line. The location of the pickup was signaled by the number of handkerchiefs she hung out to dry, which corresponded to different locations. Sometimes the information provided by female spies changed the course of the war. An example of this was when a woman (still known only as "Agent 355") provided information to the Continental Army that the British planned to attack French forces in Newport, Rhode Island. American forces then used this information to prevent the surprise attack from occurring. Anna Strong and Agent 355 are only two examples of many, which should help us remember that even before women were permitted to join national military forces in the twentieth century, they were still able to play active roles in military conflicts.

*Source:* Jeanne Munn Bracken, ed. *Women in the American Revolution* (Auburndale, MA: History Compass, 2009).

### Thinking Critically About Sources

1. How did Anna Strong Smith and "Agent 355" help to "change the course of the war?"
2. Given the strong impact of women, why weren't their contributions recorded in the history books?

## SOURCES FROM THE PAST

### Declaration of the Rights of Woman and the Female Citizen

*In 1791 Olympe de Gouges, a butcher's daughter and playwright of some note, wrote and published the Declaration of the Rights of Woman and the Female Citizen. She directly challenged the 1789 Declaration of the Rights of Man and the Citizen, which limited citizenship to males. By publicly asserting the equality of women, Gouges questioned barriers that most revolutionary leaders wanted to leave in place. Charged with treason during the rule of the National Convention, Gouges was executed by guillotine on 3 November 1793.*

**Article 1. Woman is born free** and remains the equal of man in rights. Social distinctions can only be founded on a common utility.

Article 2. The purpose of all political organisations must be the protection of the natural and imprescriptible rights of Woman and Man: these rights are liberty, property, security and above all the right to resist oppression.

Article 3. The principle of sovereignty is vested primarily in the Nation, which is but the union of Woman and Man: no body, no individual, can exercise authority that does not explicitly emanate from it.

Article 4. Liberty and justice exist to render unto others what is theirs; therefore the only limit to the exercise of the natural rights of woman is the perpetual tyranny that man opposes to it: these limits must be reformed by the laws of nature and reason . . .

Article 6. The law must embody the will of the majority; all Female and Male citizens must contribute personally, or through their representatives, to its development; it must be the same for one and all: all Female and all Male citizens, being equal in law, must be equally entitled to all public honours, positions and employment according to their capacities and with no other distinctions than those based solely on talent and virtue.

> How might Article 6 in de Gouges' Declaration have changed French society?

Article 7. No woman may be exempt; she must be accused, arrested and imprisoned according to the law. Women, like men, will obey this rigorous law . . .

Article 11. The free expression of thoughts and opinions is one of the most precious rights of woman given that this liberty ensures the legitimacy of fathers and their children. Any Female citizen can therefore freely declare 'I am the mother of your child' without a barbrous prejudice forcing them to hide the truth, unless in response to the abuse of this freedom in cases determined by the law . . .

> Why might de Gouges have included this article about acknowledging parenthood?

Article 13. Women and men are to contribute equally to the upkeep of the forces of law and order and to the costs of administration: woman shares all the labour, all the hard tasks; she should therefore have an equal share of positions, employment, responsibilities, honours and professions.

Article 14. Female and male citizens have a right to decide for themselves, or through their representatives, the necessity of public contribution. Female citizens can only subscribe to it if they are allowed an equal share not only of wealth but also of public administration and in determining the amount, assessment, collection and duration of the tax . . .

Article 17. Property belongs to both sexes, united or separated; for each it is an inviolable and sacred right; no one can be deprived of a true natural heritage unless a general necessity, legally verified, obviously requires it and on condition of a fair indemnity agreed in advance.

#### For Further Reflection

- How does Olympe de Gouges's restatement of the Declaration of the Rights of Man and the Citizen intensify its radical precepts?
- Why was the Declaration met with so much resistance, from women as well as men?

*Source:* Gouges, Olympe de. The Declaration of the Rights of Woman. Translation by Clarissa Palmer. 1791. www.olympedegouges.eu. 

revolutionary France. In the United States and the independent states of Latin America, revolution brought legal equality and political rights only for adult white men, who retained patriarchal authority over their wives and families.

**Women's Rights Movements** Nevertheless, throughout the nineteenth century social reformers pressed for women's rights as well as the abolition of slavery. The American **Elizabeth Cady Stanton** (1815–1902) was an especially prominent figure in this movement. In 1840 Stanton went to London to attend an antislavery conference but found that the organizers barred women from participation. Infuriated, Stanton returned to the United States and began to build a movement for women's rights. She organized a conference of women who met at Seneca Falls, New York, in 1848. The conference passed twelve resolutions demanding that lawmakers grant women rights equivalent to those enjoyed by men. The resolutions called specifically for women's rights to vote, attend public schools, enter professional occupations, and participate in public affairs.

Meanwhile, the movement for women's suffrage was also growing in the United Kingdom. First inspired by Mary Wollstonecraft's clear challenge to women's unequal status under the law, by the 1870s women's suffrage groups existed in most major cities and submitted numerous petitions demanding the right to vote to Parliament. By 1897 there were so many local suffrage societies that they merged together in one National Union of Women's Suffrage Societies. Elsewhere in Europe, many socialist groups also began to demand suffrage for women, and in 1889 the Second (Socialist) International included it in its platform of demands. Thereafter, women's movements flourished in places like Germany and France.

The women's rights movement experienced limited success in the nineteenth century. More women received formal education than before the American and French revolutions, and women in Europe and North America participated in academic, literary, and civic organizations. Rarely did they enter the professions, however, and nowhere did they enjoy the right to vote. Yet by seeking to extend the promises of Enlightenment political thought to people of color and women as well as white men, social reformers of the nineteenth century laid a foundation that would lead to large-scale social change in the twentieth century.

# THE NEW NATIONS AND NATIONALISM IN EUROPE

The Enlightenment ideals of freedom, equality, and popular sovereignty inspired political revolutions in much of the Atlantic Ocean basin, and the revolutions in turn helped spread Enlightenment values. The wars of the French revolution and the Napoleonic era also inspired the development of a particular type of community identity that had little to do with Enlightenment values—**nationalism.** Revolutionary wars involved millions of French citizens in the defense of their country against foreign armies and the extension of French influence to neighboring states. Wartime experiences encouraged peoples throughout Europe to think of themselves as members of distinctive national communities. Throughout the nineteenth century, European nationalist leaders worked to fashion states based on national identities and mobilized citizens to work in the interests of their own national communities, sometimes by fostering jealousy and suspicion of other national groups. By the late nineteenth century, national identities were so strong that peoples throughout Europe responded enthusiastically to ideologies of nationalism, which promised glory and prosperity to those who worked in the interests of their national communities.

A portrait of the Italian nationalist leader Giuseppe Mazzini (1805–1872). By the mid-nineteenth century, Mazzini's views had inspired nationalist movements not only in Italy but in other European states as well.
bauhaus1000/Getty Images

## Nations and Nationalism

One of the most influential concepts of modern political thought is the idea of the nation. The word *nation* refers to a type of community that became especially prominent in the nineteenth century. At various times and places in history, individuals have associated themselves primarily with families, clans, cities, regions, and religious faiths. During the nineteenth century, European peoples came to identify strongly with communities they called nations. Members of a nation considered themselves a distinctive people born into a unique community that spoke a common language, observed common customs, inherited common cultural traditions, held common values, and shared common historical experiences. Often, they also honored common religious beliefs, although they sometimes overlooked differences of faith and construed the nation as a political, social, and cultural, rather than religious, unit.

Intense feelings of national identity fueled ideologies of nationalism. Advocates of nationalism insisted that the nation must be the focus of political loyalty. Zealous nationalist leaders maintained that members of their national communities had a common destiny that they could best advance by organizing independent national states and resolutely pursuing their national interests. Ideally, in their view, the boundaries of the national state embraced the territory occupied by the national community, and its government promoted the interests of the national group, sometimes through conflict with other peoples.

**Cultural Nationalism** Early nationalist thought often sought to deepen appreciation for the historical experiences of the national community and foster pride in its cultural accomplishments. During the late eighteenth century, for example, **Johann Gottfried von Herder** (1744–1803) sang the praises of the German *Volk* ("people") and their powerful and expressive language. In reaction to Enlightenment thinkers and their quest for a scientific, universally valid understanding of the world, early cultural nationalists such as Herder focused their attention on individual communities and relished

**Johann Gottfried von Herder**
(YOH-hahn GAWT-freet fuhn HER-duhr)

their uniqueness. They emphasized historical scholarship, which they believed would illuminate the distinctive characteristics of their societies. They also valued the study of literature, which they considered the best guide to the ***Volksgeist,*** the popular soul or essence of their community. For that reason the German brothers Jakob and Wilhelm Grimm collected popular poetry, stories, songs, and tales (known in the present day as fairy tales) as expressions of the German *Volk.*

**Political Nationalism** During the nineteenth century, nationalist thought became much more strident than the cultural nationalism of Herder or the brothers Grimm. Advocates of nationalism demanded loyalty and solidarity from members of the national group. In lands where they were minorities or where they lived under foreign rule, they sought to establish independent states to protect and advance the interests of the national community.

In Italy, for example, the nationalist **Giuseppe Mazzini** (1805–1872) formed a group called **Young Italy** that promoted independence from Austrian and Spanish rule and the establishment of an Italian national state. Mazzini likened the nation to a family and the nation's territory to the family home. Austrian and Spanish authorities forced Mazzini to lead much of his life in exile, but he used the opportunity to encourage the organization of nationalist movements in other states. By the mid-nineteenth century, Young Italy had inspired the development of nationalist movements in Ireland, Switzerland, and Hungary.

While it encouraged political leaders to work toward the establishment of national states for their communities, nationalism also had strong potential to stir up conflict between different groups of people. The more nationalists identified with their own national communities, the more they distinguished themselves both from peoples in other places and from minority groups within their societies.

**Nationalism and Anti-Semitism** The divisive potential of nationalism helps to explain the emergence of **Zionism,** a political movement that holds that the Jewish people constitute a nation and have the right to their own national homeland. Unlike Mazzini's Italian compatriots, Jews did not inhabit a well-defined territory but, rather, lived in states throughout Europe and beyond. As national communities tightened their bonds, nationalist leaders often became distrustful of minority populations. Suspicion of Jews fueled **anti-Semitism** in many parts of Europe including Austria-Hungary, Germany, and eastern Europe. In Russia and in the Russian-controlled areas of Poland, anti-Semitism often turned violent, climaxing in a series of pogroms, or organized massacres. Beginning in 1881 and lasting into the early twentieth century, these massacres claimed the lives and property of thousands of Jews.

A determined Theodor Herzl (1860–1904) founded the Zionist movement, which sought to confront anti-Semitism in Europe by establishing a home for the Jews in Palestine.
The History Collection/Alamy Stock Photo

During the late nineteenth and twentieth centuries, millions of Jews migrated to other European states or to North America to escape persecution and violence. Anti-Semitism was not as violent in France as in central and eastern Europe, but it reached a fever pitch there after a military court convicted Alfred Dreyfus, a Jewish army officer, of spying for Germany in 1894. Although he was innocent of the charges and eventually had the verdict reversed on appeal, Dreyfus was the focus of bitter debates about the trustworthiness of Jews in French society.

**Zionism** Among the reporters at the Dreyfus trial was a Jewish journalist from Vienna, **Theodor Herzl** (1860–1904). As Herzl witnessed mobs shouting "Death to the Jews" in what was supposed to be the land of enlightenment and liberty, he concluded that anti-Semitism could not be solved by assimilation into the larger society. In 1896 Herzl published the pamphlet ***Judenstaat,*** which argued that the only defense against anti-Semitism lay in the mass migration of Jews from all over the world to a land that they could call their own. In the following year, Herzl organized the first Zionist Congress in Basel, Switzerland, which founded the World Zionist Organization. The delegates at Basel formulated the basic platform of the Zionist movement, declaring that "Zionism seeks to establish a home for the Jewish people in Palestine," the location of the ancient Kingdom of Israel.

---

**Giuseppe Mazzini** (joo-ZEP-peh maht-TSEE-nee)
**Theodor Herzl** (TEY-aw-dohr HER-tsuhl)
***Judenstaat*** (yoo-dehn-STAHT)

## INTERPRETING IMAGES

The charming and polished courtier Prince Klemens von Metternich (standing at left center) dominated the Congress of Vienna. Here, delegates to the Congress are gathered at the Hapsburg palace in Vienna.

**Analyze** *How was Prince von Metternich's vision of nationalism different from that of Giuseppe Mazzini (p. 535), Theodor Herzl (p. 536), and Otto von Bismarck (p. 540)?*

DeAgostini/Getty Images

## The Emergence of National Communities

The French revolution and the wars that followed it heightened feelings of national identity throughout Europe. In France the establishment of a republic based on liberty, equality, and fraternity inspired patriotism and encouraged citizens to rally to the defense of the revolution when foreign armies threatened it. Revolutionary leaders took the tricolored flag as a symbol of the French nation, and they adopted a rousing marching tune, the "Marseillaise," as an anthem that inspired pride in and identity with the national community. In Spain, the Netherlands, Austria, Prussia, and Russia, national consciousness surged in reaction to the invasions and occupations of revolutionary and Napoleonic armies. Opposition to Napoleon, and especially fears over French invasion, also inspired national feeling in Britain.

**The Congress of Vienna** After the fall of Napoleon, conservative political leaders feared that heightened national consciousness and ideas of popular sovereignty would encourage further experimentation with revolution and undermine European stability. In response, representatives of the "great powers" that defeated Napoleon—Britain, Austria, Prussia, and Russia—attempted to restore the prerevolutionary order at a meeting known as the **Congress of Vienna** (1814–1815). Under the guidance of the influential foreign minister of Austria, Prince **Klemens von Metternich** (1773–1859), the Congress dismantled Napoleon's empire, returned sovereignty to Europe's royal families, restored them to the thrones they had lost during the Napoleonic era, and created a diplomatic order based on a balance of power that prevented any one state from dominating the others. One of Metternich's central goals was to suppress national consciousness, which he viewed as a serious threat to the multicultural Austrian Empire that included Germans, Italians, Magyars, Czechs, Slovaks, Poles, Serbs, and Croats among its subjects.

The efforts of Metternich and the Congress of Vienna to restore the ancien régime had limited success. The European balance of power established at Vienna survived for almost a century, until the outbreak of World War I in 1914. Metternich and the conservative rulers installed by the Congress of Vienna took measures to forestall further revolution: they censored publications to prevent communication of seditious ideas and relied on spies to identify nationalist and republican activists. By 1815, however, it was impossible to suppress national consciousness and ideas of popular sovereignty.

**Nationalist Rebellions** From the 1820s through the 1840s, a wave of rebellions inspired by nationalist sentiments swept through Europe. The first uprising occurred in 1821 in the

**Klemens von Metternich** (kleh-men fuhn MET-er-nik)

## MAP 16.4 The unification of Italy.

The unification of Italy and Germany (see Map 28.5) as national states in the nineteenth century fundamentally altered the balance of power in Europe.

***Why did unification result from diplomacy and war conducted by conservative statesmen rather than popular nationalist action?***

Balkan peninsula, where the Greek people sought independence from the Ottoman Turks, who had ruled the region since the fifteenth century. Many western Europeans sympathized with the Greek cause. The English poet Lord Byron even joined the rebel army and in 1824 died (of a fever) while serving. With the aid of Britain, France, and Russia, the rebels overcame the Ottoman forces in the Balkans by 1827 and won formal recognition of Greek independence in 1830.

In 1830 rebellions occurred throughout Europe. In France, Spain, Portugal, and some of the German principalities, revolutionaries inspired by liberalism called for constitutional government based on popular sovereignty. In Belgium, Italy, and Poland, they demanded independence and the formation of national states as well as popular sovereignty. Revolution in Paris drove Charles X from the throne, while uprisings in Belgium resulted in independence from the Netherlands. By the mid-1830s authorities had put down the uprisings elsewhere, but in 1848 a new round of rebellions shook European states. The uprisings of 1848 brought down the French monarchy and seriously threatened the Austrian Empire, where subject peoples clamored for constitutions and independence. Prince Metternich resigned his office as Austrian foreign minister and unceremoniously fled Vienna as rebels took control of the city. Uprisings also rocked cities in Italy, Prussia, and German states in the Rhineland.

By the summer of 1849, the veteran armies of conservative rulers had put down the last of the rebellions. Advocates of national independence and popular sovereignty remained active, however, and the potential of their ideals to mobilize popular support soon became dramatically apparent.

## How the Past Shapes the Future

### The Birth of Nationalism

The consequences of the birth of nationalism for world history have been enormous, beginning in the period 1750–1914 and continuing right down to the present. From its beginnings, nationalism was intimately linked with powerful emotive phenomena such as folk traditions, songs, and literature that symbolized common heritage and common values. As a result, nationalism had the power to awaken deep feelings of love and unity, and also of hatred and ferocity, among its adherents. Such feelings often spurred individuals to work on behalf of the nation even at the expense of their own interests. They also encouraged individuals to exclude—sometimes brutally—those they defined as "outside the nation," and to see the interests of their own nation in competition with the interests of others. As a result, people around the world have done extraordinary things—both altruistic and cruel—in the name of nationalism.

In this chapter, we have already seen some of the first instances (in Italy and Germany) of individuals using the power of nationalism to create unified state governments where there were none before—a process that has been attempted multiple times (e.g., Greater Serbia, Palestine) since then. We have also seen that nationalism was used from its beginnings as a tool to exclude unwelcome groups, in this case European Jews. In fact, nationalism has often served as the double-edged sword of unity. On the one side, its symbols and myths have been used by diverse populations as the glue uniting them into one people, as in many of the newly formed North, South, and Central American nations during the nineteenth century (chapter 30). On the other side, by emphasizing particular languages and heritages, nationalism often inspires some groups to seek the exclusion of others, as people of European ancestry tried to do to Native Americans throughout the Americas (chapter 30). Nationalism has also spurred deep feelings of animosity or competition between people of different nations, which has increased the incidence of serious conflict between states (chapters 32 and 33).

A French sans-culottes holding the French tricolor flag. Behind him is the countryside of France, and his clothes indicate his common status. Images like these were used to evoke emotions in viewers about their national identity.
Heritage Images/Hulton Fine Art Collection/Getty Images

One of the hallmarks of nationalism is that its emotive power has often been exploited by state governments for self-interested purposes. In late-nineteenth-century Japan, for example, reformers tried to inculcate a strong sense of national pride in Japanese citizens in order to garner support for a rapid program of industrialization that would allow Japan to be competitive on the world stage (chapter 31). While the process did foster national identification among ordinary Japanese people as well as rapid industrialization, the result was a far stronger state buttressed by a handful of extremely powerful corporations. In Europe, meanwhile, states played upon nationalist sentiments among their citizens—especially the specter of being bested by other nations—to garner support for imperial expansion in Asia and Africa (chapter 32). Indeed, by framing expansionist programs in terms of national aggrandizement, states were able to win the support for imperial conquests. Somewhat ironically, European imperial expansion ensured that people all over the world would be introduced to the concept of nationalism during the nineteenth and twentieth centuries—with consequences that would ultimately bring all of the European empires down (chapters 31 and 32).

The birth of nationalism profoundly shaped identities, loyalties, and both individual and state actions around the world from the late eighteenth century onward, with effects that continue to be felt in the present. In subsequent chapters, think about the many and varied ways that the force of nationalism—born in the context of the Atlantic revolutions—has shaped the world we live in today.

## The Unifications of Italy and Germany

The most striking demonstration of the power that national sentiments could unleash involved the unification of Italy and of Germany. A variety of regional kingdoms, city-states, and ecclesiastical states ruled the Italian peninsula for more than a thousand years, and princes divided Germany into more than three hundred semiautonomous jurisdictions. The Holy Roman Empire claimed authority over Germany and much of Italy, but the emperors were rarely strong enough to enforce their claims.

When delegates at the Congress of Vienna dismantled Napoleon's empire and sought to restore the ancien régime, they placed much of northern Italy under Austrian rule. Southern Italy was already under close Spanish supervision because of dynastic ties between the Kingdom of the Two Sicilies and the Spanish Bourbon monarchy. As national sentiment surged throughout nineteenth-century Europe, Italian political leaders worked to win independence from foreign rule and establish an Italian national state. Mazzini's Young Italy movement attracted discontented idealists throughout the peninsula. In 1820, 1830, and 1848, they mounted major uprisings that threatened but did not dislodge foreign rule in Italy.

The German realist painter Franz von Lenbach (1836–1904) painted many leaders of his time, including the German chancellor Otto von Bismarck depicted here. Bismarck is commonly credited with the unification of Germany and the creation of the German empire in 1871. Bismarck is shown here wearing a *Pickelhaube,* a spiked helmet worn by German military, firefighters, and police in the nineteenth and twentieth centuries.
ART Collection/Alamy Stock Photo

**Cavour and Garibaldi** The **unification of Italy** came about when practical political leaders such as Count **Camillo di Cavour** (1810–1861), prime minister to King Vittorio Emanuele II of Piedmont and Sardinia, combined forces with nationalist advocates of independence. Cavour was a cunning diplomat, and the kingdom of Piedmont and Sardinia was the most powerful of the Italian states. In alliance with France, Cavour expelled Austrian authorities from most of northern Italy in 1859. Then he turned his attention to southern Italy, where **Giuseppe Garibaldi** (1807–1882), a charismatic soldier for hire and a passionate nationalist, led the unification movement. With an army of about one thousand men outfitted in distinctive red shirts, Garibaldi swept through Sicily and southern Italy, outmaneuvering government forces and attracting enthusiastic recruits. In 1860 Garibaldi met King Vittorio Emanuele near Naples. Not ambitious to rule, Garibaldi delivered southern Italy into Vittorio Emanuele's hands, and the kingdom of Piedmont and Sardinia became the kingdom of Italy. During the next decade the new monarchy absorbed several additional territories, including Venice, Rome, and their surrounding regions.

**Otto von Bismarck** In Germany as in Italy, unification came about when political leaders harnessed nationalist aspirations. The Congress of Vienna created a German Confederation composed of thirty-nine states dominated by Austria. Metternich and other conservative German rulers stifled nationalist movements, and the suppression of the rebellions of 1848 left German nationalists frustrated at their inability to found a national state. In 1862 King Wilhelm I of Prussia appointed a wealthy landowner, **Otto von Bismarck** (1815–1898), as his prime minister. Bismarck was a master of ***Realpolitik*** ("the politics of reality"). He succinctly expressed his realistic approach in his first speech as prime minister: "The great questions of the day will not be settled by speeches or majority votes—that was the great mistake of 1848 and 1849—but by blood and iron."

It was indeed blood and iron that brought about the **unification of Germany.** As prime minister, Bismarck reformed and expanded the Prussian army. Between 1864 and 1870 he intentionally provoked three wars—with Denmark, Austria, and France—and whipped up German sentiment against the enemies. In all three conflicts Prussian forces quickly shattered their opponents, swelling German pride. In 1871 the Prussian king proclaimed himself emperor of the Second Reich—meaning the Second German Empire, following the Holy Roman Empire—which embraced almost all German-speaking peoples outside Austria and Switzerland in a powerful and dynamic national state.

The unification of Italy and Germany made it clear that, when coupled with strong political, diplomatic, and military leadership, nationalism had enormous potential to mobilize

**Camillo di Cavour** (kah-MEE-loh dee kah-VOHR)
**Giuseppe Garibaldi** (juh-SEP-eh gar-uh-BAHL-dee)
**Otto von Bismarck** (oht-toh fuhn BIZ-mahrk)

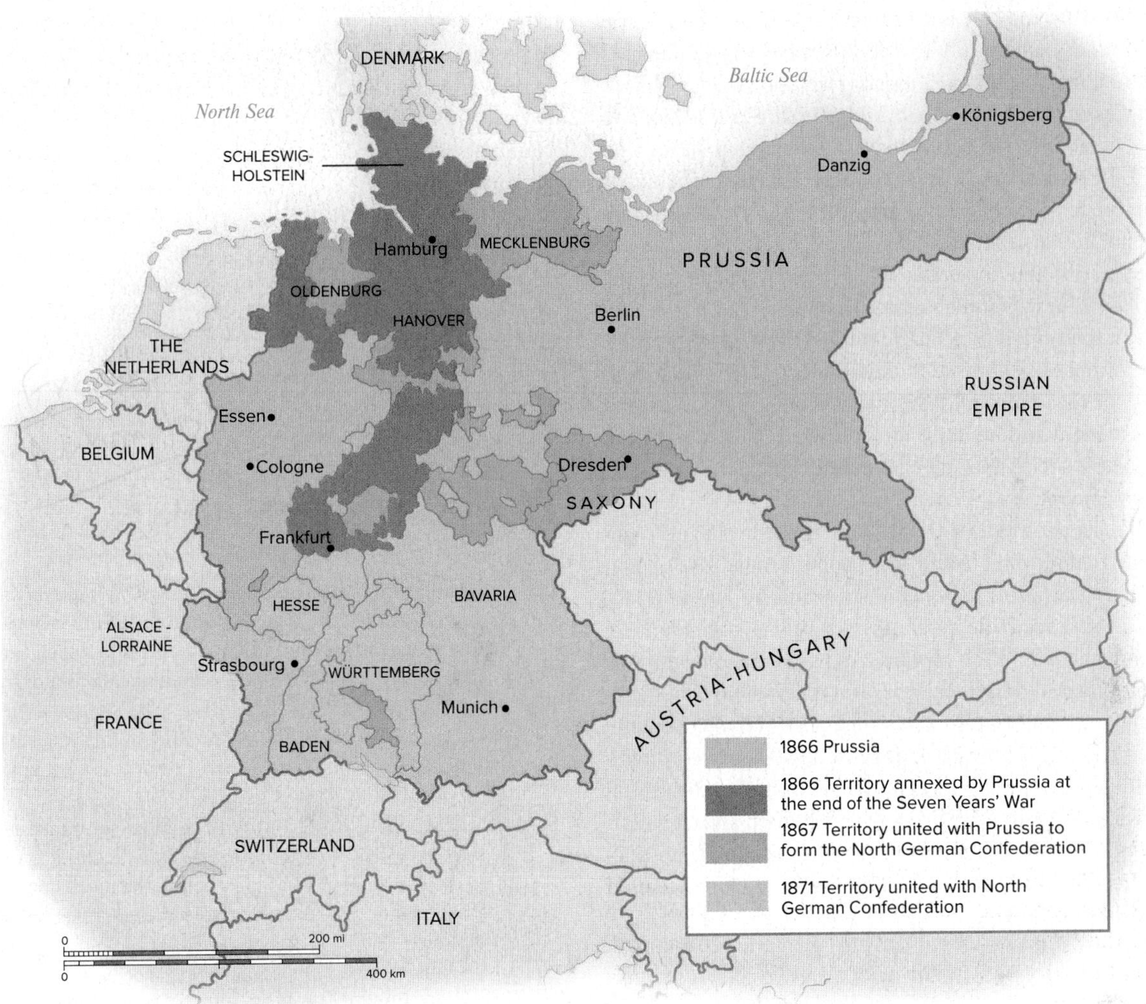


**MAP 16.5 The unification of Germany.**

Note the vast size of the territory in central Europe that united to become Germany in just five years.

***Does the map give a sense about why the state of Prussia dominated the newly unified nation?***

people who felt a sense of national kinship. Italy, Germany, and other national states went to great lengths to foster a sense of national community. They adopted national flags to serve as symbols of unity, national anthems to inspire patriotism, and national holidays to focus public attention on individuals and events of special importance for the national community. They established bureaucracies that took censuses of national populations and tracked vital national statistics involving birth, marriage, and death. They built schools that instilled patriotic values in students, and they recruited young men into armies that defended national interests and sometimes went on the offensive to enhance national prestige. By the end of the nineteenth century, the national state had proven to be a powerful model of political organization in Europe. By the mid-twentieth century, it had become nearly universal as political leaders adopted the national state as the principal form of political organization throughout the world.

## CONCLUSION

The Enlightenment ideals of freedom, equality, and popular sovereignty inspired revolutionary movements throughout much of the Atlantic Ocean basin in the late eighteenth and early nineteenth centuries. While Enlightenment ideals may have served as inspiration, war provided the opportunity and dictated the timing of the revolutions. Just as important, each successive revolution drew inspiration from the ones that went before. In North America, tensions caused by the Seven Years' War provided the context in which colonists threw off British rule and founded an independent federal republic. In France, where aid to the American revolutionaries helped to cause a massive financial crisis, revolutionaries abolished the monarchy, established a republic, and abandoned traditions to refashion the social order. In Saint-Domingue rebellious slaves who were inspired by revolutionary ideas took advantage of the chaos caused by the French Revolution to throw off French rule, establish an independent Haitian republic, and grant freedom and equality to all citizens. In Latin America creole elites led movements to expel Spanish and Portuguese colonial authorities during the power vacuum created by the invasion of Spain and Portugal by Napoleon's armies, and eventually founded independent republics. And although most of these revolutionary movements sought to extend the ideals of freedom and equality to adult white men, during the nineteenth century social reformers launched campaigns to extend them to enslaved people and women.

Meanwhile, as wars rocked the Atlantic basin in the late eighteenth and early nineteenth centuries, people around the region developed strong feelings of national identity and worked to establish states that advanced the interests of national communities. Nationalist thought was often divisive: it pitted national groups against one another and fueled tensions, especially in large multicultural states. But nationalism also had strong potential to contribute to state-building movements, and nationalist appeals played prominent roles in the unification of Italy and Germany and in the aspiration to establish a Jewish state. During the nineteenth and twentieth centuries, peoples throughout the world drew inspiration from egalitarian revolutionary ideals and nationalism when seeking to build or restructure their societies.

## STUDY TERMS

Adam Smith (515)
American revolution (518)
*ancien régime* (521)
anti-Semitism (536)
Baron de Montesquieu (515)
Camillo di Cavour (540)
*caudillos* (530)
Civil Code (525)
Congress of Vienna (537)
conservatism (531)
Continental Congress (518)
*criollos* (528)
Declaration of Independence (519)
Declaration of the Rights of Man and the Citizen (522)
Declaration of the Rights of Woman and the Female Citizen (534)
deists (516)
Elizabeth Cady Stanton (534)
Enlightenment (515)
Estates General (521)
French revolution (521)
*gens de couleur* (525)
George Washington (520)
Giuseppe Garibaldi (540)
Giuseppe Mazzini (536)
Gran Colombia (530)
Haitian revolution (525)
Jean-Jacques Rousseau (517)
Johann Gottfried von Herder (535)
John Locke (515)
*Judenstaat* (536)
Klemens von Metternich (537)
*levée en masse* (524)
liberalism (531)
Louis XVI (521)
Mary Wollstonecraft (532)
Miguel Hidalgo y Costilla (530)
Napoleon Bonaparte (524)
National Assembly (522)
nationalism (535)
Olympe de Gouges (512)
Otto von Bismarck (540)
*peninsulares* (528)
*philosophes* (515)
*Realpolitik* (540)
reign of terror (524)
Simón Bolívar (530)
*The Social Contract* (517)
suffrage (531)
Theodor Herzl (536)
Toussaint Louverture (527)
unification of Germany (540)
unification of Italy (540)
*Volksgeist* (536)
Voltaire (515)
Waterloo (525)
William Wilberforce (532)
Young Italy (536)
Zionism (536)

## FOR FURTHER READING


Benedict Anderson. *Imagined Communities: Reflections on the Origin and Spread of Nationalism.* Rev. ed. London, 1991. A pioneering work that analyzes the means and the processes by which peoples came to view themselves as members of national communities.

David A. Bell. *The First Total War: Napoleon's Europe and the Birth of Warfare as We Know It.* Boston, 2007. A fine work that argues that nearly every "modern" aspect of war was born in the Revolutionary and Napoleonic wars.

Suzanne Desan, Lynn Hunt, and William Max Nelson, eds. *The French Revolution in Global Perspective.* Ithaca, N.Y., 2013. A collection of essays that offers a new approach to the understanding of the international origins and worldwide effects of this seminal revolution.

Laurent Dubois. *Avengers of the New World: The Story of the Haitian Revolution.* Cambridge, Mass., 2005. Comprehensive study of how the French slave colony of Saint-Domingue became a unique example of a successful black revolution that challenged the boundaries of freedom, citizenship, and empire.

François Furet. *Revolutionary France 1770–1880.* Oxford, 1995. In a brilliant work of synthesis, a leading historian places the revolutions of 1789, 1830, 1848, and 1871 within the grand scheme of democratic traditions.

David Geggus, ed. *The Impact of the Haitian Revolution in the Atlantic World.* Columbia, S.C., 2001. Focuses on the wider impact of the revolution for the region in terms of ideology, economics, and precedent.

Jay Kinsbruner. *Independence in Spanish America: Civil Wars, Revolutions, and Underdevelopment.* 2nd ed. Albuquerque, 2000. A compelling reinterpretation of the independence movements of sixteen nations, their similarities, and their regional differences.

Robert Middlekauff. *The Glorious Cause: The American Revolution, 1763–1789.* 2nd ed. Oxford, 2005. Masterful exploration of the causes, events, and consequences of the revolution.

Anthony Pagden. *The Enlightenment: And Why It Still Matters.* New York, 2013. This sweeping and fascinating work is an enlightening look at the Enlightenment that argues for the continuing relevance of this intellectual movement.

# CHAPTER 16 AP EXAM PRACTICE

Questions assume cumulative knowledge from this chapter and previous chapters.

## Section I

## Multiple Choice Questions

Use the map below and your knowledge of world history to answer questions 1 – 3.

The unification of Germany
McGraw Hill

1. Which of these was a German cultural nationalist idea?
   (A) The Young German movement promoted independence from Austrian rule.
   (B) German nationalism was superior to Italian nationalism.
   (C) German culture was scientific, rational, and universally valid.
   (D) German poetry and fairy tales expressed the soul of the German people.

2. What prevented the German states from unifying sooner?
   (A) It wasn't until Camilo di Cavour became prime minister that anyone tried German unification.
   (B) The agreements made at the Congress of Vienna suppressed nationalist movements.
   (C) The Bavarian prime minister Otto von Bismarck resisted unification
   (D) The French expelled the nationalists from the German Confederation.

3. Why did Prussia dominate the newly unified German state?
   (A) Prussia had the largest territory, including much of the Baltic coastline and ports.
   (B) Prussia had access to the Silk Road trade routes.
   (C) It was thought only Prussia could prevent another French Revolution.
   (D) All the discontented idealists moved to Prussia to start the revolution.

Use the image below and your knowledge of world history to answer questions 4 and 5.

Portrait of Mary Wollstonecraft (1759–1797) in 1790–1791, painted by John Opie.
Niday Picture Library/Alamy Stock Photo

4. What might the artist be communicating with this portrait?
   (A) Mary Wollestonecraft collaborated with Olympe de Gouges to write the Declaration for the Rights of Woman and Female Citizen.
   (B) Mary Wollestonecraft was the inspiration for the Republican Revolutionary Women's patrol.
   (C) Mary Wollestonecraft accepted an absolutist theory of the family.
   (D) Mary Wollestonecraft was an avid reader and self-educated scholar who advocated for women's right to be educated.
5. Which of the following was a position held by an Enlightenment thinker about women?
   (A) John Stuart Mill thought women should not be allowed to vote.
   (B) Jean-Jacques Rousseau thought women should only be educated to become wives and mothers.
   (C) John Locke banned women from participating in antislavery organizations in London.
   (D) Mary Astell believed that a husband should be an absolute monarch like a king over a state.

## Short Answer

6. Use the image below and your knowledge of world history to answer parts A, B, and C.

Equestrian portrait of Napoleon I Bonaparte (1769–1821); painting by Jacques Louis David (1748–1825)

Leemage/Corbis/Getty Images

(A) Explain ONE way that Napoleon represented the ideals of the French Revolution.

(B) Explain ONE way that Napoleon's policies went against the ideals of the French Revolution.

(C) Identify ONE way that the Napoleonic Wars contributed to nationalism.

7. Use the map below and your knowledge of world history to answer parts A, B, and C.

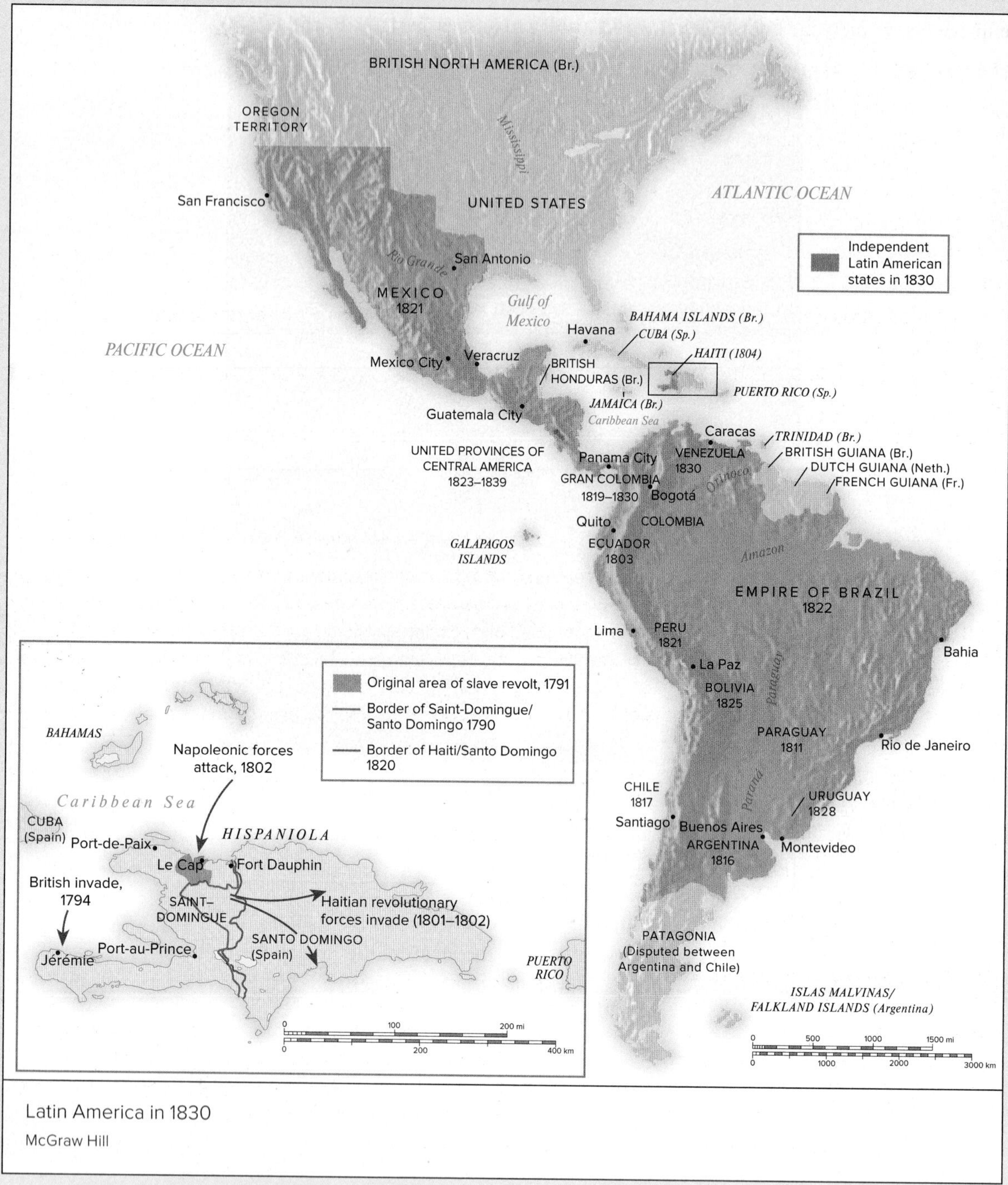


Latin America in 1830

McGraw Hill

(A) Identify ONE reason why Latin American states revolted against Spain.

(B) Identify ONE similarity between the revolutions in Latin America and the United States.

(C) Explain ONE reason why the newly independent states of Latin America on this map did not form one country.

8. Use your understanding of world history to answer parts A, B, and C.

(A) Explain ONE British policy that encouraged revolution in the North American colonies.

(B) Explain ONE Enlightenment idea that influenced the revolution in the British colonies.

(C) Explain ONE reason why some people in North America continued to support the crown during the revolution.

# Section II

## Document-Based Question

Based on the documents below and your knowledge of world history, evaluate the extent to which the Enlightenment-inspired French Revolution challenged social and economic structures.

In your response you should do the following:

- Respond to the prompt with a historically defensible thesis or claim that establishes a line of reasoning.
- Describe a broader historical context relevant to the prompt.
- Support an argument in response to the prompt using all documents.
- Use at least one additional piece of specific historical evidence (beyond that found in the documents) relevant to an argument about the prompt.
- Explain how or why the document's point of view, purpose, historical situation, and /or audience is relevant to an argument.
- Use evidence to corroborate, qualify, or modify an argument that addresses the prompt.

### Document 1

**Article 1. Woman is born free** and remains the equal of man in rights. Social distinctions can only be founded on a common utility. Article 2. The purpose of all political organisations must be the protection of the natural and imprescriptible rights of Woman and Man: these rights are liberty, property, security and above all the right to resist oppression. Article 3. The principle of sovereignty is vested primarily in the Nation, which is but the union of Woman and Man: no body, no individual, can exercise authority that does not explicitly emanate from it. Article 4. Liberty and justice exist to render unto others what is theirs; therefore the only limit to the exercise of the natural rights of woman is the perpetual tyranny that man opposes to it: these limits must be reformed by the laws of nature and reason . . .

*Source:* Gouges, Olympe de. The Declaration of the Rights of Woman. Translation by Clarissa Palmer. 1791. www.olympedegouges.eu. Translation reprinted with permission.

### Document 2

**First Article. Men are born** and remain free and equal in rights. Social distinctions may be based only on common utility. Article 2. The goal of every political association is the preservation of the natural and inalienable rights of man. These rights are liberty, property, security, and resistance to oppression. Article 3. The principle of all sovereignty resides essentially in the nation. No body and no individual can exercise authority that does not flow directly from the nation. Article 4. Liberty consists in the freedom to do anything that does not harm another. The exercise of natural rights of each man thus has no limits except those that assure other members of society their enjoyment of the same rights. These limits may be deter-mined only by law . . .

*Source: Déclaration des droits de l'homme et du citoyen (Declaration of the Rights of Man and the Citizen, 1789).* Translated by Jerry H. Bentley.

## Document 3

Jean-Jacques Dessalines (1758–1806)
Historic Images/Alamy Stock Photo

## Long Essay

Develop a thoughtful and thorough historical argument that answers the question below. Begin your essay with a thesis statement and support it with relevant historical evidence.

Using specific examples and your knowledge of world history, compare and contrast the tenets of liberalism and conservatism.

# Chapter 17 The Making of Industrial Society

Patterns of Industrialization
- Foundations of Industrialization
- The Factory System
- The Early Spread of Industrialization
- Industrial Capitalism

Industrial Society
- Industrial Demographics
- Urbanization and Migration
- Industry and Society
- The Socialist Challenge
- Global Effects of Industrialization

## ZOOMING IN ON TRADITIONS AND ENCOUNTERS

### Betty Harris, a Woman Chained in the Coal Pits

In 1827, shortly after marrying at the age of twenty-three, Betty Harris took a job as a drawer in a coal pit near Manchester, England. A drawer's job involved crawling down narrow mine shafts and hauling loads of coal from the bottom of the pit (where miners chipped it from the earth) to the surface. From there the coal went to fuel the steam engines that powered the factories and the mills of early industrial society. Drawers performed unskilled labor for low wages, but their work was essential for the emergence of industrial production.

While working, Harris wore a heavy belt around her waist. Hitched to the belt was a chain that passed between her legs and attached to the coal cart that she pulled through the mine shafts, often while creeping along on her hands and knees. The belt strained against her body, and the mine shafts were steep and slippery. Yet every workday, even when she was pregnant, Harris strapped on her belt and chain at 6:00 A.M., removing her bindings only at the end of the shift twelve hours later.

Work conditions for Betty Harris were exhausting and dangerous. She labored in the coal pit with six other women and six boys and girls. All members of the crew experienced hardships and exploitation. Harris reported that drawing coal was "very hard work for a woman," and she did not exaggerate. She and her companions often had to crawl through water that collected in the mine shafts during rainstorms, and the men who mined coal in the pits showed little respect for the ill-paid drawers. The belts and chains worn by drawers often chafed their skin raw, and miners contributed to their physical discomfort by beating them for slow or clumsy work. The miners, many of whom shed their clothes and worked naked in the hot, oppressive coal pits, also sometimes sexually abused the women and girl drawers: Harris personally knew several women who became pregnant after being raped in the coal pits.

An 1831 painting by D. O. Hill depicting the St. Rollox Chemical Works in Glasgow, Scotland, on the occasion of the opening of the Garnkirk and Glasgow railway. Note the juxtaposition between the picnicking spectators and the black smoke emanating from the St. Rollox factory chimney stacks.
FLHC 15/Alamy Stock Photo

Harris's work schedule made comfortable family life impossible. A cousin cared for her two children during the day, and Harris tended to them and her husband at night after a twelve-hour workday with only a single one-hour break to eat bread and butter. After fourteen years in the mines, at age thirty-seven, Harris put it mildly when she said, "I am not so strong as I was, and cannot stand my work so well as I used to."

# CHAPTER FOCUS

- The Atlantic revolutions were primarily *political* events with social and economic repercussions; conversely, the industrial revolution was primarily an *economic* event, with social and political implications.
- For the AP exam, you will need to know the basic causes and processes of the first industrial revolution (mostly textiles) and the second industrial revolution (steel, chemicals, electricity, precision machinery).
- You need to know what "preconditions to industry" were present in northwest Europe (but not in other places like China), and that individual entrepreneurs and investors began this revolution.
- Finally, you need to know the "high tech" inventions and processes of the second industrial revolution that ushered in the modern era.
- When factories relocated to cities, there was a staggering boom in northwestern European urbanization. Historians are particularly interested in how this new method of production (low skilled, low paid, specialized, tedious, and potentially dangerous labor) and intense urbanization affected people.
- New social classes were created to help manage and work in urban factories; family structures changed as homes were no longer the central places of production; and tremendous wealth and abject poverty coexisted in the same urban areas.
- Effects of the industrial revolution were global. As factories expanded, raw materials and markets—particularly in Africa and east Asia—became necessary.

## Historical Developments

- The development of the factory system concentrated production in a single location and led to an increasing degree of specialization of labor.
- The rapid development of steam-powered industrial production in European countries and the U.S. contributed to the increase in these regions' share of global manufacturing during the first Industrial Revolution. While Middle Eastern and Asian countries continued to produce manufactured goods, these regions' share in global manufacturing declined.
- The "second industrial revolution" led to new methods in the production of steel, chemicals, electricity, and precision machinery during the second half of the 19th century.
- Railroads, steamships, and the telegraph made exploration, development, and communication possible in interior regions globally, which led to increased trade and migration.
- In response to the social and economic changes brought about by industrial capitalism, some governments, organizations, and individuals promoted various types of political, social, educational, and urban reforms.
- New social classes, including the middle class and the industrial working class, developed.

## Reasoning Processes

- **Causation** Describe the causes and immediate effects of the industrial revolution.
- **Continuity and Change** Describe patterns of continuity and change in society and daily life as the industrial revolution advances.

## Historical Thinking Skills

- **Developments and Processes** Identify the consequences of the industrial revolution as well as its technological and ecological foundations.
- **Contextualization** Identify and describe the historical context surrounding the development of socialist ideologies.

## CHAPTER OVERVIEW

Not all industrial workers suffered as much as coal drawers, but Betty Harris's experience nonetheless illustrates some of the deep changes that industrialization wrought in patterns of work and family life. Beginning in the late eighteenth century, workers and their families had little choice but to adjust to the sometimes harsh demands of the machine age. First in Britain, then in parts of western Europe, North America, Russia, and Japan, machines and factories transformed agricultural societies into industrial societies. At the heart of this transformation were technological changes based on newly developed, inanimate sources of power—especially fossil fuels—that led to the extensive use of machinery in manufacturing. Machine production raised worker productivity, encouraged economic specialization, and promoted the growth of large-scale enterprise. Industrial machinery transformed economic production by turning out high-quality products quickly, cheaply, and efficiently. The process of industrialization encouraged rapid technological innovation and over the long term raised material standards of living in much of the world.

But the impact of industrialization went beyond economics, generating widespread environmental and social change as well. Perhaps most important, the use of fossil fuels and the transition to industrial production had enormous environmental consequences. Coal-fired furnaces pumped thick pollution into the air, while factories dumped poisonous by-products into nearby rivers, lakes, and oceans. By the turn of the twentieth century, many of the world's soils and waters were deeply polluted, and the air near industrial areas posed a serious health risk. Social change was also far-reaching. Early industrialists created a new work environment, the factory, which concentrated large numbers of workers under one roof to operate complicated machinery. Factories also enabled managers to impose work discipline and closely supervise the quality of production at their plants. By moving work outside the home, however, factories drew fathers, mothers, and children in different directions, altered traditional patterns of domestic life, and strained family relations.

Industrialization also encouraged rapid urbanization and migration. New cities mushroomed to house workers who left the countryside for jobs in factories. Millions of migrants traveled even farther, crossing the seas in search of opportunities in new lands. Often, however, early industrial workers found themselves living in squalor and toxic pollution while laboring under dangerous conditions.

Social critics and reformers worked to alleviate the social problems caused by early industrial society. Most scathing and influential of the critics were the German theorists Karl Marx and Friedrich Engels, who called for the destruction of capitalism and the establishment of a more just and equitable socialist society. Despite their appeals, capitalism and industrialization flourished and spread rapidly from Britain to continental Europe, North America, and Asia. Although industrialization spread unevenly around the globe, during the nineteenth century it became clear that it affected the entire world. This was because the industrial revolution upset the balance of power between industrialized and nonindustrialized countries, allowing industrialized countries to dominate temporarily—both economically and militarily—those that had not yet industrialized. In addition, in hindsight, it is clear that earth, air, and water in much of the world were negatively affected as a result of the demands of the industrial revolution for raw materials.

| CHRONOLOGY | |
|---|---|
| 1733 | John Kay develops the flying shuttle |
| 1765 | James Watt patents an improved steam engine |
| 1779 | Samuel Crompton develops the spinning mule |
| 1785 | Edmund Cartwright develops the power loom |
| 1797 | Eli Whitney introduces interchangeable parts to the manufacturing process |
| 1829 | George Stephenson's locomotive, the Rocket, attains a speed of 45 kilometers (28 miles) per hour |
| 1832 | Reform Bill expands electorate to House of Commons |
| 1833 | Factory Act restricts employment of women and children in textile factories |
| 1842 | Mines Act restricts employment of women and children in mines |
| 1848 | Karl Marx and Friedrich Engels publish *Manifesto of the Communist Party* |
| 1851 | Crystal Palace exhibition in London |
| 1856 | Bessemer converter developed |
| 1913 | Henry Ford introduces the assembly line to the manufacture of automobiles |

# PATTERNS OF INDUSTRIALIZATION

Industrialization refers to a process that transformed economics previously centered around agriculture and handicrafts to those distinguished by industry and machine manufacture. Critical to industrialization were productivity-increasing technological developments that made it possible to produce goods by machines rather than by hand and that harnessed inanimate sources of energy such as coal and petroleum.

Organizational changes accompanied technological developments. By the end of the nineteenth century, the factory had become the predominant site of industrial production in Europe, the United States, and Japan. Factory production strongly encouraged the emergence of new divisions of labor as interchangeable parts and belt-driven assembly lines made the mass production of goods a hallmark of industrialized societies. The need to invest in increasingly expensive equipment encouraged the formation of large businesses: by the mid-nineteenth century, many giant corporations had joined together to control trade through trusts and cartels.

## Foundations of Industrialization

By the mid-eighteenth century, several areas of the world—Great Britain in western Europe, the Yangzi Delta in China, Japan—exhibited growing and dynamic economies that shared many common features. High agricultural productivity in those regions resulted in significant population growth. High population densities in turn encouraged occupational specialization and permitted many individuals to work at tasks other than cultivation. Navigable rivers and networks of canals facilitated trade and transport, and cities and towns were home to sophisticated banking and financial institutions. At the same time, these dynamic economies ran up against difficult ecological obstacles—especially soil depletion and deforestation—that threatened continued population growth and consumption levels. First Great Britain and then the other regions of western Europe overcame those ecological constraints by exploiting coal deposits found near large centers of population and by utilizing natural resources found abroad.

**Coal and Colonies** Coal played a crucial role in the industrialization of Great Britain. Until the eighteenth century, wood had served as the primary source of fuel for iron production, home heating, and cooking. Prodigious uses of wood, however, resulted in and caused deforestation and serious wood shortages. Geographic luck had placed some of western Europe's largest coal deposits in Great Britain, within easy reach of water transport, centers of commerce, and pools of skilled labor. Humans in many parts of the world had known for at least a millennium that coal can burn. In Britain, however, it did not seem necessary to seek it out in large quantities until wood became scarce. Once it became clear that wood was in increasingly short supply, the fortunate combination of coal deposits and the skills necessary to extract it encouraged the substitution of coal for wood, thus creating a promising framework for industrialization. If coal had not been easily accessible in Britain, it is unlikely that the economy could have supported an expanding iron production and the application of steam engines to mining and industry—both crucial to the industrial process in Great Britain. In that respect, Britain's experience differed from that of China, where industrialization occurred later. In China, the largest coal deposits were hundreds of miles from the area in the Yangzi Delta where large populations of skilled laborers lived. As a result, it did not make sense to shift to a reliance on coal in China in this period.

A woman working as a drawer in a British coal mine drags her coal cart with the aid of a belt and chain, much as Betty Harris—who we met in the introduction to this chapter—would have done. Manually produced coal fueled the machines of early industrial society, though its extraction was often dangerous and difficult for workers involved in the industry.
Hulton Deutsch/Corbis Historical/Getty Images

An 1835 engraving depicts female workers at a textile factory. The shift to machine-based manufacturing commonly started with the mechanization of the textile industries not only in Great Britain but also in other industrializing lands, such as the United States and Japan. What cannot be communicated by images like this was the deafening clatter made by the machines while they were being operated throughout the day.
Bettmann/Getty Images

**Ecological Relief** The unique economic relationship between Europe and the Americas gave Great Britain in particular an additional resource to overcome ecological obstacles. After decimating the indigenous populations of the Americas and then settling the land, European colonizers overcame European land constraints by supplying European societies with a growing volume of raw materials—like sugar and cotton—that could never have been grown in the cool climate of western Europe. During the eighteenth century the slave-based plantations of northeastern Brazil, the Caribbean islands, and later the southern United States supplied Europe with huge amounts of sugar and cotton; each of which helped to fuel the industrial revolution in its own way. Sugar was high in calories and quickly converted to energy when eaten. By the mid-nineteenth century, sugar provided workers with low-cost meals that helped them work long hours. Cotton, for its part, was a vital raw material in the emerging textile industries. The plantation economies of the Caribbean islands in particular also created significant markets for manufactured imports from Europe, especially in the form of inexpensive cotton textiles to clothe enslaved people. Indeed, almost one-half of the proceeds from sugar exports paid for the importation of manufactured goods from Europe. The significance of valuable American resources grew after 1830, when large amounts of grain, timber, and beef were sent across the Atlantic to European destinations. All these products grew on colonial acreage, which expanded Europe's land base. Later in the century, American lands also served as outlets for Europe's surplus population.

**Mechanization of the Cotton Industry** Among the first industries to mechanize was British textile manufacturing. During the seventeenth century, English consumers had become fond of **calicoes**—inexpensive, brightly printed textiles imported from India, which carried on a vibrant international trade in finished cotton textiles. Cotton cloth came into demand because it was lighter, easier to wash, and quicker to dry than wool, which was the principal fabric of European clothes before the nineteenth century. Threatened by the popularity of Indian cotton products, British wool producers persuaded Parliament to pass a series of laws to protect the domestic wool industry. The Calico Acts of 1720 and 1721 prohibited imports of printed cotton cloth and restricted the sale of calicoes at home. Parliament even passed a law requiring corpses to be buried in woolen shrouds, but legislation did not dampen consumers' enthusiasm for cotton. By the 1730s, some British entrepreneurs turned their attention not to banning the use of cotton but to manufacturing their own. After the 1750s, British cotton textile producers convinced Parliament to set high tariffs on Indian textiles so their own finished goods would be less expensive. Given the demand for cotton, producers sought methods of speeding up the processes of spinning and weaving to supply growing domestic and foreign markets. To increase production, they turned to inventions that rapidly mechanized the cotton textile industry. In the early 1730s, artisans began to develop labor-saving devices for spinning and weaving cotton, thereby moving away from hand-based techniques derived from the wool and linen industries. The first important technological breakthrough came in 1733 when Manchester mechanic John Kay invented the **flying shuttle.** This device speeded up the weaving process and stimulated demand for cotton thread. Within a few years, competitions among inventors resulted in the creation of several mechanical devices to spin thread. The most important was Samuel Crompton's **"mule,"** built in 1779. Adapted for steam power by 1790, the mule became the device of choice for spinning cotton thread. A worker using a steam-driven mule could produce a hundred times more thread than a worker using a manual spinning wheel.

The new spinning machines created an imbalance in manufacturing because weavers could not keep up with the production of thread, so innovators turned their attention next to weaving. In 1785 Edmund Cartwright, a clergyman without training or experience in either mechanics or textiles, patented a water-driven **power loom** that mechanized the weaving process. Within two decades steam moved the power loom, and by the 1820s it had largely taken the place of hand weavers in the cotton industry. Collectively, these technological developments permitted the production of textile goods in great volume and variety and at low cost. By 1830 half a million people worked in the cotton business, Britain's leading industry, which accounted for 40 percent of exports.

**Steam Power** Among the most crucial technological breakthroughs of the early industrial era was the development of a general-purpose steam engine in 1765 by **James Watt,** an instrument maker at the University of Glasgow in Scotland. Steam engines burned coal to boil water and create steam, which drove mechanical devices that performed work. Even before Watt's time, primitive steam engines had powered pumps that drew water out of coal mines, but those devices consumed too much fuel to be useful for other purposes. Watt's version relied on steam to force a piston to turn a wheel, whose rotary motion converted a simple pump into an engine that had multiple uses. Watt's contemporaries used the term *horsepower* to measure the energy generated by his steam engine, which did the work of numerous animals. By 1800 more than a thousand of Watt's steam engines were in use in the British isles. They were especially prominent in the textile industry, where their application resulted in greater productivity for manufacturers and cheaper prices for consumers.

**Iron and Steel** The iron and steel industries also benefited from technological refinement in this period, and the availability of inexpensive, high-quality iron and steel reinforced the move toward mechanization. After 1709, British smelters began to use coke (a purified form of coal) rather than more expensive charcoal as a fuel to produce iron. As we know, deforestation in England had made wood—the principal source of charcoal—scarce. Besides being cheaper than charcoal, coke was a more efficient fuel and made it possible for producers to build bigger blast furnaces and turn out larger lots of iron. As a result, British iron production skyrocketed during the eighteenth century, and prices to consumers fell. Inexpensive iron fittings and parts made industrial machinery stronger, and iron soon became common in bridges, buildings, and ships.

The nineteenth century was an age of steel rather than iron. Steel is much harder, stronger, and more resilient than iron, but until the nineteenth century it was very expensive to produce. Between 1740 and 1850 a series of improvements simplified the process. In 1856 Henry Bessemer—an English inventor—built a refined blast furnace known as the Bessemer converter that made it possible to produce steel cheaply and in large quantities. Steel production rose sharply, and steel quickly began to replace iron in tools, machines, and structures that required high strength.

**Transportation** Steam engineering and metallurgical innovations both contributed to improvements in transportation technology. James Watt's steam engine did not adapt well to transportation uses because it consumed too much coal. After his patent expired, however, inventors devised high-pressure engines that required less fuel. In 1815 **George Stephenson,** a self-educated Englishman, built the first steam-powered locomotive. In 1829 his Rocket won a contest by reaching a speed of 45 kilometers (28 miles) per hour. Although they were more efficient than Watt's invention, Stephenson's engines still burned too much coal for use at sea. Sailing ships remained the most effective means of transport over the seas until the middle of the nineteenth century, when refined engines of high efficiency began to drive steamships.

Because they had the capacity to carry huge cargoes, steam trains and steamships dramatically lowered transportation costs. They also contributed to the creation of dense transportation networks that linked remote interior regions and distant shores more closely than ever before. Between 1830 and 1870, British entrepreneurs laid about 20,000 kilometers (13,000 miles) of railroads, which linked industrial centers, coalfields, iron deposits, and port cities. Railroads also carried some 322 million passengers as well as cargoes of raw materials and manufactured goods. Meanwhile, steamships proved their versatility by advancing up rivers to points that sailboats could not reach because of inconvenient twists, turns, or winds. Railroads and steamships benefited from the innovations that drove the industrialization process and in turn encouraged continuing industrialization by providing rapid and inexpensive transport.

## The Factory System

In the emerging capitalist society of early modern Europe (discussed in chapter 23), most manufacturing took place under what was known as the putting-out system. Under this system, entrepreneurs in early modern Europe paid individuals to work on materials in their households. During the seventeenth and early eighteenth centuries, new and larger units of production supplemented the putting-out system. Rising demand for certain products such as textiles and the growing use of water and wind power led to the formation of nonmechanized factories, where workers performed specialized tasks under one roof.

**The Factory** The **factory system** replaced both the putting-out system and nonmechanized factories and became the characteristic method of production in industrial economies. It began to emerge in the late eighteenth century, when technological advances transformed the British textile industry. By the mid-nineteenth century, most cotton production took place in factories. Many of the newly developed machines were too large and expensive for home use, and it became necessary to move work to locations where entrepreneurs and engineers built complicated machinery for large-scale production. This centralization of production brought together more workers doing specialized tasks than ever before. Most industrial workers came from the countryside. A combination of factors provided a plentiful supply of cheap labor for the new factories, including rural overpopulation and the land pressure and declining job opportunities that went with it.

George Stephenson's North Star engine of 1837. Although Stephenson did not invent the locomotive, his refinements of locomotive technology, his application of civil engineering to the development of efficient railroad lines, and his vision of the future impact of railway systems on commerce earned him the nickname "Father of the Railways."
Science & Society Picture Library/SSPL/Getty Images

The newly mechanized factory system became associated with a new division of labor, one that called for a production process in which each worker performed a single task rather than one in which a single worker completed the entire job, as was typical of handicraft traditions. In the first chapter of the *Wealth of Nations* (1776), Adam Smith used a pin factory to describe the new system of manufacture: "One man draws out the wire, another straights it, a third cuts it, a fourth points it, a fifth grinds it at the top for receiving the head; . . . and the important business of making a pin is, in this manner, divided into about eighteen distinct operations." Factories also enabled managers to impose strict work discipline and closely supervise employees. Thus Josiah Wedgwood (1730–1795), an Englishman who owned a pottery plant, held his employees to high standards in an effort to produce the highest quality pottery. When he spotted inferior work, he frequently dumped it on the factory floor and crushed it, saying, "This will not do for Josiah Wedgwood!"

**Working Conditions** With its new divisions of labor, the factory system allowed managers to improve worker productivity and realize spectacular increases in the output of manufactured

## What's Left Out?

How might you experience time if you had no clocks and no watches and you had no way to know the exact time to wake up, take a break, eat lunch, or go home from work? It is difficult to imagine now, but that is how most people experienced time before the industrial revolution. For almost everyone, time was dictated by the rhythm of the seasons, tasks that needed to be completed, and the progression of the day. Even if someone were wealthy enough to own their own timepiece (most were not), almost every town kept its own local time without reference to the world around it. The industrial revolution changed all that. With the advent of railroads, it became important to know exactly when a train would arrive and when a train would depart. To solve the problem of widely varying local times, in 1847 the railroads in Britain uniformly adopted Greenwich Mean Time. Over the next few decades, most towns abandoned local time for this single, standardized time. The factory system also revolutionized the way people experienced time. Unlike earlier forms of work, the scale of the workforce in factories and the expense of running complicated machines prompted factory owners to insist that workers arrive to work, take breaks, and leave from work at exact times. Suddenly, people needed to know precisely when to get up, go to work, eat, and sleep. Towns erected large clocks that loudly chimed the hour so all could hear, and those who could afford it purchased pocket watches or clocks for their homes. As a result, people began to experience time not in terms of natural rhythms but almost exclusively as something dictated by the discipline of clocks—a discipline that has become a permanent part of modern life right into the present.

*Source:* Trish Ferguson, *Victorian Time: Technologies, Standardizations, Catastrophes*, 3rd ed. (London: Palgrave Macmillan, 2013).

### Thinking Critically About Sources

1. Discuss the myriad impacts of using clocks on the lives of people and the economy. What were the positive and negative results?

goods. But the new environment also changed the nature of work in unsettling ways. The factory system led to the emergence of an owner class whose capital financed equipment and machinery that were too expensive for workers to acquire. Industrial workers themselves became mere wage earners who had only their labor services to offer and who depended on their employers for their livelihood. In addition, any broad-range skills that workers may have previously acquired as artisans often became obsolete in a work environment that rewarded narrowly defined skills. The repetitious and boring nature of many industrial jobs, moreover, left many workers alienated or estranged from their work and the products of their labor.

Equally disturbing was the new work discipline and the pace of work. Those accustomed to rural labor soon learned that the seasons, the rising and setting of the sun, and fluctuations in the weather no longer dictated work routines. Instead, clocks, machines, and shop rules established new rhythms of work. Industrial workers commonly labored six days a week for twelve to fourteen hours daily. The factory whistle sounded the beginning and the end of the working day, and throughout the day workers had to keep pace with the monotonous movements of machines. At the same time, they faced strict and immediate supervision, which made little allowance for a quick nap or socializing with friends. Floor managers pressured men, women, and children to speed up production and punished them when they did not meet expectations. Because neither the machines nor the methods of work took safety into account, early industrial workers constantly faced exposure to toxic chemicals, harmful levels of noise, and the possibility of accidents—some of which could be fatal.

**Industrial Protest** In some instances, machine-centered factories sparked violent protest. Between 1811 and 1816, organized bands of English handicraft workers known as **Luddites** went on a rampage and destroyed textile machines that they blamed for their low wages and unemployment. They called their leader King Lud, after a legendary boy named Ludlam who broke a knitting frame to spite his father. The movement broke out in the hosiery and lace industries around Nottingham (central England) and then spread to the wool and cotton mills of Lancashire in the north of the country. The Luddites usually wore masks and operated at night. Because they avoided violence against people (even though they threatened it), they enjoyed considerable popular support. Nevertheless, by hanging fourteen Luddites in 1813, the government served notice that it was unwilling to tolerate violence even against machines, and the movement gradually died out.

## The Early Spread of Industrialization

Industrialization and the technological, organizational, and social transformations that accompanied it might have originated in many parts of the world where abundant craft skills, agricultural production, and investment capital could support the industrialization process. For half a century, however, industrialization took place only in Great Britain. Aware of their head start, British entrepreneurs and government officials forbade the export of machinery, manufacturing techniques, and skilled workers.

Yet Britain's monopoly on industrialization did not last forever because enterprising entrepreneurs recognized profitable opportunities in foreign lands and circumvented government regulations to sell machinery and technical know-how abroad. Moreover, European and North American businesspeople often took such knowledge by force. European and North American entrepreneurs did not hesitate to bribe or even kidnap British engineers, and they also smuggled advanced machinery out of the British isles. Sometimes they got poor value for their investments: they found that it was difficult to attract the best British experts to foreign lands and had to make do with drunkards or second-rate specialists who demanded high pay but made little contribution to industrialization.

**Industrialization in Western Europe** Nevertheless, by the mid-nineteenth century, industrialization had spread to parts of France, Germany, Belgium, and the United States. The French revolution and the Napoleonic wars helped set the stage for industrialization in western Europe by abolishing internal trade barriers and dismantling craft guilds that discouraged technological innovation and restricted the movement of laborers. The earliest center of industrial production in continental Europe was Belgium, where coal, iron, textile, glass, and armaments production flourished in the early nineteenth century. About the same time, France also moved toward industrialization. By 1830, French firms employed about fifteen thousand skilled British workers who helped establish mechanized textile and metallurgical industries in France. By the mid-nineteenth century, French engineers and inventors were devising refinements and innovations that led to greater efficiencies in metallurgical industries. Later in the century a boom in railroad construction stimulated economic development while also leading to decreased transportation costs.

German industrialization proceeded more slowly than in Belgium and France, partly because of political instability resulting from competition between the many German states. After the 1840s, however, German coal and iron production soared, and by the 1850s an extensive railroad network was under construction. After the unification of Germany in 1871 (discussed in chapter 28), Bismarck's government sponsored rapid industrialization. In the interests of strengthening military capacity, Bismarck encouraged the development of heavy industry, and the formation of huge businesses became a hallmark of German industrialization. The giant Krupp firm, for example, dominated mining, metallurgy, armaments production, and shipbuilding.

Between 1870 and 1914, those areas in Europe that had already undergone industrialization entered a new phase of rapid technological change, standardization, and mass consumption called the ***Second Industrial Revolution***. This phase of the industrial revolution was characterized by the use of steel as well as the spread of telegraph networks, electric power lines, and telephones.

# SOURCES FROM THE PAST

## Ned Ludd's Angry Letter to a Shearing Frame Holder

*Many ordinary people in Britain were not happy with the mechanization that accompanied industrialization in the early nineteenth century. Skilled artisans like weavers rightly worried that the new machines would put them out of a job. In fact, it was true that a single person could do the work of several people by operating one of the shearing frames being introduced into the weaving industry. Between 1811 and 1816, groups of men claiming to be led by "Ned Ludd" or "General Ludd" banded together in order to destroy the new machines and to protest cuts in their wages. They sent threatening letters to business owners who utilized the new machines, broke into factories to break the machines, attacked employers, and fought with government soldiers. Although some of these protesters were caught and executed, most Luddites escaped capture because local communities seem to have protected them. The letter below was written around March 9, 1812, to a Mr. Smith, an owner of a factory with shearing frames in Yorkshire.*

**Information has just been given** in that you are a holder of those detestable Shearing Frames, and I was desired by my Men to write to you and give you fair Warning to pull them down, and for that purpose I desire you will now understand I am now writing to you. you will take Notice that if they are not taken down by the end of next Week, I will detach one of my Lieutenants with at least 300 Men to destroy them and furthermore take Notice that if you give us the Trouble of coming so far we will increase your misfortune by burning your Buildings down to Ashes and if you have Impudence to fire upon any of my Men, they have orders to murder you, & burn all your Housing, you will have the Goodness to your Neighbours to inform them that the same fate awaits them if their Frames are not speedily taken down as I understand their are several in your Neighbourhood, Frame holders.

> What will happen to Mr. Smith and his fellow industrialists if they do not voluntarily take down their shearing frames, according to the letter?

And as the Views and Intentions of me and my Men have been much misrepresented I will take this opportunity of stating them, which I desire you will let all your Brethren in Sin know of. I would have the Merchants, Master Dressers, the Government & the public to know that the Grievances of such a Number of Men are not to be made sport of for by the last Returns there were 2782 Sworn Heroes bound in a Bond of Necessity either to redress their Grievances or gloriously perish in the Attempt in the Army of Huddersfield alone, nearly double sworn Men in Leeds . . . we hope for assistance from the French Emperor in shaking off the Yoke of the Rottenest, Wickedest and most Tyranious Government that ever existed; then down come the Hanover Tyrants [the current line of British kings], and all our Tyrants from the greatest to the smallest.

And we will be governed by a just Republic, and may the Almighty hasten those happy Times is the Wish and Prayer of Millions in this Land, but we won't only pray but we will fight, the Redcoats shall know that when the proper time comes We will never lay down our Arms.

> What indication do we have that the author of this letter has only a basic education? Can that tell us anything about who he might have been?

Signed by the General of the Army of Redressers
Ned Ludd Clerk
Redressers for ever Amen,
You may make this Public
[March 9th or 10th]

### For Further Reflection

- What is the ultimate goal of Ned Ludd and his army of redressers, according to the letter above, and how will they achieve it?
- What can this document tell us about how ordinary people might have viewed the changes associated with the industrial revolution?
- How is the term "Luddite" used in contemporary society, even though it is no longer associated with violence?
- How were these protests different from outbreaks of miners and workers seeking better wages?
- Why would such aggressive and violent men be protected by the community?

Source: Clerk Ludd, Ned. Letter from "Ned Ludd Clerk" addressed "To Mr Smith Shearing Frame Holder at Hill End Yorkshire." 1812.

Workers tend to a massive steam hammer, which was used for forging metal. Note the proximity of the workers to the molten metal.
Ann Ronan Pictures/Print Collector/Getty Images

**Industrialization in North America** Industrialization transformed North America as well as western Europe in the nineteenth century. In 1800 the United States possessed abundant land and natural resources but few laborers and little money to invest in business enterprises. Both labor and investment capital came largely from Europe: migrants crossed the Atlantic in large numbers throughout the nineteenth century, and European bankers and businesspeople eagerly sought opportunities to invest in businesses that made use of American natural resources. American industrialization began in the 1820s when entrepreneurs lured British crafts workers to New England and built a cotton textile industry. By mid-century well over a thousand mills were producing fabrics from raw cotton grown in the southern states, and New England had emerged as a site for the industrial production also of shoes, tools, and handguns. In the 1870s heavy iron and steel industries emerged in areas such as western Pennsylvania and central Alabama where there were abundant supplies of iron ore and coal. By 1900 the United States had become an economic powerhouse, and industrialization had begun to spill over into southern Canada.

The vast size of the United States was advantageous to industrialists because it made abundant natural resources available to them, but it also hindered travel and communication between the regions. To facilitate transportation and distribution, state governments built canals, and private investors established steamship lines and railroad networks. By 1860 rails linked the industrial northeast with the agricultural south and the midwestern cities of St. Louis and Chicago, where brokers funneled wheat and beef from the plains to the more densely populated eastern states. As in other lands, railroad construction in the United States spurred industrialization by providing cheap transportation and stimulating the coal, iron, and steel industries. After 1870, North Americans also shared in the technological innovations that characterized the Second Industrial Revolution.

## Industrial Capitalism

**Mass Production** Cotton textiles were the major factory-made products during the early phase of industrialization, but new machinery and techniques soon made it possible to extend the factory system to other industries. Furthermore, with refined manufacturing processes, factories could mass-produce standardized items. An important contribution to the evolving factory system came from the American inventor **Eli Whitney** (1765–1825). Though best remembered as the inventor of the cotton gin (1793), Whitney also developed the technique of using machine tools to produce large quantities of interchangeable parts in the making of firearms. In conventional methods a skilled worker made a complete musket, forming and fitting each unique part; Whitney designed machine tools with which unskilled workers made only a particular part that fit every musket of the same model. Before long, entrepreneurs applied Whitney's method to the manufacture of everything from clocks and sewing machines to uniforms and shoes. By the middle of the nineteenth century, mass production of standardized items was becoming the hallmark of industrial societies.

In 1913 **Henry Ford** improved manufacturing techniques further when he introduced the assembly line to automobile

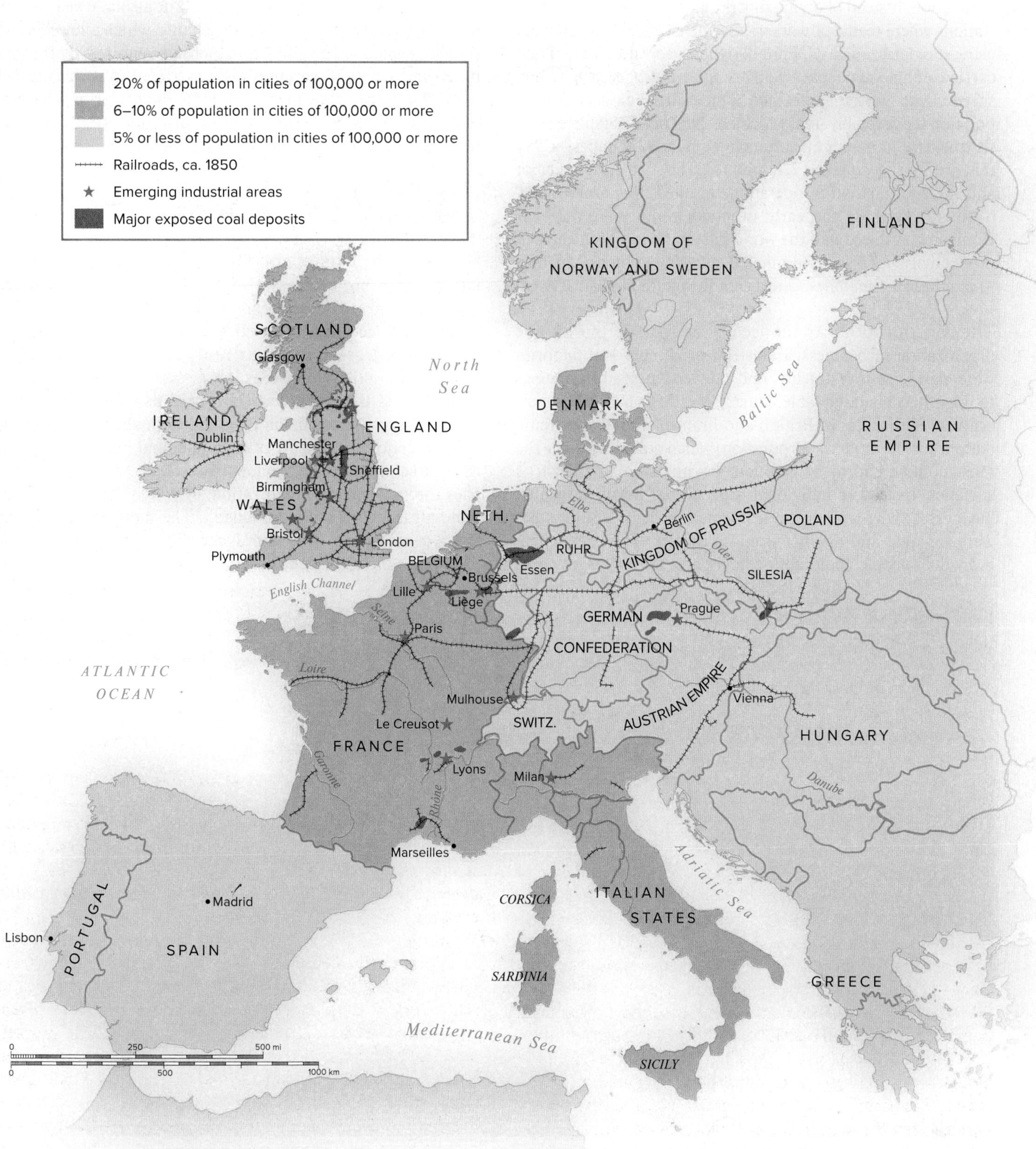


## MAP 17.1 Industrial Europe ca. 1850.

Locate the places marked as emerging industrial areas.

***Are there any features those areas have in common? If so, what are they?***

production. Instead of organizing production around a series of stations where teams of workers assembled each individual car using standardized parts, Ford designed a conveyor system that carried components past workers at the proper height and speed. Each worker performed a specialized task at a fixed point on the assembly line, which churned out a complete chassis (the base frame for an automobile) every 93 minutes—a task that previously had taken 728 minutes. The subdivision of labor and the coordination of operations resulted in enormous productivity gains. By the early twentieth century, Ford Motor Company produced half the world's automobiles. With gains in productivity, car prices plummeted, allowing millions of people to purchase automobiles. The age of the motor car had arrived.

**The Corporation** As the factory evolved, so too did the organization of business. Industrial machinery and factories were expensive investments, and they encouraged businesses to organize on a large scale. During the 1850s and 1860s, government authorities in Britain and France laid the legal foundations for the modern corporation, which quickly became the most common form of business organization in industrial societies. Instead of individual or small partnerships owning businesses, corporations were formed as legal entities that were separate and distinct from its owners. This meant that individual people could not be held liable for claims or losses incurred, thus spreading financial risk. It also allowed groups of people to raise money by selling shares, which allowed large sums of capital to be raised for expensive ventures. By the late nineteenth century, **corporations** controlled most businesses requiring large investments in land, labor, or machinery, including railroads, shipping lines, and industrial concerns that produced iron, steel, and armaments. Meanwhile, an array of investment banks, brokerage firms, and other businesses offering financial services arose to serve the needs of industrial capitalists organized in corporations.

**Monopolies, Trusts, and Cartels** To protect their investments, some big businesses of the late nineteenth century sought not only to outperform their competitors in the capitalist marketplace but also to eliminate competition. Business firms formed associations to restrict markets or establish monopolies in their industries. Large-scale business organizations formed **trusts** and **cartels.** The difference between the two was largely a technical one, and both shared a common goal: to control the supply of a product and hence its price in the marketplace. Some monopolists sought to control industries through vertical organization, by which they would dominate all facets of a single industry. The industrial empire of the American petroleum producer John D. Rockefeller, for example, which he ruled through Standard Oil Company and

This is a 1911 photograph of Standard Oil's refinery in Richmond, California. Established in 1870 as an Ohio corporation, Standard Oil was the largest oil refiner in the world at the time and operated as a major company trust. It was one of the world's first and largest multinational corporations until it was broken up by the United States Supreme Court in 1911. John D. Rockefeller, the company's founder, became the richest man in history.
Library of Congress/Corbis Historical/Getty Images

Trust, controlled almost all oil drilling, processing, refining, marketing, and distribution in the United States. Control over all aspects of the petroleum industry enabled Standard Oil to operate efficiently, cut costs, and undersell its competitors. Vertical organization of this kind offered large corporations great advantages over smaller companies.

Other monopolists tried to eliminate competition by means of horizontal organization, which involved the consolidation or cooperation of independent companies in the same business. Thus cartels sought to ensure the prosperity of their members by absorbing competitors, fixing prices, regulating production, or dividing up markets. The German firm IG Farben, the world's largest chemical company until the middle of the twentieth century, grew out of a complex merger of chemical and pharmaceutical manufacturers that controlled as much as 90 percent of production in chemical industries. By the end of the nineteenth century, some governments outlawed these combinations and broke them up because such organizations actively worked against market competition that might result in lower prices for consumers and because they tended to keep wages low for workers so profits could be maintained. When governments proved unwilling to confront large businesses or when the public remained ignorant or indifferent, monopolistic practices continued even into the present.

## INDUSTRIAL SOCIETY

Over time, industrialization brought material benefits in its train, including inexpensive manufactured products and rising standards of living. Yet industrialization also unleashed dramatic and often unsettling social and evironmental change. Massive internal and external migrations took place as millions of people moved from the countryside to work in new industrial cities, populations grew, and European migrants crossed the Atlantic by the tens of millions to seek opportunities in the less densely populated lands of the Western Hemisphere. Industrialization encouraged the emergence of new social classes—especially the middle class and the working class—and forced men, women, and children to adjust to distinctly new patterns of family and work life. Reformers sought to alleviate the social, economic, and environmental problems that accompanied industrialization. The most influential critics were the socialists, who did not object to industrialization per se but worked toward the building of a more equitable and just society.

### Industrial Demographics

Industrialization brought efficiencies in production that flooded markets with affordable manufactured goods. In 1851 the bounty of industry went on display in London at the **Crystal Palace,** a magnificent structure made of iron and glass that enclosed trees, gardens, fountains, and manufactured products from around the world. Viewers flocked to the exhibition to see industrial products such as British textiles, iron goods, and machine tools. Colt revolvers and sewing machines from the United States also attracted attention as representatives of the "American system of manufacture," which used interchangeable parts in producing large quantities of standardized goods at low prices. Observers marveled at the Crystal Palace exhibits and congratulated themselves on the achievements of industrial society.

For many people, industrialization raised material standards of living. Industrial production led to dramatic reductions in the cost of clothing, for example, so individuals were able to add variety to their wardrobes. By the early nineteenth century, all but the desperately poor could afford several changes of clothes, and light, washable underwear came into widespread use with the availability of inexpensive manufactured cotton. Industrial factories turned out tools that facilitated agricultural work, while steam-powered locomotives delivered produce quickly and cheaply to distant markets, so industrialization contributed as well to a decline in the price of food. Consumers in early industrial Europe also filled their homes with more furniture, cabinets, porcelain, and decorative objects than any but the most wealthy of their ancestors.

**Population Growth** The populations of European and Euro-American peoples rose sharply during the eighteenth and nineteenth centuries, and they reflected the rising prosperity and standards of living that came with industrialization. Between 1700 and 1800 the population of Europe increased from 105 million to 180 million, and during the nineteenth century it more than doubled to 390 million. Demographic growth in the Americas—fueled by migration from Europe—was even more remarkable. Between 1700 and 1800 the population of North America and South America rose from 13 million to 24 million and then surged to 145 million by 1900. Demographic growth was most spectacular in the temperate regions of the Western Hemisphere. In Argentina, for example, population expanded from 300,000 in 1800 to 4.75 million in 1900—a 1,583 percent increase. In temperate North America—what is now the United States—population rose from 6 million to 76 million (1,266 percent) during the 1800s.

The rapid population growth in Europe and the Americas reflected changing patterns of fertility and mortality. In most preindustrial societies fertility was high, but famines and epidemics resulted in high mortality, especially child mortality, which prevented explosive population growth.

Medical advances over time supplied the means to control disease better and reduce mortality. A case in point was smallpox, an ancient, highly contagious, and often fatal viral disease that had killed more people than any other malady in world history. The experiments of the English physician Edward Jenner dealt an effective blow against smallpox. Knowing that milkmaids—women who milked cows—often contracted cowpox, in 1797 Jenner inoculated an eight-year-old boy with cowpox and followed it six weeks later with the smallpox virus. The boy became ill but soon recovered fully, leading Jenner to deduce that cowpox conferred immunity against smallpox. Later called vaccination (from *vacca,* the Latin word for "cow"), Jenner's procedure not only created a powerful weapon in the war against smallpox but also laid the foundation for scientific

Exhibitors from around the world displayed fine handicrafts and manufactured goods at the Crystal Palace exhibition of 1851 in London. Industrial products from Britain and the United States particularly attracted the attention of visitors to the enchanting and futuristic exhibition hall.

Time Life Pictures/Mansell/The LIFE Picture Collection/Getty Images

immunology. Although it took a century and more, physicians eventually developed vaccines that prevented sickness and death from polio, tetanus, typhoid, whooping cough, and many other diseases that once plagued humankind.

Death rates fell markedly during the industrial revolution because better diets and improved disease control reduced child mortality. Since more infants survived to adulthood, the population of early industrializing societies grew rapidly. By the late nineteenth century, better diets and improved sanitation led to declining levels of adult as well as child mortality, so populations of industrial societies expanded even faster. Britain and Germany, the most active sites of early industrialization, experienced especially fast population growth. Between 1800 and 1900 the British population increased from 10.5 million to 37.5 million, while German numbers rose from 18 million to 43 million.

**The Demographic Transition** Beginning in the nineteenth century, industrializing lands experienced a social change known as the **demographic transition,** which refers to shifting patterns of fertility and mortality. As industrialization transformed societies, fertility—the number of children born—declined. In the short run, mortality fell even faster than fertility, so the populations of industrial societies continued to increase. Over time, however, declining birthrates led to lower population growth and relative demographic stability. The principal reason for declining fertility in industrial lands was voluntary birth control through contraception.

The reasons for this demographic transition are not completely clear. Some couples might have chosen to have fewer offspring because raising them cost more in industrial than in agricultural societies or because declining child mortality meant that any children born were more likely to survive to

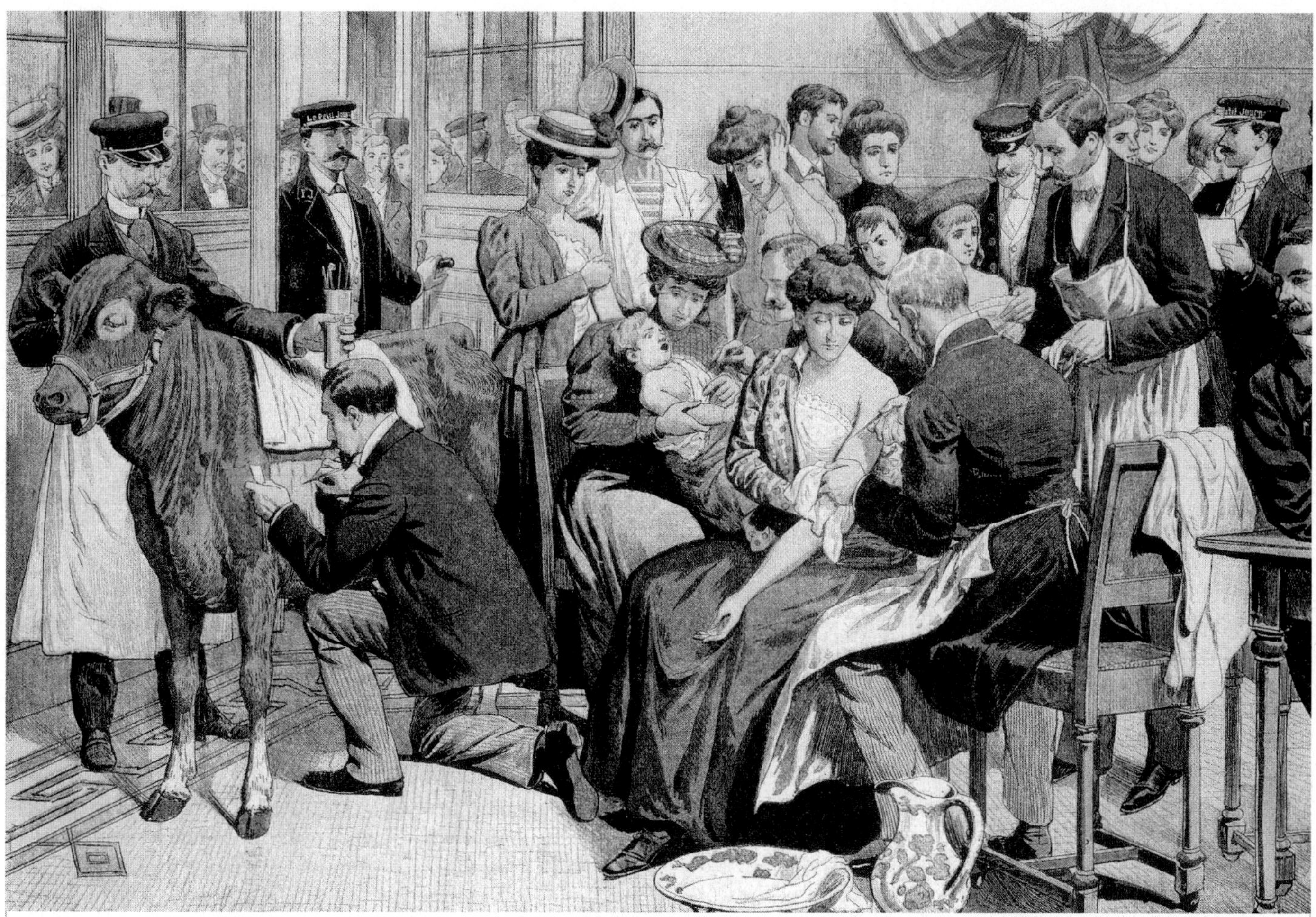

A French newspaper sponsored free smallpox vaccinations in 1905; in this image, the serum of a cow infected with cowpox is being injected into waiting Parisians.
World History Archive/Alamy Stock Photo

adulthood. Whatever the reasons, the demographic transition accompanied industrialization in western Europe, the United States, Japan, and other industrializing lands as well.

**Birth Control** For thousands of years, people tried to find deliberate ways of preventing or reducing the probability of pregnancy resulting from sexual intercourse. Some of the methods, such as withdrawal before insemination, proved not to be particularly reliable, and others, such as sexual abstinence, turned out to be unrealistic. More ingenious methods of birth control such as vaginal suppositories, cervical caps, or drinkable concoctions designed to prevent pregnancies or induce miscarriages often carried serious health risks for women. Because none of those methods proved effective, people throughout the world sometimes resorted to abortion or infanticide.

The first efficient means of contraception without negative side effects was the male condom. Initially made of animal intestines, it came into use in the seventeenth century. The effectiveness and popularity of the condom soared in the mid-nineteenth century with the arrival of the latex condom, which served both as a contraceptive device and as a barrier against syphilis, a much-feared venereal disease.

## Urbanization and Migration

Industrialization and population growth strongly encouraged migration and urbanization. Within industrial societies, migrants flocked from the countryside to urban centers in search of work. Industrial Britain led the world in urbanization. In 1800 about one-fifth of the British population lived in towns and cities of 10,000 or more inhabitants. During the following century a largely rural society became predominantly urban, with three-quarters of the population working and living in cities. That pattern repeated itself in continental Europe, the United States, Japan, and the rest of the industrialized world. By 1900 at least 50 percent of the population in industrialized lands lived in towns with populations of 2,000 or more. The increasing size of cities reflected this internal migration. In 1800 there were barely twenty cities in Europe with populations as high as 100,000, and there were none in the Western

Hemisphere. By 1900 there were more than 150 large cities in Europe and North America combined. With a population of 6.5 million, London was the largest city in the world, followed by New York with 4.2 million, Paris with 3.3 million, and Berlin with 2.7 million.

**The Urban Environment** With urbanization came intensified environmental pollution. Although cities had always been putrid and unsanitary places, the rapid increase in urban populations during the industrial age dramatically increased the magnitude and severity of water and air pollution. The widespread burning of fuels, such as wood and coal, fouled the air with vast quantities of chemicals and particulate matter. This pollution led to typical occupational diseases among some trades. Chimney sweeps, for instance, contracted cancer of the scrotum from hydrocarbon deposits found in chimney soot. Effluents from factories and mills and an increasing amount of untreated sewage dirtied virtually every major river. No part of a city was immune to the constant stench coming from air and water pollution. Worse, tainted water supplies and unsanitary living conditions led to periodic epidemics of cholera and typhus, and dysentery and tuberculosis were also common maladies. Until the latter part of the nineteenth century, urban environments remained dangerous places in which death rates commonly exceeded birthrates, and only the constant stream of new arrivals from the country kept cities growing.

Income determined the degree of comfort and security offered by city life. The wealthy typically tried to insulate themselves the best they could from urban discomforts by retreating to their elegant homes in the newly growing suburbs. The working poor, in contrast, crowded into the centers of cities to live in shoddy housing constructed especially for them. The rapid influx of people to expanding industrial cities such as Liverpool and Manchester encouraged the quick but slipshod construction of dwellings close to the mills and factories. Industrial workers and their families occupied overcrowded tenements lacking in comfort and amenities. The cramped spaces in apartments obliged many to share the same bed, increasing the likelihood of disease transmission. The few open spaces outside the buildings were usually home to herds of pigs living in their own dung or were depositories for pools of stagnant water and human waste. Whenever possible, the inhabitants of such neighborhoods flocked to parks and public gardens.

By the later nineteenth century, though, government authorities were tending to the problems of the early industrial cities. They improved the safety of municipal water supplies, expanded sewage systems, and introduced building codes that outlawed the construction of rickety tenements to accommodate poorly paid workers. Those measures made city life safer and brought improved sanitation that eventually helped to eliminate epidemic disease. City authorities also built parks and recreational facilities to encourage wholesome recreation and to make cities more livable. Nevertheless, the emissions from fossil fuel combustion that accompanied industrialization and rapid economic development were responsible for the increased amount of greenhouse gases, and hence the rise in the average temperature of earth's cities, atmosphere, and oceans: a process that has continued to the present.

**Transcontinental Migration** While workers moved from the countryside to urban centers, rapid population growth in Europe encouraged massive migration to the Americas, especially to the United States. During the nineteenth and early twentieth centuries, about fifty million Europeans migrated to the Western Hemisphere, and this flow of humanity accounts for much of the stunning demographic growth of the Americas. Many of the migrants intended to stay for only a few years and fully expected to return to their homelands with a modest fortune made in the Americas. Indeed, some did return to Europe: about one-third of Italian migrants to the Americas made the trip back across the Atlantic. The vast majority, however, remained in the Western Hemisphere.

Most of the migrants came from the British isles in the early nineteenth century; from Germany, Ireland, and Scandinavia in the middle decades; and from eastern and southern Europe in the late nineteenth century. Migration reflected difficult political, social, and economic circumstances in Europe: British migrants often sought to escape dangerous factories and the squalor of early industrial cities, most Irish migrants departed during the potato famines of the 1840s, and millions of Jews left the Russian Empire in the 1890s because of the tsar's anti-Semitic policies. Many of those migrants entered the workforce of the United States, where they settled in new industrial centers such as New York City, Pittsburgh, and Cleveland. Indeed, labor from abroad made it possible for the United States to undergo rapid industrialization in the late nineteenth century.

## Industry and Society

As millions of people moved from the countryside to industrial centers, society began a process of dramatic transformation. Before industrialization, the vast majority of the world's peoples worked in rural areas as cultivators or herders. Rulers, aristocrats, priests, and a few others enjoyed privileged status, and small numbers of people worked in cities as artisans, crafts workers, bureaucrats, or professionals. Many societies also made use of enslaved labor, occasionally on a large scale.

**New Social Classes** Industrialization helped bring new social classes into being, which eventually replaced older social structures. Owners of industry and enterprising businesspeople became fabulously wealthy and powerful enough to overshadow the military aristocracy and other traditionally privileged classes. In addition to this new class of elites, a new **middle class** emerged in this period, consisting of small business owners; factory managers; engineers; accountants; skilled employees of large corporations; and professionals such as teachers, physicians, and attorneys. Industrial production generated great wealth, and a large portion of it flowed to the middle class, which was a principal beneficiary of industrialization. Meanwhile, laborers who worked in factories and mines constituted a new **working class.** Their work did not require the

In 1872 Gustave Doré, a French book illustrator, sketched an image of Wentworth Street, Whitechapel, in London. By the middle of the nineteenth century, population shifts from rural areas to London made Whitechapel synonymous with poverty and overcrowding. Small dark avenues such as Wentworth Street epitomized the suffering of the poorest classes during the industrial revolution.
Historical Picture Archive/Corbis Historical/Getty Images

skill of artisans and craftsmen of earlier times because most of the new industries required either physical strength or the ability to tend to machines while performing a single task. Because individuals could be easily replaced by others seeking work in the growing cities, their wages tended to be quite low. By the mid-nineteenth century, the low wages and poor working conditions of the working class led them to organize for greater political rights.

**Industrial Families** The most basic unit of social organization—the family—also underwent fundamental change during the industrial age. In preindustrial societies the family was the basic productive unit. Whether engaged in agriculture, domestic manufacturing, or commerce, family members worked together and contributed to the welfare of the larger group. Industrialization challenged the family economy and reshaped family life by moving economic production outside the home and introducing a sharp distinction between work and family life. During the early years of industrialization, family economies persisted as fathers, mothers, and children pooled their wages and sometimes even worked together in factories. Over time, however, it became less common for family members to work together in the same factory. Instead, workers left their homes each day to labor an average of fourteen hours in factories, and family members led increasingly separate lives.

**A More Masculine World of Work and Play** When production moved outside the home and work increasingly dominated public life, men gained greater stature and responsibility. While western European society was patriarchal prior to the industrial revolution and women enjoyed few legal or political rights, family production had nevertheless been a joint venture to which women and children contributed. But once men began to earn the bulk of their families' income in jobs outside the home, the domestic work traditionally done by women was increasingly devalued as an economic contribution to family life. This was especially true of upper-class and middle-class men, who now set the cultural standard for their societies. These men often insisted on being the sole wage-earners in the family. Indeed, they envisioned ideal family life as one in which men went to work outside the home

The blood sport known as bear baiting had roots back to the early modern period, but was still practiced in the Victorian era. Usually, a bear was chained by the neck or leg, and trained hunting dogs were set upon it to attack. Dogs were replaced as they were wounded, killed, or became too tired to continue.
Topham Partners LLP/ Alamy Stock Photo

while women and children remained at home in comfortable surroundings.

Middle-class men also sought to instill their values about work and family life in members of the industrial workforce. They used their positions of power as factory owners and managers to threaten workers with fines, beatings, and dismissal if they did not obey factory rules against absenteeism, tardiness, and swearing. Through their support for churches and Sunday schools, factory owners also sought to persuade workers to adopt middle-class ideals of family, respectability, and morality.

Given their very low wages and substandard housing, it was impossible for all but the most skilled workers to live like the middle class. Realizing this, workers often resisted the work discipline and moral pressures they encountered at the factory. Some observed "Holy Monday" and stayed home to lengthen their weekly break from work on Sundays. They also made the most of their limited leisure time. Some joined sports teams, while others gambled, socialized at bars and pubs, or engaged in the very old tradition of "blood sports," in which spectators bet on fights between dogs, roosters, or even between dogs and bears. Although all classes had once engaged in blood sports, in the industrial era the middle and upper classes tried to suppress these activities and established urban police forces to control workers' public behavior. But efforts at regulation had limited success, and workers persistently pursued their own interests.

**Women at Home and Work** Industrialization dramatically changed the terms of work for women. When industry moved production from the home to the factory, married women were unable to work unless they left their homes and children in someone else's care. At the same time, middle-class men increasingly insisted that women should not leave the household to work but, rather, that they should devote themselves to raising children and managing their homes.

By the mid-nineteenth century, one of the hallmarks of belonging to the industrial middle class was that women did not work outside the home. For these women, industrialization brought increasing confinement to the domestic sphere and pressure to conform to new models of behavior revolving around their roles as mothers and wives. In a book titled *Woman in Her Social and Domestic Character* (1833), Mrs. John Sandford—who referred to herself by her husband's name rather than her own—described the ideal British woman. "Domestic life is the chief source of her influence," Sandford proclaimed, adding that "there is, indeed, something unfeminine in independence." (By *independence* Sandford meant taking a job.) The model woman, according to Sandford, "knows that she is the weaker vessel" and takes pride in her ability to make the home a happy place for her husband and children.

But for working-class women, who formed the largest proportion of women in industrialized societies, remaining at home without working was a nearly impossible ideal. Working-class men generally made low wages and thus could not support a whole family on a single income. Young, unmarried women were expected to support themselves by going into domestic service in middle-class households or by taking low-wage factory jobs. Married women, too, often had to supplement the family income by working outside the home. During the early stages of industrialization, it was in fact easy for working-class women to find factory jobs. This was especially true for the flourishing low-wage textile industry, where labor-saving devices made their first

This 1909 photograph shows a young girl being instructed by a male supervisor on how to use a spinning machine. Women, not men, made up the bulk of the early labor force in the textile industry, principally because it was presumed that women were easier to discipline than men and because women's smaller hands allegedly made them better suited for working with machines.
Bettmann/Getty Images

appearance. Both inventors and manufacturers mistakenly believed that women (and also children) were best suited to operate the new machines because their small hands and fingers gave them superior dexterity. As a result, by the middle of the nineteenth century, women made up the majority of the British industrial workforce. But the preference for women in factory jobs was short-lived, as male workers demanded access to industrial employment. Over the last half of the nineteenth century, women were increasingly replaced by mechanized labor-saving devices, while men were hired for factory jobs.

The largest employment sector available to working-class women was in domestic service. Industrialization increased the demand for domestic servants as the middle class grew in both numbers and wealth. One of every three European women became a domestic servant at some point in her life. Rural women sometimes had to move long distances to take positions in middle-class homes in cities, where they experienced independence from family control but also hard work, exploitation, and sexual abuse. Their employers replaced their parents as guardians, but high demand for servants ensured that women could switch jobs readily in search of more attractive positions. Young women servants often sent some of their earnings home, but many also saved wages for their future lives: amassing a dowry, for example, or building funds to start careers as clerks or secretaries.

**Child Labor** Industrialization profoundly influenced children's lives as well. Like their elders, children in preindustrial societies had always worked in and around the family home. Industrial work, which took children away from home and parents for long hours with few breaks, made abuse and exploitation of **child labor** more likely. Early reports from British textile mills described overseers who forced children to work from dawn until dark and beat them to keep them awake. Yet many families needed their children's wages to survive, so they had little choice but to send them to the factories and mines. By the 1840s the British Parliament began to pass laws regulating child labor and ultimately restricted or removed children from the industrial workforce. In the long term, industrial society was responsible for removing children from the labor process altogether, even in the home. Whereas agricultural settings continued to demand that children make a contribution to the family income, urban industrial societies redefined the role of children. Motivated in part by moral concerns and in part by the recognition that modern society demanded a highly skilled and educated labor force, governments established the legal requirement that education, and not work for monetary gain, was the principal task of childhood. In England, for instance, education for children age five to ten became mandatory by 1881.

## The Socialist Challenge

Among the most vocal and influential critics of early industrial society were the socialists, who worked to alleviate the social and economic problems generated by capitalism and industrialization. Socialists deplored economic inequalities, as represented by the vast difference in wealth between a

# SOURCES FROM THE PAST

## Testimony for the Factory Act of 1833: Working Conditions in England

*During the 1830s and 1840s, deplorable conditions in England's factories and mines led the British Parliament to conduct a series of investigations on the subject. Investigators asked doctors, workers, and factory owners many questions about working conditions and their effects on laborers. The results of these investigations led to parliamentary legislation, such as the Factory Act of 1833, designed to protect workers from the worst effects of industrialization.*

**Testimony of John Wright.**

How long have you been employed in a silk-mill?—More than thirty years.

Did you enter it as a child?—Yes betwixt five and six.

How many hours a day did you work then?—The same thirty years ago as now.

What are those hours?—Eleven hours per day and two over-hours: over-hours are working after six in the evening until eight. The regular hours are from six in the morning to six in the evening, and two others are two over-hours. . . .

If one worked thirteen hours a day, six days a week, how might this have affected family life?

Why, then, are those employed in them said to be in such a wretched condition?—In the first place, the great number of hands congregated together, in some rooms forty, in some fifty, in some sixty, and I have known some as many as 100, which must be injurious to both health and growing. In the second place, the privy [toilet] is in the factory, which frequently emits an unwholesome smell; and it would be worth while to notice in the future erection of mills, that there be betwixt the privy door and the factory wall a kind of a lobby of cage-work. 3dly, The tediousness and the everlasting sameness in the first process preys much on the spirits, and makes the hands spiritless. 4thly, the extravagant number of hours a child is compelled to labour and confinement, which for one week is seventy-six hours. . . . 5thly, About six months in the year we are obliged to use either gas, candles, or lamps, for the longest portion of that time, nearly six hours a day, being obliged to work amid the smoke and soot of the same; and also a large portion of oil and grease is used in the mills.

What are the effects of the present system of labor? —From my earliest recollections, I have found the effects to be awfully detrimental to the well-being of the operative; I have observed frequently children carried to factories, unable to walk, and that entirely owing to excessive labour and confinement. The degradation of the workpeople baffles all description: frequently have two of my sisters been obliged to be assisted to the factory and home again, until by-and-by they could go no longer, being totally crippled in their legs. And in the next place, I remember some ten or twelve years ago working in one of the largest firms in Macclesfield, . . . with about twenty-two men, where they were scarce one half fit for His Majesty's service. Those that are straight in their limbs are stunted in their growth; much inferior to their fathers in point of strength. 3dly, Through excessive labour and confinement there is often a total loss of appetite; a kind of langour steals over the whole frame—enters to the very core—saps the foundation of the best constitution—and lays our strength prostrate in the dust. In the 4th place, by protracted labour there is an alarming increase of cripples in various parts of this town, which has come under my own observation and knowledge.

In addition to the extremely difficult physical conditions, what kinds of emotional toll did working in the silk mills take on workers, according to John Wright?

Are all these cripples made in the silk factories?—Yes, they are, I believe. . . .

### For Further Reflection

- In Wright's opinion, what aspect of labor in the silk factories was the most damaging for children?
- The Factory Act was one of the first reform bills passed to address the difficult working conditions of the Industrial Revolution. The man being interviewed supposed the same "wretched conditions" for thirty years. Why did the government delay make appropriate changes?
- What prompted the reform?

*Source:* Commission for Inquiry into the Employment of Children in Factories, Second Report, with Minutes of Evidence and Reports by the Medical Commissioners, vol. V, Session 29 January–20 August, 1833. London: His Majesty's Printing Office, 1833, pp. 5, 26–28.

captain of industry and a factory laborer, and they condemned the system that permitted the exploitation of laborers, including women and children. Early socialists sought to expand the Enlightenment understanding of equality: they understood equality to have an economic as well as a political, legal, and social dimension, and they looked to the future establishment of a just and equitable society. Although most socialists shared this general vision, they held very different views on the best way to establish and maintain an ideal socialist society.

**Utopian Socialists** The term ***socialism*** first appeared around 1830, when it referred to the ideas of social critics such as Charles Fourier (1772–1837) and Robert Owen (1771–1858). Often called **utopian socialists,** Fourier, Owen, and their

Robert Koehler's 1886 painting *The Strike* depicts a situation verging toward violence as workers mill about in a confrontation with factory owners and one angry laborer crouches to pick up a stone.
Art Collection 2/Alamy Stock Photo

followers worked to establish ideal communities that would point the way to an equitable society. Fourier spent most of his life as a salesman, but he loathed the competition of the market system and called for social transformations that would better serve the needs of humankind. He painstakingly planned model communities that were supposed to be held together by love rather than coercion, in which everyone performed work in accordance with personal temperament and inclination. Owen, a successful businessman, transformed a squalid Scottish cotton mill town called New Lanark into a model industrial community. At New Lanark, Owen raised wages, reduced the workday from seventeen to ten hours, built spacious housing, and opened a store that sold goods at fair prices. Despite the costs of those reforms, the mills of New Lanark generated profits. Out of the two thousand residents of the community, five hundred were young children from the poorhouses of Glasgow and Edinburgh, and Owen devoted special attention to their education. He kept young children out of the factories and sent them to a school that he opened in 1816. Owen's indictment of competitive capitalism, his stress on cooperative control of industry, and his advocacy of improved educational standards for children left a lasting imprint on the socialist tradition.

## How the Past Shapes the Future

### The Birth of Nationalism

One of the attractions of nationalism was a sense of belonging to a defined community based on language, heritage, and culture. But revolutionary socialism as expressed in the ***Communist Manifesto*** saw the main division between peoples not in terms of nationality but in terms of membership in either the capitalist or proletariat classes. Capitalists and proletarians could be from any nation and theoretically would have more in common with others in their same group—from any nation—than with members of the opposing group, even if they were of the same nationality. Consider how revolutionary socialism could exist side by side with nationalism, and why revolutionary socialism did not replace nationalism in the areas where it developed.

The ideas of the utopian socialists resonated widely in the nineteenth century, and their disciples established experimental communities from the United States to Romania. But in spite of the enthusiasm of the founders, most of the communities soon encountered economic difficulties and political problems that forced them to fold. By the mid-nineteenth century, most socialists looked not to utopian communities but to large-scale organization of working people as the best means to bring about a just and equitable society.

Contemporary photograph of Karl Marx (1818–1883), German political philosopher and founder of modern socialism. His most important theoretical work, *Das Kapital* (*Capital,* in the English translation), is an extensive treatise on political economy that offers a highly critical analysis of capitalism. Bettmann/Getty Images

**Marx and Engels** Most prominent of the nineteenth-century socialists were the German theorists **Karl Marx** (1818–1883) and **Friedrich Engels** (1820–1895). They scorned the utopian socialists as unrealistic dabblers whose ideal communities had no hope of resolving the problems of the early industrial era. Marx and Engels believed that the social problems of the nineteenth century were inevitable results of a capitalist economy. They held that capitalism divided people into two main classes, each with its own economic interests and social status: the capitalists, who owned industrial machinery and factories (which Marx and Engels called the means of production), and the proletariat, consisting of wageworkers who had only their labor to sell. Intense competition between capitalists trying to realize a profit resulted in ruthless exploitation of the working class. To make matters worse, according to Marx and Engels, the state and its coercive institutions, such as police forces and courts of law, were agencies of the capitalist ruling class. Their function was to maintain capitalists in power and enable them to continue their exploitation of the proletariat. Even music, art, literature, and religion served the purposes of capitalists, according to Marx and Engels, since they amused the working classes and diverted attention from their misery. Marx once referred to religion as "the opiate of the masses" because it encouraged workers to focus on a hypothetical realm of existence in heaven rather than the difficulties they faced in the world of the living.

**The *Communist Manifesto*** Marx developed those views fully in a long, theoretical work called *Capital.* Together with Engels, Marx also wrote a short, spirited tract titled *Manifesto of the Communist Party* (1848). This work, which became popularly known as the *Communist Manifesto,* Marx and Engels aligned themselves with the communists, who worked toward the abolition of private property and the institution of a radically egalitarian society. The *Manifesto* asserted that all human history has been the history of struggle between social classes. It argued that the future lay with the working class because the laws of history dictated that capitalism would inexorably grind to a halt. Crises of overproduction, underconsumption, and diminishing profits would shake the foundations of the capitalist order. Meanwhile, members of the constantly growing and thoroughly exploited proletariat would come to view the forcible overthrow of the existing system as the only alternative available to them. Marx and Engels believed that a socialist revolution would result in a "dictatorship of the proletariat," which would abolish private property and destroy the capitalist order. After the revolution was secure, the state would wither away. Coercive institutions would also disappear because there would no longer be an exploiting class. Thus socialism would lead to a fair, just, and egalitarian society infinitely more humane than the capitalist order.

The doctrines of Marx and Engels came to dominate European and international socialism, and socialist parties grew rapidly throughout the nineteenth century. Political parties, trade unions, newspapers, and educational associations all worked to advance the socialist cause. Yet socialists disagreed strongly on the best means to reform society. Revolutionary socialists such as Marx, Engels, and other communists urged workers to seize control of the state, confiscate the means of production, and distribute wealth equitably throughout society. Doubting that a revolution could succeed, evolutionary socialists placed their hopes in representative governments and called for the election of legislators who supported socialist reforms.

Once held almost exclusively by men, clerical jobs increasingly went to women as industrial society matured. This photograph features the typewriting department of a large company in Dayton, Ohio. Note the absence of men in their ranks.
Everett Collection Historical/ Alamy Stock Photo

**Social Reform** Although socialists did not win control of any government until the Russian revolution of 1917, their critiques—along with those of conservatives and liberals—persuaded government authorities to attack the abuses of early industrialization and provide at least some security for the working classes. The British Parliament prohibited underground employment for women, like the drawer Betty Harris, as well as for boys and girls under age ten. It also stipulated that children under age nine not work more than nine hours a day. The 1830s and 1840s saw the inception of laws that regulated women's working hours, while leaving men without protection and constraints. The intention behind this legislation was to protect women's family roles according to middle-class ideals, but it also reduced women's economic opportunities on the grounds of their perceived frailty. Coming under pressure from the voting public and labor unions, governments increasingly accepted that the state was responsible for the social and economic welfare of its citizens. Beginning in the late nineteenth century, European countries, led by Germany, adopted social reform programs, including retirement pensions; minimum wage laws; sickness, accident, and unemployment insurance; and the regulation of hours and conditions of work. These reforms of liberal capitalist society were a prelude to the modern welfare state that emerged in the twentieth century.

**Trade Unions** **Trade unions** also sought to advance the quest for a just and equitable society. As governments regulated businesses and enhanced social security, workers struggled to eliminate abuses of early industrial society and improve workers' lives by organizing to seek higher wages and better working conditions for their members. Through most of the nineteenth century, both employers and governments considered trade unions illegal associations whose purpose was to restrain trade. Tensions ran high when union members went on strike, especially when employers sought to keep their businesses going by hiring replacement workers. In those cases, violence frequently broke out, prompting government authorities to send in police or military forces to maintain order. Over the longer run, though, trade unions gradually improved the lives of working people and reduced the likelihood that a disgruntled proletariat would mount a revolution to overthrow industrial capitalist society. Indeed, trade unions became an integral part of industrial society because they did not seek to destroy capitalism but, rather, to make employers more responsive to their employees' needs and interests.

## Global Effects of Industrialization

Early industrialization was a British affair, which then spread to western Europe and North America by the early nineteenth century. By the late nineteenth century, Russia and Japan were also beginning to industrialize (see chapter 31). In addition to its spread beyond western Europe, industrialization had deep global implications because industrial powers used their tools, technologies, business organization, financial influence, and transportation networks to obtain raw materials from societies around the world. Many places that possessed natural resources became increasingly oriented to exporting raw materials but maintained little control over them because representatives of industrial countries dominated the commercial and financial institutions associated with the trade. Some societies saw their home markets flooded with inexpensive manufactured products from industrial states, which devastated traditional industries and damaged local economies.

**The International Division of Labor** Industrialization brought great economic and military strength to societies that now relied on mechanized production. Their power encouraged other societies to work toward industrialization. Before the mid-twentieth century, however, those efforts were hampered either by outright imperial conquests undertaken by industrial states or by deliberate attempts by the same states to discourage industrialization via economic or political pressure. In India, for example, entrepreneurs had established a thriving industry in the production of cotton textiles by the eighteenth century. But since the East India Company had conquered Bengal in 1757, by the early nineteenth century British businessmen were able to crush the industry by forcing imports of inexpensive British textiles and by raising tariffs on Indian textiles.

Indeed, industrialization tilted the global balance of power in favor of industrial states and gave rise to a new international division of labor. Industrial societies needed minerals, agricultural products, and other raw materials to power their industries and to feed their growing populations. The mechanization of the textile industry, for example, produced a demand for large quantities of raw cotton, which came mostly from India, Egypt, and the southern rim of the United States. Similarly, new industrial technologies increased demand for products such as rubber, the principal ingredient of belts and tires that were essential to industrial machinery, which came from Brazil, Malaya, and the Congo River basin. When state leaders did not wish to trade on the terms offered by representatives of industrial societies, these representatives did not hesitate to use force, the threat of force, or economic intimidation to get what they wanted.

**Economic Development** In some places, specialization in the production and export of primary goods paved the way for economic development and eventual industrialization. This pattern was especially noticeable in European settler colonies, including Canada, South Africa, Australia, and New Zealand, each of which enjoyed a special relationship with Great Britain. Britons directly controlled the government in each of these colonies, and British investors were directly and heavily invested in their infrastructure and economies. European migrants flocked to the settler colonies, where they set up businesses that exported primary products to feed the economies of the industrial states. European settlers commanded high wages, and the spending power of these incomes created flourishing markets for industrial goods within the settler colonies. Over time, European entrepreneurs in the settler colonies developed mechanized industries themselves based on technologies brought from Europe.

**Economic Interdependence** Other places did not benefit from the same advantages as European settler colonies. In most of Latin America, sub-Saharan Africa, south Asia, and southeast Asia representatives of industrialized states sought

## INTERPRETING IMAGES

This is an image of the Clermont Paddlesteamer invented by Robert Fulton and launched in 1807. Steamboats transported passengers and cargo and aided in the exploitation of raw materials around the world.

**Analyze** *Consider the photos and illustrations of inventions throughout this chapter, including the textile machines (pg. 547), steam hammer (pg. 552), oil refinery (pg. 554), and spinning machine (pg. 561). What sense do these images give you about popular feelings associated with the Industrial Revolution? Which invention would you consider the most revolutionary and why? When you think about the people most affected by an Industrial Revolution invention, does it change the way you think about its importance?*

Chronicle/Alamy Stock Photo

to impose their will either by outright colonial conquest (discussed in chapter 32) or by using economic and political pressure. In most areas, they sought raw materials—especially sugar, cotton, and rubber—and encouraged whole economies to move toward an export-oriented agricultural economy based on cash crops. They actively discouraged industrialization, seeking instead to create reliable supplies of raw materials to feed their own industrial economies. They often set controls on the prices of agricultural goods, thus keeping prices—and thus the profits for producers—artificially low.

This new geographic division of labor, in which some of the world's peoples provided raw materials while others processed and consumed them, increased the volume of world trade and led to increased transportation on both sea and land. Bigger ships, larger docks, and deeper canals facilitated trade and transport around the world. However, the benefits of this new system flowed primarily to Europe, North America, and Japan. Other places realized few benefits from the process of industrialization, even though the process increasingly linked the fortunes of all the world's peoples.

## CONCLUSION

The process of industrialization involved the harnessing of inanimate sources of energy, the replacement of handicraft production with machine-based manufacturing, and the generation of new forms of business and labor organization. Along with industrialization came demographic growth, large-scale migration, and rapid urbanization, which increased the demand for manufactured goods by working people, who formed the majority of the population. Societies that underwent industrialization enjoyed sharp increases in economic productivity: they produced large quantities of high-quality goods at low prices, and their increased productivity eventually translated into higher material standards of living. Yet industrialization brought costs, in the form of unsettling social problems. Family life changed dramatically in the industrial age as men, women, and children increasingly left their homes to work in factories and mines, often under appalling conditions. In response, socialist critics sought to bring about a more just and equitable society, and government authorities eventually responded by curtailing the worst abuses of the early industrial era. Governments and labor unions both worked to raise living standards and provide security for working people. Meanwhile, industrialization increasingly touched the lives of peoples around the world. Western European, North American, and Japanese societies followed Britain's lead into industrialization, while many African, Asian, and Latin American places had little choice but to become dependent on the export of raw materials to industrial societies.

## STUDY TERMS

calicoes (553)
cartels (560)
child labor (567)
*Communist Manifesto* (569)
corporations (560)
Crystal Palace (561)
demographic transition (562)
Eli Whitney (558)
factory system (555)
flying shuttle (554)
Friedrich Engels (570)
George Stephenson (554)
Henry Ford (558)
James Watt (554)
Karl Marx (570)
Luddites (556)
middle class (564)
mule (554)
power loom (554)
Second Industrial Revolution (556)
*socialism* (568)
trade unions (571)
trusts (560)
utopian socialists (568)
working class (564)

## FOR FURTHER READING


Daniel R. Headrick. *Power over Peoples: Technology, Environments, and Western Imperialism, 1400 to the Present*. Princeton, 2009. Explores the important relationship between technology and imperialism.

Penelope Lane, Neil Raven, and K. D. M. Snell, eds. *Women, Work and Wages in England, 1600–1850.* Rochester, N.Y., 2004. Study of women's contributions to British industrialization and how it was rewarded.

Karl Marx and Friedrich Engels. *The Communist Manifesto.* Trans. by Samuel Moore. Harmondsworth, 1967. English translation of the most important tract of nineteenth-century socialism, with an excellent introduction by historian A. J. P. Taylor.

David R. Meyer. *The Roots of American Industrialization.* Baltimore, 2003. Interdisciplinary study that ties America's industrialization to increasing agricultural productivity of the antebellum period.

Prasannan Parthasarathi. *Why Europe Grew Rich and Asia Did Not: Global Economic Divergence, 1600–1800.* Cambridge, 2011. Argues that British economic policies were crucial in crushing the thriving cotton textile industry in India.

Kenneth Pomeranz. *The Great Divergence: China, Europe, and the Making of the Modern World Economy.* Princeton, 2000. Argues that the fortuitous location of coal deposits and access to the resources of the Americas created a uniquely advantageous framework for English industrialization.

William Rosen. *The Most Powerful Idea in the World: A Story of Steam, Industry, and Invention.* New York, 2010. Dismissing traditional explanations for the origins of British industrialization, the author argues that England's patent system proved the decisive factor.

Peter N. Stearns. *The Industrial Revolution in World History*. 4th ed. Boulder, Colo., 2012. This concise account places industrialization and its effects in a global perspective.

E. P. Thompson. *The Making of the English Working Class.* New York, 1966. A classic work that analyzes the formation of working-class consciousness in England from the 1790s to the 1830s.

Louise A. Tilly. *Industrialization and Gender Inequality.* Washington, D.C., 1993. A brief historiographical survey of debates on gender and industrialization in England, France, Germany, the United States, Japan, and China.

# CHAPTER 17 AP EXAM PRACTICE

Questions assume cumulative knowledge from this chapter and previous chapters.

## Section I

## Multiple Choice Questions

Use the image below and your knowledge of world history to answer questions 1 – 3.

Image of the Clermont Paddlesteamer invented by Robert Fulton and launched in 1807.
Chronicle/Alamy Stock Photo

1. What was a global impact of the Industrial Revolution?
   (A) China expanded its traditional market in porcelain.
   (B) Some countries saw their markets flooded with cheap, manufactured imports.
   (C) Countries that supplied natural resources gained control over them by controlling financial institutions.
   (D) Europeans stopped purchasing raw materials abroad and relying on what they could produce at home.

2. Why was the steamship a significant technology during the Industrial Revolution?
   (A) Steamships allowed for riverboat travel and tourism.
   (B) Steamships reduced the time it took to ship goods to and from Europe and its settler colonies.
   (C) Steamships reduced the need for industrial countries to import raw materials.
   (D) Steamships made it easier for navies to patrol their coastlines.

3. What economic opportunities did the Industrial Revolution create outside of Europe and the United States?
   (A) The Manila galleons exchanged American silver for European textiles.
   (B) The Portuguese factory system brought financial prosperity to the Indian Ocean.
   (C) The Indian royal family manipulated European industrial states against each other.
   (D) British settler colonies benefitted from a special relationship with Great Britain, which allowed European entrepreneurs to develop industry in the colonies.

Use the images below and your knowledge of world history to answer questions 4 and 5.

Exhibitors from around the world displayed fine handicrafts and manufactured goods at the Crystal Palace exhibition of 1851 in London.
Time Life Pictures/Mansell/The LIFE Picture Collection/Getty Images

Standard Oil's Refinery in Richmond, California
Library of Congress/Corbis Historical/Getty Images

4. What differences in the era of industrialization are seen in these images?
   (A) Middle-class women stayed home while working-class women worked in factories.
   (B) European elites celebrated industrial progress while environmental pollution intensified.
   (C) European colonies provided raw materials while European countries produced manufactured goods.
   (D) Working class men tried to maintain the putting out system while their wives and children worked in factories.

5. What message do you think the artist is trying to convey with this image of the Crystal Palace?
   (A) The artist wants to show the importance of local sporting clubs in industrial society.
   (B) The artist wanted to attract French and German companies to build factories in London.
   (C) The artist wanted to promote the superiority of British manufacturing and society.
   (D) The artist wanted to encourage British industrialists to buy British raw materials.

## Short Answer

6. Use the image below and your knowledge of world history to answer parts A, B, and C.

Robert Koehler's painting *The Strike* depicts a situation verging toward violence as workers mill about in a confrontation with factory owners and one angry laborer crouches to pick up a stone.
Art Collection 2/Alamy Stock Photo

(A) Identify ONE tactic that unions used in the nineteenth century to benefit workers.
(B) Explain ONE difference between revolutionary socialists and trade unions.
(C) Identify ONE improvement for workers that trade unions accomplished.

7. Use the map below and your knowledge of world history to answer parts A, B, and C.

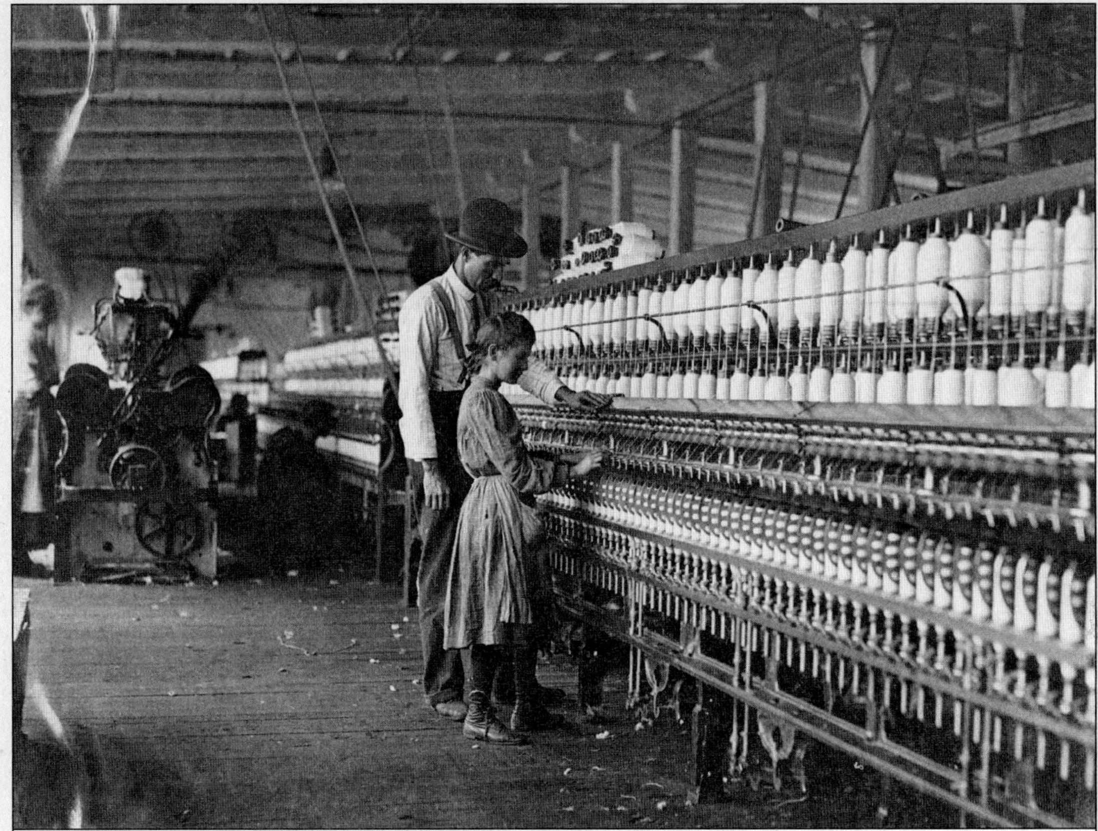

This 1909 photograph shows a young girl being instructed by a male supervisor on how to use a spinning machine.
Bettmann/Getty Images

(A) Identify ONE reason why factory owners early in the Industrial Revolution hired women and children.
(B) Explain ONE way that the lives of middle-class women were different from that of working-class women.
(C) Explain ONE way that middle-class values changed society in the era of industrialization.

8. Use your understanding of world history to answer parts A, B, and C.
(A) Identify ONE resource needed for industrial production.
(B) Explain ONE way that industrialization and colonialism worked together.
(C) Explain the importance of ONE product from the industrial revolution.

# Section II

## Document-Based Question

Based on the documents below and your knowledge of world history, analyze the extent to which industrialization brought social change to European society.

In your response you should do the following:

- Respond to the prompt with a historically defensible thesis or claim that establishes a line of reasoning.
- Describe a broader historical context relevant to the prompt.
- Support an argument in response to the prompt using all documents.
- Use at least one additional piece of specific historical evidence (beyond that found in the documents) relevant to an argument about the prompt.
- Explain how or why the document's point of view, purpose, historical situation, and /or audience is relevant to an argument.
- Use evidence to corroborate, qualify, or modify an argument that addresses the prompt.

### Document 1

**Information has just been given** in that you are a holder of those detestable Shearing Frames, and I was desired by my Men to write to you and give you fair Warning to pull them down, and for that purpose I desire you will now understand I am now writing to you. you will take Notice that if they are not taken down by the end of next Week, I will detach one of my Lieutenants with at least 300 Men to destroy them and furthermore take Notice that if you give us the Trouble of coming so far we will increase your misfortune by burning your Buildings down to Ashes and if you have Impudence to fire upon any of my Men, they have orders to murder you, & burn all your Housing, you will have the Goodness to your Neighbours to inform them that the same fate awaits them if their Frames are not speedily taken down as I understand their are several in your Neighbourhood, Frame holders.

*Source:* Clerk Ludd, Ned. Letter from "Ned Ludd Clerk" addressed "To Mr Smith Shearing Frame Holder at Hill End Yorkshire." 1812.

# Document 2

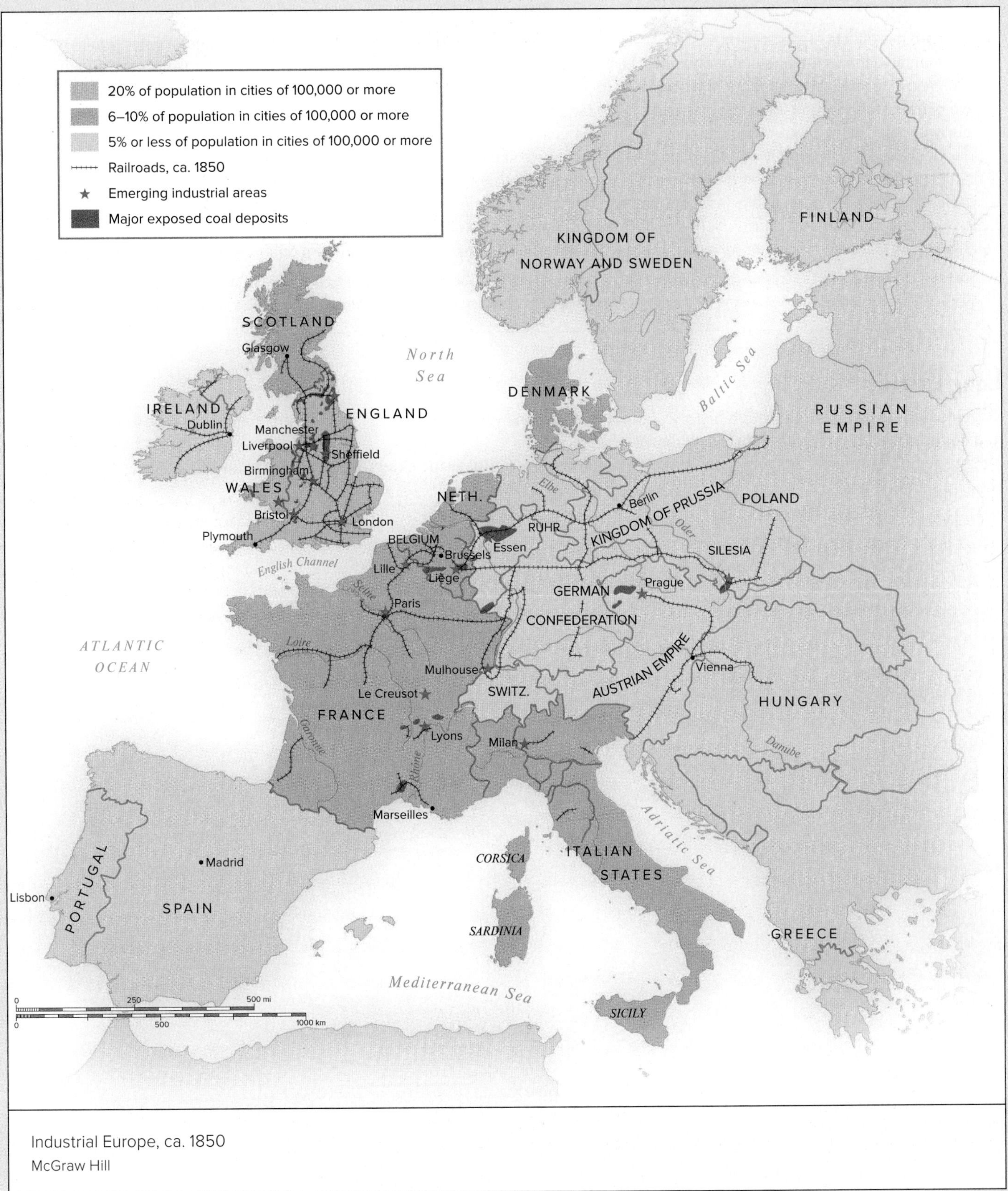


Industrial Europe, ca. 1850

McGraw Hill

## Document 3

What are the effects of the present system of labor? —From my earliest recollections, I have found the effects to be awfully detrimental to the well-being of the operative; I have observed frequently children carried to factories, unable to walk, and that entirely owing to excessive labour and confinement. The degradation of the workpeople baffles all description: frequently have two of my sisters been obliged to be assisted to the factory and home again, until by-and-by they could go no longer, being totally crippled in their legs. And in the next place, I remember some ten or twelve years ago working in one of the largest firms in Macclesfield, . . . with about twenty-two men, where they were scarce one half fit for His Majesty's service. Those that are straight in their limbs are stunted in their growth; much inferior to their fathers in point of strength. 3dly, Through excessive labour and confinement there is often a total loss of appetite; a kind of langour steals over the whole frame—enters to the very core—saps the foundation of the best constitution—and lays our strength prostrate in the dust. In the 4th place, by protracted labour there is an alarming increase of cripples in various parts of this town, which has come under my own observation and knowledge.

*Source:* Commission for Inquiry into the Employment of Children in Factories, Second Report, with Minutes of Evidence and Reports by the Medical Commissioners, vol. V, Session 29 January–20 August, 1833. London: His Majesty's Printing Office, 1833, pp. 5, 26–28.

## Long Essay

Develop a thoughtful and thorough historical argument that answers the question below. Begin your essay with a thesis statement and support it with relevant historical evidence.

Using specific examples and your knowledge of world history, evaluate the extent to which Marx and Engels were influenced by the Utopian Socialists.

# Chapter 18 The Americas in the Age of Independence



## ZOOMING IN ON ENCOUNTERS

### Fatt Hing Chin Searches for Gold from China to California

Fatt Hing Chin was a village fish peddler who lived in a coastal town in southern China. One day at the wharves, he heard people talking about a place across the ocean where the mountains were laden with gold. Chin was nineteen years old and full of energy, and he longed for the chance to see if he could find some of this gold for himself. He learned that he could purchase passage on a foreign ship, and in 1849—after reconciling his parents to his plans—he boarded a Spanish ship to sail to California and join the gold rush.

Chin felt some uncertainty once at sea. Surprised at the large number of young Chinese men crammed in with him in the ship's hold, he shared their dismay as they remained confined to the cargo areas of the ship, where the smell of vomit was overpowering. Ninety-five days and nights passed before the hills of San Francisco came into view. Upon arrival the travelers met Chinese veterans of life in the United States who explained the strategy of sticking together in order to survive and prosper.

Chin hired himself out as a gold miner and headed for the mountains of gold. After digging and sifting for two years, he had accumulated his own little pile of gold. He wrote to his brothers and cousins, urging them to join him, and thus helped fuel a large-scale overseas migration that brought 24,000 Chinese workers to California in the four years between 1849 and 1853. Having made his fortune, though, Chin decided to return to China. Now wealthy, on the way home he traveled much more comfortably in a cabin with a bunk. Although he gambled away half his gold before his ship docked in China at Guangzhou, what remained still amounted to a small fortune.

Seven miners stand near a sluice box in California around 1852. Note the four Chinese miners standing to the right.
Fotosearch/Archive Photos/Getty Images

California gold provided him with the means to take a wife, build a house, and buy some land.

Although settled and prosperous, Chin remained restless and longed to return to California. Leaving his pregnant wife, he sailed for California again after only a year. He returned to mining with his brother (who had taken his advice and made the trip to California), but the gold had become more difficult to find. Inspired by the luck of another migrant, Tong Ling, who managed to get one dollar for each meal he sold, Chin's cousins in San Francisco decided to open a restaurant. As one of them said, "If the foreign devils will eat his food, they will eat ours." Chin found the city much more comfortable than the mountains. "Let the others go after the gold in the hills," he said. "I'll wait for the gold to come to the city."

Fatt Hing Chin was one of the earliest Chinese migrants to settle in the Americas. His career path—from a miner in search of quick riches to an urban resident committed to a new homeland and hoping to profit from the service industry—was typical of Chinese migrants to the United States. Some went from mining to railroad construction or agricultural labor, but all contributed to the transformation of the Americas. Along with millions of others from Europe and Asia, Chinese migrants increased the ethnic diversity of American populations and stimulated political, social, and economic development in the Western Hemisphere.

# CHAPTER FOCUS

- Both Canada and the United States sponsored massive westward movements facilitated by railroads, worked by immigrants, and conducted over the protests of the native peoples whose lands were taken.
- In Latin American countries, a political strain also existed over the rights and lands of the native peoples, but not in the context of industrialized railroad building.
- Note that the violence of the U.S. Civil War (1861–1865), fought over slavery and the powers of the national government, pushed Canadians to establish the Canadian Dominion in 1867.
- In Latin American countries, military dictators (caudillos) worked hand in-hand with the landed creole elites to control the governments and the economies.
- Study the Mexican revolution of 1910: it is often compared to the Russian revolution of 1917 and the Chinese revolution of 1911, particularly in terms of land redistribution.
- The social history of the American multiethnic empires continued to be complex and often violent in the nineteenth and twentieth centuries.
- The demand for raw cotton to feed the new textile industry, for example, reinvigorated slavery in the United States, provoking increasing calls for its abolition, which ultimately led to the Civil War.

## Historical Developments

- The United States expanded their land holdings by conquering and settling neighboring territories.
- Migration in many cases was influenced by changes in demographics in both industrialized and unindustrialized societies that presented challenges to existing patterns of living.
- Migrants often created ethnic enclaves in different parts of the world that helped transplant their culture into new environments.
- Receiving societies did not always embrace immigrants, as seen in the various degrees of ethnic and racial prejudice and the ways states attempted to regulate the increased flow of people across their borders.

## Reasoning Processes

- **Comparison** Explain relevant similarities and differences between Canadian, U.S., and Latin American societies in the 19th century.
- **Continuity and Change** Describe the patterns of continuity and change across the Americas that resulted from mass migration.

## Historical Thinking Skills

- **Developments and Processes** Identify the major social and political transformations taking place in Canada, the United States, and Latin America in the 19th century.
- **Sourcing and Situation** Identify the point of view and historical situation surrounding Jourdan Anderson's letter to his former master.
- **Argumentation** Make a historically defensible claim describing how and why women, Native Americans, migrants, and freed slaves each struggled to establish a place in American societies.

## CHAPTER OVERVIEW

During the late eighteenth and early nineteenth centuries, almost all the territories in the Western Hemisphere won their independence from European colonial powers. American peoples then struggled throughout the nineteenth century to build states and societies that realized their potential in an age of independence. The United States embarked on a westward push that brought most of the temperate regions of North America under U.S. control. Canada built a federal state under British Canadian leadership. The varied lands of Latin America built smaller states that often fell under the sway of local military leaders. One issue that most American peoples wrestled with, regardless of their region, was the legacy of the Enlightenment. The effort to build societies based on freedom, equality, and constitutional government was a monumental challenge only partially realized in lands characterized by enormous social, economic, and cultural divisions. Both the institution of slavery and its ultimate abolition complicated the process of building societies in the Americas, particularly in regard to defining a new type of workforce for free and increasingly industrial economies. Asian and European migrants joined native-born workers and formerly enslaved people in labor systems—from plantations and factories to debt peonage—that often demonstrated the hollowness of American promises of welcome and freedom.

The age of independence for the United States, Canada, and Latin America was a contentious era characterized by continuous mass migration and explosive economic growth, occasionally followed by deep economic stagnation, and punctuated with civil war, ethnic violence, class conflict, and battles for racial and sexual equality. Independence clearly did not solve the political and social problems of the Western Hemisphere but, rather, created a new context in which American peoples struggled to build effective states, enjoy economic prosperity, and attain cultural cohesion. Those goals were elusive throughout the nineteenth century (and in many ways remain so in the present day). Nevertheless, the histories of these first territories to win independence from colonial powers inspired other peoples who later sought freedom from imperial rule. At the same time, they also served as portents of the difficulties faced by newly free states.

| CHRONOLOGY | |
|---|---|
| 1803 | Louisiana Purchase |
| 1804–1806 | Lewis and Clark expedition |
| 1812–1814 | War of 1812 |
| 1829–1852 | Rule of Juan Manuel de Rosas in Argentina |
| 1838–1839 | Trail of Tears |
| 1846–1848 | Mexican-American War |
| 1848 | Seneca Falls Convention |
| 1849 | California gold rush |
| 1850s | La Reforma in Mexico |
| 1861–1865 | U.S. Civil War |
| 1867 | Establishment of the Dominion of Canada; French troops withdraw from Mexico |
| 1867–1877 | Reconstruction in the United States |
| 1869 | Completion of the transcontinental railroad line in the United States |
| 1876 | Battle of the Little Bighorn |
| 1876–1911 | Rule of Porfirio Díaz in Mexico |
| 1885 | Completion of the Canadian Pacific Railroad; Northwest Rebellion |
| 1890 | Massacre at Wounded Knee |
| 1910–1920 | Mexican revolution |

## THE BUILDING OF AMERICAN STATES

After winning independence from Britain in 1783, the United States fashioned a government and began to expand rapidly to the west. By mid-century the new republic had forcibly absorbed almost all the temperate lands of North America. Yet the United States was an unstable society composed of varied regions with diverse economic and social structures. Differences over slavery and the rights of individual states as opposed to the federal government sparked a devastating civil war in the 1860s. That conflict resulted in the abolition of slavery and the strengthening of the federal state. The experience of Canada was very different from that of the United States. Canada gained independence from Britain without fighting a war, and, despite also being a land of great diversity, avoided fighting a civil war. Although intermittently nervous about the possibility that the United States might expand to the north, Canada established a relatively weak federal government, which presided over provinces that had considerable power over local affairs. Latin American states were even more diverse than their counterparts to the north, and in spite of the efforts of some individuals they were unable to join together in a confederation. Throughout the nineteenth century Latin America was politically fragmented, and many individual states faced serious problems and divisions within their own societies.

## The United States: Westward Expansion and Civil War

After gaining independence the United States faced the need to construct a framework of government. During the 1780s leaders from the rebellious colonies drafted a constitution that entrusted responsibility for general issues to a federal government, reserved authority for local issues for individual states, and provided for the admission of new states and territories to the confederation. Although the Declaration of Independence had declared that "all men are created equal," most individual states limited the vote to men of property. But the Enlightenment ideal of equality encouraged political leaders to extend the franchise: by the late 1820s most property qualifications had disappeared, and by mid-century almost all adult white men were eligible to participate in the political affairs of the republic.

**Westward Expansion and Manifest Destiny** While working to settle constitutional issues, residents of the United States also began to expand rapidly to the west. After the American revolution, Britain ceded to the new republic all lands between the Appalachian Mountains and the Mississippi River, and the United States doubled in size. In 1803 Napoleon Bonaparte needed funds immediately to protect revolutionary France from its enemies, and he allowed the United States to purchase France's Louisiana Territory, which extended from the Mississippi River to the Rocky Mountains. Overnight the United States doubled in size again. Between 1804 and 1806 a geographic expedition led by Meriwether Lewis and William Clark mapped the territory and surveyed its resources. Settlers soon began to flock west in search of cheap land to cultivate. By the 1840s westward expansion was well under way, and many U.S. citizens spoke of a **manifest destiny.** According to this idea, the United States was destined, even divinely ordained, to expand across the North American continent from the Atlantic seaboard to the Pacific and beyond. Manifest destiny was often invoked to justify U.S. expansion.

**Conflict with Indigenous Peoples** Although gaining territory from Britain and France gave westward expansion legal legitimacy from the American point of view, from the perspective of indigenous people it was nothing less than forcible conquest of lands on which they had lived for thousands of years. Indeed, westward expansion brought settlers and government forces into conflict with the indigenous peoples of North America, who resisted efforts to push them from their ancestral lands and hunting grounds. Native Americans forged alliances among themselves and also sought the backing of British colonial officials in Canada, but U.S. officials and military forces supported Euro-American settlers and violently forced the continent open to white expansion. Their efforts, however, did not stop at opening the land to white colonists. Instead, with the **Indian Removal Act of 1830,** the United States government determined to move all Native Americans

Sitting Bull (ca. 1831–1890) was a Hunkpapa Lakota Sioux holy man who also led his people as a war chief during years of resistance to United States government policies. The battle of the Little Bighorn, also known by the indigenous Americans as the battle of Greasy Grass Creek, was the most famous action of the Great Sioux War against the United States cavalry in 1876–1877. It was an overwhelming victory for the Lakota and Northern Cheyenne, overseen by Sitting Bull.
The Art Archive/Shutterstock

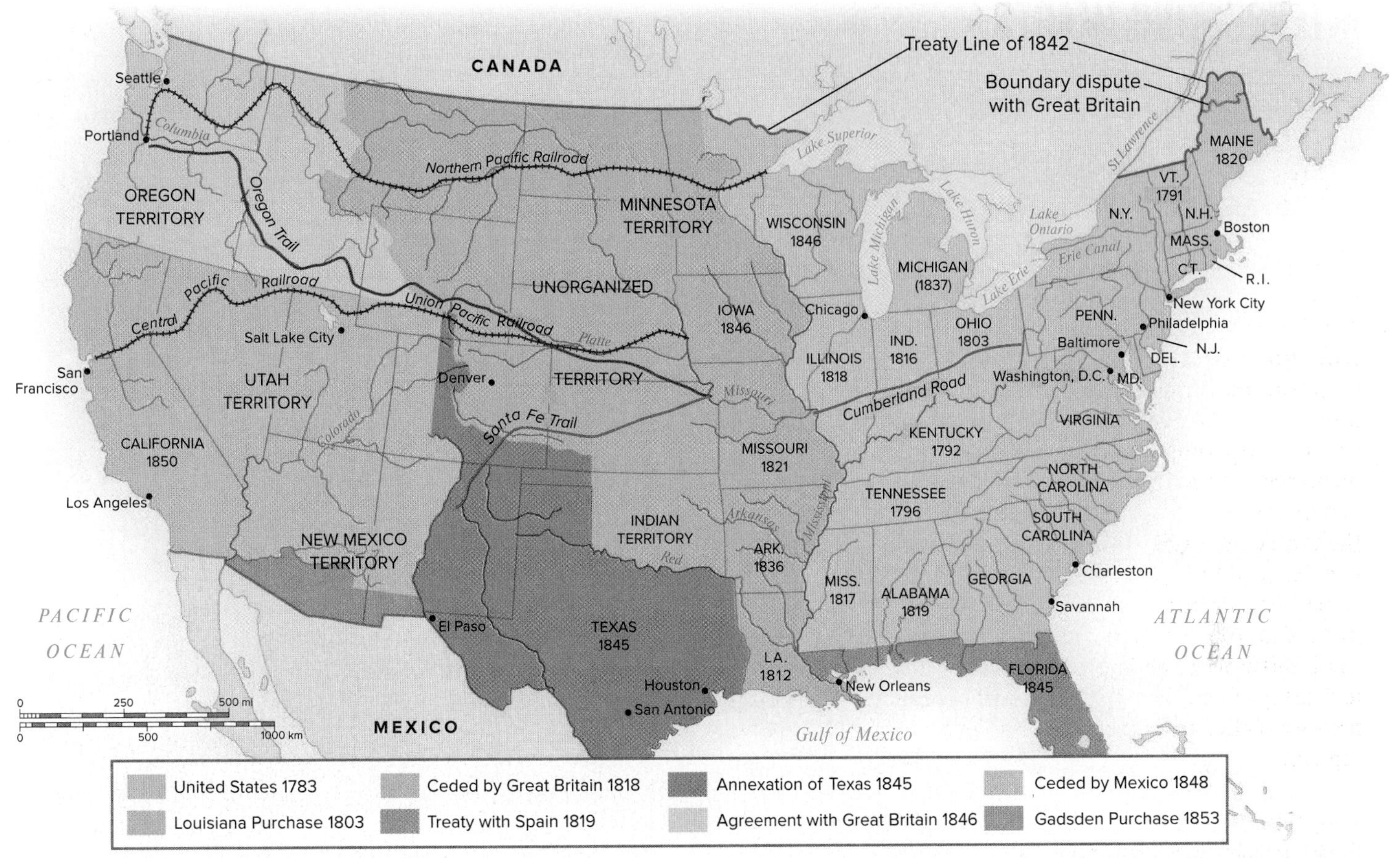


**MAP 18.1 Westward expansion of the United States during the nineteenth century.**

Note the large land claims ceded by Britain, France, and Mexico.

***Why were there no portions of North America purchased from or ceded by Native Americans?***

west of the Mississippi River onto marginal lands they called "Indian Territory" (Oklahoma). Among the tribes affected by this forced removal from the east were the Seminoles, some of whom managed to avoid capture and the long march to Oklahoma by resisting and retreating to Florida's swampy lowlands. The Cherokees also suffered a harrowing 800-mile migration from the eastern woodlands to Oklahoma on the **Trail of Tears** (1838–1839), so known because thousands died from disease, starvation, and the difficulties of relocation.

After 1840 the site of conflict between Euro-American and indigenous peoples shifted to the plains region west of the Mississippi River. Settlers and ranchers in the trans-Mississippi west encountered peoples such as the Sioux, Comanche, Pawnee, and Apache, who possessed firearms and outstanding equestrian skills. The indigenous peoples of the plains offered effective resistance to encroachment by white settlers and at times celebrated powerful victories over U.S. forces. In 1876, for example, thousands of Lakota Sioux and their allies defeated an army under the command of Colonel George Armstrong Custer in the **battle of the Little Bighorn** (in southern Montana). However, despite occasional successes in battle, Native Americans on the plains ultimately lost the war against the forces of U.S. expansionism. The weaponry employed against native peoples included cannons and deadly, rapid-fire Gatling guns. Those weapons—plus ever greater numbers of settlers and military reinforcements—aided U.S. forces in breaking Native American resistance and opened the western plains to U.S. conquest.

One last symbolic conflict took place in 1890 at Wounded Knee Creek in South Dakota. Frightened and threatened by the Sioux adoption of the Ghost Dance, an expression of religious beliefs that included a vision of an afterlife in which all white peoples disappeared, whites wanted these religious ceremonies suppressed. U.S. cavalry forces chased the Sioux who were fleeing to safety in the South Dakota Badlands. At Wounded Knee Creek, a Sioux man accidentally shot off a gun, and the cavalry overreacted badly, slaughtering more than two hundred men, women, and children with machine guns. Emblematic of harsh U.S. treatment of native peoples,

## INTERPRETING IMAGES

This photograph of an 1890s Plains Indian camp in South Dakota offers a pastoral and peaceful image of the indigenous societies in the United States who were in the process of being violently forced off their lands.

**Analyze** *John C.H. Grabill, who took this photo in 1891, was the official photographer for a few railroad and mining companies in Colorado and South Dakota. How does this information affect how you try and understand what you are seeing? Who was violently forcing these Brule and Oglala Lakota off their land and what is their relationship to the photographer?*

Buyenlarge/Archive Photos/Getty Images

**Wounded Knee** represented the place where "a people's dream died," as one Native American leader put it.

**The Mexican-American War** Westward expansion also generated tension between the United States and Mexico, whose territories included Texas, California, and New Mexico (the territory that is now the American southwest). Texas declared independence from Mexico in 1836, largely because the many U.S. migrants who had settled there wanted to run their own affairs. In 1845 the United States accepted Texas as a new state–against vigorous Mexican protest–and moved to consolidate its hold on the territory. Those moves led to conflicts that rapidly escalated into the **Mexican-American War** (1846–1848), or, as it is known in Mexico, *la intervención norteamericano* (the North American Intervention) or *la guerra del 47* (the War of 1847). U.S. forces instigated the war by sending troops into a disputed zone along the Rio Grande. When Mexican cavalry attacked U.S. soldiers in this zone, the United States sent in reinforcements and inflicted a punishing defeat on the Mexican army. By the Treaty of Guadalupe Hidalgo (1848), the United States took possession of approximately one-half of Mexico's territory, paying a mere fifteen million dollars in exchange for Texas north of the Rio Grande, California, and New Mexico. Thousands of U.S. and

Mexican soldiers died in the conflict, and thousands of Mexican families found themselves stranded in the territories annexed by the United States. Some moved to be within the new borders of Mexico, but most stayed where they were and attained U.S. citizenship. This conflict nonetheless fueled Mexican nationalism, as well as hostility toward the United States.

Westward expansion also created problems within the republic by aggravating tensions between regions. The most serious and divisive issue had to do with slavery, which had been a serious problem in American politics since independence. The Enlightenment ideal of equality clearly suggested that the appropriate policy was to abolish slavery, but the leaders of the American revolution and framers of the Constitution recognized the sanctity of private property, which legally included enslaved people. U.S. independence initially promoted a surge of antislavery sentiment, as states north of Delaware abolished slavery within their jurisdictions. Abolition did not bring full equality for former enslaved people in northern states, but it hardened divisions between what became known as "slave" and "free" states. Westward expansion aggravated tensions further by raising the question of whether settlers could extend slavery to newly acquired territories.

**Sectional Conflict** Opponents of slavery had hoped that the institution would die a natural death with the decline of tobacco cultivation. Their hopes faded, however, with the invigoration of slavery as a result of the rise of cotton as a cash crop in the early nineteenth century, and then by westward expansion. The number of enslaved people in the United States rose sharply, from five hundred thousand in 1770 to almost two million in 1820. As the numbers of enslaved people grew, antislavery forces fought to limit the spread of slavery to new territories. Beginning with the Missouri Compromise of 1820, a series of political compromises attempted to maintain a balance between slave and free states as the republic admitted new states carved out of western territories. As proslavery and antislavery forces became more strident, however, those compromises could not endure. **Abraham Lincoln** (1809–1865) predicted in 1858 that "a house divided against itself cannot stand," and he made the connection to slavery explicit: "I believe this government cannot endure permanently half *slave* and half *free*. . . . It will become *all* one thing, or *all* the other."

The election of Abraham Lincoln to the presidency in 1860 was the spark that ignited war between the states (1861–1865). Lincoln was an explicitly sectional candidate, was convinced that slavery was immoral, and was committed to the idea of free soil—territories without slavery. Although slavery stood at the center of the conflict, President Lincoln had insisted from the beginning of the war that his primary aim was the restoration of the Union, not the abolition of slavery. He was therefore reluctant to adopt an abolitionist policy. There were reasons for his hesitancy. Not only had Lincoln

*The Peacemakers*, an 1868 painting by George Healy, depicts Abraham Lincoln in a strategy session with his top army and navy commanders aboard the *River Queen* during the final days of the Civil War. From left to right are General William Tecumseh Sherman, General Ulysses S. Grant, Abraham Lincoln, and Admiral David Dixon Porter.
ARCHIVIO GBB/Alamy Stock Photo

been elected on a platform of noninterference with slavery within the states, but he also doubted the constitutionality of any federal action. He was also concerned about the difficulties of assimilating four million former enslaved people—if abolition were to go into effect—into the nation's social and political fabric. Most important, Lincoln feared that an abolitionist program would prompt Delaware, Maryland, Kentucky, and Missouri—all slave states—into leaving the Union to join the southern states in the Confederacy. The Civil War also revolved around issues central to the United States as a society: the nature of the Union, states' rights as opposed to the federal government's authority, and the imperatives of a budding industrial-capitalist system against those of an export-oriented plantation economy.

**The U.S. Civil War** Eleven southern states withdrew from the Union in 1860 and 1861, affirming their right to dissolve the Union and their support for states' rights. Slavery and the cultivation of cotton as a cash crop had isolated the southern states from economic developments in the rest of the United States. By the mid-nineteenth century, the southern states were the world's major source of cotton, and the bulk of the crop went to the British isles to feed the textile factories of the industrial revolution. Manufactured goods consumed in the southern states came mostly from Britain, and almost all food came from the region's farms. Many southerners thus considered themselves self-sufficient and believed they did not need the rest of the United States. Northerners saw the situation differently. They viewed secession as illegal insurrection and an act of betrayal. They fought not only against slavery but also against the concept of a state subject to blackmail by its constituent parts. They also fought for a way of life—their emerging industrial society—and an expansive western agricultural system based on free labor.

The first two years of the war ended in stalemate. The war changed character, however, when Abraham Lincoln signed the Emancipation Proclamation, which made the abolition of slavery an explicit goal of the war. As the war progressed, Lincoln increasingly viewed the destruction of slavery as the only way to preserve the Union. Five days after the Union victory at the battle of Antietam, President Lincoln issued a preliminary **Emancipation Proclamation.** The final version, issued January 1, 1863, freed enslaved people in the states that had rebelled. Ironically, in the states that remained loyal to the Union, slavery remained protected by the U.S. Constitution. The solution to this problem, one that Lincoln urged, was the Thirteenth Amendment to the Constitution, ratified in 1865, which completely abolished slavery throughout the United States.

Ultimately, the northern states prevailed in the Civil War, after the bloody battle at Gettysburg in July 1863 turned the military tide against southern forces. The northern states brought considerable resources to the war effort—some 90 percent of the country's industrial capacity and approximately two-thirds of its railroad lines—but still they fought four bitter years against a formidable enemy. The victory of the northern states had enormous consequences for the United States. Most immediately, it permanently ended slavery throughout the country. Moreover, it ensured that the United States would remain politically united, and it enhanced the authority of the federal government in the republic. Thus, as European lands were building powerful states on the foundations of revolutionary ideals, liberalism, and nationalism, the United States also forged a strong central government to oversee settler colonialism to the west and to deal with the political and social issues that divided the nation. That strength came at a horrible cost for both sides, however, especially in terms of the enormous human casualties. About 1,556,000 soldiers served in the Union armies and suffered a total of over 634,000 casualties,

This photograph depicts the bodies of northern soldiers who died in the bloody battle of Antietam (Maryland) in 1862. With 620,000 military deaths, the Civil War was the most costly in U.S. history in terms of lives lost.
Library of Congress, Prints & Photographs Division [LC-DIG-cwpb-01097]

360,000 of whom died. Approximately 800,000 men served in the Confederate forces, which sustained approximately 483,000 casualties, including 258,000 dead.

## The Canadian Dominion: Independence without War

**Autonomy and Division** Canada did not fight a war for independence, and in spite of deep regional divisions, it did not experience bloody internal conflict. Instead, Canadian independence came gradually as Canadians and the British government agreed on general principles of autonomy. The distinctiveness of the two dominant European ethnic groups, the British Canadians and the French Canadians, ensured that the process of building an independent society would not be smooth, but intermittent fears of U.S. expansion and concerns about the possibility of an invasion from the south helped submerge ethnic differences. By the late nineteenth century, Canada was a state in control of its own destiny, despite continuing ties to Britain and the sometimes threatening presence of the United States to the south.

Originally colonized by trappers and settlers from both Britain and France, the colony of New France was incorporated into the British Empire after the British victory in the Seven Years' War (1756-1763). Until the late eighteenth

**MAP 18.2 The Dominion of Canada in the nineteenth century.**

Note the provinces that make up the modern state of Canada and the dates in which they were incorporated into the Dominion.

***At what date were eastern and western Canada geographically united?***

century, however, French Canadians outnumbered British Canadians, so to avoid unnecessary conflict imperial officials made a number of concessions to their subjects of French descent. For example, officials recognized the Roman Catholic church and permitted continued observance of French civil law in Quebec and other areas of French Canadian settlement, which they governed through appointed councils staffed by local elites. British Canadians, in contrast, were Protestants who lived mostly in Ontario, followed British law, and governed themselves through elected representatives. Then, as the American revolution was ending in 1781, large numbers of British loyalists fled the newly formed United States to the south and sought refuge in Canada, thus greatly enlarging the size of the English-speaking community.

**The War of 1812** Ethnic divisions and political differences could easily have splintered Canada, but the **War of 1812** stimulated a sense of unity against an external threat. The United States declared war on Britain in retaliation for encroachments on U.S. rights during the Napoleonic wars, and the British colony of Canada formed one of the front lines of the conflict. U.S. military leaders assumed they could easily invade and conquer Canada to pressure their foes. Despite the greater resources of the United States, however, Canadian forces repelled U.S. incursions. Their victories promoted a sense of Canadian pride, and anti-U.S. sentiment became a means for covering over differences among French Canadians and British Canadians.

After the War of 1812, Canada experienced an era of rapid growth. Expanded business opportunities drew English-speaking migrants, who swelled the population. However, that influx threatened the identity of French Canadians in Quebec, and discontent in Canada reached a critical point in the 1830s. The British imperial governors of Canada did not want a repeat of the American revolution, so between 1840 and 1867 they defused tensions by expanding home rule in Canada and permitting the provinces to govern their own internal affairs. Inspiring this imperial move toward Canadian autonomy was the **Durham Report,** issued in 1839 by John George Lambton (1782–1840), the first earl of Durham and recent governor-general and lord high commissioner of Canada. He advocated a good deal of self-government for a united Canada, and his report became a model for later British imperial policy toward other white settler colonies, including Australia and New Zealand.

**Dominion** Over the next few decades, Canadians developed a federal structure for their developing state. The **British North America Act of 1867** joined Quebec, Ontario, Nova Scotia, and New Brunswick and recognized them as the **Dominion of Canada.** (Other provinces joined the Dominion later.) The term *dominion* signaled the continuing connection of Canada to the British government, while Canadians took control of internal affairs. Under this arrangement, each province had its own seat of government, provincial legislature, and lieutenant governor representing the British crown. The act created a federal government headed by a governor-general who acted as the British representative. An elected House of Commons and appointed Senate rounded out the framework of governance. Provincial legislatures reserved certain political matters for themselves, whereas others fell within the purview of the federal government. Without waging war, the Dominion of Canada had won control over all Canadian internal affairs, while Britain retained jurisdiction over foreign affairs until 1931.

**John A. Macdonald** (1815–1891) became the first prime minister of Canada, and he moved to incorporate all of British North America into the Dominion. He negotiated the purchase of the huge Northwest Territories from the Hudson's Bay Company in 1869, and he persuaded Manitoba, British Columbia, and Prince Edward Island to join the Dominion. Macdonald believed, however, that Canada's Dominion would remain symbolic—a mere "geographic expression," as he put it—until the government took concrete action to make Canadian unity a reality. To strengthen the union, he oversaw construction of a transcontinental railroad, completed in 1885. The railroad facilitated transportation and communications throughout Canada and eventually helped bring new provinces into the Dominion: Alberta and Saskatchewan in 1905 and Newfoundland in 1949. Internal conflicts never disappeared, but the Dominion provided a foundation for Canadian independence and unity. While maintaining ties to Britain and struggling to forge an identity distinct from that of its powerful neighbor to the south, Canada developed as a culturally diverse yet politically unified society.

## Latin America: Fragmentation and Political Experimentation

Political unity was short-lived in Latin America. Simón Bolívar (1783–1830), hailed as South America's liberator, worked for the establishment of a large confederation that would provide Latin America with the political, military, and economic strength to resist encroachment by foreign powers. The wars of independence that he led encouraged a sense of solidarity in Latin America. But Bolívar once admitted that "I fear peace more than war," and after the defeat of the common colonial enemy, solidarity proved impossible to sustain. Bolívar's Gran Colombia broke into its three constituent parts—Venezuela, Colombia, and Ecuador—and the rest of Latin America fragmented into numerous independent states.

**Creole Elites and Political Instability** Following the example of the United States, creole (people of European descent born in the Americas) elites usually established republics with written constitutions in most newly independent states of Latin America. Yet constitutions were much more difficult to frame in Latin America than in the United States. Before gaining independence, Latin American leaders had less experience with self-government because Spanish and Portuguese colonies were ruled far more directly by representatives of the crown than the British colonies in North America. Creole elites responded enthusiastically to Enlightenment

**MAP 18.3 Latin America in the nineteenth century. Date is year of independence.**

Note the many states that emerged from the independence movements early in the century.

***Why was it difficult for large, federated republics, such as the Republic of Colombia, founded by Simón Bolívar, to survive?***

***Latin American independence was relatively swift. What challenges remained after autonomous rule?***

values and republican ideals but found it difficult to put these principles into practice. As a result, several Latin American states lurched from one constitution to another as leaders struggled to create a machinery of government that would lead to political and social stability.

Creole elites themselves were part of the problem because they dominated the newly independent states and effectively prevented mass participation in public affairs. Less than 5 percent of the male population was active in Latin American politics in the nineteenth century, and millions of indigenous peoples lived entirely outside the political system. Without institutionalized means of expressing discontent or opposition, those disillusioned with the system had little choice beyond rebellion. Aggravating political instability were differences among elites. Whether they were urban merchants or rural landowners, Latin American elites divided into different camps as liberals or conservatives, centralists or federalists, secularists or Roman Catholics.

**Conflicts with Indigenous Peoples** Like their neighbors in the United States, one thing elites agreed on was the policy of claiming South American land for agriculture and ranching. That meant pushing aside indigenous peoples and establishing hegemony in Latin America. Conflict was most intense in Argentina and Chile, where cultivators and ranchers longed to take over the South American plains. During the mid-nineteenth century, as the United States was crushing indigenous resistance to western expansion in North America, Argentine and Chilean forces brought modern weapons to bear in their campaign to conquer the indigenous peoples of those states. By the 1870s, they had forced indigenous peoples on the most productive lands to retreat to marginal lands or to assimilate to Euro-American society.

**Caudillos** Although creole elites agreed on the policy of conquering indigenous peoples, division and discord in the newly independent states helped **caudillos,** or regional military leaders, come to power in much of Latin America. The wars of independence had lasted well over a decade, and they provided Latin America with military rather than civilian heroes. After independence, military leaders took to the political stage, appealing to populist sentiments and exploiting the discontent of the masses. One of the most notable caudillos was **Juan Manuel de Rosas,** who from 1829 to 1852 ruled an Argentina divided between the cattle-herding gaucho (cowboy) society of the pampas (the interior grasslands) and the urban elite of Buenos Aires. Rosas himself emerged from the world of cattle ranching, and he used his skills to subdue other caudillos and establish control in Buenos Aires. Rosas called for regional autonomy in an attempt to reconcile competing interests, but at the same time he worked to centralize the government he now controlled. He quelled rebellions, but he did so in bloody fashion. Critics often likened Rosas to well-known political manipulators or dictators

**caudillos** (KAHW-dee-yohs)
**Juán Manuel de Rosas** (HWAHN mahn-WEL deh roh-sahs)

Edouard Manet's painting (one of a series painted between 1867 and 1869) depicts the execution by firing squad of Emperor Maximilian, whose death in 1867 ended attempted French rule in Mexico.
World History Archive/ Alamy Stock Photo

from the past, calling him "the Machiavelli of the pampas" and "the Argentine Nero," and they accused him of launching a reign of terror to stifle opposition. One exiled writer compiled a chart that counted the number of Rosas's victims and the violent ways they met their ends; of the 22,404 total victims killed, most met their end in armed clashes but others died by poisoning, hanging, or assassination.

Rosas did what caudillos did best: he restored order. In doing so, however, he made terror a tool of the government, and he ruled as a despot through his own personal army. Rosas also, however, embodied the charismatic personality traits most exemplified by caudillos. He attained great popularity through his identification with the people and with gauchos, and he demonstrated his physical strength and machismo.

Emiliano Zapata (1879–1919), who hailed from the southern state of Morelos, was the very picture of a revolutionary leader, heavily armed and sporting his trademark moustache.
Cultural Heritage Images/Universal Images Group/Newscom

**Mexico: War and Reform** Independent Mexico experienced a succession of governments, from monarchy to republic to caudillo rule, but it also generated a liberal reform movement. The Mexican-American War (1846–1848) caused political turmoil in Mexico and helped the caudillo General **Antonio López de Santa Anna** (1797–1876) perpetuate his intermittent rule of the country. After the defeat and disillusion of the war, however, a liberal reform movement attempted to reshape Mexican society. Led by President **Benito Juárez** (1806–1872), a Mexican of indigenous ancestry, La Reforma of the 1850s aimed to limit the power of the military and the Roman Catholic church in Mexican society. Juárez and his followers called for reforms that were designed, in part, to create a rural middle class. The Constitution of 1857 curtailed the prerogatives of priests and military elites, and it guaranteed universal male suffrage and other civil liberties, such as freedom of speech. Land reform efforts centered on breaking up jointly held properties, which had the effect of parceling out communal Indian lands and villages as private property. However, the reforms did not have the desired effect, as much of this land ended up in the hands of large landowners rather than indigenous peoples.

**Mexico: Revolution** La Reforma challenged some of the fundamental conservatism of Mexican elites, who led a determined opposition to political, social, and economic reform. Liberals and conservatives in Mexico stayed bitterly divided, and in fact conservatives forced the Juárez government out of the capital in Mexico City. In 1861, Juarez sought to reestablish his authority and restore order to the country. To lessen Mexico's financial woes, Juárez chose to suspend loan payments to foreign powers that had invested heavily in Mexico's infrastructure, which in turn led to French, British, and Spanish intervention as Europeans sought to recover and protect their investments in Mexico. France's Napoleon III proved especially intrusive, and in 1862 he even sent an invasion force whose goal was to re-create a monarchy in Mexico, this time controlled by France. But on May 5, 1862, Mexican forces beat back the French invaders at the city of Puebla, a date thereafter celebrated as Cinco de Mayo. Napoleon III then sent tens of thousands of troops to conquer Mexico and proclaimed the creation of a Mexican empire. In 1867, however, Napoleon III had no choice but to accept defeat and withdraw his forces after a Mexican firing squad killed the man he had appointed emperor, the Austrian archduke Maximilian (1832–1867). Juárez managed to restore a semblance of liberal government following the French invasion, but Mexico remained beset by political divisions.

By the early twentieth century, Mexico was a divided land moving toward civil war. The Mexican revolution (1910–1920), a bitter and bloody conflict, broke out when middle-class Mexicans joined with peasants and workers to overthrow the powerful dictator **Porfirio Díaz** (1830–1915). The revolt in Mexico was the first major, violent effort in Latin America to attempt to topple the grossly unequal system of landed estates in which 95 percent of all peasants remained landless. As those denied land and representation armed themselves and engaged in guerrilla warfare against government forces, the revolt turned increasingly radical. The lower classes took up weapons and followed the revolutionary leaders **Emiliano Zapata** (1879–1919) and **Francisco (Pancho) Villa** (1878–1923), charismatic men of agrarian backgrounds who organized massive armies fighting for the goals of *tierra y*

**Benito Juárez** (beh-NEE-toh HWAHR-ez)
**Porfirio Díaz** (pohr-FEER-eeo DEE-ahs)
**Emiliano Zapata** (eh-mee-LYAH-no zuh-PAH-tuh)
**Francisco Villa** (frahn-SEES-kow VEE-yuh)

*libertad* (land and liberty). Zapata, the son of a mestizo peasant, and Villa, the son of a field worker, embodied the ideals and aspirations of the indigenous Mexican masses and enjoyed tremendous popular support. They discredited what they viewed as timid governmental efforts at reform and challenged governmental political control. For example, Zapata confiscated hacienda lands and began distributing the lands to the peasants, while Villa attacked and killed U.S. citizens in retaliation for U.S. support of Mexican government officials—and succeeded in eluding capture by either U.S. or Mexican forces.

Despite the power and popularity enjoyed by Zapata and Villa, they were unable to capture Mexico's major cities, and they did not command the resources and wealth to which government forces had access. The Mexican revolution came to an end soon after government forces ambushed and killed Zapata in 1919. Villa was assassinated a few years later in 1923, when his car was ambushed in the town of Hidalgo de Parral. Government forces regained control over Mexico, but the human cost of so many years of war had been appalling: as many as two million Mexicans had died during the conflicts. Although radicals such as Zapata and Villa were ultimately defeated, the Mexican government that came to power in 1917 issued a constitution that did in fact address some of the concerns of the revolutionaries. These included providing for land redistribution, universal suffrage, state-supported education, minimum wages and maximum hours for workers, and restrictions on foreign ownership of Mexican property and mineral resources. Although these constitutional provisions were not all implemented right away, they provided inspiration for the future.

Instability and conflict plagued Latin America throughout the nineteenth century in the form of division, rebellion, caudillo rule, and civil war. Many Latin American peoples continued to lack education, profitable employment, and political representation. Simón Bolívar himself once said that "independence is the only blessing we have gained at the expense of all the rest."

## AMERICAN ECONOMIC DEVELOPMENT

During the nineteenth and early twentieth centuries, two principal influences—mass migration and British financial investment—shaped economic development throughout the Americas. But American states reacted in different ways to migration and foreign investment. The United States and Canada absorbed waves of migrants, exploited British capital, built industrial societies, and established economic independence. The results of mass migration and financial investment were much more mixed in Latin America, however. In both South America and the Caribbean, migrants tended to arrive as contract or indentured laborers to take the place of enslaved people after abolition, and thus remained quite poor. In terms of foreign financial investments, in much of Latin America these tended to benefit only the investors themselves and the small elite classes that controlled most countries.

### Migration to the Americas

Underpinning the economic development of the Americas was large-scale migration of European and Asian peoples to the United States, Canada, and Latin America. Internal migration within the Americas also contributed to a new economic landscape, particularly as Latin Americans journeyed to the United States in search of work and financial opportunities. As we saw in the introduction, gold discoveries drew prospectors hoping to make a quick fortune: the California gold rush of 1849 drew the largest numbers (about three hundred thousand) but Canadian gold also lured migrants by the tens of thousands. Outnumbering gold prospectors were millions of European and Asian migrants who made their way to the factories, railroad construction sites, and plantations of the Americas. Following them were others who offered the support services that made life for migrant workers more comfortable and at the same time transformed the ethnic and cultural landscape of the Americas. Fatt Hing Chin's restaurant in San Francisco's Chinatown fed Chinese migrants, but it also helped introduce Chinese cuisine to American society. Migrants from other parts of the world found similar comforts as their foods, religious beliefs, and cultural traditions migrated with them to the Americas.

**Industrial Migrants** After the mid-nineteenth century, European migrants flocked to North America, where they filled the factories of the growing industrial economy of the United States. Their lack of skills made them attractive to industrialists seeking workers to operate machinery or perform heavy labor at low wages. By keeping labor costs down, migrants helped increase the profitability and fuel the expansion of U.S. industry.

In the 1850s 2.3 million Europeans migrated to the United States—almost as many as had crossed the Atlantic during the half century from 1800 to 1850—and the volume of migration continued to surge until the early twentieth century. Increasing rents and indebtedness drove cultivators from Ireland, Scotland, Germany, and Scandinavia to seek opportunities in North America. Some of them moved to the Ohio and Mississippi River valleys in search of cheap and abundant land, but many stayed in the eastern cities and contributed to the early industrialization of the United States. By the late nineteenth century, most European migrants were coming from southern and eastern Europe. Poles, Russian Jews, Slavs, Italians, Greeks, and Portuguese escaping either persecution or poverty were most prominent among the later migrants, and they settled largely in the industrial cities of the eastern states. They dominated the textile industries of the northeast, and without their labor, the remarkable industrial expansion that the United States experienced in the late nineteenth century would not have been possible.

Asian migrants further swelled the U.S. labor force and contributed to the construction of an American transportation infrastructure. Chinese migration grew rapidly after the 1840s,

## INTERPRETING IMAGES

Italian migrants construct a railway in New York. Italians were just one of many migrant groups coming to the Americas in the nineteenth century, including Irish and Chinese.

**Analyze** *When you think about the impacts of new waves of immigration to the Americas, how do you connect these migrants to the histories of their countries of origin? What does a world history perspective offer to histories of migration? How might this context help us tell a more accurate story about the history of the United States?*

Michael Maslan/Corbis Historical/Getty Images

when officials of the Qing government permitted foreigners to seek indentured laborers in China and approved their migration to distant lands. Between 1852 and 1875 some two hundred thousand Chinese migrated to California alone. Some, like Fatt Hing Chin, negotiated their own passage and sought to make their fortune in the gold rush, but most traveled on indentured labor contracts that required them to cultivate crops or work on the Central Pacific Railroad. An additional five thousand Chinese entered Canada to search for gold in British Columbia or work on the Canadian Pacific Railroad.

**Plantation Migrants** Whereas migrants to the United States contributed to the development of an industrial society, those who went to Latin American lands mostly worked on agricultural plantations. Some Europeans figured among these migrants. About four million Italians sought opportunities in Argentina in the 1880s and 1890s, for example, and the Brazilian government paid Italian migrants to cross the Atlantic and work for coffee growers, who experienced a severe labor shortage after the abolition of slavery in 1888. Many Italian workers settled permanently in Latin America, especially Argentina, but some, popularly known as *golondrinas* ("swallows") because of their regular migrations, traveled back and forth annually between Europe and South America to take advantage of different growing seasons in the northern and southern hemispheres.

Asian laborers also worked on plantations in the Western Hemisphere. More than fifteen thousand indentured laborers from China worked in the sugarcane fields of Cuba during the nineteenth century, and Indian migrants traveled to Jamaica, Trinidad, Tobago, and Guyana. Laborers from both China and Japan migrated to Peru, where they worked on cotton plantations in coastal regions, mined guano deposits for fertilizer, and built railroad lines. After the middle of the nineteenth century, expanding U.S. influence in the Pacific islands also led to Chinese, Japanese, Filipino, and Korean migrations to Hawai`i, where planters sought indentured laborers to tend sugarcane. About twenty-five thousand Chinese went to Hawai`i during the 1850s and 1860s, and later 180,000 Japanese also made their way to island plantations.

## Economic Expansion in the United States

**British Capital** British investment capital in the United States proved crucial to the early stages of industrial development by helping businesspeople establish a textile industry. In the late nineteenth century, it also spurred a vast expansion of U.S. industry by funding entrepreneurs, who opened coal and iron ore mines, built iron and steel factories, and constructed railroad lines. The flow of investment monies was a consequence of Britain's own industrialization, which generated enormous wealth and created a need for investors to find profitable outlets for their funds. British investors were especially keen to invest in white settler states and colonies, and this investment in turn often provided the impetus for industrial expansion and economic independence in those regions. In the case of the United States, it helped create a rival industrial power that would eventually outperform Britain's economy.

After the 1860s, U.S. businesses made effective use of foreign investment capital as the country recovered from the Civil War. The war had determined that the United States would depend on wage labor rather than enslaved labor, and entrepreneurs set about tapping American resources and building a continental economy.

**Railroads** Perhaps the most important economic development of the later nineteenth century was the construction of railroad lines that linked all U.S. regions and helped create an integrated national economy. Because of its enormous size and environmental diversity, the United States offered an abundance of natural resources for industrial exploitation. But vast distances made it difficult to maintain close economic ties between regions until a boom in railroad construction created a dense transportation, communication, and distribution network.

In this lithograph of Frances F. Palmer's well-known painting *American Express Train* (ca. 1864), the railroad is depicted as a cheerful and industrious master of the landscape.
Yale University Art Gallery

Before the U.S. Civil War, the United States had about 50,000 kilometers (31,000 miles) of railroad lines, most of them short routes east of the Mississippi River. By 1900 there were more than 320,000 kilometers (200,000 miles) of track, and the U.S. rail network stretched from coast to coast. Most prominent of the new lines was a transcontinental route, completed in 1869, running from Omaha, Nebraska (where connections provided access to eastern states), to San Francisco.

Railroads decisively influenced U.S. economic development. They provided cheap transportation for agricultural commodities, manufactured goods, and individual travelers. Railroads hauled grain, beef, and hogs from the plains states; cotton and tobacco from the south; lumber from the northwest; iron and steel from the mills of Pittsburgh; and finished products from the eastern industrial cities. In addition to the transportation services they provided, railroads spurred the development of other industries because they required huge amounts of coal, wood, glass, and rubber. Indeed, by the 1880s some 75 percent of U.S. steel went to the railroad industry. Railroads also required the development of new managerial skills to operate large, complicated businesses. In 1850 few if any U.S. businesses had more than a thousand employees. By the early 1880s, however, the Pennsylvania Railroad alone employed almost fifty thousand people, and the size of the business called for organization and coordination on an unprecedented scale. Railroads were the testing grounds where managers developed the techniques they needed to run big businesses.

**Space and Time** Railroads led to drastic changes in the ways people organized, controlled, and even thought about space and time. Railroads altered the landscape in often extreme fashion, and the transformations consequent to the building of railroads–in land control and development, the transportation of migrants and settlers to the west, and the exploitation of natural resources–only furthered the environmental impact of the railroad. The westward expansion driven by the railroad led to broadscale land clearing and the extension of farming and mining lands, and brought about both human suffering for indigenous peoples and environmental damage through soil erosion and pollution. Irrigation and the politics of water also sparked trouble, especially as settlers and farmers entered the drier plains and even desert regions. The dark smoke emanating from railroad engines undoubtedly represented progress to industrial promoters, but it also symbolized an ever-widening intrusion into the natural environment.

Railroads even shaped the sense of time in the United States. Until rapid and regular rail transportation became available, communities set their clocks by the sun. As a result, New York time was eleven minutes and forty-five seconds behind Boston time. When the clock showed 12 noon in Chicago, it was 11:50 A.M. in St. Louis and 12:18 P.M. in Detroit. Those differences in local sun times created scheduling nightmares for railroad managers, who by the 1880s had to keep track of more than fifty time standards. Observance of local time also created hazards because a small miscalculation in scheduling could bring two trains hurtling unexpectedly toward each other on the same track. To simplify matters, in 1883 railroad companies divided the North American continent into four zones in which all railroad clocks read precisely the same time. The general public quickly adopted **railroad time** in place of local sun time, and in 1918 the U.S. government legally established the four time zones as the nation's official framework of time.

**Economic Growth** Led by railroads, the U.S. economy expanded rapidly between 1870 and 1900. Inventors designed new products and brought them to market: electric lights, telephones, typewriters, phonographs, film photography, motion picture cameras, and electric motors all made their appearance during this era. Strong consumer demand for those and other products fueled rapid industrial expansion and suggested to observers that the United States had found the road to continuous progress and prosperity.

Yet the march of U.S. industrialization did not go entirely unopposed: large-scale labor unions emerged alongside big business in the period from 1870 to 1900, and confrontations between business owners seeking profits and workers seeking higher wages or job security sometimes grew ugly. A nationwide, coordinated strike of rail workers in 1877 shut down two-thirds of the nation's railroads. Violence stemming from the strike took the lives of one hundred people and resulted in ten million dollars' worth of property damage. Nevertheless, big business prevailed in its disputes with workers during the nineteenth century, often with support from federal or state governments, and by the early twentieth century the United States had emerged as one of the world's major industrial powers.

## Canadian Prosperity

British investment deeply influenced the development of the Canadian as well as the U.S. economy in the nineteenth and early twentieth centuries. Canadian leaders, like U.S. leaders, took advantage of British capital to industrialize without allowing their economy to fall under British control. During the early nineteenth century, Britain paid relatively high prices for Canadian agricultural products and minerals, partly to keep the colony stable and to discourage the formation of separatist movements. As a result, white Canadians enjoyed a high standard of living even before industrialization.

**The National Policy** After the establishment of the Dominion of Canada in 1867, politicians started a program of economic development known as the **National Policy.** The idea was to attract migrants, protect nascent industries through tariffs, and build national transportation systems. The centerpiece of the transportation network was the transcontinental **Canadian Pacific Railroad,** built largely with British investment capital and completed in 1885. The Canadian Pacific Railroad opened the western prairie lands to commerce, stimulated the development of other industries, and promoted the emergence of a Canadian national economy. The National Policy created some violent conflicts with indigenous peoples who resisted encroachment on their lands and with trappers who resented disruption of their way of life, but at the same time it also promoted economic growth and independence. In Canada as in the United States, the ability to control and direct economic affairs was crucial to limiting the state's dependence on British capital.

As a result of the National Policy, Canada experienced booming agricultural, mineral, and industrial production in the late nineteenth and early twentieth centuries. Canadian population surged as a result of both migration and natural increase. Migrants flocked to Canada's shores from Asia and especially from Europe: between 1903 and 1914 some 2.7 million eastern European migrants settled in Canada. Fueled in part by this population growth, Canadian economic expansion took place on the foundation of rapidly increasing wheat production and the extraction of rich mineral resources, including gold, silver, copper, nickel, and asbestos. Industrialists also tapped Canadian rivers to produce the hydroelectric power necessary for manufacturing.

**U.S. Investment** Canada remained wary of its powerful neighbor to the south but did not keep U.S. economic influence entirely at bay. British investment dwarfed U.S. investment throughout the nineteenth century: in 1914 British investment in Canada totaled $2.5 billion, compared with $700 million from the United States. Nevertheless, the U.S. presence in the Canadian economy grew. By 1918, Americans owned 30 percent of all Canadian industry, and thereafter the U.S. and Canadian economies became increasingly interdependent. Canada began to undergo rapid industrialization after the early twentieth century, as the province of Ontario benefited from the spillover of U.S. industry in the northeastern states.

## Latin American Investments

Latin American states did not undergo industrialization or enjoy economic development like the United States or Canada. When the colonies of Spain and Portugal became independent in the early nineteenth century, European investors from Britain, France, and Germany jumped at the chance to establish trading relationships in a region where they had long been prevented from investing. Both Central and South America offered attractive prospects for extracting raw materials such as wheat,

A contemporary photograph of the Metlac railway bridge in Mexico, constructed in 1903 during the rule of Porfirio Diaz.
George Rinhart/Corbis/Getty Images

beef, fish, and guano (bat dung—a critical source for fertilizer), and European investors were happy to supply the investment for railroads and other types of infrastructure necessary to bring raw materials to ports. Because Latin American elites retained control over local economies, European investors only needed to make sure their economic plans were attractive to them. And indeed, elites profited handsomely from European trade and investment and thus had little incentive to seek different economic policies or work toward industrialization. As a result, foreign investment and trade had more damaging effects in Latin America than in the United States or Canada. In fact, foreign investment in Latin America during this period has come to be known by scholars as "informal imperialism," meaning that foreign entities gain so much control of an economy that they are then able to exert political pressure on the governments in question as well.

**British Investment** British investors were particularly active in Latin America during the nineteenth century. Although they did not believe Latin American countries could offer attractive markets for British manufactured items, they were quite interested in their potential for producing raw materials. In Argentina, for example, British investors encouraged the development of cattle and sheep ranching. After the 1860s and the invention of refrigerated cargo ships, meat became Argentina's largest export and Britain its principal market. Because British investors controlled the industry at almost every stage; they also reaped the profits, and British business interests gained considerable control over the Argentine economy as a whole. Meanwhile, between 1880 and 1914, European migrants labored in the new export industries and contributed to the explosive growth of urban areas such as Buenos Aires: by 1914 the city's population exceeded 3.5 million. Although migrant laborers rarely shared in the profits controlled by elites, the domination of urban labor by European migrants represented yet another form of foreign influence in Latin American economic affairs.

**Attempted Industrialization** Latin American elites did make attempts to encourage industrialization in a few places, but these had limited success. The most notable of those efforts was when the dictatorial general Porfirio Díaz ruled Mexico (1876–1911). Díaz represented the interests of large landowners, wealthy merchants, and foreign investors. Under his rule, railroad tracks and telegraph lines connected all parts of Mexico, and the production of mineral resources surged. A small steel industry produced railroad track and construction materials, and entrepreneurs also established glass, chemical, and textile industries. The capital, Mexico City, underwent a transformation during the Díaz years: it acquired paved streets, streetcar lines, and electric streetlights. But the profits from Mexican enterprises did not support continuing industrial development. Instead, they went into the pockets of the Mexican elites and foreign investors who supported Díaz, while a growing and discontented urban working class seethed with resentment at low wages, long hours, and foreign managers. Even as agriculture, railroad construction, and mining were booming, the standard of living for average Mexicans had begun to decline by the early twentieth century. Frustration with that state of affairs helps explain the sudden outbreak of violent revolution in 1910.

Latin American economies expanded rapidly in the late nineteenth century. Exports geared toward foreign markets drove that growth: copper and silver from Mexico, bananas and coffee from Central America, rubber and coffee from Brazil, beef and wheat from Argentina, copper from Chile, and tobacco and sugar from Cuba. Because foreign investors controlled the markets and their infrastructure, however, they were also able to keep prices for commodities low. Latin American economies were thus subject to decisions made in the interests of foreign investors, and unstable governments could do little in the face of strong foreign intervention. Controlled by the very elites who profited from foreign intervention at the expense of their citizens, Latin American governments helped account for the region's slower economic development, despite growth in industrial and export economies.

## AMERICAN CULTURAL AND SOCIAL DIVERSITY

In his "Song of Myself" (1855), a poetic celebration of himself as well as the vast diversity of his nation, the U.S. poet Walt Whitman asked:

> Do I contradict myself?
> Very well then I contradict myself,
> (I am large, I contain multitudes.)

Much of the allure of the Americas derived from their vast spaces and diverse populations. The Americas were indeed large, and they did indeed contain multitudes. While diversity distinguished the Americas, that same diversity also provided abundant fuel for conflicts between ethnic groups, social classes, and those segregated into groups based on race and gender. The social and cultural diversity of American societies challenged their ability to achieve cultural cohesion as well as political unity and democratically inclusive states. The lingering legacies of European conquest, slavery, migration, and patriarchy highlighted contradictions between the Enlightenment ideals of freedom and equality and the realities of life for indigenous and African American peoples as well as recent migrants and women. American societies experienced abundant strife in the age of independence. In efforts to maintain their own position and preserve social stability, the dominant political forces in the Americas often repressed demands for recognition by dispossessed groups.

### Societies in the United States

By the late nineteenth century, the United States had become a boisterous multicultural society—the most culturally diverse land of the Western Hemisphere—whose population included

Apache youths at the Carlisle Indian School in Pennsylvania, where Native American children were removed from their families in an attempt to assimilate them into the larger American society.
Historical/Corbis Historical/Getty Images

indigenous peoples, Euro-Americans African Americans, and growing numbers of migrants from Europe and Asia. Walt Whitman described the United States as "not merely a nation but a teeming nation of nations." Yet political and economic power rested almost exclusively with white male elites of European ancestry. The United States experienced tension and occasional conflict as members of various constituencies worked for dignity, prosperity, and a voice in society.

**Native Peoples** As they expanded to the west, Euro-American settlers and ranchers pushed indigenous peoples off their own lands and onto marginal tracts of land called reservations. Even though the reservations were supposed to be sovereign land for Native Americans, the U.S. government nevertheless permitted settlers and railroads to encroach on the reservations, which forced indigenous people onto ever smaller and less productive territories. In the latter half of the nineteenth century the United States government embarked on a policy designed to reduce indigenous autonomy even further through laws and reforms aimed at forcibly assimilating tribes to American culture and destroying Native American cultural traditions. Some indigenous tribes on the plains, for example, had developed material cultures largely centered on the hunting of bison, or buffalo, and the skillful exploitation of those animal resources. Beginning in 1850 but accelerating after the Civil War, white migrants, railroad employees, hunters, and "wild west" men such as Buffalo Bill Cody shot and killed hundreds of thousands of bison, which deliberately exterminated the buffalo and the economy of the Plains Indians. Herds numbering at least fifteen million were reduced to a mere thousand by 1875.

A lithograph called "The First Vote" from *Harper's Weekly* in 1867. It depicts black Americans of several occupations—including an artisan, a businessman, and a Union Soldier—casting their votes for the first time in their lives.
Historical/Corbis Historical/Getty Images

Other U.S. actions also attempted to destroy Native Americans' communal traditions and cultural practices. The Dawes Severalty Act of 1887, for example, sought to lessen the influence of tribal culture by shifting land

## What's Left Out?

The practice of separating indigenous children from their parents was not just a United States policy. In fact, all of the white settler colonies—including the United States, Canada, and Australia—used child separation as a tool of colonial rule in the late nineteenth and early twentieth centuries. Although agents of these settler colonies sometimes learned from one another when implementing the practice of child separation, these policies largely originated within each colony as part of the logic of settler colonialism itself. One of the primary goals of settler colonies was to dispossess indigenous populations of their lands and then to repopulate them with settlers of European descent. Yet in spite of trying to accomplish this goal by battling with, murdering, and forcibly removing indigenous people, indigenous populations nevertheless persisted. By the late nineteenth century, this persistence led agents of the settler colonies to attempt to eradicate indigenous culture by the forcible and systematic assimilation of children. In Australia, aboriginal people were removed to isolated areas, where children were separated from their parents in segregated dormitories. In the United States, settlers founded one hundred and fifty-four boarding schools for Native American children by 1902, each located far from their home communities. In Canada, authorities studied the U.S. model and established a network of boarding schools for indigenous children. Once removed from their homes, children were taught to adopt the language and behavior of the settler culture in the hope that this would permanently eliminate their own cultures and customs. But indigenous people seldom gave up their children voluntarily. In fact, so many resisted that most were taken by force or the threat of force. In the United States, for example, authorities often withheld food rations on reservations until communities gave up their children. When thinking about this global practice of child separation, it is worth considering that the 1948 United Nations Convention on Genocide defined one of the methods of genocide as "forcibly transferring children of one group to another group."

*Source:* Margaret D. Jacobs, *White Mother to a Dark Race: Settler Colonialism, Maternalism, and the Removal of Indigenous Children in the American West and Australia, 1880–1940* (Lincoln: University of Nebraska Press, 2009).

### Thinking Critically About Sources

1. Would you consider the forcible removal of indigenous children from their homes to be "genocide"? Why or why not?
2. Although the children were given food, clothing, shelter, and education, what was the emotional and psychological toll on them? Where might you seek more information on the impact of this separation?

policies away from collective tribal reservations and toward individual tracts of land. Even more traumatic for Native Americans, government officials began a policy of removing indigenous children from their families and tribes and enrolling them in white-controlled boarding schools. These schools, such as the Carlisle Indian School and the Toledo Indian School, illustrated the extent to which white society sought to eliminate tribal influences and inculcate what they believed were Christian, U.S. values. Tribal languages as well as tribal dress and hair fashions were banned, further distancing the children from their cultures. Native Americans, however, resisted these policies designed to destroy their culture, often fleeing from boarding schools or refusing to agree to new governmental land policies. Indeed, in spite of these inhumane and concentrated efforts to deny them their heritage, Native American tribes managed not only to survive but to rebuild their communities over the following decades.

**Freed African Americans** The Civil War ended slavery, but it did not bring about equality for formerly enslaved African Americans and their descendants. In an effort to establish a place for formerly enslaved people in American society, northern forces sent armies of occupation to the southern states and forced them to undergo a program of social and political **Reconstruction** (1867–1877). Reconstruction extended civil rights to formerly enslaved people and legislated that black men would be able to vote. Black and white citizens in southern states elected biracial governments for the first time in U.S. history, and formerly enslaved people began to participate actively in the political affairs of the republic.

## How the Past Shapes the Future

### The Birth of Nationalism

The most powerful group of people in the United States during the nineteenth century—white males of European ancestry—defined the nation in terms of the legacies of the American revolution and a common western European heritage. This group often resisted incorporating other peoples from different traditions into the nation, including former enslaved people, immigrants from Asia and southern Europe, and Native Americans. Think about the methods that people of western European ancestry used to exclude people from other traditions from full participation in national life, and about the consequences of such exclusionary practices on the development of the United States from the nineteenth century all the way to the present. Why do ideas about who belongs in the nation have the potential to generate so much conflict?

After Reconstruction, however, the armies of occupation went back north, and a violent backlash soon dismantled the program's reforms. Reconstruction had not included land grants or other economic support for formerly enslaved people, so many had to work as sharecroppers for former owners of enslaved people. Under those circumstances it was relatively easy for white southerners to take away the political and civil liberties that former enslaved people had gained under Reconstruction. By the turn of the century, U.S. blacks faced violence and intimidation when they tried to vote. Southern states fashioned a rigidly segregated society that deprived the African American population of educational, economic, and political opportunities. Although freedom was better than slavery, it was far different from the hopeful visions of the enslaved people who had won their emancipation.

**Women** Even before the Civil War, a small but growing women's movement had emerged in the United States. At the **Seneca Falls Convention** in 1848, feminists—people who advocate for women's rights based on equality of the sexes—issued a "declaration of sentiments" modeled on the Declaration of Independence, and they demanded equal political and economic rights for U.S. women:

> Now, in view of this entire disenfranchisement of one-half the people of this country, their social and religious degradation—in view of the unjust laws above mentioned, and because women do feel themselves aggrieved, oppressed, and fraudulently deprived of their most sacred rights, we insist that they have immediate admission to all the rights and privileges which belong to them as citizens of the United States.

Some groups of women fought for equal rights throughout the nineteenth century, and new opportunities for education and employment slowly began to offer alternatives to marriage and domesticity. Women's colleges, reform activism, and professional industrial jobs allowed some women to pursue careers instead of marriage. Yet abundant economic and political opportunities for women awaited the twentieth century, and even these mainly benefited white women rather than women of color.

**Migrants** Between 1840 and 1914 some twenty-five million European migrants landed on American shores, and by the late nineteenth century most of them hailed from southern and eastern European countries. Migrants introduced new foods, music, dances, holidays, sports, and languages to U.S. society and contributed to the cultural diversity of the Western Hemisphere. Yet white, native-born citizens of the United States whose descendants came from western Europe often did not welcome the newer arrivals. Distaste for foreigners frequently resulted in hostility to the migrants who moved into the expanding industrial cities. Migrants and their families tended to concentrate in certain districts, such as Little Italy and Chinatown. They did this partly out of choice because they preferred neighbors with familiar cultural traditions, but partly also because native-born citizens discouraged migrants from moving into other neighborhoods. Concerns about growing numbers of migrants with different cultural and social traditions eventually led to the exclusion of new arrivals from Asia: the U.S. government ordered a complete halt to migration from China in 1882 and from Japan in 1907.

This nineteenth-century engraving provides an idealized representation of European migrants, many of them women and children, arriving in New York under the gaze of the Statue of Liberty.
Stefano Bianchetti/Corbis/Getty Images

## Canadian Cultural Contrasts

**Ethnic Diversity** British and French settlers each viewed themselves as Canada's founding people. This cleavage, which profoundly influenced Canadian political development, masked much greater cultural and ethnic diversity in Canada. French and British settlers displaced indigenous peoples, who remain a significant minority of Canada's population today. Slavery likewise left a mark on Canada. Slavery was legal in the British Empire until 1833, and many early settlers brought

# SOURCES FROM THE PAST

## The Meaning of Freedom

*Once an enslaved man in Tennessee on the plantation of Colonel P. H. Anderson, Jourdan Anderson gained his freedom in 1864, before the conclusion of the Civil War. He and his family then relocated to Dayton, Ohio. The letter below is a response to a letter from Colonel Anderson, who asked Jourdan to return to the Tennessee plantation. Jourdan's thoughtful reply, tinged with sarcastic humor, underscores his sense of dignity and self-worth.*

**Dayton, Ohio, August 7, 1865**

To my Old Master, Col. P. H. Anderson, Big Spring, Tennessee

Sir: I got your letter and was glad to find that you had not forgotten Jourdan, and that you wanted me to come back and live with you again, promising to do better for me than anybody else can. I have often felt uneasy about you. I thought the Yankees would have hung you long before this for harboring Rebs they found at your house. I suppose they never heard about your going to Col. Martin's to kill the Union soldier that was left by his company in their stable. Although you shot at me twice before I left you, I did not want to hear of your being hurt and I am glad you are still living. . . . I would have gone back to see you all when I was working in the Nashville Hospital, but one of the neighbors told me Henry intended to shoot me if he ever got the chance.

> What indications does Jourdan Anderson give here about the kind of treatment he received from Colonel Anderson while he was enslaved?

I want to know particularly what the good chance is you propose to give me. I am doing tolerably well here; I get $25 a month, with victuals and clothing; have a comfortable home for Mandy (the folks here call her Mrs. Anderson) and the children, Milly, Jane, and Grundy, go to school and are learning well; the teacher says Grundy has a head for a preacher. They go to Sunday-School, and Mandy and me attend church regularly. We are kindly treated. . . . Now, if you will write and say what wages you will give me, I will be better able to decide whether it would be to my advantage to move back again.

As to my freedom, which you say I can have, there is nothing to be gained on that score, as I got my free-papers in 1864 from the Provost-Marshal-General of the Department at Nashville. Mandy says she would be afraid to go back without some proof that you are sincerely disposed to treat us justly and kindly–and we have concluded to test your sincerity by asking you to send us our wages for the time we served you. This will make us forget and forgive old scores, and rely on your justice and friendship in the future. I served you faithfully for thirty-two years, and Mandy twenty years, at $25 a month for me, and $2 a week for Mandy. Our earnings would amount to $11,680. . . . Please send the money by Adams Express, in care of V. Winters, esq., Dayton, Ohio. If you fail to pay us for faithful labors in the past we can have little faith in your promises in the future. We trust the good Maker has opened your eyes to the wrongs which you and your fathers have done to me and my fathers, in making us toil for you for generations without recompense. . . . Surely there will be a day of reckoning for those who defraud the laborer of his hire.

> Do you think Jourdan Anderson was serious about this request or that he made it to make a point about how much the labor of enslaved people was worth?

In answering this letter please state if there would be any safety for my Milly and Jane, who are now grown up and both good looking girls. . . . I would rather stay here and starve and die if it come to that than have my girls brought to shame by the violence and wickedness of their young masters. You will also please state if there has been any schools opened for the colored children in your neighborhood, the desire of my life now is to give my children an education, and have them form virtuous habits.

From your old servant, Jourdan Anderson.

P. S.–Say howdy to George Carter, and thank him for taking the pistol from you when you were shooting at me.

### For Further Reflection

- What does Colonel Anderson's request for Jourdan Anderson to return tell us about the colonel's understanding of what slavery had been like? What does Jourdan Anderson's response tell us about what it meant to him to be free?
- In what clever ways does Jourdan Anderson test the seriousness of his former owner's offer of employment, and what does his approach say about the meaning of black freedom?
- What would prompt Colonal Anderson to request that Jourdan return to work for him?
- How does Colonel Anderson's request, read through Jourdan's letter, indicate a lack of self-reflection and understanding of Black lives by former enslavers?

*Source:* Anderson, Jordan. "Letter from a Freedman to his Old Master." *New York: New York Daily Tribune*, 22 August 1865.

enslaved people to Canada. After the 1830s, enslaved people who escaped from the United States also reached Canada by way of the Underground Railroad. Black people in Canada were free but not equal, segregated and isolated from the political and cultural mainstream. Chinese migrants also came to Canada; attracted by gold rushes such as the Fraser River rush of 1858 and by opportunities to work on the Canadian Pacific Railway in the 1880s, Chinese migrants lived mostly in segregated Chinatowns in the cities of British Columbia, and like black people they had little voice in public affairs. In the late nineteenth and early twentieth centuries, waves of migrants brought even greater ethnic diversity to Canada. Between 1896 and 1914 three million migrants from Britain, the United States, and eastern Europe arrived in Canada.

Despite the diversity of Canada's population, communities descended from British and French settlers dominated Canadian society, and conflict between the two communities was the most prominent source of ethnic tension throughout the nineteenth and twentieth centuries. After 1867, as British Canadians led the effort to settle the Northwest Territories and incorporate them into the Dominion, frictions between the two groups intensified. Westward expansion brought British Canadian settlers and cultivators into conflict with French Canadian fur traders and lumberjacks. The fur traders in particular often lived on the margins between European and indigenous societies. They frequently married or lived with indigenous women, giving rise to the métis, individuals of mixed European and indigenous ancestry.

**The Métis and Louis Riel** A major outbreak of civil strife took place in the 1870s and 1880s. Indigenous peoples and métis had moved west throughout the nineteenth century to preserve their land and trading rights, but the drive of British Canadians to the west threatened them. **Louis Riel** (1844–1885) emerged as the leader of the métis and indigenous peoples of western Canada. A métis himself, Riel abandoned his studies for the priesthood in Montreal and returned to his home in the Red River Settlement (in the southern part of modern Manitoba). Sensitive to his community's concern that the Canadian government threatened local land rights, Riel assumed the presidency of a provisional government in 1870. He led his troops in capturing Fort Garry (modern Winnipeg) and negotiated the incorporation of the province of Manitoba into the Canadian Dominion. Canadian government officials and troops soon outlawed his government and forced Riel into years of exile, during which he wandered through the United States and Quebec, even suffering confinement in asylums.

Work on the Canadian Pacific Railroad in the 1880s renewed the threat of white settlement to indigenous and métis society. The métis asked Riel to lead resistance to the railroad and British Canadian settlement. In 1885 he organized a military force of métis and indigenous peoples in the Saskatchewan river country and led an insurrection known as the **Northwest Rebellion.** Canadian forces quickly subdued the makeshift army, and government authorities executed Riel for treason.

Although the Northwest Rebellion never had a chance of success, the execution of Riel nonetheless reverberated throughout Canadian history. French Canadians took it as an indication of the state's readiness to subdue individuals who were culturally distinct and politically opposed to the drive for a nation dominated by British Canadian elites. In the very year when completion of the transcontinental railroad signified for some the beginnings of Canadian national unity, Riel's execution foreshadowed a long term of cultural conflict between Canadians of British, French, and indigenous ancestry.

A contemporary depiction of the Battle of Cut Knife during the Northwest Rebellion led by Louis Riel. Although the rebellion was defeated, Cut Knife was an early victory for Riel's forces. The History Collection/Alamy Stock Photo

## Ethnicity, Identity, and Gender in Latin America

The heritage of Spanish and Portuguese colonialism and the legacy of slavery inclined Latin American societies toward the establishment of hierarchical distinctions based on ethnicity and color. At the top of society stood the creoles, individuals of European ancestry born in the Americas, while indigenous peoples, former enslaved people, and their descendants occupied the lowest rungs of the social ladder. In between were various groups of mixed ancestry, which were known by names such as mestizos, mulattoes, zambos, and castizos. Although most Latin American states ended the legal recognition of these groups after independence, the distinctions themselves persisted and limited the opportunities available to peoples of indigenous, African, or mixed ancestry.

**Migration and Cultural Diversity** Large-scale migration brought added cultural diversity to Latin America in the nineteenth century. Indentured laborers who went from parts of Asia to Peru, Brazil, Cuba, and other Caribbean destinations carried with them many of their native cultural practices. When their numbers were relatively small, as in the case of Chinese migrants to Cuba, they mostly intermarried and assimilated into the working classes without leaving much foreign influence on the societies they joined. When they were relatively more numerous, however, as in the case of Indian migrants to Trinidad and Tobago, they formed distinctive communities in which they spoke their native languages, prepared foods from their homelands, and observed their inherited cultural and social traditions. Migration of European workers to Argentina brought a lively diversity to the capital of Buenos Aires, which was perhaps the most cosmopolitan city of nineteenth-century Latin America. With its broad avenues, smart boutiques, and handsome buildings graced with wrought iron, Buenos Aires enjoyed a reputation as "the Paris of the Americas."

Latin American intellectuals seeking cultural identity usually saw themselves either as heirs of Europe or as products of the American environment. One spokesperson who identified with Europe was the Argentine president **Domingo Faustino Sarmiento** (1811–1888). Sarmiento despised the rule of caudillos that had emerged after independence and worked for the development of a society based on European values. In his widely read book *Facundo: Civilization and Barbarism* (1845), Sarmiento argued that it was necessary for Buenos Aires to bring discipline to the disorderly Argentine countryside. Deeply influenced by the Enlightenment, he characterized books, ideas, law, education, and art as products of cities, and he argued that only when cities dominated the countryside would social stability and genuine liberty be possible.

**Gauchos** Sarmiento admired the bravery and independence of Argentina's ***gauchos*** ("cowboys"), but he thought it necessary that urban residents rather than ranchers make society's crucial decisions. Most, but not all, gauchos were of mixed race, but race was not the determining factor in becoming a gaucho. Instead, anyone who adopted gaucho ways became a gaucho, and gaucho society acquired an ethnic egalitarianism rarely found elsewhere in Latin America. Gauchos were most prominent in the Argentine pampas, but their cultural practices linked them to the cowboys, or vaqueros, found throughout the Americas. As pastoralists herding cattle and horses on

### INTERPRETING IMAGES

An 1868 photograph of an Argentinian gaucho dressed in typical gear.

**Analyze** *Compare this photograph to painted portraits in previous chapters. How does photography impact our understanding of history? What might participation in photographs mean for the subjects of these images?*

Historic Collection/Alamy Stock Photo

**Domingo Faustino Sarmiento** (doh-MING-oh fow-STEEN-oh sahr-MYEN-toh)
***gauchos*** (GOW-chohs)

the pampas, gauchos stood apart from both the indigenous peoples and the growing urban and agricultural elites who gradually displaced them with large landholdings and cattle ranches that spread to the pampas.

The gauchos led independent and self-sufficient lives that appealed broadly to many Latin Americans who lived in hierarchical societies. Legend had it that gauchos lived off their own skills and needed only their horses to survive. They dressed distinctively, with sashed trousers, ponchos, and boots. Countless songs and poems lauded their courage, skills, and romantic allure. Yet independence and caudillo rule disrupted gaucho life as the cowboys increasingly entered armies, either voluntarily or by force, and as settled agriculture and ranches surrounded by barbed wire enclosed the pampas. The gauchos did not leave the pampas without resistance. The poet José Hernandez offered a romanticized vision of the gaucho life and protested its decline in his epic poem *The Gaucho Martín Fierro* (1873). Hernandez conveyed the pride of gauchos, particularly those who resisted assimilation into Euro-American society, by having Martín Fierro proclaim his independence and assert his intention to stay that way:

> I owe nothin' to nobody;
> I don't ask for shelter, or give it;
> and from now on, nobody
> better try to lead me around by a rope.

Nevertheless, by the late nineteenth century, gauchos were mostly echoes of the Latin American past.

**Male Domination** Even more than in the United States and Canada, male domination was a central characteristic of Latin American society in the nineteenth century. Women could not vote or hold office, nor could they work or manage estates without permission from their male guardians. In rural areas, women were liable to rough treatment by men steeped in the values of ***machismo***—a social ethic that honored male strength, courage, aggressiveness, assertiveness, and cunning. A few women voiced their discontent with male domination and machismo. In her poem "To Be Born a Man" (1887), for example, the Bolivian poet Adela Zamudio lamented bitterly that talented women could not vote, but ignorant men could, just by learning how to sign their names. Although Latin American states had not yet generated a strong women's movement, they did begin to expand educational opportunities for girls and young women after the mid-nineteenth century. In large cities most girls received some formal schooling, and women usually filled teaching positions in the public schools that proliferated throughout Latin America in the late nineteenth century.

**Female Activism** Women did carve spaces for themselves outside or alongside the male world of machismo, and this was especially true in the home and in the marketplace, where Latin American women exerted great influence. In the early twentieth century, women also served in conjunction with men in the Mexican revolution, most famously as Zapatistas, or followers of Emiliano Zapata. Many women supporting Zapata labored within the domestic realm to provide food for the soldiers, but others became soldiers and officers themselves. Although those women who became ***soldaderas*** (female soldiers or supporters of soldiers) demonstrated the most extreme forms of activism during the Mexican revolution, Mexican women on the whole made major contributions to the success of the revolution and shared in the radical spirit of change that characterized much of early-twentieth-century Latin America.

## CONCLUSION

After gaining independence from European colonial powers, the states of the Western Hemisphere worked to build stable and prosperous societies. The independent American states faced difficult challenges—including vast territories, diverse populations, social tensions, and cultural differences—as they sought to construct viable societies based partly on the Enlightenment principles of freedom, equality, and constitutional government. People in the United States and Canada built large federal societies in North America, whereas people in Latin America built a series of smaller states. Encounters, at times violent, between the various groups in the Americas and their varying traditions, proved a significant challenge to the emerging states in the Western Hemisphere. The United States in particular was an expansive, colonial society, absorbing Texas, California, and the northern territories of Mexico while extending its authority from the Atlantic to the Pacific Ocean. Throughout the hemisphere, descendants of European settlers violently conquered indigenous American peoples and built societies dominated by Euro-American peoples. They established agricultural economies, exploited natural resources, and in some places launched processes of industrialization. Millions of people from Europe and Asia migrated to the Americas, contributing not only to American cultural diversity but also to the transformations in labor practices caused by the abolition of slavery and the rise of industry. All American states experienced tensions arising from social, economic, cultural, and ethnic differences, which led occasionally to violent civil conflict and often to smoldering resentments and grievances. While the making of independent American societies was not a smooth process, it nevertheless reflected the increasing interdependence of all the world's peoples.

## STUDY TERMS

Abraham Lincoln (587)
Antonio López de Santa Anna (593)
battle of the Little Bighorn (585)
Benito Juárez (593)
British North America Act of 1867 (590)
Canadian Pacific Railroad (597)
caudillos (592)
Domingo Faustino Sarmiento (605)
Dominion of Canada (590)
Durham Report (590)
Emancipation Proclamation (588)
Emiliano Zapata (593)
Francisco (Pancho) Villa (593)
*gauchos* (605)
Indian Removal Act of 1830 (584)
John A. Macdonald (590)
Juan Manuel de Rosas (592)
Louis Riel (604)
*machismo* (606)
manifest destiny (584)
Mexican-American War (586)
National Policy (597)
Northwest Rebellion (604)
Porfirio Díaz (593)
railroad time (659)
Reconstruction (601)
Seneca Falls Convention (602)
*soldaderas* (606)
Trail of Tears (585)
U.S. Civil War (650)
War of 1812 (590)
Wounded Knee (586)

## FOR FURTHER READING


David Barry Gaspar and Darlene Clark Hine, eds. *Beyond Bondage: Free Women of Color in the Americas.* Chicago, 2004. Collection of essays on free black women and their unique abilities to negotiate social and legal institutions in the era of slavery.

Pekka Hämäläinen. *The Comanche Empire.* New Haven, 2008. An ambitiously revisionist history that challenges the accepted understanding of colonial America and westward expansion.

Tom Holm. *The Great Confusion in Indian Affairs: Native Americans and Whites in the Progressive Era.* Austin, 2005. Study of Native American resistance to the American government's attempts at subjugation.

Patricia Nelson Limerick. *The Legacy of Conquest: The Unbroken Past of the American West.* New York, 1987. A provocative work exploring the influences of race, class, and gender in the conquest of the American west.

Adam McKeown. *Melancholy Order: Asian Migration and the Globalization of Borders.* New York, 2008. Documents the global scale of Asian migration in the nineteenth and twentieth centuries and argues that it triggered exclusionary border policies in the United States and Europe.

J. R. Miller. *Skyscrapers Hide the Heavens: A History of Indian-White Relations in Canada.* 3rd ed. Toronto, 2000. An important study of Canadian policies toward indigenous peoples.

Desmond Morton. *A Short History of Canada.* 6th ed. Toronto, 2006. This is a well-balanced, popular history of Canada.

Paul Ortiz. *An African American and Latinx History of the United States.* Boston, 2018. A radical revisionist exploration of U.S. history from the perspective of marginalized people in a global context.

Robert L. Scheina. *Latin American Wars.* Vol. 1: *The Age of the Caudillos, 1791–1899.* Washington, D.C., 2003. By examining the wars of independence, this work uncovers the reasons behind the failures of Latin American state building.

Allison Sneider. *Suffragists in an Imperial Age: US Expansion and the Woman Question, 1870–1929.* Oxford, 2008. Explores the women's suffrage movement in the United States and U.S. imperialism as intertwined and inseparable phenomena.

# CHAPTER 18 AP EXAM PRACTICE

Questions assume cumulative knowledge from this chapter and previous chapters.

## Section I

## Multiple Choice Questions

Use the map below and your knowledge of world history to answer questions 1-3.

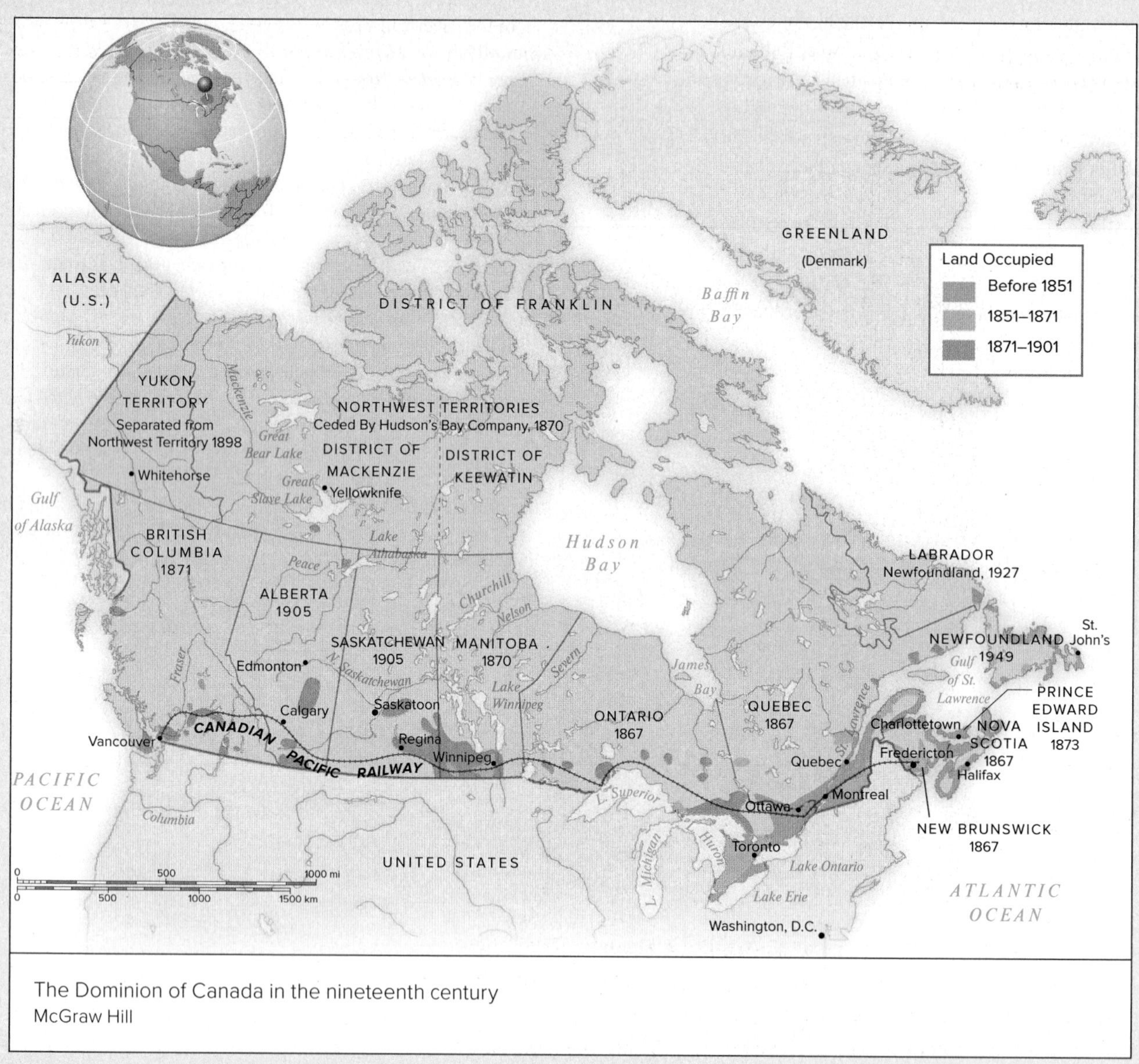


The Dominion of Canada in the nineteenth century
McGraw Hill

1. How did the Canadian Pacific Railway contribute to the unification of Canada?
   (A) The railroad facilitated transportation and communication throughout Canada and helped bring new provinces into the Dominion of Canada.
   (B) Canadians started to use the same time systems, known as "railway time."
   (C) The railway helped the Canadians fight off the Russians who were advancing through Alaska to colonize the west coast.
   (D) By allowing more frequent transportation and communication, the railroad brought together the English and Spanish speaking Canadians.

2. Which of the following is a way the United States affected developments in Canada?
   (A) Canada increased the size of their army to patrol and defend the southern border.
   (B) A former governor-general of Canada argued in the Durham Report that Canada should have no self-government to prevent a war for independence.
   (C) Canadian provinces divided themselves into slaveholding provinces and non-slaveholding provinces.
   (D) Many English loyalists moved to Canada as the US revolution ended, enlarging the English-speaking population.

3. Which of the following is a difference between the creation of Canada and of the United States?
   (A) Canadians continued to follow standardized British spelling.
   (B) The United States was created out of a war against the British while Canada achieved independence gradually.
   (C) Canadian settlers came from England and France, while settlers in the United States came only from England.
   (D) Settlers in the United States and Canada frequently intermarried with the indigenous population. Their children in the United States were known as the *métis*, but in Canada they were known as the *casta*.

Use the images below and your knowledge of world history to answer questions 4 and 5.

Revolutionary leader Emiliano Zapata (1879–1919). Cultural Heritage Images/ Universal Images Group/Newscom

4. Why was Emiliano Zapata a popular leader in the Mexican Revolution?
   (A) His superior access to weapons intimidated peasants into following him.
   (B) He was successful capturing major Mexican cities.
   (C) Zapata attacked haciendas and distributed the land to peasants.
   (D) He nationalized the Mexican oil industry.

5. Which reforms were including in the 1917 Mexican constitution?
   (A) Universal suffrage, state-supported education, and a minimum wage.
   (B) Universal suffrage, paid family leave, and health care benefits.
   (C) Health care benefits, universal life insurance, and state-supported education.
   (D) A minimum wage, paid family leave, and land redistribution.

## Short Answer

6. Use the image below and your knowledge of world history to answer parts A, B, and C.

Edouard Manet's painting (one of a series painted between 1867 and 1869) depicting the execution by firing squad of the Emperor Maximilian.
World History Archive/Alamy Stock Photo

(A) Identify ONE similarity or difference between the governments of the United States and Latin America.
(B) Explain ONE reason why Latin American states were unstable in the nineteenth century.
(C) Explain ONE way Latin American countries responded to new forms of imperialism.

7. Use the map below and your knowledge of world history to answer parts A, B, and C.

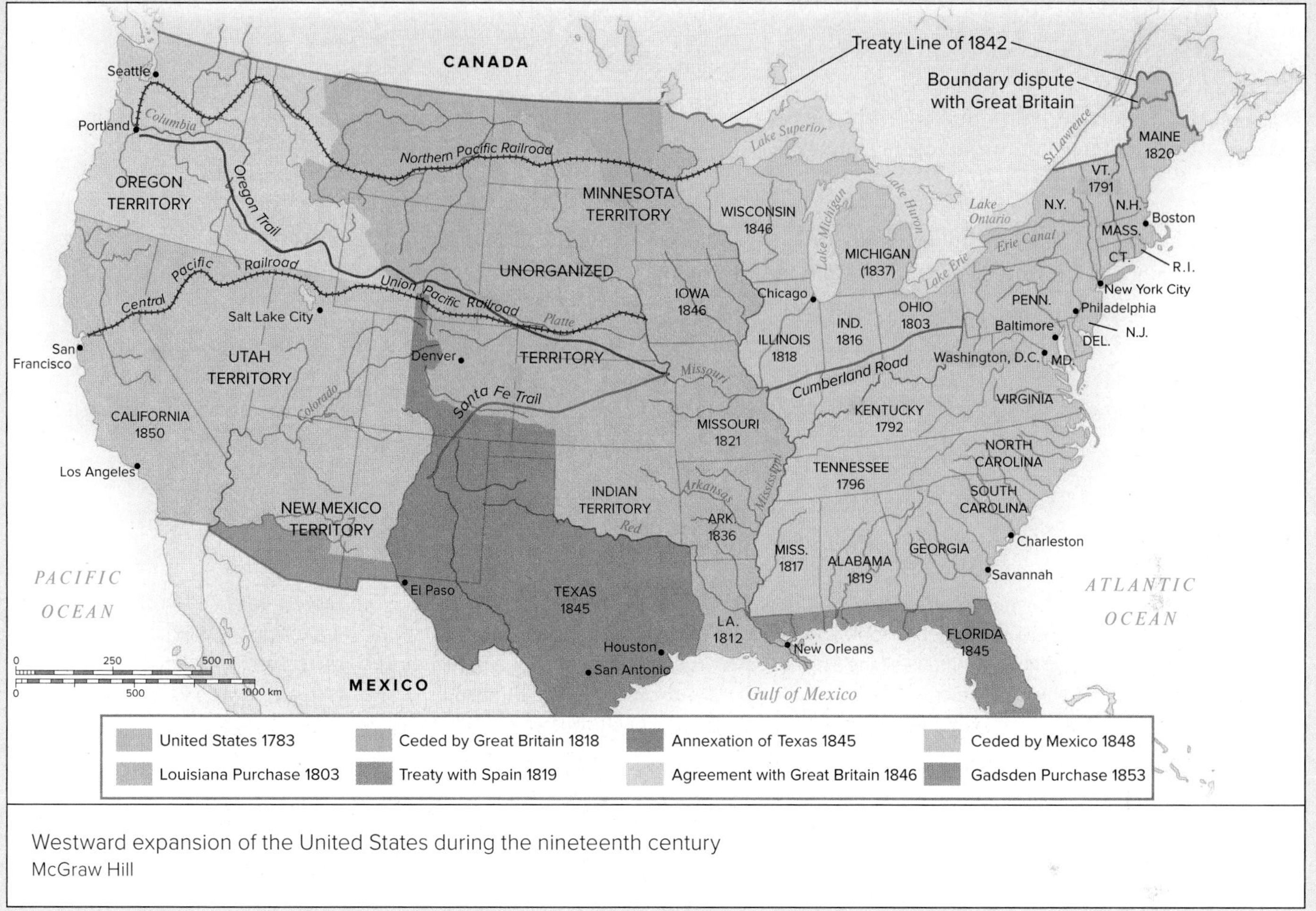


Westward expansion of the United States during the nineteenth century
McGraw Hill

(A) Explain ONE reason why the United States expanded westward.
(B) Explain ONE way that Native Americans responded to the westward expansion of the United States.
(C) Identify ONE consequence of the westward expansion of the United States.

8. Use your understanding of world history to answer parts A, B, and C.
(A) Identify ONE community where migrants maintained their cultural traditions in the Americas.
(B) Explain ONE kind of work common to immigrants in the Americas and why it was common for immigrants to do that kind of work.
(C) Explain ONE response that immigrants received from white, native-born U.S. citizens.

# Section II

## Document-Based Question

Based on the documents below and your knowledge of world history, compare and contrast the reasons for migration to and within the United States in the nineteenth century

In your response you should do the following:

- Respond to the prompt with a historically defensible thesis or claim that establishes a line of reasoning.
- Describe a broader historical context relevant to the prompt.
- Support an argument in response to the prompt using all documents.
- Use at least one additional piece of specific historical evidence (beyond that found in the documents) relevant to an argument about the prompt.
- Explain how or why the document's point of view, purpose, historical situation, and /or audience is relevant to an argument.
- Use evidence to corroborate, qualify, or modify an argument that addresses the prompt.

### Document 1

I want to know particularly what the good chance is you propose to give me. I am doing tolerably well here; I get $25 a month, with victuals and clothing; have a comfortable home for Mandy (the folks here call her Mrs. Anderson) and the children, Milly, Jane, and Grundy, go to school and are learning well; the teacher says Grundy has a head for a preacher. They go to Sunday-School, and Mandy and me attend church regularly. We are kindly treated. . . . Now, if you will write and say what wages you will give me, I will be better able to decide whether it would be to my advantage to move back again.

*Source:* Anderson, Jordan. "Letter from a Freedman to his Old Master." *New York: New York Daily Tribune*, 22 August 1865.

### Document 2

Idealized portrayal of Jewish refugees from Russia passing the Statue of Liberty; engraving by Charles Joseph Staniland. 1892.
Stefano Bianchetti/Corbis/Getty Images

## Document 3

Photograph of the forced removal of Oglala Sioux and Brule indigenous people from their land near Pine Ridge, South Dakota, in 1891.
Buyenlarge/Archive Photos/Getty Images

## Long Essay

Develop a thoughtful and thorough historical argument that answers the question below. Begin your essay with a thesis statement and support it with relevant historical evidence.

Using specific examples and your knowledge of world history, explain relevant similarities and differences between Canada's conflicts and dealings with indigenous peoples to the approach of the Latin American states in dealing with similar issues.

# Chapter 19 Societies at Crossroads



## ZOOMING IN ON TRADITIONS AND ENCOUNTERS

### "Heavenly King" Hong Xiuquan, Empress Dowager Cixi, and Qing Reform

Hong **Xiuquan,** the third son of a poor family, grew up in a farming village in southern China about 50 kilometers (31 miles) from Guangzhou. Although he was arrogant and irritable, he showed intellectual promise. His neighbors made him village teacher so that he could study and prepare for the civil service examinations, the principal avenue to government employment, because a position in the Qing bureaucracy would bring honor and wealth to both his family and his village. Between 1828 and 1837, Hong took the exams three times but failed to obtain even the lowest degree. This outcome was not surprising because thousands of candidates competed for degrees while only a few obtained one. But the disappointment was too much for Hong. He suffered an emotional collapse, lapsed into a delirium that lasted about forty days, and experienced visions.

Upon recovering from his breakdown, Hong resumed his position as village teacher and studied to take the civil service examinations again. After failing yet again in 1843,

China's Empress Dowager Cixi in 1903. Beginning her political career as a concubine in the harem of the Xianfeng emperor, she developed into a powerful and charismatic figure who became the de facto ruler of the Manchu Qing dynasty in China for over forty years, from 1861 until her death in 1908.
Art Images/Chinese School/Getty Images

**Xiuquan** (shee-OH-chew-ahn)

Hong began studying the works of a Chinese missionary who explained the basic elements of Christianity. As he pondered the religious tracts, Hong came to believe that during his illness he had visited heaven and learned from God that he was the younger brother of Jesus Christ. He believed further that God had revealed to him that his destiny was to reform China and pave the way for the heavenly kingdom. Inspired by these convictions, Hong baptized himself and worked to build a community of disciples.

Hong's personal religious vision soon evolved into a political program: Hong believed that God had charged him with the establishment of a new order, one that necessitated the destruction of the **Qing** dynasty, which had ruled China since 1644. In 1847 he emerged as the leader of the Society of God Worshipers, a religious group recently founded by his own disciples, whose supporters were poor peasants and miners from Guangxi province in southern China. In 1850, Hong led about ten thousand of these followers in rebellion against the Qing dynasty. On his thirty-seventh birthday, 11 January 1851, he assumed the title of "Heavenly King" and proclaimed his own dynasty, the Taiping tianguo ("Heavenly Kingdom of Great Peace"). Hong's followers, known as the Taipings, quickly grew from a ragtag band to a disciplined and zealous army of over one million men and women who nearly toppled the Qing dynasty. The Taiping rebellion lasted until 1864, and at its height included two million followers. Although the Taipings were eventually defeated by Qing dynasty forces under the command of the Dowager Empress **Cixi**, the rebellion—which claimed at least twenty million lives—pointed to massive turmoil within Chinese society and deep dissatisfaction with Qing rule. Given Hong's inspiration from Christianity, the Taiping rebellion also signaled the growing importance of encounters with western ideas, influence, and interference in nineteenth-century China.

**Qing** (ching)
**Taiping** (TEYE-pihng)
**Cixi** (tsuh-shee)

# CHAPTER FOCUS

- If Asian empires—the Ottoman, Russian, Chinese, and Japanese—felt compelled to industrialize to catch up to the industrialized west, the imperial governments needed to sponsor industrialization themselves—not wait for individual entrepreneurs to do it. They did not necessarily believe that industrialization was the cutting edge; after all, these empires had run the world's economy for millennia.
- These imperial governments had to respond to their own social, political, and economic circumstances when considering industrialization. The most profound argument for industrializing was that European and U.S. manufacturers were producing factory-made gunpowder weapons. Self-preservation demanded that the Ottoman, Russian, Chinese, and Japanese governments regain military equity
- Most of the ruling classes, however, wanted to choose which parts of their economies to industrialize, and leave the manufacturing of cheap, disposable, factory-made goods—and the accompanying pollution and urban problems—to the west.
- Rebellions arose over economic issues and more: public education, taxation, land redistribution, suffrage, and representational legislatures and constitutions.
- Western industrialized countries understood their advantage. By the 1850s, Europeans and U.S. businessmen controlled key parts of the Chinese, Ottoman, and Japanese economies. This indirect imperialism—allowing westerners to benefit economically without the associated costs of a complete government takeover—led to more reforms and rebellions, causing instability in all the empires but Japan's.

## Historical Developments

- The need for raw materials for factories and increased food supplies for the growing population in urban centers led to the growth of export economies around the world that specialized in commercial extraction of natural resources and the production of food and industrial crops.
- Industrialized states and businesses within those states practiced economic imperialism primarily in Asia and Latin America.
- Increasing questions about political authority and growing nationalism contributed to anticolonial movements.

- Migration in many cases was influenced by changes in demographics in both industrialized and unindustrialized societies that presented challenges to existing patterns of living.
- The older, land-based Ottoman, Russian, and Qing empires collapsed due to a combination of internal and external factors.

## Reasoning Processes

- **Causation** Describe the causes and effects of reform and modernization movements in Russia, China, Japan, and the Ottoman empire.

## Historical Thinking Skills

- **Source Claims and Evidence** Identify and describe the arguments made in the decree on opium made by China's high commissioner.
- **Making Connections** Identify patterns among and connections between Chinese and Japanese responses to contact with foreign industrial powers.

## CHAPTER OVERVIEW

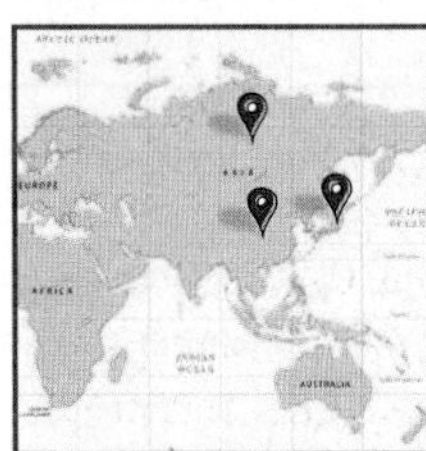

China was not the only place that faced serious turmoil in the nineteenth century: the Ottoman Empire, the Russian Empire, and Tokugawa Japan also experienced similar problems in this period. One problem common to the four societies was military weakness that left them vulnerable to foreign interference. The Ottoman, Russian, Qing, and Tokugawa armies all fought wars or engaged in military confrontations with the nations of western Europe and the United States in the nineteenth century, and all discovered suddenly and unexpectedly that industrialization had allowed their rivals to develop far more effective military weaponry than they now commanded. The result was a new power dynamic in which the industrialized states increasingly sought to impose their will on states that had not yet industrialized. Sometimes this meant that industrialized states seized territories and conquered them by force. Often, however, Euro-American states used force or the threat of force to extract favorable economic arrangements with their weaker rivals. These arrangements allowed capitalists from industrialized states to profit enormously at the expense of the weaker societies.

Other problems common to Tokugawa Japan and the Ottoman, Russian, and Qing empires were internal, including population pressure, declining agricultural productivity, famine, falling government revenue, and corruption at all levels of government. Each experienced serious domestic turmoil, especially during the second half of the nineteenth century, as peasants mounted rebellions, dissidents struggled for reform, and political factions fought among themselves or conspired to organize coups. Moreover, when leaders of the four societies were unable to respond effectively to domestic strife, this sometimes provided western European powers and the United States with an excuse to intervene to protect their business interests.

By the late nineteenth century, leaders of the Ottoman Empire, the Russian Empire, Qing China, and Tokugawa Japan recognized that their societies were at a critical crossroads: they could either institute reforms that would enable them to compete with industrial states, or they could continue to be increasingly dominated by them. Thus, reformers in all four societies

| CHRONOLOGY | |
|---|---|
| 1805–1848 | Reign of Muhammad Ali in Egypt |
| 1808–1839 | Reign of Sultan Mahmud II |
| 1814–1864 | Life of Taiping leader Hong Xiuquan |
| 1839–1842 | Opium War |
| 1839–1876 | Tanzimat era |
| 1850–1864 | Taiping rebellion |
| 1853 | Arrival of Commodore Perry in Japan |
| 1853–1856 | Crimean War |
| 1855–1881 | Reign of Tsar Alexander II |
| 1860–1895 | Self-Strengthening Movement |
| 1861 | Emancipation of the Russian serfs |
| 1868 | Meiji restoration |
| 1876 | Promulgation of the Ottoman constitution |
| 1889 | Promulgation of the Meiji constitution |
| 1894–1917 | Reign of Tsar Nicholas II |
| 1898 | Hundred Days reforms |
| 1900 | Boxer rebellion |
| 1904–1905 | Russo-Japanese War |
| 1905 | Revolution of 1905 in Russia |
| 1908–1918 | Young Turk era |

promoted plans to introduce written constitutions, limit the authority of rulers, make governments responsive to the needs and desires of the people, guarantee equality before the law, restructure educational systems, and begin processes of industrialization. Many reformers had traveled in Europe and the United States, where they experienced constitutional government and industrial society firsthand, and they sought to remodel their own societies along the lines of the industrial states.

Vigorous reform movements emerged in all four territories, but they had very different results. In the Ottoman Empire, the Russian Empire, and Qing China, ruling elites and wealthy classes opposed changes that might threaten their status. Reform in those three territories was halting and tentative, and by the early twentieth century the Ottoman, Romanov, and Qing dynasties were on the verge of collapse. In Japan, however reform, was much more thorough. By the early twentieth century, Japan was an emerging industrial power poised to expand its influence in the larger world.

# THE WEAKENING OF THE OTTOMAN EMPIRE

During the eighteenth century the Ottoman Empire experienced military reverses and challenges to its rule. By the early nineteenth century, the Ottoman state could no longer ward off extensive European economic interference or prevent territorial dismemberment. As Ottoman officials launched reforms to regenerate imperial vigor, Egypt and other north African provinces declared their independence, and European states seized territories in the northern and western parts of the Ottoman Empire. At the same time, pressure from ethnic, religious, and nationalist groups threatened to fragment the empire from within. By the late nineteenth century, the once-powerful realm found that its sovereignty was now severely compromised by the same European powers that exploited its economy.

## The Sources of Ottoman Weakness

**Military Difficulties** By the late seventeenth century, the Ottoman Empire had reached the limits of its expansion. In the late seventeenth and eighteenth centuries, Ottoman armies suffered humiliating defeats on the battlefield, especially at the hands of Austrian and Russian foes. Part of the reason for these defeats was that Ottoman forces had begun to lag behind their rivals in terms of strategy, tactics, weaponry, and training. Equally serious was a breakdown in the discipline of the elite Janissary corps (discussed in chapter 27), which had served as the backbone of the imperial armed forces since the fifteenth century. The **Janissaries** repeatedly masterminded palace coups during the seventeenth and eighteenth centuries and by the nineteenth century had become a powerful political force within the Ottoman state. The Janissaries neglected their military training and turned a blind eye to advances in weapons technology. As its military capacity declined, the Ottoman realm became vulnerable to its more powerful neighbors.

Loss of military power translated into reduced effectiveness of the central government, which was losing power in the provinces to its own officials. By the early nineteenth century, semi-independent governors and local notables had formed private armies of mercenaries and enslaved peoples to support the sultan in Istanbul in return for recognition of autonomy. Increasingly these independent rulers also turned fiscal and administrative institutions to their own interests, collecting taxes for themselves and sending only nominal payments to the imperial treasury, thus depriving the central state of revenue.

**Territorial Losses** The Ottoman government managed to maintain its authority in Anatolia (present-day Turkey), the heart of the empire, as well as in Iraq, but it suffered serious territorial losses elsewhere, especially in the nineteenth century. Russian forces took over poorly defended territories in the Caucasus and in central Asia, and the Austrian Empire nibbled away at the western frontiers. Nationalist uprisings

By the latter part of the nineteenth century, European imperialism directly affected the fortunes of the Ottoman Empire. This undated political cartoon shows England as a lion and Russia as a bear threatening Turkey (shown as a turkey). The illustration is labeled "Be my ally, or I'll give you the worst thrashing you ever had in your life."
Bettmann/Getty Images

forced Ottoman rulers to recognize the independence of Balkan provinces, notably Greece (1830) and Serbia (1867).

Most significant, however, was the loss of Egypt. In 1798 the ambitious French general Napoleon invaded Egypt in hopes of using it as a springboard for an attack on the British Empire in India. His campaign was a miserable failure: Napoleon had to abandon his army and sneak back to France, where he proceeded to overthrow the Directory. But the invasion sparked turmoil in Egypt, as local elites battled to seize power after Napoleon's departure. The ultimate victor was the energetic general **Muhammad Ali,** who built a powerful army modeled on European forces and ruled Egypt from 1805 to 1848. He drafted peasants to serve as infantry soldiers, and he hired French and Italian officers to train his troops. He also launched a program of industrialization, concentrating on cotton textiles and armaments. Although he remained technically subordinate to the Ottoman sultan, by 1820 it was clear that he had established himself as the effective ruler of Egypt, which was the most powerful land in the Muslim world. In 1839 he even invaded Syria and Anatolia, threatening to capture Istanbul and topple the Ottoman state. Indeed, the Ottoman dynasty survived only because British forces intervened out of fear that Ottoman collapse would result in a sudden and dangerous expansion of Russian influence. Nevertheless, Muhammad Ali made Egypt an essentially autonomous region within the Ottoman Empire.

**Economic Difficulties** Economic problems aggravated the military and political problems of the Ottoman state. The volume of trade passing through the Ottoman Empire declined throughout the later seventeenth and eighteenth centuries, as European merchants increasingly bypassed Ottoman territories in the Mediterranean to trade directly with their counterparts in India and China. By the eighteenth

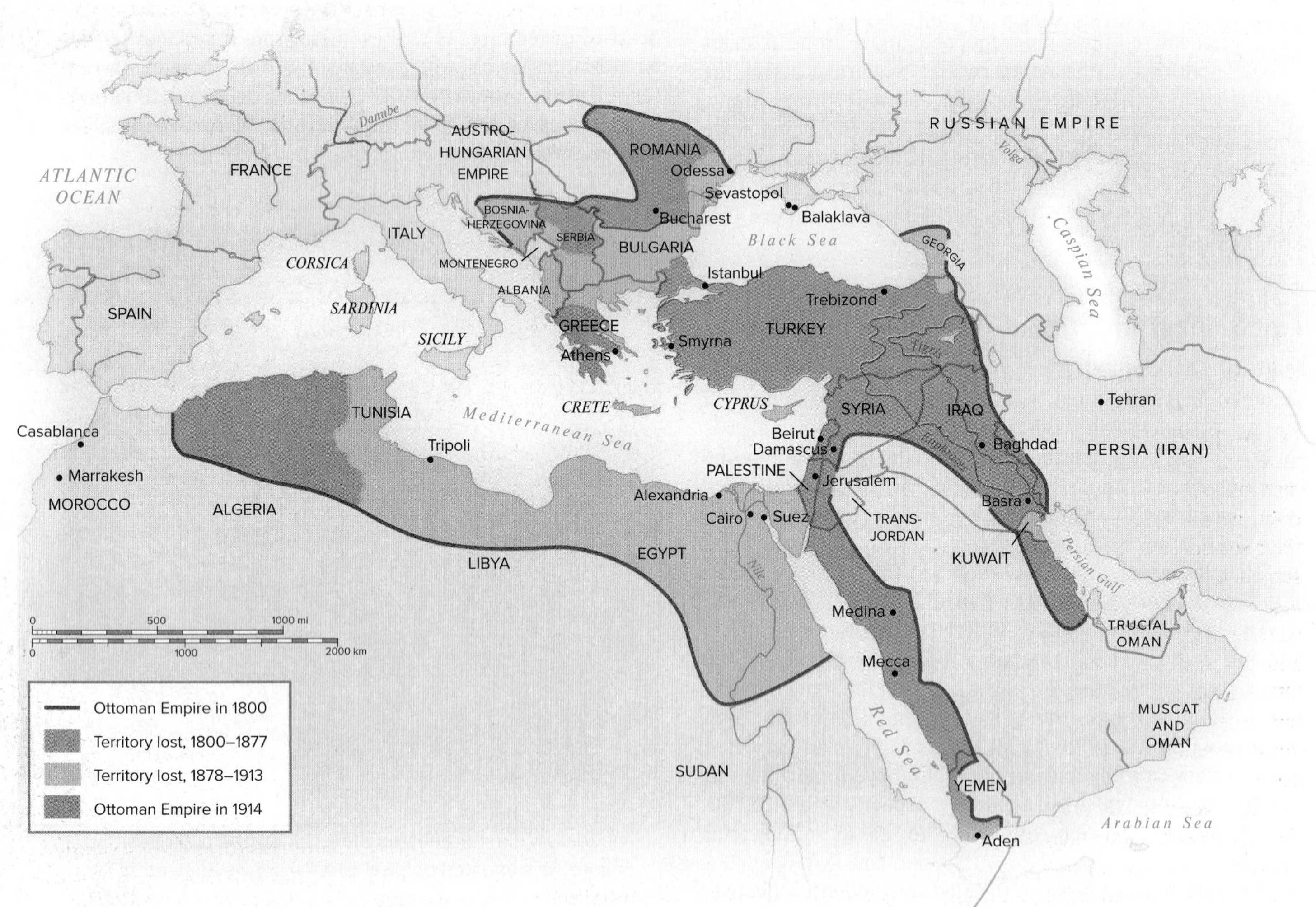


**MAP 19.1 Territorial losses of the Ottoman Empire, 1800–1923.**

Compare the borders of the Ottoman Empire in 1800 with what was left of the empire in 1914.

***What might have been the strategic value of the remaining Ottoman territories?***

century the focus of European trade had shifted to the Atlantic Ocean basin, where the Ottomans had no presence at all. Meanwhile, as European producers began to industrialize in the eighteenth and nineteenth centuries, their textiles and manufactured goods began to flow into the Ottoman Empire. Because those items were inexpensive and high-quality products, they were in high demand by Ottoman consumers. At the same time, they placed considerable pressure on Ottoman artisans and crafts workers, who frequently led urban riots to protest foreign imports. Ottoman exports consisted largely of raw materials such as grain, cotton, hemp, indigo, and opium, but they did not offset the value of imported European manufactures. Gradually, the Ottoman Empire moved toward fiscal insolvency and financial dependency. After the middle of the nineteenth century, economic development in the Ottoman Empire depended heavily on foreign loans, as European capital financed the construction of railroads, utilities, and mining enterprises. Interest payments on foreign loans grew to the point that they consumed more than half of the empire's revenues. In 1882 the Ottoman state was unable to pay interest on its loans and had no choice but to accept administration of its debts by Europeans.

**The Capitulations** Nothing symbolized foreign interference more than the **capitulations,** agreements that exempted European visitors from Ottoman law and provided European powers with extraterritoriality—the right to exercise jurisdiction over their own citizens according to their own laws. The practice dated back to the sixteenth century, when Ottoman sultans signed capitulation treaties to avoid the burden of administering justice for communities of foreign merchants. By the nineteenth century, however, Ottoman officials regarded the capitulations as humiliating intrusions on their sovereignty. Capitulations also served as instruments of economic power by European businesspeople who established tax-exempt banks and commercial enterprises in the Ottoman Empire, and they permitted foreign governments to levy duties on goods sold in Ottoman ports.

By the early twentieth century, the Ottoman state lacked the resources to maintain its costly bureaucracy. Expenditures exceeded revenues, and the state experienced growing difficulty paying the salaries of its employees in the palace household, the military, and the religious hierarchy. Declining incomes led to reduced morale, recruitment difficulties, and a rise in corruption. Increased taxation designed to offset revenue losses only led to increased exploitation of the peasantry and a decline in agricultural production. The Ottoman Empire was in trouble and it needed a major restructuring to survive.

Sultan Abdül Hamid II (1842–1918) ruled the Ottoman Empire from 1876 to 1909, when the Young Turks deposed him and sent him into exile.
Universal History Archive/UIG/Shutterstock

## Reform and Reorganization

In response to recurring and deepening crises, Ottoman leaders launched a series of reforms designed to strengthen and preserve the state. Reform efforts began as early as the seventeenth century, when sultans sought to limit taxation, increase agricultural production, and end official corruption. Reform continued in the eighteenth century, as **Sultan Selim III** (reigned 1789–1807) embarked on a program to remodel his army along the lines of European forces. But the establishment of this new fighting force, trained by European instructors and equipped with modern weapons, threatened the elite Janissary corps, which reacted violently by rising in revolt, killing the new troops, and locking up the sultan. When Selim's successor tried to revive the new military force, rampaging Janissaries killed all male members of the dynasty except one, Selim's cousin **Mahmud II,** who became sultan (reigned 1808–1839).

**The Reforms of Mahmud II** The increasing interventions by European powers and the separatist ambitions of local rulers persuaded Mahmud to launch his own reform program. Given what had happened to his predecessors, Mahmud tried to ensure that his reforms were not perceived as dangerous innovations but, rather, as a restoration of the traditional Ottoman military. Nevertheless, his proposal for a new European-style army in 1826 brought him into conflict with the Janissaries. When the Janissaries mutinied in protest, Mahmud had them massacred by troops loyal to the sultan. That incident cleared the way for a series of reforms that unfolded during the last thirteen years of Mahmud's reign.

Mahmud's program remodeled Ottoman institutions along western European lines. Highest priority went to the creation of a more effective army. European drillmasters dressed Ottoman soldiers in European-style uniforms and instructed them in European weapons and tactics. Ottoman recruits studied at military and engineering schools and learned European curricula. Mahmud's reforms also went beyond military affairs. His government created a system of secondary education for boys to facilitate the transition from mosque schools, which provided most primary education, to newly established scientific, technical, and military academies. Mahmud also tried to transfer power from traditional elites to himself and his cabinet by taxing rural landlords, abolishing the system of military land grants, and undermining the ulama, the Islamic leadership. To make his authority more effective, the sultan established European-style ministries, constructed new roads, built telegraph lines, and inaugurated a postal service. By the time of Mahmud's death in 1839, the Ottoman Empire had shrunk in size, but it was also more manageable and stronger than it had been since the early seventeenth century.

**Legal and Educational Reform** Continuing defeats on the battlefield and the rise of separatist movements among subject peoples prompted the ruling classes to undertake more radical restructuring of the Ottoman state after Mahmud's reign. The tempo of reform increased rapidly during the **Tanzimat** ("reorganization") **era** (1839–1876). Once again, the army was a principal target of reform efforts, but legal and educational reforms also had wide-ranging implications for Ottoman society. In designing their program, Tanzimat reformers drew considerable inspiration from Enlightenment thought and the constitutional foundations of western European states.

Tanzimat reformers attacked Ottoman law with the aim of making it acceptable to Europeans so they could have the capitulations lifted and recover Ottoman sovereignty. Using the French legal system as a guide, reformers issued a commercial code (1850), a penal code (1858), a maritime code (1863), and a new civil code (1870–1876). Tanzimat reformers also issued decrees designed to safeguard the rights of subjects. Key among them were measures that guaranteed public trials, rights of privacy, and equality before the law for all Ottoman subjects, whether Muslim or not. Matters pertaining to marriage and divorce still fell under religious law. But because state courts administered the new laws, legal reform undermined the ulama and enhanced the authority of the Ottoman state. Educational reforms also undermined the ulama, who controlled religious education for Muslims. A comprehensive plan for educational reform, introduced in 1846, provided for a complete system of primary and secondary schools leading to university-level instruction, all under the supervision of the state ministry of education. A still more ambitious plan, inaugurated in 1869, provided for free and compulsory primary education.

**Opposition to the Tanzimat** Although reform and reorganization strengthened Ottoman society, the Tanzimat provoked spirited opposition from several distinct quarters. Harsh criticism came from religious conservatives, who argued that reformers posed a threat to the empire's Islamic foundation. Many devout Muslims viewed the extension of legal equality to Jews and Christians as an act contrary to the basic principles of Islamic law. Even some minority leaders opposed legal equality, fearing that it would diminish their own position as intermediaries between their communities and the Ottoman state. Criticism arose also from a group known collectively as the Young Ottomans. Although they did not share a common political or religious program—their views ranged from secular revolution to uncompromising Islam—Young Ottomans agitated for individual freedom, local autonomy, and political decentralization. Many Young Ottomans desired the establishment of a constitutional government along the lines of the British system. A fourth and perhaps the most dangerous critique of Tanzimat emerged from within the Ottoman bureaucracy itself. In part because of their exclusion from power, high-level bureaucrats were determined to impose checks on the sultan's power by forcing him to accept a constitution and, if necessary, even to depose him.

## The Young Turk Era

**Reform and Repression** In 1876 a group of radical dissidents from the Ottoman bureaucracy seized power in a coup, formed a cabinet that included advocates of reform, and installed **Abdül Hamid II** as sultan (reigned 1876–1909). Convinced of the need to check the sultan's power, reformers persuaded Abdül Hamid to accept a constitution that limited his authority and established a representative government. Within a year, however, the sultan suspended the constitution, dissolved parliament, exiled many liberals, and executed others. For thirty years he ruled autocratically in an effort to rescue the empire from dismemberment by European powers. He continued, however, to develop the army and administration according to Tanzimat principles, and he oversaw the formation of a police force, educational reforms, economic development, and the construction of railroads.

Abdül Hamid's despotic rule generated many liberal opposition groups. Though intended to strengthen the state, reform and reorganization actually undermined the position of the sultan. As Ottoman bureaucrats and army officers received an education in European curricula, they not only learned modern science and technology but also became acquainted with European political, social, and cultural traditions. Many of them fell out of favor with Abdül Hamid and spent years in exile, where they experienced European society firsthand. Educated subjects came to believe that the biggest problem of the Ottoman Empire was the political structure that vested unchecked power in the sultan. For these dissidents, Ottoman society was in dire need of political reform and especially of a written constitution that defined and limited the sultan's power.

**The Young Turks** The most active dissident organization was the Ottoman Society for Union and Progress, better known as the Young Turk Party, although many of its members were neither young nor Turkish. Founded in 1889 by exiled Ottoman subjects living in Paris, the Young Turk Party vigorously

Young Turks pose for a photograph during the revolution of 1908, which forced the sultan to establish a constitutional government.
Historia/Shutterstock

promoted reform, and its members made effective use of recently established newspapers to spread their message. **Young Turks** called for universal suffrage, equality before the law, freedom of religion, free public education, secularization of the state, and the emancipation of women. In 1908 the Young Turks inspired an army coup that forced Abdül Hamid to restore parliament and the constitution of 1876. In 1909 they dethroned him and established Mehmed V Rashid (reigned 1909–1918) as a puppet sultan. Throughout the Young Turk era (1908–1918), Ottoman sultans reigned but no longer ruled.

While pursuing reform within Ottoman society, the Young Turks sought to maintain Turkish hegemony in the larger empire. They worked to make Turkish the official language of the empire, even though many subjects spoke Arabic or a Slavic language as their native tongue. As a result, Young Turk policies aggravated tensions between Turkish rulers and subject peoples outside the Anatolian heartland of the Ottoman Empire. Syria and Iraq were especially active regions of Arab resistance to Ottoman rule. In spite of their efforts to shore up the ailing empire, reformers could not adequately strengthen the empire to ward off either external or internal threats. By the early twentieth century, the Ottoman Empire survived principally because European governments could not agree on how to dismantle the empire without upsetting the European balance of power.

## THE RUSSIAN EMPIRE UNDER PRESSURE

Like the Ottoman Empire, the Russian Empire experienced battlefield reverses that exposed the economic and technological disparity between Russia and the industrialized powers of western Europe. Determined to preserve Russia's status as a great land power, the tsarist government embarked on a program of reform. The keystone of those efforts was the emancipation of Russian serfs, who were peasants tied to the land on which they were born. Social reform paved the way for government-sponsored industrialization, which began to transform Russian society during the last decades of the nineteenth century. Political liberalization did not accompany social and economic reform because the tsars refused to yield their autocratic powers. The oppressive political environment sparked opposition movements that turned increasingly radical in the late nineteenth century. In the early twentieth century, domestic discontent reached crisis proportions and exploded in revolution.

## Military Defeat and Social Reform

The nineteenth-century tsars ruled a multiethnic, multilingual, multicultural empire that stretched from Poland to the Pacific Ocean. Only about half the population spoke the Russian language or observed the Russian Orthodox faith. The Romanov tsars ruled their diverse and sprawling realm through a dictatorial regime in which all initiative came from the central administration. The tsars enjoyed the support of the Russian Orthodox church and a small but powerful class of nobles who owned most of the land and were exempt from taxes and military duty. Peasants made up the vast majority of the population, and most of them were serfs. Serfdom was in fact almost indistinguishable from slavery, but most landowners, including the state, considered it a guarantee of social stability.

**The Crimean War** During the nineteenth century the Russian Empire expanded in three directions: east into Manchuria, south into the Caucasus and central Asia, and southwest toward the Mediterranean. This last thrust led to interference in the Balkan provinces of the Ottoman Empire. After defeating Turkish forces in a war from 1828 to 1829, Russia tried to establish a protectorate over the weakening Ottoman Empire. This expansive effort threatened to upset the balance of power in Europe, which led to military conflict between Russia and a coalition including Britain, France, the kingdom of Sardinia, and the Ottoman Empire. The **Crimean War** (1853–1856) clearly revealed the weakness of the Russian Empire, which could hold its own against Ottoman and Qing forces but not against the industrial powers of western Europe. In September 1854, allied forces mounted a campaign against Sevastopol in the Crimean peninsula, headquarters of Russia's Black Sea Fleet. Unable to mobilize, equip, and transport troops to defeat European forces that operated under a mediocre command, Russian armies suffered devastating and humiliating defeats on their own territory. Russia's economy could not support the tsars' expansionist ambitions, and the Crimean War clearly demonstrated the weakness of an agrarian economy based on unfree labor. Military defeat compelled the tsarist autocracy to reevaluate the Russian social order and undertake an extensive restructuring program.

**Emancipation of the Serfs** The most significant social reform in Russia was emancipation of the serfs. Opposition to serfdom had grown steadily since the eighteenth century, not only among radicals but also among high officials. Although some Russians objected to serfdom on moral grounds, many believed that it had become an obstacle to economic development and a viable state. Besides being economically inefficient, serfdom was a source of rural instability and peasant revolt: hundreds of insurrections broke out during the first four decades of the nineteenth century. As **Tsar Alexander II** (reigned 1855–1881) succinctly suggested to the nobility of Moscow, "It is better to abolish serfdom from above than to wait until the serfs begin to liberate themselves from below." Accordingly, in 1861, the tsar issued the **Emancipation**

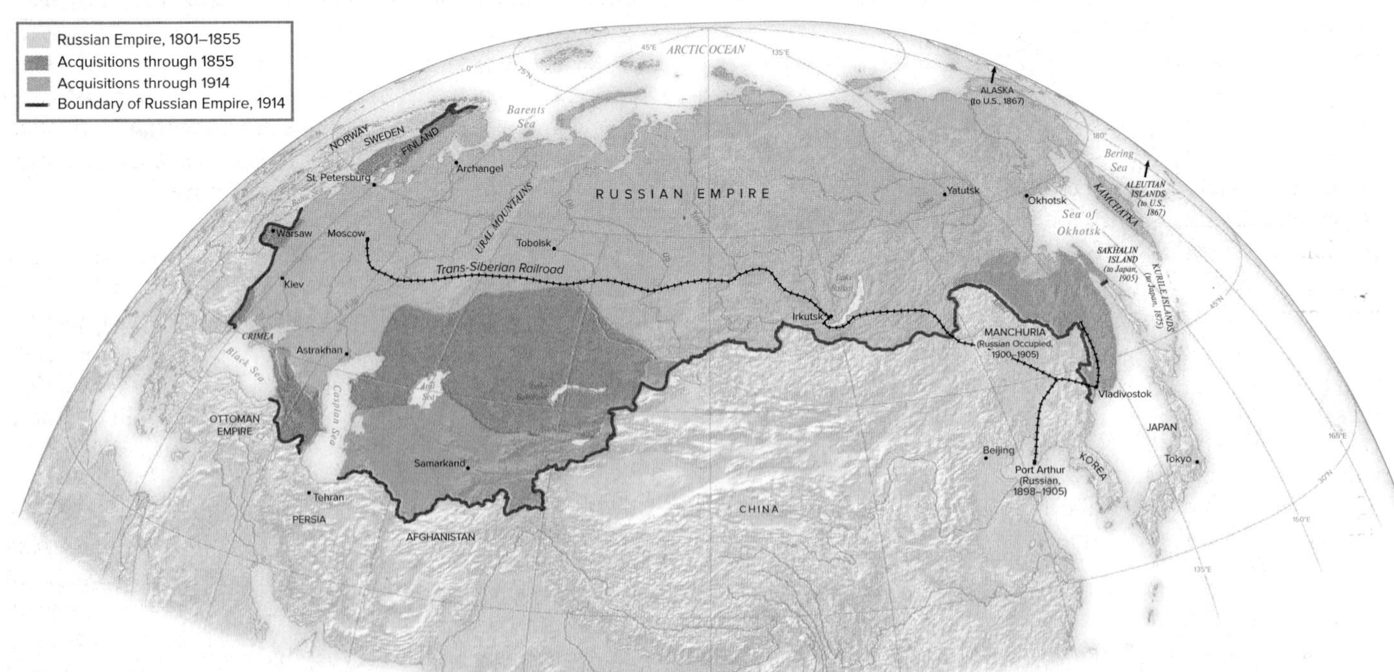


**MAP 19.2 The Russian Empire, 1801–1914.**

Note the sheer size of Russian territory in this period and that the state included parts of Europe, central Asia, and east Asia.

***How would straddling so much space and so many cultures have affected the process of industrialization and nationalism in Russia?***

**Manifesto,** which abolished the institution of serfdom and granted liberty to some twenty-three million serfs. This newfound freedom encompassed the right to full citizenship, the right to marry without consent, and the right to own property.

Although the government sought to balance the interests of nobles and serfs, on balance the terms of emancipation were unfavorable to most peasants. The government compensated landowners for the loss of their land and the serfs who had worked it. Serfs won their freedom, had their labor obligations gradually canceled, and gained opportunities to become landowners. But the peasants won few political rights, and they had to pay tax on most of the lands they received. Many disappointed peasants believed that their rulers forced them to pay for land that was theirs by right. Complicating this situation further was the fact that the majority of peasants held their land in communal ownership within a *mir* (society). Although the mir had the power to distribute land given to recently freed serfs by the government, the concept of communal ownership of the land prohibited individual peasants from selling their land. The years between 1906 and 1914 were marked by the implementation of agrarian reforms designed to break up the communes and create a class of individual peasant landowners. These so-called Stolypin reforms, named after Prime Minister Pyotr Arkadyevich Stolypin (1862–1911), ended with the outbreak of the Great War in 1914. A few peasants prospered and improved their position as the result of emancipation, but most found themselves in debt for the rest of their lives. In addition, emancipation resulted in little if any increase in agricultural production.

Tsar Alexander II of Russia (1818–1881). After signing the Treaty of Paris in 1856, ending the Crimean War, Alexander abolished serfdom in the Russian Empire in 1861.
Universal History Archive/UIG/Shutterstock

**Political and Legal Reform** Other important reforms came in the wake of the serfs' emancipation. To deal with local issues of health, education, and welfare, the government created elected district assemblies, or ***zemstvos,*** in 1864. Although all classes, including peasants, elected representatives to these assemblies, the *zemstvos* remained subordinate to the tsarist autocracy, which retained exclusive authority over national issues, and the landowning nobility, which possessed a disproportionately large share of both votes and seats. Legal reform was more fruitful than experimentation with representative government. The revision of the judiciary system in 1864 created a system of law courts based on western European models, complete with independent judges and a system of appellate courts. Legal reforms also instituted trial by jury for criminal offenses and elected justices of the peace who dealt with minor offenses. These reforms encouraged the emergence of attorneys and other legal experts, whose professional standards contributed to a decline in judicial corruption.

## Industrialization

Social and political reform coincided with industrialization in nineteenth-century Russia. Tsar Alexander II emancipated the serfs partly with the intention of creating a mobile labor force for emerging industries, and the tsarist government encouraged industrialization as a way of strengthening the Russian Empire. Thus, although Russian industrialization took place within a framework of capitalism, it differed from western European industrialization in that the motivation for development was political and military and the driving force was government policy rather than entrepreneurial initiative. Industrialization proceeded slowly at first, but it surged during the last two decades of the nineteenth century.

**The Witte System** The prime mover behind Russian industrialization was Count **Sergei Witte,** minister of finance from 1892 to 1903. His first budget, submitted to the government in 1893, outlined his aims as "removing the unfavorable conditions which hamper the economic development of the country" and "kindling a healthy spirit of enterprise." Availing himself of the full power of the state, Witte implemented policies designed to stimulate economic development. The centerpiece of his industrial policy was an ambitious program of railway construction, which linked the far-flung regions of the Russian Empire and also stimulated the development of other industries. Most important of the new lines was the trans-Siberian railway, which opened Siberia to large-scale settlement, exploitation, and industrialization. To raise domestic capital for industry, Witte remodeled the state bank and encouraged the establishment of savings banks. Witte supported infant

**Sergei Witte** (SAYR-gay VIHT-te)

Russian merchants in nineteenth-century Novgorod wear both western European and traditional Russian dress while taking tea. What does this mixed fashion suggest about Russian society at this time?
Hulton Archive/Getty Images

industries with high protective tariffs while also securing large foreign loans from western Europe to finance industrialization. His plan worked. French and Belgian capital played a key role in developing the steel and coal industries, and British funds supported the booming petroleum industry in the Caucasus.

**Industrial Discontent** For a decade the Witte system played a crucial role in the industrialization of Russia, but peasant rebellions and strikes by industrial workers indicated that large segments of the population were unwilling to tolerate the low standard of living that Witte's policies required. Recently freed serfs often did not like factory work, which forced them to follow new routines and adapt to the rhythms of industrial machinery. Industrial growth began to generate an urban working class, which endured dismal conditions similar to those experienced by workers in other societies during the early stages of industrialization. Employers kept wages of overworked and poorly housed workers at the barest minimum. The industrial sections of St. Petersburg and Moscow became notorious for the miserable working and living conditions of factory laborers. In 1897 the government limited the maximum working day to 11.5 hours, but that measure did little to alleviate the plight of workers. The government prohibited the formation of trade unions and outlawed strikes, which continued to occur in spite of the restrictions. Economic exploitation and the lack of political freedom made workers increasingly receptive to revolutionary propaganda, and underground movements soon developed among them.

Not everyone was dissatisfied with the results of intensified industrialization. Besides foreign investors, a growing Russian business class benefited from government policy that protected domestic industries and its profits. Russian entrepreneurs reaped rich rewards for their roles in economic development, and they had little complaint with the political system. In contrast to western European capitalists, who had both material and ideological reasons to challenge the power of absolute monarchs and the nobility, Russian businesspeople generally did not challenge tsarist rule.

## Repression and Revolution

**Protest** During the last three decades of the nineteenth century, antigovernment protest and revolutionary activity increased. Hopes aroused by government reforms inspired reform movements, and social tensions arising from industrialization fueled protest by groups whose aims became increasingly radical. Peasants seethed with discontent because they had little or no land, while newly mobile workers spread rebellious ideas between industrial cities. At the center of opposition were university students and a class of intellectuals collectively known as the intelligentsia. Their goals and methods varied, but they generally sought substantial political reform and comprehensive social change. Most dissidents drew inspiration from western European socialism (discussed in chapter 29), but they despised the individualism and materialism of western Europe and thus worked toward a socialist system more in keeping with Russian cultural traditions. Many revolutionaries were anarchists, who opposed all forms of government and believed that individual freedom cannot be realized until all government is abolished. Some anarchists relied on terror tactics and assassination to achieve their goals. Insofar as they had a positive political program, the anarchists wanted all authority to stem from local governing councils elected by universal suffrage.

**Repression** Some activists saw the main potential for revolutionary action in the countryside, and between 1873 and 1876 hundreds of anarchists and other radicals traveled to rural areas to rouse the peasantry. However, police soon

Japanese infantry charging during the Russo-Japanese War, 1904–1905.
Chris Hellier/Corbis NX/Getty Images

arrested the idealists. Tsarist authorities sentenced some to prison and banished others to the remote provinces of Siberia. Frightened by the increasing radicalism within their realm, tsarist authorities resorted to a campaign of repression: they censored publications and sent secret police to infiltrate and break up radical organizations. Repression, however, only served to radicalize revolutionaries further and gave them new determination to overthrow the tsarist regime.

In the Baltic provinces, Poland, Ukraine, Georgia, and central Asia, dissidents opposed the tsarist autocracy on ethnic as well as political and social grounds. In those places, subject peoples speaking their own languages often used schools and political groups as foundations for separatist movements as they sought autonomy or independence from the Russian Empire. Tsarist officials responded with a heavy-handed program of Russification to repress the use of languages other than Russian and to restrict educational opportunities only to those loyal to the tsarist state. Throughout the Russian Empire, Jews also were targets of suspicion, and tsarist authorities tolerated frequent **pogroms** (anti-Jewish riots) by subjects jealous of their Jewish neighbors' success in business affairs. To escape this violence, Jews in the Russian Empire migrated by the hundreds of thousands to western Europe and the United States in the late nineteenth century.

**Terrorism** In 1876 a recently formed group called the Land and Freedom Party began to promote the assassination of prominent officials as a means of forcing the government into political reform. In 1879 a terrorist faction of the party, the People's Will, resolved to assassinate Alexander II, who had emancipated the serfs and had launched a program of political and social reform. After several unsuccessful attempts, an assassin exploded a bomb under Alexander's carriage in 1881. The first blast did little damage, but as Alexander inspected his carriage, a second and more powerful explosion killed the reforming tsar. The attack brought the era of reform to an end and prompted the tsarist autocracy to adopt an uncompromising policy of repression.

In 1894 **Nicholas II** (reigned 1894–1917) ascended the throne. A weak ruler, Nicholas championed oppression and police control. To deflect attention from domestic issues and neutralize revolutionary movements, the tsar's government embarked on expansionist ventures in east Asia. However, Russian designs on Korea and Manchuria clashed with similar Japanese intentions, leading to a rivalry that ended in war. The Russo-Japanese War began with a Japanese surprise attack on the Russian naval squadron at Port Arthur in February 1904 and ended in May 1905 with the destruction of the Russian navy.

## What's Left Out?

We know that the Russo-Japanese War of 1904–1905 played an important role in the massive disturbances that erupted in the Russian revolution of 1905. But the effects of the war were much more far-reaching than that. Indeed, while textbooks tend to gloss over the war in favor of World War I, scholars are beginning to understand that the Russo-Japanese War represented a fundamental turning point for people in the non-Western world—especially those living under colonial rule or foreign domination. This was because the Japanese victory was interpreted by millions of people to be the first time members of an Asian "race" decisively beat members of a European "race" in a modern war. This had major consequences for the ways people of color—whether from Asia, Africa, the Middle East, or even the United States—viewed European notions of white superiority. Ordinary people in places as far flung as Egypt, India, the Dutch East Indies, Indochina, and China avidly tracked the progress of the Japanese army during the war through newspaper reports. When the Japanese emerged victorious, these same people joined in celebrations and congratulated one another, elated that an Asian nation had turned the tables on a European foe. Key revolutionaries and future nationalist leaders—including Jawaharlal Nehru of India, Sun Yat-Sen of China, and Phan Boi Chau of Indochina—were deeply inspired by the Japanese victory, and anticolonialists all over the world became more assertive and more hopeful. Some even began to send anticolonial revolutionaries to Japan so they could learn the secret to Japanese success and then use it against their colonial oppressors. So even though most textbooks do not cover the Russo-Japanese war extensively, it is worth remembering that it had profound consequences for the growing anticolonial movements that would soon convulse the world.

*Source:* Cemil Aydin, *The Politics of Anti-Westernism in Asia: Visions of World Order in Pan-Islamic and Pan-Asian Thought* (New York: Columbia University Press, 2007), chapter 4.

### Thinking Critically About Sources

1. What evidence does the passage provide that the Russo-Japanese War was a "turning point in the non-Western world"? And what evidence undermines this claim?
2. To what extent would the Japanese have been able to succeed against European countries such as Great Britain or France?

**The Revolution of 1905** Russian military defeats in the Russo-Japanese War brought to a head simmering political and social discontent and triggered widespread protests. In January 1905 a group of workers marched on the tsar's Winter Palace in St. Petersburg to petition Nicholas for a popularly elected assembly and other political concessions. Government troops met the petitioners with rifle fire, killing 130. The news of this Bloody Sunday massacre caused an angry uproar throughout the empire that culminated in labor unrest, peasant insurrections, student demonstrations, and mutinies in both the army and the navy. Organizing themselves at the village level, peasants discussed seizing the property of their landlords. Urban workers created new councils known as soviets to organize strikes and negotiate with employers and government authorities. Elected delegates from factories and workshops served as members of these soviets.

Revolutionary turmoil paralyzed Russian cities and forced the government to make concessions. Sergei Witte, whom Nicholas had appointed to conduct peace negotiations with Japan, urged the tsar to create an elected legislative assembly. The tsar reluctantly consented and permitted the establishment of the **Duma,** Russia's first parliamentary institution. Although the Duma lacked the power to create or bring down governments, from the Romanov perspective this act was a major concession. Still, the creation of the Duma did not end unrest. Between 1905 and 1907 disorder continued, and violence flared, especially in the Baltic provinces, Poland, Ukraine, Georgia, and central Asia, where ethnic tensions added to revolutionary sentiments. Through bloody reprisals the government eventually restored order, but by this time the Romanov empire had been fundamentally weakened.

## THE CHINESE EMPIRE UNDER SIEGE

The Qing dynasty in China experienced even more difficulties than did the Ottoman and Russian empires during the nineteenth century. European powers inflicted military defeats on Qing forces and compelled China's leaders to accept a series of humiliating treaties. The provisions of these treaties undermined Chinese sovereignty, carved China into spheres of influence that allowed profound economic exploitation, and handicapped the Qing dynasty's ability to deal with domestic disorder. As the government tried to cope with foreign challenges, it also faced dangerous internal upheavals, the most important of which was the Taiping rebellion, which we read about in the introduction. Caught between aggressive foreigners and insurgent rebels, China's ruling elites developed reform programs designed to maintain social order, strengthen the state, and preserve the Qing dynasty. The reforms had limited effect, however, and by the early twentieth century, China too was in a seriously weakened condition.

### The Opium War and the Unequal Treaties

In 1759 the Qianlong emperor restricted the European commercial presence in China to the waterfront at Guangzhou,

Chinese opium smokers around 1870. The Chinese government's attempt to stop the importation of opium resulted in a major defeat in the Opium War of 1839–1842. Here, opium smokers recline and sleep on the hard beds characteristic of opium dens.
Chronicle/Alamy Stock Photo

where European merchants were allowed to establish warehouses. There, Chinese authorities controlled not only European merchants but also the terms of trade. Foreign merchants could deal only with specially licensed Chinese firms known as ***cohongs,*** which bought and sold goods at set prices and operated under strict regulations established by the government. At the same time, Chinese consumers created very little demand for European products. As a result, European merchants had to pay for the Chinese products European consumers desperately wanted—including silk, porcelain, lacquerware, and tea—largely with silver.

**The Opium Trade** Seeking increased profits in the late eighteenth century, officials of the British East India Company sought alternatives to silver to exchange for Chinese goods. They gradually turned to trade in a product that was as profitable as it was criminal—opium. Using Turkish and Persian expertise, the East India Company oversaw the production of opium grown in India and shipped it to China, where company officials exchanged it for Chinese silver coin. The silver then flowed back to British-controlled Calcutta and London, where company merchants used it to buy Chinese products in Guangzhou. Once it was clear that opium was in high demand in China, the trade expanded rapidly: annual imports of opium in the early nineteenth century amounted to about 4,500 chests, each weighing 60 kilograms (133 pounds), but by 1839 some 40,000 chests of opium entered China annually to satisfy the habits of consumers. With the help of this new commodity, the East India Company easily paid for luxury Chinese products.

Trade in opium was illegal, but it continued unabated for decades because of the efforts of European and Chinese

# SOURCES FROM THE PAST

## Commissioner Lin on Banning Opium in China

*In the following passages, Commissioner Lin Zexu (1785–1850), who was appointed by the emperor to end the illegal traffic in opium, enumerated in 1839 four reasons British traders should surrender their smuggled opium. Although opium was illegal in Britain and China, the British East India Company knowingly smuggled huge quantities of opium into China in order to improve the trade deficit produced by its importation of Chinese products. Lin, whose actions touched off the Opium War that began in 1839, was a steadfast opponent of opium and its negative effects on public health and society.*

**First.** You ought to make haste and deliver up the opium, by virtue of that reason which Heaven hath implanted in all of us. . . . [W]hile you have been scheming after private advantage, with minds solely bent on profit, our people have been wasting their substance and losing their lives; and if the reason of Heaven be just, think you that there will be no retribution? If, however, you will now repent and deliver up your opium, by a well-timed repentance you may yet avert judgment and calamities; if not, then your wickedness being greater, the consequences of that wickedness will fall more fearfully upon you! . . .

Now our great emperor, being actuated by the exalted virtue of Heaven itself, wishes to cut off this deluge of opium, which is the plainest proof that such is the intention of high Heaven! . . .

**Secondly.** You ought to make immediate delivery of this opium, in order to comply with the law of your own countries, which prohibits the smoking of opium, and he who uses it is adjudged to death! . . . If, then, your laws forbid it to be consumed by yourselves, and yet permit it to be sold that it may be consumed by others, this is not in conformity with the principle of doing unto others what you would that they should do unto you. . . .

Our great emperor looks upon the opium trade with the most intense loathing, and burns to have it cut off forever; and I, the high commissioner, looking up to the great emperor, and feeling in my own person his sacred desire to love and cherish the men from afar, do mercifully spare you your lives. I wish nothing more than that you deliver up all the opium you have got, and forthwith write out a duly prepared bond, to the effect that you will henceforth never more bring opium to China, and, should you bring it, agreeing that the cargo be confiscated and the people who bring it, put to death.

When Commissioner Lin says he will spare the lives of traders here, what kind of power was he assuming over them?

**Thirdly.** You ought to make immediate delivery of this opium, by reason of your feelings as men. You come to this market of Canton to trade, and you profit thereby full threefold. Every article of commerce that you bring with you, no matter whether it be coarse or fine, in whole pieces or in small, there is not one iota of it that is not sold off and consumed; and of the produce of our country, whether it be for feeding you, for clothing you, for any kind of use, or for mere sale, there is not a description that we do not permit you to take away with you; so that not only do you reap the profit of the inner land by the goods which you bring, but, moreover, by means of the produce of our central land, do you gather gold from every country to which you transport it. Supposing that you cut off and cast away your traffic in the single article of opium, then the other business which you do will be much increased, and you will thereon reap your threefold profit comfortably.

This is the only place in the passage where Commissioner Lin discusses the economics of the trade. What does he think the economic consequences of cutting off the trade will be?

**Fourthly.** You ought to make a speedy delivery of your opium by reason of the necessity of the case. You foreigners from afar, in coming hither to trade, have passed over an unbounded ocean; your prospect for doing business depends entirely on your living on terms of harmony with your fellow-men, and keeping your own station in peace and quietness. Thus may you reap solid advantage and avoid misfortune! But if you will persist in selling your opium, and will go on involving the lives of our foolish people in your toils, there is not a good or upright man whose head and heart will not burn with indignation at your conduct; they must look upon the lives of those who have suffered for smoking and selling the drug as sacrificed by you; the simple country folk and the common people must feel anything but well pleased, and the wrath of a whole country is not a thing easily restrained: these are circumstances about which you cannot but feel anxious.

### For Further Reflection

- The Chinese high commissioner appeared to base his arguments, and those of his emperor, largely on a moral rather than an economic frame of reference. Were his points effective, and did his reasoning bring forth any hypocritical discrepancies in European beliefs?
- Commissioner Lin's treatise was written in 1839, in opposition to the nature of British trade. What earlier measures represented Chinese resistance to trade with Europe, even as early as 1630 when Zhen He explored? What was different about Lin's actions? Why were the results different?
- In what ways were European attitudes toward Opium trade similar to attitudes toward slave trade?

*Source:* Robinson, James Harvey and Charles A. Beard. *Readings in Modern European History*, vol. 3, 419–422. Boston: Ginn & Company, 1909.

smugglers and because some Chinese officials benefited personally by allowing the illegal trade to go on. By the late 1830s, however, government officials had become aware that opium had caused both a trade problem and a drug problem in China. The opium trade not only drained large quantities of silver from China but also created serious social problems, especially in southern China. When Chinese government authorities took steps in 1838 to halt the illicit trade, British merchants started losing money. In 1839 the Chinese government stepped up its campaign by charging a government official named **Lin Zexu** with the task of destroying the opium trade. Commissioner Lin acted quickly, confiscating and destroying some 20,000 chests of opium. His uncompromising policy, however, ignited a war that ended in a major defeat for China.

**The Opium War** Outraged by the Chinese action against opium (despite their awareness that the trade was illegal), British commercial agents pressed their government into a military retaliation designed to reopen the opium trade. The ensuing conflict, known as the **Opium War** (1839–1842), exposed the military power differential between Europe and China. In the initial stages of the conflict, steam-powered British naval vessels easily demonstrated their superiority on the seas. Meanwhile, equipped with antiquated muskets, swords, and spears, the defenders of Chinese coastal towns were no match for the firepower of well-drilled British infantry armed with rifles. But neither the destruction of Chinese war fleets nor the capture of coastal forts and towns persuaded the Chinese to sue for peace.

British forces broke the military stalemate when they decided to strike at China's jugular vein—the Grand Canal, which linked the Yangzi and Yellow River valleys—with the aid of steam-powered gunboats. Armed, shallow-draft steamers could travel speedily up and down rivers, projecting the military advantage that European ships enjoyed on the high seas deep into interior regions. In May 1842 a British armada of seventy ships—led by the gunboat *Nemesis*—advanced up the Yangzi River. The British fleet encountered little resistance, and by the time it reached the intersection of the river and the Grand Canal, the Chinese government had sued for peace. China experienced similar military setbacks throughout the second half of the nineteenth century in conflicts with Britain and France (1856–1858), France (1884–1885), and Japan (1894–1895).

**Unequal Treaties** In the wake of those confrontations came a series of pacts collectively known in China as **unequal treaties,** which curtailed China's sovereignty. Beginning with the **Treaty of Nanjing,** which Britain forced China to accept at the conclusion of the Opium War in 1842, these agreements guided Chinese relations with foreign states until 1943. The Treaty of Nanjing (1842) ceded Hong Kong Island to Britain; opened five Chinese ports—including Guangzhou and Shanghai—to foreign commerce and residence; compelled the Qing government to extend most-favored-nation status to Britain; and granted extraterritoriality to British subjects, which meant they were not subject to Chinese laws. The Treaty of Nanjing governed relations only between Britain and China, but France, Germany, Denmark, the Netherlands, Spain, Belgium, Austria-Hungary, the United States, and Japan later concluded similar unequal treaties with China. Collectively these treaties broadened the concessions given to foreign powers; they legalized the opium trade, permitted the establishment of Christian missions throughout China, and opened additional treaty ports. To encourage sales of foreign goods, various treaties also prevented the Qing government from levying tariffs on imports to protect domestic industries. By 1900 ninety Chinese ports were under the effective control of foreign powers, foreign merchants controlled much of the Chinese economy, Christian missionaries sought converts throughout China, and foreign gunboats patrolled Chinese waters. Several treaties also released Korea, Vietnam, and Burma (now known as Myanmar) from Chinese authority and thereby dismantled the Chinese system of tributary states.

**Lin Zexu** (lin zuh-SHOO)

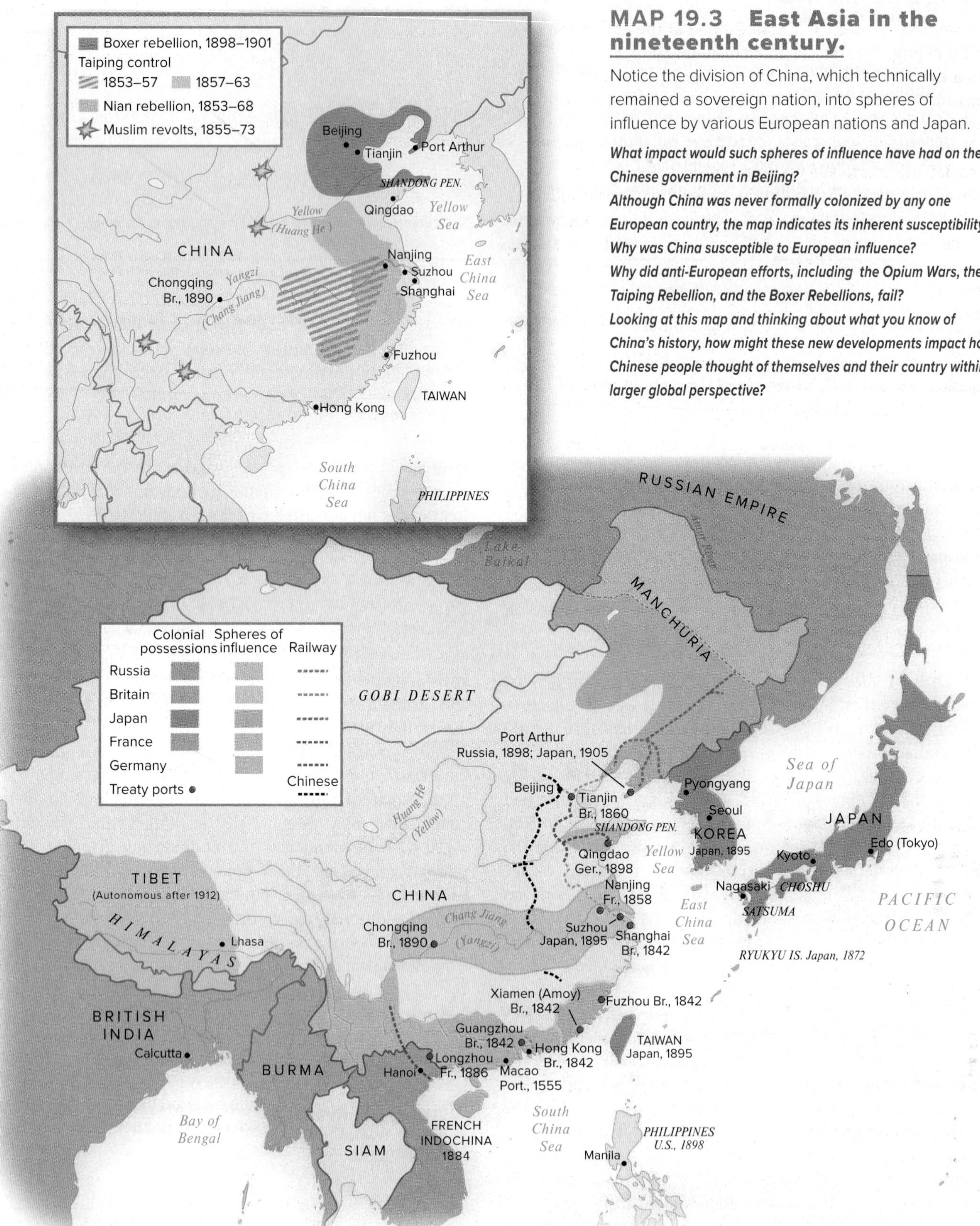


## MAP 19.3 East Asia in the nineteenth century.

Notice the division of China, which technically remained a sovereign nation, into spheres of influence by various European nations and Japan.

***What impact would such spheres of influence have had on the Chinese government in Beijing?***

***Although China was never formally colonized by any one European country, the map indicates its inherent susceptibility. Why was China susceptible to European influence?***

***Why did anti-European efforts, including the Opium Wars, the Taiping Rebellion, and the Boxer Rebellions, fail?***

***Looking at this map and thinking about what you know of China's history, how might these new developments impact how Chinese people thought of themselves and their country within a larger global perspective?***

## The Taiping Rebellion

The weakening of the Chinese Empire at the end of the nineteenth century was as much a result of internal turmoil as it was a consequence of foreign intervention. Large-scale rebellions in the later nineteenth century reflected the increasing poverty and discontent of the Chinese peasantry. Between 1800 and 1900 China's population rose by almost 50 percent, from 330 million to 475 million. But the amount of land under cultivation increased only slowly during the same period, making it difficult to feed so many more people. The concentration of land in the hands of wealthy elites aggravated peasant discontent, as did widespread corruption of government officials. After 1850, rebellions erupted throughout China: the Nian rebellion (1851–1868) in the northeast, the Muslim rebellion (1855–1873) in the southwest, and the Tungan rebellion (1862–1878) in the northwest. Most dangerous of all was the **Taiping rebellion** (1850–1864), which raged throughout most of China and brought the Qing dynasty to the brink of collapse.

**The Taiping Program** The village schoolteacher Hong Xiuquan, who we met in the introduction to this chapter, provided both inspiration and leadership for the Taiping rebellion. His call for the destruction of the Qing dynasty and his program for the radical transformation of Chinese society appealed to millions of men and women. The Qing dynasty had ruled China since 1644, and Qing elites had adapted to Chinese ways, but many native Chinese subjects despised the Manchu ruling class as foreigners. The Taiping reform program contained many radical features that appealed to discontented subjects, including the abolition of private property, the creation of communal wealth to be shared according to needs, the prohibition of foot binding and concubinage, free public edcation, simplification of the written language, and literacy for the masses. Some Taiping leaders also called for the establishment of democratic political institutions and the building of an industrial society. Although they divided their army into separate divisions of men and women soldiers, the Taipings decreed the equality of men and women. Taiping regulations prohibited sexual intercourse among their followers, including married couples, but Hong and other high leaders maintained large harems.

After sweeping through southeastern China, Hong and his followers in the Society of God Worshipers took Nanjing in 1853 and made it the capital of their Taiping ("Great Peace") kingdom. From Nanjing they campaigned throughout China, and as the rebels passed through the countryside whole towns and villages joined them—often voluntarily but sometimes under coercion. By 1855 a million Taipings were poised to attack Beijing. Qing forces repelled them, but five years later, firmly entrenched in the Yangzi River valley, the Taipings threatened Shanghai.

**Taiping Defeat** The radical nature of the Taiping program ensured that the Chinese gentry would side with the Qing government to support a regime dedicated to the preservation of the established order. After imperial forces consisting of Manchu soldiers failed to defeat the Taipings, the Qing government created regional armies staffed by Chinese instead of Manchu soldiers and commanded by members of the scholar-gentry class, a shift encouraged by the empress dowager Cixi (1835–1908), a former imperial concubine who established herself as effective ruler of China during the last fifty years of the Qing dynasty. With the aid of European advisers and weapons, these regional armies gradually overcame the Taipings. By 1862 Hong Xiuquan had largely withdrawn from public affairs, as he sought solace in religious reflection

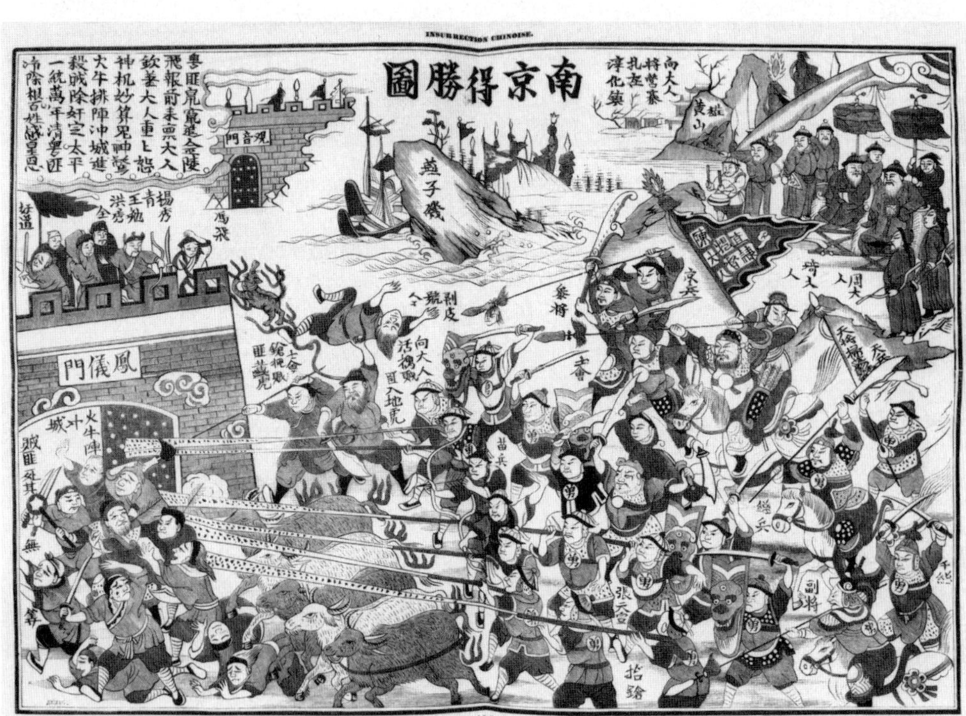


The final assault on the Taipings at Nanjing by Qing forces in 1864. Losses were devastating: about one hundred thousand Taiping soldiers were killed, and then Qing forces massacred most of the city's inhabitants after emerging victorious.
Photo12/UIG/Getty Images

## INTERPRETING IMAGES

Empress Dowager Cixi diverted government funds intended for the construction of modern warships to the construction of a huge marble vessel to decorate a lake in the gardens of the Summer Palace near Beijing.

**Analyze** *In what ways does the Empress Dowager Cixi's building of the marble ship indicate misplaced priorities and a misunderstanding of the historical moment? What underlying weaknesses did it reveal in the Qing dynasty? When you look at this marble vessel, thinking about what you've learned about Chinese history, what do you think Empress Dowager Cixi was trying to demonstrate?*

David Ball/Alamy Stock Photo

and diversion in his harem. After a lingering illness, he committed suicide in June 1864. In the following months Nanjing fell, and government forces slaughtered some one hundred thousand Taipings. By the end of the year, the rebellion was over. But the Taiping rebellion had taken a costly toll. It claimed twenty million to thirty million lives, and it caused such drastic declines in agricultural production that people in war-torn regions frequently resorted to eating grass, leather, hemp, and even human flesh.

## Reform Frustrated

The Taiping rebellion altered the course of Chinese history. Contending with aggressive foreign powers and lands ravaged by domestic rebellion, Qing rulers recognized that changes were necessary for the empire to survive. From 1860 to 1895, Qing authorities tried to fashion an efficient and benevolent Confucian government to solve social and economic problems while also adopting foreign technology to strengthen state power.

**The Self-Strengthening Movement** Most imaginative of the reform programs was the **Self-Strengthening Movement** (1860–1895), which flourished especially in the 1860s and 1870s. Empowered with imperial grants of authority that permitted them to raise troops, levy taxes, and run bureaucracies, several local leaders promoted military and economic reform. Adopting the slogan "Chinese learning at the base, Western learning for use," leaders of the Self-Strengthening Movement sought to blend Chinese cultural traditions with European industrial technology. While holding to Confucian values and seeking to reestablish a stable agrarian society, movement leaders built modern shipyards, constructed railroads, established weapons industries, opened steel foundries with blast furnaces, and founded academies to develop scientific expertise.

Although it laid a foundation for industrialization, the Self-Strengthening Movement brought only superficial change to Chinese economy and society. For one thing, it did not introduce enough industry to bring real military and economic strength to China. It also encountered obstacles in the imperial government: for example, the empress dowager Cixi diverted funds intended for the navy to build a magnificent marble boat to grace a lake in the imperial gardens. Furthermore, elites worried that industrialization would bring fundamental social change to an agrarian land and that education in European curricula would undermine the commitment to Confucian values.

**Spheres of Influence** The Self-Strengthening Movement also did not prevent continuing foreign interference into Chinese affairs. During the latter part of the nineteenth century, foreign powers began to dismantle the Chinese system of tributary states. In 1885 France incorporated Vietnam into its colonial empire, and in 1886 Great Britain detached Burma from Chinese control. In 1895 Japan forced China to recognize the independence of Korea and cede the island of Taiwan and the Liaodong peninsula in southern Manchuria. By 1898 foreign powers had carved China into spheres of economic influence. The Qing government was also forced to grant exclusive rights for railway and mineral development to Germany in Shandong Province, to France in the southern border provinces, to Great Britain in the Yangzi River valley, to Japan in the southeastern coastal provinces, and to Russia in Manchuria. Only distrust among the foreign powers prevented the total dismemberment of the Middle Kingdom.

**The Hundred Days Reforms** These setbacks sparked the ambitious but abortive **Hundred Days reforms** of 1898. The leading figures of the reform movement were the scholars Kang Youwei (1858–1927) and Liang Qichao (1873–1929), who published a series of treatises reinterpreting Confucian thought in a way that justified radical changes in the imperial system. Kang and Liang did not seek to preserve an agrarian society and its cultural traditions so much as to remake China and turn it into a powerful, modern industrial society. Impressed by their ideas, the young Emperor Guangxu (r. 1875–1898) launched a sweeping program to transform China into a constitutional monarchy, guarantee civil liberties, root out corruption, remodel the educational system, encourage foreign influence in China, modernize military forces, and stimulate economic development. The broad range of reform edicts produced a violent reaction from members of the imperial household; their allies in the gentry; and the young emperor's aunt, the ruthless and powerful empress dowager Cixi. After a period of 103 days, Cixi nullified the reform decrees, imprisoned the emperor in the Forbidden City, and executed six leading reformers. Kang and Liang, the spiritual guides of the reform movement, escaped to Japan.

Photograph of a Chinese Boxer in 1900, during the revolt.
Courtesy of Everett Collection/Shutterstock

**The Boxer Rebellion** Believing that foreign powers were conspiring to effect her retirement, Cixi threw her support behind an antiforeign uprising known as the **Boxer rebellion,** a violent movement spearheaded by militia units calling

**Kang Youwei** (kahng yoo-way)
**Liang Qichao** (lee-yahng chee-chow)

themselves the Society of Righteous and Harmonious Fists. The foreign press referred to the rebels as Boxers. In 1899 the Boxers organized to rid China of "foreign devils" and their influences. With the empress dowager's encouragement, the Boxers went on a rampage in northern China, killing foreigners and Chinese Christians as well as Chinese who had ties to foreigners. Confident that foreign weapons could not harm them, some 140,000 Boxers besieged foreign embassies in Beijing in the summer of 1900. A heavily armed force of British, French, Russian, U.S., German, and Japanese troops quickly crushed the Boxer movement in bloody retaliation for the assault. The Chinese government had to pay a punitive indemnity and allow foreign powers to station troops in Beijing at their embassies and along the route to the sea.

Because Cixi had instigated the Boxers' attacks on foreigners, many Chinese regarded the Qing dynasty as bankrupt. Revolutionary uprisings gained widespread public support throughout the country, even among conservative Chinese gentry. Cixi died in November 1908, one day after the sudden, unexpected, and mysterious death of the emperor. In her last act of state, the empress dowager appointed the two-year-old boy Puyi to the imperial throne. But Puyi never had a chance to rule: revolution broke out in the autumn of 1911, and by early 1912 the last emperor of the Qing dynasty had abdicated his throne.

## THE TRANSFORMATION OF JAPAN

In 1853 a fleet of U.S. warships steamed into Tokyo Bay and demanded permission to establish trade and diplomatic relations with Japan. Representatives of European states soon joined U.S. agents in Japan. Heavily armed foreign powers intimidated the Tokugawa shogun and his government, the bakufu, into signing unequal treaties providing political and economic privileges similar to those obtained earlier from the Qing dynasty in China. Opposition forces in Japan used the intrusion of foreigners as an excuse to overthrow the discredited shogun and the **Tokugawa bakufu.** After restoring the emperor to power in 1868, Japan's new rulers worked for the transformation of Japanese society to achieve political and economic equality with foreign powers. The changes initiated during the Meiji period turned Japan into a political, military, and economic powerhouse.

### From Tokugawa to Meiji

**Crisis and Reform** By the early nineteenth century, Japanese society was in turmoil. Declining agricultural productivity, periodic crop failures and famines, and harsh taxation contributed to economic hardship and sometimes even led to starvation among the rural population. A few cultivators prospered during this period, but many had to sell their land and become tenant farmers. Economic conditions in towns and cities, where many peasants migrated in search of a better life, were hardly better than those in the countryside. As the price of rice and other commodities rose, the urban poor experienced destitution and hunger. Even **samurai** and daimyo (discussed in chapter 26) faced hardship because they fell into debt to a growing merchant class. Under those conditions, Japan experienced increasing peasant protest and rebellion during the late eighteenth and early nineteenth centuries.

The Tokugawa bakufu responded with limited reforms. Between 1841 and 1843 the shogun's chief adviser, Mizuno Tadakuni, initiated measures to stem growing social and economic decline and to shore up the Tokugawa government. Mizuno canceled debts that samurai and daimyo owed to merchants, abolished several merchant guilds, and compelled peasants residing in cities to return to the land and cultivate rice. Most of his reforms were ineffective, and they provoked strong opposition that ultimately drove him from office.

**Foreign Pressure** Another problem facing the Tokugawa bakufu was the insistence on the establishment of diplomatic and commercial relations by foreign lands. Beginning in 1844, British, French, and U.S. ships visited Japan seeking to establish relations. The United States in particular sought ports where its Pacific merchant and whaling fleets could stop for fuel and provisions. Tokugawa officials refused all requests and stuck to the policy of excluding all European and American visitors to Japan except for a small number of Dutch merchants, who carried on a carefully controlled trade in Nagasaki. In the later 1840s the bakufu began to make military preparations to resist potential attacks.

The arrival of a U.S. naval squadron in Tokyo Bay in 1853 abruptly changed the situation. The American commander, **Commodore Matthew C. Perry,** trained his guns on the bakufu capital of Edo (modern Tokyo) and demanded that the shogun open Japan to diplomatic and commercial relations and sign a treaty of friendship. Under the pressure of force, the shogun quickly acquiesced to Perry's demands. Representatives of Britain, the Netherlands, and Russia soon won similar rights. Like Qing diplomats a few years earlier, Tokugawa officials agreed to a series of unequal treaties that opened Japanese ports to foreign commerce, deprived the government of control over tariffs, and granted foreigners extraterritorial rights.

**The End of Tokugawa Rule** The sudden intrusion of foreign powers precipitated a domestic crisis in Japan that resulted in the collapse of the Tokugawa bakufu and the restoration of imperial rule. When the shogun complied with the demands of U.S. and European representatives, he aroused

**Tokugawa** (TOH-koo-GAH-wah)
**Meiji** (MAY-jee)

Painting of Commodore Matthew Perry (1794–1858) meeting the royal commissioner at Yokahama in 1853.
Bettmann/Getty Images

the opposition of conservative daimyo and the emperor, who resented the humiliating terms of the unequal treaties and questioned the shogun's right to rule Japan as "subduer of barbarians." Opposition to Tokugawa authority spread rapidly, and the southern domains of Choshu and Satsuma became centers of discontented samurai. By 1858 the imperial court in Kyoto—long excluded from playing an active role in politics—had become the focal point for opposition. Dissidents there rallied around the slogan "Revere the emperor, expel the barbarians."

**The Meiji Restoration** Tokugawa officials did not yield power quietly. Instead, they vigorously responded to their opponents by forcibly retiring dissident daimyo and executing or imprisoning samurai critics. In a brief civil war, however, bakufu armies suffered repeated defeats by militia units trained by foreign experts and armed with imported weapons. With the Tokugawa cause doomed, the shogun resigned his office.

## Meiji Reforms

On January 3, 1868 the boy emperor **Mutsuhito**—subsequently known by his regnal name, Meiji ("Enlightened Rule")—took the reins of power. Emperor Meiji (1852-1912) reigned during a most eventful period in Japan's history. The **Meiji restoration** returned authority to the Japanese emperor and brought an end to the series of military governments that had dominated Japan since 1185. It also marked the birth of a new Japan. Determined to gain equality with foreign powers, a conservative coalition of daimyo, imperial princes, court nobles, and

**Mutsuhito** (MOO-tsoo-HEE-taw)

## INTERPRETING IMAGES

Japanese artist Miyagawa Shuntei offered a late-nineteenth-century contrast in fashion in his depiction of two women at the seaside. One wears European swimwear, and the other has donned a kimono.

**Analyze** *In what ways does the painting illustrate the success of the Meiji Reforms in "opening the door to drive out the barbarians"? Why do you think Miyagawa Shuntei chose to depict women, specifically? How does the portrayal of the women, with their clothes and poses, give you an idea of what the artist might be trying to convey about modernization?*

John Stevenson/Corbis Historical/Getty Images

samurai formed a new government dedicated to the twin goals of prosperity and strength: "rich country, strong army." The Meiji government looked to the industrial states of Europe and the United States to obtain the knowledge and expertise to strengthen Japan and reverse the unequal treaties. The Meiji government sent many students and officials abroad to study everything from technology to constitutions, and it also hired foreign experts to encourage economic development and the creation of indigenous expertise.

**Foreign Influences** Among the most prominent of the Meiji-era travelers were **Fukuzawa Yukichi** (1835–1901) and **Ito Hirobumi** (1841–1909). Fukuzawa began to study English soon after Perry's arrival in Japan, and in 1860 he was a member of the first Japanese mission to the United States. Later, he traveled in Europe, and he reported his observations of foreign lands in a series of popular publications. He applauded the constitutional government and modern educational systems that he found in the United States and western Europe, and he argued strongly for equality before the law in Japan. Ito ventured abroad on four occasions. His most important journey came in 1882 and 1883, when he traveled to Europe to study foreign constitutions and administrative systems, as Meiji leaders prepared to fashion a new government. He was especially impressed with recently united Germany, and he drew inspiration from the German constitution in drafting a governing document for Japan.

**Abolition of the Social Order** The first goal of the Meiji leaders was to centralize political power, a difficult task that required destruction of the old social order. After persuading daimyo to yield their lands to the throne in exchange for certificates of nobility, reformers replaced the old domains with prefectures and metropolitan districts controlled by the central government. Reformers then appointed new prefectural governors to prevent the revival of old loyalties. As a result, most daimyo found themselves effectively removed from power. The government also abolished the samurai class and the stipends that supported it. Gone as well were the rights of daimyo and samurai to carry swords and wear their hair in the distinctive topknot that signified their military status. When Meiji leaders raised a conscript army, they deprived the samurai of the military monopoly they had held for centuries. Many samurai felt betrayed by these actions, and Meiji officials sought to ease their discontent by awarding them government bonds. But as the bonds diminished in value because of inflation, former warriors had to seek employment or else suffer impoverishment. Frustrated by these new circumstances, some samurai rose in rebellion, but the recently created national army crushed all opposition. By 1878 the national government no longer feared internal military challenges to its rule.

**Revamping the Tax System** Japan's new leaders next put the regime on secure financial footing by revamping the tax system. Peasants traditionally paid taxes in grain, but because the value of grain fluctuated with the price of rice, so did government revenue. In 1873 the Meiji government converted the grain tax into a fixed-money tax, which provided the government with predictable revenues and left peasants to deal with

**Fukuzawa Yukichi** (foo-koo-ZAH-wah yoo-KEE-chee)
**Ito Hirobumi** (EE-toh heer-oh-BOO-mee)

market fluctuations in grain prices. The state also began to assess taxes on the potential productivity of arable land, no matter how much a cultivator actually produced. This measure virtually guaranteed that only those who maximized production could afford to hold on to their land. Others had to sell their land to more efficient producers.

## How the Past Shapes the Future

### The Birth of Nationalism

Nationalism came to Japan as a result of contact with the aggressive trade policies of the United States and other European nations. An elite group of reformers believed that, to avoid domination by western powers, they had to modernize and industrialize on the Western model—which included embracing the idea of a Japanese nation whose citizens would work together to promote the interests of the new state. In this case, then, the idea of creating a strong nation was initiated from the top down rather than from a groundswell of popular sentiment. This was accomplished in part through mandatory, state-funded education programs to teach both literacy and an appreciation of state-sanctioned national values. Consider the role mandatory public education has played in building nationalist feelings among populations around the world. Do such programs always serve the interests of states?

**Constitutional Government** The reconstruction of Japanese society continued in the 1880s under mounting domestic pressure for a constitution and representative government. Those demands coincided with the rulers' belief that constitutions gave foreign powers their strength and unity. Accordingly, in 1889 the emperor issued the Meiji constitution as "a voluntary gift" to his people. Drafted under the guidance of Ito Hirobumi, this document established a constitutional monarchy with a legislature, known as the Diet, composed of a house of nobles and an elected lower house. The constitution limited the authority of the Diet and reserved considerable power to the executive branch of government. Thus, the "sacred and inviolable" emperor commanded the armed forces, named the prime minister, and appointed the cabinet. Both the prime minister and the cabinet were responsible to the emperor rather than the lower house, unlike European parliamentary systems. The emperor also had the right to dissolve the parliament, and whenever the Diet was not in session he had the prerogative of issuing ordinances. Effective power thus lay with the emperor, whom the parliament could advise but never control. The Meiji constitution recognized individual rights, but it provided that laws could limit those rights in the interests of the state, and it established property restrictions on the franchise, ensuring that delegates elected to the lower house represented the most prosperous social classes. In the elections of 1890 less than 5 percent of the adult male population was eligible to cast ballots. Despite its conservative features, the Meiji constitution provided greater opportunity for debate and dissent than ever before in Japanese society.

**Remodeling the Economy** Economic initiatives matched efforts at political reconstruction. Convinced that a powerful economy was the foundation of national strength, the Meiji government created a modern transportation, communications, and educational infrastructure. The establishment of telegraph, railroad, and steamship lines tied local and regional markets into a national economic network. The government also removed barriers to commerce and trade by abolishing guild restrictions and internal tariffs. Aiming to improve literacy rates—40 percent for males and 15 percent for females in the nineteenth century—the government introduced a system of universal primary and secondary education. Universities provided advanced instruction for the best students, especially in scientific and technical fields. This infrastructure supported rapid industrialization and economic growth. Although most economic enterprises were privately owned, the government

This Japanese illustration of Emperor Mutsuhito demonstrates the visual and martial transformations in Meiji Japan.
The Print Collector/Print Collector/Getty Images

controlled military industries and established pilot programs to stimulate industrial development. During the 1880s the government sold most of its enterprises to private investors who had close ties to government officials. The result was a concentration of enormous economic power in the hands of a small group of people, collectively known as ***zaibatsu***, or financial cliques.

**Costs of Economic Development** Economic development came at a price, as the Japanese people bore the social and political costs of rapid industrialization. Japanese peasants, for example, supplied much of the domestic capital that supported the Meiji program of industrialization. The land tax of 1873, which cost peasants 40 to 50 percent of their crop yields, produced almost 90 percent of government revenue during the early years of Meiji development. Foreign exchange to purchase industrial equipment came chiefly from the export of textiles produced in a labor-intensive industry staffed by poorly paid workers.

The difficult lot of peasants came to the fore in 1883 and 1884 with a series of peasant uprisings aimed at moneylenders and government offices holding records of loans. The Meiji government responded by deploying military police and army units to put down these uprisings, and authorities imprisoned or executed many leaders of the rebellions. Thereafter, the government did virtually nothing to alleviate the suffering of the rural population. Hundreds of thousands of families lived in destitution—many malnourished to the point of starvation. Those who escaped rural society to take up work in the burgeoning industries learned that the state did not tolerate labor organizations that promoted the welfare of workers: Meiji law treated the formation of unions and the organization of strikes as criminal activities, and the government crushed a growing labor movement in 1901.

Nevertheless, in a single generation Meiji leaders transformed Japan into a powerful industrial society poised to play a major role in world affairs. Achieving political and economic equality with western European lands and the United States was the prime goal of Meiji leaders, who sought an end to humiliating treaty provisions. In this they were successful. In 1899 they were able to end extraterritoriality on Japanese soil for all foreign powers, and in 1902 they concluded a military alliance with Britain as an equal power. Their new status as a major military power was confirmed by stunning victories in wars first with the Chinese Empire (1894–1895) and then with the Russian Empire (1904–1905).

***zaibatsu*** (zeye-BAHT-soo)

## CONCLUSION

During the nineteenth century, Ottoman, Russian, Chinese, and Japanese societies faced severe external and internal challenges. Confrontations with western European and U.S. forces showed that the agrarian societies were militarily at a great disadvantage compared to industrial states. Ottoman, Russian, Chinese, and Japanese societies suffered also from domestic problems brought on by growing populations, the slowing of agricultural productivity, official corruption, and declining imperial revenues. To combat these problems, each of these societies embarked on ambitious reform programs that drew inspiration from western European and U.S. models to solve the crises caused by domestic discontent and foreign intrusions on their sovereignty. But reform programs had very different results in different lands. In the Ottoman, Russian, and Chinese empires, conservative ruling elites limited the scope of reform: although they generally supported industrialization and military reform, they stifled political and social reforms that might threaten their positions in society. In Japan, however, dissent led to the collapse of the Tokugawa bakufu, and reformers had the opportunity to undertake a much more thorough program of reform than did their counterparts in Ottoman, Russian, and Chinese societies. By the early twentieth century, on the basis of reforms implemented by Meiji leaders, Japan was becoming a political, military, and economic powerhouse.

## STUDY TERMS

Abdül Hamid II (620)
Boxer rebellion (633)
capitulations (619)
Cixi (615)
*cohong* (627)
Commodore Matthew C. Perry (634)
Crimean War (622)
Duma (626)
Emancipation Manifesto (622)
Fukuzawa Yukichi (635)
Hundred Days reforms (633)
Ito Hirobumi (635)
Janissaries (617)
Lin Zexu (629)
Mahmud II (619)
Meiji restoration (635)
Muhammad Ali (618)
Mutsuhito (635)
Nicholas II (625)
Opium War (629)
pogroms (625)
Qing (615)
samurai (634)
Self-Strengthening Movement (633)
Sergei Witte (623)
Sultan Selim III (619)
Taiping rebellion (631)
Tanzimat era (620)
Tokugawa bakufu (634)
Treaty of Nanjing (629)
Tsar Alexander II (622)
unequal treaties (628)
Xiuquan (614)
Young Turks (621)
*zaibatsu* (638)
*zemstvos* (623)

## FOR FURTHER READING

Michael R. Auslin. *Negotiating with Imperialism: The Unequal Treaties and the Culture of Japanese Diplomacy.* Cambridge, Mass., 2004. Diplomatic history that examines Japan's interaction with Western imperialism and the country's emergence as a world power.

David Anthony Bello. *Opium and the Limits of Empire: Drug Prohibition in the Chinese Interior, 1729–1850.* Cambridge, Mass., 2005. Explores Qing China's efforts at controlling and prohibiting the domestic opium trade.

Carter Vaughn Findley. *Turkey, Islam, Nationalism, and Modernity.* New Haven, 2011. A leading scholar examines the historical dynamics driving two centuries of Ottoman and Turkish history.

Andrew Gordon. *A Modern History of Japan: From Tokugawa Times to the Present.* Oxford, 2013. A rich and detailed narrative of the transformation of Japan since the Tokugawa period.

Peter Kolchin. *Unfree Labor: American Slavery and Russian Serfdom.* Cambridge, Mass., 1990. A remarkable and stimulating comparative study of American slavery and Russian serfdom.

Sevket Pamuk. *The Ottoman Empire and European Capitalism, 1820–1913: Trade, Investment, and Production.* Cambridge, 2010. Closely examines complex economic entanglements.

Nicolas Spulber. *Russia's Economic Transitions: From Late Tsarism to the New Millennium.* Cambridge, 2006. This massive and challenging work examines the three major transitions in Russian economic history between the early 1860s and 2000.

John W. Steinberg, ed. *The Russo-Japanese War in Global Perspective: World War Zero.* Boston, 2005. Collection of essays that examines the Russo-Japanese War as a harbinger of World War I.

Francis William Wcislo. *Tales of Imperial Russia: The Life and Times of Sergei Witte.* Oxford, 2011. Explores the life of one of the chief engineers of modern, industrial Russia prior to the 1917 revolution.

Richard Wortman. *Scenarios of Power: Myth and Ceremony in the Russian Monarchy.* Princeton, abridged, 2006. An innovative study exploring the means by which Romanov rulers held on to their autocratic prerogatives despite fundamental changes in Russian society.

# CHAPTER 19 AP EXAM PRACTICE

Questions assume cumulative knowledge from this chapter and previous chapters.

## Section I

## Multiple Choice Questions

Use the image below and your knowledge of world history to answer questions 1 - 3.

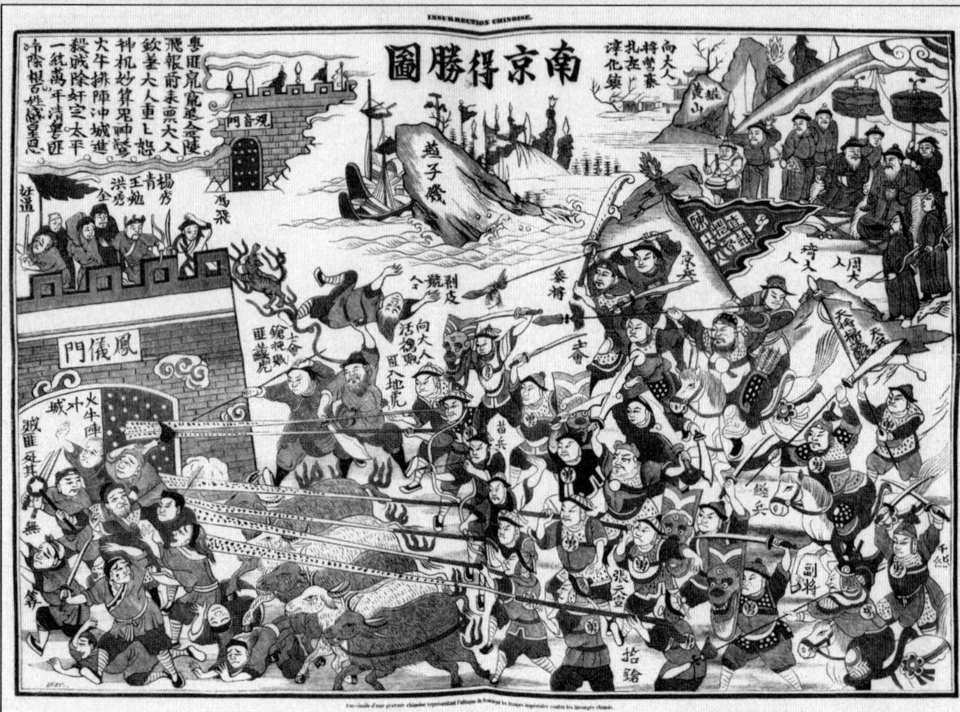


Attack of Nanjing by Qing Imperial troops against Taipings during the Boxer Rebellion, 1864.
Photo12/UIG/Getty Images

1. Which foreign religion influenced the Hong Xiuquan, the leader of the Taiping Rebellion?
   (A) Islam
   (B) Hinduism
   (C) Confucianism
   (D) Christianity

2. Why was the Taiping rebellion potentially so dangerous to the Qing dynasty?
   (A) The Taiping practiced a form of martial arts that they believed made them immune to attacks from foreigners.
   (B) Empress Cixi was manipulating the Taiping rebels to serve her own plans to overthrow the emperor.
   (C) The Taiping movement tapped into Chinese resentment of the rule of the foreign, Manchu dynasty.
   (D) Hong Xiuquan was influenced by Marxist writings and planned to build a socialist government.

3. How was the Chinese government able to finally put an end to the Taiping rebellion?
   (A) They had to discredit Hong Xiuquan so that his followers would turn on him.
   (B) They had to rely on foreign support and replacing Manchu officers with Chinese officers in the armies sent against the rebellion.
   (C) British steamship sailed up the Chinese rivers to attack the interior.
   (D) They spend one hundred days reforming the government and building a strong economy to fight the Taiping's economic reforms.

Use the image below and your knowledge of world history to answer questions 4 and 5.

Japanese infantry charging during the Russo Japanese War (1904–1905)
Chris Hellier/Corbis NX/Getty Images

4. Why do some historians consider the Russo-Japanese War of 1904–1905 a turning point in world history?
   (A) The Qing emperors started to wear European style clothing like Emperor Mutsuhito of Japan did to encourage westernizing the military.
   (B) The English and French withdrew from their Asian colonies in fear that they would lose a war with the Japanese.
   (C) The Russian royal family was deposed because they lost the war. Shortly after, they were assassinated by the Russian communists.
   (D) For the Japanese, it was the first time an Asian military defeated a modern European military, which called European notions of white supremacy into question.

5. What did anti-colonialist leaders in other countries do when Japan won the war?
   (A) They wrote newspaper articles condemning the Japanese government.
   (B) They sent revolutionaries to Japan to learn more about their successes.
   (C) They imported more Japanese products.
   (D) They reformed their governments to be like the Japanese.

## Short Answer

6. Use the image below and your knowledge of world history to answer parts A, B, and C.

"At the Seaside" by Japanese artist Miyagawa Shuntei.
John Stevenson/Corbis Historical/Getty Images

(A) Identify ONE way the Japanese government changed in the 1889 constitution.
(B) Explain ONE way that Japanese culture and society changed after the Meiji Restoration.
(C) Explain ONE way the Japanese economy changed after the Meiji Restoration.

7. Use the map below and your knowledge of world history to answer parts A, B, and C.

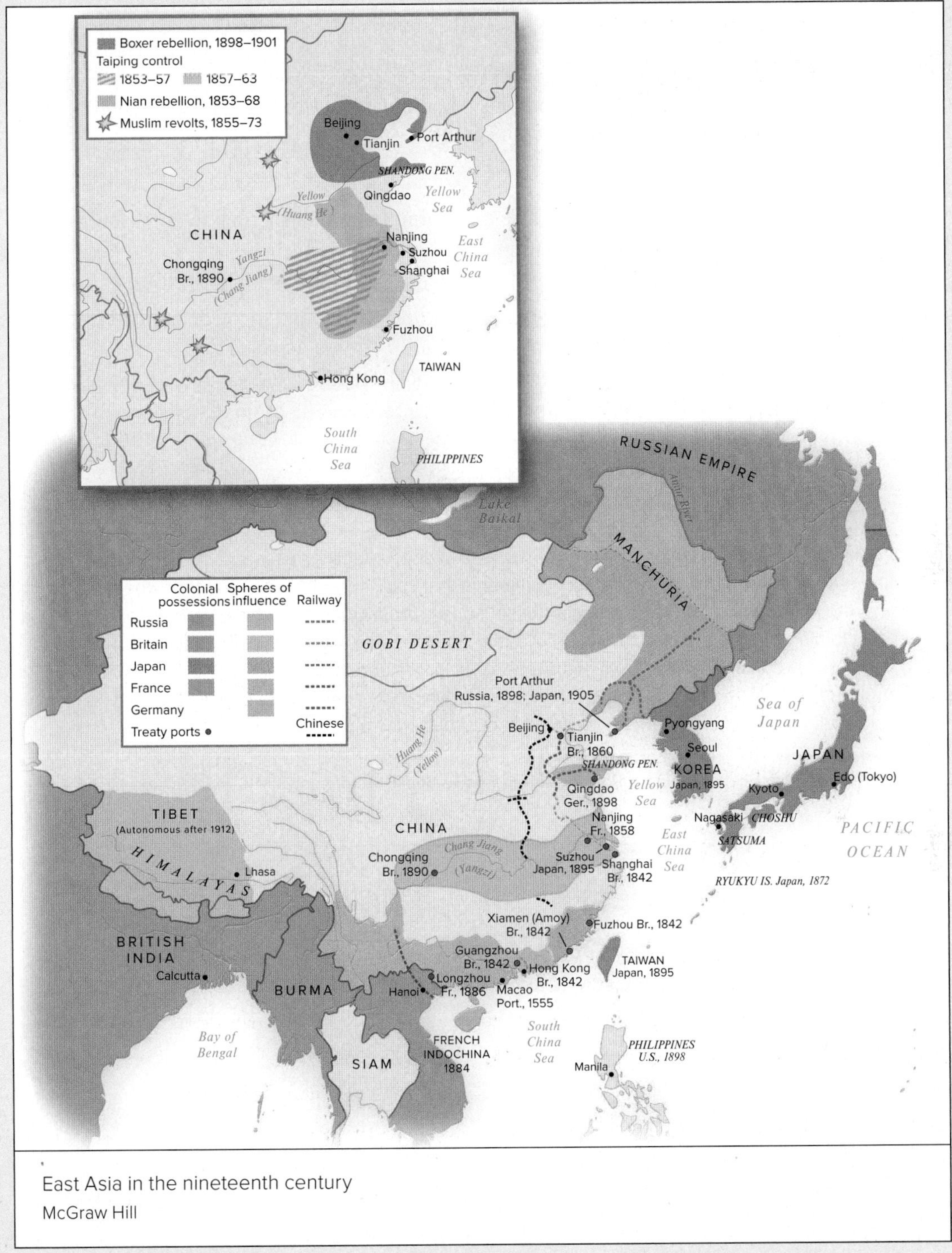


East Asia in the nineteenth century
McGraw Hill

(A) Identify ONE goal of the Self-Strengthening Movement.
(B) Explain ONE reason, based on the map, that the Boxer Rebellion was reviewed as especially dangerous.
(C) Explain ONE way that foreign spheres of influence undermined Chinese imperial rule.

8. Use your understanding of world history to answer parts A, B, and C.
(A) Identify ONE reason why the Ottoman Empire was in decline in the nineteenth century.
(B) Explain ONE reason why it was difficult for the Ottoman emperors to reform their state.
(C) Explain ONE way that local government became stronger in the Ottoman Empire.

# Section II

## Document-Based Question

Based on the documents below and your knowledge of world history, evaluate how industrialization contributed to the expansion of United States and European imperialism in the nineteenth century.

In your response you should do the following:

- Respond to the prompt with a historically defensible thesis or claim that establishes a line of reasoning.
- Describe a broader historical context relevant to the prompt.
- Support an argument in response to the prompt using all documents.
- Use at least one additional piece of specific historical evidence (beyond that found in the documents) relevant to an argument about the prompt.
- Explain how or why the document's point of view, purpose, historical situation, and /or audience is relevant to an argument.
- Use evidence to corroborate, qualify, or modify an argument that addresses the prompt.

### Document 1

**Thirdly.** You ought to make immediate delivery of this opium, by reason of your feelings as men. You come to this market of Canton to trade, and you profit thereby full threefold. Every article of commerce that you bring with you, no matter whether it be coarse or fine, in whole pieces or in small, there is not one iota of it that is not sold off and consumed; and of the produce of our country, whether it be for feeding you, for clothing you, for any kind of use, or for mere sale, there is not a description that we do not permit you to take away with you; so that not only do you reap the profit of the inner land by the goods which you bring, but, moreover, by means of the produce of our central land, do you gather gold from every country to which you transport it. Supposing that you cut off and cast away your traffic in the single article of opium, then the other business which you do will be much increased, and you will thereon reap your threefold profit comfortably.

*Source:* Robinson, James Harvey and Charles A. Beard. Readings in Modern European History, vol. 3, 419–422. Boston: Ginn & Company, 1909.

# Document 2

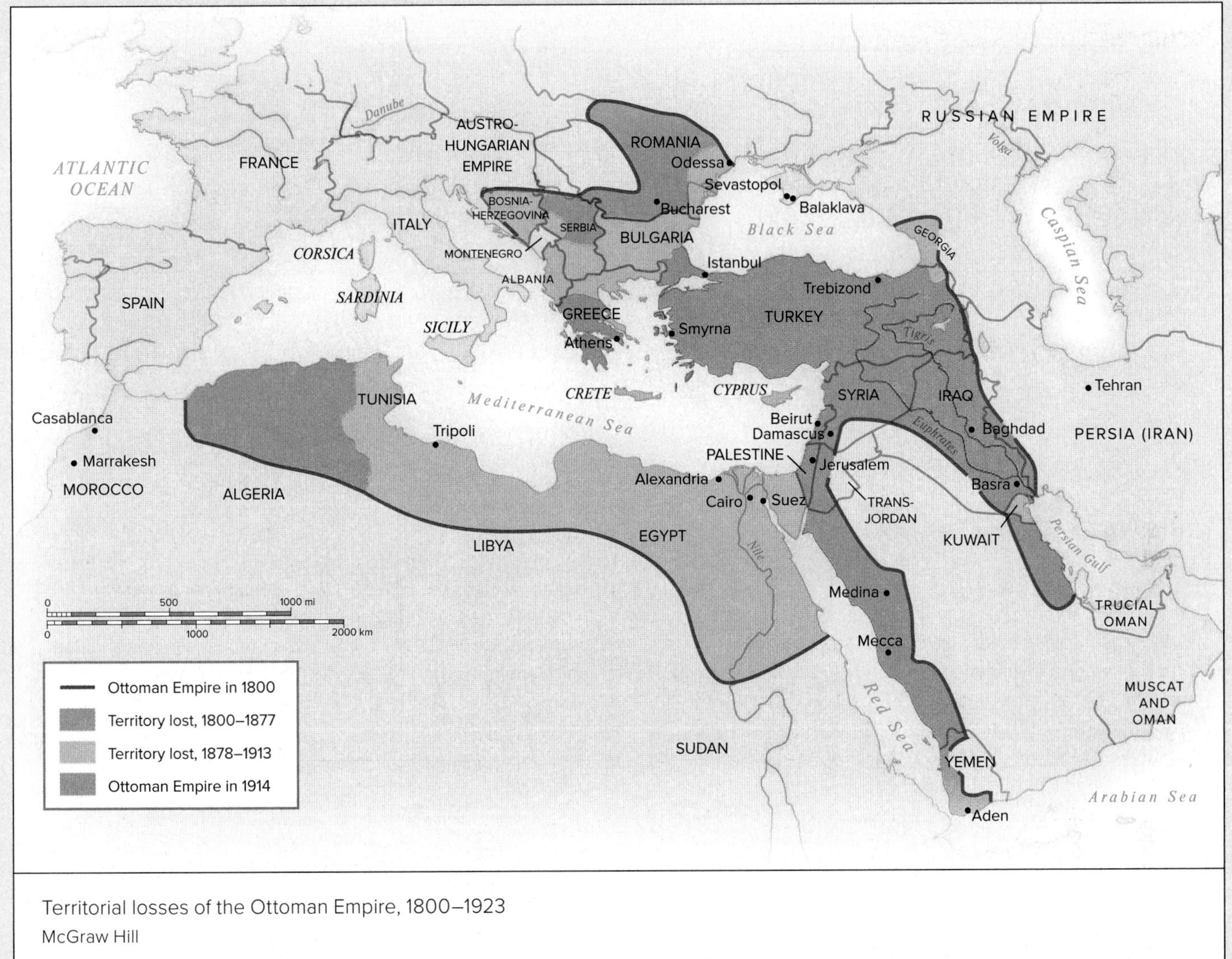


Territorial losses of the Ottoman Empire, 1800–1923
McGraw Hill

## Document 3

Painting of Commodore Matthew Perry (1794–1858) meeting the royal commissioner at Yokohama in 1853.
Bettmann/Getty Images

## Long Essay

Develop a thoughtful and thorough historical argument that answers the question below. Begin your essay with a thesis statement and support it with relevant historical evidence.

Using specific examples and your knowledge of world history, describe the similarities and differences between rebellions in the Ottoman and Russian empires.

# Chapter 20 The Apex of Global Empire Building



## ZOOMING IN ON ENCOUNTERS

### Emperor Menelik II of Ethiopia and His Warning to European Empire Builders

In 1889, Emperor Menelik II (1844–1913) came to the throne of the independent state of Ethiopia, in the horn of Africa. Long before taking the throne, Menelik had focused on obtaining the most up-to-date European firearms as a means of strengthening his power. In the wake of the Berlin West Africa Conference (1884–1885)—in which European powers divided up the continent of Africa among them—Menelik observed with increasing concern the violent conquest of huge portions of African territory. In 1891, Menelik decided to make his position about attempts to conquer Ethiopia clear by sending a letter to the European heads of state. He began the letter by informing his European readers about the current boundaries of Ethiopia, adding that he intended to expand these in the future. He continued by saying that "if powers at a distance come forward to partition Africa between them, I do not intend to be an indifferent spectator . . . As the Almighty has protected Ethiopia up to this day, I have confidence He will continue to protect her, and increase her borders in the future. I am certain He will not suffer her to be divided among other Powers."

Emperor Menelik II of Ethiopia (r. 1889–1913) on the throne in coronation garb.
MARKA/Alamy Stock Photo

Menelik did not simply rely on the power of persuasion to keep Europeans out of Ethiopia. Instead, he set about stockpiling more than eighty thousand European rifles and other weapons, including a canon. So when an Italian army—with the blessing of the British and French governments—invaded Ethiopia in 1896, the Ethiopians were ready. On March 1, they routed the Italians in the battle of Adwa, killing almost 40 percent of the force (about five thousand men), injuring another fifteen hundred, and taking a further three thousand prisoner. The battle was decisive: the Italians retreated and the European nations formally recognized Ethiopian sovereignty and independence.

But Menelik's success against European invaders was unique in the late nineteenth and early twentieth centuries. Resistance to conquest was nearly universal among African leaders and included diplomacy, seeking protection from other powers, treaties, and armed conflict. But no other state or group had been able to purchase and stockpile such a large quantity of the latest weaponry, nor had they been able to command a large, unified army to use it. As a result, Europeans maintained a technological advantage in most of the rest of Africa and used it to conquer more than 90 percent of the continent by 1910.

*Source:* Letter written by Emperor Menelik II in 1891 to the European heads of state.

# CHAPTER FOCUS

- The combination of industrialization, nationalistic attitudes, and ideologies that championed the powerful over the weak led to imperialism.
- Two sets of terms help historians analyze imperialism and its consequences: settler versus non-settler colonies (whether conquerors lived in the colony or not); and direct versus indirect imperialism (whether an imperialist power took over the government of a colony or just controlled its economy).
- In Asia, the imperial patterns varied. In established but militarily weak empires like Mughal India, the Ottoman empire, and Qing China, competing European, U.S., and Japanese imperialists imposed indirect rule and obtained concessions to control the economy.
- In contrast, Europeans generally imposed direct imperialism over their African colonies. They drew colonial borders with no attention to the native cultures living within.
- Because of imperialism, most regions in the world were brought into the industrialized web of production. People migrated along these webs to work on plantations and railroads, in factories and mines, or to take advantage of cheap and available lands.
- This globalization of labor and trade resulted in heightened cultural syncretism between the colonizers and the colonized, and between migrants and their host countries. It also fed nationalist and racist ideologies.
- Competition for colonies led to the world wars.
- Imperial conquerors brought disease, forced labor, environmental manipulation, medicines, modern transportation, governmental collapse, and ethnic warfare to their colonies.
- Imperialism created a global capitalist market that enriched the imperialist powers, and yet it also spurred nationalist movements that formed new national identities in the modern world.

## Historical Developments

- A range of cultural, religious, and racial ideologies were used to justify imperialism, including Social Darwinism, nationalism, the concept of the civilizing mission, and the desire to religiously convert indigenous populations.
- Increasing questions about political authority and growing nationalism contributed to anticolonial movements.
- Anti-imperial resistance took various forms, including direct resistance within empires and the creation of new states on the peripheries.
- Industrialized states and businesses within those states practiced economic imperialism primarily in Asia and Latin America.
- The new global capitalist economy continued to rely on coerced and semicoerced labor migration, including slavery, Chinese and Indian indentured servitude, and convict labor.
- As states industrialized, they also expanded existing overseas empires and established new colonies and transoceanic relationships.

## Reasoning Processes

- **Comparison** Explain relevant similarities and differences between settler and non-settler colonies.

## Historical Thinking Skills

- **Sourcing and Situation** Identify the purpose, historical situation, and audience of Rudyard Kipling's "The White Man's Burden."
- **Contextualization** Explain how modern imperialism relates to nationalism and industrialism.
- **Argumentation** Explain the difference between modern imperialism of the 19th and 20th centuries and earlier forms of imperialism.

# CHAPTER OVERVIEW

Throughout history strong societies have often sought to dominate their neighbors by subjecting them to imperial rule. They have built empires for various reasons: to gain control over natural resources, to subdue potential enemies, to seize wealth, to acquire territory for expansion, and to keep territories out of the hands of other powers. From the days of ancient Mesopotamia and Egypt to the present, imperialism has been a prominent theme of world history.

But in the second half of the nineteenth century, as the Ottoman and Qing empires weakened, a handful of western European states wrote a new chapter in the history of imperialism. Industrialization equipped them with the most effective tools and the most lethal weapons available anywhere in the world. Strong nationalist sentiments enabled them to mobilize their populations for purposes of overseas expansion. Three centuries of experience with maritime trade in Asia, Africa, the Americas, and Oceania provided them with extensive knowledge of the world and its peoples. With those advantages, western European peoples conquered foreign armies, overpowered local rulers, used their economic power, and imposed their hegemony throughout the world. Toward the end of the century, the United States and Japan joined European states as imperial powers with overseas territories.

The establishment of global empires in this period had far-reaching effects. In many ways, imperialism forcibly tightened links between the world's societies. Imperial powers demanded trade between dominant states and their overseas colonies, for example, and they organized mass migrations of laborers to work in agricultural and industrial ventures. Yet imperialism also fostered divisions between the world's peoples. Powerful tools, deadly weapons, and global hegemony led European peoples to consider themselves superior to their subjects throughout the world. In fact, modern racism is one of the legacies of imperialism. Another effect of imperialism was the development of anticolonial resistance in subject territories, including nationalism. Just as invasion and occupation by Napoleonic armies stimulated the development of nationalism in Europe, so the imposition of foreign rule provoked anticolonial and nationalist responses in colonized lands. Although the formal empires of this period were relatively short-lived and nearly all colonies had won their independence by 1970, the influence of global imperialism continues to shape the contemporary world.

| CHRONOLOGY | |
|---|---|
| 1772–1833 | Life of Ram Mohan Roy |
| 1838–1917 | Life of Queen Lili'uokalani |
| 1840 | Treaty of Waitangi |
| 1857 | Sepoy rebellion |
| 1859–1869 | Construction of the Suez Canal |
| 1860–1864 | Land wars in New Zealand |
| 1879–1904 | Life of Raden Adjeng Kartini |
| 1884–1885 | Berlin West Africa Conference |
| 1884–1896 | Can Vuong Movement |
| 1885 | Founding of the Indian National Congress |
| 1894–1895 | Sino-Japanese War |
| 1898–1899 | Spanish-Cuban-American War |
| 1899–1902 | South African War (Boer War) |
| 1904–1905 | Russo-Japanese War |
| 1904–1914 | Construction of the Panama Canal |
| 1906 | Founding of All-India Muslim League |

# FOUNDATIONS OF EMPIRE

Campaigns to conquer foreign territories have always been dangerous and expensive ventures. They have arisen from a sense that foreign conquest is essential, and they have entailed the mobilization of political, military, and economic resources. In nineteenth-century Europe, advocates of empire advanced a variety of political, economic, and cultural arguments to justify the conquest and control of foreign lands. The imperialist ventures they promoted enjoyed such dramatic success largely because of the military, transportation, and communications technologies developed by European industry in the first half of the nineteenth century.

## Motives of Imperialism

**Modern Imperialism** As we know, the building of empires was not a new phenomenon in world history. By the nineteenth century, however, even contemporary observers recognized that empires of their day were different from those of earlier times. By mid-century they began to speak of *imperialism,* and by the 1880s the recently coined term had made its way into popular speech and writing throughout western Europe. In contemporary usage, imperialism referred to the domination by European powers—and later by the United States and Japan as well—over subject territories overseas. Sometimes that domination was won by force of arms, but often it arose from trade, investment, and business activities that enabled imperial powers to profit from subject societies and influence their affairs without exercising direct political control.

**Modern Colonialism** Like the building of empires, the establishment of colonies in foreign territories is a practice dating from ancient times. Here, however, colonialism refers not just to the sending of colonists to settle new lands but also to the political, social, economic, and cultural structures that enabled imperial powers to dominate subject lands. In some places such as North America, Chile, Argentina, Algeria, Australia, New Zealand, and South Africa, European powers established settler colonies populated by large numbers of migrants from Europe. Yet contemporary scholars also speak of European colonies in India, southeast Asia, and sub-Saharan Africa, even though European migrants did not settle there in large numbers. European agents, officials, and businesspeople effectively turned those lands into colonies and profoundly influenced their historical development by controlling their domestic and foreign policies, integrating local economies into the network of global capitalism, introducing European business techniques, transforming educational systems according to European standards, and promoting European cultural preferences.

During the second half of the nineteenth century, many Europeans came to believe that imperial expansion and colonial domination were crucial for the survival of their states and societies—and sometimes for their personal fortunes as well. European merchants and entrepreneurs sometimes became extremely wealthy from business ventures in Asia or Africa, and they argued for their home states to pursue imperialist policies partly to secure and enhance their own enterprises. A notorious example was **Cecil John Rhodes** (1853–1902), who built a massive fortune by exploiting African laborers to mine for diamonds in southern Africa. Having made his fortune, Rhodes became a tireless advocate for the extension of British rule to the rest of the world.

**Economic Motives of Imperialism** A wide range of motives encouraged European peoples to launch imperialist campaigns of conquest and control. Some advocates argued that imperialism was in the economic interests of European societies as well as individuals. They pointed out that overseas colonies could serve as reliable sources of raw materials not available in Europe that came into demand because of industrialization: rubber, tin, and copper were vital products, for example, and by the late nineteenth century petroleum had also become a crucial resource for industrialized lands. Imperialists ruthlessly exploited wild rubber resources in the Congo River basin and established rubber plantations in Malaya. Abundant supplies of tin were available from colonies in southeast Asia and copper in central Africa. The United States and Russia supplied most of the world's petroleum in the nineteenth century, but by the early twentieth century the oil fields of southwest Asia attracted the attention of European industrialists and imperialists alike.

Proponents of imperialism also held that colonies would consume manufactured products and provide a haven for European migrants in an age of rapidly increasing population. In fact, manufactured goods did not flow to most colonies in large quantities, and European migrants went overwhelmingly to independent states in the Americas rather than to overseas colonies. Nevertheless, arguments arising from national economic interest generated considerable support for imperialism.

**Geopolitical Motives of Imperialism** In the last half of the nineteenth century, geopolitical concerns became one of the most influential motivations for imperialism. Advocates argued that even if colonies were not always economically beneficial, they were crucial for political and military reasons. Territories that occupied strategic sites on the world's sea lanes or harbors ideal for supplying commercial and naval ships attracted particular attention. Proponents of imperialism sought to acquire these sites for their own states and especially to deny them to other states. The British occupation of Egypt in 1882 is a good example of this because the British government was extremely anxious to protect the Suez Canal—the main route to India from Britain—from falling into the hands of a rival. Sometimes political motivations for imperial expansion were rooted in the desire for global power and prestige. In the late nineteenth century, for example, French enthusiasm for imperial expansion increased after its humiliating

## How the Past Shapes the Future

### The Birth of Nationalism

State governments sometimes used popular nationalist sentiment for their own purposes when it came to imperial expansion. One characteristic feature of nationalism is that nationalists often define their common bonds in opposition to other peoples and traditions: thus, national unity tends to be most strongly expressed when members feel threatened by outside forces. During the nineteenth century, some governments sought to capitalize on this characteristic of nationalism to gain popular support for imperial expansion and also to manipulate political opinion at home. The Abyssinian campaign of 1862 is but one example of this phenomenon: during an election year, the British Conservative party used an incident in which several British citizens had been taken hostage by the Ethiopian king as a way to whip up nationalist outrage against both the Ethiopians and the ruling British Liberal party. In part because of this nationalist fervor, the Liberals were defeated and the Conservatives were voted into power. What might be the short- and long-term consequences of manipulating nationalist feeling for political purposes?

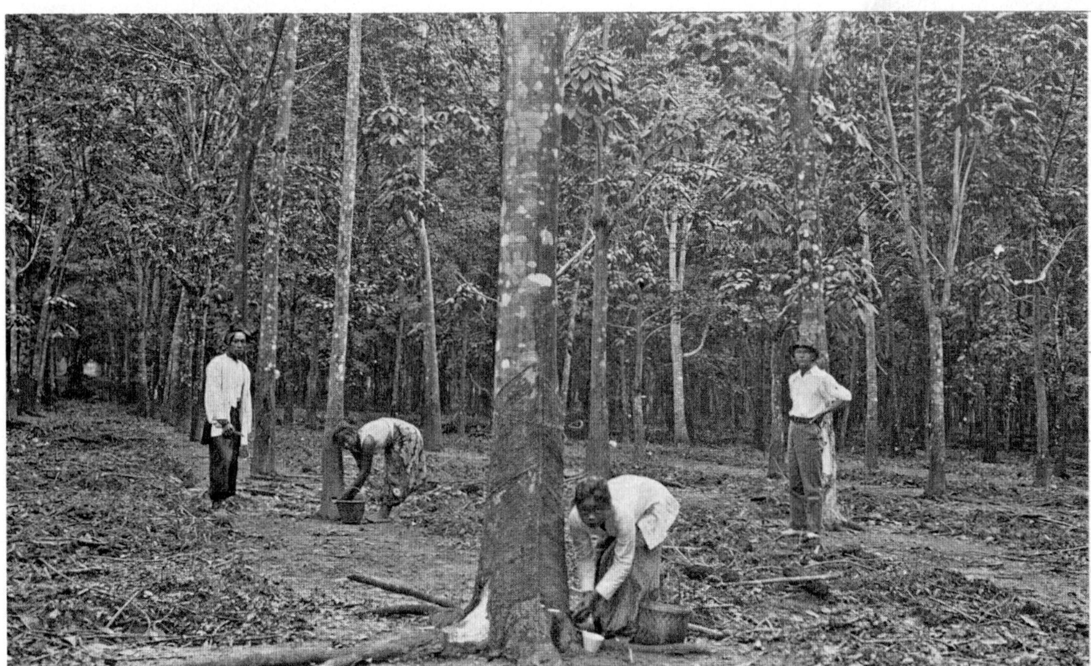

Rubber tapping on a plantation in Sumatra in the Dutch East Indies (modern Indonesia) in the early twentieth century. Sepia Times/Universal Images Group/Getty Images

defeat in the Franco-Prussian war of 1870–1871. In Germany as well, public opinion demanded colonies as a way of marking Germany's entry to great power status after the state's achievement of nationhood in 1871.

Imperialism also had its uses for domestic politics. In an age when socialists and communists directly confronted industrialists, European politicians and national leaders sought to defuse social tension and inspire patriotism by focusing public attention on imperialist ventures. Beginning in the mid-nineteenth century and continuing into the twentieth, European leaders frequently organized colonial exhibitions where they convinced or coerced colonized people to display their dress, music, and customs for tourists and the general public in imperial metropoles like London and Paris, all in an effort to win popular support for imperialist policies.

**Cultural Justifications of Imperialism** Cultural motivations also helped justify imperial expansion in this period. European missionaries, for example, believed it was their duty to seek out converts to Christianity around the world, and imperial expansion allowed them the protection of European governments as they did so. European missionaries did not always see eye to eye with European entrepreneurs or colonial officials and were sometimes deeply critical of aspects of colonial rule. Nevertheless, they often facilitated communications between imperialists and subject peoples, and they sometimes provided European officials with information they needed to maintain control of overseas colonies. Missionary settlements also served as convenient meeting places for Europeans overseas and as distribution centers for European manufactured goods.

While missionaries specifically sought to introduce Christianity to subject peoples, other Europeans thought it was their duty to bring the values and practices associated with European "civilization" to people around the world. These included ideas ranging from the establishment of European-style legal systems, modes of dress, expected gender relations, and emphasis on market consumerism. French imperialists routinely invoked the ***mission civilisatrice*** ("civilizing mission") as justification for their expansion into Africa and Asia, and the English writer and poet Rudyard Kipling (1864–1936) defined the "white man's burden" as the duty of European and Euro-American peoples to bring their ideas of order and enlightenment to distant places.

## Tools of Empire

Even the strongest motives would not have enabled imperialists to impose their rule throughout the world without the powerful technological advantages that industrialization conferred on them. Ever since the introduction of gunpowder in the thirteenth century, European states had competed vigorously to develop increasingly powerful military technologies. Industrialization enhanced those efforts by making it possible to produce huge quantities of advanced weapons and tools. During the nineteenth century, industrialists devised effective technologies of war, transportation, communication, and medicine that enabled European imperialists to exert enormous influence in the world during the nineteenth and first half of the twentieth centuries.

***mission civilisatrice*** (mih-see-on sih-vih-lees-ah-TRIHS)

**Military Technologies** The most advanced firearms of the early nineteenth century were smoothbore, muzzle-loading muskets, meaning that ammunition was projected from a smooth inner casing and that the weapon had to be loaded from the end where the ammunition was shot. When large numbers of infantry fired their muskets at once, the resulting volley could cause havoc among opponents. Yet it took a skilled musketeer about one minute to reload a weapon, and on top of that, the smoothbore interior reduced the accuracy of the musket. By mid-century European armies were using breech-loading firearms with rifled bores—in which weapons were loaded quickly from the top and ammunition was projected from a grooved interior—that were far more accurate and reliable than muskets. By the 1870s Europeans were experimenting with rifled machine guns, and in the 1880s they adopted the Maxim gun, a light and powerful weapon that fired eleven bullets per second.

Those firearms provided European armies with an arsenal vastly stronger than any other in the world. When European states sought to impose their will against others that didn't yet have the latest rifles or machine guns, as they often did in this period, they were able to inflict devastating defeats. In 1898, for example, a British army with twenty machine guns and six gunboats engaged a huge Sudanese force that sought to expel the British from the area at Omdurman, near Khartoum on the Nile River. During five hours of fighting, the British force lost a few hundred men while machine guns and explosive charges fired from gunboats killed close to twenty thousand Sudanese in a matter of hours. The battle of **Omdurman** became the first step in the establishment of British colonial rule in Sudan.

**Communications Technologies** Communications also benefited from industrialization, and in turn aided European imperial expansion. Oceangoing steamships reduced the time required to deliver messages from imperial capitals to colonial lands. In the 1830s it took as long as two years for a British correspondent to receive a reply to a letter sent to India by sailing ship. By the 1850s, however, after the introduction of steamships, correspondence could make the round-trip between London and Bombay in four months. After the opening of the Suez Canal in 1869, steamships traveled from Britain to India in less than two weeks.

The invention of the telegraph made it possible to exchange messages even faster. Telegraph wires carried communications over land beginning in the 1830s, but only in the 1850s did engineers devise reliable submarine cables for the transmission of messages across the oceans. By 1870, submarine cables carried messages between Britain and India in about five hours. By 1902, cables linked all parts of the British Empire throughout the world, and other European states maintained cables to support communications with their own colonies. Their monopoly on telegraphic communications provided imperial powers with distinct advantages over their colonial territories. Imperial officials could rapidly mobilize forces to deal with troubles, and merchants could respond quickly to developments of economic and commercial significance. Rapid communication was an integral structural element of empire.

**Medical Technologies** When Europeans traveled to the tropical and subtropical regions where they sought to impose

A British Maxim gun at Chilas Fort on India's Northwest Frontier in the late nineteenth century.
Hulton Archive/Getty Images

Thousands of spectators gathered on the banks of the Suez Canal in 1869 to watch a parade of ships that opened the canal by proceeding from the Mediterranean to the Red Sea. The Suez and Panama canals became the most strategic waterways in the world because they significantly shortened maritime routes both between Europe and the lands bordering the Indian and Pacific oceans and between one coast of North America and ports on the other side of South America. Chronicle/Alamy Stock Photo

their rule, they frequently became ill and died from malaria, a mosquito-borne disease. When they discovered an effective treatment for the disease in the form of quinine, it became a powerful weapon in the European quest to conquer and rule distant lands during the nineteenth century.

The remedy for malaria came to Europe from Peru, where indigenous peoples used the bark from the cinchona tree to treat various fevers. This "Jesuit bark," as it was known because of the missionaries' role in conveying this information to other Europeans, also worked well against malaria. When it became clear that cinchona bark could be used not only to treat malaria but also to prevent it, the bark quickly became the favored treatment for malaria. In 1820, two French chemists, Pierre Pelletier and Joseph Caventou, extracted the alkaloid of quinine from cinchona bark, and by the 1840s European colonizers kept quinine pills by their bed stands. The use of quinine proved to be a major force in the expansion of European empires and ultimately permitted small European populations to survive in tropical regions. By the time the British in India and the Dutch in Java began commercially planting cinchona trees in the 1880s to create a reliable supply of the bark, its active ingredient, quinine powder, had become crucial to the health of European colonizers wherever malaria existed.

**Transportation Technologies** The most important innovations in transportation as they related to imperial expansion involved steamships and railroads. Small steamboats plied the waters of the United States and western Europe from the early nineteenth century. During the 1830s British naval engineers adapted steam power to military uses and built large, ironclad ships equipped with powerful guns. These steamships traveled much faster than sailing vessels, and as an additional advantage they could ignore the winds and travel in any direction. Because they could travel much farther upriver than sailboats, which depended on convenient winds, steamships enabled imperialists to project power deep into the interior regions of foreign lands. For example, as we saw in chapter 31, in 1842 the British ironclad steamship *Nemesis* led an expedition up the Yangzi River that brought the Opium War to a conclusion. Steam-powered gunboats later helped to project European power to inland sites throughout Africa and Asia.

The construction of new canals enhanced the effectiveness of steamships. Both the **Suez Canal** (constructed 1859–1869) and the **Panama Canal** (constructed 1904–1914) facilitated the building and maintenance of empires by enabling naval vessels to travel more rapidly than ever before between the world's seas and oceans. They also lowered the costs of trade between imperial powers and subject lands.

Once imperialists had gained control of overseas lands, they often constructed railroads to help them maintain their hegemony and organize local economies to their own advantage. Rail transportation enabled colonial officials and armies to travel quickly through the colonies. It also facilitated the exploitation of raw materials and the distribution of European manufactured goods in the colonies.

## EUROPEAN IMPERIALISM

Aided by powerful technologies, European states launched an unprecedented round of empire building in the second half of the nineteenth century. Imperial expansion began with the British conquest of India. Competition between imperial powers led to European intrusion into central Asia and the establishment of colonies in southeast Asia. Fearful that rivals might gain control over some region that remained free of imperial control, European states embarked on a campaign of frenzied expansion in the 1880s that brought almost all of Africa and Pacific Ocean territories into their empires. Competition between imperial powers led to European intrusion into central Asia, the establishment of colonies in southeast Asia, and interference in the Ottoman and Qing empires in southwest and east Asia (discussed in chapter 31). Throughout this period, Europeans were engaged simultaneously in projects of settler colonialism, formal imperialism without large numbers of settlers, and informal imperialism in which sovereignty was compromised by widespread economic interference. Whether European powers engaged in one kind or another of imperial project depended largely on rivalries with other European powers, the strategic or economic importance of a given area, and the level and type of resistance offered by indigenous peoples.

## The British Empire in India

The British Empire in south Asia and southeast Asia grew out of the mercantile activities of the English **East India Company,** which enjoyed a monopoly on English trade with India. In 1600, the East India Company obtained permission from the Mughal emperors of India to build fortified posts on the coastlines. There, company agents traded for goods and stored commodities in warehouses until company ships arrived to transport them to Europe. In the seventeenth century, company merchants traded mostly for Indian pepper and cotton, Chinese silk and porcelain, and fine spices from southeast Asia. During the eighteenth century, tea and coffee became the most prominent trade items, and European consumers acquired a taste for both beverages that they have never lost.

**Company Rule** After the death of the emperor Aurangzeb in 1707, the Mughal state entered a period of decline, and many local authorities asserted their independence of Mughal rule. The East India Company took advantage of Mughal weakness to strengthen and expand its trading posts. In the 1750s company officials embarked on the outright conquest of India. Through diplomacy or military campaigns, the company conquered autonomous Indian kingdoms and reduced Mughal rule to only a small area around Delhi. Part of the British policy of expansion was the "doctrine of lapse," greatly resented by Indians. If an Indian ruler failed to produce a biological male heir to the throne, his territories lapsed to the company upon his death. By the mid-nineteenth century, the English East India Company had annexed huge areas of India and had established control over present-day Pakistan, Bangladesh, Burma, and Sri Lanka. Company rule was enforced by a small British army and a large number of Indian soldiers known as sepoys.

**Indian Rebellion** The British imposition of rule in south Asia was often insulting to both Hindu and Muslim religious traditions and frequently cut off the political ambitions of influential leaders without any kind of political compensation. Discontent with the British reached even to the sepoys of the East India Company, and in 1857 large portions of the army rebelled.

The rebellion in the army quickly spread to a general anti-British revolution in central and north India. Sepoys were now joined by Indian princes and their followers, whose territories had been annexed by the British, and people whose ways of life and sources of income had been disrupted by British trade, missionary activities, and misguided social reforms. What had begun as a rebellion by Indian troops in the employ of the English East India Company turned into a full-fledged war of independence against British rule. To regain control, the British waged a bloody campaign of retribution in which many thousands of Indians—including civilians not directly involved in the rebellion—were killed in summary hangings and the destruction of whole villages. After several months of inconclusive battles, British forces finally gained the upper hand by late 1857, and peace was officially declared on 8 July 1858.

**British Imperial Rule** The widespread but unsuccessful rebellion against British rule in India had far-reaching consequences. The British government officially abolished the East India Company in favor of the direct rule of India by the British government. In 1858 Queen Victoria (reigned 1837–1901) assigned responsibility for Indian policy to the newly established office of secretary of state for India. A viceroy represented British royal authority in India and administered the colony through an elite Indian civil service staffed almost exclusively by the English. Indians served in low-level bureaucratic positions, but British officials formulated all domestic and foreign policy in India.

Under both the East India Company and direct colonial administration, British rule transformed India. As they extended their authority to all parts of India and Ceylon (modern Sri Lanka), British officials cleared forests, restructured landholdings, and encouraged the cultivation of crops, such as tea, coffee, and opium, that were especially valuable trade items.

They built extensive railroad and telegraph networks that tightened links between India and the larger global economy. They also constructed new canals, harbors, and irrigation systems to support commerce and agriculture. Especially after 1857, British colonial authorities made little effort to promote Christianity, but they established English-style schools for the children of Indian elites, and they suppressed Indian customs that conflicted with European law or values. Most prominent of those customs were sati (the practice of widows burning themselves on their husbands' funeral pyres), infanticide, and slavery.

## Imperialism in Central Asia and Southeast Asia

As the East India Company and British colonial agents tightened their grip on India, competition among European

## INTERPRETING IMAGES

Troops loyal to the British hang two participants of the Indian Rebellion of 1857–59 on a makeshift gallows. During the rebellion, British forces frequently resorted to summary execution without trial for those they suspected of involvement.

**Analyze** *The Indian Rebellion of 1857 was only one of thousands of protests by colonized peoples in Africa and Asia. Like those rebellions of enslaved people in the Americas, most of these ended in brutal suppression. Why are so few of these uprisings named and described in history books? If we were able to speak to them, how might the executed men in this photograph tell this history differently?*

Felice Beato/Universal History Archive/Universal Images Group/Getty Images

states kindled further empire-building efforts. Beginning in the early nineteenth century, French and Russian strategists sought ways to undermine British power and establish their own colonial presence in India. French efforts stalled after the fall of Napoleon in 1815, but Russian interest in India fueled a prolonged contest for power in central Asia.

Russians had been interested in central Asia as early as the sixteenth century, but only in the nineteenth century did they undertake a systematic effort to extend Russian authority south of the Caucasus. The weakening of the Ottoman and Qing empires in Central Asia gave them their opportunity. By the 1860s Russians had overcome Tashkent, Bokhara, and

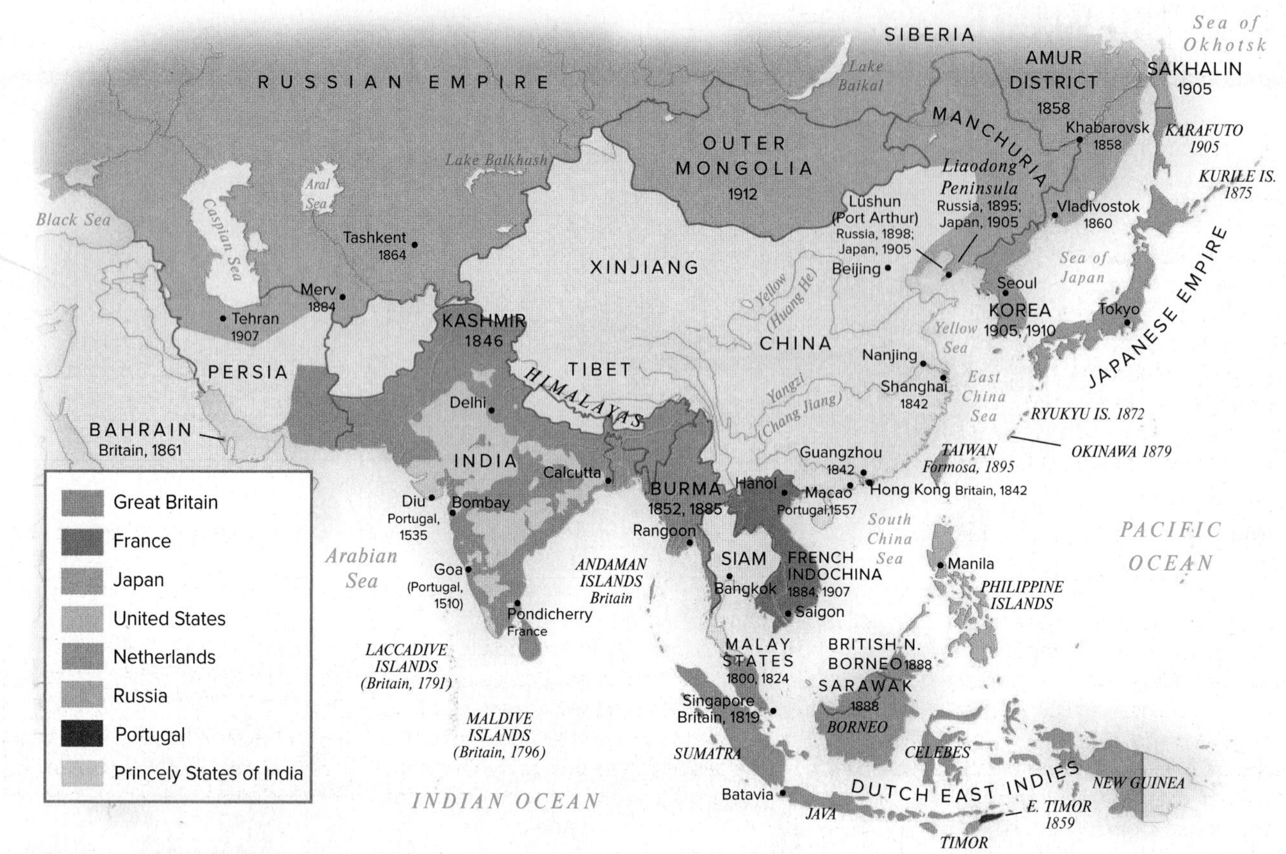


**MAP 20.1 Imperialism in Asia, ca. 1914. Date is year of conquest.**

Note the claims made by various industrial powers.

***Which territories remained unclaimed, and why? Which power claimed the most imperial territory in Asia?***

Samarkand, the great caravan cities of the Silk Roads, and approached the ill-defined northern frontier of British India. For the next half century, military officers and imperialist adventurers engaged in a risky pursuit of influence and intelligence that British agents referred to as the **"Great Game."**

**The Great Game** Russian and British explorers ventured into parts of central Asia never before visited by Europeans. They mapped terrain, scouted mountain passes, and sought alliances with local rulers from Afghanistan to the Aral Sea—all in an effort to prepare for the anticipated war for India. In fact, the outbreak of global war in 1914 and the collapse of the tsarist state in 1917 ensured that the contest for India never took place. Nevertheless, imperial expansion brought much of central Asia into the Russian empire and subjected the region to intense Russian influence that persisted until the disintegration of the Soviet Union in 1991.

Competition among European powers led also to further imperialism in southeast Asia. The Philippines had come under Spanish colonial rule in the sixteenth century, and many southeast Asian islands were conquered by the Dutch in the seventeenth century. As imperial rivalries escalated in the nineteenth century, Dutch officials tightened their control and extended their authority throughout the Dutch East Indies, the archipelago that makes up the modern state of Indonesia. Along with cash crops of sugar, tea, coffee, and tobacco, exports of rubber and tin made the Dutch East Indies a valuable colony for the Netherlands, even while Dutch colonial policy impoverished indigenous populations.

**British Colonies in Southeast Asia** In the interests of increasing trade between India, southeast Asia, and China, British imperialists moved in the nineteenth century to establish a presence in southeast Asia. As early as the 1820s, colonial officials in India came into conflict with the kings of Burma (modern Myanmar) while seeking to extend their influence to the Irrawaddy River delta. By the 1880s they had established colonial authority in Burma, which became a source of teak, ivory, rubies, and jade. In 1824 Thomas Stamford Raffles founded the port of Singapore after signing a treaty with the local rulers of the island, which soon became the busiest center of trade in the Strait of Melaka. Administered by the colonial regime in India until 1867 and then as a crown colony ruled directly from Britain, Singapore served as the base for the British conquest of Malaya (modern Malaysia) in the 1870s and 1880s. Besides offering outstanding ports that enabled the

# SOURCES FROM THE PAST

## Raden Adjeng Kartini on Life as a Colonized Subject in the Dutch East Indies

*Raden (an honorific title) Adjeng Kartini (1879–1904) was born to a noble family on the island of Java, part of the Dutch colony of the East Indies (now Indonesia). Her father worked for the Dutch government, which allowed Kartini to attend a Dutch school—a privilege reserved only for Indonesians of the highest social class and usually only for boys. In the course of her schooling, Kartini became a fierce critic of colonial racism and the oppression of women in both Dutch and Javanese culture. Yet she was forced to leave school as an adolescent because her family believed that it was inappropriate for a young, noble woman to participate in the public world. In hopes of escaping her social isolation, Kartini agreed to marry at the age of twenty-three. With the support of her husband and the Dutch government, in 1903 she opened the first primary school for Indonesian girls that did not discriminate on the basis of social class. Kartini had dreams of expanding her efforts on behalf of Indonesian women, but she died tragically from complications of childbirth only two years later, at the age of twenty-five. Below, she writes to the Dutch feminist Stella Zeehandelaar about Dutch prejudice and the coming emancipation of Indonesian men and women.*

**January 12, 1900**

The Hollanders laugh and make fun of our stupidity, but if we strive for enlightenment, then they assume a defiant attitude toward us. What have I not suffered as a child at school through the ill will of the teachers and of many of my fellow pupils? Not all of the teachers and pupils hated us. Many loved us quite as much as the other children. But it was hard for the teachers to give a native the highest mark, never mind how well it may have been deserved . . .

With heavy hearts, many Europeans here see how the Javanese, whom they regard as their inferiors, are slowly awakening, and at every turn a brown man comes up, who shows that he has just as good brains in his head, and a just as good heart in his body, as the white man . . .

> Why does Kartini say that the Europeans view the "awakening" of Javanese people with "heavy hearts"?

But we are going forward, and they cannot hold back the current of time. I love the Hollanders very, very much, and I am grateful for everything that we have gained through them. Many of them are among our best friends, but there are also others who dislike us, for no other reason than we are bold enough to emulate them in education and culture.

In many subtle ways they make us feel their dislike. "I am a European, you are a Javanese," they seem to say, or "I am the master, you the governed." Not once, but many times, they speak to us in broken Malay; although they know very well that we understand the Dutch language . . .

Why do many Hollanders find it unpleasant to converse with us in their own language? Oh yes, now I understand; Dutch is too beautiful to be spoken by a brown mouth.

A few days ago we paid a visit to Totokkers [Europeans new to the East Indies]. Their domestics were old servants of ours, and we knew that they could speak and understand Dutch very well. I told the host this, and what answer did I receive from my gentleman? "No, they must not speak Dutch." "No, why?" I asked. "Because natives ought not to know Dutch." I looked at him in amazement, and a satirical smile quivered at the corners of my mouth. The gentleman grew fiery red, mumbled something into his beard, and discovered something interesting in his boots, at least he devoted all of his attention to them.

> Why did Kartini's smile embarrass the Dutch man?

In the last few days, articles written by natives have been published in the "Locomotief," the foremost paper of India [the Dutch East Indies]. In these articles they lay bare the opinions, which have secretly been held for years about, not all, but by far the greater number of Indian officials [Dutch officials in the East Indies]. Not only the highest in the land, but also the most humble are allowing their voices to be heard. The paper calls this a good sign of the times, and rejoices. . . . It is also urged that the Dutch language be used officially in business between European and native chiefs. Splendid! . . . In July, the question of the education of women will come up too. The Javanese are emancipating themselves.

Still this is only a beginning, and it is splendid that men of influence and ability are supporting our [women's] cause. The strife will be violent, the combatants will not have to fight against opposition alone, but also against the indifference of our own countrywomen, in whose behalf they would break their lances. While this agitation among the men is on the tapis, that will be the time for the women to rise up and let themselves be heard. Poor men—you will have your hands full.

### For Further Reflection

- Kartini was a noble woman and daughter of a high-ranking official who worked for the Dutch. In what ways does the passage above give away her social status? How might Kartini's focus have been different if she had been a woman of a much lower social status?
- What gave Kartini the courage to write so candidly to a Dutch woman?
- When her efforts to move beyond the typical role of women were thwarted, what did she do?
- Why is it important to consider global and colonial contexts when analyzing movements for women's equality?

*Source:* Kartini, Raden Adjeng. *Letters of a Javanese Princess*. London: Duckworth & Co., 1921.

Warships provide covering fire as British troops prepare to storm the Burmese port of Rangoon in 1824. By the 1880s the British had established colonial authority in Burma and were using it as a source of such valuable commodities as teak, ivory, rubies, and jade.
The British Library/Robana/Getty Images

British navy to control sea lanes linking the Indian Ocean with the South China Sea, Malaya provided abundant supplies of tin and rubber.

**French Indochina** Although they were unable to oust the British and establish themselves in India, French imperialists built the large southeast Asian colony of French Indochina, consisting of the modern states of Vietnam, Cambodia, and Laos, between 1859 and 1893. Like their British counterparts in India, French colonial officials introduced European-style schools and sought to establish close connections with native elites. Unlike their rivals, French officials also encouraged conversion to Christianity, and as a result the Roman Catholic church became prominent throughout French Indochina, especially in Vietnam. By century's end, all of southeast Asia had come under European imperial rule except for the kingdom of Siam (modern Thailand), which preserved its independence largely because colonial officials regarded it as a convenient buffer state between British-dominated Burma and French Indochina.

## The Scramble for Africa

The most striking expansion of European imperialism in this period took place in Africa. As late as 1875, Europeans had only a limited presence in Africa. They held several small coastal colonies and fortified trading posts, but their only sizable possessions were the Portuguese colonies of Angola and Mozambique, the French settler colony in northern Algeria, and a cluster of settler colonies populated by British and Dutch migrants in southern Africa. After the end of the slave trade in 1807, a lively commerce developed around the exchange of African gold, ivory, and palm oil for European textiles, guns, and manufactured goods.

Between 1875 and 1900, however, the relationship between Africa and Europe dramatically changed. Within a quarter century, European imperial powers partitioned and colonized almost the entire African continent. Prospects of exploiting African resources and geopolitical rivalries between European powers help to explain this frenzied quest for empire, often referred to as the **"scramble for Africa."**

## INTERPRETING IMAGES

This photograph from around 1905 portrays Mola (seated) and Yoka (standing), two children living in the Congo Free State. Mola lost his hand from gangrene after being tied too tightly by mercenaries. Yoka's hand was amputated. Amputation was a frequent punishment for failing to meet rubber quotas.

**Analyze** *Consider earlier eras of colonization that you've read about in this course. Think about the depictions of colonized people in earlier chapters. How is this photograph different? What do you think the photographer wanted to convey?*

Cultural Heritage Images/Universal Images Group/Newscom

**Precursors to the Scramble for Africa** Europeans did not know much about the huge and diverse interior of the African continent before the mid-nineteenth century. But a series of explorers who went on to write and speak about their journeys to Africa stimulated intense interest among Europeans. The best known of these explorers was Dr. David Livingstone, a Scottish minister, who made three extremely well publicized trips to Africa to explore territories unknown to Europeans and to convert Africans to Christianity. Livingstone's books attracted many thousands of readers, and when he seemed to disappear for four years during his third journey in the African interior, the editor for the *New York Herald* ordered the American journalist Henry Morton Stanley to lead an expedition to find him. After a highly publicized journey of eight months, in 1871 Stanley found Livingstone in the town of Ujiji, Tanganyika. By that time, Europeans and Americans from many backgrounds–including merchants, missionaries, and government officials–were determined to mine Africa's potential for their own purposes.

One of these people was the King of Belgium, **Leopold II** (r. 1865–1909). By the 1870s, Leopold had become convinced that the only way for a tiny state like Belgium to play a major role in world affairs was to acquire colonies as Britain and France did. He had avidly followed Stanley's journey to find Livingstone and became convinced that Belgium could carve out a colony in the Congo River basin, whose forests were rich with natural rubber so desired by industrialized nations. Under the pretense of encouraging free trade in the area, Leopold hired Stanley to help develop commercial ventures and establish a colony called the Congo Free State (modern-day Democratic Republic of the Congo). Leopold's greed for wealth from rubber led him to establish a regime in the Congo Free State that openly used forced labor and extreme violence to induce inhabitants to collect rubber from wild vines. When inhabitants could not meet rubber quotas set by the state, colonial officials resorted to burning villages, amputations, whippings, and murder. Between four to eight million Congolese died as a result of these practices. Although all European colonial administrations used violence to enforce their will, when missionaries and journalists eventually exposed the brutality of the Congo Free State, global opinion turned sharply against Leopold. In an effort to mitigate some of the worst abuses of the regime, in 1908 the Belgian government took control of the colony away from Leopold and thereafter administered it as the Belgian Congo. While Leopold's Congo had been conceived in a climate of European fascination for Africa, it foreshadowed the many abuses that would result as Europeans sought to divide the continent between them for their own gain.

**South Africa** Long before the scramble for Africa, a European presence had grown at the southern tip of the African continent, where the Dutch East India Company had established Cape Town (1652) as a supply station for ships en route to Asia. Soon after, former company employees plus newly arrived settlers from Europe moved into territories beyond company control to take up farming and ranching. Many of these settlers, known first as Boers (the Dutch word for "farmer") and then as Afrikaners (the Dutch word for "African"), believed that God had predestined them to claim the people and resources of the Cape. The area under white settler control expanded during the eighteenth century as a steady stream of European migrants–chiefly Dutch, Germans, and French Huguenots (Protestants) fleeing religious persecution–continued to swell the colony's population. As European settlers spread beyond the reaches of the original colony, they began encroaching on lands occupied by **Khoikhoi** and **Xhosa**

**Khoikhoi** (KOY-koy)
**Xhosa** (KOH-suh)

peoples. Competition for land soon led to hostility, and by the early eighteenth century, warfare, enslavement, and smallpox epidemics had led to the virtual extinction of the Khoikhoi. After a century of intermittent warfare, the Xhosa too had been decimated, losing lives, land, and resources to European settlers.

When the British took over the Cape from the Dutch during the Napoleonic Wars (1799–1815), Afrikaners pushed further into the interior of southern Africa. The establishment of British rule in 1806 deeply disrupted Afrikaner society, for in its wake came the imposition of English law and language. The institution of slavery—a defining feature of rural Afrikaner society—developed into the most contentious issue between British administrators and Afrikaner settlers because Afrikaners believed that enslaved labor was vital to their livelihoods. Chafing under British rule, and in particular the British abolition of slavery in 1833, Afrikaners started to leave their farms in Cape Colony and gradually migrated east in what they called the Great Trek. That colonial expansion sometimes led to violent conflict with indigenous peoples, but the superior firepower of Afrikaner *voortrekkers* (Afrikaans for "pioneers") overcame first Ndebele and then Zulu resistance. The colonizers interpreted their successful expansion as evidence that God approved of their dominance in South Africa. By the mid-nineteenth century, *voortrekkers* had created several independent republics: the Republic of Natal, annexed by the British in 1843; the Orange Free State in 1854; and the South African Republic (Transvaal territories) in 1860.

French cartoon depicting the Berlin Conference of 1884–1885. Germany's Otto von Bismarck carves a large cake called "Africa" while other European delegates look on.
Historia/Shutterstock

The British in South Africa were not particularly concerned about the establishment of these states until the discovery of large mineral deposits in Afrikaner-populated territories—diamonds in 1867 and gold in 1886. When the existence of these minerals became clear, thousands of British miners and prospectors flocked to the Afrikaner states, leading to tensions between British authorities and Afrikaners. By 1899, these tensions erupted in the **South African War** (1899–1902; sometimes called the Boer War), in which Britons and Afrikaners fought over the right to control the land and resources of the Orange Free State and the Transvaal. The war was both expensive and brutal—both sides possessed modern weapons, Afrikaners engaged in guerilla warfare, and the Afrikaner lifestyle included training in marksmanship. Although the British eventually prevailed, they were forced to assemble a force of five hundred thousand men (at a cost of about two hundred million pounds) to defeat the eighty-eight thousand Afrikaners ranged against them. Moreover, to break the will of Afrikaners, the British resorted to a policy of imprisoning Afrikaner women and children in concentration camps, where at least twenty-eight thousand died. And although the war was between Britons and Afrikaners, nearly twenty thousand black Africans also died in the conflict. When Afrikaners conceded defeat in 1902, the British determined to unite their territories in the Cape and Natal with the Orange Free State and the Transvaal, creating the Union of South Africa in 1910. British attempts at improving relations between English speakers and Afrikaners after the war centered on shoring up the privileges of white colonial society over black Africans.

**The Berlin Conference** In 1882, a British army occupied Egypt in order to protect British financial and strategic interests in the Suez Canal (and its quickest sea route to India). The British government justified its actions by claiming the need to stabilize the country from military rebellion, which itself had occurred in response to high taxes imposed to pay off a crushing Egyptian debt to European lenders. In addition to provoking hostility among Egyptians, the British occupation also angered other European colonial powers who believed British control of the Suez would tip the global balance of power even further in its favor. These tenstions, and the threat of war they raised, led to the **Berlin West Africa Conference** (1884–1885), during which the delegates of twelve European states as well as the United States and the Ottoman Empire devised the ground rules for the division of African territories by outsiders. Not a single African was present. Half the nations represented, including the United States, had no colonial ambitions on the continent, but they had been invited to give the proceedings a veneer of unbiased international approval. The Berlin Conference produced agreement for future claims on African lands with the goal of avoiding war between the great powers: each colonial power had to notify the others of its claims, and each claim had to be followed up by "effective occupation" of the claimed territory. Occupation was commonly accomplished either by getting a signed agreement from a local African ruler or by military conquest. Conference participants also spelled out so-called noble-minded objectives for colonized lands: an end to the slave trade, the extension of civilization and Christianity, and increased commerce and trade. Although the conference did not parcel out African lands

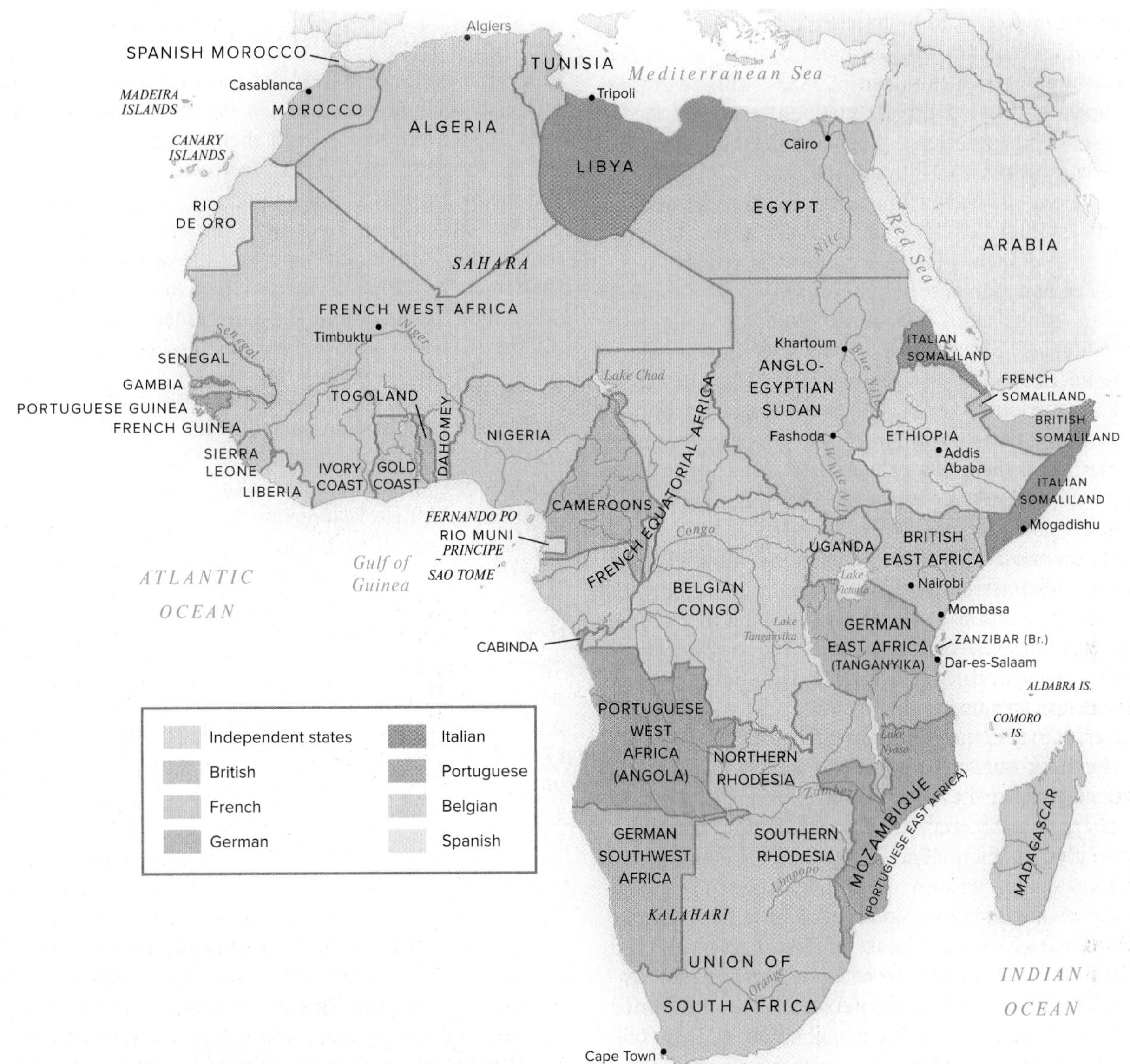


**MAP 20.2 Imperialism in Africa, ca. 1914.**

By 1914, only Ethiopia and Liberia remained free of European control.

***How was it possible for Europeans to gain such domination?***
***What motivated colonization in this era, and how did it differ from the earlier era of European colonization?***

among the participant nations, it nevertheless served public notice that European powers were poised to carve the continent into colonies.

During the next twenty-five years, European imperialists sent armies to consolidate their claims and impose colonial rule. Armed with the latest weapons technology, including the newly developed machine gun and artillery with explosive shells, they rarely failed to defeat African forces. All too often, battles were one-sided. As we have already seen, in 1898, at Omdurman (a city in central Sudan near the junction of the White and Blue Nile rivers) British forces killed close to 20,000 Sudanese in a matter of hours while suffering only minor losses themselves. As we saw in the introduction to this chapter, the only indigenous African state to resist colonization successfully was Ethiopia. Besides Ethiopia, the only African state to remain independent was Liberia, a small republic in west Africa populated by formerly enslaved people that was effectively a dependency of the United States.

**Systems of Colonial Rule** In the wake of rapid conquest came problems of colonial occupation. Imperial powers commonly assumed that, following an initial modest investment, colonial administration would become financially self-sufficient. For decades, Europeans struggled to identify the ideal system of rule, only to learn that colonial rule in Africa could be maintained only through exceedingly high expenditures.

The earliest approach to colonial rule involved "concessionary companies" such as the German Colonial Society for German Southwest Africa (founded in 1885). European governments typically granted private companies large concessions of territory and empowered them to undertake economic activities such as mining, plantation agriculture, or railroad construction. Concessionary companies also had permission to implement systems of taxation and labor recruitment. Although that approach allowed European governments to colonize and exploit immense territories with only a modest investment in capital and personnel, company rule also brought liabilities. The brutal use of forced labor, which provoked a public outcry in Europe, and profits smaller than anticipated persuaded most European governments by the early twentieth century to curtail the powers of private companies and to establish their own rule. Usually, government rule took the form of either **direct rule,** typical of French colonies, or **indirect rule,** characteristic of British colonies.

Under direct rule, colonies featured administrative districts headed by European personnel who assumed responsibility for tax collection, labor and military recruitment, and the maintenance of law and order. Administrative boundaries intentionally cut across existing African political and ethnic boundaries to divide and weaken potentially powerful indigenous groups. Direct rule aimed at removing strong kings and other leaders and replacing them with more malleable persons. Underlying the principle of direct rule was the desire to keep African populations in check and to permit European administrators to engage in a "civilizing mission." However, that approach to colonial rule presented its own difficulties. Key among them was the constant shortage of European personnel. For example, in French West Africa some thirty-six hundred Europeans tried to rule over an African population of more than nine million. The combination of long distances and slow transport limited effective communication between regional authorities and officials in remote areas. An inability to speak local languages and a limited understanding of local customs among European officials further undermined their effective administration.

The British colonial administrator Frederick D. Lugard (1858–1945) was the driving force behind the doctrine of indirect rule, which the British employed in many of their African colonies. Lugard stressed the moral and financial advantages of exercising control over subject populations through indigenous institutions. He was particularly keen on using existing "tribal" authorities and "customary laws" as the foundation for colonial rule. Forms of indirect rule worked in regions where Africans had already established strong and highly organized states, but elsewhere erroneous assumptions concerning the "tribal" nature of African societies weakened the effectiveness of indirect rule. Bewildered by the complexities of African societies, colonial officials frequently imposed their own ideas of what constituted "tribal boundaries" or "tribal authorities." The invention of rigid tribal categories and the establishment of artificial tribal boundaries became one of the greatest obstacles to nation building and regional stability in much of Africa during the second half of the twentieth century.

## European Imperialism in the Pacific

European imperial powers did not overlook opportunities to establish their presence in the Pacific Ocean basin even as they divided Africa between themselves. Imperialism in the Pacific took two main forms. In Australia and New Zealand, European powers established settler colonies and dominant political institutions. In most of the Pacific islands, however, they sought commercial opportunities and reliable bases for their operations but did not wish to go to the trouble or expense of outright colonization. Only in the late nineteenth century did they begin to impose direct colonial rule on the islands.

**Settler Colonies in the Pacific** European mariners explored the Australian coastline and made occasional landfalls from the early sixteenth century, but only after the Pacific voyages of Captain James Cook did Europeans travel to the southern continent in large numbers. In 1770 Cook anchored his fleet for a week at Botany Bay, near modern Sydney, and reported that the region would be suitable for settlement. In 1788 a British fleet with about one thousand settlers, most of them convicted criminals, arrived at Sydney harbor and established the colony of New South Wales. The migrants supported themselves mostly by herding sheep. Lured by the opportunity to acquire land, voluntary migrants outnumbered convicts by the 1830s, and the discovery of gold in 1851 brought a surge in migration to Australia. European settlers established communities also in New Zealand. Europeans first visited New Zealand while hunting whales and seals, but the islands' fertile soils and abundant stands of timber soon attracted their attention and drew large numbers of migrants.

An anonymous contemporary painting depicts the signing of the Treaty of Waitangi on 6 February 1840. British military and colonial officials look on as about fifty Maori chiefs put their names to the document.
Chronicle/Alamy Stock Photo

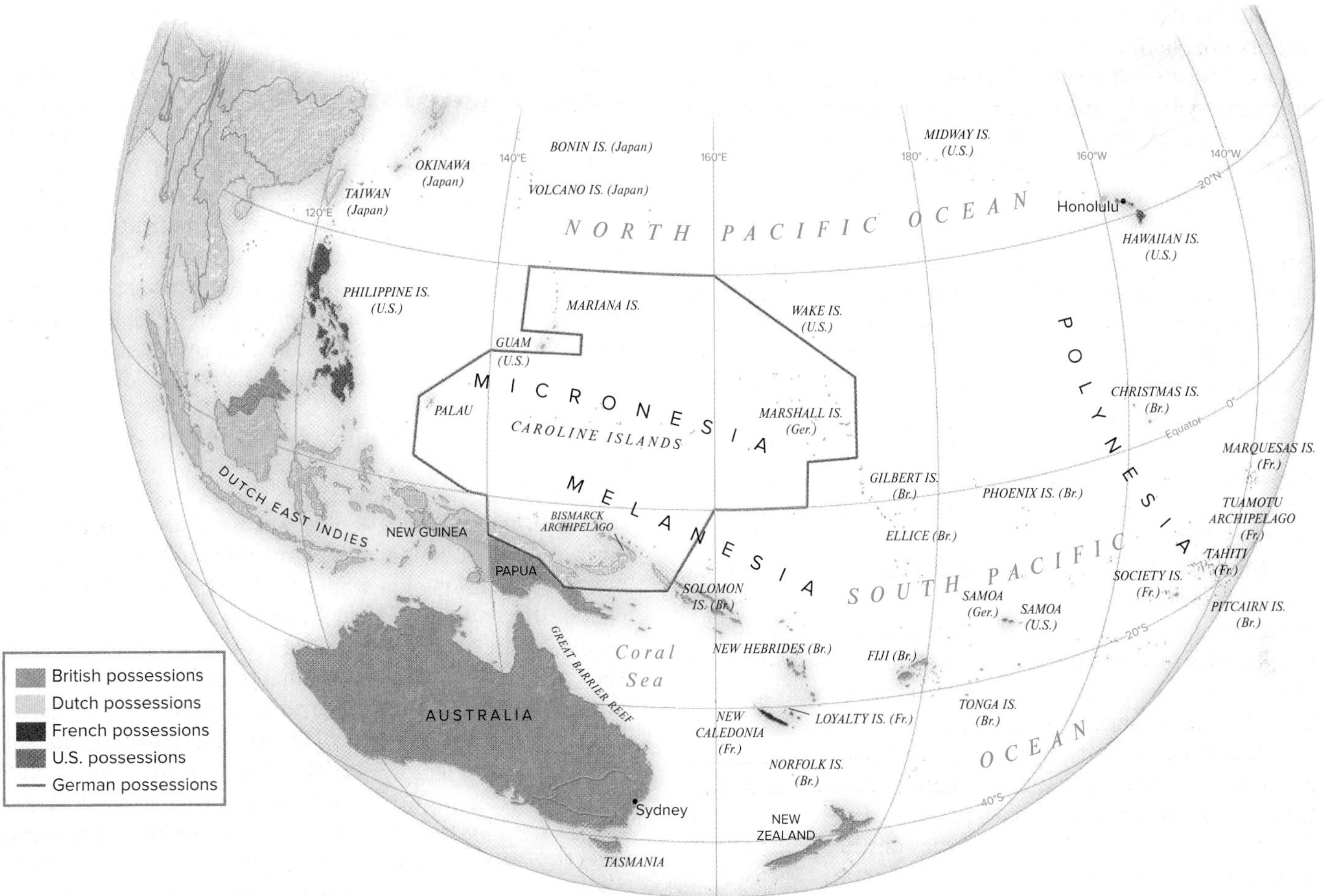


**MAP 20.3 Imperialism in Oceania, ca. 1914.**

Observe the many small, distant islands of the Pacific.

***Why would imperial powers have thought it so important to claim these islands in the late nineteenth and early twentieth centuries?***

European migration devastated the indigenous societies of Australia and New Zealand, partially as a result of the introduction of European diseases such as smallpox and measles. The aboriginal population of Australia fell from about 650,000 in 1800 to 90,000 in 1900, whereas the European population rose from a few thousand to 3.75 million during the same period. Similarly, the population of indigenous **Maori** in New Zealand fell from about 200,000 in 1800 to 45,000 a century later, while European numbers climbed to 750,000.

Increasing migration also fueled conflict between European settlers and native populations. Large settler societies pushed indigenous peoples from their lands, often following violent confrontations. Because the nomadic foraging peoples of Australia did not occupy lands permanently, British settlers considered the continent ***terra nullius***–"land belonging to no one"–that they could seize and put to their own uses. They undertook brutal military campaigns to evict aboriginal peoples from lands suitable for agriculture or herding. Despite strong resistance, by 1900 the British had succeeded in displacing most indigenous Australians from their traditional lands and dispersing them throughout the continent.

A similarly disruptive process transpired in New Zealand. Representatives of the British government encouraged Maori leaders in 1840 to sign the **Treaty of Waitangi,** which was designed to place New Zealand under British protection. Because the British underplayed the effect of the treaty on Maori sovereignty, many Maori chiefs agreed to sign it. However, the treaty actually signaled the coming of official British colonial control in New Zealand (1841) and thereafter inspired effective and long-lasting Maori opposition to British attempts to usurp their land and sovereignty. Conflicts over land confiscations and disputed land sales, for example, helped to spark the New Zealand Wars, a series of military confrontations between autonomous Maori groups and British troops and settlers that extended from the mid- to the late nineteenth century. Various Maori also cooperated in the Maori King Movement (or *Kingitanga*), beginning in 1856, as a means of forwarding Maori unity and sovereignty. While political and military battles continued, the British managed by the end of the century to force many Maori into poor rural communities separated from European settlements.

**Maori** (MAY-oh-ree)

**Pacific Islands** European diseases also ravaged indigenous populations in the Pacific islands, although most did not attract large populations of European settlers. During the nineteenth century the principal European visitors to Pacific islands were whalers, merchants, and missionaries, and for most of the century the imperialist powers had little desire to establish direct colonial rule over Pacific islands. But that situation changed in the late nineteenth century. Just as European rivalries drove the scramble for Africa, so they encouraged the imperialist powers to stake their claims in the Pacific. In an era of global imperialism, European states sought reliable coaling stations for their steamships and ports for their navies. To that end, France established protectorates in Tahiti, the Society Islands, and the Marquesas as early as 1841 and imposed direct colonial rule in 1880. France also annexed New Caledonia in 1853. Britain made Fiji a crown colony in 1874, and Germany annexed several of the Marshall Islands in 1876 and 1878. Then at the Berlin Conference in 1884–1885, diplomats agreed on a partition of Oceania as well as Africa, and Britain, France, Germany, and the United States proceeded to claim almost all of the Pacific islands. By 1900 only the kingdom of Tonga remained independent, and even Tonga accepted British protection against the possibility of encroachments by other imperial powers.

In addition to their value as ports and coaling stations, the Pacific islands offered economic benefits to imperial powers. For example, Hawai'i and Fiji were the sites of productive sugarcane plantations. Samoa, French Polynesia, and many Melanesian and Micronesian islands were sources of copra—dried coconut, which produced high-quality vegetable oil for the manufacture of soap, candles, and lubricants. New Caledonia had rich veins of nickel, and many small Pacific islands had abundant deposits of guano—bird droppings that made the world's best fertilizer.

## THE EMERGENCE OF NEW IMPERIAL POWERS

Nineteenth-century imperialism was mostly a European affair. Toward the end of the century, however, two new imperial powers joined Europeans in their efforts to divide the world into colonies: the United States and Japan. Both states experienced rapid industrialization in the late nineteenth century, and both built powerful armed forces. As European imperial powers forcibly claimed territories throughout the world, leaders of the United States and Japan decided that they too needed to establish an imperial presence overseas.

### U.S. Imperialism in Latin America and the Pacific

The very existence of the United States was due to European imperialism. After the new republic had won its independence, U.S. leaders brought almost all the temperate regions of North America under their authority. Although they purchased some of this territory from other European powers (i.e., the Louisiana Purchase in 1803) or acquired it by treaty after war (i.e., the Mexican Cession in 1848), all westward movement in the United States involved the forcible and violent removal of indigenous populations from their hereditary lands. In that sense, the settlement of the United States was no different than the settler colonialism of Australia or New Zealand, even though Americans obscured these similarities by claiming they had a "manifest destiny" to settle North America from coast to coast.

**The Monroe Doctrine** But westward expansion on the North American continent was only part of the story of U.S. imperial expansion. Early in its history as an independent republic, the fledgling United States also sought to wield power outside North America. In 1823 President James Monroe (in office 1817–1825) issued a proclamation that warned European states against imperialist designs in the Western Hemisphere. In essence Monroe claimed all of the Americas as a U.S. protectorate, and his proclamation, known as the **Monroe Doctrine,** served as a justification for later U.S. intervention in hemispheric affairs. Until the late nineteenth century, however, the United States mostly sought to ensure that other European powers did not establish new colonies in the Americas and that U.S. entrepreneurs could profit from bringing the natural resources and agricultural products of the Americas to the world market.

Queen Lili'uokalani, last monarch of Hawai'i, before her deposition in 1893. Wearing a European dress (she had received a western education by missionaries and had traveled widely in Europe and America), the queen sits on a throne covered with a traditional royal cape made of bird feathers.
Everett Collection Inc/Alamy Stock Photo

As the United States consolidated its continental holdings, U.S. leaders became interested in acquiring territories beyond the temperate regions of North America. In 1867 the United States purchased Alaska from Russia and in 1875 it claimed a protectorate over the islands of Hawai'i, where U.S. entrepreneurs had established highly productive sugarcane plantations. The Hawaiian kingdom survived until 1893, when a group of American and European planters and businesspeople overthrew

# SOURCES FROM THE PAST

## Queen Lili'uokalani's Protest against the Annexation of Hawai'i

*Queen Lili'uokalani (1838–1917) was the last monarch of the Kalakalua dynasty, which had ruled the Hawaiian Islands since 1810. Before taking the throne in 1891, Lili'uokalani had traveled extensively in the United States and Europe, and had served in the royal court. In 1887, American businessmen forced King Kalakaua, her older brother, to sign a constitution (called the "Bayonet Constitution") that limited the powers of the monarchy. Lili'uokalani adamantly opposed this constitution, and when she acceded to the throne she tried to implement a new constitution that would return her power. But in 1893, a group of European and American businessmen—with the help of U.S. Marines—staged a coup and deposed Lili'uokalani. Even after she was deposed, the queen continued to protest to the U.S. government against the loss of her power and against the rise of American power in Hawai'i. Her efforts were in vain, however, as the government of president William McKinley annexed Hawai'i in July, 1898. Below is her letter of protest to the U.S. House of Representatives from December of that year.*

**I, Liliuokalani of Hawaii,** named heir apparent on the 10th day of April, 1877, and proclaimed Queen of the Hawaiian Islands on the 29th day of January, 1891, do hereby earnestly and respectfully protest against the assertion of ownership by the United States of America of the so-called Hawaiian Crown Lands amounting to about one million acres and which are my property, and I especially protest against such assertion of ownership as a taking of property without due process of law and without just or other compensation.

Therefore, supplementing my protest of June 17, 1897, I call upon the President and the National Legislature and the People of the United States to do justice in this matter and to restore to me this property, the enjoyment of which is being withheld from me by your Government under what must be a mis-apprehension of my right and title.

Done at Washington, District of Columbia, United States of America, this nineteenth day of December, in the year one thousand eight hundred and ninety-eight.

What is the significance of the fact that Lili'uokalani went to Washington, D.C., to make this protest?

### For Further Reflection

- What, according to Lili'uokalani, is the nature of the injustices she has had to endure? Why does she say that the government must not understand her right and title?
- How does the Queen's protest reflect principles exhibited in the U.S. Declaration of Independence?
- Why did President McKinley feel justified in ignoring her plea?

*Source:* Letter from Liliuokalani, Queen of Hawaii to U.S. House of Representatives protesting U.S. assertion of ownership of Hawaii, December 19, 1898. RG 233, Records of the U.S. House of Representatives, National Archives.

the last monarch, Queen **Lili'uokalani** (reigned 1891–1893), and invited the United States to annex the islands. U.S. president Grover Cleveland (in office 1885–1889 and 1893–1897) opposed annexation, but his successor, William McKinley (in office 1897–1901), was more open to American expansion and agreed to acquire the islands as U.S. possessions in 1898.

**The Spanish-Cuban-American War** The United States emerged as an important imperial and colonial power after the brief **Spanish-Cuban-American War** (1898–1899). By the end of the nineteenth century U.S. business interests had made large investments in the Spanish colonies of Cuba and Puerto Rico. When the U.S. battleship *Maine* exploded and sank while anchored in the Cuban port of Havana in 1898, U.S. leaders claimed sabotage and declared war on Spain. The United States quickly defeated Spain and took possession of Cuba and Puerto Rico. U.S. leaders then turned their attention to Spain's Pacific colonies: Guam and the Philippines. After the U.S. navy destroyed the Spanish fleet at Manila in a single day, the United States took possession of both colonies to prevent them from falling under German or Japanese control.

The United States quickly established colonial governments in its new possessions. It also intervened directly in the affairs of Caribbean and Central American territories that were not U.S. possessions whenever it felt its business interests were threatened. U.S. military forces occupied Cuba, the Dominican Republic, Nicaragua, Honduras, and Haiti in the early twentieth century.

The consolidation of U.S. authority in the Philippines was especially brutal. The Spanish-Cuban-American War coincided with a Filipino revolt against Spanish rule, and U.S. leaders promised to support independence of the Philippines if Filipino rebels allied with the United States against Spain. After the victory over Spain, however, President William McKinley decided to bring the Philippines under American control instead. The United States paid Spain twenty million dollars for rights to the colony, which was important to American businesspeople and military leaders because of its

**Lili'uokalani** (lee-lee-oo-oh-kah-LAH-nee)

strategic position in the South China Sea. Outraged at their betrayal by the United States, Filipino rebels led by **Emilio Aguinaldo**—known to his followers as the George Washington of his country—turned their arms against the new intruders. The result was a bitter war that raged until 1902 and flared sporadically until 1906. The conflict claimed the lives of fifteen thousand rebel troops and forty-two hundred American soldiers, as well as about two hundred thousand Filipino civilians.

**The Panama Canal** To facilitate communication and transportation between the Atlantic and the Pacific oceans, the United States sought to build a canal across a narrow stretch of land in Central America. Engineers identified the isthmus of Panama in northern Colombia as the best site for a canal, but Colombia was unwilling to cede land for the project. Under President Theodore Roosevelt (in office 1901–1909), an enthusiastic champion of imperial expansion, the United States supported a rebellion against Colombia in 1903 and helped rebels establish the breakaway state of Panama. In exchange for this support, the United States won the right to build a canal across Panama and to control the adjacent territory, known as the Panama Canal Zone. Given this expansion of U.S. interests in Latin America, Roosevelt added a corollary to the Monroe Doctrine in 1904. The **Roosevelt Corollary** exerted the U.S. right to intervene in the domestic affairs of nations within the hemisphere if they demonstrated an inability to maintain the security deemed necessary to protect U.S. investments. The Roosevelt Corollary, along with the Panama Canal when it opened in 1914, strengthened U.S. military and economic claims in the region.

## Imperial Japan

Strengthened by rapid industrialization during the Meiji era, Japan also joined the ranks of imperial powers in the late nineteenth century. Japanese leaders deeply resented the unequal treaties that the United States and European powers forced them to accept in the 1860s (discussed in chapter 31). They resolved to eliminate the diplomatic handicaps imposed by the treaties and to raise Japan's profile in the world. While founding representative political institutions to demonstrate to European and American diplomats their commitment to western values, Japanese leaders also made a bid to stand alongside the world's great powers by launching a campaign of imperial expansion.

**Early Japanese Expansion** The Japanese drive to empire began in the east Asian islands. During the 1870s Japanese leaders consolidated their hold on Hokkaido and the Kurile Islands to the north, and they encouraged Japanese migrants to populate the islands to prevent Russian expansion there. By 1879 they had also established their hegemony over Okinawa and the Ryukyu Islands to the south.

In 1876 Japan purchased modern warships from Britain, and the newly strengthened Japanese navy immediately began to pursue military intervention in Korea. After a confrontation between the Korean navy and a Japanese surveying vessel, Meiji officials dispatched a gunboat expedition and forced Korean leaders to submit to the same kind of unequal treaty that the United States and European states had imposed on Japan. As European and U.S. imperialists divided up the world in the 1880s and 1890s, Meiji political and military leaders made plans to project Japanese power abroad. They developed contingency plans for a conflict with China, staged maneuvers in anticipation of a continental war, and built a navy with the capacity to fight on the high seas.

**The Sino-Japanese War** In 1894, conflict erupted between Japan and China over the status of Korea. Taking advantage of the unequal treaty of 1876, Japanese businesses had developed substantial interests in Korea. When an antiforeign rebellion broke out in Korea in 1893, Meiji leaders feared that the land might fall into anarchy and become an inviting target of European or U.S. imperialism. Qing rulers sent an army to restore order and reassert Chinese authority in Korea, but Meiji leaders were unwilling to recognize Chinese control over a place so important to Japanese business interests. Thus in August 1894 they declared war on China. The Japanese navy quickly gained control of the Yellow Sea and demolished the Chinese fleet in a battle lasting a mere five hours. The Japanese army then pushed Qing forces out of the Korean peninsula. Within a few months the conflict was over. When the combatants made peace in April 1895, Qing authorities recognized the independence of Korea, thus making it essentially a dependency of Japan. They also ceded Taiwan, the Pescadores Islands, and the Liaodong peninsula, which strengthened Japanese control over east Asian waters. Alongside territorial acquisitions, Japan gained unequal treaty rights in China like those enjoyed by European and American powers.

The unexpected Japanese victory startled European imperial powers, especially Russia. Tensions between Japan and Russia soon mounted, as both imperial powers had territorial ambitions in the Liaodong peninsula (in northeastern China), Korea, and Manchuria. During the late 1890s Japanese military leaders vastly strengthened both their navy and their army with an eye toward a future conflict with Russia.

**The Russo-Japanese War** War broke out in 1904, and Japanese forces overran Russian outposts before reinforcements could arrive from Europe. The enhanced Japanese navy destroyed the Russian Baltic fleet, which had sailed halfway around the world to support the war effort. By 1905 the war was over, and Japan won international recognition of its colonial authority over Korea and the Liaodong peninsula. Furthermore, Russia ceded the southern half of Sakhalin

---

**Emilio Aguinaldo** (eh-MEE-lyoh AH-gee-NAHL-doh)

Japanese painting of a Japanese naval victory over a Chinese vessel. China's defeat in the Sino-Japanese War showed how the Qing dynasty had been weakened militarily, especially by the Opium War, and demonstrated how successful modernization had been for Japan since the Meiji restoration.
The Artchives/Alamy Stock Photo

island to Japan, along with a railroad and economic interests in southern Manchuria. Victory in the **Russo-Japanese War** transformed Japan into a major imperial power.

## LEGACIES OF IMPERIALISM

Imperialism and colonialism profoundly influenced the development of world history. In some ways, they tightened links between the world's peoples: trade and migration increased dramatically as imperial powers exploited the resources of subject territories and recruited laborers to work in colonies throughout the world. Yet imperialism and colonialism also brought peoples into conflict and heightened senses of difference between peoples. European, Euro-American, and Japanese imperialists all came to think of themselves as superior to the peoples they conquered. Meanwhile, foreign intrusion stimulated the development of anticolonial and nationalist identities in colonized territories, and over time these identities served as a foundation for anticolonial independence movements.

### Empire and Economy

One of the principal motives of imperialism was the desire to gain access to natural resources and agricultural products. As imperial powers consolidated their hold on foreign territories, colonial administrators reorganized colonized societies so they would become efficient suppliers of timber, rubber, petroleum, gold, silver, diamonds, cotton, tea, coffee, cacao, and other products. As a result, global trade in those commodities surged during the nineteenth and early twentieth centuries. However, profits from that trade went mostly to the colonial powers, who exported raw materials for processing in the industrialized societies of Europe, North America, and Japan.

**Economic and Social Changes** Sometimes colonial rule transformed the production of crops and commodities that had long been prominent in subject societies. In India, for example, the cultivation of cotton began probably before 5000 B.C.E. For most of history, cultivators spun thread and wove their own cotton textiles or else supplied local artisans with raw materials. Beginning in the late eighteenth century, however, colonial administrators reoriented the cultivation of cotton to serve the needs of the emerging British textile industry. They encouraged cultivators to produce cotton for export rather than for local consumption, and they built railroads deep into the subcontinent to transport raw cotton to the coast quickly. They shipped raw cotton to England, where mechanized factories rapidly turned out large volumes of high-quality textiles. They also allowed the import of inexpensive British textiles to India, which undermined Indian cotton cloth production. The value of raw cotton exported from India went from 10 million rupees in 1849 to 60 million rupees in 1860 and 410 million rupees in

## What's Left Out?

Textbooks often overlook the fact that colonial policies seemingly unrelated to gender nevertheless frequently altered gender relations between colonized men and women. For example, the imposition of new systems of taxation often went hand in hand with European assumptions that men should be heads of households and thus the responsible parties for paying taxes to the state. In places where both women and men had held property and produced crops, such as colonial Tanganyika (modern Tanzania), these assumptions led to tax collection policies that put economic responsibility in the hands of men. This resulted in the marginalization of colonized women in public life and a rise in the political and economic power of colonized men, thus changing the gender dynamics between the sexes. The imposition of colonial law also similarly led to changes in gender relations. In Northern Ghana, for example, the implementation of the British judicial system brought about a deterioration in the legal status of indigenous women. Even though marriage practices in the region had given women an extraordinary amount of autonomy in both choosing and changing partners, British notions about the authority of husbands increasingly led to legal decisions that enforced the idea that wives were the property of their husbands. Over time, the colonial justice system allowed men to claim increasing legal control over their wives. While most textbooks do not have space to explore the many and varied ways colonialism shaped gender relations within the colonies, it is important to remember that the imposition of economic and legal policies could have an impact on seemingly unrelated—and quite intimate—issues such as gender relations.

### Thinking Critically About Sources

1. How did European imperialism deny colonized women privileges they had enjoyed before the arrival of Europeans?
2. Coupled with the treatment of colonized men, what impact would such "unintended consequences" have on people of all genders even after independence?
3. Does this understanding of the impact of colonization on gender change the way you think about global gender inequality today? Does it change the way you think about the relationship between gender equality and modernity?

*Source:* Jean Allman, Susan Geiger, and Nakanyike Musisi. *Women in African Colonial Histories* (Bloomington: Indiana University Press, 2002).

1913, whereas the value of finished cotton products imported into India rose from 50,000 rupees in 1814 to 5.2 million rupees in 1829 and 30 million rupees in 1890. Thus colonial policies transformed India from the world's principal center of cotton manufacture to a supplier of raw cotton and a consumer of textiles produced in the British isles.

In some cases, colonial rule led to the introduction of new crops that transformed both the landscape and the social order of subject lands. In the early nineteenth century, for example, British colonial officials introduced tea bushes from China to Ceylon (modern Sri Lanka) and India. The effect on Ceylon was profound. British planters felled trees in much of the island, converted rain forests into tea plantations, and recruited Ceylonese women by the thousands to carry out the labor-intensive work of harvesting mature tea leaves. Consumption of tea in India and Ceylon was almost negligible, so increased supplies met the growing demand for tea in Europe, where the beverage became accessible to individuals of all social classes. The value of south Asian tea exports rose from about 309,000 pounds sterling in 1866 to 4.4 million pounds sterling in 1888 and 6.1 million pounds sterling in 1900. Malaya and Sumatra underwent a similar social transformation after British colonial agents planted rubber trees there in the 1870s and established plantations to meet the growing global demand for rubber products.

## Labor Migrations

Efforts to exploit the natural resources and agricultural products of subject lands led imperial and colonial powers to encourage mass migrations of workers during the nineteenth and early twentieth centuries. Two patterns of labor migration were especially prominent during this period. European migrants went mostly to temperate lands, where they worked

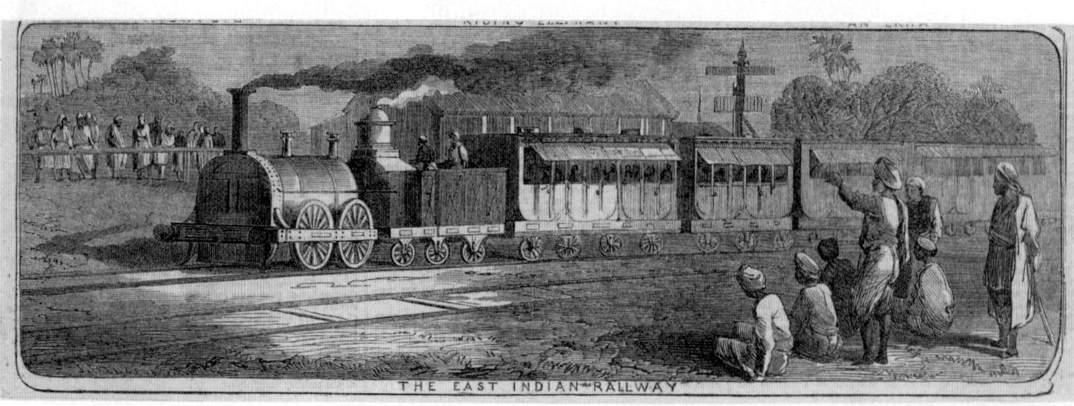


An engraving depicts the East India Railway about 1863. Though originally built to transport goods, railroads quickly became a popular means of passenger travel in India. Chronicle/Alamy Stock Photo

as free cultivators or industrial laborers. In contrast, migrants from Asia, Africa, and the Pacific islands moved largely to tropical and subtropical territories, where they worked as indentured laborers on plantations or manual laborers for mining enterprises or large-scale construction projects. Between them, these two streams of labor migration profoundly influenced the development of societies, especially in the Americas and the Pacific basin.

**European Migration** Between 1800 and 1914 some fifty million European migrants left their homes and sought opportunities overseas. Most of those migrants left the relatively poor agricultural societies of southern and eastern Europe, especially Italy, Russia, and Poland, although sizable numbers came also from Britain, Ireland, Germany, and Scandinavia. A majority of the migrants—about thirty-two million—went to the United States. Many of the early arrivals went west in search of

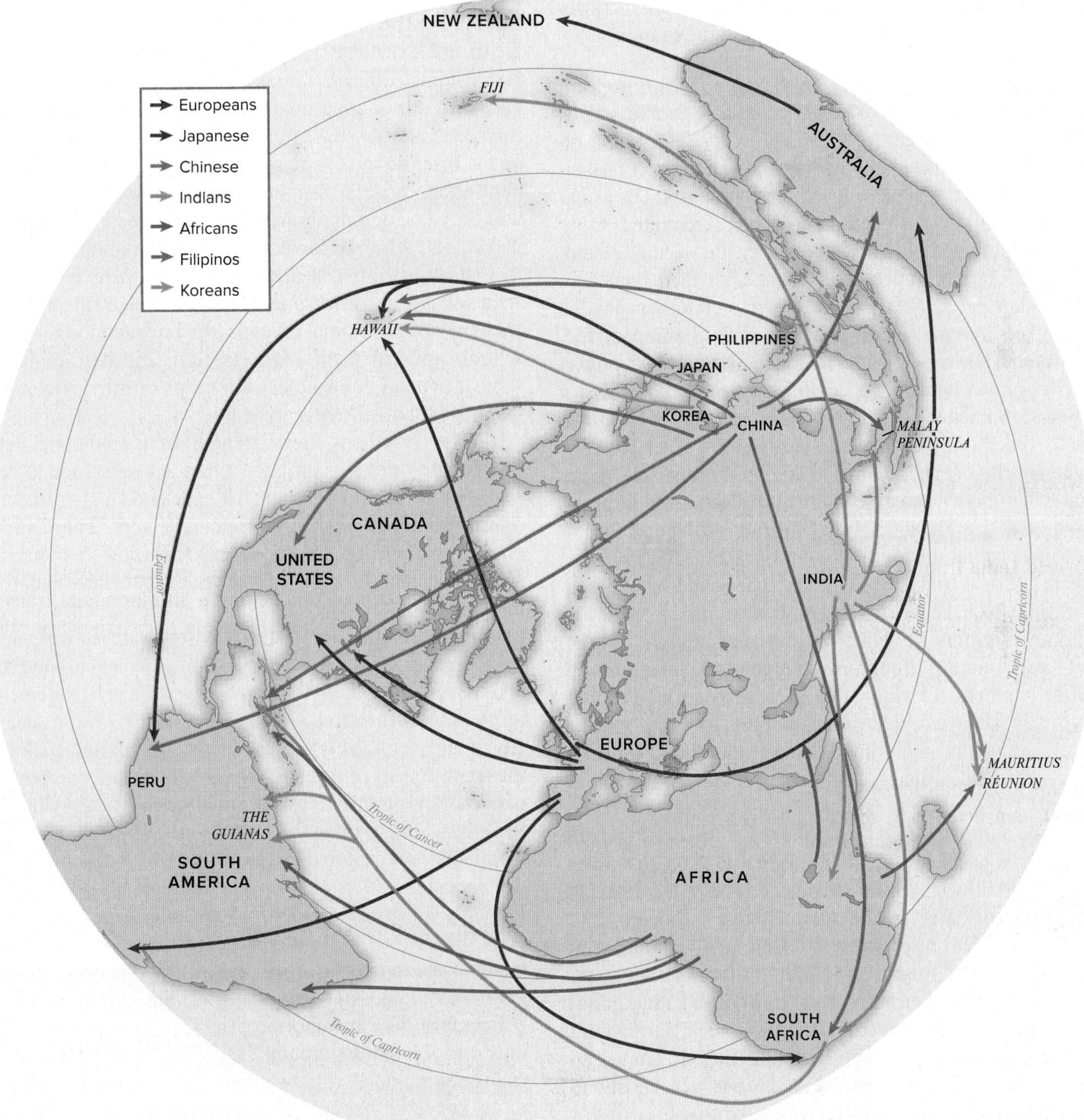


**MAP 20.4 Imperialism and migration during the nineteenth and early twentieth centuries.**

An unprecedented intercontinental migration of people characterized the age of imperialism.

*What factors encouraged and facilitated migration on this extraordinary scale?*

*Consider previous maps in this chapter. Given the patterns of imperialism you see in those maps, what motivated each of the migrations depicted on this map?*

cheap land to cultivate. Later migrants settled heavily in the northeast, where they provided the labor that drove U.S. industrialization after the 1860s. Settler colonies in Canada, Argentina, Australia, New Zealand, and South Africa also drew large numbers of European migrants, who mostly became free cultivators or herders but sometimes found employment as skilled laborers in mines or fledgling industries. Most European migrants traveled as free agents, but some went as indentured laborers. They were able to find opportunities in temperate regions of the world because of European and Euro-American imperialism in the Americas, South Africa, and Oceania.

**Indentured Labor Migration** In contrast to their European counterparts, migrants from Asia, Africa, and the Pacific islands generally traveled as indentured laborers. As the institution of slavery went into decline, planters sought large numbers of laborers to replace enslaved people who left the plantations. The planters relied primarily on indentured laborers recruited from relatively poor and densely populated places. Between 1820 and 1914 about 2.5 million indentured laborers left their homes to work in distant parts of the world. Labor recruiters generally offered workers free passage to their destinations and provided them with food, shelter, clothing, and modest compensation for their services in exchange for a commitment to work for five to seven years. Sometimes recruiters also offered free return passage to workers who completed a second term of service.

The majority of the indentured laborers came from India, but sizable numbers also came from China, Japan, Java, parts of Africa, and the Pacific islands. Indentured laborers went mostly to tropical and subtropical lands in the Americas, the Caribbean, Africa, and Oceania. The **indentured labor** trade began in the 1820s when French and British colonial officials sent Indian migrants to work on sugar plantations in the Indian Ocean islands of Réunion and Mauritius. Shortly thereafter, large numbers of Indian laborers went to work on rubber plantations in Malaya and sugar plantations in South Africa; the Pacific island of Fiji; the Guianas; and the Caribbean islands of Trinidad, Tobago, and Jamaica. After the Opium War ended in 1842, recruiters also, began to seek workers in China. Large numbers of Chinese laborers went to sugar plantations in Cuba and Hawai'i; guano mines in Peru; tin mines in Malaya; gold mines in South Africa and Australia; and railroad construction sites in the United States, Canada, and Peru. After the Meiji restoration in Japan, a large contingent of Japanese laborers migrated to Hawai'i to work on sugar plantations, and a smaller group went to work in guano mines in Peru. Indentured laborers from various parts of Africa went mostly to sugar plantations in Réunion, the Guianas, and Caribbean islands. Those from Pacific islands went mostly to plantations in other Pacific islands and Australia.

**Empire and Migration** All of the large-scale migrations of the nineteenth century reflected the global influence of imperial powers. European migrations were possible only because European and Euro-American peoples had established settler societies in temperate regions around the world. Movements of indentured laborers were possible because colonial officials were able to recruit workers and dispatch them to distant lands where their compatriots had already established plantations or opened mines. In combination the nineteenth-century migrations profoundly influenced societies around the world by establishing large communities of people with distinctive ethnic identities in places far from their original homes.

## Empire and Society

**Colonial Conflict** The policies adopted by imperial powers and colonial officials forced peoples of different societies to deal with one another on a regular and systematic basis. Their interactions often led to violent conflicts between colonizers and subject peoples. The sepoy rebellion was the most prominent effort to resist British colonial authority in India, but it was only one among thousands of insurrections organized by discontented Indian subjects between the mid-nineteenth and the mid-twentieth centuries. Colonized people in southeast Asia and Africa also strongly resisted foreign rule, the tyrannical behavior of colonial officials, the introduction of European schools and curricula, high taxation, and requirements that subject peoples cultivate certain crops or provide compulsory labor for colonists' enterprises.

Many rebellions drew strength from traditional religious beliefs, and priests or prophets often led resistance to colonial rule. Some rebellions sought to expel colonial intruders and return territories to their precolonial rulers. The Can Vuong (Loyalty to the King) movement in what is now Vietnam was one such movement. In 1884, the twelve-year-old Ham Nghi came to the throne of the Nguyen dynasty in the province of Annam (modern Vietnam). Ham Nghi's advisers watched with horror as the French began to take control of the provinces around Annam and issued regular and vehement anti-French statements. In response, a French force raided Ham Nghi's royal palace in the city of Hue, forcing the young king and his advisers to flee. From the dense forests of Annam, Ham Nghi became the centerpiece of a resistance movement whose goal was to put the king back on the throne and to drive the French out of Indochina altogether. Ham Nghi was captured and exiled in 1888, but some of his supporters continued to resist French influence until 1895 by killing French soldiers and murdering Vietnamese converts to Christianity. While the Can Vuong movement did not succeed in driving out the French, the movement did provide training for some of the most important Vietnamese revolutionaries of the twentieth century. Just as important, the Can Vuong movement was only one of hundreds around the colonized world that sought to overthrow colonial rule by force. Even when subject peoples dared not revolt because they could not match European weaponry, they resisted colonial rule by boycotting European goods, organizing political parties and pressure groups, publishing anticolonial newspapers and magazines, and pursuing anticolonial policies through churches and religious groups.

Colonial policies also led to conflicts among peoples brought together artificially into multicultural societies. When indentured laborers from different societies congregated on plantations, for example, tensions sometimes developed between workers and their supervisors and among different groups of workers themselves. In Hawai'i, which had one of the most diverse multicultural societies created by the labor migrations of the nineteenth century, workers on sugar plantations came primarily from China, Japan, and Portugal, but there were also sizable contingents from the Philippines, Korea, and other Pacific islands. Workers and their families normally lived in villages dominated by their own ethnic groups, but there were plentiful opportunities for individuals and groups to mix with one another at work or in the larger society. Although the various ethnic communities readily adopted their neighbors' foods and sometimes took spouses from other groups, linguistic, religious, and cultural differences provided a foundation for strong ethnic identities throughout the plantation era and beyond.

**Scientific Racism** Social and cultural differences were the foundation of an academic pursuit known as **scientific racism,** which became prominent especially after the 1840s. Theorists such as the French nobleman Count Joseph Arthur de Gobineau (1816–1882) took race as the most important index of human potential. In fact, there is no basis for separating humans into different races because differences such as skin color are purely physical and do not signal differences in biological makeup. Nevertheless, nineteenth-century theorists assumed that the human species consisted of several distinct racial groups. Gobineau himself divided humanity into four main racial groups, each of which had its own peculiar traits. Throughout the later nineteenth and early twentieth centuries, racial theorists sought to identify racial groups on the basis of skin color, bone structure, nose shape, cranial capacity, and other physical characteristics. Although they did not always agree on the details about racial differences, one thing they did agree on was the superiority of Europeans to all others—a belief that seemed to be justified by the dominance of European imperial powers in the larger world.

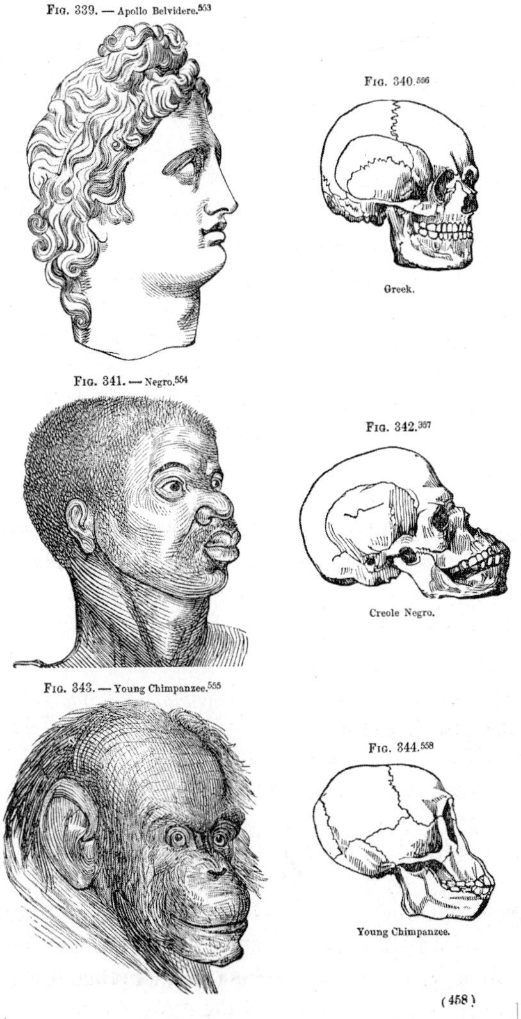

Scientific racists often argued that Europeans had reached a higher stage of evolution than other peoples. An illustration from a popular book by Josiah Clark Nott and G. R. Gliddon, *Indigenous Races of the Earth,* deliberately distorted facial and skull features to suggest a close relationship between African peoples and chimpanzees. Science Source

After the 1860s, scientific racists drew heavily from the writings of Charles Darwin (1809–1882), an English biologist whose book ***The Origin of Species*** (1859) argued that all living species had evolved over thousands of years in a ferocious contest for survival. Species that adapted well to their environment survived, reproduced, and flourished, according to Darwin, whereas others declined and went into extinction. The slogan **"survival of the fittest"** soon became a byword for Darwin's theory of evolution. Theorists known as social Darwinists seized on those ideas, which Darwin had applied exclusively to biological matters, and adapted them to explain the development of human societies. For example, the English philosopher Herbert Spencer (1820–1903) relied on theories of evolution to explain differences between the strong and the weak: successful individuals and races had competed better in the natural world and consequently evolved to higher states than did other, less fit peoples. On the basis of that reasoning, Spencer and others justified the domination of European imperialists over subject peoples as the inevitable result of natural scientific principles.

**Popular Racism** On a more popular level, there was no need for elaborate scientific theories to justify racist prejudices. Representatives of imperial and colonial powers routinely adopted racist views on the basis of personal experience, which seemed to confirm their superiority to subject peoples. For many, the simple fact of European conquest seemed to demonstrate European superiority over those they colonized since an inability to resist conquest seemed to demonstrate fundamental weakness.

Racist views were by no means a monopoly of European imperialists: U.S. and Japanese empire builders also developed a sense of superiority over the peoples they conquered and ruled. During the war to defeat Emiliano Auginaldo's independence fighters, U.S. forces in the Philippines disparaged the rebels they fought with racial slurs, and they did not hesitate to torture enemies in a conflict that was publicly justified as an effort to "civilize and Christianize" the Filipinos. In the 1890s Japanese newspapers portrayed Chinese and Korean peoples as dirty, backward, stupid, and cowardly. Some Japanese scholars concocted speculative theories that the Japanese

# Connecting the Sources

## Thinking about colonized peoples' responses to colonization

**The problem** For many years, the history of imperialism and colonialism was written from the point of view of the various colonizing powers. Colonial officials produced copious amounts of official and unofficial documents about colonial policies, their own experiences, and their opinions of colonized people. Not surprisingly, the histories written about colonialism using such sources tended to be biased in favor of the colonizers and frequently marginalized the experiences of colonized peoples themselves. In the last four decades, however, a plethora of histories have appeared that explore the colonial past from the point of view of colonized peoples, relying on previously underutilized sources such as court records, letters, memoirs, oral interviews, and fiction. Such sources have altered the way historians understand the massive imperial expansion that occurred in Asia and Africa in the nineteenth and first half of the twentieth centuries.

Let us consider two sources generated by people responding to British policies—one from China, the other from southern Africa—in order to think about what sources generated by the people who experienced colonialism can and cannot tell us.

The British Ironclad steamship HMS Nemesis destroying Chinese ships during the Opium War in 1841.
DEA Picture Library/De Agostini/Getty Images

**The documents** Read the documents below, and consider carefully the questions that follow.

### Document 1:

*The following resolution was produced in 1842—just after the defeat of the Chinese Empire by the British in the Opium War—by Chinese citizens at a large public meeting in the city of Canton (Guangzhou).*

> *Behold that vile English nation! Its ruler is at one time a woman, then a man, and then perhaps a woman again; its people are at one time like vultures, and then they are like wild beasts, with dispositions more fierce and furious than the tiger or wolf, and natures more greedy than anacondas or swine. These people having long steadily devoured all the western barbarians, and like demons of the night, they now suddenly exalt themselves here.*
>
> *During the reigns of the emperors Kien-lung [Qianlong] and Kia-king [Jiaqing] these English barbarians humbly besought an entrance and permission to deliver tribute and presents; they afterwards presumptuously asked to have Chu-san [the city of Zhoushan]; but our sovereigns, clearly perceiving their traitorous designs, gave them a determined refusal. From that time, linking themselves with traitorous Chinese traders, they have carried on a large trade and poisoned our brave people with opium.*
>
> *Verily, the English barbarians murder all of us that they can. They are dogs, whose desires can never be satisfied. Therefore we need not inquire whether the peace they have now made be real or pretended. Let us all rise, arm, unite, and go against them.*
>
> *We do here bind ourselves to vengeance, and express these our sincere intentions in order to exhibit our high principles and patriotism. The gods from on high now look down upon us; let us not lose our just and firm resolution.*

Which actions of the British caused the authors to find them so untrustworthy?

### Document 2:

*The following letter was written in 1858 by Moshweshewe I, founder of Basutoland and chief of the Basuto people in South Africa. It was directed to Sir George Grey, then governor of the Cape*

*Colony and high commissioner of South Africa, regarding Moshweshewe's treatment at the hands of white South African Afrikaners (called Boers by Moshweshewe).*

*. . . About twenty-five years ago my knowledge of the White men and their laws was very limited. I knew merely that mighty nations existed, and among them was the English. These, the blacks who were acquainted with them, praised for their justice. Unfortunately it was not with the English Government that my first intercourse with the whites commenced. People who had come from the Colony first presented themselves to us, they called themselves Boers. I thought all white men were honest. Some of these Boers asked permission to live upon our borders. I was led to believe they would live with me as my own people lived, that is, looking to me as to a father and a friend.*

*About sixteen years since, one of the [British] Governors of the [Cape] Colony, Sir George Napier, marked down my limits on a treaty he made with me. I was to be ruler within those limits. A short time after, another Governor came, it was Sir P. Maitland. The Boers then began to talk of their right to places I had then lent to them. Sir P. Maitland told me those people were subjects of the Queen, and should be kept under proper control; he did not tell me that he recognized any right they had to land within my country, but as it was difficult to take them away, it was proposed that all desiring to be under the British rule should live in that part near the meeting of the Orange and Caledon rivers.*

*Then came Sir Harry Smith, and he told me not to deprive any chief of their lands or their rights, he would see justice done to all, but in order to do so, he would make the Queen's Laws extend over every white man. He said the Whites and Blacks were to live together in peace. I could not understand what he would do. I thought it would be something very just, and that he was to keep the Boers in my land under proper control, and that I should hear no more of their claiming the places they lived on as their exclusive property. But instead of this, I now heard that the Boers consider all those farms as their own, and were buying and selling them one to the other, and driving out by one means or another my own people.*

*In vain I remonstrated. Sir Harry Smith had sent Warden to govern in the Sovereignty. He listened to the Boers, and he proposed that all the land in which those Boers' farms were should be taken from me. . . . One day he sent me a map and said, sign that, and I will tell those people . . . to leave off fighting: if you do not sign the map, I cannot help you in any way. I thought the Major was doing very improperly and unjustly. I was told to appeal to the Queen to put an end to this injustice. I did not wish to grieve Her Majesty by causing a war with her people. I was told if I did not sign the map, it would be the beginning of a great war. I signed, but soon after I sent my cry to the Queen. I begged Her to investigate my case and remove "the line," as it was called, by which my land was ruined. I thought justice would soon be done, and Warden put to rights. [Hostilities then broke out between the Boers and Moshweshewe's people, and Moshweshewe was thus requesting arbitration by Grey, the high commissioner]*

Moshweshewe I, 1786–1870.
A Short History of Lesotho by Stephen Gill

What was the main issue between Moshweshewe and the Boers (Afrikaners)?

## Questions

1. What can these documents definitively tell you about their respective writers' situations? What facts can be gleaned from these brief sources?
2. In Document 1, how do the Chinese who produced the resolution feel about the recent British victory? What have the British done to deserve such condemnation, in the group's view? How does the group propose to remedy the problem of the British in China?
3. In Document 2, why does Moshweshewe carefully recount his interactions with the various British officials who oversee the area in which Basutoland is situated? What kind of tone does Moshweshewe take in this letter, and why? Do you think Moshweshewe believes he has been treated fairly by the Boers and the British? What do you think happened when he signed the map?
4. What can these two documents tell us about the experience of colonialism in general? Do you imagine that the responses to domination suggested by these documents were common reactions to colonial expansion, or do you think responses would differ depending on the interests of the colonized group?
5. Sources such as these make up the building blocks on which historians base their interpretations of the past. How many sources do you think it would take in order to make accurate interpretations?

*Sources:* **Document 1:** "China, Japan, and the Islands of the Pacific, Vol. I." in *The World's Story: A History of the World in Story, Song, and Art,* edited by Eva March Tappan, 197. Boston: Houghton Mifflin, 1914. **Document 2:** Letter from the Chief Moshesh to the High Commissioner in 1858." in *Basutoland Records: Copies of Official Documents of Various Kinds, Accounts of Travellers, &, Volume 2,* edited by George McCall Theal, 384. Bosman Street: Government of Capetown, 1883.

people were more akin to the "Aryans," who supposedly had conquered much of the Eurasian landmass in ancient times, than to the "Mongolians" who populated China and Korea. After the Japanese victory in the Russo-Japanese War, political and military leaders came to believe that Japan had an obligation to oversee the affairs of their backward neighbors and help civilize their "little Asian brothers."

## Anticolonial and Nationalist Movements

While imperialists convinced themselves of their racial superiority, colonial rule provoked subject peoples to develop a sense of their own identities. Just as Napoleon's invasions aroused national feelings and led to the emergence of nationalist movements in Europe, so imperial expansion and colonial domination prompted the organization of anticolonial movements and the formation of national identities. In the late nineteenth and early twentieth centuries, the potential of imperialism and colonialism to push subject peoples toward nationalism was most evident in India.

**Ram Mohan Roy** During the nineteenth century, educated Indian elites helped forge a sense of Indian identity. Among the most influential of them was **Ram Mohan Roy** (1772–1833), a prominent Bengali intellectual sometimes called the "father of modern India." Roy argued for the construction of a society based on both modern European values and the Indian tradition of devotional Hinduism. He supported some British colonial policies, and he worked with Christian social reformers to improve the status of Indian women by providing them with education and property rights. Yet Roy saw himself as a Hindu reformer who drew inspiration from the Vedas and Upanishads and who sought to bring Hindu spirituality to bear on the problems and conditions of his own time. During the last two decades of his life, Roy tirelessly published newspapers and founded societies to mobilize educated Hindus and advance the cause of social reform in colonial India.

Reform societies flourished in nineteenth-century India. Many of them appealed to upper-caste Hindus, but some were Muslim organizations, and a few represented the interests of peasants, landlords, or lower castes. After mid-century, reformers increasingly called for self-government or at least greater Indian participation in government. Their leaders often had received an advanced education at British universities, and they drew inspiration from European Enlightenment values such as equality, freedom, and popular sovereignty. But they invoked those values to criticize the British colonial regime in India and to call for political and social reform.

**The Indian National Congress** The most important of the reform groups was the **Indian National Congress,** founded in 1885 as a forum for educated Indians to communicate their views on public affairs to colonial officials. Representatives from all parts of the subcontinent aired grievances about Indian poverty, the transfer of wealth from India to Britain, trade and tariff policies that harmed Indian businesses, the

Much of western India experienced severe famine in 1896–1897, and epidemics of bubonic plague broke out among weakened populations. British relief efforts were often heavy-handed and insensitive, and they did little to alleviate the problems. Historic Images/Alamy Stock Photo

inability of colonial officials to provide effective relief for regions stricken by drought or famine, and British racism toward Indians. By the end of the nineteenth century, the congress openly sought Indian self-rule within a larger imperial framework. In 1916 the congress joined forces with the All-India Muslim League, the most prominent organization working to advance the political and social interests of Muslims, who made up about 25 percent of the Indian population.

Faced with increasing demands for Indian participation in government, in 1909 colonial authorities granted a limited franchise that allowed wealthy Indians to elect representatives to local legislative councils. By that time, however, the drive for political reform had become a mass movement. Indian nationalists called for independence, mounted demonstrations to build support for their cause, and organized boycotts of British goods. Other anticolonial activists turned to violence and sought to undermine British rule by bombing government buildings and assassinating colonial officials.

Although local experiences varied considerably, Indian anticolonial and nationalist movements served as models for anticolonial campaigns in other lands. In many cases, the leaders of those movements were European-educated elites who absorbed Enlightenment values and then turned those values into an attack on European colonial rule in foreign lands.

## CONCLUSION

The construction of global empires in the nineteenth century noticeably increased the tempo of world integration. Armed with powerful transportation, communication, and military technologies, European peoples imposed their rule on much of Asia and almost all of Africa. Toward the end of the nineteenth century, the United States and Japan joined European states as global imperialists. All the imperial powers profoundly influenced the development of the societies they ruled. They shaped the economies and societies of their colonies by pushing them to supply natural resources and agricultural commodities in exchange for manufactured products, and they facilitated the movement of workers to lands where there was high demand for labor on plantations or in mines. They also developed racist ideologies that sought to justify conquest and brutal violence. In response, colonized people developed increasingly strong anticolonial and nationalist movements whose goal was to remove the imperial powers altogether. From the early twentieth century forward, much of global history has revolved around issues stemming from the world order established by imperialism and colonialism.

## STUDY TERMS

Berlin West Africa Conference (660)
Cecil John Rhodes (650)
direct rule (662)
East India Company (654)
Emilio Aguinaldo (666)
Great Game (656)
indentured labor (670)
Indian National Congress (674)
indirect rule (662)
Khoikhoi (659)
Leopold II (659)
Lili'uokalani (665)
Maori (663)
*mission civilisatrice* (651)
Monroe Doctrine (664)
Omdurman (652)
*The Origin of Species* (670)
Panama Canal (653)
Ram Mohan Roy (674)
Roosevelt Corollary (666)
Russo-Japanese War (667)
scientific racism (671)
scramble for Africa (658)
South African War (660)
Spanish-Cuban-American War (665)
Suez Canal (653)
survival of the fittest (670)
*terra nullius* (663)
Treaty of Waitangi (663)
Xhosa (659)

## FOR FURTHER READING

Clare Anderson. *Subaltern Lives: Biographies of Colonialism in the Indian Ocean World, 1790–1920.* Cambridge, 2012. Explores the experience of colonialism through the perspective of convicts, sailors, enslaved people, and indentured laborers.

Tony Ballantyne and Antoinette Burton. *Bodies in Contact: Rethinking Colonial Encounters in World History.* Durham, 2005. Collection of essays that explore the body as a critical site of cultural encounter in the context of colonialism.

Sugata Bose. *A Hundred Horizons: The Indian Ocean in the Age of Global Empires.* Cambridge, Mass., 2006. A bold interregional history that argues that the peoples of the Indian Ocean littoral shared a common historical destiny.

Jane Burbank and Frederick Cooper. *Empires in World History: Power and the Politics of Difference.* Princeton, 2010. A major study that considers modern empires in historical context.

Ken S. Coates. *A Global History of Indigenous Peoples: Struggle and Survival.* Houndmills, U.K., 2004. Stressing the active role of indigenous peoples, this work examines the dynamics of colonial encounters.

John Darwin. *Unfinished Empire: The Global Expansion of Britain.* London and New York, 2013. The author has fashioned a sweeping and sober account of one of the longest-lived and most influential empires in world history.

Daniel R. Headrick. *Power over Peoples: Technology, Environments, and Western Imperialism, 1400 to the Present.* Princeton, 2009. Explores the central role of technological innovation in the rise and fall of imperialism.

Eric T. L. Love. *Race over Empire: Racism and U.S. Imperialism, 1865–1900.* Chapel Hill, N.C., 2004. In this critical reinterpretation, the author challenges the prevailing notion that racism abetted imperialism, notwithstanding the fact that many imperialists were racists.

Heather Streets-Salter and Trevor Getz. *Empires and Colonies in the Modern World.* Oxford, 2015. Explores the structures and ideologies of imperialism and colonialism since 1400 from a global perspective.

H. L. Wesseling. *The European Colonial Empires: 1815–1919.* New York, 2004. Puts the process of colonization into a comparative and long-term perspective.

# CHAPTER 20 AP EXAM PRACTICE

Questions assume cumulative knowledge from this chapter and previous chapters.

## Section I

## Multiple Choice Questions

Use the image below and your knowledge of world history to answer questions 1-3.

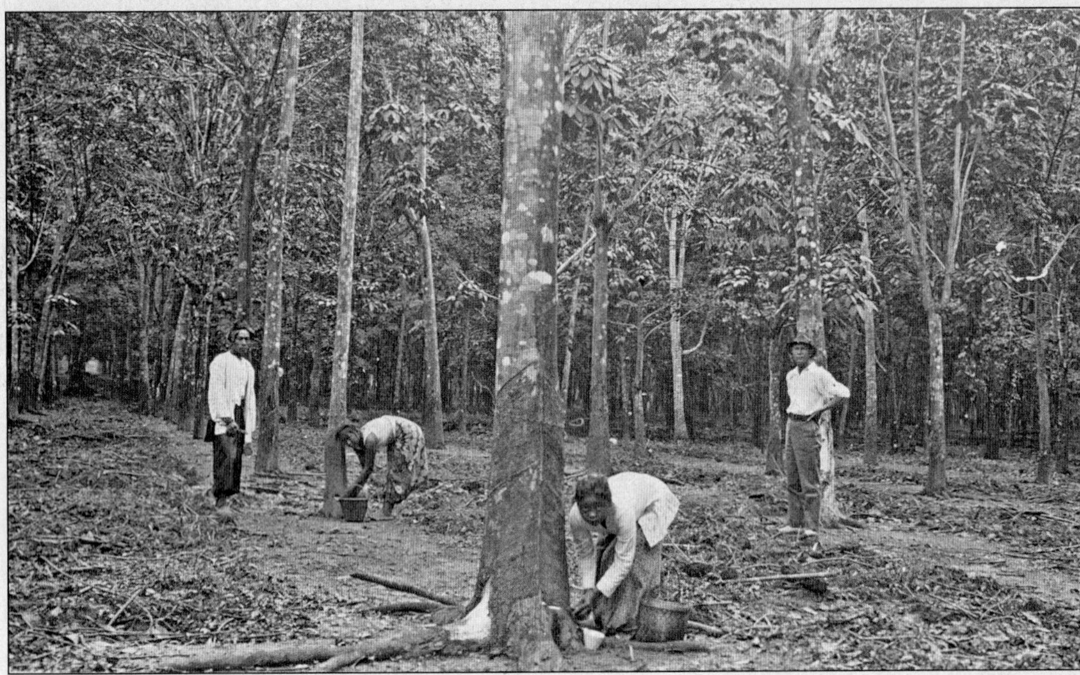

Rubber tapping on a plantation in Sumatra in the Dutch East Indies (modern Indonesia) in the early twentieth century.
Sepia Times/Universal Images Group/Getty Images

1. Which of the following is an economic reason why imperialists were interested in expanding European empires?
   (A) Industrial economies required new raw materials that could not be produced in Europe.
   (B) King Leopold II of Belgium wanted to play a larger role in world politics.
   (C) The story of Stanley and Livingstone made people excited for adventures.
   (D) Industrial economies needed to export European raw materials.

2. Which of the following was a political motivation for imperialism?
   (A) Christian missionaries believed it was their purpose to spread their faith to more areas of the world.
   (B) The French victory in the Franco-Prussian War of 1870-71 made the French government confident they could conquer more colonies.
   (C) By focusing on empire building, European politicians thought they could defuse social tensions at home.
   (D) Industrialists wanted to have new markets to purchase their products.

3. Which author celebrated imperialism?
   (A) Moshweshewe I
   (B) Ram Mohan Roy
   (C) Rudyard Kipling
   (D) Emilio Aguinaldo

Use the map below and your knowledge of world history to answer questions 4 and 5.

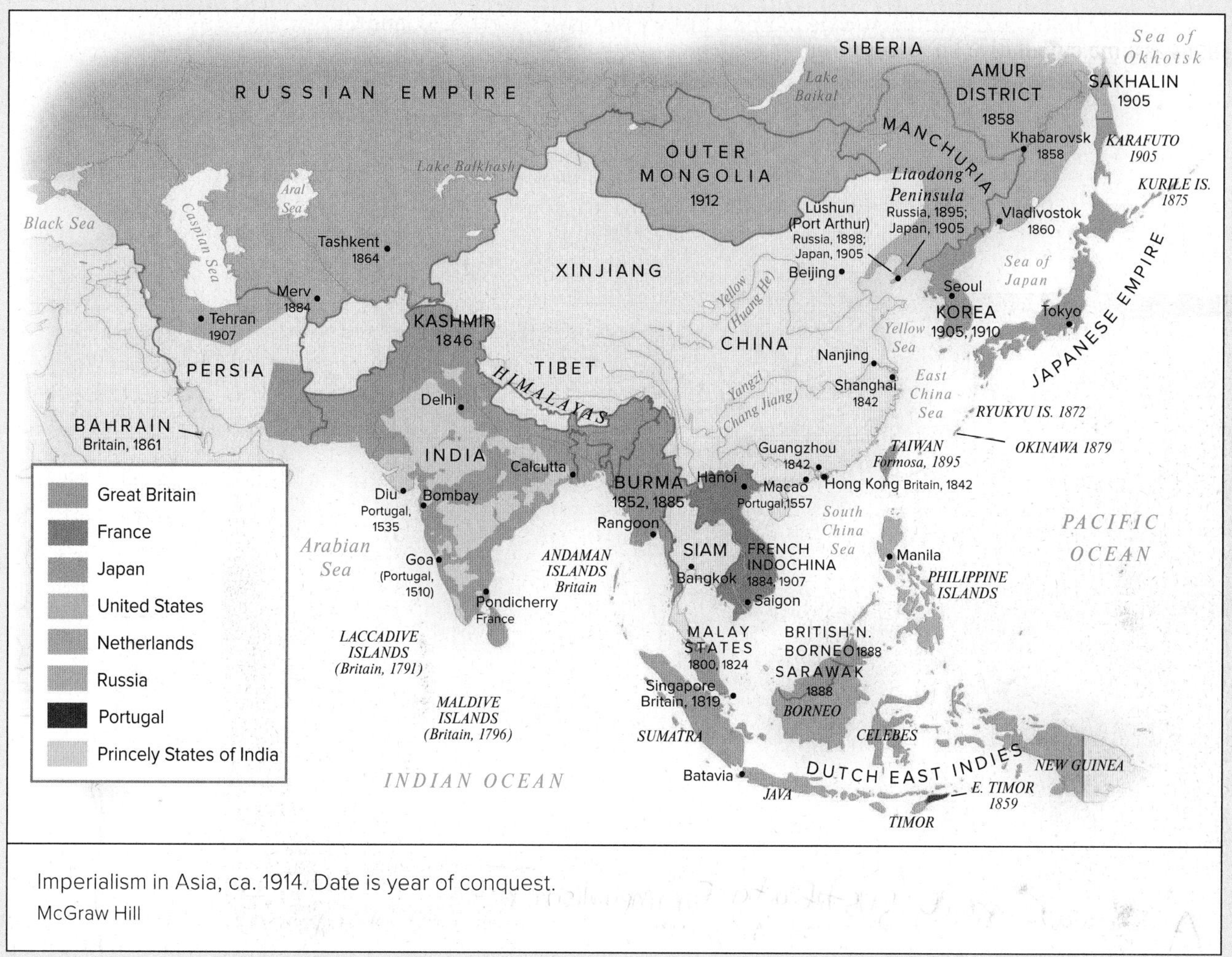


Imperialism in Asia, ca. 1914. Date is year of conquest.
McGraw Hill

4. What interest did the Russians have in Central Asia?
   (A) They were playing games with the British.
   (B) They wanted control of the caravan cities of the Silk Roads.
   (C) They wanted more ports on the Black Sea.
   (D) They wanted to compensate for the islands lost to the Japanese.

5. Why were some areas not subject to an imperial power in 1914?
   (A) The flooding of the Yellow and Yangzi rivers made them difficult to conquer.
   (B) No European state was able to prove "effective occupation" for China.
   (C) The petroleum exporting countries had formed their own empire.
   (D) While China still governed itself, much of its territory was controlled by Japan or a European state.

## Short Answer

6. Use the image below and your knowledge of world history to answer parts A, B, and C.

A British Maxim gun at Chilas Fort on India's Northwest Frontier in the late nineteenth century.
Hulton Archive/Getty Images

(A) Identify ONE way in which European racism became more institutionalized in the nineteenth century.
(B) Explain ONE way that imperialism played a role in migration.
(C) Identify ONE technological factor that helped Europeans create massive overseas empires.

A. It gave people justification for imperialism beause it gave the Europeans a sense of superiority. As racism became more institutionalized & more part of every-day European life & industries, it became evident in the eyes

B. In Australia, the Maori ppl were kicked out by british

C. "iron-clad" steamships allowed Europeans to do so.

7. Use the map below and your knowledge of world history to answer parts A, B, and C.

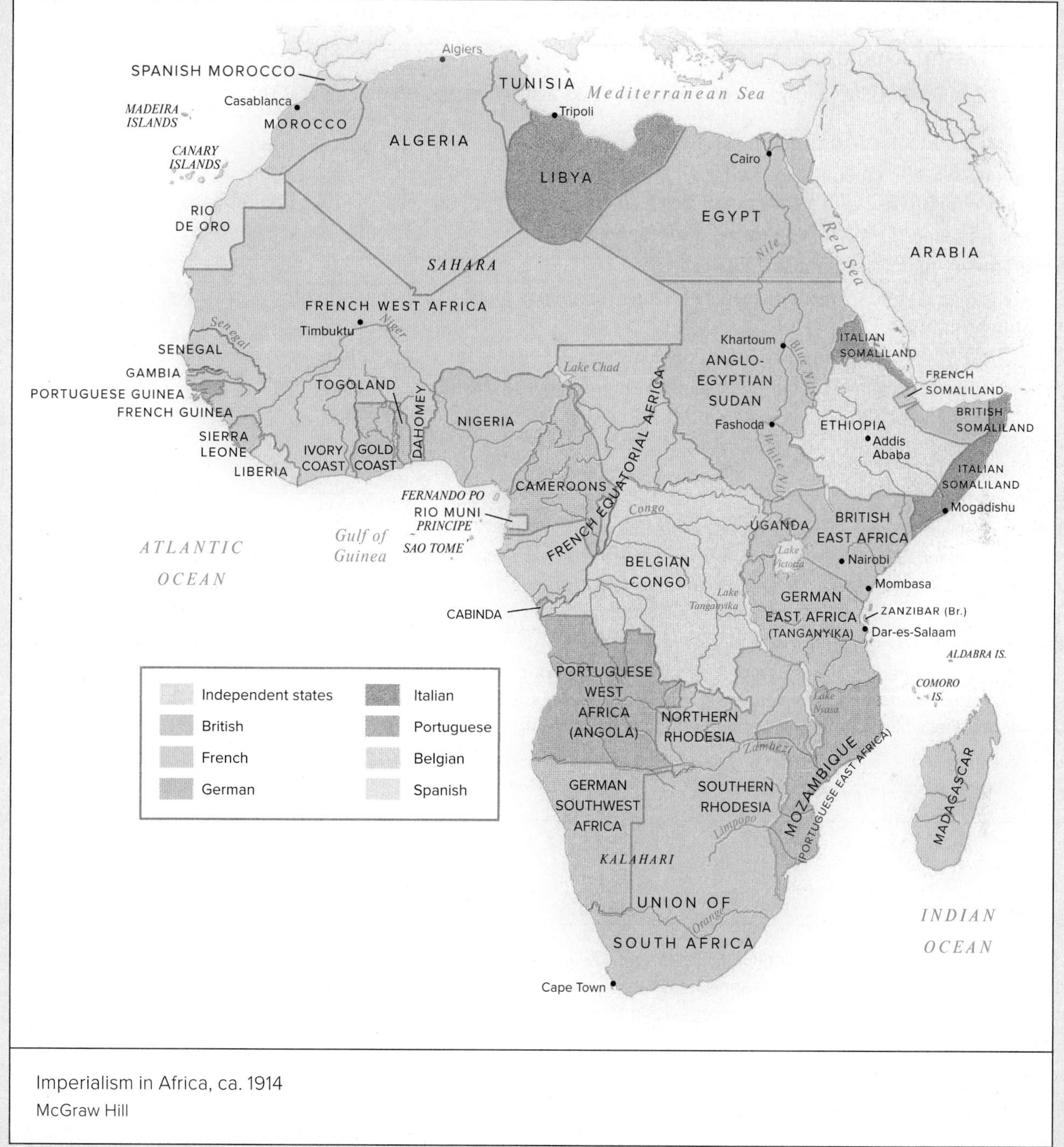


Imperialism in Africa, ca. 1914
McGraw Hill

(A) Identify ONE way this map illustrates the "Scramble for Africa."
(B) Explain ONE way the Berlin Conference affected African independence.
(C) Explain ONE reason why conflicts in South Africa were different from other African colonial situations.

8. Use your understanding of world history to answer parts A, B, and C.
(A) Identify ONE way that educated Hindus wanted to reform India. ← nationalism
(B) Explain ONE result of the Indian Rebellion in 1857. ← direct British rule
(C) Explain ONE way the Indian National Congress responded to colonialism
↑ Very negatively w/ much distaste for the famine that britain allowed.

# Section II

## Document-Based Question

Based on the documents below and your knowledge of world history, compare and contrast the responses to imperialism in the nineteenth century.

In your response you should do the following:

- Respond to the prompt with a historically defensible thesis or claim that establishes a line of reasoning.
- Describe a broader historical context relevant to the prompt.
- Support an argument in response to the prompt using all documents.
- Use at least one additional piece of specific historical evidence (beyond that found in the documents) relevant to an argument about the prompt.
- Explain how or why the document's point of view, purpose, historical situation, and /or audience is relevant to an argument.
- Use evidence to corroborate, qualify, or modify an argument that addresses the prompt.

### Document 1

I, Liliuokalani of Hawaii, named heir apparent on the 10th day of April, 1877, and proclaimed Queen of the Hawaiian Islands on the 29th day of January, 1891, do hereby earnestly and respectfully protest against the assertion of ownership by the United States of America of the so-called Hawaiian Crown Lands amounting to about one million acres and which are my property, and I especially protest against such assertion of ownership as a taking of property without due process of law and without just or other compensation.

Therefore, supplementing my protest of June 17, 1897, I call upon the President and the National Legislature and the People of the United States to do justice in this matter and to restore to me this property, the enjoyment of which is being withheld from me by your Government under what must be a mis-apprehension of my right and title.

*Source:* Letter from Liliuokalani, Queen of Hawaii to U.S. House of Representatives protesting U.S. assertion of ownership of Hawaii, December 19, 1898. RG 233, Records of the U.S. House of Representatives, National Archives.

### Document 2

During the reigns of the emperors Kien-lung [Qianlong] and Kia-king [Jiaqing] these English barbarians humbly besought an entrance and permission to deliver tribute and presents; they afterwards presumptuously asked to have Chu-san [the city of Zhoushan]; but our sovereigns, clearly perceiving their traitorous designs, gave them a determined refusal. From that time, linking themselves with traitorous Chinese traders, they have carried on a large trade and poisoned our brave people with opium.

Verily, the English barbarians murder all of us that they can. They are dogs, whose desires can never be satisfied. Therefore we need not inquire whether the peace they have now made be real or pretended. Let us all rise, arm, unite, and go against them.

*Source:* "China, Japan, and the Islands of the Pacific, Vol. I." in *The World's Story: A History of the World in Story, Song, and Art,* edited by Eva March Tappan, 197. Boston: Houghton Mifflin, 1914.

## Document 3

Emperor Menelik II of Ethiopia (r. 1889–1913) on the throne in coronation garb.
MARKA/Alamy Stock Photo

## Long Essay

Develop a thoughtful and thorough historical argument that answers the question below. Begin your essay with a thesis statement and support it with relevant historical evidence.

Using specific examples and your knowledge of world history, explain the role of nationalism in the imperial expansion of the United States and Japan.

# Part 3 Revolutions and Consequences of Industrialization (1750–1900)

At the 1781 British surrender to colonial American troops in Yorktown, the British band reputedly played the march "The World Turned Upside Down." Whether that is a true story or not, the tune's title offered an appropriate commentary on how the state of the world was indeed experiencing dramatic changes, not just by political revolutions, but also by industrialization and the new imperialism. When the underrated colonial and guerrilla forces defeated the imperial army of Great Britain, the most powerful nation in the world, that world did indeed seem upside down. A subject population of the British empire had bested its rulers and overthrown monarchy in favor of a republican form of government.

As "the people" became the source for national sovereignty in much of the Atlantic basin, revolution brought about the beheading of a king and a queen in France and the elevation of the formerly enslaved to the status of national leaders in Haiti. Throughout Europe, the Caribbean, and Latin America, old governments fell under the pressure of revolutionary ideals and a new sort of nationalism. Similarly, the economic transformations linked to industrialization contributed to a world seemingly upended, whereby machines, factories, and inanimate sources of power and energy ruled over human life and nature. Industrialization likewise promoted mass migrations of Europeans and Asians to the Americas, literally repositioning human populations across hemispheres. Migrants, indigenous peoples, people freed from slavery, and women agitated for their democratic rights and equality in these new industrial and expansionist national states, but most of the world did not immediately undergo revolution inspired by Enlightenment ideals of liberty, equality, and popular sovereignty.

Some of the oldest, most prestigious, and most powerful territories in the world, from the Ottoman empire and Africa to Russia, China, and Japan, found themselves challenged by the upstart new imperialists in Europe and the United States, their sovereignty and freedom impinged upon by the powerful combination of nationalism, industry, and militarism. Resistance to this world turned upside down persisted, however. On the foundation of thoroughgoing reform, Japan managed to attain parity with European empires. Colonial subjects from India to Africa engaged in large-scale rebellion and small acts of resistance. What North American colonists began in the late eighteenth century, colonial peoples in Africa and Asia finished in the twentieth century. After Europe imploded from within during two cataclysmic world wars, colonized peoples would turn the world upside down once again.

The world in 1900 looked very different from the world in 1750. Consider how these political, social, and economic revolutions have added to your understanding of the AP World History Themes.

Heritage Images/Hulton Fine Art Collection/Getty Images

## THEME 1: HUMANS AND THE ENVIRONMENT (ENV)

The environment shapes human societies, and as populations grow and change, these populations in turn shape their environments.

## THEME 2: CULTURAL DEVELOPMENTS AND INTERACTIONS (CDI)

The development of ideas, beliefs, and religions illustrates how groups in society view themselves, and the interactions of societies and their beliefs often have political, social, and cultural implications.

## THEME 3: GOVERNANCE (GOV)

A variety of internal and external factors contribute to state formation, expansion, and decline. Governments maintain order through a variety of administrative institutions, policies, and procedures, and governments obtain, retain, and exercise power in different ways and for different purposes.

## THEME 4: ECONOMIC SYSTEMS (ECN)

As societies develop, they affect and are affected by the ways that they produce, exchange, and consume goods and services.

## THEME 5: SOCIAL INTERACTIONS AND ORGANIZATION (SIO)

The process by which societies group their members and the norms that govern the interactions between these groups and between individuals influence political, economic, and cultural institutions and organization.

## THEME 6: TECHNOLOGY AND INNOVATION (TEC)

Human adaptation and innovation have resulted in increased efficiency, comfort, and security, and technological advances have shaped human development and interactions with both intended and unintended consequences.

Science & Society Picture Library/SSPL/Getty Images, The Art Archive/Shutterstock, DEA/G. Dagli Orti/De Agostini/Getty Images, John Stevenson/Corbis Historical/Getty Images, Dea picture library/De Agostini/Getty Images

# PART 3 AP EXAM PRACTICE

Questions assume cumulative knowledge from this Part.

## Section I

## Multiple Choice Questions

Questions 1–3 have no stimulus.

1. Which of the following was NOT and environmental factor that contributed to industrialization?
   (A) Access to rivers and canals
   (B) Lack of humidity
   (C) Access to coal, iron, and timber
   (D) Agricultural productivity

2. What did Fukuzawa Yukichi do for Japan?
   (A) He traveled to the United States and wrote about constitutional government.
   (B) He organized the overthrow of the Tokugawa *bakufu*.
   (C) He wrote the slogan "Revere the emperor, expel the barbarians."
   (D) He built the Japanese railroad system.

3. The religious movement associated with the Enlightenment is known as
   (A) Transcendentalism
   (B) Stoicism
   (C) Deism
   (D) Dispensationalism

Using the map below and your knowledge of world history, answer questions 4-6.

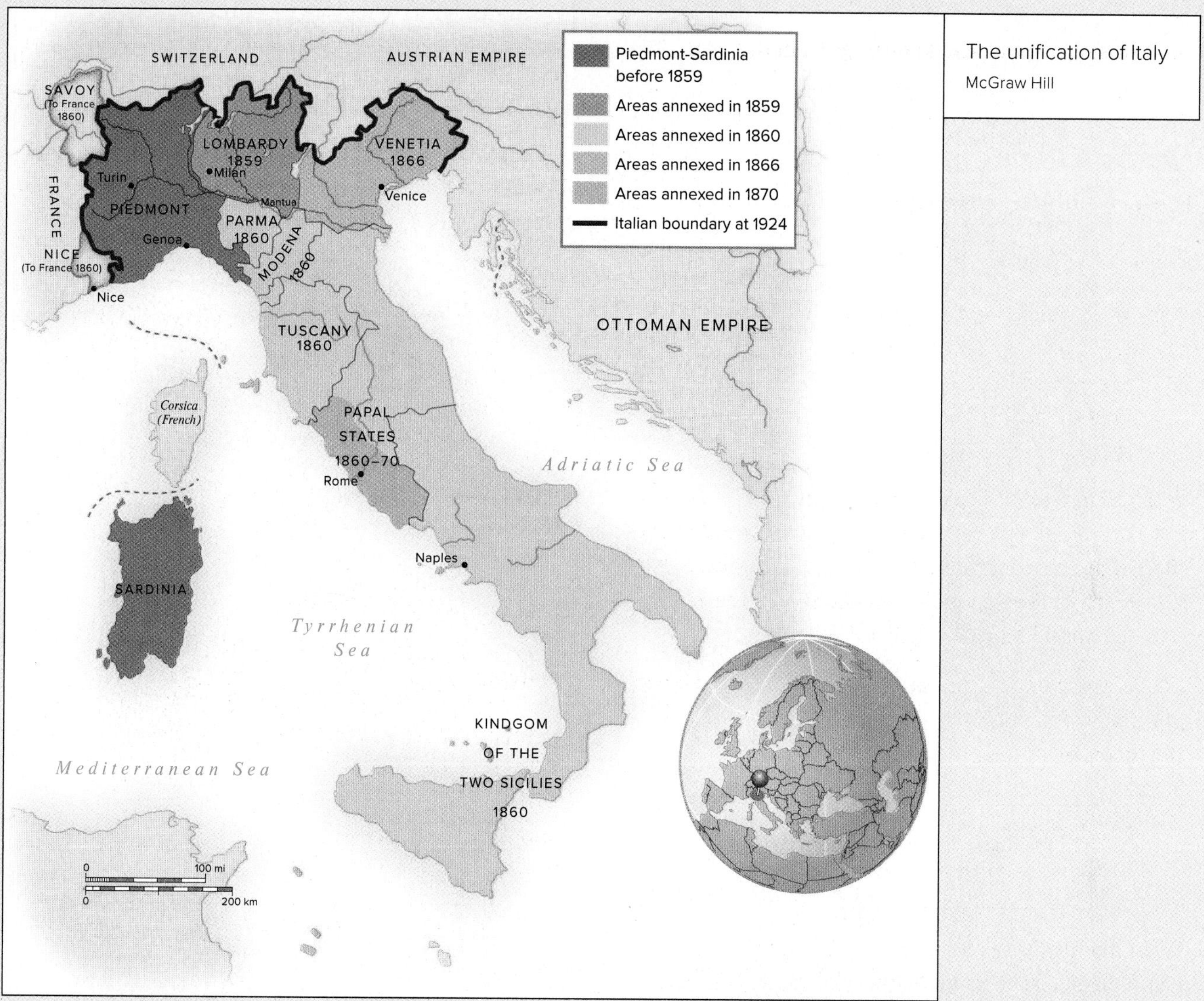


The unification of Italy

McGraw Hill

4. Why did the Congress of Vienna give northern Italy to Austria?
   (A) The Congress wanted to give Austria control of the mountain passes to Switzerland.
   (B) They planned to let Austria invade the whole Italian peninsula.
   (C) They wanted the German-speaking people of the Italian Alps to be ruled by a German-speaking state.
   (D) They wanted a strong, unified state near the French border to prevent further war.

5. What kind of nationalism was promoted by Giuseppe Mazzini and the Young Italy movement?
   (A) Political nationalism
   (B) Imperial nationalism
   (C) Cultural nationalism
   (D) Socialist nationalism

6. What did Camillo di Cavour contribute to the unification of Italy?
   (A) He made and alliance with France to expel the Spanish from Italy.
   (B) He made an alliance with France to expel the Austrians from Italy.
   (C) He persuaded to British parliament to support Giuseppe Garibaldi's revolutionaries.
   (D) He led an army of one thousand soldiers wearing red shirts to liberate Sicily.

Using the image below and your knowledge of world history, answer questions 7–9.

Apache youths at the Carlisle Indian School in Pennsylvania.
Historical/Corbis Historical/Getty Images

7. What did the Dawes Severalty Act of 1887 do?
   (A) It created schools for Native American children.
   (B) It started a land grant program for the formerly enslaved after the Civil War.
   (C) It changed collective land holding on reservations to individual land holding.
   (D) It created funding to build the railroad across Canada.

8. What was the purpose of the schools for indigenous children?
   (A) To prepare them for college and careers.
   (B) To train them for jobs in factories.
   (C) To eliminate indigenous cultures and languages.
   (D) To prepare students for missionary work.

9. What claim could a historian make about the schools based on this photograph?
   (A) Native American children were forced to assimilate by adopting Euro-American clothing and hairstyles.
   (B) The over hunting of bison forced Native Americans to move east to look for work.
   (C) The métis people of the Red River Settlement created their own school system.
   (D) The nationalist ideals that developed in the United States included non-European cultures.

Using the text selection below and your knowledge of world history, answer questions 10–12.

> In many subtle ways they make us feel their dislike. "I am a European, you are a Javanese," they seem to say, or "I am the master, you the governed." Not once, but many times, they speak to us in broken Malay; although they know very well that we understand the Dutch language . . .
>
> Why do many Hollanders find it unpleasant to converse with us in their own language? Oh yes, now I understand; Dutch is too beautiful to be spoken by a brown mouth.
>
> A few days ago we paid a visit to Totokkers [Europeans new to the East Indies]. Their domestics were old servants of ours, and we knew that they could speak and understand Dutch very well. I told the host this, and what answer did I receive from my gentleman? "No, they must not speak Dutch." "No, why?" I asked. "Because natives ought not to know Dutch." I looked at him in amazement, and a satirical smile quivered at the corners of my mouth. The gentleman grew fiery red, mumbled something into his beard, and discovered something interesting in his boots, at least he devoted all of his attention to them.
>
> *Source:* Kartini, Raden Adjeng. *Letters of a Javanese Princess*. London: Duckworth & Co., 1921.

10. What does the author dislike about the newly arrived Europeans?
    (A) They take jobs away from the local population.
    (B) The industries they create destroy the environment.
    (C) They forced the Javanese to speak Dutch.
    (D) They wanted to prevent the Javanese from learning to speak Dutch.

11. What historical development can be seen in this document?
    (A) The Portuguese rebuilt their empire in the Indian Ocean.
    (B) The British navy took control of the sea lanes linking Malaya to the Indian Ocean.
    (C) The Dutch extended their control over the East Indies to produce more cash crops.
    (D) European adventurers engaged in the "Great Game" of empire.

12. How is the author's point of view relevant to the story she tells?
    (A) The author was from a poor family who had been educated in languages, so she promotes the linguistic skills of the servants.
    (B) The author was a woman from a noble family who worked to expand education to Indonesian women, so her emphasis on knowing languages reflects her background.
    (C) The author had plans to move to the Netherlands and wanted to show that she and other Indonesians could assimilate to Dutch culture.
    (D) The author spoke fluent Dutch, but she was ashamed that working-class Indonesians could not.

Questions 13–15 have no stimulus..

13. The Egyptians build factories to produce what product?
    (A) Porcelain
    (B) Steel
    (C) Steam engines
    (D) Cotton textiles

14. What was the main issue between Moshweshewe I and the British?
    (A) The British had moved onto his land and were refusing to leave.
    (B) The British paid the Afrikaners (Boers) to build a railroad that crossed through his territory.
    (C) The British were encouraging a war between the Xhosa and Khoikhoi states.
    (D) The British were not following their agreement to enforce the law and control the Afrikaners (Boers).

15. What did granting extraterritoriality to the British in China in the Treaty of Nanjing mean?
    (A) The British took extra territories in China as their colonies.
    (B) British people in China were not subject to Chinese law.
    (C) British residents in China had to pay extra taxes.
    (D) The Chinese government doubled the number of licenses for British merchants to trade in Chinese products.

## Short Answer

16. Use the map below and your knowledge of world history to answer parts A, B, and C.

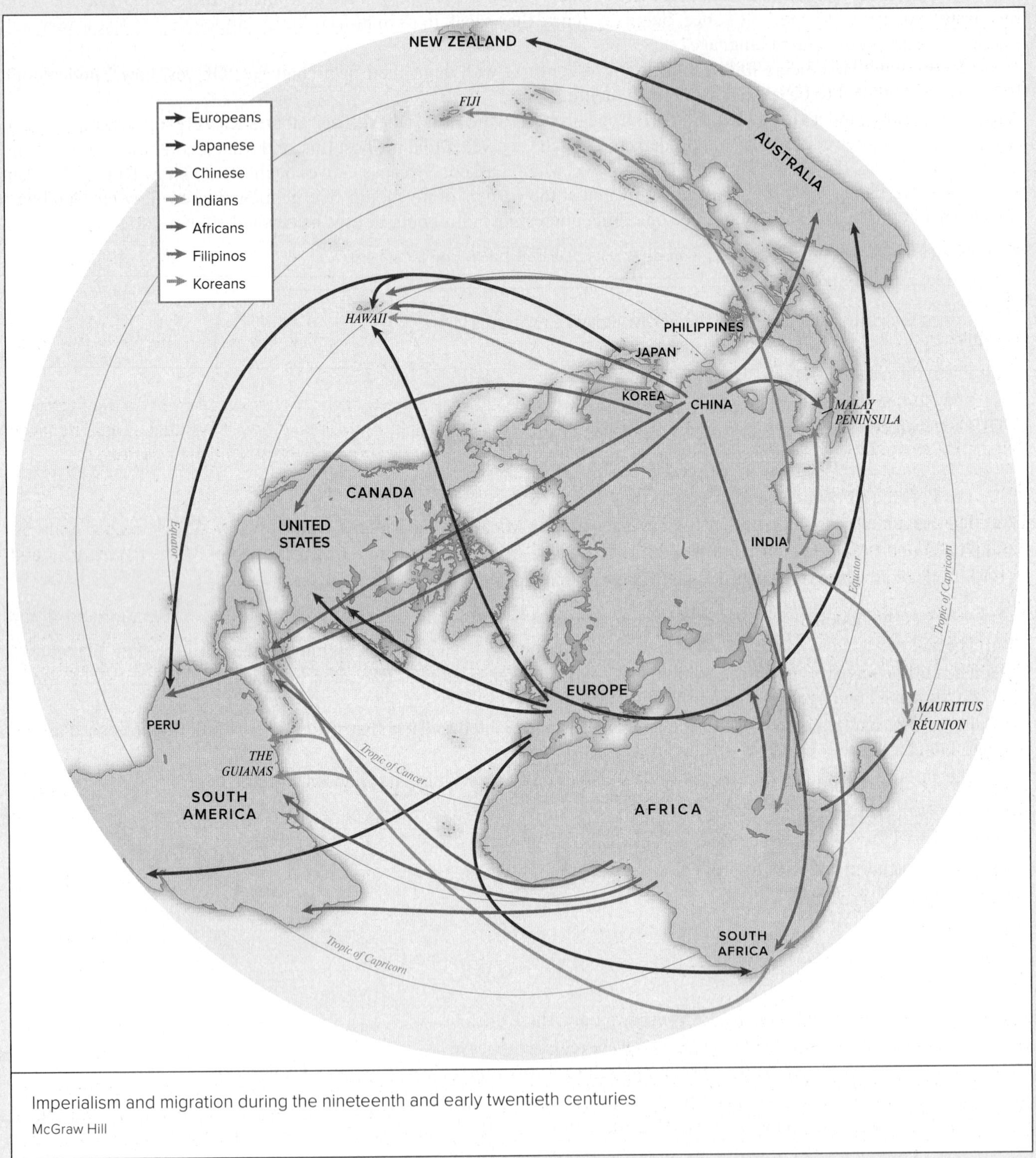


Imperialism and migration during the nineteenth and early twentieth centuries
McGraw Hill

(A) Explain ONE reason why Europeans migrated in the nineteenth and early twentieth centuries.
(B) Explain ONE reason why Asian, Africans, and Pacific Islanders migrated in the nineteenth and early twentieth centuries.
(C) Identify ONE technology that contributed to migrations.

17. Using the text excerpts below and your knowledge of world history, answer parts A, B, and C.

## Source 1

JOURNAL, Containing the Complaints, Grievances, and Claims of the Free-citizens and colored landowners of the French Islands and Colonies:

Article I. The inhabitants of the French colonies are exclusively and generally divided into two classes, Freemen and those who are born, and live, in slavery.

Article II. The class of Freemen includes not only all the Whites, but also all of the colored Creoles, the Free Blacks, Mulattos, small minorities, and others.

Article III. The freed Creoles, as well as their children and their descendants, should have the same rights, rank, prerogatives, exemptions, and privileges as other colonists.

Article IV. For that purpose, the colored Creoles request that the Declaration of the Rights of Man, decreed by the National Assembly, be applied to them, as it is to Whites. Therefore, it is requested that Articles LVII and LIX of the Edict [the Black Code] dated March 1685, be rewritten and carried out in accordance with their form and content.

Article. V. With disregard for the law, humiliating distinctions have been made until now between White men and men of color, in whichever class Nature may have placed them. To bring an end to these distinctions, resolutions must be taken that irrevocably set the respective rights and claims of those Citizens who oppress, and those who are oppressed.

Article. VI. Consequently, the National Assembly shall be requested to declare:

That Negroes and colored Creoles shall be admitted, concurrently with Whites, to all ranks, positions, responsibilities, dignities, and honors. In a word, they want to share with Whites the difficult and honorable roles of Civil government and Military service;

That in order to achieve this, they shall have access to the courts. Additionally, they shall be eligible to attain, not only the highest ranks of the Judiciary, but it would also be just that they have the freedom to fulfill the secondary roles. These functions would include: solicitor, public notary, state prosecutor, court clerk, bailiff, and any other function, regardless of title, either in France or in the Colonies.

That they shall be promoted equally with their class peers, and may try for all military positions and responsibilities, such that their color can no longer be a reason for exclusion.

That the Companies of Volunteers, Negroes, Mulattos, and small minorities, confused one with another and mixed together, shall cease as a pretext to create a distinction which should not exist between free men. That from this day on, they shall be indiscriminately made up of Whites and men of Color, without, under any pretext, the latter being excluded. . . .

8. That the priesthood, sciences, arts, professions, in a word, all of the trades, shall be accessible to citizens of color, as, to date, they have been reserved for Whites.

9. That there shall be established in the different colonies public grade schools and high schools in which Creoles of color, and even free Blacks or their children, are admitted concurrently with Whites, without any preference or any kind of predilection. . . .

Article VIII. This article shall be replaced by a disposition that simultaneously consecrates the dignity of man, the honor and safety of women slaves, their rights and the rights of their children.

For that purpose, explicit interdictions and punishments shall be given to all Citizen slave-owners of either sex and either White or of color. They shall be forbidden, under penalty, to live as husband and wife, or even cohabit in any way with their slaves. When proof of this is obtained, a fine of 1000 livres shall be given to the poor, and the slave with whom the master had lived shall be granted absolute freedom.

*(Continued)*

Article IX. These same restrictions shall apply to any free man and a female slave belonging to any other citizen.

Article X. In the case that Article VIII or IX above is breached by Free men who have cohabited with Slaves and escaped punishment heretofore indicated and who have one or more children from the cohabitation, the woman, by the sole fact of being pregnant, and the children, at the instant of their birth, shall be and shall remain free, and be masters of their own person and of their rights. . . .

Article XXII. Article VI of the Edict of 1724 forbids, as being against Natural laws, religion and civil liberties, and even contradictory to Article IX of the Edict of 1685, Whites of either sex from entering into a contract of marriage with Blacks. The National Assembly shall also be requested to revoke this, and to leave, to Whites as well as to Blacks, the freedom of being united by the bonds of Matrimony.

*Source:* Cahiers, contenant les plaintes, Doleances, et reclamations des citoyens-libre et proprietaires de couleur, des isles et colonies Françaises (Paris, 1789).

## Source 2

**First Article. Men are born** and remain free and equal in rights. Social distinctions may be based only on common utility. Article 2. The goal of every political association is the preservation of the natural and inalienable rights of man. These rights are liberty, property, security, and resistance to oppression. Article 3. The principle of all sovereignty resides essentially in the nation. No body and no individual can exercise authority that does not flow directly from the nation. Article 4. Liberty consists in the freedom to do anything that does not harm another. The exercise of natural rights of each man thus has no limits except those that assure other members of society their enjoyment of the same rights. These limits may be deter-mined only by law . . . Article 6. Law is the expression of the general will. All citizens have the right to participate either personally or through their representatives in the making of law. The law must be the same for all, whether it protects or punishes. Being equal in the eyes of the law, all citizens are equally eligible for all public honors, offices, and occupations, according to their abilities, without any distinction other than that of their virtues and talents.

*Source: Déclaration des droits de l'homme et du citoyen.* Translated by Jerry H. Bentley.

(A) Explain ONE similarity between Source 1 and Source 2.

(B) Explain ONE difference between Source 1 and Source 2.

(C) Identify ONE Enlightenment idea in either Source 1 or Source 2.

18. Use your knowledge of history to answer all parts of the questions that follow.

(A) Identify ONE movement or organization that showed workers' discontent with industrialization.

(B) Explain ONE argument Marx and Engels made against capitalism.

(C) Explain ONE assertion in *The Communist Manifesto* about the future of capitalism.

## Section II

## Document-Based Question

Suggested reading and writing time: 1 hour
It is suggested that you spend 15 minutes reading the documents and 45 minutes writing your response.

Note: You may begin writing your response before the reading period is over.
The documents have been edited for the purpose of this exercise.

Based on your analysis of the documents below, evaluate the effect of imperialism on the production and consumption of tea after 1750.

In your response you should do the following.

- Respond to the prompt with a historically defensible thesis or claim that establishes a line of reasoning.
- Describe a broader historical context relevant to the prompt.
- Support an argument in response to the prompt using at least six documents.
- Use at least one additional piece of specific historical evidence (beyond that found in the documents) relevant to an argument about the prompt.
- For at least three documents, explain how or why the document's point of view, purpose, historical situation, and/or audience is relevant to an argument.
- Use evidence to corroborate, qualify, or modify an argument that addresses the prompt.

Note: The map below is provided as a reference. The map is NOT one of the seven documents. The documents begin below the map.

### Document 1

Mary Elizabeth Braddon, *Lady Audley's Secret*, English novel, 1862

Lucy Audley looked up from her occupation among the fragile china cups and watched Robert rather anxiously as he walked softly to his uncle's room and back again to the boudoir. She looked very pretty and innocent, seated behind the graceful group of delicate opal china and glittering silver. Surely a pretty woman never looks prettier than when making tea. The most feminine and most domestic of all occupations imparts a magic harmony to her every movement, a witchery to her every glance. The floating mists from the boiling liquid in which she infuses the soothing herbs; whose secrets are known to her alone, envelope her in a cloud of scented vapor, through which she seems a social fairy, weaving potent spells with Gunpowder and Bohea [gunpowder and bohea are forms of tea]. At the tea-table she reigns omnipotent, unapproachable. What do men know of the mysterious beverage?

*Source:* Braddon, Mary Elizabeth. *Lady Audley's Secret*. Project Gutenberg, 2005.

### Document 2

Charles James Wills, "A Persian Wedding," 1885

The visitors will stop all day, only leaving to escort the bride to the home of her new husband, whither she will go after dark. Large samovars, or Russian urns, which are in use in every Persian house, are hissing like small steam-engines, ready to furnish tea for the guests on their arrival: not our idea of tea, but a pale infusion sweetened to the consistency of syrup, from the center of each cup of which will project a little island of superfluous sugar.

*Source:* Wills, Charles James. *Persia as it is: Being Sketches of Modern Persian Life and Character*. London: William Clowes and Sons, 1886.

## Document 3

Lin Zexu, "Letter to the Queen of England," February 1840

We have heard that in your own country opium is prohibited with the utmost strictness and severity:–this is a strong proof that you know full well how hurtful it is to mankind. Since then you do not permit it to injure your own country, you ought not to have the injurious drug transferred to another country, and above all others, how much less to the Inner Land! Of the products which China exports to your foreign countries, there is not one which is not beneficial to mankind in some shape or other. There are those which serve for food, those which are useful, and those which are calculated for re-sale; but all are beneficial. Has China (we should like to ask) ever yet sent forth a noxious article from its soil? Not to speak of our tea and rhubarb, things which your foreign countries could not exist a single day without, if we of the Central Land were to grudge you what is beneficial, and not to compassionate your wants, then wherewithal could you foreigners manage to exist? And further, as regards your woolens, camlets, and longells [types of fabrics], were it not that you get supplied with our native raw silk, you could not get these manufactured! If China were to grudge you those things which yield a profit, how could you foreigners scheme after any profit at all? Our other articles of food, such as sugar, ginger, cinnamon, &c., and our other articles for use, such as silk piece-goods, chinaware, &c., are all so many necessaries of life to you; how can we reckon up their number! On the other hand, the things that come from your foreign countries are only calculated to make presents of, or serve for mere amusement. It is quite the same to us if we have them, or if we have them not. If then these are of no material consequence to us of the Inner Land, what difficulty would there be in prohibiting and shutting our market against them? It is only that our heavenly dynasty most freely permits you to take off her tea, silk, and other commodities, and convey them for consumption everywhere, without the slightest stint or grudge, for no other reason, but that where a profit exists, we wish that it be diffused abroad for the benefit of all the earth!

*Source:* Lin Zexu, *Letter to the Queen of England.* In Chinese Repository, v. 8, no. 10 (February 1840), 497– 503.

## Document 4

General Notes on Tea Exports, February 7, 1908

In their review of the year, Messrs. Gow Wilson and Stanton point to the great expansion in the use of British teas abroad as one of the most remarkable features of the past two years. This rose from 129, 884,250 lbs. in 1905 to 162,461,824 lbs. in 1906, and about 171,500,000 lbs. in 1907. When it is remembered that in 1890 the total consumption of Indian and Ceylon teas abroad was only 14,001,132 lbs., the progress made it startling. The expansion is largely due to the energy with which these new markets have been exploited. No industry has done so much to push its products in foreign markets as Ceylon.

*Source:* Royal Society of Arts (Great Britain). *Journal of the Royal Society of Arts*, Volume 56. London: George Bell and Sons, 1908.

## Document 5

Nathaniel Currier, "The Destruction of Tea at Boston Harbor," lithograph depicting the 1773 Boston Tea Party, 1846

Library of Congress, Prints & Photographs Division, [LC-USZC4-523]

## Document 6

Image of women working on a Lipton tea estate in Ceylon.

Yale University Art Gallery

## Document 7

Kakuzo Okakura *The Book of Tea*, Japan, 1906.

Perhaps I betray my own ignorance of the Tea Cult by being so outspoken. Its very spirit of politeness exacts that you say what you are expected to say, and no more. But I am not to be a polite Teaist. So much harm has been done already by the mutual misunderstanding of the New World and the Old, that one need not apologise for contributing his tithe to the furtherance of a better understanding. The beginning of the twentieth century would have been spared the spectacle of sanguinary warfare if Russia had condescended to know Japan better. What dire consequences to humanity lie in the contemptuous ignoring of Eastern problems! European imperialism, which does not disdain to raise the absurd cry of the Yellow Peril, fails to realise that Asia may also awaken to the cruel sense of the White Disaster. You may laugh at us for having "too much tea," but may we not suspect that you of the West have "no tea" in your constitution?

Let us stop the continents from hurling epigrams at each other, and be sadder if not wiser by the mutual gain of half a hemisphere. We have developed along different lines, but there is no reason why one should not supplement the other. You have gained expansion at the cost of restlessness; we have created a harmony which is weak against aggression. Will you believe it?–the East is better off in some respects than the West!

Strangely enough humanity has so far met in the tea-cup. It is the only Asiatic ceremonial which commands universal esteem. The white man has scoffed at our religion and our morals, but has accepted the brown beverage without hesitation. The afternoon tea is now an important function in Western society. In the delicate clatter of trays and saucers, in the soft rustle of feminine hospitality, in the common catechism about cream and sugar, we know that the Worship of Tea is established beyond question. The philosophic resignation of the guest to the fate awaiting him in the dubious decoction proclaims that in this single instance the Oriental spirit reigns supreme.

*Source:* Okakura, Kakuzo. *The Book of Tea*. Project Gutenberg, 1997.

## Long Essay

1. Evaluate the extent to which women were involved in the Enlightenment and Atlantic revolutions.
2. Compare and contrast the effectiveness of the Boxer Rebellion in China and Sepoy Rebellion in India.
3. Describe the similarities and differences between the expansion of the United States and overland expansion of the Russian Empire.

In your response you should do the following:

- Respond to the prompt with a historically defensible thesis or claim that establishes a line of reasoning.
- Describe a broader historical context relevant to the prompt.
- Support an argument in response to the prompt using specific and relevant examples of evidence.
- Use historical reasoning (e.g. comparison, causation, continuity or change) to frame or structure an argument that addresses the prompt.
- Use evidence to corroborate, qualify, or modify an argument that addresses the prompt.

# Part 4 Global Conflict, Cold War and Decolonization, and Globalization, 1900 to present

Hulton Deutsch/Corbis Historical/Getty Images



## LEARNING OBJECTIVES

As you study Part 4 you will:

- Analyze the causes and consequences of World War I and World War II.
- Explain how the practice of "total war" affected societies.
- Analyze the continuities and changes in imperialism and colonialism.
- Analyze the historical context of the Cold War.
- Identify the causes of the end of empires.
- Explain the effects of globalization on politics, society, and economics.

One of the greatest difficulties in studying the recent past is that enough time hasn't elapsed for historians to gain a perspective on the long-term significance of recent events and see the big picture. Another related difficulty is the superabundance of information. Without a sense of long-term significance in a world flooded with print, audio-visual, and computer-based information, how can historians determine what is and what is not important? One of the ways world historians try to make sense of the recent past is to tie events to the themes and key concepts of the early eras of human history. So, as you go through this last period of world history look for themes and concepts and be certain to stay global—don't focus exclusively on Europe and the United States.

These final AP chapters address global conflict, the Cold War and decolonization, and globalization. Collectively, these chapters cover the profound global changes that have unfolded since World War I.

Rapid scientific advances in the twentieth century altered everything from how we understand the universe to how food is grown and have created a multiplicity of paradoxes. Science has made huge advances in extending the span of human life while at the same time producing technologies that threaten to destroy the delicate ecosystems on which human life depends. Advances in transportation and communication networks have made obsolete the concept of geographic distance and have enabled international trade, migration, communication, and the spread of diseases at both amazing and alarming rates. All these modern marvels and conveniences are continuities of themes you have followed since the beginning of the course.

From the very first chapter, we have seen humans migrating, traveling, and trading—processes that have fostered widespread cultural exchanges. In the following chapters we will see these same processes intensify. Look for ways in which both popular and "high" cultures have become increasingly global as communication networks get exponentially faster and widespread. Music, film, social networking sites, cell phones, and sports can reach and engage people on a global scale if they have access to necessary technologies—but not everyone has embraced the increasing globalization of culture. Many are afraid that

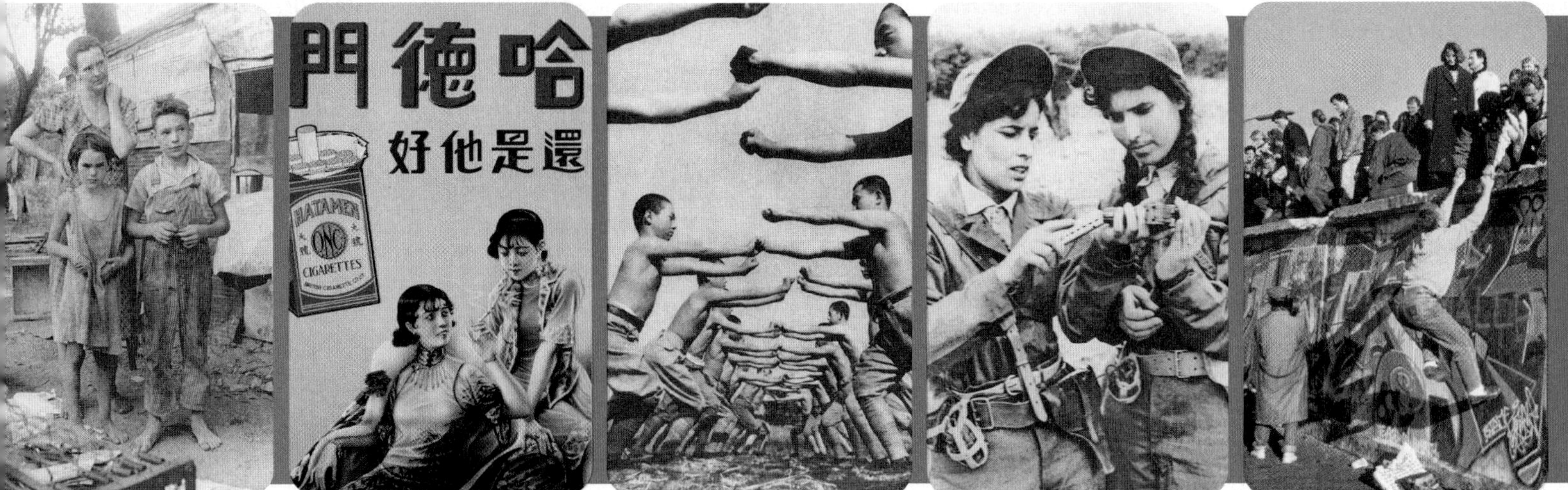


by embracing a global or common culture the viability of their own culture is threatened and the unique characteristics and traditions of their culture will lose their value. As you read these chapters, look for the conflicts that have some basis in ridding one's culture of "others." Did they succeed, and what was the cost in waging such a conflict?

Global industrial capitalism dominates the world's twentieth century economy, and yet benefits of this economic system are not evenly distributed. As you study this period, scrutinize the distribution of wealth in the global economy, particularly regarding regions, nations, and colonies. The popularity of socialist and communist ideas stem from discontent with industrial capitalism's inequities. As the nature of production changes, examine how labor does or does not change.

On a more local scale, how have the economic and political roles of women and ethnic or racial minorities changed in families, business, and politics in the twentieth and twenty-first centuries? In addition to those changes, analyze changes and continuities in social structures—who have the greatest advantages, and who are most greatly disadvantaged?

The global conflicts of the twentieth century in Part 4 are only one-third of the AP curriculum in this modern era, so don't dwell exclusively on these wars. AP students should focus on the causes and results of the two world wars, not on singular battles. Explore the "total war" aspects of these conflicts on the home fronts in great detail, since the all-consuming involvement of peoples on all continents changed the shape of much of the global community. Twentieth-century wars and modern military technologies frequently led to ethnic genocides, wartime casualties, and demands to change the dominant political power structures. The ensuing Cold War, and independence and de-colonization movements were intertwined. The U.S. and U.S.S.R. represented the new global balance of power, and AP students should be able to link postwar conflicts in Asia, Africa, and Latin America to competing superpowers' conflicts.

Some nations, especially in Asia and Africa, opposed aligning with the power blocks of either the Soviet Union or United States. You will need to explain the alternative positions offered by groups such as the Nonaligned Movement. International governing organizations like the UN, humanitarian organizations like the World Health Organization (WHO), and economic institutions like the IMF (International Monetary Fund), the European Union, and even Coca-Cola facilitated transnational or multinational economies, not merely nation-based ones.

Globalization, in its many forms, is not a new phenomenon: AP students know it started in the fifteenth century, although its roots go back much further. You have analyzed the effects of the intensification of transregional networks of communication and exchange since ca. 1200 C.E. In the twentieth and twenty-first centuries, one of the criticisms of globalization is that it comes at the expense of national or cultural identity. Some people see increasing global contact as the homogenization or the destruction of their indigenous cultures or beliefs. Others protest the economic inequalities or unevenness of the global economy, while still others focus on the destructive effects of the spread of modern technologies on the environment. There have been both peaceful and violent protests against globalization. AP students will need to be able to analyze peoples' actions in their proper historical, national, and cultural contexts. This is the challenge that historians have always faced: how to tell a story so that it does justice to the people who lived it, to the time and the context in which it took place, and to where on the globe it occurred.

## PART 4 BIG QUESTIONS:

- What forms did imperialism take around the world and how did they contribute to the first World War?
- How did the ideologies of fascism and communism develop over the course of the twentieth century?
- What role did anticolonial movements play in the end of Europe's empires?
- What does globalization mean in the twenty-first century?

# Chapter 21 The Great War: The World in Upheaval



## ZOOMING IN ON ENCOUNTERS

### An Assassination That Led to Global War

Archduke Franz Ferdinand (1863–1914) of Austria-Hungary was aware that his first official visit to Sarajevo was fraught with danger. That ancient city was the capital of Bosnia-Herzegovina, twin provinces that had been under Ottoman rule since the fifteenth century before being occupied in 1878 and finally annexed by Austria-Hungary in 1908. The provinces were home to large numbers of ethnic Serbians who sought incorporation into the neighboring kingdom of Serbia rather than into the Austro-Hungarian Empire, and as a result they became the hotbed of pan-Serbian nationalism. Even though Ferdinand himself favored diplomacy rather than hard-line tactics when it came to Serbian nationalism, most Serbian nationalists nevertheless hated the dynasty and the empire represented by the heir to the throne of Austria-Hungary.

This contemporary painting by C. R. W. Nevinson, called "The Paths of Glory," testifies to the appalling scale of death and destruction during the battles of World War I.
Photo12/Universal Images Group/Getty Images

Ferdinand and his wife Sophie arrived in Sarajevo on the warm Sunday morning of June 28, 1914. As their motorcade moved from the train station through the narrow streets of Sarajevo, seven Serbian nationalists armed with bombs and revolvers were waiting on the designated route to assassinate Ferdinand. The first would-be assassin did not take a shot, but the next man in line threw a hand grenade into the open car. Bouncing off Ferdinand's arm, the grenade exploded near another vehicle and injured dozens of spectators.

Undeterred, Ferdinand and Sophie went on to a reception at city hall; after the reception Ferdinand instructed his driver to take them to the hospital where those wounded in the earlier attack were being treated. On the way, a young Bosnian Serb named Gavrilo Princip (1894–1918) lunged at the archduke's car and fired a revolver. The first bullet blew a hole in the side of Ferdinand's neck. A second bullet intended for the governor of Bosnia went wild and entered the stomach of the expectant

Sophie. Turning to his wife, the archduke pleaded: "Sophie dear! Don't die! Stay alive for our children!" By the time medical aid arrived, however, the archduke and the duchess were dead.

In the meantime, Princip swallowed poison in an attempt to kill himself after the successful attack. But the poison was old and only made him sick. When he tried to turn the gun on himself, a crowd prevented him from doing so and held him for the police. When the police arrived, they took out their fury on Princip: they kicked him, beat him, and scraped the skin from his neck with the edges of their swords. Three months later a court found Princip guilty of treason and murder, but because he committed his crime before his twentieth birthday, he was not subject to the death penalty. Sentenced to twenty years in prison, Princip died in April 1918 from tuberculosis.

The assassination on 28 June 1914 allowed hard-liners in Austria to take control of the government, and they demanded extensive reparations from the Serbian government, which they blamed for the assassination. When the Serbian government refused the terms demanded by the Austrian government, Austria declared war on Serbia on July 28. But the stakes of the conflict quickly expanded beyond Austria and Serbia. Indeed, nationalist aspirations, international rivalries, and an inflexible alliance system transformed the conflict into a general European war and ultimately into a global struggle involving thirty-two nations and nearly all of the colonies of the various empires. Twenty-eight of those nations, collectively known as the Allies and the Associated Powers, fought the coalition known as the Central Powers, which consisted of Germany, Austria-Hungary, the Ottoman Empire, and Bulgaria. The generation that survived the carnage called this clash of arms the Great War because its scope and its casualties exceeded all previous wars. Sadly, though, a subsequent generation of survivors renamed the conflict World War I because it was only the first of two devastating wars that engulfed the world in the first half of the twentieth century

## CHAPTER FOCUS

- AP World History looks at long-term patterns. So, although military strategies in the Great War are fascinating, the sequence of battles is not required for the AP exam. Rather, historians look for causes, long-term consequences, and unique characteristics of specific wars.
- In the Great War, the industrial nature of warfare changed the way wars were fought. The bizarre combination of trench warfare and industrially-produced weaponry—a very old tradition of warfare and a very new one simultaneously—is noteworthy and was incredibly grim.
- Conflicts between different ethnic or religious groups have always occurred, but it wasn't until the twentieth century that technology could obliterate entire populations. Factories and their workers became military targets. Thus, in an industrial military economy, the enemy could argue that there were no civilians. This is what historians mean by total war, and it is an important distinction of the Great War.
- There is a growing historical argument that the Great War (World War I) and World War II should be seen as a single war with mostly the same participants and basic goals. Keep that argument in mind as you read, and decide whether you agree.
- Another argument proposes that the Great War was a civil war between Europeans; however, it is called a World War because of the involvement of colonial peoples, the entrance of industrialized Japan, and the late entry of the United States.
- For historians, the involvement of non-Europeans is particularly interesting. Many of these participants hoped that by volunteering to fight they would collectively be rewarded with the vote, legal citizenship, or independence—none of which happened.
- Four empires collapsed at the end of the Great War: the Ottoman, Russian, Austro-Hungarian, and German; and the European survivor nations were severely wounded.
- Japan and the United States were relatively unscathed, and both would take advantage of that over the subsequent two decades.
- Russia's losses would lead directly to revolution.

## Historical Developments

- The causes of World War I included imperialist expansion and competition for resources. In addition, territorial and regional conflicts combined with a flawed alliance system and intense nationalism to escalate the tensions into global conflict.
- World War I was the first total war. Governments used a variety of strategies, including political propaganda, art, media, and intensified forms of nationalism, to mobilize populations (both in the home countries and the colonies) for the purpose of waging war.
- New military technology led to increased levels of wartime casualties.
- The older, land-based Ottoman, Russian, and Qing empires collapsed due to a combination of internal and external factors. These changes in Russia eventually led to communist revolution.

## Reasoning Processes

- **Causation** Describe the causes and effects of the Great War.
- **Continuity and Change** Explain patterns of political continuity and change in Europe and European colonies over the course of the Great War.

## Historical Thinking Skills

- **Developments and Processes** Explain the causes of the Great War and identify the processes that made the war so deadly.
- **Claims and Evidence in Sources** Identify and describe the argument put forth by Walter Trier's map of Europe.
- **Contextualization** Explain how the Great War unfolded within the larger contexts of industrialization and nationalism.

## CHAPTER OVERVIEW

The Great War lasted from August 1914 to November 1918 and ushered in history's most violent century. In geographic extent the conflict surpassed all previous wars, compelling men, women, and children on five continents to participate directly or indirectly. The Great War also had the distinction of being the first total war in human history, as governments mobilized every available human and material resource for the conduct of war, including those in colonial territories. The industrial nature of the conflict meant that it was the bloodiest in the annals of organized violence. It took the lives of millions of combatants and civilians, physically maimed untold multitudes, and emotionally scarred an entire generation. The military casualties passed a threshold beyond previous experience: approximately fifteen million soldiers died, and an additional twenty million combatants suffered injuries.

The war of 1914–1918 did more than destroy individual lives. It seriously damaged national economies. The most visible signs of that damage were huge public debts and soaring rates of inflation. The international economy witnessed a shift in power away from western Europe. By the end of the conflict, the United States emerged as an economic world power that, despite its self-imposed isolation during the 1920s and 1930s, played a key role in global affairs in the coming decades. Politically, the war led to the redrawing of European boundaries and caused the demise of four dynasties and their empires—the Ottoman Empire, the Russian Empire, the Austro-Hungarian Empire, and the German Empire. The Great War also gave birth to nine new nations: Yugoslavia, Austria, Hungary, Czechoslovakia, Poland, Lithuania, Latvia, Estonia, and Finland. The war helped unleash the Bolshevik Revolution of 1917, which had profound consequences for the whole world. Finally, the Great War was responsible for an international realignment of power. It undermined the preeminence and prestige of western European society, signaling an end to Europe's global primacy.

| CHRONOLOGY | |
|---|---|
| 1914 | Assassination of Archduke Franz Ferdinand |
| 1915 | German submarine sinks the *Lusitania*;<br>Japan makes Twenty-one Demands on China;<br>Gallipoli campaign |
| 1916 | Battles at Verdun and the Somme |
| 1917 | German resumption of unrestricted submarine warfare;<br>United States declaration of war on Germany;<br>Bolshevik Revolution |
| 1918 | Treaty of Brest-Litovsk;<br>Armistice suspends hostilities |
| 1919 | Paris Peace Conference |
| 1920 | First meeting of the League of Nations |
| 1923 | Atatürk proclaims Republic of Turkey |

## THE DRIFT TOWARD WAR

As we have seen, the catalyst for war was the assassination of Archduke **Franz Ferdinand,** heir to the throne of the Austro-Hungarian Empire, by a Serbian nationalist. Yet without deeper underlying developments, Gavrilo Princip's bullets would have had limited effect. The underlying causes for the war of 1914–1918 were many, including intense nationalism, frustrated national ambitions and ethnic resentments, the pursuit of exclusive economic interests, abrasive colonial rivalries, and a general struggle over the balance of power in Europe and in the world at large. Between 1871 and 1914, European governments adopted foreign policies that steadily increased the likelihood of a general war between them. To avoid finding themselves alone in a hostile world, national leaders sought alignments with other powers. The establishment and maintenance in Europe of two hostile alliances—the Allies and the Central Powers—helped spread the war from the Balkans to most of the rest of the world.

### Nationalist Aspirations

The French revolution and subsequent Napoleonic conquests spread nationalism throughout most of Europe by the end of the nineteenth century (see chapter 28). Inherent in nationalism was the idea that peoples with the same ethnic origins, language, and political ideals had the right to form sovereign states; this concept is called **self-determination.** The dynastic and often reactionary powers that dominated European affairs during the early nineteenth century either ignored or opposed the principle of self-determination, thereby denying national autonomy to Germans, Italians, and Belgians, among others. Before long, however, a combination of powerful nationalistic movements, revolutions, and wars allowed Belgians to gain independence from the Netherlands in 1830, promoted the unification of Italy in 1861, and secured the unification of Germany in 1871. Yet at the end of the nineteenth century, the issue of nationalism remained unresolved in other areas of Europe, most notably in eastern Europe and the Balkans. There the nationalist aspirations of subject minorities threatened to tear apart the multinational empires of the Ottoman, Hapsburg, and Russian dynasties and with them the regional balance of power. In those instances, opposition to foreign rule played a large role in the construction of national identities and demands for self-determination.

The Ottoman Empire had controlled the Balkan peninsula since the fifteenth century, but after 1829 the Turkish empire lost huge portions of its territories. European powers, especially Austria and Russia, were partly responsible for these losses in Europe, but in other areas the slicing away of Turkish territory resulted mostly from nationalist revolts by the sultan's subjects. Greece was the first to gain independence (in 1830), and within a few decades Serbia, Romania, and Bulgaria followed suit.

As the Ottoman territories succumbed to the forces of nationalism, Austria-Hungary confronted the nationalist aspirations of Slavic peoples—Poles, Czechs, Slovaks, Serbs, Croats, and Slovenes. Most militant were the Serbs, who pressed for unification with the now-independent kingdom of Serbia. Russia added fuel to this volatile situation by promoting Pan-Slavism, a nineteenth-century movement that stressed the ethnic and cultural kinship of the various Slav peoples of eastern and east central Europe and that sought to unite those peoples politically. Pan-Slavism, as advocated by Russian leaders, supported Slav nationalism in lands occupied by Austria-Hungary. The purpose behind that policy was to promote secession by Slav areas, thereby weakening Austrian rule and perhaps preparing territories for future Russian annexation. Russia's support of Serbia, which supported Slav nationalism, and Germany's backing of Austria-Hungary, which tried desperately to counter the threat of national independence, helped set the stage for international conflict.

### National Rivalries

Aggressive nationalism was also manifest in economic competition and colonial conflicts, fueling dangerous rivalries among the major European powers. The industrialized nations of Europe competed for foreign markets and engaged in tariff wars, but the most unsettling economic rivalry involved Great Britain and Germany. By the twentieth century, Germany's rapid industrialization threatened British economic predominance. In 1870 Britain, the first industrial nation, produced almost 32 percent of the world's total industrial output, compared with Germany's share of 13 percent, but by 1914 Britain's share had dropped to 14 percent, roughly equivalent to that of Germany. British reluctance to accept the relative decline of British industry vis-à-vis German industry strained relations between the two economic powers.

**The Naval Race** An expensive naval race worsened tensions between the two nations. Germans and Britons convinced themselves that naval power was vital for securing and protecting merchant shipping. Military leaders and politicians also saw powerful navies as a means of controlling the seas in times of war, a control they viewed as decisive in determining the outcome of any war. Thus, when Germany's political and military leaders announced their program to build a fleet with many large battleships, they seemed to undermine British naval supremacy. The British government moved to meet the German threat through the construction of battleships known as **dreadnoughts.** Dreadnoughts represented an entirely new generation of warships, characterized in part by the high speed supplied by steam turbines. Rather than discouraging the Germans from their naval buildup, the British determination to retain naval superiority stimulated the Germans to build their own flotilla of dreadnoughts. This expensive naval race contributed further to international tensions and hostilities between nations.

**Colonial Disputes** Economic rivalries also encouraged colonial competition. During the late nineteenth and early twentieth centuries, European nations searched aggressively for new colonies or dependencies to bolster economic performance. In their haste to conquer and colonize, the imperial powers sometimes stumbled over each other, repeatedly clashing in one corner of the globe or another: Britain and Russia competed for influence in Persia (modern-day Iran) and Afghanistan; Britain and France both sought a controlling influence in Siam (modern-day Thailand) and the Nile valley; Britain and Germany competed for territory in east and southwest Africa; and Germany and France almost came to blows over attempts to influence affairs in Morocco and west Africa.

Virtually all the major powers engaged in the scramble for empire, but the competition between Britain and Germany and between France and Germany were the most intense. Germany, a unified nation only since 1871, embarked on the colonial race belatedly but aggressively, insisting that it too must have its "place in the sun." German imperial efforts were frustrated, however, by the simple fact that British and French imperialists had already carved up much of the world. German-French antagonisms and German-British rivalries were important in shaping the international alliances that contributed to the spread of war after 1914.

Between 1905 and 1914, a series of international crises and two local wars raised tensions and almost precipitated a general European war. The first crisis resulted from a French-German confrontation over Morocco in 1905. French influence had been growing in the area, and to counter this the German government announced its support of Moroccan independence. The French responded to German interference by threatening war. An international conference in Algeciras, Spain, in the following year prevented a clash of arms, but similar crises threatened the peace in subsequent years. Contributing to the growing tensions in European affairs were the Balkan wars. Between 1912 and 1913, the states of the Balkan peninsula—including Bulgaria, Greece, Montenegro, Serbia, and Romania—fought two consecutive wars for possession of

## INTERPRETING IMAGES

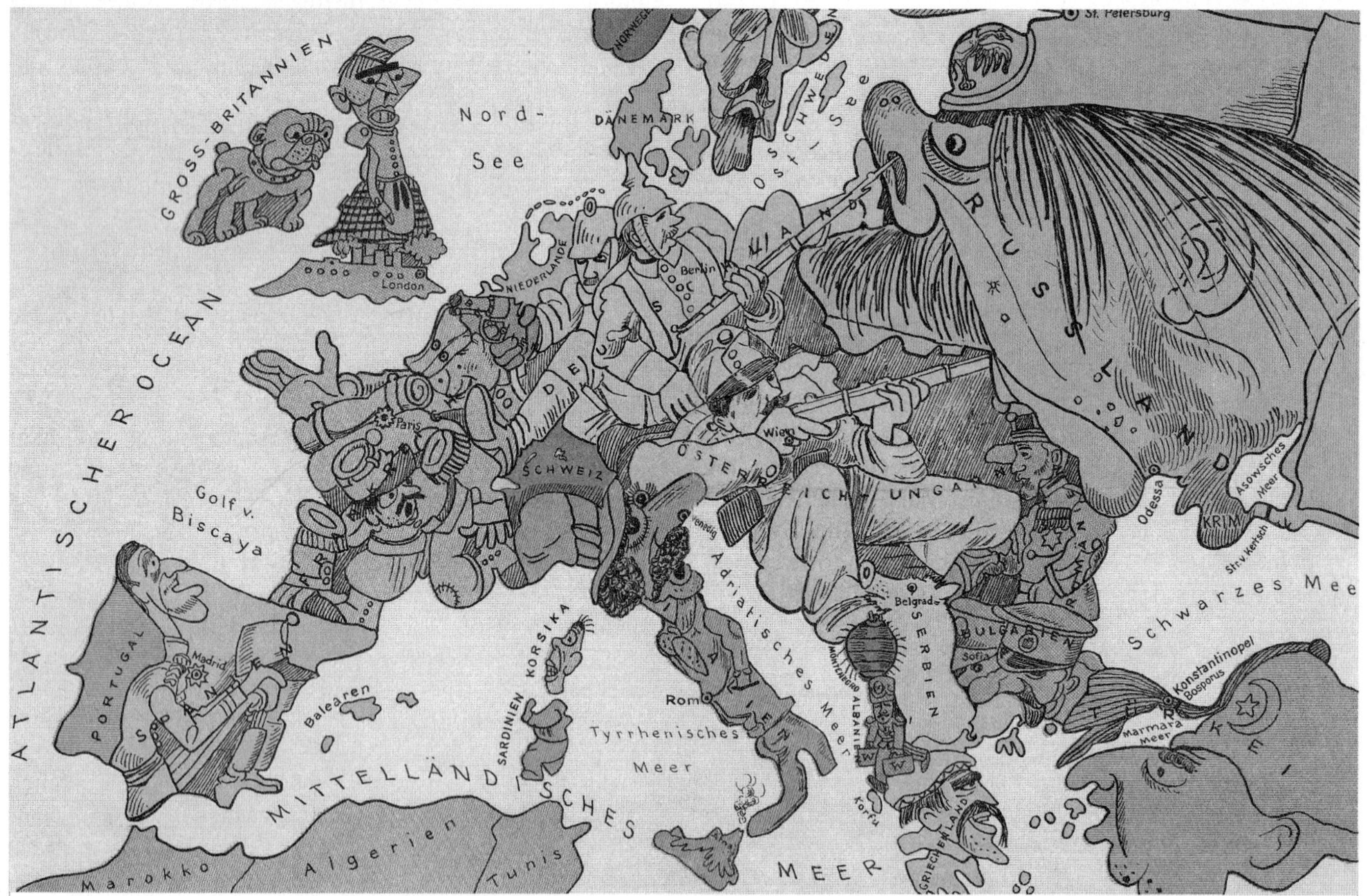


Dissident German cartoonist Walter Trier's satirical map of Europe in 1914. Trier's work stands in stark contrast to the press of the time, which fueled the chauvinist desires of competing national publics. What message was Trier trying to convey with this map?

**Analyze** *What evidence do you detect that the cartoon was created from the German perspective? What are the signs of satire?*

akg-images/Alamy Stock Photo

the remaining European territories held by the Ottoman Empire. The Balkan wars strained European diplomatic relations and helped shape the tense circumstances that led to the outbreak of the Great War.

**Public Opinion** Public pressure also contributed to national rivalries. Many European societies were characterized by a high degree of political participation and chauvinism (excessive patriotism) on the part of citizens who identified strongly with the state. These citizens wanted their nation to outshine others, particularly in the international arena. New means of communication nourished the public's desire to see their country "come in first," whether in the competition for colonies or in the race to the South Pole. The content of inexpensive, mass-produced newspapers, pamphlets, and books fueled feelings of national arrogance and aggressive patriotism. However, public pressure calling for national greatness placed policymakers and diplomats in an awkward situation. Compelled to achieve headline-grabbing foreign policy successes, these leaders ran the risk of paying for short-lived triumphs with long-lasting hostility from other countries.

## Understandings and Alliances

Escalating national rivalries and nationalist aspirations of subject minorities led to a system of entangling alliances. Fundamental to all of these alliances was that they outlined the circumstances under which countries would go to war to support one another. Although they were meant to preserve the peace, in fact rival alliance systems created a framework whereby even a small international crisis could set off a chain reaction leading to a much larger war. In 1914, the Great War erupted in large part because Europe's major powers had aligned themselves into two hostile camps—the Triple Alliance and the Triple Entente.

**The Central Powers** The Triple Alliance, also known as the **Central Powers,** grew out of the close relationship that developed between the leaders of Germany and Austria-Hungary during the last three decades of the nineteenth century. In 1879 the governments of the two empires entered into the Dual Alliance, a defensive pact that ensured reciprocal protection from a Russian attack and neutrality in case of an attack from any other power. Fear of a hostile France motivated Germans to enter into this pact, whereas Austrians viewed it as giving them a free hand in pursuing their Balkan politics without fear of Russian intervention. Italy, fearful of France, joined the Dual Alliance in 1882, thereby transforming it into the Triple Alliance. From the outset, however, the Italian policy of expansion at the expense of the Ottoman Empire and Italy's rivalry with Austria-Hungary in the Balkans threatened to wreck the alliance. Thus the Italian declaration of war on the Ottoman Empire in 1911 and the subsequent drive to annex the Tripoli region of northern Africa strained the Triple Alliance because the German government was interested in cultivating friendly relations with the Ottomans.

**The Allies** The Central Powers sought to protect the political status quo in Europe, but the leaders of other nations viewed this new constellation of power with suspicion. This response was especially true of French leaders, who neither forgot nor forgave France's humiliating defeat during the Franco-Prussian War of 1870–1871. The French government was determined to curb the growing might of Germany.

The tsarist regime of Russia was equally disturbed by the new alignment of powers, especially by Germany's support of Austria, and British leaders were traditionally suspicious of any nation that seemed to threaten the balance of power on the Continent. The result was the **Triple Entente,** a combination of nations that had once been rivals, commonly referred to as the Allies. The Triple Entente originated in a series of agreements between Britain and France (1904) and between Britain and Russia (1907) that aimed to resolve colonial disputes. Between 1907 and 1914 cooperation between the leaders of Britain, France, and Russia led to the signing of a military pact in the summer of 1914. Reciprocal treaty obligations, which the governments felt compelled to honor lest they face the risk of being alone in a hostile world, made it difficult for diplomats to contain what otherwise might have been relatively small international crises.

**War Plans** The preservation of peace was also difficult because the military staffs of each nation had devised inflexible military plans and timetables to be carried out in the event of war. For example, French military strategy revolved around Plan XVII, which revolved around offensive maneuvers. The French master plan could be summed up in one word, *attack,* to be undertaken always and everywhere. This strategy viewed the enemy's intentions as inconsequential and gave no thought to the huge number of casualties that would invariably result from repeated attacks. Yet it was German war plans in particular that played a crucial role in the events leading to the Great War. Germany's fear of encirclement encouraged its military planners to devise a strategy that would avoid a war on two fronts. It was based on a strategy developed in 1905 by General Count Alfred von Schlieffen (1833–1913).

The **Schlieffen plan** called for a swift attack on France, followed by defensive action against Russia. German planners based their strategy on the knowledge that the Russians could not mobilize their soldiers and military supplies as quickly as the French, thus giving German forces a few precious weeks during which they could concentrate their full power on France. But the Schlieffen plan raised serious logistical problems, not the least of which was moving 180,000 soldiers and their supplies into France and Belgium on five hundred trains, with fifty wagons each. More important, Germany's military strategy was a serious obstacle to those seeking to preserve the peace. In the event of Russian mobilization, Germany's leaders would feel compelled to stick to their war plans of attacking France first, thereby setting in motion a military conflict of major proportions.

**Triple Entente** (ahn-TAHNT)
**Schlieffen** (SHLEE-fn)

## GLOBAL WAR

War came to Europe during harvest time, and most ordinary people heard the news as they worked in the fields. Most reacted not with enthusiasm but with shock and fear. Other people, especially intellectuals and young city dwellers, met the news with euphoria. Many of them had long expected war and saw it as a liberating release of pressure that would resolve the various political, social, and economic crises that had been building for years. The philosopher Bertrand Russell observed that the average Englishman positively wanted war, and the French writer Alain-Fournier noted that "this war is fine and just and great." In the capitals of Europe, people danced in the streets when their governments announced formal declarations of war. When the first contingents of soldiers left for the front, jubilant crowds threw flowers at the feet of departing men, who expected to return victorious after a short time.

### INTERPRETING IMAGES

This French propaganda poster, "The Heroes of Belgium, 1914," was intended to rouse French patriotism by depicting German soldiers as inhuman monsters.

**Analyze** *This cartoon could be an effective mode of gaining support for WWI. How did it also provoke memories of the Franco-Prussian War?*

National Archives

Reality crushed any expectations of a short and triumphant war. On most fronts the conflict quickly bogged down and became a war of attrition in which the firepower of modern weapons slaughtered soldiers by the millions. For the first time in history, belligerent nations (meaning those nations that entered the war) engaged in total war. Even in democratic societies, governments assumed dictatorial control to marshal the human and material resources required for continuous war. One result was increased participation of women in the labor force. Total war had repercussions that went beyond the borders of Europe. Imperial ties drew millions of Asians, Africans, and residents of the British dominions into the war to serve as soldiers and laborers. Struggles in and over colonies further underlined the global dimension of this war. Last, the war gained a global flavor through the entry of Japan, the United States, and the Ottoman Empire, nations whose leaders professed little direct interest in European affairs.

### The Guns of August

The shots fired from Gavrilo Princip's revolver on that fateful day of 28 June 1914 were heard around the world, for they triggered the greatest war in human history up to that point. By July, Austrian investigators had linked the assassins to a terrorist group known as the **Black Hand.** Centered in neighboring Serbia, this organization was dedicated to the unification of all south Slavs, or Yugoslavs, to form a greater Serbia. As far as Serbian nationalists were concerned, the principal obstacle to Slavic unity was the Austro-Hungarian Empire, which explains why the heir to the Hapsburg throne was a symbolic victim. This viewpoint also explains Austria's unyielding and violent response to the murder.

**Declarations of War** The assassination set in motion a flurry of diplomatic activity that quickly escalated into war. Austrian leaders in Vienna were determined to teach the unruly Serbs a lesson, and on 23 July the Austrians issued a nearly unacceptable ultimatum to the government of Serbia. The Serbian government accepted all the terms of the ultimatum except one, which infringed on its sovereignty. The ultimatum demanded that Austrian officials take part in any Serbian investigation of persons found on Serbian territory connected to the assassination of Franz Ferdinand. On 28 July, after declaring the Serbian reply to be unsatisfactory, Austria-Hungary declared war on Serbia. The war had begun, and politicians and generals discovered that it could not be easily limited to a local conflict. The subsequent sequence of events was largely determined by two factors: complex mobilization plans and the logic of the alliance system.

On 29 July the Russian government under Tsar Nicholas II began mobilizing its troops to defend its Serbian ally and itself from Austria. Russia then ordered mobilization against Germany. Nicholas II (1868–1918) took that decisive step reluctantly and only after his military experts convinced him that a partial mobilization against the Austrians would upset complex military plans and timetables based on the existing alliance system. Delayed mobilization might invite defeat, they advised, should the Germans enter the war to defend their Austrian allies. That action precipitated a German ultimatum to Russia on 31 July, demanding that the Russian army cease its mobilization immediately. Another ultimatum addressed to France demanded to know what France's intentions were in case Germany and Russia went to war. The Russians replied with a blunt "impossible," and the French never answered. Thus on 1 August the German government declared war on Russia, and France started to mobilize.

After waiting two more days, the Germans declared war on France, on 3 August. On the same day, German troops invaded Belgium in accordance with the Schlieffen plan. Key to this plan was an attack on the weak left flank of the French army by a massive German force through Belgium. The Belgian government, which had refused to permit the passage of German troops, called on the signatories of the treaty of 1839, which guaranteed Belgium's neutrality. On 4 August the British government, one of the signatories, sent an ultimatum to Germany demanding that Belgian neutrality be respected. When Germany's wartime leaders refused, the British immediately declared war. A local conflict had become a general European war a mere five weeks after the assassination of Archduke Franz Ferdinand.

## Mutual Butchery

Everyone expected the war to be brief. In the first weeks of August 1914, twenty million young men donned uniforms, took up rifles, and left for the front. Many of them looked forward to heroic charges, rapid promotions, and a quick homecoming. Some dreamed of glory and honor, and they believed that God was on their side. The inscription on the belt buckle of German recruits read *Gott mit uns* ("God is with us"), a sentiment echoed by Russian troops, who fought for "God and Tsar," and British soldiers, who went into battle "For God, King, and Country." Several years later Americans believed they were entering the war to "make the world safe for democracy." Similar attitudes prevailed among the political and military leaders of the belligerent nations. Unfortunately, the war strategies devised by the finest military thinkers of the time

## INTERPRETING IMAGES

Crowds of young men happily pose outside a recruiting office in Toronto, Canada, while waiting to enlist.

**Analyze** *This photo was taken in 1914. How would you describe the energy in this photograph? Do you think a photo taken in 1917 or 1918 would depict a similar image? Why or why not?*

Shawshots/Alamy Stock Photo

paid little attention to matters of defense. Instead, they were preoccupied with visions of sweeping assaults; envelopments; and, above all, swift triumphs.

**The Western Front** The German march toward Paris in August 1914 was stopped by the French army (with British support) along the river Marne. Both sides then repeatedly tried to outflank the other, which led to a series of movements that took both armies to the North Sea (later, this movement was called the "race to the sea"). By October 1914, the German and Franco-British armies faced each other along a battlefront—called the **western front**—that stretched from the border of Switzerland to the North Sea. For the next three years, the battle lines remained virtually stationary, as both sides dug vast networks of defensive trenches and slugged it out in a war of attrition that lasted until the spring of 1918. Each belligerent tried to break through the other's defensive lines and to inflict continuous damage and casualties, only to have their own forces suffer heavy losses in return. Farther south, Italy left the Triple Alliance and then entered the war on the side of the Allies in 1915. By the terms of the Treaty of London, the Allies promised, once victory was secured, to cede to Italy Austro-Hungarian-controlled territories, specifically south Tyrol and most of the Dalmatian coast. Allied hopes that the Italians would pierce Austrian defenses quickly faded. After a disastrous defeat at Caporetto in 1917, Italian forces maintained a defensive line only with the help of the French and the British.

**Stalemate and New Weapons** The stalemate on the western and southern fronts reflected technological developments that favored defensive tactics. Barbed wire, which had confined cattle on America's Great Plains, proved highly effective in frustrating the advance of soldiers across **no-man's-land,** the deadly territory between opposing trenches. The rapid and continuous fire of machine guns further contributed to the battlefield stalemate, turning infantry charges across no-man's-land into suicide missions. First deployed by Confederate troops during the U.S. Civil War, the machine gun had been a key weapon for overcoming resistance to nineteenth-century colonial expansion before Europeans trained the weapon on one another during the Great War. The machine gun represented one of the most important advances in military technology and compelled military leaders on all sides to rethink their battlefield tactics.

The immobility of trench warfare and the desire to reintroduce movement to warfare prompted the development of weapons that supplied the power necessary to break the deadly stalemate. Both sides subsequently developed many new and potent weapons. The most unconventional weapon was poisonous gas, first used by German troops in January 1915. Especially hated and much feared by troops in the trenches was **mustard gas,** a liquid agent that, when exposed to air, turned into a noxious yellow gas, hence its name. The effects of mustard gas did not appear for some twelve hours following exposure, but then it rotted the body from both within and without. After blistering the skin and damaging the eyes, the gas attacked the bronchial tubes, stripping off the mucous membrane. Death usually occurred in four to five weeks. In the meantime, victims endured excruciating pain. Like the machine gun, gas proved a potent weapon, and both sides lost a total of about 1.2 million soldiers as a result of its use. But even though chemical agents were effective in producing heavy casualties, gas attacks failed to deliver strategic breakthroughs, and the anticipated return to more fluid battle lines never materialized.

Other weapons developed to break the stalemate on the western front included tanks and airplanes. The British first introduced tanks in September 1916, and the Allies deployed them to break down German defensive trenches. Despite its effectiveness during the final offenses of the war, the tank did not produce the longed-for strategic advantage. In most cases, German counterattacks quickly regained the ground won by tanks. Military leaders also hoped that airplanes, just recently invented in 1914, would help restore mobility to the western front. However, because airplanes could not carry enough weapons to do serious damage to troops or installations on the ground, their real asset during the Great War was aerial reconnaissance. In fact, the much publicized and glamorized aerial combat of the Great War featuring "ace fighters" and "dogfights" were not large-scale battles in themselves but, rather, were attempts to prevent the enemy from conducting such reconnaissance. The plane and the tank figured more prominently as important strategic weapons during the Second World War. Other weapons systems, such as the submarine, had made earlier appearances in warfare but did not play a significant role until the Great War. It was not until the Great War, when the German navy deployed its diesel-powered submarine fleet against Allied commercial shipping, that

Poison gas was lethal for humans and animals. Millions of horses were used for military purposes by both sides during the war. When poison gas attacks were anticipated, horses near the battle lines wore gas masks too.
Photo12/UIG/Getty Images

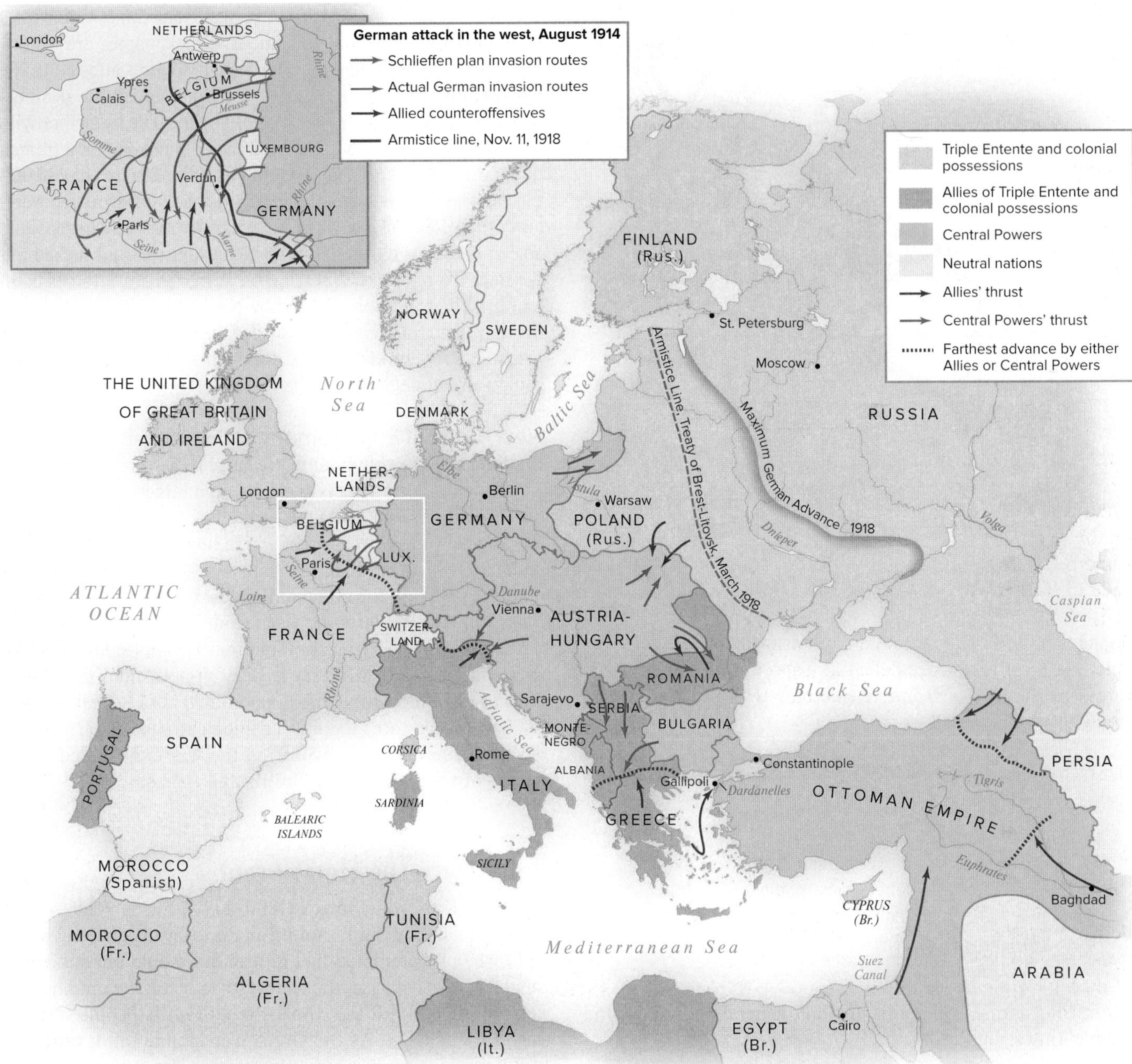


## MAP 21.1 The Great War in Europe and southwest Asia, 1914–1918.

Note the locations of both the eastern and the western fronts in Europe during the war.

***Why didn't the same kind of trench warfare immobilize opposing armies on the eastern front the way it did on the western front?***

the submarine proved its military effectiveness. Although the German navy relied more heavily on submarines, the allied navies of Great Britain and the United States also deployed their own fleets of diesel-powered submarines.

**No-Man's-Land** The most courageous infantry charges, even when preceded by pulverizing artillery barrages and clouds of poisonous gas, were no match for determined defenders. Shielded by the dirt of their trenches and by barbed wire and gas masks, they unleashed a torrent of lethal metal with their machine guns and repeating rifles. In every sector of the front, those who fought rarely found glory. Instead, they encountered death. No-man's-land was strewn with shell craters, cadavers, and body parts. The grim realities of trench warfare—the wet, cold, waist-deep mud, lice, and corpse-fed rats—contrasted sharply with the encouraging and

A dogfight (close combat between military aircraft) between German and British planes during the Great War. Dogfights as a new type of combat resulted from the attempt of each contestant to prevent the enemy from conducting aerial reconnaissance.
Historica Graphica Collection/Heritage Images/Getty Images

optimistic phrases of politicians and generals justifying the unrelenting slaughter.

**The Eastern Front** In eastern Europe and the Balkans, the battle lines were more fluid. After a staunch defense, a combination of Austrian and German forces overran Serbia, Albania, and Romania. Farther north, Russia took the offensive early by invading Prussia in 1914. The Central Powers recovered quickly, however, and by the summer of 1915 combined German and Austrian forces drove the Russian armies out of East Prussia and then out of Poland, establishing a defensive line extending from the Baltic to the Ukraine. Russian counterattacks in 1916 and 1917 collapsed amid massive casualties. The huge scale of Russian defeats in turn undermined the popularity of the tsar and his government and played a significant role in fostering revolutionary ferment within Russian society.

**Bloodletting** Many battles took place, but some were so horrific, so devastating, and so futile that their names are synonymous with human slaughter. The casualty figures attested to this bloodletting. In 1916 the Germans tried to break the deadlock with a huge assault on the fortress of **Verdun.** The French rallying cry was "They shall not pass," and they did not—but at a tremendous cost: while the defeated Germans suffered a loss of 280,000, the victorious French counted 315,000 dead. Survivors recovered fewer than 160,000 identifiable bodies. The rest were unrecognizable or had been blown to bits by high explosives and sucked into the mud. To relieve the pressure on Verdun, British forces counterattacked at the Somme, and by November they had gained a few thousand yards at the cost of 420,000 casualties. The Germans suffered similar losses, although in the end neither side gained any strategic advantage.

**New Rules of Engagement** Dying and suffering were not limited solely to combatants. Because they were crucial to the war effort, millions of civilians became targets of enemy military operations. On 30 August 1914, Parisians looked up at the sky and saw a new weapon of war, a huge, silent German zeppelin (a hydrogen-filled airship) whose underbelly rained bombs. Although the attack killed just one person, it heralded a new kind of warfare—air war against civilians. A less novel but more effective means of targeting civilian populations was the naval blockade. Military leaders on both sides used blockades to deny food to whole populations, hoping that starving civilians would force their governments to capitulate. The British blockade of Germany during the war contributed to the deaths of an estimated half-million Germans.

## Total War: The Home Front

Helmuth Karl von Moltke (1800–1891), former chief of the Prussian General Staff, showed an uncanny insight long before 1914 when he predicted that future wars would not end with a single battle because the defeat of a nation would not be acknowledged until the whole strength of its people was broken. He was right. As the Great War ground on, it became a conflict of attrition (gradually wearing down the enemy) in which the organization of material and human resources was of paramount importance. War became total, fought between entire societies, not just between armies; and total victory was the only acceptable outcome that might justify the terrible sacrifices made by all sides. The nature of total war created a military front and a home front. The term **home front** expressed the important reality that the outcome of the war hinged on how effectively each nation mobilized its economy and activated its noncombatant citizens to support the war effort.

**The Home Front** As the war continued beyond 1914 and as war weariness and a decline in economic capability set in, the response of all belligerents was to limit individual freedoms and give control of society increasingly over to military leaders.

## How the Past Shapes the Future

### The Destructive Potential of Industrial Technologies

**By the last half of the nineteenth century, a variety of European and American intellectuals believed that industrialization—which resulted in mass-produced goods, new and more rapid forms of communication, and all manner of mechanized devices—had led to a marked improvement in the human condition. Moreover, these same intellectuals were optimistic that industrialization would continue to contribute to the overall progress of humanity into the distant future. In many ways their expectations were realized: during the twentieth century industrial machinery made it possible to feed billions of people, build vast networks of roads, and create hundreds of millions of cars and airplanes. Mass-produced medicines made it possible to virtually eliminate smallpox, the plague, and a variety of other health scourges from much of the world, while mass-produced consumer goods allowed people to purchase, at relatively low cost, a bewildering variety of items designed to make them more comfortable. At an aggregate level, humans in the twentieth century lived longer, were less poor, were more connected to one another, and had access to more everyday comforts than their predecessors in previous centuries.**

### The Machinery of War

Yet the twentieth century also revealed the enormous costs of industrialization—costs that reverberate right up to the present. Indeed, although industrialization allowed the manufacture of goods and materials that brought people together or made life more convenient, it also allowed for the manufacture of items designed for destruction on a hitherto unimaginable scale. In this chapter we have already seen how the belligerent European nations involved in World War I marshaled their industrial power to manufacture deadly weapons, ammunition, chemical gases, tanks, and submarines. Few humans alive even in 1900 could have imagined the devastation—in both life and property—made possible when industrial powers put their energies toward destruction. In fact, disillusion with the destructive capacities of industrial technologies played an important role in the widespread atmosphere of anxiety that permeated intellectual and popular circles in Europe after the war—a process discussed in chapter 34. Such anxieties did not prevent industrialized nations from continuing to develop more and better ways to destroy their enemies, however. During World War II, opposing sides used industrial technology to kill ever more efficiently and quickly. In the case of Germany, Adolf Hitler took industrialized killing to a chilling new level when he authorized the use of advanced industrial techniques to kill millions of Jews, Gypsies, Slavs, dissidents, and homosexuals (chapter 36). After the war, the creation of the atom bomb used with such devastating effect in Hiroshima and Nagasaki made it clear that scientists had designed industrial weaponry capable of destroying entire populations in one blow. From that point until the dissolution of the Soviet Union in 1991, people all over the world were subjected to the threat of nuclear annihilation if the "cold" war between the United States and the Soviet Union ever erupted into a "hot" war (chapter 36). During the twentieth century, indeed, the threat of mass destruction via industrial technologies was a reality that significant segments of the world's population learned to live with, however uncomfortably.

Women at work in an English munitions factory. The Great War drew huge numbers of men out of the workforce at a time of great industrial need. Women replaced them, for the first time assuming traditionally "male" jobs.
Universal History Archive/Universal Images Group/Getty Images

### Environmental Impact

Industrial technologies also proved to be destructive during the twentieth century in terms of their environmental impact. Since the nineteenth century, industrial economies relied on fossil fuels to function. In addition, industrial manufacturing required the widespread exploitation of raw materials such as cotton and timber. During the nineteenth and much of the twentieth centuries, industrializing states operated as though fossil fuels and raw materials would be endlessly available. Over time, however, it became clear that large-scale industrialization resulted in air and water pollution as well as in deforestation, erosion, and the loss of biodiversity. During the post–World War II period, these problems intensified as a variety of new states sought to establish industrialized economies of their own—a process discussed in chapter 37. By the end of the twentieth century, moreover, the majority of the world's scientists concluded that the pollution generated by more than a century of industrialization had caused changes in climate on a planetary scale (chapter 38). The ultimate impact of these changes remains unclear, although some scientists fear that it may be too late to undo the damage that has been set in motion from industrialization.

These are only a small sampling of the destructive potential of industrial technologies, both through time and across space. When reading subsequent chapters, try to identify additional developments whose origins can be traced to the consequences of industrialization, whether of a positive or destructive nature.

Because patriotism and courage alone could not guarantee victory, the governments of belligerent nations assumed control of the home front. Initially, ministers and generals were reluctant to resort to compulsive measures, even conscription of recruits, but they quickly changed their minds. Each belligerent government eventually militarized civilian war production by subordinating private enterprises to governmental control and imposing severe discipline on the labor process.

Economic measures were foremost in the minds of government leaders because the war created unprecedented demands for raw materials and manufactured goods. Those material requirements compelled governments to institute tight controls over economic life. Planning boards reorganized entire industries, set production quotas and priorities, and determined what would be produced and consumed. Government authorities also established wage and price controls, extended work hours, and in some instances restricted the movement of workers. Because bloody battlefields caused an insatiable appetite for soldiers, nations responded by extending the age range for compulsory military service. In Germany, for example, men between the ages of sixteen and sixty were eligible to serve at the front. By constantly tapping into the available male population, the war created an increasing demand for workers at home. Unemployment—a persistent feature of all prewar economies—vanished virtually overnight.

**Women at War** As men went off to war, women replaced them at work. Conscription took men out of the labor force, and wartime leaders exhorted women to fill the gaps in the workforce. A combination of patriotism and high wages drew women into formerly "male" jobs. The lives of women changed as they left home or domestic service for the workplace. Some women took over the management of farms and businesses left by their husbands, who went off to fight. Others found jobs as postal workers and police officers. Behind the battle lines, women were most visible as nurses, physicians, and communications clerks.

Perhaps the most crucial work performed by women during the war was the making of shells. Several million women, and sometimes children, put in long, hard hours in munitions factories. This work exposed them to severe dangers. The first came from explosions because keeping sparks away from highly volatile materials was impossible. Many women died in these incidents, although government censorship during the war made it difficult to know how many. The other, more insidious danger came from working with TNT explosives. Although authorities claimed that this work was not dangerous, exposure to TNT caused severe poisoning, depending on the length of exposure. Before serious illnesses manifested themselves, TNT poisoning marked its victims by turning their skin yellow and their hair orange. Long-term health effects included damage to the eyes and skin, liver damage, reproductive problems, and severe anemia. The accepted though ineffectual

Perhaps the most crucial work performed by women during the war was the making of shells. This photograph shows a female assembly-line worker in a munitions factory in England in 1917.
Hulton Deutsch/Corbis Historical/Getty Images

# SOURCES FROM THE PAST

## Dulce et Decorum Est

*The Great War produced a wealth of poetry. The poetic response to war covered a range of moods, from early romanticism and patriotism to cynicism, resignation, and the angry depiction of horror. One of the best-known war poets was Wilfred Owen (1893–1918), whose poems are among the most poignant of the war. Owen, who enlisted for service on the western front in 1915 at the age of twenty-two, was injured in March 1917 and sent home. Declared fit for duty in August 1918, he returned to the front. German machine-gun fire killed him on 7 November, four days before the armistice that ended the war, when he tried to cross the Sambre Canal. This poem was published in 1920, two years after his death.*

Bent double, like old beggars under sacks,
Knock-kneed, coughing like hags, we cursed through sludge,
Till on the haunting flares we turned our backs
And towards our distant rest began to trudge.
Men marched asleep. Many had lost their boots
But limped on, blood-shod. All went lame; all blind;
Drunk with fatigue; deaf even to the hoots
Of gas-shells dropping softly behind.

> What is Owen trying to convey about the physical demands of service during the war?

Gas! GAS! Quick, boys!—An ecstasy of fumbling,
Fitting the clumsy helmets just in time;
But someone still was yelling out and stumbling
And floundering like a man in fire or lime.—
Dim, through the misty panes and thick green light
As under a green sea, I saw him drowning.
In all my dreams, before my helpless sight,
He plunges at me, guttering, choking, drowning.
If in some smothering dreams you too could pace
Behind the wagon that we flung him in,
And watch the white eyes writhing in his face,
His hanging face, like a devil's sick of sin;
If you could hear, at every jolt, the blood
Come gargling from the froth-corrupted lungs,
Obscene as cancer, bitter as the cud
Of vile, incurable sores on innocent tongues,—
My friend, you would not tell with such high zest
To children ardent for some desperate glory,
The old Lie: Dulce et decorum est
Pro patria mori.*

> How does Owen describe the effects of a gas attack? Is his literary depiction more or less effective than detached descriptions of war's effects?

**Author's note:* "Sweet and fitting is it to die for one's country" comes from a line by the Roman poet Horace (65–8 B.C.E.).

### For Further Reflection

- What is Owen's overall message in this poem? Do you think he intended to take a political stand on war or that he was simply describing his experience?
- How does the poem impact readers compared to a newspaper article?
- If poems such as this one had been published earlier in the war, what do you think would be the response?

*Source:* Owen, Wilfred. Dulce et Decorum Est, 1918.

remedy for TNT poisoning was rest, good food, and plenty of fresh milk.

Middle- and upper-class women often reported that the war was a liberating experience, freeing them from older attitudes that had limited their work and their personal lives. These women, who had not typically worked outside the home, frequently remarked on a sense of mission and the knowledge that they were important to the war effort. Working-class women, in contrast, had long been accustomed to earning wages, and for them war work proved far less liberating. Most of the belligerent governments promised equal pay for equal work, but in most instances that promise remained unfulfilled. Although women's industrial wages rose during the war, measurable gaps always remained between the incomes of men and women. In the end, female employment on such a large scale was a temporary phenomenon that ended when the war was over. At the end of the war, women were encouraged (and often required) to leave their wartime jobs in order to accommodate the men returning from service. Nevertheless, the extension of voting rights to women shortly after the war, in Britain (1918, for women thirty years and older), Germany (1919), and Austria (1919), was in part an acknowledgment of the important roles women assumed during the Great War.

**Propaganda** To maintain the spirit of the home front and to counter threats to national unity, governments resorted to the restriction of civil liberties, censorship of bad news, and vilification of the enemy through propaganda campaigns. While government officials busily censored war news, including letters from soldiers at the front, people who had the temerity to criticize their nation's war effort were prosecuted as traitors. In France, for example, former prime minister Joseph Caillaux spent two years in prison awaiting trial because he had publicly suggested that the best interest of France would be to reach a compromise peace with Germany.

The propaganda offices of the belligerent nations tried to convince the public that military defeat would mean the destruction of everything worth living for, and to that end they did their utmost to discredit and dehumanize the enemy. Posters, pamphlets, and "scientific" studies depicted the enemy as subhuman savages who engaged in vile atrocities. While German propaganda depicted Russians as "semi-Asiatic barbarians", French authorities chronicled the atrocities committed by the German "Hun" in Belgium. In 1917 the *Times* of London published a story claiming that Germans converted human corpses into fertilizer and food. With much less fanfare a later news story admitted that this information resulted from a sloppy translation: the German word for *horse* had been mistakenly translated as "human." German propaganda stooped equally low. One widely distributed poster invoked racist tropes by showing caricatures of black Allied soldiers raping German women, including pregnant women, to suggest the horrors that would follow if the nation's war effort failed. Most atrocity stories originated in the fertile imagination of propaganda officers, and their falsehood eventually engendered public skepticism and cynicism. Ironically, public disbelief of wartime propaganda led to skepticism about actual abominations perpetrated during subsequent wars.

## Conflict in East Asia and the Pacific

For many people outside Europe, the Great War was a murderous European civil war that quickly turned into a global conflict. There were three reasons for the war's expansion. First, European governments carried their animosities into their colonies, embroiling them—especially African societies—in their war. Second, because of massive casualties among European recruits, the British and the French augmented their ranks by recruiting men from their colonies. Millions of Africans and Asians were drawn into the war. Behind their trenches the French employed soldiers and laborers from Algeria, West Africa, and French Indochina, while the British recruited more than a million Indian soldiers as well as African troops for combat. The British also relied on troops furnished by the dominion lands, including Australia, New Zealand, Canada, Newfoundland, and South Africa. Third, the Great War assumed global significance because the desires and objectives of some principal actors that entered the conflict—Japan, the United States, and the Ottoman Empire—had little to do with the murder in Sarajevo or the other issues that drove the Europeans to battle.

**Japan's Entry into the War** On 15 August 1914 the Japanese government, claiming that it desired "to secure firm and enduring peace in Eastern Asia," sent an ultimatum to Germany demanding the handover of the German-leased territory of Jiaozhou (northeastern China) to Japanese authorities without compensation. The same note also demanded that the German navy unconditionally withdraw its warships from Japanese and Chinese waters. When the Germans refused to comply, the Japanese entered the war on the side of the Allies on 23 August 1914. With the blessing of their British allies (including the assistance of two British battalions), Japanese forces took the fortress of Qingdao, a German-held port in China's Shandong Province, in November 1914. Then, between August and November of that year, Japanese forces also took possession of the German-held Marshall Islands, the Mariana Islands, Palau, and the Carolines. Forces from New Zealand and Australia joined in the Japanese quest for German-held islands in the Pacific, capturing German-held portions of Samoa in August 1914 and German-occupied possessions in the Bismarck Archipelago and New Guinea.

**The Twenty-one Demands** After seizing German bases on the Shandong peninsula and on Pacific islands, Japan shrewdly exploited Allied support and European preoccupation to advance its own imperial interests in China. On 18 January 1915 the Japanese presented the Chinese government with twenty-one secret demands. The terms of that ultimatum, if accepted, would have reduced China to a protectorate of Japan. The most important demands were that the Chinese confirm the Japanese seizure of Shandong from Germany, grant Japanese industrial monopolies in central China, place Japanese overseers in key government positions, give Japan joint control of Chinese police forces, restrict their arms purchases to Japanese manufacturers, and make those purchases only with the approval of the Tokyo government. China submitted to most of the demands but rejected others. Chinese diplomats leaked the note to the British authorities, who spoke up for China, thus preventing total capitulation. The **Twenty-one Demands** reflected Japan's determination to dominate east Asia and served as the basis for future Japanese pressure on China.

## Africa and Africans in the War

The geographic extent of the conflict also broadened beyond Europe when the Allies targeted German colonies in Africa. When the war of 1914–1918 erupted in Europe, all of sub-Saharan Africa (except Ethiopia and Liberia) consisted of European colonies, with the Germans controlling four: Togoland, the Cameroons, German Southwest Africa, and German East Africa. Thus, one immediate consequence of war for Africans in 1914 was that the Allies invaded those German colonies. Specific strategic interests among the Allies varied. British officers and soldiers, trying to maintain naval supremacy, attempted to put German port facilities and communications systems out of action. The British also anticipated that victory in the German colonies would mean the acquisition of German territory in Africa after the war. France's objective was to recover territory in Cameroon that it had ceded to Germany in 1911. The Germans, in contrast, simply tried to hold on to what they had.

An Indian gun crew in the Somme area, 1916. During the Great War, colonial powers relied on millions of Asian and African men to fight or labor for their respective sides.
National Archives (165-BO-1602)

**Battles in Africa** Although their position in Africa was far less powerful than that of either the British or the French, by resorting to guerrilla tactics some fifteen thousand German troops tied sixty thousand Allied forces down for the duration of the war. While Togoland fell to an Anglo-French force after three weeks of fighting, it took extended campaigns ranging over vast distances to subdue the remaining German footholds in Africa. The Allied force included British, Portuguese, French, and Belgian troops and large contingents of Indian, Arab, and African soldiers. Fighting took place on land and sea; on lakes and rivers; in deserts, jungles, and swamps; and in the air. Germs were frequently more deadly than battles; tens of thousands of Allied soldiers and workers succumbed to deadly tropical diseases. The German flag did not disappear from Africa until after the armistice took effect on 11 November 1918.

**Africans in the War** More than one million African soldiers participated directly in military campaigns, in which they witnessed firsthand the spectacle of white people fighting

## What's Left Out?

For decades after the Great War, historians focused on the European causes of the Great War and its major European battlefronts. While understandable given the scale of destruction in Europe, such a focus obscured the profound ways World War I affected even neutral territories thousands of miles away. One of the reasons is because the German government established the principle of instigating revolutions in Allied colonies as an explicit war aim. Germany was especially interested in starting a revolution in India because it was Britain's most important colony and provided over a million soldiers for the war effort. For this reason, the German Foreign Office created the Committee for Indian Independence and staffed it with Indian revolutionaries who planned the immediate overthrow of British rule. Indian revolutionaries were already active before the war, but now they found common cause with a powerful state willing to provide them with money, weapons, and logistical support. During the war, the German government funded initiatives aimed at fomenting revolution in India, including establishing a secret military training base for Indians in Siam (Thailand), smuggling weapons to India from the United States via China and the Dutch East Indies, and distributing propaganda intended to whip up popular Indian support for rebellion. These efforts all required revolutionaries to move around the world and to coordinate their efforts with German consuls in neutral territories as diverse as the Dutch East Indies, the United States, Siam, and China (the latter three were neutral until 1917). These contacts, in turn, brought the politics of the war right into neutral territories because officials in those places feared they would be dragged into the war if the Central Powers were caught plotting against the Allies on their soil. As a result, each had to devote significant energy and money toward stopping German coordination with colonial revolutionaries. This example helps us to see that the enmities between the Allied and the Central Powers were not simply fought out on European battlefronts and in European colonies, but even in neutral territories halfway around the world.

*Source:* Heather Streets-Salter, *World War One in Southeast Asia* (Cambridge: Cambridge University Press, 2017).

### Thinking Critically About Sources

1. Why did Germany support independence in the Allied colonies? What strategies did they use to support them?
2. Although the colonies did not overtly rebel during WWI, how did Germany's plan help them?

## INTERPRETING IMAGES

A company of Askari riflemen fighting for the Germans march in German East Africa.

**Analyze** *Consider this photo and the one of Indian fighters at The Somme earlier in the chapter. What would motivate Asians and Africans to fight in a European war? How might these efforts backfire for Europeans after the war?*

Pictorial Press Ltd/Alamy Stock Photo

one another. They fought on African soil, in the lands of southwest Asia, and on the western front in Europe. Even more men, as well as women and children, served as carriers to support armies in areas where supplies could not be hauled by conventional methods such as road, rail, or pack animal. The colonial powers raised recruits for fighting and carrier services in three ways: on a purely voluntary basis, in levies supplied by African chiefs that consisted of volunteer and impressed (coerced) personnel, and through formal conscription. In French colonies, military service became compulsory for all males between the ages of twenty and twenty-eight, and by the end of the war more than four hundred eighty thousand colonial troops had served in the French army. The British also raised recruits in their African colonies. In 1915 a compulsory service order made all men aged eighteen to twenty-five liable for military service. In the Congo, the Belgians impressed more than half a million porters. Ultimately, more than one hundred fifty thousand African soldiers and carriers lost their lives, and many more suffered injury or became disabled.

## Battles in Southwest Asia

The most extensive military operations outside Europe took place in the southwest Asian territories of the Ottoman Empire. When war broke out between the Allied and Central powers in 1914, the Ottoman government feared that the victors would carve up what was left of its empire if it did not ally with one side or the other. After being rebuffed by the British, the Ottoman government turned to the Germans and entered into a formal alliance on October 28, 1914. Once a member of the Central Powers, the Germans convinced the Ottomans—as the seat of the caliph, or the nominal leader of Sunni Muslims around the world—to declare a *jihad* (religious war) against the Allies. This, they hoped, would undermine support for the Allies by the millions of Muslim colonial subjects ruled by Britain, France, and Russia. Although the jihadist strategy was not as effective as the Germans had hoped, the Allies viewed it with alarm and made a concerted effort to undermine the Ottoman Empire in a variety of its territories.

**Gallipoli** Ottoman entry into the war also seemed to offer a way for the Allies to break the stalemate on the western front. To accomplish this, Winston Churchill (1874–1965), first lord of the Admiralty (British navy), suggested an Allied strike against the Ottomans via the Ottoman-controlled Dardanelles Strait (see Map 33.1). Early in 1915 British and French naval forces conducted an expedition to seize the approach to the Strait in an attempt to open a warm-water supply line to Russia. After bombing the forts that defended the strait, Allied ships were damaged by floating mines and withdrew without accomplishing their mission. After withdrawing the battleships, the British high command decided to land a combined force of soldiers from Britain, Canada, Austrialia, and New Zealand on the beaches of the Gallipoli peninsula. The campaign was a disaster. Turkish defenders, ensconced in the cliffs above, quickly pinned down the Allied troops on the beaches. Trapped between the sea and the hills, Allied soldiers dug in and engaged in their own version of trench warfare. The resulting stalemate produced a total of 250,000 casualties on each side. Despite the losses, Allied leaders took nine months to admit that their campaign had failed.

**Gallipoli** was a debacle with long-term consequences. Although the British directed the ill-fated campaign, it was mostly Canadians, Australians, and New Zealanders who suffered terrible casualties. That recognition led to a weakening of imperial ties and paved the way for emerging national identities. In Australia the date of the fateful landing, 25 April 1915, became enshrined as Anzac (an acronym for Australian and New Zealand Army Corps) Day and remains the country's most significant day of public homage. On the Ottoman side, the battle for the strait helped launch the political career of the commander of the Turkish division that defended Gallipoli. Mustafa Kemal (1881–1938) went on to play a crucial role in the formation of the modern Turkish state.

**Armenian Massacres** The war provided the pretext for the Ottoman government to begin a campaign of extermination against the two million Armenians living under its rule. Armenians were the last remaining major non-Muslim ethnic group living under Ottoman rule, and like other Christians who had once been subject to Ottoman rule, they sought autonomy and eventual independence. Friction between Armenians and Ottoman authorities went back to the nineteenth century, when distinct nationalist feelings stirred many of the peoples who lived under Ottoman rule.

Initially, Armenians had relied on government reforms to prevent discrimination against non-Muslim subjects by corrupt officials and extortionist tax collectors. When abuses persisted, Armenians resorted to confrontation. Armenian demonstrations against Ottoman authorities in 1890 and 1895 led to reprisals by a government that had become increasingly convinced that the Armenians were seeking independence, as other Christian minorities of the Balkans had done in previous decades.

After 1913 the Ottoman state adopted a new policy of Turkish nationalism intended to strengthen morale within the shrinking empire. The new nationalism stressed Turkish culture and traditions, which aggravated tensions between Turkish rulers and non-Turkish subjects of the empire. In particular, the state viewed Christian minorities as an obstacle to Turkish nationalism. During the Great War, the Ottoman government branded Armenians as a traitorous internal enemy, who threatened the security of the state, and then unleashed a murderous campaign against them. Forced mass evacuations, accompanied by starvation, dehydration, and exposure, led to the death of tens of thousands of Armenians. The Ottoman government also organized massacres of Armenians through mass drowning, incineration, or assaults with blunt instruments.

The wartime Ottoman campaign against its Armenian subjects has become known as the **Armenian Genocide**. Scholars estimate that close to a million Armenians perished during the genocide. Yet the Turkish government rejects the label of genocide and claims that Armenian deaths resulted not from a state-sponsored plan of mass extermination but from disease, famine, and religious fighting between ordinary Christians and Muslims.

**The Ottoman Empire** After successfully fending off Allied forces on the beaches of Gallipoli in 1915 and in Mesopotamia in 1916, Ottoman armies retreated slowly on all fronts. The British in particular were instrumental in coordinating multiple attacks against the Ottomans, using armies that drew heavily on recruits from Egypt, India, Australia, and New Zealand to invade Ottoman territory. As the armies smashed the Ottoman state—one entering Mesopotamia and the other advancing from the Suez Canal toward Palestine—they received significant support from an Arab revolt against the Turks. In 1916, aided by the British, the nomadic bedouin of Arabia under the leadership of Hussein bin Ali, sharif of Mecca and king of the Hejaz (1856–1931), and others rose up against Turkish rule. The motivation for the Arab revolt centered on securing independence from the Ottoman Empire—a goal the British government promised to help Arabs reach—and subsequently creating a unified Arab nation spanning lands from Syria to Yemen.

The British government did not keep its promise of Arab independence after the war. Instead, the British and French governments, with the assent of Russia, forged a secret agreement, the **Sykes-Picot Treaty** of 1916, and divided Ottoman territory in southwest Asia between them in the aftermath of their victory in the war. Further complicating the issue and creating a future source of conflict was the 1917 **Balfour Declaration,** by which the British government publicly declared its support for "the establishment in Palestine of a national home for the Jewish people."

## THE END OF THE WAR

The war produced strains within all the belligerent nations, but most of them managed, often ruthlessly, to cope with food riots, strikes, and mutinies. In the Russian Empire, the war amplified existing stresses to such an extent that the Romanov dynasty was forced to abdicate in favor of a provisional government in the spring of 1917. Eight months later, **Bolshevik** revolutionaries took power from the provisional government. The Bolsheviks then promptly took Russia out of the war early in 1918. This blow to the Allies was offset by the entry of the United States into the conflict in 1917, which turned the tide of war in 1918. The resources of the United States finally compelled the exhausted Central Powers to sue for peace in November 1918.

In 1919 the victorious Allies gathered in Paris to hammer out a peace settlement. The settlements that resulted were compromises that pleased few of the parties involved. The most significant consequence of the war was Europe's diminished role in the world, though this was not immediately visible to contemporaries. The war of 1914–1918 undermined Europe's power and simultaneously promoted nationalist aspirations among colonized peoples who clamored for self-determination and national independence. For the time being, however, the major imperialist powers kept their grip on their overseas holdings.

### Revolution in Russia

**The February Revolution** The Great War had seriously undermined the Russian state. In the spring of 1917, disintegrating armies, mutinies, and food shortages provoked a series of street demonstrations and strikes in Petrograd (St. Petersburg). The inability of police forces to suppress the uprisings, and the subsequent mutiny of troops garrisoned in the capital, persuaded Tsar Nicholas II (reigned 1894–1917) to abdicate the throne in March of that year. Thus Russia ceased to be a monarchy, and the **Romanov dynasty** disappeared after more than three hundred years of uninterrupted rule. Russians called this the **February Revolution** because Russians used the Julian calendar rather than the Gregorian calendar in use by western European states.

**The Struggle for Power** After its success in Petrograd, the revolution spread throughout the country, and political power in Russia shifted to two new agencies: the provisional government and the Petrograd soviet of Workers' and Soldiers' Deputies. Soviets, which were revolutionary councils organized by socialists, appeared for the first time during the Russian revolution of 1905 (see chapter 31). In 1917, soviets of

**Sykes-Picot** (sikes pee-coh)
**Bolshevik** (BOHL-sheh-vihk)

Vladimir Lenin (1870–1924) makes a speech in Red Square on the first anniversary (1918) of the Bolshevik revolution. Hulton Deutsch/Corbis Historical/Getty Images

Workers' and Soldiers' Deputies surfaced all over Russia, wielding considerable power through their control of factories and segments of the military. The period between March and November witnessed a political struggle between the provisional government and the powerful Petrograd soviet. At first the new government enjoyed considerable public support as it disbanded the tsarist police; repealed all limitations on freedom of speech, press, and association; and abolished laws that discriminated against ethnic or religious groups. But it failed to satisfy popular demands for an end to war and for land reform. It claimed that, being provisional, it could not make fundamental changes such as confiscating land and distributing it among peasants. Any such change had to be postponed for decision by a future constituent assembly. The government also pledged itself to "unswervingly carry out the agreements made with the Allies" and promised to continue the war to a victorious conclusion. The Petrograd soviet, in contrast, called for an immediate peace. The soviets were the only ones in Russia determined to end the war and hence gained more support from the people of Russia.

**Lenin** Into this tense political situation stepped **Vladimir Ilyich Lenin** (1870–1924), a revolutionary Marxist who had been living in exile in Switzerland. Born into a warm and loving family, Lenin grew up in the confines of a moderately prosperous family living in the provincial Russian town of Simbirsk. In 1887, shortly after his father's death, the police arrested and hanged his older brother for plotting to assassinate the tsar, an event that seared Lenin's youth. Following a brief career as a lawyer, Lenin spent many years abroad, devoting himself to studying Marxist thought and writing political pamphlets. In contrast to Marx, Lenin viewed the industrial working class as incapable of developing the proper revolutionary consciousness that would lead to effective political action. To Lenin the industrial proletariat required the leadership of a well-organized and highly disciplined party, a workers' vanguard that would serve as the catalyst for revolution and for the realization of a socialist society.

In a moment of high drama, the German High Command transported Lenin and other revolutionaries in 1917 to Russia in a sealed train, hoping that this committed antiwar activist would stir up trouble and bring about Russia's withdrawal from the war. Lenin headed the Bolsheviks, the radical wing of the Russian Social Democratic Party. In April he began calling for the transfer of legal authority to the soviets and advocated uncompromising opposition to the war. Initially, his party opposed his radicalism, but he soon succeeded in converting his fellow Bolsheviks to his proposals.

**The October Revolution** The Bolsheviks, who were a small minority among revolutionary working-class parties, eventually gained control of the Petrograd soviet. Crucial to that development was the provisional government's insistence on continuing the war, its inability to feed the population, and its refusal to undertake land reform. Those policies led to a growing conviction among workers and peasants that their problems could only be solved by the soviets. The Bolsheviks capitalized on that mood with effective slogans such as "All Power to the Soviets" and, most famous, "Peace, Land, and Bread." In September, Lenin persuaded the Central Committee of the Bolshevik Party to organize an armed insurrection and seize power in the name of the All-Russian National Congress of Soviets, which was then convening in Petrograd. During the night of 6 November and the following day, armed workers, soldiers, and sailors stormed the Winter Palace, the home of the provisional government. By the afternoon of 7 November (although called the **October Revolution** in Russia because of the Julian calendar), the virtually bloodless insurrection had run its course, and power passed from the provisional government into the hands of Lenin and the Bolshevik

**Vladimir Ilyich Lenin** (VLAD-uh-meer IL-yich LEHN-in)

Party. The U.S. journalist John Reed (1887–1920), who witnessed the Bolshevik seizure of power, understood the significance of the events when he referred to them as "ten days that shook the world." Lenin and his followers were poised to destroy the traditional patterns and values of Russian society and challenge the institutions of capitalist society everywhere.

**Treaty of Brest-Litovsk** The Bolshevik rulers ended Russia's involvement in the Great War by signing the **Treaty of Brest-Litovsk** with Germany on 3 March 1918. The treaty gave the Germans possession or control of much of Russia's territory (the Baltic states, the Caucasus, Finland, Poland, and the Ukraine) and one-quarter of its population. The terms of the treaty were harsh and humiliating, but taking Russia out of the war gave the new government an opportunity to deal with internal problems. Russia's departure from the war meant that Germany could concentrate all its resources on the western front.

## U.S. Intervention and Collapse of the Central Powers

The year 1917 was crucial for another reason: it marked the entry of the United States into the war on the side of the Allies. In 1914 the American public firmly opposed intervention in a European war. Woodrow Wilson (1856–1924) was reelected president in 1916 because he campaigned on a nonintervention platform. That sentiment soon changed. After the outbreak of the war, the United States pursued a neutrality that favored the Allies, and as the war progressed, the United States became increasingly committed economically to an Allied victory.

**Economic Considerations** During the first two years of the war, the U.S. economy coped with a severe business recession that saw thousands of businesses fail and unemployment reach 15 percent. Economic recovery became dependent on sales of war materials, especially on British orders for

## INTERPRETING IMAGES

In 1915, artist Willy Stower depicted a ship sinking as a result of a submarine attack. The Germans used submarines to great effect to disrupt the shipping of essential supplies to Great Britain.

**Analyze** *Why would this painting provide a more powerful message to the public than a chart of statistics about submarine attacks?*

Bettmann/Getty Images

munitions. Because U.S. companies sold huge amounts of supplies to the Allies, insistence on neutrality seemed hypocritical at best. With the war grinding on, the Allies took out large loans with American banks, which persuaded some Americans that an Allied victory made good financial sense. Moreover, by the spring of 1917, the Allies had depleted their means of paying for essential supplies from the United States and probably could not have maintained their war effort had the United States remained neutral. An Allied victory and, hence, the ability to pay off Allied war debts could be accomplished only by direct U.S. participation in the Great War.

This 1917–1918 U.S. army recruitment poster depicts an apish monster leaving war-torn Europe and emerging on the shores of America. Wielding a club labeled Kultur, and wearing a spiked helmet associated with Prussian and German militarism, this is a less than subtle caricature of the threat emanating from a warmongering Germany.
Library of Congress Prints & Photographs Division [LC-DIG-ds-03216]

**Submarine Warfare** The official factor in the United States' decision to enter the war was Germany's resumption of **unrestricted submarine warfare** in February 1917. At the outset of the war, U.S. government officials asserted the traditional doctrine of neutral rights for American ships because they wanted to continue trading with belligerents, most notably the British and the French. With the German surface fleet bottled up in the Baltic, Germany's wartime leaders grew desperately dependent on their submarine fleet to strangle Britain economically and break the British blockade of the Central Powers. German military experts calculated that submarine attacks against the ships of Great Britain and all the ships headed to Great Britain would bring about the defeat of Great Britain in six months. German subs often sank neutral merchant ships without first giving a warning as required by international law. On 7 May 1915, a German submarine sank the British passenger liner *Lusitania* off the Irish coast, with a loss of 1,198 lives, including 128 U.S. citizens. Technically, the ship was a legitimate target because it carried 4,200 cases of ammunition and traveled through a declared war zone. Nevertheless, segments of the American public were outraged, and during the next two years the country's mood increasingly turned against Germany.

American public opinion became further enraged in 1917 when the content of a coded telegram came to light, dispatched by the foreign secretary of the German Empire, Arthur Zimmermann, to the German ambassador in Mexico. This so-called **Zimmermann telegram** was a diplomatic proposal for Mexico to join the Central Powers in the event of the United States entering World War I on the side of the Triple Entente. In return for a military alliance, Mexico was promised territories in Texas, New Mexico, and Arizona. The Mexican government was not tempted by this offer. It ignored the proposal and officially rejected it after the United States entered the war.

**America Declares War** Even though the British naval blockade directed at the Central Powers constantly interfered with American shipping, Woodrow Wilson nonetheless moved his nation to war against Germany. In January 1917, with his country still at peace, Wilson began to enumerate U.S. war aims, and on April 2 he urged the Congress of the United States to adopt a war resolution. In his ringing war message, Wilson equated German "warfare against commerce" with "warfare against mankind," intoning that "the world must be made safe for democracy." Republican senator George W. Norris, arguing for U.S. neutrality, countered by saying, "I feel that we are about to put the dollar sign upon the American flag." That protest was to no avail, and on April 6, 1917, the United States declared war against Germany. The U.S. entry proved decisive in breaking the stalemate.

**Collapsing Fronts** The corrosive effects of years of bloodletting showed. For the first two years of the conflict, most people supported their governments' war efforts, but the continuing ravages of war took their toll everywhere. In April 1916 Irish nationalists mounted the Easter Rebellion, which attempted

German prisoners of war in 1917. Over six million prisoners of war were captured by both sides during the conflict, creating strains on wartime economies. Imprisoned enlisted men were put to work to supplement labor shortages by both the Allies and the Central Powers.
GL Archive/Alamy Stock Photo

unsuccessfully to overthrow British rule in Ireland. The Central Powers suffered from food shortages as a result of the British blockade, and increasing numbers of people took to the streets to demonstrate against declining food rations. Food riots were complemented by strikes as prewar social conflicts reemerged. Governments reacted harshly to those challenges by suppressing demonstrators and jailing dissidents. Equally dangerous was the breakdown of military discipline. At the German naval base in Kiel, sailors revolted in the summer of 1917 and again, much more seriously, in the fall of 1918. In the wake of another failed offensive during the spring of 1917, which resulted in ghastly casualties, French soldiers also lost confidence in their leadership. When ordered to attack once again, they refused. The extent of the mutiny was enormous: 50,000 soldiers were involved, resulting in 23,385 courts-martial and 432 death sentences. So tight was French censorship that the Germans, who could have taken advantage of this situation, did not learn about the mutiny until the war was over.

Against the background of civilian disillusionment and deteriorating economic conditions, Germany took the risk of throwing its remaining might at the western front in the spring of 1918. The gamble failed, and as the offensive petered out, the Allies—reinforced with fresh troops from the United States—broke through the front and started pushing the Germans back. By that time Germany had effectively exhausted its human and material means to wage war. Meanwhile, Bulgaria capitulated to the invading Allies on 30 September, the Ottomans concluded an armistice on 30 October, and Austria-Hungary surrendered on 4 November. Finally, the Germans accepted an armistice, which took effect on 11 November 1918. At last the guns went silent.

## After the War

The immediate effects of the Great War were all too obvious. Aside from the physical destruction, which was most visible in northern France and Belgium, the war had killed, disabled, orphaned, or rendered homeless millions of people. Conservative estimates suggest that the war killed fifteen million people and wounded twenty million others. In the immediate postwar years, millions more succumbed to the effects of starvation, malnutrition, and epidemic diseases.

**The Influenza Pandemic of 1918** The end of the Great War coincided with the arrival of one of the worst pandemics ever recorded in human history. No one knows its origins or why it vanished in mid-1919, but by the time this virulent influenza disappeared, it had left more than twenty million dead. The disease killed more people than did the Great War, and it hit young adults—a group usually not severely affected by influenza—with particular ferocity.

The Great War did not cause the **influenza pandemic** of 1918–1919, but wartime traffic on land and sea probably contributed to the spread of the infection. It killed swiftly wherever it went. From the remotest villages in Arctic climates and crowded cities in India and the United States to the battlefields of Europe, men and women were struck down by high fever. Within a few days they were dead. One estimate puts deaths in India alone at seven million. In Calcutta, the postal service and the legal system ground to a halt. In the United States, the flu killed more Americans than all the wars fought in the twentieth century put together. In cutting a swath across west Africa, it left in its deadly path more than one million victims. The Pacific islands suffered worst of all as the flu wiped out up to 25 percent of their entire population.

There was no cure for the flu of 1918 and the influenza plague never discriminated. It struck the rich as fiercely as the poor. It decimated men and women equally. It did not distinguish between the hungry and the well nourished, and it took the healthy as well as the sick.

**The Paris Settlement** Before the costs of the war were assessed fully, world attention shifted to Paris. There, in 1919, the victorious powers convened to arrange a postwar settlement and set terms for the defeated nations. At the outset, people on both sides of the war had high hopes for the settlement, but in the end it left a bitter legacy. Because the twenty-seven nations represented at Paris had different and often conflicting aims, many sessions of the conference deteriorated into pandemonium. Ultimately, **Georges Clemenceau** (1841-1929), **Lloyd George** (1863-1945), and **Woodrow Wilson**—the representative leaders of France, Great Britain, and the United States—dominated the deliberations. The Allies did not permit representatives of the Central Powers to participate. In addition, the Allies threatened to renew the war if the terms they laid down were not accepted. Significantly, the Soviet Union was not invited to the conference. Throughout this time the British blockade of Germany remained in effect, adding a sense of urgency to the proceedings. That situation later gave rise to the charge of a dictated peace.

**Wilson's Fourteen Points** One year before the opening of the **Paris Peace Conference** in January 1918, U.S. president Woodrow Wilson forwarded a proposal for a just and enduring postwar peace settlement. Wilson's postwar vision had subsequently prompted the defeated Central Powers to announce their acceptance of his so-called Fourteen Points as the basis for the armistice. They also expected the Allies to use them as the foundation for later peace treaties. Key among Wilson's **Fourteen Points** were the following recommendations: open covenants (agreements) of peace, openly arrived at; absolute freedom of navigation on the seas in peace and war; the removal of all economic barriers and the establishment of an equality of trade conditions among all nations; adequate guarantees for a reduction in national armaments; adjustments of colonial disputes to give equal weight to the interests of the controlling government and the colonial population; and a call for "a general association of nations." The idealism expressed in the Fourteen Points gave Wilson a position of moral leadership among the Allies. Those same allies also opposed various points of Wilson's peace formula because those points compromised the secret wartime agreements by which they had agreed to distribute among themselves territories and possessions of the defeated nations. The defeated powers, in turn, later felt betrayed when they faced the harsh peace treaties that so clearly violated the spirit of the Fourteen Points.

## INTERPRETING IMAGES

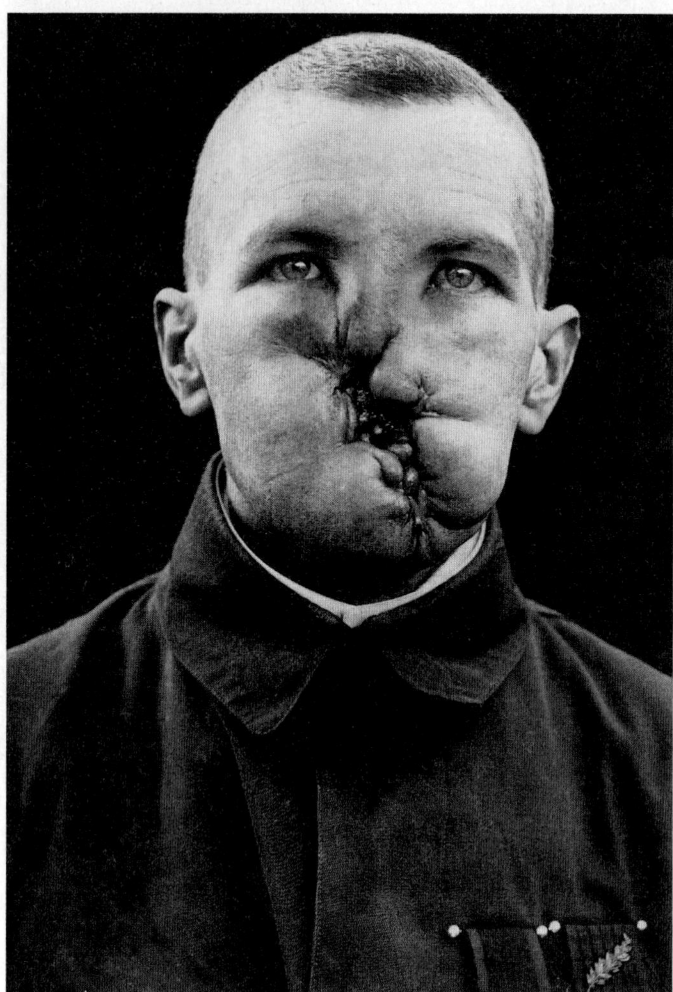

The Great War exacted an awful toll on human life, in terms of both the dead and the disfigured survivors. This brutally scarred French soldier in 1918 vividly represented the human cost of the war. Exact figures will always remain in dispute, but the best estimates suggest that the Great War claimed the lives of some 8.5 million soldiers. A far greater number, some 21 million soldiers, suffered injuries, many of them so serious they scarred people permanently, as in the case of this soldier.

**Analyze** *Consider previous portraits you have seen in this book. Would a subject like this have been captured in an artistic representation? Why or why not? How does this photograph, as well as the statistic of 21 million wounded soldiers, help to explain the post-war isolationism that allowed the expansion of Hitler twenty years later?*

adoc-photos/Corbis Historical/Getty Images

**Georges Clemenceau** (jawrj klem-uhn-SOH)

**The Peace Treaties** The final form of the treaties represented a series of compromises among the victors. The hardest terms originated with the French, who desired the destruction or the permanent weakening of German power. Thus, in addition to requiring Germany to accept sole responsibility and guilt for causing the war, the victors demanded a reduction in the military potential of the former Central Powers. For example, the **Treaty of Versailles** (1919) denied the Germans a navy and an air force and limited the size of the German army to 100,000 troops. In addition, the Allies prohibited Germany and Austria from entering into any sort of political union. The French and the British agreed that the defeated Central Powers must pay for the cost of the war and required the payment of reparations either in money or in kind. Although the German government and the public decried the Treaty of Versailles as being excessively harsh, it was no more severe in its terms than the Treaty of Brest-Litovsk that the Germans imposed on Russia in 1918.

The Paris Peace Conference resulted in several additional treaties. Bulgaria accepted the Treaty of Neuilly (1919), ceding only small portions of territory, because the Allies feared that major territorial changes in the Balkans would destabilize the region. That view did not apply to the dual monarchy of Austria-Hungary, whose imperial unity disintegrated under the impact of the war. The peacemakers recognized the territorial breakup of the former empire in two separate treaties: the Treaty of St. Germain (1919), between the Allies and the Republic of Austria, and the Treaty of Trianon (1920), between the Allies and the kingdom of Hungary. Both Austria and Hungary suffered severe territorial losses, which the Allies claimed were necessary in order to find territorial boundaries that accorded closely with the principle of self-determination. For example, the peace settlement reduced Hungarian territory to one-third of its prewar size and decreased the nation's population from twenty-eight million to eight million people.

Colonel Mustafa Kemal ("Ataturk") with Ottoman officers at the Battle of Gallipoli in 1915.
Scherl/Süddeutsche Zeitung Photo/Alamy Stock Photo

Arrangements between the defeated Ottoman Empire and the Allies proved to be a more complicated and protracted affair. The Treaty of Sèvres (1920) effectively dissolved the empire, calling for the surrender of Ottoman Balkan and Arab provinces and the occupation of eastern and southern Anatolia by foreign powers. The treaty was acceptable to the government of sultan Mohammed VI but not to Turkish nationalists, who rallied around their wartime hero Mustafa Kemal. As head of the Turkish nationalist movement, Mustafa Kemal set out to defy the Allied terms. He organized a national army that drove out Greek, British, French, and Italian occupation forces and abolished the sultanate and replaced it with the Republic of Turkey, with Ankara as its capital. In a great diplomatic victory for Turkish nationalists, the Allied powers officially recognized the Republic of Turkey in a final peace agreement, the Treaty of Lausanne (1923).

**Atatürk** As president of the republic, Mustafa Kemal, now known as **Atatürk** ("Father of the Turks"), instituted an ambitious program of modernization that emphasized economic development and secularism. Government support of critical industries and businesses, and other forms of state intervention in the economy designed to ensure rapid economic development, resulted in substantial long-term economic growth. The government's policy of secularism dictated the complete separation between the existing Muslim religious establishment and the state. The policy resulted in the replacement of religious with secular institutions of education and justice; the emancipation of women, including their right to vote; and the adoption of European-derived law, Hindu-Arabic numerals, the Roman alphabet, and Western clothing. Theoretically heading a constitutional democracy, Atatürk ruled Turkey as a virtual dictator until his death in 1938.

Turkey's postwar transformations and its success in refashioning the terms of peace proved to be something of an exception. In the final analysis, the peace settlements were strategically weak because too few participants had a stake in maintaining them and too many had an interest in revising them. German expansionist aims in Europe, which probably played a role in the nation's decision to enter the Great War, remained unresolved, as did Italian territorial designs in the

Balkans and Japanese influence in China. Those issues virtually ensured that the two decades following the peace settlement became merely a twenty-year truce, characterized by power rivalries and intermittent violence that led to yet another global war.

**The League of Nations** In an effort to avoid future destructive conflicts, the diplomats in Paris created the **League of Nations.** The League was the first permanent international security organization whose principal mission was to maintain world peace. At the urging of U.S. president Woodrow Wilson, the Covenant of the League of Nations was made an integral part of the peace treaties, and every signatory to a peace treaty had to accept this new world organization. Initially, the League seemed to be the sign of a new era: twenty-six of its forty-two original members were countries outside Europe, suggesting that it transcended European interests.

The League had two major flaws that ultimately rendered it ineffective. First, though designed to solve international disputes through arbitration, it had no power to enforce its decisions. Second, it relied on *collective security* as a tool for the preservation of global peace. The basic premise underlying collective security arrangements was the concept that aggression against any one state was considered aggression against all the other states, which had pledged to aid one another. Collective security could assume different forms, such as diplomatic pressure, economic sanctions, and ultimately force. However, the basic precondition for collective security—participation by all the great powers—never materialized because at any given time one or more of the major powers did not belong to the League. The United States never joined the organization because the U.S. Senate rejected the idea. Germany, which viewed the League as a club of Allied victors, and Japan, which saw it as an instrument of imperialism, left the League of Nations in 1933, as did some smaller powers. Italy, chastised by the League for invading Ethiopia in 1935, withdrew from it in 1937. The Soviet Union, which regarded the League as a tool of global capitalism, joined the organization in 1934, only to face expulsion in 1940. Although its failure to stop aggression in the 1930s led to its demise in 1940, the League established the pattern for a permanent international organization and served as a model for its successor, the United Nations.

**Self-Determination** One of the principal themes of the peacemaking process was the concept of self-determination, which was promoted most intensely by Woodrow Wilson. Wilson believed that self-determination was the key to international peace and cooperation. Yet Wilson's idea of self-determination was mostly directed at European populations. While Poland, Czechoslovakia, and Yugoslavia (kingdom of Serbs, Croats, and Slovenes until 1929) already existed as sovereign states by 1918, by the end of the conference the principle of self-determination had triumphed in many areas that were previously under the control of the Austro-Hungarian and Russian empires. Sometimes, however, peacemakers pushed the principle of self-determination aside for strategic and security reasons, such as in Austria and Germany, whose peoples were denied the right to form one nation. At other times, diplomats violated the notion of self-determination because they found it impossible to redraw national boundaries in accordance with nationalist aspirations without creating large minorities on one side or the other of a boundary line. Poland was a case in point, as one-third of the population did not speak Polish. A more complicated situation existed in Czechoslovakia. The peoples who gave the republic its name—the Czechs and the Slovaks—totaled only 67 percent of the population, with the remaining population consisting of Germans (22 percent), Ruthenes (6 percent), and Hungarians (5 percent). On the surface, the creation of Yugoslavia ("Land of the South Slavs") represented a triumph of self-determination because it politically united related peoples who for centuries had chafed under foreign rule. Beneath that unity, however, there lingered the separate national identities embraced by Serbs, Croats, and Slovenes. Even in Europe, the results of the application of the principle of self-determination were far from perfect.

**The Mandate System** In other parts of the world, however, peacemakers did not even try to apply the principle of self-determination. This unwillingness became most obvious when the victors confronted the issue of what to do with Germany's former colonies and the Arab territories of the Ottoman Empire. Because the United States rejected the establishment of new colonies, the European powers came up with the idea of trusteeship. Article 22 of the Covenant of the League of Nations referred to the colonies and territories of the former Central Powers as areas "inhabited by peoples not yet able to stand by themselves under the strenuous conditions of the modern world." As a result, "The tutelage of such peoples should be entrusted to the advanced nations who . . . can best undertake this responsibility." The League divided the mandates into three classes based on the presumed development of their populations in the direction of fitness for self-government. The administration of the mandates fell to the victorious powers of the Great War.

The Germans rightly interpreted the **mandate system** as a division of colonial booty by the victors, who had conveniently forgotten to apply the tutelage provision to their own colonies. German cynicism was more than matched by Arab outrage. The establishment of mandates in the former territories of the Ottoman Empire violated promises by French and British leaders during the war. They had promised Arab nationalists independence from the Ottoman Empire and had promised Jewish nationalists in Europe a homeland in Palestine. Where the Arabs hoped to form independent states, the French (in Lebanon and Syria) and the British (in Iraq and Palestine) established mandates. The Allies viewed the mandate system as a reasonable compromise between the reality of imperialism and the ideal of self-determination. To the peoples who were directly affected, the mandate system was simply continued imperial rule draped in a cloak of respectability.

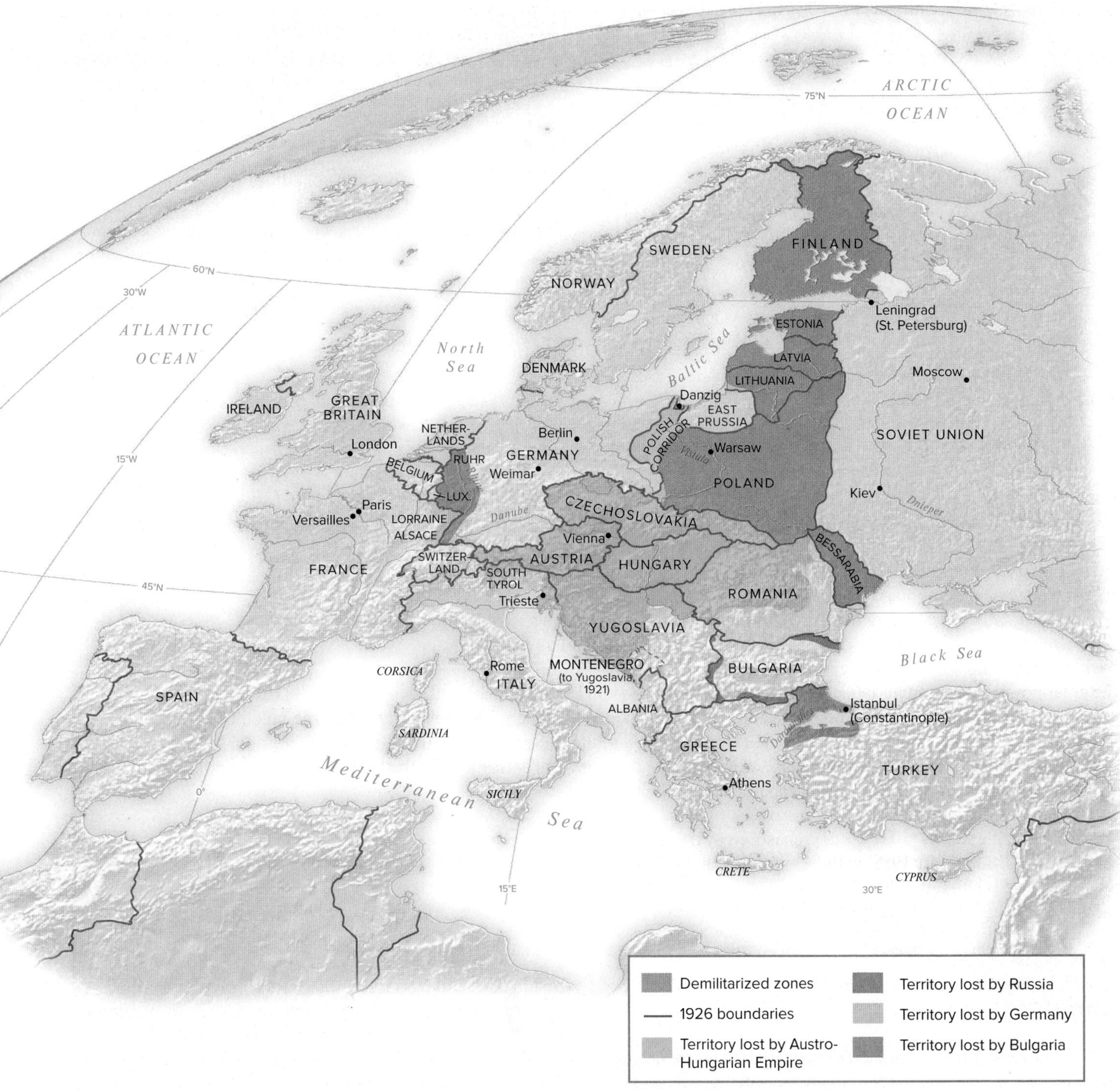


**MAP 21.2 Territorial changes in Europe after the Great War.**

Observe the territories ceded by the Central Powers and the Soviet Union.

***Which power lost the most territory, and why?***

## Challenges to European Preeminence

The Great War changed Europe forever, but most people could not see this at the war's end. With the imperial powers still ruling over their old colonies and new mandates, it appeared that European global hegemony was even more secure than it had been in 1914. In hindsight, however, it is clear that the Great War did irreparable damage to European power and prestige and set the stage for a process of decolonization that gathered momentum during and after the Second World War.

## SOURCES FROM THE PAST

### Memorandum of the General Syrian Congress

*Article 22 of the League of Nations Covenant established a system of mandates to rule the colonies and territories of the defeated powers, including parts of the former Ottoman Empire (comprising present-day Syria, Lebanon, Jordan, and Israel). The mandate system essentially substituted European mandates for Ottoman rule. The news of this arrangement came as a shock to the peoples of the defeated Ottoman Empire who had fought alongside the English and the French during the Great War and expected their independence, which they had indeed been promised. They quickly denounced the mandate system. The following selection is a memorandum addressed to the King Crane Commission, which was responsible for overseeing the transfer of Ottoman territory.*

**We the undersigned members** of the General Syrian Congress, meeting in Damascus on Wednesday, July 2nd 1919, . . . provided with the credentials and authorizations by the inhabitants of our various districts, Moslems, Christians, and Jews, have agreed upon the following statement of the desires of the people of the country who have elected us. . . .

1. We ask absolutely complete political independence for Syria. . . .
2. We ask that the Government of this Syrian country should be a democratic civil constitutional Monarchy based on broad decentralization principles, safeguarding the rights of minorities, and that the King be the Emir Feisal, who carried on a glorious struggle in the cause of liberation and merited our full confidence and entire reliance.
3. Considering that the Arabs inhabiting the Syrian area are not naturally less gifted than other more advanced races and that they are by no means less developed than the Bulgarians, Serbians, Greeks, and Romanians at the beginning of their independence, we protest against Article 22 of the Covenant of the League of Nations, placing us among the nations in their middle stage of development which stand in need of a mandatory power. . . .

Why did the Congress compare its constituents to European groups here?

6. We do not acknowledge any right claimed by the French Government in any part whatever of our Syrian country and refuse that she should assist us or have a hand in our country under any circumstances and in any place. . . .
7. We oppose the pretensions of the Zionists to create a Jewish commonwealth in the southern part of Syria, known as Israel, and oppose Zionist migration to any part of our country; for we do not acknowledge their title but consider them a grave peril to our people, from the national, economical, and political points of view. Our Jewish compatriots shall enjoy our common rights and assume the common responsibilities.

Given the tone of this memorandum, how likely does it seem that people in Syria would accept mandate rule?

#### For Further Reflection

- For what specifically was the Syrian Congress asking? Do you think the European powers expected this response to the League of Nations Covenant?
- On what basis did the Syrian government believe that their memorandum held merit and could be persuasive to the League of Nations? Why did it fail?
- In what ways did the mandate system contribute to ongoing conflict in Syria, Jordan, and Palestine?

*Source:* "United States Department of State Papers Relating to the Foreign Relations of the United States." The Paris Peace Conference, 1919, Vol. XII. Washington, DC: U.S. Government Printing Office, 1919.

The war of 1914–1918 accelerated the growth of nationalism in the European-controlled parts of the world, fueling desires for independence and self-determination.

**Weakened Europe** The decline in European power was closely related to diminished economic capacity, a result of the commitment to total war. In time, Europe overcame many war-induced economic problems, such as high rates of inflation and huge public debts, but other economic dislocations were permanent and damaging. Most significant was the loss of overseas investments and foreign markets, which had brought huge financial returns. Nothing is more indicative of Europe's reduced economic might than the reversal of the economic relationship between Europe and the United States. Whereas the United States was a debtor nation before 1914, owing billions of dollars to European investors, by 1919 it was a major creditor.

A loss of prestige overseas and a weakening grip on colonies also reflected the undermining of Europe's global hegemony. Colonial subjects in Africa, Asia, and the Pacific often viewed the Great War as a civil war among the European nations, a bloody spectacle in which the haughty bearers of an alleged superior society vilified and slaughtered one another. Because Europe seemed weak, divided, and vulnerable, the white colonizers appeared far less powerful than before.

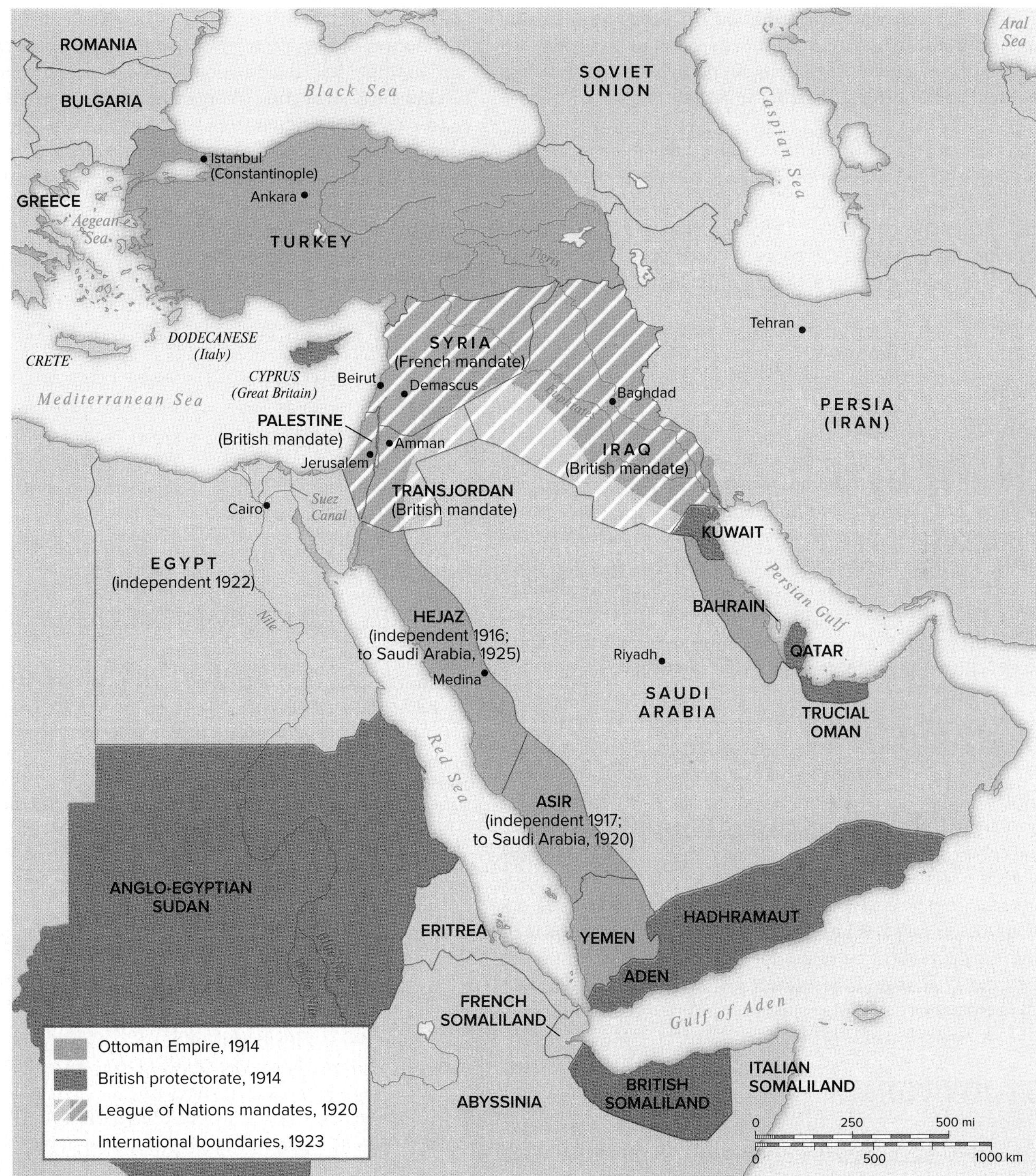


## MAP 21.3 Territorial changes in southwest Asia after the Great War.

The Great War completed the process of disintegration of the Ottoman Empire and left much of the region to be ruled as virtual colonies by the major imperial powers.

***What was the reaction in the region when European statesmen assigned former Ottoman territories to French or British control under the League of Nations mandates?***

Colonial subjects who returned home from the war in Europe and southwest Asia reinforced those general impressions with their own firsthand observations. In particular, they were less inclined to be obedient imperial subjects.

**Revolutionary Ideas** The war also helped spread revolutionary ideas to the colonies. The U.S. war aims spelled out in the Fourteen Points raised the hopes of peoples under imperial rule and promoted nationalist aspirations. The peacemakers repeatedly invoked the concept of self-determination, and Wilson publicly proposed that in all colonial questions "the interests of the native populations be given equal weight with the desires of European governments." Wilson seemed to call for nothing less than national independence and self-rule. Nationalists struggling to organize anti-imperialist resistance also sought inspiration from the Soviet Union, whose leaders denounced all forms of imperialism and pledged their support to independence movements. Taken together, these messages were subversive to imperial control and had a great appeal for colonial peoples. The postwar disappointments and temporary setbacks experienced by nationalist movements did not diminish their desire for self-rule and self-determination.

## CONCLUSION

The assassination of the Austrian archduke Franz Ferdinand had a galvanizing effect on a Europe torn by national rivalries, colonial disputes, and demands for self-determination. In the summer of 1914, inflexible war plans and a tangled alliance system transformed a local war between Austria-Hungary and Serbia into a European-wide clash of arms that also immediately entangled the colonized world. With the entry of the Ottoman Empire, Japan, and the United States, the war of 1914–1918 became a truly global conflict. Although many belligerents organized their societies for total war and drew on the resources of their overseas empires, the war in Europe remained at a bloody stalemate until the United States entered the conflict in 1917. The tide turned, and the combatants signed an armistice in November 1918. The Great War, a brutal encounter between societies and peoples, inflicted ghastly human casualties, severely damaged national economies, and discredited long-established political and cultural traditions. The war also altered the political landscape of many places as it destroyed four dynasties and their empires, fostered the creation of several new European nations, and created new protectorates called mandates. In Russia the war served as a backdrop for the world's first successful socialist revolution. In the end the Great War sapped the strength of European colonial powers while promoting nationalist aspirations among colonized peoples.

## STUDY TERMS

Armenian genocide (715)
Atatürk (721)
Balfour Declaration (715)
Black Hand (704)
Bolshevik (715)
Central Powers (703)
dreadnoughts (701)
February Revolution (715)
Fourteen Points (720)
Franz Ferdinand (701)
Gallipoli (714)
Georges Clemenceau (720)
home front (708)
influenza pandemic (719)
League of Nations (722)
Lloyd George (720)
mandate system (722)
mustard gas (706)
no-man's-land (706)
October Revolution (716)
Paris Peace Conference (720)
Romanov dynasty (715)
Schlieffen plan (703)
self-determination (701)
Sykes-Picot Treaty (715)
Treaty of Brest-Litovsk (717)
Treaty of Versailles (721)
Triple Entente (703)
Twenty-one Demands (712)
unrestricted submarine warfare (718)
Verdun (708)
Vladimir Ilyich Lenin (716)
western front (706)
Woodrow Wilson (720)
Zimmermann telegram (718)

## FOR FURTHER READING


Mustafa Aksakal. *The Ottoman Road to War in 1914: The Ottoman Empire and the First World War*. Cambridge, 2008. Uses previously untapped sources to explore how and why the Ottomans entered the Great War on the side of the Central Powers.

Christopher Clark. *The Sleepwalkers: How Europe Went to War in 1914*. New York, 2013. This is the best researched, most readable one-volume account of a most contentious subject.

Peter Gatrell. *Russia's First World War: A Social and Economic History*. London, 2005. Traces the impact of World War I on Russian society before the revolution.

Robert Gerwarth and Erez Manela. *Empires at War, 1911–1923*. Oxford, 2014. An edited collection of top-notch essays that explore the Great War as a fundamentally imperial and global conflict.

Susan R. Grayzel. *Women and the First World War*. New York, 2002. This is an excellent introduction to the experiences and contributions of women during the war.

Margaret MacMillan. *Paris 1919: Six Months That Changed the World*. New York, 2002. This is the most engaging and lucid analysis written on the subject of the peace settlement.

John H. Morrow. *The Great War. An Imperial History*. New York, 2003. A global history of the Great War that places the conflict squarely in the context of imperialism.

Michael S. Neiberg. *Fighting the Great War*. Cambridge, Mass., 2005. A good blend of narrative and analysis, this work highlights the global reach of the conflict.

Susan Pedersen. *The Guardians: The League of Nations and the Crisis of Empire*. Oxford, 2015. Comprehensive study of the history of the League of Nations and its creation and management of the mandate system.

Hew Strachan. *The First World War*. New York, 2004. One of the leading historians of World War I offers a one-volume version of his projected three-volume work, treating the war in a global rather than European context.

# CHAPTER 21 AP EXAM PRACTICE

Questions assume cumulative knowledge from this chapter and previous chapters.

## Section I

## Multiple Choice Questions

Use the image below and your knowledge of world history to answer questions 1-3.

U.S. Army recruitment poster, 1917–1918
Library of Congress Prints & Photographs Division [LC-DIG-ds-03216]

1. Which of the following is NOT a reason why the United States entered the war in 1917?
   (A) German use of unrestricted submarine warfare outraged the public in the United States when they sunk the *Lusitania*, a passenger ship.
   (B) The Zimmermann telegram included a German promise to return territories to Mexico if they entered the war.
   (C) The United States wanted the Allies to be able to repay their debts.
   (D) The United States wanted to acquire the German colonies in Asia and Africa.

2. How does this enlistment poster reinforce President Wilson's messages about the need for the war?
   (A) The German threat in the poster is shown as destroying businesses, which recalls Wilson's idea that this was "warfare against commerce."
   (B) The Germans are dehumanized, depicted as an animal, which echoes Wilson's statement that the Germans are fighting a war against mankind.
   (C) Wilson claimed that Germans were a specific threat to American women, which is seen in the poster.
   (D) Wilson claimed that American culture was superior to German culture.

3. Which of the following was a long-term consequence of the use of propaganda in the war?
   (A) Readers stopped buying newspapers, which led to many newspapers declaring bankruptcy.
   (B) When many stories of World War I atrocities were revealed to be lies, the public became skeptical about actual atrocities when they happened later.
   (C) People turned to alternative forms of media to learn the news.
   (D) Governments put extra resources into correcting errors in reporting about the war.

Use the map below and your knowledge of world history to answer questions 4 and 5.

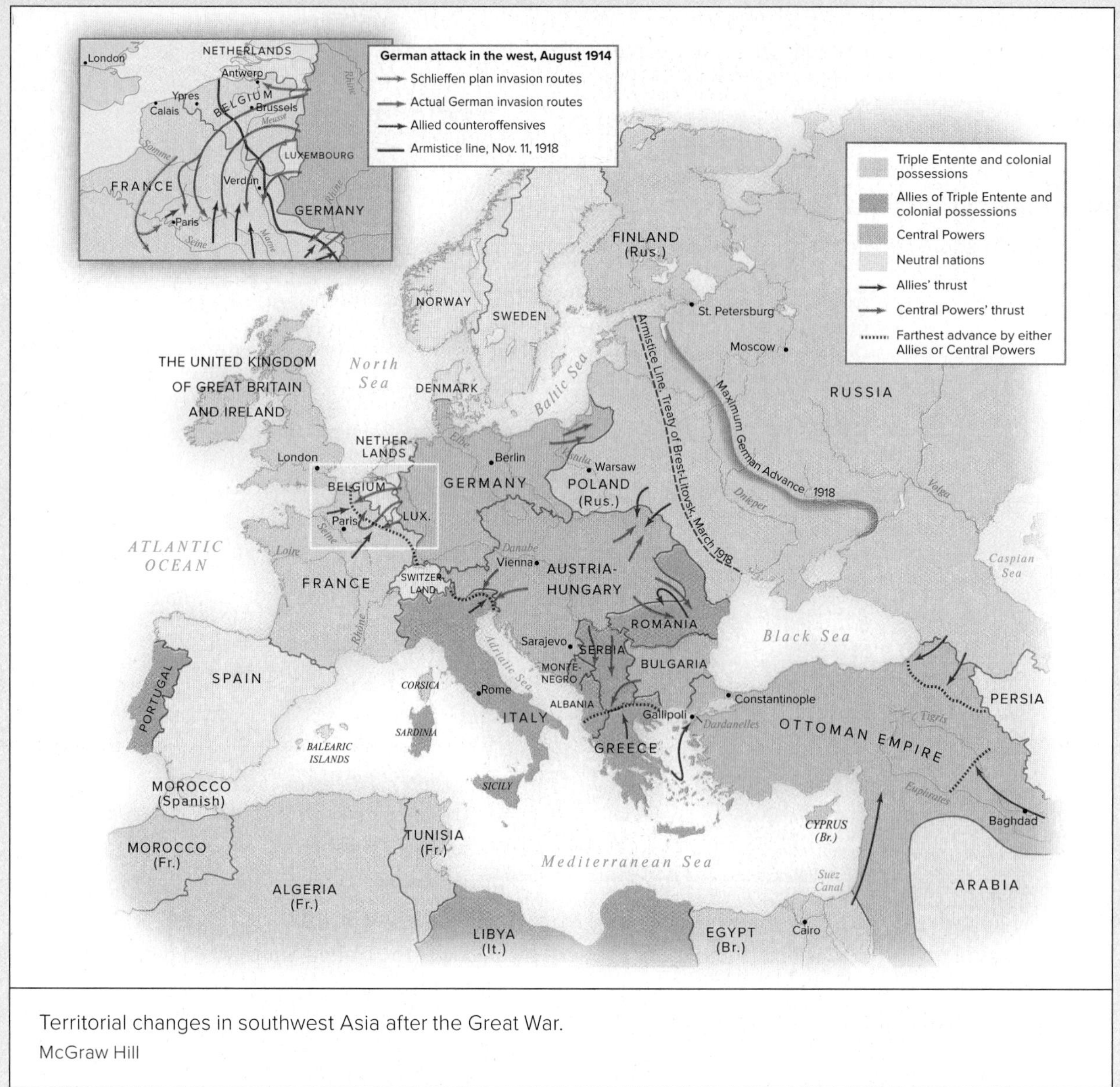


Territorial changes in southwest Asia after the Great War.
McGraw Hill

4. Based on the borders of the Ottoman empire in 1914, why might the Ottoman have entered the war on the side of the Germans and Austrians?
   (A) The Ottomans had been losing Balkan territories to nationalist movements, which gave them common cause with the Austrian empire.
   (B) They wanted to expand their control of the Silk Road trade routes.
   (C) They wanted German and Austrian support to reclaim their border with the Safavid empire.
   (D) The Ottomans felt that the French moving into Sudan was too close to the cities of Mecca and Medina.

5. What conflict did the British and French created in the mandates after the war?
   (A) The Syrians insisted that eastern Anatolia be included in their mandate.
   (B) The British promised the Turks that they would be allowed to retake the Arab provinces after twenty-five years.
   (C) The British and French had promised to include Palestine in an independent Arab state while also promising to create a Jewish nation there.
   (D) The mandates did not have natural borders and were vulnerable to German and Austrian invasions.

## Short Answer

6. Use the image below and your knowledge of world history to answer parts A, B, and C.

An Indian gun crew in the Somme area, 1916.
National Archives (165-BO-1602)

(A) Identify ONE way that non-Europeans were involved in World War I.
(B) Explain ONE way that Europe's colonies were important factors in the war.
(C) Explain ONE way that Japan's position in the war was different from that of the colonies who were part of the war effort.

7. Use the map below and your knowledge of world history to answer parts A, B, and C.

Bent double, like old beggars under sacks,
Knock-kneed, coughing like hags, we cursed through sludge,
Till on the haunting flares we turned our backs
And towards our distant rest began to trudge.
Men marched asleep. Many had lost their boots
But limped on, blood-shod. All went lame; all blind;
Drunk with fatigue; deaf even to the hoots
Of gas-shells dropping softly behind.

Gas! GAS! Quick, boys!—An ecstasy of fumbling,
Fitting the clumsy helmets just in time;
But someone still was yelling out and stumbling
And floundering like a man in fire or lime.—
Dim, through the misty panes and thick green light
As under a green sea, I saw him drowning.

In all my dreams, before my helpless sight,
He plunges at me, guttering, choking, drowning.
If in some smothering dreams you too could pace
Behind the wagon that we flung him in,
And watch the white eyes writhing in his face,
His hanging face, like a devil's sick of sin;
If you could hear, at every jolt, the blood
Come gargling from the froth-corrupted lungs,
Obscene as cancer, bitter as the cud
Of vile, incurable sores on innocent tongues,—
My friend, you would not tell with such high zest
To children ardent for some desperate glory,
The old Lie: Dulce et decorum est
Pro patria mori.*

*Source:* Owen, Wilfred. Dulce et Decorum, 1918.

(A) Identify ONE way that the author of this poem shows how military service affected soldiers physically.
(B) Explain ONE way this poem anticipated the aftermath of the war.
(C) Explain ONE consequence of the war for Europe.

8. Use your understanding of world history to answer parts A, B, and C.
(A) Identify ONE group that held power in Russia in 1917 after the tsar resigned.
(B) Explain ONE reason why the October Revolution overthrew the provisional government.
(C) Explain ONE consequence of the Treaty of Brest-Litovsk.

# Section II

## Document-Based Question

Based on the documents below and your knowledge of world history, compare and contrast the ways that World War I changed the Ottoman empire and eastern Europe.

In your response you should do the following:

- Respond to the prompt with a historically defensible thesis or claim that establishes a line of reasoning.
- Describe a broader historical context relevant to the prompt.
- Support an argument in response to the prompt using all documents.
- Use at least one additional piece of specific historical evidence (beyond that found in the documents) relevant to an argument about the prompt.
- Explain how or why the document's point of view, purpose, historical situation, and / or audience is relevant to an argument.
- Use evidence to corroborate, qualify, or modify an argument that addresses the prompt.

### Document 1

**We the undersigned members** of the General Syrian Congress, meeting in Damascus on Wednesday, July 2nd 1919, . . . provided with the credentials and authorizations by the inhabitants of our various districts, Moslems, Christians, and Jews, have agreed upon the following statement of the desires of the people of the country who have elected us. . . .

1. We ask absolutely complete political independence for Syria. . . .
2. We ask that the Government of this Syrian country should be a democratic civil constitutional Monarchy based on broad decentralization principles, safeguarding the rights of minorities, and that the King be the Emir Feisal, who carried on a glorious struggle in the cause of liberation and merited our full confidence and entire reliance.
3. Considering that the Arabs inhabiting the Syrian area are not naturally less gifted than other more advanced races and that they are by no means less developed than the Bulgarians, Serbians, Greeks, and Romanians at the beginning of their independence, we protest against Article 22 of the Covenant of the League of Nations, placing us among the nations in their middle stage of development which stand in need of a mandatory power. . . .

*Source:* "United States Department of State Papers Relating to the Foreign Relations of the United States." The Paris Peace Conference, 1919, Vol. XII. Washington, DC: U.S. Government Printing Office, 1919.

# Document 2

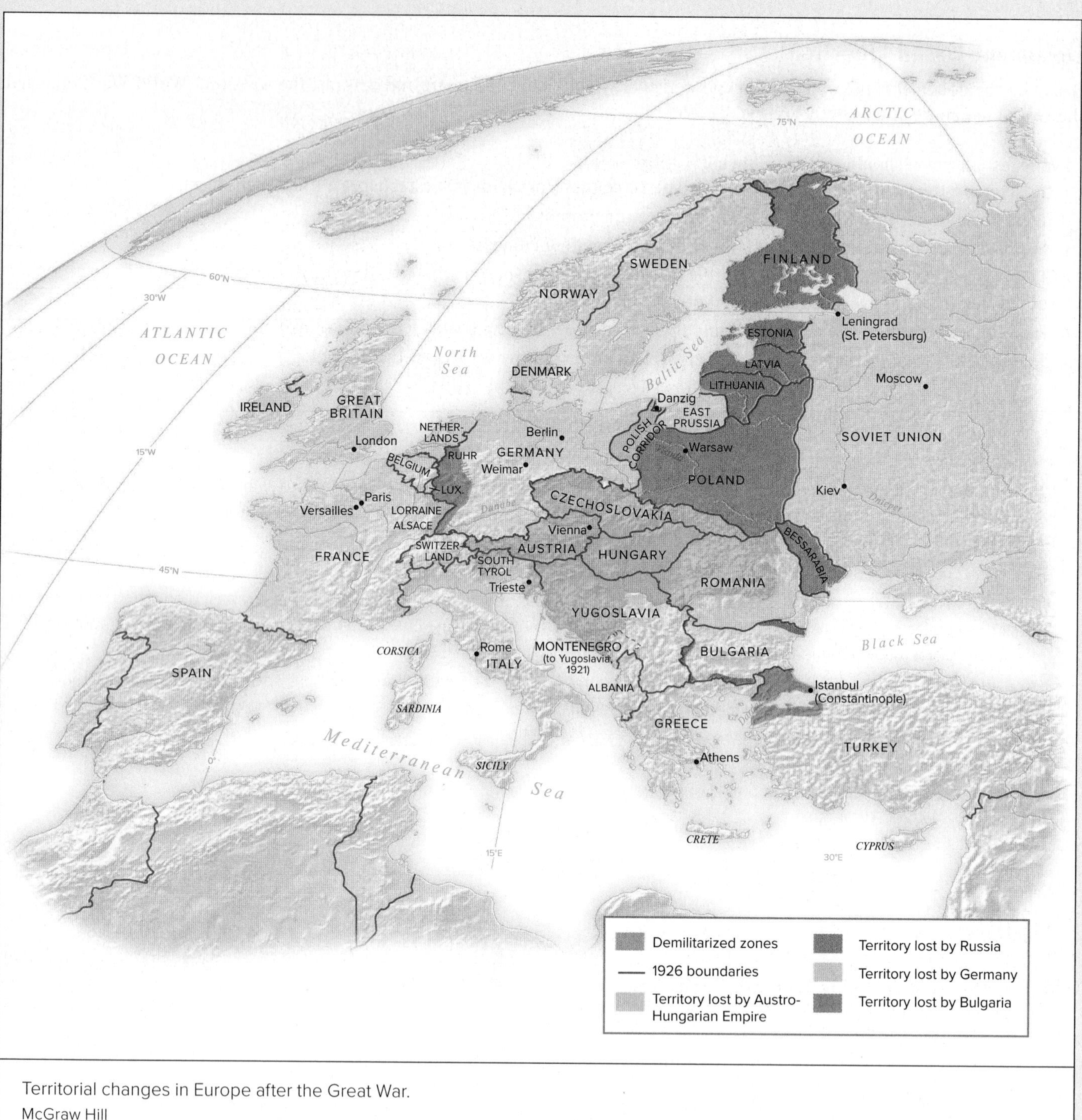


Territorial changes in Europe after the Great War.
McGraw Hill

## Document 3

Colonel Mustafa Kemal ("Ataturk") with Ottoman officers at the Battle of Gallipoli in 1915.
Scherl/Süddeutsche Zeitung Photo/Alamy Stock Photo

## Long Essay

Develop a thoughtful and thorough historical argument that answers the question below. Begin your essay with a thesis statement and support it with relevant historical evidence.

Using specific examples and your knowledge of world history, evaluate both changes and continuities in the roles of women during World War I.

# Chapter 22 Anxieties and Experiments in Postwar Europe and the United States



## ZOOMING IN ON TRADITIONS

### The Evolution of a Dictator

Born on a lovely spring day in 1889, in a quaint Austrian village, he was the apple of his mother's eye. He basked in Klara's warmth and indulgence as a youth, enjoying the fine life of a middle-class child. As he grew older, he sensed a vague anxiety that stemmed from the competing expectations of his parents. Contented with being spoiled by Klara, he bristled at the demands of his father, Alois. Alois expected him to follow in his footsteps to a career in the Austrian civil service. He had no desire to become a bureaucrat. In fact, he envisioned a completely different life for himself as an artist. His school grades slipped, and that seemed an appropriate way to express his discontent and sabotage his father's plans for his future.

Alois's unexpected death in 1903 freed him from a future as a bureaucrat. He now had the freedom to daydream and indulge his imagination. He left school in 1905 with a ninth-grade education and moved to Vienna with plans to study to become an artist. But the Vienna Academy of Fine Arts rejected him in 1907. His beloved Klara died the following year, and he meandered the city streets of Vienna, living off a pension and the money he inherited from his mother. He immersed himself in Vienna, admiring the architecture of the city and attending the opera when his funds permitted. He especially enjoyed the music of Richard Wagner, who embraced heroic German myths in his compositions.

When he finally ran through all of his money, he began staying at a homeless shelter. There, he was exposed to a variety of

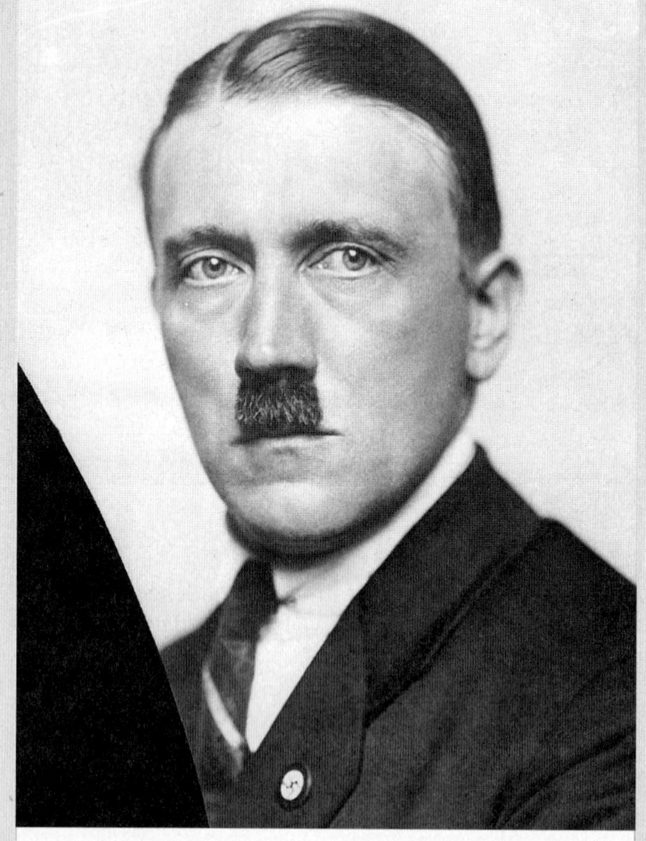

This is one of the few known photographs of a young Adolf Hitler, taken in 1923.
Bettmann/Getty Images

political ideologies held by the shelter's other inhabitants. They discussed issues such as race, and he was particularly attracted to the viewpoints of those who hailed the supremacy of the Aryan race and the inferiority of the Jews. He immersed himself in reading, particularly the newspapers and pamphlets that gave him more information about those disturbing political issues. He came to hate Jews and Marxists, whom he thought had formed an evil union with the goal of destroying the world. He also despised liberalism and democracy, and in cheap cafés he began directing political tirades at anyone who would listen. Soon, he also began to engage in public debates about these issues.

He left Vienna in 1913 for Munich, where he volunteered for service in the German army. He discovered in himself a real talent for military service, and he remained in the army for the duration of the war, 1914–1918. Twice wounded and decorated for bravery, he nonetheless found himself in despair at war's end. He learned of Germany's defeat in the war while being treated in a hospital for exposure to mustard gas. Enraged, he believed with all his being that the Jews were responsible for this humiliation, and he also knew what he had to do: he had to enter the political arena in his chosen fatherland and save the nation. **Adolf Hitler** had finally found his mission in life: a mission that would have a devastating and deadly effect for millions of people.

## CHAPTER FOCUS

- The decades of the 1920s–1930s were a time of great bitterness, hardship, and worry. The Great War and the ensuing Great Depression caused people around the globe to question the benefits of "nineteenth-century liberalism": the unregulated pursuit of wealth, none of which seemed to trickle down to the ordinary citizen; decaying and corrupt democratic governments; and power-hungry imperialists. Many people believed reforms were necessary.
- Historians often use the term *age of anxiety* to describe the feelings of authority figures and defenders of the nineteenth-century status quo. Many lamented the decline of society.
- Intellectuals believed that Sigmund Freud's work undermined Renaissance and Enlightenment ideas about the rationality of mankind, just as Einstein's and Heisenberg's works undermined the rational Newtonian universe.
- Yet many objections arose to the status quo in the west. As often happens after a cataclysm that challenges personal ideologies, the despair of the 1920s and 1930s led to change for many, especially the young.
- From the high-culture world of art emerged abstract painters, composers, and architects who created seemingly irrational or deliberately provocative works to reflect the unease and pessimism of modern life.
- Writers focused on the heartlessness of society.
- Some technological innovations—refrigerators, record players, vacuum cleaners—made their way into homes and made life a bit easier, however; and movies, radios, mass-produced cars, and planes connected people to the wider world.
- Scientific ideas (Darwin, Freud) also reached beyond the scientific community to popular levels and challenged religious ideas about the divine origins of human life.
- After the Great War, the importance of the health of *society as a whole* was replacing the liberal view of the importance of the *individual* as the basis of a strong society.
- The new weakly supported German republic was quickly taken over by the National Socialist (fascist) party, which believed that a strong national government controlling almost every aspect of public and private life would create a strong Germany.
- The new Union of Soviet Socialist Republics (U.S.S.R.) also believed in tight government control, particularly of the economy.
- In the depths of the Depression in the United States, President Franklin Roosevelt orchestrated the New Deal as a government solution to economic problems

## Historical Developments

- Following World War I and the onset of the Great Depression, governments began to take a more active role in economic life.
- The causes of World War II included the unsustainable peace settlement after World War I, the global economic crisis engendered by the Great Depression, continued imperialist aspirations, and especially the rise to power of fascist and totalitarian regimes that resulted in the aggressive militarism of Nazi Germany under Adolf Hitler.

## Reasoning Processes

- **Causation** Explain the causes and effect of the Great Depression upon states and societies.

## Historical Thinking Skills

- **Developments and Processes** Explain the emergence and consolidation of fascist and communist rule during the interwar years.
- **Making Connections** Identify patterns among and connections between U.S., German, and Russian responses to global economic depression.

## CHAPTER OVERVIEW

Badly shaken by the effects of years of war, Europeans experienced a shock to their system of values, beliefs, and traditions. Profound scientific, intellectual, and cultural transformations that came to the fore in the postwar decades also contributed to a sense of loss and anxiety. As peoples in Europe and around the world struggled to come to terms with the aftermath of war, an unprecedented economic contraction gripped the international community.

Against the background of the Great Depression, dictators in Russia, Italy, and Germany tried to translate blueprints for utopias into reality. While Joseph Stalin and his fellow communists recast the former tsarist empire into a dictatorship of the proletariat, Benito Mussolini and his fascists along with Adolf Hitler and his Nazi Party forged a new kind of national community. These political innovations unsettled many Europeans and much of the world, contributing significantly to the anxiety of the age.

| CHRONOLOGY | |
|---|---|
| 1905 | Einstein publishes special theory of relativity |
| 1918–1920 | Civil war in Russia |
| 1919 | Mussolini launches fascist movement in Italy |
| 1921–1928 | Lenin's New Economic Policy |
| 1927 | Heisenberg establishes the uncertainty principle |
| 1928–1932 | First Soviet Five-Year Plan |
| 1929 | U.S. stock market crash; Beginning of Great Depression; Ernest Hemingway and Erich Remarque publish antiwar novels |
| 1933–1945 | Hitler rules Germany |
| 1935–1938 | Stalin's Great Purge in the Soviet Union |
| 1939 | John Steinbeck publishes *The Grapes of Wrath* |

## NEW INTELLECTUAL FRONTIERS

The Great War discredited established social and political institutions and long-held beliefs about the superiority of European society. Writers, poets, theologians, and other European intellectuals lamented the decline and imminent death of their society. While some wrote obituaries, however, others embarked on bold new cultural paths that established the main tendencies of contemporary thought and taste. Most of these cultural innovators began their work before the war, but it was in the two decades following the war that a revolution in science, psychology, art, and architecture attained its fullest development and potency.

The discoveries of physicists undermined the Newtonian universe, in which a set of inexorable natural laws governed events, with a new and disturbing cosmos. Uncertainty governed this strange universe, which lacked objective reality. Equally discomforting were the insights of psychoanalysis, which suggested that human behavior was fundamentally irrational. Disquieting trends in the arts paralleled the developments in science and psychology. Especially in painting, an aversion to realism and a pronounced preference for abstraction heralded the arrival of new aesthetic standards.

### Postwar Pessimism

"You are all a lost generation," noted Gertrude Stein (1874-1946) to her fellow American writer Ernest Hemingway (1899-1961). Stein had given a label to the group of American intellectuals and literati who congregated in Paris in the postwar years. This **"lost generation"** expressed in poetry and fiction the malaise and disillusion that characterized U.S. and European thought after the Great War. The vast majority of European intellectuals had rallied enthusiastically to the war in 1914, viewing it as a splendid adventure. The brutal realities of industrialized warfare left no room for heroes, however, and most of these young artists and intellectuals quickly became disillusioned. During the 1920s they spat out their revulsion in a host of war novels such as Ernest Hemingway's *A Farewell to Arms* (1929) and Erich Maria Remarque's *All Quiet on the Western Front* (1929), works overflowing with images of meaningless death and suffering.

Postwar writers lamented the decline of Western society. A retired German schoolteacher named Oswald Spengler (1880–1936) made headlines when he published *The Decline of the West* (1918–1922). In this work, which was seen as an obituary of civilization, Spengler proposed that all societies pass through a life cycle of growth and decay comparable to the biological cycle of living organisms. His analysis of the history of western Europe led him to conclude that European society had entered the final stage of its existence. All that remained was irreversible decline, marked by imperialism and warfare. Spengler's gloomy predictions provided a kind of comfort to those who sought to rationalize their postwar despair, as did his conviction that all the nations of the world were equally doomed. In England the shock of war caused the historian Arnold J. Toynbee (1889–1975) to begin his twelve-volume classic, *A Study of History* (1934–1961), in which he analyzed the genesis, growth, and disintegration of twenty-six societies.

**Religious Uncertainty** Theologians joined the chorus of despair. In 1919 Karl Barth (1886–1968), widely recognized as one of the most notable Christian theologians, published a religious bombshell titled *Epistle to the Romans.* In his work Barth sharply attacked the liberal Christian theology that embraced the idea of progress, or the tendency of European thinkers to believe in limitless improvement as the realization of God's purpose. The Augustinian, Lutheran, and Calvinist message of original sin—the idea that humans are doomed to lives of sin as a result of Adam and Eve's disobedience—fell on receptive ears as many Christians refused to accept the idea that contemporary human society was in any way a realization of God's purpose. The Russian orthodox thinker Niokolai Berdiaev (1874–1948) summed up these sentiments: "Man's historical experience has been one of steady failure, and there are no grounds for supposing it will be ever anything else."

**Attacks on Progress** The Great War destroyed long-cherished beliefs such as belief in the universality of human progress. Many idols of nineteenth-century progress came under attack, especially those in science and technology. The scientists' dream of leading humanity to a beneficial conquest of nature seemed to have gone awry because scientists had spent the war making poisonous gas and high explosives. Democracy was another fallen idol. The idea that people should have a voice in selecting the leaders of their government had enjoyed widespread support in European societies. By the early twentieth century, the removal of property and educational restrictions on the right to vote resulted in universal male suffrage in most societies. In the years following the Great War, most European governments extended the franchise to women. These developments led to an unprecedented degree of political participation as millions of people voted in elections and referendums. However, many intellectuals came to abhor what they viewed as a weak political system that championed the tyranny of the average person. Instead, they viewed democracy as a product of decay and as lacking in positive values, and they idealized elite rule. In Germany a whole school of conservatives lamented the "rule of inferiors." Common people, too, often viewed democracy as a decaying political system because they associated it with corrupt and ineffective party politics. However, antidemocratic strains were not confined to Germany. The widely read essay "Revolt of the Masses" (1930) by the Spanish philosopher José Ortega y Gasset (1883–1955) warned readers about the masses who were destined to destroy the highest achievements of Western society.

## New Visions in Physics, Psychology, and Art

The postwar decade witnessed a revolution in physics that transformed the character of science. **Albert Einstein** (1879–1955) struck the first blow with his theory of special relativity (1905), showing that there is no single spatial and chronological framework in the universe. According to the theory, it no longer made sense to speak of space and time as absolutes because the measurement of those two categories always varies with the motion of the observer. That is, space and time are relative to the person

### How the Past Shapes the Future

**The Destructive Potential of Industrial Technologies**

World War I is an instructive example of the long-term consequences of historical events on both intellectual and popular culture. Prior to the war, many Europeans believed that the technologies associated with industrialization—while not without their problems—would ultimately lead to greater human comfort, prosperity, and happiness. Yet the role of mass-produced war matériel in the huge scale of slaughter during the war caused Europeans to wonder with horror if, with industrial technologies, humans had created a monster that would ultimately bring about more death and destruction than happiness. In effect, the realities of the war made it impossible for Europeans to return to the optimism of the nineteenth century with regard to the benefits of modern technologies. Consider how this ambivalence, in turn, became an important feature of intellectual and popular culture not only in interwar Europe but also in many parts of the world right up to the present.

One of the best-known faces of the twentieth century, Albert Einstein (1879–1955) was the symbol of the revolution in physics.
Bettmann/Getty Images

measuring them. To the layperson such notions—usually expressed in incomprehensible mathematical formulas—suggested that science had reached the limits of what could be known with certainty. A commonsense universe had vanished, to be replaced by a radically new one in which reality or truth was merely a set of mental constructs.

**The Uncertainty Principle** More disquieting even than Einstein's discoveries was the theory formulated by Werner Heisenberg (1901–1976), who in 1927 published a paper, "About the Quantum-Theoretical Reinterpretation of Kinetic and Mechanical Relationships," which established the **uncertainty principle.** According to Heisenberg, it is impossible to specify simultaneously the position and the velocity of a subatomic particle. The more accurately one determines the position of an electron, the less precisely one can determine its velocity, and vice versa. In essence, he argued that scientists cannot observe the behavior of electrons objectively because the act of observation interferes with them.

It quickly became evident that the uncertainty principle had important implications beyond physics. It also carried broader philosophical ramifications. Heisenberg's theory called into question established notions of truth and violated the fundamental law of cause and effect. Likewise, objectivity was no longer a valid concept because the observer was always part of the process under observation. Accordingly, any observer—an anthropologist studying another society, for instance—had to be alert to the fact that his or her very presence became an integral part of the study.

**Freud's Psychoanalytic Theory** Equally unsettling as the advances in physics were developments in psychology that challenged established concepts of morality and values. In an indeterminate universe governed by relativity, the one remaining fixed point was the human psyche, but the insights of **Sigmund Freud** (1856–1939) brought this into question as well. Beginning in 1896, the medical doctor from Vienna embarked on research that focused on psychological rather than

Sigmund Freud (1856–1939) formulated psychoanalysis, a theory and clinical practice to explore the mind and, by extension, its creations, such as literature, religion, art, and history.
Imagno/Getty Images

---

**Sigmund Freud** (SIG-muhnd froid)

physiological explanations of mental disorders. Through his clinical observations of patients, Freud identified a conflict between conscious and subconscious mental processes that lay at the root of neurotic (mentally unbalanced) behavior. That conflict, moreover, suggested to him the existence of a repressive mechanism that keeps painful memories or threatening events away from the conscious mind. Freud believed that dreams held the key to the deepest recesses of the human psyche. Using the free associations of patients to guide him in the interpretation of dreams, he identified sexual drives and fantasies as the most important source of repression. For example, Freud claimed to have discovered a so-called Oedipus complex in which male children develop an erotic attachment to their mother and hostility toward their father.

From dreams Freud analyzed literature, religion, politics, and virtually every other type of human endeavor, seeking always to identify the manifestations of the repressed conscious. He was convinced that his theory, known as **psychoanalysis,** provided the keys to understanding all human behavior. In the end, Freudian ideas shaped the psychiatric profession and established a powerful presence in literature and the arts. During the 1920s, novelists, poets, and painters acknowledged Freud's influence as they focused on the inner world—the hidden depths of memory and emotion—of their characters. The creators of imaginative literature used Freud's bold emphasis on sexuality as a tool for the interpretation and understanding of human behavior.

**Experimentation in Art** The sense of uncertainty and anxiety induced by advances in physics and psychology also found reflection in the arts, which in turn contributed to the unsettling atmosphere of the first half of the twentieth century. The point of departure for these developments was the brutality of the Great War, which gave birth to Dada or **Dadaism.** Although the origin of the name Dada is unclear, it is believed to be a deliberately nonsensical word. Between 1916 and 1920, the disillusioned artists of the Dada movement in Zurich, Paris, and New York used any available public forum to critique nationalism, materialism, and rationalism, which they felt had contributed to a senseless war. They consistently rejected prevailing standards of art and declared an all-out assault on the unquestioning conformity of culture and thought. They imagined themselves to be nonartists who created nonart.

Also deeply affected by the horrors of war was a German art movement of the 1920s. Known as the ***Neue Sachlichkeit*** (New Objectivity), this genre was characterized by a realistic style of painting that reflected a cynical and highly critical attitude toward war. Many proponents of the Neue Sachlichkeit aggressively attacked and satirized the evils of postwar society, especially as symbolized by those in political power, all the while illustrating the devastating effects of the Great War. Wilhelm Heinrich Otto Dix (1891–1969) was a German painter and printmaker, notorious for his merciless and bitterly realistic depictions of society in the aftermath of war. Dix had enthusiastically volunteered for the German Army in

This is one of German-Jewish artist Erwin Blumenfeld's Dadaist collages, which combined his photographs with magazine cutouts and reflected the critical changes in art and politics after the Great War.
Erwin Blumenfeld

1914, took part in the Battle of the Somme, and then became quickly and profoundly affected and disillusioned by the sights of war. Along with George Grosz (1893–1959) he is widely considered one of the most important artists of the Neue Sachlichkeit.

Not all artistic movements drew on the experiences of the Great War, but by the beginning of the twentieth century, the possibilities inherent in a new aesthetic led to the emergence of a bewildering variety of pictorial schools, all of which promised an entirely new and unsettling art. Regardless of whether they called themselves dadaists, surrealists, cubists, or abstractionists, artists generally agreed on a program "to abolish the sovereignty of appearance." Paintings no longer depicted recognizable objects from the everyday world, and beauty was expressed in pure color or shape. Some painters sought to express feelings and emotions through violent

***Neue Sachlichkeit*** (no-yuh ZACH-kleekh-kite)

distortion of forms and the use of explosive colors; others, influenced by Freudian psychology, tried to tap the subconscious mind to communicate an inner vision or a dream. By the third decade of the twentieth century, it was nearly impossible to generalize about contemporary painting. All artists were acknowledged to have a right to their own reality, and generally accepted standards that distinguished between "good" and "bad" art disappeared.

## GLOBAL DEPRESSION

After the horrors and debilitating upheavals of the Great War, much of the world yearned for a return to normality and prosperity. By the early 1920s the efforts of governments and businesses to rebuild damaged economies seemed to bear fruit. Prosperity, however, was short-lived. In 1929 the world plunged into economic depression that was so long-lasting, so severe, and so global that it has become known as the **Great Depression.** The old capitalist system of trade and finance collapsed, and until a new system took its place after 1945, a return to worldwide prosperity could not occur.

### The Great Depression

By the middle of the 1920s, some semblance of economic normality had returned, and most countries seemed on the way to economic recovery. Industrial productivity had returned to prewar levels as businesses repaired the damages the war had inflicted on industrial plants, equipment, and transportation facilities. But that prosperity was fragile, perhaps even false, and many serious problems and dislocations remained in the international economy.

**Economic Problems** The economic recovery and well-being of Europe, for example, were tied to a tangled financial system that involved war debts among the Allies, reparations paid by Germany and Austria, and the flow of U.S. funds to Europe. In essence, the governments of Austria and Germany relied on U.S. loans and investment capital to finance reparation payments to France and England. The French and British governments, in turn, depended on those reparation paymentsto pay off loans taken out in the United States during the Great War. By the summer of 1928, U.S. lenders and investors started to withdraw capital from Europe, placing an intolerable strain on the financial system.

There were other problems as well. Improvements in industrial processes reduced worldwide demand for certain raw materials, causing an increase in supplies and a drop in prices. Technological advances in the production of automobile tires, for instance, permitted the use of reclaimed rubber. The resulting glut of natural rubber had devastating consequences for the economies of the Dutch East Indies, Ceylon, and Malaysia, which relied on the export of rubber. Similarly,

Soup kitchens and breadlines became commonplace in the United States during the earliest, darkest years of the Great Depression. They fed millions of starving and unemployed people. Bettmann/Getty Images

the increased use of oil undermined the coal industry, the emergence of synthetics hurt the cotton industry, and the growing adoption of artificial nitrogen virtually ruined the nitrate industry of Chile.

One of the nagging weaknesses of the global economy in the 1920s was the depressed state of agriculture, the result of overproduction and falling prices. During the Great War, when Europe's agricultural output declined significantly, farmers in the United States, Canada, Argentina, and Australia expanded their production. At the end of the war, European farmers resumed their agricultural activity, thereby contributing to worldwide surpluses. Above-average global harvests between 1925 and 1929 aggravated the situation. As production increased, demand declined, and prices collapsed throughout the world. By 1929 the price of a bushel of wheat was at its lowest level in 400 years, and farmers everywhere became impoverished. The reduced income of farm families contributed to high inventories of manufactured goods, which in turn caused businesses to cut back production and to dismiss workers.

**The Crash of 1929** The United States enjoyed a boom after the Great War: industrial wages were high, and production and consumption increased. Many people in the United States invested their earnings and savings in speculative ventures, particularly the buying of stock on margin—putting up as little as 3 percent of a stock's price in cash and borrowing the remainder from brokers and banks or by mortgaging their homes. By October 1929, hints of a worldwide economic slowdown and warnings from experts that stock prices were overvalued prompted investors to pull out of the market. On **Black Thursday** (October 24), a wave of panic selling on the New York Stock Exchange caused stock prices to plummet. Investors who had overextended themselves in a frenzy of speculative stock purchases watched in agony. Thousands of people, from poor widows to industrial tycoons, lost their life savings, and by the end of the day eleven financiers had committed suicide. The crisis deepened when lenders called in loans, thereby forcing more investors to sell their securities at any price.

**Economic Contraction Spreads** In the wake of this financial chaos came a drastic decrease in business activity, wages, and employment. Consumer demand no longer kept up with all the goods that businesses produced, and when businesses realized that they could not sell their inventories, they responded with cutbacks in production and layoffs. With so many people unemployed or underemployed, demand plummeted further, causing more business failures and soaring unemployment. In 1930 the slump deepened, and by 1932 industrial production had fallen to half of its 1929 level. National income had dropped by approximately half. Forty-four percent of U.S. banks were out of business, and the deposits of millions of people had disappeared. Because much of the world's prosperity depended on the export of U.S. capital and the strength of U.S. import markets, the contraction of the U.S. economy created a ripple effect that circled the globe.

Most societies experienced economic difficulties throughout the 1930s. Although the severity of the economic contraction varied in intensity, virtually every industrialized society saw its economy shrivel. Nations that relied on exports of manufactured goods to pay for imported fuel and food—Germany and Japan in particular—suffered the most. The depression also spread unevenly to primary producing economies in Latin America, Africa, and Asia. Hardest hit were countries that depended on the export of a few primary products—agricultural goods, such as coffee, sugar, and cotton, and raw materials, such as minerals, ores, and rubber.

**Industrial Economies** U.S. investors, shaken by the collapse of stock prices, tried to raise money by calling in loans and liquidating investments, and Wall Street banks refused to extend short-term loans as they became due. Banking houses in Austria and Germany became vulnerable to collapse because they had been major recipients of U.S. loans. Devastated by the loss of U.S. capital, the German economy experienced a precipitous economic slide that by 1932 resulted in 35 percent unemployment and a 50 percent decrease in industrial production. As the German economy ground to a virtual halt, the rest of Europe—which was closely integrated with the German economy—sputtered and stalled. The situation in Europe deteriorated further when businesses, desperate to raise capital by exporting goods to the United States, found that U.S. markets had virtually disappeared behind tariff walls. Foreign trade fell sharply between 1929 and 1932, causing further losses in manufacturing, employment, and per capita income. Because of its great dependence on the U.S. market, the Japanese economy felt the depression's effects almost immediately. Unemployment in export-oriented sectors of the economy skyrocketed as companies cut back on production.

**Economic Nationalism** The Great Depression destroyed the international financial and commercial network of the capitalist economies. As international cooperation broke down, governments turned to their own resources and practiced **economic nationalism.** By imposing tariff barriers, import quotas, and import prohibitions, politicians hoped to achieve a high degree of economic self-sufficiency. In an age of global interdependence, however, such goals remained unobtainable, and economic nationalism invariably backfired. Each new measure designed to restrict imports provoked retaliation by other nations whose interests were affected. After the U.S. Congress passed the **Smoot-Hawley Tariff Act** in 1930, which raised duties on most manufactured products to prohibitive levels, the governments of dozens of other nations immediately retaliated by raising tariffs on imports of U.S. products. The result was a sharp drop in international trade. Instead of higher

## INTERPRETING IMAGES

In January 1932, ten thousand hunger strikers marched on Washington, D.C., seeking government relief for their misery. Human faces of the Great Depression. This 1936 photograph of a mother with her two children in Oklahoma, taken by photographer Dorothea Lange, documented the extreme poverty of the Great Depression.

**Analyze** *Consider these images as well as the photo of the soup kitchen. How do the pictures reflect problems in the U.S. severe enough to justify massive government spending on new programs? How was the U.S. government approach a contrast to Stalin's Five-Year programs? Do you think these photos accurately express the impact of the Depression in the U.S.? Who or what might be left out?*

Bettmann/Getty Images, Pictorial Press Ltd/Alamy Stock Photo

levels of production and income, economic nationalism yielded the opposite. Between 1929 and 1932, world production declined by 38 percent and trade dropped by more than 66 percent.

## Despair and Government Action

By 1933 unemployment in industrial societies reached thirty million, more than five times higher than in 1929. Men lost their jobs because of economic contraction, and a combination of economic trends and deliberate government policy caused women to lose theirs also. Unemployment initially affected women less directly than men because employers paid women two-thirds to three-quarters the wages of men doing the same work. But before long, governments enacted policies to reduce female employment, especially for married women. The notion that a woman's place was in the home was already widespread and gained even further currency during the Depression. In 1931 a British royal commission on unemployment insurance declared that "in the case of married women as a class, industrial employment cannot be regarded as the normal condition." More candid was the French Nobel Prize–winning physician Charles Richet (1850–1935), who insisted that removing women from the workforce would solve the problem of male unemployment and increase the nation's dangerously low birthrate.

**Personal Suffering** The Great Depression caused enormous personal suffering. The stark, gloomy statistics documenting the failure of economies do not convey the anguish and despair of those who lost their jobs, savings, and homes, and often their dignity and hope. For millions of people the struggle for food, clothing, and shelter grew desperate. Shantytowns appeared overnight in urban areas, and breadlines stretched for blocks. Marriage, childbearing, and divorce rates declined, while suicide rates rose. The acute physical and social problems of those at the bottom of the economic ladder often magnified social divisions and class hatreds. Workers and farmers especially came to despise the wealthy, who, despite their reduced incomes, were shielded from the worst impact of the economic downturn and continued to enjoy a comfortable lifestyle. Adolescents completing their schooling faced an almost nonexistent job market.

## SOURCES FROM THE PAST

### Franklin Delano Roosevelt: Nothing to Fear

*Franklin Delano Roosevelt (1882–1945) assumed the presidency of the United States on March 4, 1933, during the depths of the Great Depression. In his inaugural address to the nation, he conveyed both the anxiousness of the times and the seemingly unquenchable optimism that carried him—and his nation—through hard times. A vastly wealthy man serving as president during a time of devastating penury, Roosevelt nonetheless gained the admiration and respect of the people because of his warm eloquence and compassion. Although he hid his condition quite successfully during his time in public, FDR had contracted polio in the 1920s and had lost the use of his legs. This "crippled" president became a metaphor for the United States' economic collapse, but also for its ability to overcome fear itself. The excerpt below was part of Roosevelt's inaugural speech in 1933.*

**I am certain that my** fellow Americans expect that on my induction into the Presidency I will address them with a candor and a decision which the present situation of our Nation impels. This is preeminently the time to speak the truth, the whole truth, frankly and boldly. Nor need we shrink from honestly facing conditions in our country today. This great Nation will endure as it has endured, will revive and will prosper. So, first of all, let me assert my firm belief that the only thing we have to fear is fear itself—nameless, unreasoning, unjustified terror which paralyzes needed efforts to convert retreat into advance. In every dark hour of our national life a leadership of frankness and vigor has met with that understanding and support of the people themselves which is essential to victory. I am convinced that you will again give that support to leadership in these critical days.

What kind of spirit characterizes Americans during difficult times, according to Roosevelt?

In such a spirit on my part and on yours we face our common difficulties. They concern, thank God, only material things. Values have shrunken to fantastic levels; taxes have risen; our ability to pay has fallen; government of all kinds is faced by serious curtailment of income; the means of exchange are frozen in the currents of trade; the withered leaves of industrial enterprise lie on every side; farmers find no markets for their produce; the savings of many years in thousands of families are gone.

More important, a host of unemployed citizens face the grim problem of existence, and an equally great number toil with little return. Only a foolish optimist can deny the dark realities of the moment. . . .

What was Roosevelt trying to accomplish by being so frank about the difficulties facing the United States?

Happiness lies not in the mere possession of money; it lies in the joy of achievement, in the thrill of creative effort. The joy and moral stimulation of work no longer must be forgotten in the mad chase of evanescent profits. These dark days will be worth all they cost us if they teach us that our true destiny is not to be ministered unto but to minister to ourselves and to our fellow men.

#### For Further Reflection

- How does Roosevelt believe U.S. citizens can profit from the dark days of the Great Depression, and why is it that all they have to fear is fear itself?
- What conditions that formed the context of Roosevelt's speech demonstrate that his focus on "fear" was so appropriate?
- What was the purpose of his speech?
- Even though Roosevelt himself was wealthy and not suffering in the ways the American public was he was convincing?
- What characteristics of good leadership did he demonstrate?

*Source:* Roosevelt, Franklin D. First Inaugural Address of Franklin D. Roosevelt, March 4, 1933. The Avalon Project. Yale Law School Lillian Goldman Law Library..

That the Great Depression deflated economies as well as hope was especially noticeable in the literature of the period. Writers castigated the social and political order, calling repeatedly for a more just society. The U.S. writer John Steinbeck (1902–1968) chillingly captured the official heartlessness and the rising political anger inspired by the depression. In *The Grapes of Wrath* (1939), the Joad family, prototypical "Okies," migrated from Oklahoma to California to escape the "dust bowl," a period of severe and damaging dust storms. In describing their journey Steinbeck commented on the U.S. government's policy of "planned scarcity," in which surplus crops were destroyed to raise prices while citizens starved. In one of the novel's most famous passages, Steinbeck portrayed the nation's rising political anguish: The people come with nets to fish for potatoes in the river and the guards hold them back; they come in rattling cars to get the dumped oranges, but the kerosene is sprayed. And they stand still and watch potatoes float by, listen to the screaming pigs being killed in a ditch and covered with quicklime, watch the mountains of oranges slop down to a putrefying ooze; and in the eyes of the people there is the failure; and in the eyes of the hungry there is a growing wrath. In the souls of the people the grapes of wrath are filling and growing heavy, growing heavy for the vintage.

### Economic Experimentation

Classical economic thought held that capitalism was a self-correcting system that operated best when left to its own devices. Governments responded to the economic crisis in one of two ways. Initially, most governments did nothing, hoping that the crisis would resolve itself. When the misery spawned by the depression sparked calls for action, some governments assumed more active roles, pursuing deflationary measures by balancing national budgets and curtailing public spending. In either case, rather than lifting national economies out of the doldrums, the classical prescriptions for economic ills worsened the depression's impact and intensified the plight of millions of people. Far from self-correcting, capitalism seemed to be dying. Many people called for a fundamental revision of economic thought.

**Keynes** **John Maynard Keynes** (1883–1946), the most influential economist of the twentieth century, offered a novel solution. His seminal work, *The General Theory of Employment, Interest, and Money* (1936), was his answer to the central problem of the depression—that millions of people who were willing to work could not find employment. To Keynes the fundamental cause of the depression was not excessive supply, but inadequate demand. Accordingly, he urged governments to play an active role and stimulate the economy by increasing the money supply, thereby lowering interest rates and encouraging investment. He also advised governments to undertake public works projects to provide jobs and redistribute incomes through tax policy, an intervention which would result in reduced unemployment and increased consumer demand, which in turn would lead to economic revival. Such measures, Keynes argued, were necessary even if they caused governments to run deficits and maintain unbalanced budgets.

**The New Deal** Although Keynes's theories did not become influential with policymakers until after World War II, the administration of U.S. President **Franklin Delano Roosevelt** (1882–1945) applied similar ideas. Roosevelt took aggressive steps to reinflate the economy and ease the worst of the suffering caused by the depression. His proposals for dealing with the national calamity included legislation designed to prevent the collapse of the banking system, to provide jobs and farm subsidies, to give workers the right to organize and bargain collectively, to guarantee minimum wages, and to provide social security in old age. This program of sweeping economic and social reforms was called the **New Deal.** Its fundamental premise, that the federal government was justified in intervening to protect the social and economic welfare of the people, represented a major shift in U.S. government policy and started a trend toward social reform legislation that continued long after the depression years. Nevertheless, it was the enormous military spending during World War II that did more to end the Great Depression in the United States than the specific programs of the New Deal.

## CHALLENGES TO THE LIBERAL ORDER

Amid the gloom and despair of the Great Depression, it seemed to many that the capitalism and liberalism that had come to characterize much of western Europe and the United States no longer worked. At the same time, some voices promised to guide the way to more effective alternatives. Marxists, for example, believed that capitalist society was on its deathbed, and they sought to demonstrate that a new and better system based on rule by the proletariat (the working class) was being born out of the ashes of the Russian Empire. The new rulers of Russia, Vladimir Ilyich Lenin and then Joseph Stalin, transformed the former tsarist empire into the world's first communist society, the Union of Soviet Socialist Republics (1922). Once the Soviet Union was established, they also sought to export communism to the rest of the world.

Other people argued that only strong leadership from above, without the bureaucracy of democratic institutions, could build powerful societies. Fascist movements across Europe promoted their alternatives to socialism and offered revolutionary answers to the economic, social, and political problems that seemed to defy solution by traditional liberal democratic means. Among those fascist movements, the Italian and German ones figured most prominently.

### Communism in Russia

In 1917 Lenin and his fellow Bolsheviks had taken power in the name of the Russian working class, but socialist victory did not bring peace and stability to the lands of the former Russian Empire. After seizing power, Lenin and his supporters had to defend the world's first dictatorship of the proletariat against numerous enemies, including dissident socialists, anti-Bolshevik officers and troops, peasant bands, and foreign military forces.

**Civil War** Opposition to the Bolshevik takeover—by now calling itself the Russian Communist Party—erupted into a civil war that lasted from 1918 to 1920. In order to maintain power, Lenin's government in Moscow began a policy of crushing all opposition. The communists began the Red Terror campaign in which suspected anticommunists known as Whites were arrested, tried, and executed. During this period, the newly developed secret police killed some 200,000 opponents of the regime. In July 1918 the Bolsheviks executed Tsar Nicholas II, Empress Alexandra, their five children, and their remaining servants because they feared that the Romanov family would fall into the hands of the Whites, thereby strengthening counterrevolutionary forces. The peasantry, meanwhile, largely supported the Bolsheviks, fearing that a victory by the Whites would result in the return of the brutally oppressive tsarist system. And indeed, White terror was often as brutal as Red terror. But the fight between the Whites and the Reds inside Russia was only part of the conflict. Russia's former allies—Britain, France, Japan, and the United States—were deeply opposed to the assumption of Bolshevik power, partially because it threatened their economic interests in Russia and partly because Russia's exit from the war had betrayed the alliance against the Germans. Thus in 1918, just as the Great War was ending, the Allies assembled an international coalition and sent troops to support the Whites. But the coalition was poorly organized, the troops were tired from four years of war, and their numbers were small. In addition, the presence of foreign troops on the side of the Whites had the effect of uniting Russians against the Whites. After three years of brutal civil war, the Whites were decisively defeated by the Red Army in 1920. One of the lasting legacies of the civil war was that the methods of terror the Reds resorted to in order to defeat the Whites—including the creation of a powerful secret police—now became a permanent part of communist rule in Russia.

**War Communism** The need for access to funds to fight the civil war led the new Soviet government to embark on a hasty and unplanned course of nationalization, a policy known as **war communism.** After officially annulling private property, the Bolshevik government assumed ownership of banks, industry, and other privately held commercial properties. Landed estates and the holdings of monasteries and churches became national property, although the Bolsheviks explicitly exempted the holdings of poor peasants from confiscation. The government also abolished private trade, and seized crops from peasants to feed people in the cities. The policies that made up war communism were deeply unpopular with many segments of Russian society. In addition, they were disastrous for the Russian economy. By 1920 industrial production had fallen to about one-tenth of its prewar level and agricultural output to about one-half its prewar level.

In 1921, Lenin faced the daunting prospect of rebuilding a society that had been torn apart by war and civil war for the last seven years. The workers, in whose name he had taken power, were on strike. Other problems included depopulated cities, destroyed factories, and an army that demobilized soldiers faster than the workforce could absorb them. Lenin and the party tried to take strict control of the country by crushing workers' strikes, peasant rebellions, and a sailors' revolt. Yet Lenin recognized the need to make peace with those whose skills would rekindle industrial production. Faced with economic paralysis, in the spring of 1921 he decided on a radical reversal of war communism.

**The New Economic Policy** Demonstrating his pragmatism and willingness to compromise, Lenin implemented the **New Economic Policy** (NEP), which temporarily restored the market economy and some private enterprise in Russia. Large industries, banks, and transportation and communications facilities remained under state control, but the government returned small-scale industries (those with fewer than twenty workers) to private ownership. The government also allowed peasants to sell their surpluses at free market prices. Other features of the NEP included a vigorous program of electrification and the establishment of technical schools to train technicians and engineers. Lenin did not live to see the success of the NEP. After suffering three paralytic strokes, he died in 1924. His death was followed by a bitter struggle for power among the Bolshevik leaders.

**Joseph Stalin** Many old Bolsheviks continued to argue for a permanent or continuous revolution, asserting that socialism in Russia would fail if socialism did not move from a national to an international stage. Others in the Politburo, the central governing body of the Communist Party, favored establishing socialism in one country alone, thus repudiating the role of the Union of Soviet Socialist Republics as torchbearer of

Joseph Stalin (1879–1953) at a Soviet congress in 1936. By 1928 Stalin had prevailed over his opponents to become the dictator of the Soviet Union, a position he held until his death in 1953.
Bettmann/Getty Images

worldwide socialist revolution. **Joseph Stalin** (1879–1953), who served in the unglamorous but powerful bureaucratic position of general secretary of the communist party, promoted the idea of socialism in one country. A Georgian by birth, an Orthodox seminarian by training, and a Russian nationalist by conviction, Stalin spoke Russian with a heavy accent, and was an intellectual misfit among the Bolshevik elite. However, by 1928, Stalin had completely triumphed over his rivals in the party by using his influence as general secretary and had cleared the way for an unchallenged dictatorship of the Soviet Union.

**First Five-Year Plan** Stalin decided to replace Lenin's NEP with an ambitious plan for rapid economic development known as the **First Five-Year Plan.** The basic aim of this and subsequent five-year plans (the first was implemented in 1929) were to transform the Soviet Union from a predominantly agricultural country to a leading industrial power. The First Five-Year Plan set targets for increased productivity in all spheres of the economy but emphasized heavy industry—especially steel and machinery—at the expense of consumer goods. Through Gosplan, the central state planning agency, Stalin and the party attempted to coordinate resources and the labor force on an unprecedented scale. As the rest of the world teetered on the edge of economic collapse, this blueprint for maximum centralization of the entire national economy offered a bold alternative to market capitalism. Stalin repeatedly stressed the urgency of this monumental endeavor, telling his people, "We are 50 to 100 years behind the advanced countries. Either we do it, or we shall go under."

**Collectivization of Agriculture** Integral to the drive for industrialization was the **collectivization of agriculture.** The Soviet state expropriated privately owned land to create collective or cooperative farm units whose profits were supposed to be shared by all farmers. The logic of communist ideology demanded the abolition of private property and market choices, but more practical considerations also played a role. Stalin and his regime viewed collectivization as a means of increasing the efficiency of agricultural production and ensuring that industrial workers would be fed. Collectivization was extremely unpopular among peasants, but it was not a choice. Stalin's government forced peasants onto the collectivized farms and ruthlessly punished those who resisted. The government specifically attacked a group called ***kulaks*** (relatively wealthy peasants who had risen to prosperity under Lenin's New Economic Policy), who strongly opposed collectivization.

In some places, outraged peasants reacted to collectivization by slaughtering their livestock and burning their crops. The government's response was outright murder or else removal to prison camps. Millions of farmers chose to leave the land altogether to avoid collectivization and instead migrated to cities in search of work. Once in the cities, these peasants further taxed the limited supplies of housing, food, and utilities in urban areas. Collectivized farms often set unrealistic production quotas, which peasants were unable to meet. Nevertheless, the farms continued to send what they did produce to feed urban workers, leaving peasants to starve to death on the land they once owned. Stalin called a halt to collectivization in 1931, when about half of the farms in the Soviet Union had been collectivized. Although he claimed the policy had made his government "dizzy with success," in reality at least three million peasants died as a direct result of collectivization.

The Soviet Union industrialized under Stalin even though the emphasis on building heavy industry first and consumer

Men and women drive tractors out of one of the Soviet Union's Machine Tractor Stations to work fields on the new collectivized farms.
Sovfoto/Universal Images Group/Getty Images

# SOURCES FROM THE PAST

## Goals and Achievements of the First Five-Year Plan

*In the aftermath of war, revolution, and civil strife, Vladimir Lenin in 1921 adopted the New Economic Policy (NEP) to prevent the collapse of the Russian economy. The NEP was relatively successful, but it rankled Marxist purists because it permitted the return of a limited form of capitalism. Lenin's successor, Joseph Stalin, was determined to build "socialism in one country" by replacing the NEP with a planned economy, whereby a centralized bureaucracy guided and regulated production. To that end, Stalin launched a series of Five-Year Plans designed to transform the Soviet Union into a modern, powerful state. In the following report, delivered to the Central Committee of the Communist Party of the Soviet Union in January 1933, Stalin outlined the goals and the achievements of the First Five-Year Plan.*

**The fundamental task of the** five-year plan was to convert the U.S.S.R. from an agrarian and weak country, dependent upon the caprices of the capitalist countries, into an industrial and powerful country, fully self-reliant and independent of the caprices of world capitalism.

The fundamental task of the five-year plan was, in converting the U.S.S.R. into an industrial country, to completely oust the capitalist elements, to widen the front of socialist forms of economy, and to create the economic basis for the abolition of classes in the U.S.S.R., for the building of a socialist society.

The fundamental task of the five-year plan was to transfer small and scattered agriculture on to the lines of large-scale collective farming, so as to ensure the economic basis of socialism in the countryside and thus to eliminate the possibility of the restoration of capitalism in the U.S.S.R.

Finally, the task of the five-year plan was to create all the necessary technical and economic prerequisites for increasing to the utmost the defensive capacity of the country, enabling it to organize determined resistance to any attempt at military intervention from abroad, to any attempt at military attack from abroad.

What are the results of the five-year plan in four years in the sphere of industry?

We did not have an iron and steel industry, the basis for the industrialization of the country. Now we have one.

We did not have a tractor industry. Now we have one.

We did not have an automobile industry. Now we have one.

We did not have a machine-tool industry. Now we have one.

We did not have a big and modern chemical industry. Now we have one.

We did not have a real and big industry for the production of modern agricultural machinery. Now we have one.

> What areas of industry did the Soviet Union focus on during the First Five Year Plan, and what areas were neglected?

We did not have an aircraft industry. Now we have one.

In output of electric power we were last on the list. Now we rank among the first.

In output of oil products and coal we were last on the list. Now we rank among the first.

And as a result of all this the capitalist elements have been completely and irrevocably ousted from industry, and socialist industry has become the sole form of industry in the U.S.S.R.

Let us pass to the question of the results of the five-year plan in four years in the sphere of agriculture. The Party has succeeded in the course of some three years in organizing more than 200,000 collective farms and about 5,000 state farms devoted to grain growing and livestock raising, and at the same time it has succeeded during four years in expanding the crop area by 21 million hectares. The Party has succeeded in getting more than 60 per cent of the peasant farms to unite into collective farms, embracing more than 70 per cent of all the land cultivated by peasants; this means that we have fulfilled the five-year plan three times over. The Party has succeeded in converting the U.S.S.R. from a country of small-peasant farming into a country of the largest-scale agriculture in the world. Do not all these facts testify to the superiority of the Soviet system of agriculture over the capitalist system?

> Given that Stalin does not address here the three million lives lost during collectivization, is it possible that he similarly downplayed the human costs of the industrial achievements he lists above?

Finally, as a result of all this the Soviet Union has been converted from a weak country, unprepared for defense, into a country mighty in defense, a country prepared for every contingency, a country capable of producing on a mass scale all modern means of defense and of equipping its army with them in the event of an attack from abroad.

### For Further Reflection

- What were the fundamental aims and achievements of the First Five-Year Plan? What benefits, if any, did the peoples of the Soviet Union derive from this economic experiment in a planned economy?
- Why is the consideration of the audience of Stalin's report helpful in understanding the content?
- What evidence would undermine Stalin's claims to success, by describing the costs to Soviet citizens and to the long-term economy of the country?
- Offer several reasons for Stalin's strident opposition to capitalism.

*Source:* Stalin, J. V. "The Results of the First Five-Year Plan." Report Delivered at the Joint Plenum of the Central Committee and the Central Control Commission of the C.P.S.U.(B.), January 7-12, 1933. *Marxists Internet Archive (2008),* 1947, 578–630.

industries later meant that citizens postponed the gratifications of industrialization. Before refrigerators, radios, or automobiles became available, the government constructed steelworks and hydroelectric plants. The scarcity or nonexistence of consumer goods was to some degree balanced by full employment, low-cost utilities, and—when available—cheap housing and food in urban areas. Set against the collapse of the U.S. stock market and the depression-ridden capitalist world, the ability of a centrally planned economy to create more jobs than workers could fill made it appear an attractive alternative.

**The Great Purge** Nevertheless, the results of Stalin's First Five-Year Plan generated controversy as the Communist Party prepared for its seventeenth congress in 1934, the self-proclaimed "Congress of Victors." Although Stalin proclaimed that it had been a great success, the disaster of collectivization and the ruthlessness with which it was carried out had raised doubts about his administration. Although themes of unity and reconciliation prevailed, Stalin learned of a plan to bring more pluralism back into leadership. The Congress of Victors became the "Congress of Victims" as Stalin incited a civil war within the party that was climaxed by highly publicized trials of former Bolshevik elites for treason and by a purge of two-thirds of the delegates. Between 1935 and 1938, in a campaign of political repression known as the Great Purge, Stalin removed from posts of authority all persons suspected of opposition, including two-thirds of the members of the 1934 Central Committee and more than one-half of the army's high-ranking officers. The victims faced execution or long-term suffering in labor camps. According to the declassified Soviet archives, during 1937 and 1938, Soviet security forces detained 1,548,366 persons, of whom 681,692 were shot.

The outside world watched the events unfolding within the Soviet Union with a mixture of contempt, fear, and admiration. Most observers recognized that the political and social upheavals that transformed the former Russian Empire were of worldwide importance. The establishment of the world's first dictatorship of the proletariat challenged the values and institutions of liberal society everywhere and seemed to demonstrate the viability of communism as a social and political system.

## The Fascist Alternative

While socialism was transforming the former Russian Empire, another political force swept across Europe after the Great War. **Fascism,** a far-right, ultranationalist political movement and ideology that sought to create a new type of society, developed as a reaction against liberal democracy and the spread of socialism and communism. The term *fascism* derives from the word *fasces,* an ancient Roman symbol of authority consisting of a bundle of wooden rods strapped together around an axe. In 1919 Benito Mussolini adopted this symbol for the Italian Fascist movement that governed Italy from 1922 to 1943. Movements comparable to Italian fascism subsequently developed and sometimes dominated political life in many European societies, most notably in Germany in the guise of National Socialism (Nazism). Although fascism enjoyed widespread popularity in many European countries, it rarely threatened the political order and, with the exception of Italy and Germany, never overthrew a parliamentary system. Political and economic frustrations made fertile ground for fascist appeals outside Europe, and potential fascist movements sprang up during the 1930s in Japan, China, and South Africa; in Latin American societies such as Brazil and Argentina; and in several Arab territories. Nevertheless, fascism was most influential in Europe in the era between the two world wars.

**Defining Fascism** During the 1920s and 1930s, fascist movements in Europe attracted millions of followers and proved especially attractive to middle classes and rural populations. These groups became radicalized by economic and social crises and were especially fearful of class conflict and the perceived threat from the political left, especially from communism. Fascism also proved attractive to nationalists of all classes, who denounced their governments for failing to realize the glorious objectives for which they had fought during the Great War. Asserting that society faced a profound crisis, fascists sought to create a new national community, which they defined either as a nation-state or as a unique ethnic or racial group. As part of their quest, fascist movements commonly dedicated themselves to the revival of allegedly lost national traditions and, hence, differed widely. Nevertheless, most fascist movements shared certain common features, such as the veneration of the state; a devotion to a strong leader; and an emphasis on ultranationalism, ethnocentrism, and militarism.

Fascist ideology consistently invoked the central role of the state, which stood at the center of the nation's life and history and which demanded the subordination of the individual to the service of the state. Strong and often charismatic leaders, such as Benito Mussolini in Italy or Adolf Hitler in Germany, embodied the state and claimed indisputable authority. Consequently, fascists were hostile to liberal democracy; its devotion to individualism; and its institutions, which they viewed as weak. Fascism was also extremely hostile to class-based visions of the future promoted by socialism and communism. Fascist movements emphasized **chauvinism** (an aggressive form of nationalism) and **xenophobia** (a fear of foreign people). Some fascist leaders, accordingly, viewed national boundaries as artificial restraints limiting their union with ethnic or racial comrades living in other states. The typical fascist state embraced *militarism,* a belief in the rigors and virtues of military life as an individual and national ideal. In practice, militarism meant that fascist regimes maintained large and expensive military establishments; tried to organize much of public life along military lines; and generally showed a fondness for uniforms, parades, and monumental architecture.

---

**chauvinism** (SHOH-vuh-niz-uhm)
**xenophobia** (zen-uh-FOH-bee-uh)

Benito Mussolini and Adolf Hitler watch a Nazi parade staged for the Italian dictator's visit to Germany in the fall of 1937. Hitler ordered a major display of military power for Mussolini and, by the end of the visit, Mussolini was convinced that an alliance with Germany would lead to Italy becoming more powerful in Europe.
Bettmann/Getty Images

## Italian Fascism

The first fascist movement developed in Italy after the Great War. Italians in 1918 were deeply disilluisioned with their uninspired political leadership and ineffective government, extensive economic turmoil and social discontent, and what seemed like a threatening rise of socialist movements. In addition Italians were extremely disappointed with Italy's territorial spoils from the peace settlement after the Great War, as many believed Italy should have received significant chunks of Austrian territory.

**Benito Mussolini** The guiding force behind Italian fascism was **Benito Mussolini,** a former socialist and, from 1912 to 1914, editor of Italy's leading socialist daily *Avanti!* ("Forward!"). In 1914 he founded his own newspaper, *Il Popolo d'Italia* ("The People of Italy"), which encouraged Italian entry into the Great War. Mussolini was convinced that the war represented a turning point for the nation. The soldiers returning from the front, he argued, would spearhead the thorough transformation of Italian society and create a new type of state. But after the Great War, the one-time socialist advanced a political program that emphasized virulent nationalism, demanded repression of socialists, and called for a strong political leader. In 1919 he established the *Fasci Italiani di Combattimento* (Italian Combat Veteran League).

Mussolini's movement gained widespread support after 1920, and by 1921 his league managed to elect thirty-five fascists to the Italian parliament. Much of the newly found public support resulted from the effective use of violence against socialists by fascist armed squads known as Blackshirts. The Italian socialist party had organized militant strikes throughout Italy's northern industrial cities, causing considerable chaos. By early 1921 Italy hovered on the brink of civil war. In 1922, Mussolini and his followers decided the time was ripe for a fascist seizure of power, and on 28 October, they staged a march on Rome. While Mussolini stayed safely in Milan awaiting the outcome of events, thousands of his blackshirted troops converged on Rome. Rather than calling on the military to oppose the fascist threat, King Victor Emmanuel III hastily asked Mussolini on 29 October to become prime minister and form a new government. Mussolini inaugurated a fascist regime in 1922.

**The Fascist State** Between 1925 and 1931, Italy's fascists consolidated their power through a series of laws that provided the legal basis for the nation's transformation into a one-party dictatorship. In 1926 Mussolini seized total power as dictator and subsequently ruled Italy as *Il Duce* ("the leader"). The regime moved quickly to eliminate all other political parties, curb freedom of the press, and outlaw free speech and association. A Special Tribunal for the Defense of the State, supervised by military officers, silenced political dissent. Thousands of Italians were marked as antifascist subversives and found themselves imprisoned or exiled on remote islands. Others faced capital punishment. Allying himself and his movement with business and landlord interests, *Il Duce* also crushed labor unions and prohibited strikes. In an effort to harmonize the interests of workers, employers, and the state, the regime tried to establish a corporatist order. This order was based on the vague fascist concept of corporatism, which viewed society as an organic entity through which the different interests in society came under the control of the state. Thus, in theory, a National Council of Corporations settled labor disputes and supervised wage settlements, but, in reality, this scheme was little more than a propaganda effort. In 1932, on the tenth anniversary of the fascist seizure of power, Mussolini felt confident enough to announce "that the twentieth century will be a century of fascism, the century of Italian power."

Racism and antisemitism were never prominent components of Italian fascism, but in 1938 the government suddenly issued antisemitic laws that labeled Jews unpatriotic, excluded them from government employment, and prohibited all marriages between Jews and so-called Aryans. This development

***Il Duce*** (eehl DOO-cheh)

was likely occasioned by Mussolini's newfound friendship with fellow dictator Adolf Hitler. In 1936 Mussolini told his followers that from now on, world history would revolve around a Rome-Berlin Axis. In May 1939 the leaders of fascist Italy and Nazi Germany formalized their political, military, and ideological alliance by signing a ten-year Pact of Steel. This Pact of Steel illustrated the strong links between the Italian and German variants of fascism.

## German National Socialism

**Hitler and the Nazi Party** After his postwar political awakening, Adolf Hitler came into contact with an obscure political party sympathetic to his ideas. In 1921 he became chairman of the party now known as the National Socialist German Workers' Party. National Socialism (the Nazi movement) made its first major appearance in 1923 when party members and Hitler attempted to overthrow the democratic Weimar Republic that had replaced the German Empire in 1919. The revolt quickly fizzled under the gunfire of police units; Hitler was jailed, and the Nazi movement and its leader descended into obscurity. When Hitler emerged from prison in 1924, he resolved to use new tactics. Recognizing the futility of armed insurrection, he reorganized his movement and launched it on a "path of legality." Hitler and his followers were determined to gain power legally through the ballot box and, once successful, to discard democracy altogether.

**The Struggle for Power** **National Socialism** made rapid gains after 1929 because it had broad appeal. Hitler attracted disillusioned people who felt alienated from society and frightened by the growing strength of the communist party in Germany. A growing number of people blamed the young German democracy for Germany's misfortunes: a humiliating peace treaty—the Treaty of Versailles—that identified Germany as responsible for the Great War and assigned reparation payments to the Allies, the hyperinflation of the early 1920s that wiped out the savings of the middle class, the suffering brought on by the Great Depression, and the seemingly unending and bitter infighting among the nation's major political parties. Adolf Hitler promised an end to all those misfortunes by creating a new order that would lead to greatness for Germany. By stressing racial doctrines, particularly antisemitism, the Nazis added a unique and frightening twist to their ideology. Although the Nazis avoided class divisions by recruiting followers from all strata of society, National Socialism in the main appealed to the members of the lower-middle classes: ruined shopkeepers and artisans, impoverished farmers, discharged white-collar workers, and disenchanted students.

The impact of the Great Depression and political infighting led to bloody street battles, shaking the foundations of Germany's fragile young democracy. The leaders of the nation's democratic and liberal parties groped for solutions to mounting unemployment but were hindered by lack of consensus and the public's loss of faith in the democratic system. The electorate became radicalized. Fewer and fewer Germans were willing to defend a parliamentary system they considered ineffective and corrupt. Between 1930 and 1932 the Nazi Party became the largest party in parliament, and the reactionary and feeble president, Paul von Hindenburg (1847–1934), decided to offer Hitler the chancellorship. Promising to gain a majority in the next elections, Hitler lost little time in

### INTERPRETING IMAGES

"Against Starvation and Desperation—Vote for Hitler" is the translated slogan written on this election poster for the July 1932 federal election in Germany. The election resulted in great gains by the Nazi Party, which garnered 37 percent of the national vote and became the single largest party in the *Reichstag* (parliament).

**Analyze** *Hitler offered an approach to solving economic problems which was different from both Weimar democratic capitalism and communism. What was the platform? How would you describe this poster and its message?*

picture alliance/Getty Images

transforming the dying republic into a single-party dictatorship. He promised a German *Reich,* or empire, that would endure for a thousand years.

**Consolidation of Power** Under the guise of a state of national emergency, the Nazis used all available means to impose their rule. They began by eliminating all working-class and liberal opposition. The Nazis suppressed the German-communist and socialist parties and abrogated virtually all constitutional and civil rights. Subsequently, Hitler and his government outlawed all other political parties, made it a crime to create a new party, and made the National Socialist Party the only legal party. Between 1933 and 1935 the regime replaced Germany's federal structure with a highly centralized state that eliminated the autonomy previously exercised by state and municipal governments. The National Socialist state then guided the destruction of trade unions and the elimination of collective bargaining, including the prohibition of strikes and lockouts. The Nazis also purged the judiciary and the civil service, took control of all police forces, and removed enemies of the regime—both real and imagined—through imprisonment or murder.

**The Racial State** Once securely in power, the Nazi regime translated its deeply racist ideology, especially notions about racial superiority and racial purity, into practice. The leaders of the Third Reich pursued the creation of a race-based national community by introducing measures designed to improve both the quantity and the quality of the German "race." Implicit in this racial remodeling was the conviction that there was no room for the "racially inferior" or for "biological outsiders." The racial program of the Nazis, implemented as early as 1933, was based on a diffuse mixture of racial anthropological, pseudo-scientific, and antisemitic theories that harkened back to the nineteenth century.

Hitler's perception of Jews originated within a broader racist view of the world based on concepts of the "inequality" of "races" and the alleged "superiority" of the "white race" over other "races." The notion of racial superiority, in turn, was frequently buttressed by a perversion of evolutionary theory known as "social Darwinism," a theory that emerged in England and the United States in the 1870s. Proponents of "social Darwinism" applied the biological concepts of natural selection and survival of the fittest to the alleged social and political realities of human society. Thus, some "social Darwinists" argued that different races are biologically driven to struggle against one another for living space. Paralleling these racial theories was an international scientific, political, and moral ideology known as **eugenics,** which reached its peak of popularity in the first decades of the twentieth century. The term and field of modern eugenics was first formulated by Sir Francis Galton in his 1883 book *Hereditary Genius*. Reflecting a growing faith in science, especially heredity science, eugenics aimed at improving the genetic quality of the human gene

## What's Left Out?

Although Nazi Germany is most closely associated with the application of eugenics policies, in the 1920s and 1930s the United States also enacted a series of applied eugenics laws. Like Nazi Germany, eugenics in the United States—as promoted by the American Eugenics Society (founded in 1922)—focused mostly on negative eugenics, or eliminating negative traits from the population. Also like Nazi Germany, proponents of eugenics in the United States located most of these negative traits in minority populations. In the United States, poor and nonwhite populations were targeted as "undesirables," as were the mentally ill. In an effort to ensure that the most "undesirable" people within these groups did not reproduce, the eugenics movement in the United States focused on turning programs of forced sterilization into law. Indiana was the first state to enact a forced sterilization law in 1907, but by 1935 thirty-one other states had followed suit. In total, more than sixty thousand American citizens were sterilized against their will as a result of such laws. In one landmark 1927 case that made it all the way to the Supreme Court, chief justice Oliver Wendell Holmes justified the practice by writing, "It is better for all the world, if instead of waiting to execute degenerate offspring for crime, or to let them starve for their imbecility, society can prevent those who are manifestly unfit from continuing their kind. . . . Three generations of imbeciles are enough." In fact, Hitler himself boasted of studying American eugenics laws when developing his own programs of forced sterilization and euthanasia in the 1930s. When thinking about the crimes against humanity committed by Nazi Germany, it is worth remembering that these were justified by racist thinking masquerading under the guise of "scientific" ideas such as eugenics and that such racist thinking was widely believed—and put into practice—in the United States as well during the interwar period.

*Source:* Holmes, Oliver Wendell. Buck v. Bell, 274 U.S. 200 (1927). U.S. Supreme Court. May 2, 1927.

### Thinking Critically About Sources

1. Typically, scientific conclusions can be trusted. Why should people have questioned eugenics, even though it was purportedly based on "science"?
2. What questions should people have posed to challenge the assumption and conclusions of eugenics?
3. How might knowing this history affect the way we approach communicating about science today? Is it helpful to describe science as apolitical?

## INTERPRETING IMAGES

"Mother and Child" was the slogan on this poster created in the mid-1930s, idealizing and encouraging motherhood. The background conveys the Nazi predilection for the wholesome country life, a dream that clashed with the urban reality of German society.

**Analyze** *Describe the image of motherhood here. What is it advocating? What is it contrasting from? What motivated Mussolini and Hitler's fascist governments to romanticize and reward motherhood? How is motherhood politicized in other contexts?*

akg-images/Newscom

pool. As a practical matter, eugenics policies were divided into positive eugenics, the increased reproduction of those assumed to possess beneficial hereditary traits, and negative eugenics, the discouraging of reproduction among those with hereditary traits regarded as deficient. Eugenics was supported by prominent people, including Winston Churchill, Woodrow Wilson, Margaret Sanger, and Émile Zola, to mention just a few. Eugenic measures, such as the sterilization of certain mental patients, were implemented in the United States, Brazil, and Sweden, among other nations. The most infamous proponent of eugenics, however, was Adolf Hitler.

**Women and Race** Alarmed by declining birthrates in Germany, the Nazis launched a campaign to increase births of "racially valuable" children. This initiative was complementaryto Nazi ideology, which relegated women primarily to the roles of wife and mother. Through tax credits, special child allowances, and marriage loans, the government tried to encourage marriage and, they hoped, procreation among young people. Legal experts rewrote divorce laws so that a husband could get a divorce decree solely on the ground that he considered his wife sterile. At the same time, the regime outlawed abortions, closed birth control centers, restricted birth control devices, and made it difficult to obtain information about family planning. The Nazis also became enamored with pronatalist (in favor of pregnancy and childbirth) propaganda, and set in motion a veritable cult of motherhood. Annually on 12 August—the birth date of Hitler's mother—women who bore many children received the Honor Cross of the German Mother in three classes: bronze for those with more than four children, silver for those with more than six, and gold for those with more than eight. By August 1939 three million women carried this prestigious award, which many Germans cynically called the "rabbit decoration." In the long term, however, these pronatalist measures failed, and the birthrate remained below replacement level.

**Nazi Eugenics** The quantity of offspring was not the only concern of the new rulers. They were also obsessed with quality. Starting in 1933, the regime initiated a compulsory

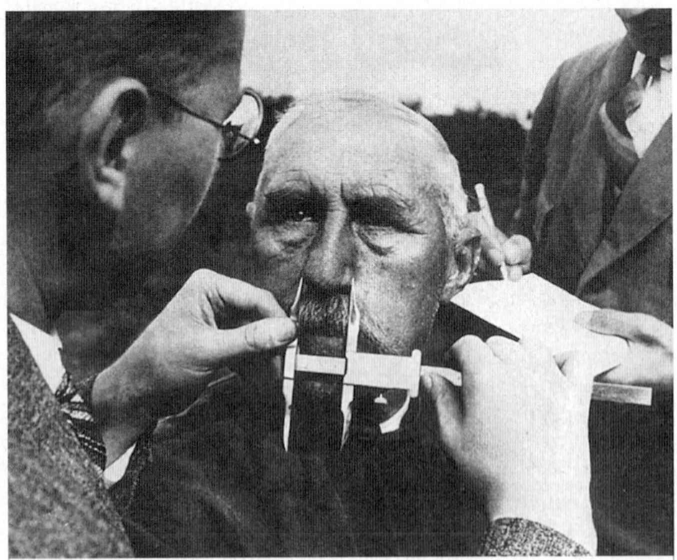

A Nazi "racial expert" uses a caliper to measure the racial purity of a German, in this case as expressed in his facial features.

Henry Guttmann Collection/Hulton Archive/Getty Images

sterilization program for men and women the regime had identified as having "hereditarily determined" sicknesses, including schizophrenia, feeblemindedness, manic depression, hereditary blindness, hereditary deafness, chronic alcoholism, and serious physical deformities. Between 1934 and 1939 more than thirty thousand men and women underwent compulsory sterilization. Beginning in 1935 the government also sanctioned abortions—otherwise illegal in Germany—of the "hereditary ill" and "racial aliens." The mania for racial health culminated in a state-sponsored euthanasia program that was responsible for the murder of approximately two hundred thousand women, men, and children. Between 1939 and 1945 the Nazis systematically killed—by gassing, lethal injections, or starvation—those people judged useless to society, especially the physically and mentally handicapped. Nazi eugenics measures served as a precursor to the wholesale extermination of peoples classified as racial inferiors, such as Roma (also called Gypsies) and Jews.

**Antisemitism** **Antisemitism,** or prejudice against Jews, was a key element in Nazi efforts to achieve a new racial order and became the hallmark of National Socialist rule. Immediately after coming to power in 1933, the Nazis initiated systematic measures to suppress Germany's Jewish population. Although Nazi antisemitism was based on biological racial theories, government authorities used religious descent to determine who was a Jew. A flood of discriminatory laws and directives designed to humiliate, impoverish, and segregate Jews from the rest of society followed. In 1935 the notorious **Nuremberg Laws** deprived German Jews of their citizenship and prohibited marriage and sexual intercourse between Jews and other Germans. The Nazi Party, in cooperation with government agencies, banks, and businesses, took steps to eliminate Jews from economic life and expropriate their wealth. Jewish civil servants lost their jobs, and Jewish lawyers and doctors lost their non-Jewish, clients. Party authorities also supervised the liquidation of Jewish-owned businesses or argued for their purchase—at much less than their true value—by companies owned or operated by non-Jews.

The official goal of the Nazi regime, at least initially, was Jewish emigration. Throughout the 1930s thousands of Jews left Germany, depriving the nation of many of its leading intellectuals, scientists, and artists. The exodus gained urgency after what came to be known as ***Kristallnacht*** ("the night of broken glass"). During the night of 9–10 November 1938, the Nazis arranged for the destruction of thousands of Jewish stores, the burning of most synagogues, and the murder of more than one hundred Jews throughout Germany and Austria. This ***pogrom*** (Yiddish for "devastation") was a signal that the position of Jews in Hitler's Reich was about to deteriorate dramatically. Although they had difficulty finding refuge, approximately 250,000 Jews left Germany by 1938. Those staying behind, especially the poor and the elderly, would face a troubling and potentially deadly future.

## CONCLUSION

In the decades after the Great War, European intellectuals questioned and challenged established traditions. While scientists and social thinkers conceived new theories that reshaped the ways humans encountered knowledge and perceptions, artists forged a contemporary aesthetic. In an age of global interdependence, the U.S. stock market crash of 1929 ushered in a period of prolonged economic contraction and social misery that engulfed much of the world and further added to a sense of crisis in Europe and the United States. As most of the industrialized world reeled under the impact of the Great Depression, the leadership of the Soviet Union embarked on a state-sponsored program of rapid industrialization. Though causing widespread human suffering, a series of five-year plans transformed the Soviet Union into a major industrial and military power and offered an alternative to liberal democracy.

European fascist regimes also offered alternatives to liberal democracy. Italians under the leadership of Mussolini rebuilt their state through fascist policies and imperial expansion. In Germany the effects of the Great Depression paved the way for the establishment of the Nazi state, which was based on the principle of racial inequality. Although many peoples suffered under the racist regime, Jews were the principal victims. Ultimately, Adolf Hitler's vision of a powerful and racially pure German state—crafted in an age of anxiety and uncertainty—helped lead to another world war less than two decades after the end of World War I.

## STUDY TERMS

Adolf Hitler (751)
Albert Einstein (737)
antisemitism (753)
Benito Mussolini (749)
Black Thursday (741)
chauvinism (748)
collectivization of agriculture (746)
Dadaism (739)
economic nationalism (741)
eugenics (751)
fascism (748)
First Five-Year Plan (746)
Franklin Delano Roosevelt (744)
Great Depression (740)
Great Purge (763)
John Maynard Keynes (744)
Joseph Stalin (746)
*Kristallnacht* (753)
*kulaks* (746)
lost generation (736)
National Socialism (750)
*Neue Sachlichkeit* (739)
New Deal (744)
New Economic Policy (NEP) (745)
Nuremberg Laws (753)
*pogrom* (753)
psychoanalysis (739)
Sigmund Freud (738)
Smoot-Hawley Tariff Act (741)
uncertainty principle (738)
war communism (745)
xenophobia (748)

## FOR FURTHER READING

H. H. Arnason and Elizabeth C. Mansfield. *History of Modern Art.* 7th ed. 2012. This is a comprehensive source for students studying the art of the late nineteenth to the twenty-first centuries.

R. J. B. Bosworth. *Mussolini's Italy: Life under the Fascist Dictatorship, 1915–1945.* New edition. New York, 2011. One of the world's leading authorities on modern Italian history successfully explores the complexities of *Il Duce* and his times.

Peter J. Bowler and Iwan Rhys Morus. *Making Modern Science: A Historical Survey.* Chicago, 2005. This work examines the relationship between science and modern thought more thoroughly than a typical survey.

Richard Evans. *The Third Reich in Power, 1933–1939.* New York, 2005. The second work in a three-volume series, this book starts with the Nazis' assumption of power and ends at the beginning of World War II in Europe.

Ian Kershaw. *Hitler: A Biography.* Reprint edition. New York, 2010. One of the foremost historians of the Nazi era pens the definitive biography of Adolf Hitler.

George Makari. *Revolution in Mind: The Creation of Psychoanalysis.* New York, 2008. A comprehensive history of the development of psychoanalysis and how it gained influence during the first half of the twentieth century.

John Moser. *Global Great Depression and the Coming of World War II.* London, 2015. Explores the ways various states responded to the crisis of the Great Depression and how these responses helped lead to World War II.

Norman Naimark. *Stalin's Genocides.* Princeton, N.J., 2010. This is a lucid analysis of Stalin's terror and brutal mass killings.

Robert Paxton. *The Anatomy of Fascism.* New York, 2004. This groundbreaking work focuses on what fascists did rather than on what they said.

Robert Service. *Stalin: A Biography.* Cambridge, Mass., 2005. The author of an acclaimed biography of Lenin provides the most complete portrait available of the Soviet ruler.

# CHAPTER 22 AP EXAM PRACTICE

Questions assume cumulative knowledge from this chapter and previous chapters.

## Section I

## Multiple Choice Questions

Use the image below and your knowledge of world history to answer questions 1–3.

Photo of a mother with her two children in Oklahoma in 1936 by photographer Dorothea Lange.
Pictorial Press Ltd/Alamy Stock Photo

1. Which of the following is a reason why the Great Depression started in 1929?
   (A) The explosive growth of the subprime mortgage market required a government bailout.
   (B) Computer driven trading models led to a panic over stock prices.
   (C) Investors overextended themselves by purchasing stocks on margin.
   (D) Excessive taxation discouraged investment.
2. How did the Great Depression affect working-class women?
   (A) Governments found ways to deny women unemployment benefits because it was believed that a woman's place should have been in the home instead of working.
   (B) Governments provided more unemployment benefits for women because they were responsible for caring for children.
   (C) Fewer women were unemployed because employers could pay them less than they paid men.
   (D) Women were sent to farms to provide extra agricultural labor.
3. How did the economist John Maynard Keynes propose to solve the economic crisis?
   (A) He encouraged industrialists to produce goods around the clock and flood the market with their products.
   (B) He argued that the Great Depression would end if states went to war and had to spend money.
   (C) He wrote the New Deal legislation that created social security.
   (D) He advised the creation of public works projects to keep people employed and purchasing consumer products.

Use the image below and your knowledge of world history to answer questions 4 and 5.

Men and women drive tractors out of one of the Soviet Union's Machine Tractor Stations to work fields where mechanization had been a rare sight.
Sovfoto/Universal Images Group/Getty Images

4. What was the New Economic Policy?
   (A) The legislation sponsored by Franklin Delano Roosevelt.
   (B) An advanced form of Keynesian economics.
   (C) Lenin's policy to temporarily restore the market economy and private enterprise.
   (D) A compromise between the Reds and the Whites.

5. Why did Stalin initiate the Great Purge?
   (A) The *kulaks* had become too influential and were threatening his position.
   (B) Stalin had come under criticism for his controversial economic policies, so there was a demand for change from within the Communist Party.
   (C) Lenin though the Five Year Plan betrayed Marxist thinking and wanted to remove Stalin from power.
   (D) Stalin feared that members of the Communist Party were spying on him and sending information to the United States and western Europe.

## Short Answer

6. Use the image below and your knowledge of world history to answer parts A, B, and C.

"Mother and Child," mid-1930s.
akg-images/Newscom

(A) Identify ONE way the Nazi government tried to increase the birthrate of Germans.
(B) Explain ONE way that ideas about race influenced the Nazis.
(C) Explain ONE way that the Nazis used eugenics when making government policies.

7. Use the image below and your knowledge of world history to answer parts A, B, and C.

Benito Mussolini and Adolf Hitler watch a Nazi parade staged for the Italian dictator's visit to Germany in the fall of 1937.
Bettmann/Getty Images

(A) Identify ONE way that fascist parties took power after World War I.
(B) Explain ONE similarity between German fascism and Italian fascism.
(C) Explain ONE difference between German fascism and Italian fascism.

8. Use your understanding of world history to answer parts A, B, and C.
(A) Identify ONE source of inspiration for Hitler's policies that did not originate in Europe.
(B) Explain ONE antisemitic action in Germany that happened before the Holocaust.
(C) Identify ONE group other than Jews who were targeted by the Nazis.

# Section II

## Document-Based Question

Based on the documents below and your knowledge of world history, compare and contrast the ways that communists, democrats, and fascists responded to the Great Depression

In your response you should do the following:

- Respond to the prompt with a historically defensible thesis or claim that establishes a line of reasoning.
- Describe a broader historical context relevant to the prompt.
- Support an argument in response to the prompt using all documents.
- Use at least one additional piece of specific historical evidence (beyond that found in the documents) relevant to an argument about the prompt.
- Explain how or why the document's point of view, purpose, historical situation, and / or audience is relevant to an argument.
- Use evidence to corroborate, qualify, or modify an argument that addresses the prompt.

## Document 1

**The fundamental task of the** five-year plan was to convert the U.S.S.R. from an agrarian and weak country, dependent upon the caprices of the capitalist countries, into an industrial and powerful country, fully self-reliant and independent of the caprices of world capitalism.

The fundamental task of the five-year plan was, in converting the U.S.S.R. into an industrial country, to completely oust the capitalist elements, to widen the front of socialist forms of economy, and to create the economic basis for the abolition of classes in the U.S.S.R., for the building of a socialist society.

The fundamental task of the five-year plan was to transfer small and scattered agriculture on to the lines of large-scale collective farming, so as to ensure the economic basis of socialism in the countryside and thus to eliminate the possibility of the restoration of capitalism in the U.S.S.R.

Finally, the task of the five-year plan was to create all the necessary technical and economic prerequisites for increasing to the utmost the defensive capacity of the country, enabling it to organize determined resistance to any attempt at military intervention from abroad, to any attempt at military attack from abroad.

What are the results of the five-year plan in four years in the sphere of industry?

We did not have an iron and steel industry, the basis for the industrialization of the country. Now we have one.

We did not have a tractor industry. Now we have one.

We did not have an automobile industry. Now we have one.

We did not have a machine-tool industry. Now we have one.

We did not have a big and modern chemical industry. Now we have one.

We did not have a real and big industry for the production of modern agricultural machinery. Now we have one.

We did not have an aircraft industry. Now we have one.

In output of electric power we were last on the list. Now we rank among the first.

In output of oil products and coal we were last on the list. Now we rank among the first.

And as a result of all this the capitalist elements have been completely and irrevocably ousted from industry, and socialist industry has become the sole form of industry in the U.S.S.R.

*Source:* Stalin, J. V. "The Results of the First Five-Year Plan." Report Delivered at the Joint Plenum of the Central Committee and the Central Control Commission of the C.P.S.U.(B.), January 7-12, 1933." *Marxists Internet Archive (2008)*, 1947, 578–630.

## Document 2

"Against Starvation and Desperation—Vote for Hitler." Election poster from the July 1932 federal election in Germany.
picture alliance/Getty Images

## Document 3

In such a spirit on my part and on yours we face our common difficulties. They concern, thank God, only material things. Values have shrunken to fantastic levels; taxes have risen; our ability to pay has fallen; government of all kinds is faced by serious curtailment of income; the means of exchange are frozen in the currents of trade; the withered leaves of industrial enterprise lie on every side; farmers find no markets for their produce; the savings of many years in thousands of families are gone.

More important, a host of unemployed citizens face the grim problem of existence, and an equally great number toil with little return. Only a foolish optimist can deny the dark realities of the moment. . . .

Happiness lies not in the mere possession of money; it lies in the joy of achieve-ment, in the thrill of creative effort. The joy and moral stimulation of work no longer must be forgotten in the mad chase of evanescent profits. These dark days will be worth all they cost us if they teach us that our true destiny is not to be ministered unto but to minister to ourselves and to our fellow men.

*Source:* Roosevelt, Franklin D. First Inaugural Address of Franklin D. Roosevelt, March 4, 1933. The Avalon Project. Yale Law School Lillian Goldman Law Library.

## Long Essay

Develop a thoughtful and thorough historical argument that answers the question below. Begin your essay with a thesis statement and support it with relevant historical evidence.

Using specific examples and your knowledge of world history, evaluate the extent to which new scientific ideas and World War I affected the larger postwar culture.

# Chapter 23 Revolutionaries and Nationalists in the Colonial and Neocolonial World

**Paths to Autonomy in South and East Asia**
- India's Quest for Home Rule
- China's Campaigns to End Foreign Domination
- Imperial and Imperialist Japan

**Sub-Saharan Africa under Colonial Domination**
- The Colonial Economy
- African Nationalism

**Latin American Struggles with Neocolonialism**
- The Impact of the Great War and the Great Depression
- The Evolution of Economic Imperialism
- Conflicts with a "Good Neighbor"

## ZOOMING IN ON ENCOUNTERS

### Shanfei Becomes a New and Revolutionary Young Woman in China

Shanfei lived in a time of great political turmoil. The daughter of a wealthy landowning man of the Chinese gentry, she grew up with luxuries and opportunities unknown to most girls. Her father reluctantly allowed her to attend school, and her mother clothed her in beautiful silk dresses. Shanfei, however, matured into a woman who rejected the rich trappings of her youth. Her formative years were marked by the unsettling cultural and political changes that engulfed the globe in the wake of the Great War. The rise of nationalism and communism in China after the revolution of 1911 and the Russian revolution in 1917 guided the transformation of Shanfei—from a girl ruled by tradition and privilege to an active revolutionary dedicated to freeing her country as a member of the Chinese Communist Party.

With the exception of Shanfei's father, the members of her family in Hunan province took in the new spirit of the first decades of the twentieth century. Her brothers returned from school with strange and compelling ideas, including some that challenged the subordinate position of women in China. Shanfei's mother, to all appearances a woman who accepted her subservience to her husband, proved instrumental to Shanfei's departure from the common destiny of Chinese girls. She listened quietly to her sons as they discussed new views, and then she applied them to her daughter. She used every means

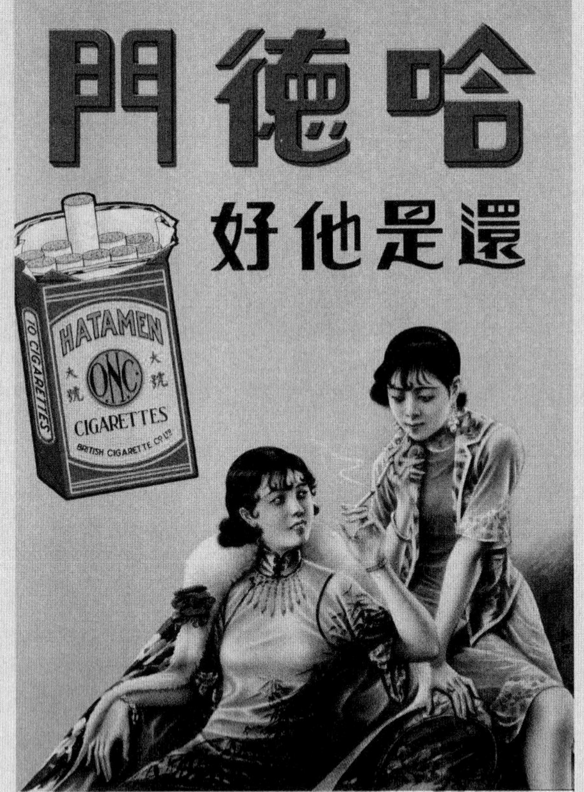


In this cigarette advertisement from 1935, Chinese women are shown wearing modern styles and smoking cigarettes. They would have been recognized around the world as "modern girls," who increasingly challenged traditional gender expectations in their choices of clothing, behavior, and occupation.
swim ink 2 llc/Corbis Historical/Getty Images

at her disposal to persuade her husband to educate their daughter. He eventually agreed but still insisted that Shanfei receive an old-fashioned education and submit to foot binding and childhood betrothal.

When Shanfei was eleven years old, her father suddenly died, and his death emboldened her mother. She ripped the bandages off Shanfei's feet and sent her to a modern school far from home. In the lively atmosphere of her school, Shanfei became an activist. At sixteen she incited a student strike against the school administration, then transferred to a more modern school, and became famous as a leader in the student movement. She attended classes with men and broke tradition in her personal and political life. In 1926 Shanfei abandoned her studies to join the Communist Youth, and she gave up the fiancé that had been arranged for her for a free marriage to the man she loved: a peasant leader in the communist movement.

# CHAPTER FOCUS

- Repercussions of World War I and the Great Depression raised demands to end imperialist
- control among Asian, African, and Latin American peoples. (Note that these events occurred when the "age of anxiety" swept Europe and the United States.).
- In British colonial India, Gandhi and others nonviolently protested for home rule and then independence.
- Intellectuals believed that Sigmund Freud's work undermined Renaissance and Enlightenment ideas about the rationality of mankind, just as Einstein's and Heisenberg's works undermined the rational Newtonian universe.
- When the Qing dynasty collapsed, the Chinese Nationalists tried to westernize but faced rebellion from peasant-farmers led by Mao Zedong and the new Chinese Communist Party (CCP).
- Deep disillusionment on the African continent, caused by failure to gain independence after World War I combined with economic collapse from the Depression, produced a nationalist movement called pan-Africanism. This transnational movement encouraged all Africans to think of themselves as a single race.
- U.S. businesses, backed by the U.S. government, had taken economic control over much of Latin America in a policy called neo-colonialism. When the Depression hit, these single-crop, export-based businesses lost their markets and failed. Many Latin Americans, especially students, demanded their governments nationalize the foreign-owned businesses and give them back to the people, as well as redistribute land to the poor.

## Historical Developments

- States around the world challenged the existing political and social order, including the Mexican Revolution that arose as a result of political crisis.
- Increasing questions about political authority and growing nationalism contributed to anticolonial movements.
- Anti-imperial resistance took various forms, including direct resistance within empires and the creation of new states on the peripheries.
- Industrialized states and businesses within those states practiced economic imperialism primarily in Asia and Latin America.
- The older, land-based Ottoman, Russian, and Qing empires collapsed due to a combination of internal and external factors. These changes in Russia eventually led to communist revolution.

## Reasoning Processes

- **Comparison** Describe similarities and differences between nationalist movements in India, Africa, and East Asia.
- **Continuity and Change** Describe patterns of continuity and change within colonial societies from the 19th to the 20th centuries.

## Historical Thinking Skills

- **Contextualization** Identify and describe the historical context for nationalist movements in Asia and Africa in the 20th century and the various ideologies that shaped nationalism and independence movements.
- **Argumentation** Make a historically defensible claim that describes the extent to which and ways in which the U.S. influenced, directly and indirectly, Latin American society in the 20th century.

## CHAPTER OVERVIEW

The twists of fate that altered the destiny of Shanfei had parallels throughout the colonial and neocolonial world after 1914. Two major events, the Great War and the Great Depression, defined much of the turmoil of those years. Disillusion and radical upheaval affected colonized and neocolonial areas all over the world, including those in Asia, Africa, and Latin America. As peoples around the world struggled to come to terms with the aftermath of war, an unprecedented economic contraction gripped the international community. The Great Depression complicated peoples' struggles for national sovereignty and financial solvency, especially in Asia, where Japan's militarist leaders sought to build national strength through imperial expansion. Latin American states worked to resist the economic domination of the United States, while people in sub-Saharan Africa suffered devastating economic consequences when European powers were no longer able to buy and use the raw materials produced in their colonies.

European empires still appeared to dominate global relations in the 1920s and 1930s, but the Great War had opened fissures within the European and U.S. spheres of influence. Nationalist and communist movements were already active in most colonial and neocolonial territories, and now they gathered strength. Indeed, in the postwar years resistance to foreign rule and a desire for national unity were stronger than ever. Movements to throw off foreign domination were especially strong in India and China, where various visions of national identity competed, but they also took on new momentum in sub-Saharan Africa and Latin America. While peoples in sub-Saharan Africa worked to become independent of outright imperial control, those in Latin America had to fight off the more indirect economic effects of postindependence colonialism, usually termed *neocolonialism*. And while we know that resistance to colonialism was as old as colonialism itself, the trauma of the Great War and the Depression that followed helped convince more people than ever before to join movements in order to secure the self-determination they desired.

| CHRONOLOGY | |
|---|---|
| 1909–1955 | Life of Carmen Miranda |
| 1912 | Taft establishes dollar diplomacy as U.S. foreign policy |
| 1919 | May Fourth Movement in China |
| 1920 | Non-Cooperation Movement in India |
| 1921 | Rivera returns to Mexico to paint |
| 1928 | Socialist Party of Peru is founded |
| 1929 | Beginning of Great Depression |
| 1930 | Civil Disobedience Movement in India |
| 1930s–1940s | Vargas's *estado novo* in Brazil |
| 1931 | Japanese invasion of Manchuria |
| 1933 | Roosevelt begins practice of the Good Neighbor Policy |
| 1934 | Long March by Chinese Communists |
| 1934 | Sandino is murdered in Nicaragua |
| 1935 | Government of India Act |
| 1938 | Cárdenas nationalizes oil industry in Mexico |

## PATHS TO AUTONOMY IN SOUTH AND EAST ASIA

In the decades following the Great War, nationalism and revolutionary anticolonialism developed into powerful political forces in Asia, especially in India and China. Achieving the twin ideals of independence from foreign powers and national unity became a goal of intellectuals, new political leaders, and ordinary people alike. Indian, Chinese, and Japanese societies underwent a prolonged period of disorder and struggle until a new order emerged. In India the quest for national identity focused on gaining independence from British rule, a pursuit that was complicated by sectarian (religious) differences between Hindus and Muslims. The Chinese path to national identity was fraught with foreign and civil war as two principal groups—the Nationalist and Communist Parties—contended for power. Deeply divided by ideologies, both parties opposed foreign domination, rejected the old order, and sought a unified Chinese state. Japanese militarists made China's quest for national unity more difficult because Japan struggled to overcome its domestic problems and enhance its national identity through conquests that focused on China.

### India's Quest for Home Rule

By the beginning of the twentieth century, Indian nationalism already threatened the British Empire's hold on India. The construction of a vast railway network across India to facilitate the export of raw materials contributed to the idea of national unity by bringing the people of the subcontinent within easy reach of one another. Moreover, because it was impossible for a small group of foreigners to control and administer such a vast country, the British had trained an elite class of English-speaking, educated Indian administrators to help in this task. A European system of education familiarized the local middle-class intelligentsia with the political and social values of European society. Those values, however—democracy, individual freedom, and equality—were the antithesis of empire, and Indians educated within this system quickly saw their fundamental contradiction with the injustices of imperial rule in India.

## INTERPRETING IMAGES

Leader of the Indian civil disobedience revolt, Mohandas Gandhi marched to the shore at Dandi, a coastal village located on the Arabian Sea, to collect salt without paying taxes. This Salt March, also known as the Salt Satyagraha, sparked large-scale acts of civil protest against the British Raj (rule) and changed both global and British attitudes about Indian independence. On his left is Sarojini Naidu (1879–1949), a feminist activist who in 1925 was elected the first female president of the Indian National Congress.

**Analyze** *Why would a protest as simple as Gandhi's Salt March have such a significant impact worldwide? What do you notice about those surrounding Gandhi in this photo?*

Bettmann/Getty Images

**Indian National Congress** Of all the associations dedicated to the struggle against British rule, the most influential was the **Indian National Congress,** founded in 1885. This organization, which enlisted the support of many prominent Hindus and Muslims, at first sought collaboration with the British to bring self-rule to India, but after the Great War the congress pursued that goal in opposition to the British. The formation of the Muslim League, established in 1906 with the encouragement of the British government, added a new current into the movement for national liberation. Both organizations were dedicated to achieving independence for India, but members of the Muslim League increasingly worried that Hindu oppression and continued subjugation of India's substantial Muslim minority might replace British rule.

During the Great War, more than one million Indians—Hindus and Muslims—served in the armies of the British at the western front and in Mesopotamia. During the war, the Indian National Congress supported the British and suspended its campaigns for self-rule. Many Indians hoped their active support in the war effort would result in British willingness to allow greater Indian autonomy. But shortages of goods and food during the war tried the patience of Indian subjects, and once the war was over the British made it clear that their ideas of sharing power fell far short of Indian expectations. In April 1919, British-led troops opened fire on a group of unarmed Indian demonstrators in the city of Amritsar, killing 379 and wounding 1200 more. This massacre shocked millions of Indians and prompted Indian political leaders—including Mohandas Gandhi—to call not just for home rule but for total independence.

**Mohandas K. Gandhi** Into this turmoil stepped **Mohandas Karamchand Gandhi** (1869–1948), a remarkable and charismatic leader. Gandhi grew up in a prosperous and pious Hindu household, married at thirteen, and left his hometown in 1888 to study law in London. In 1893 he went to South Africa, part of the British Empire, to accept a position with an Indian firm, and there he quickly became involved in organizing the local Indian community against a system of racial segregation that made Indians second-class citizens. During the twenty-five years he spent in South Africa, Gandhi embraced a moral philosophy of ***ahimsa*** (tolerance and nonviolence) and developed the technique of passive resistance that he called ***satyagraha*** ("truth and firmness"). His belief in the virtue of simple living led him to renounce material possessions, dress in the garb of a simple Indian peasant, and become a vegetarian. He renounced sex and extolled the virtues of a daily saltwater enema. He also spent an hour each morning in careful study of the *Bhagavad Gita* (Sanskrit for "The Lord's Song"), one of

---

**Mohandas Karamchand Gandhi** (moh-huhn-DAHS kuhr-uhm-CHUND GAHN-dee)

***satyagraha*** (suh-TYA-gruh-hah)

# SOURCES FROM THE PAST

## M. N. Roy: The Awakening of the East

*Narendra Nath Battacharya, who later adopted the name M. N. Roy, was born near Calcutta, India, in 1887. He began his political life as a radical Indian nationalist but became a Marxist while he lived in the United States during World War I. After helping to found the Mexican Communist Party in 1917, he was invited to Moscow to attend the Second World Congress of the Communist International (Comintern) in 1920. In Moscow, Roy became an influential leader in the Communist International. His ideas about the importance of the colonial world in the future communist revolution helped to shape Comintern policy toward the colonial world.*

***The world revolution,*** in order to accomplish its great mission, must cross the borders of the so-called Western Countries where capitalism has reached its climax. Until very recently this truth was almost entirely unknown among the revolutionaries of Europe and America, who hardly gave a moment's thought to the social and economic conditions of the Asiatic generally. It was generally maintained that, owing to their industrial backwardness, the hundreds of millions of the masses in the East would not count for anything in the great struggle between the exploiter and the exploited. Consequently the "World" of the world revolution was limited to Europe and America.

> Why does Roy think European revolutionaries never thought very much about the potential of revolutionaries in the colonized world?

But revolution is the result of objective conditions; it breaks out in the least suspected place if the dynamic forces are there. The inevitable result of oppression is that sooner or later the oppressed rebel. This is happening to-day in the Eastern countries, where the myriads of toilers have been groaning under the same exploitation against which their more fortunate and less downtrodden comrades of the Occident have been carrying on an heroic fight. The East is awakening: and who knows if the formidable tide, that will sweep away the capitalist structure of Western Europe, may not come from there . . .

During almost a century World Capitalism kept on invigorating itself by sucking the blood of the colonial toilers. But along with the bloody sword of organised exploitation, it carried in its womb the incipient forces that were destined to rise against it and build the new society upon its ruins. To-day these forces are manifesting themselves in the growing revolutionary fermentation among the Eastern peoples, who were considered till the other day negligible factors in the World Revolution. This awakening of the East must open a new vision before the revolutionary leaders of Europe. It ought to show them the way through which the retreat of the cunning enemy can be cut. A formidable upheaval of the colonial and "protected" peoples will take away from under the feet of Imperialist Capitalism, the rock of super-profit which has helped so far offset the effects of overproduction . . . The disruption of Empire is the only thing that will complete the bankruptcy of European capitalism; and the revolutionary upheavals in the Asiatic countries are destined to bring about the crumbling of the proud imperial structure of capitalism. . .

> Why does Roy believe that the awakening of the East is essential to undermining the capitalist world order?

### For Further Reflection

- Roy makes it clear that the fight against colonialism required a global strategy. How does this change our understanding of anticolonial movements in individual colonies?
- Why were M.N. Roy and others attracted to Communism?
- What are the key elements of Roy's argument?
- How does Roy couple political imperialism with economic capitalism?

*Source:* Roy, M.N. "The Awakening of the East." *The Call*, July 15, 1920, p. 5. *Marxists Internet Archive (2007).*

the most sacred writings of Hinduism, which he regarded as a spiritual dictionary.

Gandhi returned to India in 1915, where he became active in Indian politics. He succeeded in transforming the Indian National Congress from an elitist body of anglicized gentlemen into a mass organization. Although the reform program of the congress appeared remote from the needs of common people, Gandhi translated their demands in a way that was meaningful for ordinary Indians. His unique mixture of spiritual intensity and political activism appealed to a broad section of the Indian population, and in the eyes of many he quickly achieved the stature of a political and spiritual leader, their Mahatma, or "great soul."

Under Gandhi's leadership the congress launched two mass movements: the Non-Cooperation Movement of 1920–1922 and the Civil Disobedience Movement of 1930.

Convinced that economic self-sufficiency was a prerequisite for self-government, Gandhi called on the Indian people to boycott British goods and return to wearing rough homespun cotton clothing. He disagreed with those who wanted India to industrialize, advocating instead manual labor and the revival of rural cottage industries. Gandhi furthermore admonished Indians to boycott institutions operated by the British in India, such as schools, offices, and courts. Despite Gandhi's cautions against the use of force, violence often accompanied the protest movement, both by Indians who were protesting and by the British who sought to stop them.

**The India Act** For nearly two decades after the end of the Great War, the political situation in India was in constant turmoil. The Indian National Congress, led by Gandhi in the 1920s and 1930s, was only one of the movements seeking independence from Britain. Various revolutionary groups and the Indian Communist Party (founded in 1925) also agitated in favor of independence, sometimes using violence. Over time, it became clear to the British that repressive measures were simply not enough to quell such strong and sustained calls for an end to British rule. In an attempt to maintain some control over India, then, the British offered a political compromise. After years of commissions, reports, and tense conversations with Indian political leaders (including Gandhi), in 1935 the British parliament enacted the **Government of India Act**. The act established in India the institutions of a self-governing state, including the establishment of autonomous legislative bodies in the provinces of British India and the creation of a bicameral (two-chambered) national legislature. Acts of the legislature, however, were still subject to approval by the executive arm of government and remained under British control. Additionally, the British still controlled foreign policy. Although the India Act was not the independence called for by the Indian National Congress, Gandhi urged Indians to support it. A majority of Indians ended up approving the measure, which went into effect in 1937.

The India Act proved unworkable, however, because India's six hundred nominally sovereign princes refused to cooperate and because Muslims feared that Hindus would dominate the national legislature. These latter fears were exacerbated by the Great Depression because Muslims constituted the majority of indebted tenant farmers in India, and they found themselves increasingly unable to pay rents and debts during the economic crisis. And since their landlords were mainly Hindus, Muslims increasingly perceived their experiences during the Depression as stemming from economic exploitation by Hindus. They were encouraged in these perceptions by **Muhammad Ali Jinnah** (1876–1948), an eloquent and brilliant lawyer who headed the Muslim League. Jinnah and Muslim League leaders increasingly warned that a unified India represented nothing less than a threat to the Muslim faith and its Indian community. By 1940, Jinnah proposed that British India be divided into two independent states: India, for India's Hindus, and Pakistan, for India's Muslims. Thus in spite of hundreds of years of Hindus and Muslims living peacefully together in the same communities, these increasing sectarian tensions in the interwar period would come to dominate the independence process on the Indian subcontinent.

## China's Campaigns to End Foreign Domination

As Shanfei's life story suggested in the introduction to this chapter, during the first half of the twentieth century China was in a state of almost continual revolutionary upheaval. The conflict's origins dated from the nineteenth century, when the Chinese Empire came under relentless pressure from imperialist powers that rushed in to fill the vacuum created by China's internal political disintegration (see chapter 31). As revolutionary and nationalist uprisings gained widespread support, a revolution in 1911 forced the **Xuantong** emperor (also known as Puyi), to abdicate at the age of five. The Qing empire fell with relative ease. Dr. **Sun Yatsen** (1866–1925), a leading opponent of the old regime, proclaimed a Chinese republic in Nanjing in 1912 and briefly assumed the office of president. The dynasty was dead, but there remained the problems of what to put in its place.

**The Republic** The revolution of 1911 did not establish a stable government. Sun Yatsen controlled only a portion of China around Nanjing, while many others in different parts of the country had their own claim to leadership. As a result, the republic soon plunged into a state of political anarchy and economic disintegration marked by the rule of disaffected generals from the old imperial Chinese army and their troops who established themselves as provincial or regional rulers. Because the generals were responsible for the neglect of irrigation projects crucial to the survival of farmers; for the revival of the opium trade, which they protected; and for the decline of crucial economic investments, Chinese society went into economic decline in this period. Yet the rule of the generals was just one symbol of the disintegration of the political order. The fragmented relationship between Chinese authority and foreign powers was another. Since the nineteenth century, a collection of treaties, known in China as the unequal treaties, had guided Chinese relations with foreign countries. Those treaties had established a network of foreign control over the Chinese economy that effectively hindered Chinese economic development even as it greatly benefited the foreign powers. The continued sway of unequal treaties and other concessions permitted foreigners to intervene in Chinese society and protect their own interests. While foreigners did not control every aspect of the state, through their privileges they greatly impaired its sovereignty.

---

**Muhammad Ali Jinnah** (moo-HAHM-ahd ah-lee JIN-uh)
**Xuantong** (shoo-ahn-tohng)

**Chinese Nationalism** After the Great War, nationalist sentiment developed rapidly in China. Youths and intellectuals, who in the previous decade had looked to Europe and the United States for models and ideals for the reform of China, eagerly anticipated the results of the 1919 Peace Conference in Paris. They expected the U.S. government to support the termination of the treaty system and the restoration of full Chinese sovereignty. Those hopes were shattered, however, when the peacemakers did none of these things and instead approved increasing Japanese interference in China. That decision gave rise to the **May Fourth Movement.** Spearheaded by students and intellectuals in China's urban areas, the movement galvanized the country, and all classes of Chinese protested against foreign, especially Japanese, interference. In speeches, newspapers, and novels, the movement's leaders pledged themselves to rid China of imperialism and reestablish national unity. Student leaders such as Shanfei rallied their comrades to the cause.

Disillusioned by the cynical self-interest of the United States and the European powers, some Chinese became interested in Marxism (see chapter 21) and the social and economic experiments under way in the Soviet Union. The anti-imperialist rhetoric of the Soviet leadership struck a responsive chord, and in 1921 a group of Chinese activists organized the **Chinese Communist Party (CCP)** in Shanghai. Among its early members was **Mao Zedong** (1893–1976), a former teacher and librarian who viewed a Marxist-inspired social revolution as the cure for China's problems. Mao's political radicalism extended to the issue of women's equality, which he and other communists championed. As Shanfei's personal experience suggested, Chinese communists believed in divorce, opposed arranged marriages, and campaigned against the practice of foot binding.

**Sun Yatsen** Even prior to the founding of the Chinese Communist Party, Sun Yatsen—who had helped bring down the Qing government—sought to organize Chinese people into a party based on nationalism and modernization. In 1912 he founded the ***Guomindang*** (Nationalist People's Party), which became a powerful political force in the first half of the twentieth century. The Guomindang's platform was based on Sun's ideology, summarized in his *Three Principles of the People,* which called for elimination of special privileges for foreigners, national reunification, economic development, and a democratic republican government based on universal suffrage. While Sun was not a communist, he recognized the utility of forming an alliance with the powerful Soviet Union and the Chinese Communist Party in order to achieve his nationalist goals. In 1923, the Soviet Union brokered a deal in which the Guomindang and the Chinese Communist Party agreed to enter into a partnership (now known as the First United Front), in which both would work toward the common goal of uniting China and driving out foreign imperialists. To improve its chances of success, the Soviet Union agreed to provide military training, funding, and arms. This partnership was deeply alarming to the foreign powers active in China—including, especially, Britain, France, and Japan—because none of them wanted a strong Chinese state to limit their profits or privileges.

**Civil War** When Sun Yatsen died in 1925, the leadership of the Guomindang fell to **Jiang Jieshi** (Chiang Kai-shek, 1887–1975), a young general who had been trained in Japan and the Soviet

***Guomindang*** (GWOH-mihn-dahng)
**Jiang Jieshi** (jyahng jeh-she)

## INTERPRETING IMAGES

Adversaries in the struggle for power in China: at left, Jiang Jieshi (Chiang Kai-shek) (1887–1975); at right, Mao Zedong (1893–1976).

**Analyze** *How do the photos of the two leaders reflect the contrast in the people who supported them? What were the reasons Mao ultimately defeated Jiang Jieshi?*

Bettmann/Getty Images

## MAP 23.1 The struggle for control in China, 1927–1936.

Compare the continental territories controlled by Japan and the Guomindang in 1934.

***How would the size of Japan's territories in Manchuria and Korea influence Chinese abilities to challenge Japanese expansion?***

***The map demonstrates the significant power of the Japanese during the 1920s and 1930s. Why didn't Europe and the United States intervene and prevent such expansion?***

Union. Unlike Sun, Jiang distrusted the Chinese communists he was supposed to be working with and was suspicious that communists were gaining too much power in the Guomindang. In 1926, Jiang maintained the partnership of the United Front in order to wage a political and military offensive, known as the Northern Expedition, to unify the nation and bring China under Guomindang rule. But once the offensive had proven successful and Jiang's forces had taken the cities of Shanghai and Nanjing in early 1927, Jiang's forces brutally and unexpectedly turned against his former communist allies, bringing the alliance of convenience between the Guomindang and the CCP to a bloody end. On April 12, 1927, Jiang unleashed armed men on communists in the city of Shanghai, murdering thousands and arresting many more over the two weeks that followed. In the following year, nationalist forces occupied Beijing, set up a central government in Nanjing, and declared the Guomindang the official government of a unified and sovereign Chinese state. Meanwhile, the badly mauled communists retreated to a remote area of southeastern China, where they tried to reconstitute and reorganize their forces.

The nationalist government had to deal with many concerns, but Chinese leaders evaded one major global crisis—the Great Depression. China's large agrarian economy and small industrial sector were connected only marginally to the world economy. Foreign trade in such items as tea and silk, which did decline, made up only a small part of China's economy, which was otherwise dominated by its large domestic markets. Although the new government in China generally avoided having to contend with global economic devastation, it did have to confront three major problems during the 1930s. First, the nationalists actually controlled only part of China, leaving the remainder of the country in the hands of various generals. Second, by the early 1930s communist activity in China became a major threat since now communists sought to eliminate their nationalist enemies. Third, the Guomindang faced increasing Japanese aggression. In dealing with those problems, Jiang Jieshi gave priority to eliminating the CCP and its Red Army. No longer able to ward off the relentless attacks of nationalist forces, the communists took flight in October 1934 to avoid annihilation. Bursting through a military blockade around their bases in Jiangxi province in southeastern China, some eighty-five thousand troops and auxiliary personnel of the Red Army began the legendary **Long March,** an epic journey of 10,000 kilometers (6,215 miles). After traveling across difficult terrain and fighting for survival against hunger, disease, and Guomindang forces, the marchers arrived in a remote area of Shaanxi province in northwestern China in October 1935 and established headquarters at Yan'an. Although thousands died in this forced retreat, the Long March inspired many Chinese to join the Communist Party. During the Long March, Mao Zedong emerged as the leader and the principal theoretician of the Chinese communist movement. He came up with a Chinese form of Marxist-Leninism, or Maoism, an ideology grounded in the conviction that peasants rather than urban proletarians were the foundation for a successful revolution. Village power, Mao believed, was critical in a country where most people were peasants.

## Imperial and Imperialist Japan

After the Great War, Japan achieved great power status and appeared to accept the international status quo that the major powers fashioned in the aftermath of war. After joining the League of Nations as one of the "big five" powers, the Japanese government entered into a series of international agreements that sought to improve relations among countries with conflicting interests in Asia and the Pacific. As a signatory to several Washington Conference treaties in 1922, Japan agreed to limit naval development, pledged to evacuate Shandong province in China, and guaranteed China's territorial integrity. In 1928 the Japanese government signed the Kellogg-Briand Pact, which renounced war as an instrument of national policy. Concerns about earlier Japanese territorial ambitions, highlighted by the Twenty-one Demands on China in 1915, receded from the minds of the international community.

Japan's limited involvement in the Great War gave a dual boost to its economy. Japanese businesses profited from selling munitions and other goods to the Allies throughout the war, and they gained a bigger foothold in Asia as the war led Europe's trading nations to neglect Asian markets. Economic prosperity was short-lived, however, as the postwar economy of Japan faced serious challenges. Rapid inflation and labor unrest set in by 1918, followed by a series of recessions that culminated in a giant economic slump caused by the Great Depression. Like the economies of other industrial nations tied into the global economy, Japan's economy experienced plummeting industrial production, huge job layoffs, declining trade, and financial chaos. Economic contraction set the stage for social unrest and radical politics.

Public demands for sweeping political and social reforms, including a broadening of the franchise, protection for labor unions, and welfare legislation, figured prominently in Japanese domestic politics throughout the 1920s. Yet conservatives blocked any major advances beyond the suffrage law of 1925, which established universal male suffrage. By the early 1930s an increasingly frustrated public blamed its government for the nation's continuing economic problems and became more disenchanted with leading politicians tainted by bribery scandals and corrupt connections to business conglomerates. Right-wing political groups called for an end to party rule, and xenophobic nationalists dedicated themselves to the preservation of a unique Japanese culture and the eradication of Western influences. A campaign of assassinations, targeting political and business leaders, culminated in the murder of Prime Minister **Inukai Tsuyoshi** (1855–1932).

Politicians who supported Japan's role in the international industrial-capitalist system faced increasing opposition from those who were inclined toward a militarist vision of a self-sufficient Japan that would dominate east Asia. The hardships of the depression undermined support for the internationalist position, and the militarists were able to benefit from Japanese martial traditions and their own unwillingness to be constrained by international cooperation. Meanwhile, China's unification threatened Japan's economic interests in Manchuria. At the same time, China's political instability, the result of nationalists and communists vying for power, made China an inviting target. Manchuria had historically been Chinese territory, but by the twentieth century it was a sphere of influence

---

**Inukai Tsuyoshi** (ee-NO-kigh ts-yo-she)

where Japan maintained the Manchurian Railroad (built in 1906), retained transit rights, and stationed troops. In 1931 Japan's military forces in Manchuria acted to assert control over the region.

**The Mukden Incident** On the night of September 18, 1931, Japanese troops used explosives to blow up a few feet of rail on the Japanese-built South Manchuria Railway north of Mukden. They accused the Chinese of attacking their railroad. This **"Mukden incident"** became the pretext for war between Japanese and Chinese troops. Although the civilian government in Japanese tried to halt this military incursion, by 1932 Japanese troops controlled all of Manchuria, thereby ensuring Japan preeminence and protecting its long-term economic and industrial development of the region. The Japanese established a puppet state called Manchukuo, but in reality Japan had absorbed Manchuria into its empire, challenged the international peace system, and begun a war. In response to the Manchurian invasion, the Guomindang (Nationalist Party) leader Jiang Jieshi appealed to the League of Nations to halt Japanese aggression. After a lengthy investigation, the league called for the withdrawal of Japanese forces and for the restoration of Chinese sovereignty. The Japanese responded by leaving the league, and, although China gained the moral high ground in international eyes, nothing was done to stop the aggression. This reaction set the pattern for future responses to the actions of expansionist nations such as Japan. Embarking on conquests in east Asia, Japanese militarists found a sure means to promoting a new militant Japanese national identity. They also helped provoke a new global war.

The Great War and the Great Depression made signal contributions to the ongoing political upheavals taking place throughout Asia. Revolutionary and nationalist ideologies intersected with old conflicts to complicate the processes of independence and national unification in India and China. And while the global economic crisis led to some lessening of European imperial influence, it prompted an industrialized Japan to exert its imperial will on the Asian sphere.

## SUB-SAHARAN AFRICA UNDER COLONIAL DOMINATION

The Great War and the Great Depression similarly complicated quests for national independence and unity in sub-Saharan Africa. The colonial ties that bound African colonies to European powers had ensured that Africans became participants in the Great War, willing or not (see chapter 33). As in India, Africans expected that their participation in the Great War on behalf of the various colonial powers would lead to greater control over their governments and economies. But instead, colonial governments ignored African pleas for social and political reform.

## INTERPRETING IMAGES

The Victoria Falls Bridge, completed in 1905 but under construction in this photograph, is an example of the railroad infrastructure undertaken by colonial powers in sub-Saharan Africa. The bridge was constructed in Britain by British engineers and assembled mostly by African workers over the Zambezi River in what was then Rhodesia (now Zambia and Zimbabwe). The purpose of the railroad was to link coalfields with copper mining enterprises in Rhodesia.

**Analyze** *Consider the perspective of the African workers who built this bridge. Why might they have felt pride in taking part in the project? Why might they have felt hostile to it? What kind of approach to these kinds of infrastructure projects may have inspired more enthusiasm from Africans? What was the purpose of building infrastructure and deciding where to put roads and bridges?*

History and Art Collection/Alamy Stock Photo

Indeed, rather than retreating, colonialism consolidated its hold on the African continent including sub-Saharan Africa. In the decades following the Paris Peace Conference that ended the Great War in 1919, the European powers focused on the economic exploitation of their colonies. The imposition of a rapacious form of capitalism destroyed the self-sufficiency of many African economies and turned the resulting colonial economies into extensions of those of the colonizing powers. As a result, African economic life became enmeshed in the global economy. The persistence of colonialism led to the development of African anticolonial movements and the establishment of nationalist parties. During the decades following the Great War, African intellectuals searched for new national identities and looked forward to independence from colonial rule.

## The Colonial Economy

The decades following the Great War witnessed a thorough transformation of economic life in sub-Saharan Africa. Colonial powers pursued two key economic objectives in sub-Saharan Africa: they wanted to make sure that colonized people paid for the institutions—bureaucracies, judiciary, police, and military forces—that kept them in subjugation; and they developed export-oriented economies characterized by the exchange of unprocessed raw materials or minimally processed cash crops for manufactured goods from abroad. In pursuit of those goals, colonial authorities imposed economic structures that altered, subordinated, or destroyed preexisting economies in sub-Saharan Africa. In their place came colonial economies, tightly integrated into and dependent on a European-dominated global economy. The Great Depression of the 1930s exposed the vulnerability of dependent colonial economies. As international markets for primary products shrank under the impact of the depression, European companies that controlled the export of African products suffered accordingly. Trade volume often fell by half, and commodity prices dropped even more sharply.

**Infrastructure** The economic integration of sub-Saharan Africa required investment in infrastructure. Thus, during the early twentieth century, the new colonial economy first became visible in the form of port facilities, roads, railways, and telegraph wires. Transportation and communication networks not only facilitated conquest and rule but also linked the agricultural or mineral wealth of a colony to the outside world. Although Europeans later claimed that they had "given" sub-Saharan Africa its first modern infrastructure, Europeans and their businesses were its main beneficiaries. Indeed, although Africans paid for the infrastructure with their labor and taxes, Europeans did not consider the needs of local African economies.

**Farming and Mining** Colonial taxation was an important tool designed to drive Africans into the labor market. To earn the money to pay the taxes colonial powers levied on land, houses, livestock, and people themselves, African farmers had to become cash crop farmers or seek wage labor on

Two workers in a diamond mine in Northern Rhodesia. Although this photograph was taken in the 1950s, it nevertheless depicts the difficult conditions involved in the mining industries of sub-Saharan Africa in the interwar period. INTERFOTO/Alamy Stock Photo

plantations and in mines. Cash crop farming embraced the largest proportion of sub-Saharan Africans. In most colonies, farmers who had their own land specialized in one or two crops, generally destined for export to the country governing them. Farmers in sub-Saharan Africa grew a variety of cash crops for the international marketplace, among them peanuts from Senegal and northern Nigeria, cotton from Uganda, cocoa from the Gold Coast, rubber from the Congo, and palm oil from the Ivory Coast and the Niger delta. In areas with extensive European settlement, such as in Kenya, Rhodesia, and South Africa, settler agriculture was most prominent. Production of agricultural commodities intended for overseas markets remained in the hands of white settlers, whose governments saw to it that they received large and productive areas of land. In British-controlled Kenya, for example, four thousand white farmers seized the Kikuyu highlands, which comprised seven million acres of the colony's richest land. In South Africa, the government reserved 88 percent of all land for whites, who made up just 20 percent of the total population.

Colonial mining enterprises relying on African labor loomed large in parts of central and southern Africa. These enterprises usually involved the extraction of mineral wealth such as copper, gold, and diamonds, and they required vast numbers of laborers. Colonial mining companies found this labor by recruiting men from rural areas, who they paid only minimal wages. These recruitment practices set in motion a vast pattern of labor migration that persisted throughout the twentieth century. The absence of male labor and the payment of minimal wages had the effect of impoverishing the rural areas.

**Labor Practices** Colonial authorities and settlers frequently could not recruit the number of laborers they needed, in spite of the high taxes they imposed. In these cases, colonial officials resorted to outright forced labor. Indeed, forms of forced labor and barely disguised variants of slavery were prominent features of the colonial economy. A white settler in Kenya candidly expressed the view held by many colonial administrators: "We have stolen his land. Now we must steal his limbs. Compulsory labor is the corollary to our occupation of the country." Infrastructure-building projects such as the construction of railways and roads also commonly depended on forced labor regimes. When the French undertook the construction of the Congo-Ocean railway from Brazzaville to the port at Point-Noir, for example, they rounded up some ten thousand workers annually. Labor practices were so brutal that within a few years between fifteen and twenty thousand African laborers had perished from starvation, disease, and maltreatment.

## African Nationalism

In the decades following the Great War, European powers consolidated their political control over sub-Saharan Africa and imposed economies designed to exploit its natural and labor resources. Many Africans were disappointed that their contributions to the war went unrewarded. Instead, in place of anticipated social reforms or some degree of greater political participation came an extension and consolidation of the colonial system. This reality, coupled with an awareness of the demands of anticolonial movements in other parts of the

## What's Left Out?

As we have seen in this chapter, the interwar period was characterized by numerous anticolonial movements all over the world. It is impossible to capture all of these anticolonial movements in one chapter, but it is even more difficult to capture the ways in which the people involved in these movements were not only aware of each other but often knew each other personally. One of the primary reasons for this was that many anticolonial activists in this period spent time living in European cities like Paris, Berlin, and London, often while attending university. People from all over the colonized world lived in these cities, as did people from places like Latin America and China. As a result, people from diverse areas came into contact with one another through their participation in student groups, social activities, and political movements. When they interacted, they learned about colonial and neocolonial conditions in other places, thus helping them see imperialism as a global problem rather than as a problem specific to a particular imperial power. One organization designed for just this purpose was the League Against Imperialism, which held its first major conference in Brussels, Belgium, in 1927. In February of that year, 174 delegates from the colonial and neocolonial world (including India's Jawaharlal Nehru, Indonesia's Mohammad Hatta, Senegal's Lamine Senghor, and Algeria's Messali Hadj, to name just a few) gathered together with leftist Europeans to learn about global colonial oppression and to make resolutions calling for an end to imperialism. Through connections like these, anticolonial activists were inspired by each other, gained information about events happening elsewhere, and learned new techniques to fight against colonialism. When they returned home, they brought this knowledge with them and used it in their own anticolonial struggles. It was thus no accident that so many anticolonial movements flourished at roughly the same time in the interwar period.

*Source:* Rodney, Walter. How Europe Underdeveloped Africa. Washington: Howard University Press, 1981.

### Thinking Critically About Sources

1. The passage identifies several reasons that anti-colonists were empowered by interacting in European cities. In what ways would their formal education in Europe further inspire them?

# SOURCES FROM THE PAST

## Africa for Africans

*Marcus Garvey (1887–1940) is best remembered as a pivotal figure in the pan-African movement. He inspired many African leaders. A powerful orator, Garvey preached the greatness of the African heritage and called on European colonial powers to leave Africa. Convinced that blacks in the diaspora could never secure their rights as minorities, Garvey rejected the idea of integration and instead championed a "Back to Africa" movement. According to Garvey, a Jamaican who also lived for a time in the United States, only in Africa would it be possible to establish an autonomous black state that featured its own unique culture. In the excerpt below, Garvey addressed the Second International Convention of Negroes in New York City in 1921.*

**George Washington was not God Almighty.** He was a man like any Negro in this building, and if he and his associates were able to make a free America, we too can make a free Africa. Hampden, Gladstone, Pitt and Disraeli were not the representatives of God in the person of Jesus Christ. They were but men, but in their time they worked for the expansion of the British Empire, and today they boast of a British Empire upon which "the sun never sets." As Pitt and Gladstone were able to work for the expansion of the British Empire, so you and I can work for the expansion of a great African Empire. Voltaire and Mirabeau were not Jesus Christs, they were but men like ourselves. They worked and overturned the French Monarchy. They worked for the Democracy which France now enjoys, and if they were able to do that, we are able to work for a democracy in Africa. Lenin and Trotsky were not Jesus Christs, but they were able to overthrow the despotism of Russia, and today they have given to the world a Social Republic, the first of its kind. If Lenin and Trotsky were able to do that for Russia, you and I can do that for Africa. Therefore, let no man, let no power on earth, turn you from this sacred cause of liberty. I prefer to die at this moment rather than not to work for the freedom of Africa. If liberty is good for certain sets of humanity it is good for all. Black men, Colored men, Negroes have as much right to be free as any other race that God Almighty ever created, and we desire freedom that is unfettered, freedom that is unlimited, freedom that will give us a chance and opportunity to rise to the fullest of our ambition and that we cannot get in countries where other men rule and dominate.

> Why is it important to Garvey to point out that the various leaders listed here were not gods?

We have reached the time when every minute, every second must count for something done, something achieved in the cause of Africa. . . . It falls to our lot to tear off the shackles that bind Mother Africa. Can you do it? You did it in the Revolutionary War. You did it in the Civil War; You did it at the Battles of the Marne and Verdun; You did it in Mesopotamia. You can do it marching up the battle heights of Africa. Let the world know that 400,000,000 Negroes are prepared to die or live as free men. Despise us as much as you care. Ignore us as much as you care. We are coming 400,000,000 strong. We are coming with our woes behind us, with the memory of suffering behind us—woes and suffering of three hundred years—they shall be our inspiration. My bulwark of strength in the conflict of freedom in Africa, will be the three hundred years of persecution and hardship left behind in this Western Hemisphere.

> What is the three hundred years of suffering to which Garvey refers here?

### For Further Reflection

- In his speech, how does Marcus Garvey convey the significance of Africa for both Africans and those involved in the black diaspora?
- Why is it significant to consider the audience of Garvey's speech?
- Garvey uses the rhetorical device of comparing his plan to those of famous leaders, and significant events in the past. Is he persuasive?
- What obstacles would thwart Garvey's success?

*Source:* Garvey, Marcus. "Africans for Africans." *The Philosophy and Opinions of Marcus Garvey.* Edited By Amy Jacques Garvey. New Preface by Tony Martin. The Majority Press Inc. Dover, MA, pp. 73-74.

world, led Africans in sub-Saharan colonies to develop their own anticolonial movements. An emerging class of urban intellectuals, frequently educated in Europe, became especially involved in the formation of ideologies that sought freedom from colonialism and promoted new national identities.

**Sub-Saharan Africa's New Elite** Colonialism prompted the emergence of a new African social class, sometimes called the "new elite." This elite derived its status and place in society from employment and education. The upper echelons of sub-Saharan Africa's elite class contained high-ranking civil servants, physicians, lawyers, and writers, most of whom had studied abroad either in western Europe or sometimes in the United States. For example, **Jomo Kenyatta** (1895–1978), spent almost fifteen years in Europe, during which time he attended various schools and universities, including the London School of Economics. Like many other colonized subjects who lived in Europe, Kenyatta made contact with colonized subjects from other regions in sub-Saharan Africa, India, and the Caribbean. Through discussions and meetings and friendships, colonized subjects like Kenyatta were able to view imperialism as a global problem that needed to be eliminated everywhere. Later, Kenyatta led Kenya to independence from the British. Other members of the new elite included teachers, clerks, and interpreters who had obtained a European-derived primary or secondary education. Although some individuals were self-employed, such as lawyers and doctors, most held jobs with colonial governments, foreign companies, or Christian missions. In short, these were the Africans who spoke European languages and outwardly adopted European cultural norms such as wearing European-style clothes or adopting European names. It was within the ranks of this new elite that anticolonial mass movements emerged.

Portrait of the Jamaican Pan-Africanist Marcus Garvey (1887–1940), taken in 1924.
Library of Congress, Prints and Photographs Division [LC-USZ61-1854]

African nationalists frequently embraced the European concept of the nation as a means of forging unity among disparate African groups. This was partly a practical response to the artificial borders Europeans had drawn to create sub-Saharan African colonies in the first place. Even when such borders did not make sense in terms of ethnic and cultural ties, it was nevertheless true that the borders placed all the people within them under a single colonizer and a common legal and political regime. As such the idea of the nation—as defined by these borders—seemed to offer the best chance to mount effective resistance to colonialism.

**Alternatives to the Nation** Some anticolonial sub-Saharan Africans were not convinced that independent nations—especially as constituted within borders drawn by European colonizers—were what anticolonial movements should be striving for. Instead, some looked to the precolonial past for inspiration. There they found identities based on ethnicity, religion, and languages, and they believed that any future state must reconstitute institutions crucial to those identities, such as distinctively African forms of spiritual and political authority. Race had provided colonial powers with one rationale for conquest and exploitation; hence it was not surprising that some anticolonial activists used the concept of an African race as a foundation for identity, solidarity, and state building. Race figured as an important concept in another important strain of African anticolonialism, which originated in the Western Hemisphere among the descendants of slaves. Pan-Africanists thought of Africans and African-descended peoples from around the world as members of a single race and promoted the unification of all people of African descent into a single African state. Many pan-Africanists came from North America and the Caribbean, though the idea also attracted followers in Africa. Some of the most well-known representatives of this **pan-Africanism** were the black U.S. activist and intellectual **W. E. B. DuBois** (1868–1963) and the Jamaican nationalist leader **Marcus Garvey** (1887–1940), who preached black pride and called on blacks living in the African diaspora to go "Back to Africa." Collectively these ideas influenced the development of anticolonial movements in sub-Saharan Africa during the 1930s and 1940s, but the need to oppose colonial powers from within existing colonial borders made it difficult to enact proposed alternatives that moved across them.

## LATIN AMERICAN STRUGGLES WITH NEOCOLONIALISM

Having gained their independence in the nineteenth century, most sovereign nations in Latin America thereafter struggled to achieve political and economic stability in the midst of interference from foreign powers. The era of the Great War and the Great Depression proved crucial to solidifying and exposing the neocolonial structures that dominated affairs in Latin America. Generally seen as an indirect and more subtle form of imperial control, neocolonialism usually took shape as foreign economic domination but did not exclude more typically imperial actions such as military intervention and political interference. In Central and South America, as well as in Mexico and the Caribbean, this imperial influence came not from former colonial rulers in Spain and Portugal but, rather, from wealthy, industrial-capitalist powerhouses such as Great Britain and, especially, the United States. Neocolonialism impinged on the independent political and economic development of Latin American states, but it did not prevent nationalist leaders from devising strategies to combat it.

## The Impact of the Great War and the Great Depression

**Reorientation of Political and Nationalist Ideals** The Great War and the Russian revolution, along with the ongoing Mexican revolution (see chapter 27), spread radical ideas and the promise of new political possibilities throughout Latin America. The disparate ideals emerging from this time of political ferment found receptive audiences in Latin America before but especially during the global economic crisis of the Great Depression. Marxism, Vladimir Lenin's theories on capitalism and imperialism, and a growing concern for the impoverished indigenous population as well as exploited peasants and workers in Latin American societies informed the outlooks of many intellectuals and artists who sought a path to greater social and political equality. Although those revolutionary doctrines did not achieve full-scale adoption by Latin American states during the interwar era, their increasing popularity and perceived viability as political options suggested the alternatives open to nations in the future.

**University Protests and Communist Parties** The Great War had propelled the United States into a position of world economic leadership. The peoples of Latin America came to experience this increased U.S. economic power most intensely, and it was no coincidence that the capitalism embraced by the United States came under attack. One of the first institutions in many Latin American states to witness this rebelliousness were the universities. Taking their inspiration from the Mexican and Russian revolutions—both deeply anti-capitalist—students in the 1920s began to demand reforms in their own countries. Their political activism resulted in the long-term politicization of the student bodies at Latin American universities. Universities thereafter became training grounds for future political leaders, including the Cuban **Fidel Castro** (1926–2016), and the ideas explored within an academic setting—from Marxism to anti-imperialism—exerted great influence on those budding politicians.

The currency of radicalism also expressed itself in the formation of political parties that either openly espoused communism or otherwise adopted anti-capitalist and anti-imperialist agendas for change. Peruvians, for example, created a number of radical new political parties, many of which had connections to a self-educated young Marxist intellectual, **José Carlos Mariátegui** (1895–1930). Mariátegui felt particular concern for the poor and for indigenous Indians, who constituted approximately 50 percent of Peru's population. He castigated Peru's leaders in journals and newspapers for not helping the downtrodden, and he suffered exile to Europe as a result. He came back from Europe a dedicated Marxist and in 1928 established the Socialist Party of Peru. Mariátegui continued to write and rally in support of laborers, and he was in the midst of helping to create the Peruvian Communist Party when he died from cancer in 1930.

Diego Rivera (1886–1957) finishing a mural in the lobby of the Cordiac Institute, Mexico City, Mexico, circa 1930. FPG/Getty Images

The same agitation that filled José Carlos Mariátegui affected others in Peru and led in the 1920s and 1930s to violence and strikes. The *Alianza Popular Revolucionaria Americana* (Popular American Revolutionary Alliance, or APRA) gave another voice to those critical of Peru's ruling system. This party's followers, known as *Apristas,* advocated indigenous rights and anti-imperialism among other causes. *Aprismo* offered a radical but noncommunist alternative to Peruvians, and it stemmed from the ideas of **Victor Raúl Haya de la Torre** (1895–1979). Haya de la Torre began his political activism as a student protester and as a supporter of a workers' movement. Exiled like Mariátegui, Haya de la Torre nonetheless imparted his eclectic views to APRA, including both staunch anti-imperialism and a plan for capitalist development that had peasants and workers cooperating with the middle class. The more traditional power of the military and landed elites in Peru managed to contain these rebellious movements, but the cultural and political popularity of radicalism and its intellectual proponents persisted.

**Diego Rivera and Radical Artistic Visions** The ideological transformations apparent in Latin America became

**José Carlos Mariátegui** (ho-SAY car-lohs ma-ree-AH-teh-gee)

stunningly and publicly visible in the murals painted by famed Mexican artist **Diego Rivera** (1886–1957). After studying art in Mexico in his youth, Rivera went to study in Europe in 1907 and did not return to Mexico until 1921. Influenced by the art of both Renaissance artists and cubists, Rivera also experienced the turmoil and shifting political sensibilities taking place in Europe during the Great War and its aftermath. He blended his artistic and political visions in vast murals that he intended for viewing and appreciation by the masses. He believed that art should be on display for working people. Along with other Mexican muralists, such as David Alfaro Siqueiros (1896–1974) and José Clemente Orozco (1883–1949), Rivera shaped the politicized art of Mexico for decades.

Diego Rivera celebrated indigenous Mexican art and pre-Columbian folk traditions, and he incorporated radical political ideas in his style and approach to mural painting. The government commissioned him in the late 1920s and 1930s to create large frescoes for public buildings, and Rivera artistically transcribed the history of Mexico, replete with its social ills, on the walls of such structures as the National Palace and the Ministry of Education in Mexico City. An activist in the Mexican Communist Party (founded in 1917), he taught briefly in Moscow in the late 1920s. In the early 1930s the Detroit Institute of Arts commissioned him to paint murals for a U.S. audience, although this migration of his art to the United States soon caused a controversy.

In 1933 Rivera received a request to paint murals for the RCA building in Rockefeller Center in New York City. He included in one panel a portrait of Vladimir Lenin, which outraged those who had commissioned the work. John D. Rockefeller himself ordered the mural to be plastered over and replaced. Rivera in turn undertook a series of twenty-one paintings on United States history titled *Portrait of America.* He labeled one of the most pointed and critical paintings *Imperialism,* which visualized and advertised the economic interference and political repressiveness engendered by U.S. neocolonialism in Latin America. Rivera depicted massive guns and tanks extending over the New York Stock Exchange. In the foreground and at the edges of the Stock Exchange are a variety of Latin American victims of this monied-military oppression, including Central Americans laboring for the United Fruit Company and others toiling for the Standard Oil Company. Overlooking all of this in the upper-right corner is **Augusto César Sandino** (1893–1934), the martyred nationalist hero who opposed U.S. intervention in Nicaragua. Rivera made visible the impact of U.S. imperialism on Latin American societies, and by doing so he helped spread political activism in the Americas.

## The Evolution of Economic Imperialism

**United States Economic Domination** Latin American states were no strangers to foreign economic domination in the nineteenth and early twentieth centuries. Their export-oriented economies had long been tied to global finances and had long been subject to controls imposed by foreign investors, largely those from Great Britain, the United States, France, and Germany. The major evolution in economic neocolonialism during this period concerned the growing predominance of the United States in the economic affairs of Latin American nations. The Great War sealed this transition to U.S. supremacy, and U.S. investments in Latin America soared in the 1920s. Between 1924 and 1929, U.S. banks and businesses more than doubled their financial interests in Latin America as investments grew from $1.5 billion to $3.5 billion. Much of that money went toward the takeover of businesses extracting vital minerals, such as copper-mining firms in Chile and oil-drilling concerns in Venezuela.

**Dollar Diplomacy** That U.S. neocolonialism was meant to be largely economic became evident in the policies of President William Howard Taft (1857–1931). In his final address to Congress in 1912, Taft argued that the United States should substitute "dollars for bullets" in its foreign policy. He wanted businesses to develop foreign markets through peaceful commerce and believed that expensive military intervention should be avoided as much as possible. Likewise, by replacing European investments with U.S. investments, the United States would face fewer tests of the Monroe Doctrine or its 1904 Roosevelt corollary, which justified direct intervention in Latin American nations deemed unstable by the United States. This new vision of U.S. expansion abroad, dubbed **"dollar diplomacy"** by critics, encapsulated the gist of what those in Latin America perceived as "Yankee imperialism."

**Economic Depression and Experimentation** The economic crisis of the Great Depression demonstrated the extent to which Latin America had become integrated in the world economy. With some exceptions, exports had continued in the interwar period to help nations achieve basic solvency and even enough economic expansion to institute social reforms. The Great Depression, however, halted fifty years of economic growth in Latin America and illustrated the region's susceptibility to global economic crises. The increasing U.S. capital investments for budding industries and other financial concerns during the 1920s could not be maintained during this catastrophic economic downturn. Most Latin American states, because they exported agricultural products or raw materials, were further vulnerable to the effects of the depression. The prices of sugar from the Caribbean, coffee from Brazil and Colombia, wheat and beef from Argentina, tin from Bolivia, nitrates from Chile, and many other products fell sharply after 1929. Attempts by producers to raise prices by holding supplies off the market–Brazilians, for example, set fire to coffee beans or used them in the construction of highways–failed, and throughout Latin America unemployment rates increased rapidly. The drastic decline in the price of the region's exports and the drying up of foreign capital prompted Latin American governments to raise tariffs on foreign products and impose various other restrictions on foreign trade. Those same conditions

## INTERPRETING IMAGES

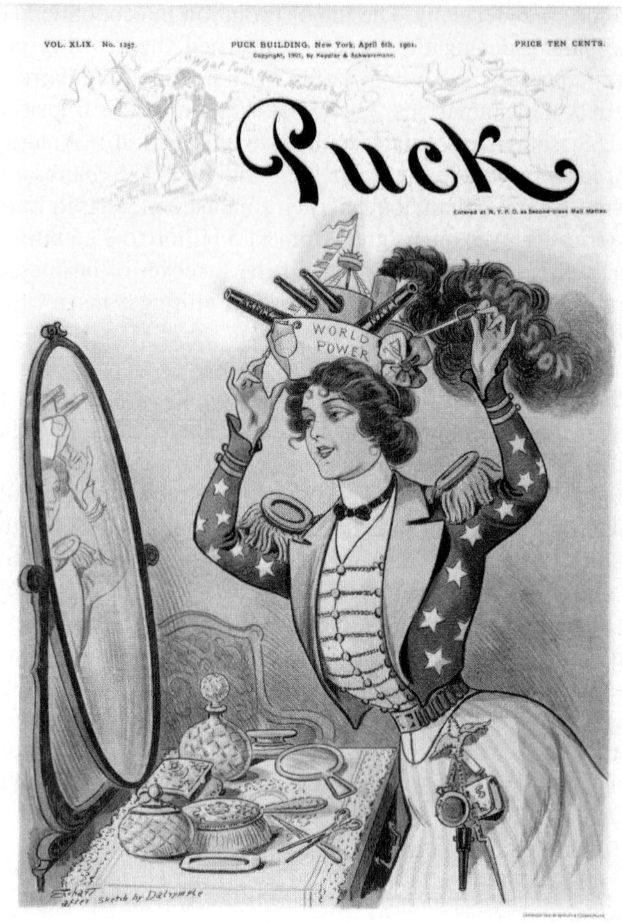


The cover of American humor and satire magazine *Puck*, from 6 April 1901, featured Columbia wearing a warship bearing the words "World Power" as her Easter bonnet. Columbia is the female personification of the United States of America.

**Analyze** *Explain the satire depicted in this cartoon. Is the artist supportive of U.S. imperialism? Why depict the U.S. as a woman instead of a man (think Uncle Sam)?*

Library of Congress, Prints and Photographs Division [LC-DIG-ppmsca-25515]

also encouraged domestic manufacturing, which made important gains in many Latin American nations in this period.

Indeed, although the weaknesses of export-oriented economies and industrial development financed by foreigners became evident during the Great Depression, the international crisis also allowed Latin American nations to take alternative paths to economic development. Economic policy stressing internal economic development was most visible in Brazil, where dictator-president (1930–1945, 1950–1954) **Getúlio Dornelles Vargas** (1883–1954) turned his nation into an ***estado novo*** (new state). Ruling with the backing of the military but without the support of the landowning elite, Vargas and his government during the 1930s and 1940s embarked on a program of industrialization that created new enterprises. Key among them was the iron and steel industry. The Vargas regime also implemented protectionist policies that shielded domestic production from foreign competition, which pleased both industrialists and urban workers. Social welfare initiatives accompanied industrial development, protecting workers with health and safety regulations, minimum wages, limits on working hours, unemployment compensation, and retirement benefits. The Great Depression contributed in many ways to the evolution of both economic neocolonialism and economic experimentation within Latin American states.

**Getúlio Dornelles Vargas** (zhi-TOO-lyoo door-NEH-lis VAHR-guhs)

## Conflicts with a "Good Neighbor"

**The "Good Neighbor Policy"** The pressures of the Great Depression and the instability of global politics led to a reassessment of U.S. foreign policy in Latin America during the late 1920s and 1930s. U.S. leaders realized the costliness and the ineffectiveness of their previous direct interventions in Latin America, especially when committing U.S. Marines as peacekeeping forces. To extricate U.S. military forces and rely more fully on dollar diplomacy, policymakers instituted certain innovations that nonetheless called into question any true change of heart among U.S. neocolonialists. They approved "sweetheart treaties" that guaranteed U.S. financial control in the Caribbean economies of Haiti and the Dominican Republic, for example, and the U.S. Marines provided training for indigenous police forces to keep the peace and maintain law and order. These national guards tended to be less expensive than maintaining forces of U.S. Marines, and the guards' leaders usually worked to keep cordial relations with the United States. This revamped U.S. approach to relations with Latin America became known as the **Good Neighbor Policy,** and it was most closely associated with the administration of Franklin D. Roosevelt (1882–1945). Although Roosevelt appeared more well-intentioned in his exercise of the policy, events in Nicaragua before and during the beginning of his administration highlighted the limits of U.S. neighborliness.

**Nicaragua and the *Guarda Nacional*** U.S. financial interests had long influenced the economy of Nicaragua, and those substantial investments–whether in the transportation industry or in bananas–served to justify U.S. intervention when revolts or civil wars broke out. The mid- and late 1920s again witnessed the outbreak of civil war in Nicaragua and the repeated insertion of U.S. Marines to restore order. Leading the opposition to Nicaraguan conservatives and the occupation of Nicaragua by U.S. Marines was Augusto César Sandino, a nationalist and liberal general who refused to accept any peace settlement that left Marines on Nicaraguan soil.

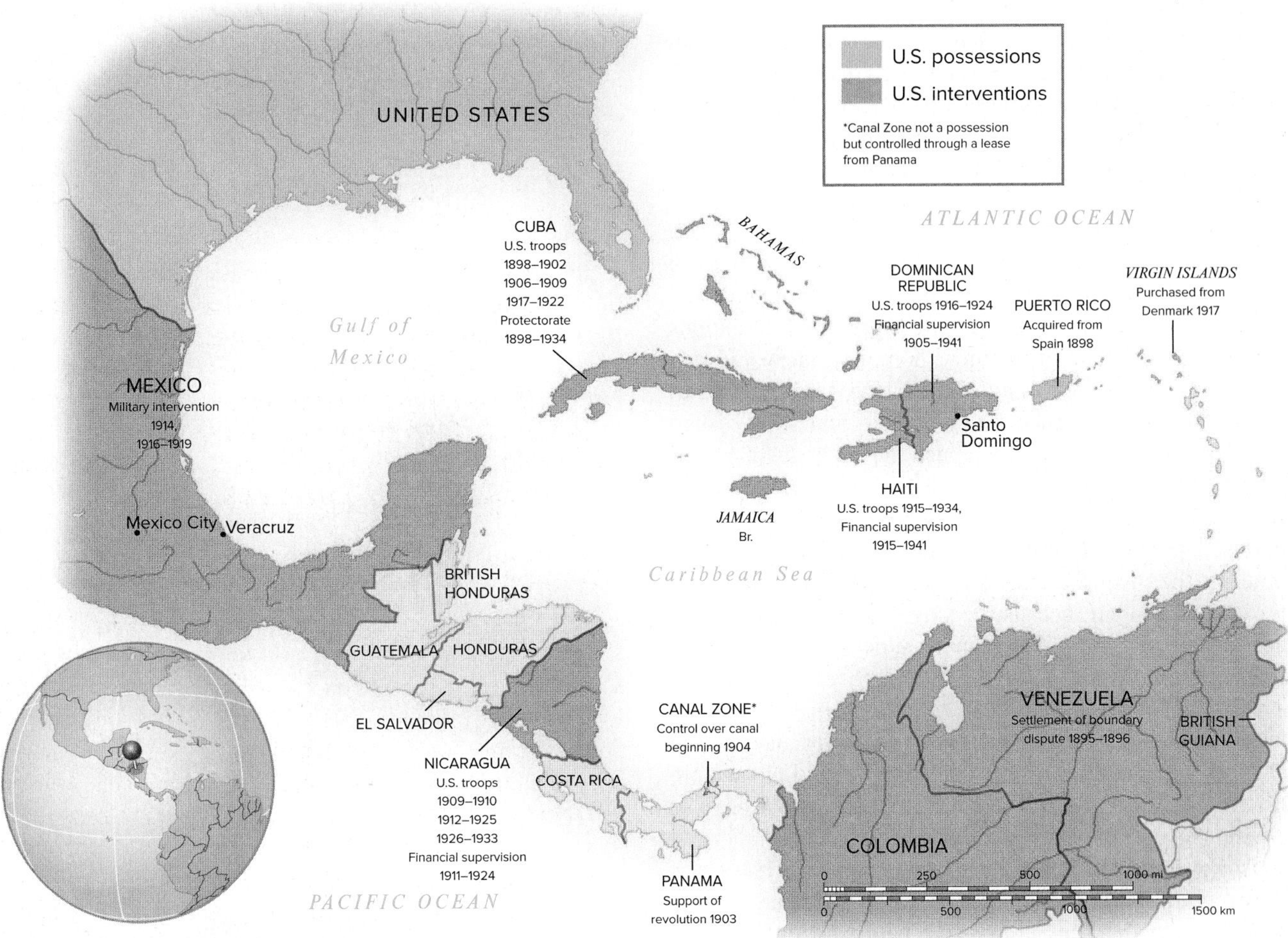


**MAP 23.2 The United States in Latin America, 1895–1941.**

Note the number of Latin American states where U.S. troops intervened in local politics.

***On what basis did U.S. policymakers justify those interventions?***

## How the Past Shapes the Future

### The Destructive Potential of Industrial Technologies

One of the features of mid-twentieth-century nationalist movements in both Brazil and China was an emphasis on economic development through industrialization. It is easy to understand the rationale behind such plans: one of the things nationalists in Asia, Africa, and Latin America agreed upon was their objection to economic exploitation by the industrial powers of Europe, Japan, or the United States. To counter such exploitation, nationalists in this period began to seek control over their economies by producing their own industrial goods and by exploiting their own natural resources. Yet the model of industrialization established by the powers that had industrialized first was one that paid little attention to the environmental consequences of resource extraction or industrial pollution. As a result, those states seeking to industrialize in the mid-twentieth century tended to perpetuate patterns of resource depletion; monocrop cultivation; soil erosion; and air, soil, and water pollution begun by the original industrial powers. Consider the aggregate environmental effects of this pattern of industrialization at the planetary level, especially as increasing numbers of states sought to escape economic domination through internal industrialization over the course of the twentieth century.

As part of a plan to remove U.S. forces, the United States established and trained the ***Guarda Nacional,*** or National Guard, in Nicaragua. The U.S.-supervised elections of 1932 brought Juan Batista Sacasa (president, 1932–1936) into power, and U.S. troops departed, having positioned the brutal but trusted **Anastacio Somoza Garcia** (1896–1956) as commander of the Guard. Even though conflicts between Sandino's forces and Somoza's Guard persisted, Sandino explored options with Sacasa and Somoza for ending the rebellion given the departure of U.S. Marines. But officers from the National Guard murdered Sandino in 1934, and Somoza soon after fulfilled his ambitions and became president of his country. Somoza endeavored successfully to maintain the loyalty of the National Guard and to prove himself a good neighbor to the United States. He visited Washington, D.C., in 1939 and renamed the Nicaraguan capital city's main thoroughfare after Roosevelt. He also began to collect what became the largest fortune in Nicaragua's history and to establish a political dynasty that ruled the nation for decades to come. In the meantime, Sandino gained heroic status as a martyr who died in part because he fought the good neighbor to the north, while ordinary Nicaraguans suffered under a brutal dictatorship supported by those same neighbors.

A 1920s photograph of Nicaraguan patriot leader Augusto César Sandino. Sandino opposed the presence of the United States in Nicaragua and fought to expel U.S. Marines in his country. He was murdered by officers from the U.S.-friendly National Guard in 1934.
Bettmann/Getty Images

**Mexico Under Cardenas's Rule** However flawed, the Good Neighbor Policy evolved under Roosevelt into a more conciliatory U.S. approach to Latin American relations. The interventionist corollary to the Monroe Doctrine enunciated previously by President Theodore Roosevelt (1859–1919) was formally renounced in December 1933, when Secretary of State Cordell Hull attended the Seventh International Conference of American States in Montevideo, Uruguay. Hull signed the Convention on the Rights and Duties of States, which held that "no state has the right to intervene in the internal or external affairs of another." That proposition faced a severe challenge in March 1938 when Mexican president **Lázaro Cárdenas** (1895–1970) nationalized the oil industry, much of which was controlled by foreign investors from the United States and Great Britain.

Given the history of tempestuous relations between the United States and Mexico, including multiple U.S. military incursions into Mexico during the revolution, there was little chance for a peaceful resolution to this move on the part of Cárdenas. Cárdenas took this step after Mexican oil workers went on strike in protest of their difficult working conditions and low pay. The Mexican government intervened and drew up a new labor agreement between Mexican workers and the foreign oil companies, but the foreign oil companies refused to abide by it. Cárdenas took this as a direct challenge to Mexican sovereignty and thus resolved to nationalize the oil industry. Despite calls for a strong U.S. and British response including those who advocated an all-out war, Roosevelt and his administration officials resisted the demands of big businesses and instead called for a cool, calm response and negotiations to end the conflict. This plan prevailed, and the foreign oil companies ultimately had to accept only $24 million in compensation rather than the $260 million that they initially demanded because Cárdenas cleverly based the compensation price on the tax value claimed by the oil companies. The nationalization of Mexican oil proved popular with Mexican people, not least because it had demonstrated Mexico's ability to stand up to the exploitative capitalist economies of the United States and western Europe.

**Lázaro Cárdenas** (LAH-sah-roh CAR-deh-nahs)

## INTERPRETING IMAGES

Chiquita Banana, an advertising icon used to promote a good image of the United Fruit Company, was a replica in fruit of the singing and acting sensation Carmen Miranda.

**Analyze** *Why is Chiquita Banana a woman? What kinds of attributes is someone supposed to notice here? How do the conditions in "Banana Republics" contrast with the ad? With the larger reach of "real life" photographs through newspapers, why are ads like this important?*

Fort Worth Star-Telegram/Tribune News Service/Getty Images

**Neighborly Cultural Exchanges?** Although the nationalization crisis in Mexico ended in a fashion that suggested the strength of the Good Neighbor Policy, a good deal of the impetus for that policy came from economic and political concerns associated with the Great Depression and the deterioration of international relations in the 1930s. The United States wanted to cultivate Latin American markets for its exports, and it wanted to distance itself from the militarist behavior of Asian and European imperial powers. The U.S. government knew it needed to improve relations with states in Latin America, if only to secure those nations' support in the increasingly likely event of another global war.

Hollywood added to this process by promoting more positive images of Latin America through its adoption of singer and dancer **Carmen Miranda** (1909–1955). Born in Portugal but raised from childhood in Brazil, Miranda found fame on a Rio de Janeiro radio station and recorded hundreds of hit songs. A Broadway producer recruited her to the United States, where she then became a popular sensation in World War II–era films such as *Down Argentine Way* (1940). Carmen Miranda appeared as an exotic Latin American woman, usually clothed in sexy, colorful costumes that featured headdresses adorned with the fruits grown in Latin America—such as bananas. She softened representations of Latin Americans for audiences in the United States, providing a less threatening counterpoint to laboring migrants or women guerrilla fighters in Mexico's revolution. She also became a source of pride for Brazilians, who reveled in her Hollywood success. At the same time, Miranda's deliberately sexualized image and her use of Latin American fruits and symbols in her costumes did not provide audiences in the United States with a realistic vision of Latin American people. Instead, Miranda's performances simply encouraged them to trade one set of stereotypes for a more palatable alternative.

And indeed, U.S. companies like the United Fruit Company—whose profits were based on the brutal exploitation of Central Americans on banana plantations—co-opted Carmen Miranda's image for their own purposes. The **United Fruit Company** owned 160,000 acres of land in the Caribbean by 1913, and already by 1918 U.S. consumers bought fully 90 percent of Nicaragua's bananas. Not content with such market control, the United Fruit Company's advertising executives in 1944 crafted "Chiquita Banana," a female banana look-alike of Carmen Miranda. In singing radio commercials, Chiquita Banana taught U.S. consumers about the storage and various uses of bananas ("I'm Chiquita Banana / And I've come to say / Bananas have to ripen / In a certain way"). This singing banana promoted the sales of United Fruit Company bananas, and for consumers in the United States, it gave the prototypical neocolonial company in Latin America a softer, less threatening image—one that challenged, for example, the more ideologically raw representation in Diego Rivera's *Imperialism*.

While Hollywood and U.S. companies were softening images of Latin American people and products for their own reasons, treatment of Mexican migrants to the United States in the same period revealed the persistence of negative attitudes toward Latin American people. During the Great War, hundreds of thousands of Mexican men, women, and children migrated to the United States to fill the labor void created when Europeans could not travel overseas to find work. In spite of the fact that their work was desperately needed, many Mexican migrants were treated poorly by U.S. citizens, who considered them "cheap Mexican labor." These attitudes hardened further during the Great Depression, when federal and local officials managed to deport thousands of Mexicans who had come to the United States at the urging of agricultural and industrial companies.

## CONCLUSION

In the decades after the Great War, and in the midst of the Great Depression, intellectuals and political activists in Asia, sub-Saharan Africa, and Latin America challenged the ideological and economic underpinnings of empire and neocolonialism. Often embracing the ideas and theories that activists encountered in their travels and around the globe as a result of the war—including self-determination, socialism, communism, and anti-imperialism—radicals and nationalists crafted new visions of a future in which political and economic independence was possible.

Meanwhile, the Japanese government embarked on a policy of militarism in East Asia, while the United States increased its efforts to intervene in Latin American economies. European colonial rulers also continued to limit, often brutally, the freedom of peoples in Asia and Africa. Yet like Shanfei, young intellectuals and older political leaders alike fought against these trends during the interwar period. Although their efforts to achieve economic and political autonomy did not come to fruition until after World War II, this period was critical to formulating their social, political, and economic responses to all forms of imperial control.

## STUDY TERMS

*ahimsa* (763)
Anastacio Somoza Garcia (778)
Augusto César Sandino (775)
Carmen Miranda (779)
Chinese Communist Party (CCP) (766)
Diego Rivera (775)
dollar diplomacy (775)
*estado novo* (785)
Fidel Castro (774)
Getúlio Dornelles Vargas (776)
Good Neighbor Policy (776)
*Guarda Nacional* (778)
*Guomindang* (766)
India Act (765)
Indian National Congress (763)
Inukai Tsuyoshi (768)
Jiang Jieshi (766)
Jomo Kenyatta (772)
José Carlos Mariátegui (774)
Lázaro Cárdenas (778)
Long March (768)
Mao Zedong (766)
Marcus Garvey (773)
May Fourth Movement (766)
Mohandas Karamchand Gandhi (763)
Muhammad Ali Jinnah (765)
Mukden incident (769)
pan-Africanism (773)
*satyagraha* (763)
Sun Yatsen (765)
United Fruit Company (779)
Victor Raúl Haya de la Torre (774)
W. E. B. DuBois (773)
Xuantong (765)

## FOR FURTHER READING

Victor Bulmer-Thomas. *The Economic History of Latin America Since Independence* (Cambridge Latin American Studies). 3rd ed. New York, 2014. This well-known classic remains the best economic history of Latin America.

Ian Buruma. *Inventing Japan, 1853–1964.* New York, 2003. A respected journalist compresses a century of complex history into a short and elegant book.

Toyin Falola. *Nationalism and African Intellectuals.* Rochester, 2002. Explores the ways African intellectuals shaped anticolonial nationalist movements in the colonial period and then state-building movements after independence.

William Gould. *Hindu Nationalism and the Language of Politics in Late Colonial India.* New York, 2004. Political history of India on the eve of independence.

Robert E. Hannigan. *The New World Power: American Foreign Policy, 1898–1917.* Philadelphia, 2002. A detailed account of U.S. foreign relations that links class, race, and gender influences to policymakers.

Michele Louro. *Comrades against Imperialism: Nehru, India, and Interwar Nationalism.* Cambridge, 2018. Argues that Jawaharlal Nehru, the first president of independent India, was deeply shaped by the internationalism of the interwar period—particularly by the League Against Imperialism.

Roland Oliver and Anthony Atmore. *Africa Since 1800.* 5th ed. Cambridge, 2005. An updated version of a well-regarded survey.

S.C.M. Paine. *The Wars for Asia, 1911–1949.* Cambridge, 2012. Explores the competing visions of Chinese, Japanese, and Russians for the future of China in the period encapsulated by the two World Wars.

Steve Striffler and Mark Moberg, eds. *Banana Wars: Power, Production, and History in the Americas.* Durham, N.C., 2003. Interdisciplinary analysis of the transformative impact of the banana industry on global trade and the consequences for Latin American societies and economies.

Odd Arne Westad. *Decisive Encounters: The Chinese Civil War, 1946–1950.* Stanford, 2003. An engaging work that introduces the reader to the salient political and military events that led to the eventual defeat of the Guomindang.

# CHAPTER 23 AP EXAM PRACTICE

Questions assume cumulative knowledge from this chapter and previous chapters.

## Section I

## Multiple Choice Questions

Use the map below and your knowledge of world history to answer questions 1-3.

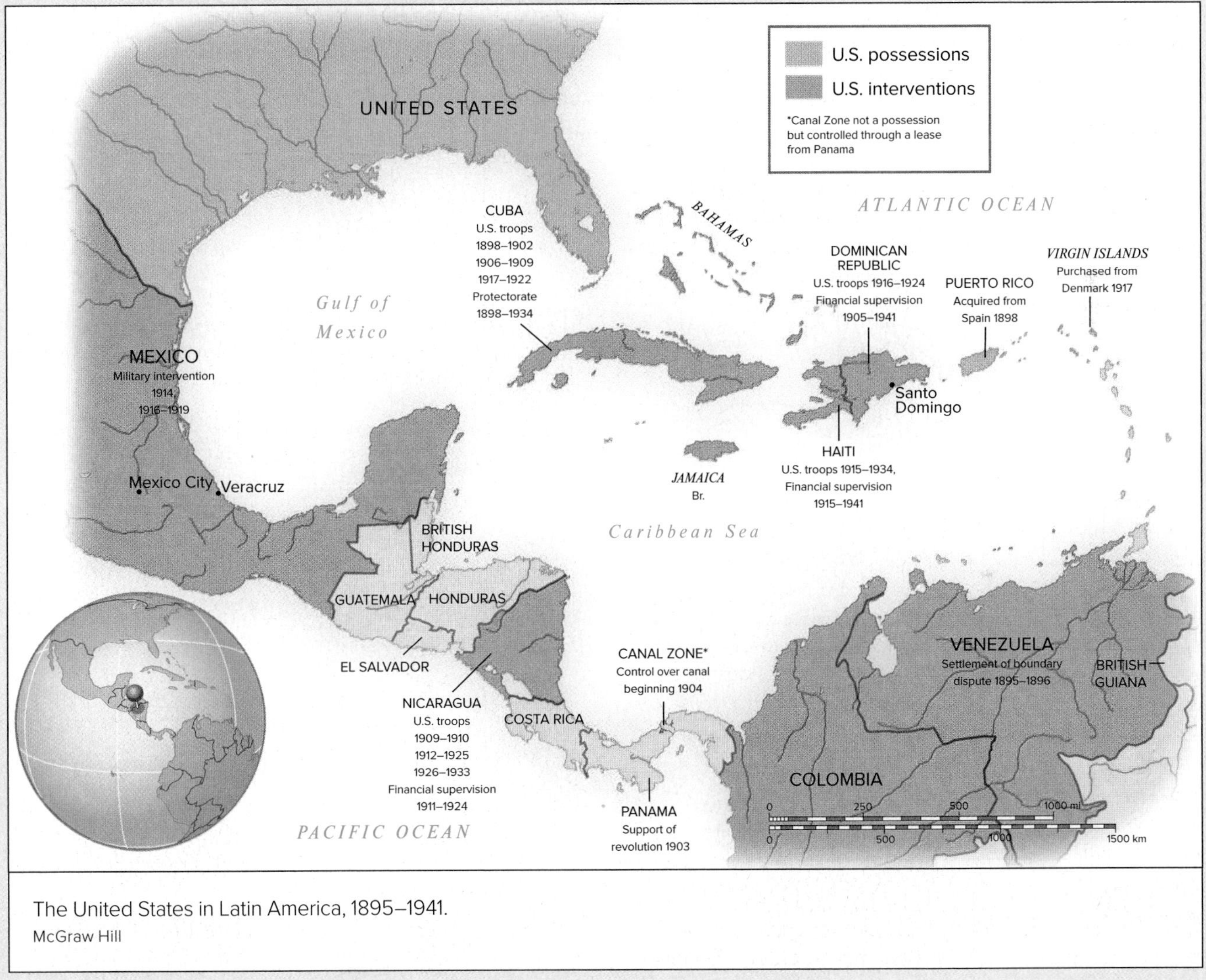


The United States in Latin America, 1895–1941.
McGraw Hill

1. What was the Good Neighbor Policy?
   (A) The United States built the border fences for Latin American countries.
   (B) This policy created inexpensive insurance policies for Latin American farmers.
   (C) The United States replaced European investments with US investments, which justified direct intervention in Latin American nations that were deemed unstable.
   (D) The United States trained Latin American police forces and their leaders protected US financial and political interests.

2. Who led the Nicaraguan opposition against the United States marines?
   (A) Augusto César Sandino
   (B) Diego Rivera
   (C) José Carlos Mariátegui
   (D) Victor Raúl Haya de la Torre

3. Why was there no US intervention in Mexico after Lázaro Cárdenas nationalized the oil industry?
   (A) The United States could not afford a military intervention because of the Great Depression.
   (B) The Zimmerman telegraph had promised the return of California and Arizona to Mexico, so the US was reluctant to involve the Germans into a conflict with Mexico.
   (C) The United States had renounced interventions earlier in Franklin Delano Roosevelt's presidency.
   (D) The United States purchased most of its oil from Saudi Arabia, so it was not concerned with Mexican oil.

Use the image below and your knowledge of world history to answer questions 4 and 5.

Chiquita Banana, used to advertise for the United Fruit Company.
Fort Worth Star-Telegram/Tribune News Service/Getty Images

4. What claim could a historian make based on the Chiquita Banana advertising icon?
   (A) American consumers were not purchasing bananas during the Great Depression, so the United Fruit Company hoped the cartoon would increase their share of the market.
   (B) Carmen Miranda was unpopular at home in Brazil because she sought success in Hollywood.
   (C) The United Fruit Company used the image and Diego Rivera's art to sell their products in the United States.
   (D) The Chiquita Banana presented a softer image of Latin American people and gave audiences in the United States an unrealistic image of Latin Americans.

5. What changed in Mexican art between the wars?
   (A) Artists used cartoon skeletons to satirize important people in Mexican politics.
   (B) Some Mexican artists celebrated indigenous people and traditions in their work.
   (C) The Dada movement broke the rules of traditional Mexican art.
   (D) Mexican muralists celebrated the close relationship between the United States and Mexico.

## Short Answer

6. Use the text selection below and your knowledge of world history to answer parts A, B, and C.

**George Washington was not God Almighty.** He was a man like any Negro in this building, and if he and his associates were able to make a free America, we too can make a free Africa. Hampden, Gladstone, Pitt and Disraeli were not the representatives of God in the person of Jesus Christ. They were but men, but in their time they worked for the expansion of the British Empire, and today they boast of a British Empire upon which "the sun never sets." As Pitt and Gladstone were able to work for the expansion of the British Empire, so you and I can work for the expansion of a great African Empire. Voltaire and Mirabeau were not Jesus Christs, they were but men like ourselves. They worked and overturned the French Monarchy. They worked for the Democracy which France now enjoys, and if they were able to do that, we are able to work for a democracy in Africa. Lenin and Trotsky were not Jesus Christs, but they were able to overthrow the despotism of Russia, and today they have given to the world a Social Republic, the first of its kind. If Lenin and Trotsky were able to do that for Russia, you and I can do that for Africa. Therefore, let no man, let no power on earth, turn you from this sacred cause of liberty. I prefer to die at this moment rather than not to work for the freedom of Africa. If liberty is good for certain sets of humanity it is good for all. Black men, Colored men, Negroes have as much right to be free as any other race that God Almighty ever created, and we desire freedom that is unfettered, freedom that is unlimited, freedom that will give us a chance and opportunity to rise to the fullest of our ambition and that we cannot get in countries where other men rule and dominate.

We have reached the time when every minute, every second must count for something done, something achieved in the cause of Africa. . . . It falls to our lot to tear off the shackles that bind Mother Africa. Can you do it? You did it in the Revolutionary War. You did it in the Civil War; You did it at the Battles of the Marne and Verdun; You did it in Mesopotamia. You can do it marching up the battle heights of Africa. Let the world know that 400,000,000 Negroes are prepared to die or live as free men. Despise us as much as you care. Ignore us as much as you care. We are coming 400,000,000 strong. We are coming with our woes behind us, with the memory of suffering behind us—woes and suffering of three hundred years—they shall be our inspiration. My bulwark of strength in the conflict of freedom in Africa, will be the three hundred years of persecution and hardship left behind in this Western Hemisphere.

*Source:* Garvey, Marcus. *The Philosophy and Opinions of Macus Garvey.* Edited by Amy Jacques Garvey. New Preface by Tony Martin. The Majority Press Inc. Dover, MA, pp. 95–96.

(A) Identify ONE way someone became part of the new African elite.

(B) Explain ONE reason why anticolonial movements all gained new momentum around the same time.

(C) Explain ONE anticolonial alternative to nationalism.

7. Use the map below and your knowledge of world history to answer parts A, B, and C.

The struggle for control in China, 1927–1936
McGraw Hill

(A) Identify ONE factor that dictated the course of the civil war in China.
(B) Explain ONE aspect of the Long March and its role in strengthening the Chinese Communist Party.
(C) Explain ONE way in which Chinese nationalism and communism impacted society in 1920s China.

8. Use your understanding of world history to answer parts A, B, and C.
(A) Identify ONE aspect of social change in interwar Japan.
(B) Explain ONE way that Japanese politics changed after joining the League of Nations.
(C) Explain ONE result of the Mukden incident in 1931.

# Section II

## Document-Based Question

Based on the documents below and your knowledge of world history, evaluate the extent to which Indian and Chinese anticolonial movements were successful between the two world wars.

In your response you should do the following:

- Respond to the prompt with a historically defensible thesis or claim that establishes a line of reasoning.
- Describe a broader historical context relevant to the prompt.
- Support an argument in response to the prompt using all documents.
- Use at least one additional piece of specific historical evidence (beyond that found in the documents) relevant to an argument about the prompt.
- Explain how or why the document's point of view, purpose, historical situation, and / or audience is relevant to an argument.
- Use evidence to corroborate, qualify, or modify an argument that addresses the prompt.

### Document 1

***The world revolution,*** in order to accomplish its great mission, must cross the borders of the so-called Western Countries where capitalism has reached its climax. Until very recently this truth was almost entirely unknown among the revolutionaries of Europe and America, who hardly gave a moment's thought to the social and economic conditions of the Asiatic generally. It was generally maintained that, owing to their industrial backwardness, the hundreds of millions of the masses in the East would not count for anything in the great struggle between the exploiter and the exploited. Consequently the "World" of the world revolution was limited to Europe and America.

But revolution is the result of objective conditions; it breaks out in the least suspected place if the dynamic forces are there. The inevitable result of oppression is that sooner or later the oppressed rebel. This is happening to-day in the Eastern countries, where the myriads of toilers have been groaning under the same exploitation against which their more fortunate and less downtrodden comrades of the Occident have been carrying on an heroic fight. The East is awakening: and who knows if the formidable tide, that will sweep away the capitalist structure of Western Europe, may not come from there . . .

During almost a century World Capitalism kept on invigorating itself by sucking the blood of the colonial toilers. But along with the bloody sword of organised exploitation, it carried in its womb the incipient forces that were destined to rise against it and build the new society upon its ruins. To-day these forces are manifesting themselves in the growing revolutionary fermentation among the Eastern peoples, who were considered till the other day negligible factors in the World Revolution. This awakening of the East must open a new vision before the revolutionary leaders of Europe. It ought to show them the way through which the retreat of the cunning enemy can be cut. A formidable upheaval of the colonial and "protected" peoples will take away from under the feet of Imperialist Capitalism, the rock of super-profit which has helped so far offset the effects of overproduction . . . The disruption of Empire is the only thing that will complete the bankruptcy of European capitalism; and the revolutionary upheavals in the Asiatic countries are destined to bring about the crumbling of the proud imperial structure of capitalism. . ..

*Source:* Roy, M.N. "The Awakening of the East." *The Call*, July 15, 1920, p. 5. *Marxists Internet Archive (2007).*

## Document 2

Jiang Jieshi (Chiang Kai-shek) (1887–1975) at left; Mao Zedong (1893–1976) at right
Bettmann/Getty Images

## Document 3

Mohandas Gandhi during the Salt March, marching with Sarojini Naidu (1879–1949), first female president of the Indian National Congress.
Bettmann/Getty Images

## Long Essay

Develop a thoughtful and thorough historical argument that answers the question below. Begin your essay with a thesis statement and support it with relevant historical evidence.

Using specific examples and your knowledge of world history, explain the similarities and differences in how the Great Depression affected Africa and Latin America.

# Chapter 24 New Conflagrations: World War II and the Cold War



## ZOOMING IN ON ENCOUNTERS

### Victor Tolley finds Tea and Sympathy in Nagasaki

On 6 August 1945, as he listened to the armed services radio on Saipan (a U.S.-controlled island in the north Pacific), U.S. marine Victor Tolley heard the news: the president of the United States announced that a "terrible new weapon" had been deployed against the city of Hiroshima, Japan. Tolley and the other marines rejoiced, realizing that the terrible new weapon—the atomic bomb—might end the war and relieve them of the burden of invading Japan. A few days later Tolley heard that the city of Nagasaki had also been hit with an atomic bomb. He remembered the ominous remarks that accompanied the news of this atomic destruction: radio announcers suggested it might be decades before the cities would be inhabitable.

Imagine Tolley's astonishment when a few weeks later, after the Japanese surrender, he and his fellow marines were assigned to the U.S. occupation forces in Nagasaki. Assured by a superior officer that Nagasaki was "very safe," Tolley lived there for three months, during which he became very familiar with the devastation wrought by the atomic bomb. As he noted, "It was just like walking into a tomb. There was total silence. You could smell this death all around ya. There was a terrible odor."

Tolley also became acquainted with some of the Japanese survivors in Nagasaki, which proved to be an eye-opening experience. After seeing "young children with sores and burns all over," Tolley, having become separated from his unit, encountered another young child. He and the boy communicated despite the language barrier between them. Tolley showed the child pictures of his wife and two daughters. The Japanese boy excitedly took Tolley home to meet his surviving family, his father and his pregnant sister. Tolley recalled,

A Japanese child cries in the rubble of Hiroshima in the aftermath of the atomic bombing, expressing the profound sadness of war and its devastating weapons.
Bettmann/Getty Images

This little kid ran upstairs and brought his father down. A very nice Japanese gentleman. He could speak English. He bowed and said, "We would be honored if you would come upstairs and have some tea with us." I went upstairs in this strange Japanese house. I noticed on the mantel a picture of a young Japanese soldier. I asked him, "Is this your son?" He said, "That is my daughter's husband. We don't know if he's alive. We haven't heard." The minute he said that, it dawned on me that they suffered the same as we did. They lost sons and daughters and relatives, and they hurt too.

Before his chance meeting with this Japanese family, Tolley had felt nothing except contempt for the Japanese. He pointed out, "We were trained to kill them. They're our enemy. Look what they did in Pearl Harbor. They asked for it and now we're gonna give it to 'em. That's how I felt until I met this young boy and his family." But after coming face-to-face with his enemies, Tolley saw only their common humanity, their suffering, and their hurt. The lesson he learned was that "these people didn't want to fight us."

# CHAPTER FOCUS

- The horrendous casualties of World War II illustrated the devastating effects of new military technologies, such as airplanes and atomic weapons, and tactics, such as firebombing.
- Other twentieth-century technologies were used to identify, transport, and sometimes destroy entire ethnic groups or wartime enemies, perceived or real.
- The leaders of industrialized nations again wreaked total war on their opponents, in which there was no distinction between armed enemy soldiers and unarmed civilians.
- As in World War I, the cold war and World War II extended far beyond official battlefields. Ethnic, religious, and nationalist prejudices became more pronounced.
- The fascists in Germany herded "undesirables" into ghettos (segregated neighborhoods), then labor camps, and then many into death camps. The U.S. uprooted Japanese Americans living on the west coast and moved them to internment camps after the bombing of Pearl Harbor. The Japanese used Chinese in Nanjing as target-practice to toughen new recruits.
- As men were drafted or pressed into military service, women's roles expanded across race and class. Women were drafted and fought for the U.S.S.R. and for China. Women volunteered to join women's auxiliary forces, were significant members of resistance movements, and moved into jobs that had been traditionally held by men.
- As in World War I, African Americans and colonized peoples around the world volunteered to fight in order to win acceptance, rights, and independence.
- This chapter traces the shift in the global balance of power from western Europe to the U.S. and U.S.S.R. in the postwar era, creating the basis for the Cold War that dominated much of the 20th century.
- Even as leaders of the Cold War worked to divide countries into a new set of antagonists, others worked toward global cooperation and a set of universally recognized human rights.
- The movement toward internationalism slowly gained traction, even as proxy wars in Africa, Asia, and Latin America threatened to pull the world's people into an eddy of a never-ending series of wars.

## Historical Developments

- The causes of World War II included the unsustainable peace settlement after World War I, the global economic crisis engendered by the Great Depression, continued imperialist aspirations, and especially the rise to power of fascist and totalitarian regimes that resulted in the aggressive militarism of Nazi Germany under Adolf Hitler.
- New military technology and new tactics, including the atomic bomb, and fire-bombing, and the waging of "total war" led to increased levels of wartime casualties.
- The global balance of economic and political power shifted during and after World War II and rapidly evolved into the Cold War. The democracy of the United States and the authoritarian communist Soviet Union emerged as superpowers, which led to ideological conflict and a power struggle between capitalism and communism across the globe.

## Reasoning Processes

- **Causation Describe** the causes of the second world war and the cold war.

## Historical Thinking Skills

- **Sourcing and Situation** Explain the point of view and historical situation expressed in first-hand accounts of the second world war.
- **Making Connections** Explain how the conclusion of the second world war led to the emergence of a global cold war.

# CHAPTER OVERVIEW

The civility that reemerged at the end of the war was barely evident during the war itself. The war began in 1931 when Japan invaded Manchuria, thereby ending the post-Great War peace, and it ended after the United States dropped atomic bombs on Hiroshima and Nagasaki. Between 1931 and 1945 the conflict expanded well beyond east Asia. By 1941 World War II was a truly global war. Hostilities spread from east Asia and the Pacific to Europe, north Africa, and the Atlantic, and people from large and small nations in North America, Asia, Europe, Africa, and Australia came into sustained contact for the duration of the war. Beyond its immense geographic scope, World War II exceeded even the Great War (1914–1918) in demonstrating the enormous sacrifices in lives and other resources required for achieving complete victory. At least sixty million people perished in the war, with civilian deaths outnumbering military casualties. In this total war, contacts with enemies, occupiers, and liberators affected populations around the world on a greater scale than any other conflict before or since. World War II also redefined gender roles and changed the shape of the colonial world, as women contributed to their nations' war efforts and as colonial peoples exploited the war's weakening of imperial nations.

Postwar recovery was complicated by the atomic and age and cold war that followed. Over time, the cold war illustrated how deep the rift between the United States of America and the Union of Soviet Socialist Republics (USSR) had grown and signaled a major realignment in international relations and the global balance of power. The cold war was a strategic struggle that, after World War II, involved the United States and its allies on the one hand and the USSR and its allied communist countries on the other. It was this clash between the forces of capitalism and communism, each armed with increasingly powerful nuclear weapons, that gave rise to a new set of global relationships, shaping the foreign policies, economic systems, and political institutions of nations throughout the world. The hostility between these new adversaries resulted in a divided world. First Europe, and Germany in particular, split into separate blocs and states. Then the cold war became global as the superpowers came into conflict in Korea and Cuba. Over the course of four decades, the cold war evolved from mutual hostility to peaceful coexistence and détente, finally coming to a close near the end of the twentieth century.

| CHRONOLOGY | |
|---|---|
| 1937 | Invasion of China by Japan; The "Rape of Nanjing" |
| 1939 | Nazi-Soviet pact; Invasion of Poland by Germany |
| 1940 | Fall of France, Battle of Britain |
| 1941 | German invasion of the Soviet Union; Attack on Pearl Harbor by Japan |
| 1942 | U.S. victory at Midway |
| 1943 | Soviet victory at Stalingrad |
| 1944 | D-Day, Allied invasion at Normandy |
| 1945 | Capture of Berlin by Soviet forces; Atomic bombing of Hiroshima and Nagasaki; Establishment of United Nations |
| 1947 | Truman Doctrine |
| 1948 | Marshall Plan |
| 1949 | Division of Berlin and Germany; Establishment of the People's Republic of China |
| 1950–1953 | Korean War |
| 1961 | Construction of Berlin Wall |
| 1962 | Cuban missile crisis |

# ORIGINS OF WORLD WAR II

In 1941 two major alliances squared off against each other. Japan, Germany, and Italy, along with their conquered territories, formed the **Axis powers.** The **Allied powers** included France and its empire, Great Britain and its empire and Commonwealth allies (such as Canada, Australia, and New Zealand), the Soviet Union, China, and the United States and its allies in Latin America. The construction of these global alliances took place over the course of the 1930s and early 1940s.

Driven in part by a desire to revise the peace settlements that followed the Great War and affected by the economic distress of the worldwide depression, Japan, Italy, and Germany engaged in a campaign of territorial expansion that ultimately broke apart the structure of international cooperation that had kept the world from violence in the 1920s. These **revisionist powers,** so called because they revised, or overthrew, the terms of the post-Great War peace, confronted nations that were committed to the international system and to the avoidance of another world war. To expand their global influence, the revisionist nations remilitarized and conquered territories they believed were central to their territorial and resource needs. The Allies did not take action against the revisionist powers' early aggressive actions, but after they had been attacked, in the late 1930s and early 1940s, the Allies engaged the Axis powers in a total war.

## Japan's War in China

The global conflict opened with Japan's attacks on China in the 1930s: the conquest of Manchuria between 1931 and 1932 was the first step in Japan's goal of expansion to meet critical strategic and resource needs. Within Japan a battle continued between supporters and opponents of the aggressive policies adopted in Manchuria, but during the course of the 1930s the militarist position dominated, and for the most part civilians lost control of the government and the military. In 1933, after the League of Nations condemned its actions in Manchuria, Japan withdrew from the league and followed an ultranationalist and promilitary policy.

Seeing territorial control as essential to its survival, Japan launched a full-scale invasion of China in 1937. A battle between Chinese and Japanese troops at the Marco Polo Bridge in Beijing in July 1937 was the opening move in Japan's undeclared war against China. Japanese troops took Beijing and then moved south toward Shanghai and Nanjing, the capital of China. Japanese naval and air forces bombed Shanghai, killing thousands of civilians, and secured it as a landing area for armies bound for Nanjing. By December 1937 Shanghai and Nanjing had fallen, and during the following six months Japanese forces won repeated victories.

### INTERPRETING IMAGES

Japanese soldiers execute Chinese prisoners in 1937. In the Japanese invasion of China that year, four hundred thousand Chinese people were brutally murdered.

**Analyze** *Even though 400,000 Chinese people were murdered in 1937, Western powers took no action against Japan. Why not?*

Hulton-Deutsch Collection/Corbis Historical/Getty Images

**The Rape of Nanjing** China became the first nation to experience the horrors of World War II in the form of brutal warfare against civilians and repressive occupation. During the invasion of China, Japanese forces used methods of warfare that led to mass death and suffering on a new, almost unimaginable level. Chinese civilians were among the first to feel the effects of aerial bombing of urban centers; the people of Shanghai died by the tens of thousands when Japanese bombers attacked the city to soften Chinese resistance. What became known as the **Rape of Nanjing** demonstrated the horror of the war as the residents of Nanjing became victims of Japanese troops inflamed by a sense of racial superiority. Over the course of two months, Japanese soldiers raped seven thousand women, murdered hundreds of thousands of unarmed soldiers and civilians, and burned one-third of the homes in Nanjing. Four hundred thousand Chinese lost their lives as Japanese soldiers used them for bayonet practice and machine-gunned them into open pits.

**Chinese Resistance** Despite Japanese military successes and the subsequent Japanese occupation of Chinese territory, Chinese resistance persisted throughout the war. Japanese aggression aroused feelings of nationalism among the Chinese that continued to grow as the war wore on. By September 1937 nationalists and communists, who had spent the past decade fighting one another, put aside their differences to fight the Japanese together. This alliance was known as the second "united front" (the first lasted from 1923 to 1927; see chapter 23), and it resulted in a combined army of 1.7 million soldiers. Although Chinese forces were not able to defeat the Japanese, who retained naval and air superiority, by 1941 the Japanese had to engage half of their land army, 750,000 soldiers, in order to maintain control in China. This was crucial because it meant these troops could not be deployed elsewhere when the Japanese army needed them.

Throughout the war, the second united front between nationalists and communists was fragile. Although neither side was willing to risk open civil war, the two groups engaged in numerous military clashes as their forces competed for both control of enemy territory and political control within China. Those clashes rendered Chinese resistance less effective, for while both sides continued the war against Japan, each understood that the alliance was temporary and thus ultimately fought for its own advantage. The nationalists suffered major casualties in their battles with Japanese forces, but they kept the Guomindang government alive by moving far inland to Chongqing. Meanwhile, the communists carried on guerrilla operations against the Japanese invaders. Lacking air force and

Japanese soldiers in 1938 engaged in strenuous physical education in order to keep fit for the challenges of war.
Bettmann/Getty Images

artillery, communist guerrillas staged hit-and-run operations from their mountain bases, sabotaged bridges and railroads, and harassed Japanese troops. While the guerrillas did not defeat the Japanese, they captured the loyalty of many Chinese peasants through their resistance to the Japanese and their moderate policies of land reform in territories they controlled.

The Japanese invasion of China met with intense international opposition, but other world powers—distracted by depression and military aggression in Europe—could offer little in the way of an effective response to Japanese actions. The government of Japan aligned itself with the other revisionist nations, Germany and Italy, by signing the Tripartite Pact, a ten-year military and economic pact, in September 1940. Japan also cleared the way for further empire building in Asia and the Pacific basin by concluding a neutrality pact with the Soviet Union in April 1941, thereby precluding hostilities on any other front, especially in Manchuria. Japan did not face determined opposition to its expansion until December 1941, when conflict with the United States created a much broader field of action for Japan and its growing empire.

## Italian and German Aggression

Italy's expansionism helped destabilize the post–Great War peace and spread World War II to the European continent. Italians suffered tremendously in World War I. Six hundred thousand Italian soldiers died, and the national economy never recovered sufficiently for Italy to function as an equal to other European military and economic powers. Many Italians expected far greater recompense and respect than they received at the conclusion of the Great War. Rather than being treated as a real partner in victory by Britain and France, Italy found itself shut out of the divisions of the territorial spoils of war.

**Italy** **Benito Mussolini** (1883–1945) promised to bring glory to Italy through the acquisition of territories that it had been denied after the Great War. Italy's conquest of Ethiopia in 1935 and 1936, when added to the previously annexed Libya, created an overseas empire. Italy also intervened in the **Spanish Civil War** (1936–1939) on the side of General Francisco Franco (1892–1975), whose militarists overthrew the republican government. Mussolini also annexed Albania in 1939 in preparation for further expansion into the Balkans. The invasion and conquest of Ethiopia in particular infuriated other nations, but, as with Japan's invasion of Manchuria, the League of Nations was not able to offer effective opposition.

Outsiders—from state leaders to ordinary people—were horrified by Italy's conquest of Ethiopia both because they feared another war and because of Italy's excessive use of force during the invasion. Mussolini sent an army of 250,000 soldiers armed with tanks, poison gas, artillery, and aircraft to conquer the Ethiopians, who were entirely unprepared for the assault. The mechanized troops mowed them down. Italy lost 2,000 soldiers while Ethiopia lost 275,000. Although the Italian government did not commit to an alliance when it invaded Ethiopia in 1935, by 1938 the Italians had made it clear that they were firmly on the side of the Axis.

**Germany** Japan and Italy were the first nations to challenge the post–World War I settlements through territorial conquest, but it was Germany that systematically undid the Treaty of Versailles and the fragile peace of the interwar years. Most Germans and their political leaders were unwilling to accept defeat and deeply resented the harsh terms imposed on their nation in 1919. In addition, even the governments of other European nations came to recognize the extreme nature of the Versailles treaty's terms, which in turn caused them to be more tolerant of the revisionist actions of **Adolf Hitler** (1889–1945) and his government. Hitler came to power in 1933, riding a wave of public discontent with Germany's postwar position of powerlessness and the suffering caused by the Great Depression. Hitler referred to the signing of the 1918 armistice as the "November crime" and blamed it on those he viewed as Germany's internal enemies: Jews, communists, and liberals of all sorts. Neighboring European states—Poland, France, Czechoslovakia, Yugoslavia, Hungary, and Austria—also shared in the blame. Hitler's scheme for ridding Germany of its enemies and reasserting its power was remilitarization—which was legally denied to Germany under the Versailles treaty. Germany's dictator abandoned the peaceful efforts of

## INTERPRETING IMAGES

Emperor Haile Selassie (1892–1975) of Ethiopia speaking at the League of Nations in 1936. Selassie strongly protested against the Italian invasion of his nation in 1935, and expressed his deep disappointment in the League for its inaction in bringing Italy to account.

**Analyze** *Why didn't the League of Nations intervene to prevent Italy from invading Ethiopia? What can you derive from Selassie's choice to take this dispute before the League of Nations?*

Scherl/Süeddeutsche Zeitung Photo/Alamy Stock Photo

his predecessors to ease the provisions of the treaty and proceeded unilaterally to destroy it step by step. Hitler's aggressive foreign policy helped relieve the German public's feeling of war shame and depression trauma. After withdrawing Germany from the League of Nations in 1933, his government carried out an ambitious plan to strengthen the German armed forces. Hitler reinstated universal military service in 1935, and in the following year his troops entered the previously demilitarized Rhineland that bordered France. Germany joined with Italy in the Spanish Civil War, during which Hitler's troops, especially the air force, honed their skills. In 1938 Hitler began the campaign of expansion that ultimately led to the outbreak of World War II in Europe.

Hitler began with the forced annexation of Austria (known as the ***Anschluss***) in March 1938. He justified this annexation as an attempt to unite all Germans into a single homeland. Europe's major powers, France and Britain, did not respond by taking action against Germany, thus enhancing Hitler's reputation in the German military. Soon thereafter, using the same rationale of uniting Germans, the Nazis attempted to gain control of the **Sudetenland,** the western portion of Czechoslovakia. This region was inhabited largely by ethnic Germans, whom Hitler conveniently regarded as persecuted minorities. Although the Czech government was willing to make concessions to the Sudeten Germans, Hitler in September 1938 demanded the immediate cession of the Sudetenland to the German Reich. Against the desires of the Czechoslovak government, the leaders of France and Britain accommodated Hitler and allowed Germany to annex the Sudetenland. Neither the French nor the British were willing to risk a military confrontation with Germany–and thus another general European war–to defend Czechoslovakian territory.

**Peace for Our Time** In September 1938, European politicians anxious to avoid war held a conference in Munich where they consolidated the policy that came to be known throughout the 1930s as **appeasement.** The **Munich Conference** was attended by representatives of Italy, France, Great Britain, and Germany and revealed how most nations outside the revisionist sphere had decided to deal with territorial expansion by aggressive nations, especially Germany. In conceding demands to Hitler, or "appeasing" him, the British and French governments extracted a promise that Hitler would not expand German territorial aims beyond the

***Anschluss*** (AHN-shloos)
**Sudetenland** (soo-DEYT-n-land)

Sudetenland. Their goal was to keep peace in Europe, even if it meant making major concessions. Britain's prime minister, Neville Chamberlain (1869–1940), arrived home from Munich to announce that the meeting had achieved "peace for our time." Unprepared for war and distressed by the depression, nations sympathetic to Britain and France also embraced peace as an admirable goal in the face of aggression by the revisionist nations.

Hitler, however, quickly broke the promises he made in the Munich agreement, and in March 1939 German troops occupied and annexed most of Czechoslovakia. But when Hitler appeared ready to invade Poland just a short time later, the European nations that had supported appeasement realized that the policy had failed. Britain and France therefore guaranteed the security of Poland, which meant that they would declare war against Germany if it decided to invade. Meanwhile, in August 1939 Hitler and the Soviet Union's **Joseph Stalin** (1879–1953) concluded the **German-Soviet Non-Aggression Pact,** an agreement that shocked and outraged the world. By the terms of the pact, the two nations agreed not to attack each other, and they promised neutrality in the event that either of them went to war with a third party. Additionally, a secret protocol divided eastern Europe into German and Soviet spheres of influence. The protocol provided for German control over western Poland while granting the Soviet Union a free hand in eastern Poland, eastern Romania, Finland, Estonia, Latvia, and Lithuania. Hitler was now ready to conquer Europe.

## TOTAL WAR: THE WORLD UNDER FIRE

Two months after the United States became embroiled in World War II, President Franklin Roosevelt (1882–1945) delivered one of his famous radio broadcasts, known as fireside chats. In it he explained the nature of the war: "This war is a new kind of war," he said. "It is warfare in terms of every continent, every island, every sea, every air lane." There was little exaggeration in FDR's analysis. Before World War II was over, almost every nation and colonial territory in the world had participated in it. Battles raged across the vast Pacific and Atlantic oceans, across Europe and northern Africa, and throughout much of Asia. Virtually every weapon known to humanity was thrown into the war. Even more than the Great War, this was a conflict in which entire societies engaged in warfare and mobilized every available material and human resource.

Japan and China had already been at war for over eight years when, between 1939 and 1941, nations and territories inside and outside Europe were drawn into the conflict. They included the French and British colonies in Africa and India as well as the British Dominion allies of Canada, Australia, and New Zealand. Germany's stunning military successes in 1939 and 1940 focused attention on Europe, but after the Soviet Union and the United States entered the war in 1941, the conflict took on global proportions.

### Blitzkrieg: Germany Conquers Europe

During World War II it became common for aggressor nations to avoid overt declarations of war. Instead, the new armed forces relied on surprise, stealth, and swiftness for their conquests. Germany demonstrated the advantages of that strategy in Poland. German forces, banking on their air force's ability to soften resistance on the ground and on their *Panzer* ("armored") columns' unmatched mobility and speed, moved into Poland unannounced on 1 September 1939. Within a month they subdued its western expanses while the Soviets took the eastern sections in accordance with the Nazi-Soviet pact. The Germans stunned the world, especially Britain and France, with their ***Blitzkrieg*** ("lightning war") and sudden victory. The term *Blitzkrieg* was coined by journalists and is still used today, although it was never an official doctrine or concept of the German armed forces.

Honoring their commitment to guarantee the security of Poland, Britain and France declared war on Germany on September 3. While they gathered their forces to defend Europe, however, the war in the Atlantic began immediately. The battle of the Atlantic was the longest-running battle of the war, lasting from September 1939 through April 1945. During that time, German submarines (***Unterseeboote***) attempted to cut off

German dive-bombers like this one dominated the early air war in World War II and played a significant role in the German technique known as Blitzkrieg.
Bettmann/Getty Images

imports of food and war material to Britain, while the British navy formed convoys of ships to protect against submarine attack. In 1942 British intelligence cracked the secret German code used by submarines, which greatly aided the Allies. Despite having the codes, however, only 10 percent of the intercepted messages were decrypted in time to prevent attacks on British ships. The battle of the Atlantic thus remained an important and dangerous theater for the duration of the war.

**The Fall of France** In April 1940 the Germans occupied Denmark and Norway, then launched a full-scale attack on western Europe. By seizing control of Norway, the Germans gained control of the eastern North Sea and prevented Britain's navy from implementing a blockade. The German offensive against Belgium, France, and the Netherlands began in May, and again the Allies were overwhelmed by Blitzkrieg tactics. Belgium and the Netherlands fell in May, while the French signed an armistice in June. The fall of France convinced Italy's Benito Mussolini that the Germans were winning the war, and it was time to enter the conflict and reap any potential benefits his partnership with the Germans might offer.

Before the battle of France, Hitler had boasted to his staff, "Gentlemen, you are about to witness the most famous victory in history!" Given France's rapid fall, Hitler was not far wrong. Field Marshal Erwin Rommel put it more colorfully: "The war has become practically a lightning Tour de France!" In a moment of exquisite triumph, Hitler had the French sign their armistice in the very railroad car in which the Germans had signed the armistice in 1918. Trying to rescue some Allied troops before the fall of France, the British engineered a retreat at the coastal town of Dunkirk, but it could not hide the bleak failure of the Allied troops in their mission to defend Europe from Germany. Britain now stood alone against the German forces.

**The Battle of Britain** The Germans next turned their attention to defeating Britain. In July 1940 they launched the **Battle of Britain,** led by the German air force, the ***Luftwaffe.*** The goal was to defeat Britain almost solely through air attacks. "The Blitz," as the British called this air war, rained bombs on heavily populated metropolitan areas, especially London, and killed more than forty thousand British civilians. The Royal Air Force staved off defeat, however, and by the end of October 1940 Hitler abandoned plans to invade Britain. But Hitler's successes continued elsewhere. By the summer of 1941, his conquests included the Balkans, and the battlefront extended to north Africa, where the British fought both the Italians and the Germans. The swastika-bedecked Nazi flag now waved from the streets of Paris to the Acropolis in Athens, and Hitler had succeeded beyond his dreams in his quest to reverse the outcome of World War I.

***Luftwaffe*** (LOOFT-vaff-uh)

**Lebensraum** (LAY-behnz-rahwm)

## INTERPRETING IMAGES

Adolf Hitler proudly walks through conquered Paris in 1940, with the Eiffel Tower as a backdrop.

**Analyze** *What strikes you about this photo? Think back to images you analyzed from WWI. How might this photo have felt to those who saw it? Why did photographs of Hitler's triumph over France create intense shock and fear in Great Britain?*

Harwood/Keystone/Hulton Archive/Getty Images

## The German Invasion of the Soviet Union

Flush with victory in the spring of 1941, Hitler next turned his attention to the Soviet Union. Notwithstanding his nonaggression pact with the Soviet Union, Hitler had long coveted Soviet territory, where Jews, Slavs, and Bolsheviks could be expelled or exterminated to create more ***Lebensraum*** ("living space") for resettled Germans. Believing firmly in the bankruptcy of the Soviet system, Hitler said of **Operation Barbarossa,** the code name for the June invasion of the Soviet Union, "You only have to kick in the door, and the whole rotten structure will come crashing down."

**Operation Barbarossa** On June 22, 1941, Adolf Hitler ordered his armed forces to invade the Soviet Union. To do so, the German military assembled the largest and most powerful invasion force in history, attacking with 3.6 million soldiers, thirty-seven hundred tanks, and twenty-five hundred planes. Military contingents from Italy, Romania, Hungary, Slovakia, Croatia, and Finland—totaling some thirty divisions—augmented the German invasion force. The invasion, along a front of 3,000 kilometers (1,900 miles), took Stalin by surprise and caught the Red Army off guard. By December 1941 the Germans had captured the Russian heartland, Leningrad had come under siege, and German troops had reached the gates of Moscow. Germany seemed assured of victory.

But the German Blitzkrieg tactics that had earlier proved so effective in Poland and western Europe failed the Germans in the vast expanses of Russia. Hitler and his military leaders underestimated Soviet personnel reserves and industrial capacity. Within a matter of weeks, the 150 German divisions faced 360 divisions of the Red Army. Also, in the early stages of the invasion Stalin ordered Soviet industry to relocate to areas away from the front. About 80 percent of firms manufacturing war matériel moved to the Ural Mountains between August and October 1941. As a result, the capacity of Soviet industry outstripped that of German industry. The Soviets also received crucial equipment from their allies, notably trucks from the United States. By the time the German forces reached the outskirts of Moscow, fierce Soviet resistance had produced eight hundred thousand German casualties.

The arrival of winter—the most severe in decades—helped Soviet military efforts and prevented the Germans from capturing Moscow. The Germans had been so sure of a quick victory that they did not bother to supply their troops with winter clothing and boots. One hundred thousand German soldiers suffered frostbite, and two thousand of them underwent amputation. The Red Army, in contrast, prepared for winter and found further comfort as the United States manufactured thirteen million pairs of felt-lined winter boots. By early December, Soviet counterattacks along the entire front had halted German advances.

German forces regrouped and inflicted heavy losses on the Red Army during the spring of 1942. The Germans briefly regained the military initiative, and by June German armies raced toward the oil fields of the Caucasus and the city of **Stalingrad.** As the Germans came on Stalingrad in September, Soviet fortunes of war reached their nadir. At this point the Soviets dug in. "Not a step back," Stalin ordered, and he called on his troops to fight a "patriotic" war for Mother Russia. Behind those exhortations lay a desperate attempt to stall the Germans with a bloody street-by-street defense of Stalingrad until the Red Army could regroup for a counterattack.

## Battles in Asia and the Pacific

The United States, though officially neutral, inched toward greater involvement in the war between 1939 and 1941. In

## INTERPRETING IMAGES

Russian prisoners captured by the Germans after the battle of Kiev in September 1941. The German military engaged in murderous policies toward Soviet prisoners of war, killing 3.3 million men (out of a total of 5.7 million) through summary execution, exposure, and starvation.

**Analyze** *Consider the scope of this photo, and the statistics in the caption. How do both the numbers and image contrast with older wars you have studied? Does this make WWII seem different to you? How?*

Heinrich Hoffmann/Mondadori/Getty Images

1939 it instituted a cash-and-carry policy of supplying the British, in which the British paid cash and carried the materials across the Atlantic on their ships. More significant was the lend-lease program initiated in 1941, in which the United States "lent" destroyers and other war goods to the British in return for the lease of naval bases. The program later extended such aid to the Soviets, the Chinese, and many others.

**Pearl Harbor** German victories over the Dutch and the French in 1940 and Great Britain's precarious military position in Europe and in Asia encouraged the Japanese to project their influence into southeast Asia. Particularly attractive were the Dutch East Indies (now Indonesia) and British-controlled Malaya, regions rich in raw materials such as tin, rubber, and petroleum. In September 1940, moving with the blessings of the German-backed Vichy government in France, Japanese forces began to occupy French Indochina (now Vietnam, Laos, and Cambodia). The government of the United States responded to that situation by freezing Japanese assets in the United States and by imposing a complete embargo on oil. Great Britain, the British Commonwealth of Nations, and the colonial government of the Dutch East Indies supported the U.S. oil embargo. Economic pressure, however, did not persuade the Japanese to comply with U.S. demands, which included the renunciation of the Tripartite Pact with Germany and Italy and the withdrawal of Japanese forces from China and southeast Asia. To Japanese militarists, given the equally unappetizing alternatives of giving in to U.S. demands or engaging the United States in war, war seemed the lesser of two evils. In October 1941, defense minister general Tojo Hideki (1884–1948) assumed the office of prime minister, and he and his cabinet set in motion plans for war against Great Britain and the United States.

The Japanese hoped to quickly destroy American naval capacity in the Pacific with an attack at **Pearl Harbor.** The attack would then clear the way for the conquest of southeast Asia and the creation of a defensive Japanese perimeter that would prevent the Allies' from striking at Japan's homeland. On December 7, 1941, Japanese pilots took off from six aircraft carriers to attack Hawai`i. More than 350 Japanese bombers, fighters, and torpedo planes struck in two waves, sinking or disabling eighteen ships and destroying more than two hundred aircraft. Except for the U.S. aircraft carriers, which were out of the harbor at the time, American naval power in the Pacific was devastated. The next day, on December 8, the United States and Great Britain declared war on Japan.

On December 11, 1941, though not compelled to do so by treaty, Hitler and Mussolini declared war on the United States. That move provided the United States with the only reason it needed to declare war on Germany and Italy. The United States, Great Britain, and the Soviet Union came together in a coalition that linked two vast and interconnected theaters of war, the European and Asian-Pacific theaters, and ensured the defeat of Germany and Japan. Adolf Hitler's gleeful reaction

Flames consumed U.S. battleships in Pearl Harbor after the Japanese attack on 7 December 1941. Bettmann/Getty Images

to the outbreak of war between Japan and the United States proved mistaken: "Now it is impossible for us to lose the war: We now have an ally who has never been vanquished in three thousand years." More accurate was **Winston Churchill** (1874–1965), prime minister of Britain, who expressed a vast sense of relief and a more accurate assessment of the situation when he said, "So we had won after all!"

**Japanese Victories** After Pearl Harbor the Japanese swept on to one victory after another. The Japanese coordinated their strike against Pearl Harbor with simultaneous attacks against the Philippines, Guam, Wake Island, Midway Island, Hong Kong, Thailand, and British Malaya. For the next year the Japanese military maintained the initiative in southeast Asia and the Pacific, capturing Borneo, Burma, the Dutch East Indies, and several Aleutian Islands off Alaska. Australia and New Zealand were now in striking distance. The Japanese navy emerged almost unscathed from these campaigns. The humiliating surrender of British-held Singapore in February 1942 dealt a blow to British prestige and shattered any myths of European military invincibility.

Singapore was a symbol of European power in Asia. The slogan under which Japan pursued expansion in Asia was "Asia for Asians," implying that the Japanese would lead Asian peoples to independence from the despised European imperialists and the international order they dominated. In this struggle for Asian independence, Japan required the region's resources and therefore sought to build what they called a **Greater East Asia Co-Prosperity Sphere.** The appeal to Asian independence at first struck a responsive chord among some anticolonial activists such as Sukarno in the Dutch East Indies, but conquest and brutal occupation made it soon obvious to most Asians that the real agenda was "Asia for the Japanese." Proponents of the Greater East Asia Co-Prosperity Sphere advocated Japan's expansion in Asia and the Pacific while cloaking their territorial and economic designs with the idealism of Asian nationalism.

## Defeat of the Axis Powers

The entry of the Soviet Union and the United States into the war in 1941 was decisive because personnel reserves and industrial capacity were the keys to the Allied victories in the European and Asia-Pacific theaters. Despite the brutal exploitation of conquered territories, neither German nor Japanese war production matched that of the Allies, who outproduced their enemies. The U.S. automotive industry alone, for instance, produced more than four million armored, combat, and supply vehicles of all kinds during the war. In the Atlantic,

## INTERPRETING IMAGES

After the Pearl Harbor attack, Americans expressed great hostility toward the Japanese nationals and Japanese Americans living in the United States, primarily on the west coast. In 1942 President Franklin Roosevelt authorized the forcible removal of approximately 120,000 Japanese and Japanese Americans to relocation or internment camps. This photograph shows interned Japanese people behind barbed wire at Santa Anita camp in California.

**Analyze** *Consider this photo in the context of the earlier image of Pearl Harbor. How might that previous photo be used to justify what is portrayed here? Why did some Americans believe this response was not justified?*

Everett Collection Historical/Alamy Stock Photo

although German submarines sank a total of 2,452 Allied merchant ships and 175 Allied warships over the course of six years, after 1942 U.S. naval shipyards simply built more "Liberty Ships" than the Germans could sink. By the end of 1943, sonar, aircraft patrols, and escort aircraft from carriers eliminated the U-boat as a strategic threat.

**Allied Victory in Europe** By 1943, German forces in Russia lost momentum and faced bleak prospects as the Soviets retook territory. Moscow never fell, and the battle for Stalingrad, which ended in February 1943, marked the first large-scale victory for Soviet forces. Desperate German counteroffensives failed repeatedly, and the Red Army, drawing on enormous personnel and material reserves, pushed the German invaders out of Russian territory. By 1944 the Soviets had advanced into Romania, Hungary, and Poland, reaching the suburbs of Berlin in April 1945. At that point, the Soviets had inflicted more than six million casualties on the German enemy—twice the number of the original German invasion force. The Red Army had broken the back of the German war machine.

With the eastern front disintegrating under the Soviet onslaught, British and U.S. forces attacked the Germans from north Africa and then through Italy. In August 1944 the Allies forced Italy to withdraw from the Axis and to join them. In the

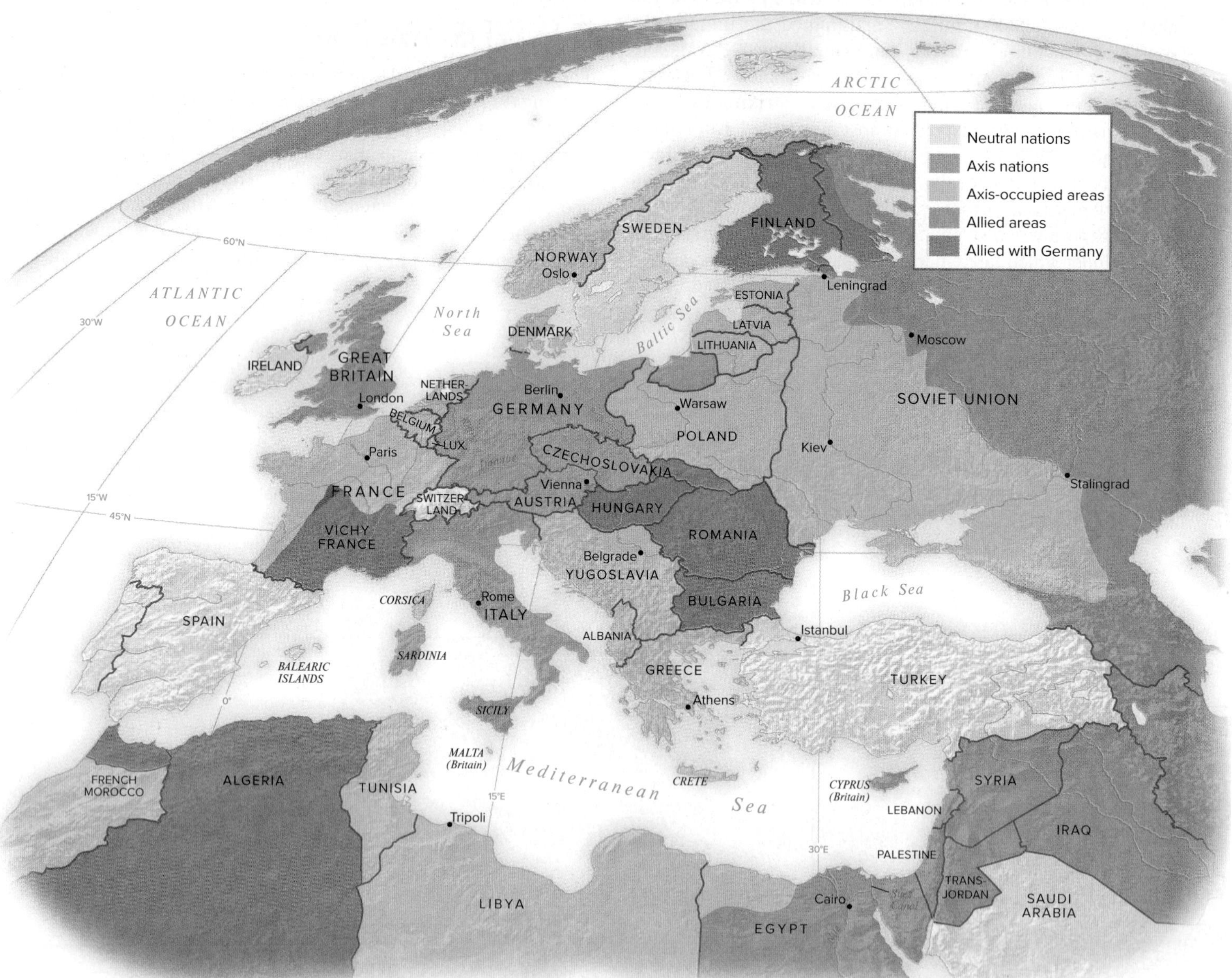


**MAP 24.1 High tide of Axis expansion in Europe and north Africa, 1942–1943.**

Observe the number of nations occupied by or allied with the Axis powers.

***Given Axis dominance in Europe, what factors finally allowed the Allies to turn the tide of war in their favor?***

meantime, the Germans also prepared for an Allied offensive in the west, where the British and U.S. forces opened a front in France. On **D-Day,** June 6, 1944, British and U.S. troops landed on the French coast of Normandy. Although the fighting was deadly for all sides, the Germans were overwhelmed. With the two fronts collapsing around them and round-the-clock strategic bombing by the United States and Britain leveling German cities, German resistance faded. Since early 1943, Britain's Royal Air Force had committed itself to area bombing in which city centers became the targets of nighttime raids. U.S. planes attacked industrial targets in daytime. The British firebombing raid on Dresden in February 1945 was particularly devastating, as one hundred thirty-five thousand German men, women, and children died in the firestorm. A brutal street-by-street battle in Berlin between Germans and Russians, along with a sweep through western Germany by British and U.S. troops, forced Germany's unconditional surrender on May 8, 1945. A week earlier, on April 30, as fighting flared right outside his Berlin bunker, Hitler committed suicide along with his mistress Eva Braun, as did many of his Nazi compatriots. He therefore did not live to see the Soviet red flag flying over the Berlin *Reichstag,* Germany's parliament building.

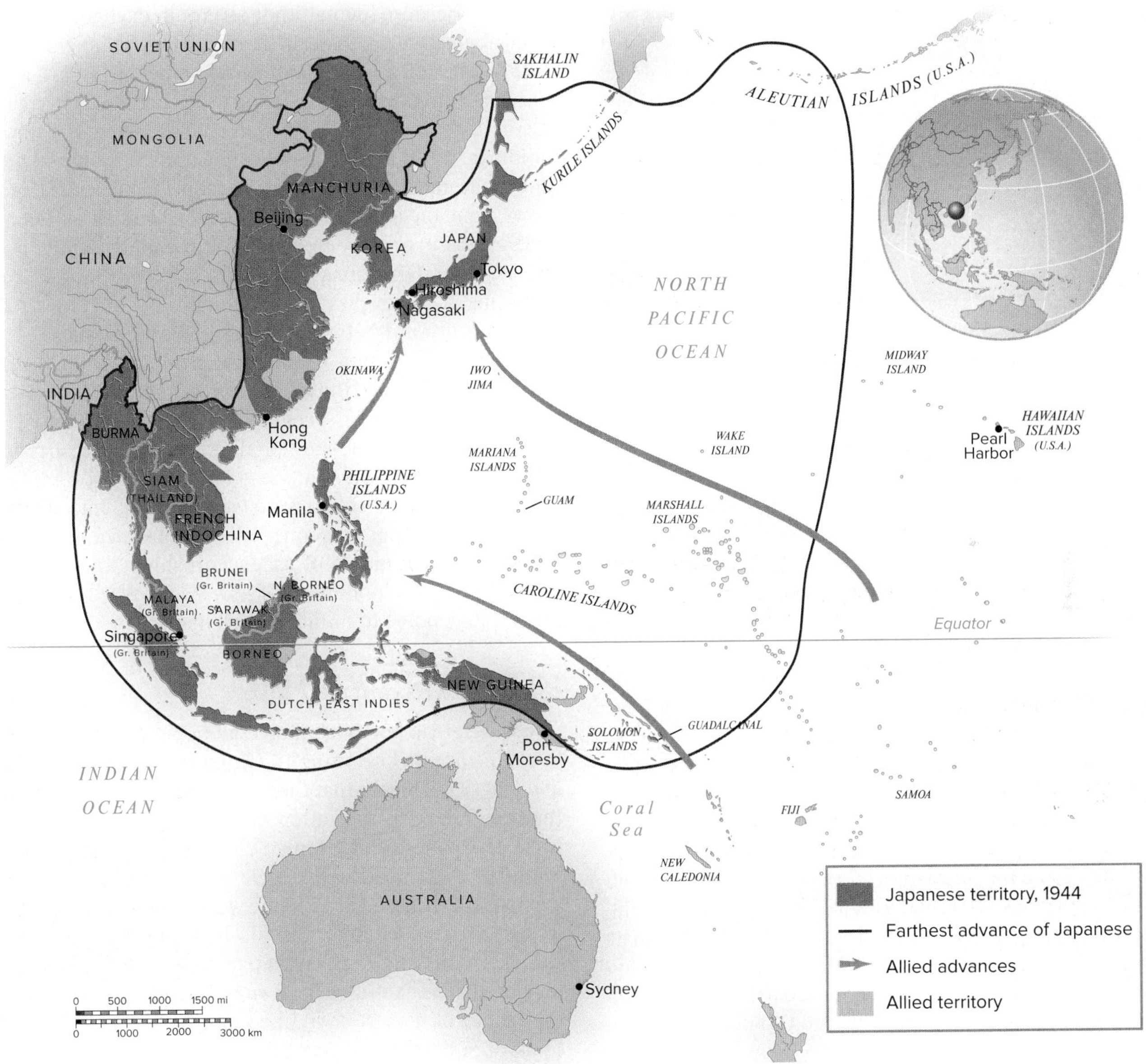


## MAP 24.2 World War II in Asia and the Pacific.

Compare the geographic conditions of the Asian-Pacific theater with those of the European theater.

***What kinds of resources were necessary to win in the Asian-Pacific theater as opposed to the European theater?***

***How do you compare and contrast the importance of Axis (Map 24.1) and Japanese victories? What was the goal of each of these empires, and how can we put these conquests in the context of our larger understandings of colonialism?***

A photograph titled *Planes over Tokyo Bay,* taken from the U.S.S. *Missouri,* visually captured a sense of U.S. power and victory on V-J Day (Victory over Japan Day), 1945.
Hulton Deutsch/Corbis Historical/Getty Images

**Turning the Tide in the Pacific** The turning point in the Pacific war came in a naval engagement near the Midway Islands on June 4, 1942. The United States prevailed there partly because U.S. aircraft carriers had survived the attack on Pearl Harbor. Although the United States had few carriers, it did have a secret weapon: a code-breaking operation known as *Magic,* which enabled a cryptographer monitoring Japanese radio frequencies to discover the plan to attack Midway. On the morning of 4 June, thirty-six carrier-launched dive-bombers attacked the Japanese fleet, sinking three Japanese carriers in one five-minute strike and a fourth one later in the day. This victory changed the character of the war in the Pacific. Although there was no immediate shift in Japanese fortunes, the Allies took the offensive. They adopted an island-hopping strategy, capturing islands from which they could make direct air assaults on Japan. Deadly fighting characterized these battles in which the United States and its allies gradually retook islands in the Marianas and the Philippines and then, early in 1945, moved toward areas more threatening to Japan: the islands of Iwo Jima and Okinawa.

**Iwo Jima and Okinawa** The fighting on **Iwo Jima** and **Okinawa** was savage. Innovative U.S. amphibious tactics were matched by the sacrifice of Japanese soldiers and pilots. On Okinawa the Japanese introduced the ***kamikaze***—pilots who "volunteered" to fly planes with just enough fuel to reach an Allied ship and dive-bomb into it. In the two-month battle, the Japanese flew nineteen hundred kamikaze missions, sinking dozens of ships and killing more than five thousand U.S. soldiers. The kamikaze, and the defense mounted by Japanese forces and the 110,000 Okinawan civilians who died refusing to surrender, convinced many people in the United States that the Japanese would never willingly surrender.

**Japanese Surrender** The fall of Saipan in July 1944 and the subsequent conquest of Iwo Jima and Okinawa brought the Japanese homeland within easy reach of U.S. strategic bombers. Because high-altitude strikes in daylight failed to do much damage to industrial sites, military planners changed tactics. The release of napalm firebombs during low-altitude missions at night met with devastating success. The firebombing of Tokyo in March 1945 destroyed 25 percent of the city's buildings, killed approximately one hundred thousand people, and made more than a million people homeless. The final blows came on August 6 and 9, 1945, when the United States used a revolutionary new weapon, the atomic bomb, against the cities of **Hiroshima** and **Nagasaki.** The atomic bombs either instantaneously vaporized or slowly killed by radiation poisoning upward of two hundred thousand people.

The Soviet Union declared war on Japan on 8 August 1945, and this new threat, combined with the devastation caused by the bombs, persuaded Emperor Hirohito (1901–1989) to surrender unconditionally. The Japanese surrendered on 15 August, and the war was officially over on 2 September 1945. When Victor Tolley—who we met in the introduction to this chapter—sipped his conciliatory cup of tea with a Nagasaki family, the images of ashen Hiroshima and firebombed Tokyo lingered as reminders of how World War II brought the war directly home to millions of civilians.

## LIFE DURING WARTIME

The widespread bombing of civilian populations during World War II, from its beginning in China to its end in Hiroshima and Nagasaki, meant that there was no safe home front during the war. The arrival of often brutal occupation forces in the wake of Japanese and German conquests in Asia and Europe reinforced this reality. Strategic bombing slaughtered men, women, and children around the world, and occupation troops forced civilians to labor and die in work and extermination camps. In this total war, civilian death tolls far exceeded military casualties. Yet alongside such terrible brutality remains the record of human endurance, personified in the contributions of resistance groups battling occupying forces, in the determination of mobilized civilians, and in the survivors of bombings or concentration camps.

### Occupation, Collaboration, and Resistance

Axis bombardments and invasion were followed by occupation, but the administration imposed on conquered territories by

***kamikaze*** (KAH-mih-kah-zee)

The writing on the board displayed by German security forces in Minsk, Belarus, reads, "We are partisans who shot at German soldiers." The Germans murdered some 700,000 civilians, mostly Belarusians and Poles, in so-called antipartisan reprisals. Women and children were included in the "reprisal" because they were considered an encumbrance. Sueddeutsche Zeitung Photo/Alamy Stock Photo

Japanese and German forces varied in character. In territories such as **Manchukuo,** Japanese-controlled China, Burma, and the Philippines, Japanese authorities installed puppet governments that served as agents of Japanese rule. Thailand remained an independent state after it aligned itself with Japan, for which it was rewarded with grants of territory from bordering Laos and Burma. Other conquered territories either were considered too unstable or unreliable for self-rule or were deemed strategically too important to be left alone. Thus territories such as Indochina (Laos, Cambodia, and Vietnam), Malaya, the Dutch East Indies, Hong Kong, Singapore, Borneo, and New Guinea came under direct military control.

In Europe, Hitler's racist ideology played a large role in determining how occupied territories were administered. As a rule, Hitler intended that most areas of western and northern Europe–populated by people he believed to be "racially valuable"–would become part of a Greater Germanic Empire. Accordingly, Denmark retained its elected government and monarchy under German supervision. In Norway and Holland, whose governments had gone into exile, the Germans left the civilian administration intact. Though northern France and the Atlantic coast came under military rule, the **Vichy** government remained the civilian authority in the unoccupied southeastern part of the country. Named for its locale in central France, the Vichy government provided a prominent place for those French willing to collaborate with German rule. The Germans had varying levels of involvement in eastern European and Balkan countries, but most conquered territories came under direct military rule as a prelude to brutal harsh occupation, economic exploitation, and German settlement.

**Exploitation** Japanese and German authorities administered their respective empires for economic gain and proceeded to exploit the resources of the lands under their control for their own benefit, regardless of the consequences for conquered peoples. The occupiers pillaged all forms of economic wealth that could fuel the German and Japanese war machines. The most notorious form of economic exploitation involved the use of slave labor. As the demands of total war stimulated an insatiable appetite for workers, Japanese and German occupation authorities used prisoners of war (POWs) and local populations to help meet labor shortages. By August 1944, more than seven million foreign workers labored inside Germany's Third Reich. And in China alone, the Japanese military mobilized more than ten million civilians and prisoners of war for forced labor. These enslaved laborers worked under horrific conditions and received little in the way of sustenance. Reaction to Japanese and German occupation varied from willing collaboration and acquiescence to open resistance.

**Atrocities** The treatment of POWs by German and Japanese authorities spoke to the horrors of the war as well. The death rate among soldiers in Japanese captivity averaged almost 30 percent, although it was even higher among Chinese POWs. The racial ideologies of Hitler's regime were reflected in the treatment meted out to Soviet prisoners of war in particular. By February 1942, 2 million out of the 3.3 million Soviet soldiers in German custody had died from starvation, exposure, disease, or outright murder.

**Vichy** (vee-shee)

Beyond the callous mistreatment of POWs, both German and Japanese authorities engaged in painful and often deadly medical experiments on thousands of unwilling subjects. In China, special Japanese military units, including the most infamous Unit 731, conducted cruel experiments on civilians and POWs. Victims, for example, became the subject of vivisection (defined as experimental surgery conducted on a living organism) or amputation without anesthesia. Tens of thousands of Chinese became victims of germ warfare experiments after they were deliberately infected with bubonic plague, cholera, anthrax, and other diseases. German physicians carried out similarly unethical medical experiments in concentration camps. Experimentation ranged from bone-grafting surgeries without anesthesia to exposing victims to phosgene and mustard gas in order to test possible antidotes. German doctors also directed painful experiments to determine how different "races" withstood various contagious diseases.

**Collaboration** The majority of people resented occupation forces but tried to go on with life as much as possible. That response was especially true in many parts of Japanese-occupied lands in Asia, where local populations found little to resent in the change from one colonial administration to another. In Asia and Europe, moreover, local notables often joined the governments sponsored by the conquerors because collaboration offered them the means to gain power. Businesspeople and companies often collaborated because they prospered financially from foreign rule. Still other people became collaborators and assisted occupation authorities by turning in friends and neighbors to get revenge for past grievances. In western Europe, anticommunism motivated Belgians, French, Danish, Dutch, and Norwegians to join units of Hitler's elite military formations, the Waffen SS, creating in the process a multinational army tens of thousands strong. In violation of its own racial policies, the SS also accepted volunteers from the Balkans, eastern Europe, and the Caucasus. In China several Guomindang generals went over to the Japanese, and local landowners and merchants in some regions of China set up substantial trade networks between the occupiers and the occupied.

**Resistance** Occupation and exploitation created an environment for resistance that took various forms. The most dramatic forms of resistance were campaigns of sabotage, armed assaults on occupation forces, and assassinations. Resistance fighters as diverse as Filipino guerrillas and Soviet partisans harassed and disrupted the military and economic activities of the occupiers by blowing up ammunition dumps, destroying communication and transportation facilities, and sabotaging industrial plants. Less conspicuously, other resisters gathered intelligence, hid and protected refugees, or passed on clandestine newspapers. Resistance also comprised simple acts of defiance such as scribbling anti-German graffiti or walking out of bars and restaurants when Japanese soldiers entered. In the Netherlands, people associated the royal House of Orange with national independence and defiantly saluted traffic lights when they turned orange.

German and Japanese citizens faced different decisions about resistance than conquered peoples did. For them, any form of noncompliance constituted an act of treason that might assist the enemy and lead to defeat. Moreover, many institutions that might have formed the core of resistance in Japan and Germany, such as political parties, labor unions, or churches, were weak or had been destroyed. As a result, there was little or no overt opposition to the state and its policies in Japan, and in Germany resistance remained generally sparse and ineffective. The most spectacular act of resistance against the Nazi regime came from a group of officers and civilians who tried to kill Adolf Hitler on July 20, 1944. The plot failed when their bomb explosion killed several bystanders but inflicted only minor injuries on Hitler.

Attempts to eradicate resistance movements often fanned the flames of rebellion because of the indiscriminate reprisals against civilians. Despite the deadly retaliation meted out to people who resisted occupation, widespread resistance movements grew throughout the war. Life in resistance movements was tenuous at best and entailed great hardship—changing identities, hiding out, and risking capture and death. Nevertheless, the resisters kept alive their nations' hopes for liberation.

## The Holocaust

By the end of World War II, the Nazi regime and its accomplices had murdered millions of Jews, Slavs, Roma (or Gypsies), and others targeted as undesirables. Jews were the primary target of Hitler's racially motivated genocidal policies. These

This photograph, taken in 2003, shows a portion of the perimeter fence at Auschwitz concentration camp. The sign in the foreground reads: "Caution. High Voltage. Danger to Life." The Auschwitz complex established in German-occupied Poland was essentially two camps in one, a labor camp and an extermination camp that took the lives of some one million Jews.
Courtesy of Herbert F. Ziegler

## How the Past Shapes the Future 

### The Destructive Potential of Industrial Technologies

World War I had demonstrated that states were willing to harness industrial technologies on a massive scale for the purpose of destroying their enemies. Many observers were horrified by this, as we know, and as a result large numbers of people around the world advocated peace as a global priority during the interwar years. But during World War II, states nevertheless unleashed even more destructive industrial technologies on their enemies than they had in World War I—and now, they specifically targeted civilian populations in addition to enemy combatants. One particularly chilling example of this was Hitler's "final solution," which sought to exterminate all the Jewish people using industrial technologies and methods. Using railways, poison gas, and a factory-like system that maximized the numbers of people who could be moved, murdered, and disposed of, the German system industrialized genocide. Consider the extent to which the use of industrial technologies during World War I might have impressed the young Adolf Hitler, who himself had fought in the war.

policies resulted in what has come to be known as the **Holocaust**, or the near elimination of European Jews by Germany, which was a human disaster on an unprecedented scale.

The murder of European Jews was preceded by a long history of vilification and persecution. For centuries Jewish communities had been singled out by Christian society as a "problem," and by the time the Nazi regime assumed power in 1933, anti-Semitism had contributed significantly to widespread tolerance for anti-Jewish measures. Marked as outsiders, Jews found few defenders in their societies. Nazi determination to destroy the Jewish population in Europe and Europeans' passive acceptance of anti-Semitism laid the groundwork for genocide.

During the 1930s through the early years of the war, the German government encouraged Jewish emigration. Although tens of thousands of Jews availed themselves of the opportunity to

FINLAND
NORWAY
SWEDEN
ESTONIA
LATVIA
North Sea
Baltic Sea
DENMARK
LITHUANIA
EAST PRUSSIA
UNITED KINGDOM
Esterwegen
Ravensbruck
Sachsenhausen
NETHER-LANDS
Bergen-Belsen
GERMANY
Sachsenburg
Buchenwald
Ohrdruf
BELGIUM
LUX.
FRANCE
Treblinka
Chelmno
POLAND
Majdanek
Sobibor
Belzec
Auschwitz/Birkenau
Theresienstadt
CZECHOSLOVAKIA
Dachau
Mauthausen
AUSTRIA
SWITZER-LAND
HUNGARY
ROMANIA
ITALY
YUGOSLAVIA
U.S.S.R.
Black Sea
0 100 200 mi
0 100 200 km

■ Major concentration camps
♦ Major extermination camps from 1942
● Euthanasia operations
Neutral countries
The high tide of Axis expansion in Europe
Territory controlled by the Allies

**Map 24.3 The Holocaust in Europe, 1933–1945.**

Observe the geographic locations of the concentration and extermination camps.

***Why were there more concentration camps in Germany and more extermination camps in Poland?***

***Given the number of death camps across Europe, why didn't the Allies prevent the Germans from killing such a large proportion of Europe's Jewish population?***

## SOURCES FROM THE PAST

### "We Will Never Speak about It in Public"

*On 4 October 1943, Heinrich Himmler, leader of the SS and chief of the German police, gave a three-hour speech to an assembly of SS generals in the city of Posen (Poznan), in what is now Poland. In the following excerpt, Himmler justified Nazi anti-Jewish policies that culminated in mass murder. The speech, recorded on tape and in handwritten notes, was entered into evidence at the Nuremberg war crimes trials in 1945.*

**I also want to speak** to you here, in complete frankness, of a really grave chapter. Amongst ourselves, for once, it shall be said quite openly, but all the same we will never speak about it in public. . . .

I am referring here to the evacuation of the Jews, the extermination of the Jewish people. This is one of the things that is easily said: "The Jewish people are going to be exterminated," that's what every Party member says, "sure, it's in our program, elimination of the Jews, extermination—it'll be done." And then they all come along, the 80 million worthy Germans, and each one has his one decent Jew. Of course, the others are swine, but this one, he is a first-rate Jew. Of all those who talk like that, not one has seen it happen, not one has had to go through with it. Most of you men know what it is like to see 100 corpses side by side, or 500 or 1,000. To have stood fast through this and except for cases of human weakness to have stayed decent, that has made us hard. This is an unwritten and never-to-be-written page of glory in our history. . . .

> What was Himmler's point here about "decent" Jews?

The wealth they possessed we took from them. I gave a strict order, which has been carried out by SS *Obergruppenfuehrer* Pohl, that this wealth will of course be turned over to the Reich in its entirety. We have taken none of it for ourselves. Individuals who have erred will be punished in accordance with the order given by me at the start, threatening that anyone who takes as much as a single Mark of this money is a dead man. A number of SS men, they are not very many, committed this offense, and they shall die. There will be no mercy. We had the moral right, we had the duty towards our people, to destroy this people that wanted to destroy us. But we do not have the right to enrich ourselves by so much as a fur, as a watch, by one Mark or a cigarette or anything else. We do not want, in the end, because we destroyed a bacillus, to be infected by this bacillus and to die. I will never stand by and watch while even a small rotten spot develops or takes hold. Wherever it may form we will together burn it away. All in all, however, we can say that we have carried out this most difficult of tasks in a spirit of love for our people. And we have suffered no harm to our inner being, our soul, our character. . . .

> Why was it so important to Himmler that individual Germans not take the wealth of murdered Jews?

#### For Further Reflection

- Himmler argued that SS officers and soldiers "stayed decent" while overseeing the extermination of the Jews; how, according to him, was this possible?
- If Himmler was so certain of the justification of the policy of extermination of the Jews, why did he claim "we will never speak about it in the public"?
- What did he consider a "page of glory in our history"? How could he claim that it was "a spirit of love for our people"?

*Source: Himmler, Heinrich. " We Will Never Speak about It in Public" (The Complete Text of the Poznan Speech), October 4, 1943, Translation used with permission of the Holocaust History Project (www.holocaust-history.org).*

escape from Germany and Austria, many more were unable to do so. Most nations outside the Nazi orbit limited the migration of Jewish refugees, especially if the refugees were impoverished (as many were because Nazi authorities had previously appropriated their wealth). This situation worsened as German armies overran Europe, bringing an ever-larger number of Jews under Nazi control. At that point Nazi "racial experts" toyed with the idea of deporting Jews to Nisko, a proposed reservation in eastern Poland, or to the island of Madagascar, near Africa. Those ideas, however, proved to be impractical.

**The Final Solution** The German occupation of Poland in 1939 and invasion of the Soviet Union in the summer of 1941 gave Hitler an opportunity to solve what he considered the problem of Jews in Germany and in Europe. When German armies invaded the Soviet Union in June 1941, the Nazis dispatched three thousand troops in mobile detachments known as SS ***Einsatzgruppen*** ("action squads") to kill entire populations of Jews, Roma (or Gypsies), and many non-Jewish Slavs in

***Einsatzgruppen*** (INE-zahts-GROO-pen)

the newly occupied territories. The action squads undertook mass shootings in ditches and ravines that became mass graves. By the spring of 1943, the special units had killed over one million Jews, and tens of thousands of Soviet citizens and Roma.

Sometime during 1941 the Nazi leadership committed to what they called the **"final solution"** of the Jewish question, a plan to murder every Jew living in Europe. At the **Wannsee Conference** on January 20, 1942, fifteen leading Nazi bureaucrats gathered to discuss and coordinate the implementation of the final solution. They agreed to evacuate all Jews from Europe to camps in eastern Poland, where they would be worked to death or exterminated. Soon after, German forces—aided by collaborating authorities in foreign countries—rounded up Jews and deported them to specially constructed concentration camps in occupied Poland. The victims, whether they were from nearby Polish ghettos or distant assembly points all across Europe, traveled to their destinations by train. On the way the sick and the elderly often perished in overcrowded freight cars. The Jewish victims packed into these suffocating railway cars never knew their destinations, but rumors of mass deportations and mass deaths nonetheless spread among Jews remaining at large and among the Allied government leaders, who were frequently apathetic to the fate of Jews.

In camps such as Kulmhof (Chelmno), Belzec, Majdanek, Sobibor, Treblinka, and Auschwitz, the final solution took on an organized and technologically sophisticated character. Here, the killers introduced gassing as the most efficient means for mass extermination, though other means of destruction were always retained, such as electrocution, phenol injections, flamethrowers, hand grenades, and machine guns. The largest of the camps was Auschwitz, where at least one million Jews perished. Nazi camp personnel subjected victims from all corners of Europe to industrial work, starvation, medical experiments, and outright extermination. The German commandant of **Auschwitz** explained proudly how his camp became the most efficient at killing Jews: by using the fast-acting crystallized prussic acid Zyklon B as the gassing agent, by enlarging the size of the gas chambers, and by lulling victims into thinking they were going through a delousing process. At Auschwitz and elsewhere, the Germans also constructed large crematories to incinerate the bodies of gassed Jews and hide the evidence of their crimes. This systematic murder of Jews constituted what war crime tribunals later termed a "crime against humanity."

**Jewish Resistance** The murder of European Jewry was carried out with the help of the latest technology and with the utmost efficiency. For most of the victims, the will to resist was sapped by prolonged starvation, disease, and mistreatment. Nevertheless, there was fierce Jewish resistance throughout the war. Thousands of Jews joined anti-Nazi partisan groups and resistance movements while others led rebellions in concentration camps or participated in ghetto uprisings from Minsk to Krakow. The best-known uprising took place in the Warsaw ghetto in the spring of 1943. Lacking adequate weapons, sixty thousand Jews who remained in the ghetto that had once held four hundred thousand rose against their tormentors. It took German security forces using tanks and flamethrowers three weeks to crush the uprising. In total, approximately 5.7 million Jews perished in the Holocaust.

## Women and the War

Observing the extent to which British women mobilized for war, the U.S. ambassador to London noted, "This war, more

### INTERPRETING IMAGES

Natalya Kravtsova (left) and Irina Sebrova (right) were pilots in the Soviet Airforce's 588th Night Bomber Regiment, and are pictured here in front of a PO 2 aircraft. Sebrova flew 825 bombing missions during World War II, and in 1945 was awarded the title "Hero of the Soviet Union" for her service.

**Analyze** *Why did Soviet women serve as pilots during WWII and women from other Allied countries did not?*

TASS/Getty Images

# Connecting the Sources

## Exploring perspective and neutrality in the historical interpretation of World War II

**The problem** More than sixty million people died in World War II. Millions more suffered intensely but ultimately survived the ordeal. Because World War II occurred within living memory, millions of individuals around the world still feel intimately connected with it—if not through their own experiences, then through the stories of their family members of an older generation. As a result, it is still understandably difficult for historians and nonhistorians alike to consider the war from a neutral perspective. Moreover, although all the countries that actively participated in the war engaged in brutalities, both the German and the Japanese states sanctioned extreme brutalities against civilian populations—which included massive campaigns of genocide, forced prostitution, forced labor, and medical experiments. These appalling events have resulted in a marked reluctance to discuss the suffering of ordinary Germans not targeted by the Holocaust or of ordinary Japanese because doing so has been associated with cheapening the experience of the millions who suffered and died as a result of German and Japanese national policies. The implication, though not usually stated explicitly, is that not all human suffering in World War II should be explored equally. Let us consider two sources as a way of considering the ways that our own proximity to traumatic historical events might affect the ways we interpret the past.

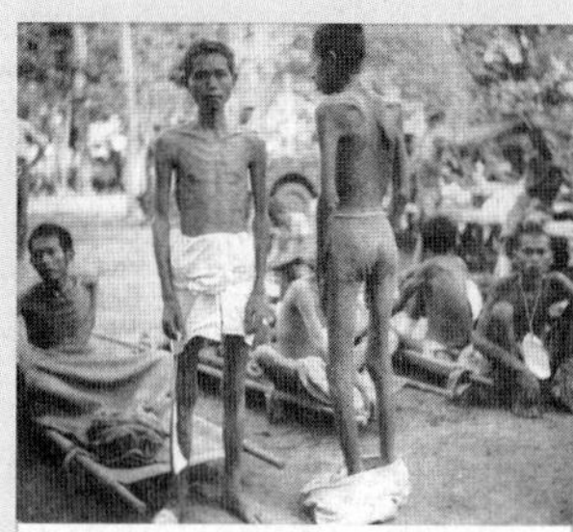

Indonesians who had been recruited by the Japanese to work as *romushas* (forced laborers).
Image bank WW2 – NIOD

**The documents** Read the documents below, and consider carefully the questions that follow.

### Document 1:

*Dulrahman, a Javanese farmer born in 1920, was one of approximately 250,000 laborers forced by the Japanese to work on various war-related projects in southeast Asia during World War II. These work battalions were called* romushas. *Although* romushas *were told they would receive pay when they were recruited, instead they found themselves working without pay in extremely difficult conditions and with little food. As a result, over half did not survive the war.*

*In June 1942, a Japanese soldier by the name of Kawakubu came to our village and asked my father if there were any people who could work, for wages, of course. My father then gave him my name. They first assigned me to help build a tunnel at Parangtritis, south of Yogya, on the coast. We didn't get paid at all, however, and they told my father they'd kill him if he'd come to fetch me. Sure, the Japanese told us repeatedly: "We've come to free you from colonial oppression." But meanwhile they forced us to work for them!*

Why did Dulrahman's father agree to let his son work for the Japanese in 1942?

*We left from Gunung Kidul for Parangtritis with about 500 people. My estimate is that about 300 survived. It's hard to be precise, for people were not buried but simply tossed into the sea. Some eight months later they shipped us out by the hundreds, including about 100 people belonging to the Gunung Kidul group. It turned out that they had taken us to Digul (in Irian Jaya, a former Dutch penal colony in what was then New Guinea) to cut trees for building a road and a prison. Compared to this place, Parangtritis had been pleasant. There at least we got a piece of cassava the size of my fist, and we could fetch water from a small mountain lake. In Digul, however, we were left to our own devices and so we had to forage for ourselves. For food, you had to look in the jungle. We ate leaves, and any snake you'd find was good for roasting.*

*Finally, they told us we could go home. Everybody was elated. . . . But about halfway, in the middle of the ocean, we began to ask ourselves: "Where on earth are they taking us this time?" There was no land to be seen anywhere. The voyage took a month. We finally arrived and got off the ship and that's when we panicked: Where on earth were we? This wasn't Indonesia, but then what country was it? After one week, I found out that we were in Burma.*

Devastation in the aftermath of the bombing of Hiroshima.
Bettmann/Getty Images

*In Burma, life for a romusha was terrible. But compared to Digul it was better. . . . if we did anything wrong, [the Japanese would] beat us up vigorously with their rubber truncheons. That was no joke. If you got beaten with that truncheon it would remove your skin when bouncing back, and that caused a lot of pain.*

*We spent exactly one year in Burma. . . . One day, our foreman let it slip that we'd be going home in two weeks. . . . When I arrived [back home], everybody cried. They thought I'd been dead long since. I certainly looked quite different. . . . During the first month, my family treated me a bit like a retiree, as it were. I was not allowed to work and they fed me very well. . . .*

*I still dream a lot about those days, especially about the work we did: dragging stones, that sort of thing. And about that voyage across the sea. Those high waves. That results in a nightmare once in a while, and then I find myself screaming out loud. . . . My gosh, to think that after 50 years I'm still dreaming about that!*

## Document 2

*Kosaku Okabe was a young Japanese soldier who had seen combat many times over the course of the war. The day after the Hiroshima bombing, on August 7, he and some fellow soldiers took the train to Hiroshima, knowing only that a bomb had been dropped on the city. The passengers were told to get out on the outskirts of the city, as the train was going no further. Once Kosaku got out, he realized it was because the train tracks had been completely destroyed. What follows is what Kosaku saw as he moved closer to the epicenter.*

*In front of me, smoke still overhung the city, and there was increasing confusion as the people leaving the city met those trying to enter it. I began to come across people with tattered clothing and injuries of a kind I had never seen before. By now the area around me was a burned-out wasteland, with no houses standing. It was when I crossed what I think was the Ota River, though, that I really seemed to step into hell . . . Dead bodies lay where they had fallen. The great cherry trees that had lined the embankment were stripped of their branches, which were now hanging down in shreds from their trunks. Looking downstream to the river mouth, I saw strange black shapes almost obliterating the sparkling sandbars . . . . as I drew nearer I realized that in reality they were dead bodies, possibly deposited there by the river . . . Farther on, in the water, floated countless bodies of men, women, and children. The misery was indescribable.*

What difference does it make to read about civilian deaths versus those of military combatants? Is it more difficult or the same for both groups? Why?

## Questions

1. What can these documents definitively tell you about their respective situations? What facts can be gleaned from these brief sources?
2. In Document 1, what was it like for Dulrahman to serve as a romusha? According to this source, how did the experience affect him after the war? Does Dulrahman's story elicit your sympathy, even though he was working in a Japanese-led work battalion? If yes, are you able to determine what factors of the story make you sympathetic? If no, are you able to determine the reasons why not?
3. In Document 2, does Kosaku's story elicit your sympathy, even though he was a Japanese soldier who had actively supported the Japanese war effort? If yes, what parts of his story make you feel sympathetic? If no, are you able to determine the reasons why not?
4. Taking both documents together, do you believe that either Dulrahman or Kosaku deserve more sympathy than the other? Do you find that your answer to this question is affected by the nationality of either person? Do you think it would be difficult for individuals who had experienced the war to be impartial about the suffering of individuals in enemy nations? Why or why not?
5. Sources such as these make up the building blocks on which historians base their interpretations of the past. When interpreting the relatively recent past, it is especially important that historians remain aware of the ways in which their own personal and national backgrounds affect both the sources they use as well as their interpretations of them.

*Source Citations:* **Document 1:** Banning, Jan. "Traces of War: Dutch and Indonesian Survivors." Open Democracy, August 18, 2005. Reprinted by permission from www.openDemocracy.net. **Document 2:** Sekinori, Gaynor and George Marshall. *Hibakusha: Survivors of Hiroshima and Nagasaki* (Kosei Publishing, 1989), pp. 33–34.

## INTERPRETING IMAGES

Four Korean "comfort women," who were forced to become military sex slaves by the Japanese during World War II, sit beside a rocky cliff in China at the end of the war in 1945.

**Analyze** *How would you describe what you see in this photo? Are there similar historical examples of other conflicts in which women were forced into roles like these? How does history deal with sexual violence in the context of war, and how might we discuss it differently?*

CPA Media Pte Ltd/ Alamy Stock Photo

than any other war in history, is a woman's war." A poster encouraging U.S. women to join the **WAVES** (Women Appointed for Volunteer Emergency Service in the navy) mirrored the thought: "It's A Woman's War Too!" While hundreds of thousands of women in Great Britain, the United States, and the Soviet Union joined the armed forces or entered war industries, women around the world were affected by the war in a variety of ways. Some nations, including Great Britain and the United States, barred women from engaging in combat or carrying weapons, but Soviet and Chinese women took up arms, as did women in resistance groups. In fact, women often excelled at resistance work because they were less suspect in the eyes of occupying security forces and less subject to searches. Nazi forces did not discriminate, though, when rounding up Jews for transport and extermination: Jewish women and girls died alongside Jewish men and boys.

**Women's Roles** Women who joined military services or took jobs on factory assembly lines gained an independence and confidence previously denied them, but so too did women who were forced to act as heads of household in the absence of husbands killed or away at war, captured as prisoners of war, or languishing in labor camps. Women's roles changed during the war, often in dramatic ways, but those new roles turned out to be temporary. After the war, especially in western Europe and the United States, women warriors and workers were expected to resume their traditional roles as wives and mothers. In the meantime, though, women made the most of their opportunities. In Britain, women served as noncombatant pilots, drove ambulances and transport vehicles, and labored in the fields to produce foodstuffs. More than 500,000 women joined British military services, and approximately 350,000 women did the same in the United States. In the Soviet Union, women recruits exceeded even these high numbers. There, about 800,000 women enlisted in the armed forces during the war. While many served as medics and nurses, thousands also served in active combat as pilots, snipers, and machine gunners.

**Comfort Women** Women's experiences in war were not always empowering. The Japanese army forcibly recruited, conscripted, and coerced as many as two hundred thousand women aged fourteen to twenty to serve in military brothels, called "comfort houses" or "consolation centers." The army presented the women to the troops as a gift from the emperor. The majority of women came from China and the Japanese colony of Korea, though others came from Japanese colonies and occupied territories in Taiwan, Manchuria, the Philippines, and elsewhere in Southeast Asia.

Once forced into this imperial sex trafficking, the **"comfort women"** catered to between twenty and thirty men each day. Stationed in war zones, the women often confronted the same risks as soldiers, and many became casualties of war.

Others were killed by Japanese soldiers, especially if they tried to escape or contracted venereal diseases. At the end of the war, soldiers massacred large numbers of these trafficking victims to cover up the operation. The impetus behind the establishment of comfort houses for Japanese soldiers came from the horrors of Nanjing, where the mass rape of Chinese women had taken place. In trying to avoid such atrocities, the Japanese army created another form of coercive horror. Comfort women who survived the war experienced deep shame and hid their past or faced being shunned by their families. They found little comfort or peace after the war.

## THE COLD WAR

The end of World War II produced moving images of peace, such as Soviet and U.S. soldiers clasping hands in camaraderie at the Elbe River, celebrating their victory over the Germans. But by the time Germany surrendered in the spring of 1945, the wartime alliance between the Soviet Union, the United States, and Great Britain was disintegrating. Within two years the alliance forged by mutual danger gave way to a cold war between two principal rivals and their allies. It was a contest in which neither side gave way; yet, in the end, a direct clash of arms was always avoided, hence the term *cold war.*

The **cold war** became a confrontation for global influence principally between the United States and the Soviet Union. The geopolitical and ideological rivalry between the Soviet Union and the United States and their respective allies lasted almost five decades and affected every part of the world. The cold war was responsible for the formation of military and political alliances, the creation of client states, and an arms race of unprecedented scope. It engendered diplomatic crises, spawned military conflicts, and at times brought the world to the brink of nuclear annihilation. Among the first manifestations of the cold war was the division of the European continent into competing political, military, and economic blocs—one dependent on the United States and the other subservient to the USSR—separated by what Winston Churchill in 1946 famously called an "iron curtain."

### Origins of the Cold War

**The United Nations** Despite their many differences, the Allies were among the nations that agreed to the creation of the **United Nations** (UN) in October 1945, a supranational organization dedicated to keeping world peace and security. The commitment to establish a new international organization derived from Allied cooperation during the war. Unlike

## What's Left Out?

Historians used to assume that antagonism between capitalist and communist systems was natural and that, therefore, the intense rivalry that emerged between the United States and the Soviet Union during the cold war needed no historical explanation. But cold war antagonisms had a history that predated the end of World War II by almost three decades. The leading capitalist powers—including Great Britain and the United States—had actively tried to put an end to the Russian revolution in 1918 when they sent troops to help overthrow the Bolsheviks as World War I was ending. In 1919 they grew even more alarmed about the Soviet state when it established the Communist International (Comintern), whose express purpose was to provide funds and strategies for colonized and marginalized people to overthrow capitalism through violent revolution. In fact, it is no exaggeration to say that metropolitan and colonial authorities—especially from Great Britain and France—were convinced that international communism posed a fundamental danger to the stability of the Euro-American global system in the interwar period. During the 1920s and 1930s, both Britain and France expended enormous energy and capital trying to root out and persecute communists around the world (especially in their colonies), and in efforts to gain allies in their anticommunist campaign. British authorities in particular were influential in shaping the anticommunist attitudes of U.S. authorities at this time, encouraging them to fear the influence of communism both in their own overseas empire and among U.S. workers. So even though the capitalist powers were able to put aside their animosity toward the Soviet Union in order to fight the Axis powers, it is hardly surprising that this decades-long rivalry flared up again at the end of the war. The difference now was that the United States, rather than Great Britain or France, was leading the campaign. What is important to remember is that the United States took over the campaign but did not invent it and that the struggle between communism and anticommunism was critical to international politics long before the United States became the primary adversary of the Soviet Union.

*Source:* Anne Foster. "Secret Police Cooperation and the Roots of Anti-Communism in Interwar Southeast Asia." *Journal of American-East Asian Relations* 4:4 (1995).

### Thinking Critically About Sources

1. How did the history of anti-Communism before World War II contribute to Western attitudes of isolationism in the midst of fascist expansion?
2. Why did the United States replace Great Britain and France in "leading the campaign" after World War II?

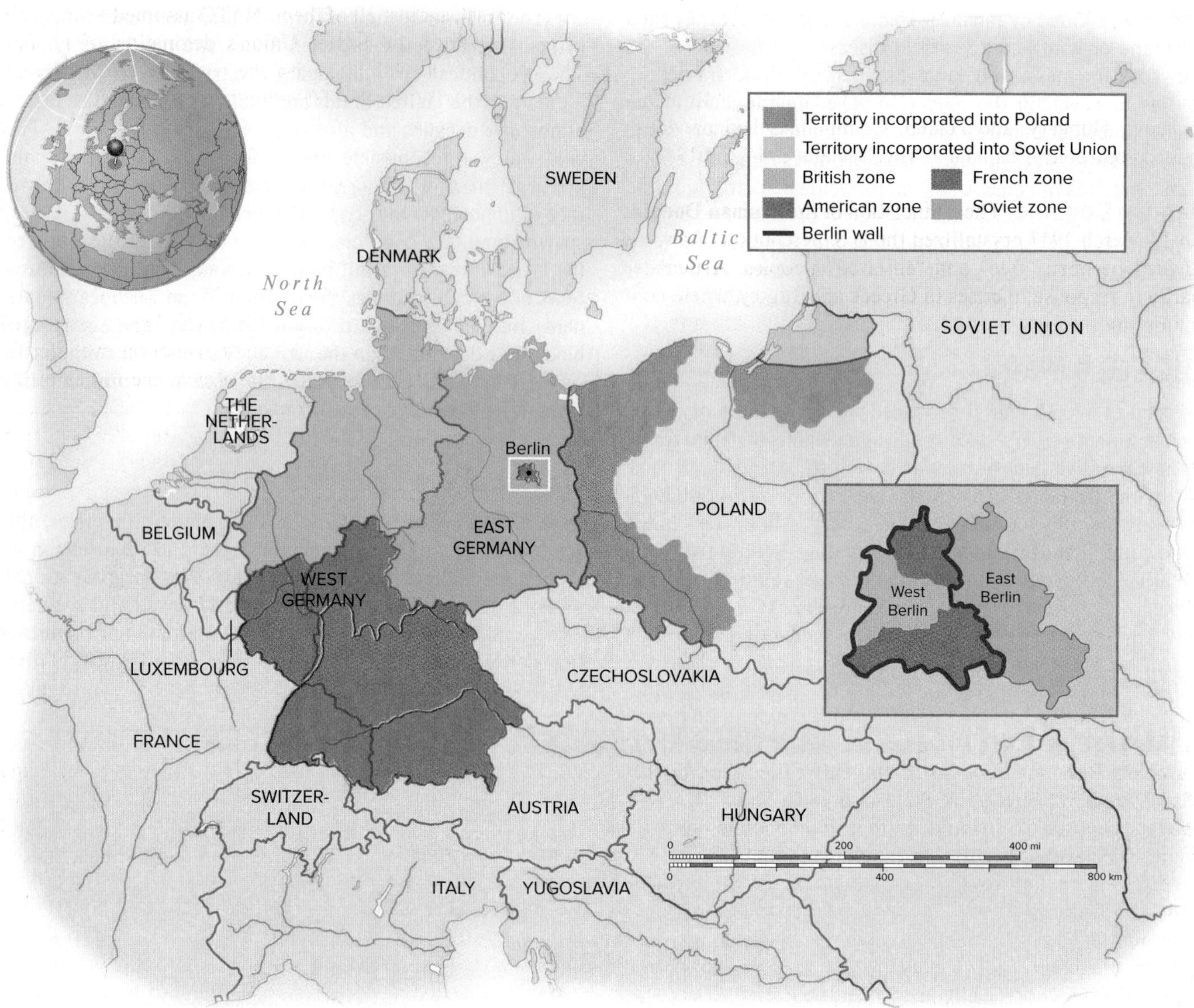


## Map 24.4 Occupied Germany, 1945–1949.

Locate the city of Berlin in Soviet-controlled territory.

***How was it possible for the British, American, and French to maintain their zones of control in Berlin, given the geographic distance from West Germany?***

its predecessor, the League of Nations (1920), which failed in its basic mission to prevent another world war, the United Nations created a powerful Security Council responsible for maintaining international peace. Recognizing that peace could be maintained only if the great powers were in agreement, the UN founders made certain that the Security Council consists of five permanent members and six rotating elected members. The United States, the Soviet Union, Great Britain, France, and China—the members of the full Allied alliance in World War II—are the five permanent powers, and their unanimous vote is required on all substantive matters. The decisions of the Security Council are binding on all members.

Despite this initial cooperation, the wartime unity of the former Allies began to crack. In addition to a long history of philosophical differences between the Soviet Union and the western European powers, at the end of the war the Allies were already expressing differences over the future of Poland and eastern European nations liberated and subsequently occupied by the Soviet Red Army. On the surface, all sides agreed at the wartime conference at Yalta (February 4-11, 1945) to "the earliest possible establishment through free elections of governments responsive to the will of the people." But the Soviet Union had just suffered a devastating invasion by the German army through this territory, and Joseph Stalin was determined that postwar governments in the region would be controlled by the Soviet Union in order to safeguard against any future threat from Germany. From the American and British perspectives, Stalin's intentions signaled the permanent Soviet domination of eastern Europe and the threat of Soviet-influenced communist parties coming to power in the democracies of western Europe. Their fears were realized in 1946 and 1947, when the Soviets helped bring communist governments to power in Romania, Bulgaria, Hungary, and Poland. Communists had previously gained control in Albania and Yugoslavia in 1944 and 1945.

**Truman Doctrine** The enunciation of the **Truman Doctrine** on 12 March 1947 crystallized the U.S. perception of a world divided between "free" and "enslaved" peoples. Articulated partly in response to crises in Greece and Turkey, where communist movements seemed to threaten democracy and U.S. strategic interests, the Truman Doctrine starkly drew the battle lines of the cold war. As President Harry Truman (1884–1972) explained to the U.S. Congress: "At the present moment in world history nearly every nation must choose between alternative ways of life. I believe that it must be the policy of the United States to support free peoples who are resisting attempted subjugation by armed minorities or by outside pressures." The United States then committed itself to an interventionist foreign policy, dedicated to the "containment" of communism, which meant preventing any further expansion of Soviet influence.

**Marshall Plan** Just after the announcement of the Truman Doctrine, the U.S. government developed a plan to help shore up the destroyed infrastructures of western Europe. The European Recovery Program, commonly called the **Marshall Plan** after U.S. Secretary of State George C. Marshall (1880–1959), proposed to rebuild European economies through cooperation and capitalism, forestalling communist or Soviet influence in the devastated nations of Europe. Proposed in 1947 and funded in 1948, the Marshall Plan provided more than $13 billion to reconstruct western Europe. Although initially included in the nations invited to participate in the Marshall Plan, the Soviet Union became infuriated over what it correctly saw as a U.S. attempt to make communism seem less attractive to Europeans devastated by the war. In response, the Soviet government came up with its own aid program for the satellite nations around it, establishing an economic Council for Mutual Economic Assistance (**COMECON**) in 1949. COMECON offered increased trade within the Soviet Union and eastern Europe as an alternative to the Marshall Plan, which Soviet officials denounced as capitalist imperialism.

**Military Alliances** The creation of the U.S.-sponsored North Atlantic Treaty Organization (**NATO**) and the Soviet-controlled **Warsaw Pact** signaled the militarization of the cold war. In 1949 the United States established NATO as a regional military alliance against Soviet aggression. The original members included Belgium, Canada, Denmark, France, Great Britain, Iceland, Italy, Luxembourg, the Netherlands, Norway, Portugal, and the United States. The intent of the alliance was to maintain peace in postwar Europe through collective security, which implied that a Soviet attack on any NATO member was an attack against all of them. NATO assumed a more military focus with the Soviet Union's detonation of its first atomic bomb in 1949 and with the outbreak of the Korean War in 1950. When NATO admitted West Germany and allowed it to rearm in 1955, the Soviets formed the Warsaw Pact as a countermeasure. A military alliance of seven communist European nations, the Warsaw Pact matched the collective defense policies of NATO.

**A Divided Germany** The fault lines of early cold war Europe were most visible in Germany. An international crisis arose there in 1948–1949 when the Soviet Union pressured the western powers to give up their jurisdiction over Berlin. After the collapse of Hitler's Third Reich, the forces of the United States, the Soviet Union, Britain, and France occupied Germany and its capital, Berlin, both of which they divided for administrative purposes into four zones. When the western powers decided to merge their occupation zones in Germany—including their sectors in Berlin—the Soviets retaliated by blockading all road, rail, and water links between Berlin and western Germany. The last thing the Soviet government wanted was a strong Germany. If it could not prevent its former allies from merging their sectors to ease German recovery, it hoped at least to force them to surrender their control over the city of Berlin, which sat deep within the Soviet sector.

**Blockade and Airlift** In the first serious test of the cold war, the Americans and the British responded with an airlift designed to keep West Berlin's inhabitants alive, fed, and warm. For eleven months, in a massive display of airpower,

Barbed wire and a concrete wall in front of the Brandenburg Gate in Berlin symbolized the cold war division of Europe.
Keystone-France/Gamma-Keystone/Getty Images

American and British aircrews flew around-the-clock missions to supply West Berlin with the necessities of life. Tensions remained high during the airlift, but the cold war did not turn hot. Stymied by British and U.S. resolve, the Soviet leadership called off the blockade in May 1949. In the aftermath of the blockade, the U.S., British, and French zones of occupation coalesced to form the Federal Republic of Germany (West Germany) in May 1949. In October the German Democratic Republic (East Germany) emerged out of the Soviet zone of occupation. A similar process repeated itself in Berlin. The Soviet sector formed East Berlin and became the capital of the new East Germany. The remaining three sectors united to form West Berlin, and the West German capital moved to the small town of Bonn.

**The Berlin Wall** By 1961 the communist East German state was hemorrhaging from a steady drain of refugees who preferred life in capitalist West Germany. Between 1949 and 1961 nearly 3.5 million East Germans—many of them young and highly skilled—left their homeland, much to the embarrassment of East Germany's communist leaders. In August 1961 the communists reinforced the border between East and West Germany, and also constructed a fortified wall that divided the city of Berlin. The wall, which began as a layer of barbed wire, quickly turned into a barrier several layers deep, with watchtowers, searchlights, antipersonnel mines, and border guards who had orders to shoot to kill. The **Berlin Wall** accomplished its purpose of stemming the flow of refugees, though at the cost of shaming a regime that seemed to be unpopular even among its own people.

**Cold War Culture and Censorship** Somewhat ironically, despite their intense competition, during the cold war societies in the Soviet Union and the United States came to resemble one another in some ways, especially in their internal censorship policies. In the United States, cold war concerns about the spread of communism reached deeply into the domestic sphere. Politicians, agents of the Federal Bureau of Investigation (FBI), educators, and social commentators warned of communist spies trying to undermine the institutions of U.S. life. Senator **Joseph McCarthy** (1909–1957) became infamous in the early 1950s for his largely unsuccessful but nonetheless intimidating quest to expose communists in the U.S. government. Thousands of citizens who supported any radical or liberal cause—especially those who were or once had been members of the Communist Party—lost their jobs and reputations after being held up as risks to their nation's security. The culture industry, and Hollywood in particular, came under great scrutiny for its suspected ties to left-wing politics, which had the effect of limiting overt criticism of the United States and its foreign policies.

In the Soviet Union and Eastern Europe, cold war ideologies also profoundly influenced domestic culture and politics. After the war, Stalin imposed Soviet economic planning on governments in Eastern Europe and expected the peoples of the Soviet Union and Eastern Europe to conform to anticapitalist ideological requirements. Rebellious artists and novelists found themselves silenced or denounced in a mirrored form of the McCarthyism evident in the United States. This policy of repression relaxed somewhat after Stalin's death in 1953, but there remained limits on Soviet liberalization. Soviet troops cracked down on Hungarian rebels in 1956, and Soviet novelist **Boris Pasternak** (1890–1960), author of *Doctor Zhivago,* was not allowed to receive his Nobel Prize in Literature in 1958. There is little doubt that societies and cultures in the Soviet Union and the United States underwent dramatic transformations as a result of the international competition between communism and capitalism, and such changes continued to engulf these societies as the cold war globalized.

## The Globalization of the Cold War

**The People's Republic of China** The establishment of a communist China in 1949 simultaneously ended a long period of imperialist intrusion in China and further transformed the cold war, as it seemed to enhance the power of the Soviet Union and its communist allies. Although China had not been formally ruled by an imperial power, many countries had impinged on its sovereignty in the nineteenth and early twentieth centuries. During the 1920s, two groups had arisen to reassert Chinese control over internal affairs: the nationalists and the communists (see chapter 23). When World War II broke out, these two groups had been engaged in a civil war, but they came together to fight against the Japanese invasion. Once World War II was over, however, the civil war resumed. In 1948 and 1949, the communists inflicted heavy military defeats on the nationalists. With the communist People's Liberation Army controlling most of mainland China, the national government under Jiang Jieshi (Chiang Kai-shek) sought refuge on the island of Taiwan, taking along most of the nation's gold reserves. Although Jiang Jieshi continued to proclaim that the government in Taiwan was the legitimate government of all China, Mao Zedong, chairman of the Chinese Communist Party, proclaimed the establishment of the People's Republic of China on 1 October 1949. That declaration brought to an end the long period of imperialist intrusion in China and spawned a close relationship between the world's largest and most powerful socialist states.

**Fraternal Cooperation** China and the Soviet Union drew closer during the early years of the cold war. This relationship was hardly surprising because the leaders of both communist states felt threatened by a common enemy, the United States, which sought to establish anticommunist bastions throughout Asia. Most disconcerting to Soviet and Chinese leaders was the American-sponsored rehabilitation of their former enemy, Japan, and the forming of client states in South Korea and

Taiwan. The Chinese-Soviet partnership matured during the early 1950s and took on a distinct form when China recognized the Soviet Union's undisputed authority in world communism in exchange for Russian military equipment and economic aid.

**Confrontations in Korea** In conjunction with the communist victory in China, the outbreak of hostilities on the Korean peninsula in the summer of 1950 shifted the focus of the cold war from Europe to east Asia. At the end of World War II, the leaders of the Soviet Union and the United States had partitioned Korea along the thirty-eighth parallel (the thirty-eighth line of latitude) into a northern Soviet zone and a southern U.S. zone. Because the superpowers were unable to agree on a framework for the reunification of the country, in 1948 they consented to the establishment of two separate Korean states: in the south, the Republic of Korea, with Seoul as its capital, and in the north, the People's Democratic Republic of Korea, with Pyongyang as its capital. After arming their respective clients, each of which claimed sovereignty over the entire country, U.S. and Soviet troops withdrew.

On the early morning of June 25, 1950, the unstable political situation in Korea came to a head. Determined to unify Korea by force, the Pyongyang regime in North Korea ordered more than one hundred thousand troops across the thirty-eighth parallel in a surprise attack, quickly pushing back South Korean defenders and capturing Seoul on June 27. Convinced that the USSR had given its blessing for the invasion, the United States persuaded the United Nations to adopt a resolution to drive the North Koreans out. Armed with a UN mandate and supported by small armed forces from twenty countries, the U.S. military went into action, and within months had pushed the North Koreans back to the thirty-eighth parallel. However, sensing an opportunity to unify Korea under a pro-U.S. government, they pushed on into North Korea and within a few weeks had occupied Pyongyang. But subsequent U.S. advances toward the Yalu River on the Chinese border brought the Chinese into the war. A combined force of Chinese and North Koreans pushed U.S. forces and their allies back into the south, and the war settled into a stalemate near the original border at the thirty-eighth parallel. After two more years of fighting that raised the number of deaths to three million—mostly Korean civilians—both sides finally agreed to a cease-fire in July 1953. The failure to conclude a peace treaty ensured that the Korean peninsula would remain in a state of suspended strife that constantly threatened to engulf the region in a new round of hostilities.

Beyond the human casualties and physical damage it wrought, the Korean conflict also encouraged the globalization of the U.S. strategy of containment. Viewing the North Korean offensive as part of a larger communist conspiracy to conquer the world, the U.S. government extended military protection and economic aid to noncommunist governments in the rest of Asia. It also entered into security agreements that culminated in the creation of the Southeast Asian Treaty Organization (SEATO), an Asian counterpart of NATO. By 1954 U.S. President Dwight D. Eisenhower (1890–1969), who had contemplated using nuclear weapons in Korea, asserted the famous **domino theory.** This strategic theory rationalized worldwide U.S. intervention on the assumption that if one country became communist, neighboring ones would collapse to communism the way a row of dominoes falls sequentially until none remains standing. Subsequent U.S. administrations extended the policy of containment to areas beyond the nation's vital interests and applied it to local or imagined communist threats in Central and South America, Africa, and Asia.

**Cracks in the Soviet-Chinese Alliance** Despite the assumptions of U.S. leaders, there was no one monolithic communist force in global politics, as was demonstrated by the divisions that developed between Chinese and Soviet communists. The Chinese had embarked on a crash program of industrialization, and the Soviet Union rendered valuable assistance in the form of economic aid and technical advisers. By the mid-1950s the Soviet Union was China's principal trading partner, annually purchasing roughly half of all Chinese exports. But the Chinese grew offended that the Soviets would not share the technology for nuclear weapons with them and were furious when the Soviet Union did not support them in their war with India in 1962. By the end of 1964, the rift between the Soviet Union and the People's Republic of China became embarrassingly public, with both sides engaging in name-calling. In addition, both nations openly competed for influence in Africa and Asia, especially in the nations that had recently gained independence. The fact that China conducted successful nuclear tests in 1964, without the help of the Soviet Union, enhanced its prestige. An unanticipated outcome of the Chinese-Soviet split was that many countries gained an opportunity to pursue a more independent course by playing capitalists against communists and by playing Soviet communists against Chinese communists. It also opened the door for an eventual truce between China and the United States because both countries now saw the Soviet Union as their principal enemy.

**The Nuclear Arms Race** A central feature of the cold war world was a costly arms race and the terrifying proliferation of nuclear weapons. The Soviet Union had broken the U.S. monopoly on atomic weaponry by testing its own atomic bomb in 1949, but because the United States was determined to retain military superiority and because the Soviet Union was equally determined to reach parity with the United States, both sides amassed enormous arsenals of nuclear weapons and developed a multitude of systems for deploying those weapons. In the 1960s and beyond, the superpowers acquired so many nuclear weapons that they reached the capacity for

A nuclear test in the Marshall Islands in 1954. Between World War II and the end of the twentieth century, nations with the capacity to produce nuclear weapons conducted more than two thousand tests. Though most tests were conducted in remote regions, they inflicted severe damage on animal populations and on the environment.
Galerie Bilderwelt/Getty Images

U.S. aerial reconnaissance photograph taken on 1 November 1962, showing clearly the existence of a medium-range ballistic missile launch site at San Cristobal, Cuba. National Archives and Records Administration

mutually assured destruction, or MAD. This balance of terror, while often frightening, tended to restrain the contestants and stabilize their relationship, with one important exception.

**Cuba: Nuclear Flashpoint** Ironically, the cold war confrontation that came closest to unleashing nuclear war took place not at the expected flashpoints in Europe or Asia but on the island of Cuba. In 1959 a revolutionary movement headed by Fidel Castro Ruz (1926–2016) overthrew the autocratic Fulgencio Batista y Zaldivar (1901–1973), whose regime had gone to great lengths to maintain the country's subservient relationship with the United States, especially with the U.S. sugar companies that controlled Cuba's economy. Fidel Castro's new regime gladly accepted a Soviet offer of massive economic aid—including an agreement to purchase half of Cuba's sugar production—and arms shipments. In return for Soviet aid, Castro declared his support for the USSR's foreign policy. In December 1961 he confirmed the U.S. government's worst suspicions when he publicly announced: "I have been a Marxist-Leninist all along, and will remain one until I die."

**Bay of Pigs Invasion** Cuba's alignment with the Soviet Union spurred the U.S. government to action. Newly elected president John F. Kennedy (1917–1963) authorized a clandestine invasion of Cuba to overthrow Castro and his supporters. In April 1961 a force of fifteen hundred anti-Castro Cubans trained, armed, and transported by the Central Intelligence Agency (CIA) landed on Cuba at a place called the **Bay of Pigs.** The arrival of the invasion force failed to incite a hoped-for internal uprising, and when the promised American air support failed to appear, the invasion quickly fizzled. Within three days, Castro's military had either captured or killed the entire invasion force. The Bay of Pigs fiasco diminished U.S. prestige, especially in Latin America. It also strengthened Castro's position in Cuba and encouraged him to accept the deployment of Soviet nuclear missiles in Cuba as a deterrent to any future invasion.

**Cuban Missile Crisis** On October 26, 1962, the United States learned that Soviet technicians were assembling launch sites for medium-range nuclear missiles on Cuba. The deployment of nuclear missiles that could reach targets in the United States within minutes represented an unacceptable threat to U.S. national security. Thus President John F. Kennedy issued an ultimatum, calling on the Soviet leadership to withdraw all missiles from Cuba and stop the arrival of additional nuclear armaments. To back up his demand, Kennedy imposed an air and naval quarantine on the island nation. The superpowers seemed poised for nuclear confrontation, and for two weeks the world's peoples held their collective breath. After two weeks, finally realizing the imminent possibility of nuclear war, the Soviet government yielded to the U.S. demands. In return, Soviet Premier Nikita Khrushchev (1894–1971) extracted an open pledge from Kennedy to refrain from attempting to overthrow Castro's regime and a secret deal to remove U.S. missiles from Turkey. The world trembled during this Cuban missile **crisis,** awaiting the apocalypse that potentially lurked behind any superpower encounter.

## Dissent, Intervention, and Rapprochement

**De-Stalinization** Even before the Cuban missile crisis, developments within the Soviet Union caused serious changes in eastern Europe. Within three years of Joseph Stalin's death in 1953, several communist leaders startled the world when they openly attacked Stalin and questioned his methods of rule. The most vigorous denunciations came from Stalin's successor, Soviet Premier Nikita Khrushchev, who embarked on a policy of **de-Stalinization,** that is, the end of the rule of terror and the partial liberalization of Soviet society. Government officials removed portraits of Stalin from public places, renamed institutions and localities bearing his name, and commissioned historians to rewrite textbooks to deflate Stalin's reputation. The de-Stalinization period, which lasted from 1956 to 1964, also brought a "thaw" in government control and resulted in the release of millions of political prisoners. With respect to foreign policy, Khrushchev emphasized the possibility of "peaceful coexistence" between different social systems and the achievement of communism by peaceful means. This change in Soviet doctrine reflected the recognition that a nuclear war was more likely to lead to mutual annihilation than to victory.

**Soviet Intervention** The new political climate in the Soviet Union tempted communist leaders elsewhere to experiment with domestic reforms and seek a degree of independence from Soviet domination. Eastern European states also tried to become their own masters, or at least to gain a measure of autonomy from the Soviet Union. The nations of the Soviet bloc did not fare well in those endeavors. East Germans staged an uprising crushed in 1953, but the most serious challenge to Soviet control came in 1956 from nationalist-minded communists in Hungary. When the communist regime in Hungary embraced the process of de-Stalinization, large numbers of Hungarian citizens demanded democracy and the breaking of ties to Moscow and the Warsaw Pact. Soviet leaders viewed those moves as a serious threat to their national security. In the late autumn of 1956, Soviet tanks entered Budapest and crushed the Hungarian uprising.

Twelve years after the Hungarian tragedy, Soviets again intervened in eastern Europe, this time in Czechoslovakia. In 1968 the Communist Party leader, Alexander Dubček (1921–1992), launched a "democratic socialist revolution." He supported a liberal movement known as the **Prague Spring** and promised his fellow citizens "socialism with a human face." The Czechs' move toward liberal communism aroused fear in the Soviet Union because such ideas could lead to the unraveling of Soviet control in eastern Europe. Intervention by Soviet and Warsaw Pact forces brought an end to the Prague Spring. Khrushchev's successor, Leonid Ilyich Brezhnev (1906–1982), justified the invasion of Czechoslovakia by the Doctrine of Limited Sovereignty. This policy, more commonly called the **Brezhnev doctrine**, reserved the right to invade any socialist country that was deemed to be threatened by internal or external elements "hostile to socialism." The destruction of the dramatic reform movement in Czechoslovakia served to reassert Soviet control over its satellite nations in eastern Europe and led to tightened controls within the Soviet Union.

**Détente** Realizing the extreme danger posed by mutually assured destruction, by the late 1960s the leaders of the Soviet Union and the United States agreed on a policy of ***détente,*** or a reduction in hostility, in which they tried to slow the costly arms race and decrease their competition in developing countries. Although détente did not resolve the deep-seated antagonism between the superpowers, it did signal a relaxation of cold war tensions and prompted a new spirit of cooperation. The spirit of détente was most visible in negotiations designed to reduce the threat posed by strategic nuclear weapons. The two cold war antagonists cooperated despite the tensions caused by the U.S. incursion into Vietnam, Soviet involvement in Angola and other African states, and continued Soviet repression of dissidents in eastern Europe. Likewise symbolic of the relaxation of tensions between democratic and communist nations were the state visits in 1972 to China and the Soviet Union made by U.S. President Richard Nixon (1913–1994). Nixon had entered politics in 1946 on the basis of his service in World War II and his staunch belief in anticommunism, and his trips to the two global centers of communism suggested a possible beginning to the end of cold war divisions.

## CONCLUSION

World War II was a total global war that forced violent encounters between peoples and radically altered the political shape of the world. Beginning in Japan and China in 1931, this global conflagration eventually engulfed Europe and its empires, the Pacific Ocean, and the rest of Asia. Men, women, and children throughout the world were subjected to the horrors of war as victims of civilian bombing campaigns, as soldiers and war workers, and as slave laborers and comfort women. When the Allies defeated the Axis powers in 1945, destroying the German and Japanese empires, the world had to rebuild just as another conflict began. The end of the war saw the breakup of the alliance that had defeated Germany and Japan, and within a short time the United States and the Soviet Union and their respective allies squared off against each other in a cold war, a rivalry waged on political, economic, and propaganda fronts. as well as via proxy wars with client states. When former colonial territories began to win their independence in the postwar period, they emerged as new nations into this bipolar world: a reality that limited their choices and shaped their futures.

## STUDY TERMS

Adolf Hitler (791)
Allied powers (798)
*Anschluss* (792)
appeasement (792)
Auschwitz (805)
Axis powers (798)
Battle of Britain (794)
Bay of Pigs (815)
Benito Mussolini (791)
Berlin Wall (812)
*Blitzkrieg* (793)
Boris Pasternak (812)
Brezhnev doctrine (816)
cold war (809)
COMECON (811)
comfort women (808)
Cuban missile crisis (817)
D-Day (799)
de-Stalinization (816)
*détente* (816)
domino theory (835)
*Einsatzgruppen* (804)
experimental surgery (804)
final solution (805)
German-Soviet Non-Aggression Pact (793)
Greater East Asia Co-Prosperity Sphere (797)
Hiroshima (800)
Holocaust (805)
Iwo Jima (800)
Joseph McCarthy (812)
Joseph Stalin (793)
*kamikaze* (800)
*Lebensraum* (794)
Luftwaffe (796)
Manchukuo (801)
Marshall Plan (811)
Munich Conference (792)
Nagasaki (800)
NATO (811)
Okinawa (800)
Operation Barbarossa (794)
Pearl Harbor (796)
Prague Spring (816)
Rape of Nanjing (792)
revisionist powers (798)
Spanish Civil War (791)
Stalingrad (795)
Sudetenland (792)
Truman Doctrine (811)
United Nations (UN) (809)
*Unterseeboote* (793)
Vichy (801)
Wannsee Conference (805)
Warsaw Pact (811)
WAVES (808)
Winston Churchill (797)

## FOR FURTHER READING

Svetlana Alexievich. *The Unwomanly Face of War: An Oral History of Women in World War II.* New York, 2017. A meticulously researched history of Soviet women's contributions to the war effort.

Christopher Bayly and Tim Harper. *Forgotten Armies: The Fall of British Asia, 1941–1945.* Cambridge, 2005. Broad study of the impact of World War II on Britain's Asian empire.

John Lewis Gaddis. *The Cold War: A New History.* New York, 2005. A fresh and concise history of the cold war by the dean of cold war historians.

Brian Masaru Hayashi. *Democratizing the Enemy: The Japanese American Internment.* Princeton, N.J., 2004. Important account of the experience of Japanese Americans in World War II.

Waldo Heinrichs and Marc Gallicchio. *Implacable Foes: War in the Pacific, 1944–1945.* Oxford, 2017. Explores both the battles and the bitter debates over strategy in the last eighteen months of the Pacific war.

Keith Lowe. *Savage Continent: Europe in the Aftermath of World War II.* New York, 2012. The author presents an absorbing and chilling picture of a continent brutalized by war.

Rana Mitter. *Forgotten Ally: China's World War II,* 1937–1945. Boston, 2013. This is an important account of how a brutal conflict shaped modern China.

Richard Overy. *The Bombers and the Bombed: Allied Air War over Europe* 1940–1945. New York, 2014. In this impressive work the author explores the military, technological, and ethical issues of strategic bombing, and challenges the notion that the Allies fought a "moral" war.

Timothy Snyder. Bloodlands: Europe between Hitler and Stalin. New York, 2010. This is a nuanced and pathbreaking study of Europe's killing fields, where the murderous regimes of Hitler and Stalin claimed the lives of fourteen million noncombatants.

Odd Arne Westad. *Global Cold War: Third World Interventions and the Making of Our Times.* New York, 2007. In a reexamination of the global conflict between the United States and the Soviet Union, the author argues that cold war interventionism helped shape present-day international affairs.

# CHAPTER 24 AP EXAM PRACTICE

Questions assume cumulative knowledge from this chapter and previous chapters.

## Section I

### Multiple Choice Questions

Use the image below and your knowledge of world history to answer questions 1–3.

Adolf Hitler proudly walks through conquered Paris in 1940, with the Eiffel Tower as a backdrop.
Harwood/Keystone/Hulton Archive/Getty Images

1. What was Neville Chamberlain's approach to negotiating with Hitler before the war?
   (A) He tried to offer Hitler a yearly stipend if he resigned.
   (B) He thought Hitler would back down if Britain bombed Dresden.
   (C) He thought he could prevent war if he agreed to many of Hitler's demands.
   (D) He presented Hitler with a series of demands that Germany could not satisfy.

2. Why did Hitler break the non-aggression pact with the Soviet Union?
   (A) He could remove all the Jews, Slavs, and communists and resettle Germans on their lands.
   (B) Hitler and Joseph Stalin disagreed over which state should dominate the pact.
   (C) He learned that Stalin was preparing his forces to invade Germany.
   (D) Soviet submarines sank merchants and passenger ships in the Baltic Sea.

3. Why would Hitler and the Nazis have had this photograph taken?
   (A) Hitler had studied architecture and admired the Eiffel Tower.
   (B) Field Marshal Rommel had compared the fall of France to winning the Tour de France.
   (C) Hitler felt that Germany had been humiliated by the Treaty of Versailles, so showing his victory over Paris was a way to erase that dishonor.
   (D) They were planning to move the capital of the new Germany empire to Paris.

Use the image below and your knowledge of world history to answer questions 4 and 5.

Japanese soldiers doing training exercises in 1938. The original caption read: "2/25/38: Japanese soldiers are pictured doing exercises to keep themselves physically fit - the better to fight the Chinese."
Bettmann/Getty Images

4. How might the Japanese government have used images like this one to justify their empire?
   (A) The Japanese would create the Greater East Asia Co-Prosperity Sphere through intense military training.
   (B) By not using weapons, the Japanese could win the war by moral force.
   (C) Training for kamikaze missions was physically difficult.
   (D) Showcasing the physical strength of the Japanese soldier reinforces the idea that Japan should take the lead in the "Asia for Asians" struggle against European imperialism.

5. How did the Japanese invasion change politics in China?
   (A) The Japanese invasion broke the alliance between the communists and the nationalists.
   (B) The communists and the nationalists stopped fighting each other so that they could fight the Japanese.
   (C) The Guomindang lost the respect of the people because they surrendered to Japan.
   (D) The Chinese Communist Party lost the respect of the people because they surrendered to Japan.

## Short Answer

6. Use the image below and your knowledge of world history to answer parts A, B, and C.

Pilots and Heroes of the Soviet Union Natalia Kravtsova (L) and Irina Sebrova (R) are pictured near PO 2 aircraft.
TASS/Getty Images

(A) Identify ONE military job open to women.
(B) Explain ONE way that the concept of a "total war" affected women during the war.
(C) Identify ONE way that women in occupied countries were targeted by occupying forces.

7. Use the map below and your knowledge of world history to answer parts A, B, and C.

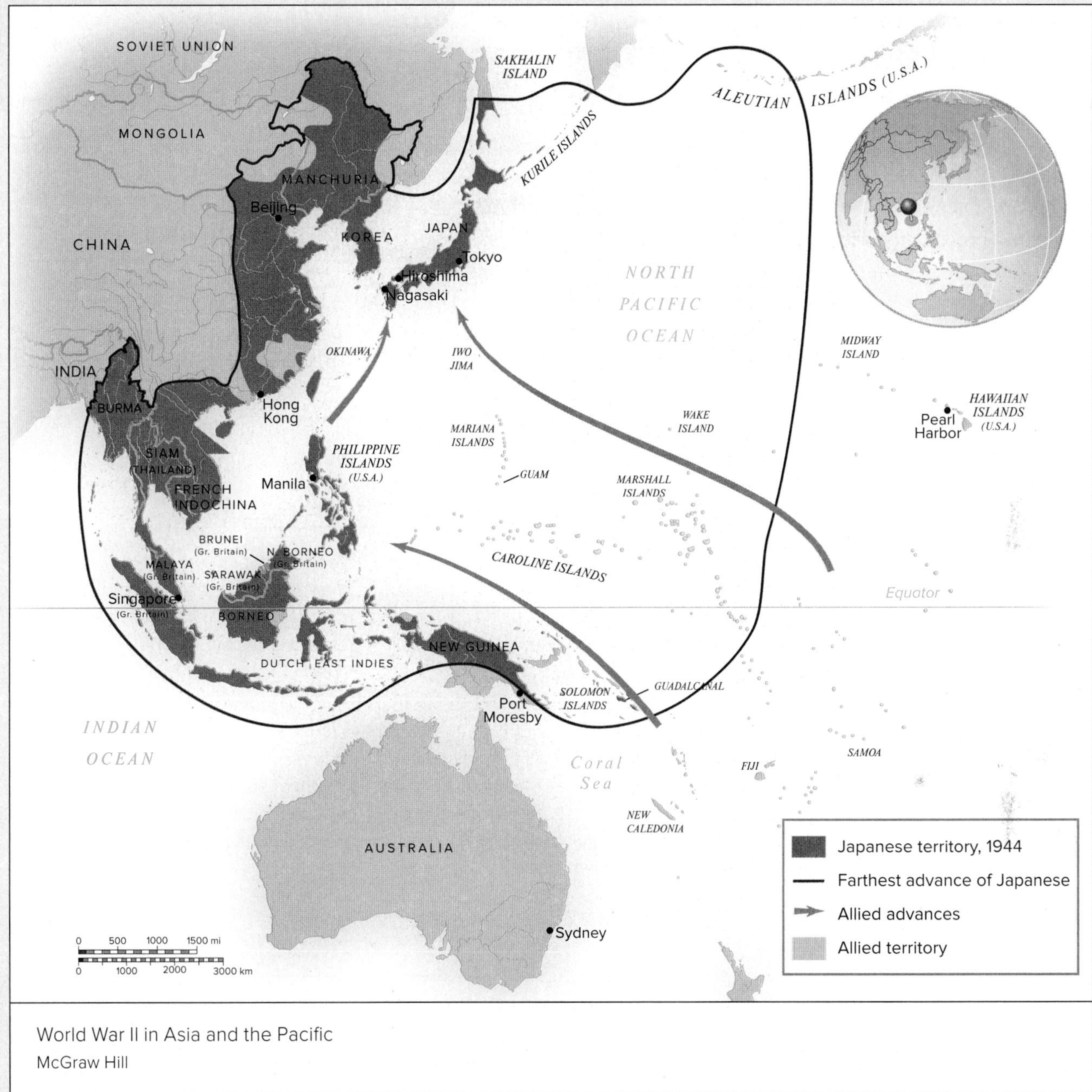


World War II in Asia and the Pacific
McGraw Hill

(A) Identify ONE geographic factor that dictated Allied strategy in the Pacific.
(B) Explain ONE factor that impacted the goals of Japanese expansion.
(C) Explain ONE impact of Japanese *kamikaze* attacks.

8. Use your understanding of world history to answer parts A, B, and C.
(A) Identify ONE way the United Nations was different from the League of Nations.
(B) Explain ONE way the Yalta Conference planned to rebuild Europe when the war ended.
(C) Explain ONE reason why the US tried to help western European states recover from the war.

# Section II

## Document-Based Question

Based on the documents below and your knowledge of world history, evaluate how World War II allowed for acts of genocide, atrocities, and ethnic violence.

In your response you should do the following:

- Respond to the prompt with a historically defensible thesis or claim that establishes a line of reasoning.
- Describe a broader historical context relevant to the prompt.
- Support an argument in response to the prompt using all documents.
- Use at least one additional piece of specific historical evidence (beyond that found in the documents) relevant to an argument about the prompt.
- Explain how or why the document's point of view, purpose, historical situation, and / or audience is relevant to an argument.
- Use evidence to corroborate, qualify, or modify an argument that addresses the prompt.

## Document 1

In June 1942, a Japanese soldier by the name of Kawakubu came to our village and asked my father if there were any people who could work, for wages, of course. My father then gave him my name. They first assigned me to help build a tunnel at Parangtritis, south of Yogya, on the coast. We didn't get paid at all, however, and they told my father they'd kill him if he'd come to fetch me. Sure, the Japanese told us repeatedly: "We've come to free you from colonial oppression." But meanwhile they forced us to work for them!

We left from Gunung Kidul for Parangtritis with about 500 people. My estimate is that about 300 survived. It's hard to be precise, for people were not buried but simply tossed into the sea. Some eight months later they shipped us out by the hundreds, including about 100 people belonging to the Gunung Kidul group. It turned out that they had taken us to Digul (in Irian Jaya, a former Dutch penal colony in what was then New Guinea) to cut trees for building a road and a prison. Compared to this place, Parangtritis had been pleasant. There at least we got a piece of cassava the size of my fist, and we could fetch water from a small mountain lake. In Digul, however, we were left to our own devices and so we had to forage for ourselves. For food, you had to look in the jungle. We ate leaves, and any snake you'd find was good for roasting.

*Source:* Banning, Jan. "Traces of War: Dutch and Indonesian Survivors." Open Democracy, August 18, 2005. Reprinted by permission from www.openDemocracy.net.

# Document 2

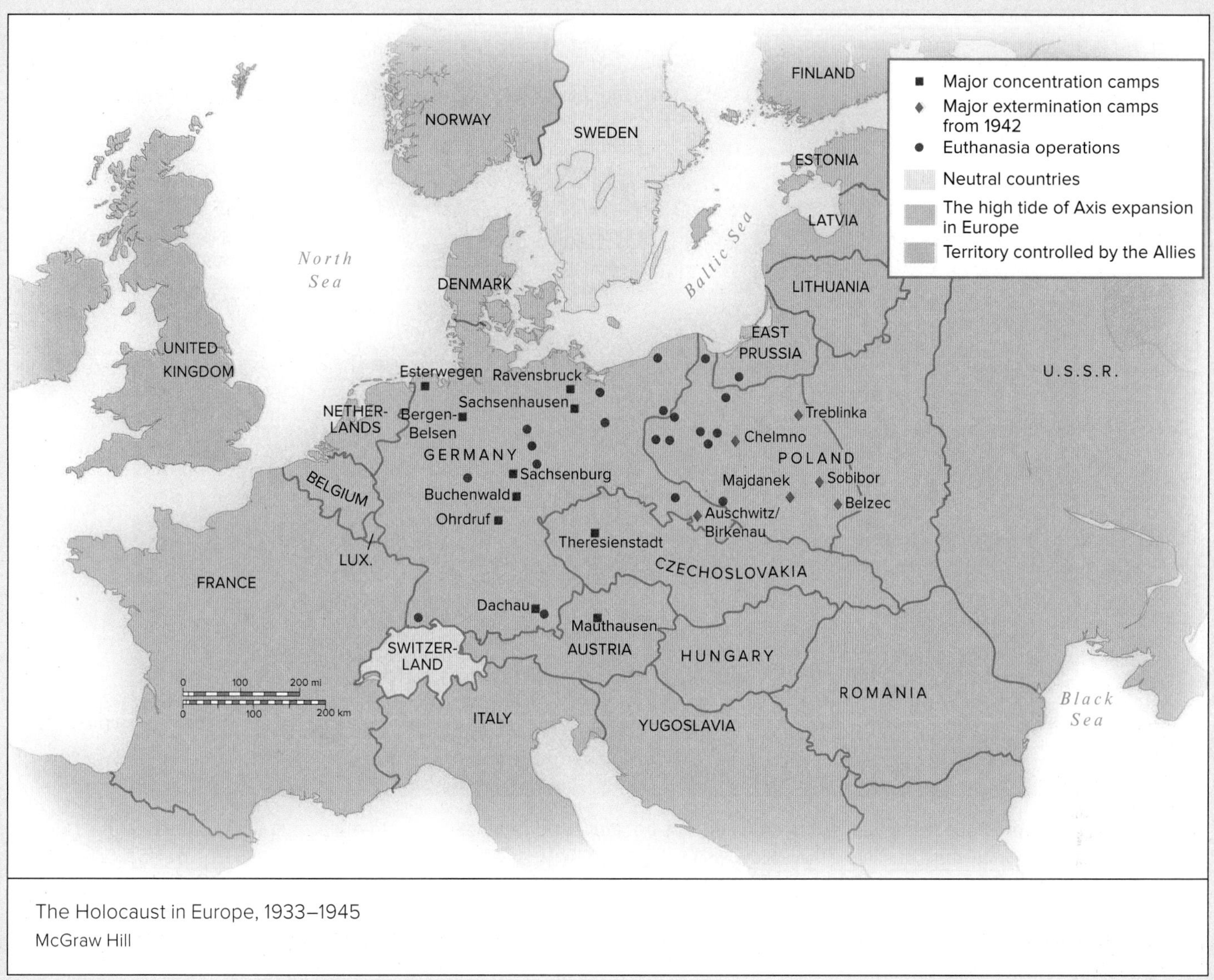


The Holocaust in Europe, 1933–1945
McGraw Hill

## Document 3

Interned Japanese and Japanese Americans behind barbed wire at the Santa Anita camp in California
Everett Collection Historical/Alamy Stock Photo

## Long Essay

Develop a thoughtful and thorough historical argument that answers the question below. Begin your essay with a thesis statement and support it with relevant historical evidence.

Using specific examples and your knowledge of world history, compare and contrast the impact of the Cold War on Korea and Cuba.

# Chapter 25 The End of Empire in an Era of Cold War



## ZOOMING IN ON ENCOUNTERS

### Mohandas Gandhi's Last Words

"Hé Ram" were the last words that escaped Gandhi's lips after three bullets ripped through his frail body. Roughly translated, he uttered, "O! God," and then died. It had begun as a day much like any other in the life of **Mohandas K. Gandhi** (1869–1948), or "Bapuji" (dear father) as he was fondly called. On January 30, 1948, a few months after India gained its independence from Great Britain, he awakened at Birla House in Delhi at an early hour, 3:00 A.M., to continue his work hammering out solutions to the problems that plagued the country. That morning, he labored on a draft of a new constitution for the **Indian National Congress,** stressing as usual his major concerns for the newly independent and strife-ridden nation: that villages be empowered, that discrimination based on the caste system be abolished, that religious intolerance and violence between Hindus and Muslims cease. Still distraught over the partitioning of his land into a Hindu India and Muslim Pakistan, he had weakened himself after independence through fasts and hunger strikes in protest against the killings of Hindus and Muslims and the mistreatment of Pakistan. He weighed a mere 107 pounds that day.

Alternating between working, talking with visitors, and napping, Gandhi finally took a meal at 4:30 P.M. He nibbled on raw and cooked vegetables and oranges, and drank goat's milk and a special brew made with aloe juice, lemons, ginger, and strained butter. A little over half an hour later, he made his way to the evening prayer meeting he was to lead. A bit late, the skies already darkening, he took a shortcut across the green, finely trimmed lawns of Birla House to reach the dais where he would speak. As he approached the dais, he stopped to press his palms together, offering the traditional Hindu

An American air strike against anti-American Viet Cong positions during the Vietnam war results in the destruction of a Vietnamese village.
Larry Burrows/Time & Life Pictures/Getty Images

greeting to the crowd waiting at the meeting. At that moment, Nathuram Godse—a Hindu extremist—stepped out of the crowd, pulled a pistol from his pants pocket, and fired the three shots that ended the life of the man many saw as the very soul and conscience of India. The force of the shots crumpled Gandhi's thin body. As he slumped to the ground, his glasses fell from his face, his sandals slipped from his feet, and large crimson bloodstains spread starkly over his white homespun shawl. After he whispered "Hé Ram," his breathing stilled. Godse's actions made it clear that not all Hindus agreed with Gandhi's lifelong rejection of violence and his insistence that Hindus and Muslims should tolerate one another's religious beliefs. Indeed, before he was executed by hanging in 1949, Godse declared Gandhi a "curse for India, a force for evil."

## CHAPTER FOCUS

- With the near destruction of western European influence, colonies began dismantling imperialism.
- Look for common elements among settler colonies and compare them to patterns in non-settler colonies; similarly, compare colonies that had been governed directly against those dominated only economically.
- Also analyze the patterns of authoritarian governments in these new postwar countries across the three continents.
- The cold war and independence movements are tightly knit together. For economic and military access, African and Asian leaders often chose to ally with either the U.S. or the U.S.S.R., but the Nonaligned Movement encouraged a third option from what some called a bipolar world.
- Independence sometimes caused problems as well as opportunities and did not guarantee a peaceful existence. This was the situation in India after independence and the creation of Pakistan.
- The creation of Israel, backed by the UN and the U.S. in 1948, sparked a political and religious reaction from many of its Arab-Muslim neighbors that grew into a popular Islamist, anti-American movement that, sadly, continues today.
- Borders that African colonies inherited from Europeans did not align with realities of identity, language, culture, land and resource claims, or religion, leading to civil wars between competing groups.
- Latin American countries were still enmeshed in colonial social and political legacies, including demands from native and poor peoples for redistribution of land and resources. These republics also wrestled with U.S. economic imperialism in the postwar era.
- Communist Party victories in China and Vietnam amplified U.S. fears about Latin American protests.

### Historical Developments

- As a result of internal tension and Japanese aggression Chinese communists seized power. These changes in China eventually led to communist revolution.
- Nationalist leaders and parties in Asia and Africa sought varying degrees of autonomy within or independence from imperial rule.
- The redrawing of political boundaries in some cases led to conflict as well as population displacement and/or resettlements, including those related to the Partition of India and the creation of the state of Israel.
- In newly independent states after World War II, governments often took on a strong role in guiding economic life to promote development.

### Reasoning Processes

- **Causation** Describe the causes and effects of decolonization in the 20th century.

### Historical Thinking Skills

- **Developments and Processes** Explain the origins and ultimate outcomes of independence movements in Africa and Asia.
- **Contextualization** Identify and describe the ways in which the Cold War was a critical context surrounding many of the independence movements around the world.
- **Making Connections** Identify patterns among or connections between independence movements in settler colonies and non-settler colonies as well as between colonies that were directly ruled and indirectly ruled.

## CHAPTER OVERVIEW

Gandhi's murder suggested the troubles and traumas faced by nations and peoples adjusting to independence from colonial rule, a process that occurred in almost every colonized territory in the three decades after World War II. Although most colonies won their independence in this period, they did not do so without a fight. Few colonial powers transferred power willingly, though the type of struggle ranged from intense negotiations to all-out war. During this period of **decolonization,** those fighting for independence not only had to actually win, but they also had to determine who would be included and excluded in the new states, whether or not established colonial borders would be adequate, how ethnic and religious minorities would be treated, and what kind of governments would be established in place of colonial rule.

European imperialism was an important theme in world history beginning in the sixteenth century. As we saw in chapter 32, by the turn of the twentieth century much of the world was dominated not only by European empires but also by empires claimed by the United States and Japan. And although we know that colonized people resisted colonial rule from its very beginnings, a series of developments in the first half of the twentieth century fundamentally undermined colonial rule around the world. One catalyst for change was the Great War (World War I), which sapped the strength and the prestige of the major colonial powers such as Great Britain and France. The Great Depression further undermined the strength of the imperialist nations, as did World War II. While the imperial powers were losing strength, anticolonial independence movements were growing stronger. The increasing ease of travel and communication that characterized the twentieth century meant that many activists seeking independence were not only aware of events outside their own colonies but that their leaders had made contact with one another in their travels to Europe and the United States. Activists fighting for independence also made use of the press, steam travel, and modern communications to spread their ideas to a very wide public. By 1994, anticolonial movements had swept away colonial rule and given birth to over ninety new nations.

This process of decolonization was aided by several factors. It became increasingly apparent that there was a significant growth of democratic and anti-imperialist sentiments within imperial countries themselves, and political leaders could no longer count on a war-weary public to make serious sacrifices to maintain overseas colonies. The short-lived Japanese Empire contributed to colonial revolutions throughout Asia, where European military prestige had been severely and permanently damaged after the Japanese defeated the British in Burma and Malaya, the French in Indochina, the Dutch in Indonesia, and the United States in the Philippines. With the emergence of the two postwar superpowers, the United States and the Soviet Union, both of which opposed European colonialism, the stage was set for a drastic overturning of colonial rule. The end of empire was one of the most important outcomes of World War II.

But decolonization frequently did not lead to the kind of freedom and stability most formerly colonized people had fought for. In some places, this was because the withdrawal of colonial rule brought religious, ethnic, or cultural divisions into high relief as once-colonized people struggled over who would take power. In other places, newly independent people realized that colonial rule had left them impoverished and without adequate infrastructure to compete on an equal footing in an increasingly globalized world. In still others, independence threw new states right into the midst of Cold War competition between the United States and the Soviet Union. This competition frequently entailed intervention and influence by one or the other Cold War powers, which limited the ability of new states to determine their own futures. Thus while freedom did not remain elusive for colonized people, peace and prosperity often did.

### CHRONOLOGY

| | |
|---|---|
| 1940s–1970 | El Milagro Mexicano |
| 1947 | Partition of India |
| 1948 | Creation of Israel |
| 1948–1989 | Apartheid in South Africa |
| 1954 | French defeat at Dien Bien Phu |
| 1954–1962 | Algerian war of liberation |
| 1955 | Bandung Conference |
| 1956 | Suez crisis |
| 1957 | Ghana gains independence |
| 1958–1961 | Great Leap Forward in China |
| 1963 | Founding of Organization of African Unity |
| 1973 | Arab-Israeli War |
| 1976 | Reunification of Vietnam |
| 1979 | Revolution in Iran |
| 1980–1988 | Iran-Iraq War |
| 1997 | Transfer of British Hong Kong to People's Republic of China |

# INDEPENDENCE IN ASIA

In the wake of World War II, the power of Asian anticolonial movements was irrepressible. In the decades that followed, new states emerged in south, southwest, and Southeast Asia. While colonized people faced different kinds of struggles in each territory, ranging from civil disobedience to guerrilla warfare, the end result across the whole region was independence from colonial rule.

## India's Partitioned Independence

In the 1930s Indians had fought for, and won, numerous reforms from the British colonial government. The most significant of these reforms was the India Act of 1935, which laid out a structure for Indian home rule (control over internal affairs). But the India Act faced challenges in the form of increasing calls for independent yet separate Hindu and Muslim states, while the eruption of World War II suspended home rule altogether.

**The Coming of Self-Rule** Under the leadership of **Winston Churchill,** who despised Gandhi and vowed never "to preside over the liquidation of the British empire," the British ordered India to support the war effort and temporarily halted thc implementation of home rule. British resistance to Indian independence evaporated after the war, however. The British people voted Churchill out of office. His conservative government was replaced with a Labour government more inclined to work with Indian nationalists, whose demands for independence had continued during the war. Faced with the necessity of waging a costly war to maintain British rule against such strong Indian resistance, the war-weary and economically weakened British government now decided to work toward independence.

The issue of Muslim separatism grew in importance as Indian independence became more certain. In particular, Muslims expressed concerns about their minority status in a free India dominated by Hindus. **Muhammad Ali Jinnah** (1876–1948), leader of the **Muslim League,** argued that these concerns could only be met through the establishment of a separate Muslim state, even as Congress Party leaders such as **Jawaharlal Nehru** (1889–1964) and Gandhi urged all Indians to act and feel as one nation, undivided by what came to be known as communalism (emphasizing religious over national identity). In August 1946, in the midst of negotiations with the British to reach terms regarding independence, the Muslim League called for a Day of Direct Action, even though the league's leaders recognized that Muslim demonstrations might lead to rioting and fighting between Muslims and Hindus. Some six thousand people died in the Great Calcutta Killing that resulted, further fueling communal feeling and adding weight to Jinnah's claim: "The only solution to India's problem is Pakistan."

**Partition and Violence** Gandhi and Nehru only reluctantly came to accept the notion of a divided and independent India. Gandhi condemned what has come to be known as the **partition of India** as a "vivisection," a term that refers to the cutting up of a living body. He avoided the celebrations on August 15, 1947, that accompanied independence for India and Pakistan, glumly prophesying that "rivers of blood" would flow in the wake of partition. Indeed, communal violence between Hindus and Muslims had already become a major problem in parts of India in the months leading up to partition

Jawaharlal Nehru (left) and Mohammad Ali Jinnah (right) sit down with the British Viceroy of India Lord Mountbatten (center) to discuss the Partition of India in 1946.
World History Archive/ Alamy Stock Photo

and independence. Both Hindus and Muslims were involved in propaganda campaigns intended to stir up animosities between the two religious traditions, while rumors about the dire consequences of remaining in the "wrong" state inspired fear and uncertainty among ordinary people. To make matters worse, the British government did not make it clear exactly where the boundaries of the new states would be, leaving that task to the new Indian government two days after independence. Hindus and Muslims who lived in the areas that would likely be affected were terrified that they would suddenly be in hostile territory once independence was declared, and thus millions began to move to what they hoped would be "safe" Muslim or Hindu territory during the summer of 1947. Muslims and Hindus who had once been neighbors and friends now began to see one another as the enemy, and in the highly charged atmosphere, individuals began to resort to violence. Acts of violence perpetrated by Hindus toward Muslims, and vice versa, spawned further violence in order to exact revenge, and quickly the cycle of violence spun out of control. By mid-1948 an estimated ten million refugees had made the torturous journey to one state or the other, and between half a million and one million people died in the violence that accompanied those massive human migrations. The hostility between migrating Hindus and Muslims spilled over into the enmity between the two states, complicating efforts to build their independent nations.

In spite of the tragic violence of partition, Indian independence became a reality with momentous consequences for the process of decolonization. India was the most important British colony, and its breakaway marked a significant turning point. Just as Gandhi's nonviolent resistance to British rule inspired anticolonial activists around the globe before and after World War II, independence in India and Pakistan further encouraged anti-imperial movements throughout Asia and Africa. Another way in which Indian independence inspired nations and set a pattern for grappling with decolonization in the midst of the Cold War was through Nehru's promotion of a nonalignment strategy. In his role as the first president of independent India, Nehru proved instrumental in fashioning a compelling position for newly independent nations caught in the Cold War and in the superpower tug-of-war contests for the loyalties of new nations. He became one of the impassioned defenders of nonalignment, especially at the Bandung Conference, where he was one of the most visible participants.

**Nonalignment** Leaders of new African and Asian countries first discussed nonalignment at the Bandung Conference. In April 1955, leaders from twenty-three Asian and six African nations met in Bandung, Indonesia, partly to find a "third path," an alternative to choosing either the United States or the Soviet Union. Bandung was the precursor of the broader **Nonaligned Movement,** which held occasional meetings so that its members could discuss matters of common interest, particularly their relations with the United States and the Soviet Union. The movement's primary goal was to maintain formal neutrality. However, the Nonaligned Movement suffered from a chronic lack of unity among its members and ultimately failed to present a genuinely united front. Although theoretically nonaligned with either Cold War superpower, many member states did in fact maintain close ties to one or the other.

## Pakistan

In the new state of Pakistan, tensions between West and East Pakistan—separated by 1000 miles with the hostile state of India between them—arose very quickly. Particularly at issue was the dominance of West Pakistan in political and economic affairs. The situation came to a head during the election of 1970, when the East Pakistani Awami League won every seat in the national assembly allotted to the East, which would have allowed the leader of the party to form a national government. Civil war erupted and, in response to massive protests in East Pakistan, an army from West Pakistan invaded on March 25, 1971 in a campaign called Operation Searchlight. For the next several months, the army targeted East Pakistani men for execution, while women were subjected to mass rape. The systematic nature of the killings and rapes have led some scholars to call Operation Searchlight a genocide. In December 1971 the Indian Army intervened on behalf of East Pakistan and forced the surrender of the West Pakistani army. East Pakistan thereafter became the independent state of Bangladesh.

## Nationalist Struggles in Vietnam

In contrast to India, the Vietnamese struggle for independence became deeply enmeshed in the politics of the Cold War. As a result, Vietnam's independence occurred only after decades of fighting bloody wars to defeat first the French and then the Americans.

**Fighting the French** Vietnamese anticolonial activists had been fighting against French rule in Indochina since the late nineteenth century. By the 1930s, the Indochinese Communist Party was among the groups fighting to drive out the French. **Ho Chi Minh** (1890–1969), the man who would become the first president of North Vietnam, had helped found the Indochinese Communist Party but spent the 1930s in exile as a wanted man in his home country. When the Japanese invaded Indochina in 1940 with the agreement of the French Vichy regime (which was collaborating with the Nazis), Ho was infuriated that after so many years of fighting French colonizers, the Vietnamese now faced another. In that year he returned to Indochina to coordinate a resistance movement against the Japanese and worked with U.S. operatives from the Office of Strategic Services to undermine their common enemy. By 1945, when it was clear that Japan was going to lose the war and before the French could return to reclaim Indochina, Ho and his party issued the Vietnamese Declaration of Independence and proclaimed Vietnam an independent republic. However, the French, humiliated by their country's easy defeat and occupation by the Germans, sought to reclaim their world-power status through their imperial possessions. By October 1945, the French had retaken Saigon and much of southern Vietnam, and by 1946, war had broken out between the French and the Vietnamese communist forces of the north, known as the Viet Minh. The French were brutal in the battles that ensued as they moved north. For example, they indiscriminately bombed the cities of Hanoi and Haiphong, killing at least ten thousand civilians. By 1947 the French appeared to have secured their power, especially in the cities, but that security proved to be temporary. Much like the Chinese communists in their battles against the Japanese and then against the nationalists in the postwar years, the Vietnamese resistance forces, led by Ho Chi Minh and former history teacher General **Vo Nguyen Giap** (1912–2013), took to the countryside and mounted a campaign of guerrilla warfare. This campaign grew even more effective after 1949, when communist China sent aid and arms to the Viet Minh. In 1954, the Viet Minh defeated French forces at their fortress at **Dien Bien Phu,** leading the French to sue for peace.

## The Geneva Conference and Partial Independence

The peace conference, held in Geneva in 1954, was dominated by Cold War concerns. Even though U.S. forces had aided Ho Chi Minh's resistance against the Japanese during World War II, by 1954 the United States was unwilling to accept that French defeat would leave Ho's communist party in control of Vietnam. As a compromise, the conference participants agreed that Vietnam should be temporarily divided at the seventeenth parallel; North Vietnam would be controlled by Ho Chi Minh and the communist forces, whereas South Vietnam would remain in the hands of noncommunists. In the context of growing tensions with the Soviet Union and China, U.S. president Dwight Eisenhower invoked the "domino theory," arguing that a communist Vietnam would lead to the spread of communism throughout Southeast Asia. The terms of the **Geneva Conference** required elections within two years in both North and South Vietnam that would reunite the country, and it seemed clear to all that Ho would easily win. Instead of allowing Ho's communist government to be fairly elected, the United States supported a South Vietnamese anti-communist leader, and together both ignored calls for new elections. But Ngo Dinh Diem (1901–1963), the first president of the Republic of (South) Vietnam, was dictatorial, corrupt, and deeply unpopular with

**Vo Nguyen Giap** (voh winn zahp)

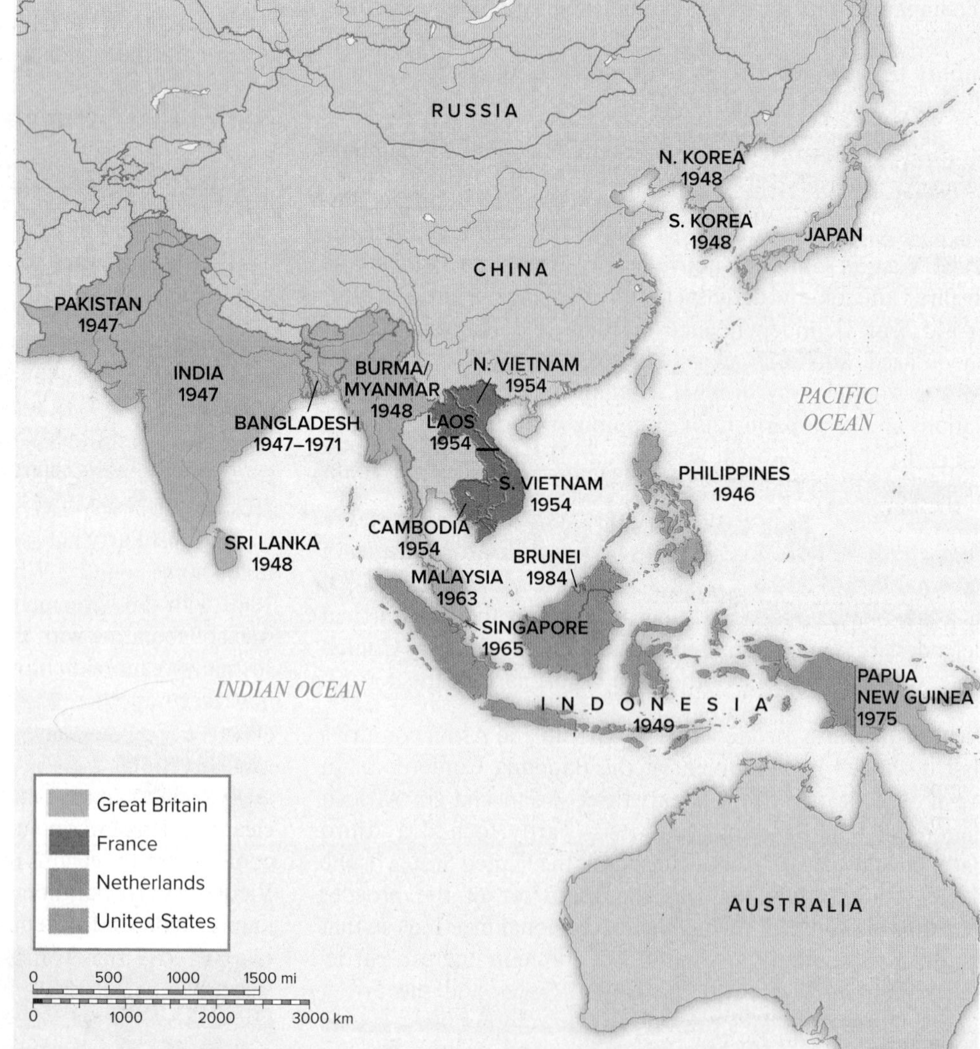


**MAP 25.1 Decolonization in Asia. Date is year of independence.**

Note the dates of independence for the colonies of Great Britain, the Netherlands, the United States, and France.

***Why did independence occur in such a short time span for most of these colonies?***

the people, and growing discontent sparked the spread of guerrilla war in the south.

In 1960, Vietnamese nationalists in the south formed the National Liberation Front (NLF) to fight for freedom from South Vietnamese rule (the military arm of the NLF became known as the **Viet Cong**). Although Vietnamese from the south made up the majority in this organization, it received direction, aid, weapons, and ultimately troops from the north. In turn, the government in the north received economic and military assistance from the Soviet Union and China, and a Cold War stalemate ensued.

Ho Chi Minh, leader of North Vietnam from 1945 to 1969 and one of southeast Asia's most influential communist leaders.
Bettmann/Getty Images

### Vietnam's "American War"

Given the lack of popular support for the U.S.-backed Diem regime, the Viet Cong's attacks against the South Vietnamese government met with continued success. Believing in the dire consequences of a communist victory for the stability of Southeast Asia, in 1965 President **Lyndon Johnson** (1908–1973) embarked on a course of action that exponentially increased U.S. involvement in Vietnam. He ordered a bombing campaign against North Vietnam and sent U.S. ground troops to augment the South Vietnamese army. Yet, even with the overwhelming firepower and military personnel, the best the United States and South Vietnam could achieve against the Viet Cong was a draw. The United States had completely underestimated the ability and the resolve of both the Viet Minh and the Viet Cong—not to mention their civilian supporters—to fight effectively for Vietnamese self-determination. But the sacrifices were terrible: between 1965 and 1975, scholars estimate that nearly 900,000 Vietnamese soldiers and civilians were killed as a result of the war.

### Vietnamese Victory

Faced with such strong and effective resistance against U.S. intervention, incensed by the loss of over 58,000 American soldiers, and shocked by daily depictions of the war's brutality on American television, public opinion in the United States began to turn against the war. In 1968, the war had become so divisive that president Lyndon Johnson pledged not to run for re-election, while Richard Nixon successfully campaigned on a pledge to end the war. After Nixon's election, he implemented his strategy of turning the war over to the South Vietnamese—termed **Vietnamization**—by escalating the conflict. Nixon extended the war into Cambodia through bombing and invasion in 1969 and 1970, and he resumed the heavy bombing of North Vietnam. He also opened diplomatic channels to the Soviet Union and China, hoping to get them to pressure North Vietnam into a negotiated end to the war. U.S. troops gradually withdrew from the conflict, and in January 1973 the "American War," as the Vietnamese termed it, ended with the negotiated Paris Peace Accords. With the Americans out of the way, forces from North Vietnam, in partnership with the Viet Cong, began to move south. In April 1975, North Vietnamese tanks rolled into Saigon. The next year, Vietnam was officially reunited as one nation, twenty-two years after the partition of the country by Cold War powers. War itself did not end, as forces from North Vietnam and the NLF continued their struggle to conquer South Vietnam and unite the nation. They achieved their goals with the military defeat of South Vietnam in 1975 and with national reunification in 1976.

## Cambodia

Cambodia, which had been part of French Indochina but became independent in 1953, was also deeply affected by the Vietnam War. During the War, United States aircraft bombed large portions of the state from 1970-1973, and government representatives interfered in its political processes. In 1975, a communist leader named Pol Pot took control of the country in the name of his party, the Khmer Rouge. In an effort to 'cleanse' the country of outside influences, Pol Pot's regime targeted for execution those who had been exposed to western education or ideas as well as Christians, Muslims, and Buddhists. Over the next four years—until the Khmer Rouge was removed from power when a Vietnamese army invaded—more than 1.7 million people died as a result of these efforts. Because the Khmer Rouge targeted groups from a variety of sectors of society, scholars disagree about whether it can be classified as a genocide under the United Nations Convention.

## Arab National States and the Problem of Palestine

With the exception of Palestine, and in stark contrast to Vietnam, the Arab states of Southwest Asia had little difficulty freeing themselves from the colonial powers of France and Britain by the end of World War II. Before World War II, anticolonial activists in Arab states had already won concessions for self-rule under the mandate system established after the Great War. For example, Egyptians had won almost complete autonomy from British rule, although this autonomy continued to be limited by British military control of the strategic Suez Canal and the oil-rich Persian Gulf.

### Arab Independence

By 1946, Syria, Iraq, Lebanon, and Jordan had gained complete independence. But as in Egypt, significant vestiges of imperial rule impeded Arab sovereignty. The battle to rid Southwest Asia of those remnants of imperialism was deeply complicated by the Cold War, as both the United States and the Soviet Union sought influence in the region because of its vast reserves of oil, the lifeblood of the Cold War's military-industrial complexes. Throughout, one ambiguous legacy of imperialism—Palestine—absorbed much of the region's energies and emotions.

**Palestine** Great Britain served as the mandate power in Palestine after the Great War and, before and during its mandate, made conflicting promises to the Palestinian Arabs and to the Jews migrating to Palestine to establish a secure homeland where they could avoid persecution. With the Balfour Declaration of 1917, the British government committed itself to the support of a homeland for Jews in Palestine, a commitment engendered in part by the vibrant Zionist movement that had been growing in Europe since the 1890s. Zionists were dedicated to combating the violent anti-Semitism prevailing in central and eastern Europe by establishing a national Jewish state. The Zionist dream of returning to Palestine, the site of the original Jewish homeland, received a boost from the Balfour Declaration and from the Allies' support for it at the Paris Peace Conference in 1919. Thus the British were compelled to allow Jewish migration to Palestine under their mandate, but they also had to respond to the fears of those in possession of the land—the Palestinian Arabs. The British therefore limited the migration and settlement of Jews and promised to protect the Arabs' political and economic rights.

At the end of World War II, a battle brewed. The Holocaust, along with the British policy of limiting Jewish migration to Palestine after the war, intensified the Jewish commitment to build a state capable of defending the world's remaining Jews. At the same time, as Arab states around Palestine gained their freedom from imperial rule, they developed a pan-Arab nationalism sparked by support for their fellow Arabs in Palestine and opposition to the possibility of a Jewish state there.

**The Creation of Israel** The British could not adjudicate the competing claims of the Arabs and the Jews in Palestine. While the Arabs insisted on complete independence under Arab rule, in 1945 the Jews embarked on a course of violent resistance to

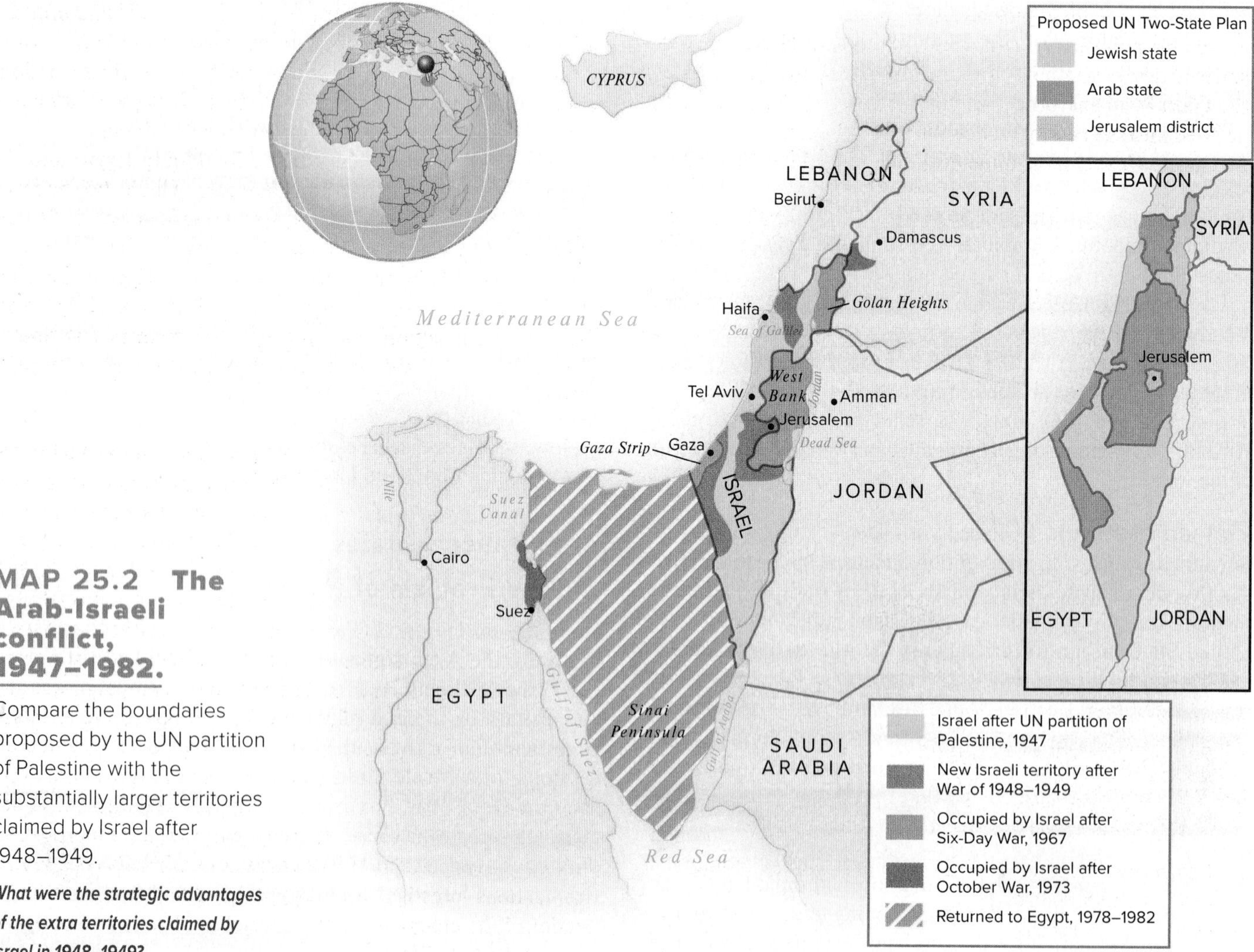


**MAP 25.2 The Arab-Israeli conflict, 1947–1982.**

Compare the boundaries proposed by the UN partition of Palestine with the substantially larger territories claimed by Israel after 1948–1949.

***What were the strategic advantages of the extra territories claimed by Israel in 1948–1949?***

the British to compel recognition of Jewish demands for self-rule and open immigration. The British gave up in 1947, stating that they intended to withdraw from Palestine and turn over the region to the newly created United Nations. Delegates to the UN General Assembly debated the idea of dividing Palestine into two states, one Arab and the other Jewish. The United States and the Soviet Union lent their support to that notion, and in November 1947 the General Assembly announced a proposal for the division of Palestine into two distinct states. Arabs inside and outside Palestine found that solution unacceptable, and in late 1947 civil war broke out. Arab and Jewish troops battled each other as the British completed their withdrawal from Palestine, and in May 1948 the Jews in Palestine proclaimed the creation of the independent state of Israel.

Israel's proclamation of statehood provoked a series of military conflicts between Israeli and various Arab forces spanning decades, most notably in 1948–1949, 1956, 1967, 1973, and 1982. As a result of those wars, Israel substantially increased the size of its territory beyond the area granted to it by the original UN partition and forced hundreds of thousands of Palestinians to become refugees outside the state of Israel. Because Arabs and Israelis could not reach a comprehensive and permanent peace agreement, hostilities continued. Beginning in 1987 a popular mass movement known as the ***intifada*** initiated a series of demonstrations, strikes, and riots against Israeli rule in the Gaza Strip and other occupied territories. Violence continues well into the twenty-first century, and the future of the occupied territories remains undetermined.

Gamal Abdel Nasser was president of Egypt from 1954 until his death in 1970.
Bettmann/Getty Images

**Egypt and Arab Nationalism** Egyptian military leaders, under the direction of **Gamal Abdel Nasser** (1918–1970), committed themselves to opposing Israel and taking command of the Arab world. When Israel had declared independence in 1948, Egypt—along with Jordan, Iraq, Syria, and Lebanon—declared war against the new state. But instead of defeating Israel, the Arab coalition was not only defeated but lost territory. Egyptians were deeply unhappy with their leadership and staged a number of riots. In July 1952 Nasser and other officers staged a bloodless coup that ended the monarchy of Egypt's King Farouk. Two years later, Nasser named himself prime minister and took control of the government. He then labored assiduously to develop Egypt economically and militarily and make it the fountainhead of pan-Arab nationalism.

In his efforts to strengthen Egypt, Nasser adopted an internationalist position based, like India's Nehru, on the idea of nonalignment (in fact, Nasser attended the Bandung Conference on nonalignment in 1955). Nasser argued that Cold War power politics were simply a new form of imperialism. Nasser condemned states that joined with either the United States or the Soviet Union in military alliances. In practice, however, Nasser played both sides off the other, and he used his political savvy to extract pledges of economic and military assistance from the United States and the Soviet Union. In so doing, Nasser demonstrated how newly independent nations could evade becoming trapped in either ideological camp and could force the superpowers to compete for influence.

Nasser also dedicated himself to ridding Egypt and the Arab world of imperial interference, which he believed included destroying the state of Israel. He also gave aid to the Algerians in their war against the French. Nasser did not neglect the remaining imperial presence in Egypt: he abolished British military rights to the Suez Canal in 1954. Through such actions and through his country's antipathy toward Israel, he laid claim to pan-Arab leadership throughout Southwest Asia and north Africa.

**The Suez Crisis** Nasser sealed his reputation during the **Suez crisis,** which left him in a dominant position in the Arab world. The crisis erupted in 1956, when Nasser decided to nationalize the Suez Canal and use the money collected from the canal to finance construction of a massive dam of the Nile River at Aswan. When he did not bow to international pressure to provide multinational control of the vital Suez Canal, British, French, and Israeli forces conspired to wrest control of the canal away from him. Their military campaign was successful, but they failed miserably on the diplomatic level and tore at the fabric of the Cold War world system. They had not consulted with the United States, which strongly condemned the attack and forced them to withdraw. The Soviet Union also objected forcefully, thereby gaining a reputation for being a staunch supporter of Arab nationalism. Nasser gained tremendous prestige, and Egypt solidified its position as leader of the charge against imperial holdovers in Southwest Asia and north Africa.

## INTERPRETING IMAGES

Two female members of the National Liberation Army in combat gear during the war for Algerian independence. Thousands of women were active participants in the fight for independence from the French.

**Analyze** *What were the various reasons for violence, even war, to be involved in decolonization movements in Africa and Asia? How does this compare to previous historical eras? Based on what you've learned in this course, what is the relationship between nationalism and violence?*

Keystone-France/Gamma-Keystone/Getty Images

Despite Nasser's successes, he did not achieve his goal of defeating Israel, which instead continued to grow stronger and gain more territory. And although Nasser succeeded in playing the Cold War powers off one another and in sowing disunity between the United States and its European allies during the Suez Crisis, the superpowers nevertheless continued to intervene in the region because of its strategic value as an oil-producing region. These interventions, along with the continuation of the Arab-Israeli conflict, contributed to long-term instability in Southwest Asia long after the end of empire.

## DECOLONIZATION IN AFRICA

Independence struggles in Africa took many forms—some peaceful and some violent—depending on the type of colony, the colonial power, and the nature of opposing anticolonial movements. In some colonies, like Angola, the colonial powers refused to relinquish their power without long and bloody wars. In others, like Ghana, decolonization was seen as an inevitability. In colonies where imperial rule had the support of European settlers, as in Algeria or Kenya, decolonization often became violent. Complicating the decolonization process were internal divisions in African societies, which undermined attempts to forge national or pan-African identities. Ethnic, religious, and linguistic divides within and between state boundaries, all of which colonial rulers had exploited, posed a challenge to African leaders. Whatever the path and in spite of many challenges, between 1957 and 1980 Africans from every region had won their independence.

### How the Past Shapes the Future

#### The Destructive Potential of Industrial Technologies

In both Algeria and Vietnam, France and the United States employed vast quantities of sophisticated weaponry—including fighter planes, helicopters, bombs, chemical agents, rifles, and grenades—to defeat the forces that opposed them. Yet even though Algerian and Vietnamese revolutionaries did not possess technological parity with French and American military might, they were not defeated. The reasons included military aid (indirect and direct) from the Soviet Union (and China, in the case of Vietnam), but also a willingness to resort to guerrilla warfare, suicide bombings, or sabotage to maximize the effectiveness of individual efforts in fighting against massive force. Consider the circumstances in which the deployment of sophisticated military technologies might not be enough to defeat a less well-armed opposition.

### Forcing the French out of North Africa

In 1956, Morocco and Tunisia peacefully won their independence from France. Four years later, thirteen French colonies in west and equatorial Africa also won their independence, leading some to dub 1960 as "the year of Africa." But in Algeria, the French resisted decolonization, sparking a brutal war that lasted eight years.

**France and Algeria** The French government treated Algeria differently than its other African colonies for two reasons. First, Algeria was a settler colony, meaning that a substantial number of Europeans had made Algeria their permanent home in the nineteenth and twentieth centuries. By the mid-1940s, two million French and other Europeans had either settled in or had been born

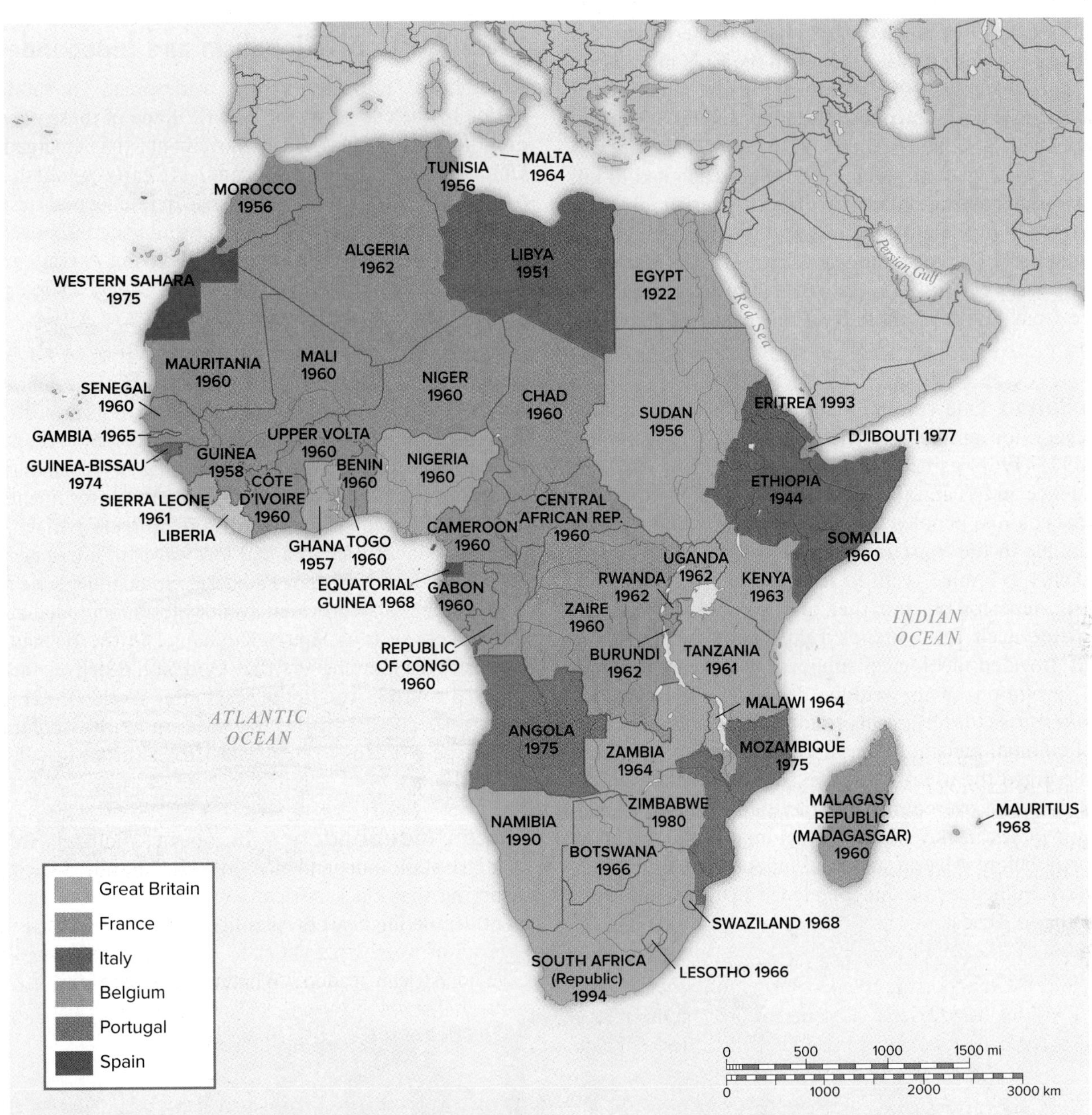


**MAP 25.3 Decolonization in Africa. Date is year of independence.**

Compare this map with Map 20.2.

***How do the borders of the newly independent African states compare with those drawn by European powers in the late nineteenth century?***

in Algeria. Second, unlike its other colonies in Africa, the French constitution of 1848 had incorporated Algeria as a region of France rather than as a separate colony. Thus, when Algerian nationalists began to advocate for independence from France and freedom from domination by white settlers just after World War II, the French government saw their actions as a threat to the integrity of France itself. The event that touched off the Algerian revolt came in May 1945.

**War in Algeria** Algerian discontent with French rule soared in May 1945. French colonial police in the town of Sétif fired shots into an otherwise peaceful demonstration in support of Algerian and Arab nationalism. Algerian rioting and French repression of the disturbances took place in the wake of the incident. In the resulting fighting more than eight thousand Algerian Muslims died, along with approximately one hundred French. Discontent simmered following the disaster, but it was only in 1954 that the Algerian war of liberation began in earnest under the command of the Front de Libération Nationale (**FLN,** or National Liberation Front). The FLN adopted tactics similar to those of nationalist liberation groups in Asia, relying on bases in outlying mountainous areas and resorting to guerrilla warfare. The French did not realize the seriousness of the challenge they faced until 1955, when the FLN moved into more urbanized areas. At that point, France sent thousands of troops to Algeria to put down the revolution, and by 1958 it had committed half a million soldiers to the war. The war was brutal and ugly: Algerians serving with the French had to kill fellow Algerians or be killed by them; Algerian civilians became trapped in the crossfire of war, often accused of and killed for aiding FLN guerrillas; thousands of French soldiers died. By the war's end in 1962, when the Algerians gained independence from France, hundreds of thousands of Algerians had died.

**Frantz Fanon** One revolutionary from the Algerian war left a legacy for anticolonial activists everywhere. **Frantz Fanon** (1925–1961) gained fame as a supporter of Algerian independence and as an influential proponent of national liberation for colonial peoples through violent revolution. Born in Martinique in the West Indies, Fanon studied psychiatry and medicine in France, went to Algeria to head a hospital's psychiatric department, and then participated in Algeria's battle to free itself from French rule. Fanon furthered his fame and provided ideological support for African nationalism and revolution in his writings. In works such as *Black Skin, White Masks* (1952), he exposed the deep and damaging effects of colonial racism. Later, in *The Wretched of the Earth* (1961), he urged the use of violence against colonial oppressors as a means of overcoming the racist degradation experienced by peoples in developing or colonial nations. Fanon died shortly before Algeria achieved independence in 1962, but his ideas influenced the independence struggles that were still ongoing in Africa.

## Black African Nationalism and Independence

Anticolonial movements were widespread in sub-Saharan Africa by the end of World War II. Some of these movements drew from the pan-African movements that emerged in the United States and the Caribbean in the early twentieth century (see chapter 22). For example, African intellectuals, especially in French-controlled west Africa, established a movement to promote ***Négritude*** ("Blackness"). Reviving Africa's great traditions, poets and writers expressed a widely shared pride in the rich and diverse cultures and histories of Africa.

**Growth of African Nationalism** This celebration of African culture was accompanied by grassroots protests against European imperialism in nearly every colony. A new urban African elite created organizations that held demonstrations and protests, and put pressure on colonial governments. Especially widespread, if sporadic, were workers' strikes against oppressive labor practices and low wages in areas such as the Gold Coast and Northern Rhodesia. Some independent Christian churches also provided avenues for anticolonial agitation, as prophets such as Simon Kimbangu in the Belgian Congo promised his churchgoers that God would deliver them from imperial control. And in the years after World War II, African poets associated with the *Négritude* movement continued to encourage Africans to turn away from European culture and colonial rule.

**African Independence** European colonizers frequently tried to stall independence in sub-Saharan Africa. Often assuming that black Africans were incapable of self-government, imperial powers planned for a slow transition to

Roadside portraits of Queen Elizabeth II (1926–) and Kwame Nkrumah (1909–1972) in Accra. The British monarch made a postindependence visit to Ghana in November 1961. Express Newspapers/ Hulton Royals Collection/ Getty Images

# SOURCES FROM THE PAST

## Kwame Nkrumah on the Future of Africa

*As the leader of the first African nation to gain independence, Kwame Nkrumah (1909–1972) became a respected spokesperson for African unity as a strategy for dealing with decolonization during the cold war. In addition to his own speeches and writings, like-minded African nationalists also sought his stamp of approval by asking him to endorse their work. In this foreward to* Africa Unbound: Reflections of an African Statesman, *Nkrumah did just that, while also reminding readers of his own vision for the future of Africa.*

**The decade following the early 1950s** may truly be regarded as Africa's decade. Breathtaking and significant changes have taken place on the African continent that were undreamed of twelve or fifteen years earlier. The independence of Ghana in March, 1957, proved to be the beginning of a great avalanche which was soon to sweep before it the "possessions" and "spheres of influence" of the colonial powers. A majority of these so called possessions have been transformed in our time into sovereign, independent states, and the process of decolonization goes on unabated.

Our next goal is to attain the political unification of the African continent so as to give form and substance to our independence through total disengagement from imperialist and colonialist entanglements . . .

Why, according to Nkrumah, was the political unification of Africa so important for its future?

Africans [are making efforts] to complete the liberation of their continent from all forms of imperialism, colonialism, racialism, and neocolonialism. In this way, we may secure the establishment of the personality of the African and the fulfillment of his destiny in an interdependent world.

### For Further Reflection

- What role do you think Nkrumah sees for Ghana in this African future? Does Nkrumah seem optimistic or pessimistic? Why?
- What does Nkrumah mean by "secure the personality of the African"?
- How did European imperialism suppress the African "personality"?

*Source:* Quaison-Sackey, Alex. *Africa Unbound: Reflections of an African Statesman.* New York: Frederick Praeger, 1963, foreword.

independence. The presence of white settlers in certain African colonies also complicated the process of decolonization. The politics of the Cold War allowed imperial powers to justify oppressive actions in the name of rooting out a subversive communist presence. Despite delays, however, sub-Saharan states slowly but surely won their independence as each newly independent nation inspired and often aided other territories to win their freedom.

## Freedom and Conflict in Sub-Saharan Africa

**Ghana** Ghana, located in west Africa, was the first sub-Saharan country to achieve independence from colonial rule. Its people had been engaged in trade with Europe since the fifteenth century. Trading originally centered on gold but then shifted to the slave trade in the seventeenth century. By the time the British established Ghana as a Crown colony in 1874 (known at that time as the Gold Coast), its economy had developed into an important center for growing and exporting cacao.

Ghana's success in achieving its freedom from British rule in 1957 served as a hallmark in Africa's end of empire. Under the leadership of **Kwame Nkrumah** (1909–1972), political parties and strategies for mass action took shape. Although the British subjected Nkrumah and other nationalists to jail terms and repressive control, they eventually conceded to reforms and negotiated the transfer of power in their Gold Coast colony.

After it became independent in 1957, Ghana emboldened and inspired other African anticolonial movements. More than thirty other African countries followed Ghana's example and won their own independence within the next decade. Nkrumah, as a leader of the first sub-Saharan African nation to gain independence from colonial rule, became a persuasive spokesperson for pan-African unity. These efforts were aided by the optimism for the future in Ghana, whose immediate postcolonial economic prospects were bright. Indeed, in 1957 Ghana's gross domestic product was roughly equal to that of South Korea and was only slightly behind Portugal. Nkrumah's leadership of this prosperous new state symbolized the changing times in Africa.

**Kwame Nkrumah** (KWAH-mee en-KROO-mah)

## INTERPRETING IMAGES

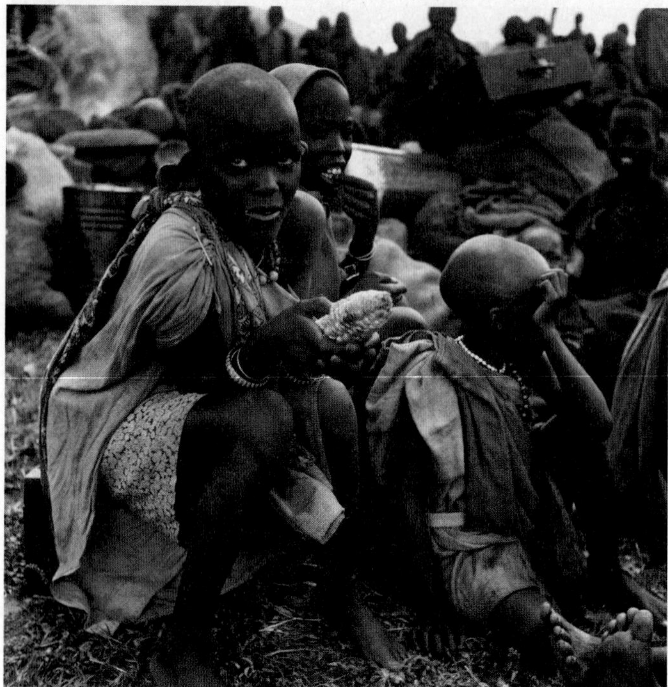

These Kikuyu children were photographed in 1952 in a British government prison camp, where most of Kenya's Kikuyu were detained without trial.

**Analyze** *Philosopher Hannah Arendt once called the twentieth century the "century of the camp." Consider images you have seen in this course of people detained in different types of camps. What is the rationale behind this detention? What do the images have in common? How are detainees portrayed in media? How do we usually think about the countries or leaders who put people in camps, and how might a photo like this affect how we understand British colonialism, especially thinking about the time period (1950s)?*

Hulton Deutsch/Corbis Historical/Getty Images

**Anticolonial Rebellion in Kenya** The process of attaining independence was sometimes extremely violent. The battle for independence that took place in the British colony of Kenya in east Africa was one of these cases. The situation in Kenya turned tense and violent in a clash between powerful white settlers and their elite, land-holding African allies on the one hand and landless Africans who had been impoverished by colonial rule on the other. Most of those involved were Kikuyu, one of Kenya's largest ethnic groups, because the British had disproportionately dispossessed the Kikuyu from their lands in the fertile Kenyan highlands. Beginning in 1947, Kikuyu seeking to drive out the British embarked on an intermittently violent campaign against both Europeans and against the Africans who had allied themselves with them. The settlers who controlled the colonial government in Nairobi refused to see the uprisings as a legitimate expression of discontent with colonial rule. Rather, they branded the Kikuyu rebels as radicals bent on a racial struggle for primacy. But it was the British settlers who displayed their own deep racism with comments such as, "Why the hell can't we fight these apes and worry about the survivors later?" Members of the militant anticolonial movements were labeled by the British government as **Mau Mau** subversives.

Kikuyu who became involved in the Mau Mau movement were deeply dissatisfied with British rule in Kenya. Their resentment originated in particular from their treatment in the 1930s and 1940s, when white settlers pushed them off the most fertile highland farm areas, often relegating them to overcrowded "tribal reserves." Resistance began in the early 1940s with labor strikes and violent direct action campaigns designed to force or frighten the white settlers off the land. In the 1950s, attacks on white settlers—and on Africans the Kikuyu believed were collaborating with them—escalated, and in 1952 the British established a state of emergency to crush the anticolonial guerrilla movement through a violent counterinsurgency program that involved rounding up and imprisoning over a hundred thousand Kikuyu in detention camps. Conditions inside the camps were dismal, and many thousands died from abuse, disease, and execution. Unable or unwilling to distinguish violent activism from nonviolent agitation, the British moved to suppress all anticolonial groups and jailed Kenyan nationalist leaders, including Jomo Kenyatta (1895–1978) in 1953. Amid growing resistance to colonial rule, the British mounted major military offenses against rebel forces, supporting their army troops with artillery, bombers, and jet fighters. By 1956 the British had effectively crushed all military resistance in a conflict that claimed the lives of twelve thousand Africans and one hundred Europeans.

Despite military defeat, Kikuyu fighters broke British resolve in Kenya and gained increasing international recognition of African grievances. The British resisted the radical white supremacism and political domineering of the settlers in Kenya and instead responded to calls for Kenyan independence. In 1959 the British lifted the state of emergency, and as political parties formed, nationalist leaders like Kenyatta reemerged to lead those parties. By December 1963 Kenya had negotiated its independence.

**Internal Colonialism in South Africa** As elsewhere in Africa, the presence of large numbers of white settlers in South Africa long frustrated, complicated, and delayed the arrival of freedom for black South Africans. Even though black South Africans made up almost 70 percent of the population by 1946, white settlers had violently driven them off the best lands and deprived them of political rights. Anticolonial agitation thus was significantly different in South Africa than in the rest of sub-Saharan Africa: it was a struggle against internal colonialism, against an oppressive white regime that denied basic human and civil rights to tens of millions of South Africans.

**Apartheid** The ability of whites to resist majority rule was aided by the South African economy, the strongest on the continent. That strength had two sources: extraction of minerals and industrial development, which received a huge boost during World War II. The growth of the industrial sector opened many jobs to black South Africans, allowing some to build wealth, to organize into labor unions, and to demand serious political reform. These changes deeply alarmed white South Africans, who had built their rule on the political and economic oppression of black South Africans. In 1948 the Afrikaner National Party, which was dedicated to quashing any move toward black equality, came to power. Under the National Party the government instituted a harsh new set of laws designed to extend their control over the increasingly organized black population; these new laws constituted the system known as **apartheid,** or "separateness."

The system of apartheid institutionalized the racial segregation established in the years before 1948. The government designated approximately 87 percent of South Africa's territory for white residents. Remaining areas were designated as homelands for black and colored citizens. Nonwhites were classified according to a variety of ethnic identifications—colored or mixed-race peoples, Indians, and "Bantu," which in turn was subdivided into numerous distinct tribal affiliations (for example, Zulu, Xhosa, Sotho). As other imperial powers had done in Africa, white South Africans divided the black and colored population in the hope of preventing the rise of unified liberation movements. The apartheid system, complex and varied in its composition, evolved into a system designed to keep blacks in a position of political, social, and economic subordination.

Black South Africans resisted apartheid, just as they had resisted oppressive laws prior to 1948. The **African National Congress** (ANC), formed in 1912, gained new young leaders such as **Nelson Mandela** (1918–2013), who inspired direct action campaigns to protest apartheid. In 1955 the ANC (itself inspired by the Indian National Congress) published its Freedom Charter, which proclaimed the ideal of multiracial democratic rule for South Africa. Because its goals directly challenged white rule, the ANC and all black activists in South Africa faced severe repression. The government declared all its opponents communists and escalated its actions against black activists. Protests increased in 1960, the so-called year of Africa when multiple African nations won their independence from European colonial powers, and on 21 March 1960 white police gunned down unarmed black South African demonstrators in Sharpeville, near Johannesburg. Sixty-nine people, among them many young adults and ten children, were killed and almost two hundred more were wounded. Sharpeville, however, only increased radical activism by black South Africans.

At the same time, the egregious use of violence and repression by the white regime in South Africa also increased international opposition to white South African rule. Newly independent nations in Asia and Africa called for UN sanctions against South Africa while anticolonial and antiracist activists sought to publicize the government's repeated human rights violations. In 1961 South Africa declared itself a republic and withdrew from the British Commonwealth. Two years later, government forces captured the leaders of the ANC's military unit, including Nelson Mandela, and sentenced them to life in prison. Thereafter, Mandela and others became symbols of oppressive white rule. Protests against the system persisted in the 1970s and 1980s, spurred especially by student activism

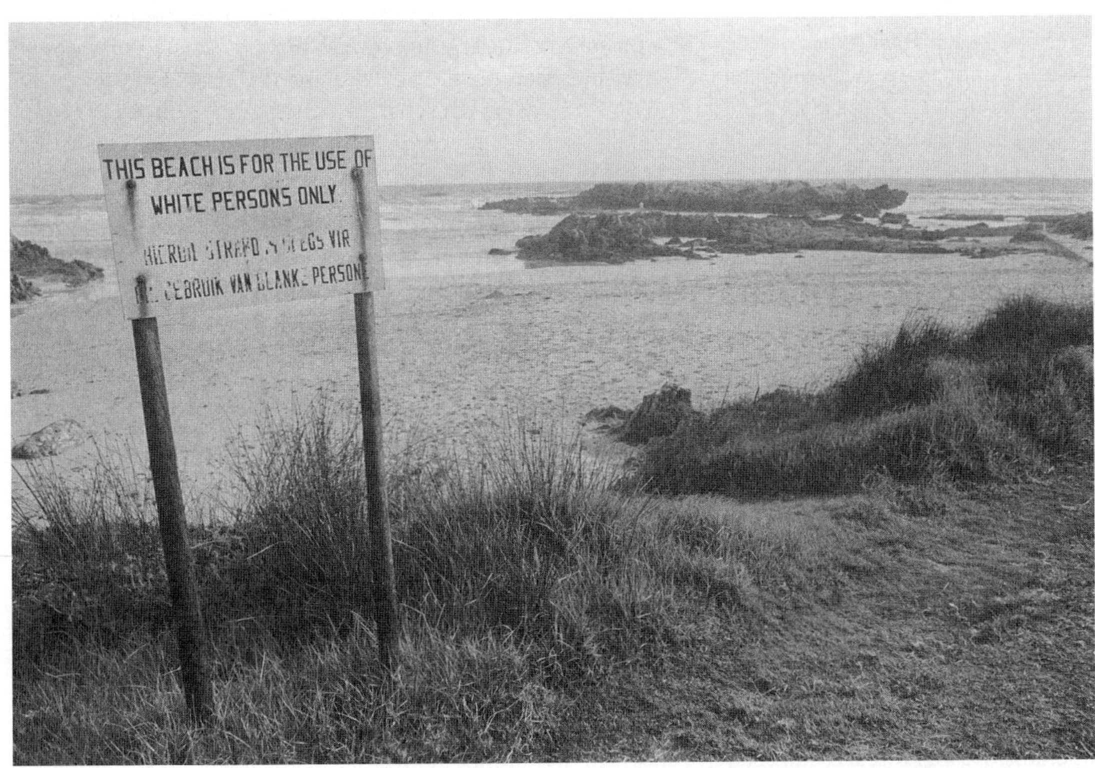


A sign in English and Afrikaans instructing visitors that the beach is for white persons only. From the Cape Province in South Africa in 1974, during the period of apartheid. Jonathan C. Katzenellenbogen/Getty Images

and awareness of successful independence struggles in neighboring states. The combined effects of widespread resistance and agitation with a powerful international anti-apartheid boycott eventually led to a growing recognition that, if it was to survive, South Africa had to change.

**The End of Apartheid** When **F. W. de Klerk** (1936-) became president of South Africa in 1989, he and the National Party began to dismantle the apartheid system. De Klerk released Mandela from jail in 1990, legalized the ANC, and worked with Mandela and the ANC to negotiate the end of white minority rule. Collaborating and cooperating, the National Party, the ANC, and other African political groups created a new constitution and in April 1994 held elections that were open to people of all races. The ANC won overwhelmingly, and Mandela became the first black president of South Africa. In 1963, at the trial that ended in his jail sentence, Mandela proclaimed, "I have cherished the ideal of a democratic and free society in which all persons live together in harmony and with equal opportunities. It is an ideal which I hope to live for and to achieve. But if needs be, it is an ideal for which I am prepared to die." Mandela lived to see his ideal fulfilled. In 1994, echoing the words of Martin Luther King Jr., President Mandela proclaimed his nation "free at last."

## The Rwandan Genocide

Another tragic event linked to the legacies of colonialism in sub-Saharan Africa was the Rwandan Genocide, which occurred between April and July, 1994. During the colonial period under first the Germans and then the Belgians, colonial administrators pursued polices that favored one of the two main ethnic groups in the territory—the Tutsi, who were a minority. This caused tensions and conflicts. In 1959, the Tutsi monarchy was abolished by a referendum and in 1960 Rwanda became a republic under elected Hutu leadership, and many Tutsi fled into exile. These exiles formed a militia in Uganda and fought a war to return to Rwanda from 1990 to 1993. In 1994, following the conclusion of a peace treaty to settle the war, a plane carrying Rwanda's Hutu president was shot down, prompting the Hutu government to blame Tutsi exiles and their kin who remained in the country. In retaliation, a Hutu military junta enlisted the cooperation of ordinary Hutu to exterminate the Tutsi in their midst, giving them lists of people, supplying them with weapons, and churning out propaganda over the radio. Over the course of 100 days, between 500,000 and 800,000 Tutsi were killed in these targeted attacks.

### INTERPRETING IMAGES

A 1966 poster shows Mao Zedong (1893–1976) inspiring young people to launch the Great Proletarian Cultural Revolution (1966–1976).

**Analyze** *What do you see in this photo that is uniquely Chinese or uniquely Communist? How would you contrast this image of patriotic young people with images from non-Communist countries? In what ways was the Chinese Cultural Revolution "cultural"?*

Hulton Archive/Getty Images

# AFTER INDEPENDENCE: LONG-TERM STRUGGLES IN THE POSTCOLONIAL ERA

Political and economic stability proved elusive after independence, particularly in those nations struggling to build political and economic systems free from the domination of more powerful nations. The legacies of imperialism, either direct or indirect, hindered the creation of democratic institutions in many parts of the world—from recently decolonized nations, such as those of Africa, to nations that won their independence a century earlier, such as those in Latin America. Continued interference by the former colonial powers or the Cold War superpowers impeded stability and prosperity all over the world. Indeed, few developing or newly independent nations escaped the legacies of imperialism or the new realities of Cold War rivalries as they sought to find their place in the postcolonial world.

## Communism and Democracy in Asia

Except for Japan and India, the developing nations in south, southeast, and east Asia adopted some form of authoritarian or militarist political system, and several followed a communist or socialist path of political development. Under Mao Zedong (1893-1976), China served as a guide and inspiration for

# SOURCES FROM THE PAST

## China's Marriage Law, 1949

*When the Chinese Communist Party came into power under Mao Zedong in 1949, the new government quickly instituted the "Marriage Law," which made Chinese men and women legal equals in marriage. This was truly revolutionary because women traditionally held very low status in China's highly patriarchal social structure. Although actual equality was more elusive than legal equality, the Marriage Law marked a significant step toward granting women more rights in Chinese society.*

**Chapter I. General Principles**

Article 1. The arbitrary and compulsory feudal marriage system, which is based on the superiority of man over woman and which ignores the children's interests, shall be abolished. The new democratic marriage system, which is based on free choice of partners, on monogamy, on equal rights for both sexes, and on protection of the lawful interests of women and children, shall be put into effect.

> Why might this article have seemed revolutionary in 1949?

Article 2. Bigamy, concubinage, child betrothal, interference with the remarriage of widows, and the exaction of money or gifts in connection with marriage shall be prohibited. . . .

**Chapter III. Rights and Duties of Husband and Wife**

Article 7. Husband and wife are companions living together and shall enjoy equal status in the home.

Article 8. Husband and wife are in duty bound to love, respect, assist, and look after each other, to live in harmony, to engage in production, to care for the children, and to strive jointly for the welfare of the family and for the building up of a new society.

Article 9. Both husband and wife shall have the right to free choice of occupation and free participation in work or in social activities.

> Why might it have seemed important to the authors of this law to include this article?

Article 10. Both husband and wife shall have equal right in the possession and management of family property.

Article 11. Both husband and wife shall have the right to use his or her own family name.

Article 12. Both husband and wife shall have the right to inherit each other's property.

### For Further Reflection

- In what ways were these marriage laws similar to or different from the demands for gender equality made by feminists in the United States and western Europe during the 1960s and 1970s?
- What was the context of the document and why was the context so significant?
- In what ways does the document reflect Communist theory and goals?

*Source:* Sherman, DennisI. *World Civilizations: Sources, Images, and Interpretations*, 3rd ed., Volume 2. New York: McGraw-Hill, 2001.

those countries seeking a means of political development distinct from the ways of the former colonial powers.

**Mao's China** Mao reunified China for the first time since the collapse of the Qing dynasty, transforming European communist ideology into a distinctly Chinese communism. After 1949 he embarked on programs designed to accelerate development in China. The economic and social transformation of Chinese society centered on rapid industrialization and the collectivization of agriculture (making landownership collective, not individual). Emulating earlier Soviet experiments, the Chinese introduced their first Five-Year Plan in 1955. Designed to speed up economic development, the Five-Year Plan emphasized improvements in infrastructure and the expansion of heavy industry at the expense of consumer goods. A series of agrarian laws promoted an unprecedented transfer of wealth among the population, virtually eliminating economic inequality at the village level. The government achieved this by confiscating the landholdings of rich peasants and landlords and redistributing the land so that virtually every peasant had at least a small plot of land. Between 1954 and 1960, however, the government oversaw the gradual collectivization of

Chinese students stage a pro-democracy sit-in at Tiananmen Square in Beijing, in June 1989, with the historic Forbidden City in the background. Such protests were repressed violently by the Chinese government.
Chris Niedenthal//Time Life Pictures/Getty Images

individual landholdings into agricultural communes in which land ownership existed only at the level of the commune. In the same period, the government took over the grain market and prohibited farmers from marketing their own crops. Collectives also became responsible for the provision of health care and primary education, which permitted the extension of social services to larger segments of the population. In the wake of economic reforms came social reforms, many of which challenged and often eliminated Chinese family traditions. Supporting equal rights for women, Chinese authorities introduced marriage laws that eliminated practices such as child or forced marriages, gave women equal access to divorce, and legalized abortion. Foot binding, a symbol of women's subjugation, was outlawed.

Mao's drive for development and revolutionary change was epitomized by the **Great Leap Forward** (1958-1961) and the **Great Proletarian Cultural Revolution** (1966-1976). These were far-reaching movements intended to bring rapid progress to China. In practice, however, they undermined the very political and economic development that Mao sought.

Mao envisioned his Great Leap Forward as a way to quickly overtake the industrial production of more developed nations. To achieve this, Mao extended the program of agricultural collectivization with the goal of collectivizing all land and managing all business and industrial enterprises collectively. Private ownership was abolished, and both farming and industry became communal. But the Great Leap Forward—or "Giant Step Backward" as some have dubbed it—failed. Most disastrous was its impact on agricultural production in China: the peasants did not meet production quotas set by the government, and a series of bad harvests contributed to one of the deadliest famines in history. Rather than face reality, Mao blamed the sparrows for the bad harvests, accusing these "counterrevolutionaries" of eating too much grain. He ordered tens of millions of peasants to kill the feathered menaces, leaving insects free to consume what was left of the crops. Between 1959 and 1962 as many as twenty million Chinese may have died of starvation and malnutrition in this crisis.

**Deng Xiaoping** (duhng show-ping)

### The Cultural Revolution

In 1966 Mao tried again to mobilize the Chinese and reignite the revolutionary spirit with the inauguration of the Great Proletarian Cultural Revolution. Designed to root out the revisionism (anti-revolutionary sentiment) Mao perceived in Chinese life, especially among Communist Party leaders and others in positions of authority, the Cultural Revolution subjected millions of people to humiliation, persecution, and death. The elite—intellectuals, teachers, professionals, managers, and anyone associated with foreign or bourgeois values—constituted the major targets of the Red Guards, teenagers Mao had empowered to cleanse Chinese society of opponents to his rule. Victims were beaten and killed, jailed, or sent to corrective labor camps or to toil in the countryside. The Cultural Revolution, which cost China years of stable development and gutted its educational system, did not end until after Mao's death in 1976. It fell to one of Mao's political heirs, Deng Xiaoping, to begin to heal the nation.

### Deng's Revolution

Although he was a colleague of Mao, **Deng Xiaoping** (1904-1997) suffered the same fate as millions of other Chinese during the Cultural Revolution: he had to recant criticisms of Mao, identify himself as a petit-bourgeois intellectual, and labor in a tractor-repair factory. When a radical faction failed to maintain the Cultural Revolution after Mao's death, China began its recovery from the turmoil. Deng came to power in 1981, and the 1980s are often referred to as the years of "Deng's Revolution." Deng moderated Mao's commitment to Chinese self-sufficiency and isolation and engineered China's entry into the international financial and trading system, a move that was facilitated by the normalization of relations between China and the United States in the 1970s.

### Tiananmen Square

To facilitate China's economic development, Deng opened the nation to the influences that had been suspect under Mao as foreign, capitalist values. His actions included sending tens of thousands of Chinese students to foreign universities to rebuild the professional, intellectual, and managerial elite needed for modern development. But Deng's openness to foreign values only extended so far. When some of the students who had studied abroad staged pro-democracy demonstrations in Beijing's **Tiananmen Square** in 1989, Deng, whose experiences in the Cultural Revolution made him wary of revolutionary movements, approved a bloody crackdown. Not surprisingly, Deng faced hostile world opinion after crushing the student movement. The issue facing China as it entered the global economy was how (or whether) to reap economic benefits without compromising its identity and its authoritarian political system. This issue gained added urgency as Hong Kong, under British administration since the 1840s and in the throes of its own democracy movement, reverted to Chinese control in 1997. Chinese leaders in the twenty-first century have managed to maintain both centralized political control over China and impressive economic growth and development, though political control has depended on swift repression of dissenting voices.

A photographer captured this image of Indira Gandhi (1917–1984) in 1976. Gandhi led India into the "green revolution," which sought to increase agricultural production to help feed the country's eight hundred million people. The campaign's mixed results, among other reasons, led to her temporarily losing power in 1977 before regaining it in 1980.
Henri Bureau/Sygma/Corbis/VCG/Getty Images

**Indian Democracy** Whereas other nations turned to dictators, military rule, or authoritarian systems, India was able to maintain its political stability and its democratic system after gaining independence in 1947. Even when faced with ethnic and religious conflict, wars, poverty, and overpopulation, India remained committed to free elections and a critical press. Its first postindependence prime minister, Jawaharlal Nehru, guided this commitment to democratic rule for seventeen years, until his death in 1964.

In 1966 **Indira Gandhi** (1917–1984), Nehru's daughter (and no relation to Mohandas K. Gandhi), became leader of the Congress Party. She served as prime minister of India from 1966 to 1977 and from 1980 to 1984, and under her leadership India embarked on the "green revolution" that increased agricultural yields for India's eight hundred million people. Although the new agricultural policies aided wealthier farmers, the masses of peasant farmers were unable to buy the high-yield seeds, chemical fertilizers, insecticides, and farm equipment central to the green revolution, and thus they fell even deeper into poverty than before. In addition to continued poverty, India during Gandhi's administration was beset by problems relating to overpopulation and sectarian conflicts.

Those problems prompted Indira Gandhi to take decidedly undemocratic action to maintain control. To quell growing opposition to her government, she declared a national emergency that suspended democratic processes from 1975 until 1977. She used her powers under the emergency to move forward with one of India's most needed social reforms, birth control. But rather than persuading or tempting Indians to control the size of their families (offering gifts of money for those who got vasectomies, for example), the government engaged in repressive birth control policies, including forced sterilization. A record eight million sterilization operations were performed in 1976 and 1977, prompting huge riots.

When Indira Gandhi allowed elections to be held in 1977, Indians voted against her because of her violation of democratic principles and her harsh birth control policies. But she was voted back into power in 1980, this time in the midst of fierce religious, ethnic, and secessionist movements. One such movement was an uprising by Sikhs who wanted greater autonomy in the Punjab region. The Sikhs, representing perhaps 2 percent of India's population, practiced a monotheistic religion, maintained a distinctive physical appearance, and had a history of serving in the Indian army. When partition occurred, the traditional Sikh homeland had been split between India and Pakistan, leaving Sikhs to desire its reunification under Sikh rule. When Sikh separatists occupied the sacred Golden Temple in Amritsar and began stockpiling weapons, Indira Gandhi ordered the Indian army to attack, killing hundreds of separatists. In retaliation, two of her Sikh bodyguards—hired for their martial skills—assassinated her a few months later in 1984.

Indira Gandhi's son **Rajiv Gandhi** (1944–1991) took over the leadership of India in 1985 and offered reconciliation to the Sikhs. However, he was assassinated by a terrorist in 1991 while attempting to win back the office he lost in 1989. Despite assassinations, violations of democratic rule, and continued problems with poverty and sectarian division, India has maintained its democratic institutions into the twenty-first century.

## Pan-Arab and Islamic Resurgence in Southwest Asia and North Africa

The geographic convergence of the Arab and Muslim worlds in Southwest Asia and north Africa encouraged the development of Arab nationalism in states of those regions that gained independence after World War II. Whether in Libya, Algeria, or Egypt in north Africa or in Syria, Saudi Arabia, or Iraq in Southwest Asia, members of Arab nations were attracted by the idea of pan-Arab unity as a way of fending off European, U.S., and Soviet influence in the region. In north Africa, Egypt's Gamal Abdel Nasser provided the leadership for this pan-Arab nationalism, and Arab opposition to the state of Israel held the dream together.

The hopes attached to pan-Arab unity did not materialize. Although Arab lands shared a common language and religion, divisions were frequent and alliances shifted over time. The

Cold War split the Arab world; some states allied themselves with the United States, while others allied with the Soviet Union. Some countries also shifted between the two, as Egypt did when it left the Soviet orbit for the U.S. sphere in 1976. Governments in these nations included military dictatorships, monarchies, and revolutionary Islamist regimes.

**Islamism** In the 1970s, **Islamism**—or the revival of Islamic values in the political and social sphere—emerged as an alternative to pan-Arab unity. Some Islamic thinkers called for the rigorous enforcement of the *sharia* (Islamic law), emphasized pan-Islamic unity, and urged the elimination of non-Muslim economic, political, or cultural influences in the Muslim world. In the view of many proponents, the Muslim world had been slipping into a state of decline, brought about by the abandonment of Islamic traditions. Many Muslims had become skeptical about European and American models of economic development and political and cultural norms, which they blamed for economic and political failure as well as for secularization and its attendant breakdown of traditional social and religious values. Disillusionment and anger with European and American societies, and especially with the United States, became widespread. The solution to the problems faced by Muslim societies lay, according to Islamists, in the revival of Islamic identity, values, and power. A small minority of Islamists argued that these goals could only be realized through violence.

**The Iranian Revolution** The **Iranian Revolution** that took place in 1979 demonstrated the power of Islam as a means of staving off secular foreign influences. Islamist influences emerged in Iran during the lengthy regime of Shah Mohammed Reza Pahlavi (1919–1980), whom the United States helped bring to power in 1953 in a CIA-engineered coup. The shah used the money from Iran's vast supply of oil to industrialize the country, and the United States provided the military equipment that enabled Iran to become a bastion of anticommunism in the region. But devout Muslim leaders despised the shah's secular regime, Iranian small businesses detested the influence of U.S. corporations on the economy, and leftist politicians rejected the shah's repressive policies. When the shah left Iran to get medical treatment in 1979, Ayatollah Ruhollah Khomeini (1900–1989) coordinated an Islamist revolution that deposed the shah.

The revolution took on a strongly anti-U.S. cast, mostly because of the long-term U.S. role in bringing the shah to power and maintaining his oppressive rule. During the revolution, Iranians captured sixty-nine hostages at the U.S. embassy in Tehran, fifty-five of whom remained captives until 1981. In the meantime, Iranian leaders shut U.S. military bases and confiscated U.S.-owned economic ventures. This Islamic power play against a developed nation such as the United States inspired other Muslims to stand up for themselves as well. Yet the resurgent Islamism of Iran did not lead to a new era of solidarity. Iranian Islam was the minority sect of Shia Islam, and one of Iran's neighbors, Iraq, attempted to take advantage of the revolution to invade Iran.

By the late 1970s Iraq had built a formidable military machine, largely owing to oil revenues and the efforts of

## INTERPRETING IMAGES

Iranian women and men protesting in favor of the revolution to remove the shah from power, Tehran 1979. Thousands of women took an active part in the Iranian revolution. Several people hold posters depicting Ayatollah Khomeini.

**Analyze** *What historical context do you need to understand what is happening here? What is motivating these people, many of whom look quite young, to rally behind an older religious leader?*

Michael Norcia/Sygma/Getty Images

**Saddam Hussein** (1937–2006), who became president of Iraq in 1979. Hussein launched his attack on Iran in 1980, believing that victory would be swift and perhaps hoping to become the new leader of a revived pan-Arab nationalism. (Iran is Muslim in religion but is not ethnically Arab.) Although they were initially successful, Iraqi troops faced a determined counterattack by Iranian forces, and the conflict became a war of attrition that did not end until 1988.

**The Iran-Iraq and Gulf Wars** The **Iran-Iraq War** killed as many as one million soldiers. In Iran the human devastation is still visible, if not openly acknowledged, in a nation that permits little dissent from Islamist orthodoxy. Young people are showing signs of a growing discontent caused by the war and by the rigors of a revolution that also killed thousands. Signs of recovery and a relaxation of Islamist strictness appeared in Iran in the late 1990s, but the destruction from war also remained visible. Islamism has reemerged in twenty-first-century Iran and has aroused some international concern, particularly for the United States. A conservative supreme leader, the Ayatollah Khamenei (1939–), and a conservative president, **Mahmoud Ahmadinejad** (1956–), represented this trend. Ahmadinejad took office in 2005 and touted Iran's nuclear program and his antipathy to the state of Israel, which had the effect of increasing his status in the Islamic world while intensifying tensions with the United States.

Iraqis continued on a militant course. Two years after the end of the Iran-Iraq War, Hussein's troops invaded Kuwait (1990) and incited the Gulf War (1991). The result was a decisive military defeat for Iraq, at the hands of an international coalition led by the United States, and further hardships for the Iraqi people.

## Colonial Legacies in Sub-Saharan Africa

The optimism that accompanied decolonization in sub-Saharan Africa faded as the prospects for political stability gave way in some areas to civil wars and territorial disputes. This condition largely reflected the impact of colonialism. As European powers departed their decolonized lands, they left behind territories whose borders were artificial conveniences that did not correspond to any indigenous economic or ethnic divisions. Historically distinct communities found themselves jammed into a single "national" state. In other instances, populations found themselves in newly independent states whose borders

**Mahmoud Ahmadinejad** (mah-MOOD ah-mah-DIH-nee-zhahd)

## What's Left Out?

While textbooks often discuss how the process of decolonization became entangled with the Cold War, few offer extended treatment of the Portuguese colony of Angola. Yet Angola endured more than thirty years of war when a local communist anticolonial movement became enmeshed in a complex web of international aid and interference during the Cold War. Anticolonial activists in Angola began a widespread rebellion against Portuguese rule in 1961, just as Britain and France were in the process of decolonizing nearby territories in sub-Saharan Africa. War broke out when it became clear that Portugal would not even consider a path to Angolan independence. But Angolans were not united in their vision of independence and broke into three factions, one of which was communist in orientation. The factions turned to outside allies for help, with the result that the communist faction drew aid from communist Cuba and Yugoslavia, while the noncommunist factions drew aid from the United States and South Africa. Outside aid ensured the war would be long and bloody. But after fourteen years of fighting, new leadership in Portgual led the government to abruptly agree to Angolan independence. Before independence could even be declared, however, the three Angolan factions erupted in civil war as each sought sole control of the new country. Seeing an opportunity to determine the ideological allegiance of independent Angola, the United States and the South African government sent weapons, advisers, and (South African) troops to support the noncommunist factions. In response, Cuba sent its own weapons and troops to support the communist faction. With Cuban help, by 1976 the communist faction had won control of now-independent Angola, but even then the South African government continued to provide weapons to noncommunists. This, in turn, led both Cuba and the Soviet Union to continue providing material and financial aid to the victorious communist factions until the Cold War ended in 1991. By then, the Angolan civil war had resulted in massive destruction to the land and infrastructure, and a half million were dead. Thanks to the politics of the Cold War, then, the struggle for Angolan independence and power in the postcolonial era ended in the virtual destruction of the country.

*Source:* Jonathan Reynolds, Sovereignty and Struggle: Africa and Africans in the Era of the Cold War, 1945–1994 (New York and Oxford: Oxford University Press, 2015).

### Thinking Critically About Sources

1. In what ways was the war in Angola similar to the War in Vietnam? In what ways was it different?
2. Why weren't there student protests in the U.S. against the support for the war in Angola?

were unacceptable to neighboring states. As a result, decolonization was sometimes accompanied or followed by civil wars and border disputes that resisted resolution.

The **Organization of African Unity** (OAU), created in 1963 by thirty-two member states, recognized some of those problems and attempted to prevent conflicts that could lead to intervention by former colonial powers. The artificial boundaries of African states, though acknowledged as problematic, were nonetheless held inviolable by the OAU to prevent disputes over boundaries. International law also treated postcolonial borders as inviolable. The OAU also promoted pan-African unity, at least in the faction headed by Kwame Nkrumah, as a vehicle for African states to resist interference and domination by foreign powers. In its early years, the OAU successfully mediated border disputes between Morocco and Algeria (1964–1965) and between Somalia and its neighbors (1965–1967). But the drive for African political unity by leaders like Kwame Nkrumah of Ghana was not always appreciated. It was so unpopular in Ghana that it contributed to Nkrumah's overthrow in a military coup in 1966. In addition, the OAU could not prevent extensive interference by the Cold War superpowers in places like the Democratic Republic of the Congo, Angola, and Mozambique. Nevertheless, in spite of continuing instability and poverty, African leaders in the early postcolonial period sought to integrate their new nations into the global economy by making the most of their rich mineral deposits, raw materials, and agricultural products.

## Politics and Economics in Latin America

The uneasy aftermath of independence visible throughout Asia and Africa also affected states on the other side of the world—states that gained their freedom from colonial rule more than a century before postwar decolonization. Nations in Central and South America along with Mexico grappled with the conservative legacies of Spanish and Portuguese colonialism, particularly the political and economic power of the landowning elite of European descent. Latin America moreover had to deal with neocolonialism because the United States not only intervened militarily when its interests were threatened but also influenced economies through investment and full or part ownership of enterprises such as the oil industry. In the nineteenth century Latin American states may have looked to the United States as a model of liberal democracy, but by the twentieth century U.S. interference provoked negative reactions. That condition was true after World War I, and it remained true during and after World War II.

**Mexico** Only President Lázaro Cárdenas (in office 1934–1940) had substantially invoked and applied the reforms guaranteed to Mexicans by the Constitution of 1917. The constitution's provisions regarding the state's right to redistribute land after confiscation and compensation, as well as its claim to government ownership of the subsoil and its products, found a champion in Cárdenas. He brought land reform and redistribution to a peak in Mexico, returning forty-five million acres to peasants, and he wrested away control of the oil industry from foreign investors. Cárdenas's nationalization of Mexico's oil industry allowed for the creation of the *Petróleos Mexicanos* (PEMEX), a national oil company in control of Mexico's petroleum products. The revenues generated by PEMEX contributed to what has been called **"El Milagro Mexicano,"** or the Mexican economic miracle, a period of prosperity that lasted until the 1970s. Conservative governments thereafter, controlled by the one-party rule of the Institutional Revolutionary Party (PRI), often acted harshly and experimented with various economic strategies that decreased or increased Mexico's reliance on foreign markets and capital. The PRI came under attack in the 1990s

In this 1950 photo taken in Buenos Aires, Eva Perón (1919–1952) waves to adoring *descamisados*, or "shirtless ones," to whose poverty she ceaselessly ministered. Although many thought of Eva Perón as a "saint," others viewed her own extravagant lifestyle as a sign of her opportunism. Keystone/Hulton Archive/Getty Images as Mexican peasants in the Chiapas district protested their political oppression. Cuauhtémoc Cárdenas, the son of Lázaro Cárdenas, took on the leadership of an opposition party, the Democratic Revolutionary Party (PRD), and this shift to democratic political competition and multiparty elections has continued into the twenty-first century.

**Argentina** Mexico served as one model for political development in Latin America, and Argentina seemed to be another candidate for leadership in South America. It had a reasonably expansive economy based on cattle raising and agriculture, a booming urban life, the beginnings of an industrial base, and a growing middle class in a population composed mostly of migrants from Europe. Given its geographic position far to the south, Argentina remained relatively independent of U.S. control and became a leader in the Latin American struggle against U.S. and European economic and political intervention in the region. A gradual shift to free elections and a sharing of political power beyond that exercised by the landowning elite also emerged. Given the military's central role in its politics, however, Argentina became a model of a less positive form of political organization: the often brutal and deadly sway of military rulers.

**Juan Perón** During World War II, nationalistic military leaders gained power in Argentina and established a government controlled by the army. In 1946 **Juan Perón** (1895–1974), a former colonel in the army, was elected president. Although he was a nationalistic militarist, his regime garnered immense popularity among large segments of the Argentine population, partly because he appealed to ordinary Argentines. He promoted a nationalistic populism, calling for industrialization, support of the working class, and protection of the economy from foreign control.

**Evita** However opportunistic Perón may have been, his popularity with the masses was real. His wife, Eva Perón (1919–1952), helped to foster that popularity, as Argentines warmly embraced their **"Evita"** (little Eva). She rose from the ranks of the desperately poor. An illegitimate child who migrated to Buenos Aires at the age of fifteen, she found work as a radio soap-opera actress. She met Perón in 1944, and they were married shortly thereafter. Reigning in the Casa Rosada (the Pink House) as Argentina's first lady from 1946 to 1952, Eva Perón transformed herself into a talented and fashionable political leader. While pushing for her husband's political reforms, she also tirelessly ministered to the needs of the poor, often the same *descamisados,* or "shirtless ones," who formed the core of her husband's supporters. Endless lines of people came to see her in her offices at the labor ministry—asking for dentures, wedding clothes, medical care, and the like. Eva Perón accommodated those demands and more: she bathed lice-ridden children in her own home, kissed lepers, and created the Eva Perón Foundation to institutionalize and extend such charitable endeavors. When she died of uterine cancer at the age of thirty-three, the nation mourned the tragic passing of a woman who came to be elevated to the status of "Santa Evita."

Some saw Eva Perón not as a saint but as a grasping social climber and a fascist sympathizer and saw her husband as a political opportunist, but after Juan Perón's ouster from office in 1955, support for the Perónist party remained strong. However, with the exception of a brief return to power by Perón in the mid-1970s, brutal military dictators held sway in Argentina for the next three decades. Military rule took a sinister turn in the late 1970s and early 1980s when dictators approved the creation of death squads that fought a "dirty war" against suspected subversives. Between six thousand and twenty-three thousand people disappeared between 1976 and 1983. Calls for a return to democratic politics increased in the aftermath of the dirty war, demands that were intensified by economic disasters and the growth of the poorest classes.

## Chile

In spite of enormous interference and pressure by the United States to prevent socialists from gaining power in Chile, in 1970 the socialist physician Salvador Allende won election to the presidency. Allende got to work quickly trying to reform the Chilean government along socialist lines. To begin, he nationalized certain industries, such as copper, as well as the health care system. He then continued work on democratizing and extending the educational system, and a program to distribute free milk to children. The Allende government also sought to redistribute land from the very wealthy to the needy, and in fact succeeded in redistributing nearly 60% of Chile's agricultural lands. But Allende's policies led to fierce resistance by landowners and those on the political right, and in 1973 a military coup (financially supported by the United States) overthrew the Allende government and replaced him with Augusto Pinochet. Under Pinochet, the Chilean government undertook a policy of state terror through the secret police, in which many thousands were interned, tortured, and killed. Pinochet's regime also reversed the socialist policies established by Allende of land redistribution and educational and social reforms.

**Liberation for Nations and Women** Revolutionary ideologies and political activism provided opportunities for Latin American women to agitate for both national and women's liberation. Nicaraguan women, for example, established the Association of Women Concerned about National Crisis in 1977 and fought as part of the Sandinista Front for National Liberation (FSLN). The **FSLN** was named in honor of the martyred Augusto Cesar Sandino (1893–1934), murdered for his opposition to U.S. intrusion in Nicaragua by the forces of Nicaraguan leader and U.S. ally Anastacio Somoza Garcia (1896–1956). Somoza's sons followed their father's brutal leadership practices, and Nicaraguan women dedicated themselves to ridding their nation of Somoza rule. In 1979 they renamed the organization the Luisa Amanda Espinoza Association of Nicaraguan Women (AMNLAE) to acknowledge the first woman who died in the battle against the Somoza regime. The group's slogan—"No revolution without women's emancipation: no emancipation without revolution"—suggested the dual goals of Nicaraguan women. By the mid-1980s, AMNLAE had over eighty thousand members. Despite facing problems typical of women's movements trying to navigate between national and personal needs, AMNLAE has been credited with forwarding women's participation in the public and political spheres, an impressive accomplishment in a region where women's suffrage had often been delayed. Although women in Ecuador attained voting rights in 1929, women in Nicaragua could not vote until 1955; Paraguay's women waited for suffrage rights until 1961, when that nation became the last in Latin America to incorporate women into the political process.

**The Search for Economic Equity** The late twentieth century witnessed a revival of democratic politics in Latin America, but economic problems continued to limit the possibility of widespread change or the achievement of economic and social equity. In many Latin American nations, the landowning elites who gained power during the colonial era were able to maintain their dominant position, which resulted in societies that remained divided between the few rich, usually backed by the United States, and the masses of the poor. It was difficult to structure such societies without either keeping the elite in power or promoting revolution on behalf of the poor, and the task of fashioning workable state and economic systems was made even more troublesome given the frequency of foreign interference by the United States. Indeed, in addition to long-standing economic interference, during the Cold War the U.S. government sanctioned either overt or covert military interference in multiple Latin American states, including Cuba, Guatemala, Brazil, the Dominican Republic, Chile, Nicaragua, and Grenada. In spite of such obstacles to stability, some Latin American states prospered in the mid-twentieth century. During World War II, many Latin American nations took advantage of world market needs and pursued greater industrial development. Profits flowed into these countries during and after the war, and nations in the region experienced sustained economic growth through expanded export trade and diversification of foreign markets. Exports included manufactured goods and traditional export commodities such as minerals and foodstuffs such as sugar, fruits, and coffee.

**Dependency Theory** Latin American nations realized the need to reorient their economies away from exports and toward internal development. One influential Argentine economist, Raul Prebisch (1901–1985), who worked for the United Nations Commission for Latin America, explained Latin America's economic problems in global terms. Prebisch crafted the **"dependency" theory** of economic development, pointing out that developed industrial nations—such as those in North America and Europe—dominated the international economy and profited at the expense of less developed and industrialized nations burdened with the export-oriented, unbalanced economies that were a legacy of colonialism. To break the unequal relationship between what Prebisch termed the "center" and the "periphery," developing nations on the periphery of international trade needed to protect and diversify domestic trade and to use strategies of import-substituting industrialization to promote further industrial and economic growth.

Prebisch's theories about the economic ills of the developing world, though influential at the time, have since declined in currency. Latin American economies have shown resilience in the late twentieth and early twenty-first centuries, and Latin American nations have maintained links to global markets and money. Their economies appeared strong enough to limit the effects of their export-oriented systems and their use of foreign investment monies. Especially since the end of the Cold War and the resulting decline in military interference by the United States, further economic growth should aid in the search for social and economic stability in Latin America.

## CONCLUSION

In the years immediately before and after World War II, a few nations claimed imperial territories that spanned much of the world. The imperial and colonial encounters between colonizers and colonized defined much of the recent history of the world before the mid-twentieth century. The decades following 1945 witnessed the stunningly rapid demise of the European, Japanese, and U.S. empires as colonized people everywhere fought for—and won—their independence. The process of decolonization was not easy and was frequently made more complicated by the presence of settlers, Cold War politics, and internal divisions. Nevertheless, by 1980 decolonization was nearly complete, and the world's peoples sought to reshape their identities and build relations with the rest of the world. This process was frequently hampered, however, by legacies of imperialism, such as lack of infrastructure, economic underdevelopment, poverty, and religious or ethnic conflict. Additionally, since decolonization occurred at precisely the same time as the Cold War, newly independent nations found their freedoms and stability compromised by the insistence of the two superpowers that they choose sides. Nevertheless, the global balance of power had been irrevocably altered by this attainment of worldwide independence and pointed to the emergence of a new kind of world order leading into the twenty-first century.

## STUDY TERMS

African National Congress (ANC) (839)
apartheid (839)
decolonization (821)
Deng Xiaoping (842)
dependency theory (848)
Dien Bien Phu (830)
El Milagro Mexicano (846)
Evita (847)
FLN (835)
FSLN (847)
Frantz Fanon (836)
F. W. de Klerk (840)
Gamal Abdel Nasser (833)
Geneva Conference (830)
Great Leap Forward (842)
Great Proletarian Cultural Revolution (842)
Ho Chi Minh (829)
Indian National Congress (825)
Indira Gandhi (843)
intifada (833)
Iran-Iraq War (845)
Iranian Revolution (844)
Islamism (844)
Jawaharlal Nehru (828)
Juan Perón (847)
Kwame Nkrumah (837)
Lyndon Johnson (831)
Mahmoud Ahmadinejad (845)
Mau Mau (838)
Mohandas K. Gandhi (825)
Muhammad Ali Jinnah (828)
Muslim League (828)
*Négritude* (836)
Nelson Mandela (839)
Nonaligned Movement (829)
Organization of African Unity (OAU) (846)
partition of India (828)
Rajiv Gandhi (843)
Saddam Hussein (845)
Suez crisis (833)
Tiananmen Square (842)
Viet Cong (831)
Vietnamization (831)
Vo Nguyen Giap (830)
Winston Churchill (828)

## FOR FURTHER READING

Abdel Monem Said Aly, Shai Feldman, and Khalil Shikaki. *Arabs and Israelis: Conflict and Peacemaking in the Middle East*. New York, 2013. An insightful book by three eyewitnesses who represent multiple perspectives on a controversial topic.

Nancy L. Clark and William H. Worger. *South Africa: The Rise and Fall of Apartheid.* New York, 2004. A survey of the history of the apartheid regime from 1948 to its collapse in the 1990s.

Prasenjit Duara, ed. *Decolonization (Rewriting Histories).* New York, 2004. The perspective of the colonized is privileged through a selection of writings by leaders of the colonizing countries.

Carlene J. Edie. *Politics in Africa: A New Beginning?* New York, 2002. Examines the domestic and external pressures that have transformed postcolonial African states and societies.

Caroline Elkins. *Imperial Reckoning: The Untold Story of Britain's Gulag in Kenya*. New York, 2005. Exposes the extreme violence and brutality of the British response to the Mau Mau rebellion in Kenya.

Rebecca Karl. *Mao Zedong and China in the Twentieth-Century World.* New Haven, 2010. Explores Mao and the Chinese revolution in a wide global context of imperialism, decolonization, and the Cold War.

Yasmin Khan. *The Great Partition: The Making of India and Pakistan*. New Haven: 2007. A thoughtful analysis of the context in which partition occurred, as well as its execution and legacy into the present.

Todd Shepherd. *Voices of Decolonization: A Brief History with Documents*. Boston, 2014. An excellent summary of decolonization with a variety of supporting documents authored by colonizers and anticolonial activists.

Martin Shipway. *Decolonization and its Impact: A Comparative Approach to the End of the Colonial Empires*. Hoboken, 2008. Explores the process of decolonization across all of the empires, with a special emphasis on under-studied areas.

Thomas E. Skidmore and Peter H. Smith. *Modern Latin America.* 8th ed. New York, 2013. A thorough and comprehensive overview of the region.

# CHAPTER 25 AP EXAM PRACTICE

Questions assume cumulative knowledge from this chapter and previous chapters.

## Section I

## Multiple Choice Questions

Use the image below and your knowledge of world history to answer questions 1–3.

Iranian women and women protesting in favor of the revolution to remove the shah from power, Tehran 1979.
michael norcia/Sygma/Getty Images

1. Which of the following groups was NOT opposed to the Shah Mohammed Reza Pahlavi?
   (A) The oil industry.
   (B) Leftist Iranian politicians.
   (C) Muslim leaders.
   (D) Iranian small business leaders

2. Why did the Iranian revolutionaries oppose the United States?
   (A) The US had tried to carry out a coup against the shah.
   (B) The US stopped purchasing Iranian oil, creating an economic crisis.
   (C) The US had brought the shah to power and helped him maintain his oppressive rule.
   (D) The US agreed to allow the Soviet Union to move into northern Iran.

3. What lead to the Iran-Iraq war of 1980–1988?
   (A) The Soviet Union started the war to prevent Iran and Iraq from leading a pan-Arab nationalist movement.
   (B) The Iraqi Shi'ites didn't want the Iranian Sunnis to be more influential.
   (C) Iran invaded Iraq to force them to withdraw from Kuwait.
   (D) Saddam Hussein, the new leader of Iraq, thought Iran was vulnerable because of the revolution.

Use the image below and your knowledge of world history to answer questions 4 and 5.

17th October 1950: Eva Peron (1919–1952), the second wife of Argentinian president Juan Peron greeting the crowds from the balcony of Government House, Buenos Aires on the fifth anniversary of the "Peronist Movement." The ceremony commemorates the day when Peron returned to power in 1945.
Keystone/Hulton Archive/Getty Images

4. Why was Juan Perón's government popular with many Argentinians?
   (A) Many Argentinians believed he would lead a revolution like the Mexican Revolution.
   (B) Argentinians thought the military should be at the center of political life.
   (C) He promised to bring in more US investment in the economy.
   (D) He supported industrialization and the working class.

5. Why was Eva Perón known as "Saint Evita?"
   (A) It was said that her singing was like the voice of a saint.
   (B) She personally worked to take care of the needs of the poor.
   (C) She played a famous saint when she was an actress.
   (D) She donated significant amounts of money to the church.

## Short Answer

6. Use the image below and your knowledge of world history to answer parts A, B, and C.

Muhammad Ali Jinnah (right) Lord Mountbatten (centre) and Jawaharlal Nehru discuss partition of India 1946

World History Archive/Alamy Stock Photo

(A) Explain ONE reason why Indian independence happened after World War II.

(B) Explain ONE reason why India was partitioned into India and Pakistan.

(C) Identify ONE reason for the ongoing conflict between Pakistan and India.

7. Use the map below and your knowledge of world history to answer parts A, B, and C.

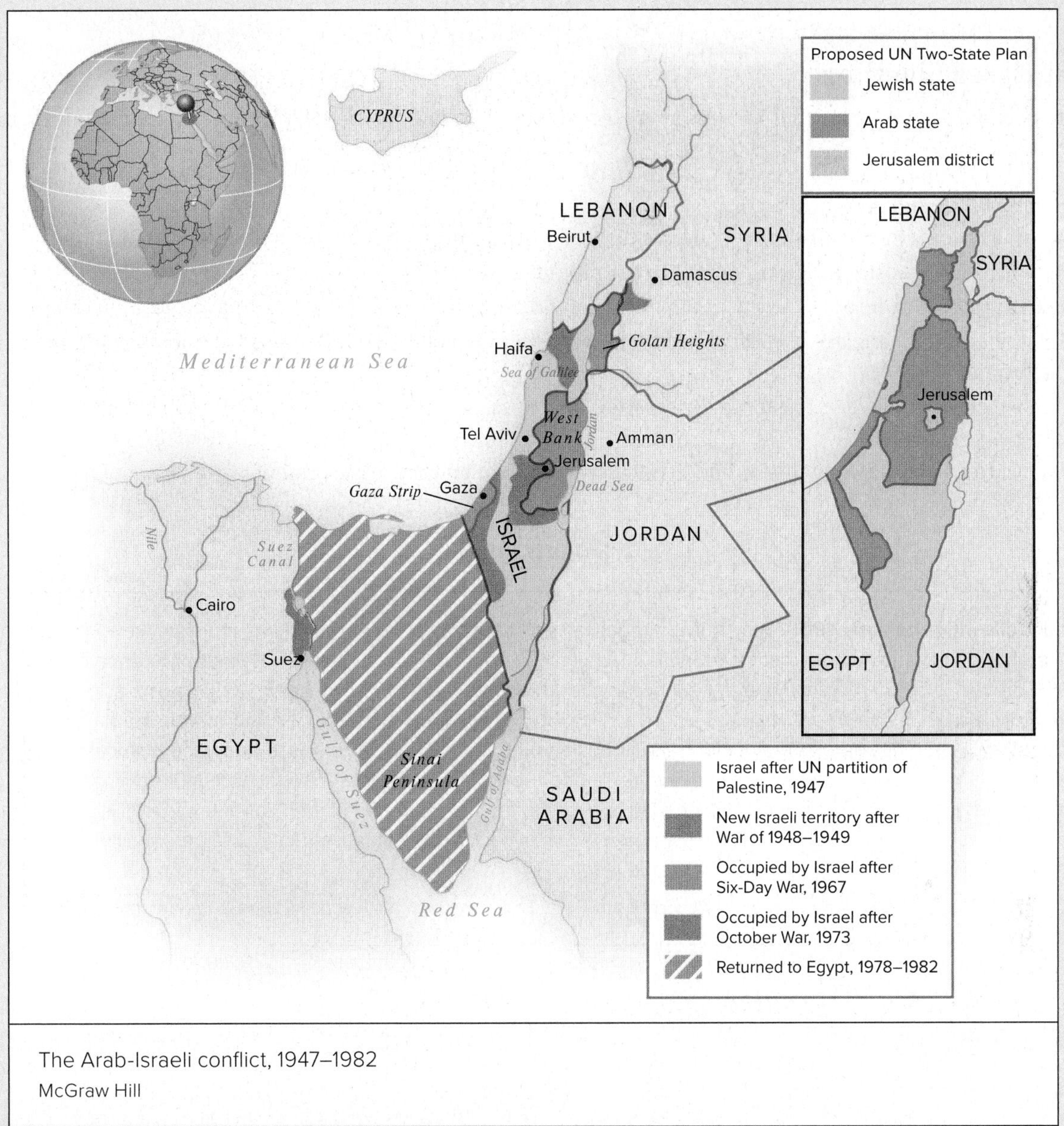


The Arab-Israeli conflict, 1947–1982
McGraw Hill

(A) Explain ONE was World War II changed British government in the Palestine Mandate.
(B) Explain ONE strategic advantage of new territories that Israel claimed in 1948-49.
(C) Identify ONE strategic advantage of Israel acquiring the Sinai Peninsula.

8. Use your understanding of world history to answer parts A, B, and C.
(A) Explain ONE factor that advanced the cause of independence in Vietnam.
(B) Explain ONE reason why the Geneva Conference did not lead to a stable, independent Vietnam.
(C) Identify ONE reason why the United States did not win in Vietnam.

# Section II

## Document-Based Question

Based on the documents below and your knowledge of world history, explain the similarities and differences in Africa's independence movements.

In your response you should do the following:

- Respond to the prompt with a historically defensible thesis or claim that establishes a line of reasoning.
- Describe a broader historical context relevant to the prompt.
- Support an argument in response to the prompt using all documents.
- Use at least one additional piece of specific historical evidence (beyond that found in the documents) relevant to an argument about the prompt.
- Explain how or why the document's point of view, purpose, historical situation, and /or audience is relevant to an argument.
- Use evidence to corroborate, qualify, or modify an argument that addresses the prompt.

### Document 1

**The decade following the early 1950s** may truly be regarded as Africa's decade. Breathtaking and significant changes have taken place on the African continent that were undreamed of twelve or fifteen years earlier. The independence of Ghana in March, 1957, proved to be the beginning of a great avalanche which was soon to sweep before it the "possessions" and "spheres of influence" of the colonial powers. A majority of these so called possessions have been transformed in our time into sovereign, independent states, and the process of decolonization goes on unabated. Our next goal is to attain the political unification of the African continent so as to give form and substance to our independence through total disengagement from imperialist and colonialist entanglements . . . Africans [are making efforts] to complete the liberation of their continent from all forms of imperialism, colonialism, racialism, and neocolonialism. In this way, we may secure the establishment of the personality of the African and the fulfillment of his destiny in an interdependent world.

*Source:* Quaison-Sackey, Alex. *Africa Unbound: Reflections of an African Statesman.* New York: Frederick Praeger, 1963, foreword.

## Document 2

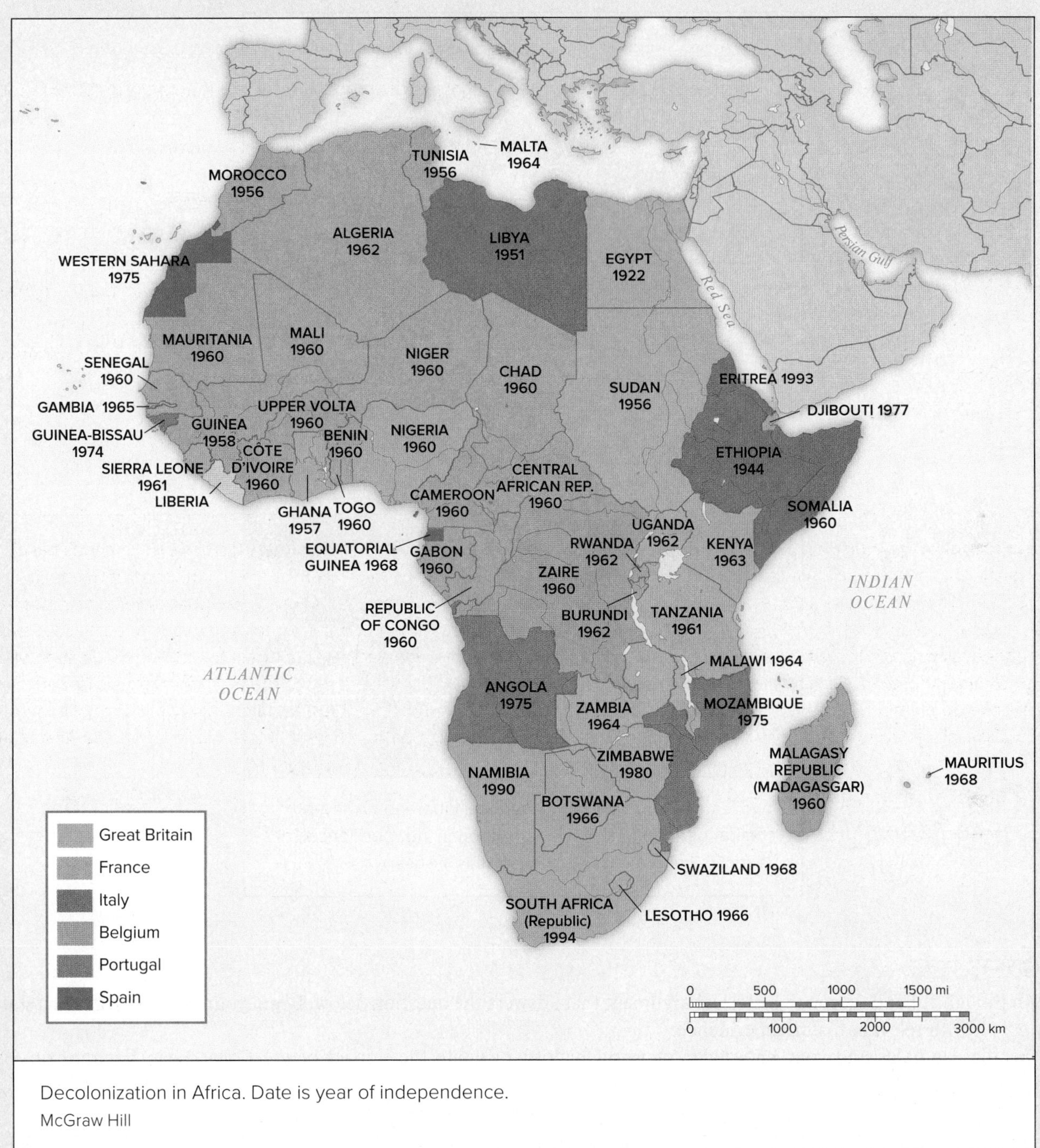


Decolonization in Africa. Date is year of independence.

McGraw Hill

## Document 3

Two female members of the National Liberation Army in combat gear during the war for Algerian independence.
Keystone-France/Gamma-Keystone/Getty Images

## Long Essay

Develop a thoughtful and thorough historical argument that answers the question below. Begin your essay with a thesis statement and support it with relevant historical evidence.

Using specific examples and your knowledge of world history, evaluate the impact of the Great Leap Forward on Chinese society.

# Chapter 26 Into the Twenty-First Century



## ZOOMING IN ON ENCOUNTERS

### Kristina Matschat and a Falling Wall

On November 9, 1989, Kristina Matschat felt excitement and tension in the night air of Berlin. She had joined thousands of other East Germans at Checkpoint Charlie, one of the most famous crossing points in the Berlin Wall. Anticipating that some momentous event was soon to occur at the wall, that the wall might come down that night, she also shivered in fear at the proximity of the *Volkspolizei* ("people's police")—the same force who since 1961 gunned down East Germans attempting

Neon McDonald's sign in Arabic, Amman, Jordan. Critics of globalization often point to the spread of McDonald's restaurants as both a sign of globalization and as a sign of the Americanization of global culture. Proponents of globalization point out that people in different cultures experience McDonald's differently, and that they make the restaurant chain their own by adding culturally specific foods and drinks to the menu. As of 2020, McDonald's had restaurants in 100 countries around the world, with over 38,000 individual locations.
A. Astes/Alamy Stock Photo

to scale the wall and escape to freedom in West Berlin. She wore running shoes in case she needed to sprint away if shooting broke out.

Matschat remembered that "everybody was full of fear—but also full of hope." Her hope overcame her fears, though, as she chanted with her fellow compatriots, "Tear the wall down! Open the gates!" She could see that on the other side of the wall massive crowds of West Berliners had gathered to join their demonstration. Thrilled by this open protest against an iconic symbol of the Cold War, she was nonetheless unprepared for how quickly victory came. Just before midnight East German soldiers suddenly began not only opening gates in the Wall but also gently helping East Germans cross to the West, many for the first time in their lives. Her near disbelief at the swift downfall of Berlin's decades-old barricade registered in the word she heard shouted over and over again by those passing through the wall: *Wahnsinn* ("craziness").

Kristina Matschat remained at the wall until 3:00 or 4:00 A.M., celebrating with the hundreds of thousands of other Berliners who now mingled, drinking champagne and dancing on top of the wall. While celebrating the fall of the barbed wire and mortar structure, she became aware of the significance of what had just happened: "Suddenly we were seeing the West for the first time, the forbidden Berlin we had only seen on TV or heard about from friends. When we came home at dawn, I felt free for the first time in my life. I had never been happier." The fall of the Berlin Wall brought down one of the world's most notorious borders and symbolized the start of a new era in the contemporary world.

## CHAPTER FOCUS

- In many ways, this chapter synthesizes all you have learned. For example, you should be able to assess how modern human migration patterns compare to migration patterns of the 1500s or 1800s C.E. You should be able to explain the historical precedents, complexities, and consequences of modern demographics. Try as best you can to connect the many demographic, technological, environmental, and economic transformations discussed in this chapter to earlier periods of world history.
- Early communities created communication networks and exchanges of people, goods, ideas, and diseases. Examine twenty-first century patterns of communication and exchange, and compare our benefits and problems with those of previous centuries.
- Globalization began in the 1400s, but what makes today seem so much more globalized than it was then? Similarly, the human-environment relationship is not new, but demographic and economic pressures have intensified in the last two centuries. With an expected population of 8 billion by 2020, imagine the environmental stresses from massive agricultural production, urbanization, and burning fossil fuels.
- International organizations flourish today, although their roots go back centuries to multiethnic empires and trading companies. Some intellectuals argue that populations are interconnected on so many levels that the definition of *nation*—a self-governed country with a common ethnicity, language, religion, history, and culture—must be changed.

## Historical Developments

- New modes of communication—including radio communication, cellular communication, and the internet—as well as transportation, including air travel and shipping containers, reduced the problem of geographic distance.
- Energy technologies, including the use of petroleum and nuclear power, raised productivity and increased the production of material goods.
- More effective forms of birth control gave women greater control over fertility, transformed reproductive practices, and contributed to declining rates of fertility in much of the world.
- The Green Revolution and commercial agriculture increased productivity and sustained the earth's growing population as it spread chemically and genetically modified forms of agriculture.
- The release of greenhouse gases and pollutants into the atmosphere contributed to debates about the nature and causes of climate change.
- Changing economic institutions, multinational corporations, and regional trade agreements reflected the spread of principles and practices associated with free-market economics throughout the world.
- Movements throughout the world protested the inequality of the environmental and economic consequences of global integration.

## Reasoning Processes

- **Continuity and Change** Describe patterns of continuity and change throughout the 20th and 21st centuries.
- **Comparison** Describe similarities and differences between globalization in the modern era and globalization in earlier periods of world history.

## Historical Thinking Skills

- **Argumentation** Corroborate, qualify, or modify the argument that the process of globalization is simply the "Americanization" of the globe using diverse and alternative evidence.

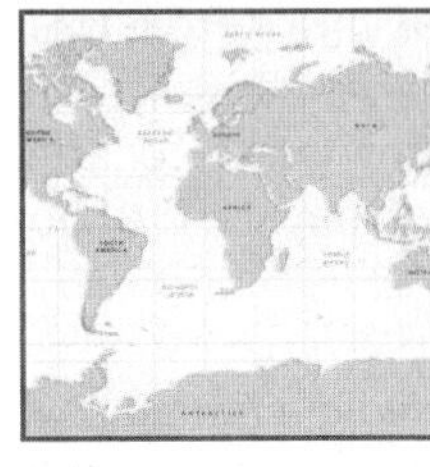

# CHAPTER OVERVIEW

The fall of the Berlin Wall signaled the end of the Cold War, a phenomenon that had shaped the world in multiple ways for more than forty years. The post–Cold War era that followed the fall of the wall was characterized by an increased level of economic interaction between countries and a tighter economic integration of the world. The forces driving the world economy in this direction, often referred to as *globalization,* included advances in communication technology, an enormous expansion of international trade, and the emergence of new global enterprises as well as governments and international organizations that favored market-oriented economics.

Cultural integration also resulted from the never-ending stream of ideas, information, and values spreading from one society to another. Consumer goods, popular culture, television, computers, and the Internet spread outward from advanced capitalist and industrialized nations but also increasingly moved the other way as well.

But the post–Cold War era was also characterized by a host of urgent issues, including climate change, women's rights, terrorism, mass migration, and global disease. Each of these issues cross national boundaries and require global, interconnected responses. Almost a quarter of the way into the twenty-first century, none have yet been solved. While no one can predict the future, the ability of the world's peoples to deal with these issues will determine how historians in the future will describe the successes and failures of the post–Cold War era.

| CHRONOLOGY | |
|---|---|
| 1947 | Establishment of GATT |
| 1948 | UN adopts Universal Declaration of Human Rights |
| 1950 | World population at 2.5 billion |
| 1960 | Introduction of birth control pill; Creation of OPEC |
| 1967 | Establishment of ASEAN; Birth of European Community |
| 1981 | Identification of AIDS |
| 1989 | Fall of Berlin Wall |
| 1991 | Collapse of the Soviet Union |
| 1992 | Beginning of socialist market economy in China |
| 2000 | World population at 6 billion |
| 2001 | Terrorist attacks against the United States and war against Afghanistan |
| 2003–2011 | U.S. war in Iraq |
| 2011 | U.S. killing of Osama bin Laden |
| 2012 | Aung San Suu Kyi elected to Burmese parliament |
| 2014 | President Obama withdraws American troops from Afghanistan |
| 2020 | World Population at 7.8 billion |

# THE END OF THE COLD WAR AND THE EMERGENCE OF A UNIPOLAR WORLD

Between 1989 and 1991, the Soviet system in Europe collapsed. In this period, through a series of mostly nonviolent revolutions, the peoples of eastern and central Europe regained their independence, instituted democratic forms of government, and adopted market-based economies.

The downfall of communist regimes in Europe was the direct consequence of interrelated economic and political developments. The United States, particularly under President **Ronald Reagan** (in office 1981–1989), kept relentless pressure on the Soviet Union to match its enormous military spending. At the same time, internal economic difficulties in the communist regimes of central Europe and the Soviet Union became so apparent as to require reforms. The policies espoused by a new Soviet leader, **Mikhail S. Gorbachev** (1931–), who came to power in 1985, represented an effort to address these massive economic challenges, but they also unleashed a tidal wave of revolution that brought down communist governments. As communism unraveled throughout eastern and central Europe, Gorbachev desperately tried to save the Soviet Union from disintegration by restructuring the economy and liberalizing society. Caught between the rising tide of radical reforms and the opposition of entrenched interests, however, there was little he could do except watch as events unfolded beyond his control. By the time the Soviet Union collapsed in 1991, the Cold War system of states and alliances had become irrelevant to international relations.

## Revolutions in Eastern and Central Europe

The inability to connect communism with national identities left communist regimes vulnerable throughout eastern and central Europe. Those regimes were born in Moscow, transplanted by the Soviet army, and shored up by tanks and bayonets. To most eastern and central Europeans, the Soviet-imposed governments lacked legitimacy from the beginning, and despite the efforts of local communist leaders, the regimes never became firmly established. The Polish intellectual **Leszek Kolakowski** echoed the sentiments of many when he bitterly complained in 1971 that "the dead and by now also grotesque creature called Marxist-Leninism still hangs at the necks of the rulers like a hopeless tumor."

Despite economic stagnation, an accelerated arms race with the United States that further strained the Soviet economy, and obvious signs of discontent, the rulers of eastern and central Europe were reluctant to confront the challenge and restructure their ailing systems. It remained for Gorbachev to unleash the forces that resulted in the disappearance of the Soviet empire in Europe. By the time Gorbachev visited East Berlin in 1989 on the fortieth anniversary of the founding of the German Democratic Republic, he had committed himself to a restructuring of the Soviet Union and to unilateral withdrawal from the Cold War. In public interviews he surprised his grim-faced hosts with the announcement that the Brezhnev Doctrine (in which the Soviet Union reserved the right to intervene in any eastern European nation if it compromised Soviet domination) was no longer in force and that from then on each country would be responsible for its own destiny. The new Soviet orientation led in rapid succession to the collapse or overthrow of regimes in Poland, Bulgaria, Hungary, Czechoslovakia, Romania, and East Germany.

**Poland, Bulgaria, and Hungary** The end of communism came first in Poland, where Solidarity—a combined trade union and nationalist movement—put pressure on the crumbling rule of the Communist Party. The Polish government legalized the previously banned Solidarity movement and agreed to multiparty elections in 1989 and 1990. The voters favored Solidarity candidates, and **Lech Walesa** (1943–), the movement's leader, became president of Poland. In Bulgaria popular unrest forced **Todor Zhivkov** (1911–1998), eastern Europe's longest-surviving communist dictator, to resign in November 1989. Two months later a national assembly began dismantling the communist state. Hungarians tore down the Soviet-style political system between 1988 and 1989. In 1990 they held free elections and launched their nation on the rocky path toward democracy and a market economy.

**Velvet and Violent Revolutions** The disintegration of communism continued elsewhere in eastern Europe. In

**Leszek Kolakowski** (LEH-shek ko-lah-KOW-skee)
**Lech Walesa** (LEHK wah-LEHN-sah)
**Todor Zhivkov** (TO-dohr JHIF-kof)

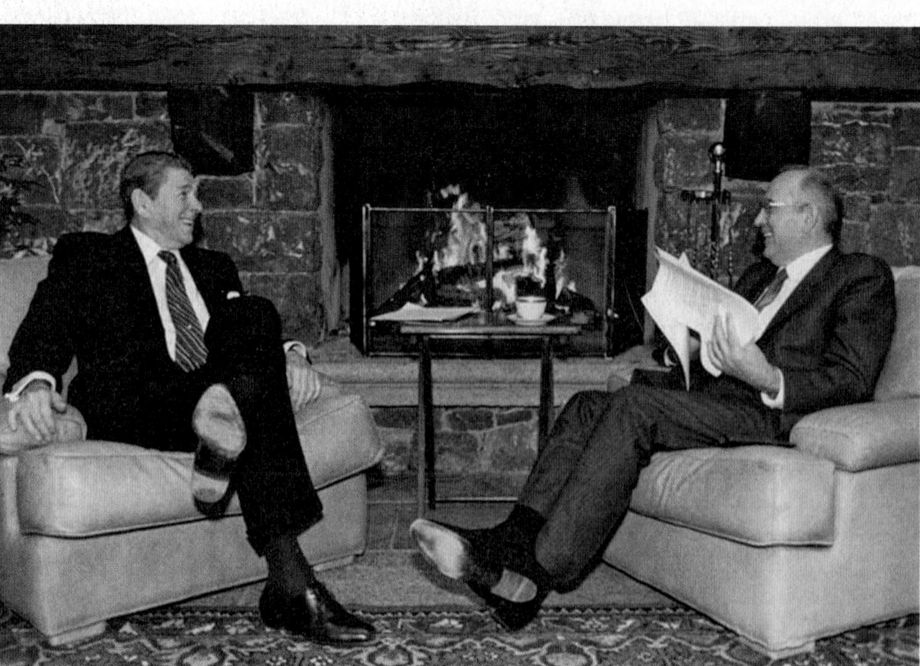

United States President Ronald Reagan and Soviet General Secretary Mikhail Gorbachev sit together at a summit meeting in Geneva, Switzerland in 1985.
Universal History Archive/Universal Images Group/Getty Images

## INTERPRETING IMAGES

Men and women climb atop the Berlin wall on November 9, 1989.

**Analyze** *How does this photo compare to images of previous revolutions or rebellions?*

picture alliance/Getty Images

Czechoslovakia a "velvet revolution" swept communists out of office and restored democracy by 1990. The term *velvet revolution* derived from the fact that aside from the initial suppression of mass demonstrations, little violence was associated with the transfer of power in societies formerly ruled by an iron fist. The communist leadership stood by and watched events take their course. In 1993, disagreements over the time frame for shifting to a market economy led to a "velvet divorce," breaking Czechoslovakia into two new nations, the Czech Republic and Slovakia. In Romania, by contrast, the regime of dictator **Nicolae Ceauşescu** (1918–1989) refused to acknowledge the necessity of reform. In 1989 *Securitate,* a brutal secret police force, savagely repressed demonstrations, setting off a national uprising that ended within four days and left Ceaus¸escu and his wife dead.

**Fall of the Berlin Wall** East Germany had long been a staunchly communist Soviet satellite. Its aging leader, Erich Honecker (1912–1994), openly objected to Gorbachev's ideas and clung to Stalinist policies. When he showed genuine bewilderment at the fact that East German citizens fled the country by the thousands through openings in the iron curtain in Hungary and Czechoslovakia, his party removed him from power. It was too late for anything other than radical changes, and when the East German regime decided to open the Berlin Wall to intra-German traffic on 9 November 1989, the end of the German Democratic Republic was in sight. The end to a divided Berlin was also in sight, literally, as thousands of east and west Berliners like Kristina Matschat tore down the Berlin Wall in the last weeks of 1989. In 1990 the two Germanies, once divided by the Cold War, formed again as a united nation.

## The Collapse of the Soviet Union

The desire to concentrate attention and resources on urgent matters at home motivated Gorbachev's decision to disengage his nation from the Cold War and its military and diplomatic extensions. When he came to power in 1985, Gorbachev was keenly aware of the need for economic reform and the liberalization of Soviet society, although he never intended the collapse of the whole system. Yet it proved impossible to fix parts of the system without undermining the whole.

**Gorbachev's Reforms** Gorbachev's reform efforts first focused on the ailing economy. Antiquated industrial plants, obsolete technologies, and inefficient government control of production resulted in shoddy and outmoded products. The diversion of crucial resources to the military in order to keep up with U.S. military spending made it impossible to produce enough consumer goods—regardless of their quality. The failure of state and collective farms to feed the population compelled the Soviet government to import grains from the United States, Canada, and elsewhere. By 1990 the government imposed rationing to cope with the scarcity of essential consumer goods and food. Economic stagnation in turn contributed to the decline of the Soviet standard of living. Ominous statistics documented the disintegration of the state-sponsored health care system: infant mortality increased while life expectancy decreased. Funding of the educational system dropped precipitously, and pollution threatened to engulf the entire country. Demoralization affected ever-larger

**Nicolae Ceauşescu** (nih-kuh-LIE chow-SHESS-koo)

numbers of Soviet citizens as divorce rates climbed, corruption intensified, and alcoholism became more widespread.

**Perestroika and Glasnost** Under the slogan of *uskorenie,* or "acceleration," Gorbachev tried to shock the economy out of its coma. Yet the old methods of boosting production and productivity through bureaucratic exhortation and harassment paid few dividends; in fact, they called attention to the drawbacks of centralized economic control. Gorbachev then contemplated different kinds of reform, using the term ***perestroika,*** or "restructuring," to describe his efforts to decentralize the economy. To make perestroika work, the Soviet leader linked it to ***glasnost,*** a term that referred to the opening of Soviet society to public criticism and admission of past mistakes.

Perestroika proved more difficult to implement than Gorbachev imagined, and glasnost unleashed a torrent of criticism that shook the Soviet state to its foundations. When Gorbachev pushed economic decentralization, the profit motive and the cost-accounting methods he instituted engendered the hostility of those whose privileged positions depended on being protected by the old system. Many of Gorbachev's comrades and certain factions of the military objected to perestroika and worked to undermine or destroy it. Glasnost also turned out to be a two-edged sword because it opened the door to public criticism of party leaders and Soviet institutions in a way unimaginable a short time earlier. While discontent with Soviet life burst into the open, long-repressed ethnic and nationalist sentiments bubbled to the surface, posing a threat to the multiethnic Soviet state. Only half of the 285 million Soviet citizens were Russian. The other half included numerous ethnic minorities, most of whom never fully reconciled themselves to Soviet dominance.

The pressures on the Soviet system were exacerbated by an ill-considered and costly Soviet military intervention in 1979 to save a Marxist regime in Afghanistan. For nine years well-equipped Soviet forces fought a brutal, unsuccessful campaign against *Afghan* ***mujahideen,*** or Islamic warriors, who gradually gained control of most of the countryside. Weapons and money from the United States, Saudi Arabia, Iran, Pakistan, and China sustained the mujahideen in their struggle. The Central Intelligence Agency of the United States supplied the decisive weapons in the war: ground-to-air Stinger missiles, which could be used to shoot down heavily armored Soviet helicopters, and thousands of mules to haul supplies from Pakistan. In 1986 the Kremlin decided to pull its troops out of the costly, unpopular, and unwinnable war. A cease-fire negotiated by the United Nations in 1988 led to a full Soviet withdrawal in 1989.

**Collapse** By the summer of 1990, Gorbachev's reforms had spent themselves. As industrial and agricultural production continued their downward slide against a backdrop of skyrocketing inflation, the Soviet economy disintegrated. Inspired by the end of the Soviet empire in eastern and central Europe, many minorities now contemplated secession from the Soviet Union. The Baltic peoples–Estonians, Latvians, and Lithuanians–were first into the fray, declaring their independence in August 1991. In the following months the remaining twelve republics of the Soviet Union followed suit. The largest and most prominent of the Soviet republics, the Russian Soviet Federated Socialist Republic, and its recently elected president, Boris N. Yeltsin (1931–2007), led the drive for independence. Soviet leaders vacillated between threats of repression and promises of better treatment, but neither option could stop the movement for independence.

Although the pace of reform was neither quick nor thorough enough for some, others convinced themselves that reforms had gone too far. While Gorbachev was vacationing in the Crimea in August 1991, a group of conspirators–including discontented party functionaries, disillusioned KGB (secret police) officials, and dissatisfied military officers–decided to seize power. Gorbachev's former friend and ally, the flamboyant Boris Yeltsin, crushed the coup with the help of loyal Red Army units. Gorbachev emerged unscathed from house arrest, but his political career had ended. He watched from the sidelines as Yeltsin dismantled the Communist Party and pushed the country toward market-oriented economic reforms. As the Soviet system disintegrated, several of its constituent regions moved toward independence. On 25 December 1991 the Soviet flag fluttered for the last time atop the Kremlin, and by the last day of that year the Union of Soviet Socialist Republics ceased to exist.

## The Unipolar Moment

With the demise of the Soviet Union, the Cold War suddenly ended. For forty years, the bipolar rivalry between the United States and the Soviet Union had dominated global politics and resulted in countless deaths as a result of "hot" proxy wars. And while millions of people rejoiced that nuclear war no longer seemed likely and the arms race could end, this massive shift in the global balance of power left a vacuum. In the three decades following 1991, the United States sought to influence world politics as the sole remaining superpower, while Russia sought to return to stability and to regain its earlier prestige. These efforts caused relations between the United States and Russia to deteriorate dramatically in the opening decades of the twenty-first century. At the same time, the end of the Cold War seemed to open space for other powers, especially China, to play major roles in global politics.

**Instability versus Overconfidence** In spite of initial optimism in and outside Russia in 1991, by the mid-1990s it was clear that the shift to a market economy could not immediately fix the country's many economic problems. Both industrial and agricultural production had dropped significantly,

***perestroika*** (pehr-eh-STROY-kuh)
***glasnost*** (GLAHS-nost)
***mujahideen*** (moo-jah-hih-deen)

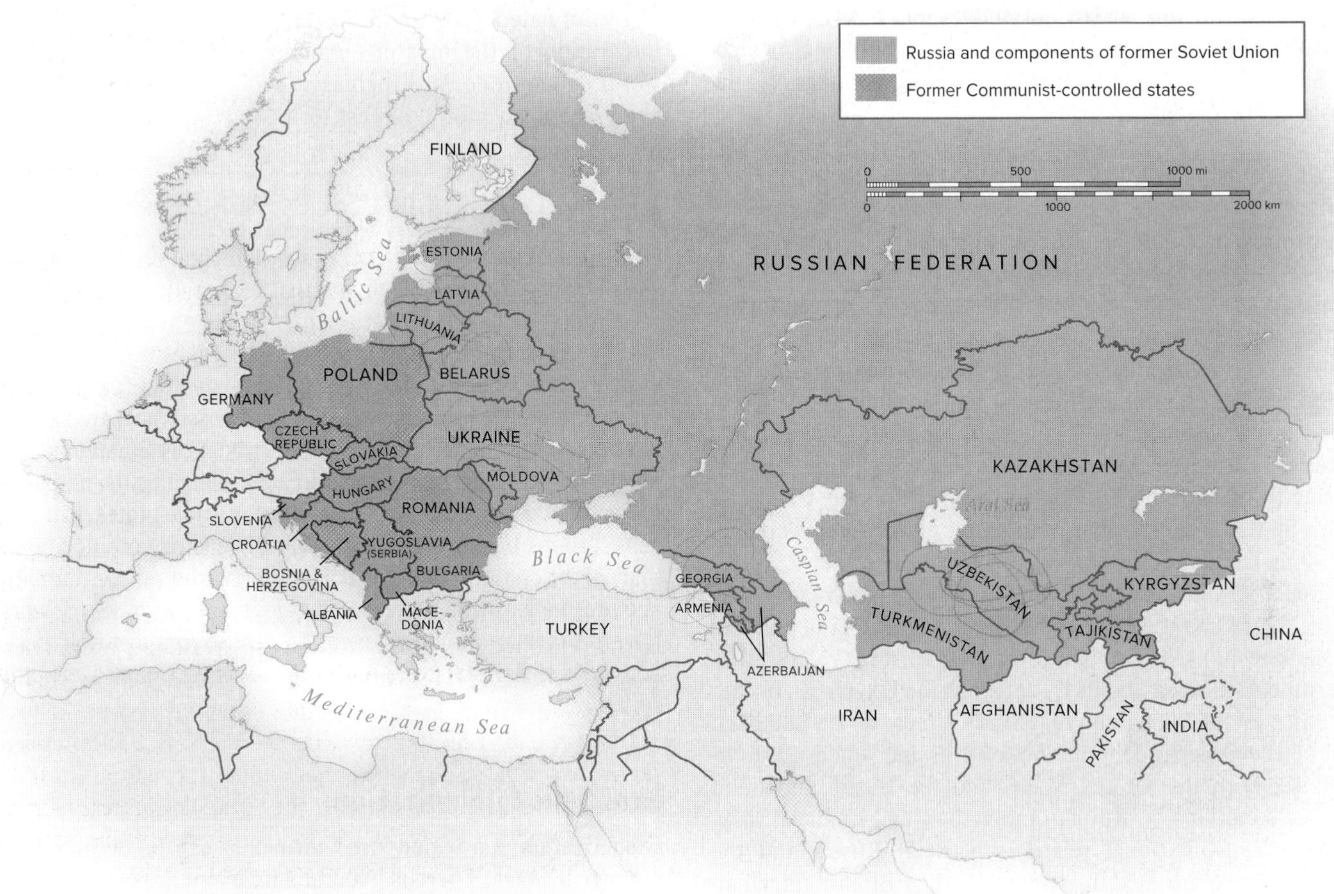


**MAP 26.1 The collapse of the Soviet Union and European communist regimes, 1991.**

Note the number of states suddenly created by the breakup of the Soviet Union.

***How would this affect the ability of each to survive, both economically and politically?***

and one-third of the Russian population had sunk below the poverty line. Crime was pervasive. To make matters worse, Boris Yeltsin—who became the first popularly elected president in Russia in 1991—proved to be an erratic ruler and badly mismanaged a war with the breakaway Chechen Republic.

In the midst of these difficulties, the U.S. government saw an opportunity to become the only world superpower and to dictate global politics on its own terms. In 1992 Paul Wolfowitz, President George H. W. Bush's undersecretary for defense, wrote a post-Cold War policy statement that advocated unilateral action and the use of the military force to prevent the reemergence of another superpower. This aggressive stance receded somewhat during President Bill Clinton's administration (1993-2001), but in this period, the United States nevertheless alarmed Russian leaders by inviting the former Soviet satellite states of Hungary, Poland, and the Czech Republic to join NATO, which they did in 1999. Given that NATO's original purpose at its founding in 1949 was to form a defensive alliance against the Soviet Union, the Russian government saw the incorporation of its traditional buffer states as a clear threat to national security.

**The Bush Doctrine** Under the administration of President George W. Bush (2001-2009), the U.S. government returned to an overtly aggressive foreign policy. The president's policies, which became known collectively as the **Bush Doctrine,** affirmed the legitimacy of the United States acting alone to pursue its own interests, even to the point of engaging in preemptive strikes. At this time the U.S. government regarded Russia as a second-rate power, and its leaders continued the policy of inviting former Soviet satellites into NATO. In 2004, NATO admitted Bulgaria, Estonia, Latvia, Lithuania, Romania, Slovakia, and Slovenia, further alarming and angering the Russian government.

**Deteriorating Relations in the Early Twenty-First Century** Meanwhile, Vladimir Putin, Boris Yeltsin's former prime minister, was elected to the Russian presidency in 2000. After serving an eight-year term, in 2008 Putin ceded the post to his protégé Dmitry Medvedev and became prime minister (all the while retaining his personal power). In 2012 he returned to the presidency, and in 2018 he was reelected for another six-year term. For the first two decades of the twenty-first century, Putin focused on winning back the prestige Russia had lost after the collapse of the Soviet Union, demonstrating to the world that Russia would not tolerate unilateral action by the United States, and gaining ever tighter control over domestic politics.

Relations between the United States and Russia hit a new low in 2014, when the pro-Russian president of Ukraine fled to Russia in response to popular protests against his rule. Putin's government then massed its forces along the Ukrainian border and annexed the Ukrainian region of Crimea, which had been part of the independent nation of Ukraine since 1991. In response, both the United States and the European Union imposed sanctions on Russian individuals and financial institutions. Confrontational relations between Russia and the United States continued in 2016, when the FBI announced an investigation of Russian hacking into the Democratic National Committee's computer system, and the Democratic Party accused Russia of meddling in the 2016 presidential election.

Tense relations between the United States and Russia in the twenty-first century have led some contemporaries to wonder if the world is experiencing a new cold war. Yet circumstances are quite different from the post–World War II era. Most important is that the world is no longer dominated by two superpower blocs. Since 1989, the United States has acted alone as the only superpower, but there are signs that this "unipolar moment" will give way to a multipolar world in the future. China in particular seems poised to take on a superpower role, which will have major consequences for the global power dynamic.

## THE GLOBAL ECONOMY

With the collapse of the Soviet Union, the potential for a truly globalized economy now expanded to the former communist world. Economists pointed to a new economic order characterized by the expansion of trade between countries, the growth of foreign investments, the unfettered movement of capital, the privatization of former state enterprises, a wave of deregulation that undermined the control that national governments once exercised over economic activity, and the emergence of a new type of corporation. Supporting the new global economy were technological developments in communications; semiconductors, fiber-optic cables, and satellites virtually eliminated geographic distances, causing an ever-faster integration of the market economy. The forces driving the world economy toward increased economic integration have been responsible for a process termed *globalization.*

### Energy Technologies

One of the forces driving economic globalization has been the use of energy sources, such as fossil fuels and nuclear energy, on a massive scale. By the last half of the twentieth century, fossil fuels were the preeminent source of power in the world, allowing the expansion of production and consumption to unprecedented levels. At the same time, fossil fuels are non-renewable, increase pollution, and contribute to climate change. Nuclear energy, once believed to be a cleaner alternative to fossil fuels, is viewed with suspicion by some states and citizens' groups because of the danger of reactor core accidents that might contaminate the environment and poison humans and animals. Both states and scientists continue to work toward other renewable, clean, and safe energy technologies—such as hydrogen—to power the world's interconnected economy.

### Economic Globalization

**Globalization** is a widely used term that can be defined in a number of ways. There is general agreement, however, that in an economic context, globalization refers to the reduction and removal of barriers between national borders to facilitate the flow of goods, capital, services, and labor. Global economic interaction and integration is not a new phenomenon. Ancient Rome and China, for example, controlled and economically integrated vast regions of the ancient world. In more recent centuries, the nations of western Europe—through their global outreach and encounters with far-flung societies—created worldwide empires in which goods and people moved with relative ease. The more recent phenomenon of globalization since 1945, however, has been different and unprecedented in both scope and speed, and it has transformed the social and political as well as the economic contours of the world.

**Free Trade** International trade proved to be a key driving force behind economic globalization. Trade across long distances especially has figured prominently in the shaping of human history, and for at least the past five hundred years it has served as an integrating force. Of more recent origin is the phrase **free trade,** meaning freedom from state-imposed limits and constraints on trade across borders. The issue of free trade engendered a debate about the extent to which free trade enhances the prosperity of a society. In the aftermath of World War II, leaders from industrialized nations, especially from the United States, took a decisive stand on the issue.

Nestlé global corporate headquarters in Vevey, Switzerland. Nestlé is the largest food company in the world and has corporate offices all over the globe. In 2018 Nestlé generated sales of $93.4 billion.
Gunter Fischer/Education Images/Universal Images Group/Getty Images

**GATT and WTO** At the end of World War II, the victors sought to establish an international trading system that would facilitate economic recovery after the destruction of the war. Believing that the protective tariffs characteristic of national policies during the Great Depression had only worsened the global economic crisis, they pushed instead for the elimination of restrictive trading practices that stood in the way of free trade. The main vehicle for the promotion of unrestricted global trade was the **General Agreement on Tariffs and Trade** (GATT), which was signed by the representatives of 23 noncommunist nations in 1947. In 1994, the member nations of GATT signed an agreement to establish the **World Trade Organization** (WTO), which took over the activities of GATT in 1995. The WTO has developed into a forum for settling international trade disputes, with the power to enforce its decisions. The WTO has 164 member nations and 23 observer nations, which accounts for 99 percent of all world trade.

**Global Corporations** The emergence of a new type of corporation played another key role in the development of the new economic order. Global corporations have increasingly replaced the more traditional international or multinational forms of corporate enterprises. International companies were born out of the desire to extend business activities across borders in pursuit of specific activities such as importation, exportation, and the extraction of raw materials. International companies evolved into multinationals, which conducted their business in several countries but had to operate within the confines of specific laws and customs of a given society. During the past twenty-five years, the transformation of the corporate landscape has resulted in the birth of some fifty thousand global corporations. In contrast to the multinational, the typical global corporation relies on a small headquarters staff while dispersing all other corporate functions around the globe in search of the lowest possible operating costs. Global corporations treat the world as a single market and act as if the nation-state no longer exists. Many multinational corporations, such as General Motors, Siemens AG, and Nestlé, have transformed themselves into global enterprises, both benefiting from and contributing to the ongoing process of globalization.

Global corporations have become the symbols of the new economy. They also have begun to transform the political and social landscape of many societies. Since the end of World War II, major corporations throughout the developed world have been required to contribute to the welfare of their respective home communities through a combination of collective bargaining agreements, tax laws, and environmental regulations. Highly mobile global corporations that are no longer bound to any particular location have managed, however, to escape those obligations. Competing with companies around the world, global corporations have moved jobs from high-wage facilities to foreign locations where wages are low and environmental laws are weak or nonexistent.

## Economic Growth in Asia

Globalization and the acceleration of worldwide economic integration also benefited from economic developments in east and southeast Asia, where the economies of Japan, China, and the so-called **little tigers** (Hong Kong, Singapore, South Korea, and Taiwan) underwent dramatic economic growth. This Asian "economic miracle" was largely a result of economic globalization.

**Japan** U.S. policies jump-started Japan's economic revival after its defeat in 1945, and by 1949 the Japanese economy had already attained its prewar level of productivity. Just as western European countries had benefited from the Marshall Plan, so Japan benefited from direct U.S. financial aid ($2 billion) and investment. In addition, the United States placed no restrictions on the entry of Japanese products into the U.S. market. Finally, because a 1952 treaty stipulated that the United States would be the military protector of Japan and that Japan could never spend more than 1 percent of its gross national product on defense, the country's postwar leaders were able to channel the savings into economic development.

At first sight, Japan's economy was ill equipped for intensive economic growth. Japan had lost its overseas empire and was hampered by a large population and a lack of natural resources. Japan's economic planners sidestepped many of those disadvantages by promoting an economic policy that emphasized export-oriented growth supported by low wages. The large workforce, willing to endure working conditions and wages considered unacceptable by organized labor in western Europe and the United States, gave Japanese employers a competitive edge over international rivals. Although Japanese industries had to pay for the import of most raw materials, the low cost of Japanese labor ensured the production of goods that could be sold inexpensively on the global market.

Initially, the Japanese economy produced labor-intensive manufactured goods such as textiles, iron, and steel slated for export to markets with high labor costs, particularly the United States. During the 1960s Japanese companies used their profits to switch to more capital-intensive manufacturing and produced radios, television sets, motorcycles, and automobiles. In the 1970s Japanese corporations took advantage of a highly trained and educated workforce and shifted their economic resources toward technology-intensive products such as random access memory chips, liquid crystal displays, and CD-ROM drives. By that time the label "Made in Japan," once associated with cheap manufactured goods, signified state-of-the-art products of the highest quality. Japan's economic achievements gave its banks, corporations, and government an increasingly prominent voice in global affairs. By the 1980s Japan seemed poised to overtake the United States as the world's largest economy. In the 1990s, however, it became clear that postwar growth rates were not sustainable, and the Japanese economy entered into a deep recession. Indeed, the recovery from this recession continued into the second decade of the twenty-first century. Nevertheless, the postwar Japanese success story served as an inspiration for other Asian countries.

**The Little Tigers** The earliest and most successful imitators of the Japanese model for economic development were Hong Kong, Singapore, South Korea, and Taiwan. Their remarkable and rapid growth rates earned them the somewhat condescending label of the "four little tigers," and by the 1980s these newly industrializing countries had become major economic powers. Like Japan, all four countries suffered from a shortage of capital, lacked natural resources, and had to cope with overpopulation. But like Japan a generation earlier, they transformed apparent disadvantages into advantages through a program of export-driven industrialization. By the 1990s the four little tigers were no longer simply imitators of Japan but had become serious competitors. As soon as new Japanese products had carved out market niches, corporations based in the four little tigers moved in and undercut the original item with cheaper versions. By the turn of the millennium, Indonesia, Thailand, and Malaysia joined the original tigers in their quest for economic development and prosperity.

**Perils of the New Economy** For the supporters of the new global economy, the spectacular economic development of so many Asian societies was proof that globalization could deliver on the promise of unprecedented prosperity. By the late 1990s, however, it seemed clear that globalization could also lead to economic ruin.

At the center of this bust was a financial crisis that came to a head in 1997. In the preceding twenty years, the developing Asian economies had started to embrace the market, opening their borders to imports and courting foreign investments. After years of generous lending and growing national debts, the international investment community suddenly lost confidence in the booming economies and withdrew support. The crisis began in Thailand in mid-1997, when the government decided to discontinue its policy of pegging the Thai national currency (the baht) to the U.S. dollar. This led many investors to turn to other markets, which in turn caused the value of the baht to plummet. The Thai stock market quickly lost 75 percent of its value, and the country found itself in the grip of a depression. For no obvious reason, the financial panic—and with it economic contraction—then moved to Malaysia, Indonesia, the Philippines, and South Korea. In each instance, the rise and fall of the individual economies resulted from their integration in the new global economy, which rewarded and punished its new participants with equal ease.

**BRICs** Contrary to all expectations, the nations hit so hard by the financial crisis recovered quickly. Their recovery was matched by other emerging economies, often identified as **BRICs** because they include the fast-growing and developing economies of Brazil, Russia, India, and China. In the aftermath of the Cold War, the governments composing the BRICs initiated political and economic reforms that embraced capitalism and allowed their countries to join the world economy. To make these nations more competitive, their leaders have simultaneously emphasized education, domestic entrepreneurship, foreign investment, and domestic consumption, with varying levels of success. China is already the leading global supplier of manufactured goods, while Brazil and Russia supply much of the world's raw materials.

**The Rise of China** After the death of Mao Zedong (see chapter 25), China's leaders launched economic reforms that opened Chinese markets to the outside world, encouraged foreign investment, and imported foreign technology. These changes promoted rapid economic growth, and in 1992 the

Chinese government labeled its new economic model a "socialist market economy." In such a model, the government retains its authoritarian control over political life while allowing a functioning market economy. In the economic realm, demand for goods and services determines production and pricing, and the role of the government is limited to providing a stable but competitive environment. Besides acting as a major exporter, China benefited from its large pool of cheap labor, while its enormous domestic markets have made the Chinese economy the destination of choice for foreign investment capital. In December 2001 China became a member of the World Trade Organization, and in 2010 it overtook Japan as the second largest economy in the world after the United States.

## Trading Blocs

In the rapidly changing global economy, some groups of nations have sought to reduce risk, achieve advantages, and gain economic strength for their partners by entering into economic alliances known as trading blocs.

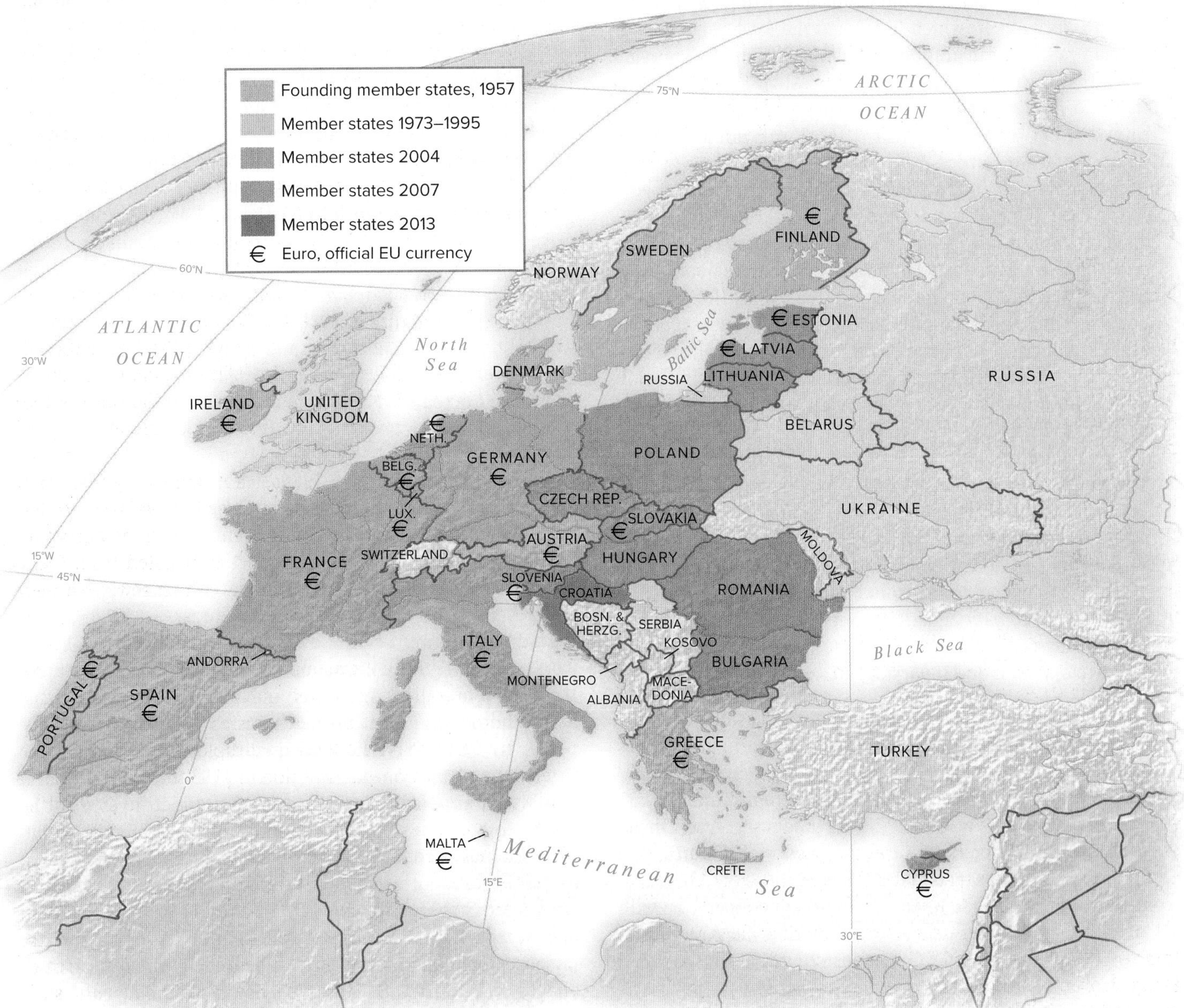


**MAP 26.2 European Union membership, 2020.**

In 2007 the European Union celebrated the fiftieth anniversary of its founding as a supranational and intergovernmental organization. The euro (sign: €) is the official currency of the eurozone, which consists of eighteen of the twenty-eight member states of the European Union. Note that Great Britain is no longer a member state, having left the European Union on January 31, 2020.

***What major challenges face the European Union in the twenty-first century?***

**European Union** The most strongly integrated regional bloc is the **European Union,** which is characterized by a common market and free trade. In March 1957, representatives of six nations–France, West Germany, Italy, the Netherlands, Belgium, and Luxembourg–took a significant step in this direction by signing the Treaty of Rome. This treaty established the European Economic Community–renamed the European Community in 1967. At the heart of this new community of nations lay the dismantling of tariffs and other barriers to free trade among member nations. Subsequent treaties created political institutions such as the Council of Ministers and the European Parliament, which facilitated the long-range goal of European political integration. The development of a supranational organization dedicated to increasing European economic and political integration culminated in the Maastricht Treaty of 1993, which established the European Union. By 2013, twenty-eight European nations submerged much of their national sovereignty in the European Union (twenty-seven as of 2020 with the exit of the United Kingdom), and since 1999 eighteen members have adopted a common currency.

Despite the European Union's many achievements, however, it has had its share of problems in the twenty-first century. Among the most serious have been concerns within member countries about the loss of control over social, political, and economic policies. Indeed, these concerns led to the first withdrawal from the EU by a member state when the United Kingdom voted to leave the union in 2016. "Brexit," as it has become known, was initiated by both economic and political concerns. Many Britons argued that the economic benefits of EU membership were no longer worth the price of a submerged British sovereignty. In addition, deep concerns over the movement of people across the European Union–particularly migrants seeking a better life from parts of Africa and the Middle East–triggered nationalist, xenophobic responses that called for reasserting control over Britain's borders. The British withdrawal became final on January 31, 2020.

**OPEC** One of the earliest and most successful economic alliances was the **Organization of Petroleum Exporting Countries** (OPEC), a producer cartel established in 1960 by the oil-producing states of Iran, Iraq, Kuwait, Saudi Arabia, and Venezuela, and later joined by Qatar, Libya, Indonesia, Abu Dhabi, Algeria, Nigeria, Ecuador, Congo, Equatorial Guinea, the United Arab Emirates, and Gabon. The purpose of OPEC is to control and negotiate the price of oil through cooperation with its mostly Arab or Muslim members. During the Arab-Israeli War of 1973, however, OPEC demonstrated that its economic control over oil prices could be used for political purposes. Because the United States supported Israel, the political enemy of many OPEC member nations, the cartel ordered an embargo on oil shipments to the United States and quadrupled the price of oil between 1973 and 1975. The huge increase in the cost of petroleum triggered a global economic downturn, as did a curtailment of oil exports in the later 1970s. OPEC's policies therefore demonstrated how the alliance could exert control over the developed world and its financial system. OPEC's influence diminished in the 1980s and 1990s as a result of overproduction and dissension among its members over the Iran-Iraq War and the Gulf War. Additionally, in the twenty-first century, the increased use of hydraulic fracturing (often called "fracking") to extract oil from shale has dramatically increased production in the United States. In 2018 the United States was the world's largest oil-producing country, with 10 million barrels a day. Since this allows the United States to be less dependent on OPEC, it has also muted the political potential of OPEC actions. Nevertheless, OPEC members continue to control around 72 percent of the world's crude oil reserves and thus remain a critically important trading bloc.

**ASEAN** Another well-established economic partnership is the **Association of Southeast Asian Nations,** or ASEAN. Established in 1967 by the foreign ministers of Thailand, Malaysia, Singapore, Indonesia, and the Philippines, its principal objectives were to accelerate economic development and promote political stability in southeast Asia. Originally conceived as a bulwark against the spread of communism in the region, the economic focus of ASEAN became sharper after it signed cooperative agreements with Japan in 1977 and the European Community in 1980. In 1992 member states agreed to establish a free-trade zone and to cut tariffs on industrial goods over a fifteen-year period. By 2020, ASEAN member states had expanded to include Brunei, Cambodia, Lao, Vietnam, and Myanmar.

**NAFTA** Beginning in the 1980s, leaders of the North American nations of the United States, Canada, and Mexico also began to discuss the creation of a trading bloc to increase their economic competitiveness in the global marketplace. The result was the **North American Free Trade Agreement** (NAFTA), which went into effect on January 1, 1994, during the administration of U.S. President Bill Clinton. NAFTA worked toward the elimination of trade barriers among the three nations, allowing goods and services to move freely across borders, and set up mechanisms to resolve trade disputes. By 2018, NAFTA had quadrupled trade among the three nations, up from $290 billion in 1993 to $1.23 trillion. It had also dramatically increased foreign direct investment by the three countries in the economies of their neighbors. But NAFTA has also been criticized, especially in the United States, for causing a loss in U.S. jobs and for keeping wages in the United States artificially low. In 2018, U.S. President Donald Trump sought the renegotiation of NAFTA for the specific purposes of reducing the U.S. trade deficit with its partners and to safeguard U.S. jobs. The new agreement, called the United States Mexico Canada Agreement (USMCA), was signed in the United States in December 2019 and was ratified by all three countries by March 2020.

**Globalization and Its Critics** The global economy is still very much a work in progress, and it is not clear what the long-term effects will be on the economies and societies it touches. To its supporters, the global economy delivers markets that operate with efficiency, speedily directing goods and services wherever there is demand for them and always expecting the highest returns possible. Proponents of globalization also argue that the new economy is the only way to bring prosperity—the kind previously enjoyed only by industrialized nations—to the developing world. To its critics the global economy is a force that rewards the few and impoverishes the many. The specific charges leveled by antiglobalization groups and coalitions are many. They assert that globalization diminishes the sovereignty of local and national governments and transfers the power to shape economic and political destinies to transnational corporations and global institutions such as the WTO. Detractors of globalization also claim that the hallmark of globalization—rapid economic development—is responsible for the destruction of the environment; the widening gap between rich and poor societies; and the worldwide homogenization of local, diverse, and indigenous cultures. It is certain that globalization has been accompanied by major social and economic changes. But it is too soon to tell if these changes will be overwhelmingly destructive for the world's lands and peoples.

## CROSS-CULTURAL EXCHANGES AND GLOBAL COMMUNICATIONS

Like trade and business organizations, cultural practices have also become globalized, thriving on a continuous flow of information, ideas, tastes, and values. At the turn of the twentieth century, local traditions—commonly derived from gender, social class, or religious affiliation—still determined the cultural identity of the vast majority of people. At the end of the twentieth century, thanks in part to advances in technology and communications, and the influence of international organizations, information and cultural practices were becoming truly global and more people than ever were aware of events and issues occurring far away. Their impact was summarized in a jingle popularized by the Walt Disney Company during the 1964–1965 World's Fair in New York City: "It's a small world after all."

### Consumption and Cultural Interaction

New communications media have tied the world together and have promoted a global cultural integration whose hallmark is consumption. Beginning in the eighteenth century, industrialization and the subsequent rise in per capita income gave birth to a type of society in which the consumption of goods and services satisfied wants and desires rather than needs or necessities. Although the desire to consume is hardly novel, the modern consumer culture means more than simple consumption. It implies that consumers want more than they need and that the items they consume take on symbolic value. Consumption, in other words, has become a means of self-expression as well as a source for personal identity and social differentiation. The peculiar shape of this consumer culture resulted from two seemingly contradictory trends: a tendency toward homogenization of cultural products and heightened awareness of local tastes and values. Critics sometimes refer to the homogenizing aspect of global culture as the "Americanization" or **"McDonaldization"** of the world.

Those terms suggest that the consumer culture that developed in the United States during the mid-twentieth century has been exported throughout the world, principally through advertising. Thus it is no accident that young people clad in blue jeans and T-shirts sing the same Usher or Eminem lyrics in San Francisco, Sarajevo, and Beijing. Still, nothing symbolizes the global marketing of U.S. mass culture more than the spread of its food and beverage products. While Pepsi and Coca-Cola fight battles over the few places on earth that their beverages have not yet dominated, fast-food restaurants such as Burger King, McDonald's, and Pizza Hut sell their standardized foods throughout the world. The closing of many bistros and cafés in France, for instance, is the result of more French people opting for fashionable fast food instead of taking the time for more traditional and lengthy lunches. So successful has the global spread of U.S. mass culture been that it seems to threaten local cultures everywhere.

The export of U.S. products and services is not the sole determinant of global cultural practices, however. Because the contemporary consumer culture stresses minute differences between products and encourages consumers to make purchase decisions based on brand names designed to evoke particular tastes, fashion, or lifestyle, it also fosters differentiation. Indeed, global marketing often emphasizes the local or indigenous value of a product. Genuinely Australian products, such as Drizabone wet-weather gear and Foster's Lager, have become international commodities precisely because they are Australian in origin. Likewise, young upwardly mobile consumers continue to prefer Rolex watches from Switzerland, Armani clothes from Italy, miniature electronics from Japan, and Perrier mineral water from France.

**Multilateral Globalization** Indeed, it would be a mistake to conceive of the globalization of culture as a one-way street emanating mainly from the United States. Rather, given the speed at which information and goods can travel, most any consumable item can gain worldwide popularity. For example, reggae music became a worldwide phenomenon after the Jamaican musician Bob Marley partnered with British-based Island Records in 1972 to produce the album *Catch a Fire.* Although reggae was a complex, hybrid musical style particular to Jamaica, its protest lyrics and beat found eager audiences in countercultures in almost every continent from North and South America to Europe and Africa, and it profoundly influenced musical traditions in the late twentieth century. Sushi consumption in the United States provides another example of the multidirectional nature of globalization. Although sushi was first introduced to the United States in the 1960s, in the 1990s sushi suddenly caught on outside major metropolitan areas as a healthy alternative to fatty, American-style food. In the last thirty years, sushi—which had been prepared in Japan since the eighth century—could be found in

# SOURCES FROM THE PAST

## The Debate over Cultural Globalization

*In 2003, Philippe Legrain tackled one of the thorniest issues related to culture and globalization: to what extent is the globalization of culture simply the Americanization of global culture? Drawing on his training as a journalist and economist, and drawing on his experiences with the World Trade Organization, Legrain rather forcefully challenged those observers and commentators who decried the omnipresence of American cultural imperialism (or what Legrain terms "Cocacolonization") in the age of globalization. In these excerpts from his article in* The Chronicle of Higher Education, *titled "Cultural Globalization Is Not Americanization," Legrain made his position in the debate clear.*

**Fears that globalization is imposing** a deadening cultural uniformity are as ubiquitous as Coca-Cola, McDonald's, and Mickey Mouse. Europeans and Latin Americans, left-wingers and right, rich and poor—all of them dread that local cultures and national identities are dissolving into a crass all-American consumerism. That cultural imperialism is said to impose American values as well as products, promote the commercial at the expense of the authentic, and substitute shallow gratification for deeper satisfaction. . . .

It is a myth that globalization involves the imposition of Americanized uniformity, rather than an explosion of cultural exchange. For a start, many archetypal "American" products are not as all-American as they seem. Levi-Strauss, a German immigrant, invented jeans by combining denim cloth (or "serge de Nîmes," because it was traditionally woven in the French town) with Genes, a style of trousers worn by Genoese sailors. So Levi's jeans are in fact an American twist on a European hybrid. Even quintessentially American exports are often tailored to local tastes. MTV in Asia promotes Thai pop stars and plays rock music sung in Mandarin. CNN en Español offers a Latin American take on world news. McDonald's sells beer in France, lamb in India, and chili in Mexico.

In some ways, America is an outlier, not a global leader. Most of the world has adopted the metric system born from the French Revolution; America persists with antiquated measurements inherited from its British-colonial past. Most developed countries have become intensely secular, but many Americans burn with fundamentalist fervor—like Muslims in the Middle East. Where else in the developed world could there be a serious debate about teaching kids Bible-inspired "creationism" instead of Darwinist evolution?

> In what ways does Legrain argue that the United States is not necessarily a leader in globalization?

America's tastes in sports are often idiosyncratic, too. Baseball and American football have not traveled well, although basketball has fared rather better. Many of the world's most popular sports, notably soccer, came by way of Britain. Asian martial arts—judo, karate, kickboxing—and pastimes like yoga have also swept the world.

People are not only guzzling hamburgers and Coke. Despite Coke's ambition of displacing water as the world's drink of choice, it accounts for less than 2 of the 64 fluid ounces the typical person drinks a day. Britain's favorite takeaway is a curry, not a burger; Indian restaurants there outnumber McDonald's six to one. For all the concerns about American fast food trashing France's culinary traditions, France imported a mere $620 million in food from the United States in 2000, while exporting to America three times that. Nor is plonk [cheap alcohol] from America's Gallo displacing Europe's finest: Italy and France together account for three-fifths of global wine exports, the United States for only a twentieth. Worldwide, pizzas are more popular than burgers, Chinese restaurants seem to sprout up everywhere, and sushi is spreading fast. By far the biggest purveyor of alcoholic drinks is Britain's Diageo, which sells the world's best selling whiskey (Johnnie Walker), gin (Gordon's), vodka (Smirnoff), and liqueur (Bailey's). . . .

> In what ways is Legrain suggesting that globalization of culture can move in multiple directions?

In pop music, American crooners do not have the stage to themselves. The three artists who were featured most widely in national Top Ten album charts in 2000 were America's Britney Spears, closely followed by Mexico's Carlos Santana and the British Beatles. Even tiny Iceland has produced a global star: Björk. Popular opera's biggest singers are Italy's Luciano Pavarotti, Spain's José Carreras, and the Spanish-Mexican Placido Domingo. Latin American salsa, Brazilian lambada, and African music have all carved out global niches for themselves. In most countries, local artists still top the charts. . . .

The evidence is overwhelming. Fears about an Americanized uniformity are overblown: American cultural products are not uniquely dominant; local ones are alive and well.

### For Further Reflection

- Do you find Legrain's arguments and examples compelling? Could cultural exchanges such as those detailed in Legrain's article be more complicated or problematic than Legrain proposed? Consider how other cultural products—perhaps those from Africa or Asia—might either uphold or undermine Legrain's thesis on globalization.
- International trade had existed for centuries. What was the context which prompted his defense of globalization?
- What would undermine his argument?

*Source:* Legrain, Philippe. "Cultural Globalization Is Not Americanization," *The Chronicle of Higher Education,* 49, no. 35 (May 9, 2003): B7. Used with permission.

local Japanese restaurants across the United States, in airports, in the prepared foods section of grocery stores, and even in the refrigerated section of gas station convenience stores. Not only that, Americans have altered and modified sushi recipes to reflect ingredients more familiar in the United States or to give the varieties American-sounding names.

The phenomenon of modification is important to remember even with products or consumables that originate in the United States. Take the case of Music Television (MTV) Latino. When MTV Latino was launched in 1993 from Miami, many critics viewed it as just another case of foreign cultural intrusion, whereby Latin video deejays speak "Spanglish" or "Chequenos" ("check us out"), mixing Spanish and English. While Latin Americans once had called for protection against such alien influence, many soon relaxed their guard. Instead of cultural domination, they saw evidence of increased cultural sharing among Latin societies, noting that MTV and cable television have come to serve as a means of communication and unity by making the nations of Latin America more aware of one another. Thus, it is important to remember that cultural dominance is limited by the ability of many societies to blend and absorb a variety of foreign and indigenous practices.

This CDC 7600 mainframe computer was built by the Control Data Corporation in the 1970s. Note its extremely large size in comparison to computers in the twenty-first century.
Science History Images/Alamy Stock Photo

## The Networked World

Throughout history, technological advances provided the means to dissolve boundaries between localities and peoples and thus allowed cultural transmission to take place. Today virtually instantaneous electronic communications have dissolved time and space. Since the mid-1990s, the rise of the Internet and smartphones has swept away the social, economic, and political isolation of the past.

Communications technologies underwent a fundamental transformation during the 1990s with the rapid spread of the Internet. The Internet had arisen from Cold War imperatives: U.S. defense specialists wanted to establish a way to disseminate information after a nuclear attack and ultimately created a network (the Advanced Research Projects Agency Network, or ARPANET) in which computers at different locations could communicate with one another. In 1983, researchers began to use a communications protocol (called TCP/IP) by which different kinds of computers on different networks could communicate, and the Internet was officially born. However, it was not until 1991 that a platform for public use, called the World Wide Web, became available. When the institution that developed the World Wide Web (CERN) announced in 1993 that the platform was free for everyone to develop, its use exploded around the world. In 1998 Google went live, changing the way millions of people searched for information, and in 2004 Facebook launched its social media platform (though only for college students). By 2008, presidential candidates were taking full advantage of the Internet to conduct their campaigns, and by the second decade of the twenty-first century, the Internet had become fully integrated into the lives of most people living in developed nations.

Although the Internet fundamentally changed the way in which people communicated around the world, at first it was only available to people or companies who owned computers or who could pay to use them in "Internet cafés." But access to the Internet gradually became more democratized by the second decade of the twenty-first century through the use of smartphones—or mobile phones that could access wireless networks and thus the Internet. Mobile phones had been available publicly since the 1980s, but these were physically heavy and expensive to use. By the early 2000s, both the size and the cost of mobile phones had shrunk, and some phones began to be developed that could access wireless networks. The introduction of the first iPhone in 2007 revolutionized smartphone use: in little more than the span of a decade, a huge percentage of the human population had access to relatively inexpensive mobile phones that could function as telephones, computers, cameras, and video recorders, with ever-increasing coverage areas in nearly every part of the world. By 2019, the Pew Research Center estimated that five billion people had mobile phones and that half of these were smartphones. And while people in developed nations are more likely to own mobile phones, 45 percent of people in developing nations own them as well.

The use of the Internet, and especially of smartphones, has not only accelerated communications and proved convenient for everyday life activities, it has also changed the way people organize social movements. For example, during the social protests that swept the Arab world during the "Arab Spring" of 2011, activists used social media to advertise the locations of protests and to communicate what was happening with the outside world. Additionally, individuals have used social media as a platform to publicize human rights abuses they have filmed on their smartphones, often leading to public outcry and even policy changes. Yet even though the Internet, smartphones, and social media have transformed the way billions of people communicate in the twenty-first century, critics worry that over-reliance on such technologies might lead people to neglect face-to-face relations or that social media in particular might be detrimental to individual self-esteem. These debates have not been settled and will likely continue as Internet-driven technologies expand around the world.

## International Organizations

As the world's peoples are becoming increasingly connected and interdependent as a result of new technologies, many have realized that they face issues that extend well beyond national borders. Since the end of World War II, this recognition has led to an increase in the number of organizations dedicated to solving global problems through international coordination and action. These institutions are important because they have the potential to tackle issues that do not respect territorial boundaries and thus cannot be effectively addressed by individual national governments.

**Intergovernmental Organizations** One type of international body is the intergovernmental organization, meaning that membership is made up of sovereign states rather than individuals or private groups. These organizations include the World Trade Organization, the North Atlantic Treaty Organization (NATO), the African Development Bank, and the European Union, to name a few. The main purposes behind intergovernmental organizations are to provide mechanisms for member states to work together to find solutions to maintain peace and security, or to enhance economic and social stability across national borders.

The best known intergovernmental organization is the United Nations (UN), which was established at the end of World War II to replace the League of Nations (1920–1946). The purpose of the UN is to find solutions to global problems and to deal with virtually any matter of concern to humanity. Unlike a national government, the UN does not legislate. Yet, in its meeting rooms and corridors, representatives of the vast majority of the world's countries (193 out of 195 total) have a voice and a vote in shaping the international community of nations. Under its charter, a principal purpose of the UN is "to maintain international peace and security." It has not been able to achieve this goal, partly because member states have often chosen to embark on wars or hostilities in spite of UN opposition. And unless all members of the UN Security Council (whose permanent members are made up of the five most powerful nations in the world) agree, the UN cannot send peacekeeping troops to help end a conflict.

But the UN has compiled an enviable record with respect to another role defined in its charter, namely, "to achieve international cooperation in solving international problems of an economic, social, cultural, or humanitarian character." Quietly and often without attracting attention from the international news media, the specialized agencies of the UN have achieved numerous successes. For example, in 1980 the World Health Organization (a division of the UN) proclaimed the worldwide eradication of smallpox as a result of its thirteen-year global program. On other fronts, UN efforts resulted in more than a 50 percent decrease in both infant and child mortality rates in developing countries between 1960 and 2002. Indeed, by 2015 the UN reported that its efforts had helped to save the lives of ninety million children worldwide since 1990. The organization's efforts also promoted an increase in female literacy, especially in Africa, where for the first time in history the majority of women—53.6 percent in 2010—were deemed to be literate. The UN also worked to provide access to safe water for over one billion people living in rural areas.

**Nongovernmental Organizations** Another type of international body is the nongovernmental organization (NGO), meaning that such an organization operates independently of any government. NGOs typically are nonprofit organizations and focus on a social, economic, environmental, or humanitarian issue that transcends national borders. Many NGOs have focused on the protection of human rights, or the notion that all persons are entitled to some basic rights, especially rights that protect an individual against state conduct prohibited by international law or custom. Universal recognition and acceptance of the concept of human rights came in the aftermath of World War II with the exposure of Nazi crimes. In 1948, the National Assembly of the UN adopted the **Universal Declaration of Human Rights,** which contributed to the codification of international human rights laws. The declaration singled out specific human rights violations such as extrajudicial or summary executions, arbitrary arrest and torture, and slavery or involuntary servitude as well as discrimination on racial, sexual, or religious grounds. Since then, concerned individuals and groups have formed human rights NGOs with the goal of ensuring these laws are upheld. For example, Amnesty International (founded 1961) seeks to expose human rights violations all over the world through massive media and lobbying campaigns, as well as to provide legal defense where possible. It is funded by individual members, which in 2020 had reached two million. Amnesty International has counted among its many victories campaigns on behalf of groups as well as individuals, from compelling Shell Oil to pay $55 million to the Nigerian government for oil spills to freeing a young woman in El Salvador who was imprisoned on suspicion of inducing an abortion.

In 2015, one organization estimated that there are ten million NGOs operating around the world. It is thus not surprising that they focus on many issues besides human rights. Many focus on global health, including organizations like Partners in Health (founded 1987), whose mission is to provide health care to the most marginalized populations in the world. Others focus on the environment and solutions to climate change. The Environmental Defense Fund (founded 1967), for example, seeks to find solutions to the most urgent environmental problems, whether in the air, in the oceans, or on land. Still others, such as Barefoot College (founded 1972), focus on education for the poor, in this case specifically by providing funding to educate and empower poor women from rural areas.

Given the intensity and acceleration of global interaction after World War II, the possibilities for solving global problems through international coordination is increasingly imaginable. And while both intergovernmental and nongovernmental international organizations are far from perfect, for the present they represent the closest thing humanity has to a global system of governance that can help the world's peoples meet the challenges of international problems.

## URGENT GLOBAL ISSUES IN THE EARLY TWENTY-FIRST CENTURY

By the twenty-first century, it had become clear that the new millennium would bring with it a multitude of issues whose solution would require both a global perspective and global responses. Each of these issues—from climate change to women's empowerment to global pandemics—have the potential to affect all the world's people, and none have easy solutions.

### Population Pressures and Climate Change

The post–World War II period has been accompanied by vast population increases. As the result of advances in agriculture, industry, science, and medicine global population has increased from 2.5 billion in 1950 to 7.9 billion in 2021. The widespread and successful use of vaccines, antibiotics, and insecticides, along with improvements in water supplies and increased agricultural yields, caused a dramatic decline in worldwide death rates in this period. The rapid decline in mortality among people who also maintained high levels of fertility led to explosive population growth in many areas of Asia and Africa in the last half of the twentieth century. In Yet the population division of the United Nations has estimated that instead of continued exponential growth of the global population, the earth's population will stabilize at around 9.8 billion in 2050. This is partly due to the fact that fertility rates in many parts of the world have fallen since the beginning of the 21st century as women have demanded, and increasingly gained, access to more effective methods of birth control. When women have the ability to limit pregnancy and childbirth, their health improves and infant mortality declines. In addition, access to birth control improves women's access to education and to paid labor, and reduces the likelihood they will live in poverty. In 2019, 57% of married women of reproductive age had access to modern methods of birth control. As more women gain such access, experts expect fertility rates to slow even further.

**Climate Change** But even if global population growth stabilizes in the short term, it is clear that human actions have dramatically altered the physical environment in ways that may prove disastrous for the survival of the planet. In recent decades one environmental issue has taken center stage: **climate change.** In the context of environmental debates and policymaking, climate change usually refers to a human-induced climate change known as **global warming.**

Global warming is the phenomenon of increasing average air temperature near the surface of the earth over the past two centuries. On the basis of detailed observations, scientists have concluded that the influence of human activities since the beginning of industrialization have altered the earth's climate. More specifically, the vast majority of scientists around the world are convinced that most of the observed temperature increases since the middle of the twentieth century are caused by increasing concentrations of greenhouse gases, which prevent solar heat from escaping from the earth's atmosphere. Like the glass panes in a greenhouse, hydrocarbon emissions from automobiles, and methane emitted from animal dung on commercial farms, trap heat within the atmosphere, leading to a rise in global temperatures. An average rise of global temperature by more than 2°C (3.6°F), would cause significant economic and ecological damage, particularly because this would cause a rise in sea levels as a result of melting in the polar ice caps.

A vigorous debate is in progress over the extent and seriousness of rising surface temperatures, their consequences for the environment, and the necessity to limit further warming. In the ancient Japanese capital of Kyoto, at a conference dedicated to climate change, the delegates from 187 nations agreed in 1997 to cut greenhouse emissions blamed for global warming. The Kyoto protocol went into force in 2005 and imposed targets for carbon emission reductions on developed countries until 2012. The protocol did not require developing countries—some of them major polluters, such as India and China—to reduce their emissions. The world's second-largest polluter after China, the United States, did not sign the protocol because it required nothing of developing countries. Since Kyoto, global carbon-dioxide emissions have risen by a third.

International efforts in dealing with climate change have been hampered by the fact that developing nations have been reluctant to commit themselves to cutting emissions. In part this is because their leaders believe that the only way to remain economically competitive in the globalized world is to continue industrializing. Additionally, some leaders resent being told they must cut back on emissions to solve environmental problems caused by developed nations over the span of more than a century. As a result, developing nations have insisted that developed nations bear the costs of reducing emissions. Efforts to find solutions have also been hampered by one of the most powerful developed nations and one of the world's greatest polluters: the United States. Politicians in the United States have worried about the economic effects of reducing emissions, and some have expressed skepticism about the existence of climate change at all. In spite of these obstacles, in December 2015 the United Nations Framework on Climate Change produced the Paris Agreement, which set global goals of capping greenhouse

Smokestacks in Siberia releasing carbon dioxide emissions into the atmosphere. Most scientists argue that emissions such as these, along with other hydrocarbon emissions and methane, contribute to global climate change.
Peter Turnley/Corbis/VCG/Getty Images

emissions. The Paris Agreement commits signatories to reducing emissions and to publicly tracking their progress in doing so. Unlike the Kyoto protocol, the Paris Agreement was signed by nearly every developing country (including China and India) as well as the United States. However, under the administration of President Donald Trump, who cited concern for American jobs and businesses, the United States withdrew from the Paris Agreement on June 1, 2017. Trump's withdrawal, however, was reversed again when President Joe Biden rejoined the Paris Agreement on his first day in office, January 20, 2021.

Family-planning programs. However, the availability and promotion of contraceptives does not guarantee effective control of fertility. Whereas China has, however stringently, significantly reduced its population growth rate and some Latin American societies also have experienced a decline in their birthrates, people in other societies have resisted efforts to reduce birthrates. In some instances, resistance stems from both religious and political motives. In India, for example, the Hindu emphasis on fertility has impeded

## How the Past Shapes the Future

### The Destructive Potential of Industrial Technologies

Nineteenth-century advocates of industrialization had envisioned a world in which mechanization and new technologies would lead to improvements in the human condition over the long term. Yet after only two centuries since industrialization began in Great Britain, it seems possible that the pollution associated with industrialization may have disastrous consequences for the whole planet if, as scientists predict, such pollution leads to global climate change. Think about how the issues associated with climate change are an excellent example of the ways historical events and processes can have consequences for the future in ways that contemporaries cannot even imagine.

birth control efforts. Thus global attempts to prevent excessive population growth have had mixed results.

## Economic Inequities and Labor Servitude

The unequal distribution of resources and income, and the resulting poverty, have materialized as key concerns of the contemporary world. Several hundred million people, especially in the developing areas of eastern Europe, Africa, Latin America, and Asia, struggle daily for sufficient food, clean water, adequate shelter, and other basic necessities. Poverty is a lack of basic human necessities, and its effects are as wide-ranging as they are devastating. Malnutrition among the poor has led to starvation and death. As one of the most persistent effects of poverty, malnutrition is also responsible for stunted growth, poor mental development, and high rates of infection. Typically, vitamin and mineral deficiencies accompany malnutrition, causing mental disorders, organ damage, and vision failure among poor children and adults. Because of inadequate shelter, lack of safe running water, and the absence of sewage facilities, the poor have been exposed disproportionally to bacteria and viruses carried by other people, insects, and rodents. Poverty has correlated strongly with higher-than-average infant mortality rates and lower-than-average life expectancies.

A rare and endangered adult woolly spider monkey in the Atlantic Forest, Brazil. This species is one of about 30,000 endangered species, 85% of which are threatened as a result of habitat loss due to human expansion.
Paulo B. Chaves/Getty Images

**The Causes of Poverty** The division between rich and poor has been a defining characteristic of all complex societies. Although relative poverty levels within a given society remain a major concern, it is the continuing division between rich and poor societies that has attracted the attention of the international community. A worldwide shortage of natural resources as well as the uneven distribution of resources have figured as major causes of poverty and have divided nations into the haves and have-nots. Excessively high population densities and environmental degradation have caused the depletion of available resources, leading to shortages of food, water, and shelter and ultimately to poverty. The other major cause of poverty, the unequal distribution of resources in the world economy, resulted from five hundred years of colonialism, defined by the appropriation of labor and natural resources. Pervasive poverty characterizes many former colonies and dependencies. All of these developing societies have tried to raise income levels and eliminate poverty through diversified economic development, but only a few, such as South Korea, Singapore, and Malaysia have accomplished their aims. In the meantime, economic globalization has generated unprecedented wealth for developed nations, creating an even deeper divide between rich and poor countries. A report issued by the antipoverty charity Oxfam noted that in 2018, 82 percent of the world's total wealth went to the richest 1 percent of the population, while the 3.7 billion people who make up the poorest half of the world saw no increase in their wealth.

**Labor Servitude** Poor economic conditions have been closely associated with forms of servitude similar to slavery. Although legal slavery ceased to exist when Saudi Arabia and Angola abolished slavery officially in the 1960s, forced and bonded labor practices continue to affect millions of poor people in the developing world. Of particular concern is child-labor servitude. According to the International Labor Organization, a specialized agency of the United Nations, more than 250 million children between ages five and fourteen work around the world, many in conditions that are inherently harmful to their physical health and emotional well-being. Child-labor servitude is most pronounced in south and southeast Asia, affecting an estimated 50 million children in India alone. Most child labor occurs in agriculture, domestic service, family businesses, and the sex trade, making it difficult to enforce existing prohibitions and laws against those practices. Many children are born into a life of bonded labor because their parents have worked in debt bondage, a condition whereby impoverished persons work for very low wages, borrow money from their employer, and pledge their labor as security.

**Trafficking** A growing and related global problem that touches societies on every continent is the trafficking of persons. In this insidious form of modern slavery, one to two million human beings annually are bought and sold across international and within national boundaries. Trafficking has appeared in many forms. In Russia and the Ukraine, for example, traffickers lure victims with the promise of well-paying jobs abroad. Once the victims arrive in the countries of their destination, they become captives of ruthless traffickers who force them into bonded labor, domestic servitude, or the commercial sex industry through threats and physical brutality—including rape, torture, starvation, incarceration, and death. Most of the victims of trafficking are girls and women, which is a reflection of the low social and economic status of women in many countries. In south Asia, for instance, it is common for poverty-stricken parents or other relatives to sell young women to traffickers for the sex trade or forced labor.

The trafficking industry is one of the fastest growing and most lucrative criminal enterprises in the world, generating billions of dollars annually in profits.

## The Continuing Inequality of Women

The status of women in many places around the world began changing after World War II. Women gained more economic, political, social, and sexual rights in highly industrialized states than in developing nations, but nowhere have they achieved full social, political, and economic equality with men. Although women have increasingly challenged cultural norms requiring their subordination to men and confinement in the family, attainment of even basic rights for many millions of women has been slow. Agitation for gender equality is often linked to women's access to employment, which is highest in industrialized nations. Women constitute 40 to 50 percent of the workforce in industrial societies, compared with only 20 percent in developing countries. Yet in all countries, the majority of women who do work for pay are engaged in low-paying jobs such as teaching, service, and clerical work. This does not include farming, as 40 percent of all farmers in the world are women. Rural African women, for example, do most of the continent's subsistence farming and produce more than 70 percent of Africa's food. Whether they are industrial, service, or agricultural workers, women earn less than men earn for the same work and are generally kept out of the highest-paid professional careers.

In addition, a report issued by the UN and the World Bank in 2017 argued that more women live in extreme poverty in the world than men. At the same time, data collected by both the UN and many NGOs have demonstrated that programs to improve overall public health, improve access to education, and promote sustainable development in societies around the world meet with greater success when steps have been taken to improve the status of women.

### The Struggle for Equality in Industrialized Nations

The discrimination that women faced in the workplace was a major stimulus for the **feminist movement** in industrialized nations. Women in most of those nations had gained the right to vote after the Great War (although women in France and Italy had to wait until 1944 and 1945), but they found that political rights did not guarantee economic or sexual equality. After World War II, when more and more women went to work, women started to protest job discrimination, pay differentials between women and men, and their lack of legal equality. In the 1960s those complaints expanded into a feminist movement that criticized all aspects of gender inequality. In the United States, the civil rights movement that demanded equality for African Americans influenced the women's movement and provided a training ground for many women activists.

Women in industrialized societies started to expose the ways in which a biologically determined understanding of gender led to their oppression. In addition to demanding equality in the workplace, women demanded full control over their bodies and their reproductive systems. Access to birth control and abortion became as essential to women's liberation as economic equality and independence. Only with birth control measures would women be able to determine whether or when to have children and thus avoid the notion that "biology is destiny." The introduction of the birth control pill in the 1960s gave millions of women the power to protect themselves from unwanted pregnancies. Shortly thereafter, beginning with the United Kingdom in 1967 and then extending to Canada (1967), the United States (1973), and many European countries, women won the fight to legalize abortion. But even though these developments provided women in industrialized nations with a measure of sexual freedom, women continued to lag behind men in terms of access to political power and equal wages for equal work. In addition, women often face sexual harassment in the workplace.

**Gender Equality in China** Legally, the position of women most closely matches that of men in communist or formerly communist countries such as the Soviet Union, Cuba, and China. "Women hold up half the sky," Mao Zedong had declared, and that eloquent acknowledgment of women's role translated into a legal commitment to fairness. The communist dedication to women's rights led to improvement in the legal status of Chinese women once the communists gained power in China. In 1950, communist leaders passed a marriage law (see chapter 37) that mandated the protection of interests of both men and women within marriage, legalized divorce, and abolished patriarchal practices such as child betrothal. It also upheld equal rights for men and women in the areas of work, property ownership, and inheritance.

Critics argue that despite such laws Chinese women have never gained true equality with men. For example, few women have gained high status in the Communist Party's leadership. And although most women in China have full-time jobs outside the home, they do not receive wages equal to those of men. They do most of the work at home as well. Nevertheless, they are able to enter most professions, although the majority of Chinese women engage in menial work. Long-standing cultural values continue to degrade the status of women, especially in rural areas. Traditionally, parents have overwhelmingly preferred boys over girls. One unintended consequence of China's population policies, which until 2016 limited couples to one child, was the mysterious statistical disappearance of a large number of baby girls. Demographers estimate that annually more than one-half million female births went unrecorded in government statistics. Although no one can with certainty account for the "missing" girls, some population experts speculate that a continued strong preference for male children caused parents to send baby girls away for adoption or to be raised secretly or, in some cases, to single them out for infanticide.

**Domesticity and Abuse** Although girls and women in industrial and communist nations are guaranteed basic if not

## INTERPRETING IMAGES

Women belonging to the U.S. feminist group the National Organization for Women (NOW) marching for equal rights in Washington, D.C., in 1992. Although American and European women have experienced many gains with respect to achieving full equality with men, they remain less powerful in many areas. Pressures against equality for women remain strong in many developing areas of the world.

**Analyze** *While a photo like this might be used to show the strength of the women's equality movement, consider the messaging you see. Is this an expression of strength or something else? Consider what you've learned about efforts for gender equality around the world. Are there substantial differences in women's equality in developed countries and in developing countries? What are they? Does gender equality exist anywhere in the world?*

Mark Reinstein/Corbis/Getty Images

fully equal legal rights and are educated in roughly the same numbers as boys and men, women in other areas of the world have long been denied access to education. Indeed, of the world's remaining 774 illiterate adults, two-thirds of these are women.

In India, for example, the literacy gap between men and women is stark, at 81.5 percent for men compared to 64.6 percent for women. Moreover, the participation of Indian women in the labor force is very low, at about 25 percent for rural women and 15 percent for urban women. At the same time, birthrates in India remain high in spite of greater access to birth control, at 2.33 births per woman as compared to 1.8 in the United States. These conditions have ensured a life of dependence for many Indian women. One indicator of the low social status of Indian women is the continued occurrence of dowry deaths. It is customary among many Indian communities to pay a dowry (gifts of money or goods) to the husband and his family upon a woman's marriage, although this requirement is difficult for many Indian families to meet. If the husband and his family perceive the dowry as inadequate, if the husband wants a new wife without returning his first wife's dowry, or in some cases if the wife has simply annoyed the husband or her in-laws, her new family douses her with kerosene and sets her on fire so that her death can be explained as a cooking accident. Although this practice is illegal and only occurs in a small minority of marriages, it is still widespread enough to make women's precarious position in society clear. In 2016 the government of India reported 7,621 dowry deaths, though unofficial estimates put the number closer to twenty-five thousand.

**Women Leaders** By 2015, women had gained the right to vote in almost every country in the world. In general, however, they do not exert political power commensurate with their numbers. Some women have nonetheless attained high political offices or impressive leadership positions. Somewhat ironically, the same south Asia that revealed so many continued barriers to women's rights on a day-to-day basis also elevated some women to positions of power. It was no accident, however, that all of these women came from powerful political

Young girls study the Qu'ran at a madrassa (school) in Pakistan, 2005.
Robert Nickelsberg/Getty Images

families. **Indira Gandhi** (1917–1984) and **Benazir Bhuto** (1953–2007), both of whose fathers had been prime ministers, served as prime minister for India and Pakistan, respectively. Yet both women were controversial figures, and both were assassinated while in office. In 1994 **Chandrika Bandaranaike Kumaratunga** (1945–) became the first female president of Sri Lanka. Both her parents had previously served as prime ministers; her mother, Sirimavo Bandaranaike (1916–2000), became the first elected woman prime minister in 1960. As president, Kumaratunga appointed her mother to serve a third term as prime minister.

In Myanmar (formerly Burma), **Aung San Suu Kyi** (1945–) has emerged as a leader, also deriving her political authority from her father, Aung San, assassinated in 1947. Assuming the leadership of the democracy movement after her return from exile in 1988, Suu Kyi called for a nonviolent revolution against what she called Myanmar's "fascist government." The government placed her under house arrest from 1989 to 1995, during which time she created a new political institution, the "gateside meeting," speaking to her followers from behind the gates of her home. In the 1990 elections Suu Kyi and her party won a landslide victory, but they were not allowed to come to power. Awarded the Nobel Peace Prize for her efforts in 1991, she could not accept the award personally because she was still under house arrest. She remained in detention or under house arrest for much of the next two decades, released from her political imprisonment only in 2010. Aung San Suu Kyi was elected to the Burmese parliament in 2012, and in 2015 she led her party, the National League for Democracy, to a landslide victory in Myanmar's first openly contested elections. Although not allowed to serve as president because she has foreign-born children, she served as de facto leader of the country from 2016 until February 2021, when the military staged a coup and overthrew her party. Since 2017, Suu Kyi has come under international criticism for her failure to stop attacks by Myanmar's army on Burma's indigenous Muslim minority, the Rohingya.

In spite of the fact that some women have served as leaders of their countries, the fact remains that by the end of the second decade of the twenty-first century, women still are vastly underrepresented as political leaders in nearly every nation. There have only been nineteen female heads of state since 2000, and in 2020 only one in five members of lower or single houses of parliament are women worldwide. Women remain a small minority of corporate managers and senior officials everywhere in the world, and only 50 percent of working age women are in the labor force compared to 77 percent of men. We have seen that women are more likely to live in poverty than men, which has clear implications for their access to adequate health care, housing, and nutrition. Additionally, a UN report indicates that about one-third of women in the world have experienced sexual or physical violence by an intimate partner or have experienced sexual violence by a nonpartner at some point in their lives. Thus, if it is true that

**Indira Gandhi** (in-DEE-rah GAHN-dee)
**Benazir Bhuto** (BEN-ah-zeer BOO-toh)
**Chandrika Bandaranaike Kumaratunga** (CHAHN-dree-kah BAHN-dah-rah-nigh-kee koo-mah-rah-TOONG-ah)
**Aung San Suu Kyi** (ong sahn soo chee)

# SOURCES FROM THE PAST

## Malala Yousafzai on Why Girls Should Go to School

*Malala Yousafzai (1997–) was eleven years old when the Taliban took control of her town in Pakistan. Malala wrote a diary protesting this, which was read by many people, and thereafter she became a target. When she dared to go to school in defiance of Taliban rules in 2012, a masked gunman boarded her school bus and shot her on the left side of the head, also wounding two of her friends. Malala survived the shooting, undergoing critical surgery in Pakistan before being flown to London for more surgeries. She and her family now live in London, where she is a vocal advocate for education, especially for girls. In 2014 she became the youngest recipient of the Nobel Peace Prize. Below are excerpts of the speech she gave at the United Nations on her sixteenth birthday.*

**I don't know where to begin my speech.** I don't know what people would be expecting me to say. But first of all, thank you to God for whom we all are equal and thank you to every person who has prayed for my fast recovery and a new life. I cannot believe how much love people have shown me. . . .

Thousands of people have been killed by the terrorists and millions have been injured. I am just one of them.

So here I stand, one girl among many . . .

Dear sisters and brothers, I am not against anyone. Neither am I here to speak in terms of personal revenge against the Taliban or any other terrorist groups. I am here to speak up for the right of education of every child. I want education for the sons and the daughters of all the extremists especially the Taliban . . .

The wise saying, "The pen is mightier than sword" was true. The extremists are afraid of books and pens. The power of education frightens them. They are afraid of women. The power of the voice of women frightens them . . . That is why they are blasting schools every day. Because they were and they are afraid of change, afraid of the equality that we will bring into our society.

> Why, according to Malala, are the Taliban so against education, and for girls in particular?

I remember that there was a boy in our school who was asked by a journalist, "Why are the Taliban against education?" He answered very simply. By pointing to his book he said, "A Talib doesn't know what is written inside this book." They think that God is a tiny, little conservative being who would send girls to the hell just because of going to school. The terrorists are misusing the name of Islam and Pashtun society for their own personal benefits. Pakistan is peace-loving democratic country. Pashtuns want education for their daughters and sons. And Islam is a religion of peace, humanity and brotherhood. Islam says that it is not only each child's right to get education, rather it is their duty and responsibility.

> In what ways does Malala argue the Taliban misrepresents Islam?

Honourable Secretary General, peace is necessary for education. In many parts of the world especially Pakistan and Afghanistan, terrorism, wars and conflicts stop children to go to their schools. We are really tired of these wars. Women and children are suffering in many parts of the world in many ways. In India, innocent and poor children are victims of child labour. Many schools have been destroyed in Nigeria. People in Afghanistan have been affected by the hurdles of extremism for decades. Young girls have to do domestic child labour and are forced to get married at early age. Poverty, ignorance, injustice, racism and the deprivation of basic rights are the main problems faced by both men and women.

Dear fellows, today I am focusing on women's rights and girls' education because they are suffering the most. There was a time when women social activists asked men to stand up for their rights. But, this time, we will do it by ourselves . . .

Dear brothers and sisters, we want schools and education for every child's bright future. We will continue our journey to our destination of peace and education for everyone. No one can stop us. We will speak for our rights and we will bring change through our voice. We must believe in the power and the strength of our words. Our words can change the world.

So let us wage a global struggle against illiteracy, poverty and terrorism and let us pick up our books and pens. They are our most powerful weapons . . .

Education is the only solution. Education first.

### For Further Reflection

- Why is education so important to Malala? What does she believe education can do to help the poor and suffering?
- Why was Malala Yousafzai's cause extraordinary enough to earn her the Nobel Peace Prize?
- Why does she claim that "peace is necessary for education"?

*Source:* United Nations, Office of the Secretary General's Envoy on Youth. Malala Yousafzai addresses United Nations Youth Assembly. https://www.un.org/youthenvoy/video/malala-yousafzai-addresses-united-nations-youth-assembly/ Used with permission of the Malala Fund.

Pro-democracy leader Aung San Suu Kyi spoke at a press conference, appearing under the flag of her political party in Yangon, Burma.
EMMANUEL DUNAND/AFP/Getty Images

programs for improving public health and sustainable development succeed best when women are empowered through access to education and work, much remains to be done.

## Global Terrorism

**Terrorism** has become a persistent feature of the globalized world since 1945. Although not a recent phenomenon, terrorism attained its greatest impact in a world distinguished by rapid technological advances in transportation, communications, and weapons development. Heightened media awareness, especially the ubiquity of worldwide television coverage, has exposed the grievances and demands of terrorists to millions of viewers, but it has also transformed the practice of terrorism. Acts of terror therefore punctuated the era following World War II, as individuals and groups the world over attempted to destabilize or overthrow political systems within or outside the borders of their countries. Terrorism figured prominently in anticolonial conflicts in Algeria and Vietnam; in struggles over a homeland between national groups such as Israelis and Palestinians; in clashes between religious denominations such as Protestants and Catholics in Northern Ireland; and between revolutionary forces and established regimes in states such as Indonesia, Iran, and Nicaragua.

**Defining Terrorism** No universally agreed-on definition of terrorism exists, but experts agree that a key feature of terrorism is the deliberate and systematic use of violence against civilians, with the aim of inspiring terror to advance political, religious, or ideological causes. Terrorists use violent means—from hijackings and hostage-taking to assassinations and mass murder—to magnify their influence and power. In contrast to the populations and institutions they fight, terrorists and their organizations are usually limited in size and resources. During the last decades of the twentieth century and the first decade of the twenty-first century, terrorism increasingly assumed a global character because instead of using terrorist techniques in local struggles, terrorist networks brought violence thousands of miles away to strike at the heart of their perceived enemies. To do this, they relied on the same sophisticated financial networks, modern modes of transportation, and communications technologies used by billions of other people in a globalized world. At the turn of the twenty-first century, this relatively novel kind of terrorism captured the attention of the world as a result of the September 11 attacks in the United States.

**September 11** On the morning of September 11, 2001, New York City and Washington, D.C., became the targets of a coordinated terrorist attack that was unprecedented in scope, sophistication, and destructiveness. Hijackers seized four passenger jetliners and used them as guided missiles. Two of the planes crashed into the World Trade Center towers in New York City, causing the collapse of the two towers, the ancillary destruction of adjacent skyscrapers, and more than twenty-five hundred deaths. Before the morning was over, another plane crashed into the Pentagon, killing one hundred twenty-five people at the nerve center of the U.S. military in Washington, D.C., and the fourth jet crashed into a field outside Pittsburgh, Pennsylvania. Intended for another Washington, D.C., landmark, the fourth jet was thwarted in its mission when passengers stormed the hijackers and forced the plane to crash. As millions around the world watched events unfold on television, the U.S. government launched an intensive investigation and identified the Islamic militant **Osama bin Laden** (1957–2011) as the mastermind behind the attacks. Officials also accused bin Laden of directing previous attacks on U.S. interests in Africa and southwest Asia. Before the dust of the collapsed World Trade towers had settled, U.S. President George W. Bush (1946–) declared war on Osama bin Laden and global terrorism itself.

Osama bin Laden headed ***al-Qaeda*** ("the base"), the core of a global terrorist network. He became a popular figure in the U.S.-backed effort to aid mujahideen (Islamic warriors) who fought Soviet forces in Afghanistan. By the end of the Persian

The north face of the south tower immediately after being struck by United Airlines flight 175 on September 11, 2001.
Laperruque/Alamy Stock Photo

Gulf War (1990–1991), however, he began to consider the United States and its allies with unqualified hatred. The stationing of U.S. troops on what he regarded as the holy soil of Saudi Arabia, the bombing of Iraq, and supporting Israeli oppression of Palestinians, bin Laden claimed, were tantamount to a declaration of war against God. His radicalism led him first to be exiled and then, in 1994, to be stripped of his Saudi Arabian citizenship. He spent time in Sudan, where he took credit for the attack on two U.S. Black Hawk helicopters in 1993. He was expelled from Sudan in 1996, at which point he went to Afghanistan at the invitation of the radical and violent **Taliban** party. From his base there in 1998, bin Laden publicly called on every Muslim to kill Americans and their allies "wherever he finds them and whenever he can." Viewed by many as the personification of evil, yet admired by some for his convictions and aims, Osama bin Laden moved to the forefront of Islamist violence.

**War in Afghanistan and Iraq** The Taliban itself emerged out of the disorder and devastation of the Afghan-Soviet war (1979–1988) and the Afghan civil war that developed in its aftermath. Promoting itself as a new force for unity and determined to create an Islamic state according to its own austere interpretation of Islam, the Taliban proclaimed its followers the liberators who brought peace to Afghanistan. In their pursuit of what they claimed would be the purest Muslim state on earth, Taliban intolerance figured prominently, and Islamist strictures quickly alienated people both inside and outside Afghanistan. Dominated by Pashtuns—the majority ethnic group of Afghanistan—the Taliban under its leading *mullah* (male religious leader), Mohammed Omar, fought a series of holy wars against other ethnic and Muslim groups, such as Afghanistan's Shia minority. At the same time, the Taliban provided sanctuary and training grounds for Islamist fighters in southwest and central Asia, most notably—as we have seen—for Osama bin Laden and al-Qaeda.

The Taliban enforced a strict interpretation of Islam that barred women from education and the workplace. As all forms of European and American dress became taboo, women had to be completely veiled in *burkas,* and men had to stop wearing neckties and grow full, untrimmed beards. The stringent form of Taliban-promoted Islam also called for a ban on television, movie theaters, photographs, and most styles of music. Some of those rules had nothing to do with Islam, but a religious police, the Ministry of the Promotion of Virtue and Prevention of Vice, nevertheless enforced them with an extremely harsh code of justice. The United Nations and most governments in the world withheld recognition of the Taliban as Afghanistan's legitimate government. Instead, they recognized a Taliban opposition force, the Northern Alliance, which was composed of the country's smaller religious and ethnic groups. The Northern Alliance became a crucial ally of the United States in its mission to find and punish those responsible for the September 11 attacks.

When the United States government announced its war against global terrorism, it also pointedly targeted "those harboring terrorists," that is, governments and states that supported and provided sanctuary for terrorists. The refusal of the Taliban government to surrender Osama bin Laden prompted the United States and its allies to begin military operations against Taliban military positions and terrorist training camps on October 7, 2001. The U.S. military and its international allies generally limited their operations to intelligence missions and massive air strikes, fighting the war on the ground through Afghan proxies, most notably the forces of the Northern Alliance. By November, U.S.-led bombardments permitted Northern Alliance troops to capture Kabul and other key Afghan cities. The United States' coalition hampered both the Taliban and al-Qaeda, but conflicts continued.

Another international action against terrorism separate from the war in Afghanistan came in March 2003, when President Bush coordinated what he termed **"Operation Iraqi Freedom."** A multinational coalition force some three hundred thousand strong, largely made up of U.S. and British troops but also including those from approximately two dozen other nations, carried out an invasion of Iraq designed to wage further war on terrorism by ousting the regime of **Saddam Hussein** and creating a democratic state. The coalition argued they had firm evidence that Hussein possessed a huge stockpile of chemical and biological weapons, otherwise termed "weapons of mass destruction," devastating implements of war that could presumably be employed by global terrorists to wreak destruction on a scale even greater than that of 11 September 2001. Hussein himself was another special target, although he eluded capture for months. Coalition forces managed to establish their military supremacy in Iraq, but they did not uncover any such cache of weapons nor did they immediately control Hussein. President Bush declared an end to major battle operations on 1 May 2003, and coalition forces since that time struggled in their efforts to occupy and stabilize Iraq. Hussein was finally caught in December 2003 and executed in 2006, but deadly resistance in Iraq persisted.

The costs of the Iraq War were enormous in terms of both casualties and expenditures. Tens of thousands of Iraqi military personnel and civilians died, as had more than 4,700 coalition soldiers by mid-2010. The United States spent approximately $4 billion per month to maintain troops in Iraq. While President Bush sustained the United States' willingness to pay such a price, some critics in the United States and around the globe balked at the president's aggressive approach to the war on terrorism. Seen as an expression of the "Bush Doctrine of Deterrence," his preemptive strike against Iraq—which had not overtly committed a terrorist act or been proven to harbor terrorists—set a troubling precedent in U.S. foreign policy. Moreover, the increased presence of foreign military personnel in Iraq appeared to intensify the sort of Islamist fervor already fanned by Osama bin Laden. U.S. President **Barack Obama** (1961–), elected in 2008 and re-elected in 2012, shifted the war on terror away from Iraq and back to Afghanistan and bin Laden. Obama announced in May 2011 that elite forces had fulfilled a major mission in the war on terror by carrying out the U.S.-sanctioned killing of Osama bin Laden in Pakistan. Further, the United States declared the war in Iraq over in December 2011, at least as far as U.S. troops were concerned, although Iraqis continued to face intense civil conflict. The Iraq War caused the deaths of almost forty-five hundred U.S. soldiers, led to the wounding of thirty thousand U.S. soldiers, cost the nation $1 trillion, and left an uncertain legacy for both the United States and Iraq.

Meanwhile, in Afghanistan President Obama announced first the draw-down (2011) and then the withdrawal of U.S. troops from Afghanistan in 2014, leaving only about ten thousand advisers. In December 2019, President Donald Trump withdrew about half of these and promised to withdraw the rest in 2020. Over nearly twenty years, the war resulted in one hundred fifty-seven thousand deaths, of which nearly forty-three thousand were civilians. The United States spent $975 billion on operations and still was unable to establish a stable government.

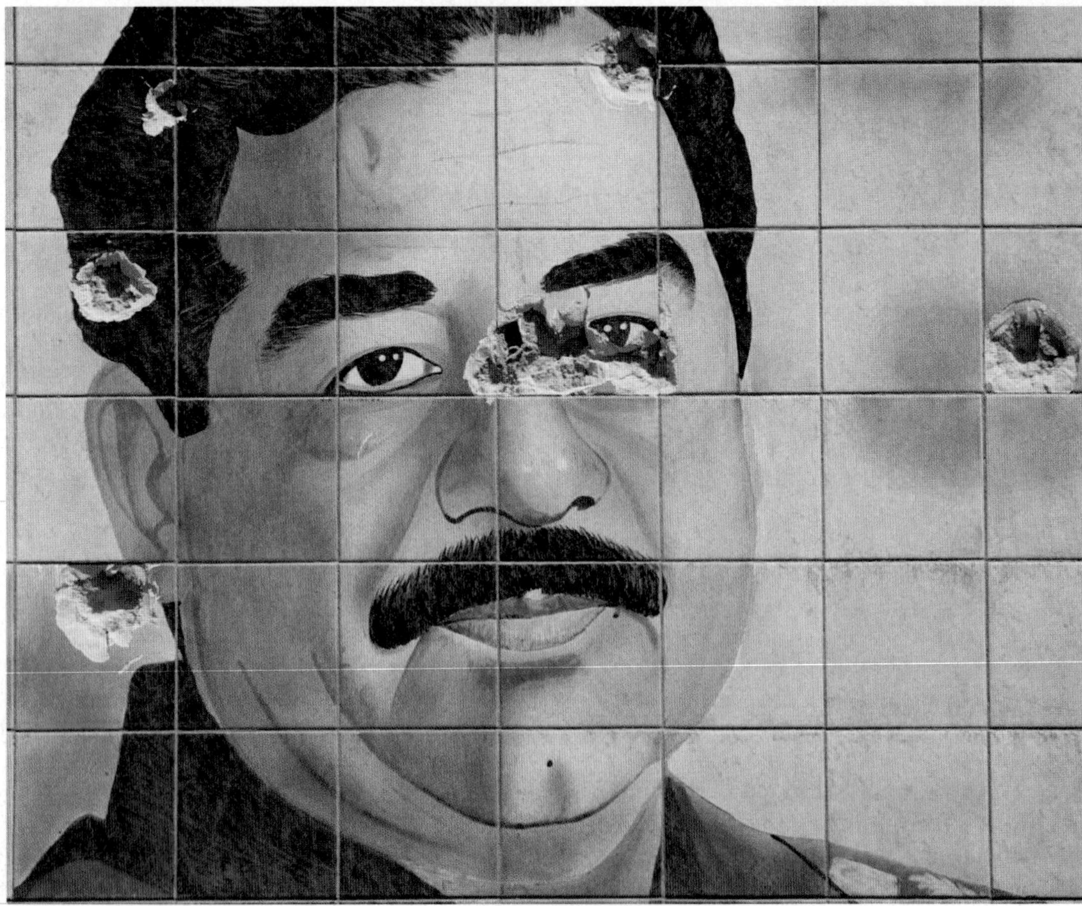

A photographer captured the ruin of Saddam Hussein in this image of a tiled mural pitted and pocked by the destruction in Baghdad as a result of Operation Iraqi Freedom.
Kevin Frayer/AP Photo

## Migration

Migration, the movement of people from one place to another, is as old as humanity and has shaped the formation and identity of societies throughout the world. The massive influx of outsiders has transformed the ethnic, linguistic, and cultural composition of indigenous populations. With the advent of industrialization during the eighteenth century, population experts distinguished between two types of migration: internal migration and external or international migration. Internal migration describes the flow of people from rural to urban areas within one society, whereas external migration describes the movement of people across long distances and international borders. Both types of migration result from push factors, pull factors, or a combination of the two. Lack of resources such as land or adequate food supplies, population pressure, religious or political persecution, or discriminatory practices aimed at ethnic minorities push people to move. Conversely, opportunities for better employment, the availability of arable land, or better services such as health care and education pull people to move.

**Internal Migration** The largest human migrations in recent history are rural-urban flows. During the second half of the twentieth century, these internal migrations led to rapid urbanization in much of the world. Today the most highly urbanized societies are those of western and northern Europe, Australia, New Zealand, and temperate South America and North America. In these societies the proportion of people living in urban areas exceeds 75 percent; in some countries, such as Belgium, it exceeds 97 percent. The societies of tropical Latin America are in an intermediate stage of urbanization, with 50 to 65 percent of the population living in cities. In many countries in Africa and Asia, the process of urbanization is at a relatively early stage. But even though most people still reside in rural areas, the rate of urbanization is very high.

**Urbanization** In Latin America, Africa, and south Asia, large numbers of people have migrated to metropolitan areas in search of relief from rural poverty. Once in the cities, though, they often find themselves equally destitute. Life is bleak in the slums outside Mumbai; in the shantytowns around Kinshasa or Nairobi; and in the *barriadas, barrios,* and *villas miserias* of Lima, Mexico City, and Buenos Aires. More than ten million people cram the environs of cities such as Calcutta, Cairo, and Mexico City, straining those cities' resources. The few services originally available to those who moved to slum areas—potable water, electricity, and medical care—have diminished with the continuous influx of new people. Among the unemployed or underemployed, disease runs rampant, and many suffer from malnutrition.

**External Migration** A combination of voluntary and forced international migrations has transformed the human landscape, especially during the past five hundred years. Between the sixteenth and the twentieth centuries, more than sixty million European migrants, for example, colonized the Americas, Australia, Oceania, and the northern half of Asia. Between 1820 and 1980, in the course of the Atlantic migration, thirty-seven million migrants of European descent made their home in the United States. Forced slave migrations supplemented those voluntary movements of people. Between the sixteenth and the nineteenth centuries, slave traders consigned about twelve million Africans to the Americas, though many died in the appalling conditions of the Atlantic voyages.

During World War II the Nazi regime initiated the largest mass expulsions of the twentieth century, deporting eight million people to forced-labor sites and extermination camps. Following the war, the Soviet regime expelled ten million ethnic Germans from eastern and central Europe and transported them back to Germany. The largest migrations in the second half of the twentieth century have consisted of refugees fleeing war. For example, the 1947 partition of the Indian subcontinent into two independent states resulted in the exchange of six million Hindus from Pakistan and seven million Muslims from India. According to recent United Nations figures, more than forty-five million people worldwide had been forcibly displaced by 2013 as a result of conflict and persecution. More than fifteen million of the uprooted were refugees who fled their home countries, while another thirty million were people who remain displaced by conflict within their homelands. These numbers have been amplified in the second decade of the twenty-first century by a new wave of migrant refugees seeking safety and stability in the wake of civil war in Syria and instability in Afghanistan and Iraq. In 2015 alone, more than one million people sought refuge in Europe, both by land and by sea, and several hundred thousand followed in the ensuing four years. Many were desperate and allowed themselves to be illegally transported by human traffickers, and more than fifteen thousand died in the process. And while a variety of European countries initially agreed to take in migrants (especially Germany but also France, Sweden, Italy, and Austria), their presence has triggered a xenophobic backlash in many countries among Europeans who worry that such a large influx of foreigners will negatively affect their national cultures. Indeed, controversy over taking in migrants is believed to have contributed to the calls for British withdrawal from the European Union in 2016, and fear of migrants has led to an upsurge in right-wing parties across Europe whose rhetoric is openly racist.

Across the Atlantic, in 2012 many tens of thousands of refugees left their home countries in El Salvador, Guatemala, and Honduras for the United States. Although migration from Central America and Mexico was not a new phenomenon (over ten million Mexican migrants have settled in the United States since 1960), the rate of migration increased in that year from Central America because of extremely dangerous internal conditions. Homicide rates were among the highest in the world, and ordinary people grew desperate enough to sacrifice everything for a chance of finding stability elsewhere. As in Europe, though, this surge in migration stimulated controversy in the United States, as many Americans began to call

Seeking relief from rural poverty, large numbers of people throughout the developing world have migrated to urban areas ill equipped to meet their needs and have had to settle in slums such as this one in Rio de Janeiro.
Vittoriano Rastelli/Corbis Historical/Getty Images

for closing the border between Mexico and the United States to prevent migration from the south. In fact, President Donald Trump ran his presidential campaign in 2016 on a promise to build a wall between Mexico and the United States to keep migrants out. Once he took office, his administration stepped up efforts to prevent immigrants seeking asylum from entering the United States and even began to separate parents from their children in detainee camps to discourage refugees from attempting to enter the country. As in Europe, fear of migrants triggered the rise of openly racist, extremist white supremacy groups in the United States.

In general, migrants leave their home countries because they seek a better life in countries with a higher standard of living and stable legal and political systems. They want better jobs and more readily available health care, educational opportunities, and a safe place to raise their children. Thus most contemporary mass migrations involve movement from developing countries to developed ones. Given the disparities and inequities between developed and developing countries, it seems likely that migration will continue to be a major issue in the short and long terms.

After their arrival on foreign shores, migrants often establish cultural and ethnic communities that maintain their social customs and native languages. The sounds of foreign languages as well as the presence of ethnic foods, arts, and music have transformed large cities into multicultural environments. Although the arrival of migrants has enriched societies in many ways, as we have seen it has also sparked resentment and conflict. People in host countries often believe that foreigners and their ways of life undermine national identity, especially if defined by language, religion, and other cultural characteristics. Beyond that, many citizens of host societies view migrants, who are often willing to work for low wages and not join labor unions, as competitors for jobs. When unemployment rates climb, there is a tendency to look for scapegoats, and all too frequently the blame falls on migrants. In many countries, governments have come under pressure to restrict immigration or even expel foreign residents. Thus, while migrants are reshaping the world outside their home countries, international mass migration poses challenges both to the migrants themselves and to the host society.

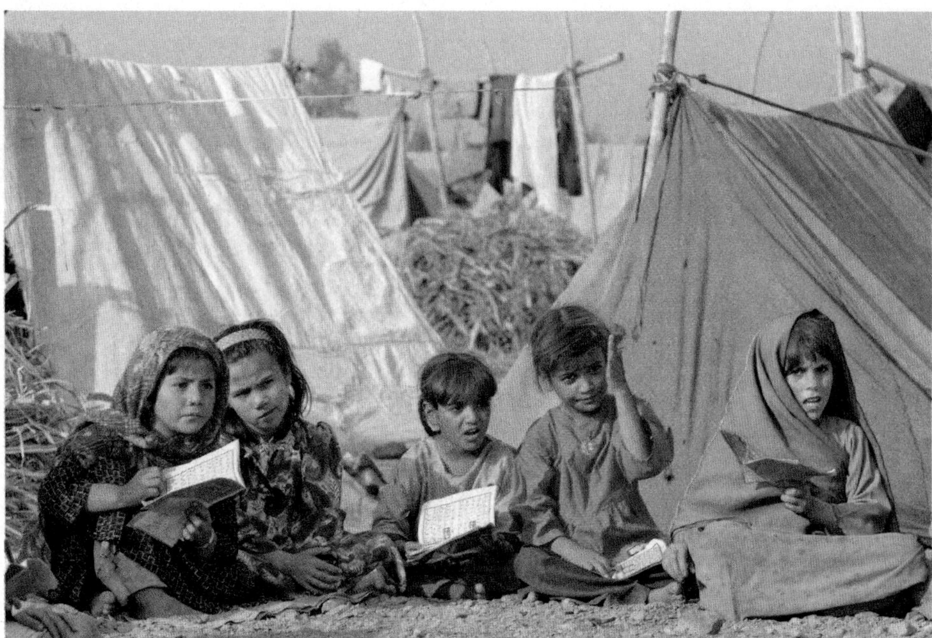

Afghan child refugees get a reading lesson at Jelozai Camp; they are just a few of the hundreds of thousands of forced displaced persons in the contemporary world.
Pascal Le Segretain/Sygma/Getty Images

## Global Diseases

For thousands of years, disease has played a significant role in the development of human communities. Its impact has been as dramatic as it has been destructive. For example, the most devastating impact of the Columbian exchange (see chapter 22) came in the wake of diseases that Europeans introduced into the Americas following the voyages of Christopher Columbus and others. The introduction of diseases to populations that lacked any form of immunity killed perhaps as many as 90 percent of Native Americans in the span of 150 years. More recently, an influenza pandemic that swept the globe in 1918 and 1919 killed between twenty and forty million people, far more than died as the result of the Great War that had just ended. Since then, medical experts, public health officials, and scientists scored major victories in their fight against diseases, eradicating smallpox and diphtheria, for example. Buoyed by those successes, the United Nations in 1978 called for the elimination of all infectious diseases by the year 2000. That goal was unrealistic and, in the meantime, ancient diseases once thought under control, such as malaria, tuberculosis, and even measles, are on the rise again. Moreover, the late twentieth century demonstrated the deadly potential of new diseases.

**HIV/AIDS** One of the most serious new diseases to emerge in this period was acquired immunodeficiency syndrome (AIDS). This fatal disorder of the immune system is caused by the human immunodeficiency virus (HIV), which slowly attacks and destroys the immune system, leaving the infected individual vulnerable to diseases that eventually cause death. AIDS is the last stage of HIV infection, during which time these diseases arise. The HIV infection is spread through sexual contact with an infected person; contact with contaminated blood; and transmission from mother to child during pregnancy and, after birth, through breast feeding.

Medical experts identified AIDS for the first time in 1981 among homosexual men and intravenous drug users in New York and San Francisco. Subsequently, evidence for an epidemic appeared among heterosexual men, women, and children in sub-Saharan Africa, and rather quickly AIDS developed into a worldwide epidemic that affected virtually every nation. At the end of 2019, the number of people living with **HIV/AIDS** was 37.9 million, and more than 32 million AIDS deaths had occurred since the beginning of the epidemic. More encouraging, both new HIV infections and the number of AIDS death have been declining during the past decade, thanks to the availability of new drug treatments. But the epidemic continues to disproportionately affect sub-Saharan Africa, home to 1.1 million new HIV infections in 2017. Equally worrisome, new infections have been on the rise in eastern Europe, central Asia, southwest Asia, and north Africa.

Although no vaccine has yet emerged to prevent or cure HIV infection, some advances have been made. When scientists first identified AIDS, there was no treatment for the disease. Existing antiviral drugs at best delayed the inevitable and at worst failed completely. By 1995, though, researchers succeeded in developing a new class of drugs known as protease inhibitors and, in combination with some of the older drugs, they produced what is now known as **highly active antiretroviral therapy,** or **HAART.** In most cases, HAART can prolong life indefinitely. Antiretroviral therapy not only prevents AIDS-related illness and death but also has the potential to significantly reduce the risk of HIV transmission and the spread of tuberculosis. The high cost of these sophisticated drugs initially prevented poor people from sharing in their benefits, but this too is changing. By 2018, 62 percent of the world's people living with HIV were receiving antiretroviral therapy.

**Present and Future Concerns** In spite of significant successes in the battle against HIV infection, global disease

## INTERPRETING IMAGES

Migrants from Libya on an overcrowded boat trying to reach Europe in 2017. These passengers were rescued by a Spanish NGO, but many thousands died trying to cross the Mediterranean from North Africa to Europe.

**Analyze** *Consider images you've seen in this text of migrants from earlier periods. How did you read them differently than this photo? Does the medium of color photography impact your interpretation of images? Which images from previous chapters would you choose to compare to this, and why?*

Samuel Nacar/SOPA Images/LightRocket/Getty Images

remains an urgent concern in the twenty-first century. Globalization has allowed ever more rapid circulations of people from one side of the globe to the other, meaning that new or mutated viruses—especially those spread through the air—can travel around the world in the space of a few hours. This was the case with the outbreak of the severe acute respiratory syndrome (SARS) virus in 2003 and the Middle East respiratory syndrome (MERS) virus in 2012. In these cases, people who had been exposed to the virus traveled in cars, trains, and planes before they knew they were sick and thus transmitted the diseases to distant locations rapidly. Viruses such as these have the potential to infect many thousands of people on every continent and require intensive international cooperation if a global pandemic is to be halted.

The incredible speed with which viruses can travel in an era of globalization was clearly demonstrated at the end of 2019, when authorities in China reported that a mysterious form of pneumonia had infected a cluster of people in the city of Wuhan. By January 7, 2020 the illness was identified as a novel coronavirus, which later became known as Covid-19. Case numbers rose quickly in China, and in an attempt to halt the spread of the epidemic, the government took drastic steps to place the city of Wuhan (with 11 million people) under strict quarantine. A week later, the United States and other nations halted travel to and from China. But these efforts were too late. The speed at which people travel ensured that individuals infected with the extremely contagious virus had already traveled to North America, Southeast Asia, Europe, and other countries in Asia. By March 11, the World Health Organization declared Covid-19 a pandemic, meaning that it was an uncontrolled disease that affected the whole world. By the beginning of June 2020, the number of people infected with the virus had reached 6.6 million, and the number of deaths exceeded 391,000. A year later, in June 2021, cases had climbed to 178 million, while the number of deaths exceeded 3.86 million.

Covid-19 revealed the weaknesses of international cooperation in halting pandemics. The World Health Organization, which was designed to coordinate international response to situations just like this, has been accused of moving too slowly to communicate the level of threat posed by the virus. Even more important, many countries—including the United States—failed to heed warnings about the virus until it had already spread widely, and thus failed to prepare by ensuring adequate levels of medical supplies or tests. Some countries sought to shift the blame for the virus to China, thus calling attention away from their own mismanagement. The pandemic also brought social inequalities into sharp relief, as it became clear that the poor and the marginalized died in far greater numbers than the rich and healthy. The worldwide lack of preparedness for dealing with a pandemic like Covid-19 meant that the only way to decrease the infection and death rates was to lock down societies by closing stores, halting gatherings and travel, and requiring people to stay at home. Indeed, by March 31 nearly one-third of humanity was living under some kind of lockdown. While lockdowns were largely successful at reducing new infections, their negative impact on both local and global economies was enormous.

Amidst the tragedies of so many lost lives and the mismanagement of the crisis by authorities around the world, the pandemic has also given us reason to be hopeful. In spite of political squabbles at the highest levels, tens of thousands of scientists, researchers, and healthcare workers have raced at

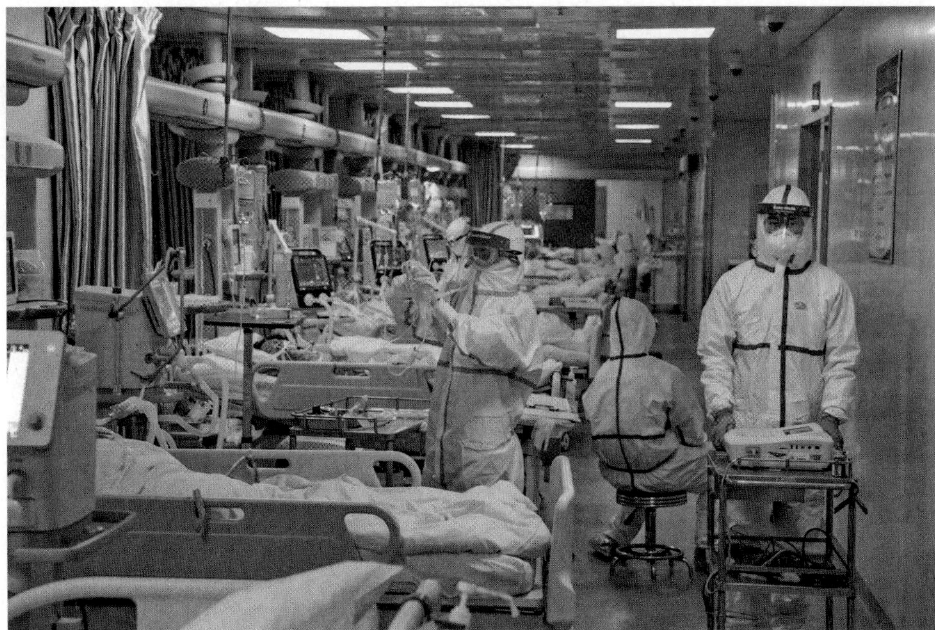

In February 2020, medical staff in Wuhan, China work in an isolated intensive care unit for the treatment of patients with Covid-19.
Feature China/Barcroft Media/Getty Images

record speed to develop effective treatments and vaccines to eliminate the threat of Covid-19. These people hail from every country, and have engaged in information-sharing and partnerships that defy national borders. Indeed, international collaboration and state sponsorship led to the creation of a vaccine for Covid-19 in record time: in December 2020, two companies were the first to win approval of their Covid-19 vaccine. Yet these vaccines have largely not been made available to countries outside of North America and Europe, leading to increased calls for vaccine equality. Let us hope that we might learn from their example, in the likely event that a global pandemic will strike again in the future.

## What's Left Out?

Historians are comfortable writing about events that happened long ago, even though they understand they can never fully comprehend the vast complexities of the past. But they are often far less comfortable writing about events that occurred in their own living memory—and grow increasingly uncomfortable as they move closer to the present. There are good reasons for this discomfort. The task of writing history is much easier when historians have perspective, which in this case means knowing what happened *after* the period under discussion. Perspective can also mean having distance from the events under discussion so that writers of history are not personally invested in the outcomes of their stories. When writing about the very recent past, it is difficult for historians to maintain either kind of perspective. This is because they might have been active participants in some of the events they write about, or because they personally knew active participants, or simply because they remember hearing about and reacting to events as they were happening. It is also because the events of the immediate past happened so recently that not enough time has elapsed to say with any certainty what their long-term effects will be. In both scenarios, it is extremely difficult for historians to maintain perspective—and especially for them to remain personally uninvolved in the way the story of the past is told. Of course, the personality and point of view of historians are always present in the histories they write. But it is worth thinking about how much more this is true when the subject matter is the very recent past. For example, although we cover the Covid-19 pandemic in this chapter, we do not yet know how the pandemic will end and what its larger effects will be in the future. And given that we lived through the pandemic, our vision of what it was like will be deeply informed by our personal experiences and where we are from. Both of these problems diminish our ability to maintain perspective.

*Source:* David Lowenthal, *The Past Is a Foreign Country Revisited*, 2nd ed. (Cambridge: Cambridge University Press, 2015), chapter 8.

### Thinking Critically About Sources

1. According to the author, what are the reasons it is difficult for historians to write about the recent past?
2. Would it be better to avoid analysis of recent events? Why or why not?

## CONCLUSION

In 1989, ordinary Germans like Kristina Matschat toppled the Berlin wall—an event that signaled the impending collapse of the Soviet Union and the end of the Cold War. The end of the Cold War changed the global balance of power in favor of the United States, although its unilateral actions in the following decades led to deteriorating relations with a variety of states, especially Russia. The decades after the end of the Cold War were also characterized by increasing globalization, which accelerated economic, political, and cultural connections between the world's peoples. While these connections and encounters in many cases aided economic growth and allowed for rich cultural exchanges, they also brought a host of urgent issues into high relief, including climate change, continuing inequalities, terrorism, migration, and global disease. Each of these issues continues to affect the whole world (although sometimes in different ways), and each appears unlikely to be solved in the short term. One thing is clear, however: if any solutions are to be found, they will require that nations work in cooperation with one another. Given the extremely violent and destructive twentieth century, in which nations killed tens of millions of people to achieve their goals, such cooperation would truly signal a new era in the history of the world.

## STUDY TERMS

*al-Qaeda* (880)
Association of Southeast Asian Nations (ASEAN) (868)
Aung San Suu Kyi (878)
Barack Obama (882)
Benazir Bhuto (866)
BRICs (866)
Bush Doctrine (863)
Chandrika Bandaranaike Kumaratunga (878)
climate change (873)
European Union (868)
feminist movement (876)
free trade (864)
General Agreement on Tariffs and Trade (GATT) (865)
*glasnost* (862)
global warming (873)
globalization (864)
Highly active antiretroviral therapy (HAART) (885)
HIV/AIDS (885)
Indira Gandhi (878)
Lech Walesa (860)
Leszek Kolakowski (860)
little tigers (865)
McDonaldization (869)
Mikhail S. Gorbachev (859)
*mujahideen* (862)
North American Free Trade Agreement (NAFTA) (868)
Nicolae Ceaușescu (861)
Organization of Petroleum Exporting Countries (OPEC) (868)
Operation Iraqi Freedom (881)
Osama bin Laden (880)
*perestroika* (862)
Ronald Reagan (859)
Saddam Hussein (881)
Taliban (881)
terrorism (880)
Todor Zhivkov (860)
Universal Declaration of Human Rights (872)
*velvet revolution* (847)
World Trade Organization (WTO) (865)

## FOR FURTHER READING

Jagdish Bhagwati. *In Defense of Globalization.* New York, 2007. A convincing rebuttal to popular fallacies about global economic integration.

Gregory C. Chow. *China's Economic Transformation.* Oxford, 2007. This stands as the most accepted reference for understanding the world's most dynamic economy.

Jussi Hanhimäki and Bernhard Blumenau. *An International History of Terrorism: Western and Non-Western Experiences*. London, 2013. Analyzes the history and uses of terrorism for the last one hundred fifty years years from a variety of perspectives.

Mark Harrison. *Contagion: How Commerce Has Spread Disease.* New Haven, 2013. A scholarly examination of the connections between trade and infectious diseases, and the measures taken to limit the spread of disease.

Jason Hickel. *The Divide: Global Inequality from Conquest to Free Markets*. New York, 2018. An anthropologist explores the complex historical reasons behind the vast global inequalities between developed and developing countries.

Edward Luce. *In Spite of the Gods: The Rise of Modern India*. New York, 2008. A keen assessment of an up-and-coming economic and geopolitical giant.

David Marples. *The Collapse of the Soviet Union, 1985–1991*. London, 2015. Revisionist look at the collapse of the Soviet Union that emphasizes the role of Soviet national republics and Boris Yeltsin instead of the arms race with the United States.

J. R. McNeill. *Something New under the Sun: An Environmental History of the Twentieth-Century World.* New York, 2000. A brilliant but dark tale of the past century's interaction between humans and the environment.

Anne Sisson Runyan and V. Spike Peterson. *Global Gender Issues in the New Millennium*. London, 2019. Looks at the ways ideologies of gender have been used to perpetuate inequalities between men and women on a global stage and also feminist resistance and action to counteract these uses.

Joseph Stiglitz, *Globalization and Its Discontents Revisited: Anti-Globalization in the Era of Trump*. New York, 2017. Updated and revised edition of the classic 2007 book that argued for the destructive impact of the International Monetary Fund (IMF), World Bank, and trade agreements on developing nations.

# CHAPTER 26 AP EXAM PRACTICE

Questions assume cumulative knowledge from this chapter and previous chapters.

## Section I

## Multiple Choice Questions

Use the image below and your knowledge of world history to answer questions 1–3.

Smokestacks in Siberia releasing carbon dioxide into the atmosphere.
Peter Turnley/Corbis/VCG/Getty Images

1. What did the delegates at the climate change conference in Kyoto in 1997 agree to do?
   (A) They decided to cap the world population at 2.5 billion.
   (B) They agreed to carbon emission reductions.
   (C) They agreed that developing nations should end their industrial development.
   (D) They decided that the claims about climate change were exaggerated.

2. Which of the following contributes to climate change?
   (A) Expanding solar ice caps.
   (B) Rising ocean levels.
   (C) Increasing concentrations of greenhouse gasses.
   (D) Old growth forests.

3. Which of these is a factor preventing more political action on climate change?
   (A) Politicians in the United States are worried about economic effects and are skeptical about climate change.
   (B) The United Nations had focused more on solving humanitarian social problems than environmental problems.
   (C) The end of the Cold War has made it difficult for the US and the Soviet Union to agree on environmental policies.
   (D) Britain's withdrawal from the European Union increased greenhouse gas emissions.

Use the image below and your knowledge of world history to answer questions 4 and 5.

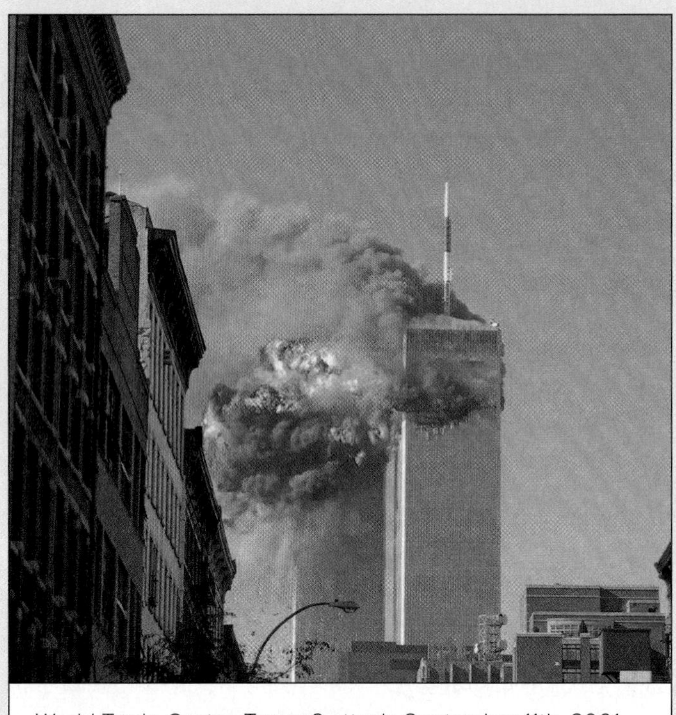

World Trade Center, Tower 2 attack. September 11th, 2001. View from the corner at West Broadway and Spring St. in SoHo, NYC North side of Tower
Laperruque/Alamy Stock Photo

4. How did terrorism change in the twenty-first century?
   (A) Terrorism was used to fight anticolonial conflicts in Algeria and Vietnam.
   (B) The Baltic states used terrorism to gain independence from the Soviet Union.
   (C) Terrorists used the financial networks, modern transportation, and communication technology that created modern globalization.
   (D) Protestants and Catholics used terrorism against each other in Northern Ireland.

5. Which of the following was falsely given as a reason to justify the invasion of Iraq in 2003?
   (A) Iraq had occupied Kuwait.
   (B) Saddam Hussein was planning to take control of the Suez Canal.
   (C) The Iraqi government was guilty of human rights abuses.
   (D) Saddam Hussein had biological weapons and other weapons of mass destruction.

## Short Answer

6. Use the image below and your knowledge of world history to answer parts A, B, and C.

**Fears that globalization is imposing** a deadening cultural uniformity are as ubiquitous as Coca-Cola, McDonald's, and Mickey Mouse. Europeans and Latin Americans, left-wingers and right, rich and poor—all of them dread that local cultures and national identities are dissolving into a crass all-American consumerism. That cultural imperialism is said to impose American values as well as products, promote the commercial at the expense of the authentic, and substitute shallow gratification for deeper satisfaction. . . .

It is a myth that globalization involves the imposition of Americanized uniformity, rather than an explosion of cultural exchange. For a start, many archetypal "American" products are not as all-American as they seem. Levi-Strauss, a German immigrant, invented jeans by combining denim cloth (or "serge de Nîmes," because it was traditionally woven in the French town) with Genes, a style of trousers worn by Genoese sailors. So Levi's jeans are in fact an American twist on a European hybrid. Even quintessentially American exports are often tailored to local tastes. MTV in Asia promotes Thai pop stars and plays rock music sung in Mandarin. CNN en Español offers a Latin American take on world news. McDonald's sells beer in France, lamb in India, and chili in Mexico.

In some ways, America is an outlier, not a global leader. Most of the world has adopted the metric system born from the French Revolution; America persists with antiquated measurements inherited from its British-colonial past. Most developed countries have become intensely secular, but many Americans burn with fundamentalist fervor—like Muslims in the Middle East. Where else in the developed world could there be a serious debate about teaching kids Bible-inspired "creationism" instead of Darwinist evolution?

America's tastes in sports are often idiosyncratic, too. Baseball and American football have not traveled well, although basketball has fared rather better. Many of the world's most popular sports, notably soccer, came by way of Britain. Asian martial arts—judo, karate, kickboxing—and pastimes like yoga have also swept the world.

People are not only guzzling hamburgers and Coke. Despite Coke's ambition of displacing water as the world's drink of choice, it accounts for less than 2 of the 64 fluid ounces the typical person drinks a day. Britain's favorite takeaway is a curry, not a burger; Indian restaurants there outnumber McDonald's six to one. For all the concerns about American fast food trashing France's culinary traditions, France imported a mere $620 million in food from the United States in 2000, while exporting to America three times that. Nor is plonk [cheap alcohol] from America's Gallo displacing Europe's finest: Italy and France together account for three-fifths of global wine exports, the United States for only a twentieth. Worldwide, pizzas are more popular than burgers, Chinese restaurants seem to sprout up everywhere, and sushi is spreading fast. By far the biggest purveyor of alcoholic drinks is Britain's Diageo, which sells the world's best selling whiskey (Johnnie Walker), gin (Gordon's), vodka (Smirnoff), and liqueur (Bailey's). . . .

In pop music, American crooners do not have the stage to themselves. The three artists who were featured most widely in national Top Ten album charts in 2000 were America's Britney Spears, closely followed by Mexico's Carlos Santana and the British Beatles. Even tiny Iceland has produced a global star: Björk. Popular opera's biggest singers are Italy's Luciano Pavarotti, Spain's José Carreras, and the Spanish-Mexican Placido Domingo. Latin American salsa, Brazilian lambada, and African music have all carved out global niches for themselves. In most countries, local artists still top the charts. . . .

The evidence is overwhelming. Fears about an Americanized uniformity are overblown: American cultural products are not uniquely dominant; local ones are alive and well.

*Source:* Legrain, Philippe. "Cultural Globalization Is Not Americanization," *The Chronicle of Higher Education*, 49, no. 35 (May 9, 2003): B7. Used with permission.

(A) Explain ONE example of McDonaldization in the late twentieth century.
(B) Explain ONE cultural product from Asia or Latin America that supports Legrain's thesis on globalization.
(C) Explain ONE political reason why globalization of consumer goods happened in the late twentieth century.

7. Use the map below and your knowledge of world history to answer parts A, B, and C.

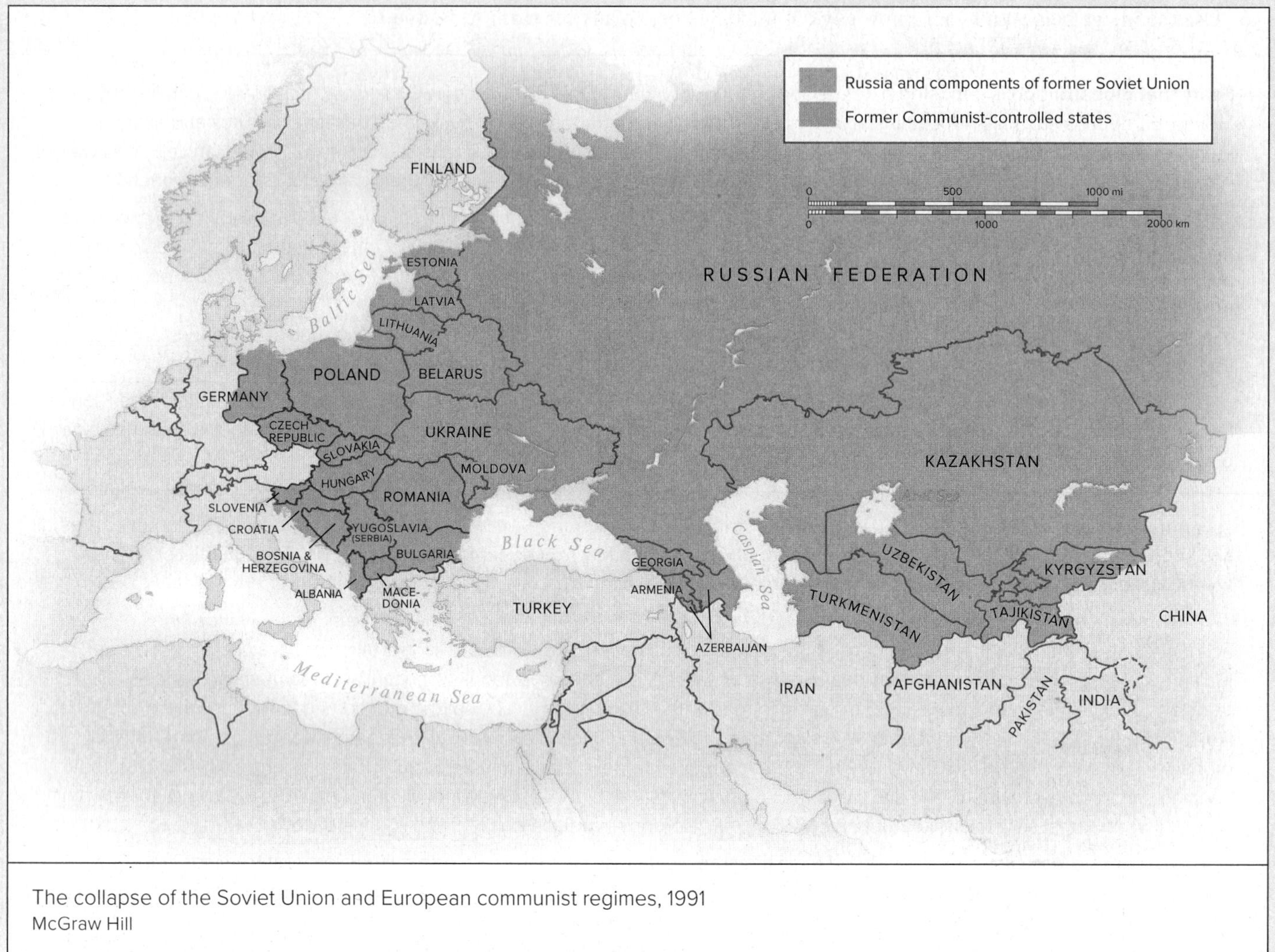


The collapse of the Soviet Union and European communist regimes, 1991
McGraw Hill

(A) Identify ONE reform policy implemented in the Soviet Union by Mikhail Gorbachev.
(B) Explain ONE way nationalism contributed to the collapse of the Soviet Union in 1991.
(C) Identify ONE consequence of the end of the Soviet Union.

8. Use your understanding of world history to answer parts A, B, and C.
(A) Identify ONE industry important to Japan's economic growth in the 1950s and 60s.
(B) Explain ONE problem the "four little tigers" had to overcome to experience rapid economic growth by the 1980s.
(C) Identify ONE reason why the Chinese economy grew in the 1990s.

# Section II

## Document-Based Question

Based on the documents below and your knowledge of world history, evaluate the barriers to equal rights for women and efforts to overcome those barriers in the second half of the twentieth century.

In your response you should do the following:

- Respond to the prompt with a historically defensible thesis or claim that establishes a line of reasoning.
- Describe a broader historical context relevant to the prompt.
- Support an argument in response to the prompt using all documents.
- Use at least one additional piece of specific historical evidence (beyond that found in the documents) relevant to an argument about the prompt.
- Explain how or why the document's point of view, purpose, historical situation, and /or audience is relevant to an argument.
- Use evidence to corroborate, qualify, or modify an argument that addresses the prompt.

### Document 1

**I don't know where to begin my speech.** I don't know what people would be expecting me to say. But first of all, thank you to God for whom we all are equal and thank you to every person who has prayed for my fast recovery and a new life. I cannot believe how much love people have shown me. . . .

Thousands of people have been killed by the terrorists and millions have been injured. I am just one of them.

So here I stand, one girl among many . . .

Dear sisters and brothers, I am not against anyone. Neither am I here to speak in terms of personal revenge against the Taliban or any other terrorist groups. I am here to speak up for the right of education of every child. I want education for the sons and the daughters of all the extremists especially the Taliban . . .

The wise saying, "The pen is mightier than sword" was true. The extremists are afraid of books and pens. The power of education frightens them. They are afraid of women. The power of the voice of women frightens them . . . That is why they are blasting schools every day. Because they were and they are afraid of change, afraid of the equality that we will bring into our society.

I remember that there was a boy in our school who was asked by a journalist, "Why are the Taliban against education?" He answered very simply. By pointing to his book he said, "A Talib doesn't know what is written inside this book." They think that God is a tiny, little conservative being who would send girls to the hell just because of going to school. The terrorists are misusing the name of Islam and Pashtun society for their own personal benefits. Pakistan is peace-loving democratic country. Pashtuns want education for their daughters and sons. And Islam is a religion of peace, humanity and brotherhood. Islam says that it is not only each child's right to get education, rather it is their duty and responsibility.

Honourable Secretary General, peace is necessary for education. In many parts of the world especially Pakistan and Afghanistan, terrorism, wars and conflicts stop children to go to their schools. We are really tired of these wars. Women and children are suffering in many parts of the world in many ways. In India, innocent and poor children are victims of child labour. Many schools have been destroyed in Nigeria. People in Afghanistan have been affected by the hurdles of extremism for decades. Young girls have to do domestic child labour and are forced to get married at early age. Poverty, ignorance, injustice, racism and the deprivation of basic rights are the main problems faced by both men and women.

Dear fellows, today I am focusing on women's rights and girls' education because they are suffering the most. There was a time when women social activists asked men to stand up for their rights. But, this time, we will do it by ourselves . . .

Dear brothers and sisters, we want schools and education for every child's bright future. We will continue our journey to our destination of peace and education for everyone. No one can stop us. We will speak for our rights and we will bring change through our voice. We must believe in the power and the strength of our words. Our words can change the world.

So let us wage a global struggle against illiteracy, poverty and terrorism and let us pick up our books and pens. They are our most powerful weapons . . .

Education is the only solution. Education first.

*Source:* United Nations, Office of the Secretary General's Envoy on Youth. Malala Yousafzai addresses United Nations Youth Assembly. https://www.un.org/youthenvoy/video/malala-yousafzai-addresses-united-nations-youth-assembly/ Used with permission of the Malala Fund.

## Document 2

1996: Myanmar pro-democracy leader Aung San Suu Kyi
EMMANUEL DUNAND/AFP/Getty Images

## Document 3

View of marchers at the March for Women's Lives rally, organized by NOW (the National Organization of Women), Washington DC, April 5, 1992. The lead banner reads 'We Won't Go Back! We Will Fight Back!'

Mark Reinstein/Corbis/Getty Images

## Long Essay

Develop a thoughtful and thorough historical argument that answers the question below. Begin your essay with a thesis statement and support it with relevant historical evidence.

Using specific examples and your knowledge of world history, evaluate the push and pull factors in late twentieth century migrations.

# Part 4 Global Conflict, Cold War and Decolonization, and Globalization (1900 to present)

The global history of the twentieth century catalogued staggering numbers of human deaths and massive amounts of material destruction. It was, to date, the world's most violent century, and that violence announced itself in assassinations of figures as diverse as the Austro-Hungarian Archduke Francis Ferdinand and the nationalist Indian hero Mohandas Gandhi. Those assassinations also symbolized the forces responsible for destroying the world as it had existed at the turn of the century: world wars of unprecedented scope and horror and the final dismantling of colonial empires in a process of decolonization that was at once liberating and sobering for those seeking national independence. Tens of millions of soldiers and civilians on both sides of mighty European and global alliances died often horrid deaths, from weapons as mundane as guns to those as bewilderingly new and appallingly destructive as the atomic bombs that demolished Hiroshima and Nagasaki. The imperial and industrial power amassed by European and North American states dissipated as a result of the human and economic cost of world wars and the relatively short-lived cold war that followed those wars. That power also diminished as colonial peoples in Asia and Africa fought for their freedom and independence and thus destroyed as surely as the world wars had the global domination of imperial nations.

The geopolitical alliances that had shaped wars and divided peoples from the time of the Great War through the cold war evaporated one by one, leaving in their wake a seemingly borderless world of both promise and peril. No longer contained by European imperial hegemony, newly independent nations from India to Ghana, from Indonesia to Vietnam, contributed to the rebirth of a world free of empire. The tearing down of literal barriers between people, such as the Berlin Wall, was matched by the fall of figurative barriers between peoples as ushered in by the process of globalization. The disintegration of the world as it existed at the beginning of this era of contemporary global realignments led to a new sort of integration at the end of the century and into the twenty-first century, led by technological and economic forces that broke through national boundaries and connected the world's peoples through a complex web of communications, transportation, and economic interconnectedness. Resisted by some and criticized by many as a new form of economic imperialism, globalization has nonetheless remade the world and undermined old divisions, underscoring in its own way the commonality of human experience.

Destruction and disaster have not disappeared in the twenty-first century, and indeed, vast natural disasters have devastated societies and reminded humans of their vulnerability to the forces of nature—a vulnerability that ties twenty-first-century humans to their earliest ancestors. The devastating Haitian earthquake of 2010 and the Covid-19 pandemic of 2020 have suggested anew that fragility of human existence. What is different about these natural disasters is the new globalized world, wherein intricate networks of communications and transportation can be used to support and help those humans in desperate need, wherein the world's common humanity can be reasserted and reaffirmed, and wherein massive destruction can be countered to some extent by a human cooperation little witnessed at the beginning of this era of contemporary global realignments.

Now that you have completed the final chapters, reflect on the developments you have seen in the six AP World History themes.

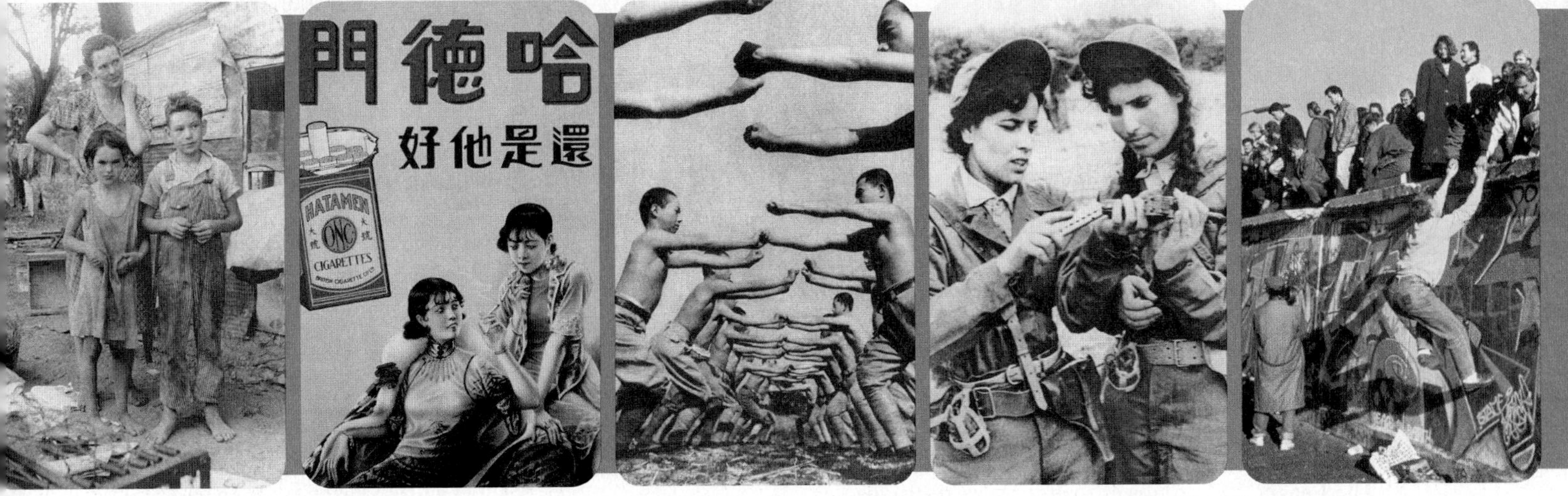


## THEME 1: HUMANS AND THE ENVIRONMENT (ENV)

The environment shapes human societies, and as populations grow and change, these populations in turn shape their environments.

## THEME 2: CULTURAL DEVELOPMENTS AND INTERACTIONS (CDI)

The development of ideas, beliefs, and religions illustrates how groups in society view themselves, and the interactions of societies and their beliefs often have political, social, and cultural implications.

## THEME 3: GOVERNANCE (GOV)

A variety of internal and external factors contribute to state formation, expansion, and decline. Governments maintain order through a variety of administrative institutions, policies, and procedures, and governments obtain, retain, and exercise power in different ways and for different purposes.

## THEME 4: ECONOMIC SYSTEMS (ECN)

As societies develop, they affect and are affected by the ways that they produce, exchange, and consume goods and services.

## THEME 5: SOCIAL INTERACTIONS AND ORGANIZATION (SIO)

The process by which societies group their members and the norms that govern the interactions between these groups and between individuals influence political, economic, and cultural institutions and organization.

## THEME 6: TECHNOLOGY AND INNOVATION (TEC)

Human adaptation and innovation have resulted in increased efficiency, comfort, and security, and technological advances have shaped human development and interactions with both intended and unintended consequences.

Pictorial Press Ltd/Alamy Stock Photo, swim ink 2 llc/Corbis Historical/Getty Images, Bettmann/Getty Images, Keystone-France/Gamma-Keystone/Getty Images, picture alliance/Getty Images

# PART 4 AP EXAM PRACTICE

Questions assume cumulative knowledge from this Part.

## Section I

## Multiple Choice Questions

Questions 1–3 have no stimulus.

1. Which of the following was a flaw in the design of the League of Nations?
   (A) The League had no power to enforce its decisions.
   (B) Some members refused to pay their membership dues.
   (C) Some members resented how much power the United States had in the League.
   (D) The Soviet Union used the League to spread communism.

2. Which of the following is not part of the "green revolution?"
   (A) High-yield seeds
   (B) Chemical fertilizers
   (C) More grasslands
   (D) Insecticides

3. What did Benito Mussolini promise the Italians?
   (A) He would have Italy join the League of Nations.
   (B) He would renegotiate the Treaty of Versailles.
   (C) He would glorify Italy by acquiring new territories.
   (D) He would only serve one term in office.

Using the image below and your knowledge of world history, answer questions 4–6.

Fall of the Berlin Wall, 1989
picture alliance/Getty Images

4. What is the name for the idea that the Soviet Union had the right to intervene in eastern European nations?
   (A) The Truman Doctrine
   (B) The Bush Doctrine
   (C) The Brezhnev Doctrine
   (D) The Gorbachev Doctrine

5. How did the communist regime in Poland come to an end?
   (A) The last communist president of Poland was kidnapped while on vacation and forced to dissolve the communist state.
   (B) The Solidarity Party was legalized and the government agreed to free elections in 1989.
   (C) The Polish government spent too much money on the invasion of Afghanistan and the economy collapsed.
   (D) The secret police brutally repressed demonstrations, causing a national uprising.

6. Based on this image, what argument could a historian make about the fall of the Berlin Wall?
   (A) The Berlin Wall fell because President Ronald Reagan demanded that Gorbachev tear down the wall.
   (B) The Berlin Wall fell when Gorbachev sent Soviet tanks into Berlin to protect the East German government. Thousands of Berliners fled to the wall to escape the Soviet army.
   (C) Mob violence caused the fall of the Berlin Wall when the east Berliners attacked the police.
   (D) The Berlin Wall fell because the East German government lost the will to fire on the people and Berliners of both sides came together to dismantle the wall.

Using the image below and your knowledge of world history, answer questions 7-9.

Egyptian President Gamal Abdel Nasser
Bettmann/Getty Images

7. Why was Gamal Abdel Nasser able to assume power in Egypt in 1952?
   (A) Egyptians were unhappy that Egypt lost territory to Israel.
   (B) He rallied the Egyptian people against the invading French army.
   (C) He promised to build a canal to connect the Red Sea to the Mediterranean.
   (D) The Egyptians wanted to join the Non-Aligned Movement.
8. How did Egypt finance the construction of the dam on the Nile River at Aswan?
   (A) Nasser promoted the Egyptian cotton textile industry.
   (B) The Egyptian government invested in the tourism industry.
   (C) They nationalized the Suez Canal and used the money for the dam.
   (D) The government allowed for the sale of more antiquities to European museums.
9. What does the Suez Crisis show about the Cold War world system?
   (A) The Suez Crisis was a proxy war between the US and the Soviet Union.
   (B) The British, French, and Israelis took the canal, but did so without Soviet or US approval. It created distrust between the US and its allies.
   (C) The Arab nationalists were unable to defend the canal, so the Arab states lost prestige and economic influence during the Cold War.
   (D) The Soviet Union supported the British and French and became known as an enemy of Arab nationalism.

Using the map below and your knowledge of world history, answer questions 10–12.

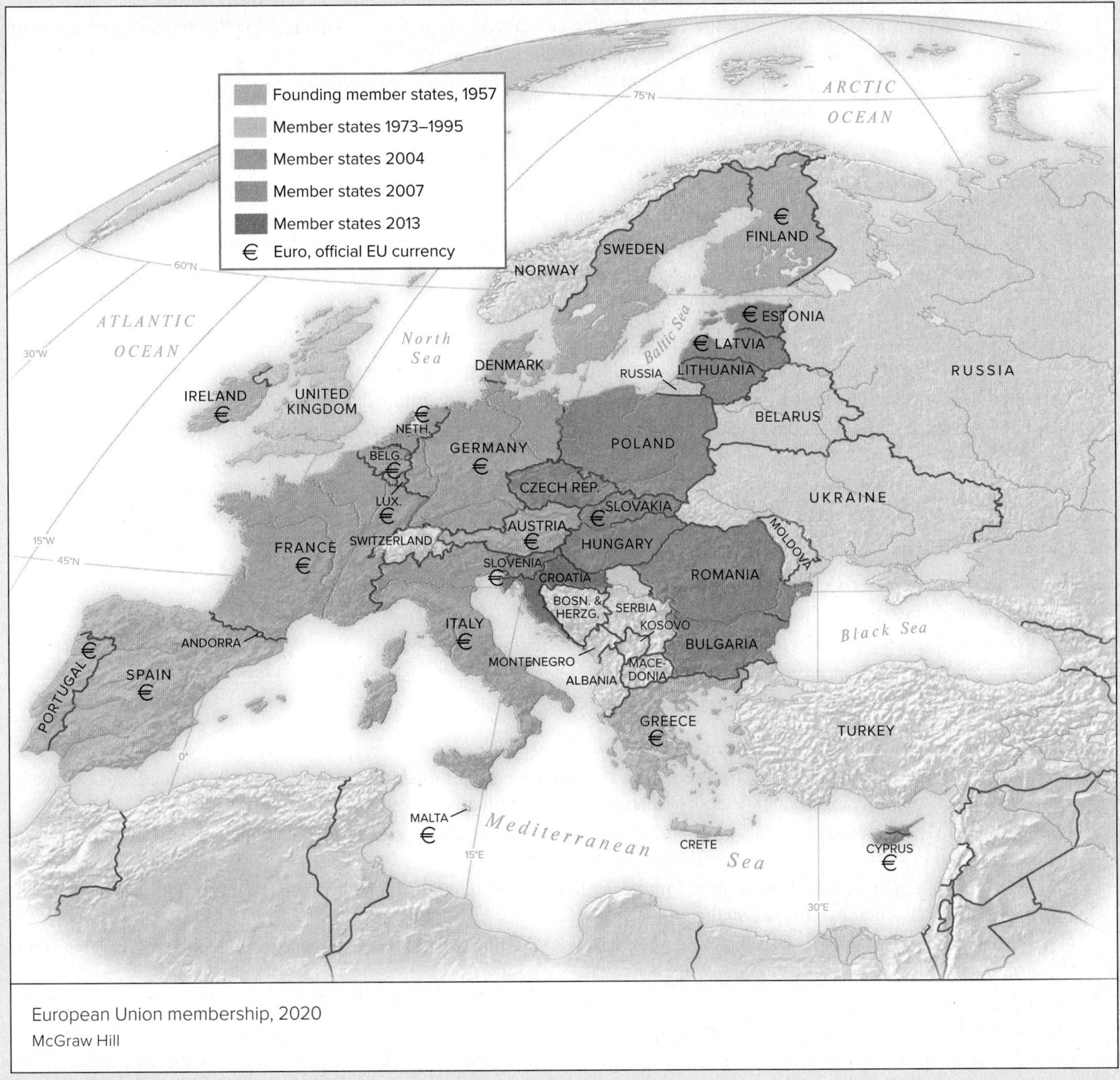


European Union membership, 2020
McGraw Hill

10. What was the purpose of the European Union?
    (A) The European Union was created to set price controls on oil.
    (B) The purpose of the European Union was to end the nationalist identities of the member states.
    (C) The European Union was created to defend Europe against Soviet aggression.
    (D) The long-term goal of the European Union was to politically integrate Europe.

11. Which of the following is a major challenge shown on the map of the European Union?
    (A) Millions of Syrians have sought refuge in Europe since 2011.
    (B) Many member states are not using the common Euro currency, presenting a challenge for the economic unity of the Union.
    (C) Climate change is pushing many Africans to move to Europe for better opportunities.
    (D) Russia controls access to fuel for most of Europe.

12. Which of the following is NOT a reason why the United Kingdom voted to leave the European Union in 2016?
    (A) The economic benefit of membership was not considered worth the loss of British sovereignty.
    (B) The British people were concerned about the movement of people across borders.
    (C) The British voters were inspired by US President Donald Trump ending the NAFTA agreement.
    (D) Refugees from Africa and the Middle East triggered a nationalist, xenophobic response to protect British borders.

Questions 13–15 have no stimulus.

13. Which of the following is reason why Germans voted the Nazi Party politicians into government?
    (A) The Nazis cheated during the elections by letting party members vote multiple times.
    (B) The Nazi Party claimed it could end economic problems for Germans by creating a racialized state that united Germans of all classes.
    (C) Hitler promised that Germany's economic problems would end if they united their economy with Austria.
    (D) Hitler and the Nazis campaigned on the idea of taking back colonies in Africa and Asia that had been lost in the Treaty of Versailles.

14. What is one reason why HIV infections continue to spread, even though there are drugs that can treat it?
    (A) HIV spreads faster than the drugs can be administered.
    (B) People who travel after infection transmit the disease to remote locations.
    (C) Some countries were more concerned with assigning blame for the disease than fighting it.
    (D) The high cost of the medication makes it difficult for poor people to access the drugs.

15. How did the Great Depression affect Japanese politics?
    (A) Because Japan was largely an agrarian economy, the worst aspects of the Great Depression were avoided, but the declining value of Japanese exports made people turn to the communist party.
    (B) The Great Depression meant that the Japanese government had to take a greater role in economic central planning. The government created a Five-Year Plan to centralize the economy.
    (C) Economic hardship undermined support for internationalist politicians, which benefited the militarists who were unwilling to be constrained by international cooperation.
    (D) The Great Depression destroyed the banking industry, so the liberal party campaigned to create a New Deal that would expand social services and create a welfare state.

## Short Answer

16. Use the map below and your knowledge of world history to answer parts A, B, and C.

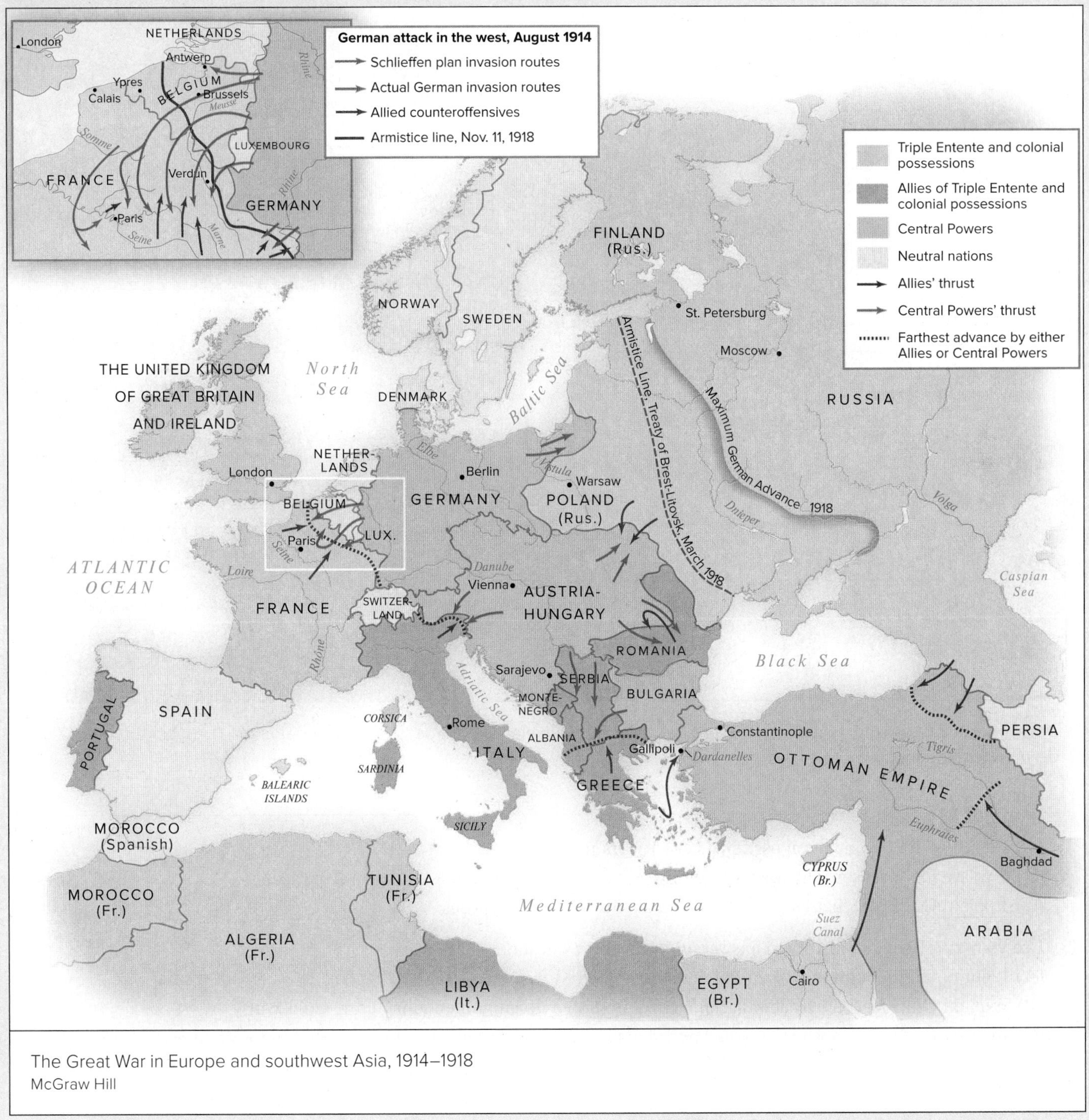


The Great War in Europe and southwest Asia, 1914–1918
McGraw Hill

(A) Explain ONE reason why trench warfare immobilized armies in the west but not on the eastern front.

(B) Explain ONE way that armies tried to end the stalemate on the western front.

(C) Explain ONE way that World War I affected life on the home front.

17. Using the image below and your knowledge of world history, answer parts A, B, and C.

Detail of Vladimir Lenin, “El hombre en el cruce de caminos” (“Man at the Crossroads”) from a larger mural, “El hombre controlador del universo” (“Man, Controller of the universe”), 1934, painted by Diego Rivera
Lucio Ruiz Pastor/agefotostock

(A) Identify ONE theme often used by Diego Rivera in his murals.
(B) Explain ONE reason why Marxist-Leninist ideas would be influential in Latin America.
(C) Explain ONE way that Diego Rivera used art for political purposes.

18. Use your knowledge of history to answer all parts of the questions that follow.
(A) Identify ONE country involved in the Non-Aligned Movement.
(B) Explain ONE reason why Jawaharlal Nehru promoted nonalignment during the Cold War.
(C) Identify ONE reason why the Non-Aligned Movement failed to create a unified front in the Cold War.

## Section II

## Document-Based Question

Suggested reading and writing time: 1 hour
It is suggested that you spend 15 minutes reading the documents and 45 minutes writing your response.

Note: You may begin writing your response before the reading period is over.
The documents have been edited for the purpose of this exercise.

Based on your analysis of the documents below, evaluate the role of the Vietnam War in decolonization and civil rights movements around the world.

In your response you should do the following.

- Respond to the prompt with a historically defensible thesis or claim that establishes a line of reasoning.
- Describe a broader historical context relevant to the prompt.
- Support an argument in response to the prompt using at least six documents.
- Use at least one additional piece of specific historical evidence (beyond that found in the documents) relevant to an argument about the prompt.
- For at least three documents, explain how or why the document's point of view, purpose, historical situation, and/or audience is relevant to an argument.
- Use evidence to corroborate, qualify, or modify an argument that addresses the prompt.

### Document 1

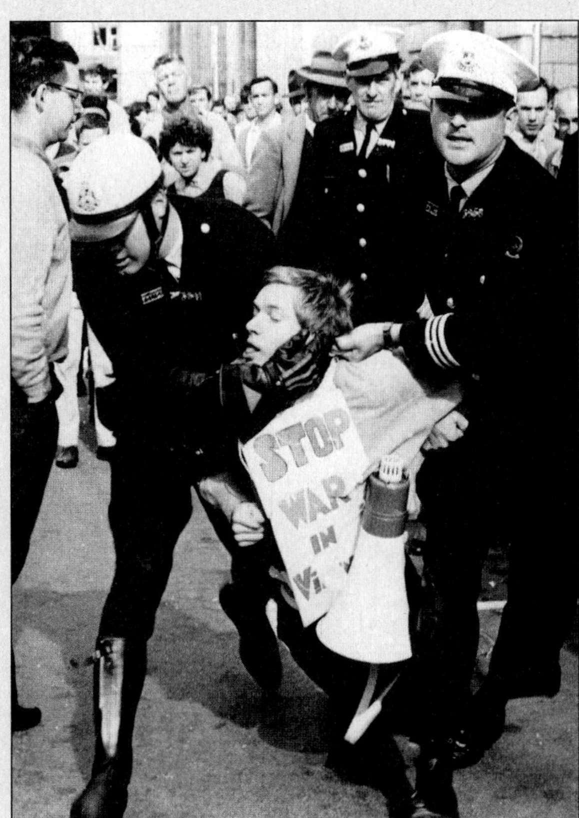


A traffic policeman and a constable, bundle off one of the four demonstrators arrested outside the General Post Office in Perth, Western Australia, June 11, 1966, during an anti-conscription and anti-Vietnam War protest.
AP Images

## Document 2

Thousands of protestors march from Place de la Republique to the Bastille on May 1, 1968 in Paris, France. On banners the demonstrators demand peace in Vietnam, higher wages and an end of the state of emergency.
STR/AP Images

## Document 3

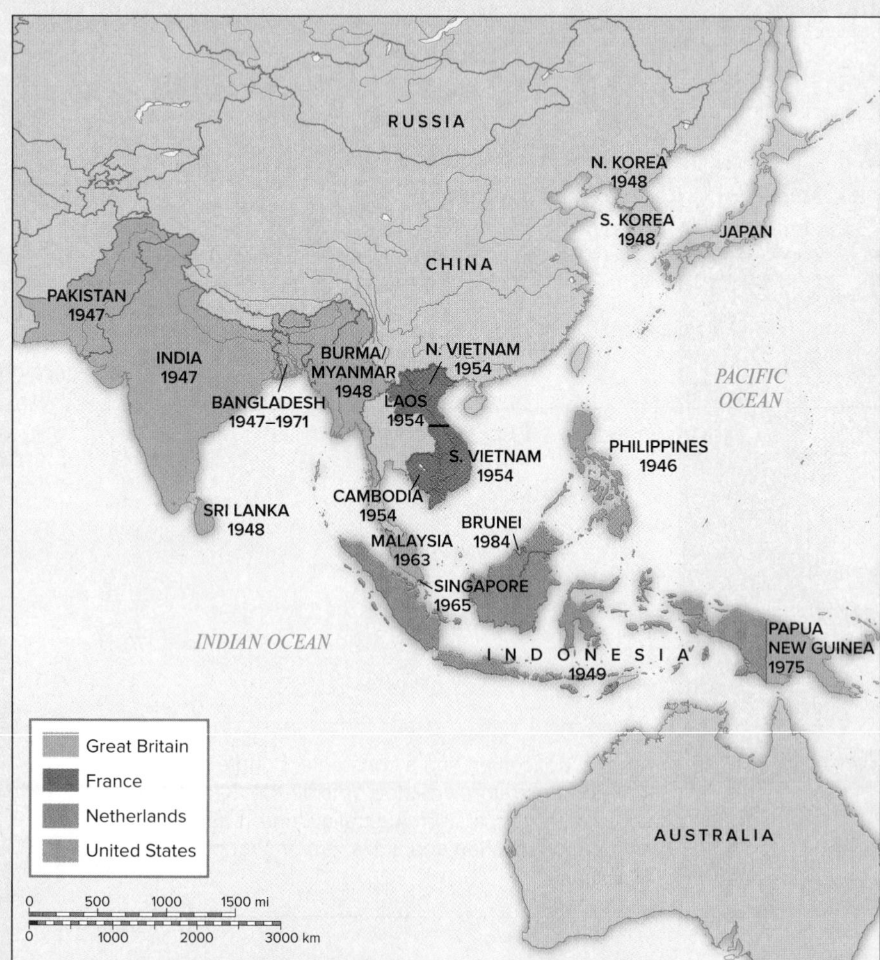


Decolonization in Asia. Date is year of independence.
McGraw Hill

## Document 4

Ho Chi Minh, Letter to President Lyndon B. Johnson, 1967

Vietnam is situated thousands of miles from the United States. The Vietnamese people have never done any harm to the United States. But, contrary to the commitments made by its representative at the Geneva Conference of 1954, the United States Government has constantly intervened in Vietnam, it has launched and intensified the war of aggression in South Vietnam for the purpose of prolonging the division of Vietnam and of transforming South Vietnam into an American neo-colony and an American military base. For more than two years now, the American Government, with its military aviation and its navy, has been waging war against the Democratic Republic of Vietnam, an independent and sovereign country.

*Source:* The Department of State Bulletin, LVI, No. 1450 (April 10, 1967), pp. 595–597.

## Document 5

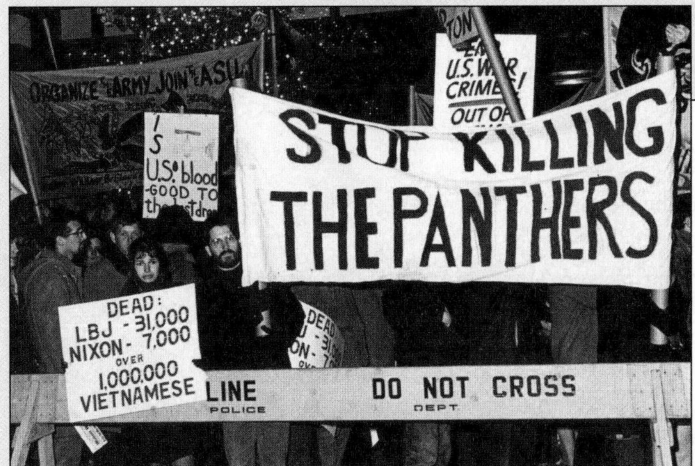


Anti-war demonstration, with small placards reading 'End US War Crimes' and 'Dead: LBJ - 31,000 NIxon - 7,000, over 1,000 Vietnamese' alongside a large banner reading 'Stop Killing the Panthers', behind a security barrier at a rally being held for George Wallace's 1968 United States presidential election campaign at Madison Square Garden in New York City, New York, 1967.

FPG/Getty Images

## Document 6

Political cartoon, "Dominos." 1964.

A 1964 Herblock Cartoon, © The Herb Block Foundation

## Document 7

Che Guevara, message to the Tricontinental, a conference for revolutionary movements from Africa, Asia, and Latin America, 1967.

There is a sad reality: Vietnam – a nation representing the aspirations, the hopes of a whole world of forgotten peoples – is tragically alone. This nation must endure the furious attacks of U.S. technology, with practically no possibility of reprisals in the South and only some of defense in the North – but always alone. . . .

When we analyze the lonely situation of the Vietnamese people, we are overcome by anguish at this illogical moment of humanity. . . .

We must ask ourselves, seeking an honest answer: is Vietnam isolated, or is it not? Is it not maintaining a dangerous equilibrium between the two quarrelling powers? . . .

What role shall we, the exploited people of the world, play? The peoples of the three continents focus their attention on Vietnam and learn their lesson. Since imperialists blackmail humanity by threatening it with war, the wise reaction is not to fear war. The general tactics of the people should be to launch a constant and a firm attack in all fronts where the confrontation is taking place.

*Source:* Guevara, Che. "Message to the Tricontinental." Transcribed by Workers' Web ASCII Pamphlet Project. The Executive Secretariat of the Organization of the Solidarity of the Peoples of Africa, Asia, and Latin America (OSPAAAL). Havana, Cuba, April 16, 1967.

## Long Essay

1. Evaluate the extent to which governments controlled their economies after 1918.
2. Evaluate the effectiveness of NATO and the Warsaw Pact.
3. Compare and contrast the ways Mohandas Gandhi and Nelson Mandela worked to bring about the end of empires in the twentieth century.

In your response you should do the following:

- Respond to the prompt with a historically defensible thesis or claim that establishes a line of reasoning.
- Describe a broader historical context relevant to the prompt.
- Support an argument in response to the prompt using specific and relevant examples of evidence.
- Use historical reasoning (e.g. comparison, causation, continuity or change) to frame or structure an argument that addresses the prompt.
- Use evidence to corroborate, qualify, or modify an argument that addresses the prompt.

## AP PRACTICE EXAM

# WORLD HISTORY

# SECTION I, Part A

## Time—55 minutes

**Directions:** Choose the best answer for each question.

**Use the excerpt to answer questions 1-3.**

> The Arab Merchant Suleiman on Business Practices in Tang China
>
> In China, commercial transactions are carried out with the aid of copper coins...These copper coins serve as money of the land. The Chinese have gold, silver, fine pearls, fancy silk textiles, raw silk, and all this in large quantities, but they are considered commodities, and only copper coins serve as money.
>
> Imports into China include ivory, incense, copper ingots, shells of sea turtles, and rhinoceros' horn, with which the Chinese make ornaments...
>
> *Source:* Jean Sauvaget, ed. *Relation de la Chine et de l'Inde.* Paris, 1948, pp. 10–11, 15–16, 19–20. (Translated into English by Jerry H. Bentley.)

1. The intended audience for this report was mostly likely
   (A) merchants.
   (B) missionaries.
   (C) explorers.
   (D) environmentalists.

2. This report would most likely stir Muslim interest in China as a source of
   (A) economic opportunity.
   (B) converts to Islam.
   (C) scientific knowledge.
   (D) cultural exchange.

3. The Ming Dynasty's (1368-1644 C.E.) reaction to the economic activity described in the passage was to
   (A) maintain the status quo of open trade.
   (B) limit trade to Silk Road routes only.
   (C) forbid all foreign trade and travel.
   (D) promote exploration of the Indian Ocean basin.

## Use the passage below to answer questions 4-6.

Historian Paul Ratchnevsky, *Genghis Khan: His Life and Legacy*

... As early as the struggle for the steppe he had spread the claim that Heaven had destined him as ruler; members of Mongol trading caravans spread stories intended to cause panic among the local populace; forged letters were fed to Sultan Muhammad which strengthened his mistrust of his Turkic units; freedom of religion was proclaimed; those who offered no resistance were promised that life and property would be spared; terrible destruction was threatened in the event of resistance; bloody examples were designed to spread fear and reduce the populace's will to resist....

*Source:* Ratchnevsky, Paul. *Genghis Khan: His Life and Legacy.* Cambridge, 1993, pg. 173.

4. Both Genghis Khan and Chinese emperors justified their right to rule based on
   (A) a decree of the deities that signaled to the general population when a ruler no longer was in their favor
   (B) popular sovereignty in which the general population got to voice its opinion as to when a ruler was no longer in its favor.
   (C) civil service patronage that encouraged support of the current ruler to maintain the status quo
   (D) support of the military that would subdue any unrest or quell any rival faction that might threaten the ruling leadership.

5. The actions described in this passage led most directly to
   (A) destruction of the Yuan Empire due to Mongol passivity throughout Asia.
   (B) establishment of the great khanates in China and Persia.
   (C) reduction in Eurasian integration of people and ideas.
   (D) increase in risk of trade and travel along the Silk Road.

6. In this excerpt the author gives an overview of Genghis Khan's reign as characterized by
   (A) religious intolerance and economic vitality.
   (B) economic stagnation and religious tolerance.
   (C) popular sovereignty and religious intolerance.
   (D) religious tolerance and brutal authoritarianism.

## Use the passage below to answer questions 7-10

*Leo Africanus on Timbuktu*

The name of this kingdom is a modern one, after a city which was built ... in the year 610 of the hegira [1232 CE] around twelve miles from a branch of the Niger River.

...In the center of the city is a temple built of stone and mortar... and, in addition, there is a large palace, ... where the king lives. The shops of the artisans, the merchants, and especially weavers of cotton cloth are very numerous. Fabrics are also imported from Europe to Timbuktu, borne by Berber merchants.

...Grain and animals are abundant, ... But salt is in very short supply because it is carried here from Tegaza, some 500 miles from Timbuktu. I happened to be in this city at a time when a load of salt sold for eighty ducats. The king has a rich treasure of coins and gold ingots. One of these ingots weighs 970 pounds.

The king is a declared enemy of the Jews. He will not allow any to live in the city. If he hears it said that a Berber merchant frequents them or does business with them, he confiscates his goods. There are in Timbuktu numerous judges, teachers, and priests, all properly appointed by the king. ... Many hand-written books imported from Barbary are also sold. There is more profit made from this commerce than from all other merchandise.

*Source:* Brians, Paul, Michael Blair, Douglas Hughes, Michael Neville, Roger Schlesinger, Alice Spitzer, and Susan Swan. *Reading About the World, Volume 2,* New York, 1999.

7. About anti-Semitism in Timbuktu, Leo Africanus point of view regarding discrimination can best be characterized as
   (A) outrightly critical.
   (B) neutrally observational.
   (C) intentionally omitted.
   (D) forcefully admonished.

8. An historian might challenge the creditability of this excerpt by citing that Leo Africanus
   (A) obtained his information through conversations with Berber merchants and therefore was a secondary source.
   (B) stressed only the economic activities of Timbuktu's trans-African gold-salt exchange, and therefore leaving out contact with other cultures.
   (C) practiced Islam and therefore may have been favorably biased towards a Muslim culture.
   (D) omitted any mention of intellectual and educational interests and therefore giving an incomplete picture of Timbuktu.

9. Which of the following audiences might have challenged Leo Africanus' description of Timbuktu?
   (A) Renaissance scholars who drew inspiration from classical Greek and Roman civilizations
   (B) The rulers of the Crusader States of the Middle East who were defeated by the Mamelukes
   (C) The scholars of Timbuktu who felt Africanus had not acknowledged their presence and contribution.
   (D) Anti-Semites whose point of view would have been in opposition to the king's policies regarding Jews.

10. The description of the king's power over church and state is evidenced by which of the following quotes?
    (A) *"The king is a declared enemy of the Jews"*
    (B) *"Judges, teachers and priests, all properly appointed by the king."*
    (C) *"Many hand-written books imported from Barbary are also sold."*
    (D) *"The king has a rich treasure of coins and gold ingots."*

## Use the passage below to answer questions 11-13.

Pedro de Cieza de Léon, a conquistador: *Chronicles of the Incas*, 1540

It was felt to be certain that those who did evil would receive punishment without fail, and that neither prayers nor bribes would avert it. At the same time, the Incas always did good to those who were under their sway, and would not allow them to be ill-treated, nor that too much tribute should be exacted from them. Many who dwelt in a sterile country where they and their ancestors had lived with difficulty, found that through the orders of the Ynca their lands were made fertile and abundant, the things being supplied which before were wanting. In other districts, where there was scarcity of clothing, owing to the people having no flocks, orders were given that cloth should be abundantly provided. In short, it will be understood that as these lords knew how to enforce service and the payment of tribute, so they provided for the maintenance of the people, and took care that they should want for nothing.

*Source:* Pedro Cieza de Léon, *The Second Part of the Chronicle of Peru*, Clements R. Markham, trans. & ed., (London: Hakluyt Society, 1883), pg. 37.

11. The tone of Pedro de Cieza de Leon's account of Incan society is best described as
    (A) condescending because he portrays a backwardness of Incan practices.
    (B) critical because he highlights the negative aspects of Incan practices.
    (C) approving because he indicates the benefits of Incan practices.
    (D) disbelieving because he doubts the efficacy of Incan practices.

12. The Incan practice of redistribution is most similar to which modern economic practice?
    (A) Laissez-faire capitalism
    (B) Welfare socialism
    (C) Anarchist Marxism
    (D) Pure communism

13. Taking into consideration Pedro de Cieza de Leon's occupation, an historian who had also studied Pizarro and Cortez might conclude that these conquerors were
    (A) solely focused on the mineral riches to be exploited from the New World.
    (B) insensitive to the cultural differences of indigenous people in the New World.
    (C) aware of and varied in their appreciation of New World cultural practices.
    (D) merciless in their treatment of indigenous people in the New World.

**Use the image below to answer questions 14-16.**

A blue and white bowl of the Ming dynasty type which was found near Kunduchi, an East African trading town dating from the 16th century.
Werner Foreman/TopFoto/The Image Works

14. Which claim is best supported by the information gleaned from this source?
    (A) East African city-states remained isolated until the arrival of the Europeans in the 16th century.
    (B) Swahili is a Bantu based language supplemented with words and ideas borrowed from Arabic.
    (C) The Indian Ocean sea lanes created a network of maritime Silk Roads and overland trade routes from Asia.
    (D) Lack of sheltered ports and dense jungle growth prohibited both east African foreign coastal trade and domestic inland trade.

15. Considering the date of this artifact, it was probably transported by which of the following?
    (A) English privateers
    (B) Dutch West Indian captains
    (C) Mughal sea commanders
    (D) Persian mariners

16. Which of the following would help authenticate the date and origin of this artifact?
    (A) a 21st century African antiquities buyers' guide with photos of items for sale
    (B) a cargo manifest from one of Vasco da Gama's exploration voyages of coastal Africa
    (C) a diary entry of 19th century Christian missionary describing Tanzanian dinner ware
    (D) a stamped engraving on the back of the artifact stating "Made in China"

## Use the passage below to answer questions 17-20.

*Excerpt from "The Twelve Articles of the Peasants," a list of peasants' demands presented during the German Peasants' War of 1525*

The First Article. ...we should have power and authority so that each community should choose and appoint a pastor, ... depose him should he conduct himself improperly.

The Third Article. ...We, therefore, take it for granted that you will release us from serfdom as true Christians, unless it should be shown us from the Gospel that we are serfs.

The Seventh Article. ...The lord should no longer try to force more services or other dues from the peasant without payment, ...

The Eighth Article. ... fix a rent in accordance with justice, so that the peasant shall not work for nothing, since the laborer is worthy of his hire.

Conclusion.—In the twelfth place it is our conclusion and final resolution, that if any one or more of the articles here set forth should not be in agreement with the word of God, as we think they are, such article we will willingly recede from when it is proved really to be against the word of God by a clear explanation of the Scripture....if more complaints should be discovered which are based upon truth and the Scriptures and relate to offences against God and our neighbor, we have determined to reserve the right to present these also.

*Source:* Thatcher, Oliver J., ed. *The Library of Original Sources.* New York, 1907., pp. 134–139.

17. Which of the following features of Western Europe in the period 1200-1500 most directly encouraged the making of the demands presented in the Twelve Articles?
    (A) Increase role of the Roman Catholic Church in religious and secular realms
    (B) Expansion of Islamic caliphates forcing sharia law on European peasants.
    (C) Decrease in population due to a global epidemic resulting in a labor shortage
    (D) Rise in the number of centers of learning in urban areas promoting scholasticism

18. The fact that the writers rely on Scripture as a justification for their demands indicates a desire to
    (A) dismantle the Roman Catholic hierarchy.
    (B) continue a religious based life.
    (C) maintain medieval feudal obligations.
    (D) uphold strict Islamic sharia law.

19. The result of the demands expressed in the Twelve Articles can best be summarized as
    (A) immediately successful and met without bloodshed.
    (B) championed by Luther and met without bloodshed.
    (C) moderately successful in that most of the demands were met.
    (D) disregarded and met with increased bloodshed.

20. The Twelve Articles was written in the vernacular which indicates that both the writers and the intended audience of nobles were
    (A) not formally educated and therefore neither group could communicate in the classical Latin.
    (B) developing a national spirit and culturally separating themselves from the medieval Holy Roman Empire political unit.
    (C) modeling Martin Luther's 95 Theses, knowing that he supported the peasants' activism and rebellion against the nobility.
    (D) irreligious and avoided using Latin, the language of the Roman Catholic Church, because they desired no connection with the Christianity.

**Use the images below to answer questions 21-23.**

Liberty on the Barricades (1830), painted by Eugène Delacroix (1798–1863);
Oleg Golovnev/Shutterstock

In Versailles, from October 5, 1789, Unknown artist
Paris Musées/Musée Carnavalet

21. Which of the following triggered the actions portrayed in these images?
    (A) Perpetuation of a medieval matriarchal based culture
    (B) Abandonment of the Catholic hierarchal structure
    (C) Persistence of the rigid Three Estate system
    (D) Continuation of Parliament with a House of Lords

22. A possible criticism leveled against these images is that they portray women as
    (A) irrational and mythical.
    (B) minor and inconsequential.
    (C) deliberate and thoughtful.
    (D) overly intellectual and astute.

23. Image #1 is Delacroix's "Liberty on the Barricades." Which of the following written works would have inspired the artist and their viewing audience?
    (A) *Two Treatises of Government* by John Locke
    (B) *Leviathan* by Thomas Hobbes
    (C) *Communist Manifesto* by Karl Marx and Frederick Engels
    (D) *Feminine Mystique* by Betty Friedan

**Use the image below to answer questions 24–27.**

Maori chiefs recognise British sovereignty by signing the Treaty of Waitangi, February 6, 1840.
Chronicle/Alamy Stock Photo

24. In what historical context was this treaty signed?
    (A) Oceania was experiencing the development of foreign settler colonies.
    (B) Oceania was experiencing the early stages of foreign exploration and charting
    (C) Oceania was experiencing the drafting of its soldiers for the Gallipoli campaign
    (D) Oceania was experiencing the pressures of the Abbasid caliphate imperialism.

25. Prior to signing the treaty, Maori chiefs signed a Declaration of Independence in 1839. Why would they have felt compelled to create such a document?
    (A) New Zealanders were aware that their nomadic lifestyles were threatened by other Pacific islanders.
    (B) New Zealanders needed Western medical care to halt diseases ravaging the indigenous population.
    (C) New Zealanders needed to be recognized as possessing its own strong land and sea defense system.
    (D) New Zealanders were concerned about European conflict over Pacific lands that could threaten their autonomy.

26. After signing a declaration of independence in 1839, why would Maori leaders have signed a treaty giving the British rights to their lands in 1840?
    (A) Maori leaders were concerned about popular uprisings amongst their people.
    (B) Maori leaders viewed partnering with the British a calculated risk to resist French incursions.
    (C) Maori leaders were impressed with Queen Victoria's rule and wanted to join her Commonwealth.
    (D) Maori leaders wanted better trade connections to Europe.

27. A timeline of subsequent events to the Treaty of Waitangi (1840), presumably to place New Zealand under British protection, includes the New Zealand Wars (1845–1872), fought between the British and Maori people of New Zealand. This series of conflicts resulted in placing New Zealand in the British Commonwealth system.

    When considering these subsequent events, which of the following seems to have been a result of the Declaration of Independence?
    (A) The Declaration was accepted by the British government with little modification.
    (B) The hereditary rulers of Britain and New Zealand worked together to maintain their political power.
    (C) New Zealand was drawn into an Oceana military alliance that safeguarded its complete independence.
    (D) New Zealand continued its efforts to achieve sovereignty for and unity among its population.

**Use the passage below to answer questions 28-30.**

William Wilberforce, member of Parliament, philanthropist and abolitionist, speech given in the House of Commons in 1789.

When I consider the magnitude of the subject which I am to bring before the House — a subject in which the interests not just of this country, nor of Europe alone, but of the whole world and of posterity are involved . . . it is impossible for me not to feel both terrified and concerned at my own inadequacy to such a task . . . the end of which is the total abolition of the slave trade.

*Source:* Schomburg Center for Research in Black Culture, Manuscripts, Archives and Rare Books Division, The New York Public Library. "The speech of William Wilberforce, esq., representative for the county of York, on Wednesday the 13th of May, 1789, on the question of the abolition of the slave trade" New York Public Library Digital Collections. Accessed October 21, 2021. https://digitalcollections.nypl.org/items/510d47e3-a708-a3d9-e040-e00a18064a99

28. The legislation that Wilberforce introduced in 1789 did not pass until 1807. Which of the following historical circumstances may have been responsible for the eventual passage of antislavery legislation?
    (A) France's reign of terror in the 1790's demonstrated the horrors of violent political change.
    (B) Napoleon's rise to power and his aggressive extension of French borders endangered British sovereignty.
    (C) Repeated slave uprisings in Latin America threatened to increase as long as there was a reliance on enslaved labor.
    (D) Congress of Vienna's liberal antislavery decree became binding on all European nation-states.

29. Which of the following writings presents an opposing point of view to Wilberforce's belief in the rightfulness of his "task"?
    (A) *The Prince* by Nicolo Machiavelli in which he details the characteristic behaviors of a successful ruler's maintenance or power
    (B) *An Inquiry into the Nature and Causes of the Wealth of Nations* by Adam Smith in which he promotes the invisible hand of market forces
    (C) *Principles of Biology* by Herbert Spencer in which he promotes the theory of survival of the fittest
    (D) *Declaration of the Rights of Woman and of the Female Citizen* by Olympe de Gouges in which she challenges the French revolutionary government

30. Which of the following actions addressed a similar human rights violation as the one Wilberforce identified?
    (A) Tiananmen Square student protest against censorship
    (B) Hong Kong campaign against Chinese oppression
    (C) North African Arab Spring uprising against theocratic rule
    (D) South African demonstration against apartheid

**Using the images below, answer questions 31-33.**

The opening of the Glasgow & Garnkirk Railway, view at St Rollox looking south east, 27 September 1831
FLHC 15/Alamy Stock Photo

Nineteenth century etching showing a woman drawing coal with the aid of a belt and chain.
Hulton Deutsch/Corbis Historical/Getty Images

31. In addition to the plentiful natural resources such as coal, which of the following factors existed in mid $19^{th}$ century England that helped foster its industrialization?
    (A) An isolationist sentiment that allowed the nation to focus upon its internal production and markets
    (B) An extremely dry climate that enabled the easy handling of cotton and wool fibers
    (C) A government that supported improvements in transportation and capitalist investment
    (D) An active reform movement that successfully championed labor rights and protections

32. Documents 1 and 2 present very different views of coal mining. Which of the following statements about the probable intended audience and purpose for each document is most correct?
    (A) Document 1 is aimed at stirring reformists and political activists' point of view.
    (B) Document 2 is aimed at strengthening laissez-faire proponents' point of view.
    (C) Document 1 is aimed at supporting reformists and political activists' point of view.
    (D) Document 2 is aimed at weakening laissez-faire proponents' point of view.

33. One of the $19^{th}$ century global consequences of the Industrial Revolution was
    (A) a decrease in interdependence as nation's concentrated on domestic production.
    (B) an increase in imperialistic ventures to secure needed raw materials and markets.
    (C) an increase in cooperation among nations to equitably proportion resources.
    (D) a decrease in environmental impact as more efficient power sources were utilized.

## Using the image and passage below, answer questions 34-36

The 3rd of May 1808 in Madrid, or "The Executions" (1814), painted by Francisco Goya
Recall Pictures/Alamy Stock Photo

Lord Byron, *The Isles of Greece*

THE isles of Greece! the isles of Greece!
Where burning Sappho loved and sung,
Where grew the arts of war and peace,—
Where Delos rose and Phoebus sprung!...

And musing there an hour alone,

I dream'd that Greece might yet be free...

*Source:* Eva March Tappan, ed., *The World's Story: A History of the World in Story, Song and Art,* 14 Vols., (Boston: Houghton Mifflin, 1914), Vol. IV: *Greece and Rome,* pp. 228–231. Scanned by Jerome S. Arkenberg, Cal. State Fullerton. The text has been modernized by Prof. Arkenberg.

34. The artistic expressions featured in Documents 1 and 2 represent which of the following 19$^{th}$ century forces?
    (A) Nationalism with its call for unity and opposition to foreign control
    (B) Imperialism with its pride in ethnic and cultural supremacy
    (C) Industrialization with its boast of efficiency and plenty
    (D) Technological progress with its display of military and civilian inventions

35. Both Goya's painting and Byron's poem are characteristic of which of the following periods of art?
    (A) Neoclassism with its subjects of antiquity
    (B) Realism with its precise detail of objects
    (C) Romanticism with its vivid sensory descriptions
    (D) Impressionism with its descriptive landscapes

36. Which of the following historical events shared a similar motivation as that expressed by Goya and Byron?
    (A) Taiping Rebellion in China
    (B) Meiji Restoration in Japan
    (C) Tet Offensive in Vietnam
    (D) Arab Spring in Tunisia

## Using the passage below, answer questions 37-39.

*An excerpt from Moshweshewe: Letter to Sir George Grey, a British colonial administrator. 1858*

. . . About twenty-five years ago my knowledge of the White men and their laws was very limited. I knew merely that mighty nations existed, and among them was the English. These, the blacks who were acquainted with them, praised for their justice. Unfortunately it was not with the English Government that my first intercourse with the whites commenced. People who had come from the Colony first presented themselves to us, they called themselves Boers. I thought all white men were honest. Some of these Boers asked permission to live upon our borders. I was led to believe they would live with me as my own people lived, that is, looking to me as to a father and a friend.

About sixteen years since, one of the [British] Governors of the [Cape] Colony, Sir George Napier, marked down my limits on a treaty he made with me. I was to be ruler within those limits. A short time after, another Governor came, it was Sir P. Maitland. The Boers then began to talk of their right to places I had then lent to them. Sir P. Maitland told me those people were subjects of the Queen, and should be kept under proper control; he did not tell me that he recognized any right they had to land within my country, but as it was difficult to take them away, it was proposed that all desiring to be under the British rule should live in that part near the meeting of the Orange and Caledon rivers.

Then came Sir Harry Smith, and he told me not to deprive any chief of their lands or their rights, he would see justice done to all, but in order to do so, he would make the Queen's Laws extend over every white man. He said the Whites and Blacks were to live together in peace. I could not understand what he would do. I thought it would be something very just, and that he was to keep the Boers in my land under proper control, and that I should hear no more of their claiming the places they lived on as their exclusive property. But instead of this, I now heard that the Boers consider all those farms as their own, and were buying and selling them one to the other, and driving out by one means or another my own people.

In vain I remonstrated. Sir Harry Smith had sent Warden to govern in the Sovereignty. He listened to the Boers, and he proposed that all the land in which those Boers' farms were should be taken from me. . . . One day he sent me a map and said, sign that, and I will tell those people . . . to leave off fighting: if you do not sign the map, I cannot help you in any way. I thought the Major was doing very improperly and unjustly. I was told to appeal to the Queen to put an end to this injustice. I did not wish to grieve Her Majesty by causing a war with her people. I was told if I did not sign the map, it would be the beginning of a great war. I signed, but soon after I sent my cry to the Queen. I begged Her to investigate my case and remove "the line," as it was called, by which my land was ruined. I thought justice would soon be done, and Warden put to rights. [Hostilities then broke out between the Boers and Moshweshewe's people, and Moshweshewe was thus requesting arbitration by Grey, the high commissioner]

*Source:* Letter from the Chief Moshesh to the High Commissioner in 1858." in Basutoland Records: Copies of Official Documents of Various Kinds, Accounts of Travellers, &c, Volume 2, edited by George McCall Theal, 384. Bosman Street: Government of Capetown, 1883.

37. At the time that this letter was written, the predominant historical force in Africa was the
    (A) imperialistic ventures of European nations that carved up Africa.
    (B) exploration and establishment of trading posts along the west African coast.
    (C) nationalist uprisings and decolonization efforts of Pan Africanism.
    (D) construction of the British trans-African Cairo to Cape Town railroad.

38. The tone of Moshweshewe letter to Sir George Grey is best described as
    (A) hostile in that he threatens war.
    (B) respectful in that he is courteous.
    (C) ambivalent in that he is uncertain.
    (D) pessimistic in that he sees no solution.

39. Moshweshewe hopes to sway his audience by an appeal to
    (A) a shared set of common cultural values.
    (B) a mutually beneficial economic arrangement.
    (C) a fulfillment of complimentary imperialistic goals.
    (D) a reciprocal military alliance and diplomatic exchange.

**Use the image below to answer questions 40-42.**

Gassed (1919), painted by John Sargent Singer
Historic Collection/Alamy Stock Photo

40. Which of the following best describes the painting?
    (A) A propaganda poster prepared by the Nazi Party
    (B) A protest poster against the atrocities of the atomic bomb.
    (C) A representation of Jewish ghetto refugees during the Holocaust
    (D) An expression of anti-war sentiment post World War I

41. Which of the following contemporaries would have most likely supported the artist's point of view regarding the "modern world"?
    (A) The poets and writers who comprised the "lost generation" with its strong disillusionment and malaise.
    (B) The signatories of the Treaty of Versailles who demanded Germany pay reparations to cover war damages
    (C) The proponents of economic nationalism who imposed trade barriers hoping to achieve economic self-sufficiency
    (D) The supporters of Zionism who saw the increasing need for Jews to have a separate homeland carved out of the Middle East.

42. Which of the following types of data could be used to counter-argue John Singer Sergeant's claim as expressed in *Gassed*?
    (A) A set of statistics compiled by the World Health Organization showing the increase in polio vaccinations administered in developing nations.
    (B) A map drawn by World Wildlife Federation indicating the increase in animal population extinction in the Eastern Hemisphere.
    (C) A graph assembled by Greenpeace depicting the 20$^{th}$ - 21$^{st}$ century increase in temperatures worldwide.
    (D) A video of a TED talk presenting information about the increase in desertification throughout sub-Saharan Africa

**Using the image below, answer questions 43-45.**

Armenian Genocide cartoon (2015)
Steven Greenberg/Cartoon Movement

43. Which of the following best describes the historical context of this cartoon?
    (A) Improvements in education about World Wars I and II.
    (B) The use of violent antisemitism by the Nazi party in Germany in the 1930s and 1940s.
    (C) Concerns about the persistence of genocide and genocide denial into the 21st century.
    (D) An effort by the United Nations to define genocide as a crime against humanity.

44. What historical problem is the cartoonist referencing?
    (A) The end of the Cold War.
    (B) UN efforts to curb the effects of climate change.
    (C) The religious conflict that resulted in the partition of India and Pakistan.
    (D) Efforts to pursue justice for the victims of forced relocation and massacres during the disintegration of the Ottoman Empire.

45. Which of the following created an international law precedent because of the historical event referred to in the cartoon?
    (A) Nuremberg Trials
    (B) Oslo Peace Accords
    (C) Versailles Treaty
    (D) Paris Climate Agreement

## Use the passage below to answer questions 46-48.

Statement by Oliver Tambo accepting the Ho Chi Minh award bestowed on the African National Congress by the World Peace Council, 15 December 1986, Luanda

The decision by the April 1986 Sofia session of the World Peace Council to present this award to our movement places our organisation in the midst of such vital forces for man's liberation as the Sandinista Liberation Front of Nicaragua, the Palestine Liberation Organisation (PLO) and the Popular Movement for the Liberation of Angola - Party of Labour (MPLA-PL) who were the earlier recipients of this singular distinction. Indeed, this poses a most serious challenge to the ANC and the people of South Africa to relentlessly pursue their struggle for the destruction of the imperialist supported apartheid system and thus make their own contribution to the promotion of peace and progress in the world. In accepting this award, we solemnly pledge never to rest until this goal is achieved. We are indeed proud to be associated with the name of Ho Chi Minh, a revolutionary giant and genius, a patriot who devoted the greater part of his life to the liberation of his fatherland. His was a life of intense struggle, hardships, simplicity, clarity of vision and sacrifices that contributed immensely to the heroic victory of the Vietnamese people over French colonialism and Japanese and American aggression. This most historic victory over a combination of colonialists and powerful imperialist forces inspired and encouraged the oppressed in South Africa and served as a spur to peoples fighting for freedom and national independence everywhere. Ho Chi Minh's devotion to the liberation struggle and his strong commitment to the ideals of peace and friendship among peoples, won him a special place of honour, high esteem and respect among Vietnamese and peace-loving peoples the world over.

*Source:* South African History Online, https://www.sahistory.org.za/archive/statement-oliver-tambo-acceptance-ho-chi-minh-award-bestowed-african-national-congress

46. Why would Oliver Tambo, a leader in the anti-apartheid movement in South Africa, receive an award named after Ho Chi Minh?
    (A) South Africa and Vietnam were both colonized by France.
    (B) Tambo became President of South Africa.
    (C) The anti-apartheid movement was viewed as part of the global decolonization movement.
    (D) China's increased investment in Africa promoting black middle class economic growth and power.

47. The anti-apartheid movement fought to do which of the following?
    (A) make South Africa a better environment to trade with southeast Asian countries.
    (B) allow white South Africans to buy property.
    (C) implement democracy and majority rule in South Africa by dismantling racist laws.
    (D) resolve the guilt that whites felt over colonization.

48. Which of the following claims about Africans prior to white settlement is a main assumption of supporters of apartheid policies in South Africa?
    (A) Black Africans had a prosperous and admirable culture in the millennium prior to the coming of the Europeans.
    (B) Black Africans were uncivilized and cruel to one another in the millennium prior to the coming of the Europeans.
    (C) Black Africans were negatively influenced by both Indian Ocean and trans-Saharan encounters in the millennium prior to the coming of the Europeans.
    (D) Black African social and cultural practices are mostly unknown and unspecified in the millennium prior to the coming of the Europeans.

## Use the passage below to answer questions 49-51.

Speech on the 1979 Uprising of Khurdad 15, Ayatollah Ruhollah Khomeini

Those who are ignorant... We must say to them: "You who imagine that something can be achieved in Iran by some means other than Islam, you who suppose that something other than Islam overthrew the Shah's regime, you who believe non-Islamic elements played a role–study the matter carefully. Look at the tombstones... All the tombstones belong to Muslims from the lower echelons of society: peasants, workers, tradesmen, committed religious scholars. As for those who oppose us because of their opposition to Islam, we must cure them by means of guidance, if it is at all possible; otherwise, we will destroy these agents of foreign powers with the same fist that destroyed the Shah's regime. It was the mosques that created this Revolution, the mosques that brought this movement into being..., do not be Western-style intellectuals, imported intellectuals; do your share to preserve the mosques!

*Source:* Tucker, Spencer C., ed. *The Cold War: The Definitive Encyclopedia and Document Collection*. Santa Barbara, 2020, pg. 2047.

49. Which of the following best identifies the goal of the Ayatollah Khomeini as expressed in this passage?
    (A) Pan Arab unity
    (B) Iranian hegemony in the Middle East
    (C) Secularization of Iran
    (D) Resurgence of Islam

50. The Ayatollah's remarks were made in what historical context?
    (A) Iran was governed by a secular, pro-Western government under the dictatorial rule of Shah Mohammed Reza Pahlavi.
    (B) Iran was controlled by the Soviet Union as one its satellite states, experiencing extreme political, economic, and military influence.
    (C) Iran was one of the non-aligned nations of the Cold War era that supported neither the United States nor the Soviet Union.
    (D) Iran was a model theocratic state that successfully balanced the practice of democratic principles with adherence to Sharia law.

51. The Ayatollah's direction in the opening paragraph to "look at the tombstones," is meant to stir which of the following in the audience?
    (A) a motivation to pursue diplomacy and negotiation over open conflict
    (B) a desire to consider syncretic religious practices and beliefs
    (C) a pride in the power and sacrifice of grassroot efforts
    (D) a rationale to promote Marxian class warfare and struggle.

## Using the graphs below, answer questions 52-54.

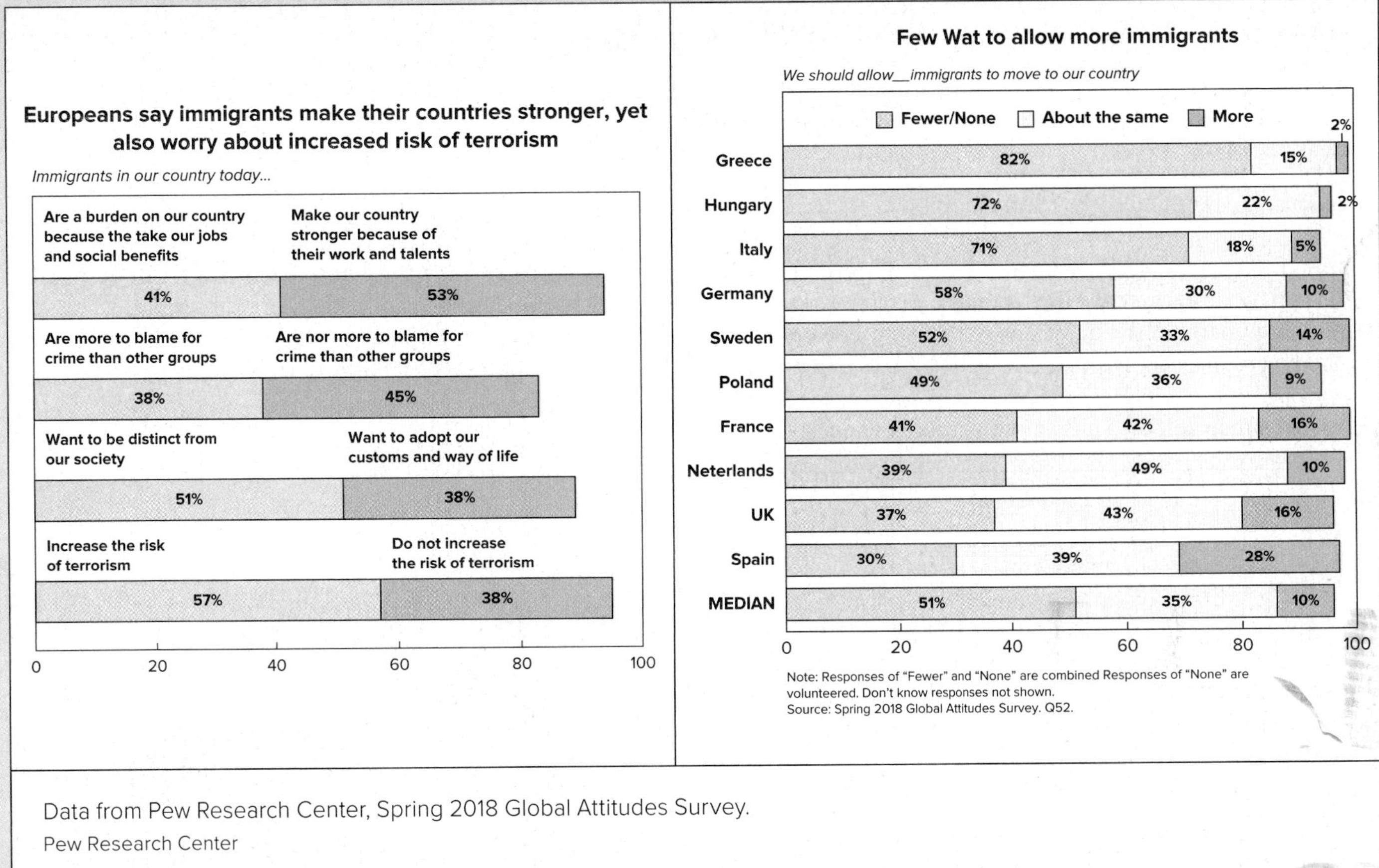


Data from Pew Research Center, Spring 2018 Global Attitudes Survey.
Pew Research Center

52. According to the survey responses presented in Document 1, which of the following claims is most accurate?
    (A) Most Europeans say immigrants make their countries stronger yet also worry about increased risk of terrorism.
    (B) Most Europeans say immigrants make their countries stronger and are not more likely to commit crime than the native population.
    (C) Most Europeans say immigrants are willing to assimilate into native cultures as they adopt new cultures and ways of life.
    (D) Most Europeans say that immigrants do not increase the risk of terrorism and often are wrongly blamed for rise in crime

53. Document 2 reveals a sentiment about immigrants that is most similar to that expressed during which of the following historical eras or events?
    (A) A welcoming sentiment as was historically shown with the initial open borders design of the European Union
    (B) A xenophobic sentiment as was historically shown in the post-World War I and Great Depression eras
    (C) A cautionary sentiment as was historically shown in the disrupted migration during the 1947 partition of India
    (D) An anti-nationalist sentiment as was historically shown at the Congress of Vienna's promotion of conservatism.

54. Which of the following socio-political behaviors reflects the surveys' results?
    (A) A surge in liberal, progressive political parties
    (B) A reduction in racist rhetoric in speech and print
    (C) A rise in solidarity among all European Union members
    (D) An increase in conservative, right-wing parties

# WORLD HISTORY

## SECTION I, Part B

### Time—40 minutes

**Directions:** Answer Question 1 and Question 2. Answer either Question 3 or Question 4.

Write your responses in the Section I, Part B: Short-Answer Response booklet. You must write your response to each question on the lined page designated for that response. Each response is expected to fit within the space provided. In your responses, be sure to address all parts of the questions you answer. Use complete sentences; an outline or bulleted list alone is not acceptable. You may plan your answers in this exam booklet, but no credit will be given for notes written in this booklet.

1. Use the map below to answer all parts of the question that follows.

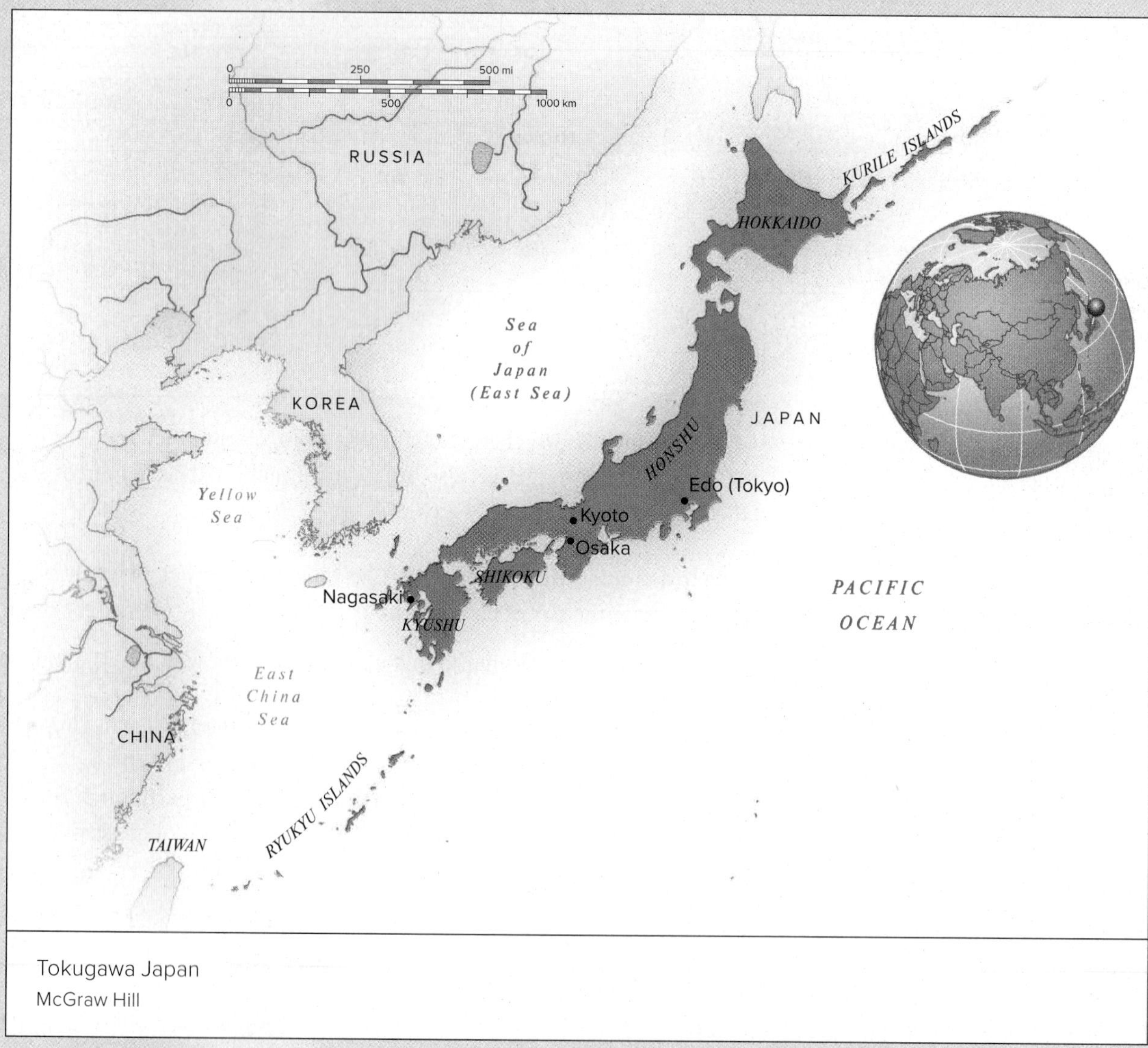


Tokugawa Japan
McGraw Hill

(A) Explain how one of Japan's major geographic features impacted its historical political development.

(B) Explain how one of Japan's major geographic features impacted its historical economic development.

(C) Identify one specific cultural influence Japan experienced due to its geographic location with neighboring mainland Asia.

2. Use the passage below to answer all parts of the question that follows.

> Below are excerpts from *The Instrument of Government,* the basis of a written constitution adopted 1653 in England.
>
> I. ...the supreme legislative authority of the Commonwealth.., shall ... reside in one person, and the people assembled in Parliament; the style of which person shall be the Lord Protector
>
> III. That all writs, processes, commissions, patents, grants, and other things, which now run in the...authority of Parliament, shall run in the name and style of the Lord Protector
>
> XV. That all such, who have advised, assisted, or abetted the rebellion of Ireland, shall be ... incapable for ever to be elected... as also all such who do or shall profess the Roman Catholic religion.
>
> XXX. That the raising of money... shall be by consent of Parliament,
>
> XXXIII. That Oliver Cromwell, Captain - shall be, and is hereby declared to be, Lord Protector of the Commonwealth ... for his life.

(A) Identify and explain how one way the design of government outlined in the excerpt reflects a continuity the predominant global political structures of the period 1450–1750.

(B) Identify and explain how one way the design of government outlined in the excerpt reflects a change in the predominant global political structures of the period 1450–1750.

(C) Identify and explain one action taken in the period 1750–1900 in opposition to the predominant global political structures of the period 1450–1750.

3. Answer all parts of the question that follows.

(A) Identify and explain in geographic terms the impact upon Africa and Asia of "old imperialism" ventures (1500–1800) as compared to those of the "new imperialism" (1800–1914).

(B) Identify and explain the economic impact upon Africa and Asia of "old imperialism" ventures (1500–1800) as compared to those of the "new imperialism" (1800–1914).

(C) Identify and explain how one technological or scientific advancement allowed for the development of "new imperialism" (1800–1914).

4. Answer all parts of the question that follows.

(A) Identify and explain one specific ethnic minority group that has surfaced because of the late $20^{th}$ century dissolution of multinational states such as the Soviet Union or Yugoslavia.

(B) Identify and explain one specific ethnic minority group that has surfaced because of nation-state creation or restructuring in the $20^{th}$ or $21^{st}$ century such as Israel or Iraq.

(C) Describe one action taken by a specific $20^{th}$- or $21^{st}$ century ethnic minority group to achieve its goal of independent nation-state recognition.

# WORLD HISTORY

# SECTION II

## Total Time—1 hour and 40 minutes

## Question 1 (Document-Based Question)

## Suggested reading and writing time: 1 hour

**It is suggested that you spend 15 minutes reading the documents and 45 minutes writing your response.**

**Note: You may begin writing your response before the reading period is over.**

**Directions:** Question 1 is based on the accompanying documents. The documents have been edited for the purpose of this exercise.

In your response you should do the following.

- Respond to the prompt with a historically defensible thesis or claim that establishes a line of reasoning.
- Describe a broader historical context relevant to the prompt.
- Support an argument in response to the prompt using at least six documents.
- Use at least one additional piece of specific historical evidence (beyond that found in the documents) relevant to an argument about the prompt.
- For at least three documents, explain how or why the document's point of view, purpose, historical situation, and/or audience is relevant to an argument.
- Use evidence to corroborate, qualify, or modify an argument that addresses the prompt.

1. Based on your analysis of the documents below, evaluate the extent to which the cultivation of the banana has affected African history.

## Document 1

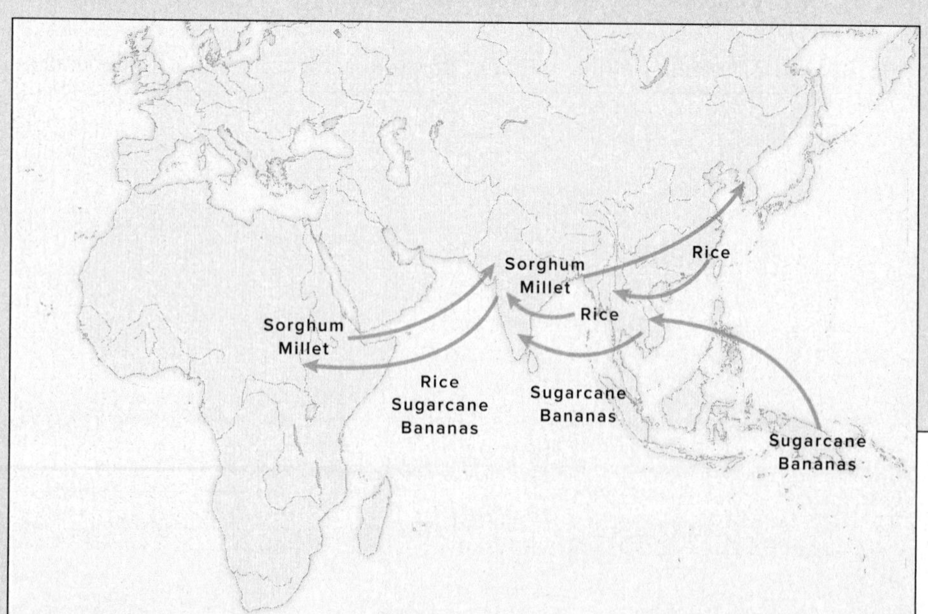


Migration of bananas from Southeast Asia to Africa, from Peter Robertshaw, "Africa's Earliest Bananas," Archaeology, Vol. 59, No. 5, pp. 25–29.
McGraw Hill

## Document 2

First domesticated in southeast Asia, bananas ...provided a nutritious supplement to Bantu diets and enabled the Bantu to expand into heavily forested regions where yams and millet did not grow well. Thus, cultivation of bananas increased the supply of food available to the Bantu, enriched their diets and allowed them to expand more rapidly than before. The population history of sub-Saharan Africa clearly reflects the significance of iron metallurgy and bananas. In 400 BE the population of sub-Saharan Africa stood at 3.5 million, by the turn of the millennium human numbers exceeded 11 million. By 800 CE after banana cultivation spread, the sub-Saharan population had climbed to 17 million. And by 1000 most regions of sub-Saharan African the population had passed 22 million.

*Source:* Jerry Bentley and Herbert Ziegler, *Traditions and Encounters: A Global Perspective on the Past,* 7th edition.

## Document 2b

Banana Harvest (1910), Henri Rousseau

Yale University Art Gallery

## Document 3

Germain Bayon, a geochemist at the French Research Institute for Exploration of the Sea in Plouzané, and his colleagues examined the weathering of sediment samples that were drawn from the mouth of the Congo River.

About 3000 years ago, a major vegetation change occurred in Central Africa when rainforest trees were abruptly replaced by savannas. Up to this point the consensus of the scientific community has been that the forest disturbance was caused by climate change. We show here that chemical weathering in Central Africa reconstructed from geochemical analyses of a marine sediment core, intensified abruptly at the same period, departing substantially from the long-term weathering fluctuations related to the Late Quaternary climate Evidence that this weathering event was also contemporaneous with the migration of Bantu-speaking farmers across Central Africa suggests that human land-use intensification at that time had already made a major impact on the rainforest.

*Source:* Germain Bayon, "Intensifying Weathering and land Use in Iron Age Central Africa," *Science* March 9, 2012

## Document 4

Thomas Malthus was graduate of Cambridge University, a member of the Royal Society, a social economist, and 19th century demographer whose writings influenced Charles Darwin.

The power of the population is indefinitely greater than the power of the earth to produce subsistence for man. Population when unchecked, increases in a geometrical ratio. Subsistence increases only in an arithmetical ratio. This implies a strong and constantly operating check on population for the difficulty of subsistence. This difficulty must fall somewhere and must necessarily be severely felt by a large portion of mankind.

During the next period of doubling, where would food be found...Where is the fresh land to turn up?

*Source: An Essay on the Principle of Population,* Thomas Malthus, 1798.

## Document 5

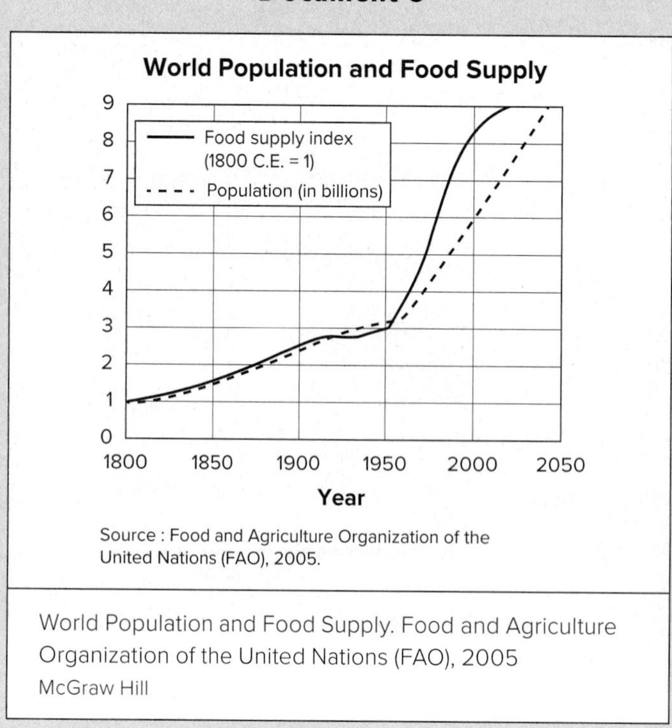


World Population and Food Supply. Food and Agriculture Organization of the United Nations (FAO), 2005

McGraw Hill

## Document 6

Bananas...play an important role as a staple food in developing countries contributing calories, nutrients and, to a limited extent, proteins to the diet. ...Most bananas are grown by small holders for self-consumption and traded in the local market providing income for the rural population in many low-income, food deficient countries. In most of sub-Saharan Africa where the Green Revolution had failed miserably, bananas are providing food security for the people. Genetic improvement of these important crops will help directly to meet the UN Millennium Development Goals, particularly those related to health and nutrition, and the reduction of poverty and hunger.

*Source: MEETING REPORT: Molecular Tools for Quality Improvement in Vegetatively Propagated Crops, Including Banana and Cassava."* Nair, Ashalatha S., and Mba Chikelu *Current Science,* 2007.

## Document 7

Archive photograph of women preparing bananas for export. The Molino De Gofio ethnographic museum in Hermigua, La Gomera, Canary Islands. 20th century.

David Lyons/Alamy Stock Photo

# Question 2, 3, or 4 (Long Essay)

## Suggested writing time: 40 minutes

**Directions:** Answer Question 2 **or** Question 3 **or** Question 4.

In your response you should do the following.

- Respond to the prompt with a historically defensible thesis or claim that establishes a line of reasoning.
- Describe a broader historical context relevant to the prompt.
- Support an argument in response to the prompt using specific and relevant examples of evidence.
- Use historical reasoning (e.g., comparison, causation, continuity or change over time) to frame or structure an argument that addresses the prompt.
- Use evidence to corroborate, qualify, or modify an argument that addresses the prompt.

1. In the period 1200–1750 C.E., advances in technology allowed for more global interaction. Opportunities increased for interactions with diverse cultures

   Develop an argument that evaluates that extent to which one or more of the these interactions involved an understanding and respect for cultural differences in this time period.

2. In the period 1750–1900 C.E., multi-ethnic and colonial empires and new nation-states developed.

   Develop an argument that evaluates the extent to which one or more of these methods achieved the goals of political and/or cultural cohesion in this time period.

3. In the period after World War II, many international and regional organizations developed, increasing the web of interactions among nations. In addition, nations decided whether to align or not with blocs representing different political and economic orientations.

   Develop an argument that evaluates the extent to which one or more individual nation -states sought to maintain and/or reestablish national sovereignty in an era of increasing global connections and interdependence.

# Glossary & Pronunciation Guide

**AH** *a* sound, as in *car, father*
**IH** short *i* sound, as in *fit, his, mirror*
**OO** long *o* sound, as in *ooze, tool, crew*
**UH** short *u* sound, as in *up, cut, color*
**A** short *a* sound, as in *asp, fat, parrot*
**EE** long *e* sound, as in *even, meet, money*
**OH** long *o* sound, as in *open, go, tone*
**EH** short *e* sound, as in *ten, elf, berry*
**AY** long *a* sound, as in *ape, date, play*
**EYE** long *i* sound, as in *ice, high, bite*
**OW** diphthong *o* sound, as in *cow, how, bow*
**AW** diphthong *a* sound, as in *awful, paw, law*

*Note on emphasis:* Syllables in capital letters receive the accent. If there is no syllable in capitals, then all syllables get equal accent.

**Abbasid dynasty** (ah-BAH-sihd) Cosmopolitan Arabic dynasty (750–1258) that replaced the Umayyads; founded by Abu al-Abbas and reached its peak under Harun al-Rashid.

**Abdül Hamid II** Reigned 1876–1909 C.E. Sultan of the Ottoman Empire whose despotic style of rule led to the creation of many opposition groups and to his deposition by dissidents in 1909.

**Abolitionism** Antislavery movement.

**Absolutism** Political philosophy that stressed the divine right theory of kingship: the French king Louis XIV was the classic example.

**Abu Bakr** (ah-BOO BAHK-uhr) First caliph after the death of Muhammad.

**Achaemenid empire** (ah-KEE-muh-nid) First great Persian empire (558–330 B.C.E.), which began under Cyrus and reached its peak under Darius.

**Adam Smith** 1723–1790. Scottish philosopher and founder of modern political economy, and a key figure in the Scottish Enlightenment. Best known for *An Inquiry into the Nature and Causes of the Wealth of Nations,* published in 1776.

**Adolf Hitler** 1889–1945 C.E. German politician and leader of the Nazi Party, who came to power in 1933. He initiated the European theater of World War II by invading Poland in 1939 and oversaw the establishment of death camps that resulted in more than ten million deaths.

**Adwa** 1896 Battle in which the Ethiopians badly defeated would-be Italian conquerors.

**Aegean Sea** Sea located between the mainlands of modern Greece and Turkey.

**Afonso d'Alboquerque** 1453–1515 C.E. Commander of the Portuguese forces in the Indian Ocean in the early sixteenth century. He was responsible for seizing Hormuz, Goa, and Malacca, which allowed the Portuguese to control Indian Ocean trade.

**African National Congress** South African political party formed in 1912 that provided consistent opposition to the apartheid state, and eventually became the majority party at the end of the apartheid era in 1994.

**Age grades** Bantu institution in which individuals of roughly the same age carried out communal tasks appropriate for that age.

**Ahimsa** (uh-HIM-suh) Jain term for the principle of nonviolence to other living things or their souls.

**Akbar** 1542–1605 C.E. The third Mughal emperor who ruled from 1556–1605 and was known for his religious tolerance.

**Al-Andalus** (al-ANN-duh-luhs) Islamic Spain.

**Albert Einstein** 1879–1955 C.E. German-born physicist who developed the theory of relativity and whose ideas had profound influence on the development of science in the twentieth century.

**Alexandria** An important city of the ancient world, founded by Alexander on the Mediterranean coast of Egypt during the fourth century B.C.E.

**Ali'i nui** Hawaiian class of high chiefs.

**Allah** (AH-lah) God of the monotheistic religion of Islam.

**al-Qaeda** Militant Islamist organization founded by Osama bin Laden in 1988, which was responsible for the September 11, 2001, attacks in the United States.

***Analects*** A collection of the sayings and teachings of the fifth century B.C.E. Chinese philosopher Confucius, collected by his students.

**Anastacio Somoza Garcia** 1896–1956. Brutal leader of the U.S.-trained Guarda Nacional in Nicaragua who became president and dictator in 1934.

**Ancien Régime** Meaning "old order," and refers to the period prior to the French Revolution in 1789.

**Angkor** (AHN-kohr) Southeast Asian Khmer kingdom (889–1432) that was centered on the temple cities of Angkor Thom and Angkor Wat.

**Anti-Semitism** Term coined in the late nineteenth century that was associated with a prejudice against Jews and the political, social, and economic actions taken against them.

**Antonianism** African syncretic religion, founded by Dona Beatriz, that taught that Jesus Christ was a black African man and that heaven was for Africans.

**Antonio López de Santa Anna** 1794–1896 C.E. Mexican army officer and politician best known for his efforts to prevent Spain from recapturing Mexico. Served as president of Mexico several times.

**Apartheid** (ah-PAHR-teyed) South African system of "separateness" that was implemented in 1948 and that maintained the black majority in a position of political, social, and economic subordination.

**Appeasement** British and French policy in the 1930s that tried to maintain peace in Europe in the face of German aggression by making concessions.

**Armenian Genocide** Campaign of extermination undertaken by the Ottomans against two million Armenians living in Ottoman territory during World War I.

**Aryans** (AIR-ee-anns) Indo-European migrants who settled in India after 1500 B.C.E.; their union with indigenous Dravidians formed the basis of Hinduism.

**Asceticism** (uh-SET-uh-siz-uhm) The practice of severe self-discipline and avoidance of all forms of indulgence, typically for religious reasons.

**Association of Southeast Asian Nations** (ASEAN) Regional organization established in 1967 by Thailand, Malaysia, Singapore, Indonesia, and the Philippines; the organization was designed to promote economic progress and political stability; it later became a free-trade zone.

**Assyrians** (uh-SEAR-ee-uhns) Southwest Asian people who built an empire that reached its height during the eighth and seventh centuries B.C.E.; it was known for a powerful army and a well-structured state.

**Astrolabe** Navigational instrument for determining latitude.

**Ataturk** 1881–1938 C.E. Meaning "Father of the Turks," his real name was Mustafa Kemal. He was a Turkish army officer, reformer, and the first president of the modern Republic of Turkey after the Ottoman defeat in World War I.

**Athens** Important city-state of ancient Greece, located in the Attica region.

**Attica** The region surrounding the ancient city of Athens.

**Audiencias** Spanish courts in Latin America.

**Augusto César Sandino** 1893–1934. Nationalist and liberal general of Nicaragua who fundamentally opposed U.S. intervention. He was murdered in 1934 by Anastacio Somoza Garcia's forces.

**Aung San Suu Kyi** 1945–. Burmese politician and author who received the 1991 Nobel Peace Prize for her opposition to Burmese military rule. Leads the National League for Democracy party.

**Aurangzeb** 1618–1707 C.E. The sixth Mughal emperor, who ruled for forty-nine years over almost all of the Indian subcontinent.

**Auschwitz** Camp established by the Nazi regime in occupied Poland, which functioned both as a concentration camp and an extermination camp. Approximately one million Jews were killed there.

**Axum** African kingdom centered in Ethiopia that became an early and lasting center of Coptic Christianity.

**Aztec empire** Central American empire constructed by the Mexica and expanded greatly during the fifteenth century during the reigns of Itzcoatl and Motecuzoma I.

**Babur** (BAH-ber) 1483–1530 C.E. Central Asian descendant of Chinggis Khan and Tamerlane who founded the Mughal dynasty in northern India in 1526.

**Bakufu** The military government of Japan from 1192 to 1868 C.E., headed by a shogun.

**Balfour Declaration** British declaration from 1917 that supported the creation of a Jewish homeland in Palestine.

**Bantu** (BAN-too) African peoples who originally lived in the area of present-day Nigeria; around 2000 B.C.E. they began a centuries-long migration that took them to most of sub-Saharan Africa; the Bantu were very influential, especially linguistically.

**Barack Obama** 1961–. Forty-fourth president of the United States, who served from 2009 to 2017. Obama was the first U.S. president of African heritage.

**Baron de Montesquieu** 1689–1755 C.E. French political philosopher who advocated the separation of legislative, executive, and judicial government powers.

**Bedouins** (BEHD-oh-ihnz) Nomadic Arabic tribespeople.

**Benazir Bhutto** 1953–2007 C.E. Pakistani politician who served twice as Pakistani prime minister: in 1988–1990 and then again in 1993–1996. She was assassinated in 2007.

**Benefice** Grant from a lord to a vassal, usually consisting of land, which supported the vassal and signified the relationship between the two.

**Benito Juárez** (beh-NEE-toh HWAHR-ez) 1806–1872 C.E. Mexican lawyer of indigenous origins who served as president of Mexico on five occasions.

**Benito Mussolini** 1883–1945 C.E. Italian politician and journalist who led the National Fascist Party and ruled as prime minister from 1922 to 1943.

**Berlin Conference** Meeting organized by German chancellor Otto von Bismarck in 1884–1885 that provided the justification for European colonization of Africa.

**Bezant** Byzantine gold coin that served as the standard currency of the Mediterranean basin from the sixth through the twelfth century.

**Bhagavad Gita** (BUH-guh-vahd GEE-tuh) "Song of the Lord," an Indian short poetic work drawn from the lengthy *Mahabharata* that was finished around 400 C.E. and that expressed basic Hindu concepts such as karma and dharma.

**Bhakti movement** (BAHK-tee) Indian movement that attempted to transcend the differences between Hinduism and Islam.

**Black Hand** Pre–World War I secret Serbian society; one of its members, Gavrilo Princip, assassinated Austrian archduke Francis Ferdinand and provided the spark for the outbreak of the Great War.

**Blitzkrieg** German style of rapid attack through the use of armor and air power that was used in Poland, Norway, Denmark, Belgium, the Netherlands, and France in 1939–1940.

**Bloodletting rituals** Ritual involving the shedding of human blood as a form of sacrifice to the gods, practiced by the Maya and Aztecs amongst many other societies.

**Bolshevik** (BOHL-shih-vehk) Russian communist party headed by Lenin.

**Bourgeoisie** Middle class in modern industrial society.

**Brahmins** (BRAH-minz) Hindu caste of priests.

**Brezhnev doctrine** Policy developed by Leonid Brezhnev (1906–1982) that claimed for the Soviet Union the right to invade any socialist country faced with internal or external enemies; the doctrine was best expressed in the Soviet invasion of Czechoslovakia.

**BRICs** Acronym for the fast-growing and developing economies of Brazil, Russia, India, and China.

**Buddha** (BOO-duh) The "enlightened one," the term applied to Siddhartha Gautama after his discoveries that would form the foundation of Buddhism.

**Buddhism** (BOO-diz'm) Religion, based on Four Noble Truths, associated with Siddhartha Gautama (563–483 B.C.E.), or the Buddha; its adherents desired to eliminate all distracting passion and reach nirvana.

**Bunraku** (boon-RAH-koo) Japanese puppet theater.

**Bush doctrine** A set of policies during the administration of American president George W. Bush (2001–2009) that advocated preemptive strikes by the United States against potential enemies instead of containment or deterrence.

**Byzantine empire** (BIHZ-ann-teen) Long-lasting empire centered at Constantinople; it grew out of the end of the Roman empire, carried the legacy of Roman greatness, and was the only classical society to survive into the early modern age; it reached its early peak during the reign of Justinian (483–565).

**Caesaropapism** Concept relating to the mixing of political and religious authority, as with the Roman emperors, that was central to the church-versus-state controversy in medieval Europe.

**Cahokia** (kuh-HOH-kee-uh) Large structure in modern Illinois that was constructed by the mound-building peoples; it was the third largest structure in the Americas before the arrival of the Europeans.

**Caliph** (KAL-ihf) "Deputy," Islamic leader after the death of Muhammad.

**Camillo di Cavour** 1810–1861 C.E. Prime Minister to King Vittorio Emmanuel II of Piedmont and Sardinia, and key figure in bringing about the unification of Italy.

**Capetian** (cah-PEE-shuhn) Early French dynasty that started with Hugh Capet.

**Capitalism** An economic system with origins in early modern Europe in which private parties make their goods and services available on a free market.

**Capitulation** Highly unfavorable trading agreements that the Ottoman Turks signed with the Europeans in the nineteenth century that symbolized the decline of the Ottomans.

**Captain James Cook** 1728–1779 C.E. British explorer, navigator, and cartographer who served in the British Royal Navy. Famous for his expeditions to the Pacific Ocean in the eighteenth century.

**Carolingians** Germanic dynasty that was named after its most famous member, Charlemagne.

**Caste** A system of social distinction that emerged in South Asia late in the second millennium B.C.E., which divides the population into a series of "classes" or varnas.

**Catherine the Great** 1729–1796 C.E. Catherine II was the longest-serving female ruler of Russia (from 1762 to 1796). She came to power by overthrowing her husband, Peter III, in a coup.

**Catholic Reformation** Sixteenth-century Catholic attempt to cure internal ills and confront Protestantism; it was inspired by the reforms of the Council of Trent and the actions of the Jesuits.

**Caudillos** (KAW-dee-ohs) Latin American term for nineteenth-century local military leaders.

**Central Powers** World War I term for the alliance of Germany, Austria-Hungary, and the Ottoman empire.

**Chaghatai** One of Chinggis Khan's sons, whose descendants ruled central Asia through the Chaghatai khanate.

**Chan Buddhism** (CHAHN BOO-diz'm) Influential branch of Buddhism in China, with an emphasis on intuition and sudden flashes of insight instead of textual study.

**Chandragupta Maurya** (chuhn-dra-GOOP-tah MORE-yuh) Founding ruler of the South Asian Mauryan Dynasty, who reigned from 321 to 297 B.C.E.

**Chang'an** (chahng-ahn) Capital city for various early Chinese dynasties, including the Qin, Han, and Tang.

**Charlemagne** Ruler of the European Carolingian Empire from 748–814 C.E.

**Charles V** Reigned 1519–1556. Emperor who inherited the Hapsburg family's Austrian territories as well as the Kingdom of Spain. When he became emperor in 1519, his empire stretched from Austria to Peru.

**Chavín culture** Mysterious but very popular South American religion (1000–300 B.C.E.).

**Chichén Itzá** (chee-CHEN eet-SAH) Major Mayan city located in the northern Yucatan Peninsula of modern Mexico.

**Chimu** Pre-Incan South American society that fell to the Incas in the fifteenth century.

**Chinampas** Agricultural gardens used by Mexica (Aztecs) in which fertile muck from lake bottoms was dredged and built up into small plots.

**Chinggis Khan** (CHIHN-gihs Kahn) 1162–1227 C.E. Founder and first Kahn (emperor) of the Mongol Empire, which became the largest contiguous land empire in the history of the world up to that time.

**Chivalry** European medieval code of conduct for knights based on loyalty and honor.

**Chola kingdom** Southern Indian Hindu kingdom (850–1267), a tightly centralized state that dominated sea trade.

**Christopher Columbus** 1451–1506 C.E. Italian explorer and navigator who made four transatlantic voyages to the islands off North America, which in turn opened the way for European colonization of the Americas.

**Chucuito** Pre-Incan South American society that rose in the twelfth century and fell to the Incas in the fifteenth century.

**City-state** Urban areas that controlled surrounding agricultural regions and that were often loosely connected in a broader political structure with other city-states.

**Civil Code** Civil law code promulgated by Napoleon Bonaparte in 1804.

**Civil service examinations** A battery of grueling tests given at the district, provincial, and metropolitan levels that determined entry into the Chinese civil service during the Ming and Qing dynasties.

**Cixi** 1835–1908 C.E. Former imperial concubine who established herself as effective ruler of the Qing dynasty in the fifty years prior to the end of Qing rule in 1908. She was hated by millions for her lavish spending, corruption, and resistance to reform.

**Cohong** Specially licensed Chinese firms that were under strict government regulation.

**Collectivization of agriculture** Process beginning in the late 1920s by which Stalin forced the Russian peasants off their own land and onto huge collective farms run by the state; millions died in the process.

**Colossal human heads** Large carved heads made of basalt, produced by the Olmec during the late-second and early-first millennia B.C.E.

**COMECON** The Council for Mutual Economic Assistance, which offered increased trade within the Soviet Union and eastern Europe; it was the Soviet alternative to the United States' Marshall Plan.

**Comfort women** Mainly Korean, Taiwanese, and Manchurian women who were forced into service by the Japanese army to serve as prostitutes to the Japanese troops during World War II.

**Communalism** A term, usually associated with India, that placed an emphasis on religious rather than national identity.

**Communism** Philosophy and movement that began in middle of the nineteenth century with the work of Karl Marx; it has the same general goals as socialism, but it includes the belief that violent revolution is necessary to destroy the bourgeois world and institute a new world run by and for the proletariat.

**Confucianism** (kuhn-FYOO-shuhn-iz'm) Philosophy, based on the teachings of the Chinese philosopher Kong Fuzi (551–479 B.C.E.), or Confucius, that emphasizes order, the role of the gentleman, obligation to society, and reciprocity.

**Congress of Vienna** Gathering of European diplomats in Vienna, Austria, from October 1814 to June 1815. The representatives of the "great powers" that defeated Napoleon—Britain, Austria, Prussia, and Russia—dominated the proceedings, which aimed to restore the prerevolutionary political and social order.

**Conquistadores** (kohn-KEE-stah-dohrayz) Spanish adventurers such as Cortés and Pizarro who conquered Central and South America in the sixteenth century.

**Constantine** Roman emperor who reigned from 306 to 337 C.E. and who moved the capital of the empire from Rome to Constantinople.

**Constantinople** The purpose-built capital of the late-Roman and Byzantine empires from the fourth to the fifteenth centuries. The name translates as "city of Constantine," the Roman emperor who founded the city.

**Constitutionalism** Movement in England in the seventeenth century that placed power in Parliament's hands as part of a constitutional monarchy and that increasingly limited the power of the monarch; the movement was highlighted by the English Civil War and the Glorious Revolution.

**Containment** Concept associated with the United States and specifically with the Truman Doctrine during the cold war that revolved around the notion that the United States would contain the spread of communism.

**Corporation** A concept that reached mature form in the 1860s in England and France; it involved private business owned by thousands of individual and institutional investors who financed the business through the purchase of stocks.

***Corpus iuris civilis*** (KOR-puhs yoor-uhs sih-VEE-lihs) *Body of the Civil Law,* the Byzantine emperor Justinian's attempt to codify all Roman law.

**Council of Trent** 1545–1563. Assembly of high Roman Catholic church officials which met over a period of years to institute reforms in order to increase morality and improve the preparation of priests.

**Crimean War** 1853–1856 C.E. War fought on the Crimean peninsula between Russia on one side and Great Britain, France, the Ottoman Empire, and Sardinia on the other.

**Criollos** (kree-OH-lohs) Creoles, people born in the Americas of Spanish or Portuguese ancestry.

**Cross staff** Device that sailors used to determine latitude by measuring the angle of the sun or the pole star above the horizon.

**Crystal Palace** Glass and iron structure that housed an exhibition in London in 1851 to display industrial products.

**Daimyo** (DEYEM-yoh) Powerful territorial lords in early modern Japan.

**Dao** Key element in Chinese philosophy that means the "way of nature" or the "way of the cosmos."

***Daodejing*** (DOW-DAY-JIHNG) Book that is the fundamental work of Daoism.

**Daoism** (DOW-i'zm) Chinese philosophy with origins in the Zhou dynasty; it is associated with legendary philosopher Laozi, and it called for a policy of noncompetition.

***Dar al-Islam*** The "house of Islam," a term for the Islamic world.

**Declaration of Independence** Drafted by Thomas Jefferson in 1776; the document expressed the ideas of John Locke and the Enlightenment, represented the idealism of the American rebels, and influenced other revolutions.

**Declaration of the Rights of Man and the Citizen** Document from the French Revolution (1789) that was influenced by the American Declaration of Independence and in turn influenced other revolutionary movements.

**Decolonization** Process by which former colonies achieved their independence, as with the newly emerging African nations in the 1950s and 1960s.

**Deism** (DEE-iz'm) An Enlightenment view that accepted the existence of a god but denied the supernatural aspects of Christianity; in deism, the universe was an orderly realm maintained by rational and natural laws.

**Deng Xiaoping** (duhng show-ping) 1904–1997 C.E. Chinese politician who led the People's Republic of China from 1978 to his retirement in 1992.

**Descamisados** "Shirtless ones," Argentine poor who supported Juan and Eva Perón.

**Détente** A reduction in cold war tension between the United States and the Soviet Union from 1969 to 1975.

**Devshirme** Ottoman requirement that the Christians in the Balkans provide young boys to be slaves of the sultan.

***Dhimmi*** (dihm-mee) Islamic concept of a protected people that was symbolic of Islamic toleration during the Mughal and Ottoman empires.

**Dhow** Indian, Persian, and Arab ships, one hundred to four hundred tons, that sailed and traded throughout the Indian Ocean basin.

**Diaspora** People who have settled far from their original homeland but who still share some measure of ethnic identity.

**Domingo Faustino Sarmiento** 1811–1888 C.E. Argentine intellectual, writer, and activist who became the seventh president of Argentina.

**Dominicans** An order of mendicants founded by St. Dominic (1170–1221 C.E.) whose purpose was to live in poverty and serve the religious needs of their communities.

**Dona Beatriz** 1684–1706 C.E. Kongo prophet and religious leader who founded her own Christian movement, Antonianism, which taught that Jesus was from the Kongo.

**Dreadnoughts** A class of British battleships whose heavy armaments made all other battleships obsolete overnight.

**Duma** Russian parliament, established after the Revolution of 1905.

**Dunhuang** Oasis in modern western China that became a site of Buddhist missionary activity by the fourth century C.E.

**Durham Report** Report issued in 1839 by the British Earl of Durham and recent governor-general of Canada, which advocated significant self-government for a united Canada.

**Dutch learning** European knowledge that reached Tokugawa Japan.

**East India Company** British joint-stock company that grew to be a state within a state in India; it possessed its own armed forces.

**Economic nationalism** Economic policies pursued by many governments affected by the Great Depression in which the nation tries to become economically self-sufficient by imposing high tariffs on foreign goods. The policy served to exacerbate the damaging effects of the Depression around the world.

**Eight-legged essay** Eight-part essays that an aspiring Chinese civil servant had to compose, mainly based on a knowledge of Confucius and the Zhou classics.

**Emancipation Manifesto** Manifesto proclaimed by the Russian Tsar Alexander II in 1861 that abolished the institution of serfdom and freed 23 million serfs.

**Emiliano Zapata** (eh-mee-LYAH-no zuh-PAH-tuh) 1879–1919 C.E. Mexican revolutionary and leader of the peasant revolution during the Mexican Revolution whose followers were called Zapatistas.

**Emilio Aguinaldo** (eh-MEE-lyoh AH-gee-NAHL-doh) 1869–1964 C.E. Filipino revolutionary who declared independence from Spain and then fought against the United States during its war of occupation.

**Emporia** Commercial establishments that specialize in products and services on a large scale, vital to the conduct of transregional trade.

***Encomienda*** (ehn-KOH-mee-ehn-dah) System that gave the Spanish settlers *(encomenderos)* the right to compel the indigenous peoples of the Americas to work in the mines or fields.

**Engenho** Brazilian sugar mill; the term also came to symbolize the entire complex world relating to the production of sugar.

**English Civil War** 1642–1649. A series of armed conflicts between the English crown and the English Parliament over political and religious differences.

**Enlightenment** Eighteenth-century philosophical movement that began in France; its emphasis was on the preeminence of reason rather than faith or tradition; it spread concepts from the Scientific Revolution.

**Epicureans** (ehp-ih-kyoo-REE-uhns) Hellenistic philosophers who taught that pleasure—as in quiet satisfaction—was the greatest good.

**Equal-field system** Chinese system during the Tang dynasty in which the goal was to ensure an equitable distribution of land.

**Eugenics** A late nineteenth- and early twentieth-century movement that sought to improve the gene pool of the human race by encouraging those deemed fit to have more children, and by discouraging those deemed unfit from reproducing. The movement was deeply tied to racism, and was eventually adopted by the German Nazi regime to justify the extermination of "undesirable" populations.

**Eunuchs** (YOO-nihks) Castrated males, originally in charge of the harem, who grew to play major roles in government; eunuchs were common in China and other societies.

**European Community (EC)** Organization of European states established in 1957; it was originally called the European Economic Community and was renamed the EC in 1967; it promoted economic growth and integration as the basis for a politically united Europe.

**European Union** Established by the Maastricht Treaty in 1993, a supranational organization for even greater European economic and political integration.

**Fascism** Political ideology and mass movement that was prominent in many parts of Europe between 1919 and 1945; it sought to regenerate the social, political, and cultural life of societies, especially in contrast to liberal democracy and socialism; fascism began with Mussolini in Italy, and it reached its peak with Hitler in Germany.

**Ferdinand Magellan** (FUR-dih-nand muh-JEHL-uhn) 1480–1521 C.E. Portuguese explorer famous for organizing the first circumnavigation of the globe, by ship, from 1519 to 1522.

**Five Pillars of Islam** The foundation of Islam: (1) profession of faith, (2) prayer, (3) fasting during Ramadan, (4) almsgiving, and (5) pilgrimage, or hajj.

**Five-year plans** First implemented by Stalin in the Soviet Union in 1928; five-year plans were a staple of communist regimes in which every aspect of production was determined in advance for a five-year period; five-year plans were the opposite of the free market concept.

**Foot binding** A practice that involved the tight wrapping of young girls' feet with strips of cloth that prevented natural growth of the bones and resulted in tiny, malformed curved feet.

**Franciscans** An order of mendicants founded by St. Francis (1182–1226 C.E.) whose purpose was to live in poverty and serve the religious needs of their communities.

**Franciso Pizarro** 1478–1541 C.E. Spanish conquistador whose military expeditions led to the fall of the Inca Empire.

**Franklin Delano Roosevelt** 1882–1945 C.E. American politician who served as the thirty-second president of the United States from 1933 until his death.

**Frederick Barbarossa** 1152–1190 C.E. Medieval emperor with lands in modern southern Germany who tried and failed to conquer Lombardy in modern Italy.

**Friedrich Engels** 1820–1895 C.E. German socialist philosopher who, with Karl Marx, founded modern communism and co-authored *The Communist Manifesto* (1848).

**Front de Libération Nationale (FLN)** The Algerian organization that fought a bloody guerrilla war for freedom against France.

**Fukuzawa Yukichi** 1835–1901. Prominent Japanese who traveled around Europe and North America after the Meiji Restoration to evaluate foreign administrative systems and constitutions.

**Fulani** (foo-LAH-nee) Sub-Saharan African people who, beginning in the seventeenth century, waged a series of wars designed to impose their own strict interpretation of Islam.

**Galileo Galilei** 1564–1642 C.E. Italian astronomer, engineer, and physicist from the town of Pisa, whose observations had a huge impact on the development of modern science.

**Gamal Abdel Nasser** 1918–1970 C.E. Second president of Egypt who led the overthrow of the monarchy in 1952 and served from 1954 until his death.

**Gauchos** (GOW-chohz) Argentine cowboys, highly romanticized figures.

**General Agreement on Tariffs and Trade (GATT)** Free-trade agreement first signed in 1947; by 1994 it had grown to 123 members and formed the World Trade Organization (WTO).

**Ghana** (GAH-nuh) Kingdom in west Africa during the fifth through the thirteenth century whose rulers eventually converted to Islam; its power and wealth was based on dominating trans-Saharan trade.

**Ghazi** (GAH-zee) Islamic religious warrior.

**Ghaznavids** Turkish tribe under Mahmud of Ghazni who moved into northern India in the eleventh century and began a period of greater Islamic influence in India.

**Glasnost** (GLAHS-nohst) Russian term meaning "openness" introduced by Mikhail Gorbachev in 1985 to describe the process of opening Soviet society to dissidents and public criticism.

**Global warming** The emission of greenhouse gases, which prevents solar heat from escaping the earth's atmosphere and leads to the gradual heating of the earth's environment.

**Globalization** The breaking down of traditional boundaries in the face of increasingly global financial and cultural trends.

**Glorious Revolution** 1688–1689. The events that led to the replacement of the Catholic English King James II by his Protestant daughter Mary II and her Dutch husband William of Orange.

**Golden Horde** Mongol tribe that controlled Russia from the thirteenth to the fifteenth century.

**Grand Canal** A huge network of canals that linked the Yangzi and Huang He river systems, and that eventually extended 2000 kilometers (1200 miles).

**Great Game** Nineteenth-century competition between Great Britain and Russia for the control of central Asia.

**Great** Zimbabwe Large sub-Saharan African kingdom in the fifteenth century.

**Greater East Asia Co-Prosperity Sphere** Japanese plan for consolidating east and southeast Asia under their control during World War II.

**Greek fire** Devastating incendiary weapon used mainly at sea by Byzantine forces in the seventh and eighth centuries C.E.

**Greenpeace** An environmental organization founded in 1970 and dedicated to the preservation of earth's natural resources.

**Griots** Professional singers, historians, and story-tellers in sub-Saharan Africa.

**Guomindang** (GWOH-mihn-dahng) Chinese nationalist party founded by Sun Yatsen (1866–1925) and later led by Jiang Jieshi; it has been centered in Taiwan since the end of the Chinese civil war.

**Gupta** (GOOP-tah) Indian dynasty (320–550 C.E.) that briefly reunited India after the collapse of the earlier Mauryan dynasty.

**Guru Kabir** 1440–1518 C.E. A blind weaver who became the most important teacher in the bhakti movement, which sought to harmonize Hinduism and Islam.

**Hacienda** (HAH-see-ehn-dah) Large Latin American estates.

***Hadith*** A collection of sayings of the Prophet Muhammad and accounts of his deeds.

**Hagia Sophia** (HAH-yah SOH-fee-uh) Massive Christian church constructed by the Byzantine emperor Justinian and later converted into a mosque.

**Hajj** (HAHJ) Pilgrimage to Mecca.

**Hammurabi's Code** (hahm-uh-RAH-beez) Sophisticated law code associated with the Babylonian king Hammurabi (r. 1792–1750 B.C.E.).

**Hangzhou** Capital of the Southern Song dynasty in the late thirteenth century.

**Hanseatic League** (han-see-AT-ik) A commercial confederation of merchant guilds and market towns in northwestern Europe that dominated Baltic trade from the thirteenth to the fifteenth centuries.

**Harsha** Ruler of northern India from 606 to 648 C.E.

**Harun al-Rashid** Powerful ruler of the Abbasid Caliphate who reigned from 789 to 809 C.E.

**Heian** (HAY-ahn) Japanese period (794–1185), a brilliant cultural era notable for the world's first novel, Murasaki Shikibu's *The Tale of Genji.*

**Hernán Cortés** 1485–1587 C.E. Spanish conquistador whose military expeditions led to the fall of the Aztec Empire.

***Hijra*** Muhammad's migration from Mecca to Medina in 622, which is the beginning point of the Islamic calendar and is considered to mark the beginning of the Islamic faith.

**Hinduism** Main religion of India, a combination of Dravidian and Aryan concepts; Hinduism's goal is to reach spiritual purity and union with the great world spirit; its important concepts include dharma, karma, and samsara.

**Hiroshima bombing** Bombing of the Japanese city on August 6, 1945 by an American bomber, which—along with the bombing of Nagasaki on August 9—led the Japanese to surrender and end World War II.

**Ho Chi Minh** 1890–1969 C.E. North Vietnamese revolutionary and politician who first fought the French and then the Americans, and then became the first prime minister of North Vietnam in 1945.

**Holocaust** German attempt in World War II to exterminate the Jews of Europe.

**Home front** Term made popular in World War I and World War II for the civilian "front" that was symbolic of the greater demands of total war.

**Hongwu** 1328–1398 C.E. Personal name Zhu Yuanzhang, was the founding emperor of the Ming dynasty in China. Reigned 1368–1398.

**Huitzilopochtli** (wee-tsee-loh-pockt-lee) Sun god and patron deity of the Aztecs.

**Hundred Days of Reform** Chinese reforms of 1898 led by Kang Youwei and Liang Qichao in their desire to turn China into a modern industrial power.

**Hundred Years' War** 1337–1453 C.E. Series of intermittent wars between France and England over the control of modern France.

**Huns** A militarized confederation of Central Asian nomads whose westward migration helped precipitate the collapse of the Western Roman Empire.

**Ibn Battuta** (ih-bun BAH-too-tah) Born 1304 in Morocco. Was the greatest Muslim traveler of his time. He covered 75,000 miles and visited almost every Muslim country and China.

**Ibn Rushd** (IB-uhn RUSHED) Known as Averroes in the West, he was an important Islamic philosopher whose intellectual contributions were also appreciated by many European scholars. He lived from 1126 to 1198 C.E.

**Iconoclasts** (eye-KAHN-oh-klasts) Supporters of the movement, begun by the Byzantine Emperor Leo III (r. 717–741), to destroy religious icons because their veneration was considered sinful.

**Ilkhanate** (EEL-kahn-ate) Mongol state that ruled Persia after abolition of the Abbasid empire in the thirteenth century.

**Imperialism** Term associated with the expansion of European powers and their conquest and colonization of African and Asian societies, mainly from the sixteenth through the nineteenth century.

**Inca empire** Powerful South American empire that would reach its peak in the fifteenth century during the reigns of Pachacuti Inca and Topa Inca.

**Indentured labor** Labor source for plantations; wealthy planters would pay the laboring poor to sell a portion of their working lives, usually seven years, in exchange for passage.

**India Act** 1935 British Act that transferred to India the institutions of a self-governing state.

**Indian Partition** Period immediately following Indian and Pakistani independence in 1947, in which millions of Muslims sought to move to Pakistan from India, and millions of Hindus sought to move from Pakistan to India. It was marked by brutal sectarian violence, and the deaths of between one half million and a million people.

**Indian Rebellion of 1857** Ultimately unsuccessful rebellion in North and Central India by a large portion of the Bengal Army and the civil population against British rule.

**Indira Gandhi** 1917–1984 C.E. Indian politician and daughter of Jawaharlal Nehru who became the first Indian female prime minister in 1966.

**Intifada** Palestinian mass movement against Israeli rule in the Gaza Strip and other occupied territories.

**Investiture** (ihn-VEHST-tih-tyoor) One aspect of the medieval European church-versus-state controversy, the granting of church offices by a lay leader.

**Iron metallurgy** The adoption and use of iron for weapons and tools.

**Iroquois** (EAR-uh-kwoi) Eastern American Indian confederation made up of the Mohawk, Oneida, Onondaga, Cayuga, and Seneca tribes.

**Isaac Newton** 1643–1727 C.E. English mathematician, physicist, and astronomer who played a key role in the Scientific Revolution.

**Isfahan** Capital city of the Safavid Empire (modern Iran), founded by Shah Abbas in the early seventeenth century.

**Islam** Monotheistic religion announced by the prophet Muhammad (570–632); influenced by Judaism and Christianity, Muhammad was considered the final prophet because the earlier religions had not seen the entire picture; the Quran is the holy book of Islam.

**Ismail.** Reigned 1501–1524. Founder of the Safavid dynasty in modern Iran.

**Jainism** (JEYEN-iz'm) Indian religion associated with the teacher Vardhamana Mahavira (ca. 540–468 B.C.E.) in which every physical object possessed a soul; Jains believe in complete nonviolence to all living beings.

**Janissaries** Highly respected, elite infantry units of the Ottoman Empire, who formed the first modern standing army in Europe.

**Jati** Indian word for a Hindu subcaste.

**Java** An island in modern Indonesia, and formerly home to the capital of the Dutch East Indies at the city of Batavia (modern Jakarta), founded 1619.

**Jawaharlal Nehru** 1889–1964 C.E. Indian activist and politician who fought for decades for Indian independence and became the first prime minister of India.

**Jenne-jeno** Settlement in the middle Niger River region in Africa that flourished from the fourth to the eighth centuries C.E. Known for iron production.

**Jews** A member of the people and cultural community whose traditional religion is Judaism and who trace their origins through the ancient Hebrew people of Israel to Abraham.

**Jiang Jieshi** (jyahng jeh-she) 1887–1975 C.E. Also known as Chiang Kai-Shek. Chinese nationalist revolutionary, military leader, and politician who led the Republic of China from 1928 to 1975, first in mainland China and then in Taiwan after the communist party won the civil war between them in 1949.

**Jihad** An Arabic term that literally translates as "struggle," and which has various meanings to Muslims, each of which refer to the imperative to spread Islam throughout the world.

**Jizya** (JIHZ-yuh) Tax in Islamic empires that was imposed on non-Muslims.

**John of Montecorvino** 1247–1328 C.E. Franciscan missionary who traveled to China in 1291 in order to win converts to Christianity.

**Joint-stock companies** Early forerunner of the modern corporation; individuals who invested in a trading or exploring venture could make huge profits while limiting their risk.

**Jomo Kenyatta** 1891–1978 C.E. Kenyan independence leader and politician who governed Kenya from its independence in 1963 until his death.

**Joseph Stalin** 1878–1953 C.E. Soviet revolutionary who led the Soviet Union from the mid-1920s to his death, whose policies resulted in the deaths of twenty million people.

**Junks** Ships used by merchants and others in the seas off China and Southeast Asia to carry commercial cargo.

**Justinian** Important early emperor of the Byzantine Empire, who reigned from 527 to 565 C.E.

**Ka'ba** (KAH-buh) Main shrine in Mecca, goal of Muslims embarking on the hajj.

**Kabuki** (kah-BOO-kee) Japanese theater in which actors were free to improvise and embellish the words.

**Kamikaze** (KAH-mih-kah-zee) A Japanese term meaning "divine wind" that is related to the storms that destroyed Mongol invasion fleets; the term is symbolic of Japanese isolation and was later taken by suicide pilots in World War II.

**Kangxi** (kahng-shee) 1654–1722 C.E. Fourth emperor of China's Qing dynasty, whose sixty-one-year rule was the longest in Chinese history.

**Kanun** (KAH-noon) Laws issued by the Ottoman Süleyman the Magnificent, also known as Süleyman Kanuni, "the Lawgiver."

**Kapu** Hawaiian concept of something being taboo.

**Karl Marx** 1818–1883 C.E. German philosopher and socialist revolutionary who founded, with Friedrich Engels, the modern communist movement and co-authored *The Communist Manifesto* (1848).

**Karma** (KAHR-mah) Hindu concept that the sum of good and bad in a person's life will determine his or her status in the next life.

**Khoikhoi** South African people referred to pejoratively as the Hottentots by Europeans.

**Khubilai Khan** (KOO-bih-lie Kahn) 1215–1294 C.E. Grandson of Chinggis Khan and founder of the Yuan dynasty in China in 1271.

**Khwarazm Shah** Ruler of Afghanistan and Persia in 1218, when Chinggis Khan sought to trade with his realm. After Khwarazm shah murdered Chingiss Khan's envoys, Chinggiss' forces devastated Persia in 1219.

**King Nzinga Mbemba** (Afonso I) (N-zinga MEHM-bah) 1456–1543 C.E. Ruler of Kongo in the first half of the sixteenth century, who became the first vassal king to Portugal.

**Knossos** City on the island of Crete that flourished during the Minoan period during the third millennium B.C.E.

**Kong Fuzi** 551–479 C.E. Original name of Confucius, Chinese philosopher and teacher of ethics.

**Kongo** Central African state that began trading with the Portuguese around 1500; although their kings, such as King Affonso I (r. 1506–1543), converted to Christianity, they nevertheless suffered from the slave trade.

**Koumbi-Saleh** Important trading city along the trans-Saharan trade route from the eleventh to the thirteenth century.

**Krishna** One of the incarnations of the Hindu god Vishnu, who appears in the Bhagavad-Gita as the teacher of Arjuna.

**Kshatriayas** (KSHAHT-ree-uhs) Hindu caste of warriors and aristocrats.

**Kulaks** Land-owning Russian peasants who benefited under Lenin's New Economic Policy and suffered under Stalin's forced collectivization.

**Kumiss** An alcoholic drink of the nomadic groups of Central Asia made of fermented mare's milk.

**Kush** Nubian African kingdom that conquered and controlled Egypt from 750 to 664 B.C.E.

**Kushan empire** Major Eurasian empire that controlled much of Central Asia and modern Pakistan and India during the first three centuries of the Common Era.

**Kwame Nkruhmah** (KWAH-mee en-KROO-mah) 1909–1972 C.E. Ghanaian politician and revolutionary who led the Gold Coast to independence in 1957 and served as the new country of Ghana's first prime minister.

**La Reforma** Political reform movement of Mexican president Benito Juárez (1806–1872) that called for limiting the power of the military and the Catholic church in Mexican society.

**Latifundia** (LAT-ih-FOON-dee-uh) Huge state-run and slave-worked farms in ancient Rome.

**Lázaro Cárdenas** 1895–1970. President of Mexico who nationalized the oil industry in 1938.

**League of Nations** Forerunner of the United Nations, the dream of American president Woodrow Wilson, although its potential was severely limited by the refusal of the United States to join.

**Lebensraum** (LAY-behnz-rowm) German term meaning "living space"; the term is associated with Hitler and his goal of carving out territory in the east for an expanding Germany.

**Lech Walesa** (LEHK WAH-lehn-sah) Leader of the Polish Solidarity movement.

**Legalism** Chinese philosophy from the Zhou dynasty that called for harsh suppression of the common people.

**Leonardo da Vinci** 1452–1519 C.E. Noted Italian painter, sculptor, architect, and engineer of the Renaissance period.

**Levée en masse** (leh-VAY on MASS) A term signifying universal conscription during the radical phase of the French revolution.

**Lili'uokalani** 1838–1917 C.E. The first and only queen of Hawaii, and the last Hawaiian sovereign to rule the islands prior to Hawai'i's annexation by the United States in 1898.

**Lin Zexu** 1785–1850 C.E. Chinese scholar and official appointed by the Qing government to destroy the illegal opium trade conducted by the British and other European and American traders.

**Linear A** Minoan written script.

**Linear B** Early Mycenaean written script, adapted from the Minoan Linear A.

**Little Ice Age** Period beginning in about 1300 C.E. when global temperatures declined for about 500 years.

**Louis Riel** 1844–1885 C.E. Leader of metis and indigenous people who organized the unsuccessful Northwest Rebellion against Canadian settlement in 1885. Riel was executed by Canadian authorities.

**Louis the Pious** 814–840 C.E. Only surviving son of Charlemagne, who held his father's empire together until his sons split it up after his death in 843.

**Louis XIV** (LOO-ee) 1638–1715 C.E. Also known as the Sun King, his seventy-two-year reign was the longest of any monarch in European history.

**Louis XVI** 1754–1793 C.E. The last king of France before the end of the French monarchy during the French Revolution, who was executed by guillotine.

**Luddites** Early-nineteenth-century artisans who were opposed to new machinery and industrialization.

**Machismo** (mah-CHEEZ-moh) Latin American social ethic that honored male strength, courage, aggressiveness, assertiveness, and cunning.

**Madrasas** (MAH-drahs-uhs) Islamic institutions of higher education that originated in the tenth century.

**Magyars** (MAH-jahrs) Hungarian invaders who raided towns in Germany, Italy, and France in the ninth and tenth centuries.

**Mahayana** (mah-huh-YAH-nah) The "greater vehicle," a more metaphysical and more popular northern branch of Buddhism.

**Maize** A plant whose domestication was crucial to the emergence of complex states in early Mesoamerica.

**Majapahit** (MAH-ja-PAHT) Southeast Asian kingdom (1293–1520) centered on the island of Java.

**Mali** (MAH-lee) West African kingdom founded in the thirteenth century by Sundiata; it reached its peak during the reign of Mansa Musa.

**Malintzin** 1500–1529 C.E. Nahua woman who acted as interpreter and advisor for Hernan Cortes.

**Manchus** Manchurians who conquered China, putting an end to the Ming dynasty and founding the Qing dynasty (1644–1911).

**Mandarin** A Chinese bureaucrat-scholar who worked for the government in Imperial China.

**Mandate of heaven** Chinese belief that the emperors ruled through the mandate, or approval, of heaven contingent on their ability to look after the welfare of the population.

**Mandate system** System that developed in the wake of World War I when the former colonies ended up mandates under European control, a thinly veiled attempt at continuing imperialism.

**Manila** City in modern Phillipines, and formerly capital of the Spanish colony of the Philippines, founded in 1565.

**Manor** Large estates of the nobles during the European middle ages, home for the majority of the peasants.

**Mansa Musa** (MAHN-suh MOO-suh) Reigned 1312–1337 C.E. Ruler of the wealthy and powerful Mali Empire in West Africa.

**Mao Zedong** 1893–1976 C.E. Chinese communist revolutionary who ruled China as the chairman of the Communist Party from 1949, when the communists defeated the nationalist Guomindang Party and forced its leaders to flee to Taiwan, until his death.

**Maori** (mow-ree) Indigenous people of New Zealand.

**Marae** Polynesian temple structure.

**Marathon** Battlefield scene of the Athenian victory over the Persians in 490 B.C.E.

**Marco Polo** 1254–1324 C.E. Italian merchant whose account of his travels to China and other lands became legendary.

**Maroons** Runaway African slaves.

**Marshall Plan** U.S. plan, officially called the European Recovery Program, that offered financial and other economic aid to all European states that had suffered from World War II, including Soviet bloc states.

**Martin Luther** 1483–1546. German monk and Catholic priest who became a critical figure in what became known as the Protestant Reformation after challenging the corruption of the church in his *Ninety-Five Theses,* published 1517.

**Mary Wollstonecraft** 1759–1797. English writer, philosopher, and advocate of women's rights, who wrote *A Vindication of the Rights of Woman* in 1792.

**Matteo Ricci** (maht-TAY-oh REE-chee) 1552–1610 C.E. Italian Jesuit who was one of the founders of the Jesuit China missions.

**Mauryan empire** Indian dynasty (321–185 B.C.E.) founded by Chandragupta Maurya and reaching its peak under Ashoka.

**May Fourth Movement** Chinese movement that began 4 May 1919 with a desire to eliminate imperialist influences and promote national unity.

**Maya ball game** Game in which Maya peoples used a hard rubber ball to propel through a ring without using their hands. Often used for ritual and ceremonial purposes.

**Maya** (Mye-uh) Brilliant Central American society (300–1100) known for math, astronomy, and a sophisticated written language.

**Mecca** Important city in modern Saudi Arabia, in which the hajj is conducted annually.

**Medes** (meeds) Indo-European branch that settled in northern Persia and eventually fell to another branch, the Persians, in the sixth century B.C.E.

**Medina** A city 345 kilometers (214 miles) north of Mecca, to which the Prophet Muhammad and his followers migrated in 622 C.E. Medina means "the city," as in "the city of the prophet."

**Meiji Restoration** (MAY-jee) Restoration of imperial rule under Emperor Meiji in 1868 by a coalition led by Fukuzawa Yukichi and Ito Hirobumi; the restoration enacted western reforms to strengthen Japan.

**Melaka** (may-LAH-kah) Southeast Asian kingdom that was predominantly Islamic.

**Mencius** (MEN-shi-us) Late-fourth/early-third century BCE Chinese philosopher recognized as one the most important followers of Confucius.

**Mesoamerica** (mez-oh-uh-MER-i-kuh) Another term for Central America.

**Mesopotamia** Term meaning "between the rivers," in this case the Tigris and Euphrates; Sumer and Akkad are two of the earliest societies.

**Mestizo** (mehs-TEE-zoh) Latin American term for children of Spanish and native parentage.

**Métis** (may-TEE) Canadian term for individuals of mixed European and indigenous ancestry.

**Mexica** (MEHK-si-kah) Nahuatl-speaking people from the Valley of Mexico who were the rulers of the Aztec Empire.

**Michaelangelo Buonarotti** 1475–1564 C.E. An Italian painter, sculptor, and architect of the Renaissance whose worked shaped the development of western art.

**Mikhail S. Gorbachev** 1931–. Soviet politician who served as the last leader of the Soviet Union from 1985 until 1991, when the Soviet Union dissolved.

**Millet** An autonomous, self-governing community in the Ottoman empire.

**Ming** Chinese dynasty (1368–1644) founded by Hongwu and known for its cultural brilliance.

**Minoan** (mih-NOH-uhn) Society located on the island of Crete (ca. 2000–1100 B.C.E.) that influenced the early Mycenaeans.

**Missi dominici** (mihs-see doh-mee-neechee) "Envoys of the lord ruler," the noble and church emissaries sent out by Charlemagne.

**Missionaries** People who travel on religious missions to help spread their faith.

**Moche** (moh-CHEE) Pre-Incan South American society (300–700) known for their brilliant ceramics.

**Modu** 210–174 B.C.E. Highly successful leader of the Xiongnu peoples of the Central Asian steppes.

**Mohandas Karamchand Gandhi** 1869–1948 C.E. Indian nationalist, politician, and lawyer who led the campaign against British rule by employing methods of nonviolent confrontation.

**Mohenjo-daro** Set of ancient cities in modern southeast Pakistan, near the Indus River, that flourished in the third millennium B.C.E.

**Monotheism** (MAW-noh-thee-iz'm) Belief in only one god, a rare concept in the ancient world.

**Monroe Doctrine** American doctrine issued in 1823 during the presidency of James Monroe that warned Europeans to keep their hands off Latin America and that expressed growing American imperialistic views regarding Latin America.

**Monsoon system** Seasonal winds that blow across the Indian subcontinent and Indian Ocean Basin that facilitated maritime trade during the early Silk Roads eras.

**Motecuzoma I** (mo-tek-oo-ZO-mah) c. 1397–1468. Fifth Aztec ruler whose conquests significantly extended Aztec rule beyond the Valley of Mexico.

**Motecuzoma II** (mo-tek-oo-ZO-mah) 1466–1520 C.E. Aztec emperor at the time of Hernan Cortes' invasion.

**Mughals** (MOO-guhls) Islamic dynasty that ruled India from the sixteenth through the eighteenth century; the construction of the Taj Mahal is representative of their splendor; with the exception of the enlightened reign of Akbar, the increasing conflict between Hindus and Muslims was another of their legacies.

**Muhammad Ali Jinnah** (moo-HAHM-ahd ah-lee JIN-uh) 1876–1948 C.E. Politician and independence fighter who led the All-India Muslim League from 1913 until the founding of Pakistan in 1947 and then served as the first leader of independent Pakistan until his death.

**Muhammad Ali** Reigned 1805–1848. Egyptian general who built a powerful army on the European model and became the effective ruler of Egypt in spite of its official status as an Ottoman territory.

**Muhammad** (muh-HAH-mehd) Prophet of Islam (570–632).

**Mujahideen** Meaning "Islamic warriors," a group who fought against Soviet intervention in Afghanistan in 1979. They were supplied and trained by United States CIA operatives, which helped lead to a Soviet withdrawal in 1989.

**Munich Conference** 1938 meeting between Germany, Great Britain, Italy, and France in which attendees agreed to German expansion in Czechoslovakia. The conference is considered part of the policy of appeasement that led Adolf Hitler to believe he had a free hand in Europe.

**Muslim** A follower of Islam.

**Mutsuhito** (MOO-tsoo-HEE-taw) 1852–1912 C.E. The first Meiji emperor of Japan who reigned from 1867 until his death. During his reign Japan transformed from a feudal to an industrial economy.

**Nam Viet** Early Chinese name for the modern nation of Vietnam.

**Napoleon Bonaparte** (nuh-POH-lee-uhn BOH-nuh-pahrt) 1769–1821 C.E. French military leader during the French Revolution who later seized power and crowned himself emperor from 1804 to 1814, and again in 1815 until he was defeated and exiled.

**National Policy** Nineteenth-century Canadian policy designed to attract migrants, protect industries through tariffs, and build national transportation systems.

**NATO** The North Atlantic Treaty Organization, which was established by the United States in 1949 as a regional military alliance against Soviet expansionism.

**Ndongo** (n'DAWN-goh) Angolan kingdom that reached its peak during the reign of Queen Nzinga (r. 1623–1663).

**Negritude** (NEH-grih-tood) "Blackness," a term coined by early African nationalists as a means of celebrating the heritage of black peoples around the world.

**Nelson Mandela** 1918–2013 C.E. South African revolutionary and politician who consistently fought against the apartheid state until its demise in 1994. He became the first black president of South Africa, and served from 1994 to 1999.

**Neo-Confucianism** (nee-oh-kuhn-FYOO-shuhn-iz'm) Philosophy that attempted to merge certain basic elements of Confucian and Buddhist thought; most important of the early Neo-Confucianists was the Chinese thinker Zhu Xi (1130–1200).

**Nestorian** (neh-STOHR-ee-uhn) Early branch of Christianity, named after the fifth-century Greek theologian Nestorius, that emphasized the human nature of Jesus Christ.

**New Economic Policy (NEP)** Plan implemented by Lenin that called for minor free-market reforms.

**Nicholas II** Reigned 1894–1917. Russian tsar who was first deposed and then executed, along with his family, in the Russian Revolution.

**Nicolaus Copernicus** 1473–1543 C.E. Polish astronomer who theorized that the Sun, rather than the Earth, lay at the center of the universe.

**Nile River** The world's longest river, it flows 6695 km (4160 mi) from Lake Victoria through Egypt to the Mediterranean Sea.

**Nonaligned Movement** Movement in which leaders of former colonial states sought to assert their independence from either Soviet or U.S. domination. The initial meeting was held in 1955 in Bandung, Indonesia.

**North American Free Trade Agreement (NAFTA)** Regional accord established in 1993 between the United States, Canada, and Mexico; it formed the world's second largest free-trade zone.

**Nubia** (NOO-bee-uh) Area south of Egypt; the kingdom of Kush in Nubia invaded and dominated Egypt from 750 to 664 B.C.E.

**Nubians** a member of one of the group of peoples that formed a powerful empire between Egypt and Ethiopia from the sixth to the fourteenth centuries.

**Oceania** Term referring to the Pacific Ocean basin and its lands.

**Olaudah Equiano** (oh-LAU-duh eh-kwee-AHN-oh) 1745–1797 C.E. Writer and abolitionist from the Kingdom of Benin who was sold into slavery but purchased his freedom in 1766.

**Olmecs** Early Mesoamerican society (1200–100 B.C.E.) that centered on sites at San Lorenzo, La Venta, and Tres Zapotes and that influenced later Maya.

**Olympe de Gouges** 1748–1793 C.E. French feminist who authored the Declaration of the Rights of Woman and the Female Citizen at the start of the French Revolution in 1789, which advocated for equal rights for women. De Gouges was later executed by the Jacobins during the Terror.

**Olympic Games** A Pan-Hellenic festival in which competitors from all over ancient Greece competed in athletic competitions, founded according to tradition in 776 B.C.E.

**Organization of African Unity (OAU)** An organization started in 1963 by thirty-two newly independent African states and designed to prevent conflict that would lead to intervention by former colonial powers.

**Organization of Petroleum Exporting Countries (OPEC)** An organization begun in 1960 by oil-producing states originally for purely economic reasons but that later had more political influence.

**Osama bin Laden** 1957–2011 C.E. Saudi Arabian-born founder of the militant pan-Islamic organization al-Qaeda responsible for planning the September 11, 2001, attacks in the United States.

**Osman** (os-MAHN) 1258–1326 C.E. Also known as Osman Gazi. Founder of the Ottoman dynasty and the Ottoman state.

**Otto von Bismarck** 1815–1898 C.E. Conservative German statesman who engineered the unification of Germany and then served as its first chancellor until 1890.

**Ottoman empire** Powerful Turkish empire that lasted from the conquest of Constantinople (Istanbul) in 1453 until 1918 and reached its peak during the reign of Süleyman the Magnificent (r. 1520–1566).

**Palestinian Liberation Organization (PLO)** Organization created in 1964 under the leadership of Yasser Arafat to champion Palestinian rights.

**Papacy** The office or authority of the pope.

**Paris Peace Accords** Agreement reached in 1973 that marked the end of the United States' role in the Vietnam War.

***Paterfamilias*** (PAH-tur fuh-MEE-lee-ahs) Roman term for the "father of the family," a theoretical implication that gave the male head of the family almost unlimited authority.

**Patriarch** (PAY-tree-ahrk) Leader of the Greek Orthodox church, which in 1054 officially split with the pope and the Roman Catholic church.

**Patricians** Roman aristocrats and wealthy classes.

***Pax romana*** (pahks roh-MAH-nah) "Roman Peace," a term that relates to the period of political stability, cultural brilliance, and economic prosperity beginning with unification under Augustus and lasting through the first two centuries C.E.

**Peninsulares** (pehn-IHN-soo-LAH-rayz) Latin American officials from Spain or Portugal.

**Perestroika** (PAYR-eh-stroy-kuh) "Restructuring," a Russian term associated with Gorbachev's effort to reorganize the Soviet state.

**Period of the Warring States** Last centuries of the Zhou dynasty (403–221 B.C.E.) when wars divided the region until the establishment of the Qin dynasty ended the disunity.

**Peter the Great** Reigned 1682–1725. Russian tsar of the Romanov family who sought to modernize Russia based on the model established by western European states.

**Pico** Pico della Mirandola, 1463–1494 C.E. Italian humanist who sought to harmonize the various religions and philosophies of the world.

**Plato** Athenian Greek philosopher, a pupil of Socrates, who lived from 430 to 347 B.C.E.

**Pogrom** Yiddish word meaning "devastation," referring to an organized massacre of a particular ethnic group—especially Jews in Eastern Europe.

**Popol Vuh** (paw-pawl vuh) Mayan creation epic.

**Porcelain** A very light, thin and adaptable type of pottery that, when fired with glazes, became a highly valuable export commodity during the Tang and Song dynasty.

**Porfirio Díaz** (pohr-FEER-eeo DEE-ahs) 1830–1915 C.E. Mexican general and politician who served seven terms as president, for a total of thirty-one years.

**Potosí** (paw-taw-SEE) City in the central highlands of modern-day Bolivia that became the world's largest silver-producing area after silver was discovered in 1545.

**Prague Spring** Period in 1968 in which the communist leader of Czechoslovakia, Alexander Dubcek, launched a reform movement aimed at softening Soviet-style rule. The movement was crushed when Russian forces invaded.

**Proletariat** Urban working class in a modern industrial society.

**Protestant Reformation** Sixteenth-century European movement during which Luther, Calvin, Zwingli, and others broke away from the Catholic church.

**Protoindustrialization** Also called the "putting-out system," in which entrepreneurs delivered raw materials to families in the countryside, who would then spin and weave the materials into garments. The entrepreneurs would then pick up the garments, pay the families, and sell them on the market.

**Putting-out system** Method of getting around guild control by delivering unfinished materials to rural households for completion.

***Qadi*** Islamic judge.

***Qanat*** (kah-NAHT) Persian underground canal.

**Qianlong** (chyahn-lawng) 1711–1799 C.E. Sixth emperor of China's Qing dynasty and grandson of Kangxi.

**Qin Shihuangdi** (chihn she-huang-dee) First emperor of the short-lived but highly influential Qin Dynasty, who reigned from 221 to 210 B.C.E.

**Qin** (chihn) Chinese dynasty (221–207 B.C.E.) that was founded by Qin Shihuangdi and was marked by the first unification of China and the early construction of defensive walls.

**Qing** (chihng) Chinese dynasty (1644–1911) that reached its peak during the reigns of Kangxi and Qianlong.

***Qizilbash*** (gih-ZIHL-bahsh) Term meaning "red heads," Turkish tribes that were important allies of Shah Ismail in the formation of the Safavid empire.

**Queen Nzinga** (N-zinga) 1583–1663 C.E. Seventeenth-century queen of the Ndongo and Matamba kingdoms in modern-day Angola.

**Quetzalcoatl** (keht-zahl-koh-AHT'l) Aztec god, the "feathered serpent," who was borrowed originally from the Toltecs; Quetzalcoatl was believed to have been defeated by another god and exiled, and he promised to return.

**Quinto** (KEEN-toh) The one-fifth of Mexican and Peruvian silver production that was reserved for the Spanish monarchy.

**Quipu** (KEE-poo) Incan mnemonic aid comprised of different-colored strings and knots that served to record events in the absence of a written text.

**Quran** (koo-RAHN) Islamic holy book that is believed to contain the divine revelations of Allah as presented to Muhammad.

**Raja** Sanskrit term for "king."

**Ram Mohan Roy** 1772–1833 C.E. Bengali intellectual who sought to harmonize aspects of European society with those of Indian society with the goal of reforming India along progressive lines.

**Rape of Nanjing** Japanese conquest and destruction of the Chinese city of Nanjing in the 1930s.

**Re** Sun god in ancient Egypt, and the chief deity among Egyptian gods.

***Realpolitik*** (ray-AHL-poh-lih-teek) The Prussian Otto von Bismarck's "politics of reality," the belief that only the willingness to use force would actually bring about change.

**Reconquista** (ray-kohn-KEE-stah) Crusade, ending in 1492, to drive the Islamic forces out of Spain.

**Reconstruction** System implemented in the American South (1867–1877) that was designed to bring the Confederate states back into the union and also extend civil rights to freed slaves.

**Relics** Physical remains of saints or religious figures assembled by churches for veneration.

**Rhapta** Port that emerged as a principal commercial center in East Africa in the centuries around the turn of the millennium.

**Roman Empire** An empire that succeeded the Roman Republic during the reign of Augustus, which dates from 27 B.C.E. to 395 C.E.

**Romanov dynasty** (ROH-mah-nahv) Russian dynasty (1610–1917) founded by Mikhail Romanov and ending with Nicholas II.

**Ronald Reagan** 1911–2004. Fortieth president of the United States, who served from 1981 to 1989. Reagan was noted for his anti-communism.

**Rubaiyat** (ROO-bee-aht) "Quatrains," famous poetry of Omar Khayyam that was later translated by Edward Fitzgerald.

**Saddam Hussein** 1937–2006 C.E. The fifth president of Iraq, who served from 1979 to 2003 until he was ousted by a coalition led by the United States.

**Safavid empire** (SAH-fah-vihd) Later Persian empire (1501–1722) that was founded by Shah Ismail and that became a center for Shiism; the empire reached its peak under Shah Abbas the Great and was centered on the capital of Isfahan.

**Sakk** Letters of credit that were common in the medieval Islamic banking world.

**Saladin** 1137–1193 C.E. Muslim leader and crusader who recaptured Jerusalem from the Christians in 1187.

**Samurai** (SAM-uhr-eye) A Japanese warrior.

**Sanskrit** Original and "sacred" language of the Indo-Aryans.

**Sasanians** (suh-SAHN-iens) Powerful empire that ruled much of Central Asia and Mesopotamia from 224 to 651 C.E.

**Sati** (SUH-TEE) Also known as *suttee,* Indian practice of a widow throwing herself on the funeral pyre of her husband.

**Satyagraha** (SAH-tyah-GRAH-hah) "Truth and firmness," a term associated with Gandhi's policy of passive resistance.

**Schism** Mutual excommunication of the Roman pope and Byzantine patriarch in 1054 over ritual, doctrinal, and political differences between the two Christian churches.

**Schlieffen plan** (SHLEE-fn) The name of German war plans to deal with a war in which battles would have to be fought on two fronts. The plan was implemented at the start of World War I, when it was clear that Germany would go to war with Russia and France.

**Scholasticism** Medieval attempt of thinkers such as St. Thomas Aquinas to merge the beliefs of Christianity with the logical rigor of Greek philosophy.

**Scientific racism** Nineteenth-century attempt to justify racism by scientific means; an example would be Gobineau's *Essay on the Inequality of the Human Races.*

**Scramble for Africa** Period between about 1875 and 1900 in which European powers sought to colonize as much of the African continent as possible.

**Self-determination** Belief popular in World War I and after that every people should have the right to determine their own political destiny; the belief was often cited but ignored by the Great Powers.

**Self-Strengthening Movement** Chinese attempt (1860–1895) to blend Chinese cultural traditions with European industrial technology.

**Seljuqs** (sahl-JYOOKS) Turkish tribe that gained control over the Abbasid empire and fought with the Byzantine empire.

**Sepoys** Indian troops who served the British.

**Serfs** Peasants who, though not chattel slaves, were tied to the land and who owed obligation to the lords on whose land they worked.

**Sergei Witte** (SAYR-gay VIHT-tee) Late-nineteenth-century Russian minister of finance who pushed for industrialization.

**Sericulture** The cultivation of silkworms for the production of silk.

**Shah Abbas the Great** 1571–1629 C.E. Fifth Safavid Shah of Iran who is generally considered the strongest of the Safavid rulers.

**Shah Jahan** 1592–1666 C.E. Fifth Mughal emperor who commissioned the building of the Taj Mahal for his wife, Mumtaz.

**Shamanism** (SHAH-mah-niz'm) Belief in shamans or religious specialists who possessed supernatural powers and who communicated with the gods and the spirits of nature.

**Shang dynasty** Dynasty of ancient China that ruled, according to tradition, from 1766–1122 B.C.E.

**Shang Yang** 390–338 B.C.E. Minister to the Duke of Qin state in Western China, and important developer of the political philosophy of Legalism.

**Sharia** (shah-REE-ah) The Islamic holy law, drawn up by theologians from the Quran and accounts of Muhammad's life.

**Shia** (SHEE-ah) Islamic minority in opposition to the Sunni majority; their belief is that leadership should reside in the line descended from Ali.

**Shintoism** (SHIHN-toh-iz'm) Indigenous Japanese religion that emphasizes purity, clan loyalty, and the divinity of the emperor.

**Shiva** (SHEE-vuh) Hindu god associated with both fertility and destruction.

**Shogun** (SHOH-gun) Japanese military leader who ruled in place of the emperor.

**Shudras** (SHOO-druhs) Hindu caste of landless peasants and serfs.

**Siberia** Region to the east of Russia in northeastern Europe, which was conquered by the Russians between 1581 and 1639.

**Siddhartha Gautama** (sih-DHAR-tuh GOW-tau-mah) Indian *kshatriya* who achieved enlightenment and became known as the Buddha, the founder of Buddhism.

**Sikhs** (SIHKS) Adherents of an Indian syncretic faith that contains elements of Hinduism and Islam.

**Silk Roads** An extensive network of trade routes that linked much of Eurasia with North Africa during the Classical Period.

**Silla dynasty** Important early Korean dynasty that flourished during the seventh and eighth centuries.

**Simón Bolívar** (see-MOHN boh-LEE-vahr) 1783–1830 C.E. Venezuelan military and political leader who led a number of Latin American states to independence from the Spanish.

**Sinicization** Process by which non–Han Chinese people come under the cultural or political domination of Han Chinese.

**Sino-Japanese War** War between China and Japan from 1897 to 1901, over the status of Korea. The Chinese were badly defeated.

**Social Darwinism** Nineteenth-century philosophy, championed by thinkers such as Herbert Spencer, that attempted to apply Darwinian "survival of the fittest" to the social and political realm; adherents saw the elimination of weaker nations as part of a natural process and used the philosophy to justify war.

**Socialism** Political and economic theory of social organization based on the collective ownership of the means of production; its origins were in the early nineteenth century, and it differs from communism by a desire for slow or moderate change compared with the communist call for revolution.

**Socrates** (SAHK-rah-teez) Athenian Greek philosopher who lived from 470 to 399 B.C.E.

**Solidarity** Polish trade union and nationalist movement in the 1980s that was headed by Lech Walesa.

**Song Taizu** (sawng tahy-zoo) First emperor of the Chinese Song dynasty who reigned from 960 to 976 C.E.

**Song** (SOHNG) Chinese dynasty (960–1279) that was marked by an increasingly urbanized and cosmopolitan society.

**Soviets** Russian elected councils that originated as strike committees during the 1905 St. Petersburg disorders; they represented a form of local self-government that went on to become the primary unit of government in the Union of Soviet Socialist Republics. The term was also used during the cold war to designate the Soviet Union.

**Spanish Inquisition** Institution organized in 1478 by Fernando and Isabel of Spain to detect heresy and the secret practice of Judaism or Islam.

**Sparta** Important city state of ancient Greece, located in the Peloponnesus region.

**Srivijaya** (sree-VIH-juh-yuh) Southeast Asian kingdom (670–1025), based on the island of Sumatra, that used a powerful navy to dominate trade.

**St. Ignatius Loyola** 1491–1556 C.E. A Basque nobleman and soldier who later devoted his life to religion and founded the missionary Society of Jesus (the Jesuits).

**St. Thomas Aquinas** (uh-KWIY-nuhs) 1225–1274 C.E. An Italian Dominican friar and Catholic priest whose religious writings became enormously influential in the school of Scholasticism.

**Stateless societies** Term relating to societies such as those of sub-Saharan Africa after the Bantu migrations that featured decentralized rule through family and kinship groups instead of strongly centralized hierarchies.

**Strategic Arms Limitation Talks (SALT)** Agreement in 1972 between the United States and the Soviet Union.

**Sufis** (SOO-fees) Islamic mystics who placed more emphasis on emotion and devotion than on strict adherence to rules.

**Sui dynasty** (SWAY) Chinese dynasty (589–618) that constructed the Grand Canal, reunified China, and allowed for the splendor of the Tang dynasty that followed.

**Sui Yangdi** (sway yahng-dee) Second emperor of the Chinese Sui Dynasty, responsible for the construction of the Chinese Grand Canal system, who reigned from 604–618 C.E.

**Süleyman** (SOO-lee-mahn) Ottoman Turkish ruler Süleyman the Magnificent (r. 1520–1566), who was the most powerful and wealthy ruler of the sixteenth century.

**Sultan Selim III** Reigned 1789–1807. Ottoman sultan whose efforts at reform threatened his elite fighting corps (the Jannissaries), who revolted and locked him up.

**Sun Yatsen** 1866–1925 C.E. Chinese physician and politician who founded the Chinese nationalist Guomindang Party and then briefly served as the first president of the Republic of China.

**Sundiata** (soon-JAH-tuh) Founder of the Mali empire (r. 1230–1255), also the inspiration for the *Sundiata*, an African literary and mythological work.

**Sunni** (SOON-nee) "Traditionalists," the most popular branch of Islam; Sunnis believe in the legitimacy of the early caliphs, compared with the Shiite belief that only a descendant of Ali can lead.

**Suu Kyi, Aung San** (SOO KEY, AWNG SAHN) Opposition leader (1945–) in Myanmar; she was elected leader in 1990 but she was not allowed to come to power; she was a Nobel Peace Prize recipient in 1991. She was finally released from house arrest in November 2010.

**Swahili** (swah-HEE-lee) East African city-state society that dominated the coast from Mogadishu to Kilwa and was active in trade. Also a Bantu language of East Africa, or a member of a group who speaks this language.

**Sykes-Picot Treaty** Secret 1917 treaty between the British and French, with the agreement of Russia, to divide the modern Middle East between them after the end of World War I.

**Taíno** (TEYE-noh) A Caribbean tribe who were the first indigenous peoples from the Americas to come into contact with Christopher Columbus.

**Taiping rebellion** (TEYE-pihng) Rebellion (1850–1864) in Qing China led by Hong Xiuquan, during which twenty to thirty million were killed; the rebellion was symbolic of the decline of China during the nineteenth century.

***Tale of Genji*** Japanese literary work written during the Heian Period (794–1185 C.E.) by the aristocratic woman Murasaki Shikibu.

**Taliban** Strict Islamic organization that ruled Afghanistan from 1996 to 2002.

**Tamerlane** (TAM-er-lane) 1336–1405 C.E. Also known as Timur. Founder of the Timurid Empire in modern-day Iran and Central Asia.

**Tang dynasty** Powerful and wealthy Chinese dynasty that ruled a vast East Asian empire from 618 to 907 C.E.

**Tang Taizong** (TAHNG TEYE-zohng) Chinese emperor (r. 627–649) of the Tang dynasty (618 to 907).

**Tanzimat era** "Reorganization" era (1839–1876), an attempt to reorganize the Ottoman empire on Enlightenment and constitutional forms.

**Temüjin** (TEM-oo-chin) Mongol conqueror (ca. 1167–1227) who later took the name Chinggis Khan, "universal ruler."

**Tenochtitlan** (the-NOCH-tee-tlahn) Capital of the Aztec empire, later Mexico City.

**Teotihuacan** (tay-uh-tee-wah-KAHN) Central American society (200 B.C.E.–750 C.E.); its Pyramid of the Sun was the largest structure in Mesoamerica.

***Terra australis incognita*** Meaning "unknown southern land," it refers to land that European explorers had speculated must exist in the world's southern hemisphere from the second to the eighteenth centuries.

***Terra Nullius*** Concept meaning "land belonging to no one" used frequently by colonial powers who sought to justify the conquest of nomadic lands.

**Theodor Herzl** 1860–1904 C.E. Jewish Austro-Hungarian writer and journalist who founded the modern Zionist movement.

**Theodora** Wife of the Emperor Justinian, who played a key role in the success of his reign.

**Third Rome** Concept that a new power would rise up to carry the legacy of Roman greatness after the decline of the Second Rome, Constantinople; Moscow was referred to as the Third Rome during the fifteenth century.

**Three estates** The three classes of European society, composed of the clergy (the first estate), the aristocrats (the second estate), and the common people (the third estate).

**Three Principles of the People** Philosophy of Chinese Guomindang leader Sun Yatsen (1866–1925) that emphasized nationalism, democracy, and people's livelihood.

**Tikal** (tee-KAHL) Maya political center from the fourth through the ninth century.

**Timbuktu** (tim-buhk-TOO) City in the Mali Empire known for its large population, wealth, and places of learning.

**Timur-i lang** (tee-MOOR-yee LAHNG) "Timur the Lame," known in English as Tamerlane (ca. 1336–1405), who conquered an empire ranging from the Black Sea to Samarkand.

**Tokugawa bakufu** Feudal style of government that ruled Japan under the direction of shoguns from 1603 until the Meiji Restoration in 1868.

**Tokugawa Ieyasu** (TOH-koo-GAH-wah) 1543–1616 C.E. Founder and first shogun of the Tokugawa dynasty in Japan.

**Tokugawa** (TOH-koo-GAH-wah) Last shogunate in Japanese history (1600–1867); it was founded by Tokugawa Ieyasu who was notable for unifying Japan.

**Toltecs** Central American society (950–1150) that was centered on the city of Tula.

**Toussaint Louverture** (too-SAHNT loo-vehr-TOOR) 1743–1803 C.E. Haitian general and leader of the Haitian Revolution against the French until his death in a French prison.

**Trail of Tears** Forced relocation of the Cherokee from the eastern woodlands to Oklahoma (1837–1838); it was symbolic of U.S. expansion and destruction of indigenous Indian societies.

**Treaty of Nanjing** 1842 Treaty forced on China by Great Britain after Britain's victory in the first Opium War, which forcibly opened China to western trade and settlement.

**Treaty of Versailles** 1919 treaty between the victorious Entente powers and defeated Germany at the end of World War I, which laid the blame for the war on Germany and exacted harsh reparations.

**Treaty of Waitangi** Treaty between British government and indigenous Maori peoples of New Zealand in 1840 that was interpreted differently by both sides and thus created substantial Maori opposition to British settlement.

**Triangular trade** Trade between Europe, Africa, and the Americas that featured finished products from Europe, slaves from Africa, and American products bound for Europe.

**Triple Alliance** Pre–World War I alliance of Germany, Austria-Hungary, and Italy.

**Triple Entente** (ahn-TAHNT) Pre–World War I alliance of England, France, and Russia.

**Troubadors** A class of traveling poets and entertainers enthusiastically patronized by Medieval aristocratic women in modern southern France and northern Italy.

**Truman Doctrine** U.S. policy instituted in 1947 by President Harry Truman in which the United States would follow an interventionist foreign policy to contain communism.

**Tsar Alexander II** 1818–1881 C.E. Emperor of Russia from 1855 until his assassination, best known for his emancipation of the serfs in 1861.

**Tsar** (ZAHR) Old Russian term for king that is derived from the term *caesar.*

**Tula** Original region of the Toltec people, located to the northwest of modern Mexico City.

**Twelver Shiism** (SHEE'i'zm) Branch of Islam that stressed that there were twelve perfect religious leaders after Muhammad and that the twelfth went into hiding and would return someday; Shah Ismail spread this variety through the Safavid empire.

**Uighurs** (WEE-goors) Turkish tribe.

**Ukiyo** Japanese word for the "floating worlds," a Buddhist term for the insignificance of the world that came to represent the urban centers in Tokugawa Japan.

**Ulaanbaatar** (OO-lahn-bah-tahr) Mongolian city.

***Ulama*** Islamic officials, scholars who shaped public policy in accordance with the Quran and the *sharia.*

**Umayyad** (oo-MEYE-ahd) Arabic dynasty (661–750), with its capital at Damascus, that was marked by a tremendous period of expansion to Spain in the west and India in the east.

***Umma*** (UM-mah) Islamic term for the "community of the faithful."

**United Nations (UN)** Successor to the League of Nations, an association of sovereign nations that attempts to find solutions to global problems.

**Untouchables** Lowest caste (or varna) in the South Asian caste system.

**Upanishads** (oo-PAHN-ee-shahds) Indian reflections and dialogues (800–400 B.C.E.) that reflected basic Hindu concepts.

**Urdu** (OOR-doo) A language that is predominant in Pakistan.

**Uruk** (OO-rook) Ancient Mesopotamian city from the fourth millennium B.C.E. that was allegedly the home of the fabled Gilgamesh.

**Utopian socialism** Movement that emerged around 1830 to establish ideal communities that would provide the foundation for an equitable society.

**Vaishyas** (VEYES-yuhs) Hindu caste of cultivators, artisans, and merchants.

**Vaqueros** (vah-KEHR-ohs) Latin American cowboys, similar to the Argentine gaucho.

***Varna*** (VAHR-nuh) Hindu word for caste.

**Velvet revolution** A term that describes the nonviolent transfer of power in Czechoslovakia during the collapse of Soviet rule.

**Venta, La** (VEHN-tuh, lah) Early Olmec center (800–400 B.C.E.).

**Vernacular** (ver-NA-kyoo-lar) The language of the people; Martin Luther translated the Bible from the Latin of the Catholic church into the vernacular German.

**Versailles** (vehr-SEYE) Palace of French King Louis XIV.

**Viet Minh** North Vietnamese nationalist communists under Ho Chi Minh.

**Vietnamization** President Richard Nixon's strategy of turning the Vietnam War over to the South Vietnamese.

**Vijayanagar kingdom** (vee-juh-yah-NAH-gahr) Southern Indian kingdom (1336–1565) that later fell to the Mughals.

**Vikings** A group that raided the British Isles from their home at Vik in southern Norway.

**Vishnu** (VIHSH-noo) Hindu god, preserver of the world, who was often incarnated as Krishna.

**Vladimir Ilyich Lenin** (VLAD-uh-meer IL yich LEHN-in) 1870–1954 C.E. Russian revolutionary and politician who led the Bolshevik Revolution in November 1917 and became the first head of state of the Soviet Union until his death.

**Vo Nguyen Giap** 1912–2013. Vietnamese general who served as Ho Chi Minh's right-hand man and is credited with the strategy behind the Vietnamese victory at the battle of Dien Bien Phu.

***Volksgeist*** (FOHLKS-geyest) "People's spirit," a term that was coined by the German philosopher Herder; a nation's volksgeist would not come to maturity unless people studied their own unique culture and traditions.

***Volta do mar*** (VOHL-tah doh MAHR) "Return through the sea," a fifteenth-century Portuguese sea route that took advantage of the prevailing winds and currents.

**Voltaire** (vohl-TAIR) 1712–1778 C.E. French Enlightenment writer and philosopher famous for his wit and criticism of the Catholic church. His real name was Francois-Marie Arouet.

**Voudou** (voh-DOW) Syncretic religion practiced by enslaved Africans and their descendants in Haiti.

**W. E. B. DuBois** 1868–1963. African American activist and intellectual who championed the movement of American blacks back to Africa.

**Wanli** (wahn-LEE) Chinese Ming emperor (r. 1572–1620) whose refusal to meet with officials hurried the decline of the Ming dynasty.

**War Communism** The Bolshevik policy of nationalizing industry and seizing private land during the civil war.

**Warsaw Pact** Warsaw Treaty Organization, a military alliance formed by Soviet bloc nations in 1955 in response to rearmament of West Germany and its inclusion in NATO.

**Wind wheels** Prevailing wind patterns in the Atlantic and Pacific Oceans north and south of the equator; their discovery made sailing much safer and quicker.

**Winston Churchill** 1874–1965 C.E. British politician who was prime minister of the United Kingdom from 1940 to 1945, during which time he led the British to victory.

**Witch hunts** Period in the sixteenth and seventeenth centuries in which about 110,000 people (mainly women) were tried as witches in western Europe.

**Woodrow Wilson** 1856–1924. President of the United States during World War I and author of the "Fourteen Points," one of which envisioned the establishment of the League of Nations.

**World Health Organization (WHO)** United Nations organization designed to deal with global health issues.

**World Trade Organization (WTO)** An organization that was established in 1995 with more than 120 nations and whose goal is to loosen barriers to free trade.

**Wu Zhao** 626–706 C.E. Concubine of Emperor Tang Taizong, who seized imperial power for herself in 690 after Taizong became debilitated.

***Wuwei*** (woo-WAY) Daoist concept of a disengagement from the affairs of the world.

**Xia** (shyah) Early Chinese dynasty (2200–1766 B.C.E.).

**Xianyang** (SHYAHN-YAHNG) Capital city of the Qin empire.

**Xiao** (SHAYOH) Confucian concept of respect for one's parents and ancestors.

**Yang Jian** (yahng jyahn) First emperor of the short-lived but effective Sui Dynasty which united China after centuries of division, reigned from 589 to 604 C.E.

**Yangzi** (YAHNG-zuh) River in central China.

**Yellow Turban Uprising** Major peasant revolt that broke out in the last decades of the Later Han Dynasty and was partly responsible for that dynasty's collapse.

**Yongle** (YAWNG-leh) Chinese Ming emperor (r. 1403–1424) who pushed for foreign exploration and promoted cultural achievements such as the *Yongle Encyclopedia.*

**Young Turks** Nineteenth-century Turkish reformers who pushed for changes within the Ottoman empire, such as universal suffrage and freedom of religion.

**Yuan dynasty** (yoo-AHN) Chinese dynasty (1279–1368) that was founded by the Mongol ruler Khubilai Khan.

**Yucatan** (yoo-kuh-TAN) Peninsula in Central America, home of the Maya.

**Yurts** (yuhrts) Tents used by nomadic Turkish and Mongol tribes.

**Zaibatsu** (zeye-BAHT-soo) Japanese term for "wealthy cliques," which are similar to American trusts and cartels but usually organized around one family.

**Zambos** (ZAHM-bohs) Latin American term for individuals born of indigenous and African parents.

**Zamudio, Adela** (ZAH-moo-dee-oh, ah-DEH-lah) Nineteenth-century Bolivian poet, author of "To Be Born a Man."

***Zemstvos*** (ZEHMST-voh) District assemblies elected by Russians in the nineteenth century.

**Zen Buddhism** Japanese version of Chinese Chan Buddhism, with an emphasis on intuition and sudden flashes of insight instead of textual study.

**Zheng He** (jung ha) 1371–1433 C.E. Chinese mariner, explorer, and admiral during the early Ming Dynasty who traveled as far as Malindi in East Africa.

**Zhou dynasty** (JOH) Chinese dynasty (1122–256 B.C.E.) that was the foundation of Chinese thought formed during this period: Confucianism, Daoism, Zhou Classics.

**Zhu Xi** (ZHOO-SHEE) Neo-Confucian Chinese philosopher (1130–1200).

**Ziggurats** (ZIG-uh-rahts) Mesopotamian temples.

**Zimbabwe** (zihm-BAHB-way) Former colony of Southern Rhodesia that gained independence in 1980.

# Index

In this index, letters following a page locater are as follows: the letter *i* denotes an illustration, *m* denotes a map, *p* denotes a photograph, and *t* denotes a table

## A

## B

## D

## H

## J

## K



## L

## N

## O

## P

## V



## W